To the IBM Hardware and Software People of the AS/400

Contents

Appendices

Preface

This book is a comprehensive text dedicated to the **RPG IV** programming language and the AS/400 environment. In addition to the general syntax of the **RPG IV** language, the following subjects are presented:

1. Most of the new **RPG IV** language operations and features are introduced, discussed, and then supported in numerous program examples.
2. Structured **RPG IV** programming is emphasized throughout the book in order to stress the importance of writing programs that may be easily maintained and debugged. **RPG IV** structured operations, where applicable, are used in all program examples.
3. The creation, syntax, and processing of ***Physical Files, Display Files, Logical Files, Subfiles,*** and ***Printer Files*** are detailed in separate chapters.
4. The procedures to use the Source Entry Utility (SEU), Data File Utility (DFU), Programmer Development Manager (PDM), and Screen Design Aid (SDA), unique to the AS/400 system, are explained in separate appendices.
5. Batch and interactive methods of debugging **RPG IV** programs are detailed in an appendix.

Specifically, this textbook offers the following advantages:

1. **RPG IV** syntax and procedures to externally process the **DB2/400** database and traditional **RPG** coding methods are discussed.
2. Students will be able to enter the source code, compile, debug, and load physical files after Chapter 2.
3. After Chapter 3 is completed, students will have the skills to write, enter, compile, and debug **RPG IV** programs that produce simple reports.

4. Over seventy complete **RPG IV** compiled programs are included to support the learning of this powerful computer language. Most of the compiled listings are supported with line-by-line explanations of the syntax and processing logic.
5. Over eight hundred figures are included in the text to explain and illustrate the syntax of **RPG IV** programs and ***Physical, Display, Logical, Printer files***, and ***Subfiles.***
6. Chapter Summaries, Questions, and Programming Assignments are included at the end of every chapter. Summaries highlight the new subjects introduced in the chapter. Questions are designed to aid in the immediate recall of chapter materials. At least three practical Programming Assignments (some chapters have six) that range in difficulty from the simple to the complex, enhance the learning of the **RPG IV** programming language.
7. Comprehensive coverage of physical file maintenance in the batch and interactive modes are detailed in separate chapters.
8. Emphasis is placed on the importance of data and its effect on the successful execution of **RPG IV** programs and accurate processing results.

This textbook introduces the sequence of subject matter outlined in the following chapters.

In order to familiarize students with the AS/400 environment, **Chapter 1** introduces basic control language commands which enable the programmer to create his or her processing environment, submit jobs and display output.

Chapter 2 explains the syntax, creation, and types of physical files. The reader is introduced to **SEU *(Source Entry Utility)*** which is needed for the entering of any source code for any file type. Specific commands are detailed which provide for the change and display of the attributes of a physical file.

Chapter 3 introduces specifics about the **RPG IV** programming language. The sequence of steps followed for the completion of an **RPG IV** program, which includes analysis of the application, design of input and output requirements, coding, compilation, debugging, and program execution are explained. The **RPG IV** syntax for the processing of *externally described* and *program described* physical files is shown. Traditional RPG II syntax is also discussed.

Chapter 4 further develops the reader's knowledge of **RPG IV** syntax and coding procedures with an introduction to report headings, editing of numeric fields, and the methods by which stand alone fields may be defined. Traditional RPG II syntax is also discussed.

RPG IV operations that support the arithmetic functions for addition, subtraction, multiplication, division, and square root are introduced in **Chapter 5.** The syntax of the **EVAL** operation (new to **RPG**) is explained with examples showing how it may simplify cumbersome calculations and be used in lieu of the traditional RPG arithmetic operations.

In addition, the syntax of the **MVR *(Move Remainder),* MOVE, MOVEL, SQRT** operations, ***Figurative Constants, Named Constants,*** and the initialization of field values is discussed in **Chapter 5.**

The syntax and processing logic of the **RPG IV** structured operations **IF/ELSE, DO, DOW *(Do While),* DOU *(Do Until),* SELECT *(Begin a Select Group),* WHEN *(When True Then Select),* OTHER *(Otherwise Select),* END** (also **ENDIF, ENDDO, ENDSL**), are discussed in **Chapter 6.** Use of the **LEAVE** and **ITER** operations within a **DO, DOU,** or **DOW** group is also covered. Programmer-controlled page overflow that provides for the printing of headings on subsequent pages is introduced. Traditional **RPG III** syntax for structured operations is also presented.

Chapter 7 introduces **RPG IV** operations, **EXSR *(Invoke Subroutine),* BEGSR *(Beginning of Subroutine),* ENDSR *(End of Subroutine),* CAS, *(Conditionally Invoke***

Subroutine) and **ENDCS** ***(End a CASxx Group),*** unique to the coding and processing of internal subroutines are discussed.

The syntax and processing logic of *programmer-controlled* control breaks that generate reports with sub-totals is also introduced in **Chapter 7.** Then, the traditional **RPG** syntax using *Control Level Indicators* (**L1–L9**) for control break processing is discussed.

Chapter 8 introduces ***Data Structures*** and ***Date Areas.*** How ***Data Structures*** are used to divide a field into subfields, change the format of a field, group noncontiguous data into a contiguous format, and define an area of storage in more than one format is covered. Special purpose ***File Information*** and ***Program Status*** data structures, used in run time error handling, are also explained.

The creation, update, and deletion of **Data Areas** is also covered in this chapter along with their *implicit* and *explicit* processing by **RPG IV** programs.

The syntax and processing of ***tables*** is introduced in **Chapter 9.** Emphasis is placed on the **RPG IV** syntax to define tables, methods of loading table data in the program cycle, alternative ways of organizing table data, and methods of processing.

Chapter 10 details the logic, syntax, and processing of arrays. Methods of loading arrays in the program cycle, organization of array data, and the editing of arrays on output are discussed. Also explained is array look up with and without an ***index.*** Multi-dimensional processing of arrays is simulated by syntax related to ***Multiple Occurrence Data Structures*** and the **RPG IV OCCUR** operation. The syntax and processing logic of the **SORTA** ***(Sort Array)*** operation is also detailed in this chapter.

Chapter 11 explains the syntax and use of the **RPG IV** character manipulation operations **CHECK, CHECKR, SCAN, SUBST, XLATE** and **SIZE.** The **%TRIM, %TRIML,** and **%TRIMR** functions are also discussed.

In addition, pointer support, new to **RPG,** is introduced in this chapter. Pointer types and the syntax and use of the **%ADDR** and **%PADDR** functions are explained.

Also included in **Chapter 11** are the **RPG IV** time and date operations **ADDDUR, SUBDUR, EXTRCT,** and **TEST.**

Data validation procedures common to the batch processing environment are introduced in **Chapter 12.** Individual **RPG IV** programs support the learning of the syntax and processing logic to control many of the commonly used validation procedures.

Chapter 13 includes a comprehensive coverage of *physical file maintenance* in the batch environment. The syntax and use of the **RPG IV** operations **CHAIN, DELETE, READ, READE, READP, READPE, SETLL, SETGT, UPDATE,** and **WRITE** are explained with numerous program examples.

The syntax and procedures related to the creation and use of Display Files, used in the interactive environment, are introduced in **Chapter 14.**

The development of interactive **RPG IV** maintenance programs is presented in **Chapter 15.** Many of the file processing operations discussed in Chapter 13 are used in the program examples in this chapter.

Chapter 16 explains the syntax and application of ***Subfiles,*** their unique keywords, and coding techniques. Separate **RPG IV** programs are included to illustrate how ***Subfiles*** are used in the maintenance and processing of physical files. The syntax for ***windowing*** within a ***Subfile*** is also included in this chapter.

The use, creation, and syntax of ***Logical Files*** is detailed in **Chapter 17.** Keywords and the processing logic of ***Non-join*** and ***Join Logical Files*** is separately discussed and supported by numerous coding examples.

Chapter 18 introduces the syntax for ***Printer Files.*** **RPG IV** coding procedures to process ***Printer Files*** is illustrated with examples.

RPG IV modular programming is introduced in **Chapter 19.** How other program objects are called using ***Dynamic*** and ***Static Binding*** is discussed. The syntax and use of the **RPG IV** operations **CALL, CALLB, PLIST, PARM,** and **RETURN** is explained with coding examples.

Chapter 20 introduces some of the **CL** commands and their syntax used in ***Control Language Programs*** **(CLP).** The basic structure of **CLPs** is discussed and example programs are reviewed in detail to explain parameter passing, variable manipulation, display, and physical file processing.

Appendices A, B, C, and **D** instruct the reader on how to use the ***SEU, PDM, DFU,*** and ***SDA*** utilities respectively. Batch and interactive debugging procedures are discussed in **Appendix E.** The ***RPG Logic Cycle*** is explained in **Appendix F.**

TEACHING TIPS

This book is only suitable for **RPG IV** language courses taught on the IBM's AS/400. For RPG courses that use other IBM systems or those of other manufacturers, refer to *RPG II, RPG III, and RPG/400 With Business Applications* by Stanley E. Myers. In addition, for users who are using RPG III (also called RPG/400), refer to *RPG/400 Programming on the AS/400* by Stanley E. Myers and Candice E. Myers.

At the option of the instructor (or reader), the sequence of chapters, or those discussed may depend on the background of the student(s). The suggested sequence for students in a two semester course with no AS/400 experience is to begin with Chapter 1 and continue through Chapter 18. As time dictates, Chapters 19 and/or 20 should ideally be covered. Any appendix should be referred to as needed. Initially, however, the material in ***Appendix A*** **(SEU)** and ***C*** **(DFU)** should be discussed.

For a one semester **RPG IV** course with students who have no previous RPG education or experience, Chapters 3 through 11, 13, and 14 through 15. If time permits, Chapters 16 and 17 should ideally be discussed.

For the professional programmer who has little or no experience in traditional RPG, this book provides an excellent reference source for the learning of **RPG IV.** Not only is the syntax discussed, but detailed program examples are included that put all of the elements of a batch and interactive processing together.

The following learning tools are available to users of this textbook:

1. An Instructor's Manual, which includes answers to all questions and compiled programming assignments listings and processing results.
2. A test bank (with separate answers) is included in the manual and on diskette.
3. Compile listings of the first **RPG IV** example program from each chapter is included on diskette.
4. Programming Assignment listings from the Instructor's Manual or example programs on diskette may be used as transparency masters.

ACKNOWLEDGMENTS

I want to extend my thanks to my children, Caroline, Megan, and Sean for providing me the time to write this textbook and supplemental Instructor's Manual.

I especially want to thank Gary W. Daniels, Vice President of Information Systems, from the Trenwick America Reinsurance Corporation in Stamford, CT for his dedicated and meticulous review of the **RPG IV** syntax introduced in this book. In addition, I want to recognize John Niski, RPG Programmer Analyst from Saint Vincent's Medical Center in Bridgeport, CT for testing the accuracy of every **RPG IV** program included in the text by rewriting each program example.

I also want to thank my wife Candice for her availability when I needed advice for her technical expertise. I more than appreciate the time that these people spent on molding this book into an excellent learning tool.

After the manuscript is completed, the production of a text of this complexity can often be a frustrating experience. However, because of the skills and patience of the production editor, Judy Winthrop, the production phase was greatly simplified. Without exception, she always had a sincere interest in the placement of figures in relationship to the supporting text, the print quality, and overall accuracy. Working with a manuscript with over eight hundred figures is not an easy task. This is my second textbook with Judy as the production editor and it will not be the last!

In addition, I want to thank Alan Apt, Prentice-Hall editor, and his staff for their timely responses to my questions and concern about the quality and marketing of this book. What a pleasure working with all of these people! Thanks to all of you!!!!

Stanley E. Myers

chapter 1

The AS/400 Environment

IBM's Application System/400 (AS/400) is a powerful family of computers intended to meet a wide range of business needs. Several types of hardware units are available: the 9402, 9404, 9406, and Advanced Series 200, 300, 310, and 320. As can be seen in Figure 1-1, the 9402, 9404, and Advanced Series 200 are compact units which, although small enough to fit under a desk, are each capable of supporting a small business. The various models of the 9406 unit (model B, model D, model E, and model F) are mounted in multiple racks, each roughly the size of a five-drawer filing cabinet, and are capable of supporting hundreds of users. The Advanced Series 300, 310, and 320, while smaller than the rack mounted units, are capable of supporting the same number of users as the 9406. To meet the needs of very large corporations, all models of the AS/400 computer may be networked together, sharing files and other resources within the same building or around the world. Indeed, it is the versatility of the AS/400 which has made it so popular.

In addition to the Advanced Series models shown in Figure 1-1, IBM has announced a new Advanced Series with 64-bit RISC (Reduced Instruction Set Computing)

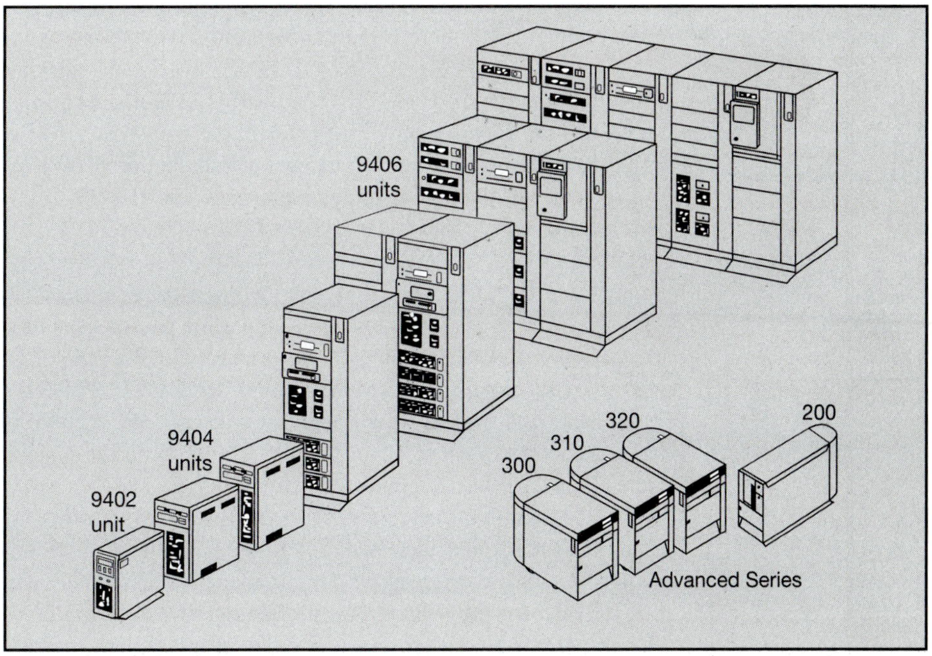

Figure 1-1 The Application System/400 models *(Courtesy of IBM)*.

technology. The new AS/400s are implemented in PowerPC AS™ microprocessors and available in Advanced Servers models 40S, 50S, 53S, 400, 500, 510, and 530. This new series processes much faster, delivers more power, and will ultimately be more functional for the user than older AS/400 models.

OS/400, the AS/400 operating system, provides the user with several tools to run the system. These tools are generally grouped together based on their functionality. *Control Language (CL)* is a set of commands which allow the user to communicate with the AS/400. *Data Management* provides the user with ways to define and access data within the AS/400's relational database. *Work Management* controls the processing of jobs in the AS/400's multiuser environment. *Programmer Services* provides development tools and utilities to assist the programmer in creating and maintaining programs and files. *System Operator Services* provides the system operator with a menu of frequently used functions. *Communication Support* provides a wide range of communication functions which allow the AS/400 to communicate with various types of systems (including, but not restricted to, other AS/400s). *Security* protects all of the data and software on the system. Together, all of these features make *OS/400* a very powerful operating system.

OS/400 keeps track of millions of *objects.* An object can be anything; programs, files, output queues, job queues, job descriptions, and libraries are all objects. All objects are accessible via a special language called *Control Language,* or *CL.* There are a number of CL commands which a programmer uses when programming on the AS/400. We will explain the most common ones as we encounter them.

THE USER'S PROFILE

Let's begin by examining the programmer's environment. When an AS/400 terminal is turned on, a sign-on screen appears. The user is prompted to enter a User ID and password. The User ID allows the system to associate a job session with information stored in a *user profile.* The user profile, which is created by the security officer, defines the executing environment to the system. If the user is a programmer, several specific aspects of this environment are of interest.

Figure 1-2 uses the **DSPUSRPRF** command to display a typical user profile for a programmer. First there is the **profile name,** which may be up to 10 characters in length; in this case, JANE. Note that JANE's password is not displayed. The AS/400 will never display a password. Passwords are encrypted and stored for use by the system. No one, not even the security officer, can display a password. If Jane forgets her password, the security officer can assign her a new one but cannot display her current password.

Many of the parameters contain the entry ***SYSVAL.** This refers to a value stored in an associated *system value.* System values contain information which controls the way in which an individual AS/400 system is run. For example, using a system value for the number of days before a user's password expires in the *Password expiration interval* parameter ensures that everyone has the same password expiration interval.

JANE has been assigned a **user class** of ***PGMR,** or programmer. This grants her two *special authorities*: ***SAVSYS** and ***JOBCTL. *SAVSYS** allows Jane to save, restore, and free storage for all objects on the system. ***JOBCTL** grants Jane the authority to hold, release, cancel, clear, or change any job on the system. She can also load the system (IPL), start writers, and stop active subsystems.

As a programmer, Jane has been associated with the **QPGMR** *group profile.* This "automatically" gives Jane authority to use a variety of system commands and access system objects which are reserved for programmers. Note that the security officer has also specified ***GRPPRF** for the *owner.* This means that any object which Jane creates will be owned by the **QPGMR** group, and the other programmers in that group will have the same

```
                    Display User Profile - *BASIC
5763SS1 V3R1M0  940909
User Profile . . . . . . . . . . . . . . . :   JANE
Previous sign-on . . . . . . . . . . . . . :   12/02/97  16:21:20
Sign-on attempts not valid . . . . . . . . :   0
Status . . . . . . . . . . . . . . . . . . :   *ENABLED
Date password last changed . . . . . . . . :   02/02/97
Password expiration interval . . . . . . . :   *NOMAX
Set password to expired  . . . . . . . . . :   *NO
User class . . . . . . . . . . . . . . . . :   *PGMR
Special authority  . . . . . . . . . . . . :   *ALLOBJ
                                               *JOBCTL
                                               *SAVSYS
Group profile  . . . . . . . . . . . . . . :   QPGMR
Owner  . . . . . . . . . . . . . . . . . . :   *GRPPRF
Group authority  . . . . . . . . . . . . . :   *NONE
Group authority type . . . . . . . . . . . :   *PRIVATE
Supplemental groups  . . . . . . . . . . . :   *NONE
Assistance level . . . . . . . . . . . . . :   *SYSVAL
Current library  . . . . . . . . . . . . . :   JANELIB
Initial program  . . . . . . . . . . . . . :   *NONE
  Library  . . . . . . . . . . . . . . . . :
Initial menu . . . . . . . . . . . . . . . :   MAIN
  Library  . . . . . . . . . . . . . . . . :     *LIBL
Limit capabilities . . . . . . . . . . . . :   *NO
Text . . . . . . . . . . . . . . . . . . . :   Jane Smith - Programmer
Display sign-on information  . . . . . . . :   *SYSVAL
Limit device sessions  . . . . . . . . . . :   *SYSVAL
Keyboard buffering . . . . . . . . . . . . :   *SYSVAL
Maximum storage allowed  . . . . . . . . . :   *NOMAX
  Storage used . . . . . . . . . . . . . . :     8
Highest scheduling priority  . . . . . . . :   3
Job description  . . . . . . . . . . . . . :   JANE
  Library  . . . . . . . . . . . . . . . . :     JANELIB
Accounting code  . . . . . . . . . . . . . :
Message queue  . . . . . . . . . . . . . . :   JANE
  Library  . . . . . . . . . . . . . . . . :     QUSRSYS
Message queue delivery . . . . . . . . . . :   *NOTIFY
Message queue severity . . . . . . . . . . :   00
Output queue . . . . . . . . . . . . . . . :   *WRKSTN
  Library  . . . . . . . . . . . . . . . . :
Printer device . . . . . . . . . . . . . . :   *WRKSTN
Special environment  . . . . . . . . . . . :   *SYSVAL
Attention program  . . . . . . . . . . . . :   QCMD
  Library  . . . . . . . . . . . . . . . . :     QSYS
Sort sequence  . . . . . . . . . . . . . . :   *SYSVAL
  Library  . . . . . . . . . . . . . . . . :
Language identifier  . . . . . . . . . . . :   *SYSVAL
Country identifier . . . . . . . . . . . . :   *SYSVAL
Coded character set identifier . . . . . . :   *SYSVAL
User options . . . . . . . . . . . . . . . :   *NONE
Object auditing value  . . . . . . . . . . :   *NONE
Action auditing values . . . . . . . . . . :   *NONE
User ID number . . . . . . . . . . . . . . :   130
Group ID number  . . . . . . . . . . . . . :   *NONE
```

Figure 1-2 DSPUSRPRF (Display User Profile) command display.

rights to that object as Jane does. For example, if Jane is on vacation and a file needs to be cleared, any of the programmers who work with Jane can clear the file.

Jane's development library, JANELIB, has been specified as her *current library*. A current library is the default library for storing any objects (programs, files, and so forth) created by the user. The system has a default library, QGPL (General Purpose Library), which may also serve as a current library. But since Jane is a programmer and is expected to create a number of new objects, it is easier to put these objects in her development library and avoid storing them with the system objects that are stored in QGPL.

The profile specifies an *initial program* for Jane. The program INLPGM in JANELIB will execute every time Jane signs onto the AS/400. Jane's initial program calls the Programmer Menu for her to work from.

The *priority limit* parameter represents the highest job scheduling and output scheduling priorities which can be assigned to a user's jobs. Zero (**0**) is the highest priority, and **9** is the lowest. Jane has been assigned a priority limit of **3**. This means that any jobs with a priority of **4** through **9** will run after Jane's jobs. However, any jobs with a priority of **0** through **2** will execute before Jane's jobs.

Jane's job description JANE in JANELIB was specified in the *job description* parameter. The job description contains information that describes the execution environment for jobs and is used by the programmer when submitting jobs to run in the batch environment.

Jane has been assigned a default *output queue* (JANE in library QGPL) for her printed output and a *message queue* (JANE in QUSRSYS) for her messages. Because the *message queue delivery* parameter specifies ***NOTIFY,** Jane will hear a beep whenever a message arrives on her message queue. Later, when it is convenient, Jane can use the **DSPMSG** *(Display Messages)* command to display her messages.

Finally, the *special environment* parameter of JANE's user profile contains the entry ***NONE.** Many companies have chosen to migrate software from an IBM System/36. The AS/400 has a special environment for running this software (***S36**). But Jane will be developing programs that are "native" to the AS/400 and will not require a special environment for execution.

When Jane logs on to the system, the information stored in her user profile is used to establish her *job* in the interactive *subsystem,* **QINTER.** A subsystem is a means of grouping and controlling jobs (including the amount of memory allocated for them to run). The AS/400 has several subsystems, but programmers are generally concerned with only two of them: **QINTER** and **QBATCH.** Most interactive jobs run in the interactive subsystem, **QINTER,** while most batch processing is done in **QBATCH.**

THE PROGRAMMER MENU

When her initial program is executed, the *Programmer Menu* is displayed on Jane's terminal (see Figure 1-3). The Programmer Menu is a system tool intended to help programmers

```
                              Programmer Menu
                                                         System:   AS400
 Select one of the following:
      1. Start AS/400 Data File Utility
      2. Work with AS/400 Query
      3. Create an object from a source file       object name, type, pgm for CMD
      4. Call a program                            program name
      5. Run a command                             command
      6. Submit a job                              (job name), , ,(command)
      7. Go to a menu                              menu name
      8. Edit a source file member                 (srcmbr), (type)
      9. Design display format using SDA           (srcmbr), ,(mode)
     90. Sign off                                  (*nolist, *list)

  Selection . . . . . ___               Parm . . . . ____________________
  Type  . . . . . . . ____________      Parm 2 . . . ____________________
  Command . . . . . . __________________________________________________
  Source file . . . . ____________      Source library . . . . . . .  *LIBL
  Object library  . . ____________      Job description  . . . . . .  *USRPRF
  F3=Exit        F4=Prompt           F6=Display messages     F10=Command entry
  F12=Cancel     F14=Work with submitted jobs                 F18=Work with output
```

Figure 1-3 The Programmer Menu.

develop and maintain software. Programmers generally use either the Programmer Menu or **PDM,** another system tool, for programming. Information on the use of **PDM** (the *Programmer Development Manager*) may be found in Appendix B.

CL commands may be entered from the Programmer Menu by selecting option **5** and typing the command on the line marked **Command**. Command prompting is available by pressing function key 4 **(F4)**. If no command has been specified and F4 is pressed, a series of easy-to-use menus will allow the individual to find the exact command he or she needs for almost any task.

Most programmers find the command-naming conventions meaningful and easy to use. The verb portion of the command is generally three consonants, such as **DSP** for *display* or **WRK** for *work with.* The remaining portion of the command describes the object type to be processed, such as **JOBD** for *job description* or **OUTQ** for *output queue.* So, to *work with* the spooled output in an *output queue,* the command to use would be **WRKOUTQ.**

LIBRARY COMMANDS

If Jane wanted to display her *library list,* she would enter a **5** on the **Selection** line and the command **DSPLIBL** on the **Command** line and press ENTER. A library list similar to the one shown in Figure 1-4 would appear. All jobs have an associated library list,

```
5763SS1 V3R1M0  940909     Library List

  Library      Type        Text Description

  QSYS         SYS         System Library
  QSYS2        SYS         System Library for CPI's
  QHLPSYS      SYS
  QUSRSYS      SYS         System Library For Users
  JANELIB      CUR         Jane's Development Library
  FILELIB      USR         Production File Library
  PGMLIB       USR         Production Software Library
  QGPL         USR         General Purpose Library
  QTEMP        USR
```

Figure 1-4 DSPLIBL (Library List) command display.

which is a list of libraries that can be searched to find any object requested. The library list of any job is composed of *four* basic parts. First there is the *System Library List.* This list contains libraries associated with the AS/400 operating system. Then comes the *Product Library.* This library is associated with the specific command in use and is necessary for its execution. When the command is initiated, the *production library* is added to the library list. When the command finishes processing, the library is removed from the library list. Next is the *Current Library* for the job. This library is used as the default library for storing any new objects created by the job and is generally the programmer's development library. Finally, there is the *User Library List.* This is a list of libraries selected by the programmer based on his or her requirements.

When a request for an object is made and a library is not specified in the request, each library in the library list is searched, in the order in which they appear in the list, until an object with the same name and type requested is found.

If Jane wanted to add a library, remove a library, or change the position of a library in her library list, she would enter the **EDTLIBL** (*Edit Library List*) command on a display with a command line and press **F4**. The screen in Figure 1-5 will be displayed showing all of the libraries in the user's portion of her library list. Within this display, she may add, remove, or reposition a library in her library list.

On the other hand, if Jane wanted to add a library to her library list without reviewing the list first, she would enter the **ADDLIBLE** (*Add Library List Entry*) command on

```
                         Edit Library List

 Type new/changed information, press Enter.
  To add a library, type name and desired sequence number.
  To remove a library, space over library name.
  To change position of a library, type new sequence number.

 Sequence             Sequence              Sequence
 Number   Library     Number    Library     Number    Library
  010     QSYS         120                   230
  020     QSYS2        130                   240
  030     QHLPSYS      140                   250
  040     QUSRSYS      150
  050     JANELIB      160
  060     FILELIB      170
  070     PGMLIB       180
  080     QGPL         190
  090     QTEMP        200
  100                  210
  110                  220

 F3=Exit          F5=Refresh          F12=Cancel
```

Figure 1-5 EDTLIBL (Edit Library List) command display.

the command line of any display and press **F4.** Figure 1-6 shows the **ADDLIBLE** command display. Note that a library must exist before it can be added to the user's library list.

```
                    Add Library List Entry (ADDLIBLE)
 Type choices, press Enter.
 Library . . . . . . . . . . . .    __________    Name
 Library list position:
   List position  . . . . . . . .   *FIRST        *FIRST, *LAST, *AFTER...
   Reference library  . . . . . .   __________    Name




 Bottom
 F3=Exit   F4=Prompt   F5=Refresh   F12=Cancel   F13=How to use this display
 F24=More keys
```

Figure 1-6 ADDLIBLE (Add Library List Entry) command display.

Furthermore, if Jane wanted to create a new library (*TEST library, for example), she must enter the **CRTLIB** (*Create Library*) command on the command line of any display and press **F4**. Figure 1-7 shows the **CRTLIB** command display.

```
                         Create Library (CRTLIB)
 Type choices, press Enter.
 Library . . . . . . . . . . . .    __________    Name
 Library type . . . . . . . . . .   *PROD         *PROD, *TEST
 Text 'description' . . . . . . .   *BLANK
 ______

                                                                  Bottom
 F3=Exit   F4=Prompt   F5=Refresh   F10=Additional parameters   F12=Cancel
 F13=How to use this display        F24=More keys
```

Figure 1-7 CRTLIB (Create Library) command display.

Display Job Description

Many of a programmer's jobs are submitted to the batch subsystem for execution. The Programmer Menu allows the programmer to specify a *job description* (or **JOBD**) to be used when submitting these jobs. The job description allows the programmer to define an environment in which jobs may be executed. Although the job description may be used to define these attributes for any job, programmers are most familiar with using the job description to control jobs which they submit for batch processing. The **CL** command **DSPJOBD** can be used to display a job description. Refer to Figure 1-8 while we discuss the parameters of most interest to programmers.

```
                    Job Description Information

Job description:   JANE            Library:   JANELIB
User profile . . . . . . . . . . . . . . . . . :    *RQD
CL syntax check  . . . . . . . . . . . . . . . :    *NOCHK
Hold on job queue  . . . . . . . . . . . . . . :    *NO
End severity . . . . . . . . . . . . . . . . . :    30
Job date . . . . . . . . . . . . . . . . . . . :    *SYSVAL
Job switches . . . . . . . . . . . . . . . . . :    00000000
Inquiry message reply  . . . . . . . . . . . . :    *RQD
Job priority (on job queue)  . . . . . . . . . :    5
Job queue  . . . . . . . . . . . . . . . . . . :    QBATCH
  Library  . . . . . . . . . . . . . . . . . . :      QGPL
Output priority (on output queue)  . . . . . . :    5
Printer device . . . . . . . . . . . . . . . . :    *USRPRF
Output queue . . . . . . . . . . . . . . . . . :    JANE
  Library  . . . . . . . . . . . . . . . . . . :      QGPL
Message logging:
  Level  . . . . . . . . . . . . . . . . . . . :    4
  Severity . . . . . . . . . . . . . . . . . . :    0
  Text . . . . . . . . . . . . . . . . . . . . :    *SECLVL
Log CL program commands  . . . . . . . . . . . :    *NO
Accounting code  . . . . . . . . . . . . . . . :    DP
Print text . . . . . . . . . . . . . . . . . . :    *SYSVAL
Routing data . . . . . . . . . . . . . . . . . :    QCMDB
Request data . . . . . . . . . . . . . . . . . :    *NONE
Device recovery action . . . . . . . . . . . . :    *SYSVAL
Time slice end pool  . . . . . . . . . . . . . :    *SYSVAL
Text . . . . . . . . . . . . . . . . . . . . . :    Jane Smith
Initial library list:
  *SYSVAL
```

Figure 1-8 DSPJOBD (Display Job Description) command display.

The **Job queue** parameter allows the programmer to specify the job queue to be used when the job is submitted. In most cases this will be **QBATCH**.

The **Job scheduling priority** and **Job output priority** parameters have a default entry of **5.** Priorities range from **0** to **9**, with **0** being the highest priority and **9** being the lowest. These entries cannot be higher in priority than the value specified in the programmer's User Profile **Highest scheduling priority** parameter. An **Accounting code** may be specified for job accounting purposes. In Figure 1-8 we see that an **accounting code** of ***USRPRF** is the default.

Routing data corresponds to special routing entries in the subsystem description. In this case, the entry **QCMDB** tells the **QBATCH** subsystem that jobs submitted with this job description should be processed in batch mode.

An **Initial library list** may be specified for use with jobs using the job description. This library list, just like the library list for the programmer's interactive job, can be searched for objects required for the job using this job description.

Message logging can be very helpful when debugging a batch job. The entry of **4** for **message level, 0** for **message severity**, and ***NOLIST** for a **message text level** means that all messages with a severity of **0** or greater will be logged during the execution of the job and, should the job end abnormally, a listing of the messages (called a *joblog*) will be produced.

The option to **Log CL statements** may also be used for debugging purposes. This parameter is usually ***NO,** but if a programmer needed to log CL statements in a CL program (CLP) as they executed, he or she could change this parameter to specify ***YES.** Then the programmer could view the executed statements in the joblog.

A default **Output queue** may be specified. Programmers frequently use this parameter to place spooled output in an output queue (**OUTQ**) not associated with a printer. In this way they can review their output via the terminal and print only selected output.

External switches may be set **ON** or **OFF** using the switch parameter of the job description. A value of **0** means "OFF." A value of **1** means "ON." The values of switches are available to both **RPG IV** programs and control language programs to condition operations.

Work with Submitted Jobs and Work with Job Spooled Files

To view a job which has been submitted, the programmer may use the **WRKSBMJOB** *(Work with Submitted Jobs)* command. This command will display a list of submitted jobs, with their current processing status, on the programmer's terminal (see Figure 1-9).

```
                        Work with Submitted Jobs                    AS400
                                                          12/08/97  08:36:43
Submitted from . . . . . . . . :    *USER
Type options, press Enter.
  2=Change   3=Hold   4=End   5=Work with   6=Release   7=Display message
  8=Work with spooled files
Opt    Job           User         Type      -----Status------    Function
__  PGM109         JANE         BATCH     OUTQ
8_  LIST_FILE      JANE         BATCH     OUTQ

                                                                     Bottom
Parameters or command
===>________________________________________________________________________
F3=Exit    F4=Prompt    F5=Refresh    F9=Retrieve    F12=Cancel
```

```
                        Work with Job Spooled Files
Job:    LIST_FILE       User:    JANE            Number:    588929
Type options, press Enter.
   1=Send   2=Change   3=Hold   4=Delete   5=Display   6=Release   7=Message
   8=Attributes          9=Work with printing status
                     Device or                        Total    Current
Opt   File           Queue         User Data   Status  Pages      Page   Copies
5_   QSYSPRT         JANE          LIST_FILE    RDY       22                 1
__   QPJOBLOG        JOBLOGS                    HLD                          1

                                                                      Bottom
Parameters for options 1, 2, 3 or command
===> _______________________________________________________________________
F3=Exit    F10=View 3    F11=View 2    F12=Cancel    F22=Printers    F24=More keys
```

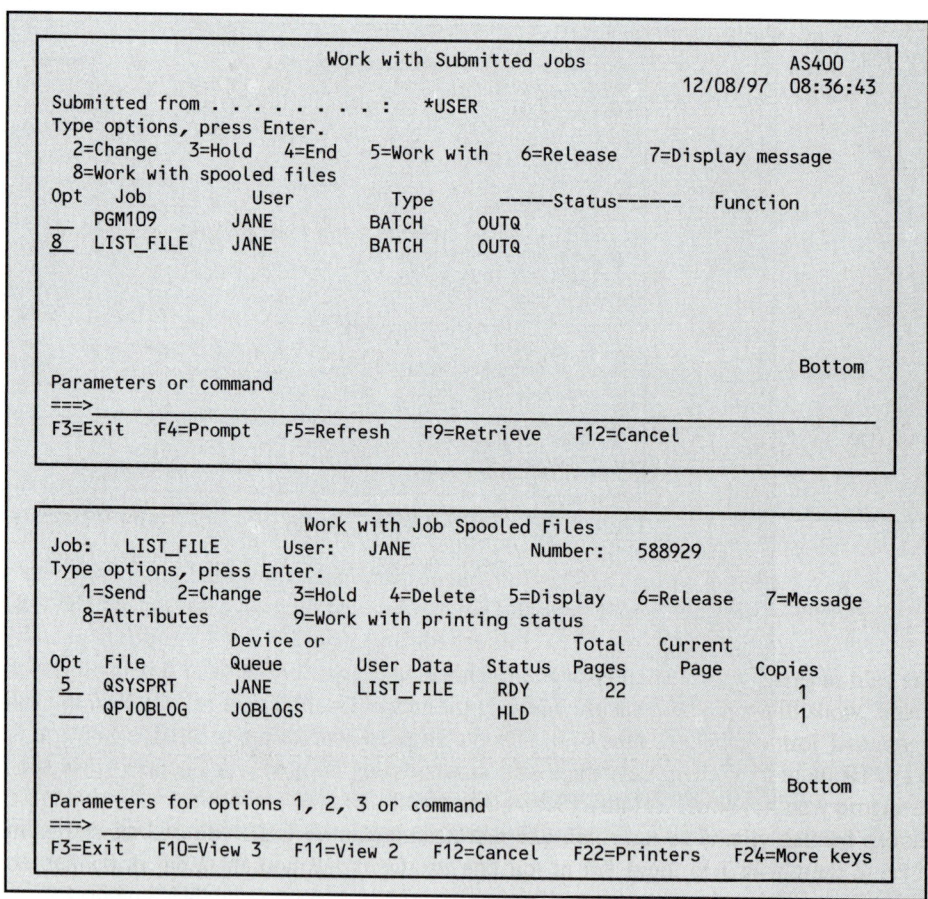

Figure 1-9 **WRKSBMJOB** (Work with Submitted Jobs) command display.

From this display the programmer may view detailed information concerning any of the jobs listed. For example, to view a report created by the LIST_FILE job, the programmer would enter an **8** in the space next to the LIST_FILE job. Then the *Work with Job Spooled Files* display would show a list of all the spooled files associated with that job.

To view the report from this display, the programmer would then enter a **5** (*view*) in the space next to the report and press **ENTER**.

Work with Output Queue

Another way to view the same report would be to look at it in the output queue. To do this the programmer would use the **WRKOUTQ** *(Work with Output Queue)* command. An output queue may be specified when executing the command. However, if a queue is not specified, the command will display a list of output queues from which to select. Once an output queue has been selected, a list of spooled files will be displayed for review (see Figure 1-10). To view the report, the programmer would enter a **5** in the space next to the report created by the LIST_FILE job and press **ENTER**.

```
                          Work with Output Queue
Queue:    JANE              Library:   QGPL             Status:   RLS/WTR
Type options, press Enter.
  1=Send   2=Change   3=Hold   4=Delete   5=Display   6=Release   7=Messages
  8=Attributes          9=Work with printing status
Opt  File        User        User Data   Sts    Pages   Copies  Form Type   Pty
 __  QSYSPRT     QSYSOPR     PGM027      RDY        1        1  *STD          5
 __  QSYSPRT     JANE        PGM109      RDY       20        1  *STD          5
 __  QSYSPRT     QSYSOPR                 RDY        1        1  *STD          5
 __  QPRINT      QSYSOPR                 RDY        1        1  *STD          5
 5_  QSYSPRT     JANE        LIST_FILE   RDY       10        1  *STD          5



                                                                       Bottom
 Parameters for options 1, 2, 3 or command
 ===>________________________________________________________________________
F3=Exit   F11=View 2   F12=Cancel   F22=Printers   F24=More keys
```

Figure 1-10 **WRKOUTQ** (Work with Output Queue) command display .

WORK WITH ALL SPOOLED FILES

A third way to view the report would be to list all of the spooled files associated with the programmer. The command **WRKSPLF** *(Work with Spooled Files)* will present the programmer with a list containing all of the spooled files on the system which he or she may have created (see Figure 1-11). Again, to view the report, the programmer would enter a **5** in the space next to the report created by the LIST_FILE job and press **ENTER**.

```
                          Work with All Spooled Files
Type options, press Enter.
  1=Send   2=Change   3=Hold   4=Delete   5=Display   6=Release   7=Messages
  8=Attributes          9=Work with printing status
                                            Device or                 Total     Cur
 Opt  File        User       Queue          User Data    Sts    Pages   Page  Copy
 __   QPJOBLOG    JANE       JOBLOGS        LIST_FILE    RDY        1           1
 __   QSYSPRT     JANE       JANE           PGM109       RDY       20           1
 5_   QSYSPRT     JANE       JANE           LIST_FILE    RDY       10           1
                                                                            Bottom
 Parameters for options 1, 2, 3 or command
 ===>________________________________________________________________________
 F3=Exit   F10=View 3   F11=View 2   F12=Cancel   F22=Printers   F24=More keys
```

Figure 1-11 **WRKSPLF** (Work with All Spooled Files) command display.

Change Spooled File Attributes

Output queues are usually associated with a printer. A special program called a *writer* manages the queue for the printer. Spooled files placed in such an output queue are automatically printed. However, in our example, Jane's output queue is not associated with a printer. Therefore, her spooled files will not print automatically. The technique of using an output queue not associated with a printer allows the programmer to review spooled output online to determine if a printed copy is necessary. Should the programmer decide to print the spooled file, he or she may place a **2** (*change*) in the space next to the file on any of the spooled file displays (**WRKSPLF, WRKOUTQ,** or the **WRKSBMJOB** spooled file display) and press the **ENTER** key. A screen similar to the one shown in Figure 1-12 will appear. The programmer may then specify the name of a printer in the

```
                     Change Spooled File Attributes (CHGSPLFA)
Type choices, press Enter.
Spooled file . . . . . . . . . . > QSYSPRT        Name, *SELECT
Job name . . . . . . . . . . . . > LIST_FILE      Name, *
  User . . . . . . . . . . . . . > JANE           Name
  Number . . . . . . . . . . . . > 588929         000000-999999
Spooled file number  . . . . . . > 1              1-9999, *ONLY, *LAST
Printer  . . . . . . . . . . . .   PRT01          Name, *SAME, *OUTQ
Print sequence . . . . . . . . .   *SAME          *SAME, *NEXT
Form type  . . . . . . . . . . .   *STD           Form type, *SAME, *STD
Copies . . . . . . . . . . . . .   1              1-255, *SAME
Restart printing . . . . . . . .   *STRPAGE       Number, *SAME, *STRPAGE...
                            Additional Parameters
Output queue . . . . . . . . . .   JANE           Name, *SAME, *DEV
  Library  . . . . . . . . . . .     QGPL         Name, *LIBL, *CURLIB
                                                                     Bottom
F3=Exit   F4=Prompt   F5=Refresh   F10=Additional parameters   F12=Cancel
F13=How to use this display        F24=More keys
```

Figure 1-12 CHGSPLFA (Change Spooled File Attributes) command display.

Printer field and press the ENTER key. The spooled file will print on the specified printer. Other attributes, such as the number of copies or the type of form on which to print the report, may be changed in the same manner.

SOURCE FILES

Numerous *source files* are included with the AS/400 software. Those that the reader of this text will be most concerned with are **QDDSSRC, QRPGLESRC, QRPGSRC,** and **QCLSRC.** When the source code for a physical file, display file, logical file, or printer file is saved via **SEU** (*Source Entry Utility*), it is stored as a member of the default **QDDSSRC** source file. Similarily, when the source for an **RPG IV** program is saved, it is stored as member of the default **QRPGLESRC** source file. To access a source *member*, the related *source file* must be specified.

The programmer may create his or her own *source file* with the **CRTSRCPF** (*Create Source Physical File*) command shown in Figure 1-13.

Unless otherwise specified, the default *source file* will be assumed when the related member is saved or accessed. To access a source *member* in a user-created *source file*, the specific *source file* must be referenced.

Note that when a program's source is compiled, the resulting object is stored in the designated library and not as a member of a *source file*.

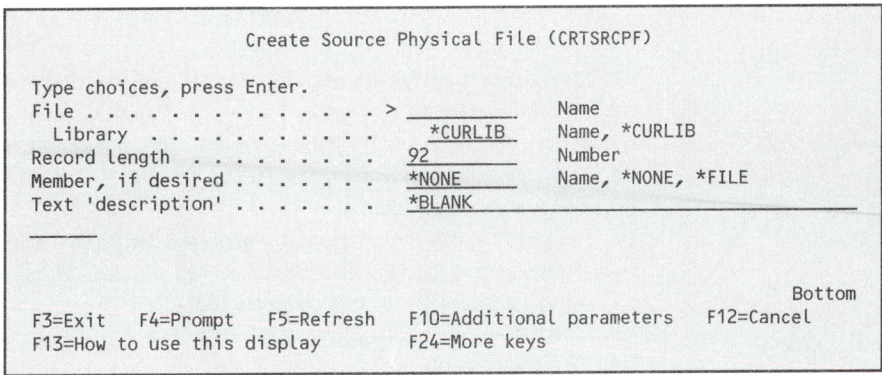

```
                    Create Source Physical File (CRTSRCPF)

Type choices, press Enter.
File . . . . . . . . . . . . . . . > __________   Name
  Library  . . . . . . . . . . .     *CURLIB      Name, *CURLIB
Record length  . . . . . . . . .   92             Number
Member, if desired . . . . . . .   *NONE          Name, *NONE, *FILE
Text 'description' . . . . . . .   *BLANK
______

                                                                     Bottom
F3=Exit   F4=Prompt   F5=Refresh   F10=Additional parameters   F12=Cancel
F13=How to use this display        F24=More keys
```

Figure 1-13 CRTSRCPF (Create Source Physical File) command display.

SUMMARY

IBM's AS/400 is a versatile computer well suited to today's business environment. Its powerful OS/400 operating system provides the programmer with an inventory of software tools with which to manage and maintain the system.

The programmer's environment is established based on parameters specified in the programmer's *user profile*. Some of the parameters rely on values maintained at the system level in *system values*. Others are maintained on the individual profile level. Parameters such as the programmer's *current library, initial program, priority limit, default message and output queues,* and *default job description* are used by the system to define the programmer's environment when the programmer signs onto the system and establishes an online session.

Job descriptions are used to define the processing environment for any job which the programmer submits to the batch subsystem for processing. They allow the programmer to specify parameters such as *run priority, job queue, output queue, message logging level* and *severity,* and a *library list* for the submitted job.

A *library list* is a list of libraries which are searched when an object is referenced. Each library, in turn, is searched until an object of the same name and type specified is found. A library list is displayed with the **DSPLIBL** (*Display Library List*) command. Libraries may be added to the user's library list with the **ADDLIBLE** (*Add Library List Entry*) command. Libraries may be removed, added, or have their position changed in the library list with the **EDTLIBL** (*Edit Library List*) command. Users may also create new libraries with the **CRTLIB** (*Create Library*) command.

A high-level computer language, known as *Control Language* (or *CL*), is used to communicate with the system. AS/400 command-naming conventions are meaningful and easy to use. The first part of a command represents the action to be taken and is generally three consonants, such as **DSP** for *display* or **WRK** for *work with.* These are followed by the *object type* to be processed, such as **OUTQ** for an *output queue* or **JOBD** for a *job description.* A few useful **CL** commands were introduced in this chapter, including **WRKOUTQ, DSPLIBL, ADDLIBLE, EDTLIBL, CRTLIB, DSPJOBD, WRKSBMJOB, WRKSPLF**, and **CRTSRCPF.** These are only a few of the more than 2,000 AS/400 **CL** commands. For a comprehensive discussion of Control Language commands and programming, refer to Chapter 20.

The AS/400 software includes numerous *source files* in which members are stored. For example, when the source for an **RPG IV** program is saved, it is stored as a member of the **QRPGLESRC** file. To access the member later, the related *source file* must be specified with the name of the program and the related library. The source for physical, logical, display, and printer files is stored in the default **QDDSSRC** *source file.* In lieu of the system-supplied default *source files,* the user may create his or her own with the **CRTSRCPF** (*Create Source Physical File*) command. All of the *source files* supplied with the AS/400 software are stored in the **QGPL** library.

QUESTIONS

1-1. Name the six groups of tools which OS/400 provides for the user to run the system.

1-2. What is an object?

1-3. What command would you use to display a user profile?

1-4. How are passwords protected on the AS/400?

1-5. What is a system value?

1-6. List five *User Profile* parameters which specified ***SYSVAL** in Figure 1-2.

1-7. There are two special authorities associated with the user class ***PGMR.** What are they and what do they allow the programmer to do?

1-8. What is a current library?

1-9. What is a priority limit?

1-10. What command may be used to display messages?

1-11. What is a library list and how is it used?

1-12. Name four commands related to the display, deletion, addition, and repositioning of libraries in a user's library list.

1-13. The job scheduling priority and job output priority specified in a job description (**JOBD**) are related to what entry on the *User Profile*? How are they related?

1-14. What is a joblog?

1-15. The job description (**JOBD**) option to log CL statements is usually set to ***NO**. When might a programmer change this option to ***YES**?

1-16. Which job description entry tells the **QBATCH** subsystem to process a job in batch mode?

1-17. What command would a programmer use to review output from a job which was submitted for batch processing?

1-18. What command would a programmer use to display all of his or her *spooled files*?

1-19. What command would a programmer use to display an *output queue*?

1-20. What are *source files*?

1-21. Name four *source files* supplied with the AS/400 software.

1-22. In what library are system-supplied *source files* initially stored?

1-23. When the source for an RPG IV program is saved, it becomes a *member* of what default *source file*?

1-24. With what command may a programmer create a *source file*?

1-25. When an RPG IV program is successfully compiled, is the object stored as a member in a *source file*? Explain.

PROGRAMMING ASSIGNMENTS

Programming Assignment 1-1: EXPLORE PROGRAMMER'S ENVIRONMENT

Sign on to the AS/400 using the user ID and password provided by your instructor. If the *Programmer Menu* is not displayed, type the command **STRPGMMNU** on the command line and press the ENTER key. Complete the following steps:

1. Type a **5** (Execute a command) in the space marked **Selection.** On the **Command** line type **DSPUSRPRF** and press command function key 4 (**F4**). Type your user ID in the **User profile** parameter and press the ENTER key.
2. Review the display of your user profile. Note the name of your default job description (**JOBD**). Press command function key 3 (**F3**) to exit the display.
3. Type a **6** (Submit a job) in the **Selection** field, and type **DSPJOBD** on the **Command** line. Press **F4**. Enter the name of the job description found in step 2 in the space labeled **JOBD.** Type ***PRINT** in the **Output** parameter and press the ENTER key.
4. Type a **5** in the **Selection** field and **WRKSBMJOB** on the **Command** line.

Programming Assignment 1-2: Working with Libraries

Step 1. With your instructor's permission, create a library using your last name (no longer than 10 characters).

Step 2. Add the library to your library list.

Step 3. Display your library list to determine if it has been added.

Step 4. Reposition your library to the first location in your library list.

Step 5. Remove your library from your library list.

Programming Assignment 1-3: Working with Source Files

Step 1. Find a list of the source files on your AS/400 system.

Step 2. Create a source file using your last name. Name the type of members that may be stored in your source file.

Step 3. Delete the source file you create in step 2.

chapter 2

Physical Files

THE DB2/400 RELATIONAL DATABASE

The database system for the AS/400 is called **DB2/400.** It is a *relational* database that is a collection of *tables* and *views*. Each table is a two-dimensional structure of *columns* and *rows*. Comparing generic relational database terminology with **DB2/400** nomenclature, a column is the same as a field and a row is the same as a record. Tables, which contain data, are called *physical files* in **DB2/400.**

A *view* must be created from one or more tables. Unlike tables, however, a view contains no data and is only a window through which the data from one or more tables pass for processing. Views are referred to as *logical files* in **DB2/400.** The creation and processing of logical files are discussed in Chapter 17.

Physical Files

Physical files in the **DB2/400** environment support only *one* record format (i.e., collection of fields). They may be organized as *keyed* or *nonkeyed* files. The organization type will determine the *access path* followed when the file is processed.

A nonkeyed physical file is similar to the traditional sequential file organization in which keys are not specified. Records, which are processed in the order in which they were loaded to the file (in *arrival sequence*), may be read, written, and updated using sequential or relative record processing methods.

Keyed physical files are similar to the traditional indexed sequential file organization in which one or more fields in the record format may be specified as a *single* or *composite* key field. Processing features unique to keyed physical files include the following:

1. Records may be accessed sequentially in key-value order or randomly by the key value.
2. Records may be processed in *arrival sequence,* ignoring the key-value order.
3. Instead of the default ascending key-value order, *physical* files may be processed in descending key-value order.
4. Records that have a common key value may be defined to process as a group of records in a default first-in, first-out (FIFO) order or in an optional last-in, first-out (LIFO) order.
5. *Composite* keys may be defined by specifying more than one field included in the body of the record format. The fields used in the composite key do not have to be contiguous within the record.

6. Any field in the body of the record format may be specified as the key field after the physical file is created. However, a logical file must be used to process the physical file in the new key order.
7. Records may be added or logically deleted without requiring a reorganization.

CREATING A PHYSICAL FILE

The steps for creating a *physical file* are the following:

1. Design a record format based on some application criteria.
2. Write the code on a *Data Description Specifications* (DDS) form (optional).
3. Enter the DDS statements via the Source Entry Utility **(SEU)** and save.
4. Compile, debug, and store the error-free physical file object format.

Record Format Design

Unlike the file organization types common to the traditional computer systems, the AS/400 physical file structure will support only *one* record format. Consequently, this restriction must be considered when a user-system is designed. Note, however, that multiple record processing may be simulated by *nonjoin* and *join* **logical files** which are related to two or more physical files. This topic will be introduced in Chapter 17.

The record format shown in Figure 2-1 will be used as the documentation to define a nonkeyed as well as a keyed sequence physical file.

```
                      PHYSICAL FILE DESCRIPTION

SYSTEM: AS/400                                   DATE: 1/10/98
FILE NAME: GLACTS                                REV NO: 0
RECORD NAME: GLACTSR                             KEY LENGTH: None
SEQUENCE: Nonkeyed                               RECORD SIZE: 58

                          FIELD DEFINITIONS

 FIELD    FIELD NAME   SIZE  TYPE    POSITION       COMMENTS
  NO                                FROM    TO

  1       ACTNUMBER       3   C        1     3
  2       ACTNAME        27   C        4    30
  3       ACT_TYPE       20   C       31    50
  4       BALANCE         8   S       51    58   2 decimals
```

Figure 2-1 Example of a physical file description.

THE DATA DESCRIPTION SPECIFICATIONS (DDS) FORM

Physical File: Nonkeyed Organization

All physical file formats (nonkeyed and keyed sequence) are usually written on *Data Description Specifications* forms before the code is entered via **SEU.**

A form completed for the example nonkeyed sequence physical file is illustrated and explained in Figure 2-2.

```
                                  Specification type
                                  Format type
                                  Record or field name
                                  Reference
                                  Field length
                                  Data type
                                  Decimal positions
                                  Usage
     .....A..........T.Name++++++RLen++TDpB......Functions++++++++++++++++

0001.00      A          R GLACTSR
0002.00      A            ACTNUMBER       3
0003.00      A            ACTNAME        27
0004.00      A            ACT_TYPE       20
0005.00      A            BALANCE         8S 2
```

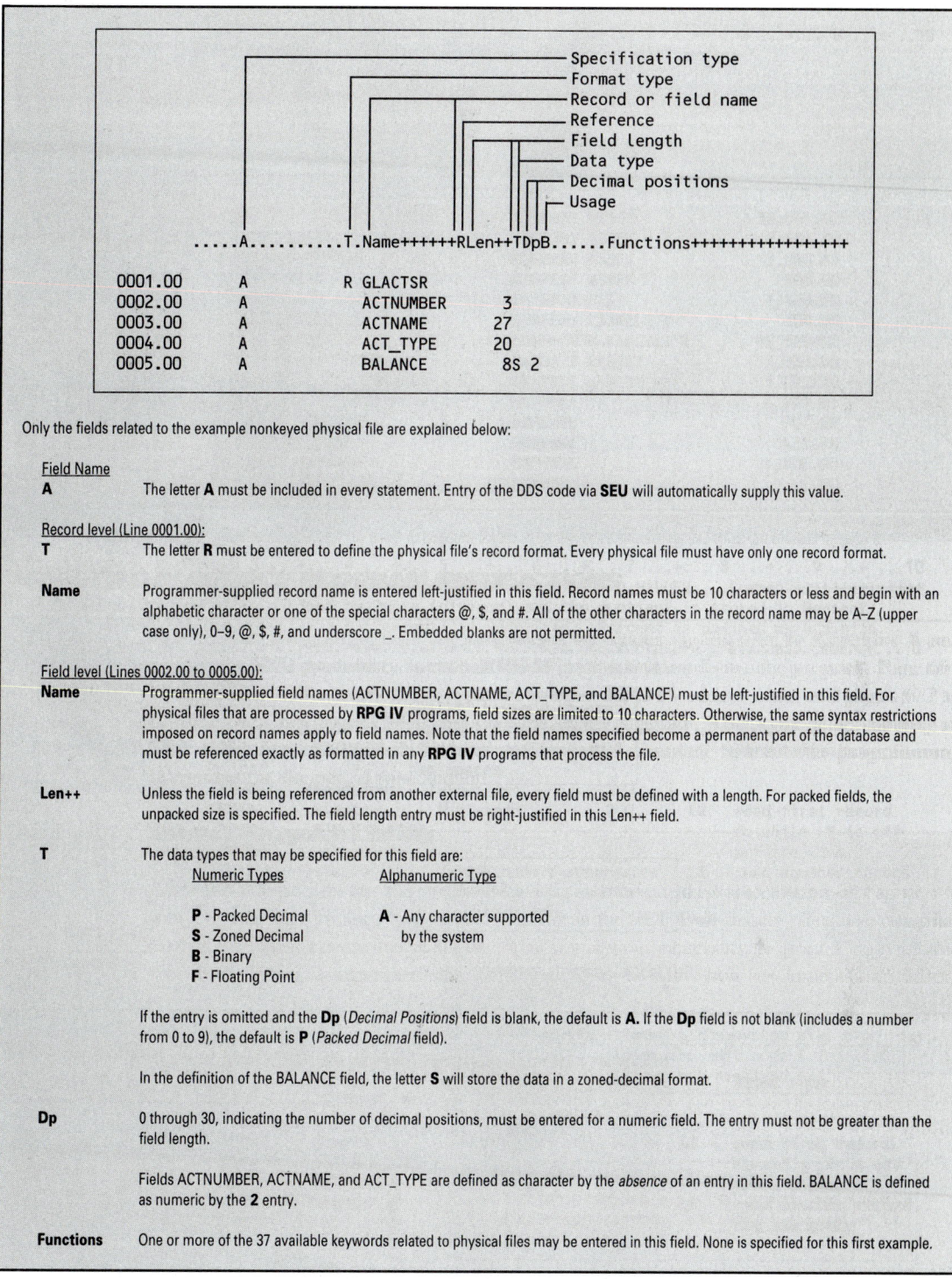

Only the fields related to the example nonkeyed physical file are explained below:

Field Name

A The letter **A** must be included in every statement. Entry of the DDS code via **SEU** will automatically supply this value.

Record level (Line 0001.00):

T The letter **R** must be entered to define the physical file's record format. Every physical file must have only one record format.

Name Programmer-supplied record name is entered left-justified in this field. Record names must be 10 characters or less and begin with an alphabetic character or one of the special characters @, $, and #. All of the other characters in the record name may be A–Z (upper case only), 0–9, @, $, #, and underscore _. Embedded blanks are not permitted.

Field level (Lines 0002.00 to 0005.00):

Name Programmer-supplied field names (ACTNUMBER, ACTNAME, ACT_TYPE, and BALANCE) must be left-justified in this field. For physical files that are processed by **RPG IV** programs, field sizes are limited to 10 characters. Otherwise, the same syntax restrictions imposed on record names apply to field names. Note that the field names specified become a permanent part of the database and must be referenced exactly as formatted in any **RPG IV** programs that process the file.

Len++ Unless the field is being referenced from another external file, every field must be defined with a length. For packed fields, the unpacked size is specified. The field length entry must be right-justified in this Len++ field.

T The data types that may be specified for this field are:

Numeric Types	Alphanumeric Type
P - Packed Decimal	**A** - Any character supported by the system
S - Zoned Decimal	
B - Binary	
F - Floating Point	

If the entry is omitted and the **Dp** (*Decimal Positions*) field is blank, the default is **A.** If the **Dp** field is not blank (includes a number from 0 to 9), the default is **P** (*Packed Decimal* field).

In the definition of the BALANCE field, the letter **S** will store the data in a zoned-decimal format.

Dp 0 through 30, indicating the number of decimal positions, must be entered for a numeric field. The entry must not be greater than the field length.

Fields ACTNUMBER, ACTNAME, and ACT_TYPE are defined as character by the *absence* of an entry in this field. BALANCE is defined as numeric by the **2** entry.

Functions One or more of the 37 available keywords related to physical files may be entered in this field. None is specified for this first example.

Figure 2-2 Data Description Specification syntax for a nonkeyed physical file.

Physical File: Keyed Sequence Organization

Except for key definition requirements, the DDS coding for a keyed sequence physical file is similar to a nonkeyed.

The *Data Description* syntax for the nonkeyed physical file shown in Figure 2-2 is modified in Figure 2-3 to define it as a keyed sequence physical file.

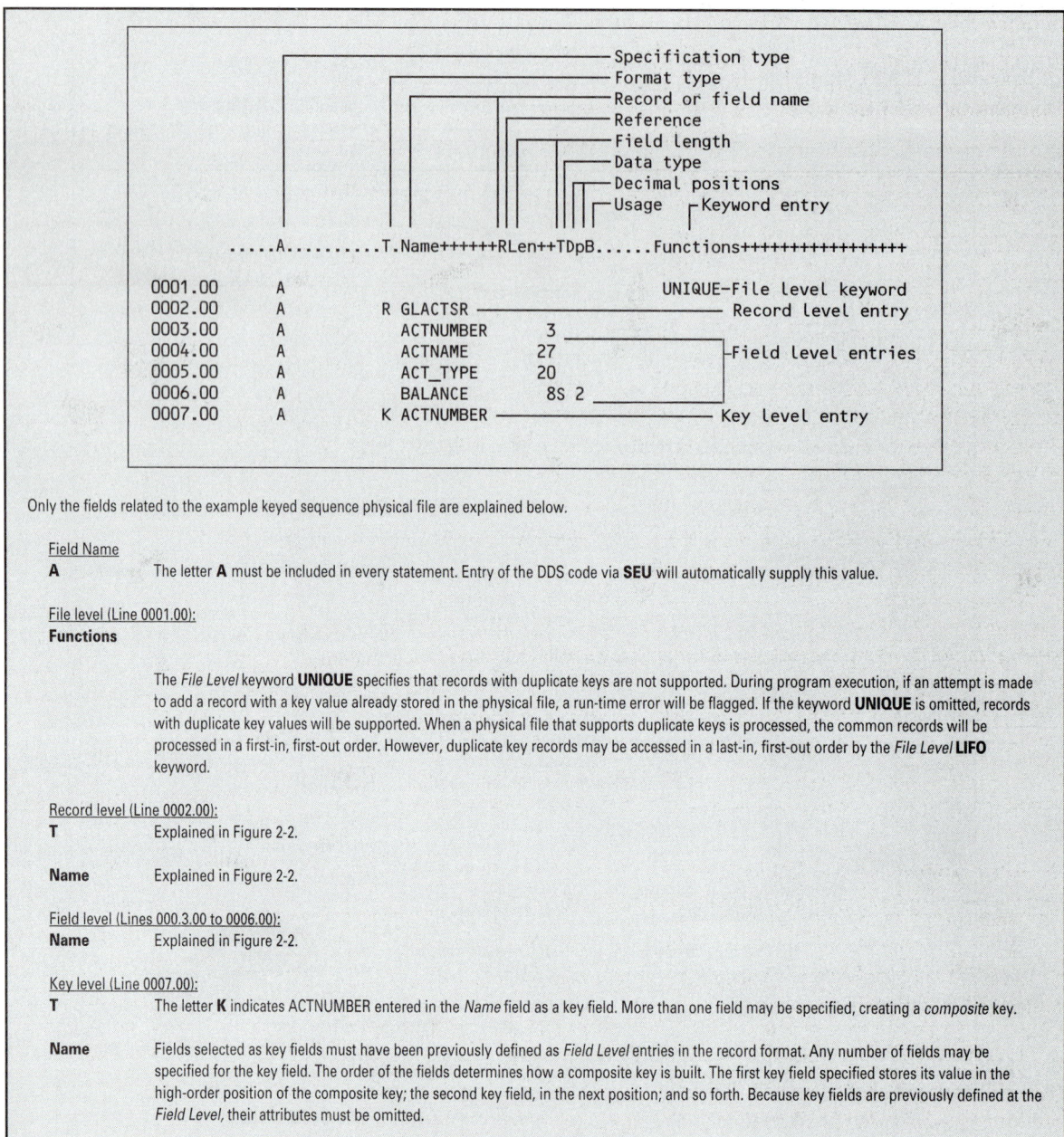

```
                                        ┌──Specification type
                                        ├──Format type
                                        ├──Record or field name
                                        ├──Reference
                                        ├──Field length
                                        ├──Data type
                                        ├──Decimal positions
                                        └──Usage    ┌Keyword entry
     .....A..........T.Name++++++RLen++TDpB......Functions++++++++++++++++

0001.00     A                                   UNIQUE-File level keyword
0002.00     A          R GLACTSR ──────────────── Record level entry
0003.00     A            ACTNUMBER       3 ──┐
0004.00     A            ACTNAME        27   ├Field level entries
0005.00     A            ACT_TYPE       20   │
0006.00     A            BALANCE        8S 2 ┘
0007.00     A          K ACTNUMBER ────────────── Key level entry
```

Only the fields related to the example keyed sequence physical file are explained below.

Field Name

A The letter **A** must be included in every statement. Entry of the DDS code via **SEU** will automatically supply this value.

File level (Line 0001.00):

Functions

The *File Level* keyword **UNIQUE** specifies that records with duplicate keys are not supported. During program execution, if an attempt is made to add a record with a key value already stored in the physical file, a run-time error will be flagged. If the keyword **UNIQUE** is omitted, records with duplicate key values will be supported. When a physical file that supports duplicate keys is processed, the common records will be processed in a first-in, first-out order. However, duplicate key records may be accessed in a last-in, first-out order by the *File Level* **LIFO** keyword.

Record level (Line 0002.00):

T Explained in Figure 2-2.

Name Explained in Figure 2-2.

Field level (Lines 000.3.00 to 0006.00):

Name Explained in Figure 2-2.

Key level (Line 0007.00):

T The letter **K** indicates ACTNUMBER entered in the *Name* field as a key field. More than one field may be specified, creating a *composite* key.

Name Fields selected as key fields must have been previously defined as *Field Level* entries in the record format. Any number of fields may be specified for the key field. The order of the fields determines how a composite key is built. The first key field specified stores its value in the high-order position of the composite key; the second key field, in the next position; and so forth. Because key fields are previously defined at the *Field Level,* their attributes must be omitted.

Figure 2-3 *Data Description Specification* syntax for a keyed sequence physical file.

Physical File Keywords

Only the **UNIQUE** keyword has been discussed for physical files. Thirty-six *File, Record, Field,* and *Key Level* keywords may be used in the definition of physical files. Figure 2-4 lists the keywords related to physical files and identifies their coding levels. For a comprehensive discussion of the function of each keyword, refer to IBM's *AS/400 DDS Reference* stored on CD-ROM or available in book form.

When included in the definition of a physical file, the keywords listed in Figure 2-4 must be entered in the *Function* field. Note that some of the keywords are only valid for

```
     ABSVAL            COMP        f FIFO        SIGNED
     ALIAS             DATFMT        FLTPCN   rf TEXT
   f ALTSEQ            DATSEP      r FORMAT      TIMFMT
     ALWNULL           DESCEND     f LIFO        TIMSEP
  ff CCSID             DFT         k NOALTSEQ  f UNIQUE
     CHECK           k DIGIT         RANGE     k UNSIGNED
     CHKMSGID          EDTCDE      f REF         VALUES
     CMP               EDTWRD        REFFLD      VARLEN
     COLHDG          f FCFO          REFSHIFT  k ZONE

  f = File Level, ff = File and Field Level, k = Key Field Level
  r = Record Level, rf = Record and Field Level,  = Field Level
```

Figure 2-4 Physical file keywords.

specified levels. Independent examples showing how some of the physical file keywords are used are illustrated and explained in Figure 2-5.

```
          .....A..........T.Name++++++RLen++TDpB......Functions++++++++++++++++++

0001.00        A                                  REF(MYERS/MASTERGL)
0002.00        A                                  LIFO
0003.00        A          R GLACTSR               TEXT('GL record format')
0004.00        A            ACTNUMBER      3      COLHDG('ACCOUNT NUMBER')
0005.00        A            ACTNAME       27
0006.00        A            LAST_UPDATL    8      DATSEP(' ')
0007.00        A            ACT_TYPE  R   20      REFFLD(ACCOUNTYPE FILE1)
0008.00        A            BALANCE        8S 2   EDTCDE(1)
0009.00        A          K ACTNUMBER             DESCEND
```

The processing results of the independent keyword examples are explained below:

Field Name

A The letter **A** must be included in every statement. Entry of the DDS code via **SEU** will automatically supply this value.

File Level keywords (Lines 0001.00 and 0002.00):

REF This *File Level* keyword has the following format:

REF([library-name/]database-file-name [record format-name])

Any entries included within [ ] are optional. However, the **database-file-name** entry must be included. When the library name is omitted, the user's library list will be searched for the referenced file. If the library in which the referenced file is stored is not in the user's library list, then the library entry must be specified. When a physical file is referenced, the **record format-name** entry is not required. However, if field attibutes are referenced from a logical, a display, or a printer file, which may have more than one record format, the **record format-name** entry may be needed.

The **REF(MYERS/MASTERGL)** entry example shown references the record and field attributes from the file **MASTERGL** stored in the **MYERS** library.

LIFO This *File Level* keyword specifies that the physical file will be processed within a common keyed group in a last-in, first-out order. This means that the last record added for the related key group will be processed first, and so forth.

COLHDG This *Field Level* keyword is used to define field labels that are referenced when the field is accessed in **SDA** (screen design aid), **DFU** (data file utility), query, or text management.

DATSEP This *Field Level* keyword specifies the separator character for a date field value. Valid separator characters are a slash (/), period (.), blank ( ), or comma (,). If this keyword is not specified, the default is the job attribute. Note that the letter **L** must be included in the *R* field for this keyword.

REFFLD This *Field Level* keyword accesses the attributes of a field defined outside the current physical file. The field name entered in the *Name* field is defined with the same attributes as the referenced field. The format of the keyword is

REFFLD([record-format-name/]referenced-field-name[{*SRC | [(library-name/]database-file-name}])

The example **REFFLD(ACCOUNTYPE FILE1)** accesses the attributes of the ACCOUNTYPE field from FILE1 which define the **ACT_TYPE** field. Because the library name was not included in the keyword format, the user's library list will be searched for FILE1. If the library in which FILE1

Figure 2-5 Examples of physical file keyword usage.

is stored is not found, a terminal error will be generated in the compilation of the physical file. Note that the letter **R** must be entered in the *R* field when the **REFFLD** keyword is specified.

EDTCDE This *Field Level* keyword uses the same edit codes as **RPG IV.** The letter **J** in the example **EDTCDE(J)** will edit the BALANCE field with high-order zero suppression, insertion of decimal, insertion of commas, and a negative sign after the low-order digit if the value is negative.

Note that the editing function will not be performed for physical file loading or maintenance functions. It is only operational for display and printer files and does not modify the physical file data.

Key Level (Line 0009.00):

DESCEND This *Key Level* keyword will process a *keyed sequence* physical file in descending key-value order instead of the default ascending order.

Figure 2-5 Examples of physical file keyword usage. (Continued)

ENTERING DDS PHYSICAL FILE CODE

The Programmer Menu

The Programmer Menu shown in Figure 2-6 provides a convenient method for accessing the utilities that control source code entry, compilation, program execution, debugging, and so forth. The numbers at the left side relate to selection criteria that perform the related function. For example, to enter DDS source code for physical files (**PF**), logical files (**LF**), display files (**DSPF**), printer files (**PRTF**), RPG programs (**RPGLE**), or Control Language Programs (**CLP**) by **SEU,** Option **8** must be selected and supplemented with the related prompt responses.

```
                          Programmer Menu
                                                        System:   AS400
Select one of the following:
     1. Start AS/400 Data File Utility
     2. Work with AS/400 Query
     3. Create an object from a source file    object name, type, pgm for CMD
     4. Call a program                         program name
     5. Run a command                          command
     6. Submit a job                           (job name), , ,(command)
     7. Go to a menu                           menu name
     8. Edit a source file member              (srcmbr), (type)
     9. Design display format using SDA        (srcmbr), ,(mode)
    90. Sign off                               (*nolist, *list)

Selection . . . . .  8              Parm . . . .  GLACTS
Type  . . . . . . .  PF             Parm 2 . . .  __________
Command . . . . . .  ________________________________________

Source file . . . .  _________      Source library . . . . . . .  *LIBL
Object library  . .  _________      Job description  . . . . . .  *USRPRF

F3=Exit        F4=Prompt                 F6=Display messages   F10=Command entry
F12=Cancel     F14=Work with submitted jobs                     F18=Work with output
```

The prompts to call **SEU** *(Source Entry Utility)* for DDS source code entry for a physical file are explained below:

Selection: **8** must be entered to call **SEU.**

Parm: A programmer-supplied physical file name (limited to 10 characters) must be entered for this prompt. GLACTS is entered for this example, which may be in upper or lower case.

Type: **PF** must be entered for a physical file that accesses the coding format for DDS source code entry in **SEU.**

Parm 2: Is not used to create a physical file. However, it is used for Selection **1** (DFU) and **2** (Query).

Figure 2-6 Programmer Menu filled in to call **SEU** for physical file code entry.

Command: Any control language command may be entered for this prompt. Execution is controlled by Selection **5** (Run a command). For example, in lieu of using Selection **3** and the Parm and Type prompts to compile a physical file, the **CRTPF** command could be entered and **F4** pressed to access a sequence of displays to define the attributes of the file. All of the defaults may be assumed or specific ones may be changed; for example, the default file size in records.

The defaults for the Source file, Source library, Object library, and Job description prompts are shown for this example. Any of these values may be changed as needed. For example, the default for the source file for physical files is **QDDSSRC;** however, if the programmer wanted to use a different source to create or access the source member, it could be entered in the Source file parameter.

The ENTER key must be pressed to display the **SEU DDS** format for the entry of the source code for a physical file.

Sign off from this menu is controlled by Selection **90.** The Parm, Type, and Parm 2 parameters must be blank to sign off.

Command-key options at the bottom of the menu provide control specific controls.

The Programmer Menu may be accessed from any AS/400 display that has a command line by **STRPGMMNU** and pressing the ENTER key.

Figure 2-6 Programmer Menu filled in to call **SEU** for physical file code entry. (Continued)

Entering the DDS Code for a Physical File with SEU

After prompts are completed to create a physical file format and the **ENTER** key is pressed, the **SEU** screen shown in Figure 2-7 will display.

```
 Columns . . . :    1  71            Edit                         SMYERS/QDDSSRC
 SEU==>                                                                   GLACTS
 FMT PF .....A..........T.Name++++++RLen++TDpB......Functions+++++++++++++++++
        *************** Beginning of data *************************************
'''''''
        ****************** End of data ****************************************
```

Figure 2-7 **SEU Edit** screen (format A) for DDS physical file code (format-line control).

Notice that the second line begins with the identifying format (FMT PF). The remainder of the line duplicates the fields on the DDS form. For example, the five dots after FMT PF represent the sequence number (columns 1–5) on the form; A in column 6 gives the form type, and so forth. Statements are entered horizontally by aligning the field entry with the column header. Pressing the **ENTER** key stores the instructions and moves the "******* End of data *******" logo down one line. Figure 2-8 illustrates the Edit screen after all of the example physical file statements have been entered.

```
 Columns . . . :    1  71            Edit                           STAN/QDDSSRC
 SEU==>                                                                   GLACTS
 FMT PF .....A..........T.Name++++++RLen++TDpB......Functions+++++++++++++++++
        *************** Beginning of data *************************************
0001.00      A                                           UNIQUE
0002.00      A          R GLACTSR
0003.00      A            ACTNUMBER      3
0004.00      A            ACTNAME       27
0005.00      A            ACT_TYPE      20
0006.00      A            BALANCE        8S 2
0007.00      A          K ACTNUMBER
        ****************** End of data ****************************************

 F3=Exit   F4=Prompt      F5=Refresh  F9=Retrieve   F10=Cursor
 F16=Repeat find          F17=Repeat change         F24=More keys
```

Figure 2-8 Filled-in **SEU Edit** screen with example PF code.

Another method that some programmers find more convenient is to use *prompt-line* control. Prompt-line entry is initiated by entering **P** on a statement line and pressing the **ENTER** key.

A prompt line (for the format type) with field headers will display at the bottom of the screen, as shown in Figure 2-9. Right-justification of number field entries is automatically supported when the **FIELD EXIT** key is pressed. After all the values for the statement are entered, the **ENTER** key is pressed, the statement is moved to its related location in the top section of the screen, and the prompt line is blanked out. This sequential

```
Columns . . . :    1  71            Edit                         STAN/QDDSSRC
SEU==>                                                                 GLACTS
FMT PF .....A..........T.Name++++++RLen++TDpB......Functions++++++++++++++++++
        *************** Beginning of data ************************************
0001.00       A                                         UNIQUE
0002.00       A              R GLACTSR
0003.00       A                ACTNUMBER       3A
'''''''
        ****************** End of data ****** ********************************

                                          When ENTER key is pressed,
                                          prompt-line values are moved
                                          to related line in listing and
                                          a new prompt line displays.

Prompt type . . .    PF       Sequence number . . .   '''''''

Name                                          Data      Decimal
Type        Name          Ref      Length     Type      Positions    Use
___       ACTNUMBER        _       ____3       A          ___         _
Functions
________________________________________

F3=Exit   F4=Prompt   F5=Refresh             F11=Previous record
F12=Cancel            F23=Select prompt      F24=More keys
```

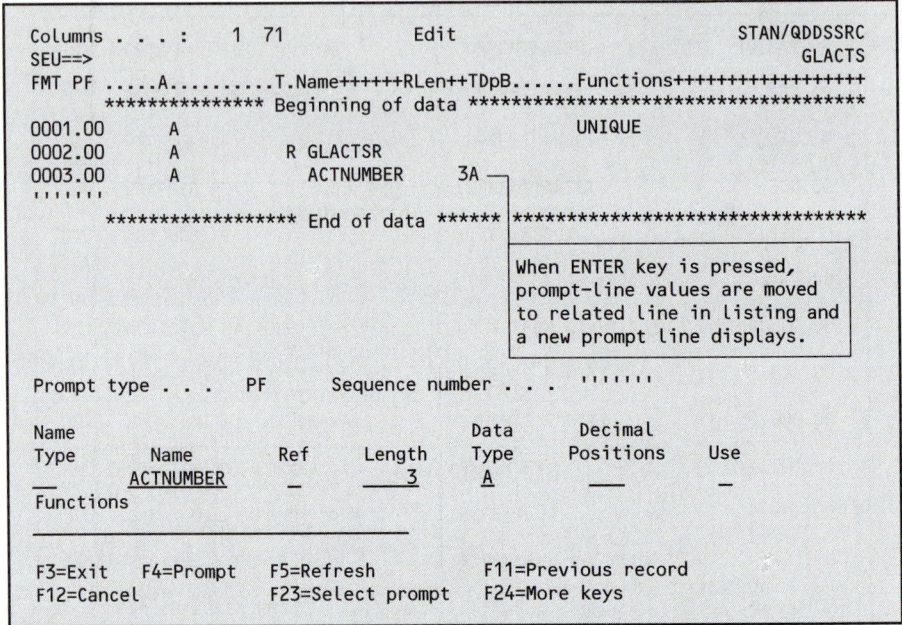

Figure 2-9 Filled-in **SEU** prompt-line format for DDS physical file code entry.

entry of the source code will continue at the programmer's option. With either method (line format or prompt), syntax errors will be displayed when the **ENTER** key is pressed. All corrections must be made before the statement is moved or stored.

The *insertion* of a line between existing lines is performed by placing the cursor above the line where the inserted line is to be entered, typing **IP** at the beginning of the statement, and pressing the **ENTER** key. After the prompt line is completed and the **ENTER** key is pressed, the new statement is inserted in the specified location. Line insertion using the line format method is executed by specifying the letter **I** at the beginning of the previous statement and pressing the **ENTER** key. A blank line will be displayed to enter the statement.

An instruction may be *moved* by entering **M** in the number area. The target position is identified by entering the letter **A** on the statement that will precede the moved instruction or the letter **B** on an instruction that will follow the moved statement. A group of instructions may be moved by entering **MM** in the number area of the first statement to be moved and **MM** on the last statement to be moved. Identical to a single instruction move, the target position is specified by an **A** or **B** entry in the number area.

Copying instructions to some other location in the source program is executed similarly to moving instructions, except that **C** or **CC** is used instead of **M** or **MM.**

A line may be *deleted* by typing the letter **D** at the beginning of a statement. Consecutive lines may be deleted from the listing by typing **DD** at the beginning of the first line and **DD** at the beginning of the last line of the group to be deleted.

After all the source code for the physical file is entered, **F3** is pressed to exit from the **SEU Edit** screen into an **SEU Exit** menu. The screen shown in Figure 2-10, which gives the programmer *exit options,* will be displayed.

```
                              Exit
Type choices, press Enter.

  Change/create member . . . . . . .  Y           Y=Yes, N=No
   Member . . . . . . . . . . . . .   GLACTS      Name, F4 for list
   File . . . . . . . . . . . . . .   QDDSSRC     Name, F4 for list
     Library . . . . . . . . . . .     STAN       Name
   Text . . . . . . . . . . . . . .   General Ledger Accounts


   Resequence member . . . . . . . . Y           Y=Yes, N=No
     Start . . . . . . . . . . . . . 0001.00     0000.01-9999.99
     Increment . . . . . . . . . . . 01.00       00.01-99.99

  Print member . . . . . . . . . . .  N           Y=Yes, N=No

  Return to editing . . . . . . . . . N           Y=Yes, N=No

  Go to member list . . . . . . . . . N           Y=Yes, N=No


F3=Exit   F4=Prompt   F5=Refresh   F12=Cancel
```

1. The Exit screen is displayed if **F3** is pressed when in **SEU.**
2. The variables shown in the Exit menu are the defaults. Member, File, and Library names are accessed by the entries on the Programmer Menu or through PDM (Programmer Development Method). A text entry provides documentation.
3. The source member currently entered (PF, LF, RPG, DSPF, PRTF, or CLP) is saved by the **Y** default for Change/create member. If an existing member is accessed by **SEU** and not changed, the default here will be an **N** (No).
4. The statements in the source file will automatically be sequenced unless the default **Y** is overridden with an **N** at the **Resequence member** prompt. Sequencing and statement incrementation may be modified by changing the Start and Increment prompts.
5. The **N** (No) default for Print member suppresses the printing of a source listing (before compilation). If a source listing is required, **Y** (Yes) must be entered for this prompt.
6. The **N** (No) default for Return to editing prevents return to **SEU** and the source file currently entered. **Y** (Yes) must be entered to return **SEU** back to the source listing.
7. The **N** (No) default for Go to member list will not display the names of any members in the current library. **Y** (Yes) must be entered to display a member list.

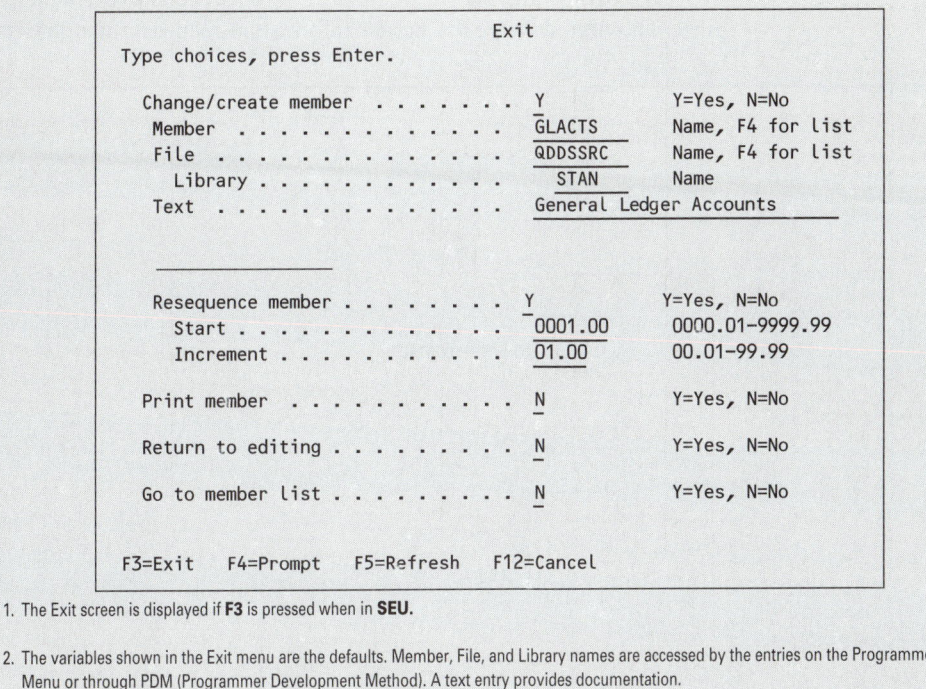

Figure 2-10 SEU Exit screen.

See Appendix A for a comprehensive discussion of the features and controls of **SEU.**

When the **ENTER** key is pressed, the member is saved and control is returned to the Programmer Menu. At this step of database development, the physical file source member is usually compiled. Again, this is a different procedure from that of the traditional computer system in which record formats are not compiled but are either hard-coded in the source program or included as a source code **COPY** member. With either method, the object will include the record format.

In the AS/400 environment, the physical file format is stored separately as a source member and the object is mutually exclusive from any high-level language program. The physical file's record format is called in during program compilation and becomes an integral part of the object.

Physical File Format Compilation

When control returns to the Programmer Menu, all the original prompt entries are retained unless changed on the **SEU Exit** menu. The physical file is compiled by entering a **3** in response to the Option prompt (Create object) and pressing the **ENTER** key.

The two listings shown in Figure 2-11 are generated when the physical file is compiled. The first includes the header information related to the physical file and lists the

```
5763SS1 V3R1M0  940909                Data Description              STAN/GLACTS              11/19/97 21:00:04        Page    1
File name . . . . . . . . . . . . . . . . . . . . . :  GLACTS
  Library name  . . . . . . . . . . . . . . . . . . :  STAN
File attribute  . . . . . . . . . . . . . . . . . . :  Physical
Source file containing DDS  . . . . . . . . . . . . :  QDDSSRC
  Library name  . . . . . . . . . . . . . . . . . . :  STAN
Source member containing DDS  . . . . . . . . . . . :  GLACTS
Source member last changed  . . . . . . . . . . . . :  11/19/97  20:59:42
Source listing options  . . . . . . . . . . . . . . :  *SOURCE     *LIST       *NOSECLVL
DDS generation severity level . . . . . . . . . . . :  20
DDS flagging severity level . . . . . . . . . . . . :  00
File type . . . . . . . . . . . . . . . . . . . . . :  *DATA
Authority . . . . . . . . . . . . . . . . . . . . . :  *LIBCRTAUT
Replace file  . . . . . . . . . . . . . . . . . . . :  *NO
Text  . . . . . . . . . . . . . . . . . . . . . . . :  Figure 2-2 - PF (nonkeyed)
Compiler  . . . . . . . . . . . . . . . . . . . . . :  IBM AS/400 Data Description Processor
                                Data Description Source
SEQNBR  *...+....1....+....2....+....3....+....4....+....5....+....6....+....7....+....8  Date
   100        A          R GLACTSR                                                    11/19/97
   200        A            ACTNUMBER     3                                            11/19/97
   300        A            ACTNAME      25                                            11/19/97
   400        A            ACT_TYPE     20                                            11/19/97
   500        A            BALANCE       8S 2                                         11/19/99
                         * * * * *   E N D   O F   S O U R C E   * * * * *
5763SS1 V3R1M0  940909                Data Description              STAN/GLACTS              11/19/97 21:00:04        Page    2
                                      Expanded Source
                                                                                     Field       Buffer position
SEQNBR  *...+....1....+....2....+....3....+....4....+....5....+....6....+....7....+....8 Length       Out      In
   100                   R GLACTSR
   200                     ACTNUMBER     3A  B      COLHDG('ACTNUMBER')               3            1        1
   300                     ACTNAME      25A  B      COLHDG('ACTNAME')                25            4        4
   400                     ACT_TYPE     20A  B      COLHDG('ACT_TYPE')               20           29       29
   500                     BALANCE       8S 2B      COLHDG('BALANCE')                 8           49       49
                 * * * * *   E N D   O F   E X P A N D E D   S O U R C E   * * * * *
5763SS1 V3R1M0  940909                Data Description              STAN/GLACTS              11/19/97 21:00:04        Page    3
                                      Message Summary
    Total         Informational       Warning        Error         Severe
                     (0-9)            (10-19)       (20-29)       (30-99)
        0              0                 0             0              0
* CPC7301        00           Message . . . . :    File GLACTS created in library STAN.
                         * * * * *   E N D   O F   C O M P I L A T I O N   * * * * *
```

Figure 2-11 Listings generated from compilation of the physical file's (GLACTS) DDS source.

source member format exactly as created. A second listing, which is printed immediately after the first, is called an *Expanded Source*. It supplements the original source with the **COLHDG** keywords for each field and identifies field lengths and the beginning position of each field in the output buffer. During program execution, *input* and *output buffers* are automatically built for all physical files processed. It is important to note that after the physical file is loaded, subsequent compilation will delete all the data in the file.

Below the Expanded Source Listing is the *Message Summary,* which identifies any *Informational, Warning, Error,* or *Severe Level* errors. *Informational* or *Warning Level* errors will not prevent successful compilation of the physical file, but *Error* and *Severe Level* errors will. After a programmer exits **SEU,** a message will be displayed at the bottom of the Programmer Menu indicating whether the object was created or an *Error* or *Severe Level* error was found.

Building a Physical File without Record or Field Definitions

A physical file may be defined without record and field descriptions by the **CRTPF** (create physical file) command. This control language statement may be entered from the Programmer Menu by specifying **5** as the option and **CRTPF** on the command line. After **F4** is pressed, the prompt screens shown in Figure 2-12 will display. Most of the prompts shown in the three screens in Figure 2-12 have default values specified. However, the programmer may change any entry as needed. For a complete explanation of each prompt line, the related *IBM AS/400 Control Language Reference* manual should be referenced.

When a physical file is built without a DDS code, two parameters to which the user must respond are the physical file name (**File**) entry on line 1 of the first screen and the *Record length* entry on line 6 of the same screen. Defaults may be taken for the remaining prompts in the other displays.

```
                    Create Physical File (CRTPF)

Type choices, press Enter.
File . . . . . . . . . . . . . .                   Name
  Library  . . . . . . . . . . .   *CURLIB         Name, *CURLIB
Source file  . . . . . . . . . .  QDDSSRC          Name
  Library  . . . . . . . . . . .    *LIBL          Name, *LIBL, *CURLIB
Source member  . . . . . . . . .  *FILE            Name, *FILE
Record length, if no DDS . . . .                   Number
Generation severity level  . . .  20               0-30
Flagging severity level  . . . .  0                0-30
File type  . . . . . . . . . . .  *DATA            *DATA, *SRC
Member, if desired . . . . . . .  *FILE            Name, *FILE, *NONE
User specified DBCS data . . . .  *NO              *NO, *YES
Text 'description' . . . . . . .  *SRCMBRTXT

                                                                More...
F9=All parameters   F11=Keywords   F14=Command string   F24=More keys
```

Roll to access next display

```
                    Create Physical File (CRTPF)

Type choices, press Enter.

                      Additional Parameters
Source listing options . . . . .                   *SRC, *NOSRC, *SOURCE...
               + for more values
System . . . . . . . . . . . . .  *LCL             *LCL, *RMT, *FILETYPE
Expiration date for member . . .  *NONE            Date, *NONE
Maximum members  . . . . . . . .  1                Number, *NOMAX
Access path maintenance  . . . .  *IMMED           *IMMED, *DLY, *REBLD
Access path recovery . . . . . .                   *NO, *AFTIPL, *IPL
Force keyed access path  . . . .  *NO              *NO, *YES
Member size:
  Initial number of records  . .  10000            1-2147483646, *NOMAX
  Increment number of records  .  1000             Number
  Maximum increments . . . . . .  3                Number
Allocate storage . . . . . . . .  *NO              *NO, *YES

                                                                More...
F9=All parameters   F11=Keywords   F14=Command string   F24=More keys
Parameter FILE required.
```

Roll to access text display

```
                      Create Physical File (CRTPF)

Type choices, press Enter.
Contiguous storage . . . . . . .  *NO              *NO, *YES
Preferred storage unit . . . . .  *ANY             1-255, *ANY
Records to force a write . . . .  *NONE            Number, *NONE
Maximum file wait time . . . . .  *IMMED           Seconds, *IMMED, *CLS
Maximum record wait time . . . .  60               Seconds, *NOMAX, *IMMED
Share open data path . . . . . .  *NO              *NO, *YES
Max % deleted records allowed  .  *NONE            1-100, *NONE
Reuse deleted records  . . . . .  *NO              *YES, *NO
Sort sequence  . . . . . . . . .  *SRC             Name, *SRC, *JOB...
  Library  . . . . . . . . . . .                   Name, *LIBL, *CURLIB
Language ID  . . . . . . . . . .  *JOB             Character value, *JOB
Coded character set ID . . . . .  *JOB             *JOB, *HEX...
Allow update operation . . . . .  *YES             *YES, *NO
Allow delete operation . . . . .  *YES             *YES, *NO
Record format level check  . . .  *YES             *YES, *NO
Authority  . . . . . . . . . . .  *LIBCRTAUT       Name, *LIBCRTAUT, *ALL...

                                                                 Bottom
F9=All parameters   F11=Keywords   F14=Command string   F24=More keys
```

Figure 2-12 CRTPF command-generated screens to create a physical file.

Note that the **CRTPF** command functions are automatically executed when the previously discussed method of building a DDS file and then creating an object member for it by selecting Option **3** on the Programmer Menu is followed. Unless some of the defaults on the parameter screens have to be changed, the create physical file **(CRTPF)** functions are transparent to the programmer.

Displaying the Attributes of a Physical File

The attributes of a physical file may be displayed by the **DSPFD** *(Display File Description)* command. Screens related to this command are accessed by entering a **5** in the Option field, typing **DSPFD** and the **file name** on the command line of the Programmer Menu or from the command line of any AS/400 display, and pressing **F4.** If the file name is omitted, a prompt screen will display in which the file name and library must be entered. Under most circumstances, the default is assumed for the library name. The user must press **ENTER** if the prompt screen is displayed first to access the first of the five displays shown in Figure 2-13. After the first screen (Page 1) is displayed, rolling

```
5763SS1 V3R1M0  940909              Display File Description                              10/02/97  22:05:15        Page    1
  File  . . . . . . . . . . . : GLACTS
    Library . . . . . . . . . : *LIBL
  Type of information . . . . : *ALL
  File attributes . . . . . . : *ALL
  System  . . . . . . . . . . : *LCL
  Processor . . . . . . . . . : IBM AS/400 Display File Description Processor

File . : GLACTS       Library . : STAN         Type of file . : Physical *DATA          Auxiliary Storage Pool ID . : 01

                                  Data Base File Attributes

  Externally described file . . . . . . . . . :                 Yes
  File level identifier . . . . . . . . . . . :                 0960213213229
  Creation date . . . . . . . . . . . . . . . :                 10/13/97
  Text 'description'  . . . . . . . . . . . . : TEXT            Figure 2-2 - PF (nonkeyed)
  DBCS capable  . . . . . . . . . . . . . . . :                 No
  Maximum members . . . . . . . . . . . . . . : MAXMBRS             1
  Number of constraints . . . . . . . . . . . :                     0
  Number of triggers  . . . . . . . . . . . . :                     0
  Number of members . . . . . . . . . . . . . :                     1
  Member size                                   SIZE
    Initial number of records . . . . . . . . :                 10000
    Increment number of records . . . . . . . :                  1000
    Maximum number of increments  . . . . . . :                     3
  Record capacity . . . . . . . . . . . . . . :                 13000
  Allocate storage  . . . . . . . . . . . . . : ALLOCATE        *NO
  Contiguous storage  . . . . . . . . . . . . : CONTIG          *NO
  Preferred storage unit  . . . . . . . . . . : UNIT            *ANY
  Records to force a write  . . . . . . . . . : FRCRATIO        *NONE
  Maximum file wait time  . . . . . . . . . . : WAITFILE        *IMMED
  Maximum record wait time  . . . . . . . . . : WAITRCD            60
  Max % deleted records allowed . . . . . . . : DLTPCT          *NONE
  Reuse deleted records . . . . . . . . . . . : REUSEDLT        *NO
  Coded character set identifier  . . . . . . : CCSID              37
  Allow read operation  . . . . . . . . . . . :                 Yes
  Allow write operation . . . . . . . . . . . :                 Yes
  Allow update operation  . . . . . . . . . . : ALWUPD          *YES
  Allow delete operation  . . . . . . . . . . : ALWDLT          *YES
  Record format level check . . . . . . . . . : LVLCHK          *YES
  Access path . . . . . . . . . . . . . . . . :                 Arrival
  Maximum record length . . . . . . . . . . . :                    58
  File is currently journaled . . . . . . . . :                 No
--------------------------------------------------------------------------------------------------------------------------
5763SS1 V3R1M0  940909              Display File Description                              10/02/97  22:05:15        Page    2
File . : GLACTS       Library . : STAN         Type of file . : Physical *DATA          Auxiliary Storage Pool ID . : 01
                                  Access Path Description
  Access path . . . . . . . . . . . . . . . . :                 Arrival
  Sort Sequence . . . . . . . . . . . . . . . : SRTSEQ          *HEX
  Language identifier . . . . . . . . . . . . : LANGID          ENU
--------------------------------------------------------------------------------------------------------------------------
5763SS1 V3R1M0  940909              Display File Description                              10/02/97  22:05:15        Page    3
File . : GLACTS       Library . : STAN         Type of file . : Physical *DATA          Auxiliary Storage Pool ID . : 01
                                  Member Description
```

Figure 2-13 DSPFD *(Display File Description)* displays.

```
  Member . . . . . . . . . . . . . . . . . . . . . : MBR         GLACTS
    Member level identifier . . . . . . . . . . :             0960213213232
    Member creation date  . . . . . . . . . . . :             10/13/97
    Text 'description'  . . . . . . . . . . . . : TEXT        Figure 2-2 - PF (nonkeyed)
    Expiration date for member  . . . . . . . . : EXPDATE     *NONE
    Member size                                   SIZE
      Initial number of records . . . . . . . . :                  10000
      Increment number of records . . . . . . . :              1000
      Maximum number of increments  . . . . . . :                 3
    Current number of increments  . . . . . . . :                      0
    Record capacity . . . . . . . . . . . . . . :                  13000
    Current number of records . . . . . . . . . :                     14
    Number of deleted records . . . . . . . . . :                      0
    Allocate storage  . . . . . . . . . . . . . : ALLOCATE    *NO
    Contiguous storage  . . . . . . . . . . . . : CONTIG      *NO
    Preferred storage unit  . . . . . . . . . . : UNIT        *ANY
    Records to force a write  . . . . . . . . . : FRCRATIO    *NONE
    Share open data path  . . . . . . . . . . . : SHARE       *NO
    Max % deleted records allowed . . . . . . . : DLTPCT      *NONE
    Data space size in bytes  . . . . . . . . . :                     3584
    Implicit access path sharing  . . . . . . . :             No
    Last change date/time . . . . . . . . . . . :             10/13/97  21:41:24
    Last save date/time . . . . . . . . . . . . :             10/17/97  15:26:19
    Last restore date/time  . . . . . . . . . . :
    Date last used  . . . . . . . . . . . . . . :             10/13/97
    Days used count . . . . . . . . . . . . . . :                1
    Date use count reset  . . . . . . . . . . . :
-------------------------------------------------------------------------------------------------------
5763SS1 V3R1M0  940909             Display File Description                   10/02/97  22:05:15     Page    4
File . : GLACTS        Library . : STAN       Type of file . : Physical *DATA      Auxiliary Storage Pool ID . : 01
                                          Record Format List
                     Record  Format Level
Format       Fields  Length  Identifier
GLACTSR          4      58   3C5057B621AD4
   Text . . . :
   Total number of formats  . . . . . . . . . :            1
   Total number of fields . . . . . . . . . . :            4
   Total record length  . . . . . . . . . . . :           58
-------------------------------------------------------------------------------------------------------
5763SS1 V3R1M0  940909             Display File Description                   10/02/97  22:05:15     Page    5
File . : GLACTS        Library . : STAN       Type of file . : Physical *DATA      Auxiliary Storage Pool ID . : 01
                                           Member List
                         Source Creation    Last Change              Deleted
 Member            Size    Type  Date       Date       Time      Records   Records     Text
 GLACTS            3584          02/13/97 02/13/97 21:41:24          14          0 Figure 2-2 - PF (nonkeyed)
   Total number of members  . . . . . . . . . :            1
   Total number of members not available  . . :            0
   Total records  . . . . . . . . . . . . . . :           14
   Total deleted records  . . . . . . . . . . :            0
   Total of member sizes  . . . . . . . . . . :         3584
```

Figure 2-13 DSPFD *(Display File Description)* displays. (Continued)

up will display the other four pages sequentially. Note that each page provides different information about the physical file:

Page 1: *Data Base File Attributes*—Identifies the current attributes of the physical file. This listing is similar to the displays generated by the **CRTPF** command used to change any default attributes when the file was created.

Page 2: *Access Path Description*—Specifies how the data in the physical file will be processed. "Arrival" indicates that the data will be processed in the order it is stored in the file. "Keyed" indicates that the data will be processed in a key-value order.

Page 3: *Member Description*—Provides information about the physical file **members. Members** are discussed in detail later in this chapter.

Page 4: *Record Format List*—Identifies the total number of record formats in the file (physical files may have only one), the total number of fields in the record format, and the total record length in bytes.

Page 5: *Member List*—Specifies the total number of members that the physical file supports, the total number of records stored in the file, the total number of logically deleted records, and the total number of member sizes.

A detailed explanation of each function may be found in the related *IBM AS/400 Control Language Reference* manual.

Displaying the Field Attributes of a Physical File

The record and field attributes of a physical file may be displayed by using the **DSPFFD** *(Display File Field Description)* command. The command may be executed by entering a **5** in the Option field, typing **DSPFFD** and the **file name** on the command line of the Programmer Menu or from the command line on any AS/400 display, and pressing **F4.** If the file name is omitted, a prompt screen will display where the library and file names must be entered. Usually the default is assumed for the library name. If the prompt screen is displayed first, press the **ENTER** key to access the **DSPFFD** display shown in Figure 2-14. Note that general information for Input parameters, File Information, and Record Format Information, with detailed *Field Level* information related to the fields in the physical file, is included.

```
5763SS1 V3R1M0  940909       Display File Field Description

Input parameters
 File . . . . . . . . . . . . . . . . . . :  GLACTS
   Library . . . . . . . . . . . . . . . . :  *LIBL

File Information
  File . . . . . . . . . . . . . . . . . . :  GLACTS
    Library. . . . . . . . . . . . . . . . :  STAN
  File location  . . . . . . . . . . . . . :  *LCL
  Externally described . . . . . . . . . . :  Yes
  Number of record formats . . . . . . . . :     1
  Type of file . . . . . . . . . . . . . . :  Physical
  File creation date . . . . . . . . . . . :  10/13/97
  Text 'description' . . . . . . . . . . . :  Figure 2-2 - PF (nonkeyed)

Record Format Information
  Record format  . . . . . . . . . . . . . :  GLACTSR
  Format level identifier  . . . . . . . . :  3C5057B621AD4
  Number of fields . . . . . . . . . . . . :     4
  Record length  . . . . . . . . . . . . . :    58

Field Level Information

             Data        Field  Buffer    Buffer         Field    Column
 Field       Type       Length  Length  Position         Usage    Heading
 ACTNUMBER   CHAR            3       3         1         Both     ACTNUMBER
   Coded Character Set Identifier  . . . . . :    37
 ACTNAME     CHAR           27      27         4         Both     ACTNAME
   Coded Character Set Identifier  . . . . . :    37
 ACT_TYPE    CHAR           20      20        31         Both     ACT_TYPE
   Coded Character Set Identifier  . . . . . :    37
 BALANCE     ZONED         8 2       8        51         Both     BALANCE
```

Figure 2-14 DSPFFD *(Display File Field Description)* screen.

PHYSICAL FILE MAINTENANCE COMMANDS

Some of the common Control Language commands used to maintain physical files are detailed in the following list.

CHGPF *(Change Physical File)*—Supports changes in the attributes of a physical file without requiring its recreation with the **CRTPF** command. The data in the physical file is *not* lost when **CHGPF** is executed.

CLRPFM *(Clear Physical File)*—Clears a physical file member of all data records without deleting the file's structure.

CPYF *(Copy File)*—Copies the data stored in a physical file to an output device or another physical file. Either all of the records or only selected records may be copied. A variety of selection criteria may be specified, such as a key or a relative record number range. When output is to a printer, either character or hexadecimal format may be specified. For readability, however, hexadecimal format is necessary if **packed numeric** values are stored in one or more fields of the record format.

DLTF *(Delete File)*—Deletes the physical file's object and any data stored in the file. A physical file cannot be deleted if a logical file has been created over it or if the file is in use.

DSPPFM *(Display Physical File Member)*—Displays the field values in the records stored in a physical file. Records are displayed in arrival sequence even if the file was created as keyed. A character or hexadecimal display of the record values may be specified. Other than printing the current display with the **Print** key, printer output is not supported.

RMVM *(Remove Member)*—Removes the specified member from the physical file and deletes all of the data stored in the member.

Any of these **CL** commands may be executed by entering the command on the command line of an AS/400 display and pressing **F4.** One or more prompt screens will display, enabling the programmer to enter command-specific data.

PHYSICAL FILE MEMBERS

Unless changed by the *Maximum number of members* option in the **CRTPF** command, a physical file will automatically be created with *one* member in which data may be stored. The physical file's name will be assigned to this member unless otherwise specified in the **CRTPF** command. A file may be initially created with no members and still include a record definition (fields and their attributes). However, if members are to be supported later, the **CHGPF** command must be executed and the **MAXMBRS** parameter changed to the required number of members. Members may be added to a physical file without destroying the data in the existing members.

When a physical file includes more than the default member, additional members are subsets of the data in the file. Each member, which must have a unique name, is automatically assigned a structure identical to the related physical file's DDS format.

Figure 2-15 illustrates the member concept. In the example shown, a separate member is created for each of the five days of a work week. When the physical file was created with the **CRTPF** command, the *Maximum number of members* **(MAXMBRS)** parameter must be assigned **5,** and DAY1 must be assigned for the member name *(MBR)* parameter. When the file is processed, DAY1 will always be considered the default member. To process the five members in any combination, a Control Language program must be written. If the physical file name were specified in an RPG IV program without a supporting **CL** program, only the data in the first member, DAY1, would be accessed.

Maintenance Commands for Physical File Members

The following functions may be performed for physical file members:

1. Members may be added to an existing physical file.
2. Any existing member may be renamed.
3. Any member may be removed from the physical file.
4. Some attributes of an existing member may be changed.

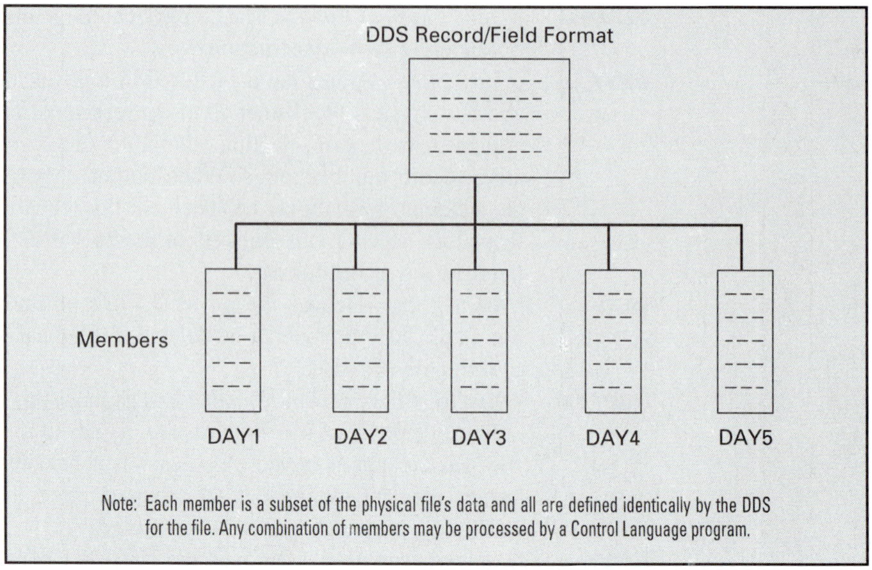

Figure 2-15 Example of a physical file member structure.

The commands to perform these maintenance functions are explained in the following paragraphs.

ADDPFM *(Add Physical File Member)*—Controls the addition of a member to the physical file after it is created.

RNMM *(Rename Member)*—Changes the name of an existing member. The name of the physical file is not changed.

RMVM *(Remove Member)*—Removes the named member and its data. The system cannot reference a removed member.

CHGPFM *(Change Physical File Member)*—Supports limited changes to a member, which include only the **EXPDATE** (the member's expiration date), **SHARE** (whether the member can be shared), and **TEXT** (text description) parameters. If extensive changes are needed, such as an increase in the maximum file size, the **CHGPF** command will change the selected attribute(s) for every member supported by the physical file.

Data File Terminology

The terms associated with the elements of a data file are *file, record, field, byte,* and *bit.* Figure 2-16 identifies the hierarchy and relationship of these items to each other. When a physical file is read, one record at a time is transferred from the storage device into an input butter area in memory. Then the field values in the record are available for processing.

Loading Data to a Physical File

After a physical file has been created and successfully compiled, a shell exists with no data records stored. Data may be written (added) to the physical file by any of the following methods:

1. **DFU** *(Data File Utility)*—Procedures to use this utility are explained in Appendix C.

2. Output from batch or interactive **RPG IV** programs.
3. Output of a **Sort** controlled by a **CL** program.
4. Output from a tape-stored file.
5. Output from the execution of the **CPYF** *(Copy File)* utility.
6. Output from a **Query** program.
7. A vendor-supplied database utility package such as **DBU.**

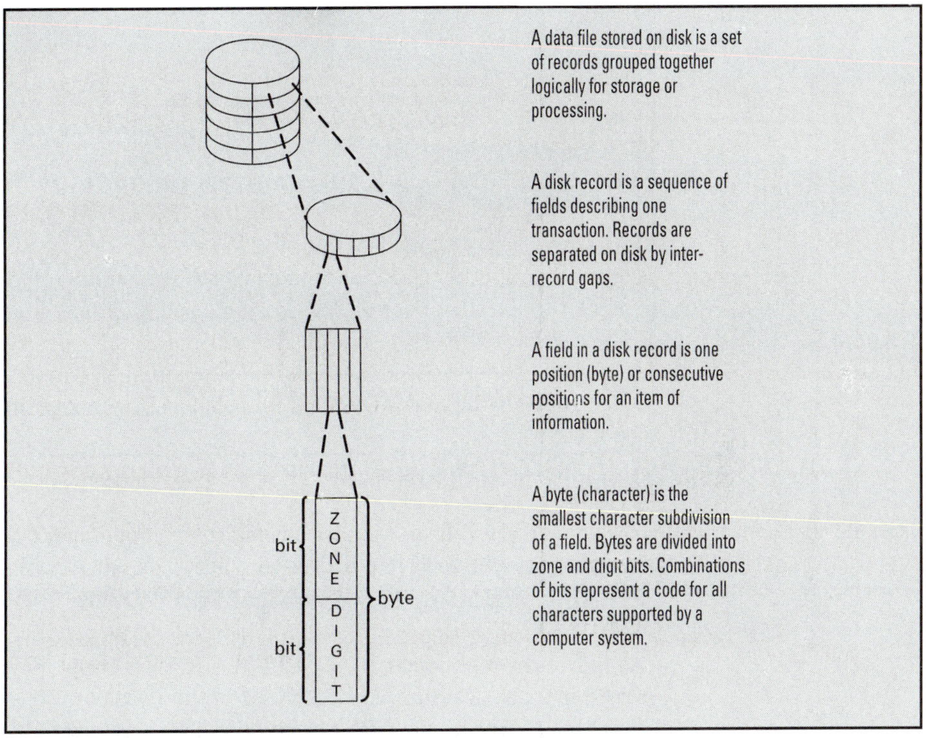

A data file stored on disk is a set of records grouped together logically for storage or processing.
A disk record is a sequence of fields describing one transaction. Records are separated on disk by inter-record gaps.
A field in a disk record is one position (byte) or consecutive positions for an item of information.
A byte (character) is the smallest character subdivision of a field. Bytes are divided into zone and digit bits. Combinations of bits represent a code for all characters supported by a computer system.
bit
bit
ZONE
DIGIT
byte

Figure 2-16 Data file terminology.

The maximum number of records that may be stored in a physical file is 2,147,485,646; the maximum number of fields in the one-record format, 8,000; and the maximum number of bytes in the record, 32,766.

Until Display Files are introduced in Chapter 14, any physical files that this text's reader creates will have to be loaded with data using the *Data File Utility* **(DFU).**

Data Entry Considerations

In the AS/400 environment, data is initially entered through a workstation under the control of a utility (for example, **DFU**) or an interactive **RPG IV** program. Regardless of the entry method, several important concepts must be understood. First, *alphabetic* and *alphanumeric* data are usually stored left-justified in their related field. Consequently, the first character of the data value is entered in the first position of the assigned field area.

Numeric data must be *right-justified* in the assigned field. Hence, the data must be entered so that the *low-order* digit of the value is stored in the low-order position of the field. When the value is stored, any unused *high-order* bytes are automatically padded with leading zeros.

Figure 2-17 illustrates the rules related to entering alphanumeric, alphabetic, and numeric data values. **RPG IV** does not distinguish between alphanumeric and alphabetic values. Any field not defined as numeric is processed as alphanumeric **(character).**

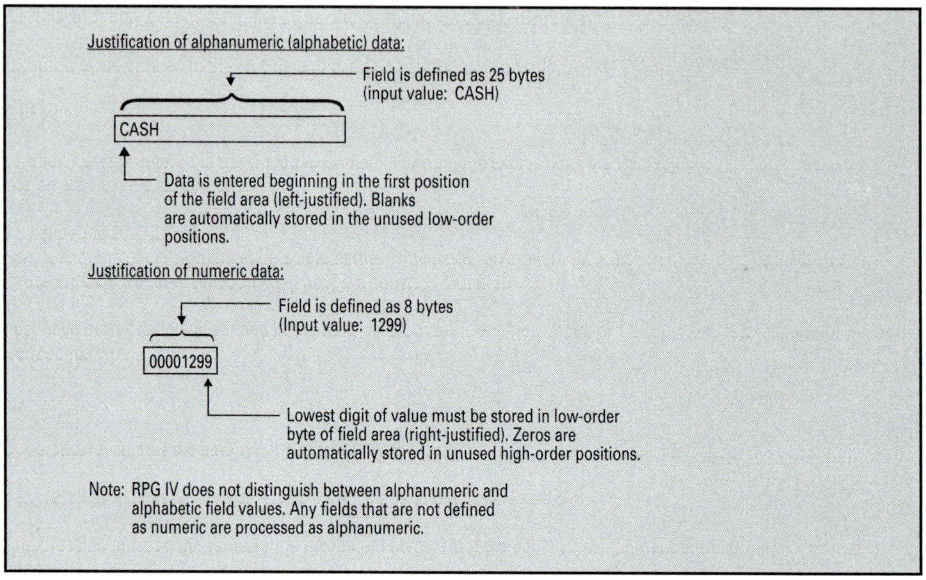

Figure 2-17 Justification rules for entering alphanumeric, alphabetic, and numeric data.

Printing a Listing of a Physical File's Data

As previously mentioned, the **DSPPFM** or **CPYF** utility may be used to review the data stored in a physical file. The **DSPFFM** utility does not support printing (except with the **Print** key), whereas the **CPYF** utility does. To access the **CPYF** utility, the programmer must enter the command **CPYF** on a command line of a display and then press **F4.** The display shown in Figure 2-18 will appear.

Options are included in the **CPYF** utility to access one or more records by their key value(s) or relative position in the file. Usually, not all of the records in the physical file will be accessed by this utility.

When output is directed to a printer (***PRINT** selected), a partial listing in ***HEX** (hexidecimal) format and one in ***CHAR** (character) format are generated by the **CPYF** command, as shown in Figure 2-19. Note that if the BALANCE field value was stored in *packed decimal* instead of *signed,* the ***CHAR** format would print unreadable characters for that field.

Field Reference Files

A *Field Reference File* is a physical file that is referenced by other externally described physical, logical, display, or printer files for names and attributes of fields. They are created and compiled exactly like other physical files but contain no data. To reduce *redundancy* (the same fields defined in multiple physical files with sometimes different attributes), all of the fields for a user's application should ideally be defined in a *Field Reference File.* Then all of the **RPG IV** programs written for the application will reference the same field names and related attributes.

```
                         Copy File (CPYF)

Type choices, press Enter.

From file . . . . . . . . . . .  GLACTS       Name
  Library . . . . . . . . . . .    SMYERS     Name, *LIBL, *CURLIB
To file . . . . . . . . . . . .  *PRINT       Name, *PRINT
  Library . . . . . . . . . . .    *LIBL      Name, *LIBL, *CURLIB
From member . . . . . . . . . .  *FIRST       Name, generic*, *FIRST, *ALL
To member or label . . . . . . . *FIRST       Name, *FIRST, *FROMMBR
Replace or add records . . . . . *NONE        *NONE, *ADD, *REPLACE
Create file . . . . . . . . . .  *NO          *NO, *YES
Print format . . . . . . . . . . *HEX         *CHAR, *HEX

                                                                  Bottom
F3=Exit   F4=Prompt   F5=Refresh   F10=Additional parameters   F12=Cancel
F13=How to use this display        F24=More keys
```

From file

Name of the physical file accessed must be entered for this prompt. The name of a logical, diskette, tape, inline, or **DDM** file may also be entered for this prompt.

Library

The library name in which the physical file is stored must be entered. If the default ***LIBL** is assumed, the user's library list will be searched for the physical file. The ***CURLIB** prompt will access the currently active library.

To file

Output may be directed either to another physical file, printer, diskette, tape, or **DDM** file by specifying the name of the file or to the printer by selecting the ***PRINT** option.

Library

When a disk file is specified for the *To file* prompt, the library name in which it is stored may be entered or the default ***LIBL** may be assumed.

From member

The default ***FIRST** specifies that the first member of the related physical file will be accessed. If the data in a specific member is to be accessed, the name of that member must be entered. If the data from all of the members supported by the physical file are to be accessed, ***ALL** must be entered for this prompt. This prompt is ignored when output is directed to a printer **(*PRINT).**

To member or label

The default ***FIRST** specifies that output is to be directed to the first member of the physical file entered for the *To file* prompt. A specific member may be specified by entering its name for this prompt. This prompt is ignored when output is direct to a printer **(*PRINT).**

Replace or add records

The default ***NONE** indicates that no records are stored in the *To file* item. The ***ADD** prompt supports the addition of records to the *To file* item. ***REPLACE** will replace records stored in the *To file* with those from the *From file.*

Create file

The default ***NO** indicates that a *To file* will not be created. A file may be created by entering ***YES** for this prompt.

Print format

In order to interpret packed numeric field values, ***HEX** is required for printed output. If packed fields are not stored in the physical file's records, ***CHAR** may be specified.

Figure 2-18 *Copy File* **(CPYF)** display.

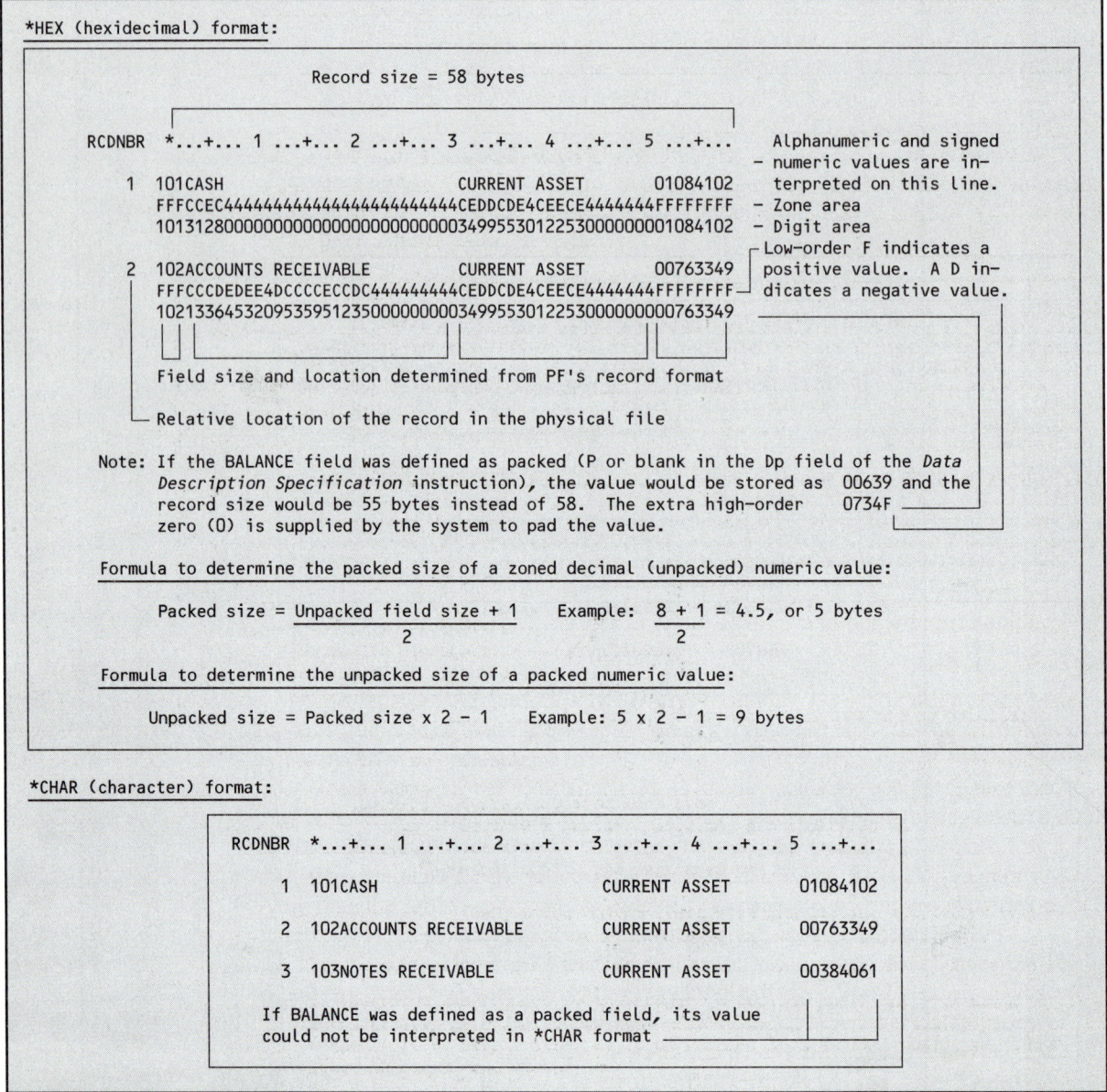

```
*HEX (hexidecimal) format:

                        Record size = 58 bytes

RCDNBR  *...+... 1 ...+... 2 ...+... 3 ...+... 4 ...+... 5 ...+...   Alphanumeric and signed
                                                                   - numeric values are in-
     1  101CASH                       CURRENT ASSET       01084102   terpreted on this line.
        FFFCCEC44444444444444444444444CEDDCDE4CEECE4444444FFFFFFFF - Zone area
        1013128000000000000000000000003499553012253000000001084102 - Digit area
                                                                   Low-order F indicates a
     2  102ACCOUNTS RECEIVABLE        CURRENT ASSET       00763349   positive value.  A D in-
        FFFCCCDEDEE4DCCCCECCDC44444444CEDDCDE4CEECE4444444FFFFFFFF   dicates a negative value.
        1021336453209535951235000000003499553012253000000000763349

        Field size and location determined from PF's record format

        Relative location of the record in the physical file

Note: If the BALANCE field was defined as packed (P or blank in the Dp field of the Data
      Description Specification instruction), the value would be stored as  00639 and the
      record size would be 55 bytes instead of 58.  The extra high-order     0734F
      zero (0) is supplied by the system to pad the value.

Formula to determine the packed size of a zoned decimal (unpacked) numeric value:

      Packed size = Unpacked field size + 1      Example:  8 + 1 = 4.5, or 5 bytes
                    -----------------------                -----
                               2                             2

Formula to determine the unpacked size of a packed numeric value:

      Unpacked size = Packed size x 2 - 1      Example: 5 x 2 - 1 = 9 bytes

*CHAR (character) format:

RCDNBR  *...+... 1 ...+... 2 ...+... 3 ...+... 4 ...+... 5 ...+...

     1  101CASH                       CURRENT ASSET       01084102

     2  102ACCOUNTS RECEIVABLE        CURRENT ASSET       00763349

     3  103NOTES RECEIVABLE           CURRENT ASSET       00384061

     If BALANCE was defined as a packed field, its value
     could not be interpreted in *CHAR format
```

Figure 2-19 Partial ***HEX** and ***CHAR** listings generated by the **CPYF** command.

Programmer Development Manager

In lieu of using the Programmer Menu to access the environments to perform source entry and compilation, execute **CL** commands, access libraries, and so forth, the programmer may prefer to use the *Programmer Development Manager* **(PDM).** The procedures to use this utility are detailed in Appendix B.

SUMMARY

The database on the AS/400 is called **DB2/400**. It is a *relational* database that modifies the generic database terminology. *Tables* are referred to as *physical files; columns* as *fields; rows* as *records;* and *views* as *logical files* in **DB2/400** databases.

Physical files may be created with or without a *Data Description Specification.* Physical files created with a *Data Description Specification* are processed by an **RPG IV** program as *externally defined* files. Those that do not have a *Data Description Specification* must be *program-described.* Chapter 3 discusses how these two physical file structures are processed in an **RPG IV** program.

The *data description* for a physical file is created by entering the source code by **SEU** *(Source Entry Utility)* according to the syntax of the *Data Description Specifications.* After the source code is entered and saved, it must be compiled. The **CRTPF** *(Create Physical File)* command compiles the source code. Numerous default attributes are included with the **CRTPF** command and may be changed as needed.

Data may be loaded to the physical file by **DFU** *(Data File Utility),* interactively, or in a batch mode by an **RPG IV** program.

Physical files may be created as *keyed* or *nonkeyed.* A keyed file will be processed in a batch mode in a default ascending key order. *Nonkeyed* files are processed in *arrival sequence.* With random processing, the records in a *keyed file* are accessed by their *key value,* whereas the records in a nonkeyed file are accessed by their *relative position in the file.*

Thirty-six keywords are available to control a related number of processing functions. Their use will depend on the requirements of the application.

Members, which use the same data structure, may be added to an existing physical file. Hence, a physical file may support more than one database file, all with the same record format.

Utilities are available to access the file and field attributes of a physical file. The *Display File Description* **(DSPFD)** command displays all of the default and user-supplied attributes of a physical file, and the **DSPFFD** *(Display File Field Description)* command displays the field attributes.

After the physical file is loaded with data, field values may be examined by the **CPYF** *(Copy File)* or **DSPPFM** *(Display Physical File Member)* command. The **CPYF** command generates a hard copy of the file in character or hexadecimal format, whereas the **DSPPFM** command displays the field values only, in either format. Software is also available that provides for many of the functions necessary for the maintenance of physical files.

QUESTIONS

2-1. What type of database is **DB2/400**?

2-2. How do tables, view, columns, and rows in generic database terminology compare with **DB2/400** names?

2-3. What is the difference between a physical file and a logical file in **DB2/400**?

2-4. In what organizational types may a physical file be defined?

2-5. Refer to Question 2-4 and explain the processing features of each organizational type.

2-6. Explain the difference between an *externally described* and a *program-described* physical file.

2-7. What is a *composite key*? How is it defined in a physical file?

2-8. Explain how a physical file may be processed by any of its fields in ascending or descending order. "Sorting" is not an acceptable answer.

2-9. Name the steps required for creating a physical file.

2-10. What specification type is used for entering the syntax for a physical file? For a *nonkeyed* file, what are the coding levels? What are they for a *keyed sequence* file?

2-11. How many record formats may be included in a physical file?

2-12. What type of physical file is shown in the following figure? Explain the meaning of each entry.

```
              .....A..........T.Name++++++RLen++TDpB......Functions+++++++++++++++++

0001.00            A          R Q212PFR
0002.00            A            DEPTNUMBER     3
0003.00            A            PARTNUMBER     6
0004.00            A            DESCRIPTON    20
0005.00            A            QTYONHAND      5P 0
0006.00            A            UNIT_COST      6  4
```

2-13. Refer to Question 2-12, and notice that some of the field definitions do not include an entry in the **T** field (after the **Len++** field). What is the default for these fields?

2-14. Refer to Question 2-12, and explain the function of the letter **P** in the **T** field for QTYON-HAND. What does the **Len++** field entry refer to?

2-15. How would the coding for Question 2-12 be modified to define a keyed sequence physical file? Assume that duplicate keys are not to be supported and that DEPTNUMBER and PARTNUMBER are to be specified as a composite key.

2-16. What is the function of the following physical file keywords?

COLHDG	**EDTWRD**	**REFFLD**
DESCEND	**LIFO**	**TEXT**
EDTCDE	**REF**	**UNIQUE**

2-17. What entries are needed on the Programmer Menu to call the utility to enter the DDS code for a physical file?

2-18. Name the utility used to enter the DDS code for a physical file. What is a prompt line in this utility?

2-19. After the source code for a physical file is entered, explain the procedures that must be followed to exit from the utility and prepare the physical file for execution.

2-20. How many listings are generated when option **3** is selected from the Programmer Menu for the compilation of a physical file? Briefly explain how the listings differ.

2-21. What Control Language command is executed when option **3** is selected from the Programmer Menu?

2-22. Under what circumstances does the **CRTPF** command have to be explicitly specified?

2-23. What **CL** command is used to display the attributes of a physical file? Name the **CL** command needed to display the field attributes of a physical file.

2-24. Explain the function of the following physical file maintenance commands:

CHGPF	**CLRPFM**	**CPYF**
DSPPFM	**RMVM**	**DLTF**

2-25. Explain the structure of a physical file that supports four members. Where are the *file, record,* and *field* attributes defined?

2-26. How many default members are assigned when a physical file is created without changing any parameters? How is a file created to support more than one member?

2-27. What is the function of each of the following maintenance commands for members?

ADDPFM	**RNMM**	**RMVM**	**CHGPFM**

2-28. If a combination of the members in a physical file is to be selectively processed, what is required to provide this control? Which member(s) is/are processed if only the file name is referenced?

2-29. By what methods may data be loaded to a physical file?

2-30. Determine the packed size of **020103456.** Present the value in an under-and-over hexidecimal format.

2-31. Determine the unpacked size of the following packed numeric value. Present the packed value in an unpacked format.

03794
0186F

2-32. Refer to Question 2-31. What does the letter **F** indicate in the packed numeric value? What would the letter **D** indicate?

Programming Assignment 2-3: CUSTOMER MAILING FILE

Physical File Record Format:

PHYSICAL FILE DESCRIPTION

SYSTEM: AS/400	DATE: Yours
FILE NAME: Yours	REV NO: 0
RECORD NAME: Yours	KEY LENGTH: None
SEQUENCE: Nonkeyed	RECORD SIZE: 44

FIELD DEFINITIONS

FIELD NO	FIELD NAME	SIZE	TYPE	POSITION FROM	POSITION TO	COMMENTS
1	CUSTNAME	15	C	1	15	
2	STREET	14	C	16	29	
3	CITY	10	C	30	39	
4	STATE	2	C	40	41	
5	ZIP_CODE	5	P	42	44	

Physical File Data:

Customer Name	Street	City	State	Zip Code
ANDREW GUMP	1 SUN AVENUE	MIAMI	FL	08881
DICK TRACY	CELL 8	ALCATRAZ	CA	07770
BEETLE BAILEY	"A" COMPANY	FORT DIX	NJ	06666
CHARLIE BROWN	8 DOGHOUSE ST.	ANYWHERE	US	00000
MOON MULLINS	16 TIDE ROAD	LAKEVILLE	CT	06497
LI`L ABNER	80 PATCH LANE	DOG PATCH	SC	99999
YOUR NAME	YOUR ADDRESS	....	..	.....

Notes: Use the **COLHDG** keyword for all fields, and provide your own field text.

chapter 3

Introduction to RPG IV Programming

DEVELOPMENT OF THE RPG PROGRAMMING LANGUAGE

In the early 1960s IBM developed **RPG** *(Report Program Generator)* as a computer language that would replace the manually wired boards of the IBM 1400 business machine. Because the jumper boards were column-oriented, this design was and still is included in **RPG.** During the next three decades IBM continued to make major enhancements to **RPG.** In 1969, **RPG II** was introduced. It supported major changes, including disk file processing, workstation access, and array processing. When IBM introduced the System/38 in 1978, **RPG III** was also announced. **RPG III** supported new features including a built-in relational database management system and structured programming operations (including **IF/ELSE, DO, DOU,** and **DOW**). With the announcement of the AS/400 in 1988, **RPG/400** was released. New features, such as **AND/OR** support for **IF** and **DO** operations, 30-digit numeric fields, and **SQL** *(Structured Query Language)* access, were some of the significant improvements incorporated in **RPG/400.**

Since 1978 and the introduction of **RPG III,** the language has become less *problem-oriented* and more *procedure-oriented* like COBOL. The programmer has the option of writing **RPG** programs that follow the built-in logic cycle that automatically controls the **OPEN, READ, WRITE,** and **CLOSE** operations or explicitly defining these operations in the program. For performance considerations, writing programs that use the logic cycle should be avoided.

In 1994 IBM released **RPG IV,** a significant change to the other versions of **RPG.** Some of the new features in **RPG IV** are as follows:

- Mixed uppercase and lowercase characters may be included in any variable names (e.g., file names, field names, array names, table names, data structure names, etc.).
- The underscore character (_) may be used in variable names.
- New *Definition* **(D)** *Specifications.*
- Wider columns may be used in the specification types.
- Keyword notation is available in many of the specifications.
- New built-in functions, date data type support, and pointer support are included.
- There is a 10-character maximum for variable names instead of 6 characters.
- There is a 10-character maximum for file names instead of 8 characters.
- Blank lines may now be included in **RPG IV** programs.

The official name for IBM's **RPG IV** is **ILE RPG IV.** The **ILE** *(Integrated Language Environment)* support allows **RPG IV** programs to be compiled and then "bound" together into an executable unit. In addition, programs written in different languages (e.g., COBOL, C, CL) may be compiled into modules and bound with one or more **RPG IV** program modules into a unit. **ILE** support enables the programmer to access reusable code, thereby reducing development time. In addition, **ILE** may also decrease the run time of an application that includes many programs that must "call" each other.

Most of the features included in the previous releases of **RPG** are supported by **RPG IV.** However, new programs should be written in **RPG IV** code and the syntax of the older versions of the language avoided.

RPG IV SPECIFICATIONS

The writing of programs in any of the previous **RPG** language versions requires a knowledge of specification forms. However, in lieu of coding on forms, which the programmer often completes before entering the instructions, **RPG IV** program syntax is entered directly using IBM's *Source Entry Utility* (**SEU**) software. The specification types used in **RPG IV** programs are explained in the following paragraphs.

- *Control Specification* (**H** in position 6)—Commonly called the *header* or *H-Spec*; is optional. Unless one or more of the functions supported by this specification is needed (such as a change in the default date and/or time format, forms alignment control, change in the default currency symbol character, and/or decimal editing), it may be omitted in the program. The compiler will automatically generate one **H-spec** and include it as the first executable instruction in the compiled **RPG IV** program.
- *File Description Specification* (**F** in position 6)—Instructions for this specification define (declare) the attributes of all input/output files (physical, logical, display, printer, tape) processed by an **RPG IV** program. Most **RPG IV** programs include one or more *File Description* instructions.
- *Definition Specification* (**D** in position 6)—Instructions for this specification define arrays, tables, data structures, data areas, named constants, and work fields. If none of those functions is included in the syntax of an **RPG IV** program, *Definition Specification* instructions are not required.
- *Input Specification* (**I** in position 6)—Many of the functions controlled by this specification type (definition of data structures, data areas, named constants, and work fields) in **RPG II** and **RPG III** programs are defined in **RPG IV** programs in the *Definition Specifications. Input Specifications* are used primarily in **RPG IV** programs to define the fields in a *program-described* physical file, rename the fields in an *externally described* physical file, and/or assign *control-level indicators* to one or more fields in the record format of a *program-* or *externally described* physical file.
- *Calculation Specification* (**C** in position 6)—Arithmetic statements, formulas, decision making, array and table processing, physical file maintenance, and display file, logical file, and printer file processing are only a few of the controls supported by this specification type.
- *Output Specification* (**O** in position 6)—Instructions to generate a *program-described* report format are defined by *Output Specification* instructions. Page and line spacing control, constants, variable fields, and numeric field editing are controlled by this specification. However, if an *externally described* printer file is processed by the **RPG IV** program, *Output Specification* instructions for the related report are not required.

In the explanation of **RPG IV** program syntax, the entries related to each specification type will be introduced as needed. Many of the field areas in the body of a specification type are special purpose and are required only when the related **RPG IV** function is specified. In any case, no attempt should be made to memorize all of the fields in the specifications. Either the **format** or **prompt** mode of **SEU** will indicate where the fields are located.

DEVELOPMENT OF AN RPG IV PROGRAM

The steps followed in the development and processing of an **RPG IV** program include

1. Program generation.
2. Program execution.

Figure 3-1 details the sequence of steps to create, save, compile, and execute an **RPG IV** program.

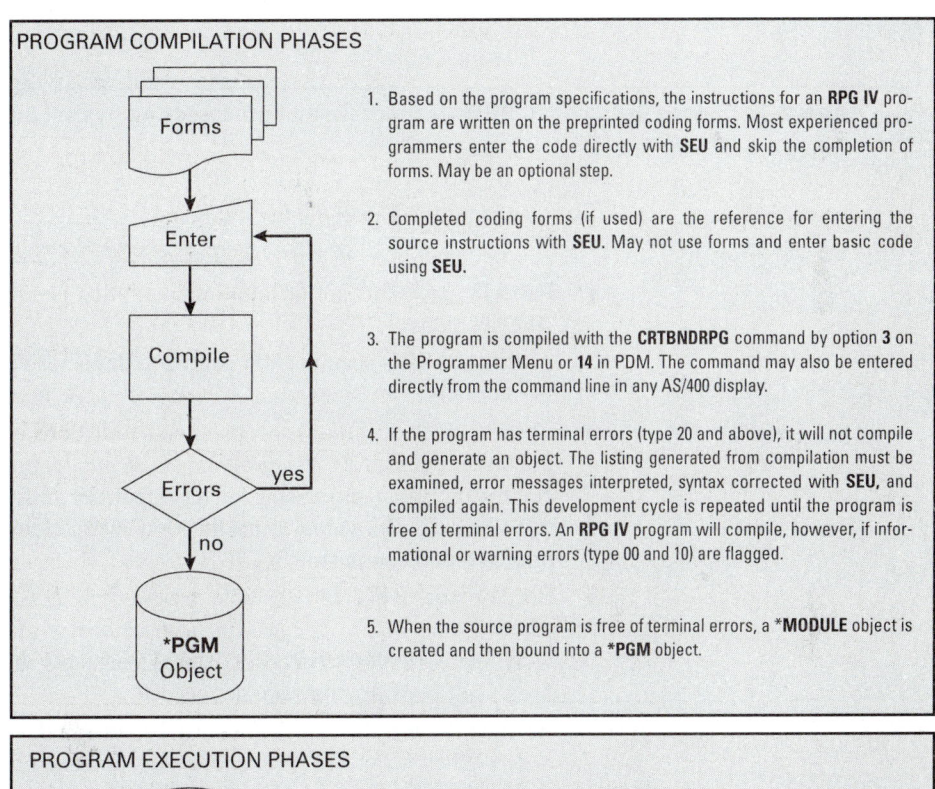

PROGRAM COMPILATION PHASES

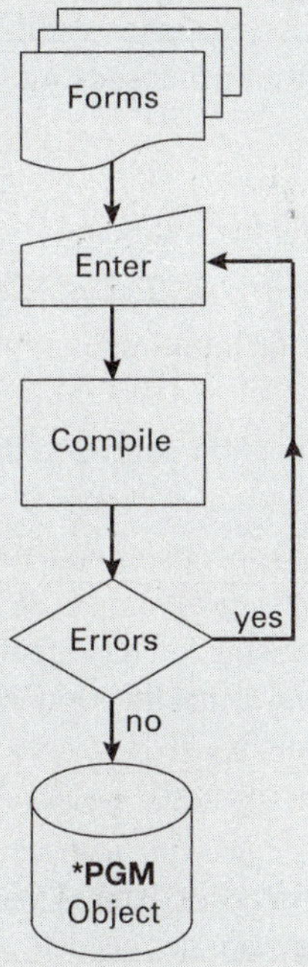

1. Based on the program specifications, the instructions for an **RPG IV** program are written on the preprinted coding forms. Most experienced programmers enter the code directly with **SEU** and skip the completion of forms. May be an optional step.
2. Completed coding forms (if used) are the reference for entering the source instructions with **SEU.** May not use forms and enter basic code using **SEU.**
3. The program is compiled with the **CRTBNDRPG** command by option **3** on the Programmer Menu or **14** in PDM. The command may also be entered directly from the command line in any AS/400 display.
4. If the program has terminal errors (type 20 and above), it will not compile and generate an object. The listing generated from compilation must be examined, error messages interpreted, syntax corrected with **SEU,** and compiled again. This development cycle is repeated until the program is free of terminal errors. An **RPG IV** program will compile, however, if informational or warning errors (type 00 and 10) are flagged.
5. When the source program is free of terminal errors, a ***MODULE** object is created and then bound into a ***PGM** object.

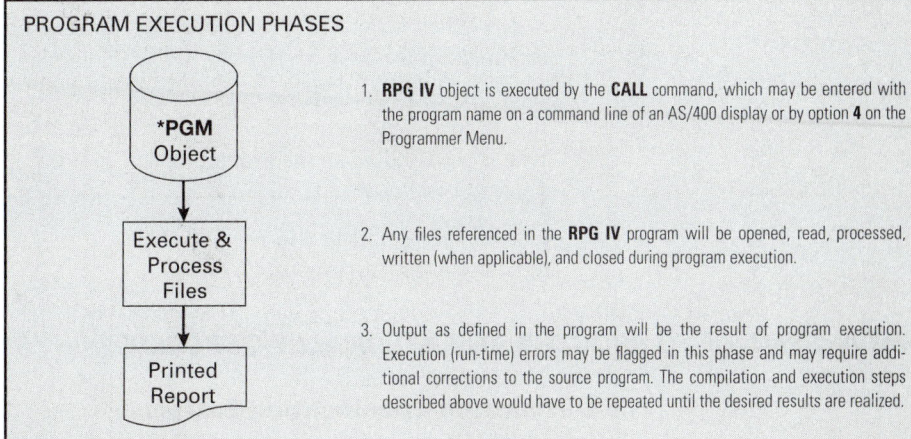

PROGRAM EXECUTION PHASES

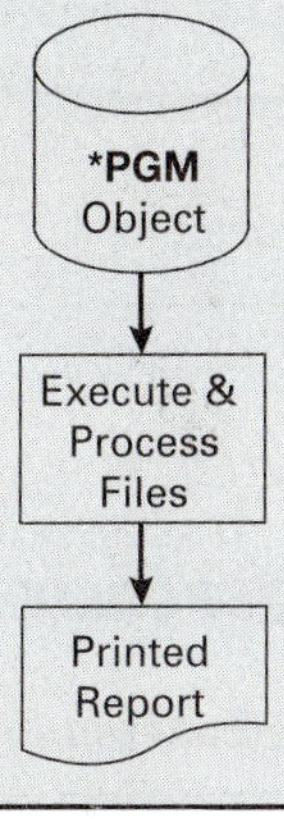

1. **RPG IV** object is executed by the **CALL** command, which may be entered with the program name on a command line of an AS/400 display or by option **4** on the Programmer Menu.
2. Any files referenced in the **RPG IV** program will be opened, read, processed, written (when applicable), and closed during program execution.
3. Output as defined in the program will be the result of program execution. Execution (run-time) errors may be flagged in this phase and may require additional corrections to the source program. The compilation and execution steps described above would have to be repeated until the desired results are realized.

Figure 3-1 RPG IV program development phases.

WHAT DOES AN RPG IV PROGRAM LOOK LIKE?

A source listing of an **RPG IV** program that reads an externally described, nonkeyed physical file, processes all of the records, and prints the field values is shown in Figure 3-2.

```
SEQNBR*...+... 1 ...+... 2 ...+... 3 ...+... 4 ...+... 5 ...+... 6 ...+... 7 ...+... 8 ...+... 9 ...+... 0
          * This program processes a PF in arrival sequence & prints a report
     FGlacts    IF   E             DISK                                    Input file
     FQsysprt   O    F  132        PRINTER

     C                   READ      Glacts                             LR   read first record
     C                   DOW       *INLR = *OFF                            do while LR is off
     C                   EXCEPT    PrintLine                               print a line
     C                   READ      Glacts                             LR   read another record
     C                   ENDDO                                             end DOW group

     OQsysprt   E            PrintLine      2
     O                       ActNumber           7
     O                       ActName            37
     O                       Act_Type           62
     O                       Balance        1   77
```

Figure 3-2 Source listing of an **RPG IV** program that processes a physical file and prints a report.

Examine Figure 3-2 and note the following:

1. **RPG IV** programs are position-oriented, that is, entries must be made in specific positions.
2. A different **SEU** specification is used to define each logical section of an **RPG IV** program.
3. The **F** *(File Description)* specification instructions define the files (physical and printer) processed by the program. **C** *(Calculation)* specification instructions control the input processing of the input file (GLACTS) and the output file (QSYSPRT). **O** *(Output)* specification instructions define the format of the printed report (output).
4. Because the **RPG IV** example program processes an externally described physical file, *Input Specification* instructions are not required. Also, because work fields, tables, arrays, or named constants are not specified, *Definition Specification* instructions are not needed.
5. Instructions for this program must be arranged in an **F, C, O** *compilation order*. When *all* of the specifications are included in an **RPG IV** program, the statements must be in an **H, F, D, I, C, O** compilation order.
6. Every **RPG IV** instruction must include the related specification letter in position 6. **SEU** will automatically supply the letter when the related specification type is accessed when the Prompt mode is used.
7. Each specification type includes special-purpose fields that are not required in every **RPG IV** instruction.

RPG IV SYNTAX TO PROCESS AN EXTERNALLY DESCRIBED PHYSICAL FILE

File Description Specification Entries

The entries included in the *File Description Specifications* are detailed in Figure 3-3.

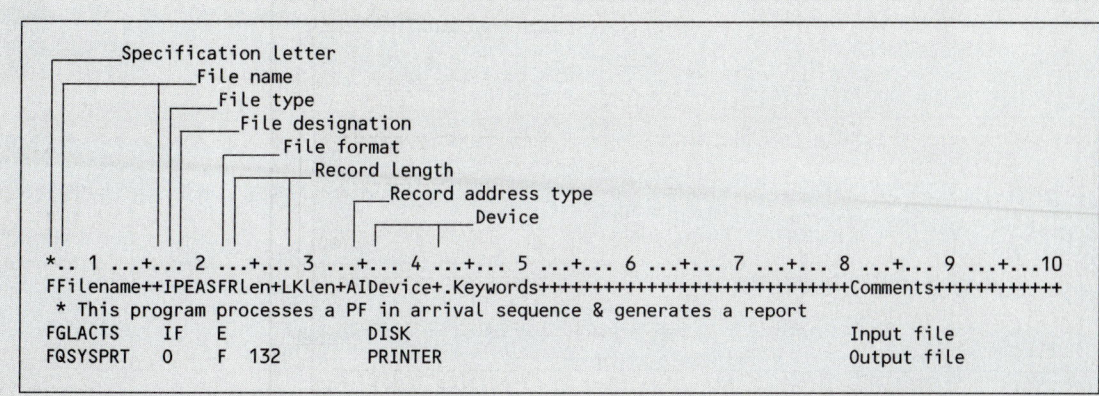

```
Specification letter
File name
File type
File designation
File format
Record length
Record address type
Device
*.. 1 ...+... 2 ...+... 3 ...+... 4 ...+... 5 ...+... 6 ...+... 7 ...+... 8 ...+... 9 ...+...10
FFilename++IPEASFRLen+LKLen+AIDevice+.Keywords+++++++++++++++++++++++++++++Comments++++++++++++
 * This program processes a PF in arrival sequence & generates a report
FGLACTS    IF   E             DISK                                       Input file
FQSYSPRT   O    F  132        PRINTER                                    Output file
```

Entries on line 1:

Comments are specified in **RPG IV** programs by an asterisk in position 7 followed by any programmer-supplied text. For readability, blank lines may be included anywhere in the program.

Entries on line 2 (Physical file definition):

Form type (position 6) — **F** is entered automatically when the *File Description Specification* format is requested in **SEU**. All of the instructions in the program must include their related specification letter in column 6 unless position 7 contains an asterisk (*).

Filename (positions 7–16) — Name of the physical file (or any other file type) must be entered left-justified in this field. The physical file (GLACTS) must have been compiled before the **RPG IV** program is compiled, or else terminal errors will be generated.

File type (position 17) — The letter **I** defines the physical file as an input file. Other file types (**C** and **U**) will be introduced in subsequent chapters.

File designation (position 18) — The letter **F** defines the physical file (GLACTS) as ***full-procedural,*** which indicates that input processing of the file will be controlled by **READ** (or **CHAIN**) instructions in the *Calculation Specifications* of the **RPG IV** program. Other position 18 entries (**blank, P, R, S, T**) will be explained in subsequent chapters.

File format (position 22) — The letter **E** defines the physical file as ***externally described.*** An **F** in this field would indicate that the file is ***program-described,*** requiring that the physical file's fields be defined in the *Input Specifications.*

Record address type (position 34) — A blank entry in this field indicates that the file will be processed in arrival sequence (order in which the records are stored). A **K** (indicating a keyed file) would indicate to process the file in a key-value order. To process the physical file directly (without a related logical file) in a key-value order, the file must have been created as a keyed file. On the other hand, keyed files may be processed in an arrival sequence (sequentially) by omitting the **K** in this field. Other record address entries (**A, D, G, P, T, Z**) will be explained in later chapters.

Device (positions 36–42) — **DISK** is the required device name for disk-stored physical files. Other device entries are **PRINTER, SEQ, SPECIAL,** and **WORKSTN.**

Entries on line 3 (Printer file definition):

Filename (positions 7–16) — **QSYSPRT** and **QPRINT** are system-supplied file names for program-described printer files. When an ***externally described*** printer file is processed, the name of the file must be entered in this field.

File type (position 18) — The letter **O** defines the file as output. Printer files may be defined only as output.

File format (position 22) — The letter **F** defines the file as ***program-described,*** which requires that the record and field descriptions be defined in the *Output Specifications* of the **RPG IV** program.

Record length (positions 23–37) — Because the file is program-described (**F** in position 22), a record length value must be entered in this field. The entry 132 (standard width for most line printers) indicates that **132** characters will be printed on a line. A smaller value may be specified; however, 132 positions will be allocated in memory for the printer file's output buffer.

Device (positions 36–42) — **PRINTER** must be used as the device name for all ***program-*** and ***externally described*** printer files.

Figure 3-3 *File Description Specifications* for an **RPG IV** program that processes a physical file and generates a report.

Calculation Specification Entries

The entries in the *Calculation Specifications* that control the processing of the physical file and the printing of the report are described in Figure 3-4.

The **RPG IV** syntax in the *Calculation Specifications* for this example program is not the only coding method possible. Many other combinations of instructions may be specified to attain the required result.

```
 ┌──Specification letter
 │                      ┌────┬──Operation code
 │                      │    │┌─────────┬──Factor 2
*.. 1 ...+... 2 ...+... 3 ...+... 4 ...+... 5 ...+... 6 ...+... 7 ...+... 8 ...+... 9 ...+...10
C                      READ      Glacts                                   LR      Read first record
C                      DOW       *INLR = *OFF                                     End of file test
C                      EXCEPT    Printline                                        Output field values
C                      READ                                               LR      Read another record
C                      ENDDO                                              │       Branch to DOW stmt
                  Indicator LR is set on when end of file is read─────────┘
```

Entries on line 500:

Operation (positions 26–35) — This **READ** operation reads the first record from the physical file GLACTS. Because of the **DOW** *(Do While* group*)*, this **READ** statement will be executed only once. The other **READ** statement on line 8 will read the remaining records in the file.

Factor 2 (positions 36–49) — The name of the physical file defined in the *File Description Specifications* as an input file must be entered in this field. The file will be processed sequentially by the two **READ** statements.

Resulting indicator (positions 75–76; Eq field) — Indicator **LR** (Last Record) will be set on when an end-of-file condition (all of the records read) for the input file is tested. When **LR** is "on," all of the files processed by the program are closed and the allocated storage in memory is released. Any attempt to read a file after an end-of-file condition is detected will cause program control to cancel.

Entries on line 600:

Operation (positions 26–35) — The **DOW** *(Do While)* statement and the related **ENDDO** operation on line 8 causes program control to perform *iterative* processing *while* the condition specified in *Factor 2* is tested as true.

Factor 2 (positions 36–49) — The **DOW** test condition is specified in this field. ***INLR** is a one-position character field where **LR** (or any other indicator) is tested for an "off" condition (in this example). The syntax of this entry is as follows:

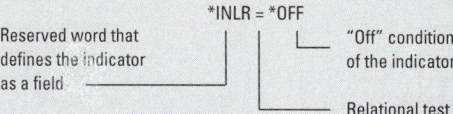

*INLR = *OFF

Reserved word that defines the indicator as a field

"Off" condition of the indicator

Relational test

The execution of instructions within the **DOW** group will be repeated *while* an end-of-fie condition (indicator **LR** is off) is not tested. When indicator **LR** is set on (the **DOW** test is not true), program control will branch to the **ENDDO** instruction on line 9 and complete execution of the program.

Entries on line 700:

Operation (positions 26–35) — The **EXCEPT** operation transfers program control to the first **E** type line defined as **Printline** in the *Output Specifications.* The example program includes only one output record format.

Factor 2 (positions 36–49) — **Printline** is the progammer-supplied name of an **E** type record format in the *Output Specifications.* Program control will search the output instructions for a record format with this name. A one-to-ten-character **EXCEPT** name may be specified. If this entry were omitted, any **E** type record in the *Output Specifications* without an exception name would be executed for every input record processed.

Entries on line 800:

Operation (positions 26–35) — This **READ** operation reads the remaining records in the physical file. Each time the loop, controlled by the **DOW** group, is executed, one record is read from the input file.

Factor 2 (positions 36–47) — Name of the physical file must be specified here.

Resulting indicator; Eq (positions 75–76) — Indicator **LR** is set on by the **READ** statement when an end-of-file condition for the input file is tested. As stated above, when **LR** is "on," all of the files processed by the program will be closed and the allocated storage in memory released.

Entries on line 900:

Operation (positions 26–35) — The **ENDDO** operation ends the **DOW** group. When this statement is executed, program control branches to the **DOW** statement on line 6, where an end-of-file test is made every time the loop is executed. An **END** operation may be specified in lieu of an **ENDDO.**

Figure 3-4 *Calculation Specifications* for an **RPG IV** program that processes a physical file and generates a printed report.

Output Specification Entries

The syntax for the example program's *Output Specifications* is explained in Figure 3-5. Note that *two* **SEU** formats, the *Record Description* and the *Field Description* sections, are used to code the statements for the program-defined printer file. Both formats are shown in Figure 3-5.

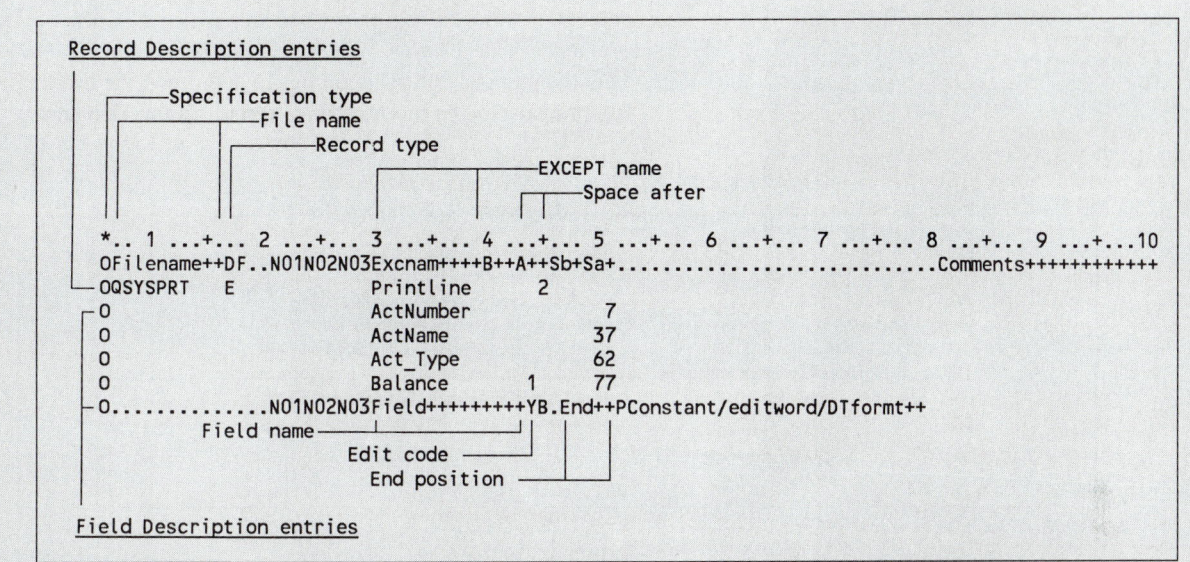

Record Description entries

```
    Specification type
    File name
    Record type
    EXCEPT name
    Space after

*.. 1 ...+... 2 ...+... 3 ...+... 4 ...+... 5 ...+... 6 ...+... 7 ...+... 8 ...+... 9 ...+...10
OFilename++DF..N01N02N03Excnam++++B++A++Sb+Sa+.............................Comments++++++++++++
OQSYSPRT        E            Printline     2
O                            ActNumber            7
O                            ActName             37
O                            Act_Type            62
O                            Balance       1     77
O..............N01N02N03Field+++++++++YB.End++PConstant/editword/DTformt++

    Field name
    Edit code
    End position
```

Field Description entries

Record Description entries:

Entries on line 1100:

Filename (positions 7–16) — Name of the PRINTER file defined in the *File Description Specifications* is entered only on the *first* output instruction.

Record type (position 17) — An **E** defines the record format as an exception type record. When the **EXCEPT** operation on line 700 is executed, program control is transferred to the first output instruction defined with an **E** in column 17 and the related *exception* name in positions 30–39. **H**, **D**, and **T** are other line types that will be discussed in subsequent chapters.

EXCEPT name (positions 30–39) — The *Factor 2* name, specified with the **EXCEPT** operation on line 700 of the calculation instruction, is entered in this field. Any output record *without* a related exception name will *not* be printed. If more than one exception type record was specified, it would have to be defined with a different name. Note that an exception record may be included on more than one line.

Space after (positions 43–45) — Line spacing in the body of a report is controlled by **Before** and/or **After** entries. **Before** specifies that spacing of the current line will occur *before* the line is printed, and **After** will cause spacing to occur *after* the line is printed. A value from **0** to **255** may be specified for **Before** or **After** spacing.

Field Description entries:

Entries on lines 1200–1500:

Field (positions 30–43) — Names of the fields from the ***externally described*** physical file (GLACTS) are entered left-justified in this field. Any field that was not defined by the physical file must be defined in the *Definition, Input, or Calculation Specifications.*

Edit code (position 44) — Edit code **1** specified in this field will suppress any leading zeros in the value in Balance, insert a comma between the thousand and hundred digits, and according to the decimal positions included in the definition of the field, insert a decimal. Other edit codes (**2–9, A–D, J–Q, X Y, Z**) will be explained in Chapter 4.

End position (47–51) — This entry indicates the location of the last byte in the field on the printed report. The last byte of the value in ActNumber will be located in position 7, the second byte in 6, and the first byte in 5. Note that if a character field is eight bytes and the value stored left-justified is only 4, the field will be located on the report by the eighth byte (a blank character) and not the fourth. Consequently, four spaces will be included after the value.

Figure 3-5 *Output Specifications* for an **RPG IV** program that processes a physical file and generates a printed report.

The *Record Description* format is accessed in **SEU** by entering **O** in the sequence number area of the Edit display and pressing the **ENTER** key. The *Field Description* format is accessed by entering **J** in the sequence number area and pressing the **ENTER** key. See Appendix A for all of the **RPG IV** specification letters. Note that the related format will display above the instruction and not at the bottom as shown for the *Field Description* entries in Figure 3-5.

Relationship of the Report Design to the Output Coding

Report designs are usually formatted on a *Printer Spacing Chart* before the *Output Specifications* are completed. This tool enables the programmer to determine the heading and field value locations and the line spacing in the body of a report. Figure 3-6 shows

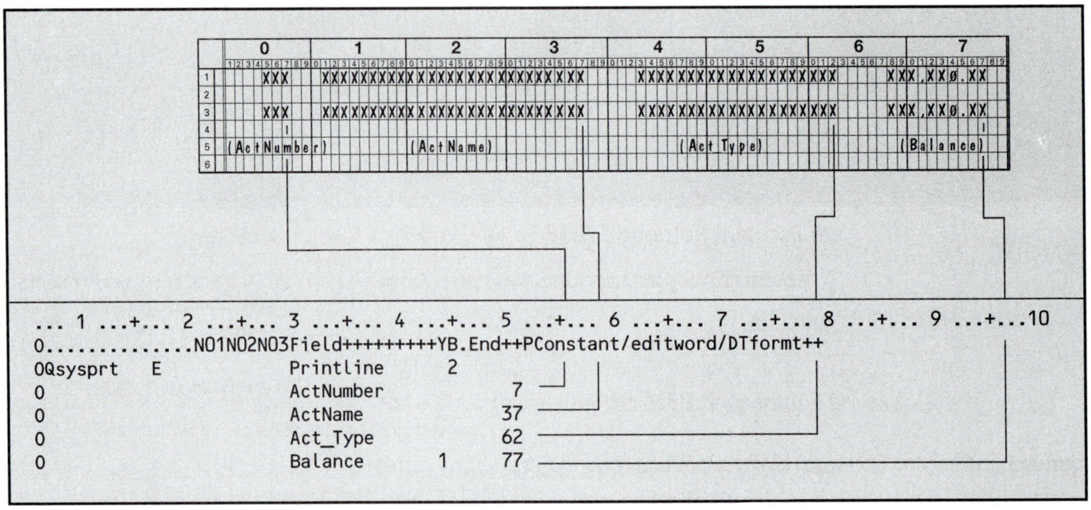

Figure 3-6 Relationship of a *Printer Spacing Chart* to the *Output Specifications* coding.

the layout characteristics of a *Printer Spacing Chart*. Note that a group of **X**s represents the maximum size of an output field that may have been defined in a physical file, in an input statement, in a definition statement, or as a result field of a calculation instruction. Any edit characters (commas, decimals, and so forth) must be included in the output format of a numeric field. A **0** in the format of the edited BALANCE field indicates where the suppression of leading zeros is to stop. An *edit code* or *edit word* is used to edit numeric fields. The relationship of the *Field Description Specification* instructions to the entries in the *Printer Spacing Chart* is also detailed in Figure 3-6.

Line spacing is indicated by two identical rows of **X**s or by a supplementary note at the bottom of the *Printer Spacing Chart.* The words enclosed in parentheses—(ActNumber), (ActName), (Act_Type), and (Balance)—identify the name of the physical file's fields and are not to be construed as headings or constants. Fields defined in the *Definition, Input,* or *Calculation Specifications* may be referenced the same way.

Figure 3-6 also shows the relationship of the *Printer Spacing Chart* to the *Output Specification's Field Description* entries for the example program.

The relationship of the *Output Specifications* coding to the report generated by execution of the **RPG IV** program is described in Figure 3-7. Because of the values stored in the physical file's character fields and the editing of the BALANCE field, the printed output may not represent the actual field size.

```
... 1 ...+... 2 ...+... 3 ...+... 4 ...+... 5 ...+... 6 ...+... 7 ...+... 8 ...+... 9 ...+...10
O.............N01N02N03Field+++++++++YB.End++PConstant/editword/DTformt++
OQsysprt   E              PrintLine       2
O                         ActNumber            7
O                         ActName             37
O                         Act_Type            62
O                         Balance        1    77
```

```
101  CASH                          CURRENT ASSET          10,841.02
102  ACCOUNTS RECEIVABLE           CURRENT ASSET           7,633.49
103  NOTES RECEIVABLE              CURRENT ASSET           3,840.61
104  PREPAID RENT                  CURRENT ASSET             300.00
110  AUTOMOBILE                    FIXED ASSET             7,120.00
201  ACCOUNTS PAYABLE              CURRENT LIABILITY         300.00
211  MORTGAGE PAYABLE              LONG-TERM LIABILITY    10,500.00
301  JOHN SMITH, CAPITAL           OWNER'S EQUITY         13,838.00
302  JOHN SMITH, WITHDRAWALS       OWNER'S EQUITY          1,000.00
400  COMMISSIONS EARNED            REVENUE                 4,201.56
500  GAS & OIL EXPENSE             EXPENSE                   707.02
501  REPAIRS EXPENSE               EXPENSE                   421.20
502  SALARIES EXPENSE              EXPENSE                 1,800.00
510  ADVERTISING EXPENSE           EXPENSE                      .00
```

Figure 3-7 Relationship of the *Output Specifications* coding to the printed report.

SEU ENTRY OF RPG IV SOURCE PROGRAM INSTRUCTIONS

Before other program options are introduced, the reader should refer to Appendix A and review the **SEU** procedures to enter **RPG IV** instructions and save the program. Page 664 of Appendix A illustrates the procedures to enter **RPG IV** source code, and pages 672 to 674 indicates how to exit **SEU** and save the source program. After some understanding of **SEU** entry and exit procedures, the reader should complete at least one programming assignment at the end of this chapter.

Source Program Listing

After the instructions for the program have been entered, the source listing in Figure 3-8 may be generated by the *Print member* option in the **SEU Exit** display. Because compilation of the program creates a listing, it is not always necessary to print a copy of the source. A listing is presented here (in Figure 3-8) to show how a source listing differs

```
SEQNBR*...+... 1 ...+... 2 ...+... 3 ...+... 4 ...+... 5 ...+... 6 ...+... 7 ...+... 8 ...+... 9 ...+... 0
      * This program processes a PF in arrival sequence & prints a report
     FGlacts    IF   E             DISK                              Input file
     FQsysprt   O    F  132        PRINTER

     C                   READ      Glacts                       LR   read first record
     C                   DOW       *INLR = *OFF                      do while LR is off
     C                   EXCEPT    PrintLine                         print a line
     C                   READ      Glacts                       LR   read another record
     C                   ENDDO                                       end DOW group

     OQsysprt   E            PrintLine      2
     O                       ActNumber            7
     O                       ActName             37
     O                       Act_Type            62
     O                       Balance        1    77
```

Figure 3-8 RPG IV source program listing.

from that generated from the compilation of an **RPG IV** program. In order to include the record formats and fields from externally described files processed by the program, compiled listings of programs will be used throughout this text.

RPG IV PROGRAM COMPILATION

An **RPG IV** source program must be compiled to generate an object that is executed for the processing of files. Program compilation is initiated by one of the following methods:

1. Enter **CRTBNDRPG** *(Create Bound RPG Program)* and the program name on a command line and press **ENTER.** This command creates an executable object if no terminal errors are generated. It is used most often with standalone programs that will not be part of a group of programs. With the exception of Chapter 19, the **CRTBNDRPG** command will be used to compile all program assignments in this text; this command is the default when **3** is selected from the Programmer Menu.
2. If the program is to be "bound" with other programs (**RPG IV, COBOL, CL**), the **CRTRPGMOD** *(Create RPG Module)* command must be used to compile an **RPG IV** source program. Successful compilation will generate an object module (type ***MODULE**) that *cannot* be executed. To execute either one or a group of object modules, the **CRTPGM** *(Create Program)* command must be used to "bind" the modules together into one callable program.

The **CRTBNDRPG, CRTRPGMOD,** and **CRTPGM** commands have parameters that are accessed by entering the command on a command line of a display and pressing **F4.** When required, any of the parameters may be changed. If none of the parameters is changed, the operating system will assume the default values.

Figure 3-9 presents the listing generated from compilation of the example **RPG IV** program.

```
5763RG1 V3R1M0  940909 RN        IBM ILE RPG/400        STAN/CH3R1             S1012CFA          12/13/97 21:55:08        Page  1
 Command . . . . . . . . . . . . :   CRTBNDRPG
   Issued by . . . . . . . . . . :     SMYERS
 Program . . . . . . . . . . . . :   CH3R1
   Library . . . . . . . . . . . :     STAN
 Text 'description' . . . . . . . :   *SRCMBRTXT
 Source Member . . . . . . . . . :   CH3R1
 Source File . . . . . . . . . . :   QRPGLESRC
   Library . . . . . . . . . . . :     STAN
   CCSID . . . . . . . . . . . . :     65535
 Text 'description' . . . . . . . :   RPG IV program - fig 3-9
 Last Change . . . . . . . . . . :   12/13/97  15:22:35
 Generation severity level  . . . :   10
 Default activation group . . . . :   *YES
 Compiler options . . . . . . . . :   *XREF      *GEN       *NOSECLVL  *SHOWCPY
                                      *EXPDDS    *EXT       *NOEVENT
 Debugging views  . . . . . . . . :   *STMT
 Output . . . . . . . . . . . . . :   *PRINT
 Optimization level . . . . . . . :   *NONE
 Source listing indentation . . . :   *NONE
 Type conversion options  . . . . :   *NONE
 Sort sequence  . . . . . . . . . :   *HEX
 Language identifier  . . . . . . :   *JOBRUN
 Replace program  . . . . . . . . :   *YES
 User profile . . . . . . . . . . :   *USER
 Authority  . . . . . . . . . . . :   *LIBCRTAUT
 Truncate numeric . . . . . . . . :   *YES
 Fix numeric  . . . . . . . . . . :   *NONE
 Target release . . . . . . . . . :   V3R1M0
 Allow null values  . . . . . . . :   *NO
5763RG1 V3R1M0  940909 RN        IBM ILE RPG/400        STAN/CH3R1             S1012CFA   12/13/97      21:55:08        Page     2
Line   <---------------------- Source Specifications ----------------------------><---- Comments ------> Do  Page  Change  Src  Seq
Number....1....+....2....+....3....+....4....+....5....+....6....+....7....+....8....+....9....+...10 Num Line  Date     Id  Number
                         S o u r c e   L i s t i n g
     1  * This program processes an externally described keyed physical file                                  971213          000100
     2  * and prints a report....                                                                             971213          000200
     3 FGLACTS    IF   E              DISK                                                                  971213          000300
       *--------------------------------------------------------------------------------------------*
       *                              RPG name         External name                                *
       * File name. . . . . . . . . :  GLACTS          STAN/GLACTS                                  *
       * Record format(s) . . . . . :  GLACTSR         GLACTSR                                      *
       *--------------------------------------------------------------------------------------------*
```

Figure 3-9 Listing generated from compilation of the example **RPG IV** program.

```
    4 FQSYSPRT   O    F  132       PRINTER                                                    971213      000400
    5                                                                                          971213      000500
*RNF2318 00      4 000400  Overflow indicator OA is assigned to PRINTER file QSYSPRT.
    6=IGLACTSR                                                                                             1000001
      *-----------------------------------------------------------------------------------*                1
      * RPG record format  . . . . :  GLACTSR                                              *                1
      * External format  . . . . . :  GLACTSR : STAN/GLACTS                                *                1
      *-----------------------------------------------------------------------------------*                1
    7=I                            A    1    3  ACTNUMBER                                                  1000002
    8=I                            A    4   30  ACTNAME                                                    1000003
    9=I                            A   31   50  ACT_TYPE                                                   1000004
   10=I                            S   51   58 2BALANCE                                                    1000005
   11 C                   READ      Glacts                        ----LR    read first record      971213      000600
   12 C                   DOW       *INLR = *OFF                            do while LR is off  B01 971213      000700
   13 C                   EXCEPT    PrintLine                               print a line         01 971213      000800
   14 C                   READ      Glacts                        ----LR    read another record  01 971213      000900
   15 C                   ENDDO                                             end DOW group       E01 971213      001000
   16                                                                                          971213      001100
   17 OQSYSPRT   E                    PrintLine      2                                         971213      001200
   18 O                               ActNumber            7                                   971213      001300
   19 O                               ActName             37                                   971213      001400
   20 O                               Act_Type            62                                   971213      001500
   21 O                               Balance        1    77                                   971213      001600
      * * * * *   E N D   O F   S O U R C E   * * * * *
 5763RG1 V3R1M0  940909 RN        IBM ILE RPG/400        STAN/CH3R1              S1012CFA        12/13/97 21:55:08        Page   3
          A d d i t i o n a l    D i a g n o s t i c    M e s s a g e s
*RNF7086 00      3 000300  RPG handles blocking for file GLACTS. INFDS is updated only
                             when blocks of data are transferred.
*RNF7066 00      3 000300  Record-Format GLACTSR not used for input or output.
 * * * * *   E N D   O F   A D D I T I O N A L   D I A G N O S T I C   M E S S A G E S   * * * * *
                O u t p u t   B u f f e r   P o s i t i o n s
 Line   Start End   Field or Constant
 Number Pos   Pos
    18      5     7 ACTNUMBER
    19     11    37 ACTNAME
    20     43    62 ACT_TYPE
    21     68    77 BALANCE
 * * * * *   E N D   O F   O U T P U T   B U F F E R   P O S I T I O N   * * * * *
 5763RG1 V3R1M0  940909 RN        IBM ILE RPG/400        STAN/CH3R1              S1012CFA        12/13/97 21:55:08        Page   4
                          C r o s s   R e f e r e n c e
      File and Record References:
         File              Device              References (D=Defined)
          Record
         GLACTS            DISK                    3D      11      14
          GLACTSR                                  0       6
         QSYSPRT           PRINTER                 4D      17      0
      Field References:
         Field             Attributes          References (D=Defined M=Modified)
         *INLR             A(1)                    12
         ACT_TYPE          A(20)                   9D      20
         ACTNAME           A(27)                   8D      19
         ACTNUMBER         A(3)                    7D      18
         BALANCE           P(8,2)                  10D     21
         PRINTLINE         EXCEPT                  13      17D
      Indicator References:
         Indicator                             References (D=Defined M=Modified)
         LR                                        11D     14D
         OA                                        0
      * * * * *   E N D   O F   C R O S S   R E F E R E N C E   * * * * *
 5763RG1 V3R1M0  940909 RN        IBM ILE RPG/400        STAN/CH3R1              S1012CFA        12/13/97 21:55:08        Page   5
                     E x t e r n a l   R e f e r e n c e s
      Statically bound procedures:
         Procedure                             References
         No references in the source.
      Imported fields:
         Field             Attributes          Defined
         No references in the source.
      Exported fields:
         Field             Attributes          Defined
         No references in the source.
   * * * * *   E N D   O F   E X T E R N A L   R E F E R E N C E S   * * * * *
 5763RG1 V3R1M0  940909 RN        IBM ILE RPG/400        STAN/CH3R1              S1012CFA        12/13/97 21:55:08        Page   6
                     M e s s a g e   S u m m a r y
 Msg id   Sv Number Message text
*RNF2318 00       1 No overflow indicator is specified; indicator assigned and
                    automatic skip to 06 generated.
*RNF7066 00       1 Record-Format name of Externally-Described file is not used.
*RNF7086 00       1 RPG handles blocking for the file. INFDS is updated only when
                    blocks of data are transferred.
      * * * * *   E N D   O F   M E S S A G E   S U M M A R Y   * * * * *
```

Figure 3-9 Listing generated from compilation of the example **RPG IV** program. (Continued)

```
5763RG1 V3R1M0  940909 RN        IBM ILE RPG/400        STAN/CH3R1            S1012CFA         12/13/97 21:55:08         Page  7
                              F i n a l   S u m m a r y
 Message Totals:
   Information  (00) . . . . . . . :        3
   Warning      (10) . . . . . . . :        0
   Error        (20) . . . . . . . :        0
   Severe Error (30+)  . . . . . . :        0
 ---------------------------------      -------
   Total . . . . . . . . . . . . . :        3
  Source Totals:
   Records . . . . . . . . . . . . :       21
   Specifications  . . . . . . . . :       17
   Data records  . . . . . . . . . :        0
   Comments  . . . . . . . . . . . :        2
        * * * * *   E N D   O F   F I N A L   S U M M A R Y   * * * * *
Program CH3R1 placed in library STAN. 00 highest severity. Created on 97/12/13 at 21:56:14.
         * * * * *   E N D   O F   C O M P I L A T I O N * * * * *
```

Figure 3-9 Listing generated from compilation of the example **RPG IV** program. (Continued)

Examine the listing, and note that it is divided into the following sections:

Prologue (page 1). This section summarizes the command parameters and their values. Seven of them are explained below.

1. Page heading—Product information is included on this line.
2. **Module** or **Program Name**—The name of the created **RPG IV** member (CH3R1) is specified if the **CRTBNDRPG** command was used to compile and create the program object. If the **CRTRPGMOD** command was used to compile the program, the name of the created module would be specified for this parameter.
3. **Source Member**—The name of the **RPG IV** source member (CH3R1) is specified for this parameter. This entry is usually the same as the module or program name explained above.
4. **Source File**—The name of the source file, which contains individual members (**RPG IV** source programs), is entered for this parameter. **QRPGLESRC** is the default source file name. If the programmer elected to create and/or use a different source file, that name would be specified.
5. **Generation severity level**—The default value **10** indicates that any compilation errors greater than **10** will generate terminal errors when the program is compiled.
6. **Compiler options**—The compiler options specified with the **CRTBNDRPG** or **CRTRPGMOD** command are listed in this parameter.
7. **Source listing indentation**—An optional programmer-supplied character to indent structured operation (**IF/ELSE, SELECT/WHEN, DO, DOW, DOU, CAS**) statements in the source section may be specified for this parameter. The default is ***NONE.**

Source Section (page 2). The instructions in the **RPG IV** source program are shown in this section. If the Compiler option (in the Prologue) is ***EXPDDS,** the record formats and related fields will be included in this section and identified with a "=" (equal sign) next to the line numbers. The DDS record formats are not shown if option ***NOEXPDDS** is specified.

The Source Section also includes the following parts:

1. Source heading—Includes Line Number heading, Ruler Line, Do number, Page line, Change Date, Source Id, and Sequence Number.

2. File/record information—Includes any externally described files' names and their record names.
3. DDS information—Identifies the externally described file from which the record and field information is extracted.
4. Generated specifications—Includes the specifications generated from the DDS files. They are identified by a "=" next to the line number.
5. Indentation—Shows how the structured operations in the program appear when indentation is specified.

Additional Diagnostic Messages Section (page 3). This section indicates the line number on which a compilation error occurred.

Field Positions in Output Buffer Section. When program-described *Output Specifications* are included in an **RPG IV** program, the line number of each variable or literal and its start and end positions will be specified in this section. Literals that are too long for this listing will be truncated.

Key Field Information. This section shows the information about the keys in a keyed file. Because the physical file processed is not keyed, this information is not included in the listing in Figure 3-9.

Cross Reference (page 4). This section identifies where files, fields, and indicators are used within the **RPG IV** program. It contains the following three separate lists:

- File and Record References
- Field References
- Indicator References

External References (page 5). Information for this section is included when one or more programs are "called" from this program. Not relevant for a single program.

Message Summary Section (page 6). This includes the error message Id, the severity level of the error, the number of statements with this error type, and the error message text.

Final Summary Section (page 7). This includes totals for the number of Information, Warning, Error, and Severe Error messages. It also includes a Source Totals section that summarizes the number of source records, specifications, data records, and comments in the **RPG IV** program. At the end of the listing, a message will be included that indicates the status of the compilation. A successful compilation includes a message indicating that the program was placed in a library and created on the current system date and time.

Four other sections—/Copy Member Table, Compile Time Data, External Reference List, and Code Generation and Binding Errors—are included in the compilation listing only when their function is used in an **RPG IV** program.

RPG IV PROGRAM EXECUTION

After the **RPG IV** program has been successfully compiled and the object has been created, the program may be executed by any of the following methods:

- Select option **4** on the Programmer Menu, enter the program name in the Parm field, and press **ENTER.**
- Enter **CALL CH3R1** (**RPG IV** program name) on the command line of any AS/400 display and press **ENTER.**
- When in the *Programmer Development Manager's Work with Objects Using PDM* display, press **F23** to display the next screen. Select and enter **16** next to the **RPG IV** object name and press **ENTER.** Refer to Appendix B for other **PDM** run-time options.

It is unlikely that the programmer's job description will support the immediate printing of a report (or compilation listing). Usually, the **WRKOUTQ** or **WRKSPLF** command (both explained in Chapter 1) is executed to view, print, copy, or delete the *spooled* output file.

The printed report generated by execution of the **RPG IV** program is shown in Figure 3-10. Note that the report does not include heading lines, page numbering, a date, or additional pages. All of these commonly used report items will be discussed in Chapters 4 and 5.

101	CASH	CURRENT ASSET	10,841.02
102	ACCOUNTS RECEIVABLE	CURRENT ASSET	7,633.49
103	NOTES RECEIVABLE	CURRENT ASSET	3,840.61
104	PREPAID RENT	CURRENT ASSET	300.00
110	AUTOMOBILE	FIXED ASSET	7,120.00
201	ACCOUNTS PAYABLE	CURRENT LIABILITY	5,114.58
211	MORTGAGE PAYABLE	LONG-TERM LIABILITY	10,500.00
301	JOHN SMITH, CAPITAL	OWNER'S EQUITY	13,838.00
302	JOHN SMITH, WITHDRAWALS	OWNER'S EQUITY	1,000.00
400	COMMISSIONS EARNED	REVENUE	4,201.56
500	GAS & OIL EXPENSE	EXPENSE	707.02
501	REPAIRS EXPENSE	EXPENSE	421.20
502	SALARIES EXPENSE	EXPENSE	1,800.00
510	ADVERTISING EXPENSE	EXPENSE	.00

Figure 3-10 Report generated from execution of the example **RPG IV** program.

RPG IV SYNTAX TO PROCESS A PROGRAM-DESCRIBED PHYSICAL FILE

For some processing scenarios, a physical file shell (no *Data Specifications* defining a record format and fields) may be created to:

1. Store the output from sorting one or more files.
2. Store the output from magnetic tape.
3. Store the output from a computer system that supports multiple record (more than one record format) files.
4. Store the output from the electronic transfer of data.
5. Store the output of the **CPYF** (*Copy File* Utility).

The physical file "shell" must be created with the **CRTPF** command and the required record length entered in the **RCDLEN** *(Record length)* parameter (see Figure 2-11).

Changes needed in the *File Description Specifications* to process a program-described physical file are detailed in Figure 3-11.

```
            ┌────────Letter F (fixed format) replaces E (externally described)
            │
            │ ┌──┬──── Record length must be specified (previously defined)
            │ │  │     in the RCDLEN parameter in the CRTPF command
*.. 1 ...+... 2 ...+... 3 ...+... 4 ...+... 5 ...+... 6 ...+... 7 ...+... 8 ...+... 9 ...+...10
FFilename++IPEASFRLen+LKLen+AIDevice+.Keywords+++++++++++++++++++++++++++++Comments++++++++++++
 * This program processes a program-described PF in arrival sequence and prints a report
FGLACTS    IF   F   58        DISK                                         Input file
FQSYSPRT   O    F  132        PRINTER                                      Output file
```

Filename (positions 7–16) — The file name specified when the physical file was created with the **CRTPF** command must be entered left-justified in this field.

File type (position 17) — The **I** specified for this entry indicates that the physical file is an input file.

File designation (position 18) — **F** defines a ***full-procedural*** file, indicating that it will be processed under the control of an **RPG IV** operation (two **READ** statements in the example program).

File format (position 22) — **F** defines the physical file as ***program-described.***

Record length (positions 23–27) — This entry must be the same as the value in the **CRTPF** command's **RCDLEN** *(Record length)* parameter. When a value is specified in the **RCDLEN** parameter, the system recognizes the physical file as ***program-described.***

Device (positions 36–42) — The device name for all physical files stored on disk is **DISK.**

Figure 3-11 *File Description Specifications* for an **RPG IV** program that processes a program-described physical file in arrival sequence and prints a report.

Input Specification Syntax

Recall that an externally described physical file does not require that record and field attributes be specified in the **RPG IV** program. Consequently, no *Input Specifications* were included in the previous program example. However, when the physical file is program-described, *Input Specification* instructions are needed to define the record format and fields. Figure 3-12 details the **RPG IV** syntax to define the record and fields in a program-described physical file.

```
 ┌──────────Filename
 │        ││┌──────────Sequence
 │        │││  ┌┬──────────────Record Identifying Indicator
*.. 1 ...+... 2 ...+... 3 ...+... 4 ...+... 5 ...+... 6 ...+... 7 ...+... 8 ...+... 9 ...+...10
IFilename++SqNORiPos1+NCCPos2+NCCPo 3+NCC..................................Comments++++++++++++
IGLACTSF    AA
I
I                                        3  ActNumber
I                                       30  ActName
I                                   3   50  Act_Type
I                                   5   58 2Balance
I.......................Fmt+SPFrom+To+++DcField+++++++++L1M1FrPlMnZr......Comments++++++++++++

Field location (From position)─────┘    │ │││          │
      Field location (To position)──────┘ │││          │
         Decimal positions────────────────┘││          │
          Programmer-supplied field name───┘└──────────┘
```

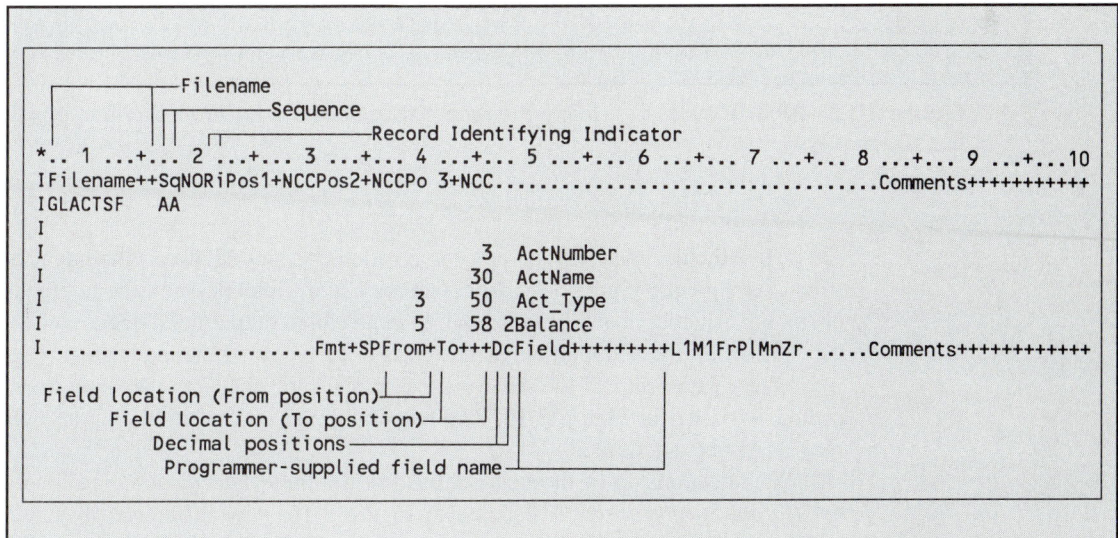

Figure 3-12 **RPG IV** syntax to define the record format of a program-described physical file.

Record Identification Section:

This section of the *Input Specifications* defines the record format of a ***program-described*** physical file. Entries must precede *Field Description* entries.

Filename (positions 7–16) — The file name entered must be identical to the input file defined in the *File Description Specifications* (GLACTSF). The rules for defining file names were explained in Chapter 2.

Sequence (positions 17–18) — Any two alphabetic characters may be entered in this field. If the entry is omitted, **AA** will be assumed by the compiler and a warning error generated. This entry is required when a file has more than one record format and sequence checking of the record order is required. Because physical files support only one record format, this option is seldom used in the AS/400 environment.

Record Identifying Indicator (positions 21–22) — A program-defined record format *may be* assigned a unique two-character indicator (e.g., **01–99, L1–L9, LR, H1–H9, U1–U8, RT**). In RPG II programs, record descriptions were commonly assigned a **01** to **99** indicator. When a record is read from the physical file, the indicator assigned will be set on for the program cycle. After the last output instruction is executed, the *Record Identifiying Indicator* will automatically be set off. When program control reads another record, the indicator is set on, and the processing sequence continues until an end-of-file condition is tested.

Record Identifying Indicators are used to condition calculations and output instructions. The status (ON or OFF) of the indicator determines whether the conditioned instruction(s) will be executed. This entry is optional in **RPG IV** programs that process program-described files. If the indicator is omitted, a warning error will be generated in compilation. On the other hand, if the indicator is specified and not used in calculations or output instructions, a warning error indicating that the indicator is not referenced will be included in compilation listing. *Record Identifying Indicators* are seldom used in **RPG IV** programs.

Record Description formats are referenced in **SEU** by the letter **I** for ***program-described*** record formats and by **IX** for ***externally defined*** record formats.

Field Description Section:

Instructions for this section are entered with a different *Input Specifications* format. When in **SEU**, entering **J** in the sequence area will access the *Field Description* format for ***program-described*** physical files. Format **JX** will reference the ***Field Description*** format for ***externally described*** physical files.

Field location (positions 37–46) — This area is divided into two separate fields: the *From* field (positions 37–41) and the *To* field (positions 42–46). The *From* field defines the beginning (high-order) position and the *To* field the last (low-order) position of the related field in the body of the record format.

The syntax rules for defining field sizes are as follows:

1. *From* and *To* entries must be right-justified in their fields.
2. Character fields have a maximum size of **32,767** characters.
3. Zones decimal numeric fields have a maximum size of **30** numbers.
4. Packed decimal numeric fields have a maximum size of **16** numbers.

Decimal positions (positions 47–48) — For character fields, no entry is required in this field. To define a field as numeric in a program-described physical file, **0** to **30** must be entered here. The number of decimal positions specified cannot be larger than the field length. Figure 3-13 illustrates how a decimal entry affects stored numeric values.

Numeric data stored on disk, diskette, and tape does not include an ***explicit*** or ***implied*** decimal. For program-described physical files, the decimal position for an input field is specified in the program and is ***implied*** in storage during execution of the program. The *Data Description Specifications* for an ***externally described*** physical file define the decimal positions for the field.

Field name (positions 49–62) — For program-described physical files, the programmer must create his or her own field names. The field names in externally described files are defined in the *Data Description Specifications*. In either case, the rules for creating field names for **RPG IV** programs are the same. Figure 3-14 summarizes the rules for assigning field names.

Figure 3-12 RPG IV syntax to define the record format of a program-described physical file. (Continued)

How the decimal position entry in positions 47 and 48 affects the numeric value in storage is shown in Figure 3-13. Note that *implied* decimal positions do not require a byte of storage, whereas an *explicit* decimal, as in an edited output field, does.

The rules for creating field names in **RPG IV** programs are explained in Figure 3-14.

The relationship of the data in the physical file “shell” to the *Input Specifications* coding is shown in Figure 3-15. The beginning and end positions of the fields in the record must be determined.

The relationship of the fields defined in the *Input Specifications* to field entries in the *Output Specifications* is detailed in Figure 3-16. Any difference in a related field name generates two compilation errors: a *warning error* identifying an **UNREFERENCED** input field and a *terminal error* for the **UNDEFINED** output field.

Decimal Position Entry	*Value in disk field*	*Value CPU storage*	*Comments*
0	12345	12345▲	Integer value
2	12345	123▲45	Decimal value with 2 implied decimals
5	12345	▲12345	Decimal value with 5 implied decimals
blank	12345	12345	Alphanumeric value

Notes: In the last example, because the decimal position field is blank, the numeric value will be processed as alphanumeric. Calculation or editing may not be performed with that field.

Symbol ▲ indicates an implied decimal (not actual). With the exception of output edited numeric fields, actual decimals are not assigned to field storage in the CPU.

Figure 3-13 Storage result of decimal position assignment on a data value.

RPG IV Rules for Creating Programmer-Supplied Field Names

1. A field name may include a maximum of 10 characters.
2. The first character of a field name must be A–Z, #, @, or $. Underscore or digits (0–9) are not permitted.
3. Other characters in a field name may be A–Z, #, @, $, 1–9, and _ (underscore).
4. Embedded blanks are not permitted.
5. Every field in the program must have a unique name.
6. Upper- or lowercase letters may be used.
7. Field names should be as descriptive as possible.
8. Field names referenced from an ***externally described*** physical, logical, display, or printer file *do not* have to be defined again in the **RPG IV** program.

Figure 3-14 RPG IV rules for creating field names.

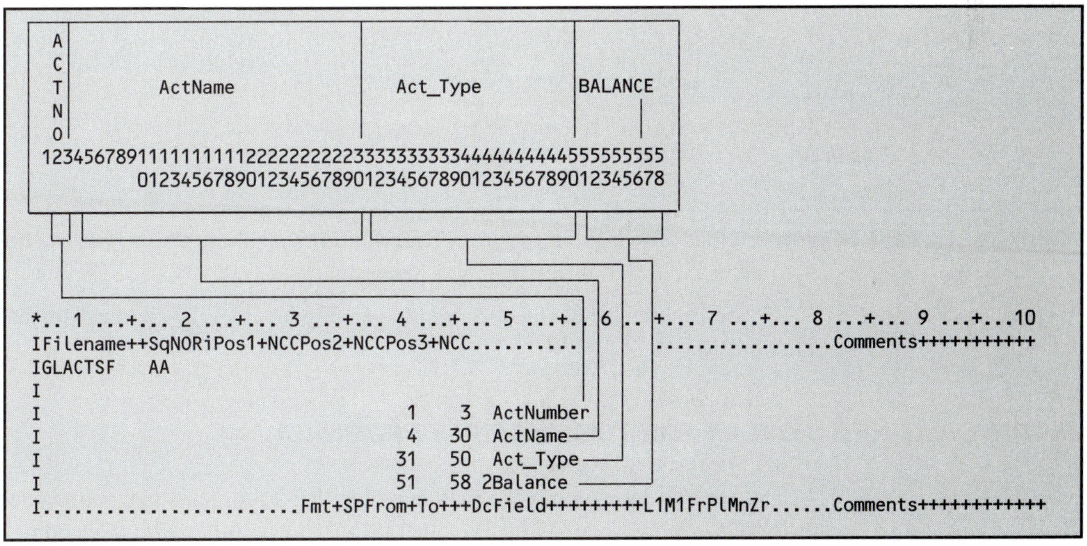

Figure 3-15 Relationship of the *Input Specification* entries to the program-described file's record format.

```
*.. 1 ...+... 2 ...+... 3 ...+... 4 ...+... 5 ...+... 6 ...+... 7 ...+... 8 ...+... 9 ...+...10
IFilename++SqNORiPos1+NCCPos2+NCCPos3+NCC..................................Comments++++++++++++
IGLACTSF    AA
I
I                                   1    3  ActNumber
I                                   4   30  ActName
I                                  31   50  Act_Type
I                                  51   58 2Balance
I.......................Fmt+SPFrom+To+++DcField+++++  ++L1M1FrPlMnZr......Comments++++++++++++

*.. 1 ...+... 2 ...+... 3 ...+... 4 ...+...5  ...+... 6 ...+... 7 ...+... 8 ...+... 9 ...+...10
O.............NO1NO2NO3Field+++++++++YB.End++PConsta  t/editword/DTformt++
OQSYSPRT    E          PrintLine       2
O                      ActNumber            7
O                      ActName             37
O                      Act_Type            62
O                      Balance         1   77
```

Figure 3-16 Relationship of the *Input Specifications* fields to the *Output Specifications.*

A source listing of the example **RPG IV** program that processes the program-described physical file is shown in Figure 3-17. Note that the calculation and output statements are identical to the previous example program that processed an externally described physical file.

```
SEQNBR*...+... 1 ...+... 2 ...+... 3 ...+... 4 ...+... 5 ...+... 6 ...+... 7 ...+... 8 ...+... 9 ...+...10
       * This program processes a program-described physical file and prints
       * a report
       FGlactsf   IF   F   58        DISK      Instruction modified       Input file
       FQsysprt   O    F  132        PRINTER   with an F in position      Output file
                                               22 and the record
       IGlactsf    SM  01                      length (58) in 23-27
       I                                    1    3  Actno
       I            Physical file           4   30  Name      Input statements define
       I            record name            31   50  Type      the fields in a program
       I                                   51   58 2Balance   described physical file

       C                   READ      GlactsF                             LR    read first record
       C                   DOW       *INLR = *OFF                              do while LR is off
       C                   EXCEPT    Printline                                 print a line
       C                   READ      GlactsF                             LR    read another record
       C                   ENDDO                                               end DOW group

       OQSYSPRT   E             Printline      2
       O                        ActNumber           7
       O                        ActName            37
       O                        Act_Type           62
       O                        Balance        1   77
```

Figure 3-17 **RPG IV** program that processes a program-described physical file and prints the field values.

The report printed by the program in Figure 3-17 is identical to that shown in Figure 3-10.

TRADITIONAL RPG SYNTAX FOR THE EXAMPLE PROGRAM

Because the reader may have to maintain older RPG programs that were coded according to **RPG's** *logic cycle*, it is important that he or she is familiar with that coding.

The **RPG** logic cycle automatically controls the opening of files, the reading and writing of records, the closing of files, and the end-of-file processing. Consequently, no calculation statements are needed to read and process the physical file. Refer to Appendix F for an explanation of the **RPG** logic cycle.

Examine the traditional **RPG** program in Figure 3-18 and note that the following coding changes have been made in the previous program example that processed an externally described physical file:

```
*.. 1 ...+... 2 ...+... 3 ...+... 4 ...+... 5 ...+... 6 ...+... 7 ...+... 8 ...+... 9 ...+...10
 * This program processes a externally described PF in arrival sequence & prints a report
 * by the RPG logic cycle.
FGLACTS    IP   E             DISK  ---------------------------------     Input file
FQSYSPRT   O    F  132        PRINTER    | Instruction modified with |     Output file
                                         | a P in position 17        |
OQSYSPRT   D    N1P----+             2   ---------------------------
O  ---------------------+ ActNumber        7
O | Instruction modified| ActName         37
O | with a D in 17 and  | Act_Type        62
O | EXCEPT name deleted | Balance      1  77
  | and N1P indicator in|
  | positions 21-23     |
```

Figure 3-18 Traditional **RPG** program that processes an externally described physical file and prints a report.

- The *File Description* instruction for the GLACTS file has been modified by replacing the letter **F** in position 18 with a **P** (for *primary file*).
- *Calculation Specification* instructions are omitted.
- *Output Specification* instructions are processed at *detail time* (**D** in position 17) instead of at *exception time* (**E** in position 17). The **EXCEPT** name in positions 30–39 has been deleted and replaced with an **N1P** indicator in positions 21–23. The **N1P** indicator prevents a blank line from printing at **1P** *(first cycle)* time.

The *File Description* instruction that defines the GLACTS file will open the input and output files. Then the accessed externally described record format will automatically read a record. Because calculation instructions are not specified, program control will "fall through" and print the field values for the current record.

This read and write process will continue until an end-of-file condition is tested, which turns on the **LR** *(Last Record)* indicator. After **LR** is set on, any calculation or output instructions conditioned with the **LR** indicator will be processed before the program is stopped and control returned to the operating system.

Because of the obvious simplicity of this program, the reader may wonder why use the more modern **RPG IV** syntax. For complex programs, the **RPG IV** method gives the programmer more control of the read, process, and write cycles. Also, the **RPG IV** syntax generates more efficient code, which decreases execution time. **RPG IV** program structure parallels the logic included in COBOL, FORTRAN, BASIC, and C programs. This may encourage use of the **ILE** *(Integrated Language Environment)*, where modules of programs written in different languages may be "bound" together into one executable unit.

SUMMARY

The functions of the six **RPG IV** specifications *(Control, File Description, Definition, Input, Calculation,* and *Output)* were discussed in this chapter. In **RPG IV** programs that process an externally described physical file, only the *File Description, Calculation,* and *Output Specifications* instructions are required. Programs that process physical files that do not have a DDS format (program-described) must define the field attributes (name, size, and type) in the *Input Specifications.*

Field names supported by **RPG IV** may be specified with a maximum of 10 characters. Numeric fields may be defined with up to 30 digits and may include no more than 30 decimal positions. Character fields may be defined with a maximum of 32,767 characters.

RPG IV instructions are entered via **SEU** *(Source Entry Utility)*, which has *format* and *prompt* lines for the complete specification type or for a section of it. Any attempt to enter invalid syntax for an instruction will be "flagged" by **SEU**.

Development of an **RPG IV** program includes the compilation and execution phases. The compilation phase, which is controlled by the **CRTBNDRPG** *(Create Bound RPG Program)* command, identifies syntax errors that may prevent an executable object from being created. After successful compilation of a program, the execution phase, which is initiated by the **CALL** command (option **4** on the Programmer Menu), runs the program and generates the required output. The results must be checked to determine if logic errors exist.

RPG IV programmers should avoid using the **RPG** *Logic Cycle*, which controls the opening of files, the reading of records, the writing of the output, and the closing of files automatically. Instead, the processing functions should be controlled by operations in calculations. Records should be read from the file by the **READ** operation, processing of the file done within a **DOU** or **DOW** group, output controlled by the **EXCEPT** operation, end-of-file condition tested in calculations, and control returned to the operating system after **LR** processing is completed.

QUESTIONS

3-1. Explain the steps involved in the development of an **RPG IV** program.

3-2. What AS/400 utility supports the entry of an **RPG IV** program's source code? What two methods of entering instructions are provided?

3-3. Name all of the **RPG IV** specifications.

3-4. Explain the function of each specification named in response to Question 3-3.

3-5. What is the compilation order of an **RPG IV** program? What is the result if the compilation order is not followed?

3-6. What Control Language command compiles an **RPG IV** source program? What other command may be used, and under what conditions must it be used?

3-7. Name four error types that may be generated in the compilation of an **RPG IV** program. Which class of errors prevents compilation of the program?

3-8. Briefly explain the information included in the listing created when an **RPG IV** program is compiled.

3-9. Refer to the specification type that defines the files processed by an **RPG IV** program, and indicate the minimum entries needed to process an externally described physical file.

3-10. Refer to the specification type that defines the files processed by an **RPG IV** program, and indicate the minimum entries needed to process a program-described physical file.

3-11. Refer to the specification type that defines the files processed by an **RPG IV** program that includes traditional code, and indicate the minimum entries needed to process an externally described physical file.

3-12. Identify any syntax errors in the following **RPG IV** syntax that processes an externally described physical file and prints a report.

```
*.. 1 ...+... 2 ...+... 3 ...+... 4 ...+... 5 ...+... 6 ...+... 7 ...+... 8 ...+... 9 ...+...10

FFilename++IPEASFRLen+LKLen+AIDevice+.Keywords+++++++++++++++++++++++++++++Comments++++++++++++
FGLACTS    I    E             DISC                                         Input file
FQSYSPRT   O    F             PRINTER                                      Output file
```

3-13. Name the minimum specification types required in an **RPG IV** program that processes an externally described physical file and prints a report.

3-14. Name the minimum specification types required in an **RPG IV** program that processes a program-described physical file and prints a report.

3-15. Name the minimum specification types required in a traditional **RPG IV** program that processes an externally described physical file and prints a report.

3-16. When are *Input Specification* instructions required in an **RPG IV** program?

3-17. What are *Record Identifying Indicators*? When are they used in an **RPG IV** program? When are they set on? When do they turn off?

3-18. Explain the term *conditioning an instruction.*

3-19. Identify any errors in the following *Input Specifications.*

```
*.. 1 ...+... 2 ...+... 3 ...+... 4 ...+... 5 ...+... 6 ...+... 7 ...+... 8 ...+... 9 ...+...10
IFilename++SqNORiPos1+NCCPos2+NCCPos3+NCC..................................Comments++++++++++++
I          AA
I
I                                  1    3  Cust-no
I                                      30  1Custnam
I                                 31   50  Cust Type
I                                 51      2$Cust_Amt
I.......................Fmt+SPFrom+To+++DcField+++++++++L1M1FrPlMnZr......Comments++++++++++++
```

3-20. When does the **LR** *(Last Record)* indicator turn on in an **RPG IV** program? When does it turn on in traditional **RPG** programs?

3-21. What is the function of calculation instructions in an **RPG IV** program that processes a physical file and prints a report?

3-22. Explain the processing features of the following **RPG IV** operations:

READ **DOW** **EXCEPT** **ENDDO**

3-23. Examine the following **RPG IV** calculation instructions and explain any syntax and logic errors.

```
*.. 1 ...+... 2 ...+... 3 ...+... 4 ...+... 5 ...+... 6 ...+... 7 ...+... 8 ...+... 9 ...+...10

C                   READ   Glacts
C                   DOW
C                   EXCEPT
C                   ENDDO
```

3-24. When does the required indicator included with the **READ** instruction turn on? What processing may be executed after the indicator is set on?

3-25. Refer to an *Output Specification* format, identify the logical sections, and explain their processing function.

3-26. What does **QSYSPRT** define? What other name(s) may be specified for this entry?

3-27. What is the function of the letter **E** in position 17 of the *Record Description* section of the *Output Specifications*?

3-28. What is an *exception* name? Where was it defined? Where is it referenced?

3-29. What does the entry in the *End position* field in the *Field Description* section of the *Output Specifications* indicate?

3-30. Examine the following *Output Specification* instructions and identify any **RPG IV** syntax errors.

```
*.. 1 ...+... 2 ...+... 3 ...+... 4 ...+... 5 ...+... 6 ...+... 7 ...+... 8 ...+... 9 ...+.. 10
OFilename++DF..N01N02N03Excnam++++B++A++Sb+Sa+.............................Comments++++++++++++
O          F            Printline
O                       ACTNUM               7
O                       ACTName              7
O                       ACT-TYPE            62
O                       BALANCE       0
O..............N01N02N03Field+++++++++YB.End++PConstant/editword/DTformt++
```

3-31. What are *Edit Codes*? On which **RPG IV** specifications are they specified? With what type of field (numeric or character, or both) may they be used?

PROGRAMMING ASSIGNMENTS

Before any **RPG IV** programs for the following assignments can be completed, the related physical file must have been compiled and loaded with data. The attributes of the physical file for each assignment are included in the Programming Assignments for Chapter 2. The related physical file may have been created by your instructor, or you may have to reference the related assignment in Chapter 2 and create and load the file. See your professor for instructions.

Your completed assignments must include:

1. The compilation listing of your **RPG IV** program.
2. A copy of the report.

Programming Assignment 3-1: ACTIVE EMPLOYEE LISTING

From the following Printer Spacing Chart, write an **RPG IV** program to generate the report format shown.

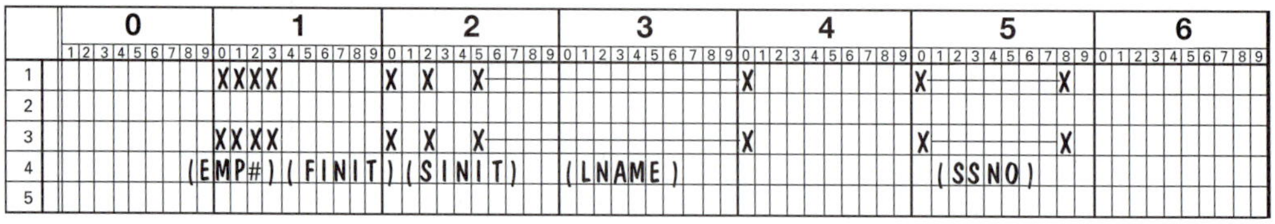

Reference Programming Assignment 2-1 for the atttributes of the physical file that this program will process.

Programming Assignment 3-2: EASTERN STATE REPORT LISTING

From the following information, write an **RPG IV** program to generate the required report.

Refer to Programming Assignment 2-2 for the attributes of the physical file. Complete a Printer Spacing Chart based on the following information. Indicate that the report is to be double-spaced.

Field	Print Positions
State letter	6–7
State name	16–35
State capital	46–70
Largest city	81–105

Programming Assignment 3-3: CUSTOMER MAILING LIST

Refer to Programming Assignment 2-3 for the attributes of the physical file that this program will process. Then, from the following Printer Spacing Chart, write an **RPG IV** program to generate the required report. Notice that *three* different output lines are printed for each record processed. Consequently, three separately formatted detail lines must be included in the program's output coding.

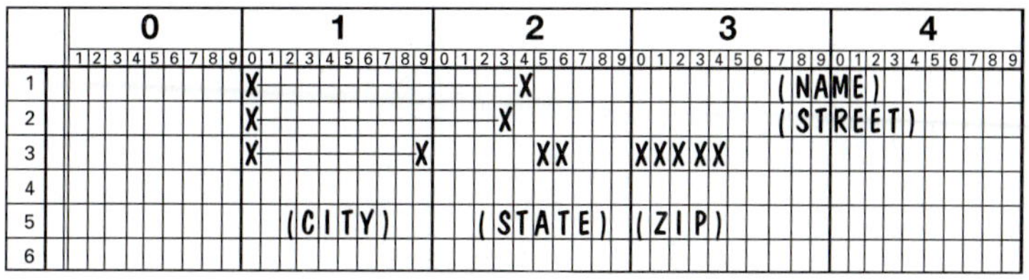

Note:
Triple-space between customer groups.

Programming Assignment 3-4: PROGRAM-DESCRIBED PHYSICAL FILE PROCESSING

If Programming Assignment 3-1, 3-2, or 3-3 was completed, modify it to process a program-described physical file. Refer to the related *Physical File Description* in the Chapter 2 assignments to determine record and field sizes. *(Hint:* To *override* the DDS external definition, the physical file must be defined with an **F** in the *File format* field and the record size included for the *Record length.)*

Programming Assignment 3-5: TRADITIONAL RPG SYNTAX

If Programming Assignment 3-1, 3-2, or 3-3 was completed, modify the instructions to process the externally described physical file and the printer file using *traditional* **RPG** syntax.

chapter 4

Report Headings and Editing

Chapter 3 presented the **RPG IV** syntax and procedures required to print a report without headings, numeric data, or editing. Generally, however, reports do have headings and include numeric values that require editing for readability. This chapter discusses the **RPG IV** syntax and processing logic needed to provide for these important features.

Examine the report shown in Figure 4-1 and notice the following:

1. The first heading line includes a date, constants, and page number.
2. The second heading line contains all constants.
3. The variable data (detail lines) is printed below the second heading line.
4. The variable spacing (triple, double, and single) is included in the body of the report.

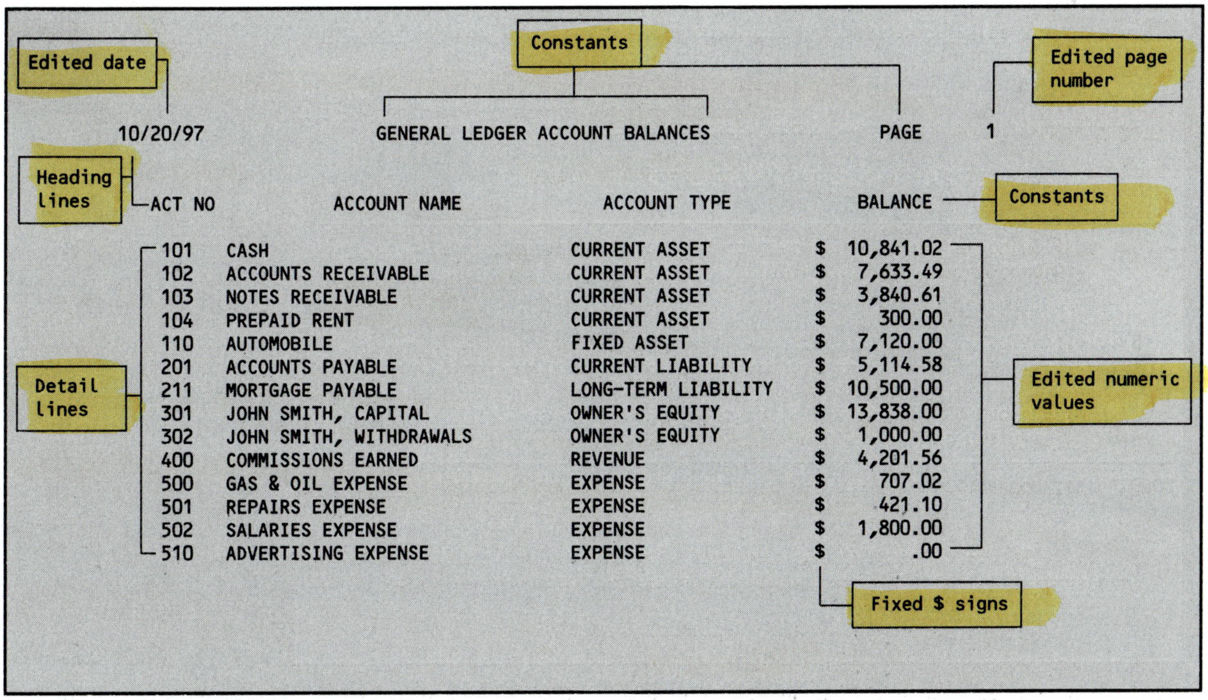

Figure 4-1 Printed report with two heading lines and edited numeric values.

5. All numeric fields (date, page number, and balance) are edited. *Editing* refers to zero suppression and the insertion of special characters in the body of a numeric value.
6. A fixed dollar sign ($) is printed before every edited balance value.

The Printer Spacing Chart related to the report (Figure 4-1) is detailed in Figure 4-2. Notice that the first heading line contains the variable field **UDATE,** the constant GENERAL LEDGER ACCOUNT BALANCES, the constant **PAGE,** and the variable field for the page number, shown as XXØX.

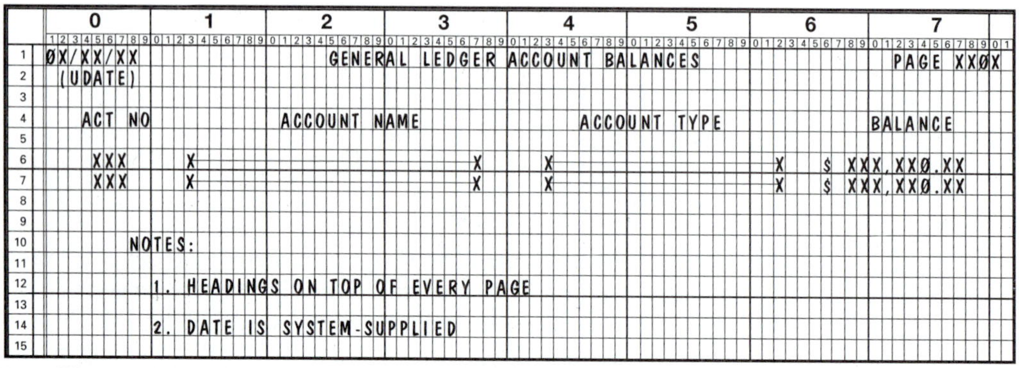

ØX/XX/XX
GENERAL LEDGER ACCOUNT BALANCES
PAGE XXØX
(UDATE)
ACT NO
ACCOUNT NAME
ACCOUNT TYPE
BALANCE
XXX X X X X $ XXX,XXØ.XX
XXX X X X X $ XXX,XXØ.XX
NOTES:
1. HEADINGS ON TOP OF EVERY PAGE
2. DATE IS SYSTEM-SUPPLIED

Figure 4-2 Printer Spacing Chart format with headings and numeric field editing requirements.

The variable field, identified as **UDATE** (positions 1–8), indicates that the system-supplied date is to be used for the report. Editing requirements for this field are indicated by the ØX/XX/XX format.

The XXØX after the constant **PAGE** is another **RPG IV** control feature that supplies an ascending page number on every page of a report. Page numbering starts at 0001 and increments to 9999.

The constants for the headings lines are coded in the **RPG IV** program to print every time the related instruction is executed. Variable field items are identified by the name enclosed in parentheses or by a related column heading.

In the **RPG IV** environment, alphanumeric and numeric field values are represented on a print chart with Xs. Editing requirements for a numeric field are indicated by the placement of insertion characters (e.g., decimal point, commas) in the body of the field. The extent of zero suppression in a numeric field is identified by a Ø (zero) in the appropriate field location, as shown in the following example.

XXX,XXØ.XX

↑ Indicates where zero suppression ends

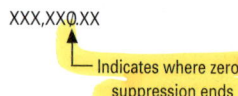

Examine Figure 4-2 and notice that the **UDATE** and page number fields also include a Ø to represent the control of zero suppression. Included in the editing of the detail lines is a fixed dollar sign printed before each balance value.

Finally, required line spacing—triple after the first heading line, double after the second heading line, and single for the detail lines—is indicated on the print chart by the location of the related lines. Notice that the two identically formatted detail lines represent single spacing and *not* that the values from every input record are to be printed twice.

The specific line types that may be included in a printed report are classified as follows:

1. Heading lines—Print lines that include only constants and/or a combination of constants and variables. Depending on the report requirements, any number of heading lines may be specified in a program.

2. Detail lines—Print lines that include variable data from an input file(s), from the result of calculations, or from a relational test.
3. Final total lines—Print lines that are generated after the end-of-file condition is tested. The variables' output often include summary totals.
4. Control total lines—Print lines that include the total for a common group of records (e.g., salesperson total, product total, store total, etc.).

The syntax to process all of the line types should be controlled in *structured* **RPG IV** programs by the **EXCEPT** operation and related **EXCEPTion** line(s) (**E** in position 17) and **EXCEPT** name (in positions 30–39) in the *Output Specifications*.

RPG IV Syntax for Headings

A constant is defined in an **RPG IV** program in positions 53–80 of the *Output Specifications* by enclosing it in apostrophes. Figure 4-3 presents examples of valid and invalid entries for the definition of constants.

```
*.. 1 ...+... 2 ...+... 3 ...+... 4 ...+... 5 ...+... 6 ...+... 7 ...+... 8
O..............N01N02N03Field+++++++++YB.End++PConstant/editword/DTformat++
O                                        55 'BALANCES' _____Valid -all required syntax specified
O                                        55 BALANCES'  _____Invalid - missing leading apostrophe
O                                           'BALANCES' _____Invalid - missing end position entry
O                                        55 'BALANCES  _____Invalid - missing ending apostrophe
O                                        58 'PAGE'     _____Invalid - according to the end position
                                                                entry of PAGE, it overlaps
                                                                BALANCES
```

Figure 4-3 Examples of valid and invalid entries for the definition of constants.

The relationship of the constants and variable fields formatted in the Printer Spacing Chart to the *Output Specifications* coding is illustrated in Figure 4-4. Locate the heading constant, GENERAL LEDGER ACCOUNT BALANCES, included in the first line of the print chart. Notice that the letter **T** is entered in column 46 of the constant ACCOUNT. Now follow the arrowed line to the output form and observe that **46** is entered in columns 42 and 43 of the *End Position in Output Record* field. This entry refers to the position in which the low-order character of a constant or field value will be placed (printed for this example). The high-order characters in the constant or field value are located accordingly in the preceding positions. The constant GENERAL LEDGER ACCOUNT will be printed as follows:

```
GENERAL LEDGER ACCOUNT
                     ▲
                     └─print position 46
```

Refer to the print chart in Figure 4-4, and notice that the constant BALANCES ends in column 55. Trace the line that connects it to the *Output Specifications* and observe that **55** is entered in the *End position* field. This entry will place the low-order S in BALANCES in print position 55 on output. Even though the space between ACCOUNT and BALANCES has not been included in either constant, the end position entry (55) for BALANCES places this constant so that it begins one space after ACCOUNT. The result of this coding is as follows:

```
GENERAL LEDGER ACCOUNT BALANCES
                     ▲        ▲
print position 46────┘        └─print position 55
```

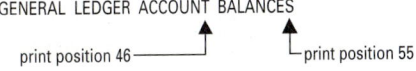

If the end position for BALANCES had been specified as 53, a space would not be included after ACCOUNT; the B in BALANCES would overlap the T in ACCOUNT, and the constant would print as follows:

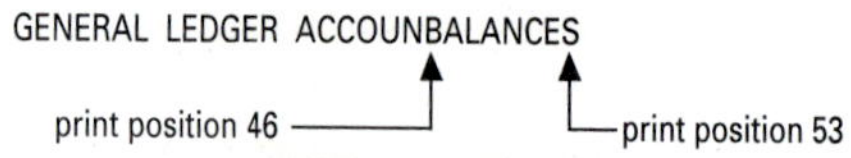

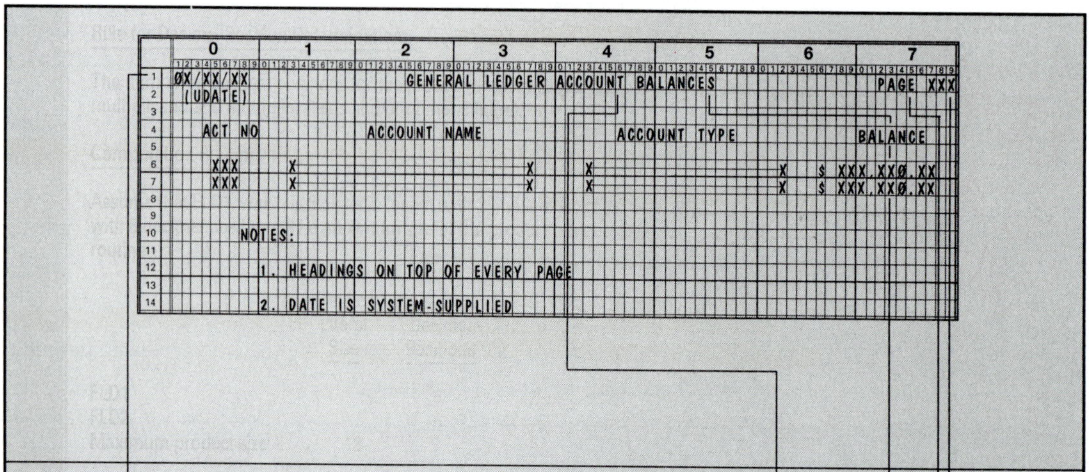


```
*.. 1 ...+... 2 ...+... 3 ...+... 4 ...+... 5 ...+... 6 ...+... 7 ...+... 8 ...+... 9 ...+...10
OFilename++DF..N01N02N03Excnam++++B++A++Sb+Sa+.............................Comments+++++++++++++
OQSYSPRT   E            Printline      301
O                       UDATE           Y      8
O                                             46 'GENERAL LEDGER ACCOUNT'
O                                             55 'BALANCES'
O                                             75 'PAGE'
O                       PAGE            Z     +2
O          E            Printline        2
O                                              9 'ACT NO'
O                                             32 'ACCOUNT NAME'
O                                             57 'ACCOUNT TYPE'
O                                             76 'BALANCE'
O          E            Detailine        1
O                       Actnum                 7
O                       Actname               37
O                       Act_Type              62
O                                             66 '$'
O                       Balance         1     77
O.............N01N02N03Field+++++++++YB.End++PConstant/editword/DTformat++Comments+++++++++++
```

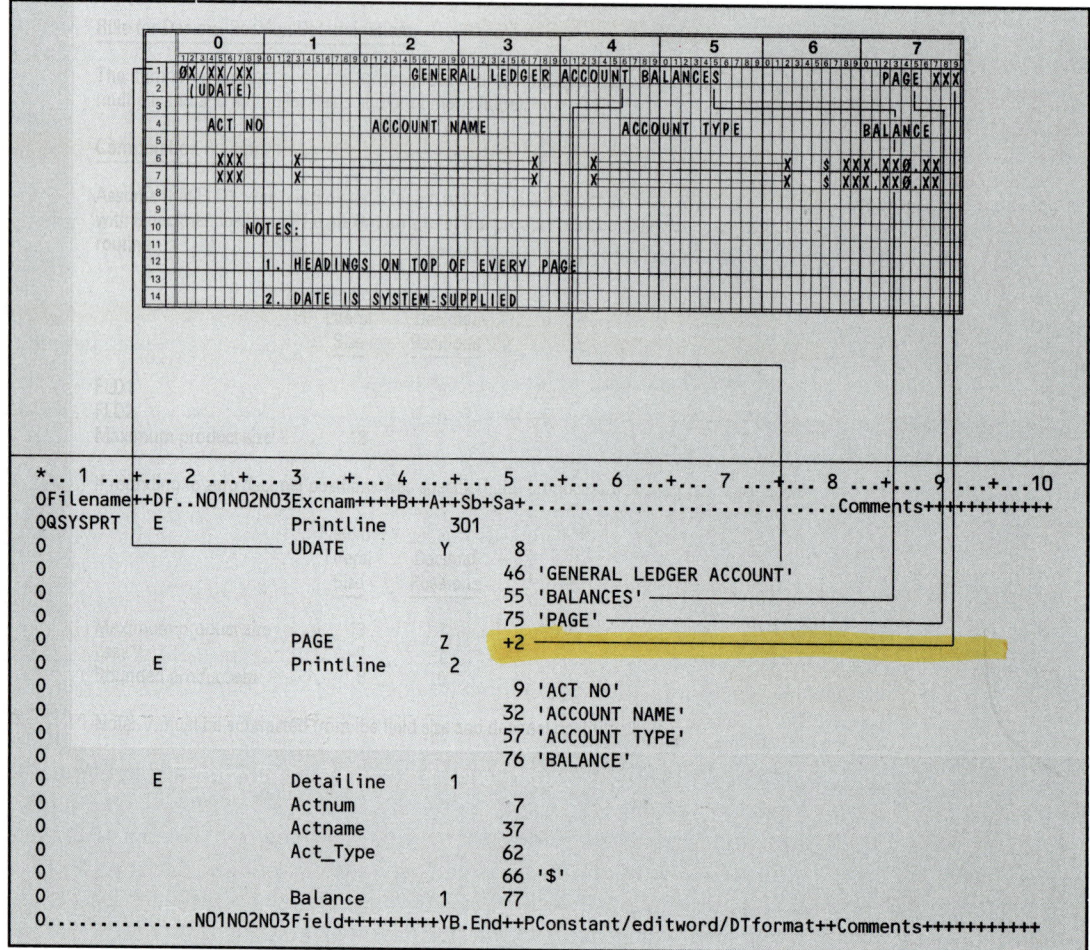

Figure 4-4 Relationship of Printer Spacing Chart entries to *Output Specifications.*

Because the constants in the first heading line could not be entered on one line of output coding, BALANCES is included on a separate line. The end position references place a constant in its required horizontal location.

Included in this example are the **RPG IV** reserved field names for **UDATE** and **PAGE.** The values for these items are also positioned on output by their end position entries. This composite of instructions completes the output record (first heading line), which is controlled during processing by the related *Record Description* entries in columns 7 to 54.

The second heading line, which includes all constants, is coded on the *Output Specifications* by enclosing each constant in apostrophes and specifying the related end positions entry.

Figure 4-4 shows another method for placing a constant or variable on output. Note how the value in the special word Page will be printed one space after the constant 'PAGE' by the +2 entry in the *End++* field. The example shown in Figure 4-4 is not to be construed as the only approach for the coding of headings in a program. Providing that the constants are enclosed in apostrophes, the end position is specified, and the items do not overlap, any coding style is acceptable. The format followed is the option of the programmer.

Session and Job Dates

The special words for user date (**UDATE, *DATE, UMONTH, *MONTH, UDAY, *UDAY, UYEAR,** and ***UYEAR**) enable the programmer to supply a session or job date at run time. **UDATE** is a six-digit numeric field in a default mmddyy format. ***DATE** is an eight-digit numeric field in a default mmddyyyy format. The **UDATE** format may be changed by including a **DATFMT** keyword with a format option in the *Header Specifications*. Figure 4-5 shows the eight options available, their valid edit characters, edited results, and an example keyword entry.

DATFMT(fmt(separator) Options	Format accessed	Valid separators	Example DATFMT keyword	Edit Code Y Result
*ISO RPG default	yyyymmdd	-	DATFMT(*ISO)	1997-12-31
*MDY	mmddyy	/ - , &	DATFMT(*MDY&)	12 31 97
*YMD	yymmdd	/ - , &	DATFMT(*YMD/)	97/12/31
*DMY	ddmmyy	/ - , &	DATFMT(*DMY,)	31,12,97
*JUL Julian	yyddd	/ - , &	DATFMT(*JUL-)	97-365
*USA IBM USA std	mmddyyyy	/ - , &	DATFMT(*USA/)	12/31/1997
*EUR IBM European std	ddmmyyyy	.	DATFMT(*EUR.)	31.12.1997
*JIS Japanese std	yyyymmdd	-	DATFMT(*JIS-)	1997-12-31

separator selected

Note: When only one valid separator is available for a format, it may be omitted from the DATFMT keyword.

Header (H) Specification entry:

```
*.. 1 ...+... 2 ...+... 3 ...+... 4 ...+... 5 ...+... 6 ...+... 7
H Keywords++++++++++++++++++++++++++++++++++++++++++++++++++++++++
H DATFMT(*USA&)
```

Figure 4-5 Summary of date formats.

UDATE may be separated into individual month, day, and year values by the special words **UMONTH, UDAY,** and **UYEAR,** respectively. Each has the related two digits assigned to its value.

Sometimes it may not be expedient to include the session date in a report. Instead, an earlier or later date may be appropriate. The session date may be overridden with a different date for the job by the **CHGJOB** *(Change Job)* command, entered at the user's workstation.

Page Numbering (PAGE)

PAGE is an **RPG IV** special word that controls the numbering of report pages. It is predefined as a four-byte numeric field with zero decimal positions (integer) that starts page numbering at 0001 and is automatically incremented by 1 for each subsequent page.

PAGE may also be defined from 1 to 15 bytes in input or calculations and may be initialized to a starting page number minus one. The incrementation of the page numbers will still be controlled automatically. Special **RPG IV** words—**PAGE1** through **PAGE7**—are also provided so that pages of a report may be numbered differently, or so that they can be used in a program that supports more than one printer file.

Figure 4-6 illustrates how **PAGE** is used in the example program and gives the values in the field for the first and second pages of the report. Use of the constant **PAGE** is optional and has no effect on the function of the special word **PAGE.**

```
*.. 1 ...+... 2 ...+... 3 ...+... 4 ...+... 5 ...+... 6 ...+... 7 ...+... 8
OFilename++DF..N01N02N03Excnam++++B++A++Sb+Sa+............................
O                                            75 'PAGE'
O                   PAGE                     +2          Constant is optional
O.............N01N02N03Field+++++++++YB.End++PConstant   and has no effect on
  Value in PAGE for the first page of the report: 0001   the function of the
                                                          special word PAGE
  Value in PAGE for the second page of the report: 0002

  Note: Edit code Z, which suppresses leading zeros in the PAGE value, is
        automatically assumed.  However, when the PAGE field is defined
        in input or calculation specifications, it is considered a field
        name and zero suppression is not automatic.
```

Figure 4-6 RPG IV syntax for the special word **PAGE.**

SUMMARY OF THIS SECTION

A source listing of the example program is presented in Figure 4-7. In addition to the newly introduced heading, **UDATE,** and **PAGE** entries in the *Output Specifications,* the program includes *one* more instruction in calculations to control the printing of the two heading lines. Note that the program example assumes that only a one-page report will be printed. *Page-overflow control,* necessary for multiple-page reports, will be introduced in Chapter 5.

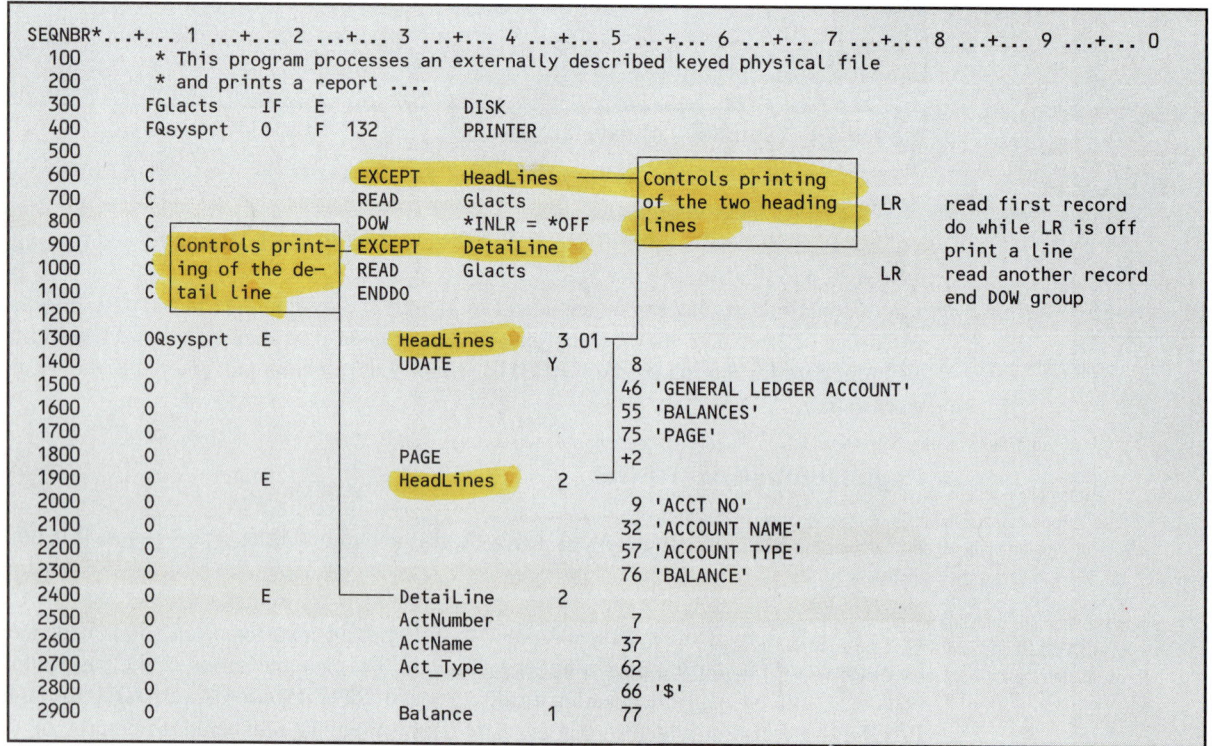

```
SEQNBR*...+... 1 ...+... 2 ...+... 3 ...+... 4 ...+... 5 ...+... 6 ...+... 7 ...+... 8 ...+... 9 ...+... 0
       * This program processes an externally described keyed physical file
       * and prints a report ....
      FGlacts     IF   E             DISK
      FQsysprt    O    F  132        PRINTER

      C                   EXCEPT    HeadLines          Controls printing
      C                   READ      Glacts             of the two heading    LR    read first record
      C                   DOW       *INLR = *OFF       lines                       do while LR is off
      C  Controls print-  EXCEPT    DetailLine                                     print a line
      C  ing of the de-   READ      Glacts                                   LR    read another record
      C  tail line        ENDDO                                                    end DOW group

      OQsysprt    E            HeadLines      3 01
      O                        UDATE         Y      8
      O                                            46 'GENERAL LEDGER ACCOUNT'
      O                                            55 'BALANCES'
      O                                            75 'PAGE'
      O                        PAGE                +2
      O           E            HeadLines      2
      O                                             9 'ACCT NO'
      O                                            32 'ACCOUNT NAME'
      O                                            57 'ACCOUNT TYPE'
      O                                            76 'BALANCE'
      O           E            DetailLine     2
      O                        ActNumber            7
      O                        ActName             37
      O                        Act_Type            62
      O                                            66 '$'
      O                        Balance       1     77
```

Figure 4-7 RPG IV program that processes a physical file and prints a report with two heading lines.

File Description Instructions:

Line No

300 The physical file (Glacts) is defined as an input (**I** in position 15) externally described file (**E** in position 22). Because it is processed by the **READ** operation, and not with the RPG Logic Cycle, an **F** is specified in position 19, indicating that it is a full-procedural file.

400 The system PRINTER file (**QSYSPRT**) is defined with this instruction.

Calculation Instructions:

600 This **EXCEPT** instruction controls the printing of the Headlines (heading lines) on lines 1300 and 1900. After printing, control will return to the **READ** instruction on line 700.

700 This **READ** instruction reads the first data record from the input file (Glacts). If no records are stored in the physical file, the **LR** indicator will turn on and end the job.

800 The **DOW** instruction performs its iterative (looping) process until the **LR** indicator is set on by the **READ** instruction on line 700 or 1000. If no records are stored in the physical file, the **READ** instruction on line 700 will turn on **LR.** The ***INLR = *OFF** relational test in the **DOW** instruction will be false and pass control to the first instruction after the **ENDDO** operation and, for this program example, end the job.

If records are stored in the physical file, the instructions with the **DOW** group will be executed.

900 This **EXCEPT** instruction controls the printing of the DetailLine on line 2400. After printing, control returns to the **READ** instruction on line 1000.

1000 This **READ** instruction reads the next record from the physical file. If end of file is tested, the **LR** indicator will be set on. When the **ENDDO** operation returns control to the **DOW** instruction on line 800, the relational test (***INLR = *OFF**) will be false and, for this program example, the job ended.

1100 The **ENDDO** operation ends the **DOW** group. When this operation is executed, control is returned to the **DOW** instruction on line 800, where the ***INLR = *OFF** test is made.

Output Instructions:

1300–1800 The first heading line is defined in these instructions.

UDATE on line 1400 accesses the session or job date value. Edit code **Y** suppresses any leading zero (for months 01–09) and inserts **/** (slashes) after the month and day values (e.g., 8/11/97).

The constants for the first heading line are defined on lines 1500–1700.

PAGE provides for page numbering beginning with 0001. Any leading zeros will automatically be suppressed without specifying an edit code or word.

1900–2300 The second heading line is defined in these instructions.

The constants for the second heading line are defined on lines 2000–2300.

2400–2900 The data from a physical file record is printed by these instructions. ActNumber through Balance are fields from the physical file, and the stored data will be printed for every record processed.

***Note:* The numbers in positions 50–52 of each instruction indicate the end position of the special word value, constant, or field when printed.**

Figure 4-7 RPG IV program that processes a physical file and prints a report with two heading lines. (Continued)

As indicated in the source listing, the **01** entry in the *Skip Before* (**Sb**) field in positions 46–47 will advance the continuous-form paper to line 1 of a new page *before* the first heading line (Headlines) is printed. This control prevents printing on the current page, which may include the output from a previous program. Note that any line number (0 to 255) may be specified in the *Space Before* (Sb) field in positions 40–42 or *Space After* (Sa) field in positions 43–45.

A compiled listing of the example program is presented in Figure 4-8. For brevity, only the Source Section of the listing is shown. However, the reader should examine and understand the content of the other sections in his or her program compilations, which were explained in Chapter 3.

```
Line   <---------------------- Source Specifications ----------------------------><---- Comments ----> Do
Number ....1....+....2....+....3....+....4....+....5....+....6....+....7....+....8....+....9....+...10 Num
                     S o u r c e   L i s t i n g
     1  * This program processes an externally described keyed physical file
     2  * and prints a report ....
     3 FGlacts    IF   E            DISK
        *------------------------------------------------------------------------------------*
        *                             RPG name          External name                        *
        * File name. . . . . . . . :  GLACTS            STAN/GLACTS                          *
        * Record format(s) . . . . :  GLACTSR           GLACTSR                              *
        *------------------------------------------------------------------------------------*
     4 FQsysprt   O    F  132         PRINTER
     5
     6=IGLACTSR
        *------------------------------------------------------------------------------------*
        * RPG record format  . . . :  GLACTSR                                                *
        * External format  . . . . :  GLACTSR : STAN/GLACTS                                  *
        *------------------------------------------------------------------------------------*
     7=I                            A    1    3  ACTNUMBER
     8=I                            A    4   30  ACTNAME
     9=I                            A   31   50  ACT_TYPE
    10=I                            S   51   58 2BALANCE
    11 C                  EXCEPT    Headlines
    12 C                  READ      GLACTS                            ----LR    read first record
    13 C                  DOW       *INLR = *OFF                                do while LR is off     B01
    14 C                  EXCEPT    Detailine                                   print a line            01
    15 C                  READ      Glacts                            ----LR    read another record     01
    16 C                  ENDDO                                                 end DOW group          E01
    17
    18 OQsysprt   E           Headlines       3 01
    19 O                      UDATE          Y        8
    20 O                                             46 'GENERAL LEDGER ACCOUNT'
    21 O                                             55 'BALANCES'
    22 O                                             75 'PAGE'
    23 O                      PAGE                   80
    24 O          E           Headlines       2
    25 O                                              9 'ACCT NO'
    26 O                                             32 'ACCOUNT NAME'
    27 O                                             57 'ACCOUNT TYPE'
    28 O                                             76 'BALANCE'
    29 O          E           Detailine       2
    30 O                      ActNumber               7
    31 O                      ActName                37
    32 O                      Act_Type               62
    33 O                                             66 '$'
    34 O                      Balance        1       77
```

Figure 4-8 Compiled program listing of the example heading program.

DEFINITION OF FIELDS

It was explained in Chapter 3 that fields related to externally described physical files are defined in *Data Description Specification* instructions. As later chapters will show, fields may also be defined in logical files, display files, printer files, and Control Language statements. Fields not defined in these external file types may be defined in an **RPG IV** program in the *Definition*, *Input*, and *Calculation Specifications*. However, new programming standards set by **RPG IV** recommend that any fields not externally defined should be defined in the *Definition Specifications* and not in the *Input* or *Calculation Specifications*. Note that fields *cannot* be defined in the *Output Specifications*. When a field is specified in an output instruction, it must have been previously defined.

Regardless of where a field is defined, numeric fields are defined as numeric by specifying a number from **0** to **30** in the decimal position field of the related specification type. Character fields are defined as character by omitting the decimal position entry. Figure 4-9 illustrates the **RPG IV** syntax for defining fields in the *Definition*, *Input*, and *Calculation Specifications*.

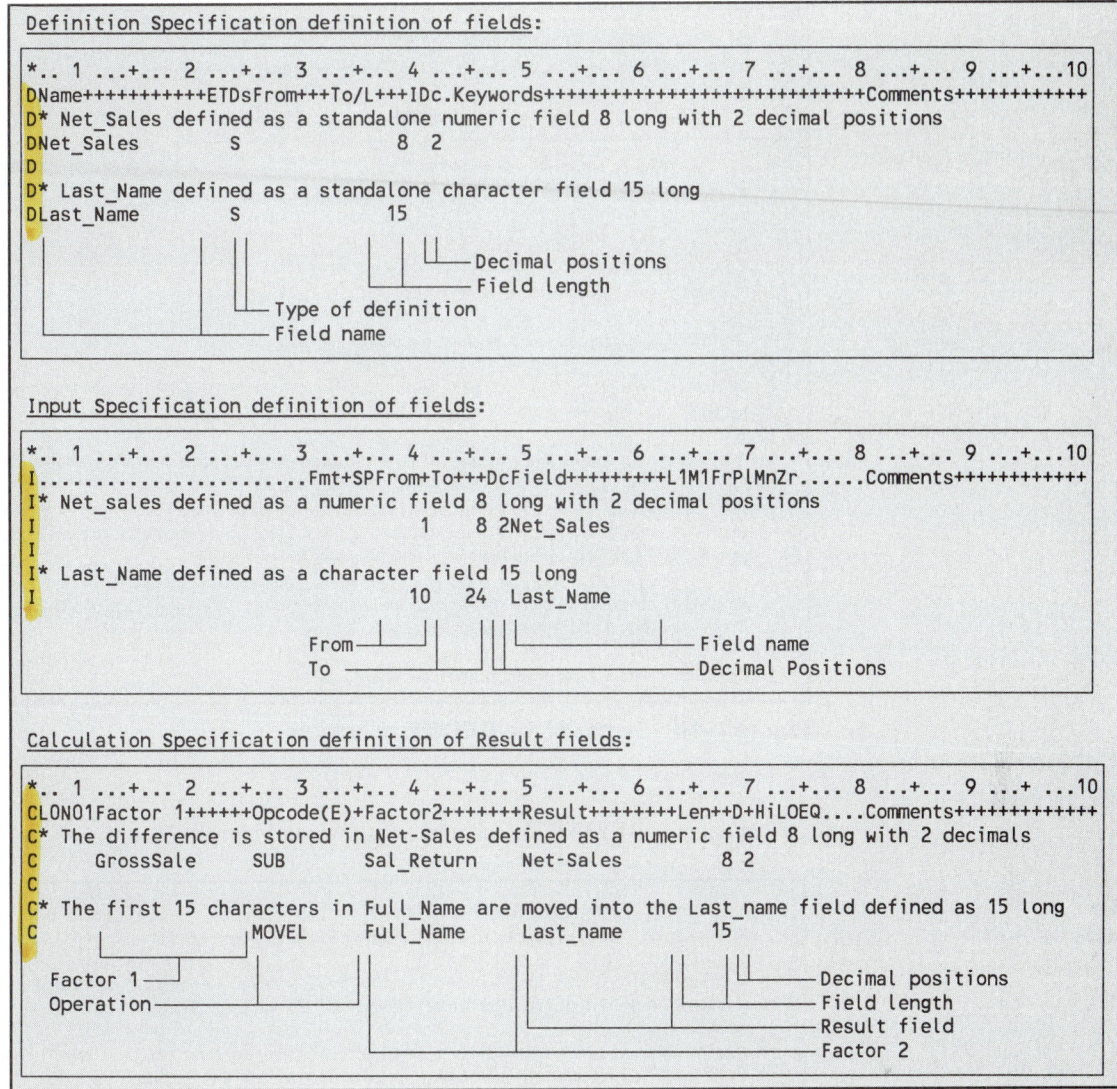

Definition Specification definition of fields:

```
*.. 1 ...+... 2 ...+... 3 ...+... 4 ...+... 5 ...+... 6 ...+... 7 ...+... 8 ...+... 9 ...+...10
DName+++++++++++ETDsFrom+++To/L+++IDc.Keywords+++++++++++++++++++++++++++++Comments++++++++++++
D* Net_Sales defined as a standalone numeric field 8 long with 2 decimal positions
DNet_Sales        S               8  2
D
D* Last_Name defined as a standalone character field 15 long
DLast_Name        S              15
```

Decimal positions
Field length
Type of definition
Field name

Input Specification definition of fields:

```
*.. 1 ...+... 2 ...+... 3 ...+... 4 ...+... 5 ...+... 6 ...+... 7 ...+... 8 ...+... 9 ...+...10
I.......................Fmt+SPFrom+To+++DcField+++++++++L1M1FrPlMnZr......Comments++++++++++++
I* Net_sales defined as a numeric field 8 long with 2 decimal positions
I                                  1    8 2Net_Sales
I
I* Last_Name defined as a character field 15 long
I                                 10   24  Last_Name
```

From
To
Field name
Decimal Positions

Calculation Specification definition of Result fields:

```
*.. 1 ...+... 2 ...+... 3 ...+... 4 ...+... 5 ...+... 6 ...+... 7 ...+... 8 ...+... 9 ...+ ...10
CL0N01Factor 1+++++++Opcode(E)+Factor2+++++++Result++++++++Len++D+HiLOEQ....Comments+++++++++++++
C* The difference is stored in Net-Sales defined as a numeric field 8 long with 2 decimals
C      GrossSale     SUB       Sal_Return    Net-Sales          8 2
C
C* The first 15 characters in Full_Name are moved into the Last_name field defined as 15 long
C                   MOVEL      Full_Name     Last_name         15
```

Factor 1
Operation
Decimal positions
Field length
Result field
Factor 2

Figure 4-9 Field definition examples in the *Definition, Input,* and *Calculation Specifications.*

A **0** entered in the decimal position field of any of the three specification types defines the field as an integer. A digit from **1** to **30** defines a field as a decimal number with the specified number of *implied* decimal positions. The decimal position assigned may *not* be greater than the length of the field.

The DEFINE Operation

Another method to define fields not defined in any of the externally described files processed by an **RPG IV** program is with a ***LIKE DEFINE** instruction. The **DEFINE** operation defines the field specified in the *Result* field of the instruction with the same attributes as the field, array element, or table name included in *Factor 2*. Entering a + or - with an integer in the *Len++* field will increase or decrease the size of the field entered in the *Result* field. Note that only the overall size of the field will be increased or decreased; the decimal positions of a numeric field *cannot* be changed. Figure 4-10 details the syntax of the **DEFINE** operation.

```
*.. 1 ...+... 2 ...+... 3 ...+... 4 ...+... 5 ...+... 6 ...+... 7 ...+... 8
CLON01Factor1+++++++Opcode(E)+Factor2+++++++Result++++++++Len++D+HiLoEq....

C        *LIKE          DEFINE    FIELDA         FIELDB

    1     2             3         4              5           6       7
```

1. A *Control Level Indicator* (**L0–L9** or **LR**) may be specified in the **L0** field.

   No entry is permitted in the **N01** field.

2. The special word ***LIKE** must be entered in *Factor 1*.

3. The **DEFINE** operation name must be entered in the *Opcode* field.

4. A field name, array element, or table name must be entered in *Factor 2*. Named constants or literals are *not* permitted.

5. A field name must be specified in the *Result* field. An array, array element, or table name is *not* permitted.

6. An entry in the *Len++* field is not required unless the *Result* field is defined larger or smaller than the *Factor 2* item. A + sign with an integer in this field will define the *Result* field integer entry larger than the Factor 2 item. A − sign with an integer will define the *Result* field integer entry smaller.

   Any decimal positions included in the *Factor 2* item will not be changed by a + or − entry. Only the overall length of the *Result* field is increased or decreased.

7. Resulting indicators (*HiLoEq* fields) are *not* permitted.

Figure 4-10 Syntax of the **DEFINE** operation.

Examples of **DEFINE** instructions are shown in Figure 4-11.

```
*.. 1 ...+... 2 ...+... 3 ...+... 4 ...+... 5 ...+... 6 ...+... 7 ...+... 8
CLON01Factor1+++++++Opcode(E)+Factor2+++++++Result++++++++Len++D+HiLoEq....
 * Given:
 *   NumField1 is defined with a length of 7 with 2 decimal positions
 *   CharField1 is defined with a length of 25 characters

 * NumField2 is defined with the same attributes as NumField1.  NumField2
 * will be 7 digits with 2 decimal positions after execution
C     *LIKE         DEFINE    NumField1     NumField2

 * NumField3 is defined 1 digit larger than NumField1.  NumField3 will be
 * 8 digits with 2 decimal positions after execution
C     *LIKE         DEFINE    NumField1     NumField3     +  1

 * NumField4 is defined 2 digits smaller than NumField1.  NumField4 will be
 * 5 digits with 2 decimal positions after execution
C     *LIKE         DEFINE    NumField1     NumField4     -  2

 * CharField2 is defined 10 characters smaller than CharField1.  CharField2
 * will be 15 characters after execution
C     *LIKE         DEFINE    CharField1    CharField2    -  10
```

Figure 4-11 Examples of **DEFINE** instructions.

ASSIGNMENT OF DECIMAL POINTS

Decimal points are not included in the numeric values stored on disk, diskette, or tape, but they are *implied* in memory during program execution. Figure 4-12 illustrates the effect of decimal position assignments on numeric values in storage during run time.

During run time, any attempt to process a numeric field that contains character data will generate a decimal data error.

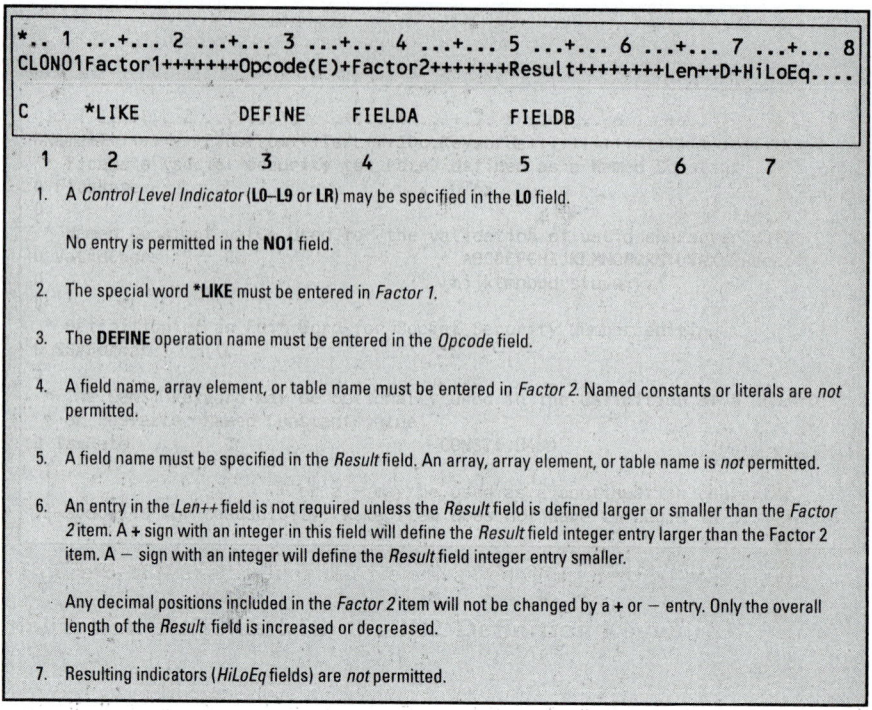

*.. 1 ...+... 2 ...+... 3 ...+... 4 .. DName+++++++++++ETDsFrom+++To/L+++IDc.	Decimal Position Entry	Value Stored on Disk	Value Stored in Memory	Comments
D				
DSales_Amt S 5 0	0	12345	12345▲	Integer value
D				
DSales_Amt S 5 2	2	12345	123▲45	Two implied decimals
D				
DSales_Amt S 5 5	5	12345	▲12345	Five implied decimals
D				
DSales_Amt S 5		12345	12345	Character value

Notes: In the last example, because the decimal position field is blank, the value will be processed as a character value. Arithmetic calculations or editing may not be performed with that field.
▲ symbol indicates the position of the implied decimal in memory.

* Only a partial *Definition Specifications* format is shown.

Figure 4-12 Effect of decimal position assignments on numeric values in memory during run time.

SIGNED NUMERIC VALUES

In the **RPG IV** environment, an unsigned numeric value is processed as positive. Negative numbers, however, must be explicitly signed as negative. When entering a negative number using an IBM workstation keyboard, the **FIELD** – keys must be pressed to define the value as negative. On the extended keyboard on microcomputers, the numeric keypad (right side of the keyboard) includes a minus (−) key that must be pressed to enter a value as negative. When stored on disk, diskette, tape, or in memory, the minus sign is stored over the low-order byte of the numeric value, which does not increase the field size.

NUMERIC FIELD EDITING

Only fields that have been defined as numeric may be edited. Editing refers to the insertion, suppression, or replacement of characters within the body of a numeric value that is printed or displayed. Editing of numeric fields in **RPG IV** programs is performed by *edit codes* and *edit words*. Each method is discussed in the following paragraphs.

Edit Codes: Simple, Combination, and User-Defined

The table in Figure 4-13 lists the available edit codes and the editing options they provide. Edit codes may be divided into three categories: simple **(X, Y, Z)**; combination **(1–4, A–D, J–Q)**; and user-defined **(5–9)**. An edit code is specified in position 44 of the *Output Specifications,* or in positions 36–37 of the DDS for a display file, or with an **EDTCDE** keyword in the DDS for a printer file.

On the editing of a numeric value, the functions of the **DECEDIT** keyword options shown in Figure 4-13 are

- '.' decimal symbol with zero suppression (e.g., **.456**),
- ',' comma symbol with zero suppression (e.g., **,456**),
- **'0.'** decimal symbol; leading zeros printed or displayed (e.g., **0.456**),
- **'0,'** comma symbol; leading zeros printed or displayed (e.g., **0,456**).

If the keyword is not specified, the default value for the decimal point is a period. The top of Figure 4-13 illustrates how a **DECEDIT** keyword instruction is coded in the *Control Specification.*

```
Example Control Specifications DECEDIT keyword:
SEQNBR*...+... 1 ...+... 2 ...+... 3 ...+... 4 ...+... 5 ...+... 6 ...+... 7 ...+... 8 ...+... 9 ...+... 0
  100       H DECEDIT('0.')
              └─ with any edit code (except Z, Y, or X), this value will control the printing of
                 a zero before the decimal point when dollar digits are all zeros (e.g.,   0.98)
```

				DECEDIT Keyword Parameter				
Edit Code	Commas	Decimal Point	Sign for Negative Balance	'.'	','	'0,'	'0.'	Zero Suppress
1	Yes	Yes	No Sign	.00 or 0	,00 or 0	0,00 or 0	0.00 or 0	Yes
2	Yes	Yes	No Sign	Blanks	Blanks	Blanks	Blanks	Yes
3		Yes	No Sign	.00 or 0	,00 or 0	0,00 or 0	0.00 or 0	Yes
4		Yes	No Sign	Blanks	Blanks	Blanks	Blanks	Yes
5–9[1]								
A	Yes	Yes	CR	.00 or 0	,00 or 0	0,00 or 0	0.00 or 0	Yes
B	Yes	Yes	CR	Blanks	Blanks	Blanks	Blanks	Yes
C		Yes	CR	.00 or 0	,00 or 0	0,00 or 0	0.00 or 0	Yes
D		Yes	CR	Blanks	Blanks	Blanks	Blanks	Yes
J	Yes	Yes	– (minus)	.00 or 0	,00 or 0	0,00 or 0	0.00 or 0	Yes
K	Yes	Yes	– (minus)	Blanks	Blanks	Blanks	Blanks	Yes
L		Yes	– (minus)	.00 or 0	,00 or 0	0,00 or 0	0.00 or 0	Yes
M		Yes	– (minus)	Blanks	Blanks	Blanks	Blanks	Yes
N	Yes	Yes	– (floating minus)	.00 or 0	,00 or 0	0,00 or 0	0.00 or 0	Yes
O	Yes	Yes	– (floating minus)	Blanks	Blanks	Blanks	Blanks	Yes
P		Yes	– (floating minus)	.00 or 0	,00 or 0	0,00 or 0	0.00 or 0	Yes
Q		Yes	– (floating minus)	Blanks	Blanks	Blanks	Blanks	Yes
X[2]								Yes
Y[3]								Yes
Z[4]								Yes

[1] These are the user-defined edit codes.

[2] The **X** edit code ensures a hexadecimal F sign for positive values. Because the system does this for you, normally you do not have to specify this code.

[3] The **Y** edit code suppresses the leftmost zeros of date fields, up to but not including the digit preceding the first separator. The **Y** edit code also inserts slashes (/) between the month, day, and year according to the following pattern:

```
   nn/n
   nn/nn
   nn/nn/n
   nn/nn/nn
  nnn/nn/nn
   nn/nn/nnnn
  nnn/nn/nnnn
 nnnn/nn/nn
nnnnn/nn/nn
```

[4] The **Z** edit code removes the sign (plus or minus) from a numeric field and suppresses leading zeros.

Figure 4-13 Table of **RPG IV** edit codes (courtesy of IBM) and **DECEDIT** keyword coding example.

Simple Edit Codes (X, Y, Z)

Because the AS/400 system provides the functions of edit code **X,** which ensures that the numeric value is positive, it is seldom used. Edit code **Y, commonly used only to edit date values,** performs the editing functions shown in the partial *Output Specifications* in Figure 4-14.

```
                                   Value in        Edited
 3 ...+... 4 ...+... 5             field           Result
 Field+++++++++YB.End++
 DATE1           Y    130          093097          9/30/97

 DATE2           Y    130          0930            9/30

 DATE3           Y    130          09301997        9/30/1997

 DATE4           Y    130          19970930        1997/09/30
                 |     |
                 |     └── Print or display position of the last number
Notes:           └──────── Edit code

   1. For Y editing to be performed, the value must be at least three
      digits.

   2. Editing is performed from left to right.

   3. If the field value is negative, the negative sign will not print
      or display.

   4. DATE1, DATE2, DATE3, and DATE4 are programmer-supplied field names
      and not special words or incidental to the field values.
```

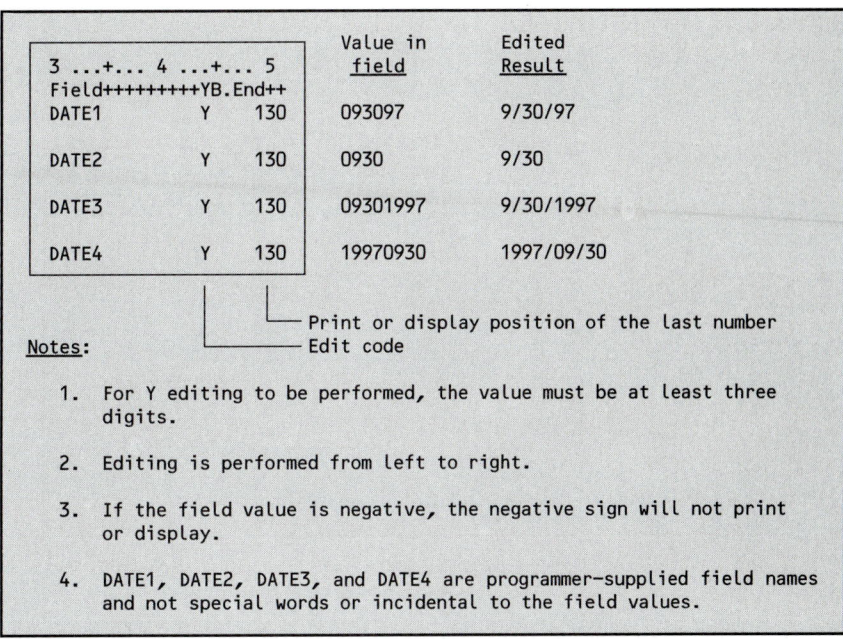

Figure 4-14 Editing results of edit code **Y** (date edit code).

Edit code **Z** performs only the suppression of leading zeros in a numeric field value. Any *implied* decimals specified for the field are *ignored,* and the value is printed or displayed as an integer. Recall that when the special word **PAGE** is used, the editing function of edit code **Z** is automatically provided.

Combination Edit Codes

Included in this classification are edit codes **1–9, A–D,** and **J–Q.** Reference to Figure 4-13 indicates that edit codes **1, 2, 3,** and **4** provide the decimal and zero suppression, but not signs for negative balances. Edit codes **1** and **2** also include one or more commas when the value is one thousand or greater.

Edit codes **5–9** are user-defined, thereby giving the programmer the opportunity to create special-purpose edit codes (e.g., for social security or telephone number editing) that would otherwise require an edit word. They are created by the **CRTEDTD** command, which is explained in the *Programming: Control Language Reference* manual.

Edit codes **A, B, C,** and **D** supply the decimal and the letters **CR** if the value is negative. One or more commas are included for **A** and **B** if the value is one thousand or greater.

Edit codes **J, K, L,** and **M** include the decimal and a minus (−) sign if the value is negative. One or more commas are included for **J** and **K** if the value is equal to or greater than one thousand.

Finally, edit codes **M, N, O,** and **P** supply the decimal and a floating minus sign if the value is negative. For **N** and **O,** commas are included if the value is one thousand or greater.

With any of the edit codes, the increase in the size of the numeric value by the decimal point, comma(s), and signs must be considered in the printed or displayed data item. The processing results of edit codes are shown in Figure 4-15.

Dollar Signs ($) Specified with Edit Codes

A dollar sign may be coded as *floating* or *fixed.* Figure 4-16 illustrates the syntax for a dollar sign and the editing result when it is specified with an edit code.

Edit Codes	Positive Number: Two Decimal Positions	Positive Number: No Decimal Positions	Negative Number: Three Decimal Positions	Negative Number: No Decimal Positions	Zero Balance: Two Decimal Positions	Zero Balance: No Decimal Positions
Unedited	1234567	1234567	00012b	00012b	000000	000000
1	12,345.67	1,234,567	.120	120	.00	0
2	12,345.67	1,234,567	.120	120		
3	12345.67	1234567	.120	120	.00	0
4	12,345.67	1234567	.120	120		
5-9						
A	12,345.67	1,234,567	.120CR	120CR	.00	0
B	12,345.67	1,234,567	.120CR	120CR		
C	12345.67	1234567	.120CR	120CR	.00	0
D	12345.67	1234567	.120CR	120CR		
J	12,345.67	1,234,567	.120-	120-	.00	0
K	12,345,67	1,234,567	.120-	120-		
L	12345.67	1234567	.120-	120-	.00	0
M	12345.67	1234567	.120-	120-		
N	12,345.67	1,234,567	-120	-120	.00	0
O	12,345,67	1,234,567	-120	-120		
P	12345.67	1234567	-120	-120	.00	0
Q	12345.67	1234567	-120	-120		
X	1234567	1234567	00012b	00012b	000000	000000
Y			0/01/20	0/01/20	0/00/00	0/00/00
Z	1234567	1234567	120	120		

Figure 4-15 Examples of edit code usage (courtesy of IBM).

```
Balance field value in memory:

     00030000
          └─ implied decimal

Fixed Dollar Sign Constant.
Edit code 1 specified:

3 ...+... 4 ...+... 5 ...+... 6 ...+... 7 ...+... 8      Printed or
Field+++++++++YB.End++PConstant/editword/DTformat++     displayed value
Balance         1     77
                      67 '$'                              $    300.00
                                   position 67
                        zeros & comma suppressed
Floating Dollar Sign Constant.
Edit code 1 specified:
                                                          Printed or
3 ...+... 4 ...+... 5 ...+... 6 ...+... 7 ...+... 8      displayed value
Field+++++++++YB.End++PConstant/editword/DTformat++
Balance         1     77 '$'                                 $300.00

                    zeros and comma suppressed
                    $ placed next to high order
                    digit greater than 0
```

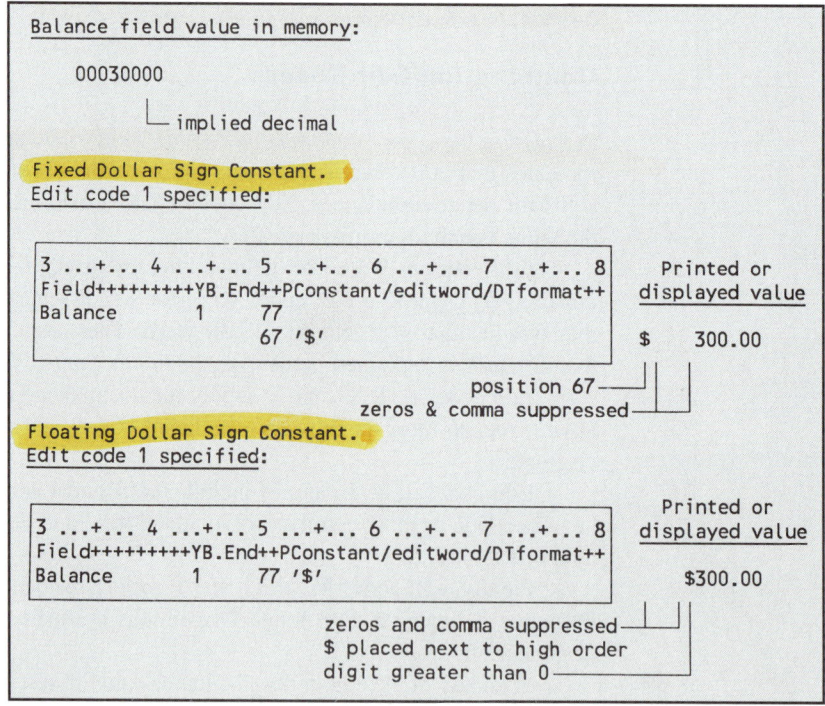

Figure 4-16 Syntax for fixed and floating dollars signs when used with an edit code.

Edit Words

When an edit code does not satisfy all editing requirements, an edit word has to be used. Figure 4-17 explains the syntax of edit words and presents coding examples.

```
| b | b | b | , | b | b | 0 | . | b | b | & | C | R | . | x | T | 0 | T |
\_____________________________________/ \_________/ \_______________/
                 Body                      Status        Expansion
```

Rules for forming an edit word:

1. An edit word must be enclosed in apostrophes.
2. A blank in the body of the edit word is replaced with the character from the corresponding position of the data field specified in *Field Name*.
3. An ampersand (&) in the body or status portion causes a blank in the edited field. It remains unchanged in the expansion portion.
4. A zero is used for zero suppression. It is placed in the rightmost position where zero suppression is to stop. It is replaced with the character from the corresponding position of the data field unless that character is zero. Column 38 (Edit Codes) must be left blank.
5. If leading zeros are desired, the edit word must contain one more position than the field to be edited. A zero must be placed in the high-order position of the edit word.
6. An asterisk in the body of the edit word is used for asterisk protection and zero suppression. It is placed in the rightmost position where zero suppression is to stop. It is replaced with the nonzero character from the corresponding position of the data field. Each suppressed zero is replaced by an asterisk. An asterisk preceding a zero is interpreted as representing asterisk protection.
7. A dollar sign in the body of the edit word written immediately to the left of the zero-suppression code causes the insertion of a dollar sign in the position to the left of the first significant digit. This is the *floating dollar* sign. A dollar sign that is entered immediately after the initial single-quote mark is fixed (printed in the same location each time). This is the *fixed dollar* sign.
8. The decimal and commas are printed in the same relative positions they were written in the edit word. If they are to the left of significant digits, they are blanked out or replaced by an asterisk.
9. All other characters used in the body of the edit word are printed if they are to the right of significant digits in the data field. If they are to the left of high-order significant digits in the data field, they are blanked out. If asterisk protection is used, they are replaced by an asterisk.
10. The letters CR or the minus symbol in the status portion of the edit word are undisturbed if the sign in the data field is minus. If the sign is plus, CR and – are blanked out.
11. Characters to the right of the status portion of the edit word are undisturbed.
12. The edit word may be larger than the field to be edited.

```
3 ...+... 4 ...+... 5 ...+... 6 ...+... 7 ...+... 8
Field+++++++++YB.End++PConstant/editword/DTformat++
Term Date           80 '0 /  /  '

SS_Number           67 '0   -  -    '
```

Comments

Zero is placed in the body of the edit word to indicate where zero suppression is to end. & inserts a space in the body of the edited value.

Extra high-order zero in edit word prevents suppression of leading zero in the value.

```
3 ...+... 4 ...+... 5 ...+... 6 ...+... 7 ...+... 8
Field+++++++++YB.End++PConstant/editword/DTformat++
Telephone           77 '0(   )-   -    '

Paymnt_Amt          90 '    ,  *.  '

Check_Amt           90 '    , $0.  '
```

Extra high-order zero in edit word prevents suppression of the (in the value.

Leading zeros and comma are replaced with asterisks.

Zeros are suppressed and a floating $ sign is printed next to first significant digit. Extra position must be included in edit word for $ sign.

```
3 ...+... 4 ...+... 5 ...+... 6 ...+... 7 ...+... 8
Field+++++++++YB.End++PConstant/editword/DTformat++
Net_Income          80 '$  ,  0  '

Gross_Sale          67 '  -   ,  0.  '
```

Fixed dollar sign must be placed immediately after leading quote mark. Extra position must be included in edit word for $ sign. Comma and decimal point are printed in their relative edit word positions. These symbols will be suppressed when value is smaller.

```
3 ...+... 4 ...+... 5 ...+... 6 ...+... 7 ...+... 8
Field+++++++++YB.End++PConstant/editword/DTformat++
Credit_Amt          80 ' ,  0.  &CR'

Gross_Sale          67 ' ,  0.  -'
```

Symbol CR will print only if value is negative. Spaces are still allocated if value is positive. End position entry for field refers to R in CR.

Minus sign will print only if value is negative. Space is still allocated if value is positive. End position entry for field refers to the – sign.

```
3 ...+... 4 ...+... 5 ...+... 6 ...+... 7 ...+... 8
Field+++++++++YB.End++PConstant/editword/DTformat++
CR_Memo             50 ' ,  0.  &THANKS'
```

Entries specified to the right of the status section (see format on top of this figure) are printed without regard to the status value.

Figure 4-17 Syntax rules for forming edit words and coding examples.

DATA ENTRY OF NUMERIC VALUES

It was explained in Chapter 3 that numeric data must be stored right-justified in its related field position when entered. Because this concept cannot be overemphasized, it is presented again as a timely review. Examine the top section of Figure 4-18 and observe what processing results occur if a numeric value is not stored right-justified. The value should be processed as 123.45, but if entered incorrectly, as shown in the figure, it will be processed as 12345.00.

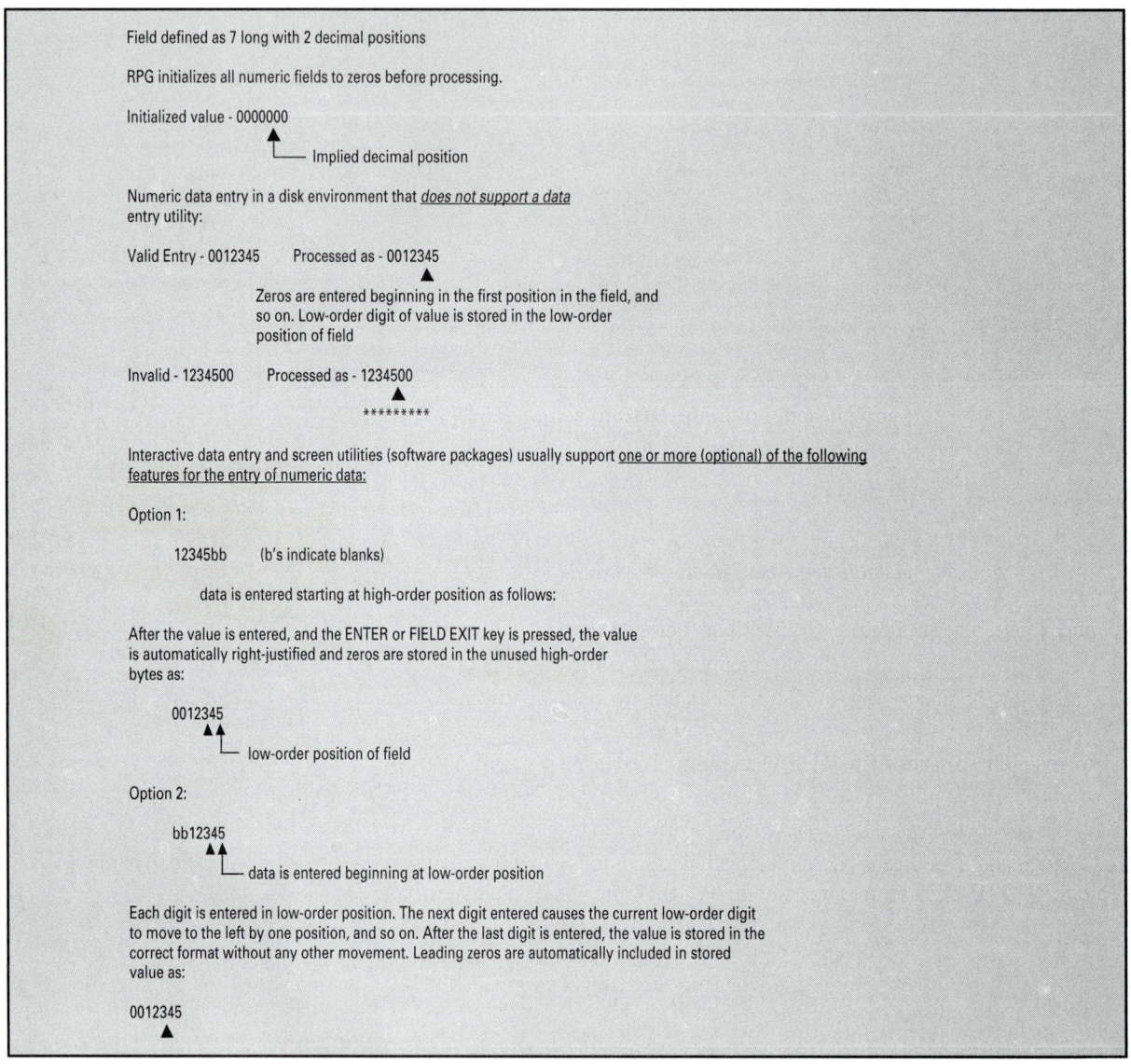

```
Field defined as 7 long with 2 decimal positions

RPG initializes all numeric fields to zeros before processing.

Initialized value - 0000000
                         ▲
                         └── Implied decimal position

Numeric data entry in a disk environment that does not support a data
entry utility:

Valid Entry - 0012345     Processed as - 0012345
                                          ▲
                   Zeros are entered beginning in the first position in the field, and
                   so on. Low-order digit of value is stored in the low-order
                   position of field

Invalid - 1234500     Processed as - 1234500
                                      ▲
                                  *********

Interactive data entry and screen utilities (software packages) usually support one or more (optional) of the following
features for the entry of numeric data:

Option 1:

   12345bb     (b's indicate blanks)

        data is entered starting at high-order position as follows:

After the value is entered, and the ENTER or FIELD EXIT key is pressed, the value
is automatically right-justified and zeros are stored in the unused high-order
bytes as:

   0012345
        ▲▲
         └── low-order position of field

Option 2:

   bb12345
        ▲▲
         └── data is entered beginning at low-order position

Each digit is entered in low-order position. The next digit entered causes the current low-order digit
to move to the left by one position, and so on. After the last digit is entered, the value is stored in the
correct format without any other movement. Leading zeros are automatically included in stored
value as:

0012345
  ▲
```

Figure 4-18 Procedures for valid numeric data entry.

In an environment that does not support a data entry or screen utility, numeric values smaller than the field size are usually entered with the required leading zeros. However, as illustrated in Figure 4-18, the entry of numeric data in an interactive environment is simplified. Two optional methods are shown. Option 1 places the CRT cursor at the high-order position of the field; as digits are entered, the cursor moves to the right. After all the numbers are entered, pressing the **ENTER** or **FIELD EXIT** key will automatically right-justify the value in its related storage area in memory. Option 2 places the CRT cursor at the low-order position of the field; as digits are entered, the number previously stored in the low-order position moves one space to the left. For either option, any unused high-order positions do not have to be filled with zeros. Zeros are automatically included when the value is moved from the screen field to the storage area. Today, most of the screen and data entry utilities support both options.

Editing Summary

A source listing of the example heading program and its relationship to the printed report shown in Figure 4-19 details the following features:

1. The BALANCE field, defined as numeric in the physical file, is edited in the *Output Specifications* by the edit code **1** entry in position 44.
2. The system date (**UDATE**) is edited by edit code **Y,** which suppresses the leading zero and inserts two spaces. Note that the default (mmddyy) date value has been changed to mmddyyyy by the **DATFMT**(***USA&**) keyword in the *Control Specifications.*
3. Because the **RPG IV** compiler provides for automatic editing (zero suppression) for edit code **Z,** it is not specified in position 44 for special word **PAGE.**

```
SEQNBR*...+... 1 ...+... 2 ...+... 3 ...+... 4 ...+... 5 ...+... 6 ...+... 7 ...+... 8 ...+... 9 ...+... 0
   100       * This program processes an externally described keyed physical file
   200       * and prints a report
   300      H DATFMT(*USA&)                        DATFMT keyword changes
   400      FGlacts    IF  E          DISK         default date format to      Input file
   500      FQsysprt   O    F  132    PRINTER      mmddyyyy and separator      Output file
   600                                             to spaces
   700      C                   EXCEPT    HeadLines
   800      C                   READ      Glacts                          LR   read first record
   900      C                   DOW       *INLR = *OFF                         do while LR is off
  1000      C                   EXCEPT    DetailLine                           print a line
  1100      C                   READ      Glacts        Edit code Y suppresses  LR   read another record
  1200      C                   ENDDO                   leading zero and in-       end DOW group
  1300                                                  serts blanks
  1400      OQsysprt   E            HeadLines      3 01
  1500      O                       UDATE          Y       8
  1600      O                                             46 'GENERAL LEDGER ACCOUNT'
  1700      O                                             55 'BALANCES'
  1800      O                                             75 'PAGE'
  1900      O                       PAGE                  80        Because the system will pro-
  2000      O          E            HeadLines      2                vide the edit code Z function,
  2100      O                                              9 'ACCT NO'   it is not required
  2200      O                                             32 'ACCOUNT NAME'
  2300      O                                             57 'ACCOUNT TYPE'
  2400      O                                             76 'BALANCE'
  2500      O          E            DetailLine     2
  2600      O                       ActNumber              7   Balance field is edited with edit code 1,
  2700      O                       ActName               37   which provides a decimal point, zero sup-
  2800      O Fixed $ will print    Act_Type              62   pression, commas, and .00 if the value is
  2900      O in position 66 for                          66 '$'  zero
  3000      O every record output   Balance        1      77
-----------------------------------------------------------------------------------------------------------
9/30/1997             GENERAL LEDGER ACCOUNT BALANCE                    PAGE    1

  ACCT NO          ACCOUNT NAME            ACCOUNT TYPE           BALANCE

   101     CASH                           CURRENT ASSET         $  10,841.02
   102     ACCOUNTS RECEIVABLE            CURRENT ASSET         $   7,633.49
```

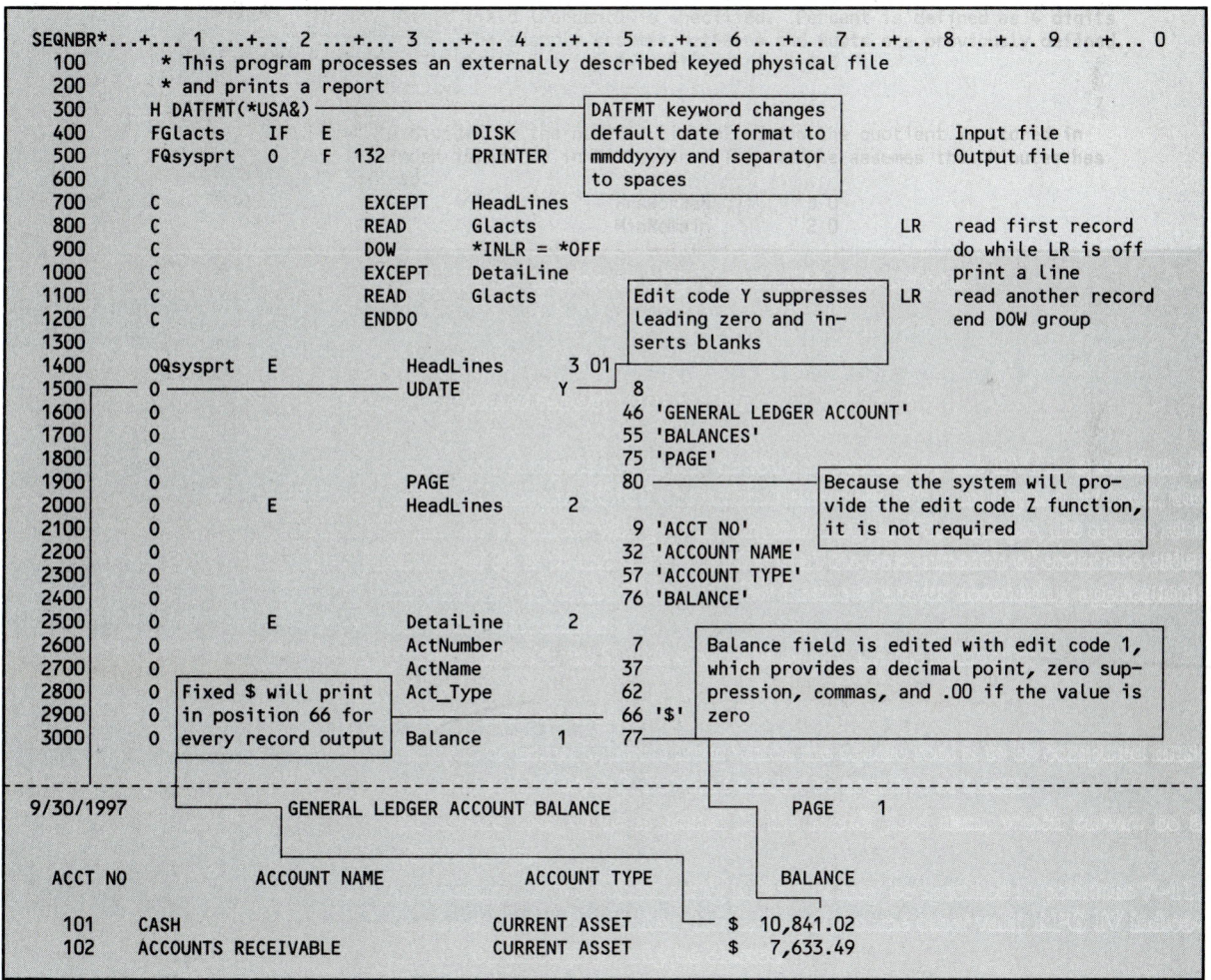

Figure 4-19 Source listing of the example heading program and its relationship to the report.

4. A fixed dollar sign, specified for the editing of the BALANCE field, will print with every record processed.

NOTE ON PRINTER TYPES

Example programs presented in this text assume that a line printer is used to generate the source and compile listings and the printed reports. Line printers print a complete line in one stroke. The standard carriage width is 132 characters. Wider models are available, however. They are noisy and do not have the print quality of *inkjet* or *laser* printers. For line printers, the standard size of the continuous-form paper is usually 14⅞ by 11 inches. Other popular printer types include serial, inkjet, and laser. *Serial printers* (also called *dot matrix*), which are commonly used with microcomputers, print one character at a time across a line. They are multidirectional in that they print a line from left to right and then print the following line from right to left. Similar to line printers, serial printers support printing on continuous forms. However, they are noisy and relatively slow, especially in the letter-quality mode.

Inkjet printers use a nozzle to shoot electronically charged droplets of ink through individual typefaces onto the paper. They are quiet and produce high-quality print. Disadvantages for some applications is that multipart paper cannot be used and they do not support the use of continuous-form paper.

Laser printers are different from the other types in that they format an entire page before printing. They have the best print quality and offer a multitude of fonts (typefaces). Continuous-form paper, however, is not supported with laser printers; the output is printed on individual sheets of paper. A disadvantage is that multipart paper cannot be used with laser printers. Regardless of the type of printer used, the syntax, page, and line controls remain the same in an **RPG IV** program.

RPG IV SYNTAX FOR FORM LENGTHS

The standard form length specified when the computer is initially configured is usually defined with a default length of 66 lines (printing at 6 lines per inch) with the default overflow on line 60. Any manual adjustment (for line and serial printers) at the top of the form, however, will determine the exact location of the page overflow line in the body of the report.

Special forms, such as labels, checks, invoices, transcripts, and so forth, are not often the standard paper length supported by the system. Three methods are available in the **RPG IV** environment for the control of variable-form lengths. One includes control by a Command Language (**CL**) instruction in a Control Language Program (**CLP**) that executes the related **RPG IV** program. A second method, discussed in Chapter 18, defines form length and overflow line in the specifications for an externally described printer file. The third method is controlled directly in the **RPG IV** program with **FORMLEN** and **FORMOFL** keywords included in the *File Description Specification* instruction for the printer file. (See Figure 4-24 for the syntax for these two keywords.)

The documentation and **RPG IV** syntax for an application program that prints customer mailing labels are presented below to illustrate how the default settings for form length and the overflow line are modified.

APPLICATION RPG IV PROGRAM: CUSTOMER MAILING LABELS

The specifications presented in Figure 4-20 describe the processing requirements for an application **RPG IV** program that prints mailing labels.

PROGRAM SPECIFICATIONS

Page 1 of 1

Program Name: Customer Mailing Labels | Program ID: CLABELS | Written by: SM

Purpose: Print customer mailing labels | Approved by: CM

Input files: CUSTMRS

Output files: QSYSPRT

Processing Requirements:

Write an **RPG IV** program to print customer mailing labels on pre-glued continuous-form labels.

Input to the program:

The externally defined physical file, CUSTMRS, contains customer names and addresses in the format shown in the attached record layout form.

Processing:

Read the physical file in arrival sequence until end of file. For every record processed, print three detail lines on a mailing label form.

Output:

A Printer Spacing Chart is attached which shows the output format for the mailing labels. Pages of continuous-form labels are used.

The following must be included in the program to control the printing of the labels:

1. Form length must be defined as 5 lines with page overflow on line 4.
2. Printer must be set at 6 lines per inch.
3. One label per form is to be printed in the format detailed in the print chart.

Figure 4-20 Specifications for the customer mailing label program.

A system flowchart indicating the files processed by the program is shown in Figure 4-21.

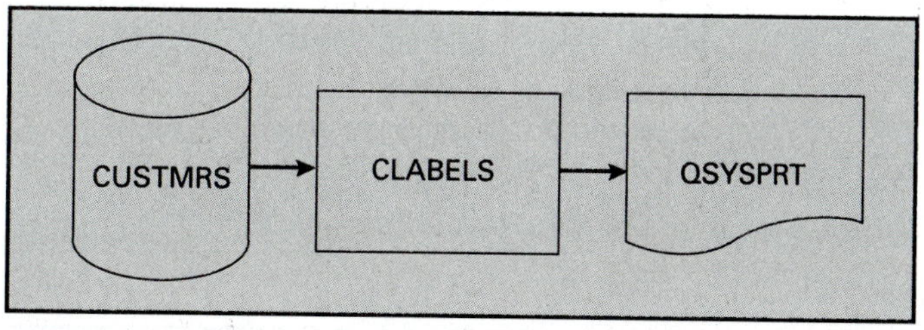

Figure 4-21 System flowchart for the customer mailing label program.

The record format of the externally described physical file **CUSTMRS** is detailed in Figure 4-22. A listing of the data file is also included.

The print format of the continuous-form labels is shown in Figure 4-23. Notice that the individual label forms are 5 lines in length, printing is to begin on line 2 of each label, and page overflow occurs on line 4.

PHYSICAL FILE DESCRIPTION

SYSTEM: AS/400 DATE: 4/10/97
FILE NAME: CUSTMRS REV NO: 0
RECORD NAME: CUSTMRSR KEY LENGTH: None
SEQUENCE: Nonkeyed RECORD SIZE: 65

FIELD DEFINITIONS

FIELD NO	FIELD NAME	SIZE	TYPE	POSITION FROM	POSITION TO	COMMENTS
1	CUST_NAME	20	C	1	20	
2	ADDRESS	20	C	21	40	
3	CITY	20	C	41	60	
4	STATE	2	C	61	62	
5	ZIP CODE	5	P	63	65	

Physical File Listing:

```
PAUL CEZANNE          44 RUE PIGALLE     STAMFORD      CT06518
EDGAR DEGAS           10 ROSE TERRACE    WESTPORT      PA07777
BUCKMINISTER FULLER  999 PARK AVENUE     GREENWICH     CT06444
```

Figure 4-22 Description of the externally described physical file processed by the customer mailing label program.

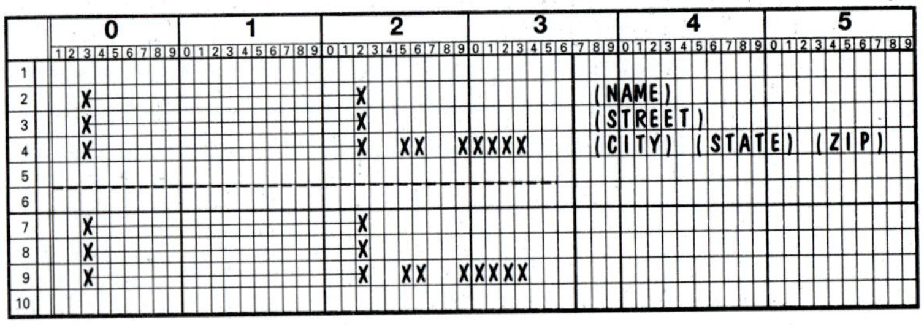

Figure 4-23 Printer Spacing Chart for customer label program.

RPG IV Syntax for Customer Labels Program

In the compiled listing in Figure 4-24, the syntax that controls the size and processing of labels is identified with comments. Also, included at the bottom is a listing of the labels with comments documenting the line references. Note that **02** in the *Skip Before* field (positions 46–48) advances the paper to line 2 for every new record processed.

```
Line    <---------------------- Source Specifications ----------------------------><---- Comments ----> Do
Number ....1....+....2....+....3....+....4....+....5....+....6....+....7....+....8....+....9....+...10 Num
                            S o u r c e   L i s t i n g
     1  * CH4R2 - customer mailing labels program - figure 4-22....
     2 FCustmrs    IF   E             DISK
       *-------------------------------------------------------------------------------------------------*
       *                                  RPG name          External name                               *
       * File name. . . . . . . . . :   CUSTMRS           STAN/CUSTMRS                                *
       * Record format(s) . . . . . :   CUSTMRSR          CUSTMRSR                                    *
       *-------------------------------------------------------------------------------------------------*
```

Figure 4-24 Compile program listing and printed labels with program-related line references.

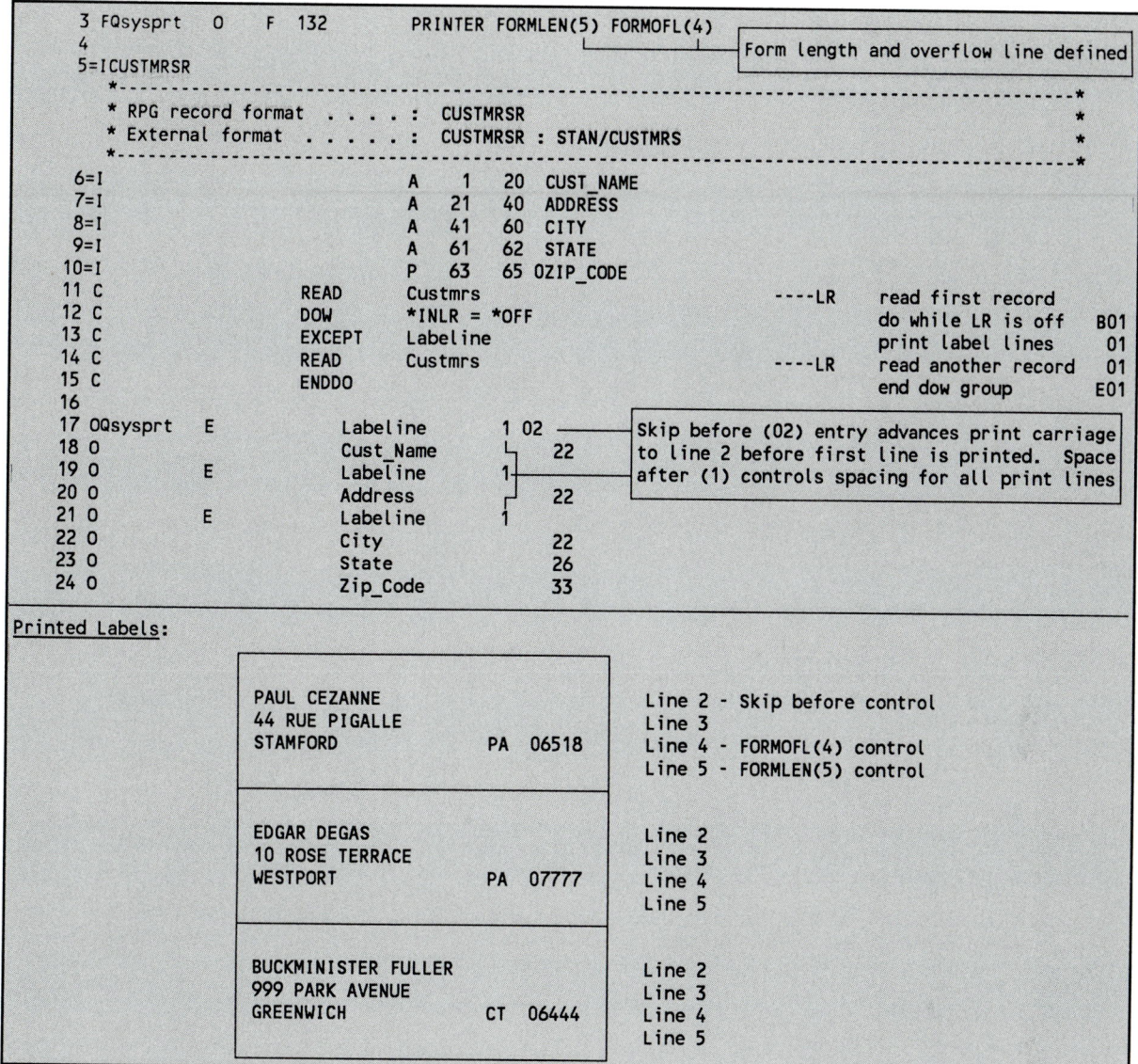

```
     3 FQsysprt   O    F  132          PRINTER FORMLEN(5) FORMOFL(4)
     4                                         Form length and overflow line defined
     5=ICUSTMRSR
       *-------------------------------------------------------------------------------------*
       * RPG record format  . . . . :  CUSTMRSR                                              *
       * External format  . . . . . :  CUSTMRSR : STAN/CUSTMRS                               *
       *-------------------------------------------------------------------------------------*
     6=I                             A    1   20  CUST_NAME
     7=I                             A   21   40  ADDRESS
     8=I                             A   41   60  CITY
     9=I                             A   61   62  STATE
    10=I                             P   63   65 0ZIP_CODE
    11 C                   READ      Custmrs                            ----LR    read first record
    12 C                   DOW       *INLR = *OFF                                 do while LR is off   B01
    13 C                   EXCEPT    Labeline                                     print label lines     01
    14 C                   READ      Custmrs                            ----LR    read another record   01
    15 C                   ENDDO                                                  end dow group        E01
    16
    17 OQsysprt   E            Labeline        1 02     Skip before (02) entry advances print carriage
    18 O                       Cust_Name            22  to line 2 before first line is printed.  Space
    19 O          E            Labeline        1        after (1) controls spacing for all print lines
    20 O                       Address              22
    21 O          E            Labeline        1
    22 O                       City                 22
    23 O                       State                26
    24 O                       Zip_Code             33
```

Printed Labels:

```
  PAUL CEZANNE                         Line 2 - Skip before control
  44 RUE PIGALLE                       Line 3
  STAMFORD                PA  06518    Line 4 - FORMOFL(4) control
                                       Line 5 - FORMLEN(5) control

  EDGAR DEGAS                          Line 2
  10 ROSE TERRACE                      Line 3
  WESTPORT                PA  07777    Line 4
                                       Line 5

  BUCKMINISTER FULLER                  Line 2
  999 PARK AVENUE                      Line 3
  GREENWICH               CT  06444    Line 4
                                       Line 5
```

Figure 4-24 Compile program listing and printed labels with program-related line references. (Continued)

TRADITIONAL RPG SYNTAX FOR EXAMPLE HEADING PROGRAM

Figure 4-25 shows a compile listing of the example heading program using traditional **RPG** syntax. Because the OPEN, READ, WRITE, and CLOSE functions are all controlled by the "built-in" **RPG** *Logic Cycle*, calculation instructions are not required to process the input and output files. An explanation of the syntax unique to traditional **RPG** is referenced by numbers and explained in the related text that supplements the compile listing.

```
Line    <--------------------- Source Specifications ---------------------------><---- Comments ----> Do
Number ....1....+....2....+....3....+....4....+....5....+....6....+....7....+....8....+....9....+...10 Num
                          S o u r c e   L i s t i n g
     1  * This program processes an externally described keyed physical file
     2  * and prints a report using traditional RPG syntax
     3 FGlacts    IP   E             DISK
```

Figure 4-25 Detailed compile listing of the example heading program modified with traditional **RPG** syntax.

```
     *-------------------------------------------------------------------------------------*
     *                                 RPG name         External name                      *
     * File name. . . . . . . . . :   GLACTS           STAN/GLACTS                         *
     * Record format(s) . . . . . :   GLACTSR          GLACTSR                             *
     *-------------------------------------------------------------------------------------*
  4 FQsysprt   O    F  132        PRINTER OFLIND(*INOF) -[1]
  5
  6=IGLACTSR
     *-------------------------------------------------------------------------------------*
     * RPG record format  . . . . :   GLACTSR                                              *
     * External format  . . . . . :   GLACTSR : STAN/GLACTS                                *
     *-------------------------------------------------------------------------------------*
  7=I                                A    1    3  ACTNUMBER
  8=I                                A    4   30  ACTNAME
  9=I                                A   31   50  ACT_TYPE
 10=I                                S   51   58 2BALANCE
[5]-11 OQsysprt   H      1P -[2]               3 01 ---------[4]
 12 O            OR     OF
 13 O                   |      UDATE-[7]      Y        8
 14 O                  [3]                            46 'GENERAL LEDGER ACCOUNT'
 15 O                                                 55 'BALANCES'
 16 O                                                 75 'PAGE'
 17 O                          PAGE-[7]               80
[5]-18 O          H      1P -[2]                 2
 19 O            OR     OF
 20 O                   |                             9 'ACCT NO'
 21 O                  [3]                            32 'ACCOUNT NAME'
 22 O                                                 57 'ACCOUNT TYPE'
 23 O                                                 76 'BALANCE'
 24 O              D    N1P -[6]                2
 25 O                               ActNumber          7
 26 O                               ActName           37
 27 O                               Act_Type          62
 28 O                                                 66 '$'
 29 O                               Balance     1     77
```

1. An overflow indicator is defined in the *File Description Specification* instruction for the printer file by the **OFLIND(*INOF)** keyword. The ***INOF** option defines the page-overflow indicator assigned. Any of the other page-overflow indicators—**OA, OB, OC, OD, OE, OG,** or **OV**—could have been specified.

   When program control senses the overflow line, the page-overflow indicator specified with the **OFLIND** keyword will be set on. Including the overflow indicator in one or more **OR** instructions in the *Output Specifications* will automatically control page overflow to any subsequent pages. Because standard-size paper is assumed, the **FORMLEN** keyword is not required for the printer file.

2. First page indicator **(1P)** controls the printing of the heading lines on the first report page. Because a record has *not* been read from the input file, any field values related to input records are not available at this "first cycle" processing time. Any *Definition, Input,* or *Calculation Specification* instructions (none in this program) are ignored during first cycle time processing. This sequence is controlled by the **RPG** logic cycle and not by the programmer. See Appendix F for an explanation of the RPG Logic Cycle.

3. The **OR** instructions on lines 12 and 19 control the printing of the heading lines on subsequent pages. Without the **OR** statements, the headings would be printed only on the first page.

4. The **01** entry in the *Skip Before* field (positions 46–48) advances the paper to line 1 on the next page at "first cycle" time and when page overflow is sensed. Any line number from 1 to 255 may be specified. Note that *Skip Before* control advances the paper to the specified line *before* printing. An entry in the *Skip After* field (positions 49–51) will advance the paper to the next page *after* printing the current line.

5. Lines 11 and 18, defined as heading lines by the **H** entry in position 17, are usually specified for output records that include constants and special **RPG IV** words. Line 24, defined as a detail line by the **D** entry in position 17, is a line type usually associated with output records that contain fields with variable data.

   Output record lines must be specified in an **H, D, T** order. However, **E** lines may be placed anywhere in the *Output Specifications* without regard to the **H, D, T** sequence.

Figure 4-25 Detailed compile listing of the example heading program modified with traditional **RPG** syntax. (Continued)

6. The **N1P** indicator in positions 21–23 conditions detail output so that it occurs only after first cycle processing is complete and the first record is read from the input file. The **N1P** entry assigns the **1P** indicator in a "not" condition. This prevents detail output from occurring at **1P** time before a record is read from the input file.

   Because the input file is externally described, no *Input Specifications* are included to define the record format. Consequently, no *Record Identifying Indicator* was specified. If the input file had been program-described, the *Record Identifying Indicator* assigned (**01–99**) could have been used to condition the detail record on line 24.

   When a page-overflow condition occurs on the output of an input record, the **OR** lines are printed first, followed by the detail record values. This sequence of processing will be executed until an end-of-file condition is sensed.

7. The syntax for the constants and special words (**UDATE** and **PAGE**) is identical to **RPG IV** coding.

Figure 4-25 Detailed compile listing of the example heading program modified with traditional **RPG** syntax. (Continued)

SUMMARY

Constants in an **RPG IV** program, which are defined in positions 53–80 of the *Output Specifications,* must be enclosed in apostrophes (single quotation marks). A Printer Spacing Chart should be prepared for the report design and referenced to determine end position locations for a constant or group of constants. The programmer has unlimited flexibility as to how constants are coded in the program.

Special **RPG IV** words that access the system or job date are **UDATE, UMONTH, UDAY,** and **UYEAR. UDATE** is accessed in a default mmddyy format unless changed by an entry in a **DATFMT** keyword specified in the *Control Specifications.* Date values are usually edited with edit code **Y.** The **CHGJOB** *(Change Job)* Control Language statement may be used to override the session date to a programmer-selected date.

PAGE is another special **RPG IV** word that provides for automatic page numbering in a report. The editing functions of edit code **Z** are provided as a default.

Top-of-page control is specified in a program by a *Skip Before* or *Skip After* entry in the first record of the *Output Specifications.* The entry refers to the line number to which the paper will advance before or after printing the current line.

Form length and the page-overflow line may be modified from default settings by **FORMLEN** and **FORMOFL** keywords specified in the *File Specification* definition of the printer file. The repetition of headings on the subsequent pages of a report is controlled by the overflow indicator.

Fields in an externally described physical file are defined as numeric by a decimal position entry in their related *Data Description Specification* (DDS) instruction. Numeric fields are defined in a program-described physical file by entering the related number for the decimal positions in positions 47–48 of the *Input Specification* instruction. By **RPG IV** standards, numeric work and other independent fields should be defined in the *Definition Specifications.* The maximum size of a numeric field in **RPG IV** is 30 digits, with a maximum of 30 decimal positions. Integer values are defined with a Ø in the decimal position field of the related specification.

Only fields defined as numeric may be edited. Editing is performed by edit codes or edit words. The function of edit codes is predetermined; therefore, edit codes are easier to use. Edit words, however, offer additional features and must be used when an edit code will not meet the editing requirements.

QUESTIONS

4-1. Where are headings defined in an **RPG IV** program?

4-2. How would the following report heading be formatted:
SALARIED EMPLOYEE PAYROLL INFORMATION

4-3. What is the function of the *Skip Before* and *Skip After* entries in an **RPG IV** program?

4-4. Is skipping specified for every output record format? Explain your answer.

4-5. What **RPG IV** keyword defines a form length? Where in the program is it specified?

4-6. Explain the page-overflow function.

4-7. What overflow indicators are provided by the **RPG IV** compiler? How and where is the indicator defined? Where is it specified?

4-8. What is the **RPG IV** special word for the system date? What is the default format?

4-9. Into what elements may the system date values be subdivided?

4-10. What **RPG IV** keyword supports modification of the system date format? Name four of the options available with the keyword. Format the result of the named options.

4-11. Explain how the page numbering in a report is provided for in an **RPG IV** program.

4-12. What, if anything, is incorrect with the following partial *Output Specification* syntax for a heading line?

```
3 ...+... 4 ...+... 5 ...+... 6 ...+... 7 ...+... 8
Field+++++++++YB.End++PConstant/editword/DTformat++
UDATE                4
                        'GENERAL LEDGER ACCOUNT
                    50  BALANCES'

PAGE                77 'PAGE'
```

4-13. On what specifications (**RPG IV** and DDS) may fields be defined as numeric?

4-14. What is the maximum numeric field length supported by **RPG IV**? What is the maximum number of decimal positions that may be defined for a numeric field? Are there any restrictions regarding the decimal positions assigned to a field?

4-15. What error will occur if character data is processed as numeric?

4-16. Define the term *implied decimal position.* Where is a decimal position *implied*?

4-17. Define the term *explicit decimal position.* Where is a decimal position formatted as *explicit*?

4-18. What fields may be edited?

4-19. Name some of the general functions provided by editing.

4-20. By what methods may editing be controlled in an **RPG IV** program?

4-21. Refer to Question 4-20, and name 12 of the short-cut options for editing.

4-22. From the following date values in storage, determine the printed output if edit code **Y** is specified for the related output field. Assume the default format.

Value in Storage	Edited Result
081198	
0811	
08	
12311998	

4-23. How and where may the default system date format be changed?

4-24. When is job date specified? How is it defined?

Note: For Questions 4-25 and 4-26, the letters J and N and the } character represent the following negative numbers in storage: J = −1; N = −5, } = −0.
The low-order character makes the numeric value negative. Because the sign is stored over the low-order digit, the combination sign and number results in a letter or character value.

4-25. Determine the edited results for the following values when the edit code specified is assigned:

Value In Storage	Edit Code Specified	Edited Result
0000000	1	
▲		
0000000	2	
▲		
0123456	1	
▲		
1000000	3	
▲		
0000099	4	
▲		
200000J	A	
▲		
0200000	B	
▲		
0001000	Z	
▲		
012459}	K	
▲		

▲ Indicates implied decimal position

4-26. On the basis of the values in storage, format the edit words to generate the indicated edited results. For all *monetary* values, the format .00 is to be printed for decimal values and 0 for integers if the value is zero. In addition, for monetary values include commas in the edit word if the size suggests them. Field sizes are indicated by the values in storage (first column).

Value In Storage	Edited Result	Required Edit Word (format on a blank output form)
012223456	012-22-3456	
▲		
010290	1/02/90	
▲		
00001000	****10.00	
▲		
00009944	$99.44	
▲		
2033334444	(203) 333 4444	
▲		
00500000	$ 5,000.00	
▲		
000187N	18.75 CR	
▲		
0213500J	$ 2,135,001–	
▲		
0015000	150.00 DEBIT	
▲		

▲ Indicates implied decimal position in storage

4-27. Must the blank positions in an edit word pattern be *equal* to the related field size? Explain your answer.

4-28. When an edit code is used, how is a fixed dollar sign specified? How is a floating dollar sign specified? If an edit word is used, how is a fixed dollar sign specified? How is a floating dollar sign specified?

4-29. What is the number of default lines for standard continuous-form paper?

4-30. On what **RPG IV** specification(s) is the default form length modified? What entries are required?

4-31. Name four printer types.

PROGRAMMING ASSIGNMENTS

For each of the following programming assignments, a physical file must have been created and loaded with the related data records. Your instructor will inform you as to whether you have to create the physical file and load it or if it has been prepared for the assignment.

Programming Assignment 4-1: SALARIED EMPLOYEE REPORT

From the following documentation, write an **RPG IV** program to generate the report formatted in the Printer Spacing Chart.

Physical File Format:

PHYSICAL FILE DESCRIPTION

SYSTEM: AS/400
FILE NAME: Yours
RECORD NAME: Yours
SEQUENCE: Nonkeyed

DATE: Yours
REV NO: 0
KEY LENGTH: None
RECORD SIZE: 36

FIELD DEFINITIONS

FIELD NO	FIELD NAME	SIZE	TYPE	POSITION FROM	POSITION TO	COMMENTS
1	EMP_NUMBER	4	C	1	4	
2	LAST_NAME	16	C	5	20	
3	FIRST_INIT	1	C	21	21	
4	SECND_INIT	1	C	22	22	
5	SSNUMBER	9	P	23	27	
6	WEK_SALARY	6	P	28	31	2 decimals
7	YTD_SALARY	8	P	32	36	2 decimals

Physical File Data:

Employee Number	Last Name	Initials 1st	Initials 2nd	SS Number	Weekly Salary	YTD Salary
0001	WASHINGTON	G	G	010731799	080000	01600000
0016	LINCOLN	A	T	018091864	110000	00440000
0018	GRANT	U	S	018221885	051599	00051599
0032	ROOSEVELT	F	D	018821945	095000	00950000
0033	TRUMAN	H	S	018841973	099999	02999970
0034	EISENHOWER	D	D	018901971	140000	02940000
0039	CARTER	J	E	019771981	023000	00920000
0040	REAGAN	R	R	020111989	200000	02000000
0045	CLINTON	W	J	030154444	400000	16000000

Report Design:

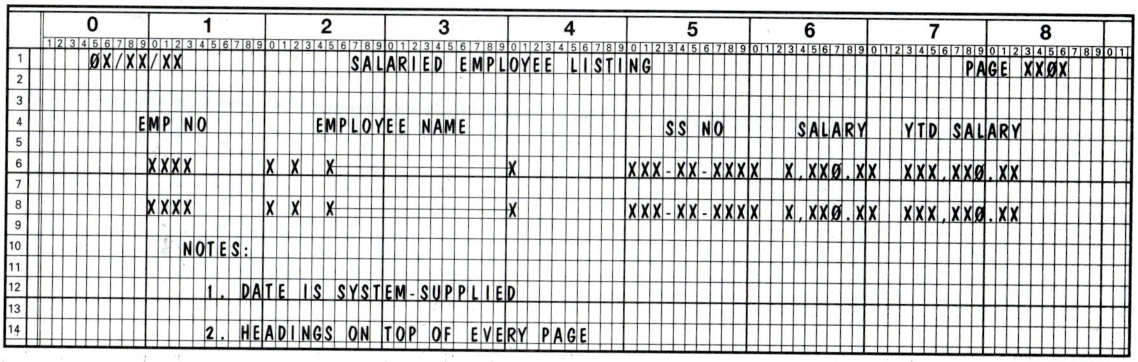

ØX/XX/XX
SALARIED EMPLOYEE LISTING
PAGE XXØX
EMP NO
EMPLOYEE NAME
SS NO
SALARY
YTD SALARY
XXXX
X X X
X
XXX-XX-XXXX
X,XXØ.XX
XXX,XXØ.XX
NOTES:
1. DATE IS SYSTEM-SUPPLIED
2. HEADINGS ON TOP OF EVERY PAGE

Programming Assignment 4-2: DATA PERSONNEL SALARY LISTING

Write an **RPG IV** program from the following documentation.

Physical File Format:

PHYSICAL FILE DESCRIPTION

SYSTEM: AS/400
FILE NAME: Yours
RECORD NAME: Yours
SEQUENCE: Nonkeyed

DATE: Yours
REV NO: 0
KEY LENGTH: None
RECORD SIZE: 30

FIELD DEFINITIONS

FIELD NO	FIELD NAME	SIZE	TYPE	POSITION FROM	TO	COMMENTS
1	JOB_TITLE	25	C	1	25	
2	AVG_SALARY	5	P	26	28	2 decimals
3	EMPLOYEES	3	P	29	30	

Physical File Data:

Job Title	Average Weekly Salary	Number of Employees
APPLICATION PROGRAMMERS	50000	010
SYSTEMS PROGRAMMERS	65000	003
COMPUTER OPERATORS	27500	008
SYSTEMS ANALYST	75000	004
DATA ENTRY CLERKS	25000	010
PROGRAMMER TRAINEES	30000	003
RECORDS CLERKS	22500	002
DATA PROCESSING MANAGER	82500	001
OPERATOR SUPERVISORS	45000	002

Report Design:

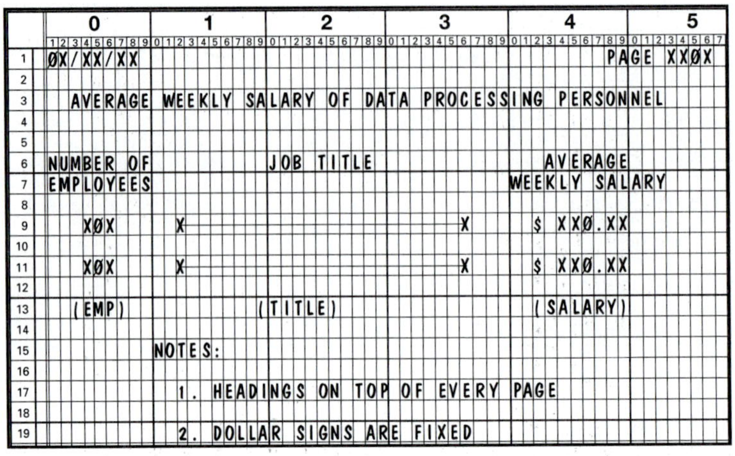

ØX/XX/XX
PAGE XXØX
AVERAGE WEEKLY SALARY OF DATA PROCESSING PERSONNEL
NUMBER OF
EMPLOYEES
JOB TITLE
AVERAGE
WEEKLY SALARY
XØX
X
X
$ XXØ.XX
XØX
X
X
$ XXØ.XX
(EMP)
(TITLE)
(SALARY)
NOTES:
1. HEADINGS ON TOP OF EVERY PAGE
2. DOLLAR SIGNS ARE FIXED

Programming Assignment 4-3: AVERAGE ITEMIZED DEDUCTIONS FOR FEDERAL INCOME TAX DETERMINATION

Write an **RPG IV** program to generate the report detailed in the Printer Spacing Chart.

Physical File Format:

PHYSICAL FILE DESCRIPTION

STEM: AS/400	DATE: Yours
FILE NAME: Yours	REV NO: 0
RECORD NAME: Yours	KEY LENGTH: None
SEQUENCE: Nonkeyed	RECORD SIZE: 30

FIELD DEFINITIONS

FIELD NO	FIELD NAME	SIZE	TYPE	POSITION FROM	POSITION TO	COMMENTS
1	DEDUCTION	12	C	1	12	
2	IR25_30	5	P	13	15	0 decimals
3	IR31_40	5	P	16	18	0 decimals
4	IR41_50	5	P	19	21	0 decimals
5	IR51_75	5	P	22	24	0 decimals
6	IR76_100	5	P	25	27	0 decimals
7	IR101_200	5	P	28	30	0 decimals

Physical File Data:

Itemized Deduction	$25,000-30,000	$30,001 40,000	$40,001-50,000	$50,001-75,000	$75,001-100,000	$100,001-200,000
MEDICAL	03306	03137	03612	04002	06003	12087
INTEREST	04662	05011	05667	06595	08847	13324
TAXES	02069	02477	03015	04049	05888	09359
CONTRIBUTIONS	01129	01213	01315	01665	02112	03442

Report Design:

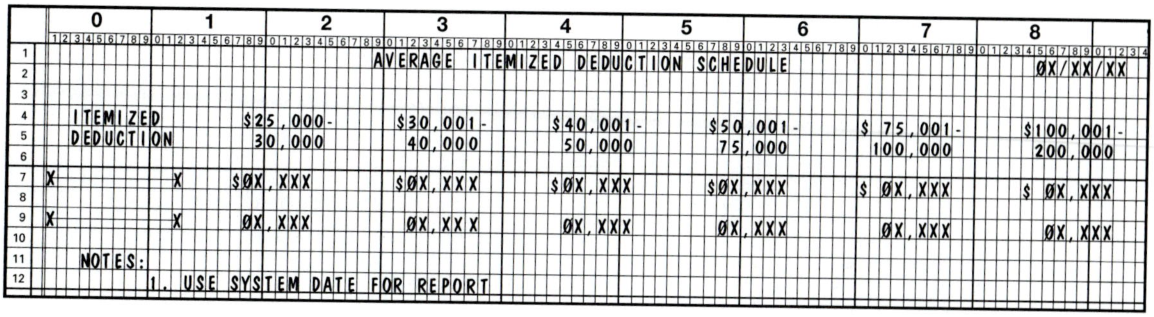

AVERAGE ITEMIZED DEDUCTION SCHEDULE
0X/XX/XX
ITEMIZED DEDUCTION
$25,000- 30,000
$30,001- 40,000
$40,001- 50,000
$50,001- 75,000
$ 75,001- 100,000
$100,001- 200,000
X X $0X,XXX $0X,XXX $0X,XXX $0X,XXX $ 0X,XXX $ 0X,XXX
X X 0X,XXX 0X,XXX 0X,XXX 0X,XXX 0X,XXX 0X,XXX
NOTES:
1. USE SYSTEM DATE FOR REPORT

Programming Assignment 4-4: STUDENT ENROLLMENT REPORT

Write an **RPG IV** program to create the report shown in the Printer Spacing Chart.

Physical File Format:

PHYSICAL FILE DESCRIPTION

SYSTEM: AS/400
FILE NAME: Yours
RECORD NAME: Yours
SEQUENCE: Nonkeyed

DATE: Yours
REV NO: 0
KEY LENGTH: None
RECORD SIZE: 59

FIELD DEFINITIONS

FIELD NO	FIELD NAME	SIZE	TYPE	POSITION FROM	POSITION TO	COMMENTS
1	SS_NUMBER	9	P	1	5	
2	SEX	1	C	6	6	
3	STU_NAME	30	C	7	36	
4	TELEPHONE	10	P	37	42	
5	TECHNOLOGY	15	C	43	57	
6	TEST_MARK	3	P	58	59	0 decimals

Physical File Data:

SS Number	Sex	Student Name	Telephone Number	Technology	Entrance Test Mark
011223333	M	LAMONT CRANSTON	2037778888	DATA	090
066445432	F	LOIS LANE	2129994322	CHEMISTRY	085
124111235	M	FRANK N STEIN	9142668413	ARCHITECTURAL	078
077889999	M	D R ACULA	9134445555	PREP PROGRAM	060
124111235	F	REDDI WATT	2033777865	MECHANICAL	100

Report Design:

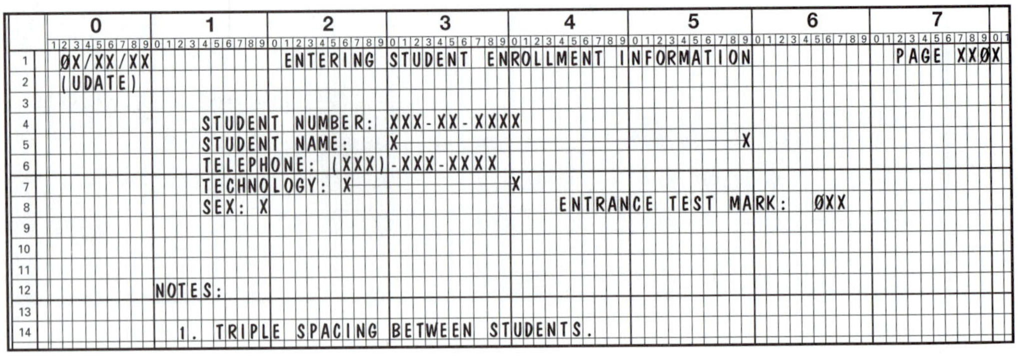

ØX/XX/XX ENTERING STUDENT ENROLLMENT INFORMATION PAGE XXØX
(UDATE)
STUDENT NUMBER: XXX-XX-XXXX
STUDENT NAME: X X
TELEPHONE: (XXX)-XXX-XXXX
TECHNOLOGY: X X
SEX: X ENTRANCE TEST MARK: ØXX
NOTES:
1. TRIPLE SPACING BETWEEN STUDENTS.

chapter 5

EVAL Expression and Arithmetic Functions

The *Calculation Specification* has two **SEU** formats as shown in Figure 5-1.

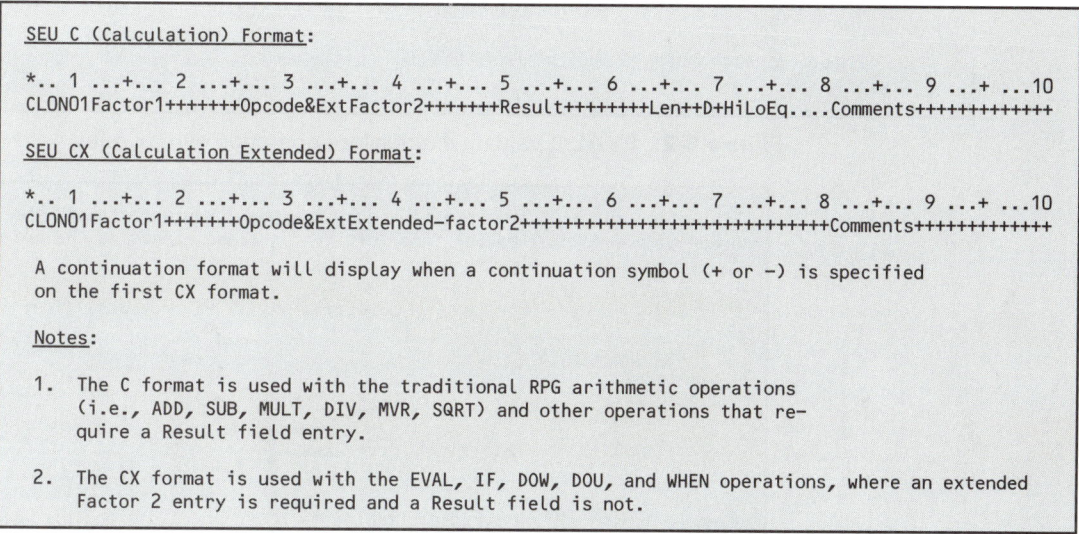

```
SEU C (Calculation) Format:

*.. 1 ...+... 2 ...+... 3 ...+... 4 ...+... 5 ...+... 6 ...+... 7 ...+... 8 ...+... 9 ...+ ...10
CLON01Factor1+++++++Opcode&ExtFactor2+++++++Result++++++++Len++D+HiLoEq....Comments+++++++++++++

SEU CX (Calculation Extended) Format:

*.. 1 ...+... 2 ...+... 3 ...+... 4 ...+... 5 ...+... 6 ...+... 7 ...+... 8 ...+... 9 ...+ ...10
CLON01Factor1+++++++Opcode&ExtExtended-factor2+++++++++++++++++++++++++++++Comments+++++++++++++

 A continuation format will display when a continuation symbol (+ or -) is specified
 on the first CX format.

 Notes:

 1.  The C format is used with the traditional RPG arithmetic operations
     (i.e., ADD, SUB, MULT, DIV, MVR, SQRT) and other operations that re-
     quire a Result field entry.

 2.  The CX format is used with the EVAL, IF, DOW, DOU, and WHEN operations, where an extended
     Factor 2 entry is required and a Result field is not.
```

Figure 5-1 *Calculation Specification* formats.

The EVAL (Evaluate Expression) Operation

Supplemental to the sometimes awkward arithmetic operations (**ADD, SUB, MULT, DIV**), **RPG IV** includes the **EVAL** (Evaluate Expression) operation, which provides for free-format numeric, logical, relational, and character expressions. Linear calculations, similar to the forms supported by COBOL, BASIC, FORTRAN, C, and so forth are now possible in **RPG IV.** The **EVAL** operation has eliminated the complexity and burden of coding multiple calculation instructions that require interim result field sizes. Figure 5-2 details the syntax for the **EVAL** operation.

Arithmetic expressions specified with the **EVAL** operation must follow the algebraic *order of operations* explained in Figure 5-3.

```
*.. 1 ...+... 2 ...+... 3 ...+... 4 ...+... 5 ...+... 6 ...+... 7 ...+... 8 ...+... 9 ...+ ...10
CLON01Factor1+++++++Opcode&ExtExtended-factor2+++++++++++++++++++++++++++++++Comments+++++++++++++
  1 2          3         4                 5
```

Note: The SEU **CX** format must be used for **EVAL** instructions.

1. An **L0–L9** or **LR** indicator may be entered in the *L0* field to condition an **EVAL** instruction at total time.

2. An **01–99** indicator may be entered in the *N01* field to condition an **EVAL** instruction.

3. *Factor 1* is not used.

4. The **EVAL** operation name is entered in the *Opcode&Ext* field. For numeric expressions the Half-adjust operation code extender **(H)** may be entered after the **EVAL** operation.

5. Entries in the *Extended-factor2* field are:
   Result field (item **left** of the equal sign) must be a field name, array name, array element, data structure, data structure subfield, or string using the **%SUBST** built-in function. May not be a constant or literal.

   Result field must have been previously defined in the **RPG IV** program *(Definition, Input,* or *Calculation Specification*—or in an *externally described* file type).

Processing Features:

- The **EVAL** operation evaluates the assignment statement and stores the result in the item specified left of the equal sign.
- Arithmetic expressions must follow the algebraic order of operations (see Figure 5-3).
- The type of expression must be the same as the result field (item left of the equal sign)—numeric with numeric or character with character.

Figure 5-2 EVAL (Evaluate expression) operation syntax rules.

```
Evaluation in the EVAL expression examines the formula following the algebraic
order of precedence: moving from left to right and executing the arithmetic
functions in the following order:

 1. (...) expression(s) within parentheses will be evaluated first

 2. ** (exponentiation) second

 3. *  (multiplication) or / (division) third

 4. + (addition) or - (subtraction) fourth
```

```
Example 1:  (Division first, multiplication second, addition third, and
             subtraction fourth)

*.. 1 ...+... 2 ...+... 3 ...+... 4 ...+... 5 ...+... 6 ...+... 7 ...+... 8
CLON01Factor1+++++++Opcode&ExtExtended-factor2+++++++++++++++++++++++++++++++

                    EVAL      Answer = FldA + FldB / FldC - FldD * FldE

 Evaluation order                          3    1    4    2
```

```
Example 2:  (Addition within parentheses is performed first, division second,
             multiplication third, and subtraction fourth)

*.. 1 ...+... 2 ...+... 3 ...+... 4 ...+... 5 ...+... 6 ...+... 7 ...+... 8
CLON01Factor1+++++++Opcode&ExtExtended-factor2+++++++++++++++++++++++++++++++

                    EVAL      Answer = (FldA + FldB) / FldC - FldD * FldE

 Evaluation order                            1     2    4    3
```

Figure 5-3 EVAL statement's algebraic order of operations.

```
Example 3:  (Subtraction within parentheses is performed first, exponentiation
             second, and division third)

*.. 1 ...+... 2 ...+... 3 ...+... 4 ...+... 5 ...+... 6 ...+... 7 ...+... 8
CLON01Factor1+++++++Opcode&ExtExtended-factor2+++++++++++++++++++++++++++++

                    EVAL      Answer = FldB / (FldC - FldD) ** FldE

 Evaluation order                           3       1        2
```

Figure 5-3 **EVAL** statement's algebraic order of operations. (Continued)

Application examples of **EVAL** expressions are shown in Figure 5-4.

```
Example 1:  Subtract Returns from Gross_Sales and store the difference in
            Net_Sales.

*.. 1 ...+... 2 ...+... 3 ...+... 4 ...+... 5 ...+... 6 ...+... 7 ...+... 8
CLON01Factor1+++++++Opcode&ExtFactor2+++++++Result++++++++Len++D+HiLoEq....

C                   EVAL      Net_Sales = Gross_Sales - Returns

Example 2:  Multiplication is performed first.  Then, the accumulated product
            is divided by 365 and the answer (quotient) stored in Daily_Int
            half-rounded.

*.. 1 ...+... 2 ...+... 3 ...+... 4 ...+... 5 ...+... 6 ...+... 7 ...+... 8
CLON01Factor1+++++++Opcode&ExtFactor2+++++++Result++++++++Len++D+HiLoEq....

C                   EVAL  (H) Daily_Int = Principal * TimeinDays *
                                      Int_Rate / 365

Example 3:  Dept_Total value is accumulated with the Dept_Sales value in
            every record processed.

*.. 1 ...+... 2 ...+... 3 ...+... 4 ...+... 5 ...+... 6 ...+... 7 ...+... 8
CLON01Factor1+++++++Opcode&ExtExtended-factor2+++++++++++++++++++++++++++++

C                   EVAL      Dept_Total = Dept_Total + Dept_Sales

Example 4:  Parentheses are required so that all multiplication will be
            performed before division.  The result stored in EconOrQty
            is half-rounded.

*.. 1 ...+... 2 ...+... 3 ...+... 4 ...+... 5 ...+... 6 ...+... 7 ...+... 8
CLON01Factor1+++++++Opcode&ExtExtended-factor2+++++++++++++++++++++++++++++

C                   EVAL  (H) EconOrQty = (2 * AnualUnits * OrderCost) /
                                      (UnitCost * CarryCost)

Example 5:  Initialization of a field with a value (figurative constant *ZEROS
            for this example)

*.. 1 ...+... 2 ...+... 3 ...+... 4 ...+... 5 ...+... 6 ...+... 7 ...+... 8
CLON01Factor1+++++++Opcode&ExtExtended-factor2+++++++++++++++++++++++++++++

C                   EVAL      Counter = *ZEROS
```

Figure 5-4 Application examples of the **EVAL** expression.

Half-Adjust (Rounding)

The **RPG IV** *half-adjust* refers to the mathematical procedure of rounding a result field value to a final size. Half-adjust is specified with the **EVAL** operation by an **(H)** code extender in the *Opcode* field. It may also be specified with any **RPG IV** arithmetic operation (e.g., **ADD, SUB, DIV, MULT, XFOOT, SQRT**) and **Z-ADD** and **Z-SUB.** Note that if the extra low-order digit is less than 5, the next-highest digit will *not* be increased by 1. Figure 5-5 details an example of the half-adjust (rounding) function.

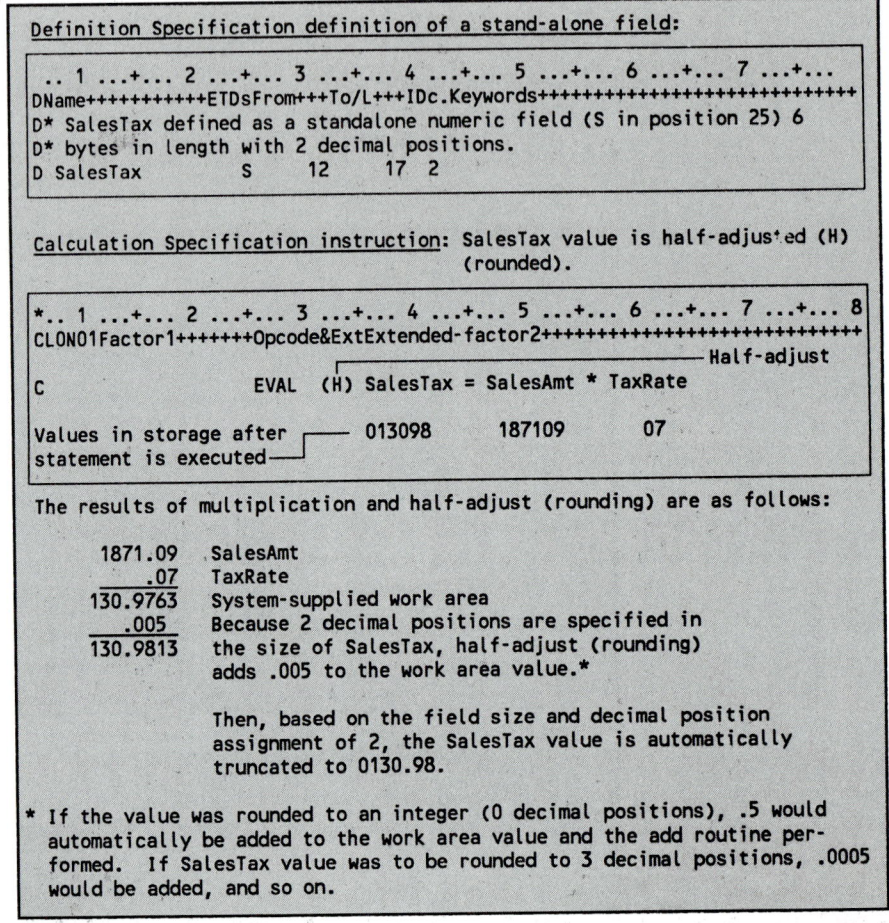

Definition Specification definition of a stand-alone field:

```
.. 1 ...+... 2 ...+... 3 ...+... 4 ...+... 5 ...+... 6 ...+... 7 ...+...
DName+++++++++++ETDsFrom+++To/L+++IDc.Keywords+++++++++++++++++++++++++++++
D* SalesTax defined as a standalone numeric field (S in position 25) 6
D* bytes in length with 2 decimal positions.
D SalesTax          S     12      17  2
```

Calculation Specification instruction: SalesTax value is half-adjusted (H) (rounded).

```
*.. 1 ...+... 2 ...+... 3 ...+... 4 ...+... 5 ...+... 6 ...+... 7 ...+... 8
CL0N01Factor1+++++++Opcode&ExtExtended-factor2+++++++++++++++++++++++++++++
                              ┌─────────────────────────────── Half-adjust
C                   EVAL    (H) SalesTax = SalesAmt * TaxRate

Values in storage after ┌── 013098      187109       07
statement is executed───┘
```

The results of multiplication and half-adjust (rounding) are as follows:

```
  1871.09   SalesAmt
      .07   TaxRate
 130.9763   System-supplied work area
     .005   Because 2 decimal positions are specified in
 130.9813   the size of SalesTax, half-adjust (rounding)
            adds .005 to the work area value.*

            Then, based on the field size and decimal position
            assignment of 2, the SalesTax value is automatically
            truncated to 0130.98.
```

* If the value was rounded to an integer (0 decimal positions), .5 would automatically be added to the work area value and the add routine performed. If SalesTax value was to be rounded to 3 decimal positions, .0005 would be added, and so on.

Figure 5-5 **EVAL** operation syntax for half-adjust (rounding).

Numeric Result Field Sizes

To avoid low-order and/or high-order truncation of result field values, their sizes must be carefully determined. The following paragraphs suggest general rules for defining result field sizes for the arithmetic functions of addition, subtraction, multiplication, and division. Furthermore, the resulting sign of the value stored in the result field for any of the arithmetic functions must be considered.

Determination of Result Field Size and Sign for Addition

The algebraic rules for sign determination of the *sum* (result field) for addition instructions are as follows:

1. Addition of two *positive* values results in a positive value for the *sum.*
2. Addition of two *negative* values results in a negative value for the *sum.*
3. Addition of two values with *different* signs results in the difference in the positive and negative values with the *sum* carrying the sign of the *largest* value.

Figure 5-6 details how the result field *(sum)* size is determined for addition instructions.

```
Determination of result field size for addition:

     9999.99    Addend
      999.99    Addend
    99999.99    Sum    Result field size should be one digit larger
                        than the largest addend (for both integer
                        and decimal positions).

    Note: If a field value is to be accumulated, common sense may
          dictate how large the result field should be for both
          the integer and decimal positions.
```

Figure 5-6 Determination of result field size for addition.

Determination of Result Field Size and Sign for Subtraction

The algebraic rule for the determination of the sign for the *difference* (result field) for subtraction instructions is as follows:

> Before subtraction, the sign of the subtrahend (bottom number) is changed. Then, the minuend (top number) and subtrahend are added to compute the difference. The result field (difference) sign follows the same rules as for addition.

Figure 5-7 details how the size of the result field (*difference*) is determined for subtraction instructions.

```
Determination of result field size for subtraction:

     9999.99 Minuend
       99.99 Subtrahend
    99999.99 Difference  To provide for possible negative values,
                         the result field size should be determined
                         using the rules followed for addition.
```

Figure 5-7 Determination of result field size for subtraction.

Determination of Result Field Size and Sign for Multiplication

The algebraic rules for the determination of the sign for the *product* (result field) in a multiplication instruction are as follows:

1. Multiplication of numbers with *like* signs results in a *product* (result field) with a positive value.
2. Multiplication of numbers with *unlike* signs results in a *product* (result field) with a negative value.

Figure 5-8 details the steps to determine the optimal result field (product) size for multiplication instructions.

Rule for Field Length Determination:

The maximum field length for the product of multiplication is the sum of the number of digits in the multiplicand and multiplier fields and/or numeric literal.

Rule for Decimal Position Determination:

The number of decimal positions for the product of the multiplication is the sum of the number of decimal positions in the multiplicand and multiplier fields and/or numeric literal.

Computation Routine:

Assume that FLD1, which is 8 digits in length with 2 implied decimals, is multiplied by FLD2, which is defined as 5 digits long with 5 decimal positions. The maximum size of the product may be determined by the following routine:

	Field or Literal Size	Decimal Positions	
FLD1		8	2
FLD2		+5	+5
Maximum product size	13	7	

If rounding to zero decimal positions was specified, the product size is computed as follows:

	Field or Literal Size	Decimal Positions
Maximum product size	13	7
Less 7	-7	-7
Rounded product size	6	0

Note: 7 must be subtracted from the field size and decimal position values.

Figure 5-8 Determination of result field (product) size for multiplication.

Determination of Result Field Size and Sign for Division

The algebraic rules for the determination of the sign for the *quotient* (result field) in a division instruction are as follows:

1. Division of numbers with *like* signs results in a quotient with a positive value.
2. Division of numbers with *unlike* signs results in a quotient with a negative value.

The factors in a division are:

xxx ———*quotient*
divisor———*xx* | *xxxx* ——*dividend*

Figure 5-9 suggests how the size of a quotient is determined. Note that a quotient size may sometimes have to be defined by trial and error and not strictly by the rules.

Move Remainder Operation (MVR)

Sometimes it may be necessary to store the remainder of a division instruction for subsequent processing. This function is performed in **RPG IV** with the **MVR** operation, which is detailed in Figure 5-10. Note that an **MVR** instruction *cannot* be used with in an **EVAL** statement. Consequently, the related **DIV** instruction must be formatted with the traditional **RPG** syntax using the **DIV** operation.

<u>The Optimum Quotient Size May Be Determined by the Following Formula:</u>

Quotient size = size of the dividend − size of the divisor + 1

<u>Example 1:</u> (divisor smaller than dividend)

Divisor size = 2 bytes with 0 decimal positions

Dividend size = 6 bytes with 2 decimal positions

Quotient size = 6 − 2 + 1

Quotient size = 5

The decimal positions in the quotient will be equal to that specified in the dividend.

<u>Example 2:</u> (divisor larger than dividend)

Divisor size = 5 bytes with 0 decimal positions

Dividend size = 3 bytes with 0 decimal positions

Quotient size = 3 − 5 + 1

Quotient size = −1 (field must be specified as 1 long with 1 decimal position)

When a larger value is divided into a smaller value, the quotient size may be specified larger than the formula indicates. The accuracy required will determine how many decimal positions are assigned.

Figure 5-9 Determination of result field (quotient) size for division.

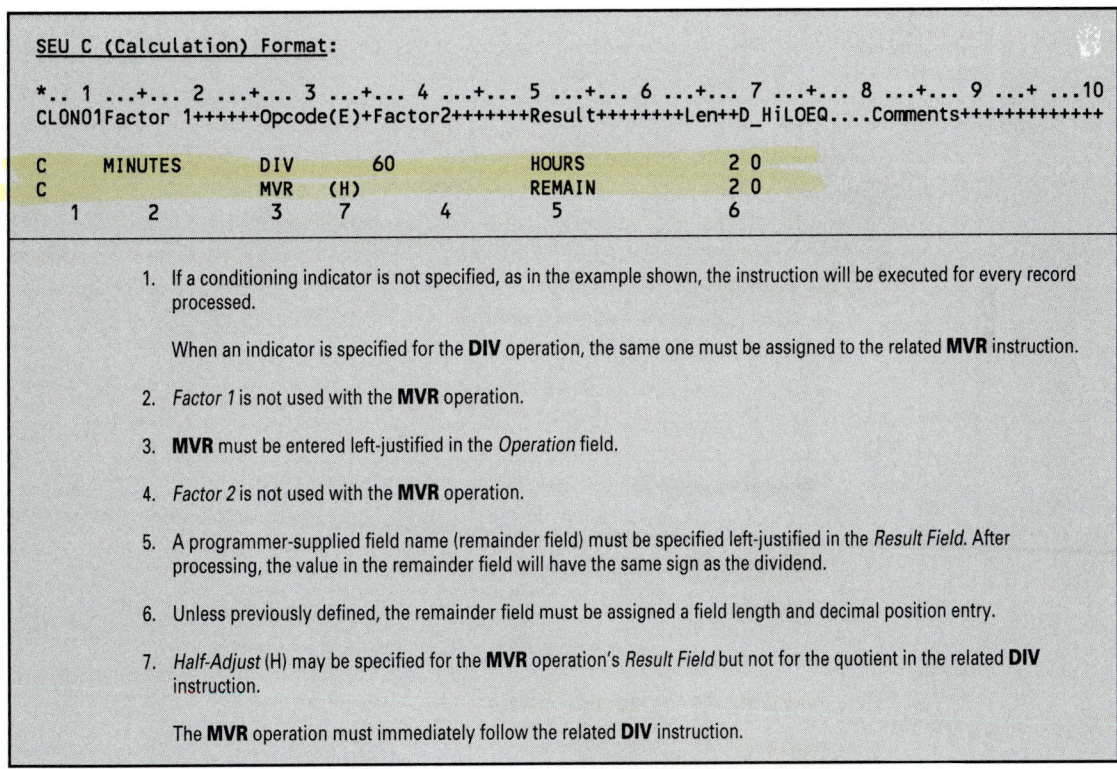

<u>SEU C (Calculation) Format:</u>

```
*.. 1 ...+... 2 ...+... 3 ...+... 4 ...+... 5 ...+... 6 ...+... 7 ...+... 8 ...+... 9 ...+ ...10
CLON01Factor 1+++++++Opcode(E)+Factor2+++++++Result++++++++Len++D_HiLOEQ....Comments+++++++++++++

C    MINUTES      DIV       60             HOURS            2 0
C                 MVR   (H)                REMAIN           2 0
  1        2         3      7       4         5             6
```

1. If a conditioning indicator is not specified, as in the example shown, the instruction will be executed for every record processed.

   When an indicator is specified for the **DIV** operation, the same one must be assigned to the related **MVR** instruction.

2. *Factor 1* is not used with the **MVR** operation.

3. **MVR** must be entered left-justified in the *Operation* field.

4. *Factor 2* is not used with the **MVR** operation.

5. A programmer-supplied field name (remainder field) must be specified left-justified in the *Result Field.* After processing, the value in the remainder field will have the same sign as the dividend.

6. Unless previously defined, the remainder field must be assigned a field length and decimal position entry.

7. *Half-Adjust* (H) may be specified for the **MVR** operation's *Result Field* but not for the quotient in the related **DIV** instruction.

   The **MVR** operation must immediately follow the related **DIV** instruction.

Figure 5-10 **RPG IV** syntax rules for the **MVR** (Move Remainder) operation.

The size and decimal positions for a remainder field may be determined by the process explained in Figure 5-11.

Division example:

```
              17.307  <------Quotient
Divisor ----->52| 900.000 <------Dividend
               52
               380
               364
                160
                156
                 400
                 364
                  36<------ Remainder
```

Rules for the determination of quotient and remainder sizes:

1. The optimal quotient size may be determined by the following formula:

   Quotient size = size of the dividend – size of the divisor + 1

2. The optimal remainder size is equal to the size of the divisor.

   The number of decimal positions for a data-item defined as a remainder may be determined by the proof computation for division as shown below:

```
  17.307 <-----------Quotient
x     52 <-----------Divisor
   34614
  86535      or     899.964
 899.964                .36    Remainder is defined with 2 decimals to equal value of dividend
                    900.000<------ Dividend
```

The decimal positions may also be determined by the following rule:

The length of a data-item used as a remainder must be equal to the number of decimal positions included in the dividend; or the sum of the decimal positions in the divisor and quotient, whichever is greater.

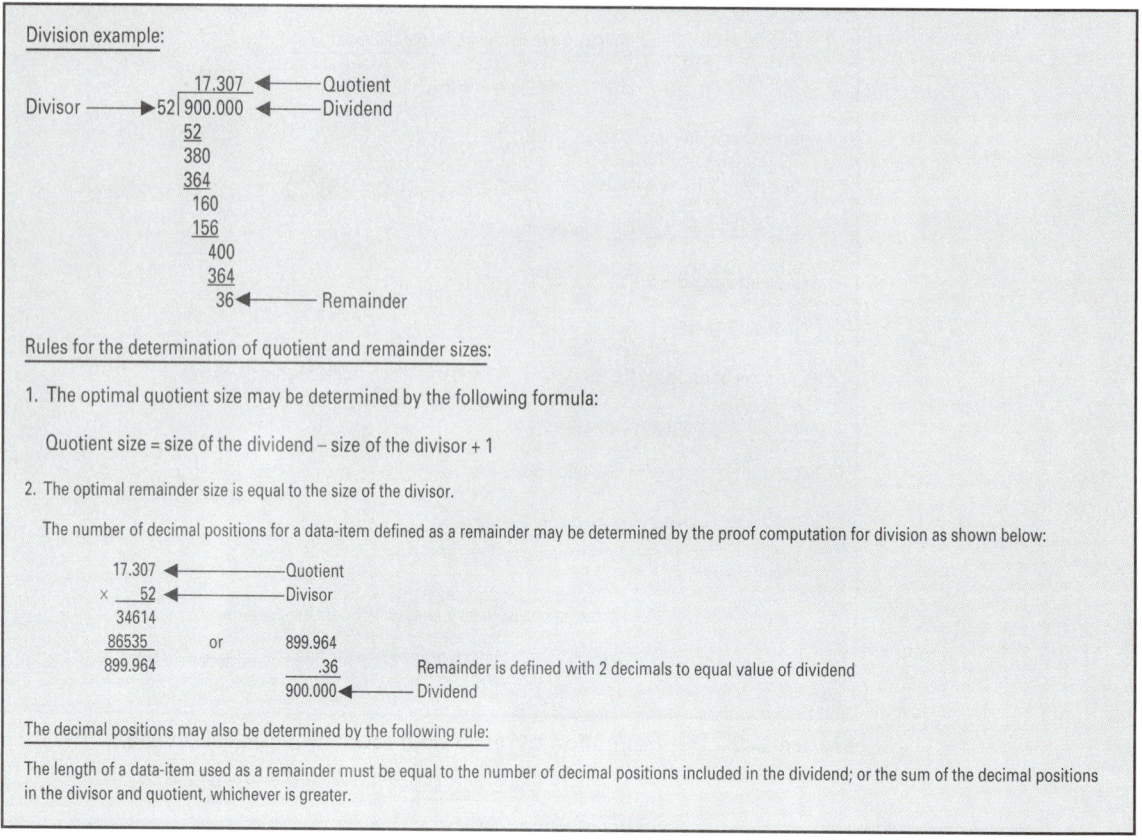

Figure 5-11 Process for determining the size and decimal positions of a remainder field.

Figurative Constants

Figurative Constants, which include ***BLANK/*BLANKS, *ZERO/*ZEROS, *HIVAL, *LOVAL, *ALL, *NULL, *IN,** and ***OFF,** are *implied literals* that are assigned a predetermined value. They are referenced without regard to length and assume the size of the field to which they relate. An explanation of each Figurative Constant is presented in Figure 5-12.

***BLANK/*BLANKS**	Indicates the constant contains all blanks (spaces). May only be used with alphanumeric fields.
***ZERO/*ZEROS**	Indicates the constant contains all zeros. May be used with any field type.
***HIVAL**	Indicates the constant contains the highest character in the collating character set of the computer. If the field in the relational test (or result field) is numeric, ***HIVAL** defaults to 9s. However, if it is alphanumeric, the constant defaults to hexadecimal FFs.
***LOVAL**	Indicates the constant contains the lowest character in the collating character set of the computer. If the field in the relational test (or result field) is numeric, ***LOVAL** is assumed to be negative 9s. However, if it is alphanumeric, the constant defaults to hexadecimal zeros.

Figure 5-12 Processing features of Figurative Constants.

***ALL'X...'**	The character string X... etc. is repeated to a length equal to the *Factor 1* or *Factor 2* field in a relational test or to the result field in a mathematical or **MOVE, MOVEL,** or **MOVEA** operation. If the relational test or result field item is numeric, all characters in the X string must be numeric. No sign or decimal point may be used in a numeric string.
***ON**	Indicates the constant contains all 1s.
***OFF**	Indicates the constant contains all 0s.
***NULL**	Used with pointers.

Figure 5-12 Processing features of Figurative Constants. (Continued)

Examples of how Figurative Constants may be used in an **EVAL** instruction are shown in Figure 5-13.

```
*.. 1 ...+... 2 ...+... 3 ...+... 4 ...+... 5 ...+... 6 ...+... 7 ...+... 8 ...+... 9 ...+ ...10
CLON01Factor1+++++++Opcode&ExtExtended-factor2+++++++++++++++++++++++++++++++Comments+++++++++++++

C                   EVAL      NAME = *BLANKS                                 Filled with blanks

C                   EVAL      TOTAL = *ZEROS                                 Filled with zeros

C                   EVAL      DOTS = *ALL'.'                                 Filled with periods

C                   EVAL      *INLR = *ON                                    Set on LR indicator

C                   EVAL      *INOF = *OFF                                   Set off OF indicator

          Note: Examples shown assume the fields NAME, TOTAL, and DOTS
                have been previously defined.
```

Figure 5-13 Examples of Figurative Constants in **EVAL** instructions.

RPG IV Reserved Words *IN and *INxx

RPG IV indicators may be set on, set off, moved, and tested by the reserved words ***IN** and ***INxx.** Their functions are explained below.

- **INxx** is a one-position character field where **xx** represents any **RPG IV** indicator.
- **IN** references a predefined **99** one-position array defining the status of indicators **01** through **99.** The format ***IN** references all **99** elements in the array. One element may be referenced by the format ***IN,xx** (**xx** for any one indicator **01** through **99**).

As shown in Figure 5-14, indicators may be individually set on and set off using the ***INxx** reserved word in an **EVAL** instruction. In lieu of using the Figurative Constant ***OFF** to set an indicator off, **'0'** (binary representation for "*off*") may be specified. Conversely, instead of using the Figurative Constant ***ON,** the binary representation **'1',** for "*on*," may be used to set on an indicator.

***IN, *IN,xx,** or ***INxx** cannot be used as a subfield in a data structure, a result field of a **PARM** operation, or in a **SORTA** operation. Each of these topics is discussed in subsequent chapters.

```
*.. 1 ...+... 2 ...+... 3 ...+... 4 ...+... 5 ...+... 6 ...+... 7 ...+... 8 ...+... 9 ...+ ...10
CLON01Factor 1+++++++Opcode(E)+Extended-factor2++++++++++++++++++++++++++++++Comments+++++++++++++
 * This instruction sets off all of the indicators in the indicator array
C                   EVAL      *IN = '0'

 * This instruction sets off indicator 10 in the indicator array
C                   EVAL      *IN,10 = *OFF

 * This instruction sets on the LR indicator
C                   EVAL      *INLR = *ON

   Notes: 1. An indicator array is built in memory for every RPG IV program executed.
          2. '0' may be specified for the figurative constant *OFF.
          3. '1' may be specified for the figurative constant *ON.
```

Figure 5-14 Examples of ***IN**, ***IN,xx**, and ***INxx** reserved words with the **EVAL** operation.

Numeric and Character Literals (Constants)

Numeric and character *literals* in **RPG IV** programs must be formatted according to the rules explained in Figure 5-15.

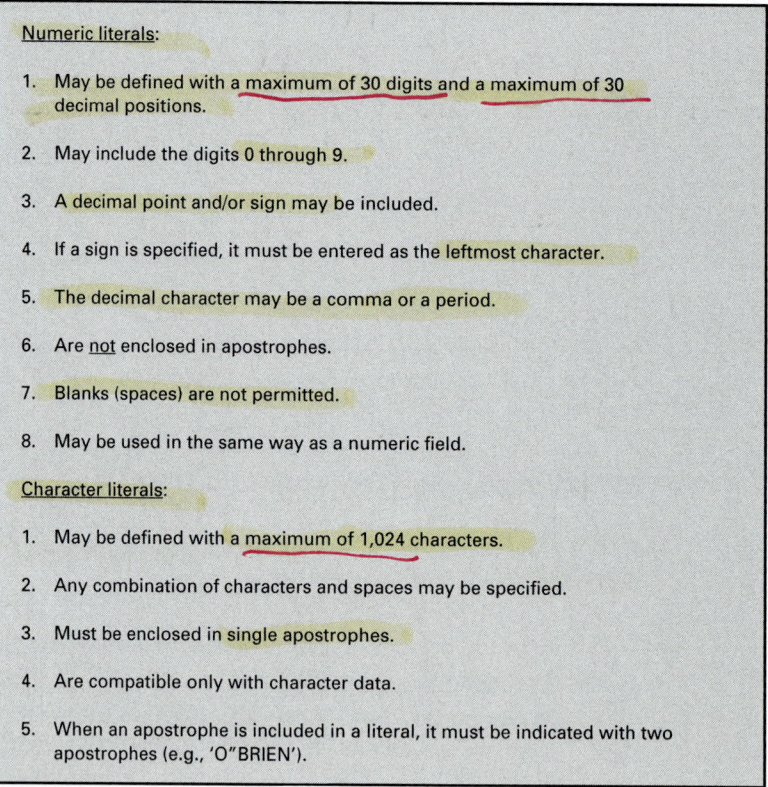

Numeric literals:

1. May be defined with a maximum of 30 digits and a maximum of 30 decimal positions.
2. May include the digits 0 through 9.
3. A decimal point and/or sign may be included.
4. If a sign is specified, it must be entered as the leftmost character.
5. The decimal character may be a comma or a period.
6. Are not enclosed in apostrophes.
7. Blanks (spaces) are not permitted.
8. May be used in the same way as a numeric field.

Character literals:

1. May be defined with a maximum of 1,024 characters.
2. Any combination of characters and spaces may be specified.
3. Must be enclosed in single apostrophes.
4. Are compatible only with character data.
5. When an apostrophe is included in a literal, it must be indicated with two apostrophes (e.g., 'O''BRIEN').

Figure 5-15 Rules for numeric and character literals.

INITIALIZATION OF FIELD VALUES

Within an **RPG IV** program it is often necessary to initialize numeric fields to zero (or some other value) and character fields to blanks (or some other value) before, during, or after a group of calculations is executed. The various methods of initializing fields are left to the preference of the programmer. However, he or she should follow **RPG IV** syntax and, for most applications, avoid the traditional **RPG** coding methods.

The methods of initializing numeric and character fields using **RPG IV** syntax are summarized in the following paragraphs.

Initialization of Field Values with the EVAL Operation

Figure 5-16 illustrates four methods of initializing numeric and character fields to zero (or some other value) using the **EVAL** operation.

```
*.. 1 ...+... 2 ...+... 3 ...+... 4 ...+... 5 ...+... 6 ...+... 7 ...+... 8 ...+... 9 ...+ ...10
CLON01Factor1+++++++Opcode&ExtExtended-factor2+++++++++++++++++++++++++++++Comments+++++++++++++
 * Initialize the RecordCnt field to zero using a figurative constant
C                   EVAL      RecordCnt = *ZERO

 * Initialize the RecordCnt field to zero using a numeric literal
C                   EVAL      RecordCnt = 0

 * Initialize the field N to 1
C                   EVAL      N = 1

 * Initialize the Dept_Total field to zero by subtracting the field from itself
C                   EVAL      Dept_Total = Dept_Total - Dept_Total

 * Initialize the StateTotal field to zero by multiplying by 0
C                   EVAL      StateTotal = StateTotal * 0

 * Initialize the character field PayStatus with a literal
C                   EVAL      PayStatus = 'OVERDUE'
```

Figure 5-16 Methods of initializing fields to a value using the **EVAL** operation.

Initialization of Fields Using Named Constants

Programmer-defined numeric or character literal values may be defined using *Named Constants*. The literal value (numeric or character) is assigned to a standalone field name on the *Definition Specification*. The field may be subsequently specified in calculation and/or output instructions. Figure 5-17 details the syntax rules for Named Constants.

NAMED CONSTANTS RULES

1. Named Constants are defined on the *Definition Specifications*.
2. The letter **C** must be entered in position 24 on the same line as the value and related field name. If the value is too long to fit in the keywords field (positions 44–80) and continues to the next line, the **C** is permitted only on the first line of the Named Constant definition.
3. Character values must be enclosed in single quotes. If the value will not fit on one line, continuation is indicated by a – (minus) sign, without a single quote, after the last character on that line. A single quote must be specified on the next continuation line. The location of the minus sign indicates the end of the value for that line. The last continuation line must include the terminating single quote. The maximum size of a character Named Constant is 1,024 characters.
4. Numeric values are specified *without* quotes. If the value will not fit on one line, continuation is indicated by a – (minus sign) *immediately* after the last digit. Negative values are defined by a *leading* – (minus sign). The maximum size of a numeric Named Constant is 30 digits. No more than 30 decimal positions may be defined.
5. Programmer-supplied Named Constant field names must be specified in the *Name* field (positions 7–21) of the first *Definition Specification* instruction for each Named Constant.

Figure 5-17 **RPG IV** syntax rules for Named Constants.

Examples of how numeric and character Named Constants are defined are detailed in Figure 5-18.

```
.. 1 ...+... 2 ...+... 3 ...+... 4 ...+... 5 ...+... 6 ...+... 7 ...+... 8
DName+++++++++++ETDsFrom+++To/L+++IDc.Keywords+++++++++++++++++++++++++++++
 * FicaRate (social security tax rate) defined as a Named Constant
D FicaRate        C                   .0765
D
 * Named Constant value used for the validation of valid character data
D ValidChars      C                   ' ABCDEFGHIJKLMNOPQRSTUVWXYZabcdefg-
D                                      hijklmnopqrstuvwxyz'
D
 * Definition of an Edit Word for Social Security Number editing
D SS#Format       C                   '0   -  -    '
D
 * The CONST keyword may be optionally used in the definition of a numeric
 * or character Named Constant value
D TaxRate         C                   CONST(.045)

                        + or a - may be used as a continuation character
 Space is for readability; Name item does not have to begin in position 7
```

Figure 5-18 Character and numeric Named Constant example instructions.

Initialization of Fields with the INZ Definition Keyword

The **INZ** keyword may be specified only as a *Definition Specification* instruction. It may be used to initialize numeric fields to zero (or some other value) and character fields to blanks (or some other value). The fields initialized with the **INZ** keyword must be defined as "standalone" fields (letter **S** in position 24 of the instruction).

Figure 5-19 presents examples of *Definition Specification* instructions using the **INZ** keyword. When character fields are initialized with a value other than blanks, the value must be enclosed in single quotes.

```
.. 1 ...+... 2 ...+... 3 ...+... 4 ...+... 5 ...+... 6 ...+... 7 ...+... 8
DName+++++++++++ETDsFrom+++To/L+++IDc.Keywords+++++++++++++++++++++++++++++
 * INZ keyword initializes Record_Cnt field (numeric) to zero
D Record_Cnt      S              5  0 INZ

 * INZ keyword initializes Loop-Ctr field (numeric) to 1
D Loop_Ctr        S              4  0 INZ(1)

 * INZ keyword initializes Message field (character) to blanks
D Message         S             12    INZ

 * INZ keyword initializes Function field (character) to INQUIRY
D Function        S              7    INZ('INQUIRY')

                  S entry defines a "standalone" field
  Space is for readability; Name item does not have to begin in column 7
```

Figure 5-19 **INZ** keyword instruction examples.

When *internal subroutines* are introduced in Chapter 7, initialization of fields using the **RPG IV** compiler-supplied subroutine ***INZSR** will be discussed.

An **RPG IV** application program will be introduced using some of the syntax introduced in the chapter.

APPLICATION PROGRAM: PROFIT ANALYSIS OF SOUP BRANDS

The specifications in Figure 5-20 summarize the processing requirements for the example application program.

PROGRAM SPECIFICATIONS

PAGE 1 of 1

Program Name: Profit Report Program-ID: SOUPS Written by: SM

Purpose: Determine profit per case for soups brands Approved by: CM

Input files: SOUPMSTR

Output files: QSYSPRT

Processing Requirements:

Write an **RPG IV** program to generate a profit report for soup brands.

Input to the program:

The externally defined physical file, SOUPMSTR, contains the selling price and cost per case information for soup brands. The physical file's record format is shown in the supplemental record layout form.

Processing:

Read the physical file in arrival sequence and perform the following for each record processed:

Detail Calculations:

Profit per case computation (in $):

Profit/case = Selling price/case – Cost/case

Percent of profit per case computation:

Step 1: $\text{Decimal profit} = \dfrac{\text{Profit/Case}}{\text{Cost/case}}$

Step 2: Percent profit = Decimal profit × 100

Step 3: Add the Percent profit (step 2) to an accumulator

Add the number of records processed to an accumulator.

Total time calculations:

Compute the average profit of all soup brands with the following formula:

$$\text{Average profit percent} = \frac{\text{Total profit percent (Step 3)}}{\text{Record count}}$$

Output:

The report design is detailed in a supplemental printer spacing chart.

Figure 5-20 Specifications for profit analysis of soup brands application program.

The system flowchart in Figure 5-21 indicates that one physical file is input and one printer file is output by the program.

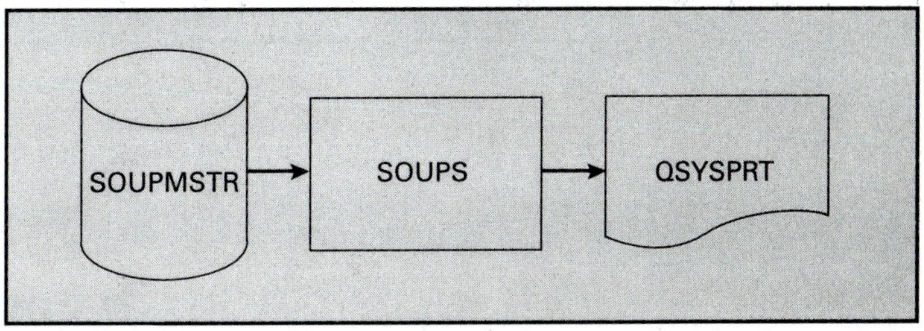

Figure 5-21 System flowchart for soup brand profit report application.

Included with the physical file description in Figure 5-22 is a listing of the data stored in the file.

```
                    PHYSICAL FILE DESCRIPTION

SYSTEM: AS/400                                      DATE: 11/30/98
FILE NAME: SOUPMSTR                                 REV NO: 0
RECORD NAME: SOUPR                                  KEY LENGTH: None
SEQUENCE: Nonkeyed                                 RECORD SIZE: 26

                          FIELD DEFINITIONS

 FIELD     FIELD NAME   SIZE  TYPE    POSITION     COMMENTS
  NO                                  FROM    TO

  1        SoupBrand     20    C        1     20
  2        SpPerCase      4    P       21     23 2 decimals
  3        CstPerCase     4    P       24     26 2 decimlas

Physical File Data:                          Selling
                                              Price       Cost
                   Soup Brand               Per Case   Per Case

          CAMPBELL TOMATO SOUP                0648       0504
          LIPTON CHICKEN                      1440       1188
          HEINZ VEGETABLE                     0792       0576
          PROGRESSO MINESTRONE                1728       1224
          PEPPERIDGE CHOWDER                  1404       1116
          STOP & SHOP TOMATO                  1476       1044
          A & P CHICKEN RICE                  0720       0792
```

Figure 5-22 Physical file description and data listing of the soup brands file.

The report design is formatted in the Printer Spacing Chart shown in Figure 5-23.

```
1   ØX/XX/XX      CASE LOT PROFIT ANALYSIS OF SOUP BRANDS        PAGE XXØX
2
3
4           BRAND               SP/CASE        COST      PROFIT      % PROFIT
5
6    X----------------------X      XØ.XX         XØ.XX     XØ.XX-      XØ.XXX-%
7
8    X----------------------X      XØ.XX         XØ.XX     XØ.XX-      XØ.XXX-%
9
10
11       AVERAGE PROFIT PERCENT = XØ.XXX-%
12
13        NOTES:
14
15           1. USE SYSTEM DATE FOR REPORT.
16
17           2. MINUS SIGN TO PRINT IF DOLLAR PROFIT OR
18              PERCENT PROFIT ARE NEGATIVE.
19
20
```

Figure 5-23 Printer Spacing Chart for soup brands profit report.

The report generated from execution of the soup brands **RPG IV** program is shown in Figure 5-24.

A detailed compile listing of the soup brands profit report program is presented in Figure 5-25. Note the following program's syntax:

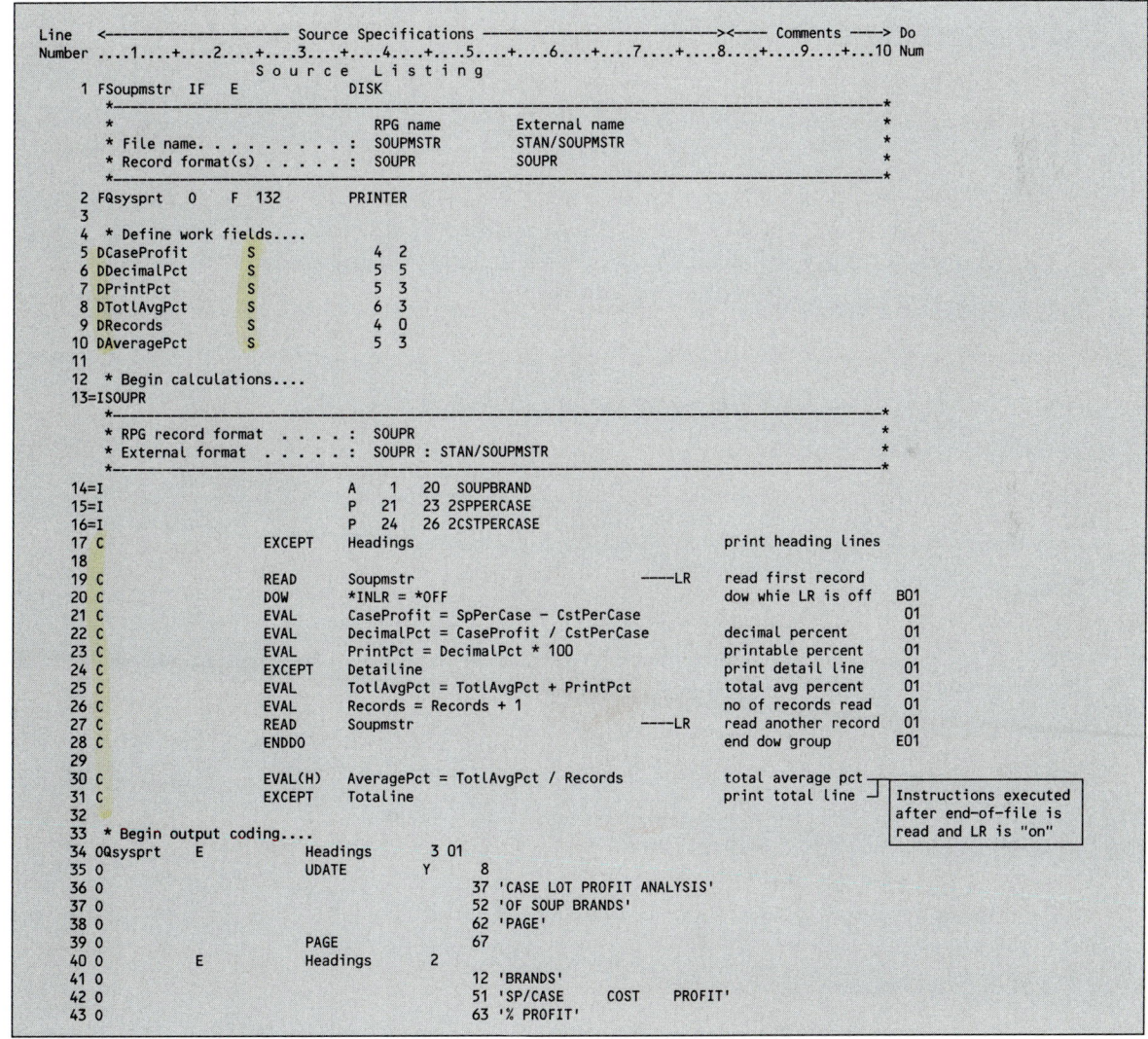

```
2/14/97      CASE LOT PROFIT ANALYSIS OF SOUP BRANDS        PAGE    1

    BRANDS                      SP/CASE      COST     PROFIT     % PROFIT

CAMPBELL TOMATO SOUP              6.48        5.04      1.44      28.571 %

LIPTON CHICKEN                   14.40       11.88      2.52      21.212 %

HEINZ VEGETABLE                   7.92        5.76      2.16      37.500 %

PROGRESSO MINESTRONE             17.28       12.24      5.04      41.176 %

PEPPERIDGE CHOWDER               14.04       11.16      2.88      25.806 %

STOP & SHOP TOMATO               14.76       10.44      4.32      41.379 %

A & P CHICKEN RICE                7.20        7.92       .72-      9.090-%


  AVERAGE PROFIT PERCENT = 26.651 %
```

Figure 5-24 Soup brands profit report listing.

```
Line   <---------------------- Source Specifications ----------------------------><---- Comments ----> Do
Number ....1....+....2....+....3....+....4....+....5....+....6....+....7....+....8....+....9....+...10 Num
                    S o u r c e   L i s t i n g
     1 FSoupmstr  IF   E              DISK
       *------------------------------------------------------------------------------------*
       *                              RPG name         External name                         *
       * File name. . . . . . . . . :  SOUPMSTR         STAN/SOUPMSTR                         *
       * Record format(s) . . . . . :  SOUPR            SOUPR                                 *
       *------------------------------------------------------------------------------------*
     2 FQsysprt   O    F  132         PRINTER
     3
     4  * Define work fields....
     5 DCaseProfit       S              4  2
     6 DDecimalPct       S              5  5
     7 DPrintPct         S              5  3
     8 DTotlAvgPct       S              6  3
     9 DRecords          S              4  0
    10 DAveragePct       S              5  3
    11
    12  * Begin calculations....
    13=ISOUPR
       *------------------------------------------------------------------------------------*
       * RPG record format  . . . . :  SOUPR                                                  *
       * External format  . . . . . :  SOUPR : STAN/SOUPMSTR                                  *
       *------------------------------------------------------------------------------------*
    14=I                              A    1   20  SOUPBRAND
    15=I                              P   21   23 2SPPERCASE
    16=I                              P   24   26 2CSTPERCASE
    17 C                    EXCEPT    Headings                               print heading lines
    18
    19 C                    READ      Soupmstr                          ----LR read first record
    20 C                    DOW       *INLR = *OFF                             dow whie LR is off   B01
    21 C                    EVAL      CaseProfit = SpPerCase - CstPerCase                           01
    22 C                    EVAL      DecimalPct = CaseProfit / CstPerCase     decimal percent      01
    23 C                    EVAL      PrintPct = DecimalPct * 100              printable percent    01
    24 C                    EXCEPT    Detailine                                print detail line    01
    25 C                    EVAL      TotlAvgPct = TotlAvgPct + PrintPct       total avg percent    01
    26 C                    EVAL      Records = Records + 1                    no of records read   01
    27 C                    READ      Soupmstr                          ----LR read another record  01
    28 C                    ENDDO                                              end dow group        E01
    29
    30 C                    EVAL(H)   AveragePct = TotlAvgPct / Records        total average pct
    31 C                    EXCEPT    Totaline                                 print total line
    32
    33  * Begin output coding....
    34 OQsysprt   E            Headings       3 01
    35 O                       UDATE         Y     8
    36 O                                          37 'CASE LOT PROFIT ANALYSIS'
    37 O                                          52 'OF SOUP BRANDS'
    38 O                                          62 'PAGE'
    39 O                       PAGE               67
    40 O          E            Headings       2
    41 O                                          12 'BRANDS'
    42 O                                          51 'SP/CASE      COST     PROFIT'
    43 O                                          63 '% PROFIT'
```

Instructions executed after end-of-file is read and LR is "on"

Figure 5-25 Compile listing of the soup brands profit report program.

```
44 O         E          Detailine      2
45 O                    SoupBrand              21
46 O                    SpPerCase      1       31
47 O                    CstPerCase     1       42
48 O                    CaseProfit     J       51
49 O                    PrintPct       J       62
50 O                                           63 '%'
51 O                    Totaline     1                                  Printed after end-of-file
52 O                                           27 'AVERAGE PROFIT PERCENT ='  is read (LR "on")
53 O                    AveragePct     J       35
54 O                                          36 '%'
```

File Description Instructions:

Line No.

1 The Soupmstr is defined as an input, full-procedural, externally described, nonkeyed physical file.

2 Qsysprt is defined as a program-described PRINTER file.

Definition Specification instructions:

5–
10 The work fields CaseProfit through AveragePct are defined as "standalone" fields (S in position 24) in *Definition Specification* instructions.

Calculation Specification instructions:

17 The **EXCEPT** instruction controls the printing of the Headings on lines 34 through 43.

19 The **READ** operation reads the first record from the Soupmstr file. If no records are stored in the file, **LR** will be set on and the test in the **DOW** operation on line 20 will cause control to branch over the **DOW** group to line 30. The coding for this program assumes that records will always be stored in the physical file.

20 The ***INLR = LR** relational test specified in the **DOW** instruction controls execution of the instructions within the **DOW** group until **LR** is set on by one of the two **READ** instructions.

21 The **EVAL** instruction computes the CaseProfit (defined as a "standalone" field) value by subtracting the value in CstPerCase from the value in SpPerCase.

22 The **EVAL** instruction computes the DecimalPct (defined as a "standalone" field) value by dividing the value in CaseProfit by the value in CstPerCase.

23 The **EVAL** instruction computes the PrintPct (defined as a "standalone" field) value by multiplying the value stored in DecimalPct by the numeric literal 100.

24 The **EXCEPT** instruction passes control to line 44, where the field values included in the Detailine record are printed.

25 The **EVAL** instruction computes the TotlAvgPct (defined as a "standalone" field) value by adding the value stored in Print Pct to the accumulator TotlAvgPct.

26 The **EVAL** instruction computes the Records (defined as a "standalone" field) value by adding the numeric literal **1** to the accumulator Records.

27 The **READ** operation reads the next record (or end-of-file) from the physical file Soupmstr. If end-of-file is read, indicator **LR** will be set on.

28 The **ENDDO** operation ends the **DOW** group and returns control back to the **DOW** instruction on line 20, where the relational test is made to continue the iterative process or exit.

30 The **EVAL** instruction computes the AveragePct (defined as a "standalone" field) value by dividing the value in TotlAvgPct by the value in Records. This operation is executed after **LR** is set on (end-of-file condition) and exit from the **DOW** group occurs.

31 The **EXCEPT** instruction passes control to the Totaline, where the constants and field value for this output record are printed.

Output Specification instructions:

34–
43 Printing of the two Headings record values is controlled by the **EXCEPT** instruction on line 17.

44–
50 Printing of the Detailine record values is controlled by the **EXCEPT** instruction on line 24.

51–
54 Printing of the Totaline record values is controlled by the **EXCEPT** instruction on line 31.

Figure 5-25 Compile listing of the soup brands profit report program. (Continued)

1. Result fields are defined in the *Definition Specification* as "standalone" fields.
2. Records are read from the physical file by two **READ** instructions.
3. A **DOW** group is specified to read the second and remaining records in the physical file.
4. **EVAL** instructions are specified for all computations.
5. **EXCEPT** instructions control printing of heading and detail output.
6. The **LR** indicator is set on by the **READ** instruction when end-of-file is read. After the remaining instructions are executed, control is returned back to the operating system.

TRADITIONAL RPG ARITHMETIC OPERATIONS

The **EVAL** operation, available only in **RPG IV,** has replaced the traditional **RPG** arithmetic operations **ADD, SUB, MULT,** and **DIV.** However, because of the maintenance requirements of existing programs, the modern programmer must have a knowledge of the syntax of these operations.

Because a *Result field* entry is needed with the **ADD, SUB, MULT,** and **DIV** operations, the **SEU C** format must be used to enter the instructions.

The ADD Operation

General syntax rules for instructions using the **ADD** operation are as follows:

1. *Factor 2* and *Result field* (sum) entries are required.
2. The *Result field* entry *cannot* be a numeric literal.
3. *Factor 1* may be omitted when a field value is accumulated (as for a record count).
4. Unless the *Result field* entry is previously defined, it must be defined in the **ADD** instruction.
5. **Half-adjust** (rounding) of the *Result field* value may be specified.
6. A maximum of two conditioning indicators may be specified in positions 7–11. One *Control Level* indicator (**L0–L9**) and/or some other valid **RPG IV** indicator (i.e., **01** through **99**) may be entered.

Coding examples of **ADD** operation instructions are shown in Figure 5-26.

```
*.. 1 ...+... 2 ...+... 3 ...+... 4 ...+... 5 ...+... 6 ...+... 7 ...+... 8 ...+... 9 ...+ ...10
CL0N01Factor 1++++++Opcode(E)+Factor2+++++++Result++++++++Len++D_HiLOEQ....Comments+++++++++++++
 * The values in two fields (addends) are added and the sum stored in a third field.  TotSales
 * is defined in the instruction (8 digits with two decimal positions).  Example assumes the
 * StoreNo1 and StoreNo2 fields have been previously defined.
C     StoreNo1      ADD       StoreNo2      TotSales           8 2

 * Because the value in RecordCnt is accumulated, it does not have to be specifed in Factor 1.
 * The default for Factor 1 is the RecordCnt field.  RecordCnt is defined as 5 digits with
 * 0 decimal positions (an integer value).
C                   ADD       1             RecordCnt          5 0
```

Figure 5-26 Examples of **ADD** operation instructions.

The SUB Operation

General syntax rules for instructions using the **SUB** operation are as follows:

1. *Factor 2* (subtrahend) and *Result field* (difference) entries are required.
2. The subtrahend (bottom) entry must be specified in *Factor 2*.

3. The *Result field* entry *cannot* be a numeric literal.
4. *Factor 1* may be omitted when the *Result field* entry is the same as the minuend (top) entry.
5. Unless the *Result field* entry is previously defined, it must be defined in the **SUB** instruction.
6. **Half-adjust** (rounding) of the *Result field* value may be specified.
7. A maximum of two conditioning indicators may be specified in positions 7–11. One *Control Level* indicator (**L0–L9**) and/or some other valid **RPG IV** indicator (i.e., **01** through **99**) may be entered.

Examples of **SUB** operation instructions are shown in Figure 5-27.

```
*.. 1 ...+... 2 ...+... 3 ...+... 4 ...+... 5 ...+... 6 ...+... 7 ...+... 8 ...+... 9 ...+ ...10
CLON01Factor 1++++++Opcode(E)+Factor2+++++++Result++++++++Len++D_HiLOEQ....Comments+++++++++++++
 * The value in Returns (subtrahend) is subtracted from the value in GrossSale (minuend) and
 * the difference is stored in NetSale, which is defined as 7 digits with 2 decimal positions.
 * The example assumes GrossSale and Returns have been previously defined.
C     GrossSale     SUB       Returns       NetSale          7 2

 * Because the value in Discount is subtracted from NetSale and NetSale is the Result field
 * entry, NetSale does not have to be specified in Factor 1.  The example assumes that Discount
 * and NetSale have been previously defined.
C                   SUB       Discount      NetSale
```

Figure 5-27 Examples of **SUB** operation instructions.

The MULT Operation

General syntax rules for instructions using the **MULT** operation are as follows:

1. *Factor 2* (multiplier or multiplicand) and *Result field* (product) entries are required.
2. The *Result field* entry *cannot* be a numeric literal.
3. *Factor 1* may be omitted when the *Result field* entry is specified with the same field name.
4. Unless the *Result field* entry is previously defined, it must be defined in the **MULT** instruction.
5. **Half-adjust** (rounding) of the *Result field* value may be specified.
6. A maximum of two conditioning indicators may be specified in positions 7–11. One *Control Level* indicator (**L0–L9**) and/or some other valid **RPG IV** indicator (i.e., **01** through **99**) may be entered.

Examples of **MULT** operation instructions are shown in Figure 5-28.

```
*.. 1 ...+... 2 ...+... 3 ...+... 4 ...+... 5 ...+... 6 ...+... 7 ...+... 8 ...+... 9 ...+ ...10
CLON01Factor 1++++++Opcode(E)+Factor2+++++++Result++++++++Len++D_HiLOEQ....Comments+++++++++++++
 * The value in GrossWages is multiplied by the numeric literal .0765 and the product is stored
 * in FicaAmt, which is defined as 6 digits with 2 decimal positions.  The example assumes that
 * GrossWages has been previously defined.  Half-adjust is specified for the FicaAmt value.
C     GrossWages    MULT (H) .0765          FicaAmt          6 2

 * Because Factor 1 is not specified, the Result field TradeDscnt is the default entry for
 * Factor 1.  The original value in TradeDscnt is replaced with the new product.  The example
 * assumes that TradePct and TradeDscnt have been previously defined.
C                   MULT (H) TradePct       TradeDscnt
```

Figure 5-28 Examples of **MULT** operation instructions.

The DIV Operation

General syntax rules for instructions using the **DIV** operation are as follows:

1. *Factor 2* (divisor) and *Result field* (quotient) entries are required.
2. The *Result field* entry *cannot* be a numeric literal.
3. *Factor 1* may be omitted when the *Result field* entry is specified with the same field name.
4. Unless the *Result field* entry is previously defined, it must be defined in the **DIV** instruction.
5. **Half-adjust** (rounding) of the *Result field* value may be specified.
6. A maximum of two conditioning indicators may be specified in positions 7–11. One *Control Level* indicator (**L0–L9**) and/or some other valid **RPG IV** indicator (i.e., **01** through **99**) may be entered.

Examples of **DIV** operation instructions are shown in Figure 5-29.

```
*.. 1 ...+... 2 ...+... 3 ...+... 4 ...+... 5 ...+... 6 ...+... 7 ...+... 8 ...+... 9 ...+ ...10
CLON01Factor 1++++++Opcode(E)+Factor2+++++++Result++++++++Len++D_HiLOEQ....Comments++++++++++++
 * NetSales (dividend) is divided by Quota (divisor) and the quotient is stored in Percent.
 * Half-adjust for the Result field (Percent) is specified.  Percent is defined as 4 digits
 * with 3 decimal positions.  The example assumes NetSales and Quota are previously defined.
C     NetSales      DIV   (H) Quota         Percent          4 3

 *
 * Minutes (dividend) is divided by the numeric literal 60 and the quotient is stored in
 * HrsWorked.  Any remainder is stored in MinRemain.  The example assumes that Minutes has
 * been previously defined.
C     Minutes       DIV       60            HrsWorked        3 0
C                   MVR                     MinRemain        2 0
```

Figure 5-29 Examples of **DIV** operation instructions.

The SQRT (Square Root) Operation

Because square root computation is not directly supported by the **EVAL** operation, it must be computed using the **SQRT** operation. Remember, when multiplied by itself, the square root value of a number will give the original number. For example, the square root of 144 is 12, that of 81 is 9, and so forth. Other than the determination of economic order quantity and standard deviation formulas, few business and/or accounting applications require square root computation.

The general rules for the **SQRT** operation syntax are the following:

1. *Factor 1* is never used.
2. The field or numeric literal from which the square root is to be computed must be specified in *Factor 2*. Its value cannot be negative or a zero.
3. The square root value is stored in the *Result field* item, which *cannot* be a numeric literal.
4. A maximum of two conditioning indicators may be specified in positions 7–11. One *Control Level* indicator (**L0–L9**) and/or some other valid **RPG IV** indicator (i.e., **01** through **99** may be entered.

An example of a **SQRT** (square root) instruction is shown in Figure 5-30.

```
*.. 1 ...+... 2 ...+... 3 ...+... 4 ...+... 5 ...+... 6 ...+... 7 ...+... 8 ...+... 9 ...+ ...10
CLON01Factor 1++++++Opcode(E)+Factor2+++++++Result++++++++Len++D_HiLOEQ....Comments+++++++++++++
 * The square root of Number is stored in the Result field Answer.  Half-adjust is specified
 * for the value in Answer.  The example assumes Number has been previously defined.  Answer is
 * defined as 6 digits with 3 decimal positions.
C                    SQRT  (H) Number        Answer              6 3
```

Figure 5-30 Example **SQRT** (square root) instruction.

The Z-ADD and Z-SUB Operations

The **Z-ADD** operation was commonly used in traditional **RPG** programs to initialize a *Result field* value to zero or some other numeric value. The **Z-SUB** operation performs the same processing functions as **Z-ADD** except that the *Factor 2* value is multiplied by −1 and the product stored in the *Result field* with a reversed sign. For both operations, the *Result field* value is first initialized to zeros and then the *Factor 2* item value is moved into it. The decimal location in the *Factor 2* value is aligned with the decimal position of the *Result* field.

The general syntax rules for the **Z-ADD** and **Z-SUB** operations are as follows:

1. Only numeric items may be used with either operation.
2. *Factor 1* is never used.
3. The field value or numeric literal that is to be moved to the *Result field* item must be entered in *Factor 2*.
4. Decimal alignment is performed between the *Factor 2* value and the *Result field* value.
5. A maximum of two conditioning indicators may be specified in positions 7–11. One *Control Level* indicator (**L0–L9**) and/or some other valid **RPG IV** indicator (i.e., **01** through **99**) may be entered.
6. If the *Result field* item is smaller (integer and/or decimal positions) than the *Factor 2* value, high- and/or low-order truncation of the moved value will occur.

Examples of **Z-ADD** and **Z-SUB** instructions are shown in Figure 5-31.

```
*.. 1 ...+... 2 ...+... 3 ...+... 4 ...+... 5 ...+... 6 ...+... 7 ...+... 8 ...+... 9 ...+ ...10
CLON01Factor 1++++++Opcode(E)+Factor2+++++++Result++++++++Len++D_HiLOEQ....Comments++++++++++++
 * The Z-ADD operation moves the zeros (figurative constant *ZERO) in Factor 2 to the Result
 *           field Amount.  Amount is defined as 6 digits with 2 decimal positions.
C                    Z-ADD     *ZEROS        Amount              6 2

 * The Z-ADD operation moves the numeric literal .15 into the Percent field defined as 3 digits
 * with 2 decimal positions.  Decimal alignment is performed; therefore, the value in Percent
 * after the instruction is executed will be 0.15.
C                    Z-ADD     .15           Percent             3 2

 * The Z-SUB operation moves the numeric value from CreditAmt into DebitAmt after automatically
 * multiplying the CreditAmt value by -1.  Decimal alignment is performed.
C                    Z-SUB     CreditAmt     DebitAmt            8 2
 *
```

Figure 5-31 Examples of **Z-ADD** and **Z-SUB** instructions.

The SETON and SETOF Operations

The **SETON** operation is used to *turn on* the (one to three) **RPG** indicators specified in the *HiLoEq* fields of a calculation instruction. On the other hand, the **SETOF** operation is used to turn off the (one to three) indicators specified in the *HiLoEq* fields of a calculation instruction. The **SETOF** operation is commonly used in traditional **RPG** programs as a "housekeeping" function to turn off all indicators before the next record is processed. Any number of **SETON** or **SETOF** instructions may be specified in a program.

The syntax rules for the **SETON** and **SETOF** operations are summarized below:

1. *Factor 1*, *Factor 2*, *Result*, *Len*, and *D* fields are *not* used with the **SETON** or **SETOF** operation.
2. The *Hi*, *Lo*, and *Eq* fields do not have any meaning for either operation. They are used only to enter the indicator(s) to be turned on or off.
3. A maximum of two conditioning indicators may be specified in positions 7–11. One *Control Level* indicator (**L0–L9**) and/or some other valid **RPG IV** indicator (i.e., **01** through **99**) may be entered.

Figure 5-32 illustrates examples of **SETOF** and **SETON** instructions.

```
*.. 1 ...+... 2 ...+... 3 ...+... 4 ...+... 5 ...+... 6 ...+... 7 ...+... 8 ...+... 9 ...+ ...10
CLON01Factor 1++++++Opcode(E)+Factor2+++++++Result++++++++Len++D_HiLOEQ....Comments++++++++++++
 * The SETON operation turns on indicator 10, which is entered in the HI field.  10 could have
 * optionally been entered in the Lo or Eq field.  Three indicators may be turned on with one
 * SETON operation.
C                   SETON                                        10

 * The SETOF operation turns off indicators 90, 80, and 50.  The order of the indicators is
 * irrelevant.
C                   SETOF                                        908050
```

Figure 5-32 Examples of **SETON** and **SETOF** instructions.

The MOVE and MOVEL Operations

In **RPG IV** programs the **MOVE** and **MOVEL** operations are used primarily to convert a character field value to a numeric field value, or vice versa. However, when a character value is moved into a numeric field, invalid numeric values may be generated, causing run-time errors when the data are processed by an **RPG IV** program. The operations are also used to move part of a field value to another field.

The syntax rules for the **MOVE** and **MOVEL** operations are summarized below.

1. *Factor 1* is not used.
2. The *Factor 2* item includes the value to be moved.
3. The *Result field* entry (cannot be a literal or constant) is the receiving field for all or part of the *Factor 2* value.
4. Decimal alignment is *not* performed.
5. The *Result field* entry is *not* initialized to blanks or zeros before the move. Consequently, if a smaller value is moved to a larger field with the **MOVE** operation, any previously stored high-order values in the *Result field* item will remain after the move is executed. Conversely, when a smaller value is moved to a larger field with the **MOVEL** operation, any previously stored low-order values in *Result field* entry will remain after the move is executed.
6. In a **MOVE** operation, high-order truncation of the *Factor 2* value will occur if the *Result field* entry is smaller. However, in a **MOVEL** operation, low-order truncation of the *Factor 2* value will occur if the *Result field* entry is smaller.
7. A maximum of two conditioning indicators may be specified in positions 7–11. One *Control Level* indicator (**L0–L9**) and/or some other valid **RPG IV** indicator (i.e., **01** through **99**) may be entered.

Examples of **MOVE** and **MOVEL** instructions are presented in Figure 5-33.

With the exception of the **SQRT, MOVE,** and **MOVEL** operations, the other traditional **RPG** operations should not be used in **RPG IV** programs. The programmer should be consistent in his or her program coding and try to avoid mixing **RPG IV** syntax with the traditional **RPG** syntax. However, in the maintenance of older **RPG** programs, that informal rule may be difficult to follow and some knowledge of traditional **RPG** is essential.

```
*.. 1 ...+... 2 ...+... 3 ...+... 4 ...+... 5 ...+... 6 ...+... 7 ...+... 8 ...+... 9 ...+ ...10
CLON01Factor 1+++++++Opcode(E)+Factor2+++++++Result++++++++Len++D_HiLOEQ....Comments+++++++++++++
 * MOVE operation moves Factor 2 characters or digits to the low-order position in the Result
 * field item.  Movement stops when Result field is full or all of the Factor 2 characters or
 * digits have been moved.
 * Value in Smaller before MOVE: ABC      Value in Larger before MOVE: DEFGH
 * Value in Smaller after MOVE: ABC       Value in Larger after MOVE: DEABC
C                   MOVE      Smaller       Larger             5

 * Value in Larger before MOVE: DEFGH   Value in Smaller before MOVE: ABC
 * Value in Larger after MOVE:  DEFGH   Value in Smaller after MOVE: FGH
C                   MOVE      Larger        Smaller            3

 * MOVEL operation moves Factor 2 characters or digits to the high-order positions in the Result
 * field item.  Movement stops when the Result field is full or all of the Factor 2 characters
 * or digits have been moved.
 * Value in Smaller before MOVEL: ABC   Value in Larger before MOVEL: DEFGH
 * Value in Smaller after MOVEL: ABC    Value in Larger after MOVEL: ABCGH
C                   MOVEL     Smaller       Larger             5

 * Value in Larger before MOVEL: DEFGH  Value in Smaller before MOVEL: ABC
 * Value in Larger after MOVEL: DEFGH   Value in Smaller after MOVEL: DEF
C                   MOVEL     Larger        Smaller            3
```

Figure 5-33 Examples of **MOVE** and **MOVEL** instructions.

SUMMARY

The **EVAL** ***(Evaluate Expression)*** operation enables the **RPG IV** programmer to write one or more arithmetic operations in one instruction. When a string of arithmetic operations is included in one **EVAL** instruction, the algebraic rules for the order of operations must be considered. The string is tested from left to right, executing any exponentiation first, multiplication and division second, and addition and subtraction third. This order may be changed by including parentheses around one or more arithmetic operations, which will cause program control to execute that operation first and then continue with the standard order of operations.

Any fields specified in an **EVAL** instruction must have been previously defined in either an *externally described* file, *Definition Specification* instructions, or *Input Specification* instructions.

The value in the answer field (left of the equal sign) may be half-adjusted (rounded) by including **(H)** in the *Opcode* field after the **EVAL** operation.

EVAL instructions may also be used to initialize field values, set on indicators, and in relational and logical statements.

The result field size (item left of the equal sign) in an **EVAL** instruction must be carefully determined to avoid any high- and/or low-order truncation of values. General rules for determining result field sizes were explained in the chapter.

If a remainder in a division instruction has to be saved, the traditional **DIV** operation must be specified followed by the **MVR** (move remainder) operation. In addition, if the **SQRT** operation is used, it must be specified as a separate instruction. The **EVAL** operation does not support either of these operations.

The *Figurative Constants* ***BLANK/*BLANKS, *ZERO/*ZEROS, *HIVAL, *LOVAL, *ALL'...',** when specified in instructions, initialize result fields to a predetermined value. ***ON** and ***OFF** *Figurative Constants* replace the binary **'1'** and **'0'** values. They are used to test the status of an indicator or to turn one or more on or off.

The **RPG IV** reserved words ***IN**, ***INxx**, and ***IN,xx** are used to set on, set off, move, and test the on and off condition of indicators. Field values may be initialized to some value in **RPG IV** programs by **EVAL** instructions, *Named Constants*, or the **INZ** keyword.

The traditional **RPG** operations **(ADD, SUB, MULT, DIV, SETON, SETOF, Z-ADD, Z-SUB, MOVE,** and **MOVEL)** discussed in this chapter should ideally not be used in **RPG IV** programs. However, for the maintenance of older programs, a knowledge of their syntax is necessary.

QUESTIONS

5-1. Name the functions the **EVAL** operation can perform.

5-2. What are the arithmetic symbols used in an **EVAL** instruction for addition, subtraction, multiplication, division, and exponentiation?

Examine the following **EVAL** *instruction, and answer Questions 5–3 through 5–6:*

```
*.. 1 ...+... 2 ...+... 3 ...+... 4 ...+... 5 ...+... 6 ...+... 7 ...+... 8
CLON01Factor1+++++++Opcode&ExtExtended-factor2+++++++++++++++++++++++++++++
C                   EVAL   (H) FLDA = FLDB + FLDC / FLDD - FLDE ** FLDF
```

5-3. Which arithmetic operation is performed first? second? third? fourth? fifth?

5-4. Where is the result stored?

5-5. What is the function of the **(H)** entry?

5-6. Where are the fields included in the **EVAL** instruction defined?

Examine the following **EVAL** *instruction and answer Questions 5–7 through 5–9:*

```
*.. 1 ...+... 2 ...+... 3 ...+... 4 ...+... 5 ...+... 6 ...+... 7 ...+... 8
CLON01Factor1+++++++Opcode&ExtExtended-factor2+++++++++++++++++++++++++++++
C                   EVAL      FLDX = FLDB * 1.5 / (FLDY + FLDZ) * FLDS
```

5-7. Which arithmetic operation is performed first? second? third? fourth?

5-8. Where is the result stored?

5-9. What is the term for the 1.5 entry? What is the maximum size of numeric and character entries?

Examine the following **EVAL** *instruction and answer Questions 5–10 through 5–12:*

```
*.. 1 ...+... 2 ...+... 3 ...+... 4 ...+... 5 ...+... 6 ...+... 7 ...+... 8
CLON01Factor1+++++++Opcode&ExtExtended-factor2+++++++++++++++++++++++++++++
C                   EVAL      FLDD = FLDE - FLDF
```

5-10. Where is the difference stored?

5-11. Which field is the subtrahend?

5-12. Which field is the minuend?

Examine the following **EVAL** *instruction and answer Questions 5–13 through 5–15:*

```
*.. 1 ...+... 2 ...+... 3 ...+... 4 ...+... 5 ...+... 6 ...+... 7 ...+... 8
CLON01Factor1+++++++Opcode&ExtExtended-factor2+++++++++++++++++++++++++++++
C                   EVAL      FLDM = FLDN * FLDO
```

5-13. Where is the product stored?
5-14. Which field is the multiplier?
5-15. Which field is the multiplicand?

Examine the following **EVAL** *instruction and answer Questions 5–16 through 5–18:*

```
*.. 1 ...+... 2 ...+... 3 ...+... 4 ...+... 5 ...+... 6 ...+... 7 ...+... 8
CLON01Factor1+++++++Opcode&ExtExtended-factor2+++++++++++++++++++++++++++++
C                   EVAL      FLDH = FLDI / FLDJ
```

5-16. Where is the quotient stored?
5-17. Which field is the divisor?
5-18. Which field is the dividend?

Examine the following **EVAL** *instruction and answer Questions 5–19 through 5–21:*

```
*.. 1 ...+... 2 ...+... 3 ...+... 4 ...+... 5 ...+... 6 ...+... 7 ...+... 8
CLON01Factor1+++++++Opcode&ExtExtended-factor2+++++++++++++++++++++++++++++
C                   EVAL      FLDQ = FLDR + FLDS
```

5-19. Where is the sum stored?
5-20. Which field is the addend?
5-21. What two **RPG IV** *arithmetic* operations cannot be used in an **EVAL** instruction?
5-22. Using the following **SEU C** format as a reference, write the instruction to divide FLDL by FLDM and store the result in FLDN. Save the remainder in FLDO.

```
*.. 1 ...+... 2 ...+... 3 ...+... 4 ...+... 5 ...+... 6 ...+... 7 ...+... 8
CLON01Factor1+++++++Opcode&ExtFactor2+++++++Result++++++++Len++D+HiLoEq....
C
C
```

5-23. Using the following **SEU C** format as a reference, write the instruction to compute the square root of FLDG and store the result in FLDJ.

```
*.. 1 ...+... 2 ...+... 3 ...+... 4 ...+... 5 ...+... 6 ...+... 7 ...+... 8
CLON01Factor1+++++++Opcode&ExtFactor2+++++++Result++++++++Len++D+HiLoEq....
C
C
```

5-24. Name the ***figurative constants*** available in **RPG IV.** Explain the function of each one.
5-25. Half-adjust the following values to two decimal positions.
(1) 45.2891 (b) 99.9959 (c) .4567

45.29 100.00 .46

Using the following SEU CX format as a reference, write the instruction to complete Questions 5–26 through 5–28:

```
*.. 1 ...+... 2 ...+... 3 ...+... 4 ...+... 5 ...+... 6 ...+... 7 ...+... 8
CLON01Factor1+++++++Opcode&ExtExtended-factor2+++++++++++++++++++++++++++++
C
```

5-26. Write an **EVAL** instruction to turn on indicator **LR.**
5-27. Write an **EVAL** instruction to fill the AmtPaid field to asterisks.
5-28. Write an **EVAL** instruction to initialize field CompTotal to zero.
5-29. Write an **EVAL** instruction to initialize field ProcesMode to spaces.

Examine the following instructions and answer Questions 5–30 through 5-32:

```
*.. 1 ...+... 2 ...+... 3 ...+... 4 ...+... 5 ...+... 6 ...+... 7 ...+... 8
CLON01Factor1+++++++Opcode&ExtExtended-factor2+++++++++++++++++++++++++++++
C                   EVAL      *IN = *ZERO

C                   EVAL      *IN,90 = *BLANK

C                   EVAL      *INLR = *ON
```

5-30. What is the processing result of the first **EVAL** instruction?
5-31. What is the processing result of the second **EVAL** instruction?
5-32. What is the processing result of the third **EVAL** instruction?
5-33. Name four methods to initialize numeric fields to zero or some other value.
5-34. Name three methods to initialize character fields to spaces or some other value.
5-35. Name the traditional **RPG** *arithmetic* operations. With which **SEU** calculation format are they coded?
5-36. What is the function of the traditional **RPG SETON** and **SETOF** operations?

*Examine the following **MOVE** and **MOVEL** instructions and answer Questions 5–37 through 5–40. Note that the field values given represent the related field size:*

```
*.. 1 ...+... 2 ...+... 3 ...+... 4 ...+... 5 ...+... 6 ...+... 7 ...+... 8
CLON01Factor1+++++++Opcode&ExtFactor2+++++++Result++++++++Len++D+HiLoEq....
C                   MOVE      FLDA          FLDB

C                   MOVE      FLDC          FLDD

C                   MOVEL     FLDP          FLDQ

C                   MOVEL     FLDR          FLDS
```

5-37. For the first **MOVE** instruction: if the value in FLDA is **12345** and the value in FLDB is **0000000** before execution, what are the values in the two fields after execution?
5-38. For the second **MOVE** instruction: if the value in FLDC is **ABCDEF** and the value in FLDD is **XYZ** before execution, what are values in the two fields after execution?
5-39. For the first **MOVEL** instruction: if the value in FLDP is **ABCDEF** and the value in FLDQ is **XYZ** before execution, what are values in the two fields after execution?
5-40. For the second **MOVEL** instruction: if the value in FLDR is **1234** and the value in FLDS is **0000000** before execution, what are values in the two fields after execution?
5-41. With a **MOVE** or **MOVEL** instruction, may a numeric field value be moved into a character field? May a character field value be moved into a numeric field?
5-42. Is decimal alignment performed with a **MOVE** or **MOVEL** instruction?

PROGRAMMING ASSIGNMENTS

For each of the following programming assignments, a physical file must have been created and loaded with the related data records. Your instructor will inform you as to whether you have to create the physical file and load it or if it has been prepared for the assignment.

Programming Assignment 5-1: COMPUTATION OF SIMPLE INTEREST

Simple interest is the rent paid to a lender for the privilege of borrowing money. It is charged on personal loans, car loans, installment loans, home mortgages, and so forth. The formula for computing simple interest is:

$$I = \frac{P \times R \times T}{365}$$

where I = dollar amount of simple interest
P = principal (amount borrowed) on which interest is computed
R = annual interest rate expressed as a decimal
T = number of days, months, or years for which the money will be loaned

Note: 365 is used as denominator in above formula if T (time) is in days. If time is in years, denominator may be 1 (or no entry needed).

Processing: Include the formula for computing simple interest in an **RPG IV** program. Process the input file consecutively, and generate the report format shown in the supplemental Printer Spacing Chart. Notice that the interest percentage value input must be multiplied by 100 for output.

Physical File Record Format:

PHYSICAL FILE DESCRIPTION

SYSTEM: AS/400	DATE: Yours
FILE NAME: Yours	REV NO: 0
RECORD NAME: Yours	KEY LENGTH: None
SEQUENCE: Nonkeyed	RECORD SIZE: 14

FIELD DEFINITIONS

FIELD NO	FIELD NAME	SIZE	TYPE	POSITION FROM	POSITION TO	COMMENTS
1	LOAN_NO	5	P	1	3	0 decimals
2	PRINCIPAL	8	P	4	8	2 decimals
3	INTRATE	5	P	9	11	5 decimals
4	LOANDATE	4	P	12	14	0 decimals

Physical File Data:

Loan No	Principal (P)	Interest Rate (R)	Time of Loan in Days (T)
10000	12000000	08500	0120
10001	00300000	07000	0185
10002	01025000	09100	0730
10003	00047500	10250	0090
10004	00100000	12125	0060

Report Design:

```
          0         1         2         3         4         5         6         7
 1234567890123456789012345678901234567890123456789012345678901234567890123456789
 1                            SIMPLE INTEREST LOAN SCHEDULES AS OF ØX/XX/XX
 2
 3
 4     LOAN                      INTEREST RATE     TIME IN     INTEREST           TOTAL
 5    NUMBER     PRINCIPAL             /ANNUM        DAYS      ON LOAN         AMOUNT DUE
 6
 7    XXXXX     $XXX,XXØ.XX          ØX.XXX%         XXØX     $XX,XXØ.XX     $X,XXX,XXØ.XX
 8
 9    XXXXX     $XXX,XXØ.XX          ØX.XXX%         XXØX     $XX,XXØ.XX     $X,XXX,XXØ.XX
10
11        NOTES:
12
13           1. USE SYSTEM DATE FOR REPORT.
14
15           2. HEADINGS ON TOP OF EVERY PAGE.
```

Programming Assignment 5-2: GROSS PROFIT ANALYSIS REPORT

A computer supply company wants a gross profit report on its best-selling printers. The listed catalog selling prices are subject to trade discounts that range from the series 10%, 5%, 5% to 30%, 10%, 5%.

Trade discounts are computed as follows:

Assume a trade discount of 30%, 10%, 5%.

Step 1: Subtract each percentage point from 1.00.

$$1.00 - 0.30 = 0.70$$
$$1.00 - 0.10 = 0.90$$
$$1.00 - 0.05 = 0.95$$

Step 2: Determine an equivalent trade discount by multiplying the percentages calculated in step 1.

$$0.70 \times 0.90 \times 0.95 = 0.5985 \text{ (carry to four decimal places)}$$

Step 3: Multiply the catalog list price by the percentage derived from step 2.

$$\$1{,}000 \times 0.5985 = \$598.50 \text{ net selling price (rounded nearest cent)}$$

Step 4: Subtract the net selling price (step 3) from the catalog list price to determine the trade discount.

Step 5: Determine the item's gross profit by subtracting cost from the net selling price calculated in step 3.

Step 6: Calculate the percentage of gross profit (decimal expression) by dividing the gross profit (step 5) by the net selling price (step 3). *Include the control that prevents a divide-by-zero error.*

Step 7: Multiply the decimal percentage derived from step 6 by 100 to calculate the percentage expression for printing.

Physical File Record Format:

PHYSICAL FILE DESCRIPTION

SYSTEM: AS/400	DATE: Yours
FILE NAME: Yours	REV NO: 0
RECORD NAME: Yours	KEY LENGTH: None
SEQUENCE: Nonkeyed	RECORD SIZE: 46

FIELD DEFINITIONS

FIELD NO	FIELD NAME	SIZE	TYPE	POSITION FROM	POSITION TO	COMMENTS
1	ITEM_NO	3	P	1	2	0 decimals
2	DESCRPTION	30	C	3	32	
3	CATALOGLST	6	P	33	36	2 decimals
4	DISCOUNT1	2	P	37	38	2 decimals
5	DISCOUNT2	2	P	39	40	2 decimals
6	DISCOUNT3	2	P	41	42	2 decimals
7	ITEM_COST	6	P	43	46	2 decimals

Physical File Data:

Item Number	Item Description	Catalog List	Trade Discount %	Item Cost
720	BROTHER JR-35 PRINTER	140000	30 10 05	061000
776	EXP-770 SILVER REED PRINTER	149500	25 10 05	073000
789	JUKI 6100 PRINTER	059900	10 05 05	037500
799	P12 DIABLO SYSTEMS PRINTER	069900	15 05 00	034500
820	H-P LASERJET+ PRINTER	349500	10 10 05	226800

Report Design:

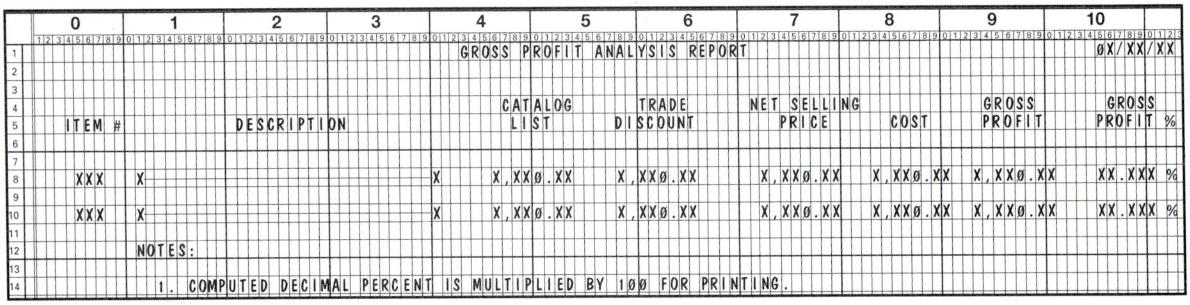

GROSS PROFIT ANALYSIS REPORT
ØX/XX/XX
CATALOG LIST
TRADE DISCOUNT
NET SELLING PRICE
GROSS PROFIT
GROSS PROFIT %
ITEM #
DESCRIPTION
COST
XXX X X X,XXØ.XX X,XXØ.XX X,XXØ.XX X,XXØ.XX X,XXØ.XX XX.XXX %
XXX X X X,XXØ.XX X,XXØ.XX X,XXØ.XX X,XXØ.XX X,XXØ.XX XX.XXX %
NOTES:
1. COMPUTED DECIMAL PERCENT IS MULTIPLIED BY 1ØØ FOR PRINTING.

Programming Assignment 5-3: DETERMINATION OF ECONOMIC ORDER QUANTITY

The costs of carrying an item in inventory include deterioration, obsolescence, handling, clerical labor, taxes, insurance, storage, and reasonable return on investment. These costs are weighed against the costs of inadequate inventory, which may lead to loss of sales, loss of customer goodwill, production stoppage, extra purchasing costs, and a higher item cost for small-quantity purchases. Because of these inventory considerations, companies often rely on mathematical models as guidelines for the decision-making process of determining how much to order and when. A useful quantitative tool is the *economic order quantity formula,* which calculates the optimum quantity to order of any one item.

Before an item's *economic order quantity* is calculated, the number of units needed annually, cost per order, unit cost of the item, and its carrying cost must be determined. Then, the following formula may be used.

$$\text{Economic Order Quantity} = \sqrt{\frac{2 \times \text{units needed annually} \times \text{ordering cost}}{\text{item unit cost} \times \text{inventory carrying cost \%}}}$$

$$\text{EOQ} = \sqrt{\frac{2 \times U \times OC}{UC \times ICC}}$$

Note: Round EOQ answer to a whole number.

Physical File Record Format:

PHYSICAL FILE DESCRIPTION

SYSTEM: AS/400 DATE: Yours
FILE NAME: Yours REV NO: 0
RECORD NAME: Yours KEY LENGTH: None
SEQUENCE: Nonkeyed RECORD SIZE: 36

FIELD DEFINITIONS

FIELD NO	FIELD NAME	SIZE	TYPE	POSITION FROM	POSITION TO	COMMENTS
1	ITEMNO	25	C	1	25	
2	ANULUSAGE	5	P	26	28	0 decimals
3	ORDNGCOST	3	P	29	30	0 decimals
4	UNITCOST	5	P	31	33	2 decimals
5	CARRYCOST	4	P	34	36	4 decimals

Physical File Data:

Item Name	Annual Usage	Order Cost	Unit Cost	Carrying Cost %
LEFT-HAND MONKEY WRENCH	10000	025	01250	0250
MEN'S DIESEL SHAVER	20000	018	01800	1000
ATOMIC TOOTHBRUSH	40000	020	11290	1400
FUEL-INJECTED LAWN MOWER	00200	050	29000	9000
LASER TOOTHPICKS	30000	024	00650	0856

Report Design: Complete a Printer Spacing Chart according to the following report format.

```
0X/XX/XXXX    ECONOMIC ORDER QUANTITIES OF INVENTORY ITEMS    PAGE XX0X

         ITEM NAME               ANNUAL USAGE     EOQ     ORDERS PER YEAR

XXXXXXXXXXXXXXXXXXXXXXXXX          XX,XX0        X,XX0          XX0

XXXXXXXXXXXXXXXXXXXXXXXXX          XX,XX0        X,XX0          XX0

  Note:  Use system date for report.
```

Programming Assignment 5-4: UNION PROPOSAL FOR HOURLY EMPLOYEES

A company is engaged in union negotiations for its hourly employees. The union is proposing a 7% increase in the hourly rate based on a 35-hour workweek. The company wants a report generated in the format shown in the attached printer spacing chart. Note, the 7% rate and 35-hour workweek are "hard-coded" in the **RPG IV** program and not field values from the physical file.

Physical File Record Format:

```
                    PHYSICAL FILE DESCRIPTION

SYSTEM: AS/400                                  DATE: Yours
FILE NAME: Yours                                REV NO: 0
RECORD NAME: Yours                              KEY LENGTH: 9
SEQUENCE: Keyed                                 RECORD SIZE: 28

                        FIELD DEFINITIONS

 FIELD    FIELD NAME    SIZE  TYPE    POSITION     COMMENTS
   NO                                FROM    TO

   1      SS_NUMBER        9   P        1     5  Key field
   2      EMPLOYEE        20   C        6    25
   3      HRLY_RATE        4   P       26    28  2 decimals
```

Physical File Data:

Social Security No	Employee Name	Current Hourly Rate
019203344	HENRY WADWORTH	1000
110407700	JOHN BYRON	1250
023902345	EDGAR POE	1025
110557777	JAMES LONGFELLOW	1500
030224444	WILLIAM SHAKESPEARE	1600

Report Design:

```
         1         2         3         4         5         6         7         8
12345678901234567890123456789012345678901234567890123456789012345678901234567890
0X/XX/XXXX            UNION PROPOSAL FOR HOURLY EMPLOYEES                PAGE XX0X

         WORK WEEK: 35 HOURS                      PROPOSED INCREASE: X.X%


                               CURRENT        CURRENT         PROPOSED        PROPOSED
     EMPLOYEE NAME          HOURLY RATE     WEEKLY PAY     HOURLY RATE      WEEKLY PAY

XXXXXXXXXXXXXXXXXXXX           0X.XX         X,XX0.XX          0X.XX          X,XX0.XX

XXXXXXXXXXXXXXXXXXXX           0X.XX         X,XX0.XX          0X.XX          X,XX0.XX

--------------------------------------------------------------------------------

   SUMMARY:

   TOTAL PROPOSED WEEKLY PAY: $ XXX,XX0.XX
   TOTAL CURRENT WEEKLY PAY:    XXX.XX0.XX

   PROPOSED WEEKLY INCREASE:  $ XXX,XX0.XX

  Note:
       Print row of hyphens two spaces after the last detail (employee) record.
```

Programming Assignment 5-5: CERTIFICATES OF DEPOSIT ANALYSIS REPORT

Write an **RPG IV** program to calculate the compound interest on depositor's certificates of deposit and generate the report detailed in the supplemental printer spacing chart.

Processing: Read the physical file in arrival sequence and for every record processed perform the following steps:

Step 1: Complete the calculation instructions for the following compound interest formula:

$a = (i + 1)^{-n}$ where: a = Compound amount of $1

i = Annual interest rate (must be divided by 365 for the daily interest rate)

n = Number of interest periods (input from physical file − field TIMEINDAYS)

Step 2: Compute the **compound amount** based on the PRINCIPAL by multiplying the PRINCIPAL (input field) by the value in **a** (computed in the previous formula). *Note*: you may prefer to include this step in the compound interest formula.

Step 3: Subtract the principal (input from physical file) from the compound amount (a) determined in step 2 or 1.

Step 4: Multiply the daily and annual interest rates by 100 for printing of the two percent values.

Physical File Record Format:

PHYSICAL FILE DESCRIPTION

SYSTEM: AS/400	DATE: Yours
FILE NAME: Yours	REV NO: 0
RECORD NAME: Yours	KEY LENGTH: None
SEQUENCE: Nonkeyed	RECORD SIZE: 17

FIELD DEFINITIONS

FIELD NO	FIELD NAME	SIZE	TYPE	POSITION FROM	POSITION TO	COMMENTS
1	ACCTNO	4	C	1	4	
2	PRINCIPAL	8	P	5	9	2 decimals
3	ANNRATE	5	P	10	12	5 decimals
4	ANNPERDS	3	P	13	14	0 decimals
5	TIMEINDAYS	5	P	15	17	0 decimals

Physical File Data:

Account Number	Principal	Annual Rate	Interest Periods Per Annum	Total Periods
1000	00100000	10000	365	0365
2000	00100000	10000	365	0180
3000	00100000	06500	365	0365
4000	00100000	06500	365	0180

Report Design:

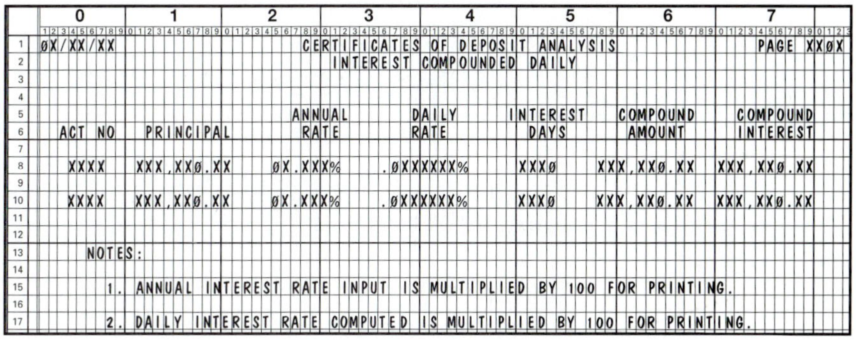

ØX/XX/XX
CERTIFICATES OF DEPOSIT ANALYSIS
PAGE XXØX
INTEREST COMPOUNDED DAILY
ANNUAL RATE
DAILY RATE
INTEREST DAYS
COMPOUND AMOUNT
COMPOUND INTEREST
ACT NO
PRINCIPAL
XXXX XXX,XXØ.XX ØX.XXX% .ØXXXXXX% XXXØ XXX,XXØ.XX XXX,XXØ.XX
XXXX XXX,XXØ.XX ØX.XXX% .ØXXXXXX% XXXØ XXX,XXØ.XX XXX,XXØ.XX
NOTES:
1. ANNUAL INTEREST RATE INPUT IS MULTIPLIED BY 100 FOR PRINTING.
2. DAILY INTEREST RATE COMPUTED IS MULTIPLIED BY 100 FOR PRINTING.

chapter 6

RPG IV Structured Operations for Decision Making, Branching, and Looping Control

Decision making (without iterative processing) may be controlled in an **RPG IV** program by the following **structured** operations:

1. **IF/ELSE**
2. **SELECT/WHEN/OTHER**

Regardless of the operation(s) used in a decision-making instruction, a relational test must be made. The relational tests include *equal to* **(EQ)**, *less than* **(LT)**, *greater than* **(GT)**, *less than or equal to* **(LE)**, *greater than or equal to* **(GE)**, and *not equal to* **(NE)**. The tests are made in an **IF/ELSE** or **SELECT/WHEN/OTHER** group with the signs **= (EQ), < (LT), > (GT), <= (LE), >= (GE),** and **<> (NE).**

The logical test result from the relational comparison of the values in two fields or a field and a literal is controlled by the collating sequence of the computer. IBM mainframe and the mid-range AS/400 computer systems support *Extended Binary Coded Decimal Interchange Code* **(EBCDIC).** Others, including IBM's microcomputers, support an **ASCII** *(American National Standard Code for Information Interchange)* code structure. Figure 6-1 presents a partial listing of the two code sets. Any character lower in the hier-

EBCDIC	ASCII	
(blank)	(blank)	lowest
.	"	
<	$	
(	:	
+	(	
$	)	
*	*	
)	+	
;	'	
-	-	
/	.	
,	/	
>	0 through 9	
:	;	
=	<	
"	=	
A through Z	>	
0 through 9	A through Z	highest

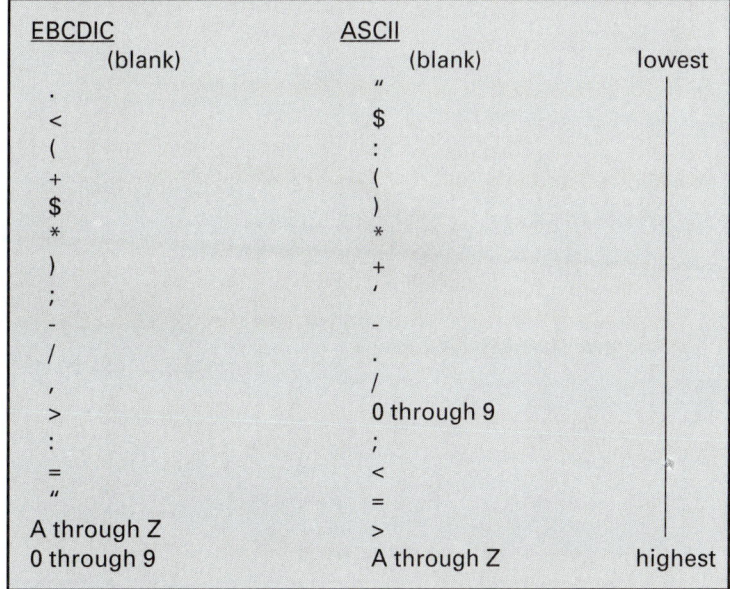

Figure 6-1 EBCDIC and ASCII code set collating sequences.

archy than another character will test as *less than* in a relational instruction. Notice that a **blank** is the lowest character in both code sets, with **9** being the highest in EBCDIC and **Z** the highest in ASCII.

IF/ELSE OPERATIONS

The **IF** *(If)* and **ELSE** *(Else)* operations are used to control **relational** testing. The **IF** operation evaluates a condition and, depending on whether the relational test is true or false, directs program control to a specific instruction within the **IF/ELSE** group. An **ELSE** operation, which must be related to an **IF** instruction, provides for an alternative action when the **IF** test is not true. An **IF** or **IF/ELSE** group of instructions is ended by an **ENDIF** operation. Figure 6-2 explains the **RPG IV** syntax for the **IF, ELSE,** and **ENDIF** operations.

```
*.. 1 ...+... 2 ...+... 3 ...+... 4 ...+... 5 ...+... 6 ...+... 7 ...+... 8 ...+... 9 ...+...10
CLON01Factor 1+++++++Opcode&ExtExtended-factor2+++++++++++++++++++++++++++++Comments++++++++++++
 * IF group without a related ELSE operation:
C  1      2         IF         expression
C                   3              4
C                   .
C                   ENDIF
                      5
 * IF group with a related ELSE operation:
C                   IF         expression
C                    .
C                    .
C 7 8   8           ELSE       8
C                    6
C                    .
C  9    9           ENDIF     9
                      5
```

IF operation syntax rules:

1. Conditioning indicators may be specified in the *LO* and/or *NO1* fields (positions 7–11).
2. *Factor 1* is not used.
3. The **IF** operation name must be entered in the *Opcode* field (positions 26–34).
4. Any relational expression may be specified in the *Extended-factor 2* field (positions 36–80). A numeric expression may be continued on the next line (starting in at least position 36) without a continuation character. Character literals are continued to the next line by ending the current line with a + or – and starting the continuation line in at least position 36.
5. The logical operations **AND** and **OR** may be used to combine one or more expressions. In any case, the **AND** or **OR** relationship is tested from left to right after other tests have been performed.

ELSE operation syntax rules:

6. **ELSE** operation must be related to one **IF** instruction; it cannot be specified by itself.
7. Indicators (**LO** through **LR**) are permitted in the *LO* field (positions 7–8).
8. Indicators are not permitted in the *NO1* field (positions 9–11). *Factor 1* and the *Extended-factor 2* fields are not used.

Figure 6-2 **RPG IV** syntax rules for the **IF, ELSE,** and **ENDIF** operations.

ENDIF operation syntax rules:

An **ENDIF** (or **END**) operation must close an **IF** or **IF/ELSE** group.

9. The **ENDIF** operation must be specified by itself.

10. *LONO1, Factor 1*, and *Extended-factor 1* fields are not used.

Figure 6-2 **RPG IV** syntax rules for the **IF, ELSE,** and **ENDIF** operations. (Continued)

Examples of **IF** and **IF/ELSE** groups are shown in Figure 6-3.

```
*.. 1 ...+... 2 ...+... 3 ...+... 4 ...+... 5 ...+... 6 ...+... 7 ...+... 8 ...+... 9 ...+ ...10
CLONO1Factor 1++++++Opcode&ExtExtended-factor2+++++++++++++++++++++++++++++Comments+++++++++++++
 * This IF group controls a true-only action:
C                   IF        Yrs_Emp >= 5
C                   EVAL      Tenured = Tenured + 1
C                   ENDIF

 * This IF/ELSE group controls a true/false action.  When the expression for the IF instruction
 * is not true, the instruction(s) following the ELSE operation are automatically executed.
C                   IF        Yrs_Emp >= 5
C                   EVAL      Tenured = Tenured + 1
C                   ELSE
C                   EVAL      NonTenured = NonTenured + 1
C                   ENDIF
```

Figure 6-3 Examples of simple **IF** and **IF/ELSE** instruction groups.

Nested IF Instructions

Nested **IF**'s are classified as those that pair more than one **IF** instruction within an **IF** group. The syntax and processing logic related to this structure are detailed in Figure 6-4.

```
*.. 1 ...+... 2 ...+... 3 ...+... 4 ...+... 5 ...+... 6 ...+... 7 ...+... 8 ...+... 9 ...+ ...10
CLONO1Factor 1++++++Opcode&ExtExtended-factor2++++++++++++
 * This IF/ELSE example illustrates "nested" IF's            This IF instruction is executed if
C                   IF        Emply_Code = 'H'               the previous IF test is true
C  When this test   EVAL      Hourly = Hourly + 1
C  is false, con-   IF        Emp_Status = 'FT'              This ELSE instruction is executed
C  trol branches    EVAL      FullTime = FullTime + 1        only when the inner IF instruction
C  to the last      ELSE                                     test is false
C  ELSE operation   EVAL      PartTime = PartTime + 1
C                   ENDIF
C                   ELSE                                     Closes the inner IF/ELSE group
C                   EVAL      Salaried = Salaried + 1
C Control branches  ENDIF
  to here when the                                           Closes the outer IF/ELSE group
  first IF instruc-
  tion test is false
```

Figure 6-4 Example of nested **IF/ELSE** instructions.

Complex IF Instructions

A *complex* **IF** instruction includes two or more relational tests specified in an **AND** and/or **OR** relationship. When an **AND** relationship is specified, *all* of the conditions must be "true" to execute the action. For **IF** instructions in an **OR** relationship, only one of the test conditions has to be true to execute the action. The syntax and processing logic related to complex **IF** instructions are shown in Figure 6-5.

```
*.. 1 ...+... 2 ...+... 3 ...+... 4 ...+... 5 ...+... 6 ...+... 7 ...+... 8 ...+... 9 ...+ ...10
CLON01Factor 1++++++Opcode&ExtExtended-factor2+++++++++++++++++++++++++++++Comments+++++++++++++
 * Example of an AND relationship.  Both relational tests must be true to execute the
 * instructions within the IF group.
C                   IF        FieldA = FieldB AND FieldC > FieldD
C                    .
C                    .
C                   ENDIF

 * Example of an OR relationship.  Only one relational test has to be true to execute the
 * instructions within the IF group.  When the first test is true, the second (OR) test
 * is not made.
C                   IF        FieldA <= FieldM OR FieldK = FieldS
C                    .
C                    .
C                   ENDIF

 * Example using AND and OR relationships.  When the AND relationship is true, the OR
 * relationship is not tested.  On the other hand, when the AND relationship is false,
 * the OR relationship is tested.  Note that a continuation symbol is not required
 * for fields; only for character literals.
C                   IF       FieldF > FieldG
C                             AND FieldH = FieldJ
C                             OR FieldN <= FieldP
C                    .
C                    .
C                   ENDIF
```

Figure 6-5 Examples of complex **IF** instructions using **AND** and **OR** logical operators.

PAGE OVERFLOW CONTROL

Because the **IF** operation was not introduced until this chapter, previous example programs and programming assignments have not included *page overflow control*. However, many reports extend to more than one page, which usually requires that all or some of the heading lines be printed on subsequent pages. Any of the **RPG IV** overflow indicators—**OA, OB, OC, OD, OE, OF, OG,** and **OV**—may be specified in a program to test and control a page overflow condition (when the overflow line is sensed). Unless changed in the **RPG IV** program with a **FORMOF** keyword specified in the *File Description Specification* instruction for the printer file, the default overflow line for the computer's standard form length will be assumed.

When the overflow line is sensed, the overflow indicator assigned will automatically be turned on; the overflow line printed; and the paper advanced to the top of the next page. Any top-of-page information (headings, page number, system date, etc.) controlled by the status of the overflow indicator will be printed on the following page.

An example of the *File Description* and *Calculation Specification* instructions to control page overflow and print any heading information on every page is shown in Figure 6-6.

File Description Specification page overflow keyword entry:

```
*.. 1 ...+... 2 ...+... 3 ...+... 4 ...+... 5 ...+... 6 ...+... 7 ...+... 8 ...+... 9 ...+...10
FFilename++IPEASFRLen+LKlen+AIDevice+.Keywords+++++++++++++++++++++++++++++Comments++++++++++++
 * Overflow indicator OF assigned to the printer file with the keyword OFLIND
FQSYSPRT   O    F  132         PRINTER OFLIND(*INOF)
```

Figure 6-6 *File Description* and *Calculation Specifications* entries for page overflow control.

Calculation Specification instructions for overflow control:

```
*.. 1 ...+... 2 ...+... 3 ...+... 4 ...+... 5 ...+... 6 ...+... 7 ...+... 8 ...+... 9 ...+ ...10
CLON01Factor1+++++++Opcode&ExtExtended-factor2+++++++++++++++++++++++++++++Comments+++++++++++++
 * The following page overflow control instructions are part of a DOW, DOU, or DO group that
 * includes other instructions to control the reading, end-of-file control, and closing processes.

 * The IF instruction tests the status of the overflow indicator (OF).  When the test is true,
 * (OF on), program control will pass to the next instruction.
 * The first EXCEPT instruction branches program control to output where the exception lines
 * named HeadLines will be printed.
 * The EVAL instruction turns off the OF indicator after the HeadLines are printed.
 * The ENDIF operation ends the IF group.
 * The second EXCEPT instruction controls the printing of the exception line named DetailLine.
 * DetailLine will be printed regardless of the status of the overflow indicator.
                    .
                    .
C                   IF        *INOF = *ON
C                   EXCEPT    HeadLines
C                   EVAL      *INOF = *OFF
C                   ENDIF
C                   EXCEPT    DetailLine
                    .
                    .
```

Figure 6-6 *File Description* and *Calculation Specifications* entries for page overflow control. (Continued)

APPLICATION PROGRAM: WEEKLY PAYROLL REPORT

Documentation

The specifications in Figure 6-7 summarize the processing requirements for the **RPG IV** Weekly Payroll Report program.

PROGRAM SPECIFICATIONS — Page 1 of 1

Program Name: Weekly Payroll Report — Program-ID: PAYROLL — Written by: SM

Purpose: Generate a weekly payroll report — Approved by: CM

Input files: EMPPAYFL

Output files: QSYSPRT

Processing Requirements:

Write a structured RPG IV program to generate a weekly payroll report for day- and night-shift employees.

Input to the program:

An externally defined physical file, EMPPAYFL, stores the weekly payroll data for each employee. The supplemental record layout form details the record format.

Processing:

Read the Weekly Payroll File, EMPPAYFL, in key-value order and perform the following computations:

Step 1: Test the shift code field to determine if the employee worked the day or night shift. An additional 15% hourly rate bonus is added for the night shift.

Figure 6-7 Specifications for Weekly Payroll Report program.

Step 2: Convert minutes to hours. Any remainder less than 30 is considered a 1/2 hour (.5) and if equal to or greater than 30 is processed as 1 hour.

Step 3: Compute the regular pay as follows:
HOURLY RATE × HOURS WORKED = REGULAR PAY

Step 4: Determine if the employee worked overtime (over 35 hours):
HOURS WORKED − 35 = OVERTIME HOURS (if greater than 0)

Step 5: Compute overtime premium as follows:
HOURLY RATE/2 = OVERTIME PREMIUM RATE (rounded to 2 decimals)
Then:
OVERTIME HOURS × OVERTIME PREMIUM RATE = OVERTIME PAY

Step 6: Compute each employee's total week's pay as follows:
REGULAR PAY + OVERTIME PAY = TOTAL WEEK'S PAY

Step 7: Provide totals for the hours worked, regular pay, overtime pay, and total pay.

Output:

Complete the report detailed in the supplemental printer spacing chart.

Figure 6-7 Specifications for Weekly Payroll Report program. (Continued)

The system flowchart in Figure 6-8 indicates that one physical file is processed by an **RPG IV** program to generate the report.

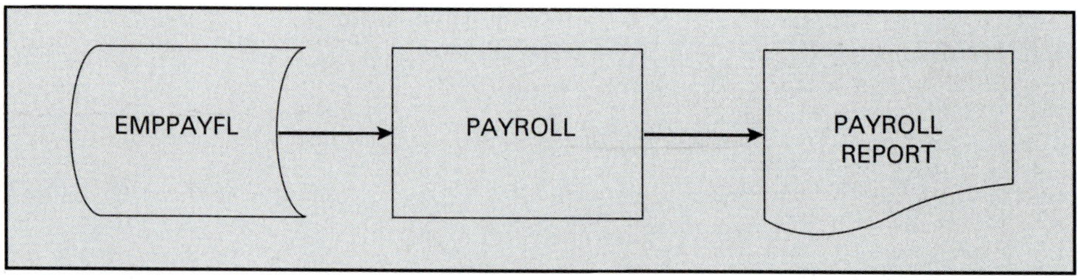

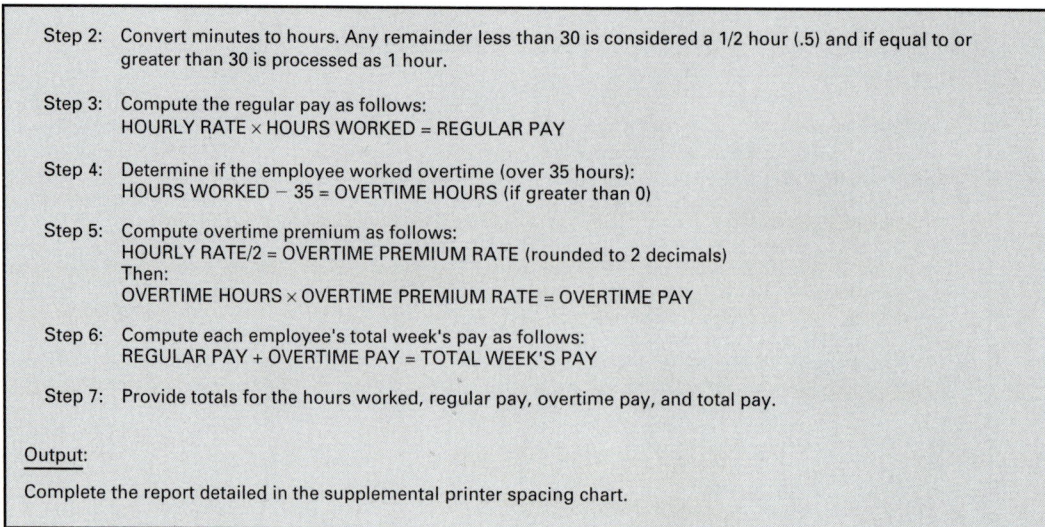

Figure 6-8 System flowchart for Weekly Payroll Report program.

The record format of the physical file is shown in Figure 6-9 with a listing of the data.

PHYSICAL FILE DESCRIPTION

SYSTEM: AS/400 DATE: 8/11/97
FILE NAME: EMPPAYFL REV NO: 0
RECORD NAME: EMPPAYR KEY LENGTH: 4
SEQUENCE: Keyed RECORD SIZE: 31

FIELD DEFINITIONS

FIELD NO	FIELD NAME	SIZE	TYPE	POSITION FROM	POSITION TO	COMMENTS
1	EMP_NUMBER	4	C	1	4	Key field
2	EMP_NAME	20	C	5	24	
3	SHIFT	1	C	25	25	
5	HRLYRATE	4	P	26	28	2 decimals
4	MINUTES	4	P	29	31	0 decimals

Figure 6-9 Physical file record format and listing of the data.

Physical File Data:

Employee Number	Employee Name	Shift	Hourly Rate	Minutes Worked
1234	LEONARDO DA VINCI	D	2250	2226
2345	ALEXANDER G BELL	N	2000	1800
3456	ROBERT FULTON	D	1275	2450
4567	CHARLES S GOODYEAR	N	1425	2100
5678	MARCHESE MARCONI	D	1500	2130

Figure 6-9 Physical file record format and listing of the data. (Continued)

The printer spacing chart shown in Figure 6-10 details the design of the report. Also included is a listing of the report generated from execution of the **RPG IV** program.

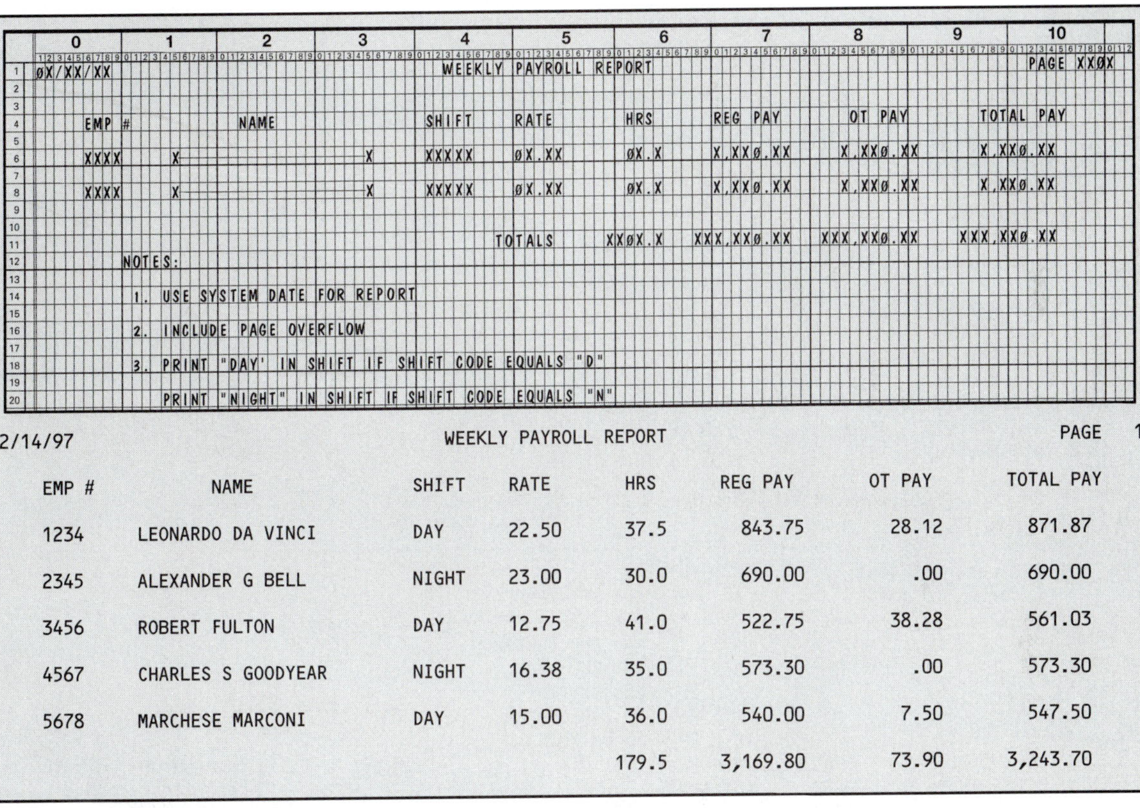

2/14/97 WEEKLY PAYROLL REPORT PAGE 1

EMP #	NAME	SHIFT	RATE	HRS	REG PAY	OT PAY	TOTAL PAY
1234	LEONARDO DA VINCI	DAY	22.50	37.5	843.75	28.12	871.87
2345	ALEXANDER G BELL	NIGHT	23.00	30.0	690.00	.00	690.00
3456	ROBERT FULTON	DAY	12.75	41.0	522.75	38.28	561.03
4567	CHARLES S GOODYEAR	NIGHT	16.38	35.0	573.30	.00	573.30
5678	MARCHESE MARCONI	DAY	15.00	36.0	540.00	7.50	547.50
				179.5	3,169.80	73.90	3,243.70

Figure 6-10 Printer spacing chart for Weekly Payroll Report program and report listing.

RPG IV Program for the Weekly Payroll Report

Figure 6-11 presents a detailed compile listing of the **RPG IV** program that generates a weekly payroll report. After an examination of the compiled program listing in Figure 6-11, the following should be noted:

1. The **OF** overflow indicator is defined in the *File Description* for the printer file.
2. A test routine for page overflow is included.

3. The work fields (not from the physical file) are defined as "standalone" fields in the *Definition Specifications*.
4. **IF** groups include the instructions related to a specific function for the application.
5. One "nested" **IF** group is included.
6. Compiler-"supplied" **IF/ELSE** references are included at the right side of the listing, indicating the beginning and ending instructions for each **IF** and **IF/ELSE** group.

```
Line   <---------------------- Source Specifications ----------------------------><---- Comments ----> Do
Number ....1....+....2....+....3....+....4....+....5....+....6....+....7....+....8....+....9....+...10 Num
                             S o u r c e   L i s t i n g
     1  * Weekly Payroll Report For Hourly Employees...
     2 FEmppayfl  IF   E           K DISK
        *------------------------------------------------------------------------------------------------*
        *                                 RPG name              External name                            *
        * File name. . . . . . . . . :   EMPPAYFL              STAN/EMPPAYFL                            *
        * Record format(s) . . . . . :   EMPPAYR               EMPPAYR                                  *
        *------------------------------------------------------------------------------------------------*
     3 FQsysprt   O    F  132        PRINTER OFLIND(*INOF)
     4
     5  * Definition of work fields....
     6 D OverTimPay      S              6  2
     7 D ShiftOut        S              5
     8 D HrsWorked       S              2  0
     9 D Remainder       S              2  0
    10 D TotEmpHrs       S              3  1
    11 D OTHours         S              3  1
    12 D OTimeRate       S              4  2
    13 D RegularPay      S              6  2
    14 D WeeksPay        S              6  2
    15 D TotalHours      S              5  1
    16 D TotlRegPay      S              8  2
    17 D TotalOTPay      S              8  2
    18 D TotalPay        S              8  2
    19
    20  * Begin calculations....
    21=IEMPPAYR
        *------------------------------------------------------------------------------------------------*
        * RPG record format  . . . . :  EMPPAYR                                                          *
        * External format  . . . . . :  EMPPAYR : STAN/EMPPAYFL                                          *
        *------------------------------------------------------------------------------------------------*
    22=I                              A    1    4  EMP_NUMBER
    23=I                              A    5   24  EMP_NAME
    24=I                              A   25   25  SHIFT
    25=I                              P   26   28 2HRLYRATE
    26=I                              P   29   31 0MINUTES
    27 C                   EVAL      *INOF = *ON                        turn on OF indicator
    28 C                   READ      Emppayfl                     ----LR read first record
    29 C                   DOW       *INLR = *OFF                       do while LR is off     B01
    30
    31  * Page overflow control....
    32 C                   IF        *INOF = *ON                        overflow ind on?       B02
    33 C                   EXCEPT    Hdglines                           print heading lines     02
    34 C                   EVAL      *INOF = *OFF                       turn off OF indicatr    02
    35 C                   ENDIF                                        end IF group           E02
    36
    37 C                   EVAL      OverTimPay = *ZERO                                         01
    38 C                   IF        Shift > 'D'                                               B02
    39 C                   EVAL      HrlyRate = HrlyRate * 1.15         night shift rate        02
    40 C                   EVAL      ShiftOut = 'NIGHT'                 load for printing       02
    41 C                   ELSE                                                                X02
    42 C                   EVAL      ShiftOut = 'DAY  '                 load for printing       02
    43 C                   ENDIF                                        end IF group           E02
    44
```

References beginning and end of a structured group

Figure 6-11 Compile listing of the Weekly Payroll Report program.

```
 45 C      Minutes       DIV       60            HrsWorked                compute hrs worked     01
 46 C                    MVR                     Remainder                save remainder         01
 47
 48
 49 C                    IF        Remainder = *ZERO                      remainder zero?       B02
 50 C                    Z-ADD     HrsWorked     TotEmpHrs                initial. TotEmpHrs     02
 51 C                    ELSE                                                                   X02
 52 C                    IF        Remainder < 30                         remainder < 30?       B03
 53 C                    EVAL      TotEmpHrs = HrsWorked + .5             add 1/2 hour           03
 54 C                    ELSE                                                                   X03
 55 C                    EVAL      TotEmpHrs = HrsWorked + 1              add 1 hour             03
 56 C                    ENDIF                                            end inner IF          E03
 57 C                    ENDIF                                            end outer IF          E02
 58
 59 C                    EVAL      RegularPay = TotEmpHrs * HrlyRate      compute regular pay    01
 60
 61 C                    IF        TotEmpHrs > 35                         hrs > 35?             B02
 62 C                    EVAL      OTHours = TotEmpHrs - 35               compute OT hours       02
 63 C                    EVAL(H)   OTimeRate = HrlyRate / 2               compute OT rate        02
 64 C                    EVAL      OverTimPay = OTHours * OTimeRate       compute OT pay         02
 65 C                    ENDIF                                            end IF group          E02
 66
 67 C                    EVAL      WeeksPay = RegularPay + OverTimPay     compute week's pay     01
 68 C                    EXCEPT    DetailLine                             print detail line      01
 69 C                    EVAL      TotalHours = TotalHours + TotEmpHrs    total of all hours     01
 70 C                    EVAL      TotlRegPay = TotlRegPay + RegularPay   total of all pays      01
 71 C                    EVAL      TotalOTPay = TotalOTPay + OverTimPay   compute total OT pay   01
 72 C                    EVAL      TotalPay = TotalPay + WeeksPay         total of all emps      01
 73 C                    READ      Emppayfl                        ----LR read another record    01
 74 C                    ENDDO                                            end dow group         E01
 75
 76 C                    EXCEPT    TotalLine                              print total line
 77
 78 OQsysprt   E            Hdglines       3 01
 79 O                       UDATE          Y     8
 80 O                                           64 'WEEKLY PAYROLL REPORT'
 81 O                                          105 'PAGE'
 82 O                       PAGE               110
 83 O          E            Hdglines       2
 84 O                                           10 'EMP #'
 85 O                                           25 'NAME'
 86 O                                           45 'SHIFT'
 87 O                                           53 'RATE'
 88 O                                           63 'HRS'
 89 O                                           76 'REG PAY'
 90 O                                           89 'OT PAY'
 91 O                                          105 'TOTAL PAY'
 92
 93 O          E            DetailLine     2
 94 O                       Emp_Number           9
 95 O                       Emp_Name            34
 96 O                       ShiftOut            45
 97 O                       HrlyRate       1    54
 98 O                       TotEmpHrs      1    64
 99 O                       RegularPay     1    77
100 O                       OverTimPay     1    90
101 O                       WeeksPay       1   104
102
103 O          E            TotalLine    1
104 O                       TotalHours     1    64
105 O                       TotlRegPay     1    77
106 O                       TotalOTPay     1    90
107 O                       TotalPay       1   104
```

File Description instructions:

Line No.

2 Emppayfl is defined as an input, full-procedural, externally described, keyed physical file.

3 Qsysprt is defined as a program-described printer file. The **OFLIND(*INOF)** keyword defines the **OF** page overflow indicator.

Figure 6-11 Compile listing of the Weekly Payroll Report program. (Continued)

Definition Specification instructions:

6–18 The work fields OverTimPay through TotalPay are defined as "standalone" fields (**S** in position 24) in *Definition Specification* instructions.

Calculation Specification instructions:

27 The **EVAL *INOF = *ON** instruction turns "on" the **OF** overflow indicator so that the **IF *INOF = *ON** instruction on line 32 will test as "true" and pass control to the exception records on lines 78–91, causing the Hdglines records to be printed.

28 The **READ** instruction reads the first record from the Emppayfl file. If no records are stored in the file, **LR** will be set on and the test in the **DOW** operation on line 29 will cause control to branch over the **DOW** group to line 76. The coding for this program assumes that records will always be stored in the physical file.

29 The ***INLR = LR** relational test specified in the **DOW** instruction controls execution of the instructions within the **DOW** group until **LR** is set on by one of the two **READ** instructions.

32–35 The **IF *INOF = *ON** instruction tests the status of the **OF** overflow indicator. If it is "on," which it will be for the first record read (turned on line 27), the instructions in the **IF** group (lines 33–35) will be executed.

When the **IF** test on line 32 is "true," the **EXCEPT** instruction on line 33 will pass control to output and print the two Hdglines record formats.

33 The **EXCEPT** instruction controls the printing of the Hdglines on lines 78 through 91.

34 The **EVAL *INOF = *OFF** instruction turns off the **OF** indicator, preventing the Hdglines from being printed when the next iteration of the **DOW** is performed.

35 The **ENDIF** operation ends the **IF** group that began on line 32.

37 The **EVAL** instruction initializes the OverTimPay field to zeros before the payroll values for the next employee are computed.

38 The **IF** instruction tests the value in the physical file field Shift. If the value in Shift is greater than **D** (day shift), the **EVAL** instructions on lines 39 and 40 will be executed. When the relational test is not "true," control will branch to the **EVAL** instruction on line 42.

39 The **EVAL** instruction computes the HrlyRate value for "night" Shift employees, which is 15% greater than "day" Shift employees.

40 The **EVAL** instruction initializes the ShiftOut field with the constant NIGHT.

41 The **ELSE** (false) action is executed when the **IF** test on line 38 is "false."

42 The **EVAL** instruction initializes the ShiftOut field with the constant DAY.

43 The **ENDIF** operation ends the **IF** group that began on line 38.

45 The value in the physical file field Minutes is divided by the numeric literal 60 to compute the HrsWorked value for the employee.

46 Any remainder calculated by the **DIV** instruction on line 45 will be stored in the "standalone" Remainder field with this **MVR** instruction.

49–50 The **IF** instruction tests the Remainder field value for zero. When the test is "true," the **Z-ADD** instruction on line 50 will move the value in HrsWorked to the "standalone" TotEmpHrs field.

51 The **ELSE** operation begins the "false" action for the **IF** instruction test on line 49.

52–53 The "nested" **IF** instruction tests the Remainder field for a value less than 30. When the test is "true," the **EVAL** instruction on line 53 adds .5 to the HrsWorked value and stores the sum in TotEmpHrs.

54 This **ELSE** operation begins the "false" action for the related **IF** instruction on line 52.

55 The **EVAL** instruction adds 1 to the HrsWorked value and stores the sum in TotEmpHrs.

56 This **ENDIF** operation ends the "nested" **IF** group that began on line 52.

57 This **ENDIF** operation ends the **IF** group that began on line 49.

Figure 6-11 Compile listing of the Weekly Payroll Report program. (Continued)

59	The **EVAL** instruction computes the RegularPay value for an employee by multiplying TotEmpHrs by the HrlyRate.
61	The **IF** instruction determines if the employee has overtime hours by comparing TotEmpHrs with 35. If TotEmpHrs is greater than 35, the instructions within this **IF** group (lines 62–65) will be executed.
62	The **EVAL** instruction determines the OTHours by subtracting the numeric literal 35 from TotEmpHrs.
63	The **EVAL** instruction computes the OTimeRate (rounded) by dividing the employee's HrlyRate by the numeric literal 2.
64	The **EVAL** instruction computes the OverTimPay by multiplying OTHours by the OTimeRate.
65	This **ENDIF** operation ends the **IF** group that began on line 61.
67	The **EVAL** instruction computes the employee's WeeksPay by adding RegularPay to the OverTimPay. It was important that the OverTimPay field was initialized to zeros on line 37 before the WeeksPay value for an employee is computed. Otherwise, if the previous employee had OverTimPay, that amount would be added to the next employee's WeeksPay value who did not have OverTimPay.
68	This **EXCEPT** instruction passes control to output, where the values for the DetailLine record are printed.
69	The **EVAL** instruction accumulates TotalHours by adding TotEmpHrs to its value.
70	The **EVAL** instruction accumulates TotRegPay by adding RegularPay to its value.
71	The **EVAL** instruction accumulates TotalOTPay by adding OverTimPay to its value.
72	The **EVAL** instruction accumulates TotalPay by adding WeeksPay to its value.
73	This **READ** instruction reads another record from the Emppayfl. If end of file is read, the **LR** indicator will be turned on.
74	The **ENDDO** operation ends the **DOW** group that began with the **DOW** instruction on line 29. If the **READ** instruction on line 73 turned on **LR** (end of file), the **DOW** test line 29 will be "false" and control will leave the **DOW** group and branch to line 76. If **LR** was not "set on," the iterative process will continue.
76	The **EXCEPT** instruction passes control to output line 103, where the values for the total fields (TotalHours through TotalPay) are printed.
78–91	The constants and reserved field values in these HdgLines record formats are printed when the **EXCEPT** instruction on line 33 is executed. The **01** entry in the *Space Before* field advances the paper to a new page before the values in this record format are printed.
93–101	The values for the physical and "standalone" fields in the DetailLine record format are printed when the **EXCEPT** instruction on line 68 is executed.
103–107	The values for the "standalone" (total) fields are printed when the **EXCEPT** instruction on line 76 is executed at **LR** time.

Figure 6-11 Compile listing of the Weekly Payroll Report program. (Continued)

SELECT Operation *(Begin a Select Group)*

A **SELECT** group conditionally processes a sequence of one or more relational **WHEN** or **WHENxx** *(When True Then Select)* instructions. It may include some or all of the following:

- A **SELECT** operation (required)
- **WHEN** instruction(s) (optional)
- **OTHER** operation and related instruction group (optional)
- An **ENDSL** *(End Select)* operation (required)

The syntax and processing logic of a **SELECT** group are detailed in Figure 6-12.

```
*.. 1 ...+... 2 ...+... 3 ...+... 4 ...+... 5 ...+... 6 ...+... 7 ...+... 8 ...+... 9 ...+ ...10
CLON01Factor 1++++++Opcode&ExtExtended-factor2+++++++++++++++++++++++++++++Comments+++++++++++++
 *  SELECT group with two WHEN instructions and OTHER operation.
                           3
C  1         2         SELECT       2
C                      WHEN       expression
C                       .
C     entry            WHENxx     entry
C                       .
C                      OTHER
C                       .
C                      ENDSL
                         4
```

SELECT operation syntax rules:

1. Conditioning indicators may be specified in the *LO* (positions 7–8) and *NO1* (positions 9–11) fields.
2. *Factor 1* and *Extended-factor2* fields are not used.
3. **SELECT** operation must be entered in the *Opcode* field.
4. **ENDSL** operation must end a **SELECT** group.

Processing logic of a **SELECT** group:

- Within a **SELECT** group, control passes to the first instruction following the first **WHEN** instruction that tested as true. After the instructions for the **WHEN** group are executed, control branches to the first executable instruction following the related **ENDSL** operation.
- If none of the **WHEN** or **WHENxx** instructions within the **SELECT** group tests as true, instructions following the **OTHER** operation are automatically executed. After the instructions within the **OTHER** group are executed, control will pass to the first executable instruction following the **ENDSL** operation.
- If an **OTHER** operation is not specified and the previous **WHEN** or **WHENxx** tests are not true, control will branch to the first executable instruction following the **ENDSL** operation.

Figure 6-12 Syntax and processing logic of a **SELECT** group.

WHEN Operation *(When True Then Select)*: Expression Format

The two formats for this operation are **WHEN** and **WHENxx.** Either instruction must be included within a **SELECT** group after the **SELECT** operation and before, if included, an **OTHER** operation.

Figure 6-13 explains the syntax for the **WHEN** operation format.

```
*.. 1 ...+... 2 ...+... 3 ...+... 4 ...+... 5 ...+... 6 ...+... 7 ...+... 8 ...+... 9 ...+ ...10
CLON01Factor 1++++++Opcode&ExtExtended-factor2+++++++++++++++++++++++++++++Comments+++++++++++++
 * WHEN operation format with logical expression
                         :
C 1 2       3          WHEN       expression
C                       4             5
```

WHEN operation syntax rules:

1. An **L0–L9** or **LR** conditioning indicator may be specified in the *L0* field (positions 7–8).
2. Indicators are not permitted in the *N01* field.
3. *Factor 1* is not used.
4. **WHEN** must be entered in the *Opcode* field, entered within a **SELECT** group, and placed before any **OTHER** operation.
5. A logical expression must be specified in the *Extended-factor2* field.

Figure 6-13 Syntax and processing logic of the **WHEN** operation.

Processing logic of the **WHEN** operation:

- If the relational test is true, the instructions following the **WHEN** expression are processed until the next **WHEN, OTHER,** or **ENDSL** operation is encountered.
- After the instructions included in the **WHEN** group are executed, control passes to the instruction after the **ENDSL** operation. Any other **WHEN** groups will be ignored.
- If none of the **WHEN** expressions within the **SELECT** group tests as true, control will pass to the instruction following the **ENDSL** operation. If an **OTHER** operation is included in the **SELECT** group, control will pass to the instruction following the **OTHER.**
- For **WHEN** expressions combined with **AND** conditions, all logical tests must be true to execute the instructions within the **WHEN** group. However, for **OR** conditions, only one logical test must be true. **AND** and **OR** tests may be combined in a **WHEN** expression.

Figure 6-13 Syntax and processing logic of the **WHEN** operation. (Continued)

Examples of the **WHEN** instruction are shown in Figure 6-14.

```
*.. 1 ...+... 2 ...+... 3 ...+... 4 ...+... 5 ...+... 6 ...+... 7 ...+... 8 ...+... 9 ...+ ...10
CLON01Factor 1+++++++Opcode&ExtExtended-factor2+++++++++++++++++++++++++++++++Comments+++++++++++++
 * WHEN operation format example instructions....
                    :
C                  WHEN      Shift = 'D'
C                   :
C                  WHEN      Hours > 35 AND Shift = 'N'
C                   :
```

Figure 6-14 **WHEN** operation example instructions.

WHENxx Operation *(When True Then Select)*: Decision Format

Figure 6-15 details the syntax of the **WHENxx** operation.

```
*.. 1 ...+... 2 ...+... 3 ...+... 4 ...+... 5 ...+... 6 ...+... 7 ...+... 8 ...+... 9 ...+ ...10
CLON01Factor 1+++++++Opcode(E)+Factor2+++++++Result++++++++Len++D_HiLoEq....Comments+++++++++++++
 * WHENxx operation format with decision logic.....
                    :
C 1 2    3         WHENxx      5           6                  6
C                   4
```

WHENxx operation syntax rules:

1. An **L0-L9** or **LR** conditioning indicator may be specified in the *L0* field (positions 7–8).
2. Indicators are not permitted in the *N01* field (positions 9–11).
3. *Factor 1* must include a field name, numeric literal, named constant, or array element.
4. The **WHENxx** operation must be left-justified in the *Opcode* field, included within a **SELECT** group, and specified before any **OTHER** operation. The **xx** entry must be an **EQ, LT, GT, LE, GE,** or **NE** relational test.
5. *Factor 2* must include a field name, numeric literal, named constant, or array element. It must be defined as the same type as the *Factor 1* item (both numeric or character).
6. *Result* field or *Resulting Indicators* are not used.

Figure 6-15 Syntax and processing logic of the **WHENxx** operation.

Processing logic of the **WHENxx** operation:

- If the relational test (**xx** entry) is true, the instructions following the **WHEN** expression are processed until the next **WHEN** (or **WHENxx**), **OTHER**, or **ENDSL** operation is encountered.
- After the instructions included in the **WHENxx** group are executed, control passes to the instruction after the **ENDSL** operation. Any other **WHEN** groups will be ignored.
- If none of the **WHENxx** expressions within the **SELECT** group tests as true, control will pass to the instruction following the **ENDSL** operation. If an **OTHER** operation is included in the **SELECT** group, control will pass to the instruction following the **OTHER** operation.
- For **WHENxx** expressions combined with **ANDxx** conditions, all logical tests must be true to execute the instructions within the **WHENxx** group. However, for **ORxx** conditions, only one logical test must be true. **ANDxx** and **ORxx** tests may be combined in a **WHENxx** expression.

Figure 6-15 Syntax and processing logic of the **WHENxx** operation. (Continued)

Examples of the **WHENxx** instructions are shown in Figure 6-16.

```
*.. 1 ...+... 2 ...+... 3 ...+... 4 ...+... 5 ...+... 6 ...+... 7 ...+... 8 ...+... 9 ...+ ...10
CLON01Factor 1+++++++Opcode(E)+Factor2+++++++Result++++++++Len++D_HiLoEq....Comments+++++++++++++
 * WHENxx operation example instructions....
                       :
C     Shift            WHENEQ     'D'
C                      :
C     Hours            WHENGT     35
C     Shift            ANDEQ      'N'
C                      :
```

Figure 6-16 **WHENxx** operation example instructions.

The programmer will usually determine whether to use the **WHEN** or **WHENxx** format of this operation. However, the **WHEN** format is more consistent with **RPG IV** syntax.

OTHER *(Otherwise Select)*

The **OTHER** operation is optional in a **SELECT** group. If none of the previous **WHEN** expressions is true, control will branch to the first instruction after the **OTHER** operation. Figure 6-17 details the syntax and processing logic of the **OTHER** operation.

```
*.. 1 ...+... 2 ...+... 3 ...+... 4 ...+... 5 ...+... 6 ...+... 7 ...+... 8 ...+... 9 ...+ ...10
CLON01Factor 1+++++++Opcode&ExtExtended-factor2+++++++++++++++++++++++++++++++Comments+++++++++++++
 * SELECT group with one WHEN instruction and OTHER operation

C                    SELECT
C                    WHEN      expression
C                     :
C 1 2    3           OTHER             3
C                     4
C                    ENDSL
```

OTHER operation syntax rules:

1. An **L0–L9** or **LR** conditioning indicator may be specified in the *L0* field (positions 7–8).
2. An indicator is not permitted in the *N01* (positions 9–11) field.
3. The *Factor 1* and *Extended-factor2* fields are not used.
4. The **OTHER** operation must be entered in the *Opcode* field and placed after any **WHEN** or **WHENxx** instruction(s). Only one **OTHER** operation is permitted in a **SELECT** group.

Figure 6-17 Syntax and processing logic of the **OTHER** operation.

Processing logic of the **OTHER** operation:

- If the **WHEN** or **WHENxx** expression(s) before the **OTHER** operation test is/are false, the instructions included after the **OTHER** operation (and before the **ENDSL** operation) will be executed.
- After the instruction(s) included in the **OTHER** group is/are executed, control passes to the first executable instructions following the **ENDSL** operation.

Figure 6-17 Syntax and processing logic of the **OTHER** operation. (Continued)

Weekly Payroll Report Program Using a SELECT Group

The Weekly Payroll Report program shown in Figure 6-11 is modified in Figure 6-18 with the **SELECT** group syntax. Note that **IF/ELSE** groups are included in the program to control the processing logic.

```
Line   <---------------------- Source Specifications ----------------------------><---- Comments ----> Do
Number ....1....+....2....+....3....+....4....+....5....+....6....+....7....+....8....+....9....+...10 Num
                          S o u r c e   L i s t i n g
     * Weekly Payroll Report for hourly employees using SELECT/WHEN/OTHER operations....
   FEmppayfl  IF   E           K DISK
      *----------------------------------------------------------------------------------------*
      *                                  RPG name         External name                        *
      * File name. . . . . . . . :       EMPPAYFL         STAN/EMPPAYFL                        *
      * Record format(s) . . . . :       EMPPAYR          EMPPAYR                              *
      *----------------------------------------------------------------------------------------*
   FQsysprt   O    F  132        PRINTER OFLIND(*INOF)

     * Definition of work fields....
   D OverTimPay      S               6  2
   D ShiftOut        S               5
   D HrsWorked       S               2  0
   D Remainder       S               2  0
   D TotEmpHrs       S               3  1
   D OTHours         S               3  1
   D OTimeRate       S               4  2
   D RegularPay      S               6  2
   D WeeksPay        S               6  2
   D TotalHours      S               5  1
   D TotlRegPay      S               8  2
   D TotalOTPay      S               8  2
   D TotalPay        S               8  2

     * Begin calculations....
  =IEMPPAYR
      *----------------------------------------------------------------------------------------*
      * RPG record format  . . . . :     EMPPAYR                                              *
      * External format  . . . . . :     EMPPAYR : STAN/EMPPAYFL                              *
      *----------------------------------------------------------------------------------------*
  =I                            A    1    4  EMP_NUMBER
  =I                            A    5   24  EMP_NAME
  =I                            A   25   25  SHIFT
  =I                            P   26   28 2HRLYRATE
  =I                            P   29   31 0MINUTES
   C                   EVAL      *INOF = *ON                               turn on OF indicator
   C                   READ      Emppayfl                          ----LR  read first record
   C                   DOW       *INLR = *OFF                              do while LR is off    B01

     * Page overflow control....
   C                   IF        *INOF = *ON                               overflow ind on?      B02
   C                   EXCEPT    Hdglines                                  print heading lines    02
   C                   EVAL      *INOF = *OFF                              turn off OF indicator  02
   C                   ENDIF                                               end IF group          E02
```

Figure 6-18 Compile listing of the Weekly Payroll Program modified with a **SELECT** group.

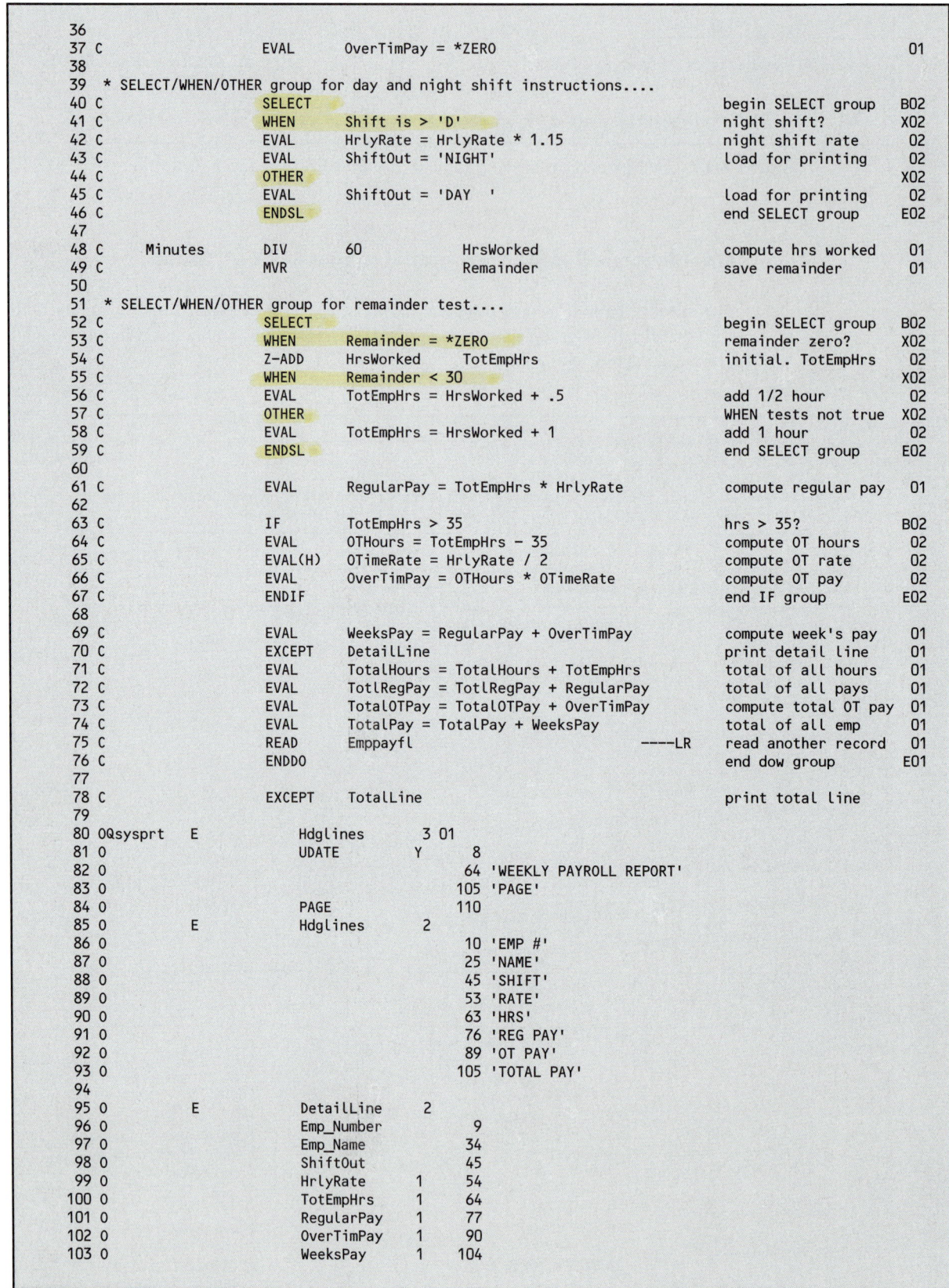

```
C                   EVAL      OverTimPay = *ZERO                                  01
 * SELECT/WHEN/OTHER group for day and night shift instructions....
C                   SELECT                                  begin SELECT group   B02
C                   WHEN      Shift is > 'D'                night shift?         X02
C                   EVAL      HrlyRate = HrlyRate * 1.15    night shift rate      02
C                   EVAL      ShiftOut = 'NIGHT'            load for printing     02
C                   OTHER                                                        X02
C                   EVAL      ShiftOut = 'DAY  '            load for printing     02
C                   ENDSL                                   end SELECT group     E02
C     Minutes       DIV       60            HrsWorked       compute hrs worked    01
C                   MVR                     Remainder       save remainder        01
 * SELECT/WHEN/OTHER group for remainder test....
C                   SELECT                                  begin SELECT group   B02
C                   WHEN      Remainder = *ZERO             remainder zero?      X02
C                   Z-ADD     HrsWorked     TotEmpHrs       initial. TotEmpHrs    02
C                   WHEN      Remainder < 30                                     X02
C                   EVAL      TotEmpHrs = HrsWorked + .5    add 1/2 hour          02
C                   OTHER                                   WHEN tests not true  X02
C                   EVAL      TotEmpHrs = HrsWorked + 1     add 1 hour            02
C                   ENDSL                                   end SELECT group     E02
C                   EVAL      RegularPay = TotEmpHrs * HrlyRate compute regular pay 01
C                   IF        TotEmpHrs > 35                hrs > 35?            B02
C                   EVAL      OTHours = TotEmpHrs - 35      compute OT hours      02
C                   EVAL(H)   OTimeRate = HrlyRate / 2      compute OT rate       02
C                   EVAL      OverTimPay = OTHours * OTimeRate compute OT pay      02
C                   ENDIF                                   end IF group         E02
C                   EVAL      WeeksPay = RegularPay + OverTimPay compute week's pay 01
C                   EXCEPT    DetailLine                    print detail line     01
C                   EVAL      TotalHours = TotalHours + TotEmpHrs total of all hours 01
C                   EVAL      TotlRegPay = TotlRegPay + RegularPay total of all pays 01
C                   EVAL      TotalOTPay = TotalOTPay + OverTimPay compute total OT pay 01
C                   EVAL      TotalPay = TotalPay + WeeksPay total of all emp     01
C                   READ      Emppayfl                      ----LR read another record 01
C                   ENDDO                                   end dow group        E01
C                   EXCEPT    TotalLine                     print total line
OQsysprt   E            Hdglines       3 01
O                       UDATE         Y      8
O                                           64 'WEEKLY PAYROLL REPORT'
O                                          105 'PAGE'
O                       PAGE               110
O          E            Hdglines       2
O                                           10 'EMP #'
O                                           25 'NAME'
O                                           45 'SHIFT'
O                                           53 'RATE'
O                                           63 'HRS'
O                                           76 'REG PAY'
O                                           89 'OT PAY'
O                                          105 'TOTAL PAY'
O          E            DetailLine     2
O                       Emp_Number           9
O                       Emp_Name            34
O                       ShiftOut            45
O                       HrlyRate      1     54
O                       TotEmpHrs     1     64
O                       RegularPay    1     77
O                       OverTimPay    1     90
O                       WeeksPay      1    104
```

Figure 6-18 Compile listing of the Weekly Payroll Program modified with a **SELECT** group. (Continued)

```
104
105 O          E          TotalLine   1
106 O                     TotalHours    1     64
107 O                     TotlRegPay    1     77
108 O                     TotalOTPay    1     90
109 O                     TotalPay      1    104
```

File Description instructions:

Line No.

2 Emppayfl is defined as an input, full-procedural, externally described, keyed physical file.

3 Qsysprt is defined as a program-described printer file. The **OFLIND(*INOF)** keyword defines the **OF** page overflow indicator.

Definition Specification instructions:

6–18 The work fields OverTimPay through TotalPay are defined as "standalone" fields (**S** in position 24) in *Definition Specification* instructions.

Calculation Specification instructions:

27 The **EVAL *INOF = *ON** instruction turns "on" the **OF** overflow indicator so that the **IF *INOF = *ON** instruction on line 32 will test as "true" and pass control to the exception records on lines 80–93, causing the Hdglines records to be printed.

28 The **READ** instruction reads the first record from the Emppayfl file. If no records are stored in the file, **LR** will be set on and the test in the **DOW** operation on line 29 will cause control to branch over the **DOW** group to line 78. The coding for this program assumes that records will always be stored in the physical file.

29 The ***INLR = LR** relational test specified in the **DOW** instruction controls execution of the instructions within the **DOW** group until **LR** is set on by one of the two **READ** instructions.

32–35 The **IF *INOF = *ON** instruction tests the status of the **OF** overflow indicator. If it is "on," which it will be for the first record read (turned on line 27), the instructions in the **IF** group (lines 33–35) will be executed.

When the **IF** test on line 32 is "true," the **EXCEPT** instruction on line 33 will pass control to output and print the two Hdglines record formats.

33 The **EXCEPT** instruction controls the printing of the Hdglines on lines 80 through 93.

34 The **EVAL *INOF = *OFF** instruction turns off the **OF** indicator, preventing the Hdglines from being printed when the next iteration of the **DOW** is performed.

35 The **ENDIF** operation ends the **IF** group that began on line 32.

37 The **EVAL** instruction initializes the OverTimPay field to zeros before the payroll values for the next employee are computed.

40 The **SELECT** operation begins the select group (lines 40–46).

41 The **WHEN** instruction tests the value in the physical file field Shift. If the value in Shift is greater than **D** (day shift), the **EVAL** instructions on lines 42 and 43 will be executed. When the relational test is not "true," control will branch to the **EVAL** instruction on line 45 after the **OTHER** operation.

42 The **EVAL** computes the HrlyRate value for "night" Shift employees, which is 15% greater than "day" Shift employees.

43 The **EVAL** instruction initializes the ShiftOut field with the constant NIGHT.

44 The **OTHER** operation provides the "false" action when the **WHEN** test on line 41 is not "true."

45 The **EVAL** instruction initializes the ShiftOut field with the constant DAY.

46 The **ENDSL** operation ends the **SELECT** group included on lines 40–46.

48 The value in the physical file field Minutes is divided by the numeric literal 60 to compute the HrsWorked value for the employee.

49 Any remainder calculated by the **DIV** instruction on line 45 will be stored in the "standalone" Remainder field with this **MVR** instruction.

52 The **SELECT** operation begins the select group on lines 52–59.

53–54 The **WHEN** instruction tests the Remainder field value for zero. When the test is "true," the **Z-ADD** instruction on line 54 will move the value in HrsWorked to the "standalone" TotEmpHrs field.

Figure 6-18 Compile listing of the Weekly Payroll Program modified with a **SELECT** group. (Continued)

55 If the **WHEN** instruction test on line 53 is "false," this **WHEN** instruction is executed in which the value in Remainder is tested for less than 30.

56 If the **WHEN** test on line 54 is "true," the **EVAL** instruction on line 56 adds .5 to the HrsWorked value and stores the sum in TotEmpHrs.

57 If none of the **WHEN** instructions in this **SELECT** group tests as "true," the instruction following this **OTHER** operation will be executed.

58 The **EVAL** instruction adds 1 to the HrsWorked value and stores the sum in TotEmpHrs.

59 This **ENDSL** operation ends the **SELECT** group on lines 52–59.

61 The **EVAL** instruction computes the RegularPay value for an employee by multiplying TotEmpHrs by the HrlyRate.

63 The **IF** instruction determines if the employee has overtime hours by comparing TotEmpHrs with 35. If TotEmpHrs is greater than 35, the instructions within this **IF** group (lines 62–65) will be executed.

64 The **EVAL** instruction computes the OTHours by subtracting the numeric literal 35 from TotEmpHrs.

65 The **EVAL** instruction computes the OTimeRate (rounded) by dividing the employee's HrlyRate by the numeric literal 2.

66 The **EVAL** instruction computes the OverTimPay by multiplying OTHours by the OTimeRate.

67 This **ENDIF** operation ends the **IF** group that began on line 63.

69 The **EVAL** instruction computes the employee's WeeksPay by adding RegularPay to the OverTimPay. It was important that the OverTimPay field was initialized to zeros on line 37 before the WeeksPay value for an employee is computed. Otherwise, if the previous employee had OverTimPay, that amount would be added to the next employee's WeeksPay value who did not have OverTimPay.

70 This **EXCEPT** instruction passes control to output, where the values for the DetailLine record are printed.

71 The **EVAL** instruction accumulates TotalHours by adding TotEmpHrs to its value.

72 The **EVAL** instruction accumulates TotRegPay by adding RegularPay to its value.

73 The **EVAL** instruction accumulates TotalOTPay by adding OverTimPay to its value.

74 The **EVAL** instruction accumulates TotalPay by adding WeeksPay to its value.

75 This **READ** instruction reads another record from the Emppayfl. If end of file is read, the **LR** indicator will be turned on.

76 The **ENDDO** operation ends the **DOW** group that began with the **DOW** instruction on line 29. If the **READ** instruction on line 75 turned on **LR** (end of file), the **DOW** test line 29 will be "false" and control will leave the **DOW** group and branch to line 78. If **LR** was not **"set on,"** the iterative process will continue.

78 The **EXCEPT** instruction passes control to output line 105, where the values for the total fields (TotalHours through TotalPay) are printed.

80–93 The constants and reserved field values in these HdgLines record formats are printed when the **EXCEPT** instruction on line 33 is executed. The **01** entry in the *Space Before* field advances the paper to a new page before the values in this record format are printed.

95–103 The values for the physical and "standalone" fields in the DetailLine record format are printed when the **EXCEPT** instruction on line 70 is executed.

105–109 The values for the "standalone" (total) fields are printed when the **EXCEPT** instruction on line 78 is executed at **LR** time.

Figure 6-18 Compile listing of the Weekly Payroll Program modified with a **SELECT** group. (Continued)

RPG IV LOOPING CONTROL (ITERATIVE PROCESSING)

Looping in a computer program is defined as the branching of program control to a preceding statement and executing the included instruction(s) one or more times. This process is required for *iterative* calculations, where the result is determined after repeating the same instructions a predetermined number of times. Typical business applications that require *iterative* processing are the raising of a number to a power, compound interest computations, mortgage payment calculations, depreciation of an asset over its useful life, and so forth.

RPG IV supports three structured operations to control looping *(iterative)* processing. Included are the **DO** *(Do)*, **DOU** *(Do Until)*, and **DOW** *(Do While)* operations, which are discussed individually in the following sections.

The DO *(Do)* Operation

The **DO** operation controls the processing of a group of calculation instructions (within the **DO** group) a predetermined number of times. How many times the group of instructions within the **DO** group are performed is determined by specifying a starting value (or a default value of 1), a limit value, and an index value. The syntax and processing logic of the **DO** operation are explained in Figure 6-19.

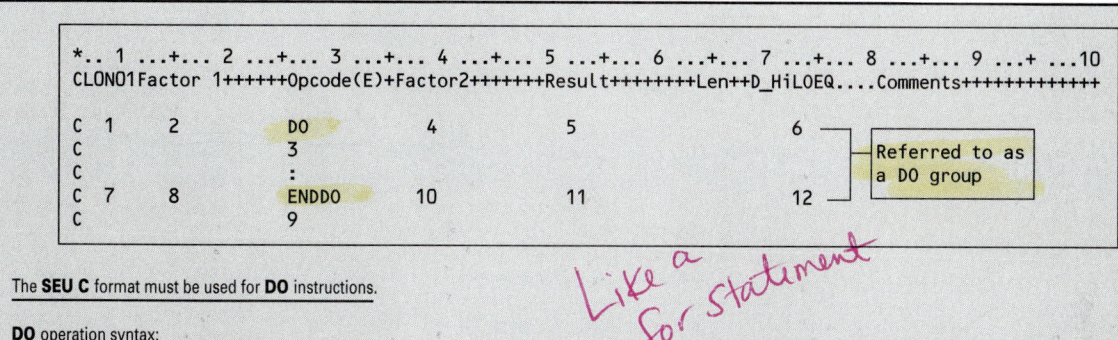

```
*.. 1 ...+... 2 ...+... 3 ...+... 4 ...+... 5 ...+... 6 ...+... 7 ...+... 8 ...+... 9 ...+ ...10
CLON01Factor 1+++++++Opcode(E)+Factor2+++++++Result++++++++Len++D_HiLOEQ....Comments+++++++++++++

C  1     2            DO            4               5                      6 ─┐
C                     3                                                       ├─ Referred to as
C                     :                                                       │  a DO group
C  7     8            ENDDO        10               11                     12 ─┘
C                     9
```

The **SEU C** format must be used for **DO** instructions.

DO operation syntax:

1. *Conditioning indicators* may be specified at *total time* (columns 7–8) and/or *detail time* (columns 9–11). If the indicator(s) specified is (are) not **"ON,"** control will branch to the statement following the **ENDDO** (or **END**) operation. *Conditioning indicators* specified are tested only when the **DO** statement is initially executed. For subsequent loops, the indicator status is ignored.

2. *Factor 1* (starting index value) entry is optional. It may include a numeric literal, field name, array element, table name, or data structure subfield. Any of these numeric items must be defined as an integer (no decimal positions). The value stored in the *Factor 1* entry initializes the index *(Result Field)* to its starting value. If the *Factor 1* entry is omitted, the starting value of the index is a default value of 1.

3. The **DO** operation name must be left-justified in the *Operation* field. It controls automatic looping and exit from the **DO** group when the index value (*Result Field* item) is greater than the limit value (*Factor 2* entry).

4. *Factor 2* (limit value) entry is optional. It may include a numeric literal, field, array name, table name, or data structure subfield. Any of these numeric entries must be defined as an integer. The value stored in the *Factor 2* item specifies the number of times the loop will be executed. If this entry is omitted, the limit value is 1. Note that the limit value must be equal to or greater than the starting value in *Factor 1* (when specified).

5. *Result Field* entry is optional. This entry may be a numeric literal, field, array element, table name, or a data structure subfield. When specified, it defines the index (counter) value, which is automatically incremented by 1, or by the value included in *Factor 2* of the related **ENDDO** (or **END**) statement. If this entry is omitted, the **RPG IV** compiler will supply an index.

6. *Resulting Indicators* are not permitted.

ENDDO operation:

7. Optional *conditioning indicators* may be assigned to an **ENDDO** (or **END**) statement which determine if the looping process is to continue. If an indicator is assigned and it is ON, control will pass to the **DO** statement. However, if the indicator is not ON, control will pass to the first executable instruction following the **ENDDO** (or **END**) operation.

8. *Factor 1* is not used.

9. **ENDDO** (or **END**) operation name must be entered left-justified in the *Operation* field.

10. By default, the index will be automatically incremented by 1. It may be incremented with some other value by specifying a numeric literal, field, array element, table name, or data structure subfield in *Factor 2*.

Figure 6-19 **DO** operation syntax and processing logic.

11. *Result Field* is not used.

12. *Resulting Indicators* are not permitted.

Processing logic:

1. The **DO** operation begins execution by moving the value from *Factor 1* entry (when specified) to the index item *(Result Field)*. If a *Factor 1* entry is not specified, the index is initialized to 1.

2. When the index value (*Result Field* item if specified) is greater than the limit value (*Factor 2* item), control branches to the first statement following the related **ENDDO** (or **END**) operation.

Figure 6-19 **DO** operation syntax and processing logic. (Continued)

An example program that prints two labels for each customer is presented in Figure 6-20 to illustrate an application of the **DO** operation. A line-by-line explanation of each instruction follows the compile listing.

```
Line    <--------------------- Source Specifications ----------------------------><---- Comments ----> Do
Number ....1....+....2....+....3....+....4....+....5....+....6....+....7....+....8....+....9....+...10 Num
                        S o u r c e   L i s t i n g
     1   * Customer labels program using DO operation control....
     2 FCh6pf4    IF   E             DISK
        *---------------------------------------------------------------------------------------*
        *                              RPG name          External name                           *
        * File name. . . . . . . . . : CH6PF4            STAN/CH6PF4                             *
        * Record format(s) . . . . . : CH6PF4R           CH6PF4R                                 *
        *---------------------------------------------------------------------------------------*
     3 FQsysprt   O    F  132        PRINTER FORMLEN(8) FORMOFL(7)
     4
     5   * Do while LR is off....
     6=ICH6PF4R
        *---------------------------------------------------------------------------------------*
        * RPG record format  . . . . : CH6PF4R                                                   *
        * External format  . . . . . : CH6PF4R : STAN/CH6PF4                                     *
        *---------------------------------------------------------------------------------------*
     7=I                             A    1    5  CUSTNUMBER
     8=I                             A    6   25  CUSTNAME
     9=I                             A   26   40  ADDRESS1
    10=I                             A   41   55  ADDRESS2
    11=I                             A   56   74  CITY
    12=I                             A   75   76  STATE
    13=I                             P   77   79 0ZIP
    14 C                   READ      Ch6pf4                             ----LR   read first record
    15 C                   DOW       *INLR = *OFF                                do while LR is off    B01
    16
    17   * Exit DO group when index is greater than 2....
    18 C                   DO        2                                           DO until index > 2    B02
    19 C                   EXCEPT    Lines1_2                                    print lines1_2         02
    20 C                   IF        Address2 > *BLANKS                          field not blank?      B03
    21 C                   EXCEPT    Line3                                       print line3            03
    22 C                   EXCEPT    Line4                                       print line4            03
    23 C                   ELSE                                                                        X03
    24 C                   EXCEPT    Line4                                       print line4            03
    25 C                   ENDIF                                                 end IF group          E03
    26 C                   ENDDO                                                 end DO group          E02
    27
    28 C                   READ      Ch6pf4                             ----LR   read next record       01
    29 C                   ENDDO                                                 end DO group          E01
    30
    31 OQsysprt   E            Lines1_2       1 03
    32 O                       CustName            30
    33 O                       CustNumber          40
    34 O          E            Lines1_2       1
    35 O                       Address1            25
```

Figure 6-20 Compile listing of a program that uses the **DO** operation to generate multiple labels for each customer.

```
36 O          E             Line3          1
37 O                        Address2            25
38 O          E             Line4          1
39 O                        City                29
40 O                        State               32
41 O                        Zip                 39
```

Printed Report:

```
ENRICO FERMI              10000
10 NEUTRON LANE
CHICAGO              IL  04010
- - - - - - - - - - - - - - - -
ENRICO FERMI              10000
10 NEUTRON LANE
CHICAGO              IL  04010
- - - - - - - - - - - - - - - -
EDWARD TELLER             20000
ATOMIC LANE
PO BOX 239
LOS ALAMOS           NM  08803
- - - - - - - - - - - - - - - -
EDWARD TELLER             20000
ATOMIC LANE
PO BOX 239
LOS ALAMOS           NM  08803
```

File Description Specifications:

Line No.

2 Ch6pf4 is defined as an input, full-procedural, externally described, nonkeyed physical file.

3 Qsysprt is defined as a program-described printer file. The default form length is changed to 8 by the **FORMLEN(8)** keyword. Page overflow is defined so that it will occur on line 7 by the **FORMOFL(7)** keyword.

Calculation Specifications:

14 The **READ** instruction reads the first record from the Ch6pf4 physical file. If no records are stored in the file, the **LR** indicator will be set on.

15 The **DOW *INLR = *OFF** instruction tests the status of the **LR** indicator. If it is "off," the iterative process will continue. However, if **LR** is "on," indicating an end-of-file condition, the job will end.

18 The numeric literal **2** in the **DO** instruction controls the number of iterations that the **DO** group will perform. Because the **RPG IV** compiler will supply an index, a programmer-supplied field name (index) is not required in the *Result* field. When the value in the compiler-supplied index is greater than **2,** an automatic exit from the **DO** group will occur.

19 The **EXCEPT** instruction controls the printing of the two Lines1_2 record formats on lines 31 through 35.

20–21 After Lines1_2 are printed, control returns to this **IF** instruction. The **IF** instruction tests the Address2 field for blanks. When the value in Address2 is greater than blanks (indicating a second address as P.O. Box or apartment number), the following **EXCEPT** instruction will control the printing of the Line3 record format on lines 36 through 37.

22 This **EXCEPT** instruction will control the printing of the Line4 record format. Within the "true" action of the **IF** instruction, the Line4 record format on lines 44 through 47 will be printed after the Address2 record values. Consequently, four lines are printed on a label when a value is stored in the Address2 field greater than blanks.

Figure 6-20 Compile listing of a program that generates multiple labels for each customer using the **DO** operation. (Continued)

23 When the **IF** instruction test on line 20 is "false," this **ELSE** operation begins the "false" action.

24 This **EXCEPT** controls the printing of the Line4 record format after the Address1 record values when the Address2 field is blank (no second address).

25 The **ENDIF** operation ends the **IF** group that began on line 20.

26 This **ENDDO** operation ends the **DO** group and returns control back to the **DO** instruction on line 18.

28 This **READ** instruction reads another record from the Ch6pf4 physical file. If end-of-file is read, the **LR** indicator will be set on.

29 This **ENDDO** operation ends the **DOW** group that began on line 15 and transfers control back to the **DOW** instruction, where the status of the **LR** indicator is tested. If **LR** is "off," the iterative process will continue. When it is "on," the job will end.

Output Specifications:

31–35 The printing of the two Lines1_2 record formats is controlled by the **EXCEPT** instruction on line 19.

36–37 The printing of the Line3 record formats is controlled by the **EXCEPT** instruction on line 21. The values for this output record are printed only if the Address2 field has a value greater than blanks.

38–41 Depending on the value in the Address2 field, the printing of the Line4 record format is controlled by the **EXCEPT** instruction on line 22 or the one on line 24. If the value in Address2 is greater than blanks, the **EXCEPT** instruction on line 22 will be executed. However, if the value in Address2 is blanks, the **EXCEPT** instruction on line 24 will be executed.

Figure 6-20 Compile listing of a program that generates multiple labels for each customer using the **DO** operation. (Continued)

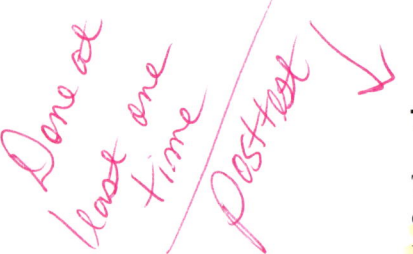

The DOU *(Do Until)* Operation

The **DOU** operation is another structured **RPG IV** instruction that controls iterative processing. This operation differs, however, from the **DO** operation in that it requires a programmer-supplied counter to exit from the looping sequence. The syntax and processing logic related to the **DOU** operation are detailed in Figure 6-21.

```
*.. 1 ...+... 2 ...+... 3 ...+... 4 ...+... 5 ...+... 6 ...+... 7 ...+... 8 ...+... 9 ...+ ...10
CLON01Factor 1++++++Opcode&ExtExtended-factor2+++++++++++++++++++++++++++++Comments+++++++++++++
 * Instructions within the DOU group are executed at least once.  The status of the logical
 * expression determines whether subsequent "loops" are performed.
C 1     2          DOU       logical expression
C                   3             4
C                   :
C 5     6          ENDDO          8
                    7
```

SEU CX format must be used when an expression is specified with the **DOU** operation.

DOU operation syntax:

1. Conditioning indicator(s) may be specified at total time *(L0* field) or at detail time *(N01)* field. If the indicator(s) specified is/are on, control will branch to the first executable instruction following the **ENDDO** operation. The status of the indicator is tested every time the **DOU** operation is executed.
2. *Factor 1* is not used.
3. The **DOU** operation must be entered in the *Opcode* field.
4. A logical expression must be specified in the *Extended-factor2* field.

Figure 6-21 **DOU** operation syntax and processing logic.

5. Conditioning indicators are optional for an **ENDDO** operation.

6. *Factor 1* is not used.

7. An **ENDDO** or **END** operation entered in the *OpCode* field must end a **DOU** group.

8. *Factor 2* is not used with an **ENDDO** operation that delimits a **DOU** group.

Processing logic:

- The **DOU** operation executes the instructions within the group at least once. Subsequent looping depends on the status of the logical expression specified in the **DOU** instruction.
- Unlike the **DO** operation, a **DOU** operation does not include an automatic counter (index). Looping must be controlled by a programmer-supplied counter within the **DOU** group that is tested in the logical expression.

Figure 6-21 **DOU** operation syntax and processing logic. (Continued)

The example customer label program using the **DO** operation is modified in Figure 6-22 with the **DOU** operation.

```
Line   <---------------------- Source Specifications ----------------------------><---- Comments ----> Do
Number ....1....+....2....+....3....+....4....+....5....+....6....+....7....+....8....+....9....+...10 Num
                       S o u r c e   L i s t i n g
     1  * Customer labels program using DOU operation control....
     2 FCh6pf4    IF   E             DISK
       *--------------------------------------------------------------------------------------------*
       *                             RPG name          External name                                *
       * File name. . . . . . . . :  CH6PF4            STAN/CH6PF4                                  *
       * Record format(s) . . . . :  CH6PF4R           CH6PF4R                                      *
       *--------------------------------------------------------------------------------------------*
     3 FQsysprt   O    F  132        PRINTER FORMLEN(8) FORMOFL(7)
     4
     5  * work field....
     6 D Count           S              2  0                            DOU counter control
     7=ICH6PF4R
       *--------------------------------------------------------------------------------------------*
       * RPG record format  . . . . :  CH6PF4R                                                      *
       * External format  . . . . . :  CH6PF4R : STAN/CH6PF4                                        *
       *--------------------------------------------------------------------------------------------*
     8=I                             A    1    5  CUSTNUMBER
     9=I                             A    6   25  CUSTNAME
    10=I                             A   26   40  ADDRESS1
    11=I                             A   41   55  ADDRESS2
    12=I                             A   56   74  CITY
    13=I                             A   75   76  STATE
    14=I                             P   77   79 0ZIP
    15 C                   READ      Ch6pf4                          ----LR   read first record
    16
    17  * Process while LR is off....
    18 C                   DOW       *INLR = *OFF                             do while LR is off   B01
    19 C                   Z-ADD     *ZERO         Count                      initialize counter    01
    20
    21  * Print label lines....
    22 C                   DOU       Count = 2                                DO until Count = 2   B02
    23 C                   EXCEPT    Lines1_2                                 print lines 1 & 2     02
    24 C                   IF        Address2 > *BLANKS                       field not blank?     B03
    25 C                   EXCEPT    Line3                                    print Address2 line   03
    26 C                   EXCEPT    Line4                                    print city etc line   03
    27 C                   ELSE                                               Address2 blank       X03
    28 C                   EXCEPT    Line4                                    print city etc line   03
    29 C                   ENDIF                                              end IF group         E03
```

Figure 6-22 Compile listing of a program that uses the **DOU** operation to generate multiple labels for each customer.

```
30 C                                                                          E03
31 C                  EVAL       Count = Count + 1          increment counter  02
32 C                  ENDDO                                 end DOU group     E02
33
34 C                  READ       Ch6pf4             ----LR  read next record   01
35 C                  ENDDO                                 end DOU group     E01
36
37 OQsysprt   E           Lines1_2       1 03
38 O                      CustName          30
39 O                      CustNumber        40
40 O          E           Lines1_2       1
41 O                      Address1          25
42 O          E           Line3          1
43 O                      Address2          25
44 O          E           Line4          1
45 O                      City              29
46 O                      State             32
47 O                      Zip               39
```

Printed Report:

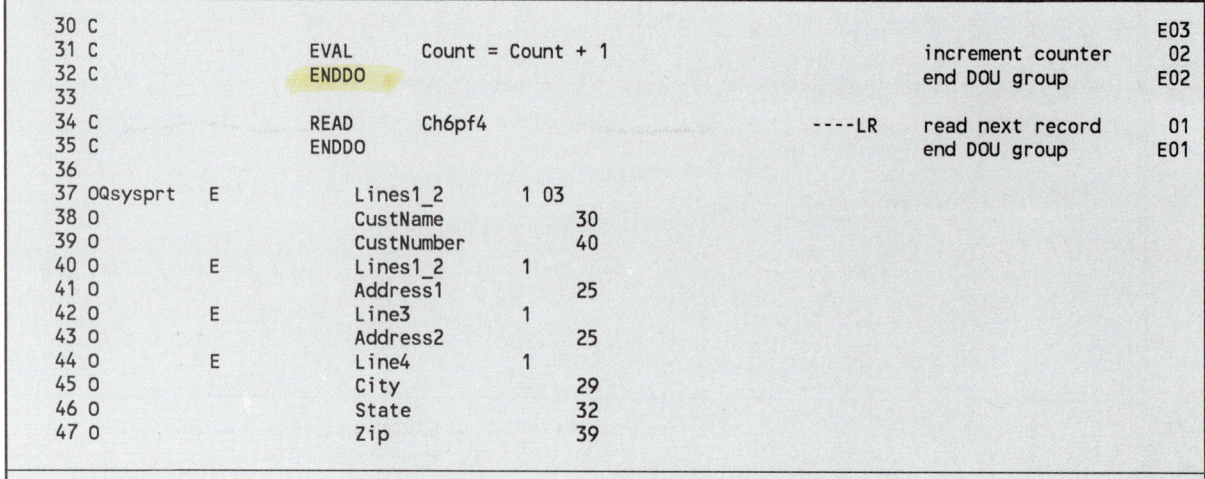

```
ENRICO FERMI              10000
10 NEUTRON LANE
CHICAGO               IL  04010
- - - - - - - - - - - - - - - -
ENRICO FERMI              10000
10 NEUTRON LANE
CHICAGO               IL  04010
- - - - - - - - - - - - - - - -
EDWARD TELLER             20000
ATOMIC LANE
PO BOX 239
LOS ALAMOS            NM  08803
- - - - - - - - - - - - - - - -
EDWARD TELLER             20000
ATOMIC LANE
PO BOX 239
LOS ALAMOS            NM  08803
```

File Description Specifications:

Line No.

2 Ch6pf4 is defined as an input, full-procedural, externally described, nonkeyed physical file.

3 Qsysprt is defined as a program-described printer file. The default form length is changed to 8 by the **FORMLEN(8)** keyword. Page overflow is defined so that it will occur on line 7 by the **FORMOFL(7)** keyword.

Definition Specifications:

6 Count is defined as a "standalone" field. The field is used within the **DOU** group to increment a counter that determines when to exit from the iterative process.

Figure 6-22 Compile listing of a program that uses the **DOU** operation to generate multiple labels for each customer. (Continued)

Calculation Specifications:

15 The **READ** instruction reads the first record from the Ch6pf4 physical file. If no records are stored in the file, the **LR** indicator will be set on.

18 The **DOW *INLR = *OFF** instruction tests the status of the **LR** indicator. If it is "off," the iterative process will continue. However, if **LR** is "on," indicating an end-of-file condition, the job will end.

19 The Count field is initialized to zero before the next record is processed.

22 When the **DOW** test on line 18 is "true," this **DOU** instruction will be executed. The expression Count = **2** in *Factor 2* controls when to exit from the **DOU** group. With this control, exit will occur after two labels are printed for the customer. Ideally, the *numeric literal 2 in the expression* would be accessed from a *data area* or entered via a *display file* and not "hard-coded" in the program. Because neither of these subjects has been introduced, the numeric literal method is used in this program.

23 The **EXCEPT** instruction controls the printing of the two Lines1_2 record formats on lines 37 through 41.

24–25 After Lines1_2 are printed, control returns to this **IF** instruction. The **IF** instruction tests the Address2 field for blanks. When the value in Address2 is greater than blanks (indicating a second address as P.O. Box or apartment number), the following **EXCEPT** instruction will control the printing of the Line3 record format on lines 42 through 43.

26 This **EXCEPT** instruction will control the printing of the Line4 record format. Within the "true" action of the **IF** instruction, the Line4 record format on lines 44 through 47 will be printed after the Address2 record values. Consequently, four lines are printed on a label when a value is stored in the Address2 field greater than blanks.

27 When the **IF** instruction test on line 24 is "false," this **ELSE** operation begins the "false" action.

28 This **EXCEPT** controls the printing of the Line4 record format after the Address1 record values when the Address2 field is blank (no second address).

29 The **ENDIF** operation ends the **IF** group that began on line 24.

31 The **EVAL** instruction increments the Count field (used as a "delimiter" in the **DOU** instruction) by **1.**

32 This **ENDDO** operation ends the **DOU** group that began on line 22. The relational test for the **DOU** instruction on line 22 is made at this operation. When the value in Count is equal to 2, exit from the **DOU** group will occur.

34 This **READ** instruction reads another record from the Ch6pf4 physical file. If end-of-file is read, the **LR** indicator will be set on.

35 This **ENDDO** operation ends the **DOW** group that began on line 18 and transfers control back to the **DOW** instruction where the status of the **LR** indicator is tested. If **LR** is "off," the iterative process will continue. When it is "on," the job will end.

Output Specifications:

37–41 The printing of the two Lines1_2 record formats is controlled by the **EXCEPT** instruction on line 23.

42–43 The printing of the Line3 record formats is controlled by the **EXCEPT** instruction on line 25. The values for this output record are printed only if the Address2 field has a value greater than blanks.

44–47 Depending on the value in the Address2 field, the printing of the Line4 record format is controlled by the **EXCEPT** instruction on line 26 or the one on line 28. If the value in Address2 is greater than blanks, the **EXCEPT** instruction on line 26 will be executed. However, if the value in Address2 is blanks, the **EXCEPT** instruction on line 28 will be executed.

Figure 6-22 Compile listing of a program that uses the **DOU** operation to generate multiple labels for each customer. (Continued)

The `DOW` *(Do While)* Operation

The **DOW** operation differs from **DOU** in that the **DOW** group is performed only if the logical expression is initially true (unlike the **DOU** operation, where the group is executed *at least once*). Similar to the **DOU** operation, a programmer-supplied counter must be included within the **DOW** group to control exit from the looping sequence. Figure 6-23 details the syntax and processing logic of the **DOW** operation.

```
*.. 1 ...+... 2 ...+... 3 ...+... 4 ...+... 5 ...+... 6 ...+... 7 ...+... 8 ...+... 9 ...+ ...10
CLON01Factor 1+++++++Opcode&ExtExtended-factor2+++++++++++++++++++++++++++++++Comments++++++++++++
 * Instructions within the DOW group are executed only when the logical expression is
 * initially true.  A programmer-supplied counter determines if subsequent "loops" are
 * performed.

C  1       2            DOW        logical expression
                         3                 4
C                        :
C  5       6            ENDDO              8
                          7
```

SEU CX format must be used when an expression is specified with the **DOW** operation.

DOW operation syntax:

1. Conditioning indicator(s) may be specified at total time (*L0* field) or at detail time (*N01* field). If the indicator(s) specified is/are on, control will branch to the first executable instruction following the **ENDDO** operation. The status of the indicator is tested every time the **DOW** operation is executed.
2. *Factor 1* is not used.
3. The **DOW** operation must be entered in the *Opcode* field.
4. A logical expression must be specified in the *Extended-factor2* field.
5. Conditioning indicators are optional for an **ENDDO** operation.
6. *Factor 1* is not used.
7. An **ENDDO** or **END** operation entered in the *OpCode* field must end a **DOW** group.
8. *Factor 2* is not used with an **ENDDO** operation that delimits a **DOW** group.

Processing logic:

- The **DOW** operation executes the instructions within the group only if the relational test in the expression is initially "true."
- Unlike the **DO** operation, a **DOW** operation does not include an automatic counter (index). Looping must be controlled by a programmer-supplied counter within the **DOW** group that is tested in the logical expression.

Figure 6-23 **DOW** operation syntax and processing logic.

The original example customer label program using the **DO** operation is modified in Figure 6-24 with the **DOW** operation.

```
Line    <---------------------- Source Specifications ----------------------------><---- Comments ----> Do
Number ....1....+....2....+....3....+....4....+....5....+....6....+....7....+....8....+....9....+...10 Num
                         S o u r c e   L i s t i n g
     1  * Customer labels program using DOW operation control....
     2 FCh6pf4    IF   E             DISK
       *--------------------------------------------------------------------------------------------*
       *                              RPG name          External name                               *
       * File name. . . . . . . . :   CH6PF4            STAN/CH6PF4                                 *
       * Record format(s) . . . . :   CH6PF4R           CH6PF4R                                     *
       *--------------------------------------------------------------------------------------------*
     3 FQsysprt   O    F  132        PRINTER FORMLEN(8) FORMOFL(7)
     4
     5  * work field....
     6 D Count           S              2 0                                    DOW counter control
     7=ICH6PF4R
```

Figure 6-24 Compile listing of a program that uses the **DOW** operation to generate multiple labels for each customer.

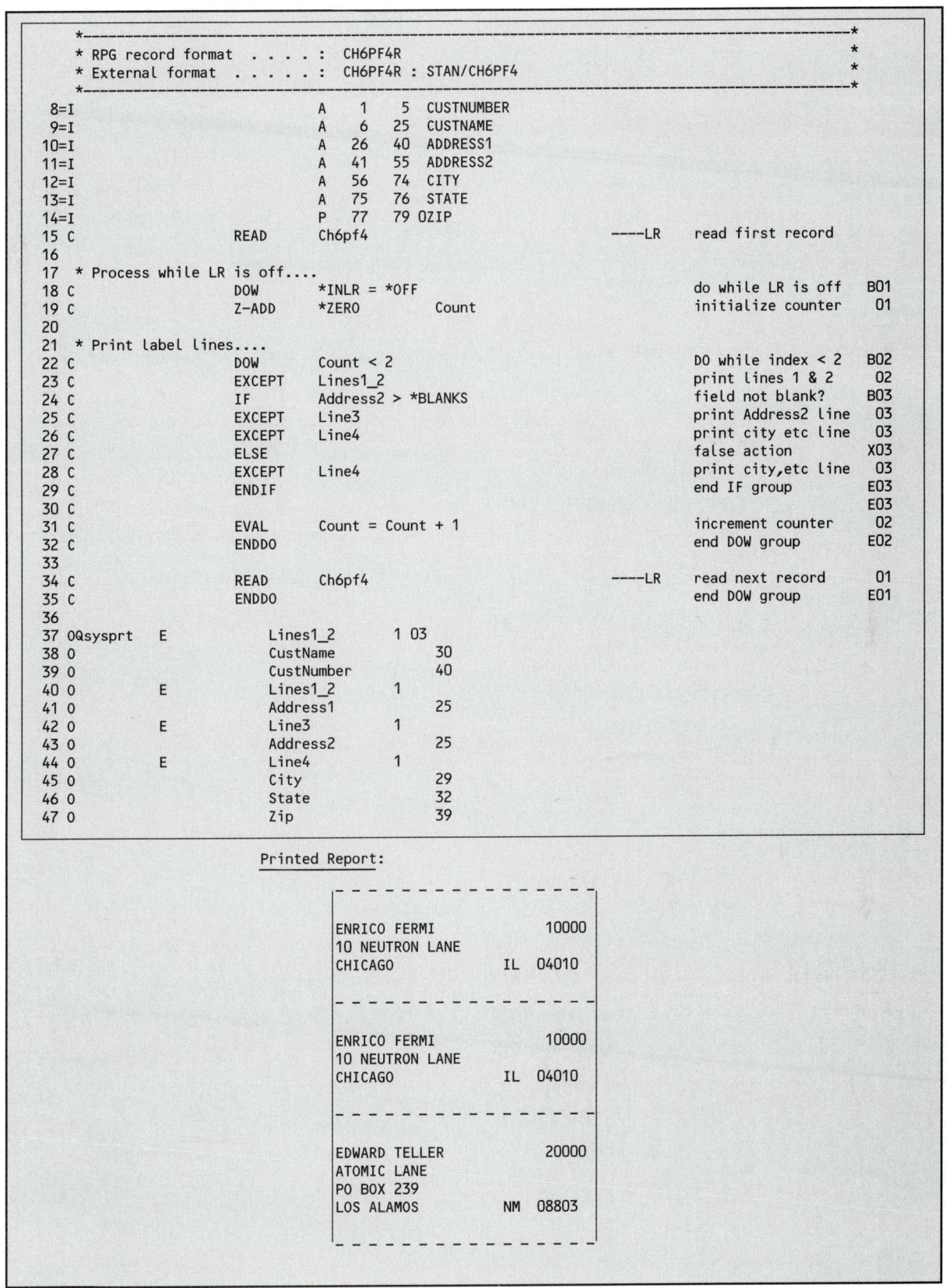

```
     *------------------------------------------------------------------------------------*
     * RPG record format  . . . . :  CH6PF4R                                              *
     * External format  . . . . . :  CH6PF4R : STAN/CH6PF4                                *
     *------------------------------------------------------------------------------------*
 =I                          A    1    5 CUSTNUMBER
 =I                          A    6   25 CUSTNAME
 =I                          A   26   40 ADDRESS1
 =I                          A   41   55 ADDRESS2
 =I                          A   56   74 CITY
 =I                          A   75   76 STATE
 =I                          P   77   79 0ZIP
 C                 READ      Ch6pf4                            ----LR     read first record

   * Process while LR is off....
 C                 DOW       *INLR = *OFF                                 do while LR is off    B01
 C                 Z-ADD     *ZERO         Count                          initialize counter     01

   * Print label lines....
 C                 DOW       Count < 2                                    DO while index < 2    B02
 C                 EXCEPT    Lines1_2                                     print lines 1 & 2      02
 C                 IF        Address2 > *BLANKS                           field not blank?      B03
 C                 EXCEPT    Line3                                        print Address2 line    03
 C                 EXCEPT    Line4                                        print city etc line    03
 C                 ELSE                                                   false action          X03
 C                 EXCEPT    Line4                                        print city,etc line    03
 C                 ENDIF                                                  end IF group          E03
 C                                                                                              E03
 C                 EVAL      Count = Count + 1                            increment counter      02
 C                 ENDDO                                                  end DOW group         E02

 C                 READ      Ch6pf4                            ----LR     read next record       01
 C                 ENDDO                                                  end DOW group         E01

 OQsysprt   E            Lines1_2       1 03
 O                       CustName            30
 O                       CustNumber          40
 O          E            Lines1_2       1
 O                       Address1            25
 O          E            Line3          1
 O                       Address2            25
 O          E            Line4          1
 O                       City                29
 O                       State               32
 O                       Zip                 39
```

Printed Report:

```
 - - - - - - - - - - - - - - - - -

ENRICO FERMI                10000
10 NEUTRON LANE
CHICAGO               IL  04010

 - - - - - - - - - - - - - - - - -

ENRICO FERMI                10000
10 NEUTRON LANE
CHICAGO               IL  04010

 - - - - - - - - - - - - - - - - -

EDWARD TELLER               20000
ATOMIC LANE
PO BOX 239
LOS ALAMOS            NM  08803

 - - - - - - - - - - - - - - - - -
```

Figure 6-24 Compile listing of a program that uses the **DOW** operation to generate multiple labels for each customer. (Continued)

```
EDWARD TELLER            20000
ATOMIC LANE
PO BOX 239
LOS ALAMOS            NM  08803

- - - - - - - - - - - - - - - - -
```

File Description Specifications:

Line No.

2 Ch6pf4 is defined as an input, full-procedural, externally described, nonkeyed physical file.

3 Qsysprt is defined as a program-described printer file. The default form length is changed to 8 by the **FORMLEN(8)** keyword. Page overflow is defined so that it will occur on line 7 by the **FORMOFL(7)** keyword.

Definition Specifications:

6 Count is defined as a "standalone" field. The field is used within the **DOW** group to increment a counter that determines when to exit from the iterative process.

Calculation Specifications:

15 The **READ** instruction reads the first record from the Ch6pf4 physical file. If no records are stored in the file, the **LR** indicator will be set on.

18 The **DOW *INLR = *OFF** instruction tests the status of the **LR** indicator. If it is "off," the iterative process will continue. However, if **LR** is "on," indicating an end-of-file condition, the job will end.

19 The Count field is initialized to zero before the next record is processed.

22 When the **DOW** test on line 18 is "true," this **DOW** instruction will be executed. The expression Count < **2** in *Factor 2* controls when to exit from the **DOW** group. With this control, exit will occur after two labels are printed for the customer. Ideally, the *numeric literal* **2** *in the expression* would be accessed from a *data area* or entered via a *display file* and not "hard-coded" in the program. Because neither of these subjects has been introduced, the numeric literal method is used in this program.

23 The **EXCEPT** instruction controls the printing of the two Lines1_2 record formats on lines 37 through 41.

24–25 After Lines1_2 are printed, control returns to this **IF** instruction. The **IF** instruction tests the Address2 field for blanks. When the value in Address2 is greater than blanks (indicating a second address as P.O. Box or apartment number), the following **EXCEPT** instruction will control the printing of the Line3 record format on lines 42 through 43.

26 This **EXCEPT** instruction will control the printing of the Line4 record format. Within the "true" action of the **IF** instruction, the Line4 record format on lines 44 through 47 will be printed after the Address2 record values. Consequently, four lines are printed on a label when a value is stored in the Address2 field greater than blanks.

27 When the **IF** instruction test on line 24 is "false," this **ELSE** operation begins the "false" action.

28 This **EXCEPT** controls the printing of the Line4 record format after the Address1 record values when the Address2 field is blank (no second address).

29 The **ENDIF** operation ends the **IF** group that began on line 24.

31 The **EVAL** instruction increments the Count field (used as a "delimiter" in the **DOW** instruction) by **1**.

32 This **ENDDO** operation ends the **DOW** group that began on line 22. Unlike the **DOU** operation, the relational test is made at the **DOW** instruction on line 22.

34 This **READ** instruction reads another record from the Ch6pf4 physical file. If end-of-file is read, the **LR** indicator will be set on.

35 This **ENDDO** operation ends the **DOW** group that began on line 18 and transfers control back to the **DOW** instruction, where the status of the **LR** indicator is tested. If **LR** is "off," the iterative process will continue. When it is "on," the job will end.

Output Specifications:

37–41 The printing of the two Lines1_2 record formats is controlled by the **EXCEPT** instruction on line 23.

42–43 The printing of the Line3 record format is controlled by the **EXCEPT** instruction on line 25. The values for this output record are printed only if the Address2 field has a value greater than blanks.

44–47 Depending on the value in the Address2 field, the printing of the Line4 record format is controlled by the **EXCEPT** instruction on line 26 or the one on line 28. If the value in Address2 is greater than blanks, the **EXCEPT** instruction on line 26 will be executed. However, if the value in Address2 is blanks, the **EXCEPT** instruction on line 28 will be executed.

Figure 6-24 Compile listing of a program that uses the **DOW** operation to generate multiple labels for each customer. (Continued)

Additional Structured Operations

The **LEAVE** *(Leave a DO Group)* and **ITER** *(Iterate)* operations support additional control within a **DO, DOU,** or **DOW** group. When a **LEAVE** operation is executed within any of the "DO groups," control is transferred to the instruction *following* the related **ENDDO** (or **END**) operation. The **ITER** operation passes control to the related **ENDDO** or **END** operation and performs the next iteration.

Figure 6-25 illustrates how the **LEAVE** and **ITER** operations are used. Other than the *Opcode* field entry and optional conditional indicators in the *L0* and *N01* fields, no additional entries are supported for either operation.

Note that the **LEAVE** and **ITER** operations may be entered with either the **SEU C** or **CX** format.

```
*.. 1 ...+... 2 ...+... 3 ...+... 4 ...+... 5 ...+... 6 ...+... 7 ...+... 8 ...+... 9 ...+ ...10
CLON01Factor 1++++++Opcode(E)+Factor2+++++++Result++++++++Len++D_HiLOEQ....Comments+++++++++++++
CLON01Factor 1++++++Opcode&ExtExtended-factor2+++++++++++++++++++++++++++++Comments+++++++++++++
 * When indicator 04 is on, the ITER operation transfers control to the ENDDO operation and the
 * next iteration of the DOW group is performed.
 * When indicator 05 is on, the LEAVE operation causes an "early" exit from the DOW group by
 * transferring control to the first executable instruction following the ENDDO operation.
C                   :
C                   DOW       *IN03 = *OFF    Transfers control to the ENDDO
C                   :                         operation and next iteration
C                   IF        *IN04 = *ON     of the DOW group is performed
C                   ITER      ----------------
C                   ENDIF
C                   :
C                   IF        *IN05 = *ON
C                   LEAVE     ----------------Transfers control to the first
C                   ENDIF                     executable instruction follow-
C                   :                         ing the ENDDO operation. Con-
C                   ENDDO                     trols "early exit" from the
C                   :                         DOW group.
```

Figure 6-25 Examples of the **LEAVE** and **ITER** operations.

TRADITIONAL RPG SYNTAX FOR STRUCTURED OPERATIONS

Traditional **RPG III** syntax for the **IF/ELSE, SELECT/WHxx/OTHER, DOUxx,** and **DOWxx** groups are explained in the following sections. All of these operations require the **SEU C** format be used to enter the instructions.

Traditional IFxx/ELSE Operations

Figure 6-26 illustrates and explains the syntax of the traditional **RPG III IFxx** operation. Note that entries must always be made in the *Factor 1*, *Opcode*, and *Factor 2* fields.

```
*.. 1 ...+... 2 ...+... 3 ...+... 4 ...+... 5 ...+... 6 ...+... 7 ...+... 8 ...+... 9 ...+ ...10
CLON01Factor 1++++++Opcode(E)+Factor2+++++++Result++++++++Len++D_HiLOEQ....Comments+++++++++++++
 * Simple IF instruction. If the value in ItemA is equal to the value in ItemB, the instructions
 * within the IF group will be executed.
C     ItemA         IFEQ      ItemB
C                   :
C                   ENDIF
```

Figure 6-26 Traditional **IFxx** and **ELSE** operations syntax and example instructions.

```
 * Example IF/ELSE group.  If the value in ItemA is greater than or equal to the value in ItemB,
 * the instructions within the IFGE group will be executed.  If the relational test is false,
 * the instructions after the ELSE operation (and before the ENDIF operation) will be executed.

C      ItemA           IFGE      ItemB
C  1     2              3          4
                        :
C                      ELSE
C                       5
                        :
C                      ENDIF
                        6
```

IF operation syntax:

1. Conditioning indicators may be specified in the *LO* and/or *NO1* fields.
2. *Factor 1* and *Factor 2* must contain either a literal, field name, array element, table name, or data structure subfield and be the same type (numeric or character).
3. The **IFxx** operation must be left-justified in the *Opcode* field. The **xx** entry must include one of the following:

xx Option	Relational Test
EQ	Value in *Factor 1* is equal to the value in *Factor 2.*
GE	Value in *Factor 1* is greater than or equal to the value in *Factor 2.*
GT	Value in *Factor 1* is greater than the value in *Factor 2.*
LE	Value in *Factor 1* is less than or equal to the value in *Factor 2.*
LT	Value in *Factor 1* is less than the value in *Factor 2.*
NE	Value in *Factor 1* is not equal to the value in *Factor 2.*

Relational tests may be compounded with **AND** and/or **OR** instructions. Each related **AND/OR** instruction(s) must include a *Factor 1* and *Factor 2* entry.

4. *Result* and *HiLOEQ* fields are not used.
5. An **ELSE** operation must be specified after its related **IFxx** group of instructions. The instructions within the related **ELSE** group are executed only when the related **IFxx** instruction test is false.
6. **ENDIF** (or **END**) operation must end an **IFXX** or **IFxx/ELSE** group.

IFxx and **IFxx/ELSE** groups may be nested within each other.

Figure 6-26 Traditional **IFxx** and **ELSE** operations syntax and example instructions. (Continued)

The Traditional RPG III DOU and DOW Operations

Figure 6-27 illustrates and explains the syntax of the traditional **DOUxx** and **DOWxx** operations. Note that the **SEU C** format must be used to enter traditional instructions.

```
*.. 1 ...+... 2 ...+... 3 ...+... 4 ...+... 5 ...+... 6 ...+... 7 ...+... 8 ...+... 9 ...+ ...10
CL0N01Factor 1++++++Opcode(E)+Factor2+++++++Result++++++++Len++D_HiLOEQ....Comments+++++++++++++
 * Entries of the same type must be included in Factors 1 and 2.  Because the relational test is
 * made at the ENDDO operation, the instructions within the DOU group will be executed at least
 * once.
```

Figure 6-27 Traditional **DOUxx** and **DOWxx** operations syntax and example instructions.

```
C      ItemA          DOUEQ     ItemB
C  1       2            3          4              5                    5
C                       :
C                     ENDDO
                        6
C                       :
 * Entries of the same type must be included in Factors 1 and 2.  Because the relational test is
 * made at the DOWLT operation, the instructions within the DOW group will be executed only if
 * the test is true.

C      ItemA          DOWLT     ItemB
C  1       2            3          4              5                    5
C                       :
C                     ENDDO
                        6
```

DOU operation syntax:

1. Conditioning indicators may be specified in the *LO* and/or *NO1* fields.
2. *Factor 1* must contain either a literal, field name, array element, table name, or data structure subfield and be the same type (both numeric or both character) as the *Factor 2* entry.
3. The relational tests may be **EQ, GE, GT, LE, LT,** and **NE** with the **DOU** operation **xx** entry.
4. *Factor 2* must contain either a literal, field name, array element, table name, or data structure subfield and be the same type (both numeric or both character) as the *Factor 1* entry.
5. The *Result* and *HiLOEQ* fields are not used.

   A counter, defined as either the *Factor 1* or *2* entry, must be included within the **DOU** group to control exit from the iteration.

   Because the relational test is made at the required **ENDDO** (or **END**) operation, a **DOU** group of instructions will execute at least once.
6. An **ENDDO** (or **END**) operation must end a **DOU** group.

DOW operation syntax:

1. Conditioning indicators may be specified in the *LO* and/or *NO1* fields.
2. The relational tests may be **EQ, GE, GT, LE, LT,** and **NE** with the **DOW** operation.
3. *Factor 2* must contain either a literal, field name, array element, table name, or data structure subfield and be the same type (both numeric or both character) as the *Factor 1* entry.
4. The *Result* and *HiLOEQ* fields are not used.

   A counter, defined as either the *Factor 1* or *2* entry, must be included within the **DOW** group to control exit from the iteration.

   Because the relational test is made at the **DOW** instruction, the instructions within the **DOW** group will be executed if the test is initially "true."
5. An **ENDDO** (or **END**) operation must end a **DOW** group.

Figure 6-27 Traditional **DOUxx** and **DOWxx** operations syntax and example instructions. (Continued)

The Traditional COMP Operation

The **COMP** operation was used in the earliest version of **RPG** to control relational testing. It has been replaced by the **IF/ELSE** and **WHENxx/OTHER** operations and should not be used in today's structured **RPG IV** programs. However, because maintenance of existing **RPG** programs is a common function of the programmer, an understanding of the **COMP** operation's syntax is essential. Figure 6-28 shows coding examples of the **COMP** operation and explains its syntax.

```
*.. 1 ...+... 2 ...+... 3 ...+... 4 ...+... 5 ...+... 6 ...+... 7 ...+... 8 ...+... 9 ...+ ...10
CLON01Factor 1++++++Opcode(E)+Factor2+++++++Result++++++++Len++D_HiLOEQ....Comments++++++++++++
 * The value in ItemX is compared to the value in ItemY.  If the value in ItemX is greater than
 * the value in ItemY, indicator 30 (Hi field) will be turned on.  Any subsequent instructions
 * conditioned by indicator 30 (or without any indicator) will be executed.
C      ItemX          COMP      ItemY                            30
C  30                 :
C  1       2          3         4          5                        6

 * The value in ItemS is compared to the value in ItemT.  If the value in ItemS is greater than
 * the value in ItemT, indicator 20 in the Hi field will be turned on.  If the value in ItemS
 * is less than the value in ItemT, the indicator 21 in the LO field will be turned on. If ItemS
 * is equal to the value in ItemT, indicator 22 in the EQ field will be turned on.
C      ItemS          COMP      ItemT                            202122
C   20                :
C   21                :
C   22                :
```

COMP operation syntax:

1. Conditioning indicators may be specified in the *LO* and/or *N01* fields.
2. Entry in *Factor 1* must be the same type (numeric or character) as the *Factor 2* entry.
3. The **COMP** operation must be entered left-justified in the *Opcode* field.
4. Entry in *Factor 2* must be the same type (numeric or character) as the *Factor 1* entry.
5. *Result* field is not used.
6. One to three indicators must be specified in the *HiLOEQ* fields. The related indicator is turned on if the relational test is true (i.e., *Hi – Factor 1* value greater than the *Factor 2* value; *LO – Factor 1* value less than the *Factor 2* value; *EQ – Factor 1* value equal to the *Factor 2* value. The indicator turned on may be used to condition calculations and/or output instructions. Any instructions not conditioned by an indicator(s) will be executed.

Figure 6-28 Traditional **COMP** operation syntax and example instructions.

The Traditional GOTO Operation

The **GOTO** operation should *not* be used in today's structured **RPG IV** programs. It encourages "spaghetti" coding that is difficult to maintain. However, in the maintenance of older **RPG** programs, it will be seen and, therefore, must be understood. Figure 6-29 shows coding examples of the **GOTO** operation and explains its syntax.

```
*.. 1 ...+... 2 ...+... 3 ...+... 4 ...+... 5 ...+... 6 ...+... 7 ...+... 8 ...+... 9 ...+ ...10
CLON01Factor 1++++++Opcode(E)+Factor2+++++++Result++++++++Len++D_HiLOEQ....Comments++++++++++++
 * If indicator 02 is "on," the GOTO Skip instruction will branch control to the Skip TAG in-
 * struction.  Any instruction between the GOTO and TAG operations will not be executed.  If 02
 * is not "on," the GOTO instruction will be ignored and the instructions following the GOTO
 * operation executed.

C   02                GOTO      Skip                             30
C                     :
C                     :
C      Skip           TAG

 * Looping example.  If indicator 20 is on, the GCTO instruction will transfer control back to
 * the Loop TAG instruction and repeat the instructions between the GOTO and TAG operations.

C      Loop           TAG
C                     :              Without the conditioning indicator on the
C                     :              GOTO instruction, a perpetual loop would
C   20                GOTO      Loop occur, requiring a user's response
```

Figure 6-29 **GOTO/TAG** operations syntax and example instructions.

GOTO operation syntax:

1. Conditioning indicators may be specified in the *LO* and/or *NO1* fields. If one or more indicators are entered, the instruction is referred to as a conditional **GOTO.** If no indicator(s) is/are specified, the instruction is called an unconditional **GOTO.**
2. The *Factor 1* field is not used.
3. The **GOTO** operation name must be entered left-justified in the *Opcode* field.
4. The *Factor 2* entry must be a programmer-supplied **TAG** name that follows **RPG IV** field-naming conventions. Any number of **GOTO** instructions may include the same **TAG** name in *Factor 2*.
5. The *Result* and *HiLOEQ* fields are not used.

TAG operation syntax:

6. An **LO-L9** or **LR** indicator may be specified in the *LO* field. Indicators are not permitted in the *NO1* field.
7. *Factor 1* must include the name of the entry in *Factor 2* of the related **GOTO** instruction(s).
8. The **TAG** operation name must be left-justified in the *OpCode* field.
9. *Factor 2, Result,* and *HiLOEQ* fields are not used.

Figure 6-29 GOTO/TAG operations syntax and example instructions. (Continued)

The Traditional CABxx *(Compare and Branch)* Operation

The **CABxx** *(Compare and Branch)* operation includes a relational test (**EQ, GT, LT, GE, LE,** or **NE** for the **xx** entry) and the **GOTO** operation in one instruction. Again, because **CABxx** is not a structured operation, it should not be used in **RPG IV** programs. Figure 6-30 details the syntax of the **CABxx** operation and illustrates how it is used to control branching and looping.

```
*.. 1 ...+... 2 ...+... 3 ...+... 4 ...+... 5 ...+... 6 ...+... 7 ...+... 8 ...+... 9 ...+ ...10
CL0N01Factor 1+++++++Opcode(E)+Factor2+++++++Result++++++++Len++D_HiLOEQ....Comments+++++++++++++
 * When the CABEQ instruction is executed, the relational test (EQ) is made between the values
 * in ItemC and ItemD (which must be the same type).  If the test is true, control will branch
 * to the related Over/TAG instruction and the instructions between the CABEQ and TAG operations
 * will not be executed.  However, if the relational test is false, the instructions following
 * the CABEQ statement will be executed.

C     ItemC          CABEQ     ItemD          Over
C                      :
C                      :
C     Over           TAG

 * Looping example.  If the value in ItemE is less than the value in ItemF, the CABLT
 * instruction will transfer control back to the Again/TAG statement and the iteration
 * (looping) process continued.  Exit from the loop will occur when the value in ItemE
 * is not less than the value in ItemF.

C     Again          TAG
C                      :
C                      :
C     ItemE          CABLT     ItemF          Again
```

Figure 6-30 CABxx operation syntax and example instructions.

CABxx operation syntax:

1. Conditioning indicators may be specified in the *LO* and/or *NO1* fields. If one or more indicators are entered, the instruction is referred to as a conditional **CABxx.** If no indicator(s) is/are specified, the instruction is called an unconditional **CABxx.**

2. *Factor 1* and *Factor 2* must contain the items to be compared. Both items must be the same type (numeric or character).

3. The **xx** entry in the **CABxx** operation may be **EQ, LT, GT, GE, LE,** or **NE.** The **CABxx** operation name must be entered left-justified in the *Opcode* field.

4. The *Result* field entry must be a programmer-supplied **TAG** name that follows **RPG IV** field-naming conventions. Any number of **CABxx** instructions may include the same **TAG** name in the *Result* field.

5. *Resulting indicator* entries in the *HiLOEQ* fields are optional. An indicator specified in the *Hi* field will turn on if *F1 > F2;* an indicator in the *LO* field will turn on if *F1 < F2;* and an indicator in the *EQ* field will turn on if *F1 = F2.*

TAG operation syntax:

6. An **LO–L9** or **LR** indicator may be specified in the *LO* field. An indicator entry in the *NO1* field is not permitted.

7. *Factor 1* must include the name of the entry in the *Result* field of the related **CABxx** instruction(s).

8. The **TAG** operation name must be left-justified in the *OpCode* field.

9. *Factor 2, Result,* and *HiLOEQ* fields are not used.

Figure 6-30 CABxx operation syntax and example instructions. (Continued)

SUMMARY

The structured **RPG IV** operations discussed in this chapter include **IF** *(If Then),* **ELSE** *(Else Do),* **ENDIF** *(End If Group),* **SELECT** *(Begin a Select Group),* **ENDSL** *(End a Select Group),* **WHEN** *(When True Then Select),* **OTHER** *(Otherwise Select),* **DO** *(Do),* **DOU** *(Do Until),* **DOW** *(Do While),* and **ENDDO** *(End Do Group).* An **END** operation may be substituted for an **ENDDO, ENDIF,** or **ENDSL** instruction. Any **IF, DO, DOU, DOW,** or **SELECT** group must be ended by the related "End" operation.

The relational tests >, <, =, >=, <=, or <> must be specified with an **IF, DOU,** and **DOW** operation. In any case, the two items being compared must be the same type. The **WHEN** instruction must also include one of the relational operators. **IF, DOU, DOW,** and **WHEN** instructions may be coded as complex statements using the **AND** and/or **OR** logical operators.

Iterative processing is controlled by the structured operations **DO, DOU,** and **DOW.** The **DO** operation supports an index (either programmer- or system-defined) that is automatically incremented for every iteration. On the other hand, the **DOU** and **DOW** operations require a programmer-defined counter that must be incremented or decremented by one or more instruction(s) within the **DO** group. **ITER** and **LEAVE** operations may be included in **DO, DOU,** or **DOW** groups to control "early" branching. The **ITER** operation transfers control to the related **ENDDO** operation, and the iteration continues. The **LEAVE** operation causes control to exit from the **DO** group by branching to the first executable instruction following the related **ENDDO** operation.

Because most programmers will be required to maintain older **RPG** programs, the syntax for the **RPG III** format of the **IFxx, DOUxx,** and **DOWxx** structured operations was explained. In addition, the syntax of the *unstructured* operations **COMP, GOTO,** and **CABxx** was introduced.

QUESTIONS

6-1. Name eight **RPG IV** structured operations.

6-2. Explain the functions of the **IF** and **ELSE** operations.

6-3. What relational tests may be made in an **IF** operation?

6-4. How are complex **IF** instructions formatted?

6-5. May an **IF** instruction be specified without a related **ELSE** operation? May an **ELSE** operation be specified without a related **IF** instruction?

6-6. What operation(s) flags the end of an **IF** group?

Examine the following coding and answer Questions 6-7 to 6-11:

```
.... *.. 1 ...+... 2 ...+... 3 ...+... 4 ...+... 5 ...+... 6 ...+... 7 ...+... 8
     CLON01Factor 1++++++Opcode(E)+Extended-factor2++++++++++++++++++++++++++++++

   1 C                   IF        Sex = 'F'
   2 C                   EVAL      Female = Female + 1
   3 C                   ELSE
   4 C                   EVAL      Male = Male + 1
   5 C                   ENDIF
   6 C                     :
```

6-7. When the test on line 1 is true, what instructions are executed?

6-8. When the test on line 1 is false, what instructions are executed?

6-9. What is the function of the **ENDIF** operation? Is it required when an **IF** instruction is specified without a related **ELSE** operation?

6-10. Name the structure of the **IF/ELSE** group shown in the preceding example.

6-11. Name any syntax restrictions related to the entries to the "left" and the "right" of the relational operator (e.g., >, <, =, >=, <=, and <>).

Examine the following coding and answer Questions 6-12 to 6-16:

```
.... *.. 1 ...+... 2 ...+... 3 ...+... 4 ...+... 5 ...+... 6 ...+... 7 ...+... 8
     CLON01Factor 1++++++Opcode(E)+Extended-factor2++++++++++++++++++++++++++++++

   1 C                   IF        Sex = 'F'
   2 C                             AND Age < 21
   3 C                   EVAL      Group1 = Group1 + 1
   4 C                   ELSE
   5 C                   EVAL      Group2 = Group2 + 1
   6 C                   ENDIF
   7 C                     :
```

6-12. When the relational tests on lines 1 and 2 are true, what instructions are executed?

6-13. When the relational test on line 1 is true and the test on line 2 is false, what instructions are executed?

6-14. When the relational test on line 1 is false and the test on line 2 is true, what instructions are executed?

6-15. Under what test conditions will the instructions on lines 4 and 5 be executed?

6-16. When is the instruction on line 7 executed?

6-17. Are both relational tests made in an **AND** relationship? Explain.

Examine the following coding and answer Questions 6-18 to 6-24:

```
..... *.. 1 ...+... 2 ...+... 3 ...+... 4 ...+... 5 ...+... 6 ...+... 7 ...+... 8
      CLON01Factor 1++++++Opcode&ExtExtended-factor2+++++++++++++++++++++++++++++

    1 C                   IF        Code = 'T'
    2 C                             OR Code = 'X'
    3 C                   EVAL      Count1 = Count1 + 1
    4 C                   ELSE
    5 C                   EVAL      Count2 = Count2 + 1
    6 C                   ENDIF
    7 C                     :
```

6-18. When the relational tests on lines 1 and 2 are true, what instructions are executed?

6-19. When the relational test on line 1 is true and the test on line 2 is false, what instructions are executed?

6-20. When the relational test on line 1 is false and the test on line 2 is true, what instructions are executed?

6-21. Under what test conditions will the instructions on lines 4 and 5 be executed?

6-22. When is the instruction on line 7 executed?

6-23. Are both relational tests made in an **OR** relationship? Explain.

6-24. Name the **RPG IV** structured operations that support *iterative* processing. Identify the operation that *does not* require a programmer-supplied counter for loop control.

Examine the following coding and answer Questions 6-25 to 6-30:

```
..... *.. 1 ...+... 2 ...+... 3 ...+... 4 ...+... 5 ...+... 6 ...+... 7 ...+... 8
      CLON01Factor 1++++++Opcode&ExtFactor2+++++++Result++++++++Len++D_HiLOEQ....

    1 C     2             DO        IntPeriods    Times
    2 C                   :
    3 C                   ENDDO     2
    4 C                   :
```

6-25. Explain the function of the *Factor 1* entry (numeric literal **2**).

6-26. What is the function of the *Factor 2* entry (IntPeriods)?

6-27. Explain the function of the *Result* field entry (Times).

6-28. What is the function of the **ENDDO** operation and the numeric literal (**2**) specified in *Factor 2?*

6-29. Under what conditions will an exit occur from a **DO** group?

6-30. What relational tests are included in a **DO** instruction?

Examine the following coding and answer Questions 6-31 to 6-33:

```
..... *.. 1 ...+... 2 ...+... 3 ...+... 4 ...+... 5 ...+... 6 ...+... 7 ...+... 8
      CLON01Factor 1++++++Opcode&ExtExtended-factor2+++++++++++++++++++++++++++++

    1 C                   DOU       Count = IntPeriods
    2 C                    :
    3 C                   ENDDO
```

6-31. If the value in Count is equal to the value in IntPeriods when the **DOU** instruction is initially tested, what instruction is executed next?

6-32. At which instruction is the relational test made?

6-33. How is exit from a **DOU** group controlled?

6-34. How does the processing logic for the **DOW** operation differ from the **DOU** operation?

Examine the following coding and answer Questions 6-35 to 6-38:

```
..... *.. 1 ...+... 2 ...+... 3 ...+... 4 ...+... 5 ...+... 6 ...+... 7 ...+... 8
      CLON01Factor 1+++++++Opcode&ExtExtended-factor2+++++++++++++++++++++++++++++

    1 C                   DOW       Count = IntPeriods
    2 C                    :
    3 C                   ENDDO
```

6-35. If the value in Count is equal to the value in IntPeriods when the **DOW** instruction is initially tested, what instruction is executed next?

6-36. In which instruction is the relational test made?

6-37. How is exit from a **DOW** group controlled?

6-38. With the **DOU** or **DOW** instruction, are there any restrictions for the entries specified before and after the relational operator?

6-39. What operations may be included in a **SELECT** group?

6-40. In a **SELECT** group, what operation does the relation test(s)?

Examine the following coding and answer Questions 6-41 to 6-45:

```
..... *.. 1 ...+... 2 ...+... 3 ...+... 4 ...+... 5 ...+... 6 ...+... 7 ...+... 8
      CLON01Factor 1+++++++Opcode&ExtExtended-factor2+++++++++++++++++++++++++++++

    1 C                   SELECT
    2 C                   WHEN      WHEN Status = 'FT'
    3 C                    :
    4 C                   WHEN      WHEN Status = 'PT'
    5 C                    :
    6 C                   OTHER
    7 C                    :
    8 C                   ENDSL
```

6-41. When the relational test on line 2 is true, which instruction(s) is/are executed?

6-42. When the relational test on line 2 is false, which instruction(s) is/are executed?

6-43. When the relational test on line 4 is true, which instruction(s) is/are executed?

6-44. When the relational test on line 4 is false, which instruction(s) is/are executed?

6-45. If all of the **WHEN** tests are false, which instruction(s) is/are executed?

6-46. What is the format of the **RPG IV** *structured* **IF, ELSE, SELECT, WHEN, OTHER, DO, DOU,** and **DOW** operations in **RPG III** syntax?

6-47. What *unstructured* **RPG** operation supports relational testing?

6-48. What *unstructured* **RPG** operation supports branching and looping?

6-49. What *unstructured* **RPG** operation supports relational testing, branching, and looping?

PROGRAMMING ASSIGNMENTS

For each of the following programming assignments, a physical file must have been created and loaded with the related data records. Your instructor will inform you if you have to create the physical file and load it or if it has been prepared for the assignment.

Programming Assignment 6-1: SALES JOURNAL

Write an **RPG IV** program to generate a Sales Journal that summarizes all of a month's sales on account.

Processing: Read the input file consecutively, and for every record processed perform the following calculations:

1. Test the Sales Amount field on input for a negative and zero value. If one of those conditions is tested, *do not* perform any calculations for that record. Depending on the error condition, one of the two messages shown in the printer spacing chart that follows is to be printed with the transaction date, customer name, and invoice number from the related record.

For Valid Records:

2. Compute the sales tax by multiplying the sales amount by the numeric literal .0750.
3. Compute the total sale for the record by adding the sales tax to the sales amount.
4. Accumulate the sales amount, sales tax, and total sale into separate total fields.

Physical File Record Format:

PHYSICAL FILE DESCRIPTION

SYSTEM: AS/400	DATE: Yours
FILE NAME: Yours	REV NO: 0
RECORD NAME: Yours	KEY LENGTH: None
SEQUENCE: Nonkeyed	RECORD SIZE: 41

FIELD DEFINITIONS

FIELD NO	FIELD NAME	SIZE	TYPE	POSITION FROM	POSITION TO	COMMENTS
1	SALEDATE	6	P	1	4	
2	CUSTNAME	29	C	5	33	
3	INVOICE#	6	P	34	37	
4	SALEAMOUNT	7	P	38	41	2 decimals

Physical File Data:

Sales Date	Customer Name	Invoice Number	Sales Amount
080196	HUDSON MOTOR CAR COMPANY	40000	081200
080996	PACKARD COMPANY	40001	000000
081196	THE HUPMOBILE COMPANY	40002	857010
081696	THE TUCKER CAR COMPANY	40003	000212
082196	AUBURN INCORPORATED	40004	004500
082796	BRICKLIN LIMITED	40005	106891
083096	THE LOCOMOBILE CAR COMPANY	40006	214000
083196	STUDEBAKER CARS INCORPORATED	40007	005050

Report Design:

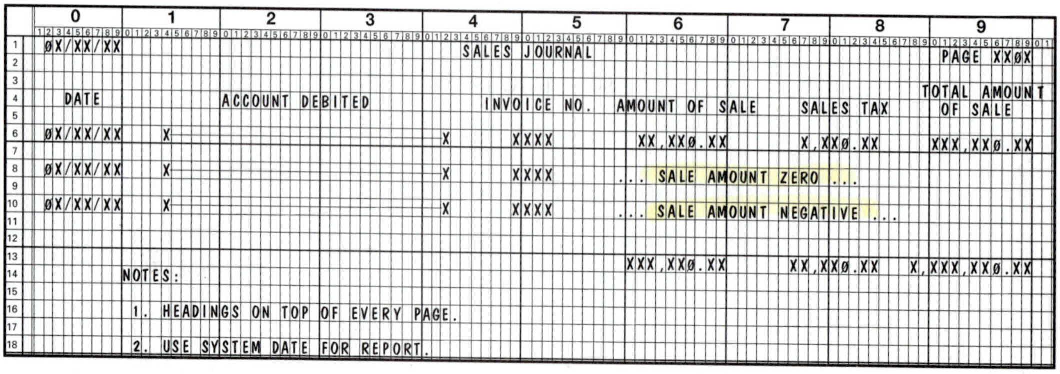

Programming Assignment 6-2: SALESPERSON SALARY/COMMISSION REPORT

From the following documentation, write an **RPG IV** program to generate the report detailed in the supplemental print chart.

The Happy Sales Company pays its sales employees salary plus a commission on net sales. Payments are based on the following:

1. All sales employees are paid a base salary regardless of their sales. Those with less than two years' employment are paid a $600 monthly base salary. Employees with two or more years are guaranteed a $1,000 monthly salary.
2. Net sales over $2,000 are eligible for a commission that is added to the base salary. In any case, no commission is paid on the first $2,000 of net sales.

The commission amount is determined as follows:

1. Two or More Years' Employment. Twenty percent (0.20) commission is paid on net sales (sales − returns) over $2,000. Any commission sales over $30,000 are paid an additional 5% commission.
2. Less Than Two Years' Employment. Twelve percent (0.12) commission is paid on net sales (sales − returns) over $2,000. Any commission sales over $25,000 are paid an additional 2% commission.

Summary:

Net Sales = Monthly Sales − Sales Return

Commission Sales = Net Sales − $2,000

All commission computations are based on commission sales.

Physical File Record Format:

PHYSICAL FILE DESCRIPTION

SYSTEM: AS/400	DATE: Yours
FILE NAME: Yours	REV NO: 0
RECORD NAME: Yours	KEY LENGTH: None
SEQUENCE: Nonkeyed	RECORD SIZE: 41

FIELD DEFINITIONS

FIELD NO	FIELD NAME	SIZE	TYPE	POSITION FROM	POSITION TO	COMMENTS
1	SALEPERSN#	5	C	1	5	
2	SALEPNAME	25	C	6	30	
3	YRSEMPLYED	2	P	31	32	
4	SALEAMOUNT	8	P	33	37	2 decimals
5	SALERETURN	7	P	38	41	2 decimals

Physical File Data:

Salesperson Number	Salesperson Name	Yrs Emp	Sales Amount	Sales Returns
11111	SIEGFRIED HOUNDSTOOTH	4	01125050	0100000
11112	FELIX GOODGUY	1	02800000	0000000
22222	OTTO MUTTENJAMMER	6	10000000	0000000
33333	HANS OFFENHAUSER	1	00250000	0070000
44444	BARNEY OLDFIELD	3	00190000	0000000
55555	WILLIAM PETTY	2	02200000	0000000

Report Design:

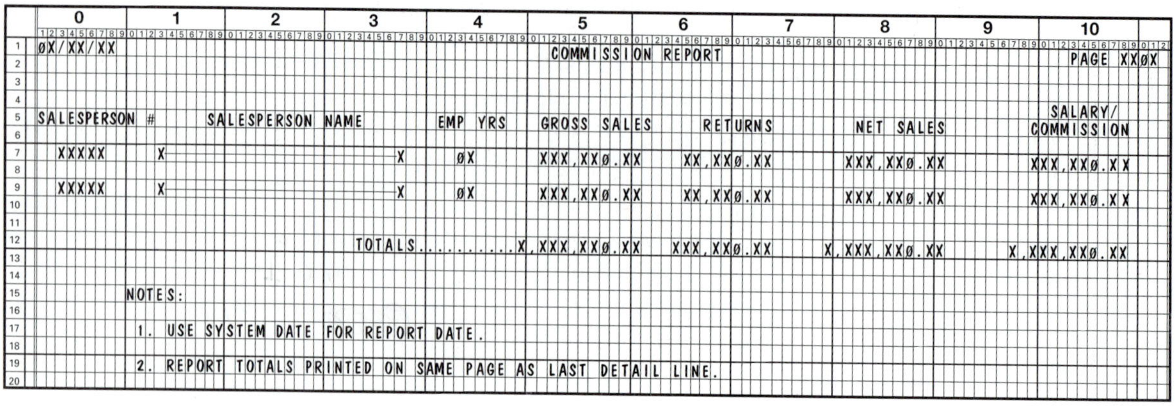

ØX/XX/XX
COMMISSION REPORT
PAGE XXØX
SALESPERSON #
SALESPERSON NAME
EMP YRS
GROSS SALES
RETURNS
NET SALES
SALARY/ COMMISSION
XXXXX X X ØX XXX,XXØ.XX XX,XXØ.XX XXX,XXØ.XX XXX,XXØ.XX
XXXXX X X ØX XXX,XXØ.XX XX,XXØ.XX XXX,XXØ.XX XXX,XXØ.XX
TOTALS..........X,XXX,XXØ.XX XXX,XXØ.XX X,XXX,XXØ.XX X,XXX,XXØ.XX
NOTES:
1. USE SYSTEM DATE FOR REPORT DATE.
2. REPORT TOTALS PRINTED ON SAME PAGE AS LAST DETAIL LINE.

Programming Assignment 6-3: PAYROLL REGISTER

A payroll register records the year-to-date and weekly payroll information for each employee. Federal income and social security taxes withheld to date and for the current week are included in the report. In addition, the week's gross and net pay amounts are also specified. Other deductions, such as hospitalization, retirement, union dues, and so forth, may also be subtracted from an employee's paycheck. From the record layout form, processing logic flowchart, and printer spacing chart that follow, write a structured **RPG IV** program to generate the required report.

Processing Logic Flowchart:

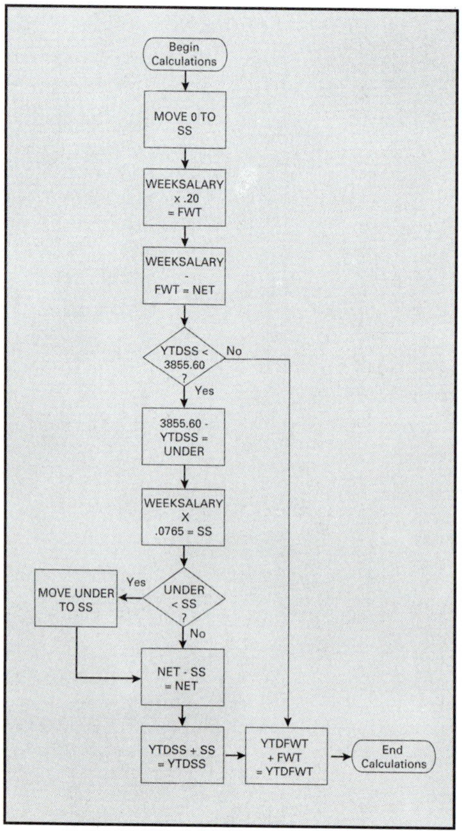

Physical File Record Format:

```
                        PHYSICAL FILE DESCRIPTION

SYSTEM: AS/400                                DATE: Yours
FILE NAME: Yours                              REV NO: 0
RECORD NAME: Yours                            KEY LENGTH: None
SEQUENCE: Nonkeyed                            RECORD SIZE: 41

                            FIELD DEFINITIONS

 FIELD    FIELD NAME    SIZE  TYPE     POSITION      COMMENTS
   NO                                 FROM    TO

   1      SSNO            9    P        1      5
   2      EMPNAM         20    C        6     25
   3      YTDWAG          7    P       26     29   2 decimals
   4      YTDFWT          7    P       30     33   2 decimals
   5      YTDSS           6    P       34     37   2 decimals
   6      WEKSAL          6    P       38     41   2 decimals
```

Physical File Data:

SS Number	Employee Name	Wages	YTD FWT	YTD SS	Week's Salary
050446666	BETTY BURPO	0250000	0050000	019125	050000
001012345	DICK TRACY	4965000	0993000	379823	075000
100709876	SHERLOCK HOLMES	6000000	1200000	385560	100000
020324321	JAMES BOND	5000000	1000000	382500	080000
020400050	INSPECTOR GADGET	5040000	1008000	385560	090000
110889999	PERRY MASON	0011000	0002200	000842	027500

Report Design:

```
    1  ØX/XX/XX                                         PAYROLL REGISTER                                      PAGE XXØX
    2
    3
    4     SS#           EMPLOYEE NAME          YTD WAGES       YTD FWT      YTD SS     WEEK PAY     WEEK EWT     WEEK SS    NET PAY
    5
    6   XXX-XX-XXXX X--------------------X    XX,XXØ.XX     XX,XXØ.XX    X,XXØ.XX    X,XXØ.XX     X,XXØ.XX     XXØ.XX    X,XXØ.XX
    7
    8   XXX-XX-XXXX X--------------------X    XX,XXØ.XX     XX,XXØ.XX    X,XXØ.XX    X,XXØ.XX     X,XXØ.XX     XXØ.XX    X,XXØ.XX
    9
   10      NOTES:
   11
   12         1. DATE IS SYSTEM SUPPLIED.
   13
   14         2. HEADINGS ON TOP OF EVERY PAGE.
```

Programming Assignment 6-4: STOCKBROKER'S COMMISSION REPORT

Write an **RPG IV** program to generate the stockbroker's commission report illustrated in the supplemental printer spacing chart.

Calculations:

Step 1: Multiply the number of shares purchased by the cost per share (input values) to calculate the total dollars of stock purchased.

Step 2: Test the stock exchange input field to determine on which exchange the stock is listed. The stock exchange codes are as follows:

NY New York Stock Exchange
AM American Stock Exchange
OV Over-the-Counter Exchange

Step 3: On the basis of the following individual stock exchange rates, compute the broker commission on the total dollars of stock purchased:

NY 5.1% AM 4.2% OV 3.5%

Step 4: Accumulate separate totals for the number of transactions related to each stock exchange, and print at LR time.

Step 5: Test the stock exchange input field, and print the related code on each detail line as shown in the printer spacing chart.

Physical File Record Format:

PHYSICAL FILE DESCRIPTION

SYSTEM: AS/400	DATE: Yours
FILE NAME: Yours	REV NO: 0
RECORD NAME: Yours	KEY LENGTH: None
SEQUENCE: Nonkeyed	RECORD SIZE: 35

FIELD DEFINITIONS

FIELD NO	FIELD NAME	SIZE	TYPE	POSITION FROM	POSITION TO	COMMENTS
1	ACTNUMBER	5	C	1	5	
2	STOCKNAME	20	C	6	25	
3	NO_SHARES	6	P	26	29	0 decimals
4	SHARECOST	6	P	30	33	3 decimals
5	EXCHANGE	2	C	34	35	

Physical File Data:

Acct#	Stock Name	Number of Shares	Cost/ Share	Stock Exchange
10000	IBM CORPORATION	001000	057125	NY
12000	ECHLIN MFG	000050	025500	OV
13000	BENQUET INC	010000	004250	NY
14000	BIC CORPORATION	000300	002600	AM
15000	BLACK & DECKER	001500	023750	OV
16000	TRANS-LUX	100000	009125	AM
17000	ALCIDE CORPORATION	025000	003125	OV
18000	PEOPLE'S BANK	004000	009500	OV
19000	XEROX	000100	051375	NY
20000	DU PONT	000300	088125	NY

Report Design:

```
ØX/XX/XX                        STOCK BROKER COMMISSION REPORT                            PAGE XXØX

                                    SHARES     PRICE/      PURCHASE IN     STOCK      BROKER
   ACT#       STOCK PURCHASED     PURCHASED    SHARE         DOLLARS      EXCHANGE COMMISSION

   XXXXX   X------------------X    XXX,XØX    X,XXØ.XX    XX,XXX,XXØ.XX      XX    XX,XXX,XXØ.XX

   XXXXX   X------------------X    XXX,XØX    X,XXØ.XX    XX,XXX,XXØ.XX      XX    XX,XXX,XXØ.XX


             NUMBER OF XX EXCHANGE TRANSACTIONS: XXØX
             NUMBER OF XX EXCHANGE TRANSACTIONS: XXØX
             NUMBER OF XX EXCHANGE TRANSACTIONS: XXØX
```

Programming Assignment 6-5: STRAIGHT-LINE DEPRECIATION SCHEDULE

Write an **RPG IV** program to generate a report that details a depreciation schedule for a company's fixed assets. Depreciation is a tax-deductible expense for assets that are used in the production of income. It may be defined as the "allocation of the cost of an asset over its useful life." Because of its simplicity and acceptance by the Internal Revenue Service, one of the most popular determinations of annual depreciation expense is the straight-line method, which is computed by the following formula:

$$\text{Annual Depreciation} = \frac{\text{Cost} - \text{Salvage (Trade-In)}}{\text{Estimated Useful Life}}$$

where:

Annual Depreciation = the amount of depreciation expense computed for each year of the asset's life,
Cost = the original cost of the asset plus any capital improvements,
Salvage Value (also called Trade-In) = the amount the asset will realize as scrap or trade-in at the end of its estimated useful life,
Estimated Useful Life = the expected life of the asset based on its estimated productivity. The tax laws have established useful life by general categories of assets. For example, autos and light-duty trucks are assigned a three-year life, whereas all other capital goods (machinery, equipment, and so forth) have a five-year life.

Physical File Record Format:

PHYSICAL FILE DESCRIPTION

SYSTEM: AS/400	DATE: Yours
FILE NAME: Yours	REV NO: 0
RECORD NAME: Yours	KEY LENGTH: None
SEQUENCE: Nonkeyed	RECORD SIZE: 40

FIELD DEFINITIONS

FIELD NO	FIELD NAME	SIZE	TYPE	POSITION FROM	POSITION TO	COMMENTS
1	ASSETNAME	25	C	1	25	
2	PURCHDATE	6	P	26	29	
3	COST	9	P	30	34	2 decimals
4	EUL	2	P	35	36	0 decimals
5	SALVALUE	6	P	37	40	0 decimals

Physical File Data:

Asset Name	Date of Purchase	Cost	EUL	Salvage Value
BPT MILLING MACHINE	051497	001500000	07	003000
IBM AS/400 - MODEL E	021097	037500000	05	020000
IBM MICRO - PENTIUM	011197	000280000	03	000400
OFFICE FURNITURE	100197	000900000	10	000600
FACTORY BUILDING	061597	120000000	18	000000

Processing: Read the physical file and for every record processed compute the annual depreciation expense for the asset based on the formula that has been given. Notice that the accumulated depreciation and book value must be computed each year for the life of the asset. The printer spacing chart indicates the field sizes for these items. The annual depreciation, accumulated depreciation, and book value amounts are rounded to the nearest dollar. Because of rounding, the book value after the last year's depreciation as calculated may not equal the cost of the asset. Any dollar difference must be added to the last year's annual depreciation amount, so the book value is zero for the last year.

Report Design: Page overflow is to be specified in the report for the two heading lines for the columns (i.e., YEAR, ANNUAL, ACCUMULATED, BOOK, and so forth) only and not for the first four report lines.

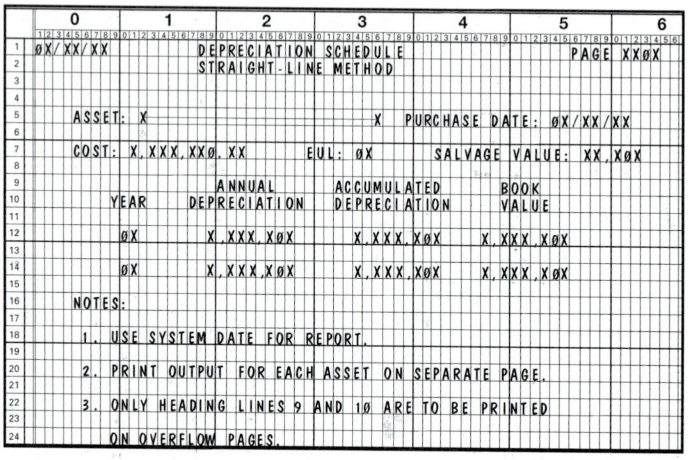

ØX/XX/XX
DEPRECIATION SCHEDULE
STRAIGHT-LINE METHOD
PAGE XXØX
ASSET: X
X PURCHASE DATE: ØX/XX/XX
COST: X,XXX,XXØ.XX
EUL: ØX
SALVAGE VALUE: XX,XØX
YEAR
ANNUAL
DEPRECIATION
ACCUMULATED
DEPRECIATION
BOOK
VALUE
ØX
X,XXX,XØX
X,XXX,XØX
X,XXX,XØX
ØX
X,XXX,XØX
X,XXX,XØX
X,XXX,XØX
NOTES:
1. USE SYSTEM DATE FOR REPORT.
2. PRINT OUTPUT FOR EACH ASSET ON SEPARATE PAGE.
3. ONLY HEADING LINES 9 AND 1Ø ARE TO BE PRINTED
ON OVERFLOW PAGES.

The depreciation schedule is complete when the accumulated depreciation value is equal to the depreciable amount (i.e., when the remainder is zero).

chapter 7

Internal Subroutines and Control Breaks

As programs become larger or more complex, they are usually difficult to debug and maintain. One method of keeping any program readable is to separate the calculations into *internal subroutines* (also called *modules*), which may or may not be independent of other coding. Ideally, any instructions related to a select program function should be included in a separate subroutine. The size and number of internal subroutines specified will depend on the program logic, the program complexity, and/or the programmer's coding preferences. In addition, internal subroutines support the current trend of structured **RPG IV** programming, where calculations are modularized and performed in a top–down sequence.

Internal Subroutine Operations

Internal subroutines are specified in the *Calculation Specifications* and include the following operation names:

EXSR *(Invoke Subroutine)* Causes program control to branch to the internal subroutine identified by the programmer-supplied name entered in *Factor 2*. The subroutine name must be formatted according to the syntax related to field names.

BEGSR *(Beginning of Subroutine)* Identifies the entry point for the subroutine named in *Factor 2* of the related **EXSR** instruction. The entry in *Factor 1* must be identical to the *Factor 2* entry of the related **EXSR** operation.

ENDSR *(End of Subroutine)* Indicates the end of the internal subroutine. When this operation is encountered, program control branches back to the instruction immediately following the related **EXSR** operation.

Figure 7-1 shows how the internal subroutine operations are used. Internal subroutines must follow all *detail* and *total time* calculations. They may be specified in any order and do not have to be coded in the same sequence as their related **EXSR** operations. Note that the **SEU C** format must be used to enter internal subroutine instructions.

Other than conditioning indicators in the *L0* and *N01* fields, the only valid entries in the body of the subroutine is **SR,** to optionally identify the subroutine's instructions, and **AN** and **OR,** to code complex relational statements (e.g., **IF, WHEN, DOU, DOW**).

The syntax rules for internal subroutines are listed in Figure 7-2.

```
*.. 1 ...+... 2 ...+... 3 ...+... 4 ...+... 5 ...+... 6 ...+... 7 ...+... 8 ...+... 9 ...+ ...10
CLON01Factor 1++++++Opcode(E)+Factor2+++++++Result++++++++Len++D_HiLOEQ....Comments+++++++++++++
 * EXSR instruction branches program control to the subroutine named in Factor 2
C                  EXSR      SubrOne
C                    :
C                    :
 * Entry point for the subroutine named in Factor 2 of the related EXSR statement
C     SubrOne      BEGSR
C                    :
C                    :
C                  ENDSR  End of subroutine branches program control to the instruction
                          immediately following the related EXSR operation
```

Figure 7-1 **RPG IV** coding example of an internal subroutine.

The syntax for rules 1, 6, 7, 8, and 9 in Figure 7-2 are applied in the subroutine instructions shown in Figure 7-3.

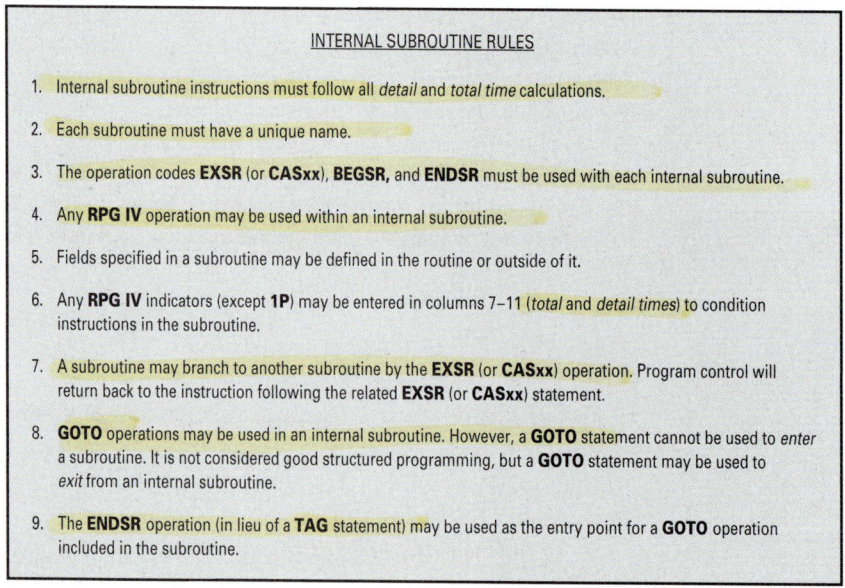

INTERNAL SUBROUTINE RULES

1. Internal subroutine instructions must follow all *detail* and *total time* calculations.
2. Each subroutine must have a unique name.
3. The operation codes **EXSR** (or **CASxx**), **BEGSR,** and **ENDSR** must be used with each internal subroutine.
4. Any **RPG IV** operation may be used within an internal subroutine.
5. Fields specified in a subroutine may be defined in the routine or outside of it.
6. Any **RPG IV** indicators (except **1P**) may be entered in columns 7–11 (*total* and *detail times*) to condition instructions in the subroutine.
7. A subroutine may branch to another subroutine by the **EXSR** (or **CASxx**) operation. Program control will return back to the instruction following the related **EXSR** (or **CASxx**) statement.
8. **GOTO** operations may be used in an internal subroutine. However, a **GOTO** statement cannot be used to *enter* a subroutine. It is not considered good structured programming, but a **GOTO** statement may be used to *exit* from an internal subroutine.
9. The **ENDSR** operation (in lieu of a **TAG** statement) may be used as the entry point for a **GOTO** operation included in the subroutine.

Figure 7-2 Internal subroutine rules.

```
*.. 1 ...+... 2 ...+... 3 ...+... 4 ...+... 5 ...+... 6 ...+... 7 ...+... 8 ...+... 9 ...+ ...10
CLON01Factor 1++++++Opcode(E)+Factor2+++++++Result++++++++Len++D_HiLOEQ....Comments+++++++++++++
C                    :
C          detail time calculations
C                    :
C                  EXSR      Routine1                                Exit to a subroutine
C                    :
C          total time calculations
C                    :
C     Routine1     BEGSR    [1]                                      Begin subroutine
C                    :
C                    :
C                  EXSR      Routine2    [7]                         Exit to a subroutine
C                    :
C                    :
C   30  [6]        GOTO      End     [8]                             Branch to ENDSR
C                    :
C                    :
C     End     [9]  ENDSR                                             End subroutine
```

Figure 7-3 Coding examples for internal syntax rules 1, 6, 7, 8, and 9.

THE CASxx (Conditionally Invoke Subroutine) OPERATION

When a *relational* test is required before exiting to an internal subroutine, the **CASxx** operation should be used. The functions provided by the **COMP** and **EXSR** operations are included in a **CASxx** instruction. Because of its functions, the **CASxx** operation eliminates the need for *Resulting Indicators* required in a **COMP** statement and their use in conditioning a related **EXSR** statement. The syntax for the **CASxx** operation is detailed in Figure 7-4.

```
*.. 1 ...+... 2 ...+... 3 ...+... 4 ...+... 5 ...+... 6 ...+... 7 ...+... 8 ...+... 9 ...+ ...10
CLON01Factor 1+++++++Opcode(E)+Factor2+++++++Result++++++++Len++D_HiLOEQ....Comments+++++++++++++
C                       :
C 1  2        3        CASxx  4       5            6                 7
C                8      ENDCS
C                       :
C             9        BEGSR
C                       :
C            10        ENDSR
```

1. A *total time* indicator may condition a **CASxx** instruction.
2. A *detail time* indicator may condition a **CASxx** instruction.
3. Unless the **xx** entry in the **CASxx** operation is blank, a field name or literal must be entered in *Factor 1*. The item entered in this field must be the same type as the entry in *Factor 2*.
4. The **CASxx** operation name is entered in the *Operation* field. Entries for the **xx** value may be **GT, LT, EQ, NE, GE, LE,** or **blanks** (*Factor 1* not compared to *Factor 2*).
5. *Factor 2* must include a literal or field name and be defined as the same type as the *Factor 1* field or literal. If the **xx** entry in the **CASxx** operation is blank, an entry in the field is not required.
6. A programmer-supplied internal subroutine name must be entered in the *Result* field.
7. One or more *Resulting Indicators* are required if the **CASxx** operation is specified without a relational test condition and the *Factor 1* and *2* entries are included. Otherwise, the indicator(s) is (are) optional.
8. A required **ENDCS** (or **END**) operation indicates the end of a single **CASxx** statement or group.
9. A **BEGSR** operation indicates the beginning of an internal subroutine. The name specified in the *Result* field of the related **CASxx** statement must be entered left-justified in *Factor 1*. Internal subroutines must follow all *detail* and *total time* calculations.
10. An **ENDSR** operation indicates the end of the internal subroutine. It may be used as a **TAG** operation for a **GOTO** or **CABxx** statement within the internal subroutine.

Notes:

1. After a **CASxx** statement is executed, control returns to the statement following the related **ENDCS** (or **END**) operation. Consequently, when a **CASxx** instruction is executed, any subsequent **CASxx** statements within the group will be ignored.
2. Only **CASxx** statements may be included in a **CASxx** group.
3. The normal placement of a **CASbb (b = blanks)** instruction (no relational test specified) is after any other **CASxx** statements within the group.

Figure 7-4 Syntax for the **CASxx** operation.

The processing logic related to a **CASxx** group is detailed in Figure 7-5. When a **CASxx** instruction within a *Case Group* is executed, any following **CASxx** statements will be ignored. Program control returns to the statement following the related **ENDCS** (or **END**) operation, which must always terminate *one* or *more* **CASxx** instructions. This processing logic differs from the **EXSR** operation, where program control returns to the statement immediately following the related **EXSR** instruction.

```
*.. 1 ...+... 2 ...+... 3 ...+... 4 ...+... 5 ...+... 6 ...+... 7 ...+... 8 ...+... 9 ...+ ...10
CLON01Factor 1++++++Opcode(E)+Factor2+++++++Result++++++++Len++D_HiLOEQ....Comments+++++++++++++
 * If the CASEQ instruction is true, control will branch to the RoutineA BEGSR instruction.
 * If the CASLT instruction is true, control will branch to the RoutineB BEGSR instruction.
 * If the CASEQ and CASLT instructions are false, the CAS instruction will be executed and
 * control will automatically branch to the RoutineC BEGSR instruction.
C     FieldA         CASEQ     FieldB         RoutineA
C     FieldA         CASLT     FieldB         RoutineB
C                    CAS                      RoutineC
C                    ENDCS
 * After a subroutine is executed, control returns to the instruction after the ENDCS operation.
C                      :
C     RoutineA       BEGSR
C                      :
C                    ENDSR
C            other subroutines
C                      :
```

Figure 7-5 Processing logic of a **CASxx** group.

Common to all of the **RPG IV** structured operations, a **CASxx** statement may be complex by including one or more **AND** and/or **OR** conditions in the relational test.

SYSTEM TIME

Access of System Time with the `TIME` Operation

Unlike other **RPG IV** special words, such as **PAGE, UDATE, UDAY, UMONTH,** and **UYEAR,** which are predefined, the system time has to be accessed explicitly. One method is with the **TIME** operation. Depending on the *Result* field size (e.g., 6, 12, or 14), the system time may be accessed in a 6-byte **hhmmss** time format, or in a 12-byte **hhmmssmmddyy** time/date format, or in a 14-byte **hhmmssmmddyyyy** time/date format. In any case, the **TIME** value is extracted in a 24-hour clock format. For example, a time value of **141530** is equal to **2:15:30 PM** for the equivalent 12-hour clock format. The **CHGJOB** (*Change Job*) command or *Control Specification* **TIMEFMT** keyword may be used to change the default system time format for a job. Figure 7-6 illustrates three examples of accessing the system time with the **TIME** operation.

The format of the system date part for a 12- or 14-byte **TIME** value is a default **mmddyy** or **mmddyyyy.** However, this may be changed by the *Control Specification* keyword **DATFMT** or with the **CHGJOB** command.

```
*.. 1 ...+... 2 ...+... 3 ...+... 4 ...+... 5 ...+... 6 ...+... 7 ...+... 8 ...+... 9 ...+ ...10
CLON01Factor 1++++++Opcode(E)+Factor2+++++++Result++++++++Len++D_HiLOEQ....Comments+++++++++++++
 * When the TIME operation is specified with a 6-byte Result field, the hhmmss format is stored.
 *
C                    TIME                     Hhmmss             6 0
 * When the TIME operation is specified with a 12-byte Result field, the hhmmssmmddyy (TIME/
 * DATE) format is stored.  The first 6 digits are the time and the last 6, the system date.

C                    TIME                     TimeMdyy          12 0
 * When the time operation is specified with a 14-byte Result field, the hhmmssmmddyyyy (TIME/
 * DATE) format is stored.  The first 6 digits are the time and the last 8, the system date.

C                    TIME                     TimeMdyyyy        14 0
```

Figure 7-6 **RPG IV** syntax to access the system time with the **TIME** operation.

Access of System Time in Definition Specification

In addition to accessing the system time value with the previously discussed **TIME** operation, the *Definition Specification* instruction shown in Figure 7-7 may be used.

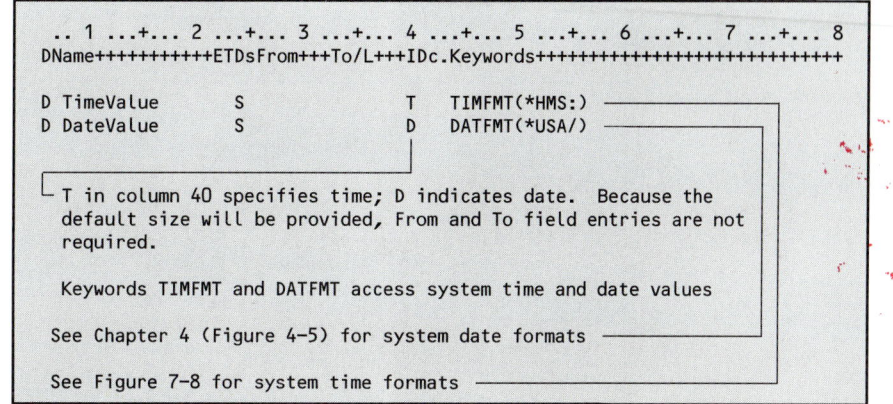

```
.. 1 ...+... 2 ...+... 3 ...+... 4 ...+... 5 ...+... 6 ...+... 7 ...+... 8
DName+++++++++++ETDsFrom+++To/L+++IDc.Keywords+++++++++++++++++++++++++++++

D TimeValue       S                T    TIMFMT(*HMS:)
D DateValue       S                D    DATFMT(*USA/)

  T in column 40 specifies time; D indicates date.  Because the
  default size will be provided, From and To field entries are not
  required.

  Keywords TIMFMT and DATFMT access system time and date values

 See Chapter 4 (Figure 4-5) for system date formats

 See Figure 7-8 for system time formats
```

Figure 7-7 *Definition Specification* syntax to access system **TIME** (and **DATE** value(s)).

The system time and date values may also be accessed by instructions in the *Input Specification* or with **CL** commands. A table of valid time formats is presented in Figure 7-8.

	TIME FORMATS			
OPTION	EXPLANATION	FORMAT	VALID SEPARATORS	EDITED EXAMPLE
***HMS**	Hours:minutes:seconds	**hhmmss**	: or , or **&**	15:45:30
***ISO**	International Standards Organization	**hhmmss**	.	15.45.30
***USA**	IBM USA standard	**hhmm AM**	:	3:45 PM
***EUR**	IBM European standard	**hhmmss**	.	15.45.30
***JIS**	Japanese industrial standard	**hhmmss**	:	15:45:30
Note: Except for the ***USA** 12-hour value, the others are 24-hour values.				

Figure 7-8 Table of **TIME** formats.

An application program that illustrates how internal subroutines and **TIME** are used in an **RPG IV** program is discussed in the following paragraphs. Understand, however, that internal subroutines are not a coding requirement but are used only to enhance the readability of a program and support and encourage structured design.

APPLICATION PROGRAM: ELECTRIC BILLING REPORT

The specifications for an **RPG IV** program that generates a billing report for an electric company are presented in Figure 7-9. Other program documentation is supported by the system flowchart in Figure 7-10.

PROGRAM SPECIFICATIONS — Page 1 of 1

Program Name: Electric Bill Report — Program-ID: ELBILLS — Written by: SM

Purpose: Generate an electric bill report — Approved by: CM

Input files: ELCUSTRS

Output files: QSYSPRT

Processing Requirements:

Write an RPG IV program to generate a billing report for an electric company's customers.

Input to the program:

The externally defined physical file, ELCUSTRS, includes the record format shown in the supplemental record layout form. The file is to be processed in arrival sequence.

Processing:

The company has different base and usage rates for industrial customers and homeowners, which are detailed below:

Rates for homeowners:
Base usage = 1,000 kilowatt hours
Base charge = $40
Additional rate for usage over 1,000 kwh = $.042/kwh

Rates for industrial customers:
Base usage = 5,000 kilowatt hours
Base charge = $175
Additional rate for usage over 5,000 kwh = $.035/kwh

Test the user code field in each record processed. If the value is H, branch to an internal subroutine for homeowners' calculations. If the value is I, branch to a separate routine for industrial users.

For either user, if the kilowatt hours used is equal to or less than the base usage (1,000 or 5,000), the related base charge (40 or 175) is billed for the month.

If more than the base amount is used, then the excess usage over the base amount is multiplied by the applicable additional rate (.042 or .035). The base charge and additional amount are added to determine the amount billed.

In addition, all users are subject to a tax based on $.015 per 100 kwh used. The tax is added to the amount billed. Add the total amount billed to an accumulator.

Output:

Complete the report format detailed in the supplemental print chart.

Figure 7-9 Specifications for an **RPG IV** program that generates an electric billing report.

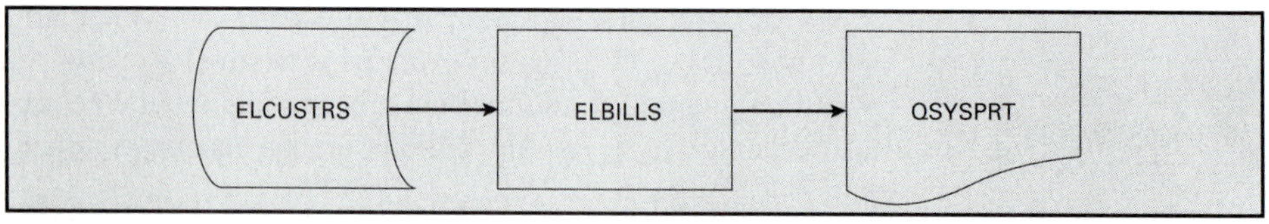

Figure 7-10 System flowchart for an **RPG IV** program that generates an electric billing report.

The physical file's record format and data listing are shown in Figure 7-11.

The report design is detailed in the printer spacing chart in Figure 7-12 with a report listing.

```
                    PHYSICAL FILE DESCRIPTION

SYSTEM: AS/400                                 DATE: 9/20/97
FILE NAME: ELCUSTRS                            REV NO: 0
RECORD NAME: ELCUSTR                           KEY LENGTH: None
SEQUENCE: Nonkeyed                             RECORD SIZE: 25

                        FIELD DEFINITIONS

FIELD    FIELD NAME    SIZE  TYPE    POSITION     COMMENTS
 NO                                 FROM    TO

  1      CUSTNAME       20    C        1    20
  2      KWHOURS         6    P       21    24   0 decimals
  3      USER            1    C       25    25   H - Home
                                                 I - Indust

Physical File Data:
                                 Kilowatt
        Customer Name           Hours Used   User

        IVAN PATZIK               000945      H
        MANAGEMENT COMPANY        011000      I
        CHRIS LENTZ               001400      H
        TAYCO INCORPORATED        004500      I
        FRANZ ECKART              001050      H
        COMPUTER SERVICES CO      150000      I
```

Figure 7-11 Physical file's record format and data listing for the Electric Billing Report program.

```
            0         1         2         3         4         5
   1234567890123456789012345678901234567890123456789012345678
 1 ØX/XX/XXXX          EDISON ELECTRIC COMPANY          PAGE XXØX
 2 XX:XX:XX       CUSTOMER USAGE AND BILLING REPORT
 3
 4              NAME              USER TYPE    KWH HRS      TOTAL BILL
 5
 6 X------------------X   INDUSTRIAL   XXX,XØX      XX,XXØ.XX
 7
 8 X------------------X         HOME   XXX,XØX      XX,XXØ.XX
 9
10
11                TOTAL BILLINGS                    XXX,XXØ.XX
12
13   NOTES:
14
15     1. HEADINGS ON TOP OF EVERY PAGE.
16
17     2. USE SYSTEM DATE FOR REPORT.
```

```
10/01/95            EDISON ELECTRIC COMPANY          PAGE    1
13:26:47        CUSTOMER USAGE AND BILLING REPORT

              NAME            USER TYPE   KWH HRS      TOTAL BILL

IVAN PATZIK                        HOME       945           40.14

MANAGEMENT COMPANY           INDUSTRIAL    11,000          386.65

CHRIS LENTZ                        HOME     1,400           57.01

TAYCO INCORPORATED           INDUSTRIAL     4,500          175.68

FRANZ ECKART                       HOME     1,050           42.25

COMPUTER SERVICES CO         INDUSTRIAL   150,000        5,272.50


                  TOTAL BILLINGS                         5,974.23
```

Figure 7-12 Printer spacing chart and report generated by the Electric Billing Report program.

The flowchart in Figure 7-13 details the processing logic for the Electric Billing Report program.

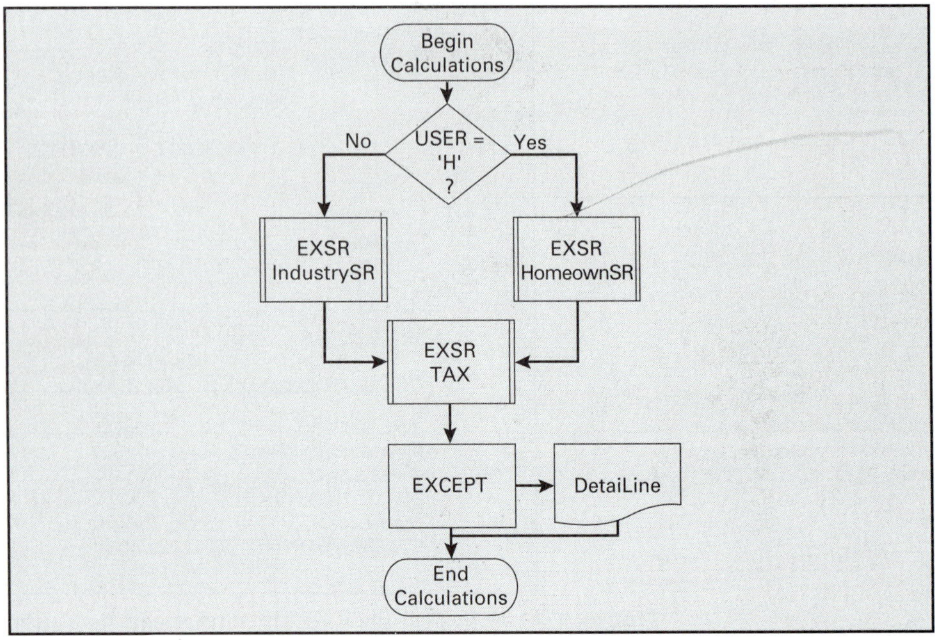

Figure 7-13 Processing logic for internal subroutines included in the Electric Billing Report program.

Compile Program Listing

Examine the compile listing in Figure 7-14. Observe that four internal subroutines, system time, and *exception* time output are included in the **RPG IV** program.

```
Line   <--------------------- Source Specifications ----------------------------><---- Comments ----> Do
Number ....1....+....2....+....3....+....4....+....5....+....6....+....7....+....8....+....9....+...10 Num
                               S o u r c e   L i s t i n g
     1  * This program computes and generates a billing report for an
     2  * electric company's homeowner and industrial customers....
     3
     4 FCh7p1     IF   E             DISK
        *--------------------------------------------------------------------------------------------*
        *                                RPG name         External name                                *
        * File name. . . . . . . . :    CH7P1            STAN/CH7P1                                   *
        * Record format(s) . . . . :    CH7P1R           CH7P1R                                       *
        *--------------------------------------------------------------------------------------------*
     5 FQsysprt   O    F  132        PRINTER OFLIND(*INOF)
     6
     7  * Define work fields....
     8 D HhMmSs          S              6  0
     9 D User_Type       S             10
    10 D Bill_Amt        S              7  2
    11 D Excess_Kwh      S              6  0
    12 D Extra_Amt       S              7  2
    13 D TaxableKwh      S              4  0
    14 D Tax_Amt         S              6  2
    15 D TotalBills      S              8  2
    16
    17  * Exit to housekeeping subroutine...
    18=ICH7P1R
```

Figure 7-14 Compile listing of the Electric Billing Report program.

```
     *---------------------------------------------------------------------------------*
     * RPG record format  . . . . :  CH7P1R                                            *
     * External format  . . . . . :  CH7P1R : STAN/CH7P1                               *
     *---------------------------------------------------------------------------------*
  I                          A    1   20  CUSTNAME
  I                          P   21   24 OKWHOURS
  I                          A   25   25  USER
  C                EXSR      HouseKepSR                                 exit to HouseKepSR

   * Read first record - execute DOW group until end of file is read...
  C                READ      Ch7p1                           ----LR     read first record
  C                DOW       *INLR = *OFF                               do while LR is off   B01

   * Test for page overflow condition (*INOF "on")
  C                IF        *INOF = *ON                                OF indicator "on"?   B02
  C                EXCEPT    Heading                                    print headLine        02
  C                EVAL      *INOF = *OFF                               turn off OF indicatr  02
  C                ENDIF                                                end IF group         E02

   * Test for User....
  C   User         CASEQ     'H'           HomeOwnSR                    exit to HomeOwnSR     01
  C                CAS                     IndustrySR                   exit to IndustrySR    01
  C                ENDCS                                                end CAS group         01

  C                EXSR      TaxCompSR                                  exit to tax SR        01
  C                EXCEPT    DetaiLine                                  print DetaiLine       01
  C                READ      Ch7p1                           ----LR     read next record      01
  C                ENDDO                                                end DOW group        E01

   * Print total billings record and end the job....
  C                EXCEPT    TotaLine                                   print TotaLine

   * Begin subroutines....
  C   HouseKepSR   BEGSR                                                begin HouseKepSR
  C                TIME                    HhMmSs                       access system time
  C                EVAL      *INOF = *ON                                turn on OF indicator
  C                ENDSR                                                end HouseKepSR

  C   HomeOwnSR    BEGSR                                                begin HomeOwnSR
  C                EVAL      User_Type = '    HOME    '                 initialize User_Type
  C                EVAL      Bill_Amt = 40                              initialize Bill_Amt
  C                IF        KWHours > 1000                             KwHours > 1000?      B01
  C                EVAL      Excess_Kwh = KWHours - 1000                compute Excess_Kwh    01
  C                EVAL(H)   Extra_Amt = Excess_Kwh * .042              compute Extra_Amt     01
  C                EVAL      Bill_Amt = Bill_Amt + Extra_Amt            compute Bill_Amt      01
  C                ENDIF                                                end IF group         E01
  C                ENDSR                                                end HomeOwnSR

  C   IndustrySR   BEGSR                                                begin
  C                EVAL      User_Type = 'INDUSTRIAL'                   initialize User_Type
  C                EVAL      Bill_Amt = 175                             initialize Bill_Amt
  C                IF        KWHours > 5000                             KwHours > 5000?      B01
  C                EVAL      Excess_Kwh = KWHours - 5000                compute Excess_Kwh    01
  C                EVAL(H)   Extra_Amt = Excess_Kwh * .035              compute Extra_Amt     01
  C                EVAL      Bill_Amt = Bill_Amt + Extra_Amt            compute Bill_Amt      01
  C                ENDIF                                                end IF group         E01
  C                ENDSR                                                end IndustrySR

  C   TaxCompSR    BEGSR                                                begin TaxCompSR
  C                EVAL      TaxableKwh = KWHours / 100                 compute TaxableKwh
  C                EVAL      Tax_Amt = TaxableKwh * .015                compute Tax_Amt
  C                EVAL      Bill_Amt = Bill_Amt + Tax_Amt              add tax to bill_amt
  C                EVAL      TotalBills = TotalBills + Bill_Amt         compute TotalBills
  C                ENDSR                                                end IndustrySR

   * Begin output....
  OQsysprt   E                 Heading          1 01
  O                            *DATE          Y      10
  O                                                  51 'PAGE'
```

Figure 7-14 Compile listing of the Electric Billing Report program. (Continued)

```
 84 O                        PAGE                56
 85 O                                            40 'EDISON ELECTRIC COMPANY'
 86 O          E             Heading        2
 87 O                        HhMmSs               8 ' : : '
 88 O                                            30 'CUSTOMER USAGE AND'
 89 O                                            45 'BILLING REPORT'
 90 O          E             Heading        2
 91 O                                            11 'NAME'
 92 O                                            31 'USER TYPE'
 93 O                                            41 'KWH HRS'
 94 O                                            56 'TOTAL BILL'
 95 O          E             DetailLine     2
 96 O                        CustName            20
 97 O                        User_Type           32
 98 O                        KWHours        2    41
 99 O                        Bill_Amt       1    56
100
101 O          E             TotaLine      1
102 O                                            28 'TOTAL BILLINGS'
103 O                        TotalBills     1    56
```

File Description Specifications

Line No.

4 Ch7p1 is defined as an input, full-procedural, externally described, nonkeyed physical file.

5 Qsysprt is defined as an output, program-described printer file. The page overflow indicator **OF** is assigned to the file by the **OFLIND(*INOF))** keyword.

Definition Specifications

8–15 "Standalone" fields, HhMmSs through TotalBills, are defined by these instructions.

Calculation Specifications

22 The **EXSR** instruction branches control to the HouseKepSR subroutine.

25 This **READ** instruction reads the first record from the physical file Ch7p1. If no records are stored in the file, the **LR** indicator will be set on.

26 The **DOW** instruction tests the status of the **LR** indicator. If it is *not on*, another iteration of the **DOW** group will be executed. If it is *on*, program control will branch to line 45, print the TotaLine, and end the job.

29 The **IF** instruction tests the status of the **OF** indicator. Because **OF** is set on the HouseKepSR (line 50) before the first record is processed, the relational test will be "true" and the instructions in the **IF** group executed.

30 The **EXCEPT** instruction controls the printing of the Heading recofds (lines 81–93).

31 This **EVAL** instruction turns off the **OF** indicator, so that page overflow will not occur on the next iteration of the **DOW** group. After the Heading lines are printed on the first page, the Heading lines on subsequent pages will be printed when page overflow is detected and the **OF** indicator automatically turned on.

32 The **ENDIF** operation ends the **IF** group.

35 The **CASEQ** instruction tests the physical file User field for the literal H. When the test is "true," control will branch to the HomeOwnSR subroutine.

36 The **CAS** instruction will cause control to branch to the IndustrySR subroutine if the **CASEQ** relational test on line 35 was "false."

37 The **ENDCS** operation ends the **CAS** group.

39 The **EXSR** instruction branches control to the TaxCompSR subroutine.

40 This **EXCEPT** instruction controls the printing of the DetaiLine record on lines 95–99.

41 The **READ** instruction reads the next record from the Ch7p1 physical file. If end of file is read, the **LR** indicator will be turned on. When control branches back to the **DOW** instruction on line 26, the test will be false. Control will then branch to the **EXCEPT** instruction on line 45, the TotaLine record printed, and the job ended.

Figure 7-14 Compile listing of the Electric Billing Report program. (Continued)

42	The **ENDDO** operation ends the **DOW** group that began on line 26.
45	This **EXCEPT** instruction controls the printing of the TotaLine record on lines 101–103 after **LR** is turned on by one of the **READ** instructions.
48	This **BEGSR** instruction begins the HouseKepSR subroutine that was accessed by the **EXSR** instruction on line 22.
49	The **TIME** operation accesses the system time and stores it in the HhMmSs field.
50	This **EVAL** instruction turns on the **OF** overflow indicator, which controls the printing of the Heading lines in the **IF** group on lines 29–32. This forces the Heading lines to be printed after the first record is read. After the Heading lines are printed, the **OF** indicator is turned off by the **EVAL** instruction on line 31.
51	This **ENDSR** operation ends the HouseKepSR subroutine.
53	This **BEGSR** operation begins the HomeOwnSR subroutine that was accessed by the **CASEQ** instruction on line 35.
54	This **EVAL** instruction stores the character literal ' HOME ' in the User_Type field.
55	This **EVAL** instruction initializes the Bill_Amt field to 40, the base charge for a homeowner.
56	This **IF** instruction tests the KWHours field for a value greater than 1,000. If the relational test is "true," the instructions within the **IF** group will be executed.
57	This **EVAL** instruction computes the Excess_Kwh value by subtracting the numeric literal 1000 from KWHours field value.
58	This **EVAL** instruction computes the Extra_Amt value by multiplying the Excess-Kwh value by the numeric literal .042.
59	This **EVAL** instruction increases the Bill_Amt value by adding the Extra_Amt computed on line 58 to the Bill_Amt value computed on line 55.
60	This **ENDIF** operation ends the **IF** group that began on line 56.
61	This **ENDSR** operation ends the HomeOwnSR subroutine that began on line 53.
63	This **BEGSR** operation begins the IndustrySR subroutine that was accessed by the **CAS** instruction on line 36.
64	This **EVAL** instruction stores the character literal 'INDUSTRIAL' into the User_Type field.
65	This **EVAL** instruction initializes the Bill_Amt field to 175, the base charge for an Industrial user.
66	This **IF** instruction tests the KWHours field for a value greater than 5,000. If the relational test is "true," the instructions within this **IF** group will be executed.
67	This **EVAL** instruction computes the Excess_Kwh value by subtracting the numeric literal 5000 from the KWHours field value.
68	This **EVAL** instruction computes the Extra_Amt value by multiplying the Excess-Kwh value by the numeric literal .035.
69	This **EVAL** instruction increases the Bill_Amt value by adding the Extra_Amt computed on line 68 to the Bill_Amt value computed on line 65.
70	This **ENDIF** operation ends the **IF** group that began on line 66.
71	This **ENDSR** operation ends the IndustrySR subroutine that began on line 63.
73	This **BEGSR** instruction begins the TaxCompSR subroutine that was accessed by the **EXSR** instruction on line 39.
74	This **EVAL** instruction computes the TaxableKwh field value by dividing KWHours by the numeric literal 100.
75	This **EVAL** instruction computes the Tax_Amt field value by multiplying the TaxableKwh field value by the numeric literal .015.
76	This **EVAL** instruction increases the Bill_Amt field value, computed for either the homeowner or industrial user, by the Tax_Amt field value.
77	This **EVAL** instruction increments the TotalBills field value by the previously computed Bill_Amt field value.
78	This **ENDSR** operation ends the TaxCompSR subroutine that began on line 73.

Figure 7-14 Compile listing of the Electric Billing Report program. (Continued)

Output Specifications

81–94	The four Heading line record formats are printed by the **EXCEPT** instruction on line 30. After the initial printing, subsequent Heading lines are printed only when page overflow is detected and the overflow indicator **(OF)** is automatically turned on.
95–99	The DetailLine record format, printed for every record processed, is controlled by the **EXCEPT** instruction on line 40.
101–103	The TotaLine record format is printed after end of file is read and **LR** turned on by the **READ** instruction on line 41. Printing is controlled by the **EXCEPT** instruction on line 45.

Figure 7-14 Compile listing of the Electric Billing Report program. (Continued)

CONTROL BREAK PROCESSING

Reports generated by example programs and programming assignments discussed to date have included, when required, only final totals printed when the end-of-file (**LR** time) condition was tested. Many applications require subtotals in the body of a report. Figure 7-15 shows a report that includes subtotals for salesperson groups. Notice that when a salesperson number changes (from 1000 to 1100, 1100 to 1200, and so forth), a total line for the related salesperson is printed. In addition, at end of file (**LR** time) the total for the last salesperson group is printed before the TOTAL STORE SALES sum.

An examination of the report in Figure 7-15 will show that the data is in ascending order by date (*minor* field), which is within the ascending salesperson number (*major* field) order. The logic of *control break* processing requires that the data file, defined as input (or update), be *sorted* in ascending or descending order by one or more *control fields* (salesperson number and date) before processing. In lieu of *sorting*, a *logical file* may be created to process the related physical file(s) in the required *Control field(s)* order.

```
                     WEEKLY SALES REPORT AS OF  9/30/1997    PAGE    1

  DATE      SALESPERSON        WEEKLY SALES

 9/08/97        1000               256.12 ─┐
 9/15/97        1000             1,441.70  ├── Control group (same
 9/22/97        1000               384.20  │   salesperson number)
 9/29/97        1000               302.44 ─┘

                        SALESPERSON 1000 SALES..... 2,384.46 *── Control group total
                                                                  (generated when sales-
 9/08/97        1100               189.76 ─┐                      person number changes)
 9/15/97        1100               500.38  │
 9/22/97        1100             2,198.37  ├── Control group
 9/29/97        1100               246.18 ─┘

                        SALESPERSON 1100 SALES..... 3,134.69 *── Control group total

 9/08/97        1200             1,612.55 ─┐
 9/15/97        1200               800.00  │
 9/22/97        1200               999.19  ├── Control group
 9/29/97        1200             3,737.47 ─┘
```

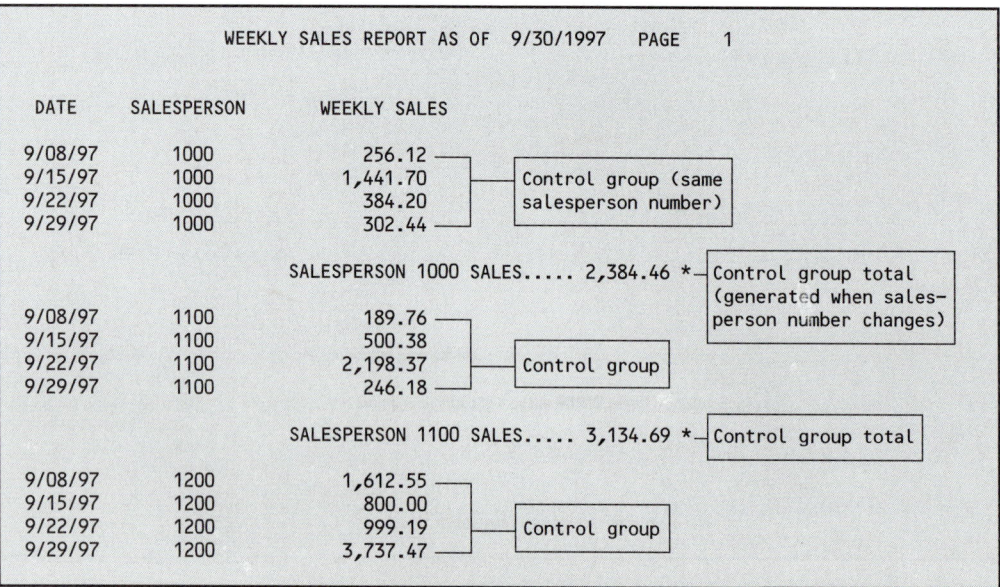

Figure 7-15 Detail report with subtotals.

```
                         SALESPERSON 1200 SALES..... 7,149.21 * - Control group total

9/08/97       1300              645.33 ┐
9/15/97       1300              301.76 │
9/22/97       1300            2,868.88 ├── Control group
9/29/97       1300            1,532.86 ┘

                         SALESPERSON 1300 SALES..... 5,348.83 * - Control group total

9/08/97       1400              184.79 ┐
9/15/97       1400              733.74 │
9/22/97       1400              472.52 ├── Control group
9/29/97       1400            4,900.09 ┘

                         SALESPERSON 1400 SALES..... 6,291.14 * - Last control group total
                                                                  generated at LR time

                            TOTAL STORE SALES....   24,308.33 ** - LR total
```

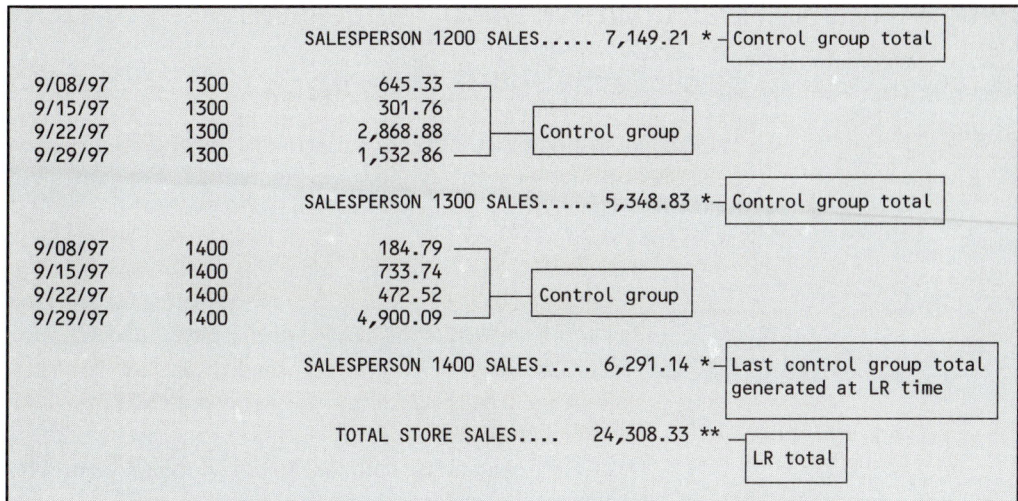

Figure 7-15 Detail report with subtotals. (Continued)

Structure of the Data File

Figure 7-16 lists the data file that was processed for the report in Figure 7-15. Comments identify the new terms associated with *control break* processing including *control field(s)*, *control groups*, *control break(s)*, and *control group totals*.

```
Control field ─────────              Sales amount
(salesperson number)                 Week ending date

First record ────────── 10000301025612090897
                        10000301144170091597
                        10000301038420092297
                        10000301030244092997     238446 ┐
Control break ───────── 11000301018976090897            │
  1000 to 1100          11000301050038091597            │
                        11000301219837092297            │
                        11000301024618092997     313469 ┤
Control break ───────── 12000501161255090897            │
  1100 to 1200          12000501080000091597            │
                        12000501099919092297            │
                        12000501373747092997     714921 ├── Control group
Control break ───────── 13001202064533090897            │   totals
   1200 to 1300         13001202030176091597            │
                        13001202286888092297            │
                        13001202153286092997     534883 ┤
Control break ───────── 14000803018479090897            │
   1300 to 1400         14000803073374091597            │
                        14000803047252092297            │
                        14000803490009092997     629114 ┘
LR (end-of-file) ──────
(Control break for last control
 group total must be provided)

Note:

 1. The physical file was created as in ascending composite key order with
    salesperson number as the major key, and date as the minor key element.
```

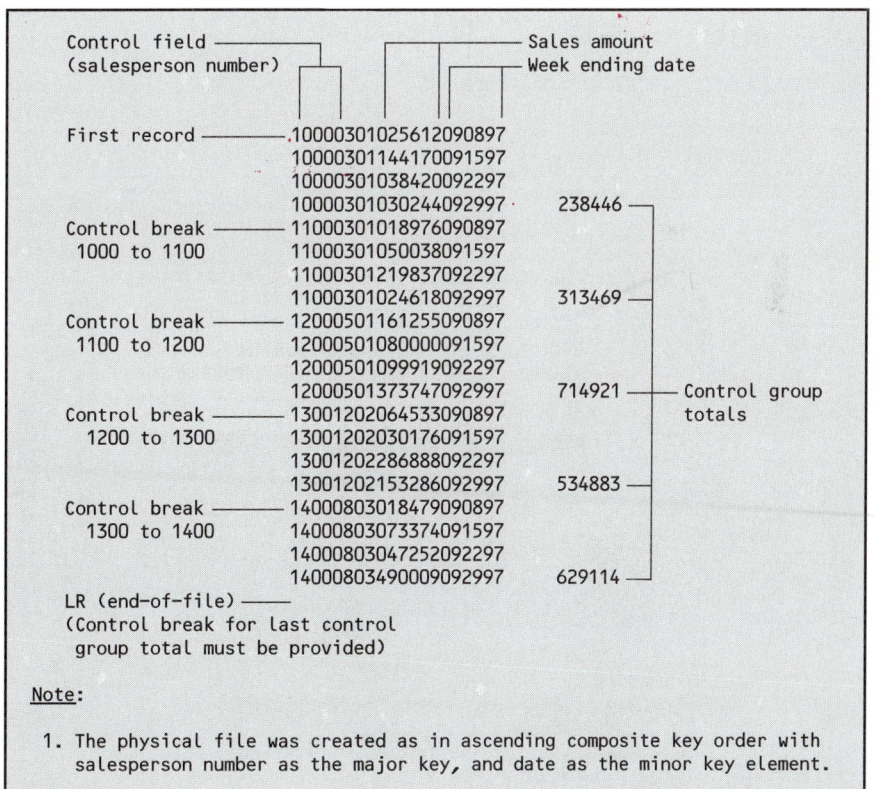

Figure 7-16 Listing of the physical file processed by the one control break **RPG IV** program.

PROGRAMMER-DEFINED CONTROL BREAK PROCESSING

Single Control Break Program

The compile listing of an **RPG IV** program that generates a report with a single control group (salesperson number) is shown in Figure 7-17. Examine the listing and note the following features:

1. One *holding field* is defined in the *Calculation Specification* with the **DEFINE** operation equal to the size of the salesperson field. The input salesperson number will be moved to the *holding field* for every record processed.
2. Three *internal subroutines* are included: one for housekeeping; a second for salesperson control break processing; and a third for control break processing after end of file is read.
3. **EXCEPT** operations control all *Heading*, *Detail*, control break, and *end-of-file* output.

```
Line   <--------------------- Source Specifications ---------------------------><---- Comments ----> Do
Number ....1....+....2....+....3....+....4....+....5....+....6....+....7....+....8....+....9....+...10 Num
                         S o u r c e   L i s t i n g
     1  * This program prints a report with one control group on
     2  * Salesperson number....
     3
     4 FCh7P2     IF   E           K DISK
        *----------------------------------------------------------------------------------*
        *                           RPG name            External name                      *
        * File name. . . . . . . . :  CH7P2             STAN/CH7P2                         *
        * Record format(s) . . . . :  CH7P2R            CH7P2R                             *
        *----------------------------------------------------------------------------------*
     5 FQsysprt   O    F  132         PRINTER OFLIND(*INOF)
     6
     7=ICH7P2R
        *----------------------------------------------------------------------------------*
        * RPG record format  . . . . :  CH7P2R                                             *
        * External format  . . . . . :  CH7P2R : STAN/CH7P2                                *
        *----------------------------------------------------------------------------------*
     8=I                            A    1    4  SALESPERNO
     9=I                            A    5    6  DEPTNO
    10=I                            A    7    8  STORENO
    11=I                            P    9   12 2SALES_AMT
    12=I                            P   13   16 0SALES_DATE
    13 C     *LIKE         DEFINE    SalesPerNo    HoldSalPNo                    define HoldSalpNo
    14 C     *LIKE         DEFINE    Sales_Amt     SalesPSum          +1         define SalesPSum
    15 C     *LIKE         DEFINE    Sales_Amt     State_Sum          +2         define StateSum
    16
    17 C                   READ      Ch7P2                              ----LR   read first record
    18 C                   EXSR      HouseKepSR
    19
    20 C                   DOW       *INLR = *OFF                                do while LR is off   B01
    21
    22  * Heading control....
    23 C                   IF        *INOF = *ON                                 OF "on" ?            B02
    24 C                   EXCEPT    Heading                                     print heading lines   02
    25 C                   EVAL      *INOF = *OFF                                turn off OF indicatr  02
    26 C                   ENDIF                                                 end IF group         E02
    27
    28  * Begin processing....
    29 C     SalesPerNo    CASNE     HoldSalPNo    SalpSR                        control break?        01
    30 C                   ENDCS                                                 end CAS group         01
    31 C                   EVAL      SalesPSum = SalesPSum + Sales_Amt           Accumulate SalesPSum  01
    32 C                   EXCEPT    DetailLine                                  print detail line     01
    33 C                   READ      Ch7P2                              ----LR   read next record      01
    34 C                   ENDDO                                                 end DOW group        E01
```

Figure 7-17 Compile listing of a single control break **RPG IV** program.

```
35
36  * End of file processing....
37 C                    EXSR      EofSR                                 branch to EOF SR
38
39  * Begin subroutines....
40 C      HouseKepSR    BEGSR                                           Begin HouseKepSR
41 C                    EVAL      HoldSalPNo = SalesPerNo               Initialize HoldSalPNo
42 C                    EVAL      *INOF = *ON                           turn on OF indicator
43 C                    ENDSR                                           end HouseKepSR
44
45 C      SalpSR        BEGSR                                           begin SalPBrakSR
46 C                    EVAL      State_Sum = State_Sum + SalesPSum     accumulate State_Sum
47 C                    EXCEPT    SPBrakLine                            print break total
48 C                    EVAL      HoldSalPNo = SalesPerNo               initialize HoldSalPNo
49 C                    EVAL      SalesPSum = *ZERO                     initialize SalesPSum
50 C                    ENDSR                                           end SalPBrakSR
51
52 C      EofSR         BEGSR                                           begin EOFSR
53 C                    EXSR      SalpSR                                branch to SalPBrakSR
54 C                    EXCEPT    EofLine                               print last totals
55 C                    ENDSR                                           end EofSR
56
57  * Begin output....
58 OQsysPrt   E            Heading        3 01
59 O                                          42 'WEEKLY SALES REPORT AS'
60 O                                          45 'OF'
61 O                       *DATE          Y   56
62 O                                          63 'PAGE'
63 O                       PAGE               68
64 O          E            Heading        2
65 O                                           6 'DATE'
66 O                                          20 'SALESPERSON'
67 O                                          41 'WEEKLY SALES'
68 O          E            DetailLine     1
69 O                       Sales_Date     Y    8
70 O                       SalesPerNo         19
71 O                       Sales_Amt      1   39
72 O          E            SPBrakLine   1 2
73 O                                          37 'SALESPERSON'
74 O                       HoldSalPNo         42
75 O                                          53 'SALES.....'
76 O                       SalesPSum      1   63
77 O                                          65 '*'
78 O          E            EofLine      1
79 O                                          51 'TOTAL STATE SALES.....'
80 O                       State_Sum      1   63
81 O                                          66 '**'
```

File Description Specifications

Line No.

4 Ch7P2 is defined as an input, full procedural, externally described, keyed physical file.

5 Qsysprt is defined as an output, program-described printer file. The page overflow indicator **OF** is assigned to the file by the **OFLIND(*INOF)** keyword.

Calculation Specifications

13–15 The three ***LIKE DEFINE** commands define three work fields. HoldSalPNo is defined with the same attributes as SalesPerNo. SalesPSum is defined one integer greater than Sales_Amt. State_Sum is defined two integers greater than Sales_Amt.

17 This **READ** instruction reads the first record from the physical file. If no records are stored in the file, the **LR** indicator (*Eq* field) will be turned on. The **DOW** relational test on line 20 will be "false," which will transfer control out of the **DOW** group and end the job. Note that the program is coded with the assumption that at least one record is stored in the physical file.

18 This **EXSR** instruction branches control to the HouseKepSR that begins on line 40.

20 The **DOW** instruction begins the iterative process of reading the physical file and the related calculations for each record. When indicator **LR** is turned on by the **READ** instruction on line 17 or 33, control will exit from the **DOW** group and complete end-of-file-processing, and end the job.

23 This **IF** instruction tests the status of the **OF** indicator. Because an **EVAL** instruction in the HouseKepSR (line 42) turned on the **OF** indicator, page overflow will occur for the first record processed and the Heading records will be printed. Subsequent page overflow processing will automatically occur when the overflow line is detected.

Figure 7-17 Compile listing of a single control break **RPG IV** program. (Continued)

24	This **EXCEPT** instruction transfers control to output, where the Heading line records are printed.
25	This **EVAL** instruction turns off the **OF** indicator so that page overflow will not occur for the next record processed.
26	The **ENDIF** operation ends the **IF** group that began on line 23.
29	The value in SalesPerNo is compared to the value in the HoldSalPNo field. If they are not equal (indicating a control break), this **CASNE** instruction transfers control to the SalpSR subroutine.
30	The **ENDCS** operation ends the one instruction **CAS** group.
31	This **EVAL** instruction accumulates the current record's Sales_Amt value in the SalesPSum field.
32	This **EXCEPT** instruction transfers control to output, where the DetaiLine record values are printed (lines 68–71).
33	This **READ** instruction reads the next record in the physical file. If end of file is read, the **LR** indicator will be turned on.
34	The **ENDDO** operation ends the **DOW** group that began on line 20.
37	This **EXSR** instruction transfers control to the EofSR subroutine. It is executed only after end of file is read and control exits from the **DOW** group.
40	This **BEGSR** instruction begins the HouseKepSR subroutine that was accessed by the **EXSR** instruction on line 18.
41	This **EVAL** instruction initializes the HoldSalPNo field with the value in the input field SalesPerNo. This will prevent a "null" break for the first record processed.
42	This **EVAL** instruction turns on the **OF** indicator, which will cause page overflow to occur for the first record processed.
43	This **ENDSR** operation ends the HouseKepSR subroutine.
45	This **BEGSR** instruction begins the SalpSR subroutine that was accessed by the **CASNE** instruction on line 29 after a control break (change in SalesPerNo) was detected.
46	This **EVAL** instruction adds the SalesPSum control field total to the State_Sum accumulator.
47	This **EXCEPT** instruction transfers control to output, where the SPBrakline record (control break total) is printed.
48	This **EVAL** instruction initializes the HoldSalNo field with the SalesPerNo value from the current record (the one that caused the control break).
49	This **EVAL** instruction initializes the SalesPSum field to zero so that the next SalesPSum total will not include the control field total from the previous SalesPerson.
50	This **ENDSR** operation ends the SalpSR subroutine.
52	This **BEGSR** instruction begins the EofSR that was accessed by the **EXSR** instruction on line 37 that was executed after end of file was detected by the **READ** instruction on line 33 and exit from the **DOW** group.
53	This **EXSR** instruction transfers control to the SalpSR subroutine, where the State_Sum is accumulated for the last SalesPerNo control group, the SPBrakLine printed, the HoldSalPNo field initialized with the current SalesPerNo value, and the SalesPSum initialized to zero.
54	This **EXCEPT** instruction transfers control to output, where the EofLine record format is printed.
55	This **ENDSR** operation ends the EofSR subroutine.
58–67	The Heading record formats are defined in these instructions and the values printed when the **EXCEPT** instruction on line 24 is executed.
68–71	The DetaiLine record format is defined in these instructions and the values are printed when the **EXCEPT** instruction on line 32 is executed.
72–77	The SPBrakLine record format is defined in these instructions and the values are printed after a control break is detected and the **EXCEPT** instruction on line 47 is executed.
78–81	The EofLine record format is defined in these instructions and the values are printed after end of file is read and the **EXCEPT** instruction on line 54 is executed.

Figure 7-17 Compile listing of a single control break **RPG IV** program. (Continued)

A line-by-line explanation of the program instructions is included at the end of the compile listing.

The report generated by the single control group program was shown in Figure 7-1. A condensed processing logic flowchart for the **RPG IV** program is detailed in Figure 7-18. Included is the logic flow that occurs when a control break *is not* detected, when a control break *is* detected, and end-of-file processing. Note that the line numbers alongside the symbols relate to the instruction(s) in the program.

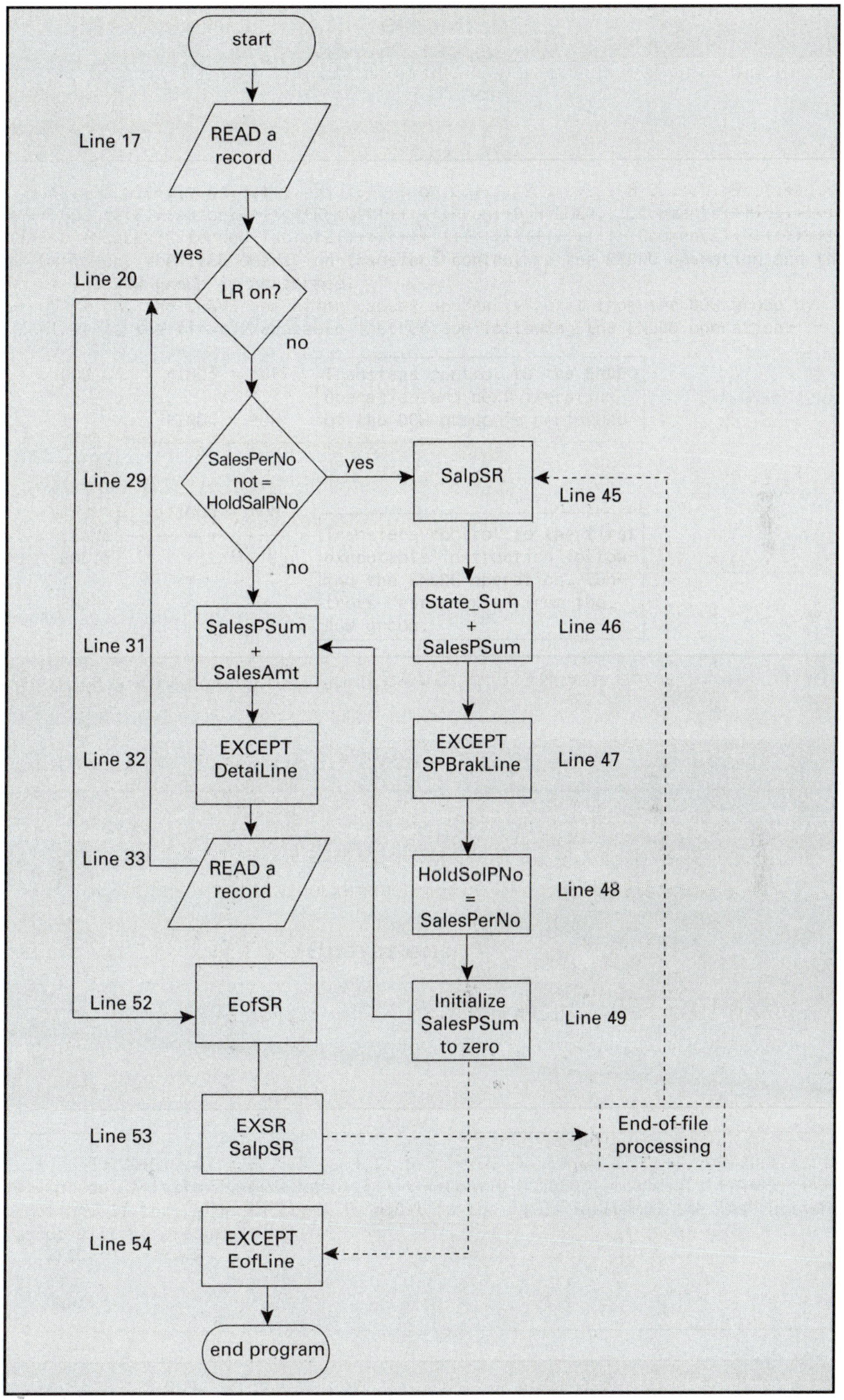

Figure 7-18 Condensed processing logic flowchart for single control break **RPG IV** program.

Multiple Control Break Program

The compile listing for a *multiple* control break **RPG IV** program is detailed in Figure 7-19. Note the following summary of the program's structure as related to multiple control break processing.

1. For the first record processed, the programmer-selected control field values from the physical file **(SalesPerNo, DeptNo,** and **StoreNo)** are moved into their related holding fields **(HoldSalPNo, HoldDeptNo,** and **HoldStorNo)** in the **HouseKepSR** subroutine (lines 56–58).
2. The largest control field **(StoreNo)** is tested first (line 35). If a change in the **StoreNo** value is detected, the **SalpSR** subroutine for the salesperson group is processed, followed by the department **(DeptSR)** and then store **(StoreSR)** subroutines.
3. If a change in the **StoreNo** is not detected, the next-lower control field **(DeptNo)** is tested (line 39). If a change in the **DeptNo** value is sensed, the internal subroutine, **SalpPSR,** for the salesperson group is processed followed by the department **(DeptSR)** subroutine.
4. If a change in the **DeptNo** is not detected, then a change in the value of the lowest control field **(SalesPerNo)** is tested (line 42). If a change in the **(SalesPerNo)** value is detected, the **SalpSR** subroutine for the salesperson group is processed.
5. When end of file is read (**LR** time), the **EofSR** subroutine is executed, from which the **SalpSR, DeptSR,** and **StoreSR** subroutines are consecutively processed before the state total **(State_Sum)** is printed. The instruction controls the printing of the last *three* control group totals before the state total is printed.
6. Output for each control group total (lines 109–126) is processed at *exception time*.
7. After a control group is executed, the record currently processed (which caused the control break) is printed at exception time (lines 103–108).

```
Line     <---------------------- Source Specifications ----------------------------><---- Comments ----> Do
Number ....1....+....2....+....3....+....4....+....5....+....6....+....7....+....8....+....9....+...10 Num
                        S o u r c e   L i s t i n g
     1   * This program prints a report with control group breaks on
     2   * salesperson number, department number, and store number....
     3
     4 FCh7p2     IF   E             K DISK
       *--------------------------------------------------------------------------------------------*
       *                            RPG name        External name                                    *
       * File name. . . . . . . . :  CH7P2           STAN/CH7P2                                       *
       * Record format(s) . . . . :  CH7P2R          CH7P2R                                           *
       *--------------------------------------------------------------------------------------------*
     5 FQsysprt   O    F  132        PRINTER OFLIND(*INOF)
     6
     7
     8=ICH7P2R
       *--------------------------------------------------------------------------------------------*
       * RPG record format  . . . . :  CH7P2R                                                        *
       * External format  . . . . . :  CH7P2R : STAN/CH7P2                                           *
       *--------------------------------------------------------------------------------------------*
     9=I                                A    1    4  SALESPERNO
    10=I                                A    5    6  DEPTNO
    11=I                                A    7    8  STORENO
    12=I                                P    9   12 2SALES_AMT
```

Figure 7-19 Compile listing of a multiple control group **RPG IV** program.

```
=I                                P    13   16 0SALES_DATE
C       *LIKE        DEFINE    SalesPerNo     HoldSalPNo                       define HoldSalpNo
C       *LIKE        DEFINE    DeptNo         HoldDeptNo                       define HoldDeptNo
C       *LIKE        DEFINE    StoreNo        HoldStorNo                       define HoldStoreNo
C       *LIKE        DEFINE    Sales_Amt      SalesP_Sum      +1               define SalesPSum
C       *LIKE        DEFINE    SalesP_Sum     Dept_Sum        +1               define dept sum
C       *LIKE        DEFINE    Dept_Sum       Store_Sum       +1               define StoreSum
C       *LIKE        DEFINE    Store_Sum      State_Sum       +1               define StateSum

C                    READ      Ch7P2                                 ----LR    read first record
C                    EXSR      HouseKepSR

C                    DOW       *INLR = *OFF                                    do while LR is off   B01

 * Heading control....
C                    IF        *INOF = *ON                                     OF "on" ?            B02
C                    EXCEPT    Heading                                         print heading lines   02
C                    EVAL      *INOF = *OFF                                    turn off OF indicatr  02
C                    ENDIF                                                     end IF group         E02

 * Begin processing....
C                    SELECT                                                    begin select group   B02
C                    WHEN      StoreNo <> HoldStorno                           branch to SalpSR     X02
C                    EXSR      SalpSR                                                                02
C                    EXSR      DeptSR                                          branch to DeptSR      02
C                    EXSR      StoreSR                                         branch to StoreSR     02
C                    WHEN      DeptNo <> HoldDeptNo                            dept break?          X02
C                    EXSR      SalpSR                                          branch to SalBrakSR   02
C                    EXSR      DeptSR                                                                02
C                    WHEN      SalesPerNo <> HoldSalPNo                        control break?       X02
C                    EXSR      SalpSR                                                                02
C                    ENDSL                                                     end CAS group        E02

C                    EVAL      SalesP_Sum = SalesP_Sum + Sales_Amt             Accumulate SalesPSum  01
C                    EXCEPT    DetaiLine                                       print detail line     01
C                    READ      Ch7P2                                 ----LR    read next record      01
C                    ENDDO                                                     end DOW group        E01

 * End of file processing....
C                    EXSR      EofSR                                           branch to EOF SR

 * Begin subroutines....
C       HouseKepSR   BEGSR                                                     begin HouseKepSR
C                    EVAL      HoldSalPNo = SalesPerNo                         initialze HoldSalPNo
C                    EVAL      HoldDeptNo = DeptNo                             initialze HoldDeptNo
C                    EVAL      HoldStorNo = StoreNo                            initialze HoldStorNo
C                    EVAL      *INOF = *ON                                     turn on OF indicator
C                    ENDSR                                                     end HouseKepSR

C       SalpSR       BEGSR                                                     begin SalpSR
C                    EVAL      Dept_Sum = Dept_Sum + SalesP_Sum                accumulate State_Sum
C                    EXCEPT    SPBrakLine                                      print break total
C                    EVAL      HoldSalPNo = SalesPerNo                         initialze HoldSalPNo
C                    EVAL      SalesP_Sum = *ZERO                              initialize SalesPSum
C                    ENDSR                                                     end SalpSR

C       DeptSR       BEGSR                                                     begin SalpSR
C                    EVAL      Store_Sum = Store_Sum + Dept_Sum                accumulate State_Sum
C                    EXCEPT    DpBrakLine                                      print break total
C                    EVAL      HoldDeptNo = DeptNo                             initialze HoldSalPNo
C                    EVAL      Dept_Sum = *ZERO                                initialize SalesPSum
C                    ENDSR                                                     end SalpSR

C       StoreSR      BEGSR                                                     begin SalpSR
C                    EVAL      State_Sum = State_Sum + Store_Sum               accumulate State_Sum
C                    EXCEPT    StBrakLine                                      print break total
C                    EVAL      HoldStorNo = StoreNo                            initialze HoldSalPNo
C                    EVAL      Store_Sum = *ZERO                               initialize SalesPSum
C                    ENDSR                                                     end SalpSR
```

Figure 7-19 Compile listing of a multiple control group **RPG IV** program. (Continued)

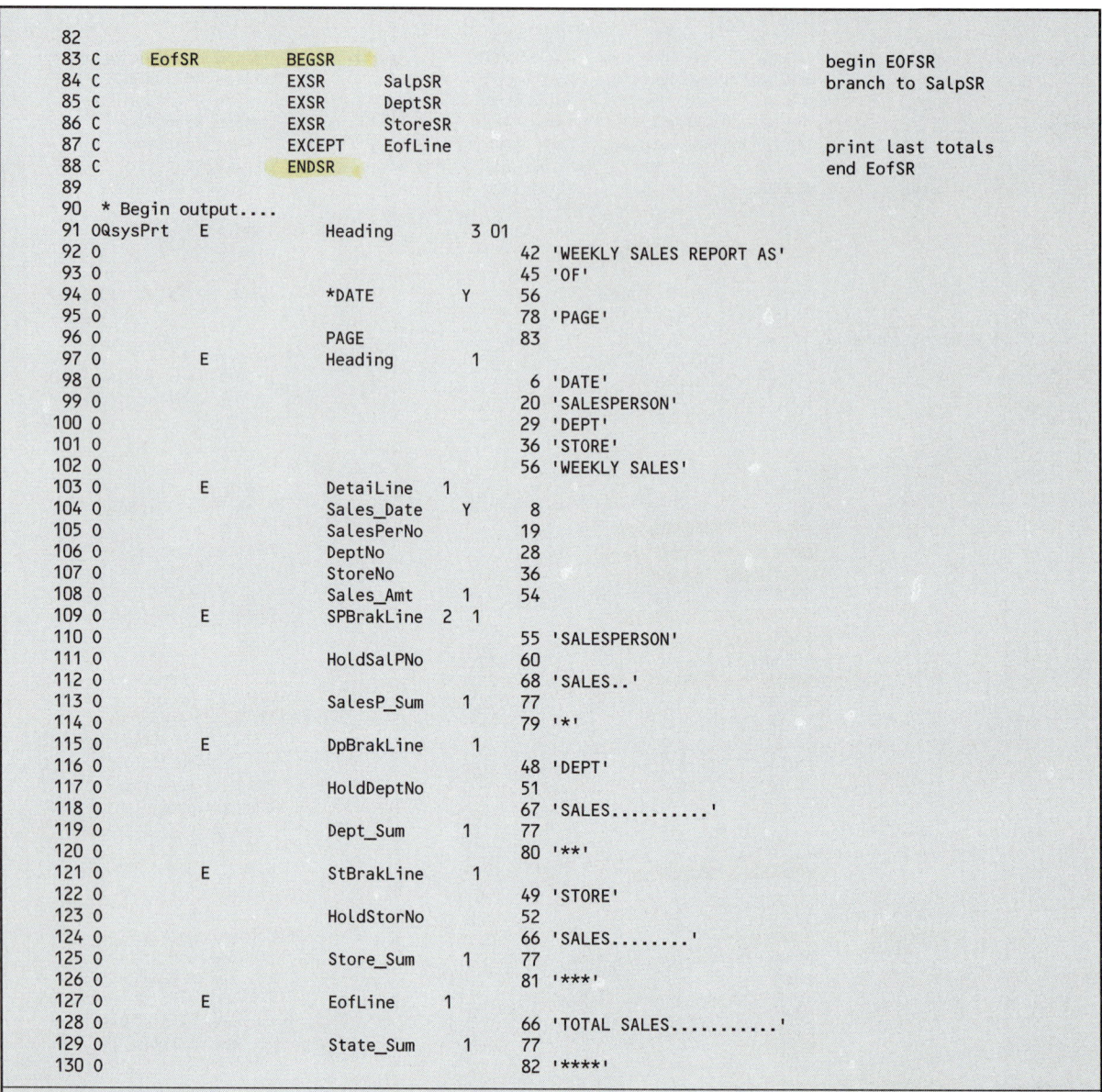

```
 82
 83 C     EofSR         BEGSR                                                   begin EOFSR
 84 C                   EXSR      SalpSR                                        branch to SalpSR
 85 C                   EXSR      DeptSR
 86 C                   EXSR      StoreSR
 87 C                   EXCEPT    EofLine                                       print last totals
 88 C                   ENDSR                                                   end EofSR
 89
 90  * Begin output....
 91 OQsysPrt   E            Heading        3 01
 92 O                                          42 'WEEKLY SALES REPORT AS'
 93 O                                          45 'OF'
 94 O                       *DATE         Y    56
 95 O                                          78 'PAGE'
 96 O                       PAGE               83
 97 O          E            Heading        1
 98 O                                           6 'DATE'
 99 O                                          20 'SALESPERSON'
100 O                                          29 'DEPT'
101 O                                          36 'STORE'
102 O                                          56 'WEEKLY SALES'
103 O          E            DetailLine   1
104 O                       Sales_Date    Y     8
105 O                       SalesPerNo         19
106 O                       DeptNo             28
107 O                       StoreNo            36
108 O                       Sales_Amt     1    54
109 O          E            SPBrakLine   2  1
110 O                                          55 'SALESPERSON'
111 O                       HoldSalPNo         60
112 O                                          68 'SALES..'
113 O                       SalesP_Sum    1    77
114 O                                          79 '*'
115 O          E            DpBrakLine      1
116 O                                          48 'DEPT'
117 O                       HoldDeptNo         51
118 O                                          67 'SALES..........'
119 O                       Dept_Sum      1    77
120 O                                          80 '**'
121 O          E            StBrakLine      1
122 O                                          49 'STORE'
123 O                       HoldStorNo         52
124 O                                          66 'SALES........'
125 O                       Store_Sum     1    77
126 O                                          81 '***'
127 O          E            EofLine      1
128 O                                          66 'TOTAL SALES...........'
129 O                       State_Sum     1    77
130 O                                          82 '****'
```

File Description Specifications

Line No.

4 Ch7p2 is defined as an input, full-procedural, externally described, keyed physical file.

5 Qsysprt is defined as an output, program-described printer file. The page overflow indicator **OF** is assigned to the file by the **OFLIND(*INOF)** keyword.

Calculation Specifications

14–20 The three ***LIKE DEFINE** instructions on lines 14–16 define three work fields: HoldSalPNo is defined with the same attributes as SalesPerNo; HoldDeptNo the same as Dept_No; and HoldStorNo the same as StoreNo.

The four ***LIKE DEFINE** instructions on lines 17–20 define three control group total fields and a field for State_Sum. Note that the next-larger control group total field is defined one integer larger than the preceding one.

Figure 7-19 Compile listing of a multiple control group **RPG IV** program. (Continued)

22 This **READ** instruction reads the first record from the physical file. If no records are stored in the file, the **LR** indicator (*Eq* field) will be turned on. The **DOW** relational test on line 25 will be "false," which will transfer control out of the **DOW** group, execute end-of-file processing, and end the job. Note that the program is coded with the assumption that at least *one* record is stored in the physical file.

23 This **EXSR** instruction branches control to the **HouseKepSR** that begins on line 55.

25 The **DOW** instruction begins the iterative process of reading the physical file and executing the related calculations for each record processed. When indicator **LR** is turned on by the **READ** instruction on line 22 or 48, control will exit from the **DOW** group, complete end-of-file processing, and end the job.

28 This **IF** instruction tests the status of the **OF** indicator. Because an **EVAL** instruction in the **HouseKepSR** (line 59) turned on the **OF** indicator, page overflow will occur for the first record processed and the Heading records will be printed. Subsequent page overflow processing will occur automatically when the overflow line is detected.

29 This **EXCEPT** instruction transfers control to output, where the values in the Heading line records are printed.

30 This **EVAL** instruction turns off the **OF** indicator so that page overflow will not occur for the next record processed.

31 The **ENDIF** operation ends the **IF** group that began on line 28.

34 The **SELECT** operation begins the **SELECT** group.

35 This **WHEN** instruction compares the value in StoreNo to HoldStorNo. If they are *not* equal, indicating a control break, the three **EXSR** instructions on lines 36–38 will be executed. Note that the largest control field is tested first for a control break, followed by the next largest (DeptNo), and then the smallest (SalesPerNo).

36 This **EXSR** instruction transfers control to the **SalpSR** subroutine.

37 This **EXSR** instruction transfers control to the **DeptSR** subroutine.

38 This **EXSR** instruction transfers control to the **StoreSR** subroutine.

Because the control group totals are printed with the salesperson group first, department group second, and store group last, the related subroutines are accessed in the same order.

39 If the **WHEN** instruction test on line 35 is not "true," the relational test for this **WHEN** instruction will be executed. When the value in DeptNo is *not* equal to the value in HoldDeptNo, a control break will be detected, and the **SalpSR** and **DeptSR** subroutines accessed.

40 This **EXSR** instruction transfers control to the **SalpSR** subroutine.

41 This **EXSR** instruction transfers control to the **DeptSR** subroutine.

42 If the **WHEN** instruction test on line 39 is not "true," the relational test for this **WHEN** instruction will be executed. When the value in SalesPerNo is *not* equal to the value in HoldSalPNo, a control break will be detected, and the **SalpSR** subroutine accessed.

43 This **EXSR** instruction transfers control to the **SalpSR** subroutine.

44 The **ENDSL** operation ends the **SELECT** group that began on line 34.

After the instructions included in a **WHEN** group are executed, control is transferred to the first executable instruction following the **ENDSL** operation.

If none of the three **WHEN** instruction tests is "true," indicating no control break, program control will automatically begin processing with the first executable instruction following the **ENDSL** operation.

46 This **EVAL** instruction adds the Sales_Amt value from the current record to the SalesPSum control group total field.

47 This **EXCEPT** instruction transfers control to output, where the DetailLine record values are printed (lines 103–108).

48 This **READ** instruction reads the next record in the physical file. If end of file is read, the **LR** indicator will be turned on.

49 The **ENDDO** operation ends the **DOW** group that began on line 25.

52 This **EXSR** instruction transfers control to the **EofSR** subroutine. It is executed only after end of file is read (**LR** set on) and control has exited from the **DOW** group.

55 This **BEGSR** instruction begins the **HouseKepSR** subroutine that was accessed by the **EXSR** instruction on line 23.

Figure 7-19 Compile listing of a multiple control group **RPG IV** program. (Continued)

56	This **EVAL** instruction initializes the HoldSalPNo field with the value from the input field SalesPerNo.
57	This **EVAL** instruction initializes the HoldDeptNo field with the value from the input field DeptNo.
58	This **EVAL** instruction initializes the HoldStorNo field with the value from the input field StoreNo.
59	This **EVAL** instruction turns on the **OF** (overflow) indicator so that page overflow will occur for the first record processed and the Heading lines printed.
60	The **ENDSR** operation ends the **HouseKepSR** subroutine that began on line 55.
62	This **BEGSR** instruction begins the **SalpSR** subroutine that was accessed by the **EXSR** instruction on line 36 after a control break (change in StoreNo) was detected; or by the **EXSR** instruction on line 40 after a change in DeptNo occurred; or by the **EXSR** instruction on line 43 after a change in SalesPerNo occurred; or by the **EXSR** instruction on line 84 after end of file was read.
63	This **EVAL** instruction adds the SalesP_Sum value to the Dept_Sum, the next-highest control group total field.
64	This **EXCEPT** instruction transfers control to output, where the SPBrakline record (control break total) is printed.
65	This **EVAL** instruction initializes the HoldSalNo field with the SalesPerNo value from the current record (the one that caused the control break).
66	This **EVAL** instruction initializes the SalesPSum field to zero so that the next SalesPSum total will not include the control field total from the previous SalesPerson.
67	This **ENDSR** operation ends the **SalpSR** subroutine.
69	This **BEGSR** instruction begins the **DeptSR** subroutine that was accessed by the **EXSR** instruction on line 37 after a change in StoreNo was detected; or by the **EXSR** instruction on line 41 after a change in DeptNo occurred; or by the **EXSR** instruction on line 85 after end of file is read.
70	This **EVAL** instruction adds the Dept_Sum value to the Store_Sum, the next-highest control group total field.
71	This **EXCEPT** instruction transfers control to output, where the DpBrakline record (control break total) is printed.
72	This **EVAL** instruction initializes the HoldDeptNo field with the DeptNo value from the current record (the one that caused the control break).
73	This **EVAL** instruction initializes the Dept_Sum field to zero so that the next Dept_Sum total will not include the control field total from the previous department group.
74	This **ENDSR** operation ends the **DeptSR** subroutine.
76	This **BEGSR** instruction begins the **StoreSR** subroutine that was accessed either by the **EXSR** instruction on line 38 after a change in StoreNo was detected or by the **EXSR** instruction on line 86 after end of file was read.
77	This **EVAL** instruction adds the Store_Sum value to the State_Sum.
78	This **EXCEPT** instruction transfers control to output, where the StBrakline record (control break total) is printed.
79	This **EVAL** instruction initializes the HoldStorNo field with the StoreNo value from the current record (the one that caused the control break).
80	This **EVAL** instruction initializes the Store_Sum field to zero so that the next Store_Sum total will not include the control field total from the previous store group.
81	This **ENDSR** operation ends the **StoreSR** subroutine.
83	This **BEGSR** instruction begins the **EofSR** subroutine that was accessed by the **EXSR** instruction on line 52 after the end of file was read by the **READ** instruction on line 48; the **LR** indicator turned on; and exit from the **DOW** group was executed.
84	This **EXSR** instruction transfers control to the **SalpSR** subroutine from which the control group total for the last SalesPerNo group will be printed before the other control group totals (Dept_Sum and Store_Sum) and the State_Sum are printed.
85	This **EXSR** instruction transfers control to the **DeptSR** subroutine from which the control group total for the last DeptNo group will be printed before the other control group total (Store_Sum) and the State_Sum are printed.
86	This **EXSR** instruction transfers control to the **StoreSR** subroutine from which the control group total for the last StoreNo group will be printed before the State_Sum is printed.
87	This **EXCEPT** instruction transfers control to output, where the EofLine record (control break total) is printed.
88	This **ENDSR** operation ends the **EofSR** subroutine.

Figure 7-19 Compile listing of a multiple control group **RPG IV** program. (Continued)

91–102	The Heading record formats are defined in these instructions and the values printed when the **EXCEPT** instruction on line 29 is executed.
103–108	The DetailLine record format is defined in these instructions and the values are printed when the **EXCEPT** instruction on line 47 is executed. Printing occurs for every record processed.
109–114	The SPBrakLine record format is defined in these instructions and the values are printed after a control break is detected and the **EXCEPT** instruction on line 64 is executed.
115–120	The DpBrakLine record format is defined in these instructions and the values are printed after a control break is detected and the **EXCEPT** instruction on line 71 is executed.
121–126	The StBrakLine record format is defined in these instructions and the values are printed after a control break is detected and the **EXCEPT** instruction on line 78 is executed.
127–130	The EofLine record format is defined in these instructions and the values are printed after end of file is read and the **EXCEPT** instruction on line 87 is executed.

Figure 7-19 Compile listing of a multiple control group **RPG IV** program. (Continued)

A flowchart that indicates the processing sequence of the internal subroutines for the multiple control group **RPG IV** program is presented in Figure 7-20. Note the following structure of the **SELECT** group:

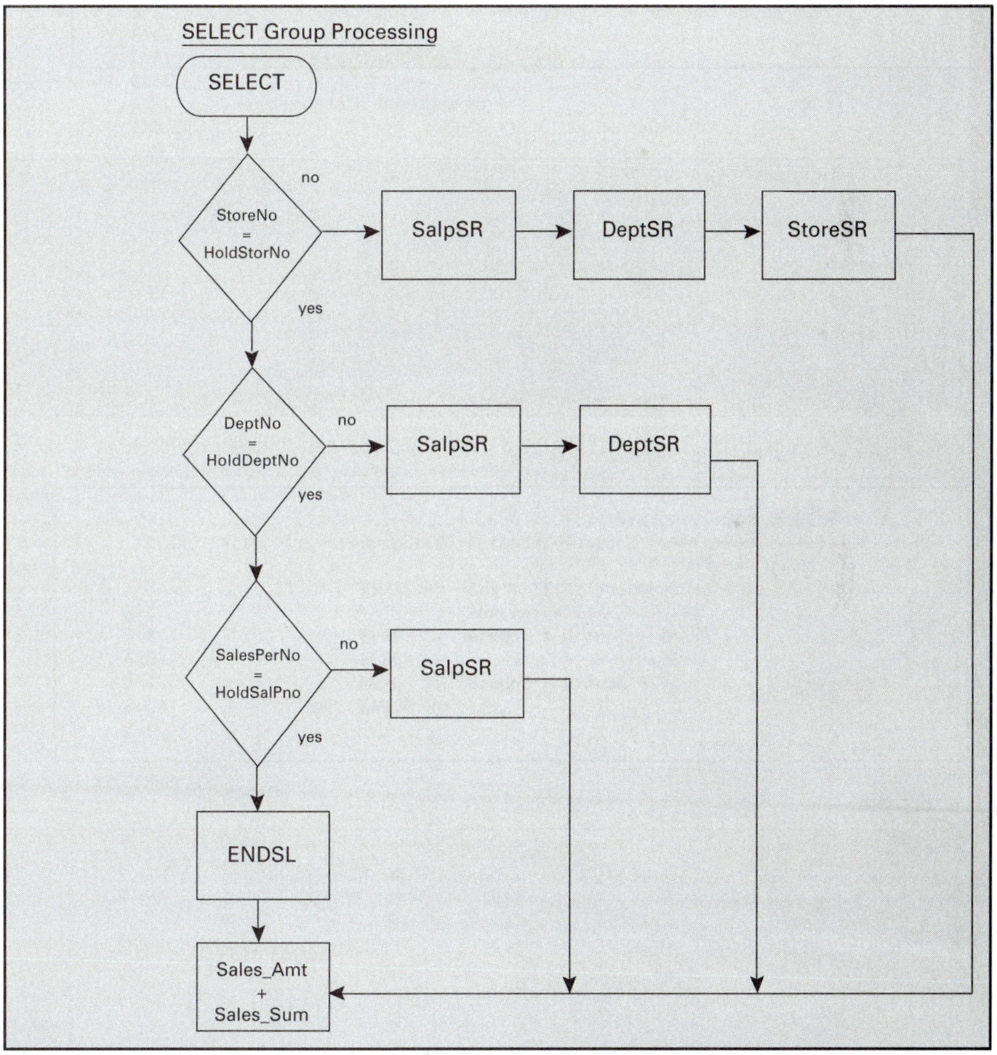

Figure 7-20 Flowchart showing **SELECT** group control of control breaks in the multiple control group program.

1. Control break tests are made in a *higher-to-lower* order. A control break for store (**StoreNo**) is tested first; department (**DeptNo**), second; and salesperson (**SalesPerNo**), last.
2. Within the **StoreSR** and **DeptSR** subroutines, however, the related control group subroutines are processed in a *lowest-to-highest* order.
3. After a control break is detected and the related subroutine(s) executed, control returns to the instruction in which the Sales_Amt from the current record is added to the Sales_Sum control group total field.

The report generated by the multiple conrol break program is shown in Figure 7-21. Note that the single, double, triple, and quadruple asterisks at the end of a control group total line are included in the report for the identification of the related total lines.

```
                         WEEKLY SALES REPORT AS OF  9/30/97                        PAGE   1

 DATE        SALESPERSON  DEPT     STORE      WEEKLY SALES

 9/08/97         1000       03       01             256.12
 9/15/97         1000       03       01           1,441.70
 9/22/97         1000       03       01             384.20
 9/29/97         1000       03       01             302.44

                                              SALESPERSON 1000 SALES.. 2,384.46 *

 9/08/97         1100       03       01             189.76
 9/15/97         1100       03       01             500.38
 9/22/97         1100       03       01           2,198.37
 9/29/97         1100       03       01             246.18

                                              SALESPERSON 1100 SALES.. 3,134.69 *
                                              DEPT 03   SALES......... 5,519.15 **

 9/08/97         1200       05       01           1,612.55
 9/15/97         1200       05       01             800.00
 9/22/97         1200       05       01             999.19
 9/29/97         1200       05       01           3,737.47

                                              SALESPERSON 1200 SALES.. 7,149.21 *
                                              DEPT 05   SALES......... 7,149.21 **
                                              STORE 01   SALES........ 12,668.36 ***

 9/08/97         1300       12       02             645.33
 9/15/97         1300       12       02             301.76
 9/22/97         1300       12       02           2,868.88
 9/29/97         1300       12       02           1,532.86

                                              SALESPERSON 1300 SALES.. 5,348.83 *
                                              DEPT 12   SALES......... 5,348.83 **
                                              STORE 02   SALES........ 5,348.83 ***

 9/08/97         1400       08       03             184.79
 9/15/97         1400       08       03             733.74
 9/22/97         1400       08       03             472.52
 9/29/97         1400       08       03           4,900.09

                                              SALESPERSON 1400 SALES.. 6,291.14 *
                                              DEPT 08   SALES.......... 6,291.14 **
                                              STORE 03   SALES......... 6,291.14 ***

                                              TOTAL SALES...........   24,308.33 ****
```

Figure 7-21 Report generated by the multiple control break **RPG IV** program.

TRADITIONAL RPG SYNTAX FOR INTERNAL SUBROUTINES

Except for the fact that internal subroutine names may now be a maximum of 10 characters instead of 6, the syntax for traditional (**RPG** and **RPG III**) programs is identical to the **RPG IV** coding discussed in this chapter.

TRADITIONAL RPG SYNTAX FOR CONTROL BREAK PROCESSING

Traditional **RPG** syntax for control break processing required the use of *Control Level Indicators*, **L1–L9.** As needed, one or more *Control Level Indicators* (L1–L9) are defined and assigned to one or more control fields in the *Input Specifications*. Then, select calculation and/or output instructions are conditioned with the related **L1** to **L9** indicator(s). Included in Figure 7-22 is a compile listing of a traditional **RPG** single control break program using a **L1** *Control Level Indicator* supplemented with a line-by-line explanation of the syntax.

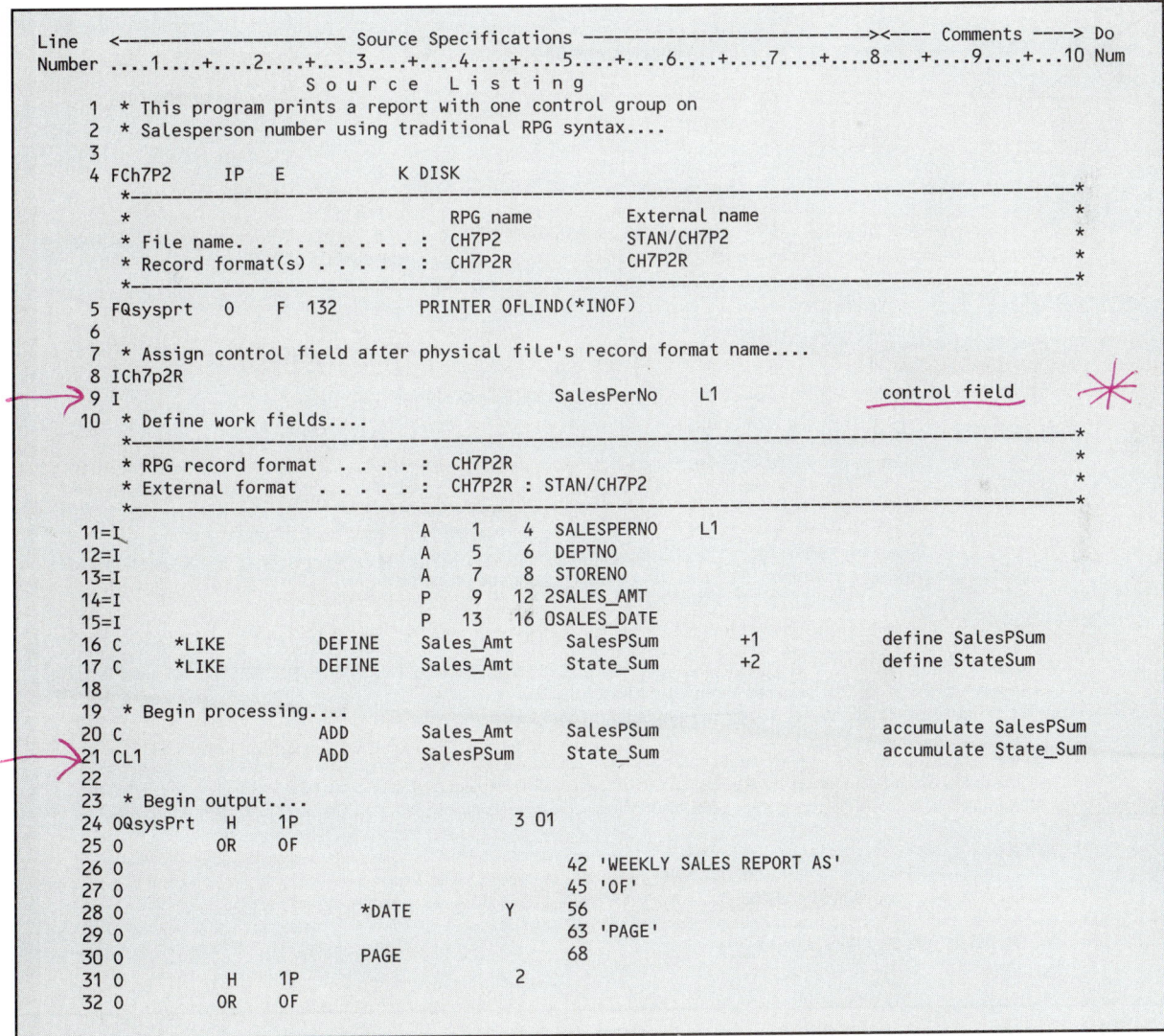

```
Line   <---------------------- Source Specifications ----------------------------><---- Comments ----> Do
Number ....1....+....2....+....3....+....4....+....5....+....6....+....7....+....8....+....9....+...10 Num
                          S o u r c e   L i s t i n g
       * This program prints a report with one control group on
       * Salesperson number using traditional RPG syntax....

      FCh7P2     IP   E           K DISK
       *--------------------------------------------------------------------------------------*
       *                              RPG name          External name                          *
       * File name. . . . . . . . . :  CH7P2             STAN/CH7P2                             *
       * Record format(s) . . . . . :  CH7P2R            CH7P2R                                 *
       *--------------------------------------------------------------------------------------*
      FQsysprt   O    F  132         PRINTER OFLIND(*INOF)

       * Assign control field after physical file's record format name....
      ICh7p2R
      I                                       SalesPerNo    L1                 control field
       * Define work fields....
       *--------------------------------------------------------------------------------------*
       * RPG record format  . . . . :  CH7P2R                                                   *
       * External format  . . . . . :  CH7P2R : STAN/CH7P2                                      *
       *--------------------------------------------------------------------------------------*
      I                           A    1    4  SALESPERNO    L1
      I                           A    5    6  DEPTNO
      I                           A    7    8  STORENO
      I                           P    9   12 2SALES_AMT
      I                           P   13   16 0SALES_DATE
      C     *LIKE         DEFINE    Sales_Amt     SalesPSum          +1           define SalesPSum
      C     *LIKE         DEFINE    Sales_Amt     State_Sum          +2           define StateSum

       * Begin processing....
      C                   ADD       Sales_Amt     SalesPSum                       accumulate SalesPSum
      CL1                 ADD       SalesPSum     State_Sum                       accumulate State_Sum

       * Begin output....
      OQsysPrt   H    1P                 3 01
      O          OR   OF
      O                                      42 'WEEKLY SALES REPORT AS'
      O                                      45 'OF'
      O                       *DATE       Y  56
      O                                      63 'PAGE'
      O                       PAGE           68
      O          H    1P                 2
      O          OR   OF
```

Figure 7-22 Compile listing of a traditional **RPG** program that generates a report with one control break.

```
33 0                                          6 'DATE'
34 0                                         20 'SALESPERSON'
35 0                                         41 'WEEKLY SALES'
36 0         DF   N1P                   1
37 0                     Sales_Date     Y     8
38 0                     SalesPerNo          19
39 0                     Sales_Amt      1    39
40 0         TF   L1                1  2
41 0                                         37 'SALESPERSON'
42 0                     SalesPerNo          42
43 0                                         53 'SALES.....'
44 0                     SalesPSum      1B   63
45 0                                         65 '*'
46 0         TF   LR                1
47 0                                         51 'TOTAL STATE SALES.....'
48 0                     State_Sum      1    63
49 0                                         66 '**'
```

The syntax for this program follows the **RPG** Logic Cycle, which automatically controls the opening of all files, the reading of the records from the input files, control break processing, and the closing of files. Note that *Heading* **(H)**, *Detail* **(D)**, and *Total* **(T)** time instructions control the sequence of the output instructions.

File Description Specifications

Line No.

4 Ch7P2 is defined as an input, primary, externally described, keyed physical file.

5 Qsysprt is defined as an output, program-described printer file. The page overflow indicator **OF** is assigned to the file by the **OFLIND(*INOF))** keyword.

Input Specifications

8 Because the physical file is externally described, its record format name (CH7P2R) must be specified in the *Record* name field (positions 7–16).

9 The **L1** *Control Level Indicator* (positions 63–64) is assigned to the SalesPerNo control field. When a change in SalesPerNo is detected, the **L1** *Control Level Indicator* is automatically turned on. This will also occur for the first and last records processed from the physical file.

Calculation Specification Syntax:

16 This ***LIKE DEFINE** instruction defines the SalesPSum field **1** integer larger than the Sales_Amt field.

17 This ***LIKE DEFINE** instruction defines the State_Sum field **2** integers larger than the Sales_Amt field.

20 For each record read from the physical file, the Sales_Amt field value is added to the SalesPSum field. When a change in the SalesPerNo is detected (control break and **L1** turned on), this instruction will be ignored and the following instruction conditioned by the **L1** indicator in positions 7 and 8 (Total Time) will be executed. After the *Total* time instruction on line 21 is executed and **L1** *Total* time output (**T** in position 17) printed (lines 40–45), this instruction will be executed for the current record (the one that caused the control break) being processed.

21 The *Control Level Indicator* **L1** in positions 7–8 turns on at *Total* time when a change in the SalesPerNo field value is detected, causing a control break. If a change in the SalesPerNo value is not detected (no control break), this instruction will be ignored for the current record processed.

Output Specification Syntax:

24 The system-supplied printer file name **QSYSPRT** (defined in the *File Description*) is specified in positions 7–16. The **H** in position 17 defines this instruction as a "header" type output record. Triple spacing is specified with the **3** in the *Space after* field (positions 43–45). The **01** entry in the *Skip before* field controls the skipping of the paper to line 1 of a new page after page overflow is sensed and the current line printed.

The **1P** (First Page) indicator is automatically turned on after the files are opened and before a record is read from the input file(s). Any *Definition, Input,* and/or *Calculation Specification* instructions will be ignored. *Output Specification* instructions conditioned by the **1P** indicator (or no indicator) will be executed. After this "first cycle" processing is completed, the **1P** indicator is permanently turned off and the first record is read from the input file.

25 The **OR** entry in positions 16–17 indicates that this instruction is in an "**OR**" relationship with the previous instruction on line 24. The **OF** overflow indicator, which was defined with the keyword **OFLIND(*INOF)** in positions 44–80 of the *File Description* instruction for the printer file, is entered in positions 22–23. When page overflow is detected, the overflow indicator defined is turned on, the current line is printed, and the paper is advanced to the next page, where any output records conditioned by the **OF** overflow indicator are printed. Any one of the available page overflow indicators (i.e., **OA, OB, OC, OD, OE, OF,** or **OV**) may be specified.

Figure 7-22 Compile listing of a traditional **RPG** program that generates a report with one control break. (Continued)

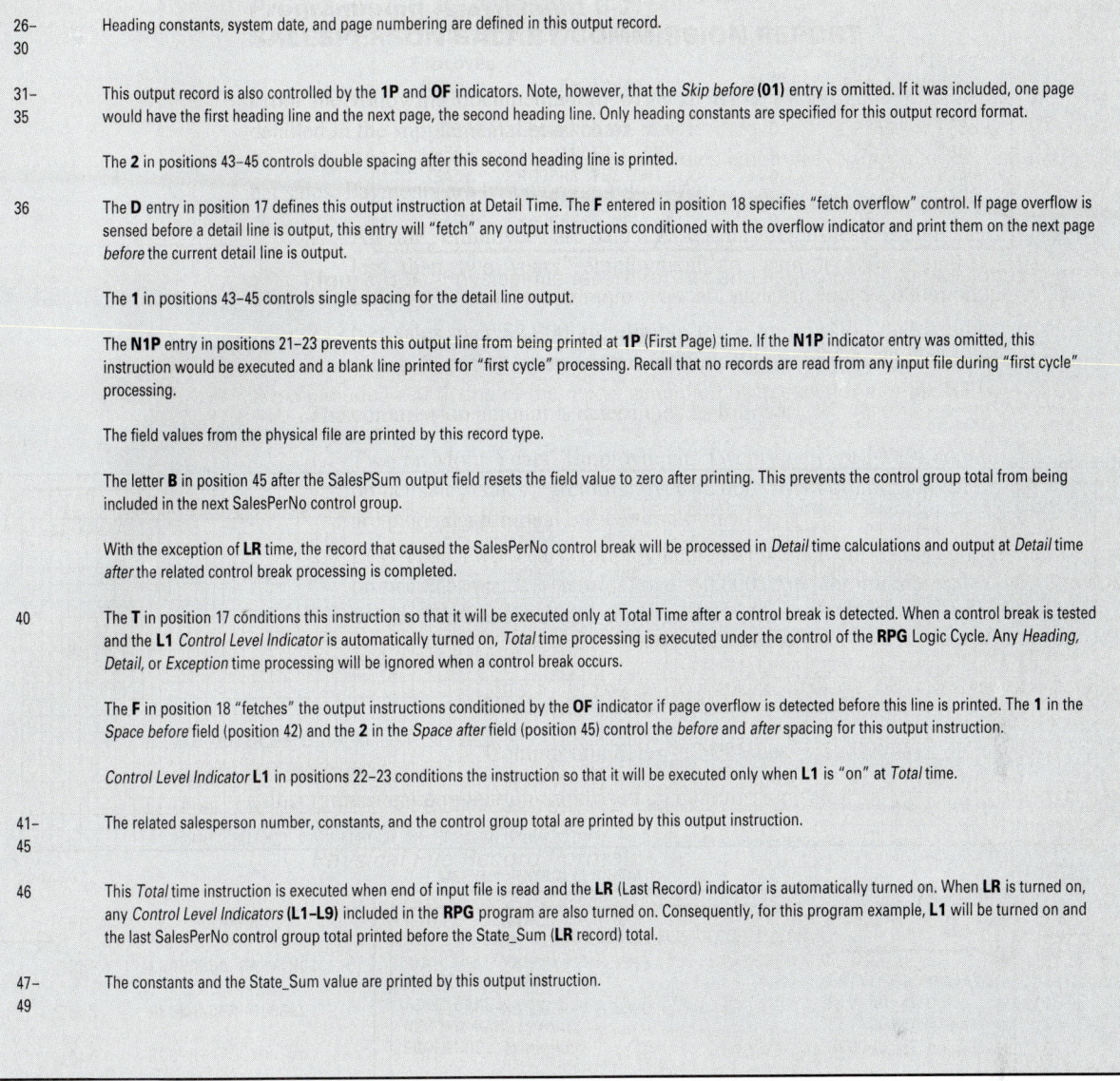

26–30	Heading constants, system date, and page numbering are defined in this output record.
31–35	This output record is also controlled by the **1P** and **OF** indicators. Note, however, that the *Skip before* **(01)** entry is omitted. If it was included, one page would have the first heading line and the next page, the second heading line. Only heading constants are specified for this output record format.
	The **2** in positions 43–45 controls double spacing after this second heading line is printed.
36	The **D** entry in position 17 defines this output instruction at Detail Time. The **F** entered in position 18 specifies "fetch overflow" control. If page overflow is sensed before a detail line is output, this entry will "fetch" any output instructions conditioned with the overflow indicator and print them on the next page *before* the current detail line is output.
	The **1** in positions 43–45 controls single spacing for the detail line output.
	The **N1P** entry in positions 21–23 prevents this output line from being printed at **1P** (First Page) time. If the **N1P** indicator entry was omitted, this instruction would be executed and a blank line printed for "first cycle" processing. Recall that no records are read from any input file during "first cycle" processing.
	The field values from the physical file are printed by this record type.
	The letter **B** in position 45 after the SalesPSum output field resets the field value to zero after printing. This prevents the control group total from being included in the next SalesPerNo control group.
	With the exception of **LR** time, the record that caused the SalesPerNo control break will be processed in *Detail* time calculations and output at *Detail* time *after* the related control break processing is completed.
40	The **T** in position 17 conditions this instruction so that it will be executed only at Total Time after a control break is detected. When a control break is tested and the **L1** *Control Level Indicator* is automatically turned on, *Total* time processing is executed under the control of the **RPG** Logic Cycle. Any *Heading, Detail,* or *Exception* time processing will be ignored when a control break occurs.
	The **F** in position 18 "fetches" the output instructions conditioned by the **OF** indicator if page overflow is detected before this line is printed. The **1** in the *Space before* field (position 42) and the **2** in the *Space after* field (position 45) control the *before* and *after* spacing for this output instruction.
	Control Level Indicator **L1** in positions 22–23 conditions the instruction so that it will be executed only when **L1** is "on" at *Total* time.
41–45	The related salesperson number, constants, and the control group total are printed by this output instruction.
46	This *Total* time instruction is executed when end of input file is read and the **LR** (Last Record) indicator is automatically turned on. When **LR** is turned on, any *Control Level Indicators* **(L1–L9)** included in the **RPG** program are also turned on. Consequently, for this program example, **L1** will be turned on and the last SalesPerNo control group total printed before the State_Sum (**LR** record) total.
47–49	The constants and the State_Sum value are printed by this output instruction.

Figure 7-22 Compile listing of a traditional **RPG** program that generates a report with one control break. (Continued)

The report generated by this traditional single control break **RPG** program is identical to the one previously shown in Figure 7-20.

Traditional RPG Multiple Control Break Program

A compile listing of a traditional **RPG** program that controls multiple (three) control breaks is detailed in Figure 7-23. Examine the program and note the following syntax:

1. Three control fields (SalesPerNo, DeptNo, and StoreNo) assigned **L1, L2,** and **L3** *Control Level Indicators* are specified in the *Input Specifications.*

2. Three *Total* time instructions, conditioned by **L1, L2,** and **L3** *Control Level Indicators*, control the control level break processing in the *Calculation Specifications*.
3. Three *Total* time instructions (**T** in position 17) define the three control group total records in the *Output Specifications*.

```
Line   <---------------------- Source Specifications ----------------------------><---- Comments ----> Do
Number ....1....+....2....+....3....+....4....+....5....+....6....+....7....+....8....+....9....+...10 Num
                        S o u r c e   L i s t i n g
     1  * This program prints a report with control group breaks on
     2  * salesperson number, department number, and store number....
     3
     4 FCh7p2     IP   E           K DISK
        *------------------------------------------------------------------------------------------*
        *                                  RPG name          External name                         *
        * File name. . . . . . . . . :   CH7P2             STAN/CH7P2                              *
        * Record format(s) . . . . . :   CH7P2R            CH7P2R                                  *
        *------------------------------------------------------------------------------------------*
     5 FQsysprt   O    F  132          PRINTER OFLIND(*INOF)
     6
     7  * Assign control fields after physical file record format name....
     8 ICh7p2r
     9 I                                          SalesPerNo    L1
    10 I                                          DeptNo        L2
    11 I                                          StoreNo       L3
    12
    13  * Define work fields....
        *------------------------------------------------------------------------------------------*
        * RPG record format  . . . . :   CH7P2R                                                    *
        * External format  . . . . . :   CH7P2R : STAN/CH7P2                                       *
        *------------------------------------------------------------------------------------------*
    14=I                               A    1    4 SALESPERNO    L1
    15=I                               A    5    6 DEPTNO        L2
    16=I                               A    7    8 STORENO       L3
    17=I                               P    9   12 2SALES_AMT
    18=I                               P   13   16 0SALES_DATE
    19 C     *LIKE       DEFINE    Sales_Amt     SalesP_Sum          +1            define SalesPSum
    20 C     *LIKE       DEFINE    SalesP_Sum    Dept_Sum            +1            define dept sum
    21 C     *LIKE       DEFINE    Dept_Sum      Store_Sum           +1            define StoreSum
    22 C     *LIKE       DEFINE    Store_Sum     State_Sum           +1            define StateSum
    23
    24  * Begin processing....
    25 C                 ADD       Sales_Amt     SalesP_Sum                        accumulate SalesPSum
    26 CL1               ADD       SalesP_Sum    Dept_Sum                          accumulate DeptSum
    27 CL2               ADD       Dept_Sum      Store_Sum                         accumulate StoreSum
    28 CL3               ADD       Store_Sum     State_Sum                         accumulate state sum
    29
    30  * Begin output....
    31 OQsysPrt   H    1P                 3 01
    32 O         OR    OF
    33 O                                      42 'WEEKLY SALES REPORT AS'
    34 O                                      45 'OF'
    35 O                     *DATE        Y   56
    36 O                                      78 'PAGE'
    37 O                     PAGE             83
    38 O          H    1P                 1
    39 O         OR    OF
    40 O                                       6 'DATE'
    41 O                                      20 'SALESPERSON'
    42 O                                      29 'DEPT'
    43 O                                      36 'STORE'
    44 O                                      56 'WEEKLY SALES'
```

Figure 7-23 Compile listing of a traditional **RPG** program that generates a report with multiple control breaks.

```
45 O          D   N1P                   1
46 O                        Sales_Date     Y    8
47 O                        SalesPerNo         19
48 O                        DeptNo             28
49 O                        StoreNo            36
50 O                        Sales_Amt      1   54
51 O          T    L1                  2  1
52 O                                           55 'SALESPERSON'
53 O                        SalesPerNo         60
54 O                                           68 'SALES..'
55 O                        SalesP_Sum    1B   77
56 O                                           79 '*'
57 O          T    L2                     1
58 O                                           48 'DEPT'
59 O                        DeptNo             51
60 O                                           67 'SALES..........'
61 O                        Dept_Sum      1B   77
62 O                                           80 '**'
63 O          T    L3                     1
64 O                                           49 'STORE'
65 O                        StoreNo            52
66 O                                           66 'SALES........'
67 O                        Store_Sum     1B   77
68 O                                           81 '***'
69 O          T    LR                  1
70 O                                           66 'TOTAL SALES...........'
71 O                        State_Sum      1   77
72 O                                           82 '****'
```

The syntax for this program follows the **RPG** Logic Cycle, (see Appendix F), which automatically controls the opening of all files, the reading of the records from the input files, control break processing, and the closing of files. Note that *Heading* **(H)**, *Detail* **(D)**, and *Total* **(T)** time instructions control the sequence of the output instructions.

File Description Specification

Line No.	
4	Ch7P2 is defined as an input, primary, externally described, keyed physical file.
5	Qsysprt is defined as an output, program-described printer file. The page overflow indicator **OF** is assigned to the file by the **OFLIND(*INOF)** keyword.

Input Specifications

8	Because the physical file is externally described, its record format name (CH7p2r) must be specified in the *Record* name field (positions 7–16).
9–11	Three *Control Level Indicators,* **L1, L2,** and **L3,** are assigned to the control fields, SalesPerNo, DeptNo, and StoreNo, respectively. When a change in the StoreNo value is detected, **L3** will turn on, which will also set on **L2** and **L1.** If no change in the StoreNo value is tested but a change in the DeptNo value is, *Control Level Indicators* **L2** and **L1** will be set on. Then, if no change is detected in the StoreNo or DeptNo values but *is* tested for SalesPerNo, only **L1** will be turned on. Consequently, when a higher *Control Level Indicator* (e.g., **L3**) is set on, it will automatically set on any lower *Control Level Indicators,* (e.g., **L1** and **L2**) specified in the program.

Calculation Specifications

19–22	The four ***LIKE DEFINE** instructions define the three control group total fields and the State_Sum field. SalesP_Sum is defined 1 integer larger than Sales_Amt; Dept_Sum is defined 1 integer larger than SalesP_Sum; Store_Sum is defined 1 integer larger than Dept_Sum; and State_Sum is defined 1 integer larger than Store_Sum.
25–26	For each record read from the physical file, the Sales_Amt field value is added to the SalesP_Sum field. When a change in the SalesPerNo (**L1** control break) is sensed, this instruction will be ignored and the instruction on line 26 executed, where the SalesP_Sum total is added to the Dept_Sum field.
27	When a change in DeptNo is detected, *Control Level Indicator* **L2** will be set on, which will also turn on **L1.** This will execute the instruction on line 26 conditioned at *Total* time (positions 7–8) with the **L1** *Control Level Indicator* and the instruction on line 27 conditioned at *Total* time with the **L2** *Control Level Indicator,* where the Dept_Sum total is added to the Store_Sum field.

Figure 7-23 Compile listing of a traditional **RPG** program that generates a report with multiple control breaks. (Continued)

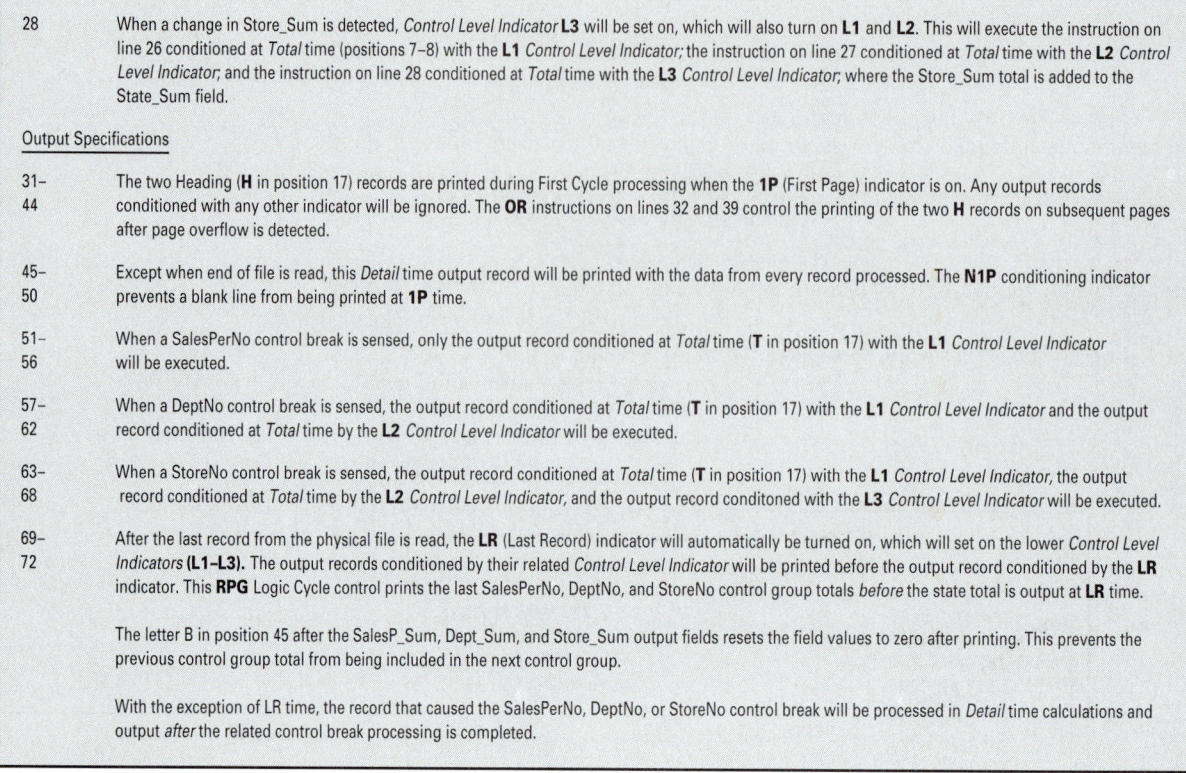

28	When a change in Store_Sum is detected, *Control Level Indicator* **L3** will be set on, which will also turn on **L1** and **L2**. This will execute the instruction on line 26 conditioned at *Total* time (positions 7–8) with the **L1** *Control Level Indicator;* the instruction on line 27 conditioned at *Total* time with the **L2** *Control Level Indicator*; and the instruction on line 28 conditioned at *Total* time with the **L3** *Control Level Indicator*, where the Store_Sum total is added to the State_Sum field.
Output Specifications	
31–44	The two Heading (**H** in position 17) records are printed during First Cycle processing when the **1P** (First Page) indicator is on. Any output records conditioned with any other indicator will be ignored. The **OR** instructions on lines 32 and 39 control the printing of the two **H** records on subsequent pages after page overflow is detected.
45–50	Except when end of file is read, this *Detail* time output record will be printed with the data from every record processed. The **N1P** conditioning indicator prevents a blank line from being printed at **1P** time.
51–56	When a SalesPerNo control break is sensed, only the output record conditioned at *Total* time (**T** in position 17) with the **L1** *Control Level Indicator* will be executed.
57–62	When a DeptNo control break is sensed, the output record conditioned at *Total* time (**T** in position 17) with the **L1** *Control Level Indicator* and the output record conditioned at *Total* time by the **L2** *Control Level Indicator* will be executed.
63–68	When a StoreNo control break is sensed, the output record conditioned at *Total* time (**T** in position 17) with the **L1** *Control Level Indicator,* the output record conditioned at *Total* time by the **L2** *Control Level Indicator,* and the output record conditoned with the **L3** *Control Level Indicator* will be executed.
69–72	After the last record from the physical file is read, the **LR** (Last Record) indicator will automatically be turned on, which will set on the lower *Control Level Indicators* **(L1–L3).** The output records conditioned by their related *Control Level Indicator* will be printed before the output record conditioned by the **LR** indicator. This **RPG** Logic Cycle control prints the last SalesPerNo, DeptNo, and StoreNo control group totals *before* the state total is output at **LR** time.
	The letter B in position 45 after the SalesP_Sum, Dept_Sum, and Store_Sum output fields resets the field values to zero after printing. This prevents the previous control group total from being included in the next control group.
	With the exception of LR time, the record that caused the SalesPerNo, DeptNo, or StoreNo control break will be processed in *Detail* time calculations and output *after* the related control break processing is completed.

Figure 7-23 Compile listing of a traditional **RPG** program that generates a report with multiple control breaks. (Continued)

SUMMARY

Internal subroutines logically group calculation instructions into separate modules. They are controlled in an **RPG IV** program by four operations: **EXSR** *(Invoke Subroutine)*; **CASxx** *(Compare and Branch to a Subroutine)*; **BEGSR** *(Beginning of Subroutine)*; and **ENDSR** *(End of Subroutine)*. When the end of an internal subroutine is encountered, program control returns to the instruction following the related **EXSR** or **ENDCS** operation and any *detail* or *total time* processing continues. Then, within the sequence of instructions, when the first **BEGSR** operation is read without an **EXSR**-controlled branch, all of the subroutines are ignored and program control "falls through" to the first *implied* or *explicit* output instruction.

The instructions included in each internal subroutine must follow all detail and total time calculations. The order of the subroutines does not indicate the processing sequence; that is conrolled by the order of the **EXSR** and/or **CASxx** instructions.

The **CASxx** operation combines the functions of the **COMP** and **EXSR** operations. One or more **CASxx** instructions in a consecutive order are referred to as a *case group*, which must be ended by an **ENDCS** or **END** operation. If more than one **CASxx** instruction is included in a case group, and one is executed, any subsequent ones are ignored. Regardless of how a subroutine is executed, after the **ENDSR** operation is read, program control returns to the instruction following the related **EXSR** operation or the **ENDCS** operation for a **CAS** group.

The system time value may be accessed by the **TIME** operation. It may be accessed in an **hhmmss** format or in a system time/date (**hhmmssmmddyy** or **hhmmss-mmddyyyy**) format. An alternative method of accessing the system time value is with a "standalone" *Definition Specification* instruction. Similar to the system date, the default system time may be changed for a job by the **CHGJOB** command.

In addition to end-of-file totals, many reports require subtotals. Structured **RPG IV** programs should avoid the use of the traditional *Control Level Indicators* (**L1–L9**) and instead use programmer-controlled *control break* processing. Before a physical file is processed for subtotals, it must be in the related *control field* value order. The required sequencing of the file's data may be performed by sorting or a logical file.

QUESTIONS

7-1. Define *internal subroutines*. When should they be included in an **RPG IV** program?

7-2. What **RPG IV** operations control the processing of *internal subroutines?* Explain the function of each operation.

7-3. Where in the body of an **RPG IV** program are the instructions for an internal subroutine placed?

7-4. If more than one internal subroutine is included in an **RPG IV** program, what controls the order in which they will be processed?

7-5. What is the sequence of processing after an internal subroutine is executed?

7-6. What **RPG IV** operations and indicators may be included in an internal subroutine?

7-7. Explain the function of the **CASxx** operation. What must be substituted for the **xx** entry?

7-8. What is a *case group*? How is it ended?

Examine the following coding and answer Questions 7-9 through 7-11:

```
..... *.. 1 ...+... 2 ...+... 3 ...+... 4 ...+... 5 ...+... 6 ...+... 7 ...+... 8
      CLON01Factor 1++++++Opcode(E)+Factor2+++++++Result++++++++Len++D_HiLOEQ....

   10 C      FieldA        CASEQ     FieldB        Subroutin1
   20 C      FieldA        CASGT     FieldC        Subroutin2
   30 C                    CAS                     Subroutin3
   40 C                    ENDCS
   50 C                      :
```

7-9. If the instruction on line 10 is true, where does program control branch? Where does it return?

7-10. If the instruction on line 10 is false, what processing occurs?

7-11. When is the **CAS** operation on line 30 executed? Where does program control return?

7-12. By what methods may the system time be accessed in an **RPG IV** program?

7-13. With the operation named in Question 7-12, in what formats may system time be accessed?

Examine the following coding and answer Questions 7-14 through 7-16:

```
.. *.. 1 ...+... 2 ...+... 3 ...+... 4 ...+... 5 ...+... 6 ...+... 7 ...+... 8
   CLON01Factor 1++++++Opcode(E)+Factor2+++++++Result++++++++Len++D_HiLOEQ....

10 C                    TIME                    Time1               6 0
20 C                    TIME                    Time2              12 0
30 C                    TIME                    Time3              14 0
```

7-14. In what format will the system time be accessed by the **TIME** instruction on line 10?

7-15. In what format will the system time be accessed by the **TIME** instruction on line 20?

7-16. In what format will the system time be accessed by the **TIME** instruction on line 30?

Examine the following coding and answer Questions 7-17 through 7-22:

```
.. 1 ...+... 2 ...+... 3 ...+... 4 ...+... 5 ...+... 6 ...+... 7 ...+... 8
DName+++++++++++ETDsFrom+++To/L+++IDc.Keywords+++++++++++++++++++++++++++++

DSystemTime       S                T    TIMFMT(*HMS:)
```

7-17. What does the **SystemTime** entry in the *Name* field define?

7-18. What is the function of the **S** entered in position 24?

7-19. What is the function of the **T** entered in position 40?

7-20. What is the function of the **TIMFMT(*HMS:)** keyword?

7-21. What other entries may be substituted for the ***HMS**: entry in the **TIMFMT** keyword?

7-22. In the **HMS:** entry of the **TIMFMT** keyword, what is the function of the **:** (colon) entry?

7-23. Define the following terms: *control field, control group, control break,* and *control group total.*

7-24. How must the data in a physical file be organized before an **RPG IV** program that processes one control break is executed?

7-25. Refer to Question 7-24. By what methods may the data in the physical file be organized for control group processing?

7-26. When the first record is read from a physical file, what housekeeping is necessary for a programmer-controlled group report program that supports two control breaks?

7-27. In a programmer-controlled group report program that supports three control groups (state, county, and town), in what order should the control fields be tested?

7-28. Refer to Question 7-27. In what order will the internal subroutines be processed after the control break for the largest control group is detected?

7-29. What function(s) must be performed after a control group total is printed?

7-30. What are *Control Level Indicators*? Where are they defined in an **RPG IV** program? On which specification may they be used to condition instructions?

7-31. When do *Control Level Indicators* turn on?

Examine the following traditional **RPG** *coding and answer Questions 7-32 through 7-40:*

```
.. *.. 1 ...+... 2 ...+... 3 ...+... 4 ...+... 5 ...+... 6 ...+... 7 ...+... 8
   CL0N01Factor 1++++++Opcode(E)+Factor2+++++++Result++++++++Len++D_HiLOEQ....

10 C                   ADD       PiecesMade    SectionSum
20 C                   ADD       SectionSum    DeptSum
30 C                   ADD       DeptSum       PlantSum
40 C                   ADD       PlantSum      CompanySum
```

7-32. Assume that **SectionNo, DeptNo,** and **PlantNo** are the control fields specified in an **RPG** program. On which instructions will the *Control Level Indicators* **L1, L2, L3,** and **LR** be assigned and in what *Calculation Specification* field?

7-33. If *no* control break occurs for the current record processed, which *Calculation Specification* instruction(s) is/are executed? Use instruction number(s) for your answer.

7-34. If a **SectionNo** control break occurs for the current record processed, which *Calculation Specification* instruction(s) is/are executed? Use instruction number(s) for your answer.

7-35. If a **DeptNo** control break occurs for the current record processed, which *Calculation Specification* instruction(s) is/are executed? Use instruction number(s) for your answer.

7-36. If a **PlantNo** control break occurs for the current record processed, which *Calculation Specification* instruction(s) is/are executed? Use instruction number(s) for your answer.

7-37. When end of file is read and the **LR** *(Last Record)* indicator is turned on, what other indicators will be set on? What output is printed?

7-38. If a **SectioNo** control break occurs, what *Output Specification* instruction(s) will be executed?

7-39. If a **DeptNo** control break occurs, what *Output Specification* instruction(s) will be executed?

7-40. If a **PlantNo** control break occurs, what *Output Specification* instruction(s) will be executed?

7-41. At what time in the **RPG** Logic Cycle does Control Break processing occur?

PROGRAMMING ASSIGNMENTS

For each of the following programming assignments, a physical file must have been created and loaded with the related data records. Your instructor will inform you if you have to create the physical file and load it or if it has been prepared for the assignment.

Programming Assignment 7-1: VOTER REPORT BY TOWN AND STATE TOTALS

Write an **RPG IV** program to generate the report detailed in the supplemental printer spacing chart.

Physical File Record Format:

```
                    PHYSICAL FILE DESCRIPTION

SYSTEM: AS/400                                  DATE: Yours
FILE NAME: Yours                                REV NO: 0
RECORD NAME: Yours                              KEY LENGTH: 9
SEQUENCE: Keyed                                 RECORD SIZE: 13

                       FIELD DEFINITIONS

 FIELD    FIELD NAME    SIZE  TYPE    POSITION     COMMENTS
  NO                                 FROM    TO

  1       DISTRICTNO      4    C        1     4   3rd key
  2       TOWNNO          3    C        5     7   2nd key
  3       COUNTYNO        2    C        8     9   1st key
  4       VOTERS          6    P       10    13   0 decimals
```

Physical File Data:

District Number	Town Number	County Number	Number of Voters In District
1000	100	10	215625
1010	100	10	082784
1020	100	10	104716
1030	100	10	012899
1040	100	10	267004
2000	200	10	057800
2010	200	10	014111
2020	200	10	118923
2030	200	10	073807
3000	300	30	200749
3010	300	30	111111
4000	400	40	067242
4010	400	40	104338
4020	400	40	099917
4030	400	40	178615
4040	400	40	222234
4050	400	40	033845
4060	400	40	117871
4070	400	40	064899
4080	400	40	045348
4090	400	40	888888

Note: A field is included for county number that is not referenced for this assignment. It is, however, required for the multiple control group report for Assignment 7-3.

Processing: Process the input file consecutively, and accumulate the number of voters in each district into a control total. Also, maintain a total for all the voters in the state that is to be printed after end of file is tested. Refer to the following printer spacing chart result field sizes. Print the report in a *detail* format.

Report Design:

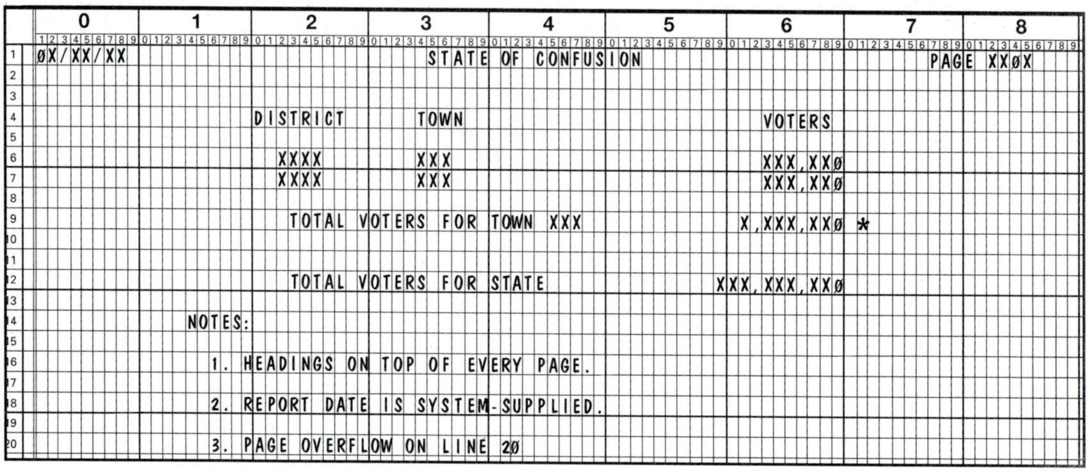

Because of the limited number of data records, page overflow will not be tested. Therefore, with *permission from the instructor*, use the **FORMLEN** keyword to change the page length to 22 lines and the **FORMOFL** keyword to change the page overflow line to 20.

Programming Assignment 7-2: VOTER REPORT BY TOWN, COUNTY, AND STATE TOTALS

If Assignment 7-1 was previously completed, supplement it to include the changes in the modified printer spacing chart shown below. On the other hand, if Assignment 7-1 was not completed, refer to that assignment for input record format and data.

Physical File Record Format: Refer to the record format in Assignment 7-1. Define town number and county number as the two control fields.

Processing: Read the file consecutively and accumulate a town total. When the town number changes, add the accumulated town total to a county total field. Then, when the county number changes, add the accumulated county total to a state total. Print related output according to the report format detailed in the print chart.

Report Design:

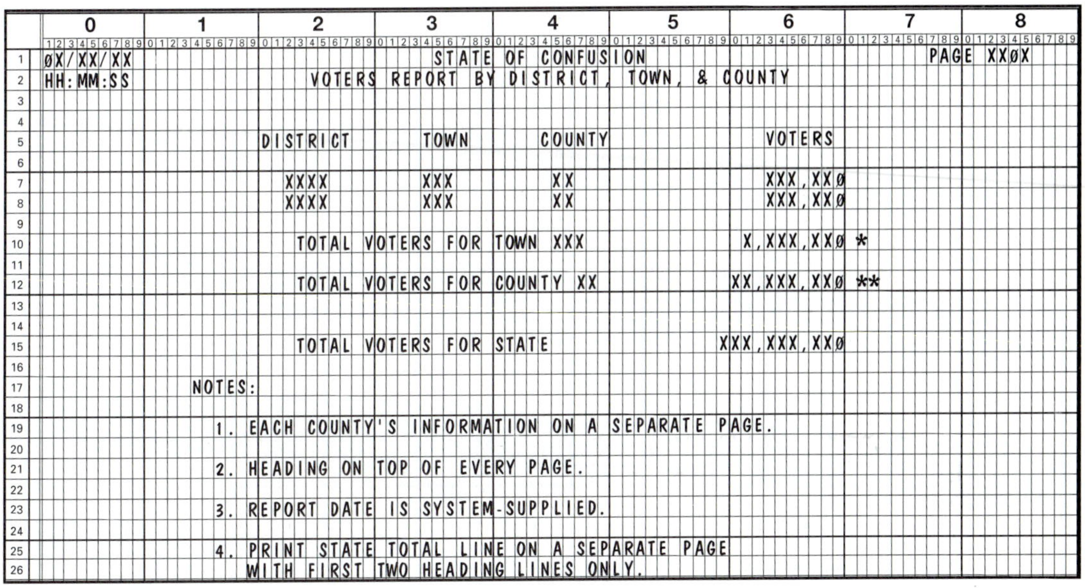

```
ØX/XX/XX                          STATE OF CONFUSION                          PAGE XXØX
HH:MM:SS               VOTERS REPORT BY DISTRICT, TOWN, & COUNTY


                   DISTRICT      TOWN      COUNTY                 VOTERS

                     XXXX        XXX         XX                   XXX,XXØ
                     XXXX        XXX         XX                   XXX,XXØ

                      TOTAL VOTERS FOR TOWN XXX                X,XXX,XXØ *

                      TOTAL VOTERS FOR COUNTY XX              XX,XXX,XXØ **


                      TOTAL VOTERS FOR STATE                 XXX,XXX,XXØ

             NOTES:

               1. EACH COUNTY'S INFORMATION ON A SEPARATE PAGE.

               2. HEADING ON TOP OF EVERY PAGE.

               3. REPORT DATE IS SYSTEM-SUPPLIED.

               4. PRINT STATE TOTAL LINE ON A SEPARATE PAGE
                  WITH FIRST TWO HEADING LINES ONLY.
```

Programming Assignment 7-3: PLANT RAW MATERIALS REPORT

From the following information, write an **RPG IV** program (either traditional or programmer-controlled) to generate the detail report shown in the supplemental printer spacing chart.

Physical File Record Format:

```
                     PHYSICAL FILE DESCRIPTION

SYSTEM: AS/400                                    DATE: Yours
FILE NAME: Yours                                  REV NO: 0
RECORD NAME: Yours                                KEY LENGTH: 11
SEQUENCE: Keyed                                   RECORD SIZE: 37

                         FIELD DEFINITIONS

FIELD     FIELD NAME    SIZE  TYPE    POSITION      COMMENTS
 NO                                  FROM   TO

 1        PARTNO          4    C       1     4   4th key
 2        JOBNO           3    C       5     7   3rd key
 3        SECTIONNO       2    C       8     9   2nd key
 4        DEPTNO          2    C      10    11   1st key
 5        DESCRIPTON     20    C      12    31
 6        PARTSUSED       4    P      32    34   0 decimals
 7        PARTCOST        5    P      35    37   2 decimals
```

Physical File Data:

Part#	Job#	Section#	Dept#	Part Description	Qty Used	Part Cost
6278	100	200	10	CLOSER-WHITE	0024	00550
6280	100	200	10	JAMB BRACKET-WHITE	0024	00073
6284	100	200	10	DOOR BRACKET-WHITE	0024	00049
6349	101	200	10	PHILP 12 X 1 SCREWS	0192	00008
6350	101	200	10	PHILP 8 X 1 SCREWS	0144	00006
6355	101	200	10	PHILP 6 X 1/2 SCREWS	0096	00050
6364	101	200	10	THUMB SCREW	0384	00117
6461	102	210	20	36" SCREEN-WHITE	0012	02999
6462	102	210	20	36" SCREEN-BLACK	0024	02999
6463	102	210	20	32" SCREEN-ALMOND	0010	03299
6573	103	300	20	INSIDE HANDLE	0024	00320
6574	103	300	20	OUTSIDE HANDLE	0024	00305
6576	103	300	20	LATCH ASSEMBLY	0024	01244

For each detail record processed, the quantity used is multiplied by the cost per item to obtain the total cost for the part. Three control fields must be specified with job number the lowest; section number, second; and department, third. The plant total, which must include the cost of all the parts, is to be printed at last record time.

Report Design:

```
1   ØX/XX/XX           PART USAGE REPORT            PAGE XXØX
2   HH:MM:SS       BY JOB, SECTION, & DEPT
3
4
5       PART NO      DESCRIPTION           TOTAL COST
6
7        XXXX     X------------------X    X,XXX,XXØ.XX
8        XXXX     X------------------X    X,XXX,XXØ.XX
9
10
11               JOB NO XXX TOTAL        XX,XXX,XXØ.XX *
12
13               SECTION XX TOTAL       XXX,XXX,XXØ.XX **
14
15               DEPT XX TOTAL      X,XXX,XXX,XXØ.XX ***
16
17               PLANT TOTAL       XX,XXX,XXX,XXØ.XX
18
19
20           NOTE: HEADINGS ON TOP OF EVERY PAGE.
```

Programming Assignment 7-4: HOSPITAL BILLING REPORT

Write an **RPG IV** program using internal subroutines to generate the Hospital Billing Report detailed in the attached printer spacing chart.

Physical File Record Format:

PHYSICAL FILE DESCRIPTION

SYSTEM: AS/400	DATE: Yours
FILE NAME: Yours	REV NO: 0
RECORD NAME: Yours	KEY LENGTH: 5
SEQUENCE: Keyed	RECORD SIZE: 40

FIELD DEFINITIONS

FIELD NO	FIELD NAME	SIZE	TYPE	POSITION FROM	POSITION TO	COMMENTS
1	PATIENTNO	5	C	1	5	Key field
2	PATNTNAME	20	C	6	25	
3	ADMITDATE	6	P	26	29	Admit date
4	OUTDATE	6	P	30	33	Out date
5	DAYSIN	3	P	34	35	
6	ROOMTYPE	1	C	36	36	I, P, S
7	PRIVTNURSE	1	C	37	37	N
8	ROOMTV	1	C	38	38	T
9	OXYGEN	1	C	39	39	O
10	IVFEEDING	1	C	40	40	V

Physical File Data:

Patient#	Patient Name	Admit Date	Out Date	Days	Room Type	PrIvate Nurse	TV	Oxygen	IV
10000	WALTER WINCHELL	010595	011595	10	P		T		
11000	EDGAR BERGEN	010895	011395	5	S		T		
12000	ZAZU PITTS	010295	011995	17	I			O	
13000	LON CHANEY	010695	011595	9	I	N			V
14000	FANNY BRICE	011095	011495	4	P		T		
15000	W.C. FIELDS	012095	013195	11	S		T		
16000	JACK BENNY	012295	013095	8	I	N	T	O	V

Processing: The following steps are required to determine a patient's bill:

Step 1: Include the following rate information in the calculations:

Room Type	*Input Code*	*Daily Rate*
Intensive care	I	$400
Private room	P	$300
Semi-private room	S	$200

Extra Services	*Input Code*	*Daily Rate*
Private nurse	N	$110
Oxygen	O	$250
I.V. feeding	V	$105
Television	T	$ 10

Step 2: Test the room type code (**I, P, S**) and multiply the related rate by the number of days the patient was in the hospital. Accumulate each room-type billing amount to a separate total field.

Report Design:

```
HH:MM:SS                                   GET WELL HOSPITAL                                    PAGE XXØX
                                          ROOM BILLING REPORT
                                             AS OF ØX/XX/XX


PATIENT                          ADMIT     CHECKOUT    BILLING                      ROOM    EXTRA SERVICES
NUMBER      PATIENT NAME         DATE        DATE       DAYS      ROOM TYPE        CHARGE       CHARGE

XXXXX  X--------------------X   ØX/XX/XX   ØX/XX/XX     XØX    X------------X   XXX,XXØ.XX  XXX,XXØ.XX

XXXXX  X--------------------X   ØX/XX/XX   ØX/XX/XX     XØX    X------------X   XXX,XXØ.XX  XXX,XXØ.XX

     TOTALS:

       NUMBER OF PATIENTS:..........X,XØX
       PRIVATE ROOM BILLING:........$X,XXX,XXØ.XX
       INTENSIVE CARE ROOM BILLING:..$X,XXX,XXØ.XX
       SEMI-PRIVATE ROOM BILLING:....$X,XXX,XXØ.XX
       EXTRA SERVICES BILLING:.......$X,XXX,XXØ.XX

  NOTE: Use system date for this report.
```

For the room type output, print INTENSIVE CARE, PRIVATE, or SEMI-PRIVATE. Because two of the room constants are too long to fit in *Factor 2* of a **MOVE** operation, define them as Named Constants. Depending on the room type, move the related field value to *one* output field defined for room type.

chapter 8

Data Structures and Data Areas

Data structures, which are specified in the *Definition Specifications* of an **RPG IV** program, define an area in storage and the layout of related subfields. Data structures may be used to:

1. Divide a field into subfields.
2. Change the format of a field.
3. Group noncontiguous data in a contiguous format.
4. Define an area of storage in more than one format.
5. Define multiple occurrences of a data structure (discussed in Chapter 10).

The following three special-purpose data structures may also be included in an **RPG IV** program:

1. *Data Area Data Structure*
2. *File Information Data Structure* **(INFDS)**
3. *Program Status Data Structure*

Data structures may be *program-* or *externally* defined and must include two parts: the data structure statement and at least one related *subfield.* Figure 8-1 details the syntax for data structures.

```
.. 1 ...+... 2 ...+... 3 ...+... 4 ...+... 5 ...+... 6 ...+... 7 ...+... 8 ...+... 9 ...+...+...10
DName+++++++++++ETDsFrom+++To/L+++IDc.Keywords+++++++++++++++++++++++++++++Comments++++++++++++++++
 * Data structure with subfields defined with absolute notation.

DDsName          DS                        From and To/L posi-
D  Subfield1                 1      4  2   tions are specified
D  Subfield2                 5      7  2   for absolute notation

 * Data structure with subfields defined with length notation

DDsName          DS                        Only the To/L entry
D  Subfield1                        4  2   is specified for
D  Subfield2                        3  2   length notation
```

Figure 8-1 Data structure syntax rules.

Data Structure Field Entries:

Field Name/ Positions	Explanation
7– 21	The name of the data structure (maximum of 10 characters) may be entered in this field. Entry is optional for *program-described* data structures and required for *data area, file information,* and *externally-described* data structures.
E 22	**Blank** for *program-described* and **E** for *externally described* data structures.
T 23	**Blank** for *program-described* data structures. **U** for *data area* data structures; and **S** for *Program Status* Data Structures.
Ds 24–25	**DS** must be entered for *all* data structure types.
From+++ 26–32	Not used.
To/L 33–39	The length of the data structure may be optionally entered in this field. If the entry is omitted, the system will determine the length from the subfield sizes.
I 40	Not used.
Dc 41–42	Not used.
• 43	Not used.
Keywords 44– 80	**Blank** for *single-occurrence, data area, File Information,* and *Program Status* Data Structures. *Multiple-occurrence* Data Structures (discussed in Chapter 10) require a numeric integer entry (1 to 32,767) in this field indicating the number of occurrences.
	The keyword **INZ** will initialize all of the numeric subfields included in the data structure to zeros and all of the character subfields to blanks.

Subfield Entries:

Field Name/ Positions	Explanation
7– 21	**Subfield** name (maximum 10 characters) must be entered in this field. The subfield name may begin in any position in the field. At least *one* subfield must be specified in any data structure.
ETDs 22–25	Three fields are not used.
From 26–32	For subfields defined with the *absolute notation,* an entry indicating the beginning position of the subfield within the data structure must be specified. *No* entry is required for subfields defined with the *length notation.*
To/L+++ 33–39	For subfield defined with the *absolute notation,* an entry indicating the end position (33–39) of the subfield within the data structure must be specified. An entry, indicating the length of the subfield, is required for subfields defined with the *length notation.*
I 40	Not used.
Dc 41–42	A **0** through **30** entry the subfield as numeric. A **blank** defines the subfield as character.
Keywords 44– 80	The keyword **DIM** may be specified to define the subfield as an array. The entry **DIM(12)** indicates that the array has 12 elements. Chapter 10 discusses arrays.
	When the *length notation* of a subfield is specified, the keyword **OVERLAY** is required to indicate that the subfield is part of the previous subfield. Otherwise, it would be considered *adjacent* to the previous subfield.
	The **INZ** keyword may be used to initialize numeric subfields to zero or character subfields to blanks. In lieu of these defaults, any value may be specified by enclosing it within parentheses after the **INZ** keyword. Within the parentheses, character values must be enclosed in single quotes and numeric values with only digits and any required decimal points.

Figure 8-1 Data structure syntax rules. (Continued)

Subfield Syntax Rules

The syntax rules that must be followed when defining the **subfields** in a data structure are detailed in Figure 8-2.

DATA STRUCTURE SUBFIELD RULES

1. An input field name cannot
   *be specified both as a subfield and a data structure name,
   *be used more than once in a data structure.
2. If a subfield is defined elsewhere in the program (e.g., as a field in a physical file), it must match the attributes of the other definition.
3. A subfield cannot be larger than the length of the related field or larger than the length of the data structure (when specified in positions 33–39).
4. Overlapping subfields cannot be used as an element of a calculation instruction.
5. A subfield may redefine another subfield.
6. Numeric subfields must be initialized with numeric data before they can be used in calculations or output editing.
7. Subfields defined with the length notation must include the **OVERLAY** keyword to extract part of another subfield.

Figure 8-2 Data structure subfield syntax rules.

Examples of data structure types will be discussed in the following sections.

Data Structure to Separate a Field into Subfields

Figure 8-3 illustrates two methods of separating a field from a physical file record into subfields using a data structure. The first example uses the *absolute notation* method and the second, the *length notation* option. In both examples, the **ActNumber** field is subdivided into its logical parts with the subfields: **Region, State, Division,** and **Store.** A limitation of this method is that the data structure name **(ActNumber)** cannot be used as a numeric field. However, by redefining the data structure name **ActNumber** as the subfield **AcctNo,** it may be defined as numeric providing that the value of **ActNumber** is numeric.

```
.. 1 ...+... 2 ...+... 3 ...+... 4 ...+... 5 ...+... 6 ...+... 7 ...+... 8
DName+++++++++++ETDsFrom+++To/L+++IDc.Keywords+++++++++++++++++++++++++++++
 * Data structure with subfields defined with absolute notation.

DActNumber        DS
D  Region                     1      2
D  State                      3      4
D  Division                   5      8
D  Store                      9     11
D  AcctNo                     1     11  0

 * Data structure with subfields defined with length notation. Field being
 * subdivided must be defined as a subfield--not as a data structure name
```

Figure 8-3 Defining subfields with a data structure.

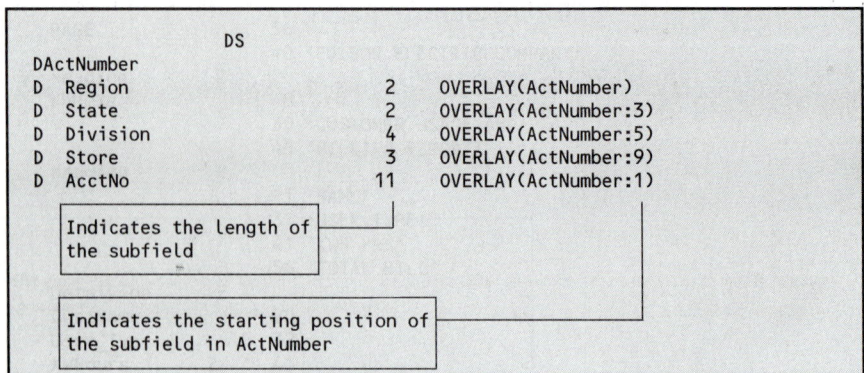

```
                  DS
DActNumber
D  Region                      2     OVERLAY(ActNumber)
D  State                       2     OVERLAY(ActNumber:3)
D  Division                    4     OVERLAY(ActNumber:5)
D  Store                       3     OVERLAY(ActNumber:9)
D  AcctNo                     11     OVERLAY(ActNumber:1)

   Indicates the length of
   the subfield

   Indicates the starting position of
   the subfield in ActNumber
```

Figure 8-3 Defining subfields with a data structure. (Continued)

Data Structure to Reorganize the Fields from an Input Record

Figure 8-4 shows the coding for a data structure that reorganizes a field from a *program-described* physical file. The input **DATE** field is in an **MMDDYY** format, but the processing logic requires that it be arranged into a **YYMMDD** format. First, the input field is subdivided into its related elements **(MM, DD, YY).** Then, the data structure rearranges the **MM, DD, YY** elements into a **YY, MM, DD** order and stores their values in the **YYMMDD** subfield. This is a more efficient approach than using either a mathematical formula or **MOVE** and **MOVEL** operations to separate and reorganize the data elements.

```
*.. 1 ...+... 2 ...+... 3 ...+... 4 ...+... 5 ...+... 6 ...+... 7 ...+... 8
IFilename++SqNORiPos1+NCCPos2+NCCPos3+NCC
I.......................Fmt+SPFrom+To+++DcField+++++++++L1M1FrPlMnZr......

 * Input Specification instructions to define the elements of the Date
 * field from a program-described physical file
IInputPf    SM  01
I                                     1    6  Date
i                                     1    2  Mm
I                                     3    4  Dd     Parts of the Date field
I                                     5    6  Yy
```

```
 .. 1 ...+... 2 ...+... 3 ...+... 4 ...+... 5 ...+... 6 ...+... 7 ...+... 8
DName+++++++++++ETDsFrom+++To/L+++IDc.Keywords+++++++++++++++++++++++++++++

 * Definition Specification instructions for a data structure that reorgan-
 * izes the parts of an input field subdivided in the Input Specification
D                 DS
DYyMmDd                  1      6
D  Yy                    1      2      Fields were defined in the
D  Mm                    3      4      Input Specifications
D  Dd                    5      6
```

Figure 8-4 Reorganizing parts of an input field with a data structure.

Data Structure to Group Fields

Contiguous or noncontiguous fields from a physical file may be grouped for processing by a data structure. The building of a *composite key* field from the fields of one physical file to randomly access the records from another physical file is one example where this data structure method may be required. Figure 8-5 illustrates a data structure that groups fields. Note that the physical file's record and field names must be entered in *uppercase* letters but may be specified in *mixed case* in the **RPG IV** program.

```
*.. 1 ...+... 2 ...+... 3 ...+... 4 ...+... 5 ...+... 6 ...+... 7 ...+... 8
A..........T.Name++++++RLen++TDpB......Functions++++++++++++++++++++++++++++
 * Physical file record format

A           R EMPRECORD
A             EMPNUMBER      6 0
A             EMPNAME       20
A             SECTION        3 0
A             DEPARTMENT     2 0
A             PLANT          3 0
```

```
 .. 1 ...+... 2 ...+... 3 ...+... 4 ...+... 5 ...+... 6 ...+... 7 ...+... 8
DName+++++++++++ETDsFrom+++To/L+++IDc.Keywords+++++++++++++++++++++++++++++
 * Physical file's fields grouped in a different order to load the EmpKey
 * data structure value

DEmpKey           DS
D  EmpNumber                    1      6  0
D  Plant                        7      9  0
D  Department                  10     11  0
D  Section                     12     14  0
```

Figure 8-5 Physical file record format and a data structure that groups the fields.

Furthermore, the subfields in the data structure must be referenced with the same name, type, and size as the related fields from the physical file.

Data Structure That Defines a Memory Area in More Than One Format

An example of defining the same area in memory for more than one record format is illustrated in Figure 8-6. The *Input Specification* entries shown [file name, sequence entry, *Record Identifying Indicator, Record Identification Codes* (see explanation in Figure 8-7), and *From+* and *To+++* field locations] indicate that the physical file is *program-described.* Recall that physical files that are formatted with *Data Description Specification* entries support only *one* record format (if needed, refer to Chapter 2). Therefore, to illus-

```
*.. 1 ...+... 2 ...+... 3 ...+... 4 ...+... 5 ...+... 6 ...+... 7 ...+... 8
IFilename++SqNORiPos1+NCCPos2+NCCPos3+NCC
I........................Fmt+SPFrom+To+++DcField+++++++++L1M1FrPlMnZr......

 * Four record formats included in the program-described physical file
 * Each record format is identified by a Record Identification Code

ICh9Pf1    SM  01     1 CN                              Record Identifica-
I                                1   55  SundryRcd      tion Code
i          SM  02     1 CC
I                                1   56  ARPayRcd       Record formats are
I          SM  03     1 CS                              defined as prog-
I                                1   52  CashRcd        rammer-described
I          SM  04                                       fields
i                                1   46  ErrorRcd
```

```
 .. 1 ...+... 2 ...+... 3 ...+... 4 ...+... 5 ...+... 6 ...+... 7 ...+... 8
DName+++++++++++ETDsFrom+++To/L+++IDc.Keywords+++++++++++++++++++++++++++++

 * Data structure subdivides the four record formats defined in the Input
 * Specification into their related subfields.  Each subfield must have a
 * unique name.
```

Figure 8-6 Data structure that defines one area in memory for four data record formats.

```
D                 DS
 * N type (Sundry amount) record field definition......
DSundryRcd                     1     55
D  Date1                       2      7  0
D  ActName1                    8     26
D  Explan1                    27     46
D  Folio                      47     49
D  SundryAmt                  50     55  2

 * C type (Accounts Receivable payment) record field definition......
DARPayRcd                      1     56
D  Date2                       2      7  0
D  ActName2                    8     26
D  Explan2                    27     46
D  Terms                      47     50
D  DiscntPct                  47     47  0
D  ARPayment                  51     56  2

 * S type (Cash Sales amount) record field definition......
DCashRcd                       1     52
D  Date3                       2      7  0
D  ActName3                    8     26
D  Explan3                    27     46
D  CashSale                   47     52  2

 * Error Record -- No record Identification Code prevents program execution
 * from halting if a record is read that does not include an N, C, or S in
 * position 1.
DErrorRcd                      1     46
D  Date4                       2      7  0
D  ActName4                    8     26
D  Explan4                    27     46
```

Figure 8-6 Data structure that defines one area in memory for four data record formats. (Continued)

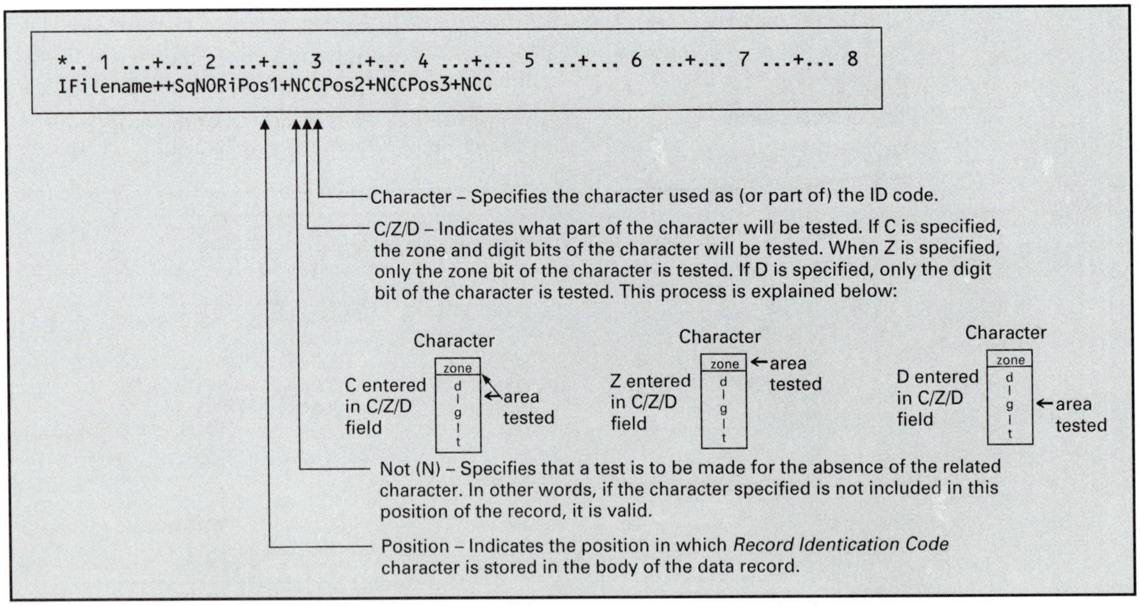

Figure 8-7 *Record Identification* Code syntax.

trate the function of this data structure type, the data is stored in a physical file that does not have a **DDS** record format.

Because only one memory area is reserved for the record formats in this program-described physical file, each record read overrides the record that was previously stored. The record formats are identified by their *Record Identification Codes* entered in position 1. The ErrorRcd, which has no *Record Identification Code* specified, is a "catch-all" record that prevents program execution from halting (or aborting) if a record is read that does not include an **N, C,** or **S** in position 1.

Record Identification Codes

Because externally described physical files support only one record format, *Record Identification Codes* are seldom included in the record design. However, for program-described physical files that may include more than one record format, *Record Identification Codes* are needed to identify one record type from another. Figure 8-7 explains the syntax related to *Record Identification Codes.* Any number of positions in a record may be allocated for a code, and any characters may be specified. Note that three codes may be specified on a *Record Identification* instruction with additional codes, as needed, entered in an **OR** or **AND** relationship on the following line(s).

Data Area Data Structures

When an **RPG IV** program is executed, the AS/400 system automatically creates a **local data area (LDA)** that is 1,024 bytes in size and defined as character (not numeric). The **LDA** may be used to transfer data from one program to another in the job. When the job ends, the **LDA** is deleted.

Permanent **data areas** may be created by the **CRTDTAARA** *(Create Data Area)* **CL** command. A data area created by this method remains an *object* until *explicitly* deleted by the **DLTDTAARA CL** command. A data area may be thought of as a file with one record that has a maximum size of 2,000 bytes. It is independent of any other files and may be accessed by any **RPG IV** program during run time.

Permanent data areas are typically used to store small amounts of data that must be referenced and sometimes frequently updated. The last payroll check number, next check date, batch totals, and current tax rates are a few of the many values that may be stored in a data area.

Data areas may be *implicitly* or *explicitly* retrieved and updated. When the data area is defined in an **RPG IV** program as a **data area data structure,** its data is *implicitly* retrieved for processing and automatically updated at the end of the program. The *explicit* processing of data areas and data area data structures will be discussed later in this chapter. Figure 8-8 shows an example of a data area data structure and explains the syntax.

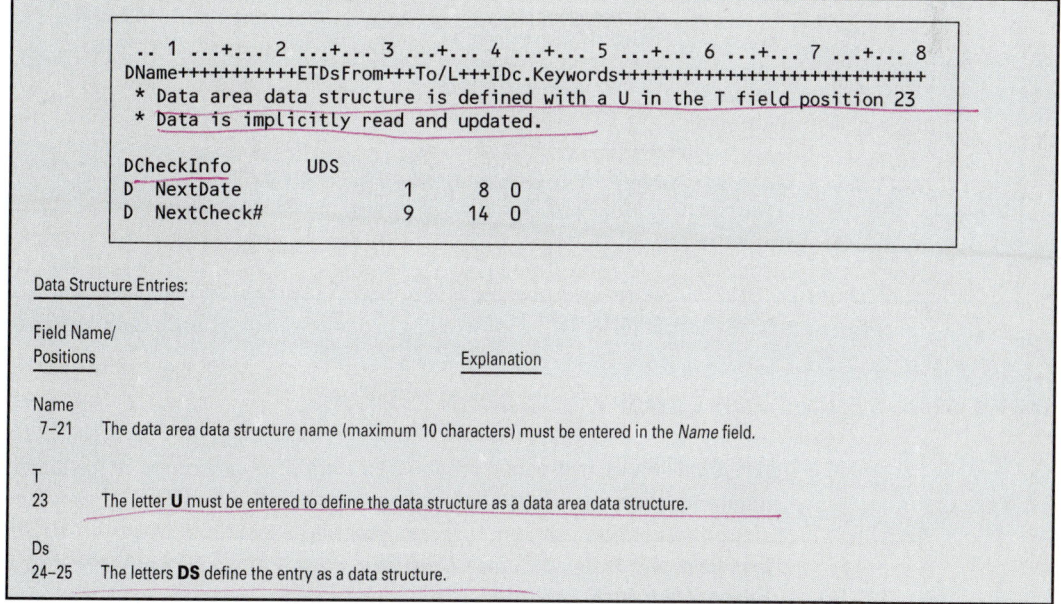

```
.. 1 ...+... 2 ...+... 3 ...+... 4 ...+... 5 ...+... 6 ...+... 7 ...+... 8
DName+++++++++++ETDsFrom+++To/L+++IDc.Keywords+++++++++++++++++++++++++++++
 * Data area data structure is defined with a U in the T field position 23
 * Data is implicitly read and updated.

DCheckInfo      UDS
D  NextDate                1      8 0
D  NextCheck#              9     14 0
```

Data Structure Entries:

Field Name/ Positions	Explanation
Name 7–21	The data area data structure name (maximum 10 characters) must be entered in the *Name* field.
T 23	The letter **U** must be entered to define the data structure as a data area data structure.
Ds 24–25	The letters **DS** define the entry as a data structure.

Figure 8-8 Data area data structure syntax.

Subfield Entries:

Name 7–21	Subfield names (maximum 10 characters) must begin on a new line. For readability, they may be indented within the *Name* field. Unlike externally described physical files, data areas have no **DDS** definition, which requires that the subfields be program-defined.
From+++ 26–32	The *beginning* position of the related subfield value in the data area must be specified.
To/L+++ 33–39	The **end** position of the related subfield value in the data area must be specified. Because the values stored in a data area are contiguous, the *From* and *To* field positions are required to extract the related values. Character subfields may be defined with a maximum of **256** bytes and numeric **30.**
Dc 41–42	The data area and subfields must be defined as *character* for a data area data structure. Consequently, no decimal position entry is permitted.

Figure 8-8 Data area data structure syntax. (Continued)

An example **RPG IV** program that illustrates the syntax for a data area data structure is shown in Figure 8-9. To simplify the program, no input file is specified. The result of processing generates a report with the original value in the data area and automatically updates the date area (Ch8dal) with the new value moved into **Date** (see line 10) at the end of the job. Note that the value in the Ch8dal data area must have been defined as character (***CHAR).**

```
Line    <---------------------- Source Specifications ----------------------------><---- Comments ----> Do
Number ....1....+....2....+....3....+....4....+....5....+....6....+....7....+....8....+....9....+...10 Num
                             S o u r c e   L i s t i n g
     1  * Data area update using a data area data structure....
     2 FQsysprt   O    F  132          PRINTER

     4  * Define Data Area Data Structure....
     5 DCh8da1           UDS
     6 D Date                          1      8
     7
     8 C                   MOVE      Date          DateOut           8 0         move to numeric fld
     9 C                   EXCEPT    DetailLine                                  print detailLine
    10 C                   MOVE      *DATE         Date                          update data area
    11 C                   EVAL      *INLR = *ON                                 end the job
    12
    13 OQsysprt   H    1P                       2 06
    14 O                                            20 'DATA AREA EXAMPLE 1'
    15 O          E            DetailLine     1
    16 O                       DateOut       Y      15

Note: Data area (Ch8da1) is automatically updated with new Date value at end of job.
```

UDS defines the data area as a data area data structure. Data area value must be defined as character in data area and program.

```
Report:                        DATA AREA EXAMPLE 1

                                   11/30/1997
```

Figure 8-9 Example **RPG IV** program that processes a data area data structure.

DATA STRUCTURES FOR EXCEPTION/ERROR CONTROL

Exception errors that cause program execution to cancel are not uncommon in the programming environment. Routines may be included in an **RPG IV** program to identify and control *exception/errors* and prevent program execution "aborts." *File Information Data Structures* and *Program Status Data Structures* are two **RPG IV** run-time methods to control exception/error processing.

File Information Data Structure (INFDS)

A *File Information Data Structure* provides exception/error information that may have occurred when processing a file during program execution. This type of data structure contains predefined subfields that identify:

1. The name of the file for which the error occurred
2. The record processed when the error occurred
3. The operation being processed when the error occurred
4. The status code number
5. The **RPG IV** routine in which the error occurred

Specifically, keywords including ***FILE, *STATUS, *OPCODE, *ROUTINE,** and ***RECORD** provide the previously named information for any file selected for error control and processed by the **RPG IV** program. Other information, including the open status of the file, end-of-file status, **RPG IV** source listing number, error on a **SPECIAL** file, and machine or system message number, may be accessed by defining the location of the information in the *From* and *To* fields in the related *Definition Specification* instructions and assigning a programmer-supplied name to the location of the item within the fixed 66-byte record size. Because the keywords are supplied by the compiler, their location in the body of the record does not have to be specified.

The **RPG IV** *File Description* and *Definition Specification* coding to support a *File Information Data Structure* **(INFDS)** is detailed in Figure 8-10. Note that a *file exception/error subroutine (INFSR*PSSR)* is specified on a second instruction, which

```
.. 1 ...+... 2 ...+... 3 ...+... 4 ...+... 5 ...+... 6 ...+... 7 ...+... 8 ...+... 9 ...+...10
FFilename++IPEASFRLen+LKLen+AIDevice+.Keywords+++++++++++++++++++++++++++++Comments++++++++++++
 * File information data structure (Infds1) is assigned to this input file with the INFDS key-
 * word. An internal subroutine (*PSSR) is provided by the INFSR keyword.  *PSSR is an RPG IV
 * compiler-supplied subroutine that is automatically processed when an error occurs.

FCH9PF1    IF   E             DISK    INFDS(Infds1)
F                                     INFSR(*PSSR)
```

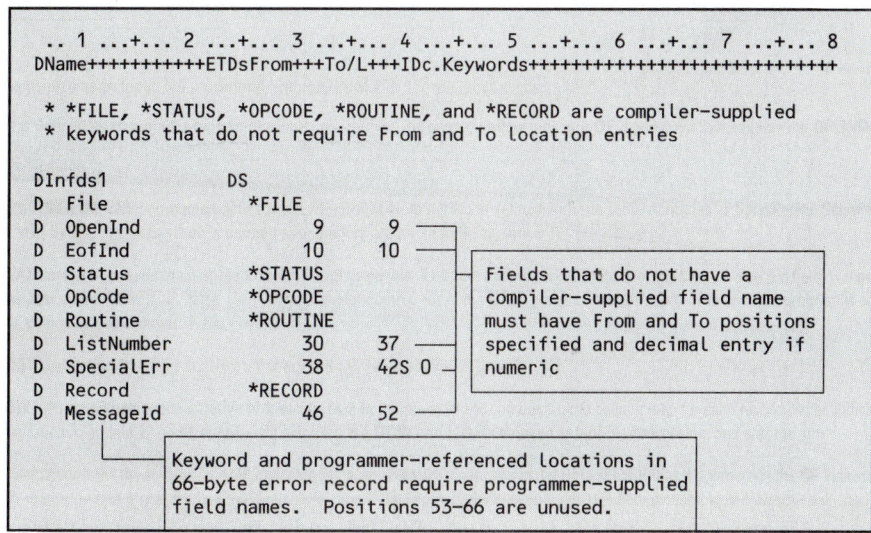

```
.. 1 ...+... 2 ...+... 3 ...+... 4 ...+... 5 ...+... 6 ...+... 7 ...+... 8
DName+++++++++++ETDsFrom+++To/L+++IDc.Keywords+++++++++++++++++++++++++++++

 * *FILE, *STATUS, *OPCODE, *ROUTINE, and *RECORD are compiler-supplied
 * keywords that do not require From and To location entries

DInfds1          DS
D File             *FILE
D OpenInd                 9      9
D EofInd                 10     10
D Status           *STATUS
D OpCode           *OPCODE
D Routine          *ROUTINE
D ListNumber             30     37
D SpecialErr             38     42S 0
D Record           *RECORD
D MessageId              46     52
```

Fields that do not have a compiler-supplied field name must have From and To positions specified and decimal entry if numeric

Keyword and programmer-referenced locations in 66-byte error record require programmer-supplied field names. Positions 53-66 are unused.

Figure 8-10 Definition Specification syntax for a file information data structure.

accesses the **RPG IV**-supplied ***PSSR** internal subroutine. When an error is detected, control will automatically pass to this subroutine. Based on the error type, programmer-supplied instructions in the ***PSSR** routine will determine the action to be taken (i.e., end the job or ignore the error and continue processing).

The *Definition Specification* in Figure 8-10 defines the information record that is to be accessed if an exception/error occurs. One, or all ten, of the available information fields may be included to identify a select error condition. The ***PSSR** routine (or a programmer-defined routine) will be executed only if the ***STATUS** code value is *greater than* **00099.** All of the files, or only select files, processed by an **RPG IV** program may be assigned a file information data structure. If this control is not included in an **RPG IV** program, the system will generate a message on the user's screen which provides for cancel, go, dump, or system dump options. This system-supplied exception/error control is *not* advisable in a batch environment.

The ***STATUS** keyword errors that may be identified with a *file information data structure* are listed in Figure 8-11.

Many of the **RPG IV** file operations (e.g., **CHAIN, WRITE, UPDATE, DELETE, READ, READC, READE, READP, READPE, SETLL, SETGT,** and **EXFMT**) identify and control processing errors by specifying an indicator in positions 73–74 of the related calculation instruction. The "on" or "off" status of the indicator will determine the action that the programmer includes in the **RPG IV** program. Under those circumstances, a file information data structure may not be needed.

Other *field feedback information,* available in a file information data structure for **display files,** may be accessed by the keywords ***SIZE, *INP, *OUT,** and ***MODE.** For a comprehensive discussion of the fields in the record format of a file information data structure, refer to IBM's *ILE RPG/400 Reference* manual.

Table 7 (Page 1 of 2). Exception/Error Codes

Code	Device[1]	RC[2]	Condition
01011	W,D,SQ	n/a	Undefined record type (input record does not match record identifying indicator).
01021	W,D,SQ	n/a	Tried to write a record that already exists (file being used has unique keys and key is duplicate, or attempted to write duplicate relative record number to a subfile).
01031	W,D,SQ	n/a	Match field out of sequence.
01041	n/a	n/a	Array/table load sequence error.
01051	n/a	n/a	Excess entries in array/table file.
01052	n/a	n/a	Clearing of table prior to dump of data failed.
01071	W,D,SQ	n/a	Numeric sequence error.
01121[4]	W	n/a	No indicator on the DDS keyword for Print key.
01122[4]	W	n/a	No indicator on the DDS keyword for Roll Up key.
01123[4]	W	n/a	No indicator on the DDS keyword for Roll Down key.
01124[4]	W	n/a	No indicator on the DDS keyword for Clear key.
01125[4]	W	n/a	No indicator on the DDS keyword for Help key.
01126[4]	W	n/a	No indicator on the DDS keyword for Home key.
01201	W	34xx	Record mismatch detected on input.
01211	all	n/a	I/O operation to a closed file.
01215	all	n/a	OPEN issued to a file already opened.
01216[3]	all	yes	Error on an implicit OPEN/CLOSE operation.
01217[3]	all	yes	Error on an explicit OPEN/CLOSE operation.
01218	D,SQ	n/a	Record already locked.

Figure 8-11 RPG IV run-time ***STATUS** codes for a file information data structure.

01221	D,SQ	n/a	Update operation attempted without a prior read.
01231	SP	n/a	Error on SPECIAL file.
01235	P	n/a	Error in PRTCTL space or skip entries.
01241	D,SQ	n/a	Record number not found (Record number specified in record address file is not present in file being processed.)
01251	W	80xx 81xx	Permanent I/O error occurred.
01255	W	82xx 83xx	Session or device error occurred. Recovery may be possible.
01261	W	n/a	Attempt to exceed maximum number of acquired devices.
01281	W	n/a	Operation to unacquired device.
01282	W	0309	Job ending with controlled option.
01285	W	0800	Attempt to acquire a device already acquired.
01286	W	n/a	Attempt to open shared file with SAVDS or IND options.
01287	W	n/a	Response indicators overlap IND indicators.
01299	W,D,SQ	yes	Other I/0 error detected.
01331	W	0310	Wait time exceeded for READ from WORKSTN file.

Note: "Device" refers to the devices for which the condition applies. The following abbreviations are used: P = PRINTER; D = DISK; W = WORKSTN; SP = SPECIAL; SQ = Sequential. The major/minor return codes under column RC apply only to WORKSTN files. [2]The formula mmnn is used to described major/minor return codes: mm is the major and nn the minor. [3]Any errors that occur during an open or close operation will result in a *STATUS value of 1216 or 1217 regardless of the major/minor return code value.

Figure 8-11 RPG IV run-time ***STATUS** codes for a file information data structure. (Continued) (Courtesy of IBM)

Program Example Using a File Information Data Structure

Figure 8-12, which includes a compile listing of an example **RPG IV** program that computes the square root of numbers, illustrates the use of a file information data structure. Note that the program processes a program-described physical file that includes a *Record Identification Code* in position 1 of each input record. The error control in the compiler-supplied internal subroutine ***PSSR** prevents program execution from canceling when an invalid code is tested.

Program Status Data Structure

As we have discussed, a *File Information Data Structure* identifies exception/error conditions associated with file processing and includes its own set of ***STATUS** error codes. *Program Data Structures*, however, identify exception/error conditions that are generated by instructions in the **RPG IV** program and not by the processing of physical, logical, display, or printer files.

Four keywords—***PROC, *STATUS, *ROUTINE,** and ***PARMS**—are supported by a *Program Status Data Structure*. Twenty-nine other fields in the 429-byte error record identify other processing errors. Any or all of these *other* error conditions may be determined by specifying a programmer-supplied field name and the related *From* and *To* field positions in one or more *Definition Specification* instructions.

The eight-character ***ROUTINE** keyword contains the name of the **RPG IV** routine (e.g., ***INIT, *DETL, *GETIN, *TOTC, *TOTL, *DETC, *OFL, *TERM, *ROUTINE**) in which the exception/error condition occurred. Note that the value in the ***ROUTINE** may not be valid for programmer-controlled processing that does not use the normal **RPG IV** cycle.

The ***PROC** keyword is a 10-byte character field that identifies the procedure being processed when the exception/error condition occurred. The ***PARMS** keyword is a

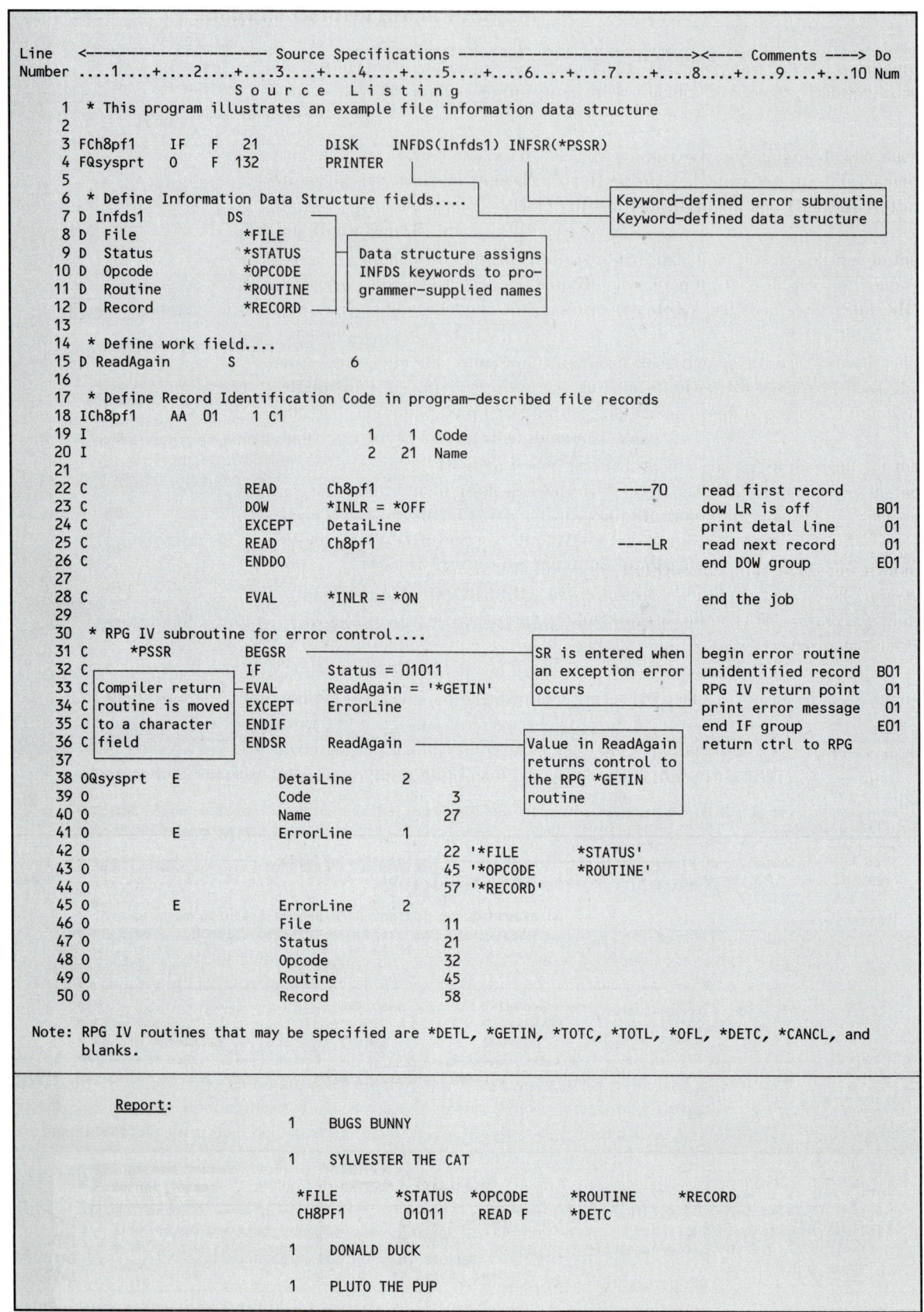

```
Line   <---------------------- Source Specifications ----------------------------><---- Comments ----> Do
Number ....1....+....2....+....3....+....4....+....5....+....6....+....7....+....8....+....9....+...10 Num
                          S o u r c e   L i s t i n g
   * This program illustrates an example file information data structure

  FCh8pf1    IF   F   21           DISK    INFDS(Infds1) INFSR(*PSSR)
  FQsysprt   O    F  132           PRINTER

   * Define Information Data Structure fields....
  D Infds1           DS
  D  File                  *FILE
  D  Status                *STATUS
  D  Opcode                *OPCODE
  D  Routine               *ROUTINE
  D  Record                *RECORD

   * Define work field....
  D ReadAgain        S               6

   * Define Record Identification Code in program-described file records
  ICh8pf1    AA  01     1 C1
  I                                  1    1  Code
  I                                  2   21  Name

  C                   READ      Ch8pf1                             ----70    read first record
  C                   DOW       *INLR = *OFF                                 dow LR is off          B01
  C                   EXCEPT    DetailLine                                   print detal line        01
  C                   READ      Ch8pf1                             ----LR    read next record        01
  C                   ENDDO                                                  end DOW group          E01

  C                   EVAL      *INLR = *ON                                  end the job

   * RPG IV subroutine for error control....
  C     *PSSR         BEGSR                                                  begin error routine
  C                   IF        Status = 01011                               unidentified record    B01
  C                   EVAL      ReadAgain = '*GETIN'                         RPG IV return point     01
  C                   EXCEPT    ErrorLine                                    print error message     01
  C                   ENDIF                                                  end IF group           E01
  C                   ENDSR     ReadAgain                                    return ctrl to RPG

  OQsysprt   E             DetailLine     2
  O                        Code                 3
  O                        Name                27
  O          E             ErrorLine      1
  O                                        22 '*FILE        *STATUS'
  O                                        45 '*OPCODE      *ROUTINE'
  O                                        57 '*RECORD'
  O          E             ErrorLine      2
  O                        File                11
  O                        Status              21
  O                        Opcode              32
  O                        Routine             45
  O                        Record              58
```

Keyword-defined error subroutine

Keyword-defined data structure

Data structure assigns INFDS keywords to programmer-supplied names

SR is entered when an exception error occurs

Compiler return routine is moved to a character field

Value in ReadAgain returns control to the RPG *GETIN routine

Note: RPG IV routines that may be specified are *DETL, *GETIN, *TOTC, *TOTL, *OFL, *DETC, *CANCL, and blanks.

Report:

```
          1    BUGS BUNNY

          1    SYLVESTER THE CAT

           *FILE       *STATUS  *OPCODE     *ROUTINE     *RECORD
           CH8PF1       01011    READ F     *DETC

          1    DONALD DUCK

          1    PLUTO THE PUP
```

Figure 8-12 Compile listing of an **RPG IV** program that includes a *File Information Data Structure.*

3-byte zoned decimal integer field that specifies the number of parameters passed to this program from a calling program. Five-digit integer exception/error condition codes stored in the ***STATUS** field are summarized in Figure 8-13.

Program Status Codes

Any code placed in the subfield location *STATUS that is greater than 99 is considered to be an exception/error condition. If the status code is greater than 99, the error indicator, if specified in positions 73 and 74, is set on, or the program exception/error subroutine receives control. Location *STATUS is updated when an exception/error occurs.

The following codes are placed in the subfield location *STATUS for the program status data structure:

Normal Codes

Code	Condition
00000	No exception/error occurred.
00001	Called program returned with the LR indicator on.

Exception/Error Codes

Code	Condition
00100	Value out of range for string operation.
00101	Negative square root.
00102	Divide by zero.
00103	An intermediate result is not large enough to contain the result.
00112	Invalid Date, Time, or Timestamp value.
00113	Date overflow or underflow. (For example, when the result of a Date calculation results in a number greater than *Hival or less than *Loval.)
00114	Date mapping errors, where a Date is mapped from a 4-character year to a 2-character year and the date range is not 1940–2039.
00120	Table or array out of sequence.
00121	Array index not valid.
00122	OCCUR outside of range.
00123	Reset attempted during initialization step of program.
00202	Called program or procedure failed; halt indicator (*H1 through H9) not on.
00211	Error calling program or procedure.
00221	Called program tried to use a parameter not passed to it.
00222	Pointer or parameter error.
00231	Called program or procedure returned with halt indicator on.
00232	Halt indicator on in this program.
00233	Halt indicator on when RETURN operation run.
00299	RPG IV formatted dump failed.
00333	Error on DSPLY operation.
00401	Data area specified on IN/OUT not found.
00402	*PDA not valid for non-prestart job.
00411	Data area type or length does not match.
00412	Data area not locked for output.
00413	Error on IN/OUT operation.
00414	User not authorized to use data area.
00415	User not authorized to change data area.
00421	Error on UNLOCK operation.
00431	Data area previously locked by another program.
00432	Data area locked by program in the same process.
00450	Character field not entirely enclosed by shift-out and shift-in characters.
00501	Failure to retrieve sort sequence.
00502	Failure to convert sort sequence.
00802	Commitment control not active.
00803	Rollback operation failed.
00804	Error occurred on COMMIT operation.
00805	Error occurred on ROLBK operation.
00907	Decimal data error (digit or sign not valid).
00970	The level number of the compiler used to generate the program does not agree with the level number of the RPG IV run-time subroutines.
09998	Internal failure in RPG IV compiler or in run-time subroutines.
09999	Program exception in system routine.

Figure 8-13 Program status data structure exception/error codes (courtesy of IBM).

The *File Description* and *Definition Specification* syntax for a *Program Status Data Structure* is detailed in Figure 8-14. In lieu of the compiler-supplied ***PSSR** routine, a programmer-named exception/error condition routine may be specified as shown.

```
.. 1 ...+... 2 ...+... 3 ...+... 4 ...+... 5 ...+... 6 ...+... 7 ...+... 8 ...+... 9 ...+...10
FFilename++IPEASFRLen+LKLen+AIDevice+.Keywords+++++++++++++++++++++++++++++Comments++++++++++++
 * A program status data structure is assigned to the input file with the INFSR keyword.  A
 * programmer-named internal subroutine (ErrorSR) is defined with the INFSR keyword.  When an
 * exception/error condition occurs, control is automatically passed to the subroutine for
 * programmer-controlled processing.

FNumbers   IP   E             DISK    INFSR(ErrorSR)
FQsysPrt   O    F  132        PRINTER
```

```
.. 1 ...+... 2 ...+... 3 ...+... 4 ...+... 5 ...+... 6 ...+... 7 ...+... 8
DName+++++++++++ETDsFrom+++To/L+++IDc.Keywords+++++++++++++++++++++++++++++
 * S in the T field (position 23) defines the data structure as a program
 * status data structure.  Only the four RPG IV-supplied keywords are
 * specified for this example.  The other 29 fields may be included by
 * defining their related positions in the error record with a From and
 * To entry and a programmer-supplied field name.

D                   SDS                    Programmer-supplied names
D  Procedure           *PROC               must redefine each keyword
D  Statuscode          *STATUS
D  RPGRoutine          *ROUTINE
D  Parameters          *PARM
```

Figure 8-14 *File Description* and *Definition Specification* syntax for a *Program Status Data Structure.*

The **RPG IV** program that computes the square root of numbers, shown in Figure 8-15, illustrates how a program status data structure *controls run-time errors and prevents program abends*. Note that the **RPG IV *GETIN** routine was used in this example; however, any of the other routines may be used to test for one or more related exception/error conditions. As previously mentioned, **RPG IV** operation indicator control for error processing may not always be accurate for programmer-controlled programs. Consequently, this program example uses the *RPG IV Logic Cycle* to illustrate program status data structure error processing.

```
Line   <---------------------- Source Specifications ----------------------------><---- Comments ----> Do
Number ....1....+....2....+....3....+....4....+....5....+....6....+....7....+....8....+....9....+...10 Num
                       S o u r c e   L i s t i n g
     * This program uses a program status data structure to control errors
    FCh8pf2    IP   E             DISK    INFSR(*PSSR)
     *--------------------------------------------------------------------------------------------*
     *                                RPG name          External name                             *
     * File name. . . . . . . . . :  CH8PF2            STAN/CH8PF2                               *
     * Record format(s) . . . . . :  CH8PF2R           CH8PF2R                                   *
     *--------------------------------------------------------------------------------------------*
    FQsysprt   O    F  132        PRINTER OFLIND(*INOF)

     * Define Program Status Data Structure keywords....
    DPSDS            SDS
    D Procedure          *PROC
    D StatusCode         *STATUS
    D Routine            *ROUTINE
    D LineNo                21     28

     * Define work fields....
    D SquareRoot      S              6  0
    D ReadAgain       S              6
```

Figure 8-15 Example Square Root program with *Program Status Data Structure* control.

```

 * Begin calculations....
=ICH8PF2R
    *--------------------------------------------------------------------------------------*
    * RPG record format  . . . . :  CH8PF2R                                                *
    * External format  . . . . . :  CH8PF2R : STAN/CH8PF2                                  *
    *--------------------------------------------------------------------------------------*
=I                            P    1    3 0NUMBER
 C                    SQRT      Number        SquareRoot                  compute square root
 C                    EXCEPT    GoodRecord                                print good record

 * Begin error routine....
 C     *PSSR          BEGSR                                               begin error routine
 C                    IF        StatusCode = 00101                        negative numbr error B01
 C                    EVAL      ReadAgain = '*GETIN'                      compiler return pt    01
 C                    EXCEPT    ErrorRecrd                                print error line      01
 C                    ENDIF                                               end IF group         E01
 C                    ENDSR     ReadAgain                                 end SR & Return

 * Begin output instructions....
 OQsysprt   H    1P                    2 01
 O                                          47 'SQUARE ROOT OF NUMBERS'
 O          H    1P                    1
 O                                          47 'NUMBER           SQUARE'
 O          H    1P                    2
 O                                          46 'ROOT'
 O          E            GoodRecord    2
 O                       Number        J    30
 O                       SquareRoot    3    46
 O          E            ErrorRecrd    1
 O                       Number        J    30
 O                                          57 'NUMBER NEGATIVE OR ZERO'
 O          E            ErrorRecrd    2
 O                                          12 'Procedure = '
 O                       Procedure          22
 O                                          37 'StatusCode = '
 O                       StatusCode         42
 O                                          54 'Routine = '
 O                       Routine            62
 O                                          73 'Lineno = '
 O                       LineNo             81
```

Figure 8-15 Example Square Root program with *Program Status Data Structure* control. (Continued)

DATA AREAS

Data areas, which were defined when *data area data structures* were discussed in this chapter, are objects used to transfer data to one or more programs with a job or between jobs. A *data area* may be considered as a one-record permanent storage area from which its value is extracted for processing by an **RPG IV** or **CL** program.

Data areas are created with the **CRTDTAARA** *(Create Data Area)* command, their values changed with the **CHGDTAARA** *(Change Data Area)* command, viewed with the **DSPDTAARA** *(Display Data Area)* command, and deleted with the **DLTDTAARA** *(Delete Data Area)* command. Figure 8-16 shows the display generated by entering **CRTDTAARA** on a command line and pressing **F4.** Note the example shown is after the variables are entered.

The **CRTDTAARA** display in Figure 8-16 named the data area Ch8da2, which will be stored in the current library **(*CURLIB)** and defined as ***DEC** type with a length of 8 digits with 0 decimal positions. 12311997 is entered on the *Initial value* line. If character **(*CHAR)** is specified, the value must be enclosed in single apostrophes.

A data area defined with a ***DEC**-type parameter may be a maximum of 24 digits with a maximum of 9 decimal positions. ***CHAR** type may store a maximum character

```
                     Create Data Area (CRTDTAARA)

Type choices, press Enter.

Data area . . . . . . . . . . . > Ch8da2____     Name
  Library . . . . . . . . . . . >   *CURLIB___   Name, *CURLIB
Type . . . . . . . . . . . . . . > *DEC_          *DEC, *CHAR, *LGL
Length:
  Length . . . . . . . . . . . . > 8_____         1-2000
  Decimal positions  . . . . . . > 0_____         0-9
Initial value  . . . . . . . . . > 12311997_________________________
Text 'description' . . . . . . . > ch8 - data area example__________________
_____

                                                                    Bottom
F3=Exit   F4=Prompt   F5=Refresh   F10=Additional parameters   F12=Cancel
F13=How to use this display        F24=More keys
```

Figure 8-16 CRTDTAARA *(Create Data Area)* command display.

string of 2,000 characters. ***LGL** (logical) type may contain a 1 or 0, indicating an on/off, true/false, or yes/no condition, respectively. For a comprehensive discussion of all the parameters, refer to the appropriate IBM *Control Language Reference* manual on CD-ROM or in hardcopy.

The value in a *data area* may be changed by an **RPG IV** program, by a **CL** program, or by the **CHGDTAARA** command. Identical to the access of the parameters of any **CL** command, **CHGDTAARA** is entered on a command line and then **F4** is pressed. Figure 8-17 illustrates the display after the value 12311997 has been changed to 01011998.

```
                     Change Data Area (CHGDTAARA)

Type choices, press Enter.

Data area specification:

  Data area  . . . . . . . . . . > Ch8da1____     Name, *LDA, *GDA, *PDA
    Library  . . . . . . . . . . >   *CURLIB___   Name, *LIBL, *CURLIB
  Substring specifications:
  Substring starting position  .   *ALL__         1-2000, *ALL
  Substring length . . . . . . .   ______         1-2000
New value  . . . . . . . . . . .   01011998_________________________

                                                                    Bottom
F3=Exit   F4=Prompt   F5=Refresh   F12=Cancel   F13=How to use this display
F24=More keys
```

Figure 8-17 CHGDTAARA *(Change Data Area)* command display.

The old value may be replaced with a new value entirely, or it may be partially changed by entering the related starting location in the *Substring starting position* parameter. The ***ALL** default indicates that all of the current value may be changed. If a new value is larger, the new length must be entered in the *Substring length* parameter.

The value stored in a *data area* may be reviewed by the **DSPDTAARA** *(Display Data Area)* command. A display of the Ch8da2 data area is shown in Figure 8-18.

```
                         Display Data Area
                                                    System:   AS/400

Data area . . . . . . . :   Ch8da2
  Library . . . . . . . :     SMYERS
Type  . . . . . . . . . :   *DEC
Length  . . . . . . . . :   8 0
Text  . . . . . . . . . :   ch8 - data area example
Value . . . . . . . . . :   01011998




Press Enter to continue.

F3=Exit   F12=Cancel
```

Figure 8-18 **DSPDTAARA** *(Display Data Area)* command.

A *data area* may be deleted by the **DLTDTAARA** command illustrated in Figure 8-19.

```
                      Delete Data Area (DLTDTAARA)

Type choices, press Enter.
Data area  . . . . . . . . . .   Ch8da2        Name, generic*
  Library  . . . . . . . . . .     *LIBL       Name, *LIBL, *CURLIB...





                                                                 Bottom
F3=Exit   F4=Prompt   F5=Refresh   F12=Cancel   F13=How to use this display
F24=More keys
```

Figure 8-19 **DLTDTAARA** *(Delete Data Area)* command.

Processing of Data Areas

The *data area data structure* previously explained (Figure 8-9) illustrated how the data stored in a *data area* may be *implicitly* retrieved and updated by an **RPG IV** program. *Data areas* may be *explicitly* retrieved and updated with **IN** and **OUT** operations in an **RPG IV** program. The operations and reserved words related to the *explicit* processing of *data areas* are summarized in Figure 8-20.

RPG IV OPERATIONS AND RESERVED WORDS FOR DATA AREA PROCESSING

Operation	Function
IN *(Retrieve a Data Area)*	Explicitly retrieves a data area and optionally permits the programmer to "lock" it so that the data cannot be updated by another program during execution of the controlling program. For a data area to be retrieved by the **IN** operation, its name must be entered in the *Result* field of the ***DTAARA DEFINE** instruction. It may also be retrieved by an **IN** operation by using the ***DTAARA** keyword with the *Definition Specification* definition of the data area.

Figure 8-20 **RPG IV** operations and reserved words for the explicit processing of data areas.

OUT *(Write a Data Area)*	The **OUT** operation updates the data area specified in *Factor 2* of an **OUT** instruction. The data area must have been explicitly retrieved by an **IN** operation or by the ***DTAARA** keyword in the *Definition Specifications.* In addition, the data area must have been "locked" by entering the reserved word ***LOCK** in *Factor 1* of the related **IN** operation.
DEFINE *(Field Definition)*	When used with a ***DTAARA** reserved word in *Factor 1,* it accesses the data area specified in the *Result* field. If a program-defined field, data structure, or data structure subfield is specified in the *Result* field, the external data area name must be entered in *Factor 2.*
UNLOCK *(Unlock a Data Area)*	The **UNLOCK** operation is used to "unlock" one or more data areas. *Factor 2* must contain the name of the data area specified in the related ***DTAARA DEFINE** instruction. Entering the **DTAARA** keyword in *Factor 2* will "unlock" *all* of the data areas processed by the program that were previously "locked."
Reserved Words	
***LOCK**	When used as a *Factor 1* entry with an **IN** operation, this reserved word places an object "lock" on the specified data area. When used as a *Factor 1* entry with an **OUT** operation, the data area is written to but retains its object lock.
***DTAARA**	When used with a **DEFINE** operation, associates the external data area specified in *Factor 2* with the field, data structure, or data structure subfield in the *Result* field. The external data area name may be entered in the *Result* field if specified with the length and decimal position (when numeric) entries identical to those in the related data area.

Figure 8-20 **RPG IV** operations and reserved words for the explicit processing of data areas. (Continued)

EXPLICIT ACCESS OF A DATA AREA

Data Area Accessed Without a Data Structure

The compile listing of the **RPG IV** program in Figure 8-21 illustrates the syntax required to access the value from a data area defined as ***DEC** when the data area name is speci-

```
Line   <---------------------- Source Specifications ----------------------------><---- Comments ----> Do
Number ....1....+....2....+....3....+....4....+....5....+....6....+....7....+....8....+....9....+...10 Num
                        S o u r c e   L i s t i n g
   1  * Data area access using explicit processing....   ┌Data area name may be entered in the
   2 FQsysprt   O    F  132          PRINTER              │Result field if it is defined exactly
   3                                                      │as specified in the external definition
   4  * Access data area....
   5 C      *DTAARA       DEFINE                 Ch8da2 ────────  8 0           define data area
   6 C                    IN        Ch8da2                                       access data area
   7 C                    MOVE      Ch8da2       DateOut          8 0           move to out fld
   8 C                    EXCEPT    DetaiLine                                    print detaiLine
   9 C                    EVAL      *INLR = *ON                                  end the job
  10
  11 OQsysprt   H    1P                   2 06
  12 O                                        20 'DATA AREA EXAMPLE 2'
  13 O          E             DetaiLine      1
  14 O                        DateOut     Y       15

 Note: * To be retrieved by an IN instruction, the data area name must be specified in the Result field;
         or it may be defined by a DTAARA keyword in a Definition Specification instruction.

 Report:
                                  DATA AREA EXAMPLE 2

                                      12/31/1997
```

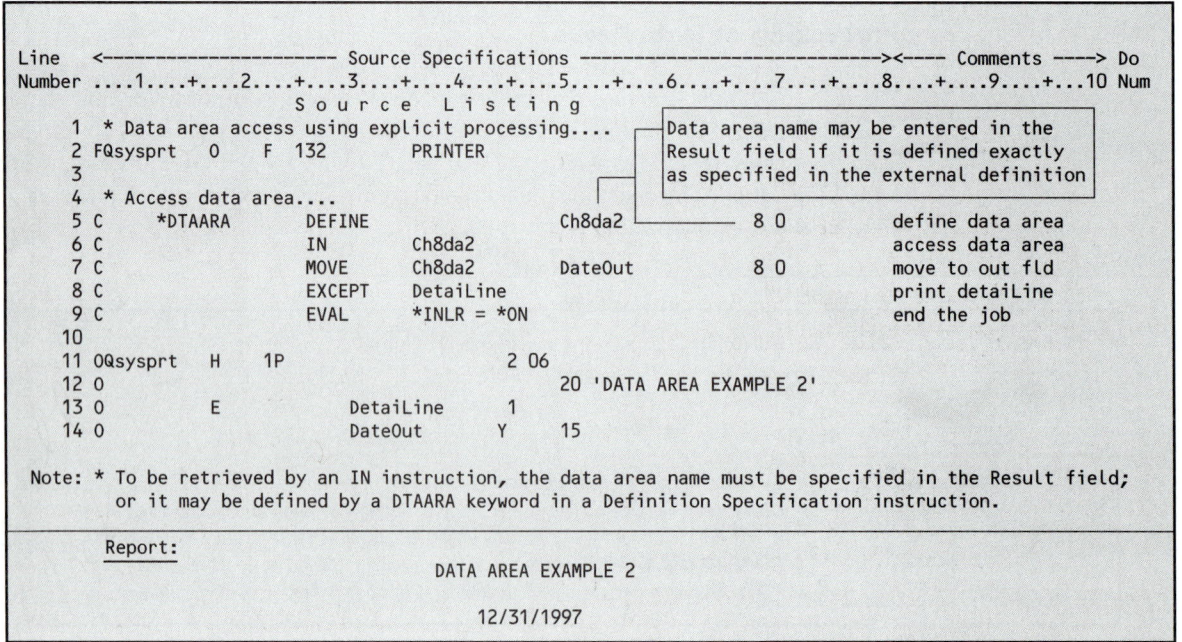

Figure 8-21 Explicit access of the value in a data area without subfields.

fied in the *Result* field of a ***DTAARA DEFINE** instruction. Note the following features of the example program:

1. An input file is not specified. This has nothing to do with the processing of a data area. The program is simplified to emphasize data area processing rather than other **RPG IV** syntax.
2. The data area's external name **(Ch8da2)** is specified in the *Result* field of a ***DTAARA DEFINE** instruction. When accessed by this method, the data area's external attributes (size and decimal positions when ***DEC** type) must be specified.
3. An **IN** instruction accesses the value stored in the data area **(Ch8da2).**
4. Because only one numeric value is stored in the data area, its value does not have to be subdivided into separate fields by a data structure for processing.

The report is included only to show that the value stored in the data area was accessed by the program.

Data Area Accessed with a Data Structure

When the value stored in a data area is a composite of more than one item, it usually has to be subdivided into its related elements for processing. One method of doing this is with a data structure. The example **RPG IV** program in Figure 8-22 illustrates the syntax for this method of the *explicit* processing of a data area.

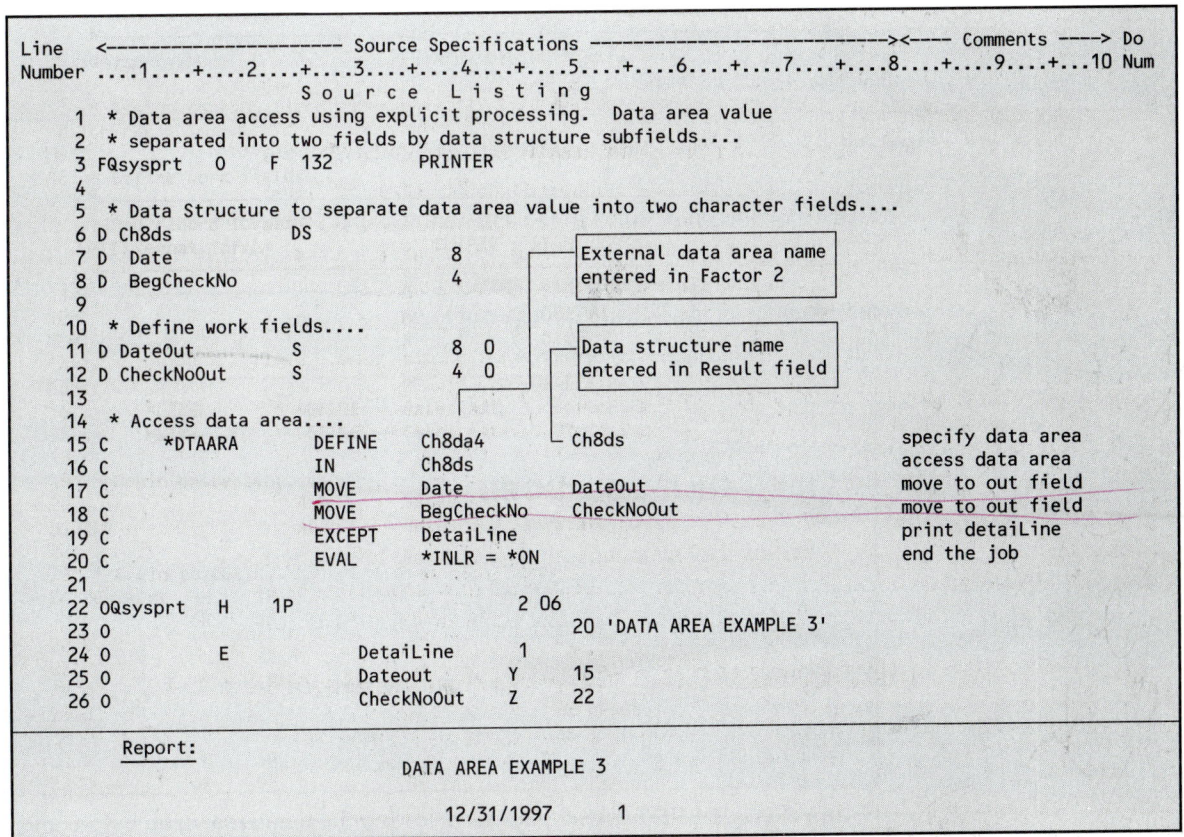

```
Line   <--------------------- Source Specifications ---------------------------><---- Comments ----> Do
Number ....1....+....2....+....3....+....4....+....5....+....6....+....7....+....8....+....9....+...10 Num
                          S o u r c e   L i s t i n g
     * Data area access using explicit processing.  Data area value
     * separated into two fields by data structure subfields....
     FQsysprt   O    F  132        PRINTER

     * Data Structure to separate data area value into two character fields....
     D Ch8ds           DS
     D  Date                          8
     D  BegCheckNo                    4

     * Define work fields....
     D DateOut         S              8  0
     D CheckNoOut      S              4  0

     * Access data area....
     C     *DTAARA       DEFINE    Ch8da4        Ch8ds              specify data area
     C                   IN        Ch8ds                            access data area
     C                   MOVE      Date          DateOut            move to out field
     C                   MOVE      BegCheckNo    CheckNoOut         move to out field
     C                   EXCEPT    DetaiLine                        print detaiLine
     C                   EVAL      *INLR = *ON                      end the job

     OQsysprt   H    1P                 2 06
     O                                       20 'DATA AREA EXAMPLE 3'
     O          E            DetaiLine    1
     O                       Dateout      Y   15
     O                       CheckNoOut   Z   22
```

External data area name entered in Factor 2

Data structure name entered in Result field

Report:

```
                    DATA AREA EXAMPLE 3

                    12/31/1997      1
```

Figure 8-22 Explicit access of the value in a data area with a data structure.

The data area (Ch8da4) accessed by the program in Figure 8-22 was defined as ***CHAR** type with a value of **'123119970001'.** Note that the ***DTAARA DEFINE** instruction on line 15 assigns the data structure to the data area. The **IN** instruction on line 16 loads the data structure's subfields with the value from the data area. The function of the **MOVE** instructions on lines 17 and 18 is to move the character-type subfields to numeric fields so that editing may be performed. Because the data area was created as ***CHAR** type, the data structure's subfields *cannot* be defined as numeric.

EXPLICIT UPDATE OF A DATA AREA VALUE

The two previous program examples that *explicitly* accessed a data area did not change the stored value. To change the value in a data area, the **OUT** operation is required. For the **OUT** operation to be functional, the related **IN** instruction must include the reserved word ***LOCK** in *Factor 1.* Data areas are "unlocked" with the **UNLOCK** operation. Figure 8-23 presents an **RPG IV** program that *explicitly* updates a data area. Note that the *File Description* and *Output Specification* instructions have been deleted from this program example. Its function is to update the data area with the eight-character system date value (***DATE**).

```
Line   <--------------------- Source Specifications ----------------------------><---- Comments ----> Do
Number ....1....+....2....+....3....+....4....+....5....+....6....+....7....+....8....+....9....+...10 Num
                           S o u r c e   L i s t i n g
       * Data area update with explicit processing....

       * Access data area....
     C      *DTAARA       DEFINE                   Ch8da2             8 0       specify data area
     C      *LOCK         IN        Ch8da2                                      access data area
     C                    MOVE      *DATE          Ch8da2                       move to data area
     C                    OUT       Ch8da2                                      udate data area
     C                    UNLOCK    Ch8da2                                      unlock data area
     C                    EVAL      *INLR = *ON                                 end the job
```

Figure 8-23 RPG IV program that explicitly updates a data area.

Because the value stored in the data area (Ch8da2) represents the data for only one field, it does not have to be subdivided for processing. The two **DSPDTAARA** *(Display Data Area)* displays presented in Figure 8-24 show the data area before and after update by the execution of the **RPG IV** program in Figure 8-23.

```
Before:                         Display Data Area
                                                            System:   AS/400

Data area . . . . . . . :   Ch8da2
  Library . . . . . . . :     *LIBL
Type  . . . . . . . . . :   *DEC
Length  . . . . . . . . :   8 0
Text  . . . . . . . . . :   ch8 - data area example
Value . . . . . . . . . :   1231997




Press Enter to continue.

F3=Exit    F12=Cancel
```

Figure 8-24 DSPDTAARA displays showing the data area value before and after updating by an **RPG IV** program.

```
After:                          Display Data Area
                                                          System:   AS/400

Data area . . . . . . . :    Ch8da2
  Library . . . . . . . :      *LIBL
Type  . . . . . . . . . :    *DEC
Length  . . . . . . . . :    8 0
Text  . . . . . . . . . :    ch8 - data area example
Value . . . . . . . . . :    0101998


Press Enter to continue.

F3=Exit   F12=Cancel
```

Figure 8-24 **DSPDTAARA** displays showing the data area value before and after updating by an **RPG IV** program. (Continued)

SUMMARY

Data structures, which are defined in the *Definition Specifications* of an **RPG IV** program, divide a temporary storage area into one or more subfields. They are commonly used to divide a field into subfields, change the format of a field, group noncontiguous data in a contiguous format, define an area of storage in more than one format, and define multiple occurrences of a data structure.

Data Area Data Structures, File Information Data Structures **(INFDS),** and *Program Status Data Structures* are special-purpose data structures. *Data Area Data Structures* assign a data area to an **RPG IV** program and implicitly input the stored value and output the original or changed value automatically at job end. *File Information Data Structures* identify a class of exception/error codes and, when coded accordingly, prevent cancellation of program execution. *Program Status Data Structures* identify a different class of exception/error codes and prevent run-time "abends."

Data areas are objects used to transfer data to one or more programs within a job or between jobs. A data area may be considered a one-record/field storage area whose value may be accessed by an **RPG IV** program. A beginning check number, a report date, and a batch total are some of the many data items that may be stored in a data area.

Data areas are created by the **CRTDTAARA** command, their value is changed with the **CHGDTAARA** command, they are viewed with the **DSPDTAARA** command, and they are deleted with the **DLTDTAARA** command. Data areas may be *implicitly* or *explicitly* processed by an **RPG IV** program. The Data Area value is accessed with a ***DTAARA DEFINE** instruction and an **IN** instruction. Updating of data areas is performed with an **OUT** operation.

QUESTIONS

8-1. What are the functions of a data structure in an **RPG IV program?** May more than one data structure be included in a program?

8-2. Where in an **RPG IV** program are data structures defined?

8-3. Explain some of the syntax rules that must be followed when defining a data structure in an **RPG IV** program.

8-4. Name three special-purpose data structures. What is the function of each?

8-5. Write the coding required to define a data structure to separate CUSTNO into its STATE, COUNTY, and CITY elements.

8-6. Using a different coding method, modify Question 8-5 to accomplish the same results.

8-7. Write a data structure to format a DATE field stored in the physical file INVMSTR from its YYYYMMDD format to an MMDDYYYY format. Remember the physical field entries!

8-8. Write a data structure to format CUSTNO, STATE, COUNTY, and CITY fields from the physical file record format CUSTRCD into the field CUSKEY for processing. Remember the physical file's record entries!

8-9. In an **RPG IV** program, what is the function of *Record Identification Codes?* Where are they specified in the program? Where are they included in a physical file record format?

8-10. How many characters may be used as *Record Identification Codes* in a physical file record format?

8-11. In the coding for *Record Identification Codes,* what does the letter **C** entered in the **C/Z/D** field(s) indicate? What does **Z** indicate? What does **D** indicate?

8-12. Explain the advantage of a data structure that defines an area of storage into more than one record format.

8-13. If a physical file stores data in more than one record format, how is it defined in the **RPG IV** program?

8-14. Write the coding needed to access a data area data structure named TERMDT to extract the term date (six-byte field) for student records processing.

8-15. What ***STATUS** error codes indicate an exception/error?

8-16. By what methods may exception/errors be controlled in an **RPG IV** program?

8-17. Write the required coding to define a file information data structure for the physical file STUMSTR. Only the value stored in ***STATUS** is to be accessed. Include the coding that will transfer control to the **RPG IV** routine ***PSSR** if an exception/error is detected.

8-18. Name some of the ***STATUS** codes identified by a program status data structure.

8-19. Write the required coding to define a program status data structure for the physical file ACTMSTR. The values in all of the keywords are to be accessed. Include the coding that will transfer control to the **RPG IV** routine ***PSSR** if an exception/error is detected.

8-20. Define a data area.

8-21. What **CL** command creates a data area? What entries must be made on the display to create the data area?

8-22. Which **CL** command supports changes to a data area? What command displays the stored value?

8-23. What **RPG IV** statement *explicitly* assigns a data area to a field or data structure? Which **RPG IV** operation accesses the value from the data area? Which operation changes the value in a data area?

8-24. Which **RPG IV** operation *explicitly* prevents other programs from using the data area after it has been accessed by a program? What operation *explicitly* releases the data area?

8-25. Write the required **RPG IV** coding to assign the data area RPTDAT to the field DATE, access the value for processing, and change the data area value with **UDATE.** *Explicitly* lock the data area and release it after processing.

PROGRAMMING ASSIGNMENTS

For each of the following programming assignments, a physical file must have been created and loaded with the related data records. Your instructor will inform you if you have to create the physical file and load it or if it has been prepared for the assignment.

Programming Assignment 8-1: Schedule of Accounts Receivable

Write an **RPG IV** program to generate the report shown in the supplemental printer spacing chart.

A physical file must be created *without* a **DDS** format and loaded with the following data:

Record ID Code	Customer Number	Customer Name	Acct Balance
AR	11111	ALWAYS ABLE	00219215
AR	11121	MARY BEST	00051322
AF	11444	I. M. CURRENT	00020010
AR	12345	LARS DEFICIT	00797788
AR	12356	HUGH DENT	00011154
AR	13344	NEVER EARLY	00485673
AR	14455	ONA TIME	00061487
AT	15376	I. C. GUNN	01065936
AR	16443	Y. HOLD	00004128
AR	17777	I. ITCH	00613366
AR	18123	H. I. JUMP	00032446
AR	19996	E. Z. KIDD	00444444
AR	20019	I. M. A. LUMOX	00056784

Processing: Code your **RPG IV** program to process the file as a *program-described* file and include the *Record Identification Code* entries to test for valid records. Any records that do not include **AR** in positions 1 and 2 are unidentified and must generate an error message of your design on the printed report.

Include a file information data structure that accesses only the five keywords and not the other programmer-defined field areas. Test for ***STATUS** code **01011** (unidentified record type) exception/error and include an internal subroutine to process the error. Modify the existing report format to include an output line for the error record(s).

Create a data area and define its size as 13 characters. Store the report date value **12311997** in the first *eight* positions of the data area; in the other *five* positions, store **00000** for the total number of records processed by the program. At the end of the file, update the report date to **03311998** and the five positions record count field with the number of *valid* records processed.

Report Design: Note that the dollar sign is specified only on the first detail line and the total line. As shown below, appropriate underlining is to be included.

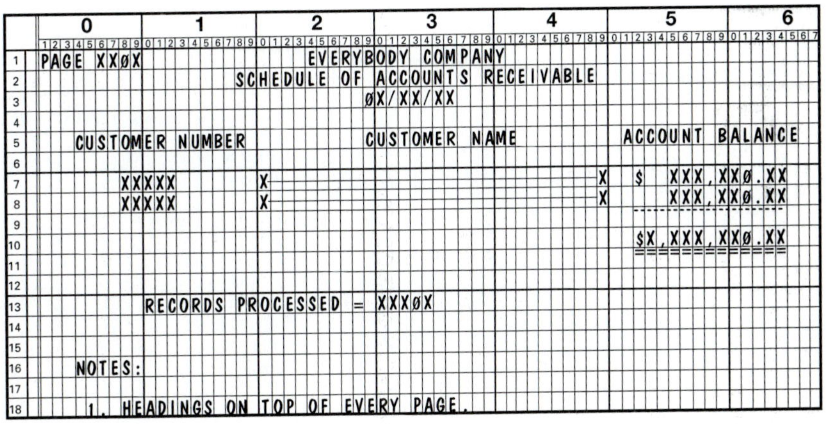

The completed assignment must include the following:

1. Display of the **CRTDTAARA** display with original values included. Use the **Print Screen** key to obtain a printout, or demonstrate to your instructor as requested.
2. A **DSPDTAARA** display after the data area is updated. Use the **Print Screen** key to obtain a printout, or demonstrate to your instructor as requested.
3. A **DLTDTAARA** display to delete the data area *after* the **RPG IV** program is successfully executed and output checked.
4. **RPG IV** compile listing.
5. Printed report.

Programming Assignment 8-2: INCLUDING A PROGRAM STATUS DATA STRUCTURE IN AN RPG IV PROGRAM

If Programming Assignment 6-5 was not previously completed, refer to its documentation in Chapter 6 (page 169). In any case, modify the program to include a program status data structure, specifying only the five keywords and not the programmer-defined field areas.

Modify the physical file data using **DFU** so that one or two records include a zero value for the **EUL** (estimated useful life) field. Test for ***STATUS** code **00102** (divide by zero) exception/error. Include a subroutine in the program to process the error and add an error message line of your own design to the report format.

Programming Assignment 8-3: CASH DISBURSEMENTS JOURNAL

A *cash disbursements journal* is used in an accounting system to record all cash disbursements. Special columns are included in the journal for the elements of each transaction. Write an **RPG IV** program to generate the journal format shown in the supplemental printer spacing chart.

Physical File Record Format:

PHYSICAL FILE DESCRIPTION

SYSTEM: AS/400	DATE: Yours
FILE NAME: Yours	REV NO: 0
RECORD NAME: Yours	KEY LENGTH: 3
SEQUENCE: Keyed	RECORD SIZE: 53

FIELD DEFINITIONS

FIELD NO	FIELD NAME	SIZE	TYPE	POSITION FROM	POSITION TO	COMMENTS
1	TRANSCODE	1	C	1	1	S or P
2	CHECKDATE	6	P	2	5	
3	CHECKNUM	3	P	6	7	key field
4	PAYEE	20	C	8	27	
5	ACTDEBIT	20	C	28	47	
6	FOL_PCT	3	P	48	49	3 decimals
7	TRANSAMT	6	P	50	53	2 decimals

Physical file data:

Record ID	Check Date	Check#	Payee	Account Debited	Dis Pct or Folio	Acts Pay or Sundry Amount
S	010297	100	APEX REALTY	RENT EXPENSE	503	250000
P	010397	101	EAST SALES CO	EAST SALES CO	020	100000
S	010497	102	SAVO AND SONS	OFFICE EQUIPMENT	110	050000
S	010597	103	JERRY HALE	SALARIES EXPENSE	505	066000
P	011097	104	ACME MFG CO	ACME MFG CO	020	200000
S	011497	105	ELSIE TRUCKING CO	DELIVERY EXPENSES	590	005798
P	011897	106	SMITH AND SONS	SMITH AND SONS	025	030000
P	012297	107	ARIZONA SUPPLY CO	ARIZONA SUPPLY CO	015	095010
D	012397	108	ABC REPAIR SERVICE	OFFICE REPAIRS	508	007825
P	012597	109	WESTERN SUPPLY CO	WESTERN SUPPLY CO	010	089045
S	012997	110	SHELTON FORD	CAR EXPENSE	511	045093
P	013197	111	MATCHLESS TOOL CO	MATCHLESS TOOL CO	030	060000
A	013197	112	STAPLES SUPPLY	OFFICE SUPPLIES	100	034967

Note that the two record formats are logically supported by the physical file. They are identical in field sizes but differ for the related **S** or **P** type transaction. Record type **S** uses the **FOL_PCT** field for a Folio value and **TRANSAMT** for a Sundry value. Record type **P** uses the **FOL_PCT** field for a discount percent value and **TRANSAMT** for an Accounts Payable value.

For this assignment, define the data file in the **RPG IV** program as *program-described* (**F** in column 19 of the *File Description* statement) and define the **S** and **P** record formats in the *Input Specifications*. Use *Record Identification Codes* to identify the **S** and **P** record types.

Processing: Include a file information data structure in the program to identify and process unidentified record types (without an **S** or **P**) and prevent cancellation of program execution.

Because the **FOL_PCT** field is defined in the record format as three bytes with three decimal positions, it must be redefined as an integer for the Folio value in **S** type records. Consequently, multiply the **FOL_PCT** field by 1,000 and store the value in a three-byte integer field for printing. Note that for **S** records the **TRANSAMT** field value is printed in two columns in the report.

For **P** type records, multiply the discount **TRANSAMT** field by the **FOL_PCT** field to determine the purchase discount. Then subtract the purchase discount from the **TRANSAMT** field to determine the cash credit value (last column in printer spacing chart).

Accumulate totals for the sundry, accounts payable, purchase discount, and cash credit columns, and print them at **LR** time.

Report Design:

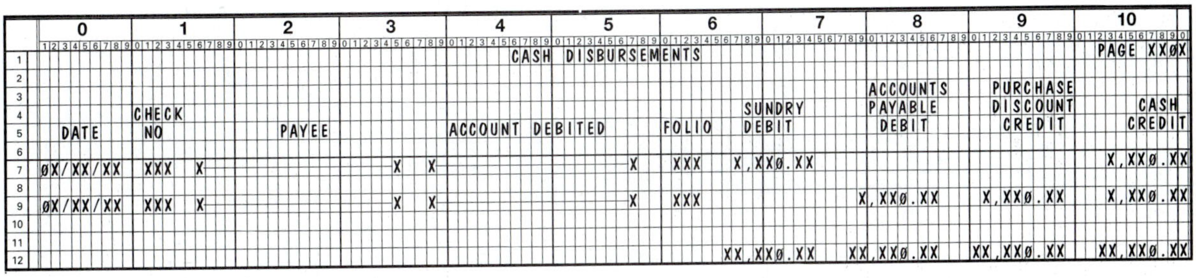

CASH DISBURSEMENTS
PAGE XXØX
DATE
CHECK NO
PAYEE
ACCOUNT DEBITED
FOLIO
SUNDRY DEBIT
ACCOUNTS PAYABLE DEBIT
PURCHASE DISCOUNT CREDIT
CASH CREDIT
ØX/XX/XX XXX X X X X XXX X,XXØ.XX X,XXØ.XX
ØX/XX/XX XXX X X X X XXX X,XXØ.XX X,XXØ.XX X,XXØ.XX
XX,XXØ.XX XX,XXØ.XX XX,XXØ.XX XX,XXØ.XX

chapter 9

Table Processing

In the **RPG IV** environment, a *table* may be defined as a list of data stored in memory. The storage positions for a table are built and loaded during program execution before any other input files are read and processed. Tables include relatively *fixed* data that is referenced by other data. Tax rates, transaction codes, pay grades, pay rates, month names, and so forth are examples of data commonly included in tables.

TABLE STRUCTURE

Argument and Function Tables

Figure 9-1 illustrates six examples of table structures. A single table is referred to in **RPG IV** as a *simple table*. A table may be processed as a standalone table or used to relate to one or more other simple tables.

Illustration 1

Pay Code	Hourly Rate
A	500
B	550
C	610
D	675
E	735
F	800
Argument Table	Function Table

Related tables sorted in ascending order.

Illustration 2

Item Number	Price
1234	00056
5678	00188
9123	00239
8321	00751
1789	01051
Argument Table	Function Table

Smaller numeric table entries must be padded with high-order zeros. Both tables are in an unordered sequence.

Illustration 3

SS No.	Name
040000009	DROPOUT A
222222222	FAIL Y
789665555	HONORS HI
820801234	SUCCEED I
934202601	TOPP ON
Argument Table	Function Table

Smaller alphabetic (or alphanumeric) entries are padded with low-order blanks. SS No. table is in ascending order and related Name table in unordered sequence.

Illustration 4

Taxable Amount	Fixed Amount	Tax Percent
035	0336	18
073	1020	21
202	3729	23
231	4396	27
269	5422	31
333	7406	35

Illustration 5

Item #	Brand
300	COCA COLA
500	SPRITE
400	7-UP
550	SLICE
600	FRESCA
900	HIRES ROOT BEER
100	WELCH'S GRAPE

Illustration 6

Special Characters
&
*
#
:
@
?
/

Figure 9-1 Examples of table structures.

Argument Table | Function Table 1 | Function Table 2 | Argument Table | Function Table | Argument Table

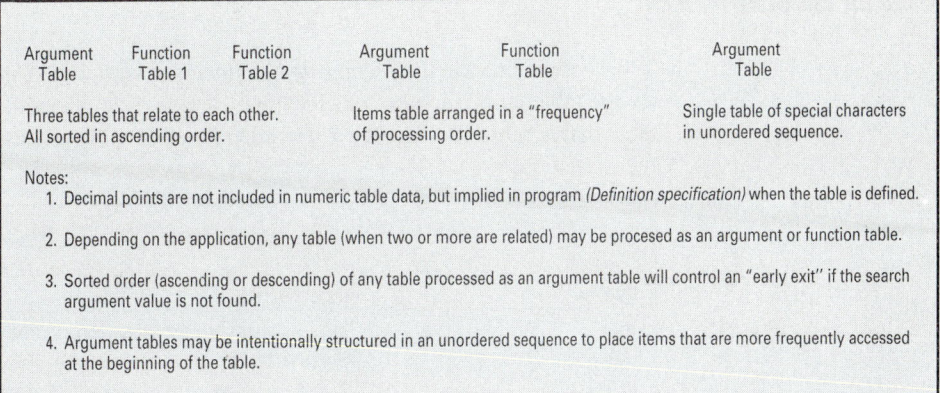

Three tables that relate to each other. All sorted in ascending order.

Items table arranged in a "frequency" of processing order.

Single table of special characters in unordered sequence.

Notes:

1. Decimal points are not included in numeric table data, but implied in program *(Definition specification)* when the table is defined.
2. Depending on the application, any table (when two or more are related) may be procesed as an argument or function table.
3. Sorted order (ascending or descending) of any table processed as an argument table will control an "early exit" if the search argument value is not found.
4. Argument tables may be intentionally structured in an unordered sequence to place items that are more frequently accessed at the beginning of the table.

Figure 9-1 Examples of table structures. (Continued)

Two new terms, *argument* and *function*, are introduced in Figure 9-1. An *argument table* is the one that is "looked up" by a data item called the *search argument*. A *function table* relates physically and logically to an argument table. For example, the first entry in an argument table relates to the first entry in a corresponding function table. Any number of function tables may relate to an argument table; and, depending on the application, any table may be referenced as an argument or function table.

LOADING TABLES

"Loading a table" refers to the time in the program cycle when table data is read, moved, and stored into the memory positions defined and built by an **RPG IV** program. Tables may be loaded at *compile* time or at *prerun* time. Figure 9-2 details the processing logic associated with the loading of a table each time in the program cycle.

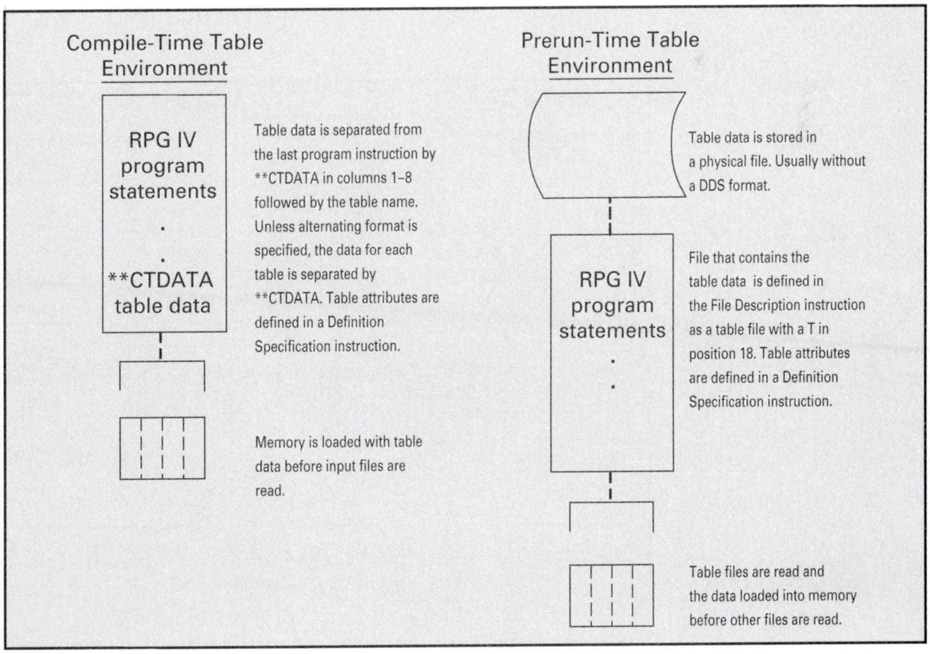

Figure 9-2 Processing logic for loading tables at compile and prerun times.

TABLE DESCRIPTION

Tables are defined in the *Definition Specification* with one or more instructions that specify the table name, number of elements, element size, element type, and sequence of the table data. Figure 9-3 lists the keywords related to table processing and an explanation of their function.

TABLE KEYWORDS USED IN THE DEFINITION SPECIFICATION

Table Keyword	Function
ALT	Table elements are in an alternating format with another table
ASCEND	Specifies that the table data is in ascending order
CTDATA	Specifies the beginning of a compile-time table
DESCEND	Specifies that the table data is in descending order
DIM	Defines the number of table elements
FROMFILE	Specifies the input table file in which the table data is stored
PERRCD	Specifies the number of table elements per record
TOFILE	Specifies the file to which the table data will be written

Figure 9-3 Table keywords used in *Definition Specification* instructions.

The syntax for compile- and prerun-time tables will be discussed in the following sections. *Note that all table names must begin with the letters* **TAB** *with one to seven additional programmer-supplied characters.*

RPG IV SYNTAX FOR COMPILE-TIME TABLES

Compile-time table data is an extension of the **RPG IV** program. The data for each compile-time table (except for alternating sequence of the table data) must be separated from each other with a ****CTDATA** keyword format (in positions 1–8) followed by a space and the related table name. Figure 9-4 details the syntax for a compile-time table. Note that the **TabMonth** table has all of the data elements stored on *one* record. The number of data elements stored on a compile-time table record is at the option of the programmer.

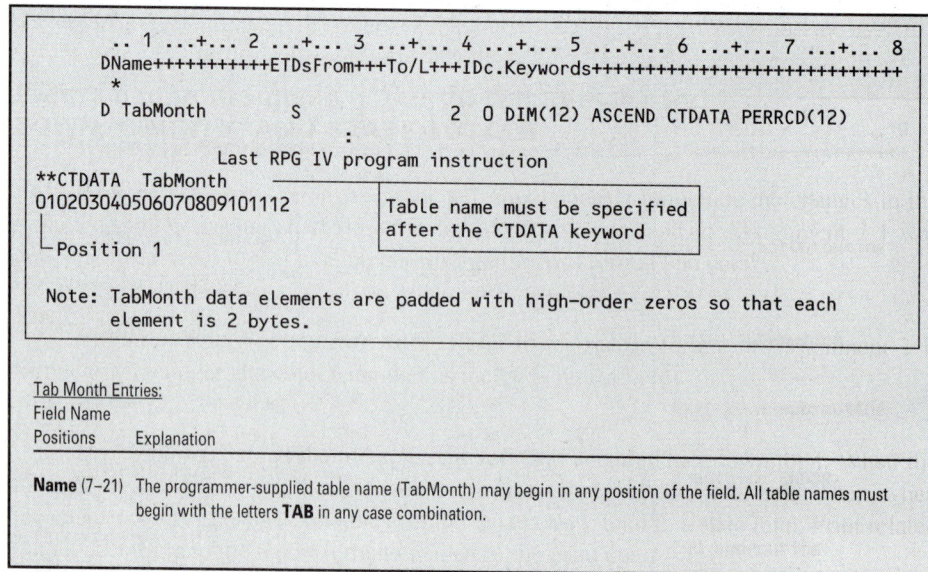

```
          .. 1 ...+... 2 ...+... 3 ...+... 4 ...+... 5 ...+... 6 ...+... 7 ...+... 8
          DName+++++++++++ETDsFrom+++To/L+++IDc.Keywords+++++++++++++++++++++++++++++
          *
          D TabMonth        S               2  0 DIM(12) ASCEND CTDATA PERRCD(12)
                                                 :
                     Last RPG IV program instruction
**CTDATA  TabMonth  ──────────────────────────
010203040506070809101112          Table name must be specified
|                                 after the CTDATA keyword
└Position 1

 Note: TabMonth data elements are padded with high-order zeros so that each
       element is 2 bytes.
```

Tab Month Entries:

Field Name Positions	Explanation
Name (7–21)	The programmer-supplied table name (TabMonth) may begin in any position of the field. All table names must begin with the letters **TAB** in any case combination.

Figure 9-4 *Definition Specification* syntax for a compile-time table.

S (24)	**S** indicates the entry is a standalone field. For tables, multiple entries are supported.
L+++ (36–39)	Defines the length of the table's elements. All of the elements (data items) in a table must be the same size. Smaller numeric elements are padded with high-order zeros and smaller character elements are padded with low-order blanks. The **2** entered defines this table's elements with a length of two bytes.
Dc (41–42)	Defines the table element as numeric. A **0** to **30** may be entered to indicate the number of implied decimals for the elements. If an entry is not made in this field, the table elements are defined as character. The **0** entered indicates that the elements are defined as numeric integers.
DIM(12)	Specifies the number of elements stored in the table. The **12** in parentheses defines the table with 12 elements.
ASCEND	Defines the table data as stored in ascending order. If this entry is omitted, the table data will be defined as stored in an unordered sequence.
CTDATA	Compile-time tables require this entry, which specifies that the data is an extension of the **RPG IV** program.
PERRCD	Indicates the number of elements stored on each table record. If this entry is omitted, **RPG IV** will assume that one element is stored on a table record. The **12** in parentheses for this example specifies that **12** elements are stored on one or more table records. Note that when table data is stored on more than one record, the last record may have less than the **PERRCD** keyword indicates.

Figure 9-4 *Definition Specification* syntax for a compile-time table. (Continued)

RPG IV Syntax for Related Compile-Time Tables

More than often, tables are not "standalone" but are related to the data in one or more other tables. Figure 9-5 explains the syntax for two related compile-time tables. Understand that each table may be processed without referring to the other table. However, for this example, the TabMonth table *(argument table)* would be searched first to extract the related value from the TabName *(function)* table.

```
      .. 1 ...+... 2 ...+... 3 ...+... 4 ...+... 5 ...+... 6 ...+... 7 ...+... 8
      DName+++++++++++ETDsFrom+++To/L+++IDc.Keywords+++++++++++++++++++++++++++++
       * Definition of two related compile-time tables
      D TabMonth        S              2  0 DIM(12) ASCEND CTDATA PERRCD(12)
      D TabName         S              9    DIM(12) CTDATA PERRCD(6)
                                 :
                Last RPG IV program instruction
**CTDATA TabMonth
010203040506070809101112                        Table names must be
**CTDATA TabName                                specified after the
JANUARY  FEBRUARY MARCH    APRIL    MAY      JUNE      CTDATA delimiters
JULY     AUGUST   SEPTEMBEROCTOBER  NOVEMBER DECEMBER
|
└─ Position 1

 Note: TabName data elements are padded with low-order blanks so that each
       is nine bytes in length.
```

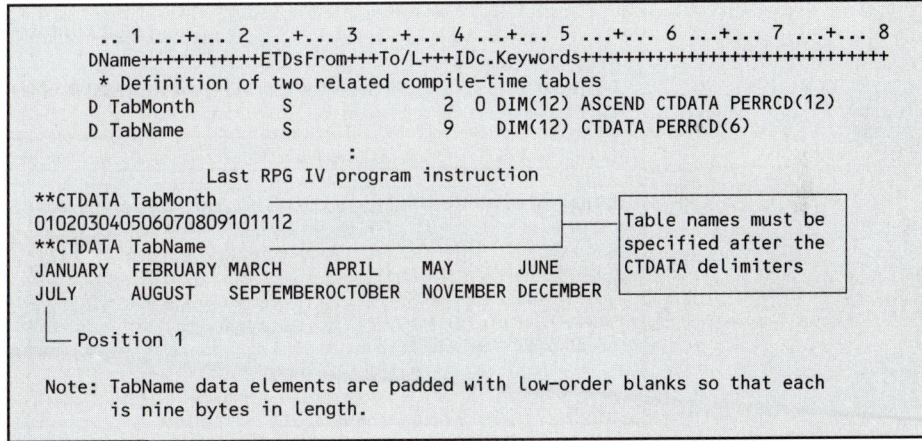

Figure 9-5 *Definition Specification* syntax for two related compile-time tables.

The syntax for the TabMonth table is identical to that shown in Figure 9-4. However, the syntax for the TabName table has the following changes:

- The TabName elements are defined as nine characters.
- The **PERRCD(6)** keyword specifies that six elements are stored on each table record.

- Because the table data is in an unordered sequence, an **ASCEND** or **DESCEND** keyword entry is omitted.
- A second ****CTDATA** delimiter is included in the table data to separate the data for one compile-time table from the other.

RPG IV Syntax for Compile-Time Table Elements Stored in an Alternating Format

Figure 9-6 shows the table data from Figure 9-5 arranged in an alternating format with the modified *Definition Specification* entries. Note the following changes in the *Definition Specification* syntax:

- Because only one TabMonth table entry is stored on a record, the **PERRCD** keyword may be omitted in the table definition.
- Because the elements for TabName are in an alternating format with the elements for TabMonth, the **CTDATA** keyword, indicating a compile-time table, is not required.
- The **ALT(TabMonth)** keyword specifies that the elements for TabName are in an alternating format with TabMonth.

```
          .. 1 ...+... 2 ...+... 3 ...+... 4 ...+... 5 ...+... 6 ...+... 7 ...+... 8
          DName+++++++++++ETDsFrom+++To/L+++IDc.Keywords+++++++++++++++++++++++++++++
           * Definition of two related compile-time tables with elements stored in
           * an alternating format
          D TabMonth        S              2  0 DIM(12) ASCEND CTDATA
          D TabName         S              9    DIM(12) ALT(TabMonth)
                                      :
                     Last RPG IV program instruction
**CTDATA TabMonth
01JANUARY         The name of the primary table (first defined)
02FEBRUARY        must be specified with the **CTDATA delimiter
03MARCH
04APRIL
05MAY
06JUNE            The data for TabMonth and TabName are stored
07JULY            in an alternating format with one element
08AUGUST          for each table on a record
09SEPTEMBER
10OCTOBER
11NOVEMBER
12DECEMBER

Position 1
```

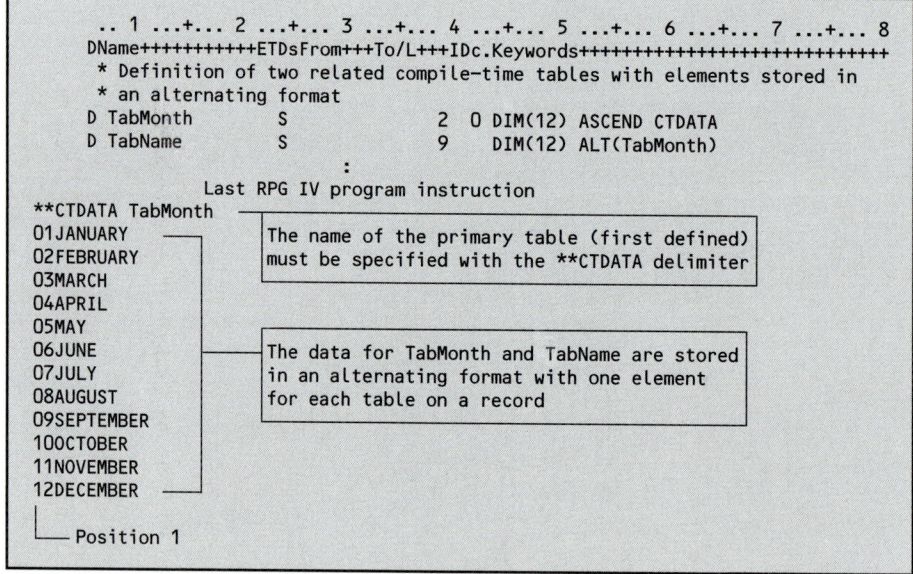

Figure 9-6 *Definition Specification* and related data for two compile-time tables stored in an alternating format.

No *File Description, Input,* or *Output Specification* instructions are required to define and process compile-time tables. However, to access the elements from a compile-time or prerun-time table, *Calculation Specification* instructions are needed. The access of table data will be discussed later in this chapter.

RPG IV SYNTAX FOR PRERUN-TIME TABLES

Data for prerun-time tables is stored externally, usually in a physical file without a DDS format. When the **RPG IV** program is executed, a storage area is built in memory and the elements loaded with data before any other data files are read. The table remains in memory for the complete program cycle and, unless updated, is not changed. When required, an updated prerun-time table data may be written back to the physical file and/or printed.

Figure 9-7 illustrates the *File Description* and *Definition Specification* syntax to define a prerun-time table. The example uses the table data processed by the previously discussed compile-time tables. Note that the letter **T** is specified in position 18 to define the input file as a table file. In addition, the input file is defined with an **F** in position 22, indicating that it is program-described. Because the file is defined as program-described, the record length (11 for this example) must be entered in positions 23–27.

```
.. 1 ...+... 2 ...+... 3 ...+... 4 ...+... 5 ...+... 6 ...+... 7 ...+... 8
FFilename++IPEASFRLen+LKLen+AIDevice+.Keywords+++++++++++++++++++++++++++++
 * Letter T in position 18 defines the file as a table file.  F in position
 * 22 defines a program-described file.  Record length (11) in positions
 * 23-27 must be specified for a program-described file.

FTableFile IT   F   11         DISK
FQsysPrt   O    F  132         PRINTER
```

```
.. 1 ...+... 2 ...+... 3 ...+... 4 ...+... 5 ...+... 6 ...+... 7 ...+... 8
DName+++++++++++ETDsFrom+++To/L+++IDc.Keywords+++++++++++++++++++++++++++++
 * The FROMFILE keyword must be specified for a prerun-time table.  The
 * file name (defined in the File Description as a table file) must be
 * entered in parentheses after the FROMFILE keyword.  Other syntax is
 * identical to compile-time tables.

D TabMonth        S              2  0 DIM(12) ASCEND FROMFILE(TableFile)
D TabName         S              9    DIM(12) ALT(TabMonth)
```

Figure 9-7 *File Description* and *Definition Specification* syntax for prerun-time tables. Data is stored in the physical file in an alternating format.

Note that the syntax in Figure 9-7 is for two related tables with the data stored in an alternating format. This is not a requirement for prerun-time tables; the data may be stored in separate files. However, the data for only *two* tables may be stored in any table file.

Update of Prerun-Time Tables

Compile-time table data may be updated only by accessing the related **RPG IV** source program, changing the table data with **SEU,** saving the changed program, and recompiling. Prerun-time table data, however, may be updated during program execution. Figure 9-8

```
.. 1 ...+... 2 ...+... 3 ...+... 4 ...+... 5 ...+... 6 ...+... 7 ...+... 8
FFilename++IPEASFRLen+LKLen+AIDevice+.Keywords+++++++++++++++++++++++++++++
 * Letter C (for combined file) must replace the letter I in position 17
 * when the prerun-time table data is to be updated by the RPG IV program.

FTableFile CT   F   11         DISK
FQsysPrt   O    F  132         PRINTER
```

Figure 9-8 *File Description* and *Definition Specification* syntax to update the data in a prerun-time table.

```
.. 1 ...+... 2 ...+... 3 ...+... 4 ...+... 5 ...+... 6 ...+... 7 ...+... 8
DName+++++++++++ETDsFrom+++To/L+++IDc.Keywords+++++++++++++++++++++++++++++
 * The TOFILE(TableFile) keyword entry must be included when the prerun-
 * time table data is to be updated at the end of program execution.

D TabMonth        S              2  0 DIM(12) ASCEND FROMFILE(TableFile)
D                                     TOFILE(TableFile)
D TabName         S              9    DIM(12) ALT(TabMonth)
```

Figure 9-8 *File Description* and *Definition Specification* syntax to update the data in a prerun-time table. (Continued)

details the syntax for updating prerun-time table data. In the *File Description Specification* definition for the table file, the letter **C,** for combined file (i.e., both input and output), must replace the **I** in position 17. In the *Definition Specification* definition for the prerun-time table, the **TOFILE** keyword must be included followed by the related prerun-time table file name in parentheses (e.g., **TOFILE(TableFile)**).

Instead of updating the prerun-time table file in which the data is stored, the table data may be written to another physical file that does not have a DDS format or to the printer. In any case, the update process, or printing, occurs automatically at the end of program execution.

The decision on whether to use a compile- or prerun-time table in an **RPG IV** program generally depends on the following factors:

1. Compile-time tables are most often used when the table contains few entries, the data is not likely to change, and/or the data is not shared by other programs. The month number/name tables previously discussed are an example of the type of data stored in compile-time tables.
2. Prerun-time tables are used when the tables contain many entries, and/or the data is frequently updated, and/or the data is accessed by other programs.

FORMAT OF TABLE DATA

The records that store the data for compile-time and prerun-time tables must be formatted according to the rules explained in Figure 9-9.

RULES FOR FORMATTING TABLE DATA

1. The data must begin in the first position of each record.
2. Entries for a table must all be the same size.
3. Smaller numeric elements must be padded with high-order zeros; smaller character elements must be padded with low-order blanks.
4. When an alternating format is used for the data for two tables, the values for the tables must be included on a record based on the entry with the **PERRCD** keyword. If the **PERRCD** keyword is omitted, the default format will be one entry per record from each table. In any case, the data cannot be separated onto two records; it must be stored in pairs.
5. The order of the compile-time table data does not have to be in the same sequence as their related *Definition Specification* descriptions.

Figure 9-9 Rules for formatting the data for compile- and prerun-time tables.

PROCESSING TABLES

So far the **RPG IV** syntax to define tables has been explained without a discussion of how the tables are processed. A table is searched consecutively by the **LOOKUP** operation; depending on the application, the table may be searched until an equal, high-range, or low-range condition is tested. The following sections will explain how table data is accessed for processing.

Single (Standalone) Table Processing

An *argument* table may be processed by an **RPG IV** program without any relationship to other tables, or it may be related to one or more *function* tables. Single table processing is commonly used in data validation procedures. An example is shown in Figure 9-10 where

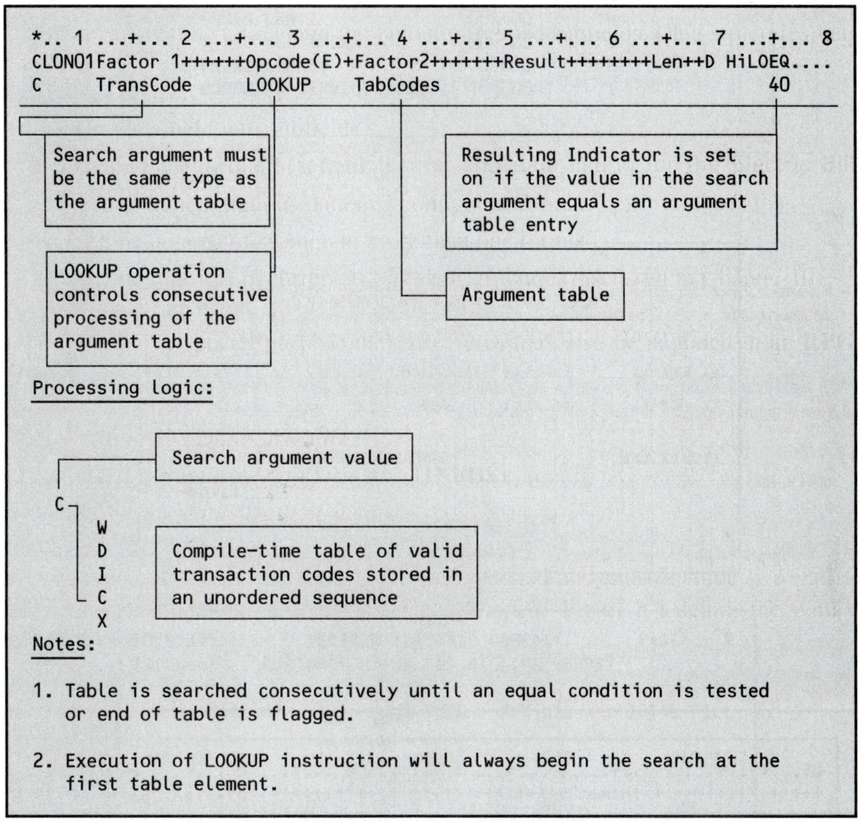

Figure 9-10 Syntax and processing logic for an equal lookup of one table.

a field value from a physical file "looks up" a compile-time table of acceptable codes with the **LOOKUP** operation. If the *search argument* value is found in the table, the *Resulting Indicator* in the **Eq** field will be set on. Depending on the program logic, subsequent calculations will be executed by the "on" and/or "off" status of the indicator. Because *Factor 1* and *Factor 2* entries of the **LOOKUP** instruction are required, the **SEU C** format or prompt option must be used to enter the coding.

Related Table Processing

In addition to single table processing, two or more tables may relate to each other. An argument table (*Factor 2* entry) is searched; when the lookup condition is satisfied, the related value from a function table (*Result* entry) is accessed automatically. Figure 9-11 details the *Calculation Specification* syntax and logic associated with the processing of three related tables.

```
*.. 1 ...+... 2 ...+... 3 ...+... 4 ...+... 5 ...+... 6 ...+... 7 ...+... 8
CL0N01Factor 1+++++++Opcode(E)+Factor2+++++++Result++++++++Len++D_HiLOEQ....
CL0N01Factor 1+++++++Opcode(E)+Extended-factor2+++++++++++++++++++++++++++++

C     MthNumber     LOOKUP    TabMthNo       TabMonth                 30
C                   IF        *IN30 = *ON
C     MthNumber     LOOKUP    TabMthNo       TabDays                  30
C                   ENDIF
C                     :
```

Second LOOKUP instruction accesses related TabDays element

First LOOKUP instruction accesses related TabMonth element

Indicator must be specified in both LOOKUP instructions. Same indicator may be used.

Processing logic:

Search argument value: 08

TabMthNo	TabMonth	TabDays
01	JANUARY	31
02	FEBRUARY	28
03	MARCH	31
04	APRIL	30
05	MAY	31
06	JUNE	30
07	JULY	31
08	AUGUST	31
09	SEPTEMBER	30
10	OCTOBER	31
11	NOVEMBER	30
12	DECEMBER	31

Notes:

1. Because of the search argument value, the TabMonth table is specified as the argument table for both LOOKUP instructions.
2. Search argument (MthNumber) consecutively searches the argument table (TabMthNo) until an equal condition is tested. Because TabName is specified in the Result Field in the first LOOKUP instruction, its related element value is also accessed. This logic is the same for the second LOOKUP instruction.
3. Because the TabMthNo table data is in ascending order (assume it is defined in the Definition Specification instruction with the ASCEND keyword), an "early exit" will automatically be controlled if 00 or a minus number was entered for the MthNumber value. However, if the MthNumber value is greater than 12, the TabMthNo table would be processed to the end.

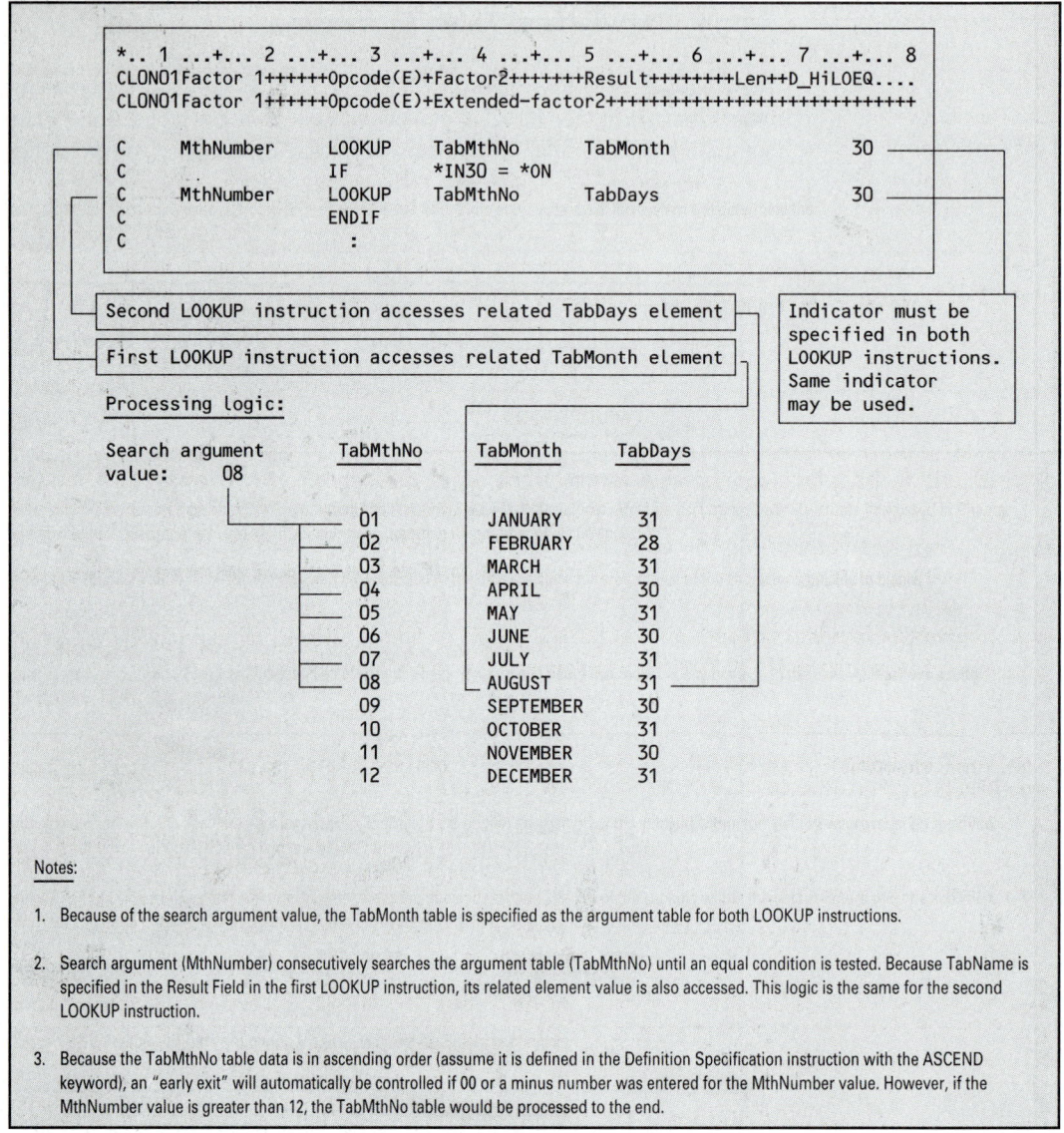

Figure 9-11 Syntax and processing logic for an equal lookup of three related tables.

"EARLY EXIT" CONTROL OF TABLE LOOKUP

For an unsuccessful search, an unordered sequence of table data will cause program control to process to the end of the table. With small tables this is not significant; it is, however, for large tables that have hundreds or thousands of elements. More efficient processing is provided if the argument table data is sorted in either ascending or descending order.

A sorted order supports an "early exit" for an unsuccessful "equal" table lookup condition. For tables in *ascending* order, a search argument value *less than* an argument table element will prompt an early exit and stop the search. Tables in *descending* order will cause an early exit when the search argument value is *greater than* an argument table element.

To provide early exit control, the **ASCEND** or **DESCEND** keyword (as appropriate) must be included in the *Definition Specification* instruction that defines the related argument table.

When a compile-time table is defined in the *Definition Specification* as sorted (either **ASCEND** or **DESCEND** keyword) and the table data is unordered, a terminal error will be generated during compilation. For prerun-time tables, however, sequence errors are flagged only during program execution.

APPLICATION PROGRAM: WEEKLY PAYROLL REPORT

Documentation

The specifications presented in Figure 9-12 explain the processing requirements for an application program that generates a weekly payroll report. The system flowchart in

PROGRAM SPECIFICATIONS

Page 1 of 1

Program Name: Weekly Payroll Report

Program - ID: CH9P1

Written by: SM

Purpose: Weekly payroll report for hourly employees

Approved by: CM

Input files: PAYROLL

Output files: QSYSPRT

Processing Requirements:

Write an RPG IV program to generate a weekly payroll report for day- and night-shift employees.

Input to the program:

The externally defined physical file, PAYROLL, contains the weekly payroll data for day- and night-shift hourly employees. A supplemental record layout form details the physical file's record format.

Processing:

Include the following compile-time tables in the RPG IV program:

1. A table for month numbers and a related table for month names
2. Tables for labor grades, day-shift rates, and night-shift rates with the following values:

Labor Grade	Day Rate	Night Rate
A	0800	0900
B	1000	1150
C	1275	1525
D	1600	1800
E	1950	2300

Figure 9-12 Specifications for an application program using tables that generates a weekly payroll report.

Look up the month number table with the month value from the WKDATE field in the first record processed to access the month name from the related month name table. Include the month name on the second heading line. Use the month and year values from the WKDATE field for the third heading line.

For each input record, test the shift field for a D or N and look up the labor grade table to access the related shift rate. Two **LOOKUP** statements must be provided, one to access the day-rates table and the other to access the night-rates table.

For a successful search of the grade table, compute the week's pay for an employee by multiplying the hours worked by the accessed rate table value. If the search is unsuccessful, print the error messag ....LABOR GRADE NOT VALID... .Refer to the print chart for the location of this message.

Add each employee's wages to an accumulator and print the value at LR time.

Output:

Refer to the supplemental printer spacing chart and code the output accordingly.

Figure 9-12 Specifications for an application program using tables that generates a weekly payroll report. (Continued)

Figure 9-13 indicates that one physical file and one output printer file are processed by

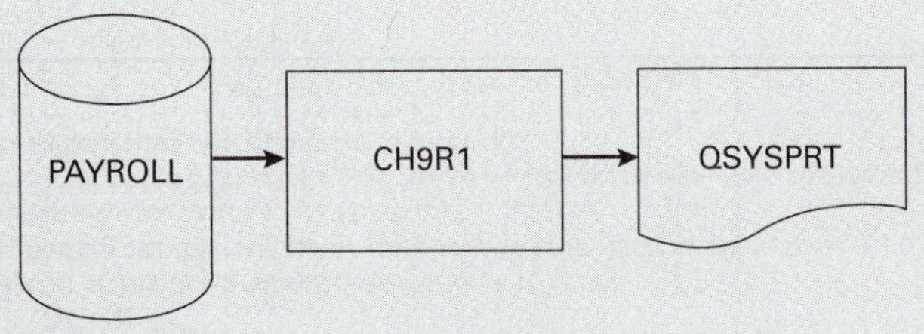

Figure 9-13 System flowchart for Weekly Payroll Report program.

the program. Figure 9-14 details the record format of the input file. The *Labor Grade* field will be used as the search argument in the **LOOKUP** operations. The design of the

PHYSICAL FILE DESCRIPTION

SYSTEM: AS/400 DATE: 8/01/97
FILE NAME: PAYROLL REV NO: 0
RECORD NAME: PAYROLLR KEY LENGTH: 9
SEQUENCE: Keyed RECORD SIZE: 33

FIELD DEFINITIONS

FIELD NO	FIELD NAME	SIZE	TYPE	POSITION FROM	POSITION TO	COMMENTS
1	SSNUMBER	9	P	1	5	Key field
2	EMPNAME	20	C	6	25	
3	LABORGRADE	1	C	26	26	
4	SHIFT	1	C	27	27	
5	WEEKLY_HRS	3	P	28	29	0 decimals
6	PAY_DATE	6	P	30	33	

Figure 9-14 Physical file record format and data listing.

Physical file data:

SS Number	Employee Name	Labor Grade	Shift	Weekly Hours	Payroll Date
011111111	DONALD DRAKE	E	D	40	091597
022222222	LAMONT CRANSTON	A	N	32	091597
033333333	MICKEY MOUSE	C	D	37	091597
044444444	RICHARD TRACY	F	N	40	091597
055555555	PAUL VALIANT	D	N	35	091597
066666666	MORTIMER SNERD	B	D	30	091597
077777777	ANDREW GUMP	E	N	40	091597

Figure 9-14 Physical file record format and data listing. (Continued)

Weekly Payroll Report is shown in Figure 9-15, and the report generated by it is shown in Figure 9-16.

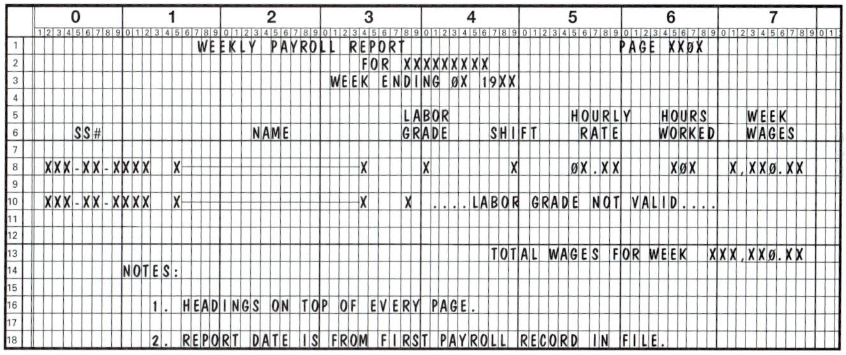

Figure 9-15 Design of Weekly Payroll Report.

```
                          WEEKLY PAYROLL REPORT                      PAGE    1
                             FOR SEPTEMBER
                           WEEK ENDING  9/15/97

                                       LABOR             HOURLY   HOURS    WEEK
    SS#                 NAME           GRADE    SHIFT     RATE    WORKED   WAGES

011-11-1111  DONALD DRAKE                E        D      19.50      40     780.00

022-22-2222  LAMONT CRANSTON             A        N       9.00      32     288.00

033-33-3333  MICKEY MOUSE                C        D      12.75      37     471.75

044-44-4444  RICHARD TRACY               F   ....LABOR GRADE NOT  VALID....

055-55-5555  PAUL VALIANT                D        N      18.00      35     630.00

066-66-6666  MORTIMER SNERD              B        D      10.00      30     300.00

077-77-7777  ANDREW GUMP                 E        N      23.00      40     920.00

                                              TOTAL WAGES FOR WEEK     3,389.75
```

Figure 9-16 Report generated by Weekly Payroll Report program.

Source Program Coding

A compile listing of the Weekly Payroll Report program is detailed in Figure 9-17.

```
Line   <--------------------- Source Specifications ----------------------------><---- Comments ----> Do
Number ....1....+....2....+....3....+....4....+....5....+....6....+....7....+....8....+....9....+...10 Num
                          S o u r c e   L i s t i n g
     1  *             WEEKLY PAYROLL REPORT FOR HOURLY EMPLOYEES
     2  *  Program includes the folowing compile-time tables:
     3  *    1. Table of month numbers and related month names
     4  *    2. Table of labor grade codes
     5  *    3. Related tables for hourly day- and night-shift rates
     6  *  Labor grade code is the search argument for the LOOKUP in the
     7  *  grade table.
     8
     9
    10 FPayroll   IF   E           K DISK
       *--------------------------------------------------------------------------------------------*
       *                              RPG name          External name                               *
       * File name. . . . . . . . :   PAYROLL           STAN/PAYROLL                                *
       * Record format(s) . . . . :   PAYROLLR          PAYROLLR                                    *
       *--------------------------------------------------------------------------------------------*
    11 FQsysprt   O    F  132         PRINTER OFLIND(*INOF)
    12
    13  * Define compile-time tables....
    14 D TabMthNo        S              2  0 DIM(12) ASCEND CTDATA PERRCD(2)
    15 D TabName         S              9    DIM(12) ALT(TabMthNo)
    16 D TabGrade        S              1    DIM(5) ASCEND CTDATA PERRCD(5)
    17 D TabDayRate      S              4  2 DIM(5) ASCEND CTDATA PERRCD(5)
    18 D TabNitRate      S              4  2 DIM(5) ASCEND CTDATA PERRCD(5)
    19
    20  * Define work fields....
    21 D MonthNo         S              2  0
    22 D WeeksPay        S              6  2
    23 D TotalPay        S              8  2
    24 D HourlyRate      S              4  2
    25
    26  * Begin calculations....
    27=IPAYROLLR
       *--------------------------------------------------------------------------------------------*
       * RPG record format  . . . . :   PAYROLLR                                                    *
       * External format  . . . . . :   PAYROLLR : STAN/PAYROLL                                     *
       *--------------------------------------------------------------------------------------------*
    28=I                             P    1    5 0SSNUMBER
    29=I                             A    6   25  EMPNAME
    30=I                             A   26   26  LABORGRADE
    31=I                             A   27   27  SHIFT
    32=I                             P   28   29 0WEEKLY_HRS
    33=I                             P   30   33 0PAY_DATE
    34 C                   EVAL      *INOF = *ON                                 turn on OF
    35 C                   READ      Payroll                            ----LR   Read first record
    36 C                   MOVEL     Pay_Date      MonthNo                       extract month number
    37 C     MonthNo       LOOKUP    TabMthNo      TabName              ----20   get month name
    38
    39  * Begin DOW group....
    40 C                   DOW       *INLR = *OFF                                Do while LR is off     B01
    41
    42  * Test for page overflow....
    43 C     *INOF         CASEQ     *ON           HeadingSR                                            01
    44 C                   ENDCS                                                 end case group         01
    45
    46 C                   EXSR      ProcessSR                                   exit to subroutine     01
    47 C                   READ      Payroll                            ----LR   read next record       01
    48 C                   ENDDO                                                 end DOW group         E01
    49 C                                                                                              E01
    50 C                   EXCEPT    TotalLine                                   print total line
```

Figure 9-17 Compile listing of the Weekly Payroll Report program.

```
C                    EVAL      *INLR = *ON                                        end the job

 * Begin internal subroutines....
C     HeadingSR      BEGSR                                                        begin subroutine
C                    EXCEPT    HeadLine                                           print heading lines
C                    EVAL      *INOF = *OFF                                       turn off OF indicatr
C                    ENDSR                                                        end IF group

C     ProcessSR      BEGSR                                                        begin subroutine
C                    SELECT                                                       begin SELECT group   B01
C                    WHEN      Shift = 'D'                                        test for day shift   X01
C     LaborGrade     LOOKUP    TabGrade       TabDayRate                 ----20   look up table         01
C                    IF        *IN20 = *ON                                        successful lookup    B02
C                    EVAL      WeeksPay = Weekly_Hrs * TabDayRate                 compute weekspay      02
C                    EVAL      TotalPay = TotalPay + WeeksPay                     accumulate weekspay   02
C                    EVAL      HourlyRate = TabDayRate                            initial. HourlyRate   02
C                    EXCEPT    GoodLine                                           print good record     02
C                    ELSE                                                         false action         X02
C                    EXCEPT    ErrorLine                                          print error record    02
C                    ENDIF                                                        end IF group         E02

C                    OTHER                                                        test for day shift   X01
C     LaborGrade     LOOKUP    TabGrade       TabNitRate                 ----20   look up table         01
C                    IF        *IN20 = *ON                                        successful lookup    B02
C                    EVAL      WeeksPay = Weekly_Hrs * TabNitRate                 compute weekspay      02
C                    EVAL      TotalPay = TotalPay + WeeksPay                     accumulate weekspay   02
C                    EVAL      HourlyRate = TabNitRate                            initial. HourlyRate   02
C                    EXCEPT    GoodLine                                           print good record     02
C                    ELSE                                                         false action         X02
C                    EXCEPT    ErrorLine                                          print error record    02
C                    ENDIF                                                        end IF group         E02

C                    ENDSL                                                        end IF group         E01
C                    ENDSR                                                        end subroutine

OQsysprt   E            HeadLine       1 06
O                                           50 'WEEKLY PAYROLL REPORT'
O                                           75 'PAGE'
O                       PAGE                80
O          E            HeadLine       1
O                                           36 'FOR'
O                       TabName             46
O          E            HeadLine       2
O                                           41 'WEEK ENDING'
O                       Pay_Date      Y     50
O          E            HeadLine       1
O                                           42 'LABOR'
O                                           76 'HOURLY   HOURS    WEEK'
O          E            HeadLine       2
O                                            7 'SS#'
O                                           26 'NAME'
O                                           59 'GRADE    SHIFT    RATE'
O                                           77 'WORKED   WAGES'
O          E            GoodLine       2
O                       SSNumber            12 '0   -  -    '
O                       EmpName             34
O                       LaborGrade          40
O                       Shift               49
O                       HourlyRate     1    59
O                       Weekly_Hrs     2    67
O                       WeeksPay       2    78
O          E            ErrorLine      2
O                       SSNumber            12 '0   -  -    '
O                       EmpName             34
O                       LaborGrade          40
O                                           62 '....LABOR GRADE NOT '
O                                           72 'VALID....'
O          E            TotalLine    1
O                                           66 'TOTAL WAGES FOR WEEK'
```

Figure 9-17 Compile listing of the Weekly Payroll Report program. (Continued)

```
  120 0                        TotalPay      1     78
      * * * * *   E N D   O F   S O U R C E   * * * * *

 5763RG1 V3R1M0  940909 RN        IBM ILE RPG/400          STAN/CH9R1                    S1012CFA
           A d d i t i o n a l   D i a g n o s t i c   M e s s a g e s
*RNF7086 00     10 001000  RPG handles blocking for file PAYROLL. INFDS is updated
                           only when blocks of data are transferred.
*RNF7066 00     10 001000  Record-Format PAYROLLR not used for input or output.
 * * * * *   E N D   O F   A D D I T I O N A L   D I A G N O S T I C   M E S S A G E S   * * * * *
                 O u t p u t   B u f f e r   P o s i t i o n s
Line    Start End   Field or Constant
Number Pos    Pos
    87    30    50 'WEEKLY PAYROLL REPORT'
    88    72    75 'PAGE'
    89    77    80 PAGE
    91    34    36 'FOR'
    92    38    46 TABNAME
    94    31    41 'WEEK ENDING'
    95    43    50 PAY_DATE
    97    38    42 'LABOR'
    98    55    76 'HOURLY   HOURS    WEEK'
   100     5     7 'SS#'
   101    23    26 'NAME'
   102    38    59 'GRADE    SHIFT    RATE'
   103    64    77 'WORKED   WAGES'
   105     1    12 SSNUMBER
   106    15    34 EMPNAME
   107    40    40 LABORGRADE
   108    49    49 SHIFT
   109    55    59 HOURLYRATE
   110    65    67 WEEKLY_HRS
   111    71    78 WEEKSPAY
   113     1    12 SSNUMBER
   114    15    34 EMPNAME
   115    40    40 LABORGRADE
   116    43    62 '....LABOR GRADE NOT '
   117    64    72 'VALID....'
   119    47    66 'TOTAL WAGES FOR WEEK'
   120    69    78 TOTALPAY
 * * * * *   E N D   O F   O U T P U T   B U F F E R   P O S I T I O N   * * * * *
                         C o m p i l e   T i m e   D a t a
   121 **CTDATA TabMthNo
        *---------------------------------------------------------------------*
        * Table . . . : TABMTHNO     Alternating Table  . . . . : TABNAME     *
        *---------------------------------------------------------------------*
   122 01JANUARY  02FEBRUARY
   123 03MARCH    04APRIL
   124 05MAY      06JUNE
   125 07JULY     08AUGUST
   126 09SEPTEMBER10OCTOBER
   127 11NOVEMBER 12DECEMBER
   128 **CTDATA TabGrade
        *---------------------------------------------------------------------*
        * Table . . . : TABGRADE                                              *
        *---------------------------------------------------------------------*
   129 ABCDE
   130 **CTDATA TabDayRate
        *---------------------------------------------------------------------*
        * Table . . . : TABDAYRATE                                            *
        *---------------------------------------------------------------------*
   131 0800100012751600195O
   132 **CTDATA TabNitRate
        *---------------------------------------------------------------------*
        * Table . . . : TABNITRATE                                            *
        *---------------------------------------------------------------------*
   133 09001150152518002300
    * * * * *   E N D   O F   C O M P I L E   T I M E   D A T A   * * * * *
```

Figure 9-17 Compile listing of the Weekly Payroll Report program. (Continued)

File Description Specifications

Line No.

10 Payroll is defined as an input, full-procedural, externally described, keyed physical file.

11 Qsysprt is defined as an output, program-described printer file. The page overflow indicator **OF** is assigned to the file by the **OFLIND(*INOF)** keyword.

Definition Specifications

14–18 Five compile-time tables are defined with these instructions. The **CTDATA** keyword defines the tables as compile time.

21–24 Four "standalone" fields, MonthNo through HourlyRate, are defined by these instructions.

Calculation Specifications

34 This **EVAL** instruction turns on the **OF** overflow indicator so that the **CASEQ** test on line 43 will be "true," branch control to the HeadingSR, and print the heading lines before the first record is processed and a GoodLine or ErrorLine is printed.

35 This **READ** instruction reads the first record from the physical file Payroll. If no records are stored in the file, the **LR** indicator will be set on.

36 The **MOVEL** instruction moves the month value from the Pay_Date field to the MonthNo field left-justified.

37 The two-digit MonthNo value used as the search argument to "look up" an equal value in the TabMthNo table. If the **LOOKUP** is successful, the value in the related TabName table will be extracted for processing and *Resulting Indicator* 20 will be turned on.

40 The **DOW** instruction tests the status of the **LR** indicator. If it is *not on*, another iteration of the **DOW** group will be executed. If it is *on*, program control will branch to line 50, print the TotalLine, and end the job.

43 This **CASEQ** instruction tests the status of the **OF** indicator. Because **OF** is turned on in line 34 before the first record is processed, the relational test will be "true" and control will branch to the HeadingSR subroutine.

44 This **ENDCS** operation ends the **CASEQ** group.

46 This **EXSR** instruction branches control to the ProcessSR for every input record read.

47 This **READ** instruction reads the next record from the Payroll physical file. If end of file is read, the **LR** indicator will be turned on. When control branches back to the **DOW** instruction on line 40, the test will be false. Control will then branch to the **EXCEPT** instruction on line 50, the TotalLine record printed, and the program ended.

48 The **ENDDO** operation ends the **DOW** group that began on line 40.

50 This **EXCEPT** instruction controls printing of the TotalLine record on lines 118–120 after **LR** is turned on by one of the **READ** instructions.

51 This **EVAL** instruction turns on the **LR** indicator that ends the program.

54 This **BEGSR** instruction begins the HeadingSR subroutines.

55 This **EXCEPT** instruction prints the HeadLine output records.

56 This **EVAL** instruction turns off the **OF** indicator, so that page overflow will not occur on the next iteration of the **DOW** group. After the Heading lines are printed on the first page, the Heading lines on subsequent pages will be printed when page overflow is detected and the **OF** indicator is automatically turned on.

57 This **ENDSR** operation ends the HeadingSR subroutine.

59 This **BEGSR** instruction begins the ProcessSR subroutine.

60 The **SELECT** operation begins a **SELECT** group.

61 This **WHEN** instruction tests the Shift field value for **D.** If the test is true, the instructions within the **WHEN** group (lines 62–70) will be executed.

62 The value in the input field LaborGrade is used as the search argument to "look up" the TabGrade table. If the **LOOKUP** is successful, the value from the TabDayRate table will be extracted and indicator 20 turned on.

Figure 9-17 Compile listing of the Weekly Payroll Report program. (Continued)

63 This **IF** instruction tests the status of indicator 20, which was either turned on by a *successful* table **LOOKUP** or *not* turned on by an *unsuccessful* **LOOKUP.** When the test is "true," the instructions on lines 64–67 will be executed. If the test is not "true," the instruction on 69 will be executed.

64 This **EVAL** instruction computes the WeeksPay value by multiplying the input field Weekly-Hrs by the value in the TabDayRate table element.

65 This **EVAL** instruction adds the WeeksPay value to the TotalPay field accumulator.

66 This **EVAL** instruction initializes the HourlyRate field with the value from the TabDayRate table.

67 This **EXCEPT** instruction prints the GoodLine output record.

68 When the **IF** test on line 63 is "false," the instruction following this **ELSE** operation will be executed.

69 This **EXCEPT** instruction prints the ErrorLine output record.

70 This **ENDIF** operation ends the **IF** group that began on line 63.

72 If the **WHEN** instruction test on line 61 is "false," the instructions following the **OTHER** operation (lines 73–81) will be executed.

73 The value in the input field LaborGrade is used as the search argument to "look up" the TabGrade table. If the **LOOKUP** is successful, the value from the TabNitRate table will be extracted and indicator 20 turned on.

74 This **IF** instruction tests the status of indicator 20, which was either turned on by a *successful* table **LOOKUP** or *not* turned on by an *unsuccessful* **LOOKUP.** When the test is "true," the instructions on lines 75–78 will be executed. If the test is not "true," the instruction on 80 will be executed.

75 This **EVAL** instruction computes the WeeksPay value by multiplying the input field Weekly-Hrs by the value in the TabNitRate table element.

76 This **EVAL** instruction adds the WeeksPay value to the TotalPay field accumulator.

77 This **EVAL** instruction initializes the HourlyRate field with the value from the TabNitRate table.

78 This **EXCEPT** instruction prints the GoodLine output record.

79 When the **IF** test on line 74 is "false," the instruction following the **ELSE** operation will be executed.

80 This **EXCEPT** instruction prints the ErrorLine output record.

81 This **ENDIF** operation ends the **IF** group that began on line 74.

83 The **ENDSL** operation ends the **SELECT** group that began on line 60.

84 This **ENDSR** operation ends the ProcessSR subroutine that began on line 59.

Output Specifications

86–103 The HeadLine record formats, defined in these instructions, are executed by the **EXCEPT** instruction on line 55.

104–111 The GoodLine record format, defined in these instructions, is executed by the **EXCEPT** instruction on line 67 or 78.

112–117 The ErrorLine record format, defined in these instructions, is executed by the **EXCEPT** instruction on line 69 or 80.

118–120 The TotalLine record format, defined in these instructions, is executed by the **EXCEPT** instruction on 50.

121–133 The data for the five compile-time tables is defined in these instructions. Note that between the last output instruction (line 120) and the first compile-time table entry line (line 121), the **RPG IV** compiler has included *Additional Diagnostic Messages* and *Output Buffer Positions* entries.

Note: To enter the ****CTDATA** delimiter for a compile-time table and the related table data, enter **IF**** in the sequence number area and press **Enter.** Then enter **W1** (window over 1 position) followed by a space in the sequence number area and press **Enter.** The screen will move to the right so that the compile-time table entries can be entered beginning in the required position 1 and *not* in position 6. Recall that other **RPG IV** line formats begin in position 6.

Figure 9-17 Compile listing of the Weekly Payroll Report program. (Continued)

TABLE RANGE LOOKUP

The examples and application program presented have all used an *equal* test condition for table processing. Some tables, however, are structured in a format that requires a *range* **LOOKUP.** Federal and state income tax tables are generally accessed by this processing method.

Figure 9-18 illustrates a state's tax tables used to determine the tax liability on dividends and interest income. The taxpayer's Adjusted Gross Income (AGI) determines the percentage of tax on dividends and interest income. No tax is applied to this income for any AGI below $54,000.

The tables shown in Figure 9-18 require processing by *range* **LOOKUP** control. Table format restrictions to support this processing method are as follows:

ADJUSTED GROSS INCOME

At Least	But Less Than	
$ 54,000	$ 58,000	1%
58,000	62,000	2%
62,000	66,000	3%
66,000	70,000	4%
70,000	74,000	5%
74,000	78,000	6%
78,000	82,000	7%
82,000	86,000	8%
86,000	90,000	9%
90,000	100,000	11%
100,000 AND OVER		12%
Low range	High range	Rate (function table)

Low-range values may be used as the argument table. However, because the upper amount of each group specifies "But Less Than," the values have to be reduced by 1 to support high-range processing.

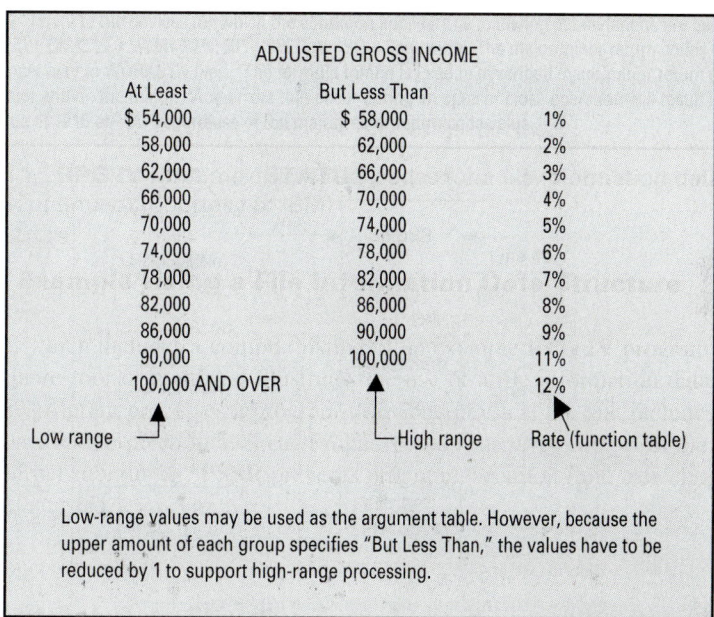

Figure 9-18 Tax tables for a state's dividends and interest income.

1. Argument table data *must* be sorted in an ascending or descending order. Compile-time tables that are unordered will be flagged by a terminal error during program compilation. The unordered sequence of prerun-time tables will not be identified until program execution, which will cause processing to abort.
2. The keyword **ASCEND** or **DESCEND,** as appropriate, must be included in the *Definition Specification* instruction for the related table. If sequence is not specified with range processing, ascending order of the table data is the default. A warning error will be generated if the keyword is omitted and the data is in ascending order. However, if the table data is in descending order and the **DESCEND** keyword is omitted in the definition of the table, a terminal error will occur during compilation for compile-time tables and at execution time for prerun-time tables.

Low-Range LOOKUP Control

In Figure 9-19, the data from Figure 9-18 has been formatted into *two* tables for processing. Notice that the *At Least* values (low range) have been used as the argument table data

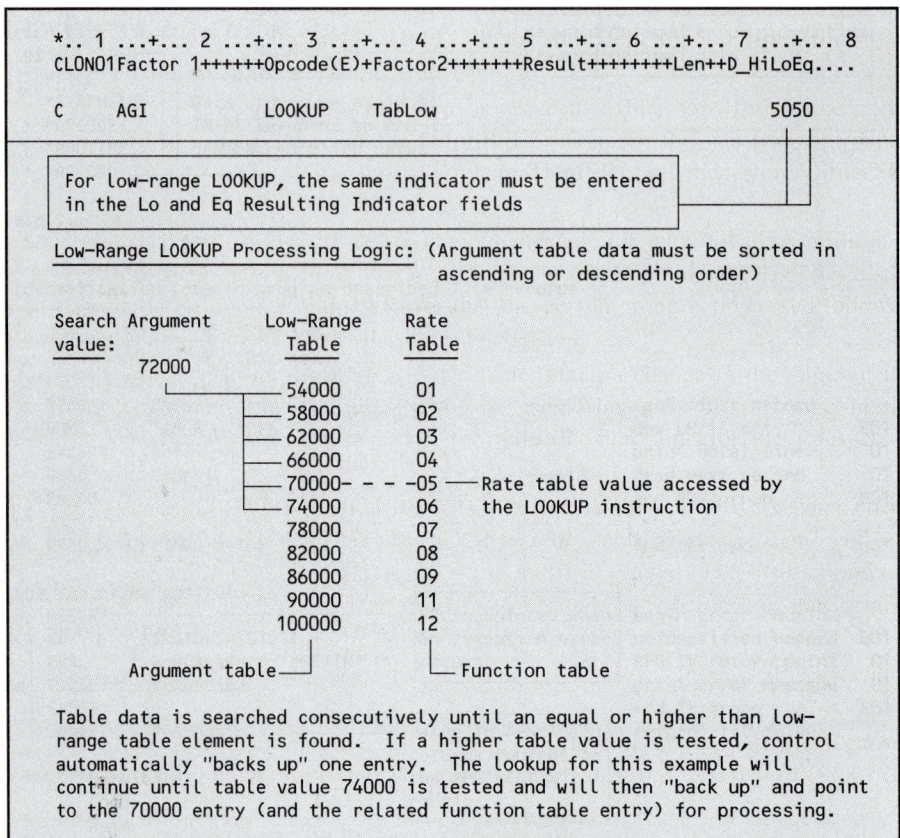

```
*.. 1 ...+... 2 ...+... 3 ...+... 4 ...+... 5 ...+... 6 ...+... 7 ...+... 8
CLON01Factor 1+++++++Opcode(E)+Factor2+++++++Result++++++++Len++D_HiLoEq....

C     AGI            LOOKUP    TabLow                                 5050

 For low-range LOOKUP, the same indicator must be entered
 in the Lo and Eq Resulting Indicator fields

Low-Range LOOKUP Processing Logic: (Argument table data must be sorted in
                                    ascending or descending order)

Search Argument     Low-Range      Rate
value:                Table        Table
       72000
                      54000         01
                      58000         02
                      62000         03
                      66000         04
                      70000- - - -05 ---Rate table value accessed by
                      74000         06    the LOOKUP instruction
                      78000         07
                      82000         08
                      86000         09
                      90000         11
                     100000         12

      Argument table                  Function table

Table data is searched consecutively until an equal or higher than low-
range table element is found.  If a higher table value is tested, control
automatically "backs up" one entry.  The lookup for this example will
continue until table value 74000 is tested and will then "back up" and point
to the 70000 entry (and the related function table entry) for processing.
```

Figure 9-19 LOOKUP instruction for low-range table processing, related table structure, and processing logic.

and the related percentages used for the function table entries. When low-range processing is specified, the high-range *(But Less Than)* values are not required.

High-Range LOOKUP Control

An examination of Figure 9-20 indicates that the data from Figure 9-18 has been formatted for high-range table **LOOKUP** processing. Because the high amount of a range relates to values *less than* those specified in Figure 9-18, the original table amounts must be reduced accordingly. Consequently, the *But Less Than* values have all been reduced by 1. Also, to compute the tax for search argument values equal to or greater than **100000,** table value **999999** is included as the last element.

Range table processing will be discussed further in the following application program, which determines a taxpayer's federal income tax liability.

```
*.. 1 ...+... 2 ...+... 3 ...+... 4 ...+... 5 ...+... 6 ...+... 7 ...+... 8
CLON01Factor 1++++++Opcode(E)+Factor2+++++++Result++++++++Len++D_HiLoEq....

C     AGI          LOOKUP    TabHigh                                 50  50

 For high-range LOOKUP, the same indicator must be entered
 in the Hi and Eq Resulting Indicator fields

High Range LOOKUP Processing Logic: (Argument table data must be sorted in
                                     in ascending or descending order)

Search Argument      High-Range   Rate
value:                 Table      Table
         72000
                      057999       01
                      061999       02
                      065999       03
                      069999       04
                      073999- - - -05    Rate table value accessed by the
                      077999       06    LOOKUP instruction. Because "But
                      081999       07    less than" entries are specified
Entry needed for      085999       08    for the high range (see Figure 9-
search argument       089999       09    18), the value for each element
values = or >         099999       11    has to be reduced by 1 (i.e., from
1000000 ------------- 999999       12    58000 to 57999.

          Argument table              Function table

Table data is searched consecutively until an equal to or higher table
value is found.  Search for this example will continue until table value
73999 is tested.  Then, the related function table value is accessed in the
LOOKUP instruction.  No additional movement of the "pointer" occurs with
high-range LOOKUP.
```

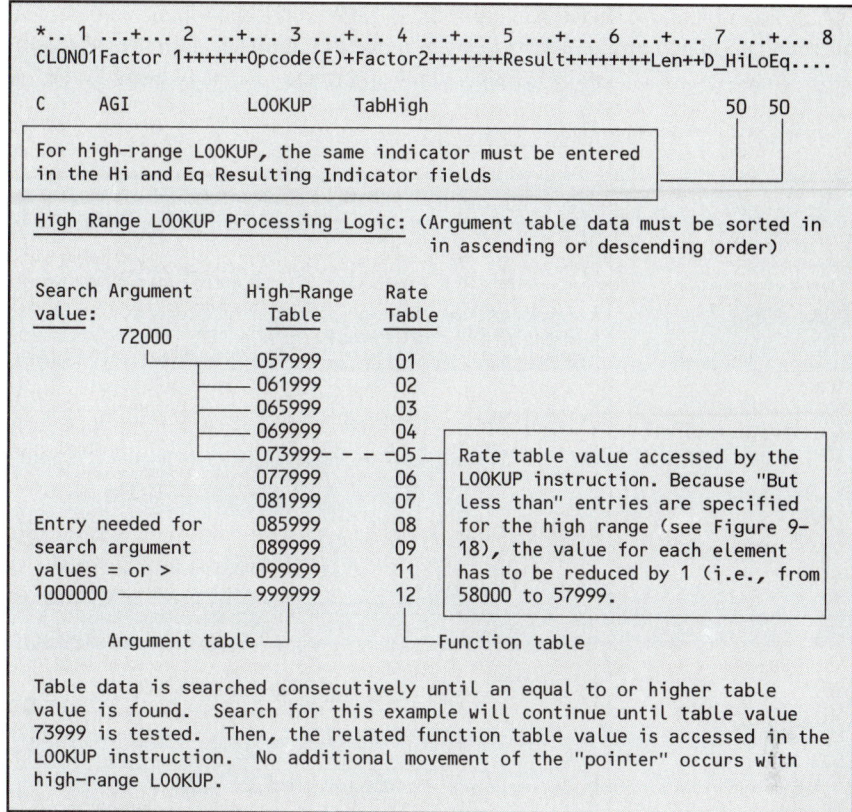

Figure 9-20 LOOKUP instruction for high-range table processing, related table structure, and processing logic.

APPLICATION PROGRAM: FEDERAL INCOME TAX COMPUTATION

Documentation

The specifications shown in Figure 9-21 detail the processing requirements for an application program that computes the federal income tax liability for taxpayers who have a filing status of Single, Married–Filing Jointly, Married–Filing Separately, or Head of Household. Input and output files processed by the program are identified in the

PROGRAM SPECIFICATIONS — Page 1 of 1

Program Name: Federal Tax Report — Program - ID: CH9R2 — Written by: SM

Purpose: Federal Income Tax Liability Report — Approved by: CM

Input files: INCOME

Output files: QSYSPRT

Figure 9-21 Specifications for the Federal Income Tax Liability Report program.

Processing Requirements:

Write an RPG IV program to generate a Federal Income Tax Liability Report for individual taxpayers.

Input to the program:

The externally defined physical file, INCOME, contains records with the information for individual taxpayers. The attached record layout form identifies the fields in the physical file's record format. Note that the taxable income amount was previously computed and is not a function of this program.

Processing:

Format the following four rate schedules into nine compile-time tables. Because the range of percents is the same for all filing classifications (i.e., 15% 28%, 31%), only one percent table has to be specified. Use the Over amount as the argument table with the related fixed and percent values as the related function tables.

Table values:

Schedule X — Use if your filing status is Single

If the amount on Form 1040, line 37, is: *Over—*	*But not over—*	Enter on Form 1040, line 38	*of the amount over—*
$0	$21,450	.... 15%	$0
21,450	51,900	$3,217.50 + 28%	21,450
51,900	....	11,743.50 + 31%	51,900

Schedule Y-1—Use if your filing status is Married filing jointly or Qualifying widow(er)

If the amount on Form 1040, line 37, Is: *Over—*	*But not over—*	Enter on Form 1040, line 38	*of the amount over—*
$0	$35,800	.... 15%	$0
35,800	86,500	$5,370.00 + 28%	35,850
86,500	....	19,566.00 + 31%	86,500

Schedule Y-2—Use if your filing status is Married filing separately

If the amount on Form 1040, line 37, is: *Over—*	*But not over—*	Enter on Form 1040, line 38	*of the amount over—*
$0	$17,900	.... 15%	$0
17,900	43,250	$2,685.00 + 28%	17,900
43,250	....	9,783.00 + 31%	43,250

Schedule Z—Use if your filing status is Head of household

If the amount on Form 1040, line 37, is: *Over—*	*But not over—*	Enter on Form 1040, line 38	*of the amount over—*
$0	$28,750	.... 15%	$0
28,750	74,150	$4,312.50 + 28%	28,750
74,150	....	17,024.50 + 31%	74,150

Figure 9-21 Specifications for the Federal Income Tax Liability Report program. (Continued)

Test the input filing status field (STATUS) for S (single), J (married–filing jointly), M (married–filing separately), and H (head of household), and execute the related internal subroutine to look up the argument table with the TAXINC field.

The following calculations are required:

1. Look up the appropriate low-range table (Over— amounts) with the taxable income field (TAXINC), and extract the fixed amount from the related function table.
2. Look up the same low-range (Over—) argument table, and extract the percent value from the common percent table.
3. Subtract the "of the amount over—" (same as Over— table value) from the taxable income field (TAXINC), and store the difference in a work field.
4. Multiply the difference in step 3 by the table percent from step 2 and store in an output field for the tax due.
5. Add the fixed table amount (step 1) to the tax due field (step 4) to compute the total Federal Income Tax due for the taxpayer.

With the exception of the different tables, the five steps detailed are identical for each filing status.

Output:

Generate the report shown in the attached printer spacing chart. Note that the tax year is accessed from the first data record processed.

Figure 9-21 Specifications for the Federal Income Tax Liability Report program. (Continued)

system flowchart shown in Figure 9-22. The format of the records in the physical file and a listing of the data are detailed in Figure 9-23. The printer spacing chart in

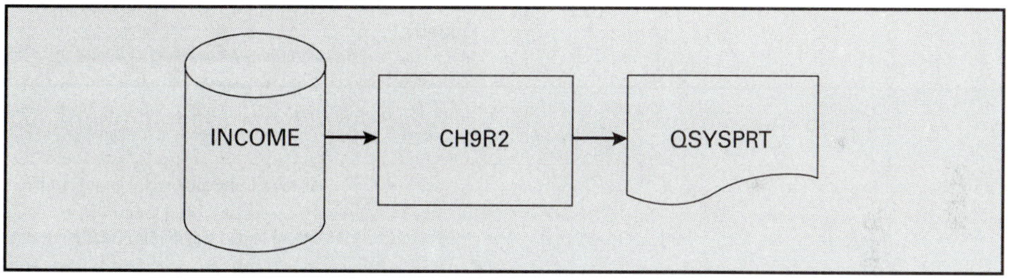

Figure 9-22 System flowchart for Federal Income Tax Liability Report program.

PHYSICAL FILE DESCRIPTION

SYSTEM: AS/400 DATE: 1/31/95
FILE NAME: INCOME REV NO: 0
RECORD NAME: INCOMER KEY LENGTH: 9
SEQUENCE: Keyed RECORD SIZE: 32

FIELD DEFINITIONS

FIELD NO	FIELD NAME	SIZE	TYPE	POSITION FROM	POSITION TO	COMMENTS
1	SS#	9	P	1	5	Key field
2	NAME	20	C	6	25	
3	TAXINC	6	P	26	29	0 decimals
4	STATUS	1	C	30	30	S, J, M, H
5	TAXYR	2	C	31	32	

Figure 9-23 Record layout and data processed by the Federal Income Tax Liability Report program.

```
Physical file data:
                                     Taxable   Filing   Tax
   SS#        Taxpayer's Name        Income    Status   Year

0111111111 DONALD & DAISY DRAKE      050000      J       95
0222222222 LAMONT CRANSTON           080000      H       95
0333333333 MIKE & MINA MOUSE         200000      J       95
0444444444 RICHARD TRACY             010000      M       95
0555555555 PAUL VALIANT              023901      H       95
0666666666 MORTIMER SNERD            014875      M       95
0777777777 ANDREW GUMP               100000      S       95
```

Figure 9-23 Record layout and data processed by the Federal Income Tax Liability Report program. (Continued)

Figure 9-24 details the design of the report. A listing of the printed report generated by the program is shown in Figure 9-25.

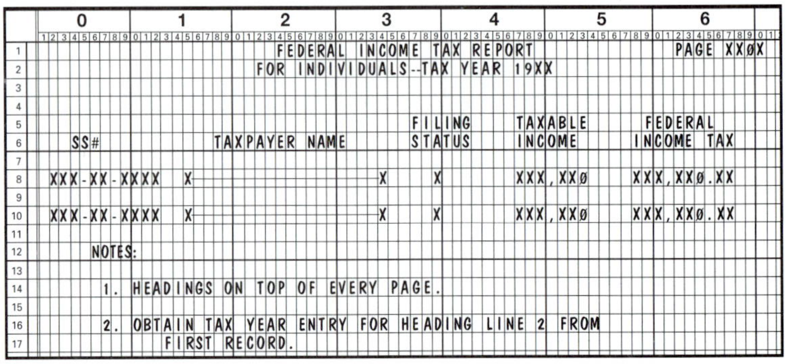

Figure 9-24 Design of the Federal Income Tax Liability Report.

```
                    FEDERAL INCOME TAX REPORT                  PAGE    1
                 FOR INDIVIDUALS--TAX YEAR 1997


                                    FILING    TAXABLE       FEDERAL
   SS#           TAXPAYER NAME      STATUS    INCOME      INCOME TAX

011-11-1111  DONALD & DAISY DRAKE     J        50,000       9,346.00

022-22-2222  LAMONT CRANSTON          H        80,000      18,838.00

033-33-3333  MIKE & MINA MOUSE        J       200,000      54,751.00

044-44-4444  RICHARD TRACY            M        10,000       1,500.00

055-55-5555  PAUL VALIANT             H        23,901       3,585.15

066-66-6666  MORTIMER SNERD           M        14,875       2,231.25

077-77-7777  ANDREW GUMP              S       100,000      26,654.50
```

Figure 9-25 Report generated by Federal Income Tax Liability Report program.

Source Program Coding

A commented compile listing of the federal income tax report application program is presented in Figure 9-26.

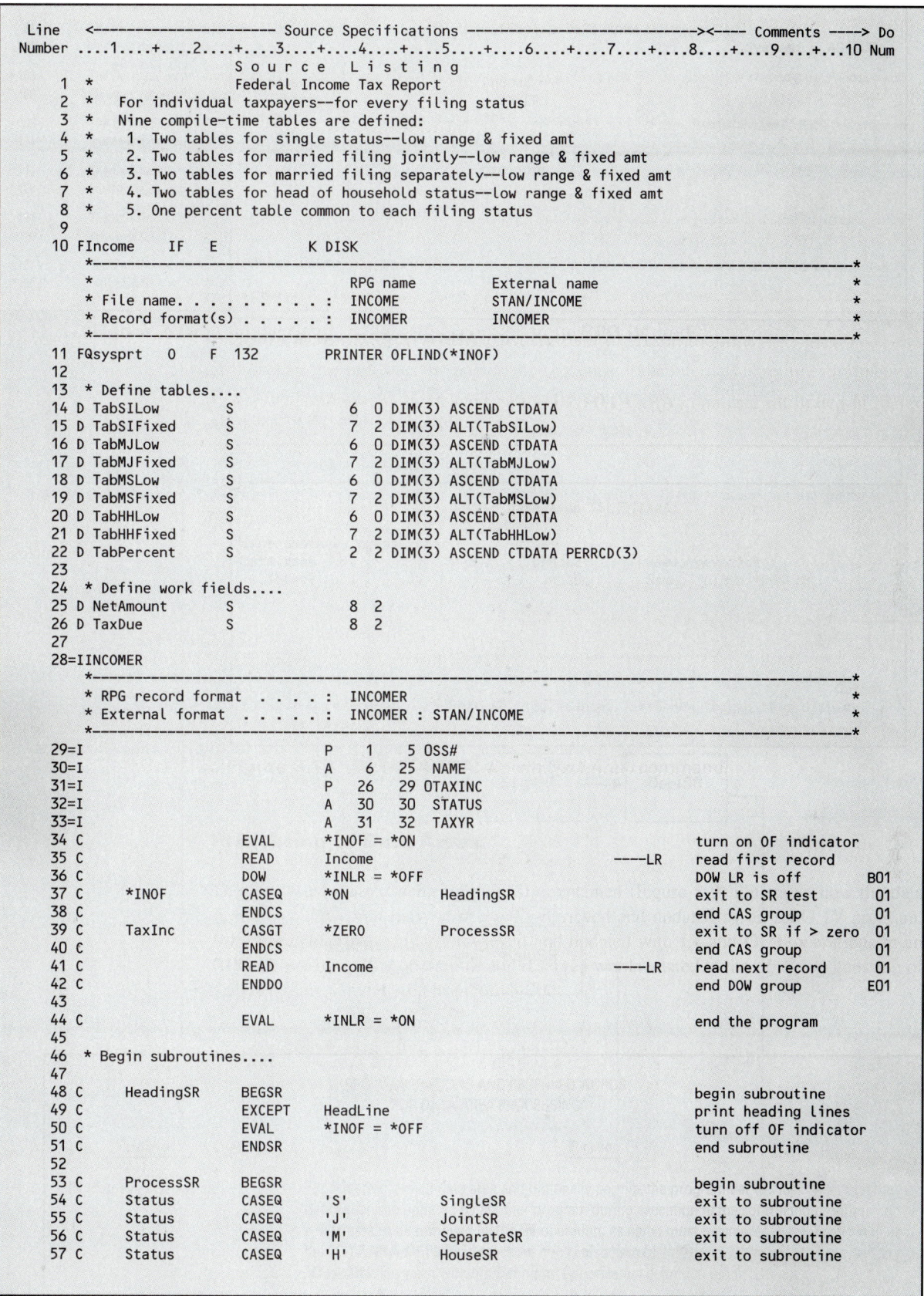

```
 Line   <---------------------- Source Specifications ----------------------------><---- Comments ----> Do
Number ....1....+....2....+....3....+....4....+....5....+....6....+....7....+....8....+....9....+...10 Num
                      S o u r c e   L i s t i n g
        *             Federal Income Tax Report
        *    For individual taxpayers--for every filing status
        *    Nine compile-time tables are defined:
        *      1. Two tables for single status--low range & fixed amt
        *      2. Two tables for married filing jointly--low range & fixed amt
        *      3. Two tables for married filing separately--low range & fixed amt
        *      4. Two tables for head of household status--low range & fixed amt
        *      5. One percent table common to each filing status

       FIncome    IF   E             K DISK
        *--------------------------------------------------------------------------------------*
        *                                  RPG name          External name                      *
        * File name. . . . . . . . . :   INCOME            STAN/INCOME                        *
        * Record format(s) . . . . . :   INCOMER           INCOMER                            *
        *--------------------------------------------------------------------------------------*
       FQsysprt   O    F  132              PRINTER OFLIND(*INOF)

        * Define tables....
       D TabSILow        S                  6  0 DIM(3) ASCEND CTDATA
       D TabSIFixed      S                  7  2 DIM(3) ALT(TabSILow)
       D TabMJLow        S                  6  0 DIM(3) ASCEND CTDATA
       D TabMJFixed      S                  7  2 DIM(3) ALT(TabMJLow)
       D TabMSLow        S                  6  0 DIM(3) ASCEND CTDATA
       D TabMSFixed      S                  7  2 DIM(3) ALT(TabMSLow)
       D TabHHLow        S                  6  0 DIM(3) ASCEND CTDATA
       D TabHHFixed      S                  7  2 DIM(3) ALT(TabHHLow)
       D TabPercent      S                  2  2 DIM(3) ASCEND CTDATA PERRCD(3)

        * Define work fields....
       D NetAmount       S                  8  2
       D TaxDue          S                  8  2

       IINCOMER
        *--------------------------------------------------------------------------------------*
        * RPG record format . . . . :   INCOMER                                               *
        * External format . . . . . :   INCOMER : STAN/INCOME                                 *
        *--------------------------------------------------------------------------------------*
       I                               P    1     5 OSS#
       I                               A    6    25  NAME
       I                               P   26    29 OTAXINC
       I                               A   30    30  STATUS
       I                               A   31    32  TAXYR
       C                   EVAL      *INOF = *ON                                turn on OF indicator
       C                   READ      Income                           ----LR    read first record
       C                   DOW       *INLR = *OFF                               DOW LR is off        B01
       C     *INOF         CASEQ     *ON           HeadingSR                    exit to SR test       01
       C                   ENDCS                                                end CAS group         01
       C     TaxInc        CASGT     *ZERO         ProcessSR                    exit to SR if > zero  01
       C                   ENDCS                                                end CAS group         01
       C                   READ      Income                           ----LR    read next record      01
       C                   ENDDO                                                end DOW group        E01

       C                   EVAL      *INLR = *ON                                end the program

        * Begin subroutines....

       C     HeadingSR     BEGSR                                                begin subroutine
       C                   EXCEPT    HeadLine                                   print heading lines
       C                   EVAL      *INOF = *OFF                               turn off OF indicator
       C                   ENDSR                                                end subroutine

       C     ProcessSR     BEGSR                                                begin subroutine
       C     Status        CASEQ     'S'           SingleSR                     exit to subroutine
       C     Status        CASEQ     'J'           JointSR                      exit to subroutine
       C     Status        CASEQ     'M'           SeparateSR                   exit to subroutine
       C     Status        CASEQ     'H'           HouseSR                      exit to subroutine
```

Figure 9-26 Compile listing of the Federal Income Tax Liability Report program.

```
C                   ENDCS                                                     end CAS group
C                   EXCEPT    DetailLine                                      print detail line
C                   ENDSR                                                     end subroutine

C     SingleSR      BEGSR                                                     begin subroutine
C     TaxInc        LOOKUP    TabSILow      TabSIFixed               --5050  get fixed table amt
C                   IF        *IN50 = *ON                                     entry found?        B01
C     TaxInc        LOOKUP    TabSILow      TabPercent               --5050  get table percent   01
C                   EVAL      NetAmount = TaxInc - TabSILow                   compute difference  01
C                   EVAL      TaxDue = NetAmount * TabPercent                 compute tax due     01
C                   EVAL      TaxDue = TaxDue + TabSIFixed                    total tax due       01
C                   ENDIF                                                     end IF group        E01
C                   ENDSR                                                     end subroutine

C     JointSR       BEGSR                                                     begin subroutine
C     TaxInc        LOOKUP    TabMJLow      TabMJFixed               --5050  get fixed table amt
C                   IF        *IN50 = *ON                                     entry found?        B01
C     TaxInc        LOOKUP    TabMJLow      TabPercent               --5050  get table percent   01
C                   EVAL      NetAmount = TaxInc - TabMJLow                   compute difference  01
C                   EVAL      TaxDue = NetAmount * TabPercent                 compute tax due     01
C                   EVAL      TaxDue = TaxDue + TabMJFixed                    total tax due       01
C                   ENDIF                                                     end IF group        E01
C                   ENDSR                                                     end subroutine

C     SeparateSR    BEGSR                                                     begin subroutine
C     TaxInc        LOOKUP    TabMSLow      TabMSFixed               --5050  get fixed table amt
C                   IF        *IN50 = *ON                                     entry found?        B01
C     TaxInc        LOOKUP    TabMSLow      TabPercent               --5050  get table percent   01
C                   EVAL      NetAmount = TaxInc - TabMSLow                   compute difference  01
C                   EVAL      TaxDue = NetAmount * TabPercent                 compute tax due     01
C                   EVAL      TaxDue = TaxDue + TabMSFixed                    total tax due       01
C                   ENDIF                                                     end IF group        E01
C                   ENDSR                                                     end subroutine

C     HouseSR       BEGSR                                                     begin subroutine
C     TaxInc        LOOKUP    TabHHLow      TabHHFixed               --5050  get fixed table amt
C                   IF        *IN50 = *ON                                     entry found?        B01
C     TaxInc        LOOKUP    TabHHLow      TabPercent               --5050  get table percent   01
C                   EVAL      NetAmount = TaxInc - TabHHLow                   compute difference  01
C                   EVAL      TaxDue = NetAmount * TabPercent                 compute tax due     01
C                   EVAL      TaxDue = TaxDue + TabHHFixed                    total tax due       01
C                   ENDIF                                                     end IF group        E01
C                   ENDSR                                                     end subroutine

 * Begin output....
OQsysprt   E            HeadLine       1 01
O                                           42 'FEDERAL INCOME TAX'
O                                           49 'REPORT'
O                                           65 'PAGE'
O                       PAGE                70
O          E            HeadLine       3
O                                           37 'FOR INDIVIDUALS-'
O                                           48 'TAX YEAR 19'
O                       TaxYr               50
O          E            HeadLine       1
O                                           53 'FILING     TAXABLE'
O                                           65 'FEDERAL'
O          E            HeadLine       2
O                                            6 'SS#'
O                                           30 'TAXPAYER NAME'
O                                           42 'STATUS'
O                                           52 'INCOME'
O                                           67 'INCOME TAX'
O          E            DetailLine     2
O                       SS#                 12 '0   -  -    '
O                       Name                34
O                       Status              39
O                       TaxInc         2    53
O                       TaxDue         1    67
  * * * * *   E N D   O F   S O U R C E   * * * * *
```

Figure 9-26 Compile listing of the Federal Income Tax Liability Report program. (Continued)

```
 5763RG1 V3R1M0  940909 RN         IBM ILE RPG/400          STAN/CH9R2                S1012CFA    05/19/97
               A d d i t i o n a l    D i a g n o s t i c    M e s s a g e s
*RNF7086 00        10 001000  RPG handles blocking for file INCOME. INFDS is updated only
                              when blocks of data are transferred.
*RNF7066 00        10 001000  Record-Format INCOMER not used for input or output.
 * * * * *   E N D   O F   A D D I T I O N A L   D I A G N O S T I C   M E S S A G E S   * * * * *
                    O u t p u t   B u f f e r   P o s i t i o n s
Line     Start End    Field or Constant
Number Pos     Pos
   104     25     42 'FEDERAL INCOME TAX'
   105     44     49 'REPORT'
   106     62     65 'PAGE'
   107     67     70 PAGE
   109     22     37 'FOR INDIVIDUALS-'
   110     38     48 'TAX YEAR 19'
   111     49     50 TAXYR
   113     37     53 'FILING    TAXABLE'
   114     59     65 'FEDERAL'
   116      4      6 'SS#'
   117     18     30 'TAXPAYER NAME'
   118     37     42 'STATUS'
   119     47     52 'INCOME'
   120     58     67 'INCOME TAX'
   122      1     12 SS#
   123     15     34 NAME
   124     39     39 STATUS
   125     47     53 TAXINC
   126     58     67 TAXDUE
 * * * * *   E N D   O F   O U T P U T   B U F F E R   P O S I T I O N   * * * * *
                        C o m p i l e   T i m e   D a t a
   127 **CTDATA TabSILow
        *---------------------------------------------------------------------*
        * Table . . . : TABSILOW      Alternating Table  . . . . : TABSIFIXED *
        *---------------------------------------------------------------------*
   128 0000000000000
   129 0214500321750
   130 0519001174350
   131 **CTDATA TabMJLow
        *---------------------------------------------------------------------*
        * Table . . . : TABMJLOW      Alternating Table  . . . . : TABMJFIXED *
        *---------------------------------------------------------------------*
   132 0000000000000
   133 0358000537000
   134 0865001956600
   135 **CTDATA TabMSLow
        *---------------------------------------------------------------------*
        * Table . . . : TABMSLOW      Alternating Table  . . . . : TABMSFIXED *
        *---------------------------------------------------------------------*
   136 0000000000000
   137 0179000268500
   138 0432500978300
   139 **CTDATA TabHHLow
        *---------------------------------------------------------------------*
        * Table . . . : TABHHLOW      Alternating Table  . . . . : TABHHFIXED *
        *---------------------------------------------------------------------*
   140 0000000000000
   141 0287500431250
   142 0741501702450
   143 **CTDATA TabPercent
        *---------------------------------------------------------------------*
        * Table . . . : TABPERCENT                                            *
        *---------------------------------------------------------------------*
   144 152831
 * * * * *   E N D   O F   C O M P I L E   T I M E   D A T A   * * * * *
```

File Description Specifications

Line No.

10 Income is defined as an input, full-procedural, externally described, keyed physical file.

11 Qsysprt is defined as an output, program-described printer file. The page overflow indicator **OF** is assigned to the file with the **OFLIND(*INOF)** keyword.

Figure 9-26 Compile listing of the Federal Income Tax Liability Report program. (Continued)

Definition Specifications

14–22 Nine compile-time tables are defined (**CTDATA** keyword) in these instructions. The low range of the tax tables are assigned to tables TabSILow, TabMJLow, TabMSLow, and TabHHLow. One table element is included on each compile-time record. Three elements are defined for each table, six integers long.

The fixed amount value for each filing status is assigned to tables TabSIFixed, TabMJFixed, TabMSFixed, and TabHHFixed. Note that these tables are specified in an alternating sequence (**ALT** keyword) with their related Low tables. They are defined as seven digits long with two decimal positions.

The TabPercent table has values common to each filing status. Consequently, a separate table is not required for each. The table data is stored with three elements on one record with a length of two bytes with two decimal positions.

25–26 Two work fields, NetAmount and TaxDue, are defined as "standalone" fields.

Calculation Specifications

34 This **EVAL** instruction turns on the **OF** overflow indicator so that the **CASEQ** test on line 37 will branch control to the Heading SR subroutine and print the heading lines before the first record is processed and a DetailLine printed.

35 This **READ** instruction reads the first record from the Income file. If no records are stored in the file, the **LR** indicator will be set on. The program's coding logic assumes that at least one record is stored in the file.

36 The **DOW** instruction tests the status of the **LR** indicator. If it is *not on*, another iteration of the **DOW** group will be executed. If it is on, program control will branch to line 44 and end program execution.

37 This **CASEQ** instruction tests the status of the **OF** overflow indicator. Because **OF** was turned on in line 34 before the first record was processed, the relational test will be "true" and control will branch to the HeadingSR subroutine.

38 This **ENDCS** operation ends the **CASEQ** group.

39 This **CASGT** instruction determines if the TaxInc field value is greater than 0. If it is, program control will branch to the ProcessSR subroutine. If TaxInc is not greater than 0, control will branch to the **READ** instruction on line 41.

40 This **ENDCS** operation ends the **CASEQ** group.

41 This **READ** instruction reads the next record from the Income physical file. If end of file is read, the **LR** indicator will be turned on. When control returns back to the **DOW** instruction on line 36, the test will be false. Control will then branch to the **EVAL** instruction on line 44 and end program execution.

48 This **BEGSR** instruction begins the HeadingSR subroutine.

49 This **EXCEPT** instruction prints the four HeadLine output records on lines 103–120.

50 This **EVAL** instruction turns off the **OF** indicator so that page overflow will not occur on the next iteration of the **DOW** group. After the HeadLines are printed on the first page, the Heading lines on subsequent pages will be printed only when page overflow is detected and the **OF** indicator is automatically turned on.

51 This **ENDSR** operation ends the HeadingSR subroutine.

53 This **BEGSR** instruction begins the ProcessSR subroutine.

54–57 If the value of the input field Status is equal to **S,** control will branch to the SingleSR subroutine. If Status is equal to **J,** control will branch to the JointSR subroutine. If Status is equal to **M,** control will branch to the SeparateSR subroutine. If Status is equal to **H,** control will branch to the HouseSR subroutine.

58 This **ENDCS** operation ends the **CASEQ** group.

59 After control returns from processing one of the subroutines, this **EXCEPT** instruction prints the DetailLine record on lines 121–126 for each record processed.

60 This **ENDSR** operation ends the ProcessSR subroutine.

62 This **BEGSR** instruction begins the SingleSR subroutine.

63 This **LOOKUP** instruction uses the TaxInc field from the physical file to "look up" the TabSILow table and extract the related fixed value from the TabSIFixed table. Indicator 50, which is included in the *Lo* and *Eq Resulting Indicator* fields, will turn on if the lookup is successful.

64 This **IF** instruction tests the status of indicator 50. If it is "on," indicating a successful **LOOKUP** on line 63, the instructions on lines 65–68 will be executed.

65 This **LOOKUP** instruction uses the TaxInc field again to "look up" TabSILow to extract the related percent value from the TabPercent table. Indicator 50, in the *Lo* and *Eq Resulting Indicator* fields, is specified again to satisfy the syntax requirements of the **RPG IV** compiler.

66 This **EVAL** instruction computes the intermediate value for NetAmount by subtracting the TabsSILow table value from TaxInc.

67 This **EVAL** instruction computes the value for TaxDue by multiplying NetAmount by the TabPercent table value.

Figure 9-26 Compile listing of the Federal Income Tax Liability Report program. (Continued)

68	This **EVAL** instruction computes the final value for TaxDue by adding the TabSIFixed table value to the TaxDue field.
69	This **ENDIF** operation ends the **IF** group.
70	This **ENDSR** operation ends the SingleSR subroutine.
72–80	The instructions in the JointSR subroutine follow the same sequence of instructions discussed in the SingleSR subroutine. The only difference is that the tables (TabMJLow and TabMJFixed) for married filing jointly status are used in the computations.
82–90	The instructions in the SeparateSR subroutine follow the same sequence of instructions discussed in the SingleSR subroutine. The only difference is that the tables (TabMSLow and TabMSFixed) for married filing separately status are used in the computations.
92–100	The instructions in the HouseSR subroutine follow the same sequence of instructions discussed in the SingleSR subroutine. The only difference is that the tables (TabHHLow and TabHHFixed) for head of hosuehold filing status are used in the computations.
Output Specifications	
103–120	The HeadLine output record formats defined in these instructions are executed by the **EXCEPT** instruction on line 49.
121–126	The DetaiLine output record format defined in these instructions is executed by the **EXCEPT** instruction on line 59.
127–144	The data for the nine compile-time tables is defined in these instructions. Note that between the last output instruction (line 126) and the first compile-time table entry (line 127), the **RPG IV** compiler has included **Additional Diagnostic Messages** and **Output Buffer Positions** entries.
Note:	To enter the ****CTDATA** delimiter for a compile-time table and the related table data, enter **IF**** in the sequence number area and press **Enter.** Then enter **W1** (window over 1 position) followed by a space in the sequence number area and press **Enter.** The screen will move to the right so that the compile-time table entries can be entered beginning in the required position 1 and *not* in position 6. Recall that other **RPG IV** formats begin in position 6.

Figure 9-26 Compile listing of the Federal Income Tax Liability Report program. (Continued)

Processing Logic for the Federal Income Tax Liability Report Program (Low-Range LOOKUP)

The mathematical steps to compute the tax liability for married taxpayers filing jointly is shown in Figure 9-27. With the exception of different table values, the other three filing statuses follow the same **LOOKUP** operation logic and related calculations.

```
Processing logic for any filing status (Married Filing Jointly) shown:

                                     (Over-)
        Taxable                     TabMJLow  TabMJFixed  TabPercent
         income:  050000
                                     00000     0000000        15
                                     35800     0537000        28
Table search continues               86500     1956600        31
until higher value is
tested, then control
"backsup" to previous
entry. Argument and any
one function table entry
are available for process-
ing.

The following steps are required to compute the tax due:

Step 1: Subtract bracket low amount (TabMJLow) from Taxable Income:

                  50,000 - 35,800 = 14,200
```

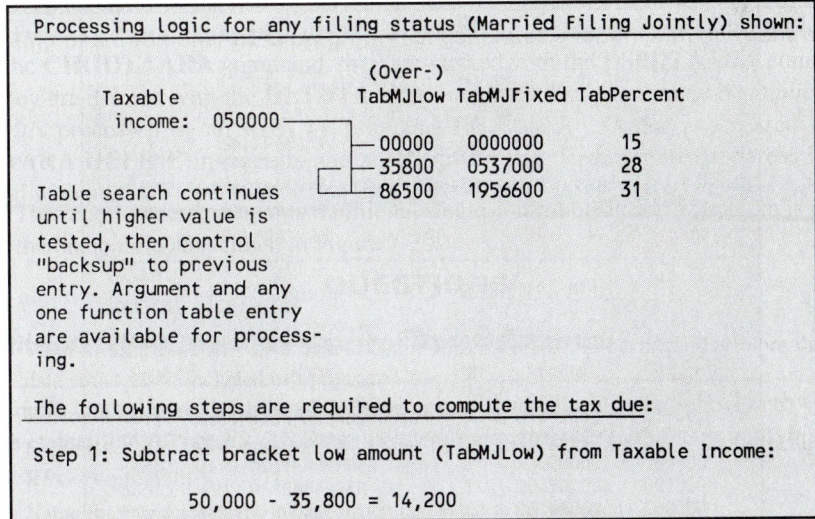

Figure 9-27 Processing logic for Federal Income Tax Liability Report program using low-range **LOOKUP** and mathematical steps to compute the tax due.

```
Step 2: Multiply difference from step 1 by bracket percent (TabPercent):

             14,200 x .28 = 3,976

Step 3: Add product from Step 2 to bracket fixed amount (TabMJFixed)
        for total tax amount due:

             3,976 + 5,370.00 = 9,346.00
```

Figure 9-27 Processing logic for Federal Income Tax Liability Report program using low-range **LOOKUP** and mathematical steps to compute the tax due. (Continued)

Calculations for the Federal Income Tax Liability Report Program (Married Filing Jointly Status)

The instructions included in the program for married taxpayers filing jointly status is detailed in Figure 9-28. Because the same sequence of instructions is used for each filing status, understanding one will apply to the others. Refer back to Figure 9-25 for a review of the report generated by the **RPG IV** program.

```
Processing logic for any filing status (Married Filing Jointly) shown:

                         (Over-)
  Taxable                TabMJLow  TabMJFixed  TabPercent
   income:  050000 ───┐
                      ├── 00000    0000000       15
                    ┌─┼── 35800    0537000       28
                    └─┴── 86500    1956600       31

Calculations:  LOOKUP instruction on lines 73 and 75 use the processing logic
               shown above.

SEQUENCE
NUMBER      ....1....+....2....+....3....+....4....+....5....+....6....+....7....+

      72 C       Joint          BEGSR
      73 C       TAXINC         LOOKUP    TabMJLow       TabMJFixed            5050
      74 C                      IFEQ      *IN50 = *ON
      75 C       TAXINC         LOOKUP    TabMJLow       TabPercent            5050
      76 C                      EVAL      NetAmount = TaxInc - TabMJLow
      77 C                      EVAL      TaxDue = NetAmount * TabPercent
      78 C                      EVAL      TaxDue = TaxDue + TabMJFixed
      79 C                      ENDIF
      80 C                      ENDSR
```

Figure 9-28 Calculations for Federal Income Tax Liability program using low-range table **LOOKUP** for Married Filing Jointly status.

TRADITIONAL RPG SYNTAX FOR TABLES

Tables are defined in the *Extension Specification* (not used in **RPG IV**) in traditional **RPG II** and **RPG III** programs. The syntax for compile- and prerun-time tables in those environments is summarized in Figure 9-29.

```
*.. 1 ...+... 2 ...+... 3 ...+... 4 ...+... 5 ...+... 6 ...+... 7 ...+... 8
E....FromfileTofile++Name++N/rN/tbLenPDSArrnamLenPDSCComents+++++++++*
 1    2    3      4    5   6  7 891  11  12 891
                                 0         0
```

Figure 9-29 Fields used in the *Extension Specifications* to define tables at compile and prerun times (traditional **RPG**).

* All *Extension Specification* instructions must include an **E** in column 6 and immediately follow the last *File Description* statement.

1. Columns 7–10 are not used.
2. **From Filename** (columns 11–18): Required for *prerun-time* tables. File name, defined in a *File Description* statement, must be entered left-justified in this field.
3. **To Filename** (columns 19–26): Optional for *prerun-time* tables. If the table data is to be written to an output device at the end of the program, the name of the output file must be entered left-justified in this field.
4. **Table Name** (columns 27–32): All table names must begin with the letters **TAB.** The one, two, or three additional characters must be programmer-supplied.
5. **Number of Entries Per Record** (columns 33–35): Specifies how many individual table elements are stored on a record.
6. **Number of Entries Per Table** (columns 36–39): Specifies how many table elements are stored in the table.
7. **Length of Entry** (columns 40–42): Specifies the size of the table entries. All elements of a table must be the same size. Elements in character tables may be defined from 1 to 256 bytes. Numeric table elements may be defined from 1 to 30 bytes.
8. **P/B/L/R** (column 43): If the numeric data in a ***prerun-time*** table is stored in packed decimal format, the letter **P** must be specified in this field. If the data is stored in binary format, a **B** must be specified. If no entry is specified, the numeric table data is stored as zoned decimal. ***Compile-time*** table data is entered in a zoned decimal format. An **L** entered in this field indicates that a separate sign is stored to the left of the value and an **R** to the right.
9. **Decimal Positions** (columns 44): A blank in this field indicates that the table is character. A number from 0 to 9 defines the table elements as numeric with the indicated implied decimal positions. The entry cannot be larger than the *Length of Entry* size.
10. **Sequence (A/D)** (column 45): If the table is not in a sorted order, this field must be blank. If the data is in an ascending order, an **A** may be entered. If the table data is in a descending order, a **D** may be specified. If sequence is specified, an "early exit" is provided for an unsuccessful equal lookup condition, reducing run times.
11. **Table Name (Alternating Format)** (columns 46–51): A table name entered in this field indicates that two or more entries from two related tables are stored in each record, for example, data for a TAB1 element followed by the data for a TAB2 element. *Number of Entries Per Record* specifies how many "pairs" are included on a record.
12. Columns 52–57: These four fields relate to the attributes of the alternating table. Refer to items 7, 8, 9, and 10 for an explanation of these fields.

Figure 9-29 Fields used in the *Extension Specifications* to define tables at compile and prerun times (traditional **RPG**). (Continued)

Traditional RPG Syntax for Compile-Time Tables

The syntax for traditional **RPG II** and **RPG III** compile-time tables is shown in Figure 9-30. Note that the table delimiter is an ** entry, which separates the data for the first compile table from the last **RPG** instruction. The data for other compile-time tables must each follow an ** control statement.

```
     *.. 1 ...+... 2 ...+... 3 ...+... 4 ...+... 5 ...+... 6 ...+... 7 ...
     E....FromfileTofile++Name++N/rN/tbLenPDSArrnamLenPDSCComents++++++++*

     E                    TABMM  12  12  2 0A
     E                    TABNAM  6  12  9
                                  :
                           Last RPG Instruction
  **
  010203040506070809101112
  **
  JANUARY  FEBRUARY MARCH    APRIL    MAY      JUNE
  JULY     AUGUST   SEPTEMBEROCTOBER NOVEMBER DECEMBER

     Position 1

Related table data must be entered in the order that the tables are defined
in the Extension Specification.
```

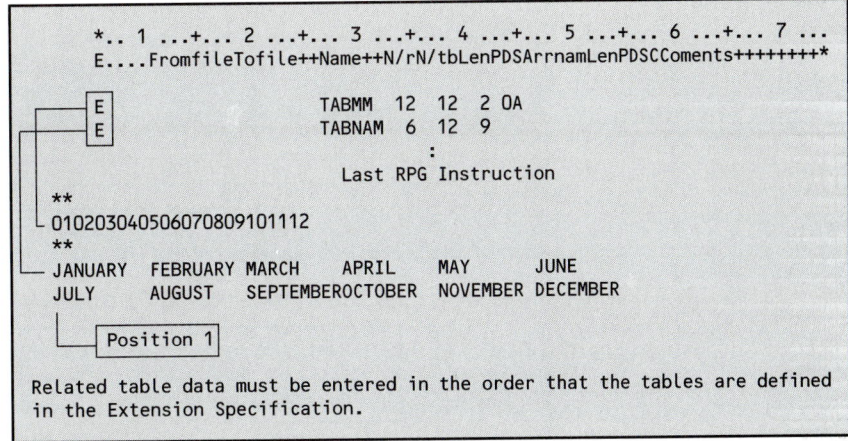

Figure 9-30 *Extension Specification* syntax and related data for two compile-time tables.

Traditional RPG Syntax for Compile-Time Tables Stored in an Alternating Format

Figure 9-31 shows the table data from Figure 9-30 rearranged in an alternating format with the modified *Extension Specification* coding.

```
*.. 1 ...+... 2 ...+... 3 ...+... 4 ...+... 5 ...+... 6 ...+... 7 ...
E....FromfileTofile++Name++N/rN/tbLenPDSArrnamLenPDSCComents++++++++*

E                   TABMM   1  12  2 0ATABNAM  9

   Position 1                      :
                          Last RPG Instruction
**
01JANUARY
02FEBRUARY
03MARCH
04APRIL
05MAY            Alternating table data defined in
06JUNE           the Extension Specification with 12
07JULY           elements for each table with 1 entry
08AUGUST         per record
09SEPTEMBER
10OCTOBER
11NOVEMBER
12DECEMBER
```

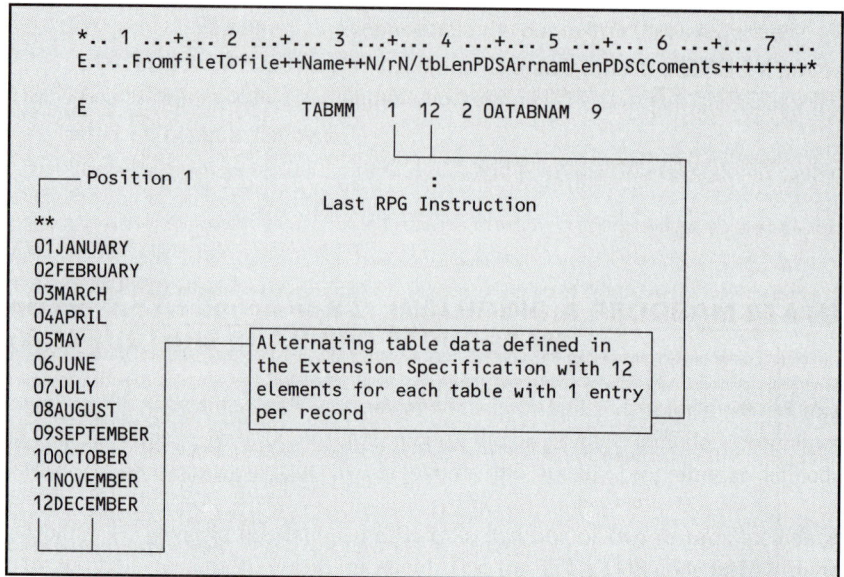

Figure 9-31 *Extension Specification* syntax and related table data for two compile-time tables arranged in an alternating format (traditional **RPG**).

Traditional RPG Syntax for Prerun-Time Tables

Figure 9-32 illustrates the traditional **RPG** syntax to define a prerun-time table. This example uses the same month number and name table data stored for the previously explained compile-time tables. A *File Description Specification* instruction must define the input file that

```
*.. 1 ...+... 2 ...+... 3 ...+... 4 ...+... 5 ...+... 6 ...+... 7 ...
FFilenameIPEAF....RlenLK1AIOvKlocEDevice+......KExit++Entry+A....U1.*

FTablfileIT  F      11          EDISK

        Physical file must       Indicates table attributes
        be defined as a          are defined in the Extension
        table file               Specification
```

```
*.. 1 ...+.. 2 ...+... 3 ...+... 4 ...+... 5 ...+... 6 ...+... 7 ...
E....FromfileTofile++Name++N/rN/tbLenPDSArrnamLenPDSCComents++++++++*

E   Tablfile        TABMM   1  12  2 0ATABNAM  9

       Physical file defined with a T in position 16 in the
       related File Description instruction must be entered
       in the Fromfile field.
```

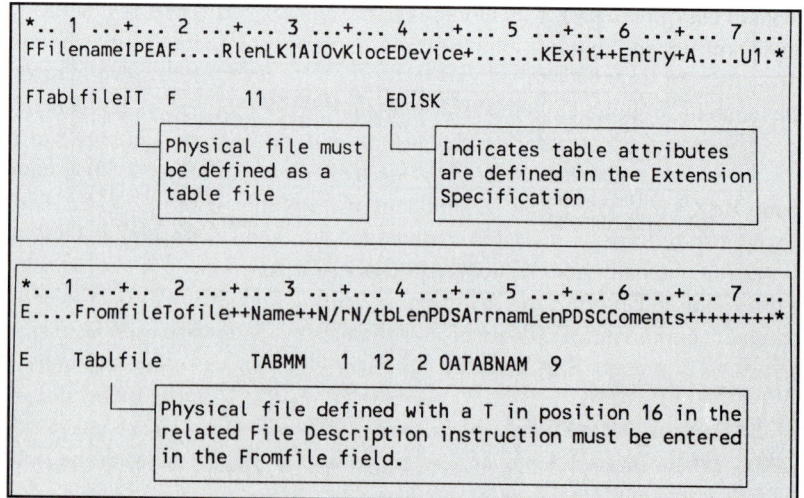

Figure 9-32 Traditional **RPG** *File Description* and *Extension Specification* syntax for prerun-time tables. Data is stored in alternating sequence.

contains the table data. In addition to the letter **I** in position 15, the letter **T** must be entered in position 16 and an **E** in position 39. **T** indicates to the program that the file is to be processed as a table file and that the table data is to be loaded before other input files are read. **E** specifies that the attributes of the tables are defined in *Extension Specification* instructions. Because the physical file in which the table data is stored is usually created without a DDS format, the record length must be specified in the Rlen field, positions 24–27.

Processing of Traditional RPG Tables

With the exception of the lookup operation, which must be **LOKUP** instead of **LOOKUP,** the *Calculation Specification* syntax for the processing of tables with traditional **RPG** is identical to that previously discussed for **RPG IV.**

SUMMARY

In the **RPG IV** programming environment, tables are lists of data stored in a computer's memory. A table may stand alone or relate to one or more other tables.

Tables are defined in *Definition Specification* instructions, which are entered in the program after the *File Description* statements. Tables may be defined as **compile time** or **prerun time.** The data for **compile-time tables** is stored in an **RPG IV** program after the last source program instruction and the delineating ****CTDATA** delimiter. **Prerun-time** table data is stored in a data file and requires that a table file be defined in a *File Description Specification* instruction with the letter **T** in position 18.

Tables, which are always processed consecutively, are accessed by the **LOOKUP** operation. The entry in *Factor 1*, referred to as the *search argument*, must be the same type as the *argument table* entry in *Factor 2*. One related *function table* may be specified in the *Result* field. If more than one function table is required for the application, additional **LOOKUP** instructions must be provided.

For an equal **LOOKUP** condition, an indicator must be specified in the *Eq* field (positions 75–76) of the calculation instruction. When the value in the **search argument** (*Factor 1* entry) equals the value in the **argument table** *(Factor 2* entry*)*, the indicator will be set on. A low-range table condition may be tested by including the same indicator in the *Lo* and *Eq* fields. High-range conditions may be controlled by specifying the same indicator in the *Hi* and *Eq* fields. For either range table processing, an argument table value is found even though an equal condition is not tested.

For processing efficiency, an "early exit" from an equal table **LOOKUP** may be controlled by storing the table data in either ascending or descending order. Then, when a search argument value is not found in the related argument table, **LOOKUP** processing is terminated before the table is searched to its end.

QUESTIONS

9-1. When should tables be included in an **RPG IV** program?

9-2. Name two business applications that require the use of tables.

9-3. On which **RPG IV** specifications are tables defined? Where are these instructions placed in the source program?

9-4. How is a table stored in memory?

9-5. When in the program cycle may tables be loaded with data? Where is the data stored (before processing) for each loading method?

9-6. Reference a blank *Definition Specification*. Identify and explain the function of the fields used to define a table. Indicate the fields used (and not used) for each loading method.

9-7. What new entries are needed in the *File Descriptions* to support each loading method? What new entries are needed on the input form to define and/or process tables?

9-8. What are some of the syntax rules regarding the assignment of a table name?

9-9. Define the following table terms:

SEARCH ARGUMENT	**ARGUMENT TABLE**
FUNCTION TABLE	**LOOKUP**

9-10. Reference a *Calculation Specifications*, and answer the following:

a. Entry in *Factor 1* is referred to as the ________________.

b. Entry in *Factor 2* is referred to as the ________________.

c. Entry in the *Result Field* is referred to as the ________________.

d. What are the minimum entries that must be specified with a **LOOKUP** operation?

e. How many tables may be accessed in one **LOOKUP** operation?

9-11. Explain the rules for formatting table data.

9-12. What are *alternating tables*? How many tables may be defined in an alternating format?

9-13. Answer the following questions about table processing:

a. Where in a table does a search begin?

b. Does the search begin at the same table entry for successive **LOOKUP** operations?

c. Are tables consecutively or randomly processed?

d. If the table data is in an unordered sequence and a search is unsuccessful, at which entry in the table does processing stop? Does this cancel program execution?

9-14. Explain the table processing term *early exit*. How is it provided for in an **RPG IV** program?

9-15. If a table is defined as sorted and the data is not in the required sequence, when is this error identified?

9-16. Explain the following table processing terms:

EQUAL lookup **HIGH RANGE**
LOW RANGE

9-17. What additional entries are needed in the *Definition* and *Calculation Specifications* to support low-range table processing? High-range table processing?

9-18. If a low-range **LOOKUP** is specified, which table entry will be accessed if the *search argument* value is 07000? What table entry will be accessed if a high-range **LOOKUP** is specified and the *search argument* value is 07000?

00000
02480
03670
04750
07010
09170

9-19. Following are three simple tables that relate to one another. Format the **TABCDE** and **TABSTA** entries in an alternating format with one entry per record. Include all the related percentages on one record. Assuming they are compile time, format the tables (with required control statement(s)) as they would be entered in a program.

TABCDE	*TABSTA*	*TABTAX*
NJ	NEW JERSEY	6.0%
CT	CONNECTICUT	7.5%
NY	NEW YORK	7.0%
MA	MASSACHUSETTS	6.0%
VT	VERMONT	5.0%
CA	CALIFORNIA	8.0%

Note: **TABCDE data must be sorted in ascending order.**

9-20. Refer to Question 9-19, and complete the *Extension* and *Calculation Specifications* coding to define and access the three tables. Assume that the search argument STATE is defined as a two-byte alphanumeric input field.

9-21. Refer to Questions 9-19 and 9-20, and include and/or make any additional changes to define and process the tables as prerun time.

9-22. Given below are a state's sales tax percentage tables. All sales over $1.07 are subject to a 7% sales tax. If the sales amount is

Over	But Not Over	The Tax Is
$ .00	$ .07	$ .00
.07	.21	.01
.21	.35	.02
.35	.49	.03
.49	.64	.04
.64	.78	.05
.78	.92	.06
.92	1.07	.07

Format the table entries so that all the entries for a table are included on one record. Assume that the tables are to be loaded at compile time. Use *low-range* processing for the amount of sales (argument) table.

9-23. Refer to Question 9-22, and complete the *Definition* and *Calculations Specifications* to define and process the tables. Assume SALES is the search argument item.

9-24. Refer to Question 9-22, and format the table data for *high-range* processing. Complete the *Definition* and *Calculation Specifications* to define and process the tables. Assume that the search argument is SALES.

PROGRAMMING ASSIGNMENTS

For each of the following programming assignments, a physical file must have been created and loaded with the related data records. Your instructor will inform you if you have to create the physical file and load it or if it has been prepared for the assignment.

Programming Assignment 9-1: REAL PROPERTY TAX REPORT

A county wants a report of selected real property owners in some of the cities within its jurisdiction.

Physical File Record Format:

```
                    PHYSICAL FILE DESCRIPTION

SYSTEM: AS/400                                   DATE: Yours
FILE NAME: Yours                                 REV NO: 0
RECORD NAME: Yours                               KEY LENGTH: None
SEQUENCE: Nonkeyed                               RECORD SIZE: 28

                       FIELD DEFINITIONS

 FIELD   FIELD NAME   SIZE  TYPE    POSITION    COMMENTS
  NO                               FROM    TO

  1      CITYCODE        2   C        1     2
  2      TAXPAYER       20   C        3    22
  3      ASSESSMENT      8   P       23    27  0 decimals
  4      VETERAN         1   C       28    28  V or blank
```

Physical file data:

City Code	Taxpayer Name	Assessed Amount	Vet Code
NL	W.C. FIELDS	00125000	V
SD	CLARK GABLE	01050000	
ST	MARILYN MONROE	12495000	
GH	CHARLIE CHAPLIN	09896500	V
BT	STANLEY LAUREL	00700590	
MN	BETTY BOOP	10456330	V
NK	JOHN WAYNE	15000000	
NH	JAYNE MANSFIELD	08750900	
HD	TYRONE POWELL	00500788	V
ST	ERROL FLYNN	20598500	

Table Data (Include as compile-time tables):

City Code	City Name	Mill Rate
GH	GREENWICH	57.2
SD	STAMFORD	52.1
NK	NORWALK	50.7
BT	BRIDGEPORT	48.8
ST	STRATFORD	46.5
NH	NEW HAVEN	47.0
MN	MIDDLETOWN	39.6
HD	HARTFORD	42.3
NL	NEW LONDON	38.4

Processing: The following steps are required:

1. Look up the City Code table with the code field from each input record, and access the City Name table for the related city's name.
2. Look up the City Code table again to get the related value from the Mill Rate table.
3. Divide the assessed amount by 1,000 to determine the multiples of \$1,000.

   Example:

   $$\text{Assessed amount } \frac{\$60{,}000}{1{,}000} = 60 \text{ multiples of } \$1{,}000$$

   Veterans are allowed a \$1,000 tax exemption that is subtracted from the assessed amount before the multiple is computed. A **V** in the Veteran Status field of a physical file record indicates that the taxpayer is a veteran.
4. Multiply the related Mill Rate table value from step 2 by the multiple computed in step 3 to determine the property tax liability for the taxpayer.

Report Design: Format the report shown in the printer spacing chart. Note that a **YES** or **NO** is printed by testing the Veteran Status field for a **V** and moving a **YES** or **NO** literal to an output field.

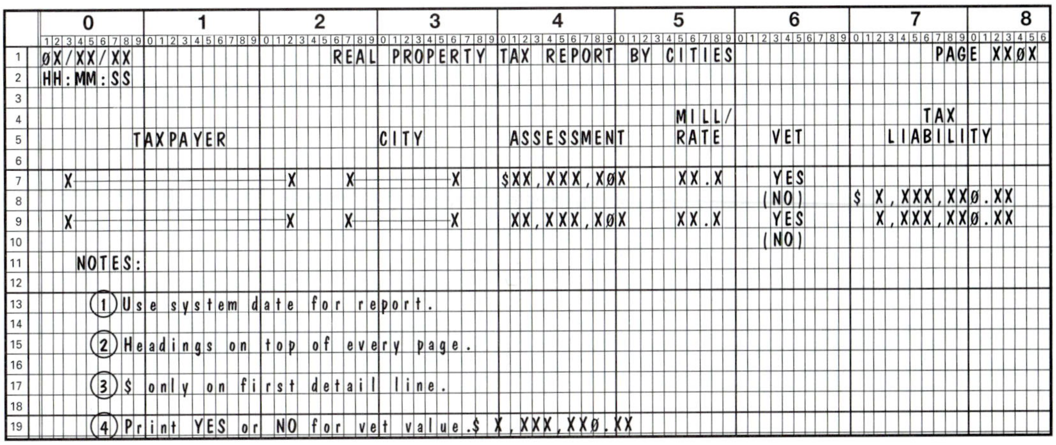

ØX/XX/XX REAL PROPERTY TAX REPORT BY CITIES PAGE XXØX
HH:MM:SS
MILL/ TAX
TAXPAYER CITY ASSESSMENT RATE VET LIABILITY
X X X X $XX,XXX,XØX XX.X YES (NO) $ X,XXX,XXØ.XX
X X X X XX,XXX,XØX XX.X YES (NO) X,XXX,XXØ.XX
NOTES:
1 Use system date for report.
2 Headings on top of every page.
3 $ only on first detail line.
4 Print YES or NO for vet value.$ X,XXX,XXØ.XX

Programming Assignment 9-2: WEEKLY SHIPPING REPORT

A company needs a weekly report of the shipping charges it incurs. All deliveries are made FOB destination (seller pays shipping cost).

Physical File Record Format: A physical file of customers is maintained with the following attributes:

PHYSICAL FILE DESCRIPTION

SYSTEM: AS/400 DATE: Yours
FILE NAME: Yours REV NO: 0
RECORD NAME: Yours KEY LENGTH: 4
SEQUENCE: Keyed RECORD SIZE: 32

FIELD DEFINITIONS

FIELD NO	FIELD NAME	SIZE	TYPE	POSITION FROM	POSITION TO	COMMENTS
1	CUSTNAME	20	C	1	20	
2	INVOICENO	4	P	21	23	Key field
3	INVOICEAMT	6	P	24	27	2 decimals
4	POUNDS	2	P	28	29	0 decimals
5	OUNCES	2	P	30	31	0 decimals
6	COD	1	C	32	32	Y or blank

Physical file data:

Customer Name	Invoice Number	Invoice Amount	Invoice Weight PDS	Invoice Weight OZ	COD
HENRY JACKSON	1244	002400	05	08	
DOROTHY PARTON	1235	010000	20	00	
ROBERT WARFIELD	1236	004500	08	09	Y
MARIO LANZA	1237	120000	70	00	Y
ENZIO PINZA	1238	245000	82	12	
NELSON EDDY	1239	001000	01	00	Y

Table Data: Include the following as ***compile-time*** tables in the program:

Weight (PDS)	Rate (2 decimal positions)
01	129
02	137
03	146
04	154
05	163
06	171
07	180
08	188
09	197
10	205
11	214
12	222
13	231
14	239
15	248
16	256
17	265
18	273
19	282
20	290

Processing: Use the invoice shipping weight field as the search argument, and look up the weight table to access the related shipping charge. For weights that contain any ounces over a pound, round to the next-higher pound. All shipments over 20 pounds are charged the table amount for that weight plus an additional 6 cents for each pound over 20.

A maximum shipping limit of 70 pounds is imposed by the parcel delivery firm. Identify this condition on the report by the message OVER WEIGHT, and skip any additional calculations.

For invoice amounts under $25, the shipping charge is absorbed by the buyer and added to the invoice total. Identify these transactions on the report by asterisks in place of the shipping charge amount.

For COD sales, a flat charge of $1.50 is added to the invoice on all invoices under $50. COD shipments are identified by the letter **Y** in the related input field.

Report Design:

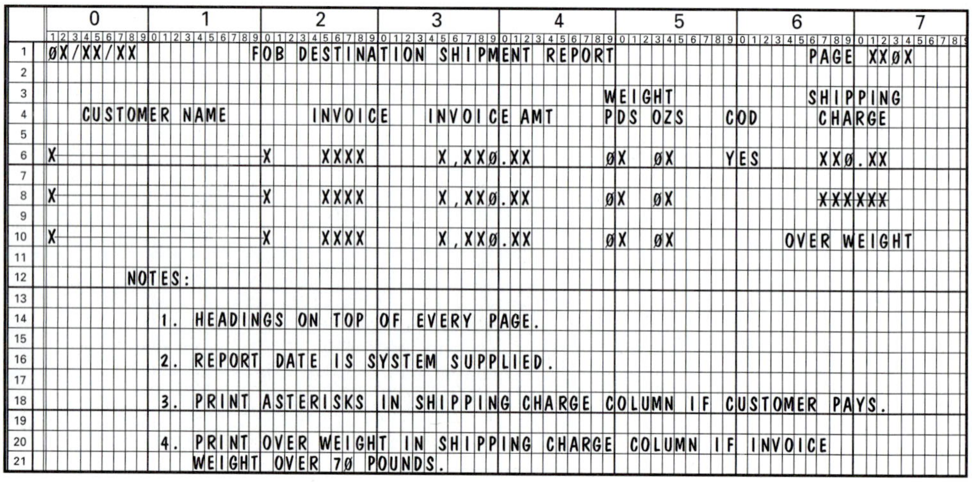

Programming Assignment 9-3: FLEXIBLE BUDGET REPORT

A company has a flexible budget formula for its factory overhead expenses. Each expense item has a fixed dollar amount plus a variable rate based on the standard direct labor hours (hours budgeted for the level of production attained). The formula is expressed as

Budget amount for overhead expense item = Fixed \$ amount
+ (variable rate × std direct hrs)

At the end of each accounting period, the company wants to determine the flexible budget amount for each expense item and compare it with the actual dollars incurred to identify a *favorable* or *unfavorable variance*. A favorable variance occurs when the actual costs incurred for the expense are less than the budget allowance. An unfavorable variance results when the actual costs are more than the budget amount.

Physical File Record Format:

PHYSICAL FILE DESCRIPTION

SYSTEM: AS/400	DATE: Yours
FILE NAME: Yours	REV NO: 0
RECORD NAME: Yours	KEY LENGTH: 3
SEQUENCE: Keyed	RECORD SIZE: 8

FIELD DEFINITIONS

FIELD NO	FIELD NAME	SIZE	TYPE	POSITION FROM	POSITION TO	COMMENTS
1	ACCOUNTNO	3	C	1	3	Key field
2	ACTUALCOST	8	P	4	8	2 decimals

Physical file data:

Account Number	Actual Cost Incurred
600	03000090
601	05100010
602	00550068
603	00840000
604	01500025
605	00550010
606	01000000
607	00950000
608	00705078
609	00420015

Table Data: Include the following data in compile-time tables:

Account Number	Account Name	Fixed Amount	Variable Rate Per Direct Labor Hours (2 decimals)
600	INDIRECT LABOR	20000	015
601	FACTORY SUPPLIES	02000	100
602	FACTORY ELECTRICITY	03000	006
603	MACHINE REPAIRS	01000	010
604	PLANT MAINTENANCE	04000	020
605	FACTORY HEATING OIL	02700	004
606	FACTORY CUSTODIAL	05000	010
607	TOOL CRIB LABOR	04500	011
608	COST CLERKS	04000	008

Data Area Requirements: Create a data area that includes the accounting period date—113098—and 50,000 for standard direct labor hours. The date is to be used as the report date and the standard direct labor hours in the computation of the total budget amount.

Processing: Use the Account Number field from the input records as the search argument, and look up the related Account Number table for an equal condition. Provide for an early exit if the account number is not found in the table.

If the table search is successful, multiply the standard direct labor hours input by the related variable rate table entry. Add this amount to the fixed amount table entry for the item for the total flexible budget amount allowed for the level of activity (standard direct labor hours input).

The favorable or unfavorable variance for each expense item is determined by subtracting the total flexible budget amount from the actual cost incurred. A positive difference indicates an unfavorable variance; a negative, favorable.

Examine the printer spacing chart, and notice that the letter **F** (favorable) or **U** (unfavorable) is printed next to the variance amount. *Do not print a negative sign.*

Report Design:

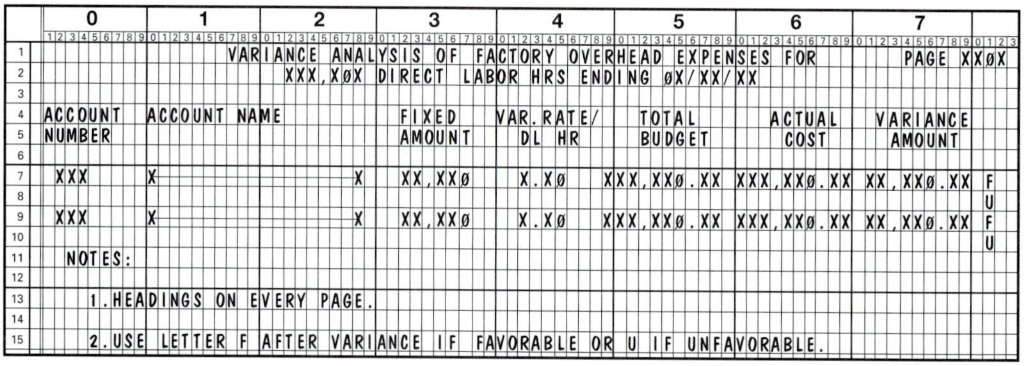

VARIANCE ANALYSIS OF FACTORY OVERHEAD EXPENSES FOR
PAGE XXØX
XXX,XØX DIRECT LABOR HRS ENDING ØX/XX/XX
ACCOUNT NUMBER
ACCOUNT NAME
FIXED AMOUNT
VAR. RATE/ DL HR
TOTAL BUDGET
ACTUAL COST
VARIANCE AMOUNT
XXX
X X
XX,XXØ
X.XØ
XXX,XXØ.XX
XXX,XXØ.XX
XX,XXØ.XX
F
U
NOTES:
1. HEADINGS ON EVERY PAGE.
2. USE LETTER F AFTER VARIANCE IF FAVORABLE OR U IF UNFAVORABLE.

Programming Assignment 9-4: WEEKLY PAYROLL CHECKS

The XYZ Company needs an **RPG IV** program to print the weekly payroll checks (with stubs) on preprinted check forms for its employees.

General Information: By federal law all employee wages are subject to federal withholding tax (FWT) and Social Security/Medicare Tax deductions. There are many acceptable methods to compute the federal tax that must be withheld under the pay-as-you-earn system. The percentage method, which requires the use of tables, is popular for computerized systems and will be used for this program.

Earnings, number of exemptions, marital status, and payroll period (weekly, biweekly, and so forth) determine the amount of federal income tax withheld. Based on the company's payroll, this program requires computations only for a weekly payroll period for single and married wage earners.

Processing: The steps needed to compute the Federal Withholding Tax (FWT) to be withheld from an employee's weekly pay using the percentage method are detailed below. Note that the value determined in step 1 is used as the search argument to look up the low-range table.

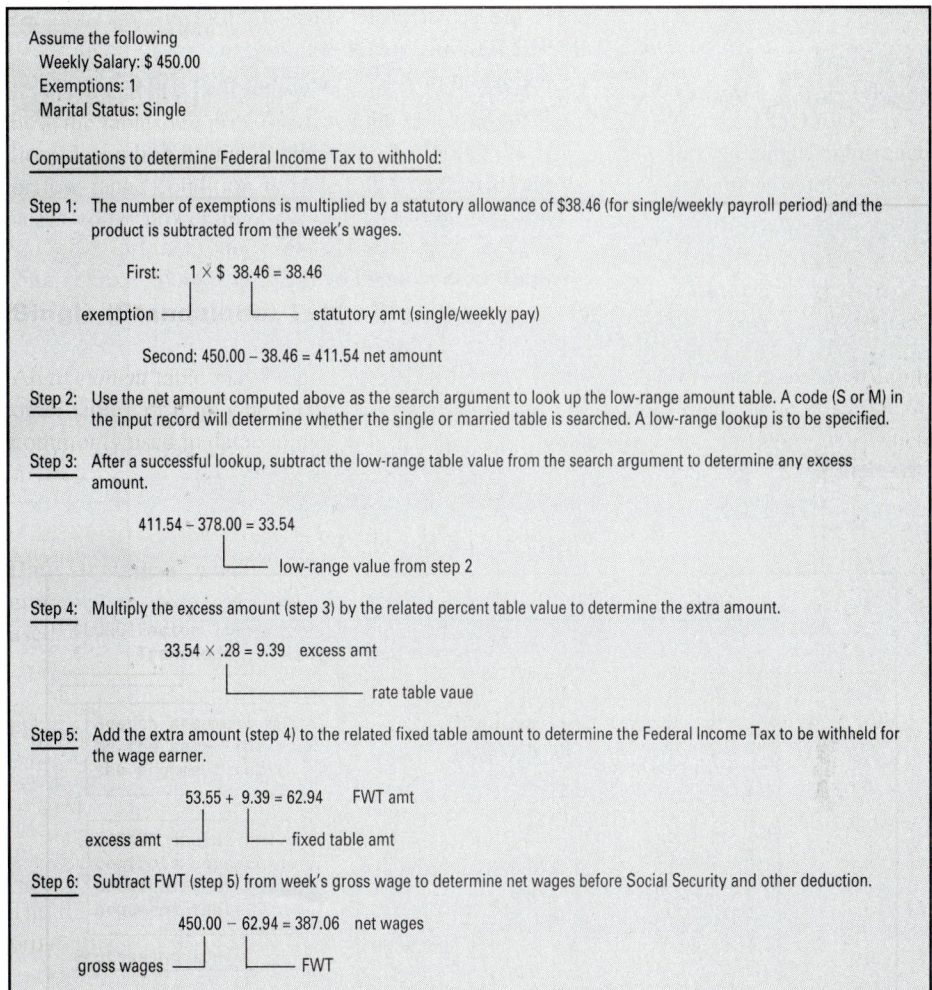

Assume the following
Weekly Salary: $ 450.00
Exemptions: 1
Marital Status: Single

Computations to determine Federal Income Tax to withhold:

Step 1: The number of exemptions is multiplied by a statutory allowance of $38.46 (for single/weekly payroll period) and the product is subtracted from the week's wages.

First: 1 × $ 38.46 = 38.46

exemption — statutory amt (single/weekly pay)

Second: 450.00 – 38.46 = 411.54 net amount

Step 2: Use the net amount computed above as the search argument to look up the low-range amount table. A code (S or M) in the input record will determine whether the single or married table is searched. A low-range lookup is to be specified.

Step 3: After a successful lookup, subtract the low-range table value from the search argument to determine any excess amount.

411.54 – 378.00 = 33.54

low-range value from step 2

Step 4: Multiply the excess amount (step 3) by the related percent table value to determine the extra amount.

33.54 × .28 = 9.39 excess amt

rate table vaue

Step 5: Add the extra amount (step 4) to the related fixed table amount to determine the Federal Income Tax to be withheld for the wage earner.

53.55 + 9.39 = 62.94 FWT amt

excess amt — fixed table amt

Step 6: Subtract FWT (step 5) from week's gross wage to determine net wages before Social Security and other deduction.

450.00 – 62.94 = 387.06 net wages

gross wages — FWT

Table Data:

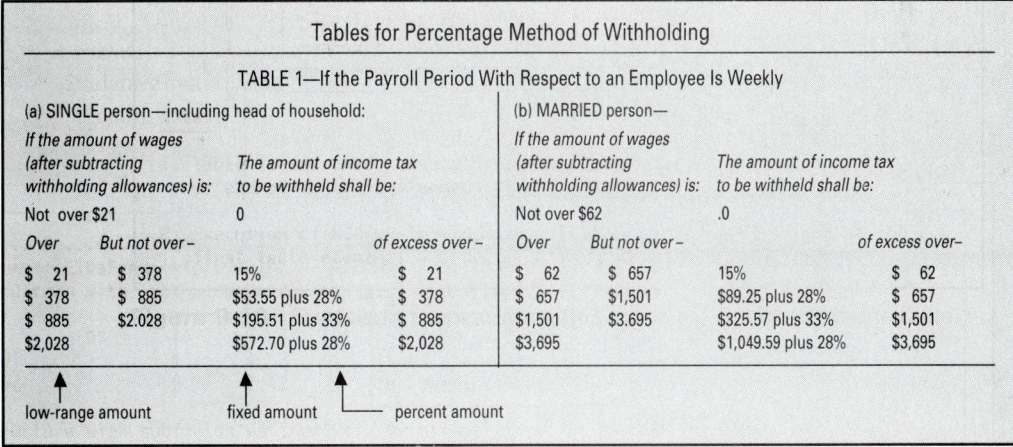

Tables for Percentage Method of Withholding

TABLE 1—If the Payroll Period With Respect to an Employee Is Weekly

(a) SINGLE person—including head of household:

If the amount of wages (after subtracting withholding allowances) is:		*The amount of income tax to be withheld shall be:*	
Not over $21		0	
Over	*But not over–*		*of excess over–*
$ 21	$ 378	15%	$ 21
$ 378	$ 885	$53.55 plus 28%	$ 378
$ 885	$2.028	$195.51 plus 33%	$ 885
$2,028		$572.70 plus 28%	$2,028

(b) MARRIED person—

If the amount of wages (after subtracting withholding allowances) is:		*The amount of income tax to be withheld shall be:*	
Not over $62		.0	
Over	*But not over–*		*of excess over–*
$ 62	$ 657	15%	$ 62
$ 657	$1,501	$89.25 plus 28%	$ 657
$1,501	$3.695	$325.57 plus 33%	$1,501
$3,695		$1,049.59 plus 28%	$3,695

low-range amount — fixed amount — percent amount

As of 1994, the *Social Security Tax* **(FICA)** is computed at 7.65% on the first $62,700 paid to an employee. A *Medicare Tax* of 1.45%, which is not limited by the amount of income, is included in the 7.65%. The following must be considered in the computation of the *Social Security/Medicare Tax*:

1. If the year-to-date wages (before adding the current week) are greater than \$62,700, no social security tax is computed. However, the *Medicare Tax* deduction of 1.45% continues on all additional earnings.
2. If the year-to-date wages are not \$62,700 or greater, then it must be determined if all, or only part, of the current week's pay is subject to the Social Security part (6.20%) of the 7.65% total tax. For example, if the year-to-date wages are \$62,500 and the current week's pay is \$600, only \$200 will be subject to the FICA 7.65% rate. However, any additional amounts and future pay will continue to be reduced by the 1.45% Medicare Tax rate.
3. Note that there is no limit on the *Federal Withholding Tax* (**FWT**) withheld.

Create a data area to store the week ending date and the beginning check number. Use 12171998 for the date value and 1000 as the beginning check number.

Physical File Record Format:

PHYSICAL FILE DESCRIPTION

SYSTEM: AS/400	DATE: Yours
FILE NAME: Yours	REV NO: 0
RECORD NAME: Yours	KEY LENGTH: 9
SEQUENCE: Keyed	RECORD SIZE: 51

FIELD DEFINITIONS

FIELD NO	FIELD NAME	SIZE	TYPE	POSITION FROM	POSITION TO	COMMENTS
1	SSNUMBER	9	P	1	5	Key Field
2	EMPNAME	22	C	6	27	
3	YTDWAGES	9	P	28	32	2 decimals
4	YTDFWT	7	P	33	36	2 decimals
5	YTDSS	6	P	37	40	2 decimals
6	YTDMEDICAR	6	P	41	44	2 decimals
7	WEEKWAGES	6	P	45	48	2 decimals
8	EXEMPTIONS	2	P	49	50	0 decimals
9	MAR_STATUS	1	C	51	51	

Physical file data:

Employee Name	SS Number	YTD Wages	YTD FWT	YTD SS	YTD Med	Week's Wages	Exemp-tions	Marital Status
ROBERT FULTON	040503871	06250000	0905210	387500	090625	125000	2	M
THOMAS EDISON	030216532	03000000	0524200	186000	043500	060000	1	S
ALEXANDER BELL	020315555	13470000	3332450	388740	195315	269400	4	M
HENRY FORD	060548754	06500000	1505150	388740	094250	130000	1	S
WALTER CHRYSLER	050703302	06000000	1098750	372000	087000	120000	2	M

Report Design: Output is to be printed on simulated preprinted check forms. Assume that all of the *constants* shown in the printer spacing chart are preprinted. The **RPG IV** program is to output only the variable data (shown with the **X**'s). Control page overflow so that only one check and stub will print per page *(see your instructor, however, before you execute your program and change the standard form length).*

```
         1         2         3         4         5         6
123456789012345678901234567890123456789012345678901234567890
XXX-XX-XXXX             XYZ COMPANY                     XXXX
                        ALCATRAZ, CA
                                     WEEK ENDING: 0X/XX/XXXX
 PAY TO THE
  ORDER OF   XXXXXXXXXXXXXXXXXXXXXX

         PAY EXACTLY  $ *,***.XX

                 ALWAYS ACCURATE BANK
                        HOPE, CA
                                         JOHN DIDIT, JR
                                          CONTROLLER
- - - - - - - - - - - - - - - - - - - - - - - - - - - - - -
 DO NOT CASH - CHECK STUB                               XXXX

 XXX-XX-XXXX                         WEEK ENDING: 0X/XX/XXXX

   GROSS PAY     FWT         SS       MEDICARE     NET PAY

   X,XX0.XX   X,XX0.XX    X,XX0.XX     XX0.XX     X,XX0.XX


       YTD WAGES    YTD SS   YTD MEDICARE     YTD FWT

      XXX,XX0.XX   X,XX0.XX    X.XX0.XX      XXX,XX0.XX
```

Correct alignment of the variables may be determined by a transparency master of this report design, supplied by the instructor, or with a forms ruler.

chapter 10

Array Processing

COMPARISON OF ARRAYS TO TABLES

Because *arrays* and *tables* are similar, you may be confused about when to use an array instead of a table, or vice versa. Two broad considerations may help you to determine whether to use an array or a table in an **RPG IV** program:

1. The way the data for loading the array or table is arranged in the records
2. The way the array or table will be processed

The structural and processing differences of arrays and tables are explained in the comparison detailed in Figure 10-1.

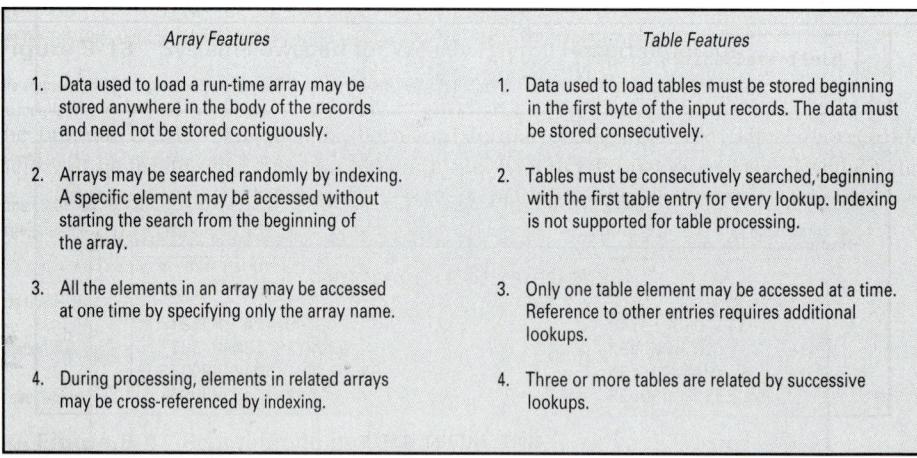

Array Features	*Table Features*
1. Data used to load a run-time array may be stored anywhere in the body of the records and need not be stored contiguously.	1. Data used to load tables must be stored beginning in the first byte of the input records. The data must be stored consecutively.
2. Arrays may be searched randomly by indexing. A specific element may be accessed without starting the search from the beginning of the array.	2. Tables must be consecutively searched, beginning with the first table entry for every lookup. Indexing is not supported for table processing.
3. All the elements in an array may be accessed at one time by specifying only the array name.	3. Only one table element may be accessed at a time. Reference to other entries requires additional lookups.
4. During processing, elements in related arrays may be cross-referenced by indexing.	4. Three or more tables are related by successive lookups.

Figure 10-1 Comparison of the structural and processing features of arrays and tables.

ARRAY STRUCTURE

As related to computers, an *array* may be defined as an arrangement of computer memory positions in one (or multiple) dimension with each position having the same attributes. Figure 10-2 illustrates the structures of one- and two-dimensional arrays.

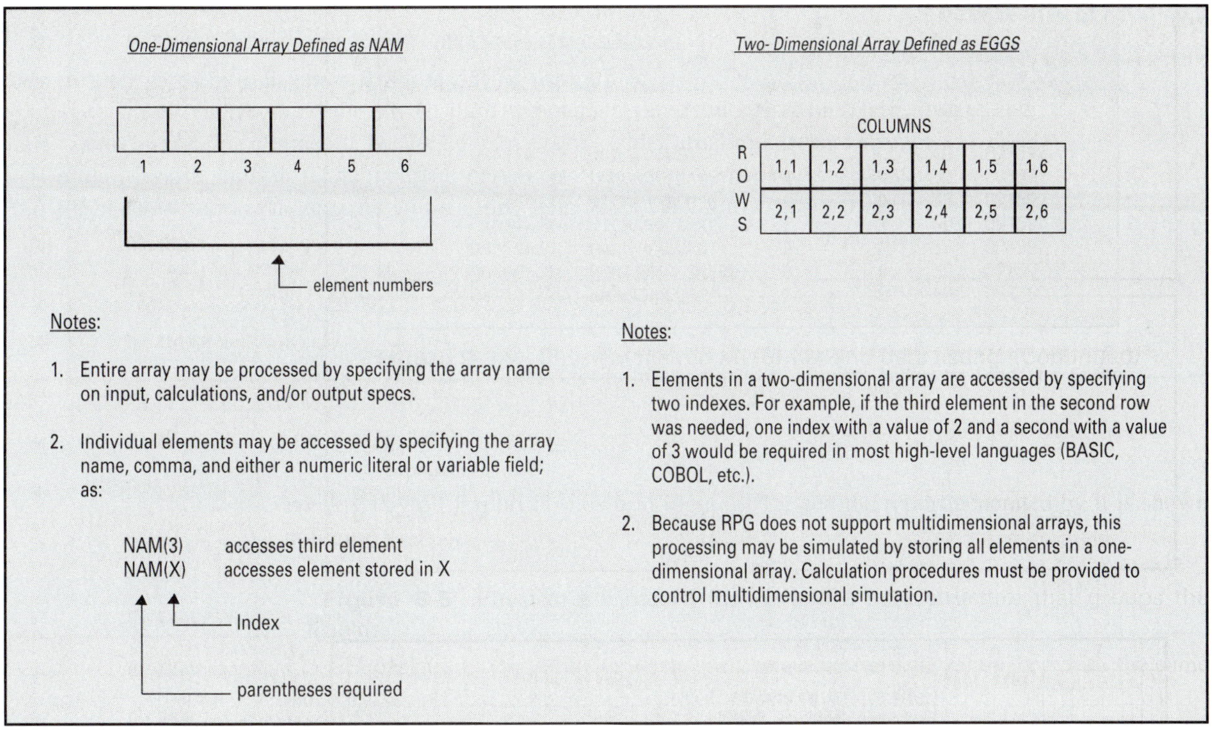

Figure 10-2 Structure of one- and two-dimensional arrays.

One-Dimensional Arrays

The storage positions built for an array are referred to as *elements*. The array NAM, shown in Figure 10-2, was built with six elements. All elements may be accessed at one time by specifying only the array name. Individual elements may be accessed by including a literal or variable field index in parentheses with the array name. Program requirements will determine how the array is processed.

Multidimensional Arrays

Refer to Figure 10-2 for an example of a two- (multi-) dimensional array. This structure may be better understood if the array shown is thought of as an egg carton with two rows of six eggs each. In languages such as COBOL and BASIC, the third egg (column 3) from row 2 would be accessed by specifying two indexes. For example, the coding in COBOL would be

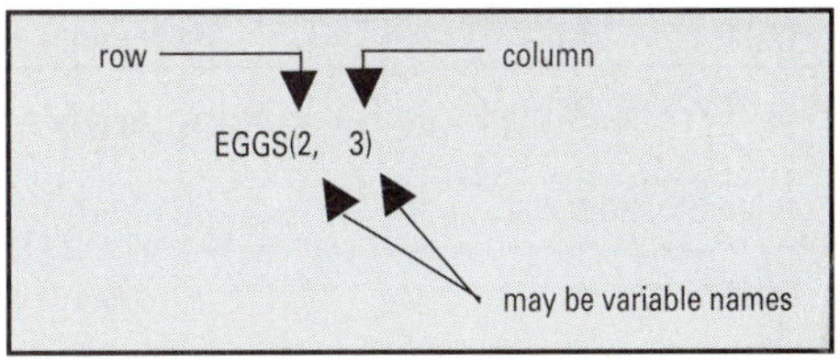

RPG IV does not directly support multidimensional arrays. However, they may be simulated by defining one or more **Multiple Occurrence Data Structures** in a program and processing them with one or more **OCCUR** statements. An example program that includes these features is discussed later in this chapter.

LOADING AN ARRAY

"Loading an array" refers to the time in the program cycle during which data is read, moved, and stored in the array elements built by the attributes defined in the *Definition Specifications*. Similar to tables, arrays may be loaded at compile and prerun times. They may also be loaded by input and calculation instructions as run-time arrays. Figure 10-3 details the processing logic associated with loading an array at various times in the program cycle.

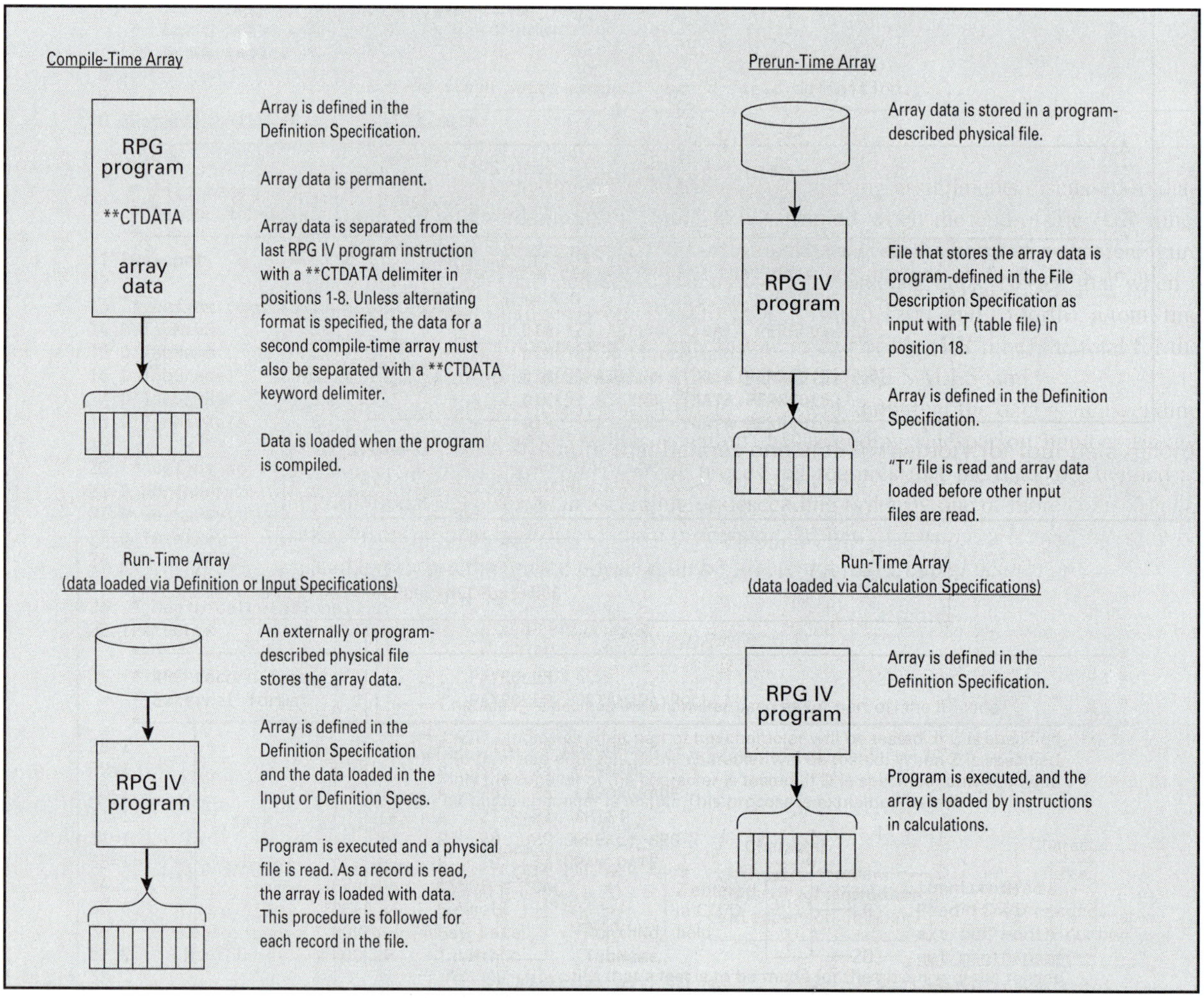

Figure 10-3 Processing logic for loading arrays at compile, prerun, and run times.

ARRAY DESCRIPTION

Arrays are defined in the *Definition Specification* with one or more instructions that specify the array name, number of elements, element size, element type, and sequence of the array data. Figure 10-4 lists the keywords related to array processing and an explanation of their functions.

ARRAY KEYWORDS USED IN THE DEFINITION SPECIFICATION

Array Keyword	Function
ALT	Array elements are in an alternating format with another array
ASCEND	Specifies that the array data is in ascending order
CTDATA	Specifies the beginning of a compile-time array
DESCEND	Specifies that the array data is in descending order
DIM	Defines the number of array elements
FROMFILE	Specifies the input table file in which the array data is stored
PERRCD	Specifies the number of array elements per record
TOFILE	Specifies the file to which the array data will be written

Figure 10-4 Array keywords used in *Definition Specification* instructions.

RPG IV SYNTAX FOR COMPILE-TIME ARRAYS

Figure 10-5 shows that compile-time array data is an integral ("hard-coded") extension of an **RPG IV** program. The data must be included after a ****CTDATA** delimiter keyword entered in positions 1–8 following the last **RPG IV** program instruction. Unless the arrays are stored in alternating format, the data for two or more arrays must be separated by a ****CTDATA** delimiter. Figure 10-5 shows the relationship of the *Definition Specification* syntax and the data for two compile-time arrays.

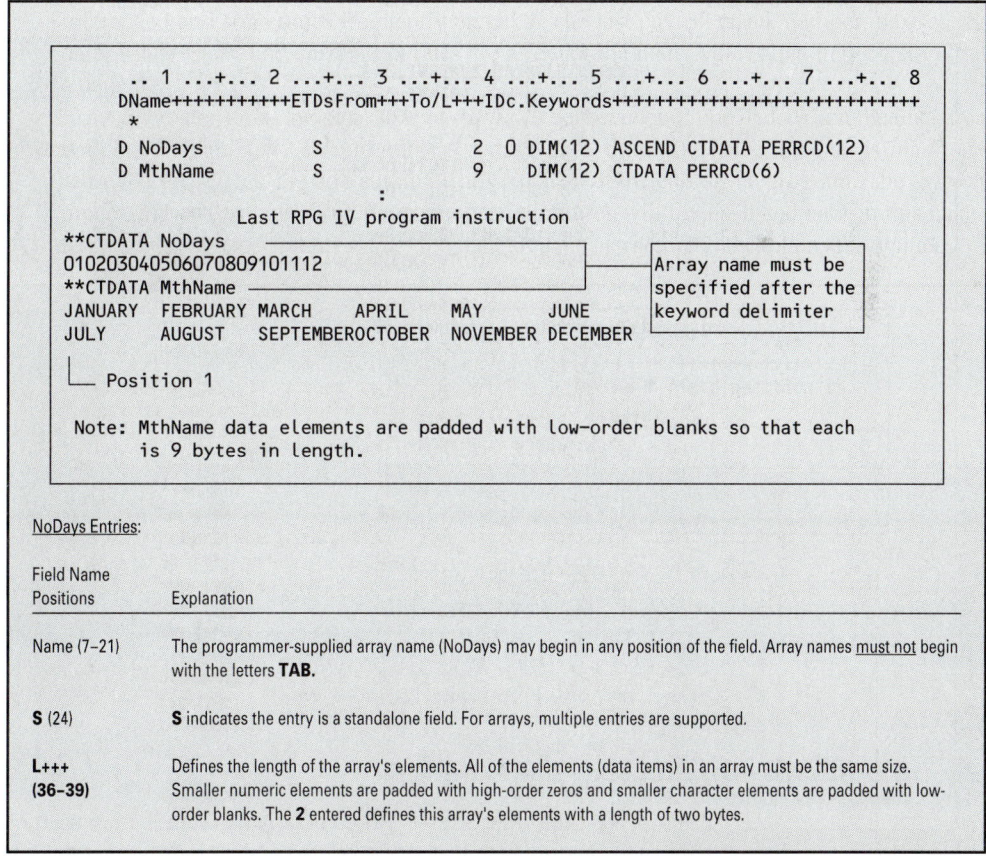

```
      .. 1 ...+... 2 ...+... 3 ...+... 4 ...+... 5 ...+... 6 ...+... 7 ...+... 8
      DName+++++++++++ETDsFrom+++To/L+++IDc.Keywords+++++++++++++++++++++++++++++
       *
      D NoDays          S              2  0 DIM(12) ASCEND CTDATA PERRCD(12)
      D MthName         S              9    DIM(12) CTDATA PERRCD(6)
                                   :
                Last RPG IV program instruction
**CTDATA NoDays ---------------------------------
010203040506070809101112                        |-------Array name must be
**CTDATA MthName --------------------------------       specified after the
JANUARY  FEBRUARY MARCH    APRIL    MAY      JUNE       keyword delimiter
JULY     AUGUST   SEPTEMBEROCTOBER  NOVEMBER DECEMBER
|
L__ Position 1

 Note: MthName data elements are padded with low-order blanks so that each
       is 9 bytes in length.
```

NoDays Entries:

Field Name Positions	Explanation
Name (7–21)	The programmer-supplied array name (NoDays) may begin in any position of the field. Array names must not begin with the letters **TAB.**
S (24)	**S** indicates the entry is a standalone field. For arrays, multiple entries are supported.
L+++ (36–39)	Defines the length of the array's elements. All of the elements (data items) in an array must be the same size. Smaller numeric elements are padded with high-order zeros and smaller character elements are padded with low-order blanks. The **2** entered defines this array's elements with a length of two bytes.

Figure 10-5 *Definition Specification* syntax for two related compile-time arrays.

Dc (41-42)	Defines the array elements as numeric. A **0** to **30** may be entered, indicating the number of implied decimals for the elements. If an entry is not made in this field, the array elements are defined as character. The **0** entered indicates that the elements are defined as numeric integer.
DIM(12)	Specifies the number of elements stored in the array. The **12** in parentheses defines the array with 12 elements.
ASCEND	Defines the array data as being in ascending order. If this entry is omitted, the array data will be defined as in an unordered sequence.
CTDATA	Compile-time arrays require this entry. It specifies that the data is an extension of the **RPG IV** program.
PERRCD	Indicates the number of elements stored on each array record. If this entry is omitted, **RPG IV** will assume that one element is stored on an array record. The **12** in parentheses for this example specifies that 12 elements are stored on one or more array records. Note: When array data is stored on more than one record, the last record may have fewer elements than the **PERRCD** keyword indicates.
MthName Entries:	The explanation for this array follows the same syntax as the NoDays array except for the following: * The MthName array elements are defined as character with a length of 9. * The **PERRCD(6)** keyword specifies that 6 elements are included on an array record.

Figure 10-5 *Definition Specification* syntax for two related compile-time arrays. (Continued)

RPG IV Syntax for Compile-Time Arrays; Data Stored in an Alternating Format

Figure 10-6 shows the data for two compile-time arrays arranged in an alternating format with the modified *Definition Specification* syntax.

```
   .. 1 ...+... 2 ...+... 3 ...+... 4 ...+... 5 ...+... 6 ...+... 7 ...+... 8
  DName+++++++++++ETDsFrom+++To/L+++IDc.Keywords+++++++++++++++++++++++++++++
   *
  D MthNumber       S              2  0 DIM(12) ASCEND CTDATA
  D MthName         S              9    DIM(12) ALT(MthNumber)
                                  :
            Last RPG IV program instruction
**CTDATA MthNumber ----------
01JANUARY                    Name of base array entered
02FEBRUARY
03MARCH
04APRIL
05MAY
06JUNE
07JULY
08AUGUST
09SEPTEMBER
10OCTOBER
11NOVEMBER
12DECEMBER
| |
| └------MthName entries
└--------MthNumber entries
```

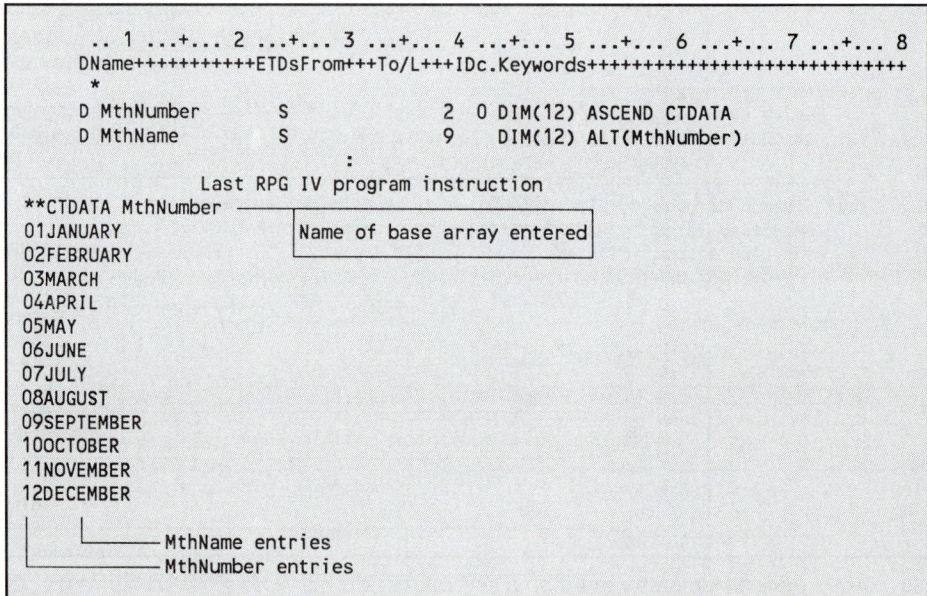

Figure 10-6 *Definition Specification* syntax and related data for two compile-time arrays arranged in an alternating format.

RPG IV SYNTAX FOR PRERUN-TIME ARRAYS

Data for a prerun-time array is stored externally from the program in a physical file. When processed, the array is created and loaded with data from the physical file *before* any other files are processed. The array data remains in storage for the complete program cycle.

Figure 10-7 illustrates the syntax required in an **RPG IV** program to define and load a prerun-time array.

```
.. 1 ...+... 2 ...+... 3 ...+... 4 ...+... 5 ...+... 6 ...+... 7 ...+... 8
FFilename++IPEASFRLen+LKLen+AIDevice+.Keywords+++++++++++++++++++++++++++++
 * Letter T in position 18 defines the file as a table file. F in position
 * 22 defines a program-described file.  Record length (11) in positions
 * 23-27 must be specified for a program-described file.

FArrayFile IT   F   11          DISK
FQsysPrt   O    F  132          PRINTER
```

```
.. 1 ...+... 2 ...+... 3 ...+... 4 ...+... 5 ...+... 6 ...+... 7 ...+... 8
DName+++++++++++ETDsFrom+++To/L+++IDc.Keywords+++++++++++++++++++++++++++++
 * The FROMFILE keyword must be specified for a prerun-time array.  The
 * file name (defined in the File Description as a table file) must be
 * entered in parentheses after the FROMFILE keyword.  Other syntax is
 * identical to compile-time arrays.

D MthNumber       S              2  0 DIM(12) ASCEND FROMFILE(ArrayFile)
D MthName         S              9    DIM(12) ALT(MthNumber)
```

Figure 10-7 *File Description* and *Definition Specifications* syntax for prerun-time arrays.

If the array data was to be updated and written back to the physical file, the keyword **TOFILE** and the file name in parentheses (i.e., **TOFILE(ArrayFile)**) would be required in the definition of the MthNumber array.

Format of Data for Compile- and Prerun-Time Arrays

Data for compile and prerun-time arrays must be formatted according to the rules explained in Figure 10-8.

RULES FOR FORMATTING THE DATA FOR
COMPILE- AND PRERUN-TIME ARRAYS

1. The data must begin in the first position of each record.
2. Elements for an array must be the same size.
3. Smaller numeric elements must be padded with high-order zeros and smaller character elements must be padded with low-order blanks.
4. When alternating sequence is used for the data for two arrays, the values for the two arrays must be included on a record based on the **PERRCD** keyword entry. The values may not be separated onto two records.
5. The compile-time array data does *not* have to be in the same order in which the arrays were defined in the *Definition Specifications.*

Figure 10-8 Rules for formatting the data records for compile- and prerun-time arrays.

When to Use Compile- or Prerun-Time Arrays

The decision about whether to use a compile- or prerun-time array in an **RPG IV** program usually depends on the following:

1. Compile-time arrays are commonly used when an array has few elements, the data is not likely to change, and/or the data is not shared with other programs.

2. Prerun-time arrays are commonly used when an array has many elements, the data is frequently updated, and/or the data is shared with other programs.

RPG IV SYNTAX FOR RUN-TIME ARRAYS (LOADED IN DEFINITION *OR* INPUT SPECIFICATIONS*)*

Similar to prerun-time arrays, the data for run-time arrays (loaded by *Definition* or *Input Specification* instructions) is stored in an externally or program-described physical file. However, there are significant storage and processing differences, which are identified in the comparison in Figure 10-9.

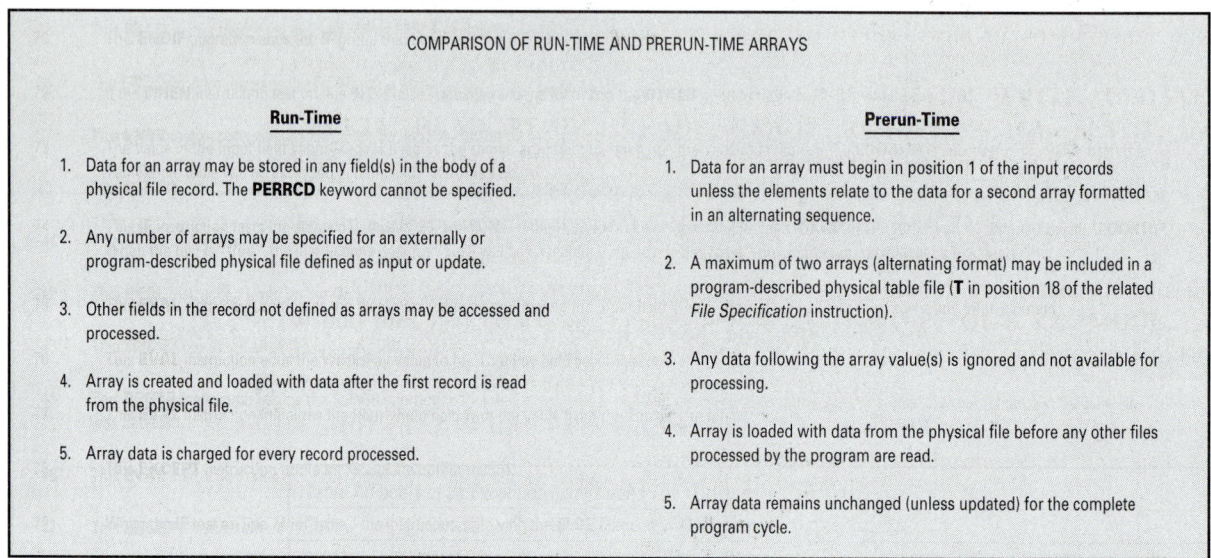

COMPARISON OF RUN-TIME AND PRERUN-TIME ARRAYS

Run-Time

1. Data for an array may be stored in any field(s) in the body of a physical file record. The **PERRCD** keyword cannot be specified.
2. Any number of arrays may be specified for an externally or program-described physical file defined as input or update.
3. Other fields in the record not defined as arrays may be accessed and processed.
4. Array is created and loaded with data after the first record is read from the physical file.
5. Array data is charged for every record processed.

Prerun-Time

1. Data for an array must begin in position 1 of the input records unless the elements relate to the data for a second array formatted in an alternating sequence.
2. A maximum of two arrays (alternating format) may be included in a program-described physical table file (**T** in position 18 of the related *File Specification* instruction).
3. Any data following the array value(s) is ignored and not available for processing.
4. Array is loaded with data from the physical file before any other files processed by the program are read.
5. Array data remains unchanged (unless updated) for the complete program cycle.

Figure 10-9 Comparison of the storage and processing features for run-time and prerun-time arrays.

Run-Time Array (Loaded in *Definition Specifications*): Data Stored in an Externally Defined Physical File

When the data for a run-time array is stored in an externally defined physical file in contiguous or noncontiguous fields, the data may be loaded into the array elements with *Definition Specification* instructions as shown in Figure 10-10.

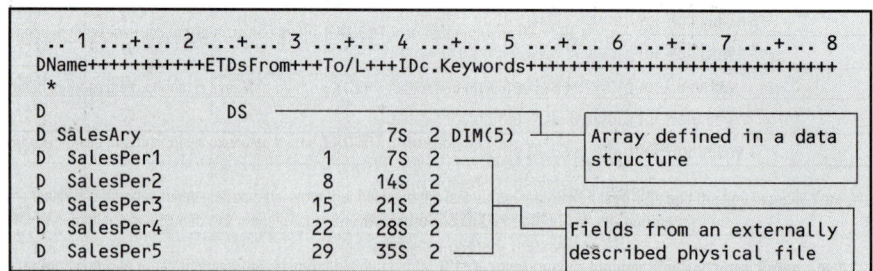

```
.. 1 ...+... 2 ...+... 3 ...+... 4 ...+... 5 ...+... 6 ...+... 7 ...+... 8
DName+++++++++++ETDsFrom+++To/L+++IDc.Keywords+++++++++++++++++++++++++++++
 *
D                 DS
D SalesAry                       7S 2 DIM(5)
D  SalesPer1              1      7S 2
D  SalesPer2              8     14S 2
D  SalesPer3             15     21S 2
D  SalesPer4             22     28S 2
D  SalesPer5             29     35S 2
```

Array defined in a data structure

Fields from an externally described physical file

Figure 10-10 Loading a run-time array with *Definition Specification* instructions.

Note that the array's definition and the fields from the physical file are both included in a data structure. The size of the fields specified in the data structure must be identical to the related fields in the physical file.

Run-Time Array (Loaded in *Input Specifications*): Data Stored in an Externally Described Physical File

Another method of loading the data in contiguous or noncontiguous fields from an externally described physical file into the elements of a run-time array is with *Input Specification* instructions. Figure 10-11 illustrates the syntax for this method. Note that the

```
Definition Specification: Defines the array

.. 1 ...+... 2 ...+... 3 ...+... 4 ...+... 5 ...+... 6 ...+... 7 ...+.
DName+++++++++++ETDsFrom+++To/L+++IDc.Keywords+++++++++++++++++++++++++
D SalesAry                       7S   2 DIM(5)

Input Specification: Loads the array elements-SEU JX format accessed

*.. 1 ...+... 2 ...+... 3 ...+... 4 ...+... 5 ...+... 6 ...+... 7 ...+.
I..............Ext-field+..................Field+++++++++L1M1..PlMnZr..
I              SalesPer1                   SalesAry(1)
I              SalesPer2                   SalesAry(2)
I              SalesPer3                   SalesAry(3)
I              SalesPer4                   SalesAry(4)
I              SalesPer5                   SalesAry(5)

   Fields from the externally        Individual array elements
   described physical file           referenced by indexing

 Note: When the RPG IV program is executed, the value in each of the
       physical file's fields will be moved into the related array
       element.
```

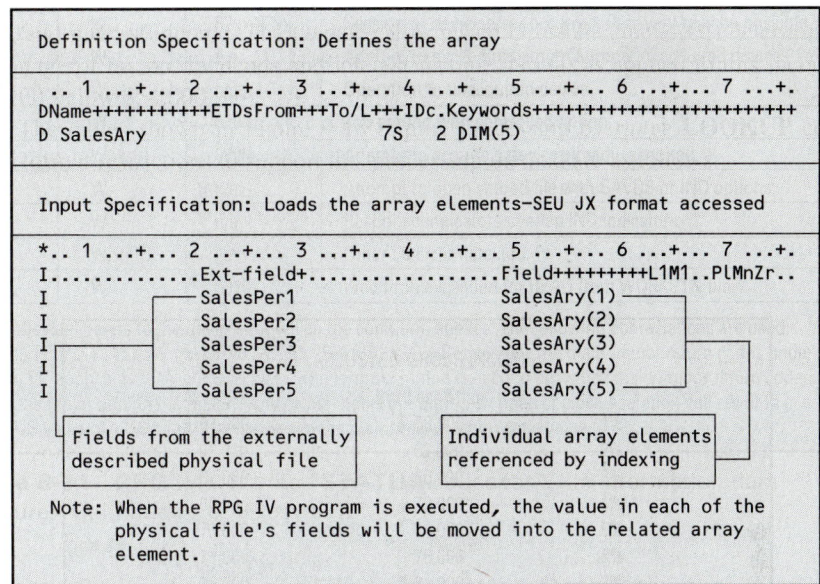

Figure 10-11 Loading a run-time array with *Input Specification* instructions.

SalesAry array is defined in a *Definition Specification* instruction and the fields from the physical file are specified in the *External field* name field (positions 21–30) in the *Input Specifications*. The five fields from the physical file are "redefined" as array elements in the *Field name* field (positions 49–62) by **indexing.**

Individual array elements are referenced by indexing, which is specified by entering a left parenthesis after the array name, followed by a related digit or integer variable, and closed by a right parenthesis. Note that the syntax for an **index** is an *extension* to the array name. Consequently, with indexing, the array name may be defined with a maximum of 10 characters plus the parentheses and the index.

Run-Time Array (Loaded in *Input Specifications*): Data Stored in a One Field in the Records of an Externally Described Physical File

The coding example in Figure 10-12 illustrates how a run-time array is loaded when the data for all of the elements is stored in *one* field in the records of an externally described

```
.. 1 ...+... 2 ...+... 3 ...+... 4 ...+... 5 ...+... 6 ...+... 7 ...+... 8
DName+++++++++++ETDsFrom+++To/L+++IDc.Keywords++++++++++++++++++++++++++++
 *
D                DS
D SalesAry                       7S   2 DIM(5)      Array defined in a data
D  SalesAmts              7     41A   2             structure

   Field from the physical file defined as
   character (A in position 40)
```

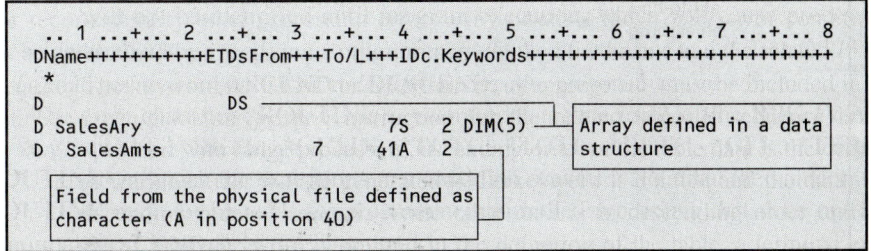

Figure 10-12 Run-time array loaded from one contiguous field in an externally described physical file.

physical file. Note that SalesAmt is a field from the file and the *From* and *To* (i.e., positions 7–41) field entries define the location of the contiguous array data in the body of the records.

Run-Time Array Loaded in Calculations

Run-time arrays may be loaded in calculation instructions by an arithmetic operation and **EVAL, Z-ADD, Z-SUB, MOVE, MOVEL,** and **MOVEA** (discussed later) instructions. The syntax is identical to **run-time** arrays loaded from *Definition* or *Input* instructions in that the **PERRCD** keyword is not used. Figure 10-13 details the syntax for loading a run-time array in calculations from another run-time array that is loaded from *Input* instructions.

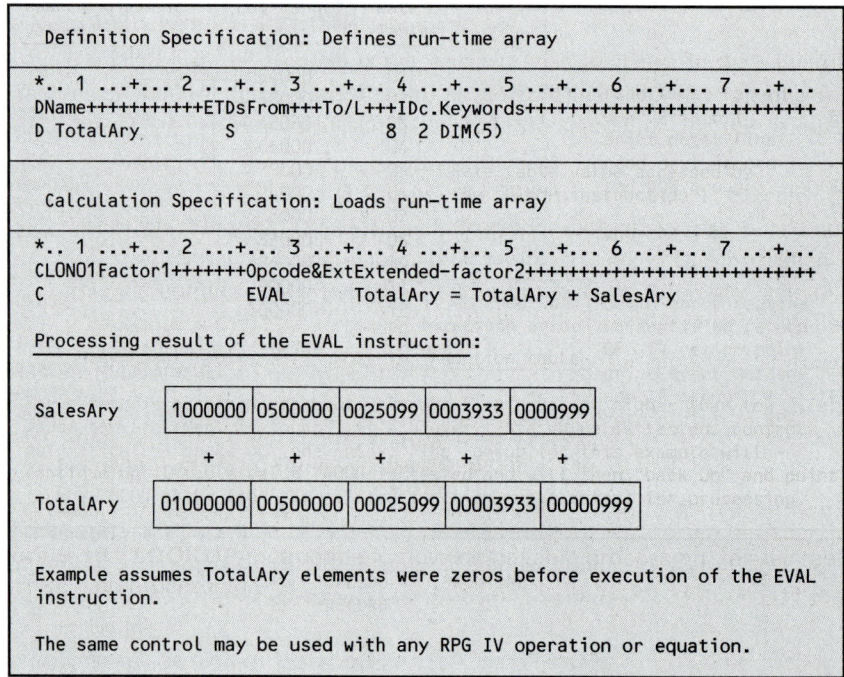

Definition Specification: Defines run-time array

```
*.. 1 ...+... 2 ...+... 3 ...+... 4 ...+... 5 ...+... 6 ...+... 7 ...+...
DName+++++++++++ETDsFrom+++To/L+++IDc.Keywords+++++++++++++++++++++++++++++
D TotalAry        S               8  2 DIM(5)
```

Calculation Specification: Loads run-time array

```
*.. 1 ...+... 2 ...+... 3 ...+... 4 ...+... 5 ...+... 6 ...+... 7 ...+...
CL0N01Factor1+++++++Opcode&ExtExtended-factor2+++++++++++++++++++++++++++++
C                   EVAL      TotalAry = TotalAry + SalesAry
```

Processing result of the EVAL instruction:

SalesAry	1000000	0500000	0025099	0003933	0000999
	+	+	+	+	+
TotalAry	01000000	00500000	00025099	00003933	00000999

Example assumes TotalAry elements were zeros before execution of the EVAL instruction.

The same control may be used with any RPG IV operation or equation.

Figure 10-13 Run-time array loaded with a calculation instruction.

PROCESSING ARRAYS

The **RPG IV** syntax used to define all of the array types has been explained in the preceding subsections without any discussion of how the arrays are processed. Compile-, prerun-, or run-time arrays may be processed consecutively or randomly. All of the elements in an array may be accessed at one time, or individual elements may be randomly accessed, or the array may be consecutively processed.

Extracting select elements randomly from an array requires the use of indexes. Indexing and other processing methods are explained in the following text and program examples. The first application program illustrates the consecutive processing of two run-time arrays.

APPLICATION PROGRAM: SALESPERSON MONTHLY PERFORMANCE REPORT

Documentation

The specifications presented in Figure 10-14 explain the processing requirements for the first application program that generates a monthly sales performance report by salesperson.

PROGRAM SPECIFICATIONS — Page 1 of 1

Program Name: Performance Report — Program - ID: CH10-P1 — Written by: SM

Purpose: Salesperson monthly performance report — Approved by: CM

Input files: CH10P1

Output files: QSYSPRT

Processing Requirements:

Write an RPG IV program to generate a monthly performance report by salesperson.

Input to the program:

The externally defined monthly sales file (CH10P1) contains the sales transactions for the company's salespersons for one month of the current year. A supplemental record layout form details the format of the physical record.

Processing:

Define a run-time array that will be loaded in the *Input Specifications* from the data stored in the externally defined physical file. Also, define a second run-time array that will be loaded in calculations from the data loaded in the run-time input array.

For every record processed, cross-foot the five salesperson elements to accumulate the total sales for the week. Add the five salesperson amounts (loaded for each record read in the run-time input array) to the five elements in the run-time calculation array. At **LR** time, cross-foot the run-time calculation array for the total company's monthly sales.

Output:

Generate the report detailed in the attached printer spacing chart.

Figure 10-14 Specifications for the monthly sales performance report program that processes two run-time arrays.

The system flowchart in Figure 10-15 indicates that one physical file and one program-defined printer file are processed by the program.

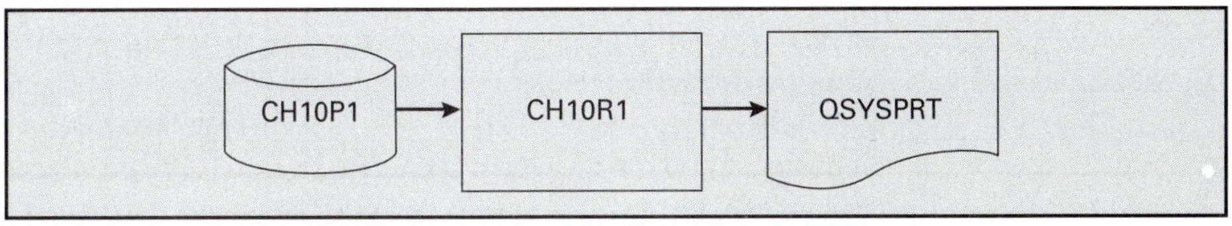

Figure 10-15 System flowchart for monthly sales performance report program.

Figure 10-16 details the physical file's record format. The five salesperson fields will be loaded into the five-element SalesAry array for each record processed.

```
                    PHYSICAL FILE DESCRIPTION

SYSTEM: AS/400                                  DATE:  6/1/97
FILE NAME: CH10P1                               REV NO: 0
RECORD NAME: CH10P1R                            KEY LENGTH: 6
SEQUENCE: Keyed (unique)                        RECORD SIZE: 24

                        FIELD DEFINITIONS

FIELD    FIELD NAME    SIZE  TYPE    POSITION      COMMENTS
 NO                                  FROM   TO

 1       WEEKENDING     6     P         1    4   Key field
 2       SALESPER1      7     P         5    8   2 decimals
 3       SALESPER2      7     P         9   12   2 decimals
 4       SALESPER3      7     P        13   16   2 decimals
 5       SALESPER4      7     P        17   20   2 decimals
 6       SALESPER5      7     P        21   24   2 decimals

Physical file data:

Week
Ending    Sales-      Sales-     Sales-     Sales-     Sales-
 Date     person 1    person 2   person 3   person 4   person 5

060497    0008000     0014530    0035140    0012400    0005224
061197    0054300     0057000    0580001    0058500    0063000
061897    0009000     0040000    0052500    0053500    0754000
062597    0050000     0045300    0012099    0085000    0086000
063097    0012000     0012300    0014000    0150800    0003000
```

Figure 10-16 Physical file record format and data listing for the monthly performance report program.

The design of the sales performance report and the listing generated by the **RPG IV** program are shown in Figure 10-17.

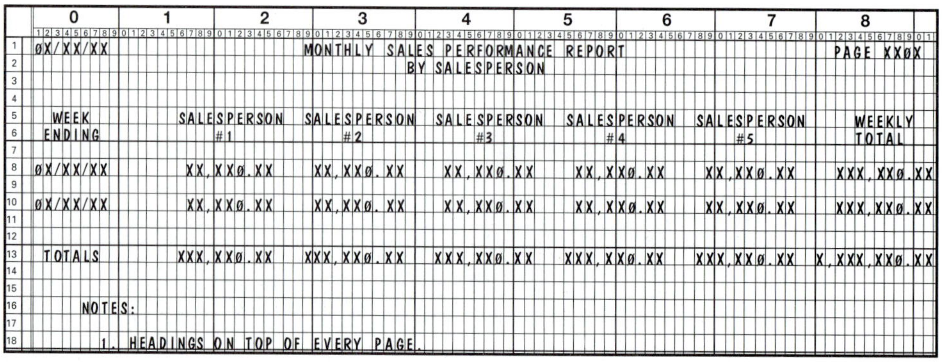

Figure 10-17 Report design and listing for the monthly sales performance report program.

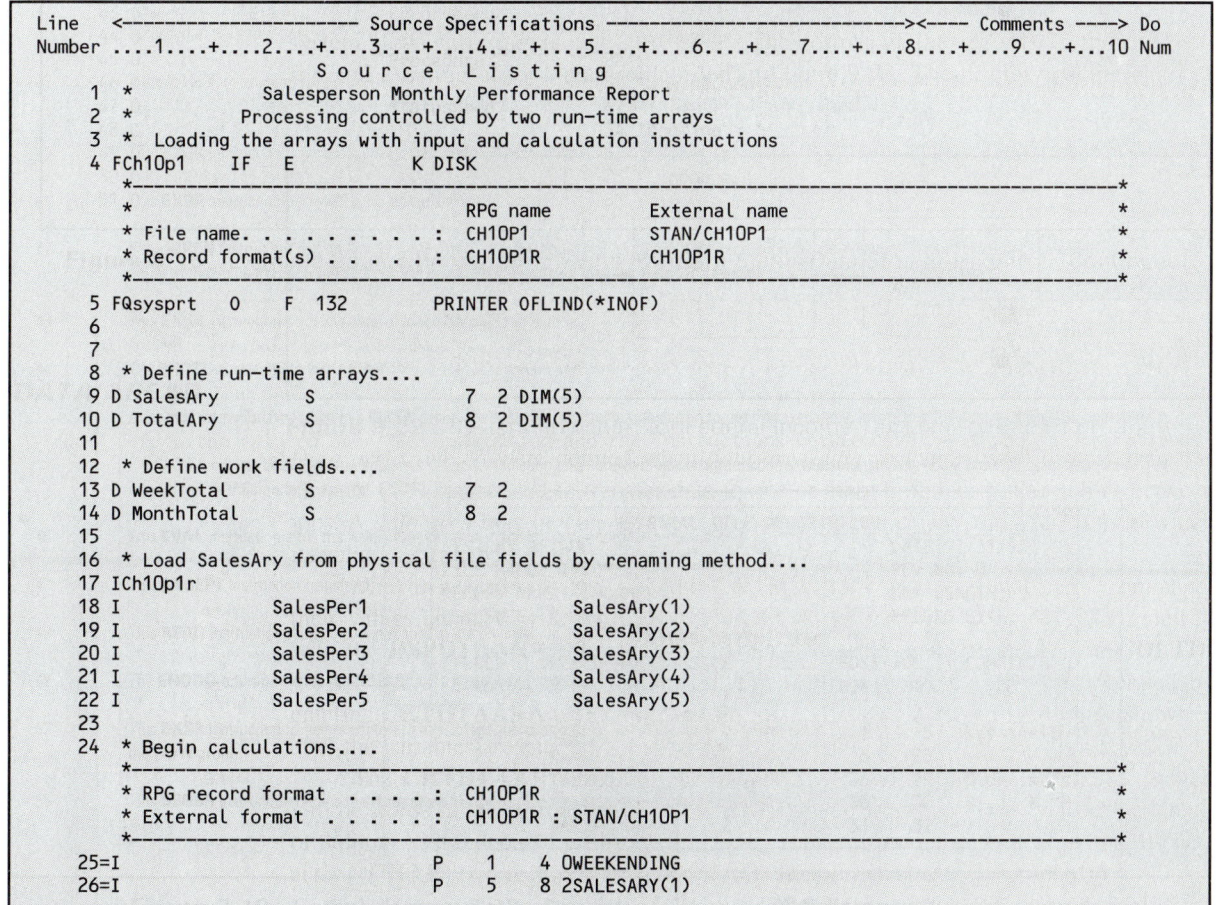

```
6/30/97                      MONTHLY SALES PERFORMANCE REPORT                  PAGE    1
                                      BY SALESPERSON
```

WEEK ENDING	SALESPERSON #1	SALESPERSON #2	SALESPERSON #3	SALESPERSON #4	SALESPERSON #5	WEEKLY TOTAL
6/04/97	80.00	145.30	351.40	124.00	52.24	752.94
6/11/97	543.00	570.00	5,800.01	585.00	630.00	8,128.01
6/18/97	90.00	400.00	525.00	535.00	7,540.00	9,090.00
6/25/97	500.00	453.00	120.99	850.00	860.00	2,783.99
6/31/97	120.00	123.00	140.00	1,508.00	30.00	1,921.00
TOTALS	1,333.00	1,691.30	6,937.40	3,602.00	9,112.24	22,675.94

Figure 10-17 Report design and listing for the monthly sales performance report program. (Continued)

RPG IV Syntax for the Monthly Sales Performance Report Program

A compile listing of the monthly sales performance report program presented in Figure 10-18 is supplemented with a line-by-line explanation of the instructions.

```
Line   <--------------------- Source Specifications ----------------------------><---- Comments ----> Do
Number ....1....+....2....+....3....+....4....+....5....+....6....+....7....+....8....+....9....+...10 Num
                       S o u r c e   L i s t i n g
     1  *            Salesperson Monthly Performance Report
     2  *          Processing controlled by two run-time arrays
     3  *  Loading the arrays with input and calculation instructions
     4 FCh10p1    IF   E             K DISK
        *------------------------------------------------------------------------------------------*
        *                               RPG name          External name                            *
        * File name. . . . . . . . :   CH10P1            STAN/CH10P1                              *
        * Record format(s) . . . . :   CH10P1R           CH10P1R                                  *
        *------------------------------------------------------------------------------------------*
     5 FQsysprt   O    F  132        PRINTER OFLIND(*INOF)
     6
     7
     8  * Define run-time arrays....
     9 D SalesAry        S              7  2 DIM(5)
    10 D TotalAry        S              8  2 DIM(5)
    11
    12  * Define work fields....
    13 D WeekTotal       S              7  2
    14 D MonthTotal      S              8  2
    15
    16  * Load SalesAry from physical file fields by renaming method....
    17 ICh10p1r
    18 I              SalesPer1                 SalesAry(1)
    19 I              SalesPer2                 SalesAry(2)
    20 I              SalesPer3                 SalesAry(3)
    21 I              SalesPer4                 SalesAry(4)
    22 I              SalesPer5                 SalesAry(5)
    23
    24  * Begin calculations....
        *------------------------------------------------------------------------------------------*
        * RPG record format  . . . . :  CH10P1R                                                    *
        * External format  . . . . . :  CH10P1R : STAN/CH10P1                                      *
        *------------------------------------------------------------------------------------------*
    25=I                            P    1    4 0WEEKENDING
    26=I                            P    5    8 2SALESARY(1)
```

Figure 10-18 Compile listing of the monthly sales performance program with line-by-line explanation.

```
27=I                          P    9   12 2SALESARY(2)
28=I                          P   13   16 2SALESARY(3)
29=I                          P   17   20 2SALESARY(4)
30=I                          P   21   24 2SALESARY(5)
31 C               EVAL       *INOF = *ON                                      turn on OF indicator
32 C               READ       Ch10p1                                 ----LR    read first record
33 C               DOW        *INLR = *OFF                                     dow LR is off        B01
34
35 C               IF         *INOF = *ON                                      OF on?               B02
36 C               EXCEPT     Heading                                          print heading lines   02
37 C               EVAL       *INOF = *OFF                                     turn off OF indicatr  02
38 C               ENDIF                                                       end IF group         E02
39
40 C               XFOOT      SalesAry      WeekTotal                          cross-foot array      01
41 C               EXCEPT     DetaiLine                                        Print DetaiLine       01
42 C               EVAL       TotalAry = TotalAry + SalesAry                   accumulate TotalAry   01
43 C               READ       Ch10p1                                 ----LR    read next record      01
44 C               ENDDO                                                       end DOW group        E01
45
46 C               XFOOT      TotalAry      MonthTotal                         crossfoot TotalAry
47 C               EXCEPT     TotaLine                                         print TotaLine
48
49   * Begin output....
50 OQsysprt  E          Heading        1 01
51 O                    UDATE        Y      8
52 O                                       40 'MONTHLY SALES'
53 O                                       59 'PERFORMANCE REPORT'
54 O                                       85 'PAGE'
55 O                    PAGE                90
56 O         E          Heading        3
57 O                                       51 'BY SALESPERSON'
58 O         E          Heading        1
59 O                                        6 'WEEK'
60 O                                       39 'SALESPERSON  SALESPERSON'
61 O                                       65 'SALESPERSON  SALESPERSON'
62 O                                       89 'SALESPERSON     WEEKLY'
63 O         E          Heading        2
64 O                                        7 'ENDING'
65 O                                       34 '#1            #2'
66 O                                       60 '#3            #4'
67 O                                       88 '#5          TOTAL'
68 O         E          DetaiLine      2
69 O                    WeekEnding   Y      8
70 O                    SalesAry            81 '  ,  0.  &&&&'
71 O                    WeekTotal     1     91
72 O         E          TotaLine    1
73 O                                        7 'TOTALS'
74 O                    TotalAry            80 '   ,  0.  &&&'
75 O                    MonthTotal    1     91
```

File Description Specifications

Line No.

4 Ch10p1 is defined as an input, full-procedural, externally described, keyed physical file.

5 QSYSPRT is defined as an output, program-described printer file. The page overflow indicator **OF** is assigned to the file by the **OFLIND(*INOF)** keyword.

Definition Specifications

9 The SalesAry is defined as a standalone array (**S** in position 24) with 5 elements – **DIM(5)** – each 7 digits long with 2 decimal positions.

10 The TotalAry is defined as a standalone array (**S** in position 24) with 5 elements – **DIM(5)** – each 8 digits long with 2 decimal positions.

13–14 WeekTotal and MonthTotal are defined as standalone fields that are used as work fields in calculation instructions.

Input Specifications

17 The record format name, Ch10p1r, from the physical file Ch10p1 is specified to access the values from the fields SalesPer1 through SalesPer5.

18–22 The physical file fields SalesPer1 through SalesPer5, entered in the *External field name* field (positions 21–30), are "redfined" as elements of the SalesAry array by the SalesAry(1) through SalesAry(5) entries in the *Field name* field (positions 49–62). Note that the (1) through (5) characters supplementing the five SalesAry name entries access the related element in the array by indexing.

Figure 10-18 Compile listing of the monthly sales performance program with line-by-line explanation. (Continued)

Calculation Specifications

31 This **EVAL** instruction turns on the **OF** overflow indicator so that the **IF** instruction test on line 35 will be "true," will execute the **EXCEPT** instruction on line 36, and will print the Heading lines before any DetailLine lines are printed.

32 This **READ** instruction reads the first record from the Ch10p1 physical file. If no records are stored in the file, **LR** will be set on.

33 The **DOW** instruction tests the status of the **LR** indicator. If it is not on, another iteration of the **DOW** group will be performed. If **LR** is on, program control will branch to line 46, "cross-foot" the TotalAry array, print the TotalLine record format, and end the program.

35–36 This **IF** instruction tests the status of the **OF** indicator. Because the **OF** indicator was turned on on line 31, the test will be "true." The **EXCEPT** instruction on line 36 will be executed and the Heading line record formats printed.

37 This **EVAL** instruction turns off the **OF** indicator so that page overflow will not occur for each record processed. Subsequent page overflow will occur automatically when the page overflow line is sensed and **OF** is turned on.

38 The **ENDIF** operation ends the **IF** group.

40 This **XFOOT** instruction "cross-foots" (adds) the values in the five elements in the SalesAry array and stores the sum in the work field WeekTotal.

41 This **EXCEPT** instruction controls the printing of the DetailLine record format.

42 This **EVAL** instruction adds the values in the five elements of the SalesAry array to the five elements in the TotalAry array.

43 This **READ** instruction reads the next record from the physical file. If end of file is read, the **LR** indicator will be turned on.

44 The **ENDDO** operation ends the **DOW** group.

46 The **XFOOT** instruction "cross-foots" (adds) the values in the five elements in the TotalAry array and stores the sum in the work field MonthTotal.

47 This **EXCEPT** instruction prints the TotaLine record format.

Note: The instructions on lines 46 and 47 are executed after end of file is read and exit from the **DOW** group occurs.

Output Specifications

50–67 The Heading record formats, defined in these instructions, are printed by the **EXCEPT** instruction on line 36.

68–71 The DetailLine record format, defined in these instructions, is printed by the **EXCEPT** instruction on line 41.

72–75 The TotaLine record format, defined in these instructions, is printed by the **EXCEPT** instruction on line 47.

Figure 10-18 Compile listing of the monthly sales performance program with line-by-line explanation. (Continued)

THE XFOOT *OPERATION*

The syntax of the **XFOOT** operation, used on lines 40 and 46 of the application program in Figure 10-18, is detailed in Figure 10-19.

```
*.. 1 ...+... 2 ...+... 3 ...+... 4 ...+... 5 ...+... 6 ...+... 7 ...+.
CLON01Factor1+++++++Opcode&ExtFactor2+++++++Result++++++++Len++D+HiLoEq

C  1        2       XFOOT           4           5           6      7
                     3
```

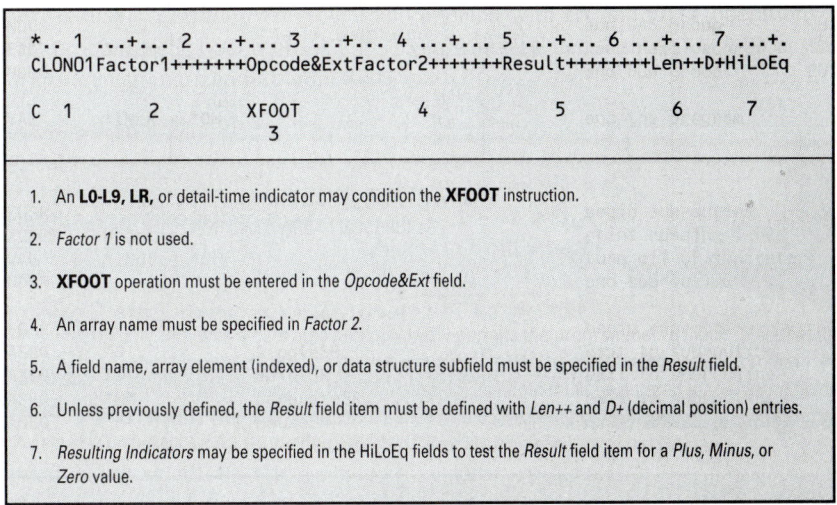

1. An **L0-L9, LR,** or detail-time indicator may condition the **XFOOT** instruction.
2. *Factor 1* is not used.
3. **XFOOT** operation must be entered in the *Opcode&Ext* field.
4. An array name must be specified in *Factor 2.*
5. A field name, array element (indexed), or data structure subfield must be specified in the *Result* field.
6. Unless previously defined, the *Result* field item must be defined with *Len++* and *D+* (decimal position) entries.
7. *Resulting Indicators* may be specified in the HiLoEq fields to test the *Result* field item for a *Plus, Minus,* or *Zero* value.

Figure 10-19 Syntax of the **XFOOT** operation.

The processing result of the **XFOOT** instruction on line 40 of the program in Figure 10-18 is detailed in Figure 10-20.

```
*.. 1 ...+... 2 ...+... 3 ...+... 4 ...+... 5 ...+... 6 ...+... 7 ...+.
CL0N01Factor1+++++++Opcode&ExtFactor2+++++++Result++++++++Len++D+HiLoEq

C                   XFOOT     SalesAry       WeekTotal

Result after first record is processed:
                                                 WeekTotal
                    SalesAry values                value

0008000 + 0014530 + 0035140 + 0012400 + 0005224 = 0075294
```

Figure 10-20 Processing result of the **XFOOT** instruction on line 40 of the salesperson monthly performance report program in Figure 10-18.

SEPARATION AND EDITING OF ARRAY ELEMENTS FOR PRINTING OR DISPLAY

The following two considerations must be given to the printing or display of arrays:

1. Separation of the elements
2. Spacing and editing requirements for each element

Numeric array elements may be separated and edited by edit words, edit codes, or indexing. The separation of character arrays into individual elements is controlled only by indexing. Each of these separation and editing functions is discussed in the following subsections.

Editing Numeric Arrays with Edit Words

The syntax to edit the SalesAry array using an edit word and the processing results are shown in the output instruction in Figure 10-21. (For a review of the syntax for edit words, refer to Chapter 4, pages 74–75.)

```
*.. 1 ...+... 2 ...+... 3 ...+... 4 ...+... 5 ...+... 6 ...+... 7 ...+... 8
O.............N01N02N03Field+++++++++YB.End++PConstant/editword/DTformat++
O                       SalesAry          81 '  ,  0.  &&&&'

Storage value in the SalesAry (first record processed):    End position is four
                                                            spaces after the
00080000014530003514000124000005224                         last array element

Result of processing the SalesAry with an edit word:

     80.00       145.30       351.40       124.00       52.24

Note: Because of zero suppression, more than four spaces are included between
      the elements.
```

Figure 10-21 Output instruction for editing a numeric array using an edit word and the printed result.

Editing of Numeric Arrays with Edit Codes

Editing numeric arrays with edit codes is less flexible than doing so with edit words because only *two* spaces are provided between the array elements. Figure 10-22 shows the syntax and result of using an edit code to separate and edit the elements of the SalesAry array. Edit code 1 is used in the example; however, any of the other edit codes may be used to edit a numeric array for printing or display.

```
*.. 1 ...+... 2 ...+... 3 ...+... 4 ...+... 5 ...+... 6 ...+... 7 ...+... 8
O.............N01N02N03Field+++++++++YB.End++PConstant/editword/DTformat++
O                       SalesAry      1     77

                                                    End position of the
                                                    last array element

Storage value in the SalesAry (first record processed):

000800000145300035140001240000005224

Result of processing the SalesAry with an edit code:

    80.00     145.30     351.40     124.00     52.24

Note: Because of zero suppression, more than two spaces are included between
      the elements.  The two spaces for an edit code are automatically inclu-
      ded before each element.
```

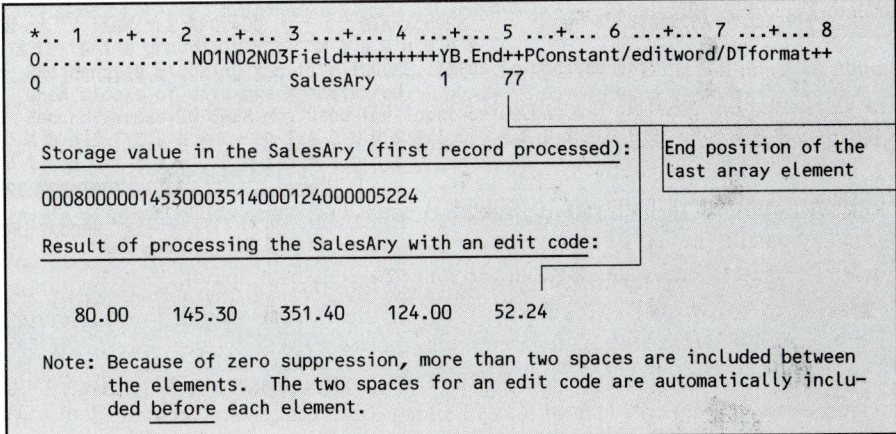

Figure 10-22 Output instruction for editing a numeric array using an edit code and the printed result.

Editing Numeric and Character Arrays by Indexing

The most flexibility in the separation and editing of arrays is provided by indexing. As mentioned, indexing is the method by which individual array elements are randomly accessed. An index may be a numeric literal, field, or data structure subfield. The index item must be enclosed in parentheses and immediately follow the last character of the array name as shown in Figure 10-23.

```
*.. 1 ...+... 2 ...+... 3 ...+... 4 ...+... 5 ...+... 6 ...+... 7 ...+... 8
O.............N01N02N03Field+++++++++YB.End++PConstant/editword/DTformat++
O                       SalesAry(1)   1     25
O                       SalesAry(2)   1     38
O                       SalesAry(3)   1     51
O                       SalesAry(4)   1     64      End position of each
O                       SalesAry(5)   1     77      array element

Storage value in the SalesAry (first record processed):

000800000145300035140001240000005224

Result of processing the SalesAry with indexing:

    80.00       145.30        351.40        124.00        52.24

Note: Each element is extracted separately by its related index (i.e. (1))
```

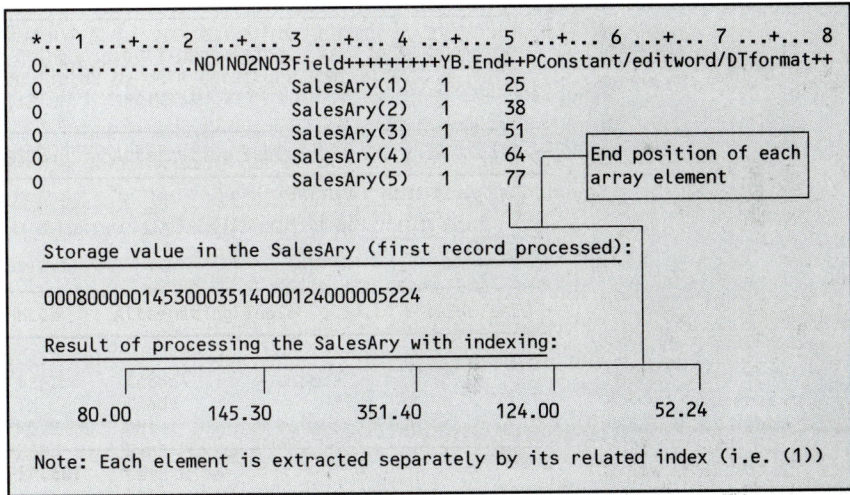

Figure 10-23 Output instruction for editing a numeric array using indexing and the printed result.

LOADING AN ARRAY FROM MORE THAN ONE INPUT RECORD

The data for loading an array may not always be conveniently stored on one data record, as the previous examples demonstrated. Instead, the data may be stored on separate records. For example, the input file listed in Figure 10-24 shows that the sales data for the

```
              SalesAmt
999999999999999
123456789111111
|-----| |-| 012345
      |
      |___ SalesPerNo
|_________ WeekEnding

Partial data file listing:

060497010008000 — first record in file
060497020014530
060497030035140
060497040012400
060497050005224
       .
       .
063097010012000
063097020012300
063097030014000
063097040150800
063097050003000 — last record in file
|     ||  |__|___ SalesAmt
|     ||_________ SalesPerNo
|_________________ WeekEnding
```

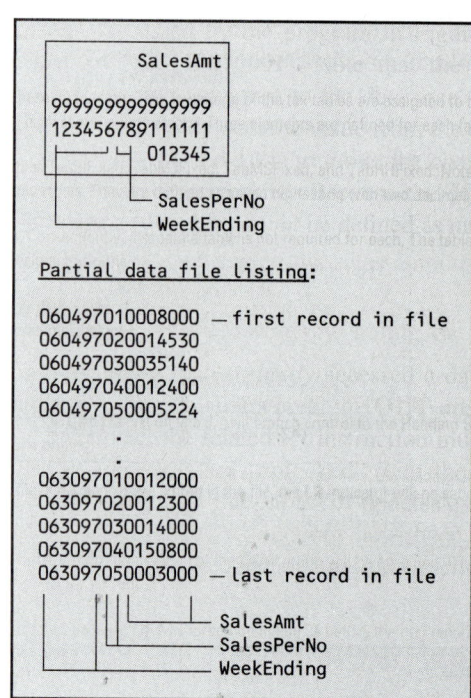

Figure 10-24 Modified record format and file listing of array data stored on separate records.

five salespersons for each week is stored on five records. Hence, the data for the entire month is now stored on 25 records instead of 5, as in the file processed by the previous program. Also, notice that the record format has been modified to include a salesperson number field. This addition is needed in the record format to determine which record belongs to which salesperson.

Furthermore, if the data in the physical file was not in the required week-ending date/salesperson number order, a logical file (or sort) would have to be created to access the data in the sequence required for the report. For this program example, the data is stored in an externally described physical file with WeekEnding (week-ending date) as the major key field and SalesPerNo (salesperson number) as the minor key field. A detailed compile listing of the modified program is presented in Figure 10-25.

The report generated by the **RPG IV** program in Figure 10-25 is identical to the one shown in Figure 10-17.

```
Line   <---------------------- Source Specifications ----------------------------><---- Comments ----> Do
Number ....1....+....2....+....3....+....4....+....5....+....6....+....7....+....8....+....9....+...10 Num
                         S o u r c e   L i s t i n g
     1 *              Salesperson Monthly Performance Report
     2 *            Processing controlled by two run-time arrays
     3 *              Array data stored on separate pf records
     4 FCh10p1x   IF   E           K DISK
       *--------------------------------------------------------------------------------------------*
       *                                  RPG name          External name                          *
       * File name. . . . . . . . :   CH10P1X           STAN/CH10P1X                            *
       * Record format(s) . . . . :   CH10P1XR          CH10P1XR                                *
       *--------------------------------------------------------------------------------------------*
     5 FQsysprt   O    F  132        PRINTER OFLIND(*INOF)
     6
     7
```

Figure 10-25 Compile listing of a salesperson monthly performance report program modified to process array data stored on separate records in a physical file.

```
  * Define run-time arrays....
 D SalesAry        S               7  2 DIM(5)
 D TotalAry        S               8  2 DIM(5)

  * Define work fields....
 D WeekTotal       S               7  2
 D MonthTotal      S               8  2
 D X               S               1  0

  * Begin calculations....
=ICH10P1XR
    *-------------------------------------------------------------------------------*
    * RPG record format  . . . . :  CH10P1XR                                        *
    * External format  . . . . . :  CH10P1XR : STAN/CH10P1X                        *
    *-------------------------------------------------------------------------------*
=I                                 P    1     4 0WEEKENDING
=I                                 P    5     6 0SALESPERNO
=I                                 P    7    10 2SALESAMT
 C                   EVAL      *INOF = *ON                                turn on OF indicator
 C                   READ      Ch10p1x                        ----LR      read first record
 C                   DOW       *INLR = *OFF                               dow LR is off         B01

 C                   IF        *INOF = *ON                                OF on?                B02
 C                   EXCEPT    Heading                                    print heading lines    02
 C                   EVAL      *INOF = *OFF                               turn off OF indicatr   02
 C                   ENDIF                                                end IF group          E02

  * Load array elements...
 C                   EVAL      X = X + 1                                  increment index        01
 C                   MOVE      SalesAmt      SalesAry(x)                                         01
 C                   IF        X = 5                                      array loaded?         B02
 C                   XFOOT     SalesAry      WeekTotal                    cross-foot array       02
 C                   EVAL      TotalAry = TotalAry + SalesAry             accumulate SalesAry    02
 C                   EXCEPT    DetailLine                                 Print DetailLine       02
 C                   EVAL      X = 0                                      initialize index       02
 C                   ENDIF                                                end IF group          E02

 C                   READ      Ch10p1x                        ----LR      read next record       01
 C                   ENDDO                                                end DOW group         E01

 C                   XFOOT     TotalAry      MonthTotal                   cross-foot TotalAry
 C                   EXCEPT    TotalLine                                  print TotalLine

  * Begin output....
 OQsysprt   E            Heading        1 01
 O                       UDATE         Y     8
 O                                          40 'MONTHLY SALES'
 O                                          59 'PERFORMANCE REPORT'
 O                                          85 'PAGE'
 O                       PAGE               90
 O          E            Heading        3
 O                                          51 'BY SALESPERSON'
 O          E            Heading        1
 O                                           6 'WEEK'
 O                                          39 'SALESPERSON  SALESPERSON'
 O                                          65 'SALESPERSON  SALESPERSON'
 O                                          89 'SALESPERSON     WEEKLY'
 O          E            Heading        2
 O                                           7 'ENDING'
 O                                          34 '#1                #2'
 O                                          60 '#3                #4'
 O                                          88 '#5              TOTAL'
 O          E            DetailLine     2
 O                       WeekEnding    Y     8
 O                       SalesAry           81 '  ,  0.  &&&&'
 O                       WeekTotal     1    91
 O          E            TotalLine     1
 O                                           7 'TOTALS'
 O                       TotalAry           80 '  ,  0.  &&&'
 O                       MonthTotal    1    91
```

Figure 10-25 Compile listing of a salesperson monthly performance report program modified to process array data stored on separate records in a physical file. (Continued)

File Description Specifications

Line No.

4 Ch10p1x is defined as an input, full-procedural, externally described, keyed physical file.

5 QSYSPRT is defined as an output, program-described printer file. The page overflow indicator **OF** is assigned to the file by the **OFLIND(*INOF)** keyword.

Definition Specifications

9 The SalesAry is defined as a standalone array (**S** in position 24) with 5 elements – **DIM(5)** – each 7 digits long with 2 decimal positions.

10 The TotalAry is defined as a standalone array (**S** in position 24) with 5 elements – **DIM(5)** – each 8 digits long with 2 decimal positions.

13–15 WeekTotal, MonthTotal, and X are defined as standalone fields that are used as work fields in calculation instructions. X is used as the index to load the physical file field value to the related array element (see line 33).

Calculation Specifications

22 This **EVAL** instruction turns on the **OF** indicator so that the **IF** instruction test on line 26 will be "true," will execute the **EXCEPT** instruction on line 27, and will print the Heading lines before any DetailLine lines are printed.

23 This **READ** instruction reads the first record from the Ch10p1x physical file. If no records are stored in the file, **LR** will be set on.

24 The **DOW** instruction tests the status of the **LR** indicator. If it is not on, another iteration of the **DOW** group will be performed. If **LR** is on, program control will branch to line 46, "cross-foot" the TotalAry array, print the TotaLine record format, and end the program.

26–27 This **IF** instruction tests the status of the **OF** indicator. Because the **OF** indicator was turned on on line 22, the test will be "true." The **EXCEPT** instruction on line 27 will be executed and the Heading line record formats printed.

28 This **EVAL** instruction turns off the **OF** indicator so that page overflow will not occur for each record processed. Subsequent page overflow will occur automatically when the page overflow line is sensed and **OF** is turned on.

29 The **ENDIF** operation ends the **IF** group that began on line 26.

32 This **EVAL** instruction increments field X, which is used as the SalesAry array index on line 33.

33 The **MOVE** instruction moves the value in the physical file field to the related SalesAry element. For the first record processed, the value of X will be 1. Consequently, the first element of the SalesAry array will be loaded.

34 This **IF** instruction tests the value of the X. If it is 5, indicating that the 5 elements have been loaded from 5 records from the physical file, the instructions within the **IF** group will be processed.

35 This **XFOOT** instruction "cross-foots" (adds) the values in the five elements in the SalesAry array and stores the sum in the work field WeekTotal.

36 This **EVAL** instruction adds the values in the five elements of the SalesAry array to the five elements in the TotalAry array.

37 This **EXCEPT** instruction controls the printing of the DetailLine record format.

38 This **EVAL** instruction initializes field X (used as the index) to zero, so that the next five records from the physical file will load the SalesAry, beginning with the first element. If the index was not initialized, a run-time error would occur, indicating that the index was "out of range." Note that the SalesAry was defined to store five elements (i.e., DIM(5)). Any index value greater than 5 will cause a severe run-time error.

39 This **ENDIF** operation ends the **IF** group that began on line 34.

41 This **READ** instruction reads the next record from the physical file. If end of file is read, the **LR** indicator will be turned on.

42 The **ENDDO** operation ends the **DOW** group.

44 The **XFOOT** instruction "cross-foots" (adds) the values in the five elements in the TotalAry array and stores the sum in the work field MonthTotal.

45 This **EXCEPT** instruction prints the TotaLine record format.

Note: The instructions on line 46 and 47 are executed after end of file is read and exit from the **DOW** group occurs.

Output Specifications

48–65 The Heading record formats, defined in these instructions, are printed by the **EXCEPT** instruction on line 27.

66–69 The DetailLine record format, defined in these instructions, is printed by the **EXCEPT** instruction on line 37.

70–73 The TotaLine record format, defined in these instructions, is printed by the **EXCEPT** instruction on line 45.

Figure 10-25 Compile listing of a salesperson monthly performance report program modified to process array data stored on separate records in a physical file. (Continued)

RANDOM PROCESSING OF ARRAYS

Similar to tables, the access to individual array elements may be controlled by the **LOOKUP** operation. However, array and table "lookup" processing differ greatly, as Figure 10-26 indicates.

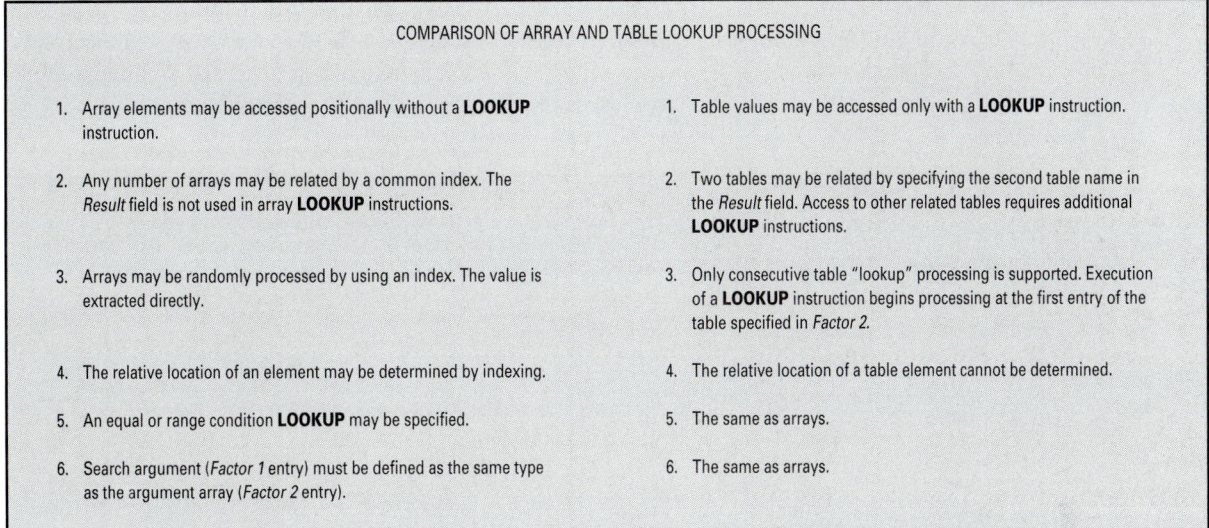

COMPARISON OF ARRAY AND TABLE LOOKUP PROCESSING

Array	Table
1. Array elements may be accessed positionally without a **LOOKUP** instruction.	1. Table values may be accessed only with a **LOOKUP** instruction.
2. Any number of arrays may be related by a common index. The *Result* field is not used in array **LOOKUP** instructions.	2. Two tables may be related by specifying the second table name in the *Result* field. Access to other related tables requires additional **LOOKUP** instructions.
3. Arrays may be randomly processed by using an index. The value is extracted directly.	3. Only consecutive table "lookup" processing is supported. Execution of a **LOOKUP** instruction begins processing at the first entry of the table specified in *Factor 2.*
4. The relative location of an element may be determined by indexing.	4. The relative location of a table element cannot be determined.
5. An equal or range condition **LOOKUP** may be specified.	5. The same as arrays.
6. Search argument (*Factor 1* entry) must be defined as the same type as the argument array (*Factor 2* entry).	6. The same as arrays.

Figure 10-26 Comparison of array and table **LOOKUP** processing.

Array Lookup Without Indexing

An array is processed without using an index when an element value does not have to be extracted after it is found. Checking a transaction code from an input record by searching a compile-time array of valid codes is one example of an array lookup that does not require indexing. Figure 10-27 details the syntax and processing logic of this type of array lookup.

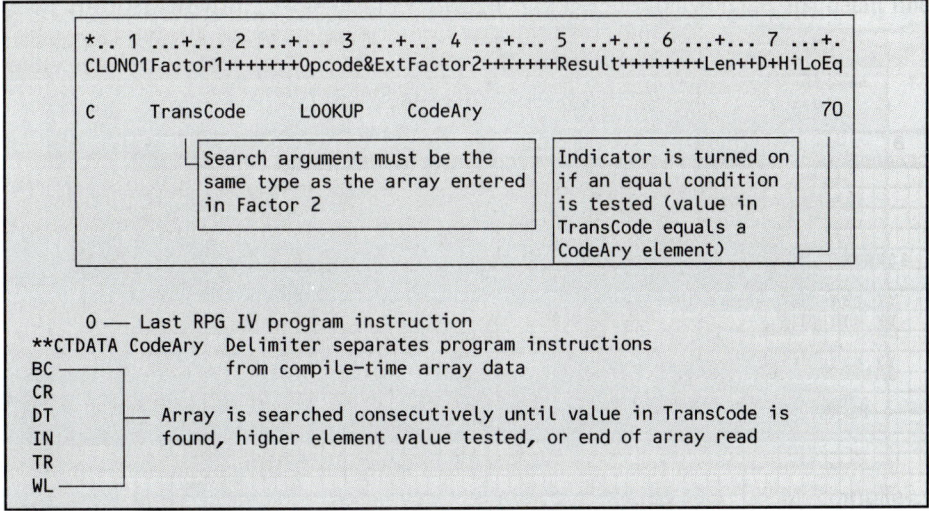

```
*.. 1 ...+... 2 ...+... 3 ...+... 4 ...+... 5 ...+... 6 ...+... 7 ...+.
CLON01Factor1+++++++Opcode&ExtFactor2+++++++Result++++++++Len++D+HiLoEq

C     TransCode      LOOKUP    CodeAry                                70

        Search argument must be the      Indicator is turned on
        same type as the array entered   if an equal condition
        in Factor 2                      is tested (value in
                                         TransCode equals a
                                         CodeAry element)

  0 —— Last RPG IV program instruction
**CTDATA CodeAry  Delimiter separates program instructions
BC                from compile-time array data
CR
DT         —— Array is searched consecutively until value in TransCode is
IN            found, higher element value tested, or end of array read
TR
WL
```

Figure 10-27 Syntax and processing logic of array **LOOKUP** without indexing.

Array Lookup by Indexing

*Processing Without a **LOOKUP** Instruction.* Indexing must be used in an array lookup if an element value is to be extracted and used in subsequent processing. Access of an element is controlled by indexing with or without the **LOOKUP** operation. An example of processing an array by the relative location (position) of the elements (no **LOOKUP** instruction) is shown in Figure 10-28. A month name is accessed by specifying the array and index names (i.e., **MthName(MM)**). The example assumes that the array is defined in the *Definition Specifications* and the MM index is defined as a data structure subfield. Note that access of the array is with an output instruction; however, any definition, input, or calculation instruction may access any array positionally with an index.

Value in MM index: 08

```
*.. 1 ...+... 2 ...+... 3 ...+... 4 ...+... 5 ...+... 6 ...+... 7 ...+... 8
O..............N01N02N03Field+++++++++YB.End++PConstant/editword/DTformat++
O                               MthName(MM)        70

**CTDATA MthName
JANUARY
FEBRUARY
MARCH
APRIL
MAY
JUNE
JULY
AUGUST
SEPTEMBER
OCTOBER
NOVEMBER
DECEMBER
```

Based on the value in the MM index, element value is extracted directly (positionally) without a consecutive search of the array

Figure 10-28 Syntax and processing logic to access an array element positionally with an index.

*Processing an Array with the **LOOKUP** Instruction.* Processing an array by indexing *with* the **LOOKUP** operation is used to extract an element when its position in the array is not known or to relate the values from two or more arrays. Recall that in table lookup, a *function table* name may be entered in the *Result* field, and its value is automatically extracted with a successful *argument table* **LOOKUP.** Array **LOOKUP** does not support this processing feature (refer to Figure 10-26). Any relationship between the arrays must be controlled by a common index. The processing logic unique to array **LOOKUP** processing is summarized in Figure 10-29.

ARRAY LOOKUP OPERATION WITH INDEXING

1. Index must be defined as a numeric integer.
2. Index must be initialized before the **LOOKUP** instruction is executed.
3. Search of the array begins at the element specified in the value in the index.
4. End-of-array control is automatically provided.
5. An array element found is not retained from the **LOOKUP** but may be accessed by specifying the array name and index name (enclosed in parentheses) after the **LOOKUP** condition is satisfied.

Figure 10-29 Array **LOOKUP** operation with index processing features.

Figure 10-30 contains the syntax and control for processing two related arrays by the **LOOKUP** operation with indexing. Item numbers are stored in the ItemNumber array and the related item name in the ItemName array; both are defined as compile-time arrays.

```
    Value in ItemNo = 180

    *.. 1 ...+... 2 ...+... 3 ...+... 4 ...+... 5 ...+... 6 ...+... 7 ...+.
    CLON01Factor1+++++++Opcode&ExtFactor2+++++++Result++++++++Len++D+HiLoEq
                        EVAL      X = 0
    C     ItemNo        LOOKUP    ItemNumber(X)                          60
    C                   IF        *IN60 = *ON
    C                   MOVE      ItemName(X)   NameOfItem
    C                   ENDIF
               .....last program instruction....

 **CTDATA ItemNumber   Index value
 100COCA COLA              01
 110PEPSI COLA             02
 1207 UP                   03
 130SPRITE                 04
 140TAB                    05
 150PEPSI LITE             06
 160DIET COKE              07
 170SLICE APPLE            08
 180SLICE                  09    Index is incremented automatically without
 190DR PEPPER                    a programmer-supplied counter
 200HIRES ROOT BEER
```

Figure 10-30 Syntax and logic for processing two related arrays with the **LOOKUP** operation and index control.

The MOVEA (*Move Array*) Operation

The **MOVEA** operation transfers character, graphic, or numeric values from the *Factor 2* item to the *Result* field item. Either or both the *Factor 2* and/or *Result* field item(s) must contain an array name with or without indexing. The syntax of the **MOVEA** operation is described in Figure 10-31.

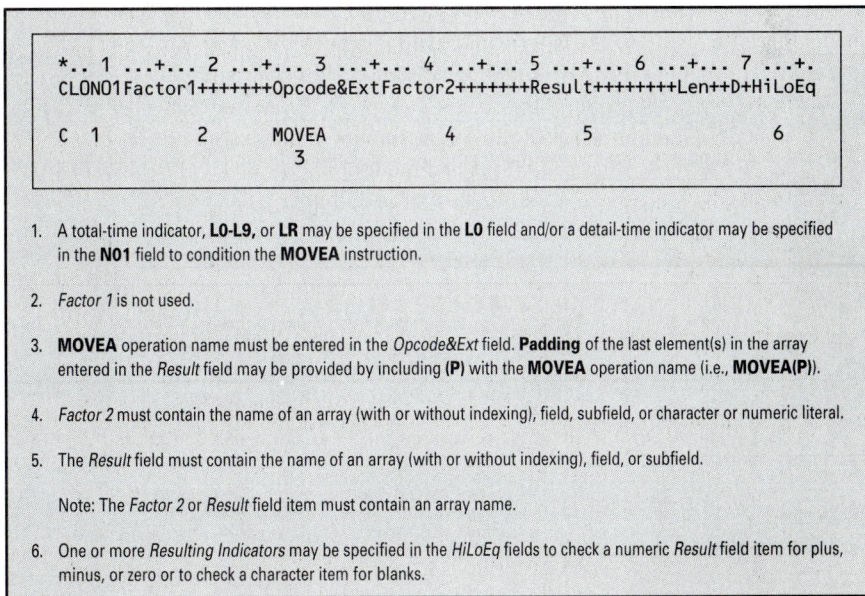

```
*.. 1 ...+... 2 ...+... 3 ...+... 4 ...+... 5 ...+... 6 ...+... 7 ...+.
CLON01Factor1+++++++Opcode&ExtFactor2+++++++Result++++++++Len++D+HiLoEq

C 1           2       MOVEA        4            5              6
                        3
```

1. A total-time indicator, **L0-L9,** or **LR** may be specified in the **LO** field and/or a detail-time indicator may be specified in the **N01** field to condition the **MOVEA** instruction.
2. *Factor 1* is not used.
3. **MOVEA** operation name must be entered in the *Opcode&Ext* field. **Padding** of the last element(s) in the array entered in the *Result* field may be provided by including **(P)** with the **MOVEA** operation name (i.e., **MOVEA(P)**).
4. *Factor 2* must contain the name of an array (with or without indexing), field, subfield, or character or numeric literal.
5. The *Result* field must contain the name of an array (with or without indexing), field, or subfield.

   Note: The *Factor 2* or *Result* field item must contain an array name.
6. One or more *Resulting Indicators* may be specified in the *HiLoEq* fields to check a numeric *Result* field item for plus, minus, or zero or to check a character item for blanks.

Figure 10-31 Syntax and processing logic of the **MOVEA** *(Move Array)* operation.

Processing Logic:

* Character, graphic, or numeric values are transferred from the *Factor 2* item to the *Result* field item.
* If an array name is specified in *Factor 2* and it is not indexed, movement of the data starts with the first element in the array and continues until all elements in the array have been moved or the *Result* field item is filled.
* If an array name is specified in *Factor 2* and it is indexed, movement of the data starts with the element specified by the index and continues until all elements in the array have been moved or the *Result* field item is filled.
* If a field name is specified in *Factor 2*, movement of the data starts with the first character in the field.
* If the *Result* field contains an array name or field, the data storage begins at the first position.
* If the *Result* field contains an indexed array, the data storage begins at the specified element.
* Decimal positions are ignored in the move. Consequently, there is no alignment of any decimal positions in the *Factor 2* or *Result* field items.
* The *figurative constants* ***BLANK, *ALL, *ON,** and ***OFF** may not be specified in *Factor 2*.

Figure 10-31 Syntax and processing logic of the **MOVEA** *(Move Array)* operation. (Continued)

Five examples of **MOVEA** operation instructions are shown in Figure 10-32.

Example 1:

```
*.. 1 ...+... 2 ...+... 3 ...+... 4 ...+... 5 ...+... 6 ...+... 7 ...+.
CLON01Factor1+++++++Opcode&ExtFactor2+++++++Result++++++++Len++D+HiLoEq

 * Array-to-array move.  No indexing specified, different-length arrays
 * with same element length (2 characters)....

C                   MOVEA     ARRAYA          ARRAYB

          ARRAYA      values before MOVEA        ARRAYB

      |AA|BB|CC|DD|                          |12|34|56|78|90|

          ARRAYA      values after MOVEA         ARRAYB

      |AA|BB|CC|DD|                          |AA|BB|CC|DD|90|

  Because ARRAYB is larger than ARRAYA, last element in ARRAYB
  is not replaced.
```

Example 2:

```
*.. 1 ...+... 2 ...+... 3 ...+... 4 ...+... 5 ...+... 6 ...+... 7 ...+.
CLON01Factor1+++++++Opcode&ExtFactor2+++++++Result++++++++Len++D+HiLoEq

 * Array-to-array move with an indexed array in the result field. Same-
 * length elements (2 characters)....

C                   MOVEA     ARRAYA          ARRAYB(4)

          ARRAYA      values before MOVEA        ARRAYB

      |AA|BB|CC|DD|                          |12|34|56|78|90|

          ARRAYA      values after MOVEA         ARRAYB

      |AA|BB|CC|DD|                          |12|34|56|AA|BB|

  Transfer ARRAYA elements beginning at the fourth element in ARRAYB
```

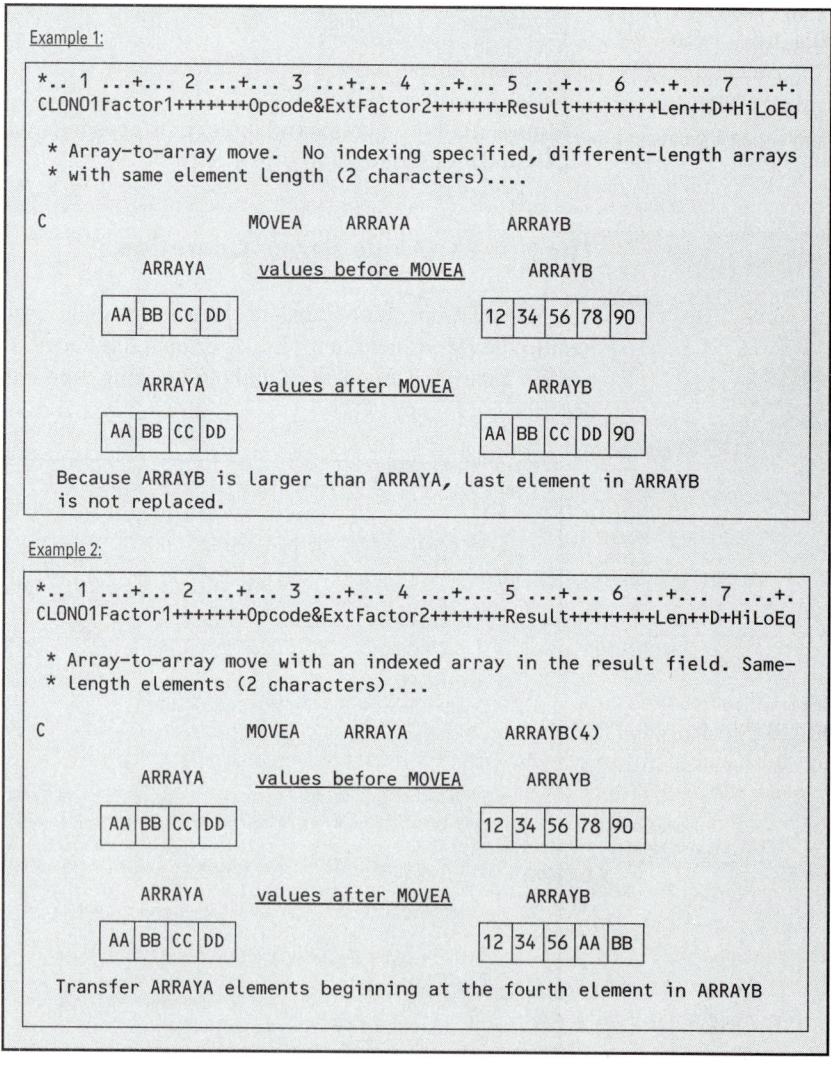

Figure 10-32 **MOVEA** instruction examples.

Example 3:

```
*.. 1 ...+... 2 ...+... 3 ...+... 4 ...+... 5 ...+... 6 ...+... 7 ...+.
CLON01Factor1+++++++Opcode&ExtFactor2+++++++Result++++++++Len++D+HiLoEq

 * Array-to-field move -- field smaller than the array....
C                   MOVEA     ARRAYA         FIELDX

         ARRAYA      values before MOVEA      FIELDX

       |AA|BB|CC|DD|                         |12|34|56|

         ARRAYA      values after MOVEA       FIELDX

       |AA|BB|CC|DD|                         |AA|BB|CC|

  Elements from the array begin loading a field at the first character
```

Example 4:

```
*.. 1 ...+... 2 ...+... 3 ...+... 4 ...+... 5 ...+... 6 ...+... 7 ...+.
CLON01Factor1+++++++Opcode&ExtFactor2+++++++Result++++++++Len++D+HiLoEq

 * Array-to-array move -- both numeric arrays with different decimal
 * positions defined....
C                   MOVEA     ARRAYC         ARRAYD

         ARRAYC      values before MOVEA       ARRAYD

       |1.0|2.0|3.0|                         |22.|33.|44.|

         ARRAYC      values after MOVEA        ARRAYD

       |1.0|2.0|3.0|                         |1.0|2.0|3.0|

  Decimal alignment is not performed with a MOVEA instruction
```

Example 5:

```
*.. 1 ...+... 2 ...+... 3 ...+... 4 ...+... 5 ...+... 6 ...+... 7 ...+.
CLON01Factor1+++++++Opcode&ExtFactor2+++++++Result++++++++Len++D+HiLoEq

 * Array-to-array move -- different-length numeric arrays with padding
 * specified....
C                   MOVEA(P) ARRAYE          ARRAYF

         ARRAYE      values before MOVEA         ARRAYF

       |1.0|2.0|3.0|                         |22.|33.|44.|55.|

         ARRAYC      values after MOVEA          ARRAYF

       |1.0|2.0|3.0|                         |1.0|2.0|3.0|0.0|

                     Last element padded with zeros ---------┘

 Note: A character array would be padded with blanks
```

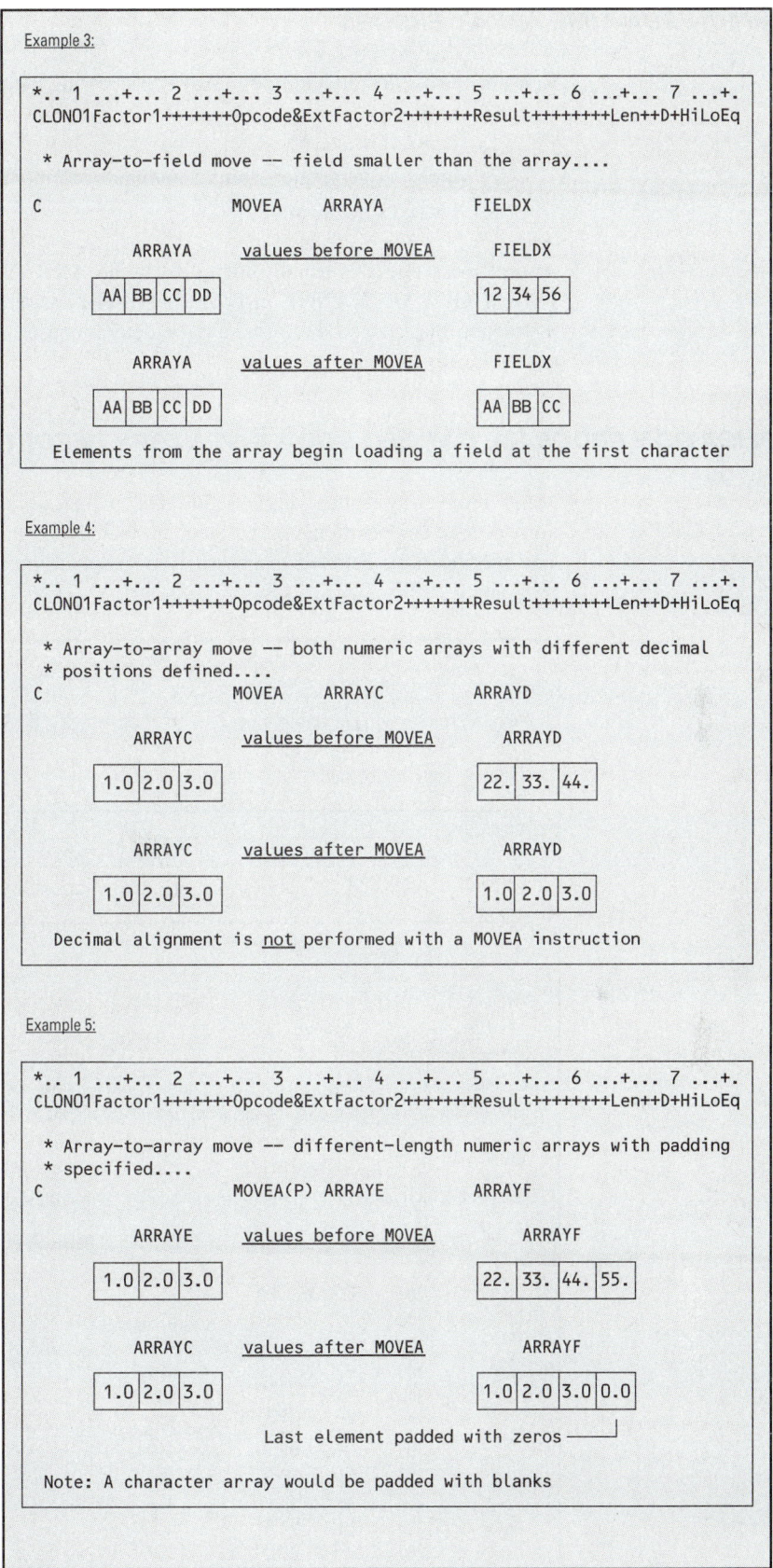

Figure 10-32 MOVEA instruction examples. (Continued)

COMMON RUN-TIME ARRAY ERRORS

Run-time errors that are common in array processing include the following:

1. Index value zero
2. Index value greater than the number of elements in the array
3. Index value negative

Any of these errors is usually identified by an **ARRAY INDEX ERROR** or **ARRAY INDEX OUT OF RANGE** error message. The specific error and the related program instruction that caused the error may be determined by several debugging methods discussed in Appendix E.

APPLICATION PROGRAM: CANNED SODA INVENTORY REPORT

Many of the array features discussed in this chapter, such as **LOOKUP**, indexing, related array access, and positional processing, are included in this **RPG IV** application program. The specifications detailed in Figure 10-33 explain the processing requirements for the program.

PROGRAM SPECIFICATIONS — Page 1 of 1

Program Name: Soda Inventory Report — Program - ID: CH10R3 — Written by: SM

Purpose: Generate a canned soda inventory report — Approved by: CM

Input files: CH10P3

Output files: QSYSPRT

Processing Requirements:

Write an RPG IV program to generate a canned soda inventory report.

Input to the program:

A canned soda inventory physical file includes a field for soda numbers and the related quantity of cans on hand. A supplemental layout form details the record format.

Table Data:

Include the following three compile-time array data in the program:

Item#	Description	Cost/Can (2 decimals)
100	COCA COLA	45
110	PEPSI COLA	47
120	7-UP	41
130	SPRITE	49
140	TAB	51
150	PEPSI LITE	50
160	DIET COKE	44
170	SLICE APPLE	48
180	SLICE	43
190	DR PEPPER	63
200	HIRES ROOT BEER	56

Figure 10-33 Specifications for the Canned Soda Inventory Report program.

Also include an error message array with the following value:

.. ITEM NOT FOUND ..

Processing:

Use the *ITEMNUMBER* field from the physical file's records as the search argument to look up (with indexing) the item number array. For a successful search, use the same index value to access the related values from the description and cost per can arrays. Then, multiply the input quantity (QTYONHAND) by the cost per can array value to determine the dollar amount on hand.

If an item number from the input record is not found in the item number array, print the error message in the location shown on the printer spacing chart.

Output:

Generate the report detailed in the attached printer spacing chart.

Figure 10-33 Specifications for the Canned Soda Inventory Report program. (Continued)

A system flowchart in Figure 10-34 indicates that the program processes one physical file to generate the Canned Soda Inventory Report.

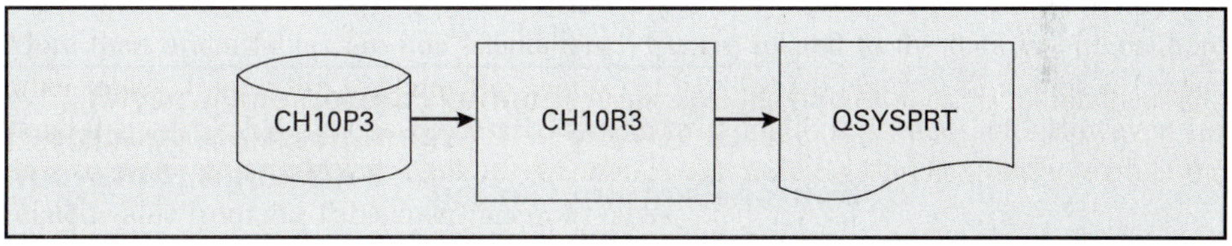

Figure 10-34 System flowchart for the Canned Soda Inventory Report program.

The format of the records in the physical file is presented in Figure 10-35 with a listing of the stored data.

```
                    PHYSICAL FILE DESCRIPTION

SYSTEM: AS/400                                 DATE: 8/19/97
FILE NAME: CH10P3                              REV NO: 0
RECORD NAME: CH10P3R                           KEY LENGTH: None
SEQUENCE: Nonkeyed                             RECORD SIZE: 6

                        FIELD DEFINITIONS

 FIELD    FIELD NAME   SIZE  TYPE    POSITION     COMMENTS
   NO                               FROM    TO

   1      ITEMNUMBER      3   C        1     3
   2      QTYONHAND       4   P        4     6  0 decimals
```

Physical file data:

Item Number	Qty On Hand
150	2400
210	0000
100	2000
200	0600
155	0000

Figure 10-35 Physical file record format and data file listing.

The design of the Canned Soda Inventory Report is detailed in the printer spacing chart in Figure 10-36 with a listing of the report generated by the program.

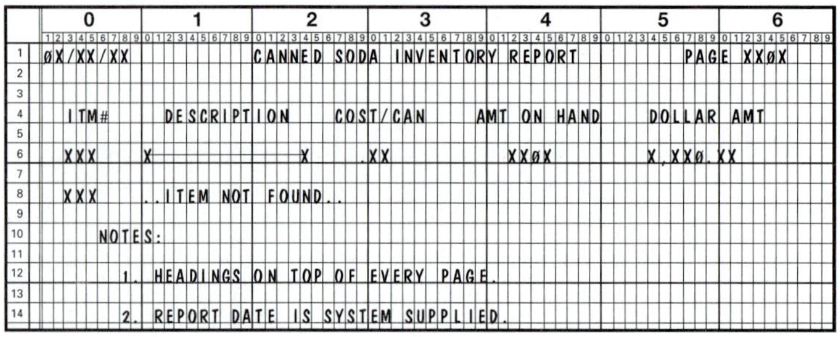

0 1 2 3 4 5 6
ØX/XX/XX CANNED SODA INVENTORY REPORT PAGE XXØX
ITM# DESCRIPTION COST/CAN AMT ON HAND DOLLAR AMT
XXX X X .XX XXØX X,XXØ.XX
XXX ..ITEM NOT FOUND..
NOTES:
1. HEADINGS ON TOP OF EVERY PAGE.
2. REPORT DATE IS SYSTEM SUPPLIED.


```
 8/30/97            CANNED SODA INVENTORY REPORT            PAGE    1

  ITEM#     DESCRIPTION      COST/CAN     AMT ON HAND     DOLLAR AMT

  150     PEPSI LITE       .50             2,400          1,200.00

  210     ..ITEM NOT FOUND..

  100     COCA COLA        .45             3,000          1,350.00

  200     HIRES ROOT BEER  .56               600            336.00

  155     ..ITEM NOT FOUND..
```

Figure 10-36 Design of the Canned Soda Inventory Report and printed report.

Source Program Coding

A compile listing of the Canned Soda Inventory Report program and a detailed line-by-line discussion of the instructions are presented in Figure 10-37.

```
Line   <---------------------- Source Specifications ----------------------------><---- Comments ----> Do
Number ....1....+....2....+....3....+....4....+....5....+....6....+....7....+....8....+....9....+...10 Num
                          S o u r c e   L i s t i n g
     1  *                      Canned Soup Inventory Report
     2  * Three related compile-time arrays are included: ItemNo, CostPerCan, and
     3  * Description.  A one-element ErrorMsg compile-time array is also defined
     4
     5 FCh10p3    IF   E             DISK
        *--------------------------------------------------------------------------------------------*
        *                             RPG name              External name                              *
        * File name. . . . . . . . :  CH10P3                STAN/CH10P3                                *
        * Record format(s) . . . . :  CH10P3R               CH10P3R                                    *
        *--------------------------------------------------------------------------------------------*
     6 FQsysprt   O    F  132        PRINTER OFLIND(*INOF)
     7
     8 D ItemNo          S              3    DIM(11) ASCEND CTDATA
     9 D Descrip         S             15    DIM(11) ALT(ItemNo)
    10 D CanCost         S              2  2 DIM(11) CTDATA PERRCD(11)
    11 D ErrorMsg        S             18    DIM(1) CTDATA
    12
    13  * Define work field & index....
    14 D TotalAmt        S              7  2
    15 D X               S              2  0
    16
    17=ICH10P3R
```

Figure 10-37 Compile listing of the Canned Soda Inventory Report program.

```
       *------------------------------------------------------------------------------------------------*
       * RPG record format  . . . . :  CH10P3R                                                          *
       * External format  . . . . . :  CH10P3R : STAN/CH10P3                                            *
       *------------------------------------------------------------------------------------------------*
    18=I                            A     1    3  ITEMNUMBER
    19=I                            P     4    6  OQTYONHAND
    20 C                  EVAL      *INOF = *ON                                 turn on OF indicator
    21 C                  READ      Ch10p3                           ----LR     read first record
    22
    23 C                  DOW       *INLR = *OFF                                dow LR is off         B01
    24 C                  EVAL      X = 1                                       initialize index       01
    25 C                  IF        *INOF = *ON                                 OF indicator on?      B02
    26 C                  EXCEPT    Heading                                     print heading lines    02
    27 C                  EVAL      *INOF = *OFF                                turn off OF indicatr   02
    28 C                  ENDIF                                                 end IF group          E02
    29
    30 C     ItemNumber   LOOKUP    ItemNo(X)                        ----50     look up array          01
    31 C                  IF        *IN50 = *ON                                 look up successful?   B02
    32 C                  EVAL      TotalAmt = QtyOnHand * CanCost(X)           compute total $ amt    02
    33 C                  EXCEPT    DetailLine                                  print detail line      02
    34 C                  ELSE                                                  look up no good       X02
    35 C                  EXCEPT    ErrorLine                                   print error message    02
    36 C                  ENDIF                                                 end IF group          E02
    37
    38 C                  READ      Ch10p3                           ----LR     read next record       01
    39 C                  ENDDO                                                 end DOW group         E01
    40
    41 OQsysprt   E            Heading        3    01
    42 O                       UDATE         Y       8
    43 O                                            40 'CANNED SODA INVENTORY'
    44 O                                            47 'REPORT'
    45 O                                            60 'PAGE'
    46 O                       PAGE                 65
    47 O          E            Heading        2
    48 O                                            22 'ITEM#    DESCRIPTION'
    49 O                                            34 'COST/CAN'
    50 O                                            49 'AMT ON HAND'
    51 O                                            63 'DOLLAR AMT'
    52 O          E            DetailLine     2
    53 O                       ItemNumber            5
    54 O                       Descrip(X)           24
    55 O                       CanCost(X)     1     31
    56 O                       QtyOnHand      2     45
    57 O                       TotalAmt       1     61
    58 O          E            ErrorLine      2
    59 O                       ItemNumber            5
    60 O                       ErrorMsg             27
    61
      * * * * *   E N D   O F   S O U R C E   * * * * *
          A d d i t i o n a l   D i a g n o s t i c   M e s s a g e s
 *RNF7086 00       5 000500  RPG handles blocking for file CH10P3. INFDS is updated only
                             when blocks of data are transferred.
 *RNF7066 00       5 000500  Record-Format CH10P3R not used for input or output.
  * * * * *   E N D   O F   A D D I T I O N A L   D I A G N O S T I C   M E S S A G E S   * * * * *
                 O u t p u t   B u f f e r   P o s i t i o n s
 Line    Start End    Field or Constant
 Number  Pos   Pos
     42      1     8 UDATE
     43     20    40 'CANNED SODA INVENTORY'
     44     42    47 'REPORT'
     45     57    60 'PAGE'
     46     62    65 PAGE
     48      3    22 'ITEM#    DESCRIPTION'
     49     27    34 'COST/CAN'
     50     39    49 'AMT ON HAND'
     51     54    63 'DOLLAR AMT'
     53      3     5 ITEMNUMBER
     54     10    24 DESCRIP
     55     29    31 CANCOST
     56     41    45 QTYONHAND
```

Figure 10-37 Compile listing of the Canned Soda Inventory Report program. (Continued)

```
   57    53    61 TOTALAMT
   59     3     5 ITEMNUMBER
   60    10    27 ERRORMSG
* * * * *   E N D   O F   O U T P U T   B U F F E R   P O S I T I O N   * * * * *
                    C o m p i l e   T i m e   D a t a
   62 **CTDATA ItemNo
        *---------------------------------------------------------------------*
        * Array . . . : ITEMNO        Alternating Array  . . . . : DESCRIP   *
        *---------------------------------------------------------------------*
   63 100COCA COLA
   64 110PEPSI COLA
   65 1207-UP
   66 130SPRITE
   67 140TAB
   68 150PEPSI LITE
   69 160DIET COKE
   70 170SLICE APPLE
   71 180SLICE
   72 190DR PEPPER
   73 200HIRES ROOT BEER
   74 **CTDATA CanCost
        *---------------------------------------------------------------------*
        * Array . . . : CANCOST                                               *
        *---------------------------------------------------------------------*
   75 4547414951504448436356
   76 **CTDATA ErrorMsg
        *---------------------------------------------------------------------*
        * Array . . . : ERRORMSG                                              *
        *---------------------------------------------------------------------*
   77 ..ITEM NOT FOUND..
   * * * * *   E N D   O F   C O M P I L E   T I M E   D A T A   * * * * *
```

File Description Specifications

Line No.

5 Ch10p3 is defined as an input, full-procedural, externally described, nonkeyed physical file.

6 Qsysprt is defined as an output, program-described printer file. The page overflow indicator **OF** is assigned to the file by the **OFLIND(*INOF)** keyword.

Definition Specifications

9 The ItemNo, Descrip, CanCost, and ErrorMsg are defined as compile-time arrays. The ItemNo array is defined with its elements in ascending order (**ASCEND** keyword). Descrip is defined as in an alternating format (**ALT** keyword) with the ItemNo array. The CanCost array is defined with all 11 of its elements on one record **(PERRCD(11)** keyword). ErrorMsg is a one-element array with the error message **..ITEM NOT FOUND..**.

14–15 TotalAmt and X are defined as standalone fields. X is used as the index to extract the related elements from the Descrip and CanCost arrays.

Calculation Specifications

20 This **EVAL** instruction turns on the **OF** overflow indicator so that the **IF** instruction test on line 25 will be "true," will execute the **EXCEPT** instruction on line 26, and will print the Heading lines before a DetaiLine line is printed.

21 This **READ** instruction reads the first record from the Ch10p3 physical file. If no records are stored in the file, **LR** will be set on.

23 The **DOW** instruction tests the status of the **LR** indicator. If it is not on, another iteration of the **DOW** group will be performed. If **LR** is on, program control will branch to line 40 and end the program.

24 This **EVAL** instruction initializes the X index to 1.

25–26 This **IF** instruction tests the status of the **OF** indicator. Because the **OF** indicator was "turned on" on line 20, the test will be "true." The **EXCEPT** instruction on line 26 will be executed and the two Heading line record formats printed.

27 This **EVAL** instruction turns off the **OF** indicator so that page overflow will not occur for the next record processed. Subsequent page overflow will occur automatically when the page overflow line is sensed and **OF** is turned on.

28 The **ENDIF** operation ends the **IF** group that began on line 25.

30 The input field ItemNumber is specified as the search argument in the **LOOKUP** of the ItemNo array. If an equal lookup occurs, the location of the related element in the ItemNo array will be stored in the index X.

Figure 10-37 Compile listing of the Canned Soda Inventory Report program. (Continued)

31	If a successful lookup occurred in the **LOOKUP** instruction on line 30, indicator 50 was turned on and the instructions within this **IF** group will be executed.
32	This **EVAL** instruction multiplies the input field QtyOnHand by indexed CanCost(X) array element to compute the TotalAmt value. The value in the index X was determined by the **LOOKUP** instruction on line 30.
33	This **EXCEPT** instruction prints a DetailLine record format.
34	When the **LOOKUP** instruction on line 30 is not successful (ItemNumber value not found in the ItemNo array), the instruction following this **ELSE** operation will be executed.
35	This **EXCEPT** instruction prints the ErrorLine record format.
36	This **ENDIF** operation ends the **IF** group that began on line 31.
38	This **READ** instruction reads the next record from the physical file. If end of file is read, the **LR** indicator will be turned on.
39	The **ENDDO** operation ends the **DOW** group.

Output Specifications

41–51	The Heading record formats, defined in these instructions, are printed by the **EXCEPT** instruction on line 26.
52–57	The DetailLine record format, defined in these instructions, is printed by the **EXCEPT** instruction on line 33.
58–60	The ErrorLine record format, defined in these instructions, is printed by the **EXCEPT** instruction on line 35.

Compile-Time Table Data

62–77	The elements for the four compile-time arrays are included in these instructions.

Note: The source program included the array elements after the last output instruction. In a compile listing, Additional Diagnostic Messages and Output Buffer Positions statements are inserted between the last output instruction and the compile-time data.

Figure 10-37 Compile listing of the Canned Soda Inventory Report program. (Continued)

MULTIDIMENSIONAL PROCESSING WITH MULTIPLE-OCCURRENCE DATA STRUCTURES

OCCUR (SET/GET Occurrence of a Data Structure)

It was emphasized at the beginning of this chapter that **RPG IV** does not directly support multidimensional (more than one index) array processing. When needed, however, it may be simulated by a combination of **multiple-occurrence data structures** and one or more **OCCUR** operations. The data structures build the **occurrences** (relative positions) of the data in storage, and the **OCCUR** instructions load and access the values of select occurrences.

All of the data for multiple-occurrence data structures must be loaded into memory before an **OCCUR** instruction is executed. The data may be stored externally in a physical file, or if a small number of records with fixed values are required, the data may be "hard-coded" in the program's calculations. For simplicity, the "hard-coded" method is used in the example program discussed later in this chapter.

Definition Specifications Syntax for a Multiple-Occurrence Data Structure

Figure 10-38 details the *Definition Specification* syntax required to define two multiple-occurrence data structures that support 20 occurrences each. Note that the **OCCURS** key-

```
.. 1 ...+... 2 ...+... 3 ...+... 4 ...+... 5 ...+... 6 ...+... 7 ...+... 8
DName+++++++++++ETDsFrom+++To/L+++IDc.Keywords+++++++++++++++++++++++++++++
 *
D Dstr1           DS                  OCCURS(20)
D  FieldA                          5
D  FieldB                          5
D Dstr2           DS                  OCCURS(20)
D  FieldC                          4
D  FieldD                          4
```

The OCCURS keyword defines the DS as a multiple-occurrence data structure

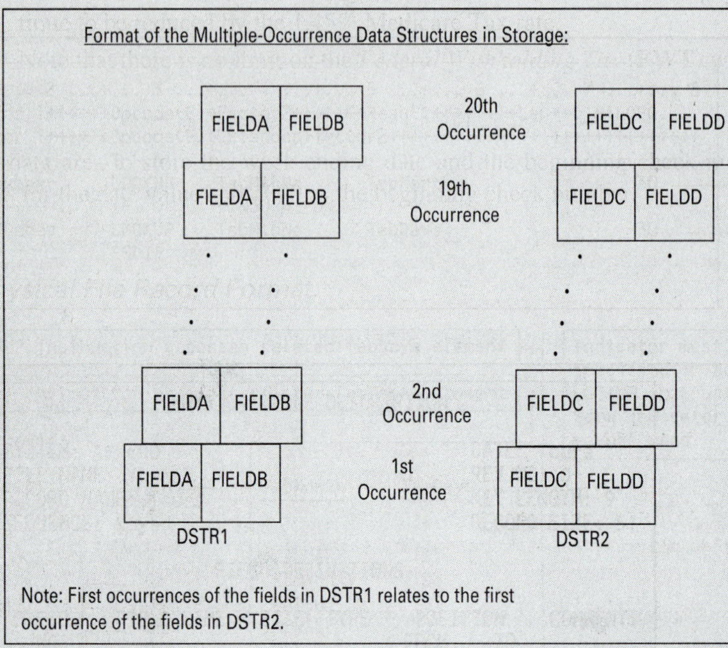

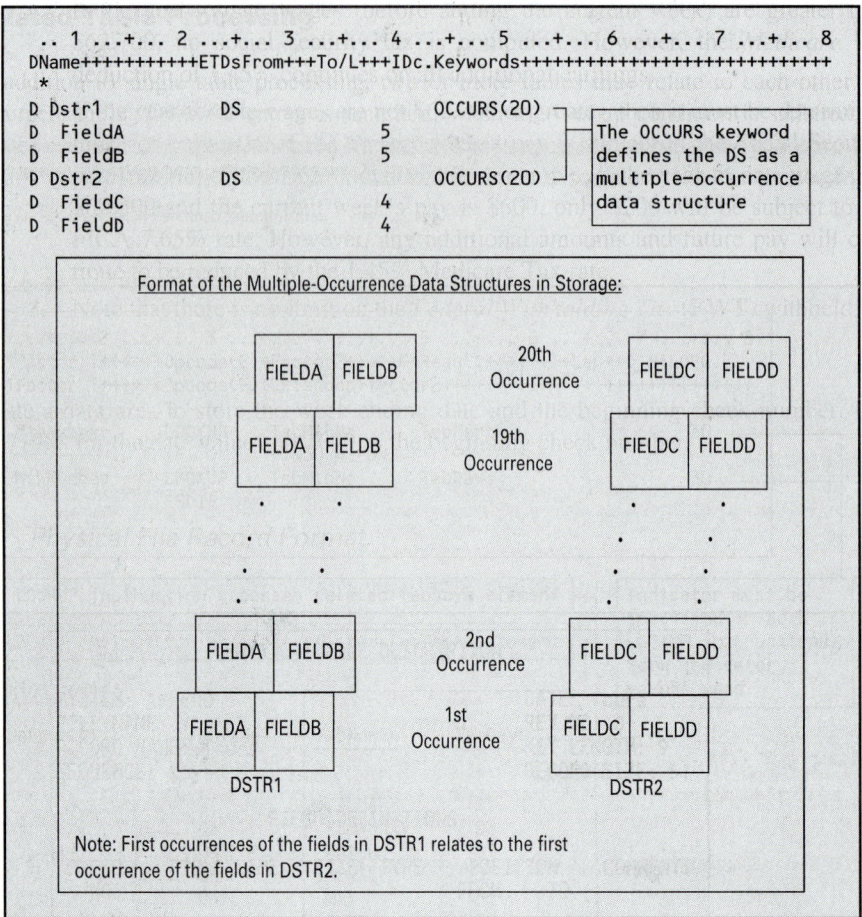

Figure 10-38 *Definition Specification* syntax to define a multiple-occurrence data structure and the storage results.

word defines the data structure as a multiple-occurrence data structure. Also shown are the storage results from building the data structures when the related **RPG IV** program is executed.

OCCUR (SET/GET Occurrence of a Data Structure) Operation

The **OCCUR** operation determines which occurrence of a multiple-occurrence data structure is used next in an **RPG IV** program. The syntax for the **OCCUR** operation is explained in Figure 10-39.

```
*.. 1 ...+... 2 ...+... 3 ...+... 4 ...+... 5 ...+... 6 ...+... 7 ...+.
CLON01Factor1+++++++Opcode&ExtFactor2+++++++Result++++++++Len++D+HiLoEq

C 1           2     OCCUR           4           5                  6
                      3
```

1. A total time indicator, **L0–L9**, or **LR** may be specified in the **L0** field and/or a detail-time indicator may be specified in the **N01** field to condition the **OCCUR** instruction.

Figure 10-39 Syntax rules for the **OCCUR** operation.

2. *Factor 1* is an optional entry. If specified, it may contain a numeric field, literal, named constant, or data structure name defined with no decimal positions.

3. The **OCCUR** operation name must be entered in the *Opcode&Ext* field.

4. *Factor 2* is required and must contain the name of a multiple-occurrence data structure.

5. A *Result* field entry is optional. When used, it must be a numeric field defined with no decimal positions. The field will contain the value of the current occurrence of the data structure references in *Factor 2*. For example, if program control points to the 15th occurrence, 15 will be stored in the *Result* field.

6. A *Resulting Indicator* may be specified in the *Lo* field (positions 73–74), which is set on if the occurrence specified is outside of the range specified (number of occurrences defined by the **OCCUR** keyword in the related *Definition Specification* instruction).

Figure 10-39 Syntax rules for the **OCCUR** operation. (Continued)

Calculation instructions detailing some of the methods by which the multiple-occurrence data structures defined in Figure 10-38 may be processed with **OCCUR** instructions are shown in Figure 10-40.

```
     *.. 1 ...+... 2 ...+... 3 ...+... 4 ...+... 5 ...+... 6 ...+... 7 ...+.
     CLON01Factor1+++++++Opcode&ExtFactor2+++++++Result++++++++Len++D+HiLoEq
1    C         10        OCCUR     Dstr1
2    C         TransCode OCCUR     Dstr2          FieldD              90
3    C         Dstr2     OCCUR     Dstr1
4    C                   OCCUR     Dstr1        WorkOne
5    C         Dstr1     OCCUR     Dstr2        WorkTwo
```

Line No.

1. Multiple-occurrence data structure, Dstr1, is set to the tenth occurrence by the numeric literal 10. The values in FieldA and FieldB, defined in Dstr1, are accessed for processing.

2. The value in the TransCode field (must be defined as an integer) sets the occurrence in the multiple-occurrence data structure Dstr2. If the value in TransCode is within the limits of Dstr2, the value in FieldD is accessed from Dstr2. *Resulting Indicator* 90 specified in the *Lo* field (positions 73–74) is turned on if the TransCode value is zero or greater than the number of occurrences in Dstr2.

3. Multiple-occurrence data structure, Dstr1 is set to the current occurrence of Dstr2. If Dstr2 had been previously set to the 18th occurrence, Dstr1 would also be set to the 18th occurrence.

4. The current occurrence of Dstr2 is stored in WorkOne field. Any field specified in the *Result* field of an **OCCUR** instruction must be defined as a numeric integer.

5. Multiple-occurrence data structure, Dstr2 is set to the current occurrence of the multiple-occurrence data structure Dstr1. If Dstr2 had been previously set to the 12th occurrence, Dstr2 would also be set to the 12th occurrence. The value of the Dstr2 occurrence is stored in the WorkTwo field.

Figure 10-40 **OCCUR** operation processing examples.

APPLICATION RPG IV PROGRAM THAT PROCESSES A MULTIPLE-OCCURRENCE DATA STRUCTURE

The specifications for an **RPG IV** program that processes a multiple-occurrence data structure to access the stored data in a two-dimensional format are given in Figure 10-41.

PROGRAM SPECIFICATIONS — Page 1 of 1

Program Name: Weekly Payroll Report   Program - ID: CH10R4   Written by: SM

Purpose: Weekly payroll report of day/night employees   Approved by: CM

Input files: CH10P4

Output files: QSYSPRT

Processing Requirements:

Write an RPG IV program to print a weekly payroll report of day- and night-shift employees.

Input to the program:

The externally defined physical file, CH10P4, contains the information shown in the attached record layout form.

Processing:

Define a multiple-occurrence data structure in the program that includes three occurrences with the following values:

Grade	Day Rate	Night Rate
1	2000	2300
2	1700	1950
3	1400	1600

Occurrence (Grade column) — Values in multiple-occurrence data structure (day- and night-rate fields)

Hard-code the day- and night-rate data for multiple-occurrence data structure in the program and load it into the three occurrences before any other processing functions are executed. Use the LABORGRADE field (values of 1, 2, or 3) from each physical file record read to position the **OCCUR** statement at the related occurrence in the data structure. After data structure is "set" to the related occurrence (by the value in the LABORGRADE field), test WORKSHIFT field (**D** or **N**) in the physical file's record to determine whether a day- or night-shift employee is being processed. Access the related field from the multiple-occurrence data structure to extract the day- or night-shift employee's hourly rate.

Output:

A supplemental printer spacing chart details the report requirements.

Figure 10-41 Specifications for an **RPG IV** program that processes a multiple-occurrence data structure.

The system flowchart in Figure 10-42 indicates that one physical file is processed to generate a report.

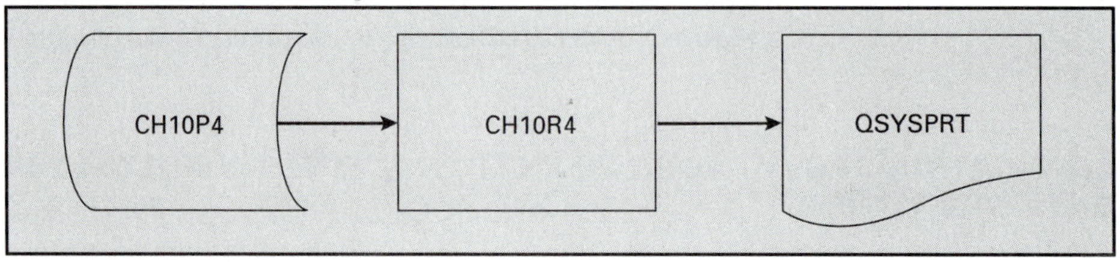

Figure 10-42 System flowchart for an **RPG IV** program that processes a multiple-occurrence data structure.

The record layout form in Figure 10-43 shows the field structure of the physical file. A listing of the data is also included in the figure.

```
                    PHYSICAL FILE DESCRIPTION

SYSTEM: AS/400                                     DATE: 9/20/97
FILE NAME: CH10P4                                  REV NO: 0
RECORD NAME: CH10P4R                               KEY LENGTH: 9
SEQUENCE: Keyed (Unique)                           RECORD SIZE: 9

                        FIELD DEFINITIONS

 FIELD    FIELD NAME    SIZE  TYPE    POSITION     COMMENTS
  NO                                 FROM    TO

  1       SSNUMBER        9    P        1     5  Key field
  2       LABORGRADE      1    P        6     6  0 decimals
  3       WORKSHIFT       1    C        7     7
  4       HRSWORKED       3    P        8     9  0 decimals

Physical file data:

               SSNO       Grade    Shift    Hours

             011111111      3        N       40
             022222222      1        D       35
             033333333      2        D       50
             044444444      3        D       30
             055555555      1        N       40
             066666666      2        N       25
```

Figure 10-43 Physical file record format for the **RPG IV** program that processes a multiple-occurrence data structure.

Included in Figure 10-44 is a printer spacing chart showing the report design and the printed output generated by the multiple-occurrence data structure program.

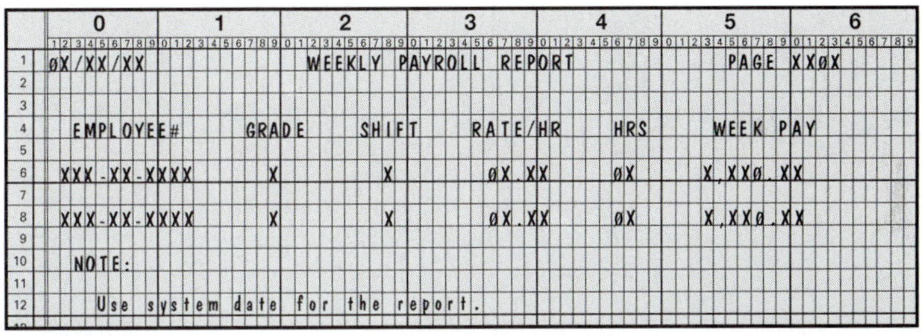

0X/XX/XX
WEEKLY PAYROLL REPORT
PAGE XXØX
EMPLOYEE#
GRADE
SHIFT
RATE/HR
HRS
WEEK PAY
XXX-XX-XXXX
X
X
ØX.XX
ØX
X,XXØ.XX
NOTE:
Use system date for the report.


```
9/30/97              WEEKLY PAYROLL REPORT              PAGE    1

 EMPLOYEE#      GRADE     SHIFT     RATE/HR     HRS     WEEK PAY

011-11-1111       3         N        16.00      40       640.00

022-22-2222       1         D        20.00      35       700.00

033-33-3333       2         D        17.00      50       850.00

044-44-4444       3         D        14.00      30       420.00

055-55-5555       1         N        23.00      40       920.00

066-66-6666       2         N        19.50      25       487.50
```

Figure 10-44 Report design and listing generated by the mutiple-occurrence data structure program.

Source Program Syntax

A compile listing of the **RPG IV** program that processes a multiple-occurrence data structure that simulates two-dimensional array processing is presented in Figure 10-45. A line-by-line discussion explains the program's instructions.

```
Line   <---------------------- Source Specifications ----------------------------><---- Comments ----> Do
Number ....1....+....2....+....3....+....4....+....5....+....6....+....7....+....8....+....9....+...10 Num
                         S o u r c e   L i s t i n g
     1  *                      Weekly Payroll Report
     2  *           With A Multiple-Occurrence Data Structure
     3 FCh10p4    IF   E             K DISK
        *--------------------------------------------------------------------------------------------*
        *                                RPG name          External name                             *
        * File name. . . . . . . . :   CH10P4            STAN/CH10P4                                 *
        * Record format(s) . . . . :   CH10P4R           CH10P4R                                     *
        *--------------------------------------------------------------------------------------------*
     4 FQsysprt   O    F  132         PRINTER OFLIND(*INOF)
     5
     6  * Define work fields....
     7 D HourlyRate      S               4 2
     8 D WeeksPay        S               6 2
     9
    10  * Define multiple-occurrence data structure....
    11 D Rates          DS                        OCCURS(3)
    12 D  DayRate                    1   4 2
    13 D  NightRate                  5   8 2
    14
    15  * Begin calculations....
    16=ICH10P4R
        *--------------------------------------------------------------------------------------------*
        * RPG record format  . . . . :  CH10P4R                                                      *
        * External format  . . . . . :  CH10P4R : STAN/CH10P4                                        *
        *--------------------------------------------------------------------------------------------*
    17=I                               P    1     5 OSSNUMBER
    18=I                               P    6     6 OLABORGRADE
    19=I                               A    7     7  WORKSHIFT
    20=I                               P    8     9 OHRSWORKED
    21 C                   EXSR      LoadSR                                   branch to subroutine
    22 C                   EVAL      *INOF = *ON                              turn on OF indicator
    23 C                   READ      Ch10p4                             ----LR read first record
    24
    25 C                   DOW       *INLR = *OFF                             dow LR is off         B01
    26 C                   IF        *INOF = *ON                              OF indicator on?      B02
    27 C                   EXCEPT    Heading                                  print heading lines    02
    28 C                   EVAL      *INOF = *OFF                             turn off OF indicatr   02
    29 C                   ENDIF                                              end IF group          E02
    30
    31 C     LaborGrade    OCCUR     Rates                                    get workshift data     01
    32 C                   IF        WorkShift = 'D'                          day workshift?        B02
    33 C                   EVAL      HourlyRate = DayRate                     init. with DayRate     02
    34 C                   ELSE                                               not DayShift          X02
    35 C                   EVAL      HourlyRaTE = NightRate                   init. with NightRate   02
    36 C                   ENDIF                                              end IF group          E02
    37
    38 C                   EVAL      WeeksPay = HrsWorked * HourlyRaTE        compute weekspay       01
    39 C                   EXCEPT    DetaiLine                                print DetaiLine        01
    40 C                   READ      Ch10p4                             ----LR read next record       01
    41 C                   ENDDO                                              end dow group         E01
    42
    43  * Begin subroutine....
    44 C     LoadSR        BEGSR                                              begin subroutine
    45 C     1             OCCUR     Rates                                    find 1st occurrence
    46 C                   MOVE      20002300      Rates                      load 1st occurrence
    47 C     2             OCCUR     Rates                                    find 2nd occurrence
    48 C                   MOVE      17001950      Rates                      load 2nd occurrence
    49 C     3             OCCUR     Rates                                    find 3rd occurrence
```

Figure 10-45 Compile listing of the multiple-occurrence data structure program.

```
50 C                   MOVE      14001600      Rates                          Load 3rd occurrence
51 C                   ENDSR                                                  end subroutine
52
53 OQsysprt   E            Heading        2 01
54 O                       UDATE          Y      8
55 O                                            42 'WEEKLY PAYROLL REPORT'
56 O                                            58 'PAGE'
57 O                       PAGE                 63
58 O          E            Heading        2
59 O                                            11 'EMPLOYEE#'
60 O                                            30 'GRADE    SHIFT'
61 O                                            48 'RATE/HR     HRS'
62 O                                            61 'WEEK PAY'
63 O          E            DetaiLine      2
64 O                       SSNumber             12 '0   -  -    '
65 O                       LaborGrade           19
66 O                       WorkShift            28
67 O                       HourlyRate     1     40
68 O                       HrsWorked      2     47
69 O                       WeeksPay       1     60
```

File Description Specifications

Line No.

3 Ch10p4 is defined as an input, full-procedural, externally described, keyed physical file.

4 QSYSPRT is defined as an output, program-described printer file. The page overflow indicator **OF** is assigned to the file by the **OFLIND(*INOF)** keyword.

Definition Specifications

7–8 HourlyRate and WeeksPay are defined as standalone fields.

11–13 Line 11 defines Rates as a multiple-occurrence data structure by the **OCCURS(3)** keyword. DayRate and NightRate are defined as subfields of the data structure.

Calculation Specifications

21 The **EXSR** instruction branches program control to the internal subroutine beginning on line 44. Data for the multiple-occurrence data structure Rates is "hard-coded" in the program and loaded to the three occurrences.

22 This **EVAL** instruction turns on the **OF** overflow indicator so that the **IF** instruction test on line 25 will be "true," will execute the **EXCEPT** instruction on line 27, and will print the Heading lines before a DetaiLine is printed.

23 This **READ** instruction reads the first record from the Ch10p4 physical file. If no records are stored in the file, **LR** will be set on.

25 The **DOW** instruction tests the status of the **LR** indicator. If it is not on, another iteration of the DOW group will be performed. If **LR** is on, program control will branch to line 42 and end the program.

26–27 This **IF** instruction tests the status of the **OF** indicator. Because the **OF** indicator was "turned on" on line 22, the test will be "true." The **EXCEPT** instruction on line 27 will be executed and the two Heading line record formats printed.

28 This **EVAL** instruction turns off the **OF** indicator so that page overflow will not occur for the next record processed. Subsequent page overflow will occur automatically when the page overflow line is sensed and **OF** is turned on.

29 The **ENDIF** operation ends the **IF** group that began on line 26.

31 Depending on the value in the input field LaborGrade, the values from first, second, or third occurrence will be accessed from the multiple-occurrence data structure rates by this **OCCUR** instruction. Note that the values in both the DayRate and NightRate subfields for the related occurrence are accessed by this instruction.

32 This **IF** instruction tests the value in the input field WorkShift for the uppercase character **D** (DayRate test).

33 When the **IF** instruction test on line 32 is "true," this **EVAL** instruction stores the DayRate value into the work field HourlyRate.

34 When the **IF** instruction on line 26 is "false," the instruction on line 35 will be executed.

Figure 10-45 Compile listing of the multiple-occurrence data structure program. (Continued)

35	This **EVAL** instruction stores the NightRate subfield value into the HourlyRate work field.
36	This **ENDIF** operation ends the **IF** group that began on line 32.
38	This **EVAL** instruction multiplies the value in HrsWorked by the value in HourlyRate and stores the product in the WeeksPay work field.
39	This **EXCEPT** instruction prints a DetaiLine record format.
40	This **READ** instruction reads the next record from the physical file. If end of file is read, the **LR** indicator will be turned on.
41	The **ENDDO** operation ends the **DOW** group. When this instruction is executed, program control branches back to the **DOW** instruction on line 25 where the relational test is made.
44	The **BEGSR** instruction begins the LoadSr internal subroutine.
45–46	The numeric literal **1** in *Factor 1* accesses the first occurrence of the multiple-occurrence data structure Rates. The **MOVE** instruction on line 46 moves the "hard-coded" data into the first occurrence.
47–48	The numeric literal **2** in *Factor1* accesses the second occurrence of the multiple-occurrence data structure Rates. The **MOVE** instruction on line 48 moves the "hard-coded" data into the second occurrence.
49–50	The numeric literal **3** in *Factor 1* accesses the third occurrence of the multiple-occurrence data structure Rates. The **MOVE** instruction on line 50 moves the "hard-coded" data into the third occurrence.
	Note: Unless changed during program execution, the "hard-coded" data will remain undisturbed in the multiple-occurrence data structures memory positions.
Output Specifications	
53–62	The Heading record formats, defined in these instructions, are printed by the **EXCEPT** instruction on line 27.
63–69	The DetaiLine record format, defined in these instructions, is printed by the **EXCEPT** instruction on line 39.

Figure 10-45 Compile listing of the multiple-occurrence data structure program. (Continued)

SORTING ARRAYS

The data in the elements of an array may be sorted by the following methods:

Prerun- and Run-Time (Loaded on Input) Arrays

1. External from the **RPG IV** program by a logical file or sort utility.
2. Internal in the **RPG IV** program by the **SORTA** operation.

Compile- and Run-Time (Loaded in Calculation) Arrays

1. Internal in the program by a **SORTA** operation.

Only the internal sorting of arrays with the **SORTA** operation is discussed. For the procedures and syntax related to the external sorting of data, refer to the *RPG/400 Programming on the AS/400* text by this author or IBM's sort manual.

The SORTA Operation

During program execution, the data in the elements of an array may be sorted in either an ascending or descending order by the **SORTA** operation. Figure 10-46 details the syntax of the **SORTA** operation.

```
*.. 1 ...+... 2 ...+... 3 ...+... 4 ...+... 5 ...+... 6 ...+... 7 ...+.
CLON01Factor1+++++++Opcode&ExtFactor2+++++++Result++++++++Len++D+HiLoEq

C 1          2      SORTA            4            5             6
                      3
```

1. A total time indicator, **L0–L9,** or **LR** may be specified in the **L0** field and/or a detail-time indicator may be specified in the **N01** field to condition the **SORTA** instruction.
2. *Factor 1* is not used.
3. The **SORTA** operation name must be entered in the *Opcode&Ext* field.
4. *Factor 2* is required and must contain the name of the array to be sorted.
5. *Result* field is not used.
6. *Resulting Indicator* may not be specified.

Processing logic:

* If no sequence is specified in the definition **(ASCEND** or **DESCEND)** keyword, the array is sorted in an ascending order beginning at the first character in each element.
* Sorting an array does not save any previous order. The result of the last sort will be the order of the elements.
* If an array is defined with the **OVERLAY** keyword, the base array will be sorted in the sequence defined by the **OVERLAY** array.

Figure 10-46 Syntax of the **SORTA** operation.

An example of the **RPG IV** syntax to sort an array beginning at the first character of each element is shown in Figure 10-47.

Definition Specification instruction

```
*.. 1 ...+... 2 ...+... 3 ...+... 4 ...+... 5 ...+... 6 ...+... 7 ...+.
DName+++++++++++ETDsFrom+++To/L+++IDc.Keywords+++++++++++++++++++++++++

D ABCArray        S               4A   DIM(6) ASCEND
```

Calculation Specification instruction

```
*.. 1 ...+... 2 ...+... 3 ...+... 4 ...+... 5 ...+... 6 ...+... 7 ...+.
CLON01Factor1+++++++Opcode&ExtFactor2+++++++Result++++++++Len++D+HiLoEq

C                   SORTA     ABCArray
```

ABCArray Before Sorting

40NY	10AZ	30MA	20CT

ABCArray After Sorting

10AZ	20CT	30MA	40NY

Notes: Sort is performed beginning at the first character in each of the array's elements.

If the ASCEND keyword was omitted in the definition of the array, the default would be ascending order.

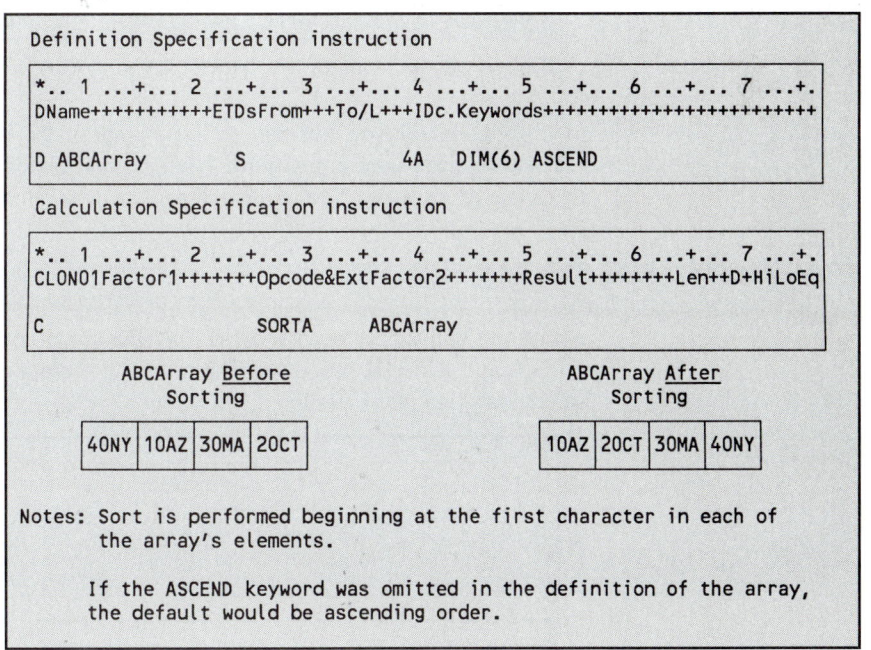

Figure 10-47 Syntax and result of sorting an array.

Sorting an Array Beginning on a Select Element Position

The **SORTA** example shown in Figure 10-47 will always begin the sort on the first character stored in each element. Sometimes a sort may be required beginning on a position in the elements other than the first character. Figure 10-48 explains the **RPG IV** syntax to

Definition Specification instructions

```
*.. 1 ...+... 2 ...+... 3 ...+... 4 ...+... 5 ...+... 6 ...+... 7 ...+.
DName+++++++++++ETDsFrom+++To/L+++IDc.Keywords+++++++++++++++++++++++++
 * Another array (ABCOverAry) must be defined to store the characters
 * to be sorted.  The overlay array will automatically be defined with
 * the same number of elements as the base array (ABCArray).  Arrays
 * must be defined as subfields in a data structure....

D ABCArray        S              4A   DIM(6) ASCEND
D ABCOverAry      S              2A   OVERLAY(ABCArray:3)

                   begins sort on the third position
                   within the ABCArray elements
```

Calculation Specification instruction

```
*.. 1 ...+... 2 ...+... 3 ...+... 4 ...+... 5 ...+... 6 ...+... 7 ...+.
CL0N01Factor1+++++++Opcode&ExtFactor2+++++++Result++++++++Len++D+HiLoEq

                    SORTA     ABCOverAry
```

ABCArray Before Sorting

4ONY	1OAZ	3OMA	2OCT

ABCArray After Sorting

1OAZ	2OCT	3OMA	4ONY

Notes: Sort is performed beginning at the third character in the base array's elements (ABCArray). After the sort, the ABCArray will be in the element order specified by the overlay array (ABCOverAry). The array is specified in Factor 2 of the SORTA instruction.

If the ASCEND keyword was omitted in the definition of the array, the default would be ascending order.

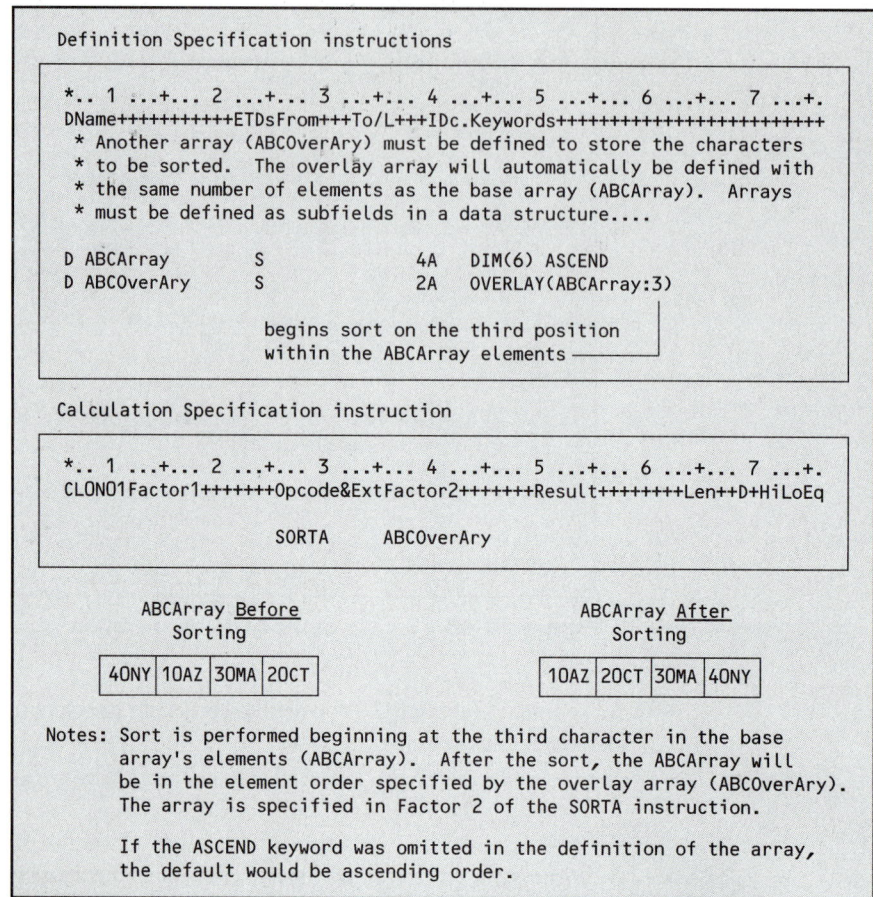

Figure 10-48 Use of the **OVERLAY** keyword in the sorting of an array.

modify the default sort position 1. The format of the **OVERLAY** keyword is: **OVERLAY(base array name:position).** The base and overlay arrays *must* be defined as subfields in a data structure. Note that the base array is referenced for output of the sort.

TRADITIONAL RPG SYNTAX FOR ARRAYS

Arrays are defined in the *Extension Specifications* (not used in **RPG IV**) in traditional **RPG II** and **RPG III** programs. The syntax for compile-, prerun-, and run-time arrays is summarized in Figure 10-49.

```
*.. 1 ...+... 2 ...+... 3 ...+... 4 ...+... 5 ...+... 6 ...+... 7 ...+... 8
E....FromfileTofile++Name++N/rN/tbLenPDSArrnamLenPDSCComents++++++++*
  1     2      3       4    5   6  7 891   11   12 891
                                           0          0
```

Figure 10-49 Fields used in the *Extension Specifications* to define arrays at compile, prerun, and run times.

* All *Extension Specification* instructions must include an **E** in column 6 and immediately follow the last *File Description* statement.

1. Columns 7–10 - not used.

2. **From Filename** (columns 11–18) - Required for prerun-time arrays. File name, specified in a *File Description* statement (**T** in column 16) as program-defined (**F** in column 19), must be entered left-justified in this field.

3. **To Filename** (columns 19–26) - Optional for prerun-time arrays. If the array data is to be written to an output device at the end of the program, the name of the output file must be entered left-justified in this field.

4. **Array Name** (columns 27–32) - Programmer-supplied array name must be entered in this field. If the array is to be indexed, the required comma and index name or literal must be considered in the arrays specified in the program.

5. **Number of Entries Per Record** (columns 33–35) - Specifies how many individual array elements are stored on a record. Entry is only for compile- and prerun-time arrays.

6. **Number of Entries Per Array** (columns 36–39) - Specifies how many array elements are stored in the array. Required for all array types.

7. **Length of Entry** (columns 40–42) - Specifies the size of the array elements. All elements of an array must be the same size. Elements in character arrays may be defined from 1 to 256 bytes long. Numeric array elements may be defined from 1 to 30 bytes long.

8. **P/B/L/R** (column 43) - If the numeric data in a prerun- or run-time array is stored in packed decimal format, the letter **P** must be specified in this field. If the data is stored in binary format, a **B** must be specified. If no entry is specified, the numeric array data is stored as zoned decimal. *Compile-time* array data is entered in a zoned decimal format. An **L** entered in this field indicates that a separate sign is stored to the left of the value and an **R** to the right.

9. **Decimal Positions** (column 44) - A blank in this field indicates that the array is character. A number from 0 to 9 defines the array elements as numeric with the indicated implied decimal positions. The entry cannot be larger than the **Length of Entry** size.

10. **Sequence (A/D)** (column 45) - If the array is not in a sorted order, this field must be blank. If the data is in an ascending order, an **A** may be entered. On the other hand, if the array data is in a descending order, a **D** may be specified. If sequence is specified, an "early exit" is provided for an unsuccessful equal lookup condition, reducing run times.

11. **Array Name (Alternating Format)** (columns 46–51). An array name entered in this field indicates that two or more entries from two related arrays are stored in each record; for example, data for an SSNO element followed by the data for a NAME element. **Number of Entries Per Record** specifies how many "pairs" are included on a record. Only valid for compile- and prerun-time arrays.

12. Columns 52–57 - These four fields relate to the attributes of the alternating array. Refer to items 7, 8, 9, and 10 for an explanation of these fields.

Figure 10-49 Fields used in the *Extension Specifications* to define arrays at compile, prerun, and run times. (Continued)

Traditional RPG Syntax for Compile-Time Arrays

The syntax for traditional **RPG II** and **RPG III** compile-time arrays is shown in Figure 10-50. Note that the array delimiter is an ** (positions 1 and 2), which separates the data for the first compile-time array from the last **RPG** instruction. The data for other compile-time arrays must each follow a ** control statement.

```
*.. 1 ...+... 2 ...+... 3 ...+... 4 ...+... 5 ...+... 6 ...+... 7 ...
E....FromfileTofile++Name++N/rN/tbLenPDSArrnamLenPDSCComents++++++++*

E                      NOARY  12  12  2 0A
E                      NAMARY  6  12  9
                               :
                        Last RPG Instruction
**
010203040506070809101112
**
JANUARY  FEBRUARY MARCH    APRIL    MAY      JUNE
JULY     AUGUST   SEPTEMBEROCTOBER  NOVEMBER DECEMBER
└──Position 1

Related array data must be entered in the order that the arrays are defined
in the Extension Specification.
```

Figure 10-50 *Extension Specification* syntax and related data for two compile-time arrays.

Traditional RPG Syntax for Compile-Time Arrays Stored in an Alternating Format

Figure 10-51 shows the array data from Figure 10-50 rearranged in an alternating format with the modified *Extension Specification* coding.

```
*.. 1 ...+... 2 ...+... 3 ...+... 4 ...+... 5 ...+... 6 ...+... 7 ...
E....FromfileTofile++Name++N/rN/tbLenPDSArrnamLenPDSCComents++++++++*

E                      NOARY   1  12  2 0ANAMARY  9
                               :
┌── Position 1
                        Last RPG Instruction
**
01JANUARY
02FEBRUARY
03MARCH
04APRIL
05MAY              Alternating array data defined in
06JUNE             the Extension Specification with 12
07JULY             elements for each table, with 1 entry
08AUGUST           per record
09SEPTEMBER
10OCTOBER
11NOVEMBER
12DECEMBER
```

Figure 10-51 *Extension Specification* syntax and related array data for two compile-time arrays arranged in alternating format (traditional **RPG**).

Traditional RPG Syntax for Prerun-Time Arrays

Figure 10-52 illustrates the traditional **RPG** syntax to define a prerun-time array. This example uses the same month number and name array data stored for the previously explained compile-time arrays. A *File Description Specification* instruction must define the input file that contains the table data. In addition to the letter **I** in position 15, the letter **T** must be entered in position 16, and an **E** in position 39. **T** indicates to the program that the file is to be processed as a "table" file and that the array data is to be loaded before other input files are read. **E** specifies that the attributes of the arrays are defined in *Extension Specifications* instructions. Because physical files in which prerun-time array data is stored are usually created without a DDS format, the record length must be specified in the *Rlen* field, positions 24–27.

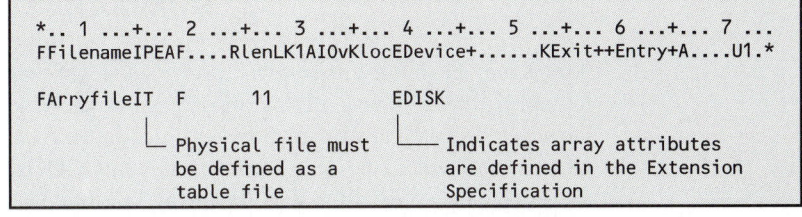

```
*.. 1 ...+... 2 ...+... 3 ...+... 4 ...+... 5 ...+... 6 ...+... 7 ...
FFilenameIPEAF....RlenLK1AIOvKlocEDevice+......KExit++Entry+A....U1.*

FArryfileIT  F       11             EDISK

              Physical file must      Indicates array attributes
              be defined as a         are defined in the Extension
              table file              Specification
```

```
*.. 1 ...+... 2 ...+... 3 ...+... 4 ...+... 5 ...+... 6 ...+... 7 ...
E....FromfileTofile++Name++N/rN/tbLenPDSArrnamLenPDSCComents++++++++*

E    Arryfile       NOARY   1  12  2 OANAMARY  9

              Physical file defined with a T in position 16 in the
              related File Description instruction must be entered in
              the Fromfile field
```

Figure 10-52 *File Description* and *Extension Specification* syntax for prerun-time arrays—data stored in an alternating format (traditional RPG).

Traditional RPG Syntax for Run-Time Arrays

Run-time arrays are defined in the *Extension Specifications* without a *Number of Entries Per Record* entry. The data is loaded into a run-time array with *Input* or *Calculation Specification* instructions. Figure 10-53 details the syntax for loading an array with *Input Specification* instructions.

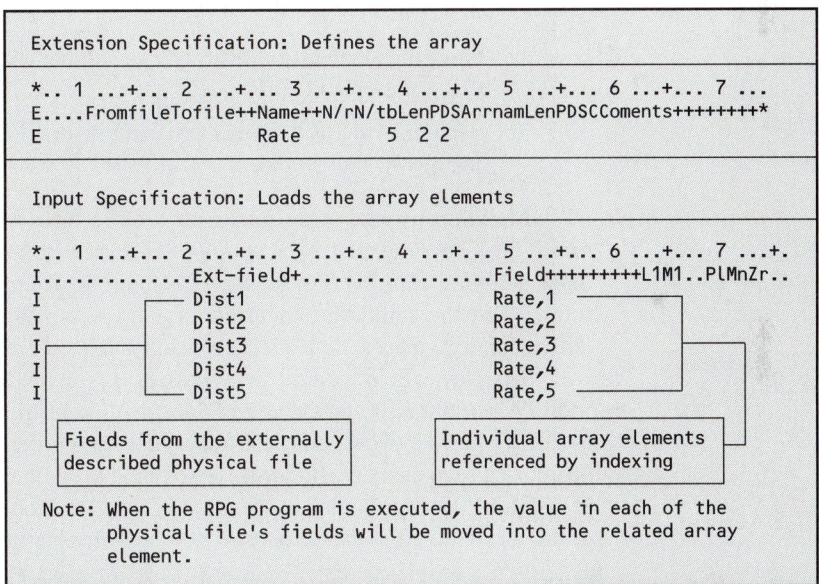

```
Extension Specification: Defines the array

*.. 1 ...+... 2 ...+... 3 ...+... 4 ...+... 5 ...+... 6 ...+... 7 ...
E....FromfileTofile++Name++N/rN/tbLenPDSArrnamLenPDSCComents++++++++*
E                    Rate         5  2 2

Input Specification: Loads the array elements

*.. 1 ...+... 2 ...+... 3 ...+... 4 ...+... 5 ...+... 6 ...+... 7 ...+.
I..............Ext-field+..................Field+++++++++L1M1..PlMnZr..
I              Dist1                       Rate,1
I              Dist2                       Rate,2
I              Dist3                       Rate,3
I              Dist4                       Rate,4
I              Dist5                       Rate,5

  Fields from the externally            Individual array elements
  described physical file               referenced by indexing

 Note: When the RPG program is executed, the value in each of the
       physical file's fields will be moved into the related array
       element.
```

Figure 10-53 *Extension* and *Input Specification* syntax to define and load a run-time array with input instructions.

Run-time arrays may be loaded in calculations with any of the arithmetic functions and **MOVE, MOVEL,** and **MOVEA** instructions with single or multiple statements.

Processing Traditional RPG Arrays

With the exception of the "lookup" operation, which must be specified as **LOKUP** instead of **LOOKUP,** the *Calculation Specification* syntax for the processing of arrays with traditional **RPG** is identical to that previously discussed for **RPG IV.**

SUMMARY

Arrays may be defined as *compile*, *prerun*, and *run time* in an **RPG IV** program. Similar to tables, the elements of an array may be accessed by the **LOOKUP** operation. However, a related array cannot be specified in the *Result* field. If related arrays are to be processed together, the *index* from a previous **LOOKUP** instruction must be used to access element values from the other array(s). Unlike tables, the elements of an array may also be accessed positionally or randomly by *indexing*. In addition, *all* elements in an array may be accessed at one time by specifying only the array name.

Arrays are defined in an **RPG IV** program in the *Definition Specifications*. An array, defined as a "standalone" field, is identified as an array by the **DIM** keyword. Other keywords, such as **CTDATA, ALT, PERRCD, ASCEND, DESCEND, FROMFILE, TOFILE,** and **OVERLAY,** are provided to define the array type, attributes, and sequence.

The **CTDATA** keyword defines an array as compile time. The **FROMFILE** and **TOFILE** keywords define an array as prerun time. The omission of these keywords defines an array as a run-time array.

The **XFOOT** operation "cross-foots" all of the elements in a numeric array and stores the sum in the item specified in the *Result* field. Any arithmetic function **(ADD, SUB, MULT, DIV, MVR,** and **SQRT**) may be performed on all of the elements in one instruction. For example, the elements in one numeric array may be added to the elements in another numeric array.

The elements of a numeric array may be separated and edited for printing or display by *edit words*, *edit codes*, or indexing. Character array elements may be separated (not edited) only by indexing.

The functions of the **MOVEA** operation include the following:

1. Move the elements of an array into another array or field.
2. Move a field value into an array.
3. Begin moving from a select element in an array into a select starting element of an array or into a field.

Multidimensional array processing (more than one index to extract an array element) may be simulated by a *multiple-occurrence data structure*. A data structure is defined in the *Definition Specifications* as multiple occurrence with the **OCCUR** keyword followed by the number of occurrences (storage positions) enclosed in parentheses. The individual occurrences are loaded with data and accessed by **OCCUR** operations.

The elements in an array may be sorted in ascending or descending order with the **SORTA** operation. In the *Definition Specification* instruction for the array, the **ASCEND** or **DESCEND** keyword will determine the sorted order. An array sort begins at the first position of each element. If the sort is to begin at some other position in the elements, the **OVERLAY** keyword must be specified in the definition of a *second* related array. Output of the sort is stored in the base array, not the overlay array.

QUESTIONS

10-1. What is an array in the **RPG IV** programming environment?

10-2. Describe the logical structure of a one-dimensional array and also that of a two-dimensional array. How many dimensions does **RPG IV** support?

10-3. What factors should be considered in deciding whether to use an array or a table?

10-4. Compare the processing features of arrays to those of tables.

10-5. When may arrays be loaded in the program cycle?

10-6. Refer to Question 10-5, and explain where the array data is stored and the loading process for each method.

10-7. Refer to Question 10-5, and explain under what conditions each loading method should be used.

10-8. On which **RPG IV** specification are arrays defined?

10-9. Explain the function of the following keywords and operations used in the definition and processing of arrays:

DIM	**PERRCD**	**CTDATA**
ALT	**FROMFILE**	**ASCEND**
DESCEND	**OVERLAY**	**TOFILE**
XFOOT	**LOOKUP**	

Examine the following Definition Specifications *instructions and answer Questions 10-10 to 10-12:*

```
 .. 1 ...+... 2 ...+... 3 ...+... 4 ...+... 5 ...+... 6 ...+... 7 ...+
DName+++++++++++ETDsFrom+++To/L+++IDc.Keywords+++++++++++++++++++++++++
 *
D ArrayOne        S              6  0 DIM(50) DESCEND CTDATA PERRCD(5)
D ArrayTwo        S             20    DIM(50) ALT(ArrayOne)
D ArrayThree      S              2    DIM(15)
```

10-10. Explain the function of the keyword entries for ArrayOne.

10-11. Explain the function of the keyword entries for ArrayTwo.

10-12. What type of array is ArrayThree? When will the data for the array be loaded in the program cycle?

Examine the following Definition Specifications *instruction and answer Questions 10-13 to 10-16:*

```
 .. 1 ...+... 2 ...+... 3 ...+... 4 ...+... 5 ...+... 6 ...+... 7 ...+
DName+++++++++++ETDsFrom+++To/L+++IDc.Keywords+++++++++++++++++++++++++
 *
D ArrayFour       S             10  0 DIM(200) FROMFILE(ArrayFile)
D                                     TOFILE(ArrayFile)
```

10-13. What type of array is ArrayFour?

10-14. What is the function of the **FROMFILE** keyword?

10-15. Where is the data for the array stored?

10-16. What is the function of the **TOFILE** keyword?

10-17. Name three methods of loading data to a run-time array.

10-18. What is the function of the **XFOOT** operation?

Examine the following Calculation Specifications *instruction and answer Questions 10-19 and 10-20:*

```
*.. 1 ...+... 2 ...+... 3 ...+... 4 ...+... 5 ...+... 6 ...+... 7 ...+.
CL0N01Factor1+++++++Opcode&ExtFactor2+++++++Result++++++++Len++D+HiLoEq

C                   XFOOT     Amount        Final
```

10-19. The *Factor 2* entry must be: (a) a field name; (b) an array name; (c) either a field or an array name.

10-20. The *Result* field entry must be: (a) a field name; (b) an array name; (c) either a field or array name.

10-21. What arithmetic operations may be used with numeric arrays? Are all of the elements accessed in one instruction, or does each element have to be specified individually?

10-22. In terms of array processing, what is an index? How must it be defined? Where may an index be defined?

10-23. Explain the meaning of the following entry in an output instruction: **CustName(X).**

10-24. What is the function of the **LOOKUP** operation with arrays? How does it differ from table **LOOKUP** processing?

10-25. When an array is processed with the **LOOKUP** operation, how is the index incremented?

10-26. If three arrays, MthNo, MthName, and MthDays, are related and **N** is specified as the index, how many **LOOKUP** instructions are needed to access all three arrays at one time?

10-27. Define positional array processing. Does this type of array access require a **LOOKUP** instruction?

10-28. Name and explain the run-time errors common to the processing of arrays.

10-29. How does the function of a **MOVEA** operation differ from the **MOVE** and **MOVEL** operations?

10-30. Refer to the following and determine the value in the *Result* field items after the related **MOVEA** operation is executed.

Entries in Factor 2	Entries in Result	Values in before MOVEA Factor 1	Values in before MOVEA Result	Value in Result after MOVEA
Array1	Array2	123456	789000	
Field	Array(6)	DONALD	DUCK,bbbbbb	
States(3)	Name(7)	CTNYNJ	DEVONbbb	
AmtArray	Field	010000	9999999	
AmtArray(3)	Field	001400	88	

Notes: Items defined as Field are not arrays
Letter b indicates a blank character
Factor 1 and Result field values indicate the array or field size

10-31. What is the function of a multiple-occurrence data structure? What coding is required to define this type of data structure?

10-32. What **RPG IV** operation loads and processes a multiple-occurrence data structure?

10-33. Refer to the data given below, and complete the instructions required to define it as a multiple-occurrence data structure. Use Model as the data structure name and Deluxe and Standard as the subfield names.

Model	Deluxe	Standard
1	1200	1000
2	1350	1175
3	1600	1450
4	1900	1790

10-34. Refer to Question 10-33 and complete the *Calculation Instructions* to "hard-code" the data into the occurrences and process the data structure. Assume Models is the input field.

10-35. What fields are used in calculations for a **SORTA** instruction?

10-36. On what position in the element values does a sort begin? How may the sort be modified to begin at some other element position?

10-37. Name the keywords that may be used in the definition of an array that is to be sorted.

10-38. Examine the following array definition and explain the function of each field entry and keyword.

```
*.. 1 ...+... 2 ...+... 3 ...+... 4 ...+... 5 ...+... 6 ...+... 7 ...+.
DName+++++++++++ETDsFrom+++To/L+++IDc.Keywords+++++++++++++++++++++++++

D DEFArray        S              6A   DIM(3) ASCEND
D HIGArray        S              3A   OVERLAY(DEFArray:4)
```

10-39. Refer to Question 10-38. If the value in DEFArray was before the sort, what is the value in DEFArray after the sort?

456XYZ	234MNO	123ABC

PROGRAMMING ASSIGNMENTS

For each of the following programming assignments, a physical file must have been created and loaded with the related data records. Your instructor will tell you if you have to create the physical file and load it or if it has been prepared for the assignment.

Programming Assignment 10-1: FACTORY OVERHEAD BUDGET

Write an **RPG IV** program using arrays to generate the report shown in the printer spacing chart.

Physical File Record Format:

Define the fields QTRONE through QTRFOUR as the four elements of a run-time array.

PHYSICAL FILE DESCRIPTION

SYSTEM: AS/400 DATE: Yours
FILE NAME: Yours REV NO: 0
RECORD NAME: Yours KEY LENGTH: None
SEQUENCE: Nonkeyed RECORD SIZE: 40

FIELD DEFINITIONS

FIELD NO	FIELD NAME	SIZE	TYPE	POSITION FROM	POSITION TO	COMMENTS
1	ACTNAME	24	C	1	24	
2	QTRONE	6	P	25	28	0 decimals
3	QTRTWO	6	P	29	32	0 decimals
4	QTRTHREE	6	P	33	36	0 decimals
5	QTRFOUR	6	P	37	40	0 decimals

Physical file data:

Account Name	1st Quarter Sales	2nd Quarter Sales	3rd Quarter Sales	4th Quarter Sales
INDIRECT LABOR	250000	190000	201910	186750
FACTORY SUPPLIES	086000	070000	103480	093100
HEAT, LIGHT, POWER	067440	079000	080500	071330
SUPERVISION	150000	150000	165000	167000
MAINTENANCE	090000	087000	089000	077900
TAXES AND INSURANCE	110000	110000	110000	110000
DEPRECIATION	125000	125000	125000	125000

Calculations: For every record processed, each expense account's quarterly amounts are to be cross-footed to calculate the sum for the year. In addition, the quarterly amounts are added to calculate the sum for each quarter. At end of file, the quarter totals are to be cross-footed for the year's total.

Report Design:

```
            PROJECTO MANUFACTURING COMPANY                              PAGE XXØX
        BUDGETED FACTORY OVERHEAD COST BY QUARTERS
                     FOR BUDGET YEAR 19XX


   EXPENSE ACCOUNT               1Q          2Q          3Q          4Q           YEAR

X                       X    XXX,XXØ     XXX,XXØ     XXX,XXØ     XXX,XXØ    X,XXX,XXØ

X                       X    XXX,XXØ     XXX,XXØ     XXX,XXØ     XXX,XXØ    X,XXX,XXØ

  TOTAL OVERHEAD COST      X,XXX,XXØ   X,XXX,XXØ   X,XXX,XXØ   X,XXX,XXØ   XX,XXX,XXØ



      NOTES:

        1. HEADINGS ON TOP OF EVERY PAGE.
```

Programming Assignment 10-2: INCOME STATEMENT BY QUARTERS

Write an **RPG IV** program to generate the income statement shown in the printer spacing chart.

Define *one* four-element run-time array that will be loaded in the *Input* or *Definition Specifications* with the four quarterly amounts for each input record processed. Also, define *seven* other four-element run-time arrays—one each for Sales, Cost of Goods Sold, Gross Profit, Operating Expenses, Net Income, Decimal Percentage of Net Income to Sales, and Percentage of Net Income to Sales—that will be loaded in calculations.

Physical File Record Format:

PHYSICAL FILE DESCRIPTION

SYSTEM: AS/400	DATE: Yours
FILE NAME: Yours	REV NO: 0
RECORD NAME: Yours	KEY LENGTH: None
SEQUENCE: Nonkeyed	RECORD SIZE: 19

FIELD DEFINITIONS

FIELD NO	FIELD NAME	SIZE	TYPE	POSITION FROM	POSITION TO	COMMENTS
1	ACTCODE	1	C	1	1	S, C, E
2	YEAR	2	P	2	3	
3	QTR1AMT	6	P	4	7	0 decimals
4	QTR2AMT	6	P	8	11	0 decimals
5	QTR3AMT	6	P	12	15	0 decimals
6	QTR4AMT	6	P	16	19	0 decimals

Physical file data:

ID Code	Year	1Q	2Q	3Q	4Q
S	98	200000	175000	210000	309000
C	98	100000	092000	120000	209000
E	98	070000	052000	089000	105000

The **run-time** array loaded on input and the Sales, Cost of Sales, Gross Profit, Operating Expenses, and Net Income arrays must be defined with four six-byte elements with no decimal positions.

The Decimal Percentage of Net Income to Sales array must be defined with four five-byte elements with five decimal positions. The Percentage of Net Income to Sales array must be defined with four four-byte elements with two decimal positions.

Processing: For each record read from the physical file, the run-time array will automatically be loaded. In calculations, test the ACTCODE field and load the related array. For the "S" record, load the Sales array; for the "C" record, load the Cost of Sales array; and for the "E" record, load the Operating Expenses array.

After the three records from the physical file are read and the three arrays loaded, complete the following steps at **LR** time:

1. Subtract the Cost of Sales array from the Sales array, and store the differences in the Gross Profit array.
2. Subtract the Operating Expenses array from the Gross Profit array, and store the differences in the Net Income array.
3. Divide the Net Income array by the Sales array, and store the quotients in the Decimal Percentage of Net Income to Sales array.
4. Multiply the Decimal Percentage of Net Income to Sales array by 100, and store the products in the Percentage of Net Income to Sales array.
5. Cross-foot the Sales, Cost of Sales, Gross Profit, Operating Expenses, and Net Income arrays to compute the totals for the four quarters.
6. The Percentage of Net Income *total* cannot be calculated by cross-footing. The value must be determined by dividing the total for the Net Income array by the total for the Sales array.
7. Print the entire report at **LR** time.

Report Design:

```
 1                                  DAGWOOD COMPANY
 2                                 INCOME STATEMENT
 3                              FOR YEAR ENDING 12/31/XX
 4
 5                                   1Q            2Q            3Q            4Q           TOTAL
 6
 7  SALES                         $ XXX,XXØ     $ XXX,XXØ     $ XXX,XXØ     $ XXX,XXØ     $ X,XXX,XXØ
 8  LESS COST OF SALES              XXX,XXØ       XXX,XXØ       XXX,XXØ       XXX,XXØ       X,XXX,XXØ
 9     GROSS PROFIT               $ XXX,XXØ     $ XXX,XXØ     $ XXX,XXØ     $ XXX,XXØ     $ X,XXX,XXØ
10  LESS OPERATING EXPENSE          XXX,XXØ       XXX,XXØ       XXX,XXØ       XXX,XXØ       X,XXX,XXØ
11     NET INCOME (LOSS--)        $ XXX,XXØ     $ XXX,XXØ     $ XXX,XXØ     $ XXX,XXØ     $ X,XXX,XXØ
12
13  PCT OF NET INCOME TO SALES      XØ.XX         XØ.XX         XØ.XX         XØ.XX           XØ.XX
14
15
16       NOTES:
17
18            1. PERCENT DECIMAL COMPUTED IN CALCULATIONS IS MULTIPLIED BY 1ØØ
19               FOR PRINTING.
20
21            2. DOLLAR SIGNS ARE ALL FIXED.
```

Programming Assignment 10-3: SHIPPING CHARGE REPORT (Multiple-Occurrence Data Structure)

Write an **RPG IV** program to generate the report shown in the supplemental printer spacing chart.

Physical File Record Format:

PHYSICAL FILE DESCRIPTION

SYSTEM: AS/400	DATE: Yours
FILE NAME: Yours	REV NO: 0
RECORD NAME: Yours	KEY LENGTH: 4
SEQUENCE: Keyed	RECORD SIZE: 33

FIELD DEFINITIONS

FIELD NO	FIELD NAME	SIZE	TYPE	POSITION FROM	POSITION TO	COMMENTS
1	CUSTNAME	20	C	1	20	
2	INVNUMBER	4	C	21	24	Key field
3	INVAMOUNT	6	P	25	28	2 decimals
4	POUNDS	2	P	29	30	0 decimals
5	OUNCES	2	P	31	32	2 decimals
6	DELDAYS	1	P	33	33	0 decimals

Physical file data:

Customer Name	Invoice Number	Invoice Amount	Shipping Weight PDS	Shipping Weight OZS	1 or 2 Day Delivery
HENRY JACKSON	1234	002400	05	08	1
DOROTHY PARTNER	1235	010000	10	00	2
ROBERT WARFIELD	1236	004500	09	09	1
MARIO LANZA	1237	120000	20	00	1
ENZIO PINZA	1238	245000	20	12	2
NELSON EDDY	1239	001000	01	00	2

Processing: Load the following as hard-coded data into a multiple-occurrence data structure:

Weight in Pounds	1-day Rate	2-day Rate
01	129	161
02	137	171
03	146	183
04	154	192
05	163	204
06	171	213
07	180	225
08	188	235
09	197	246
10	205	257

(1-day and 2-day rates: 2 decimal positions)

Use the invoice shipping pounds to access the related multiple-occurrence data structure's field entries. Increase any shipping weights over a pound to the next-higher pound. Test the delivery field in each physical file record for 1 or 2. An entry of **1** indicates one-day delivery and a **2,** two- or more day delivery. Extract the 1- or 2-day delivery rate from the related multiple-occurrence data structure's field.

Any package weighing over 10 pounds is charged the 1- or 2-day delivery amount for 10 pounds plus an additional 6 cents for each pound over 10.

A maximum shipping weight limit of 20 pounds is imposed by the parcel delivery firm. Any packages over 20 pounds cannot be shipped. Identify this on the report by the message OVER WEIGHT in the position shown on the printer spacing chart.

For any invoice amounts under $25, the shipping charge is added to the invoice amount. Print asterisks in place of the shipping charge.

Report Design:

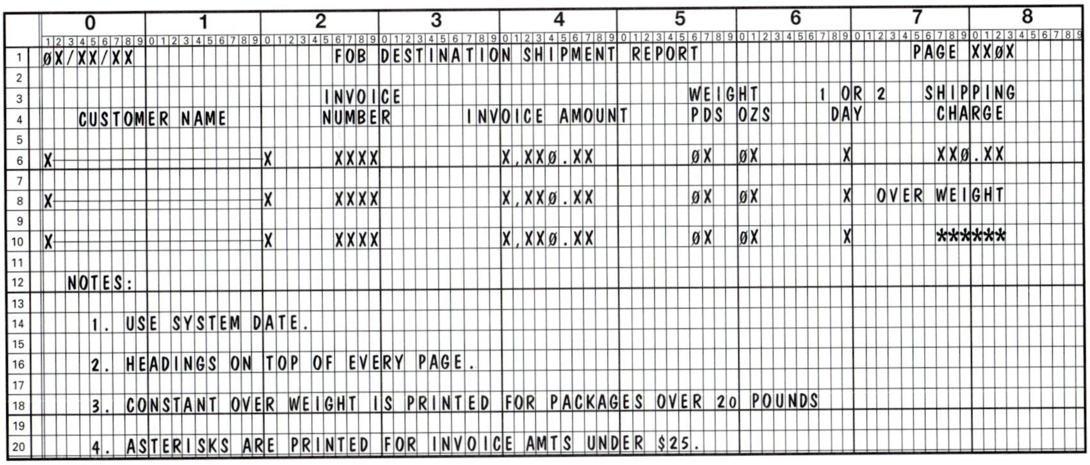

Programming Assignment 10-4: MAILING LABELS

A mail-order company needs a program written to generate mailing labels for the shipment of goods to its customers. The labels are gummed and mounted on standard size ($14\frac{1}{2}$ inch × 11 inch) continuous-forms paper in the format shown in the printer spacing chart ahead.

Processing: Define four-element arrays for the following input fields:

1. CUSTOMER NAME
2. STREET
3. APARTMENT NUMBER (or other second address information)
4. CITY/STATE/ZIP (all items in one array).

After an input record is read, move the field values into their related arrays. A counter must be incremented for use as an index to load the input record values into their individual array elements. When the counter is equal to 4 (four elements in each array loaded), output a detail line of labels and initialize the counter back to 0 before the next group of four customer records is processed. Because the counter may not always be equal to 4 when the end of file is sensed, the printing of the last line of labels must be separately controlled.

Notice in the following record layout form that there are two address fields. ADDRESS2 is for supplemental information such as apartment number, office number, and blank value. If the input value for this field is blank, the CITY/STATE/ZIP line will be printed on the third line so that a blank line will not be included after the ADDRESS1 value. If the ADDRESS2 field is not blank, all four lines are to be printed for the label.

Physical File Record Format:

PHYSICAL FILE DESCRIPTION

SYSTEM: AS/400	DATE: Yours
FILE NAME: Yours	REV NO: 0
RECORD NAME: Yours	KEY LENGTH: None
SEQUENCE: Nonkeyed	RECORD SIZE: 78

FIELD DEFINITIONS

FIELD NO	FIELD NAME	SIZE	TYPE	POSITION FROM	POSITION TO	COMMENTS
1	CUSTNAME	18	C	1	18	
2	ADDRESS1	18	C	19	36	
3	ADDRESS2	11	C	37	47	
4	CITYSTZIP	31	C	48	78	

Physical File Data:

Name	Address 1	Address 2	City/State/Zip
KAREL APPEL	20 AMSTERDAM AVE	APT 35	NEW YORK, NY 074500000
GEORGES BRAQUE	300 ST CLAIR ST		NEW JERSEY, NJ 055011234
PAUL CEZANNE	44 RUE PIGALLE	BLDG 10	STAMFORD, CT 065180010
MARC CHAGALL	222 QUAIL AVENUE		BRIDGEPORT, CT 066661000
EDGAR DEGAS	10 ROSE TERRACE		WESTPORT, PA 077770000
MAX ERNST	1 FRANKFURT DRIVE	LOT 14	FRANKFORT, KY 055510111
BUCKMINSTER FULLER	999 PARK AVENUE	APT 201	NEW YORK, NY 075500000
JULIO GONZALEZ	101 SMITH LANE		GREENWICH, CT 064440000
HECTOR HYPPOLITE	888 PEACHTREE AVE		ATLANTA, GA 033322200
PIERRE JEANERET	90 CHATEAU DRIVE		GENEVA, NY 077774000
WASSILY KANDINSKY	13 WARSAW LANE		LOS ANGELES, CA 099900000
CHARLES CORBUSIER	10 PARIS PLACE		ENGLEWOOD CLIFFS, NJ 076320000
PABLO PICASSO	1784 BASTILLE BLD		FRANCE, KY 088800000

Format of the Labels:

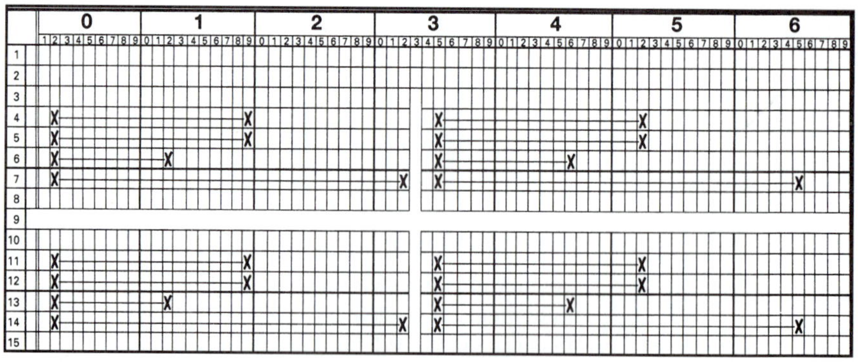

Note: Four labels are printed per line (one label per customer).

Programming Assignment 10-5: SORTING AN ARRAY

Write an **RPG IV** program to process a program-described physical file as a table file. Load the data from the table file to a prerun-time array. Sort the prerun-time array in ascending salesperson number order, and generate the report shown in the supplemental printer spacing chart. For printing, separate the salesperson number, year-to-date sales, and the salesperson name into three separate fields with **MOVEA** instructions.

The following data is to be loaded into a program-described physical file:

```
440003468562MARGARET STERN
110001256784HENRY SMITH
550000498855JOSE GONZALEZ
220010003219WALTER CHANG
660006758974KALMAN COHEN
330000310986JEROME WALDRON
```

Salesperson name
Year-to-date sales
Salesperson number

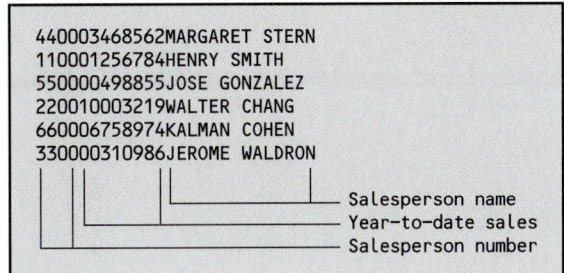

Report Design:

```
            1         2         3         4         5
   12345678901234567890123456789012345678901234567890
 1           SALESPERSON PERFORMANCE REPORT      000X
 2                  AS OF 0X/XX/XXXX
 3
 4
 5   SALESPERSON                           YEAR-TO-DATE
 6     NUMBER        SALESPERSON NAME          SALES
 7
 8      XXXX         XXXXXXXXXXXXXXX       XXX,XX0.XX
 9
10      XXXX         XXXXXXXXXXXXXXX       XXX,XX0.XX
11
12    Notes: 1. Use run date for the report.
13           2. Headings on top of every page.
14
```

Programming Assignment 10-6: SORTING AN ARRAY BEGINNING ON A SELECT POSITION IN AN ELEMENT

If Programming Assignment 10-5 was completed, modify the **RPG IV** program to sort the base array on Year-to-date sales in ascending order. If Programming Assignment 10-5 was not completed, refer to the specifications for that assignment.

chapter 11

RPG IV Character Manipulation Operations, Built-In Functions (BIFs), and Date/Time Operations

RPG IV CHARACTER MANIPULATION OPERATIONS

RPG IV character manipulation operations include **CHECK** *(Check)*, **CHECKR** *(Check Reverse)*, **SCAN** *(Scan String)*, **SUBST** *(Substring)*, and **XLATE** *(Translate)*.

CHECK *(Check)* Operation

The **CHECK** operation verifies that each character in the base string (*Factor 2* item) (from left to right) is included in the comparator string (*Factor 1* item). The *Factor 1* and *Factor 2* items must be the same type (both character). Figure 11-1 details the syntax of the **CHECK** operation.

```
*.. 1 ...+... 2 ...+... 3 ...+... 4 ...+... 5 ...+... 6 ...+... 7 ...+... 8 ...+... 9 ...+ ...10
CLON01Factor1+++++++Opcode&ExtFactor2+++++++Result++++++++Len++D+HiLoEq....Comments++++++++++++
   1         2       CHECK          4              5                  6 5
                       3
```

1. *Total-* and/or *detail-time* indicators may condition a **CHECK** instruction.
2. The *Factor 1* item must be defined as character (not numeric) and may include a field name, array element, named constant, data structure name, table name, or literal.
3. The **CHECK** operation name must be specified in the *Opcode&Ext* field.
4. *Factor 2* must include the name of the string to be checked. The entry may be a field name, array element, named constant, data structure name, table name, or literal defined as character. The entry may be specified with or without a colon and start location. The start location, which must be defined as an integer, indicates where checking for the *Factor 1* characters is to begin in the *Factor 2* string. The entry may be a field name, array element, named constant, table name, or literal. If no start location is specified (colon and entry omitted after the string item), checking will begin at the first character in the *Factor 2* value.
5. The optional *Result* field entry must be defined as an integer and may be a field, array element, array name, or table name. If it is not specified, a *Resulting Indicator* in the *Eq* field (positions 75–76) must be included.

   If the *Result* field contains an array name, the location of every *Factor 2* character field that does not equal a *Factor 1* character will be stored in the array elements. If the *Result* field is not an array, only the location of the first invalid character will be stored in the *Result* field item.
6. A *Resulting Indicator* may be specified in the *Lo* field (positions 73–74), which will be set on if an execution error occurs.

Figurative Constants cannot be used in *Factor 1, Factor 2,* or the *Result* field.

Figure 11-1 Syntax of the **CHECK** operation.

Processing Logic:

Each character in the *Factor 1* item checks the *Factor 2* string for an invalid character (not equal to the character(s) in *Factor 1*). If an invalid character is found in the *Factor 2* string, its location is stored in the *Result* field item. If the *Result* field is not specified, the *Resulting Indicator* in the *Eq* field (positions 75–76) will be set on when the first invalid character is found in the *Factor 2* string.

The **CHECK** operation begins at the leftmost character (or the starting position specified) in the *Factor 2* string and continues character by character from left to right until a character not equal to a *Factor 1* character is found or the end of the *Factor 2* string is encountered. If the *Factor 1* character(s) is/are found in the *Factor 2* string, the *Result* field item is set to zero.

If an array name is specified in the *Result* field, the checking will continue and store the location of every invalid character in the *Factor 2* string. If the *Factor 1* characters are found in the *Factor 2* string, the array elements are all set to zero.

Figure 11-1 Syntax of the **CHECK** operation. (Continued)

Coding examples of the **CHECK** operation are shown in Figure 11-2.

```
*.. 1 ...+... 2 ...+... 3 ...+... 4 ...+... 5 ...+... 6 ...+... 7 ...+... 8
CLON01Factor1+++++++Opcode&ExtFactor2+++++++Result++++++++Len++D+HiLoEq....

 * The CHECK operation checks the Factor 2 string for invalid characters
 * with characters from the Factor 1 value.  In the example shown below,
 * 'bMOUSE' is stored in the Factor 2 string (NAME). The string will be
 * checked from left to right with the blank literal in Factor 1. The
 * position (2) of the first nonblank character (M) will be stored in
 * the Result Field X.
C      ' '           CHECK     NAME          X

 * When an array is specified in the Result Field, the position of every
 * invalid character in the Factor 2 string will be stored in the elements.
 * In the example shown below, 0123456789 is stored in the Named Constant
 * NUMBERS.  The DATE field specified as the Factor 2 string has a value of
 * b8/11/97.  After execution of the instruction, 1, 3, 6 (the location of
 * b, /, and /) will be stored in the first three elements of the array.
C      NUMBERS       CHECK     DATE          ARRAY

 * When a starting location is specified with the Factor 2 string, check-
 * ing for the Factor 1 characters in the Factor 2 string will begin at
 * that Factor 2 string position.  In the example shown below, the 26
 * letters of the alphabet and a blank are stored in the Named Constant
 * ALPHA.  The CITYST string in Factor 2 has a value of NEW YORK, NY.
 * After execution of the instruction, 9 (the location of the comma) will
 * be stored in the Result Field N.
C      ALPHA         CHECK     CITYST:3      N
  Note: b indicates a blank character.
        Assumes that all Result field items have been previously defined.
```

Figure 11-2 Coding examples of the **CHECK** operation.

CHECKR *(Check Reverse)* Operation

The **CHECKR** operation verifies that each character in the base string (*Factor 2* item) (from right to left) is included in the comparator string (*Factor 1* item). The *Factor 1* and *Factor 2* items must be the same type (both character). Figure 11-3 details the syntax of the **CHECKR** operation.

```
*.. 1 ...+... 2 ...+... 3 ...+... 4 ...+... 5 ...+... 6 ...+... 7 ...+... 8 ...+... 9 ...+ ...10
CLON01Factor1+++++++Opcode&ExtFactor2+++++++Result++++++++Len++D+HiLoEq....Comments++++++++++++
    1         2       CHECKR         4             5                6 5
                        3
```

Figure 11-3 Syntax of the **CHECKR** operation.

1. *Total-* and/or *detail-time* indicators may condition a **CHECKR** instruction.
2. The *Factor 1* item must be defined as character (not numeric) and may include a field name, array element, named constant, data structure name, table name, or literal.
3. The **CHECKR** operation name must be specified in the *Opcode&Ext* field.
4. *Factor 2* must include the name of the string to be checked. The entry may be a field name, array element, named constant, data structure name, table name, or literal defined as character. The entry may be specified with or without a colon and start location. The start location, which must be defined as an integer, indicates where checking for the *Factor 1* characters is to begin in the *Factor 2* string. The entry may be a field name, array element, named constant, table name, or literal. If no start location is specified (colon and entry omitted after the string item), checking will begin at the last character in the *Factor 2* value.
5. The optional *Result* field entry must be defined as an integer and may be a field, array element, array name, or table name. If it is not specified, a *Resulting Indicator* in the *Eq* field (positions 75–76) must be included.

   If the *Result* field contains an array name, the location of every *Factor 2* character field that does not equal a *Factor 1* character will be stored in the array elements. If the *Result* field is not an array, only the location of the first invalid character will be stored in the *Result* field item.
6. A *Resulting Indicator* may be specified in the *Lo* field (positions 73–74), which will be set on if an execution error occurs.

   Figurative Constants cannot be used in *Factor 1, Factor 2,* or the *Result* field.

   Processing Logic:

   Each character in the *Factor 1* item checks the *Factor 2* string for an invalid character (not equal to the character or characters in *Factor 1*). If an invalid character is found in the *Factor 2* string, its location is stored in the *Result* field item. If the *Result* field is not specified, the *Resulting Indicator* in the *Eq* field (positions 75–76) will be set on when the first invalid character is found in the *Factor 2* string.

   The **CHECKR** operation begins at the rightmost character (or the starting position specified) in the *Factor 2* string and continues character by character from right to left until a character not equal to a *Factor 1* character is found or the end of the *Factor 2* string is encountered. If the *Factor 1* character(s) is/are found in the *Factor 2* string, the *Result* field item is set to zero.

   If an array name is specified in the *Result* field, the checking will continue and store the location of every invalid character in the *Factor 2* string. If the *Factor 1* characters are found in the *Factor 2* string, the array elements are all set to zero.

Figure 11-3 Syntax of the **CHECKR** operation. (Continued)

Coding examples of the **CHECKR** operation are shown in Figure 11-4.

```
*.. 1 ...+... 2 ...+... 3 ...+... 4 ...+... 5 ...+... 6 ...+... 7 ...+... 8
CL0N01Factor1+++++++Opcode&ExtFactor2+++++++Result++++++++Len++D+HiLoEq....

 * The CHECKR operation checks the Factor 2 string for invalid characters
 * with characters from the Factor 1 value.  In the example shown below,
 * 'MOUSEb' is stored in the Factor 2 string (NAME). The string will be
 * checked from right to left with the blank literal in Factor 1. The
 * position (5) of the first nonblank character (E) will be stored in
 * the Result Field X.
C     ' '           CHECKR    NAME          X

 * When an array is specified in the Result Field, the position of every
 * invalid character in the Factor 2 string will be stored in the elements.
 * In the example shown below, 0123456789 is stored in the Named Constant
 * NUMBERS.  The DATE field specified as the Factor 2 string has a value of
 * b8/11/97.  After execution of the instruction, 6, 3, 1 (the location of
 * /, /, and b) will be stored in the first three elements of the array.
C     NUMBERS       CHECKR    DATE          ARRAY

 * When a starting location is specified with the Factor 2 string, check-
 * ing for the Factor 1 characters in the Factor 2 string will begin at
 * that Factor 2 string position.  In the example shown below, the 26
 * letters of the alphabet and a blank are stored in the Named Constant
 * ALPHA.  The CITYST string in Factor 2 has a value of NEW YORK, NY.
 * After execution of the instruction, 9 (the location of the comma from
 * the low-order position) will be stored in the Result field N.
C     ALPHA         CHECKR    CITYST:11     N

  Note: b indicates a blank character.
        Assumes that all Result field items have been previously defined.
```

Figure 11-4 Coding examples of the **CHECKR** operation.

SCAN *(Scan String)* Operation

The **SCAN** operation scans the characters (base string) specified in *Factor 2* for the characters stored in *Factor 1*. When the **SCAN** condition is satisfied, the *location* of the *Factor 1* item value in the character string in *Factor 2* is stored in the *Result* field. If an array name (defined with one-byte elements in a size equal to or greater than the *Factor 2* string) is entered in the *Result* field, every incidence of the *Factor 1* value in the *Factor 2* string will be stored in the array elements. Figure 11-5 explains the syntax of the **SCAN** operation.

```
*.. 1 ...+... 2 ...+... 3 ...+... 4 ...+... 5 ...+... 6 ...+... 7 ...+... 8 ...+... 9 ...+ ...10
CLON01Factor1+++++++Opcode&ExtFactor2+++++++Result++++++++Len++D+HiLoEq....Comments++++++++++++
   1        2       SCAN            4              5                 6 5
                     3
```

1. *Total-* and/or *detail-time* indicators may condition a **SCAN** instruction.

2. *Factor 1* must contain a character string (not numeric) defined as a field name, array element, named constant, data structure name, literal, or table name. The *Factor 1* item may be specified with or without a low-order colon (:). When the item is specified without the colon, the full value stored in the *Factor 1* entry is compared to the *Factor 2* character string. If the colon is included at the end of the *Factor 1* entry, followed by an item defined as a numeric integer, the compare will begin at the first character in the *Factor 1* item and compare only the number of characters specified. Thus, if the *Factor 1* entry is 10 characters in length and a 5 is specified after the colon, only the first five characters will be used to scan the *Factor 2* item.

3. The **SCAN** operation must be left-justified in the *Opcode&Ext* field.

4. *Factor 2* must contain a base string entry or a base string entry followed by a colon (:) and the start location for the **SCAN.** The base string entry must be defined as character and may be a field name, array element, named constant, data structure name, literal, or table name. If no start lcoation is specified, the **SCAN** begins at the first character in the base string. When a colon follows the entry and an item defined as a numeric integer, the start location begins at that value.

5. The *Result* field may contain a field name, array element, array name, or table name defined as a numeric integer. If a *Result* field is not specified, a *Resulting Indicator* must be specified in the *Eq* field (positions 75–76). When the *Result* field contains an array, the location of each occurrence is stored in the array beginning with the leftmost occurrence in element 1 of the array. The array should be defined with elements equal to the size of the base string.

6. A *Resulting Indicator* may be included in the *Eq* field (positions 75–76), which is set on if the string scanned for is found in the base string. An indicator may also be specified in the *Lo* field (positions 73–74), which will be set on if an error occurs during execution of the **SCAN** operation.

Processing Logic:

The **SCAN** begins at the leftmost (high-order) character of the *Factor 2* base string. If a colon and numeric integer are included after the base string item, the **SCAN** begins at that position. Then scanning continues character by character from left to right, comparing the characters in *Factor 2* with those in *Factor 1*. If the *Result* field is not an array, only the location of the first occurrence will be stored. On the other hand, if the *Result* field entry is an array, every occurrence of the *Factor 1* entry in the *Factor 2* base string will be stored in the array elements. If no occurrences are found, the *Result* field entry is set to zero.

Note that the **SCAN** operation is case-sensitive. Consequently, an uppercase character will not be equal to the related lowercase character.

Figure 11-5 Syntax of the **SCAN** operation.

Coding examples of the **SCAN** operation appear in detail in Figure 11-6.

```
*.. 1 ...+... 2 ...+... 3 ...+... 4 ...+... 5 ...+... 6 ...+... 7 ...+... 8
CLON01Factor1+++++++Opcode&ExtFactor2+++++++Result++++++++Len++D+HiLoEq....
*
* The SCAN operation searches the base string in Factor 2 (beginning
* with the first character) for the value in Factor 1.  XYZ is found
* in the Factor 2 string beginning in position 3.  The integer 3 will
* be stored in HOLD.  Because the scan is successful, indicator 70 is
* set on.
C     'XYZ'         SCAN      'ABXYZCD'     HOLD                      70
```

Figure 11-6 Coding examples of the **SCAN** operation.

```
 *
 *
 * The SCAN operation searches the string stored in Factor 2 (FIELD1)
 * starting in position 1 for the value stored in Factor 1 (FIELD2).
 * Because the Result Field of the SCAN instruction is an array, 2 and
 * 3, the positions of G in the Factor 2 entry, are stored in the first
 * and second elements of the array (ARRAY).  Indicator 70 will be set
 * on if the scan is successful.
C                    MOVE      'EGGS'        FIELD1
C                    MOVE      'G'           FIELD2
C     FIELD2         SCAN      FIELD1        ARRAY                  70
 *
 *
 * The SCAN operation searches the string in Factor 2, starting in posi-
 * tion 2, for an occurrence of the string in Factor 1 for a length of
 * 3 characters.  Because the scan is not successful, HOLD is set to
 * zero and indicator 70 is not turned on.
C                    MOVE      'ANYTHING'    FIELD1
C                    MOVE      'NYG'         FIELD2
C     FIELD2:3       SCAN      FIELD2:2      HOLD                   70
```

Figure 11-6 Coding examples of the **SCAN** operation. (Continued)

The SUBST *(Substring)* Operation

The **SUBST** operation extracts characters included in the substring in *Factor 2*, starting at the location specified in *Factor 2*, and moves the specified number of characters to the *Result* field based on the value in the *Factor 1* entry. Figure 11-7 explains the syntax of the **SUBST** operation.

```
*.. 1 ...+... 2 ...+... 3 ...+... 4 ...+... 5 ...+... 6 ...+... 7 ...+... 8 ...+... 9 ...+ ...10
CLON01Factor1+++++++Opcode&ExtFactor2+++++++Result++++++++Len++D+HiLoEq....Comments++++++++++++
    1        2        SUBST           4             5               6
                        3
```

1. *Total-* and/or *detail-time* indicators may condition a **SUBST** instruction.

2. *Factor 1* must include the length of the string to be extracted from the string specified in *Factor 2.* The entry may be a literal, field name, named constant, array element, or table name defined as a numeric integer.

3. The **SUBST** operation name must be entered in the *Opcode&Ext* field.

4. *Factor 2* must include a base character string with or without a following colon (:) and a starting location. The base string entry must be character and may contain a literal, field name, table name, named constant, data structure name, or an array element.

   When specified, the entry following the colon must be defined as a numeric integer and have a value greater than zero and not greater than the length of the base string. The start location may be a literal, field name, named constant, array element, or table name. If the starting location is omitted, execution of a **SUBST** instruction begins in position 1 of the *Factor 2* base string.

5. The *Result* field must be defined as character and may contain a field name, table name, array element, or data structure. The substring passed from the *Factor 2* entry is left-justified in the *Result* field item. Its length should be no less than that specified in *Factor 1.* If the substring passed is longer than the *Result* field entry, low-order characters in the string will be truncated.

   If the *Factor 1* entry is shorter than the *Result* field item, a **P** entered in the operation extender position (i.e., **SUBST(P)**) will pad the low positions in the *Result* field entry with blanks.

6. An indicator may be entered in positions 73–74, which will set on if an error occurs when the **SUBST** instruction is executed. An error may occur if the start position is greater than the length of the *Factor 2* entry or if the *Factor 1* entry is larger than the *Result* field item.

Figure 11-7 Syntax of the **SUBST** operation.

Processing Logic:

The **SUBST** operation moves the string value entered in *Factor 2* to the *Result* field item. If a colon and numeric integer item are not included after the string entry, movement begins at the first character in the *Factor 2* string. If a colon and numeric integer item are included, movement begins at that position in the *Factor 2* string. The number of characters moved from the *Factor 2* string to the *Result* field item is controlled by the *Factor 1* entry.

A **P** included with the **SUBST** operation will pad any low-order positions in the *Result* field with blanks when the characters moved from the *Factor 2* string are less than the size of the *Result* field.

Figure 11-7 Syntax of the **SUBST** operation. (Continued)

Coding examples of the **SUBST** operation are shown in Figure 11-8.

```
*...1....+....2....+....3....+....4....+....5....+....6....+....7...*
CLON01N02N03Factor1+++OpcdeFactor2+++ResultLenDHHiLoEqComments++++++
 *
 * The SUBST operation extracts the substring from Factor 2 beginning at
 * position 3.  The 5 in Factor 1 indicates that five characters from
 * the Factor 2 string (BASE) will be moved into LAST. Because the
 * move is successful, indicator 70 will not be set on.  LAST will cont-
 * ain MOUSE after the SUBST is executed.
C                    MOVEL     'M MOUSE'     BASE              7
C     5              SUBST     BASE:3        LAST              5    70
 *
 *
 * The SUBST operation extracts the substring from Factor 2 (YY) begin
 * ning at default position 1.  The 4 in Factor 1 indicates that four
 * characters starting in position 1 of YY will be moved left-justified
 * into YYMMDD.  The Result field YYMMDD will have value of 20000930 after
 * the SUBST statement is executed.  Because the operation is successful,
 * indicator 70 will not be set on.  The example assumes the value in DATE
 * is 09301999.
C                      MOVE '2000'     YY       4
C                      MOVELDATE       MMDD     4
C                      MOVE MMDD       YYMMDD   8
C           4          SUBSTYY         YYMMDD         70
 *
 *
 * The SUBST operation moves the value in the YY substring to the four
 * high-order positions in YYMMDD.  The P entry in column 53 stores blanks
 * in the four low-order positions.  YYMMDD will have a value of 2000bbbb
 * (b = blank) after the SUBST statement is executed.
C                      MOVE '2000'     YY       4
C           4          SUBSTYY         YYMMDD   8 P  70
```

Figure 11-8 Coding examples of the **SUBST** operation.

The XLATE *(Translate)* Operation

The **XLATE** operation translates a *Factor 2* source string according to the *From* and *To* strings formats (both *Factor 1* entries separated by a colon) and stores the translated *Factor 2* value into the *Result* field. Figure 11-9 explains the syntax of the **XLATE** operation.

```
*.. 1 ...+... 2 ...+... 3 ...+... 4 ...+... 5 ...+... 6 ...+... 7 ...+... 8 ...+... 9 ...+ ...10
CLON01Factor1+++++++Opcode&ExtFactor2+++++++Result++++++++Len++D+HiLoEq....Comments+++++++++++++
   1       2       XLATE          4            5                  6
                     3
```

Figure 11-9 Syntax of the **XLATE** operation.

1. *Detail-* and/or *total-time* indicator(s) may condition an **XLATE** instruction.

2. *Factor 1* must contain the *From* string, followed by a colon, followed by the *To* string. The *From* and *To* strings may each be a field name, array element, table name, named constant, data structure name, or literal.

3. The **XLATE** operation name must be entered in the *Opcode&Ext* field. (P) (i.e., **XLATE(P)**) specified with the **XLATE** operation will pad the *Result* field with low-order blanks if the *Factor 2* value is shorter.

4. *Factor 2* must contain either the source string or the source string followed by a colon and the start location. The source string must be defined as character or graphic and may contain a field name, array element, named constant, data structure name, data structure subfield, literal, or table name.

   When a start position is specified (entry after the colon), it must be defined as an integer, named constant, array element, field name, literal, or table name. If no start position is specified, the default position is 1.

5. The *Result* field may be a character or graphic field, character or graphic array element, character or graphic table, or data structure name. The *Result* field should be as large as the *Factor 2* entry. If the *Result* field is larger than the source string, the value from the *Factor 2* item will be left-justified in the *Result* field. If the *Result* field is smaller than the *Factor 2* item, the *Result* field will contain the truncated high-order characters of the *Factor 2* item.

6. A *Resulting Indicator* may be specified in the *Lo* field (positions 73–74), which will turn on if an error occurs when the operation is executed.

   Figurative Constants cannot be used in *Factor 1* or the *Result* field. No overlapping in a data structure is permitted for *Factor 1* and the *Result* field or for *Factor 2* and the *Result* field.

Figure 11-9 Syntax of the **XLATE** operation. (Continued)

Coding examples of the **XLATE** operation are shown in Figure 11-10.

```
*.. 1 ...+... 2 ...+... 3 ...+... 4 ...+... 5 ...+... 6 ...+... 7 ...+... 8
CL0N01Factor1+++++++Opcode&ExtFactor2+++++++Result++++++++Len++D+HiLoEq....

 * The following example translates the comma in the City field value
 * (i.e., NORWALK,CT) from the comma to a blank and stores NORWALK CT in
 * the Result field NewCity.  Resulting Indicator 80 will turn on if an
 * error is detected.

C     ',':' '       XLATE     City          NewCity                  80

 *  The following example translates the characters in the CustName field
 *  from uppercase to lowercase based on the values in the two Named
 *  Constants.  The original value in CustName was MICKEY MOUSE; the value
 *  in NewName after execution of the XLATE instruction is mickey mouse.

*.. 1 ...+... 2 ...+... 3 ...+... 4 ...+... 5 ...+... 6 ...+... 7 ...+... 8
DName+++++++++++ETDsFrom+++To/L+++IDc.Keywords+++++++++++++++++++++++++++++

D UpCase          C                   'ABCDEFGHIJKLMNOPQRSTUVWXYZ'
D Locase          C                   'abcdefghijklmnopqrstuvwxyz'

CL0N01Factor1+++++++Opcode&ExtFactor2+++++++Result++++++++Len++D+HiLoEq....

C     UpCase:LoCase XLATE     CustName      NewName
```

Figure 11-10 Coding examples of the **XLATE** operation.

Application RPG IV Program Using the SCAN, SUBST, and XLATE Operations

An **RPG IV** program that extracts the state code value from a CityState field in the records of a physical file and converts the lowercase CustName field value to uppercase is detailed in the compile listing in Figure 11-11.

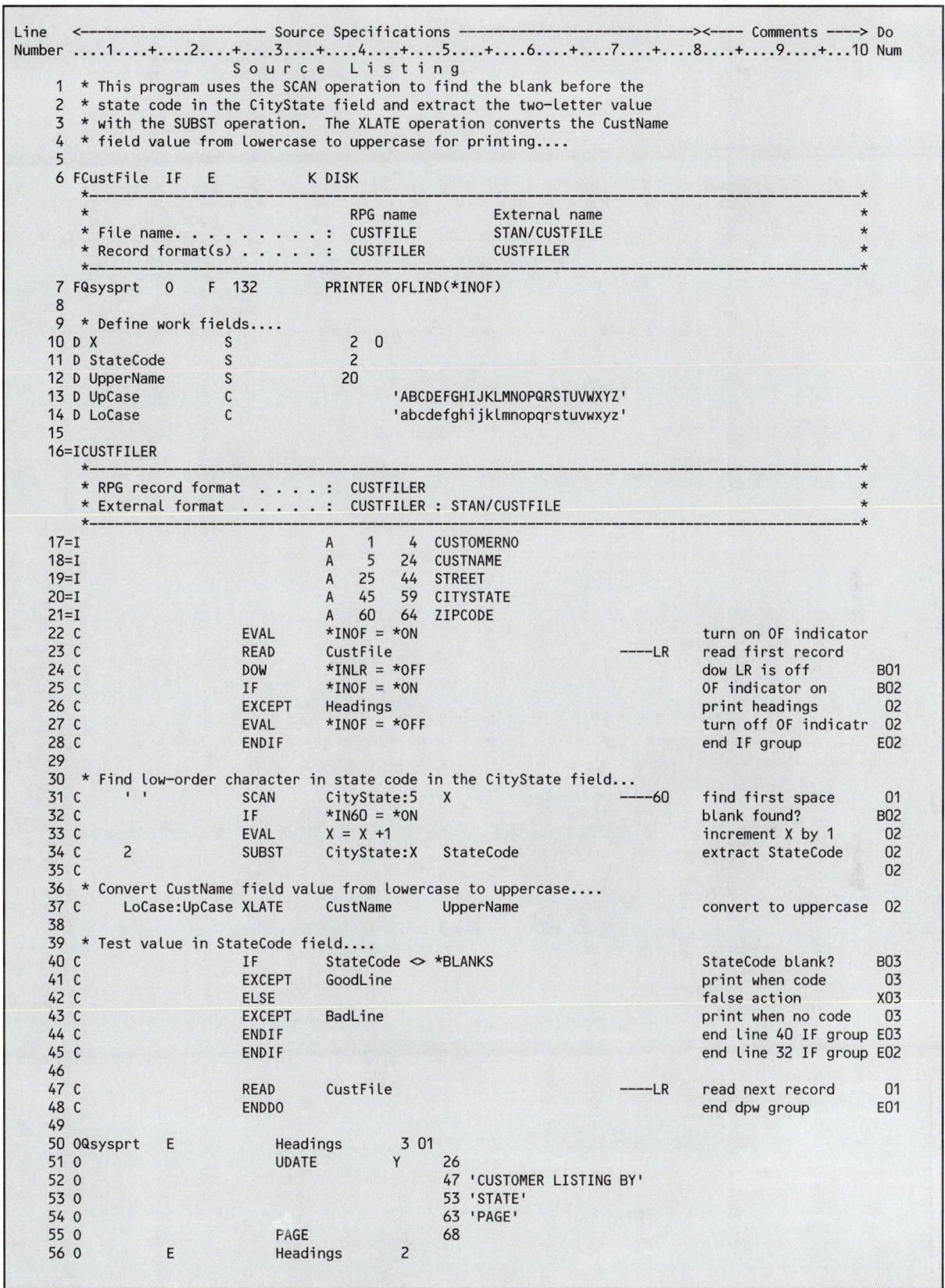

```
Line   <---------------------- Source Specifications ----------------------------><---- Comments ----> Do
Number ....1....+....2....+....3....+....4....+....5....+....6....+....7....+....8....+....9....+...10 Num
                           S o u r c e   L i s t i n g
     1  * This program uses the SCAN operation to find the blank before the
     2  * state code in the CityState field and extract the two-letter value
     3  * with the SUBST operation.  The XLATE operation converts the CustName
     4  * field value from lowercase to uppercase for printing....
     5
     6 FCustFile  IF   E           K DISK
        *--------------------------------------------------------------------------------------------*
        *                             RPG name          External name                                 *
        * File name. . . . . . . . :  CUSTFILE          STAN/CUSTFILE                                 *
        * Record format(s) . . . . :  CUSTFILER         CUSTFILER                                     *
        *--------------------------------------------------------------------------------------------*
     7 FQsysprt   O    F  132        PRINTER OFLIND(*INOF)
     8
     9  * Define work fields....
    10 D X               S              2  0
    11 D StateCode       S              2
    12 D UpperName       S             20
    13 D UpCase          C                   'ABCDEFGHIJKLMNOPQRSTUVWXYZ'
    14 D LoCase          C                   'abcdefghijklmnopqrstuvwxyz'
    15
    16=ICUSTFILER
        *--------------------------------------------------------------------------------------------*
        * RPG record format  . . . :  CUSTFILER                                                       *
        * External format  . . . . :  CUSTFILER : STAN/CUSTFILE                                       *
        *--------------------------------------------------------------------------------------------*
    17=I                             A    1    4  CUSTOMERNO
    18=I                             A    5   24  CUSTNAME
    19=I                             A   25   44  STREET
    20=I                             A   45   59  CITYSTATE
    21=I                             A   60   64  ZIPCODE
    22 C                   EVAL      *INOF = *ON                            turn on OF indicator
    23 C                   READ      CustFile                         ----LR  read first record
    24 C                   DOW       *INLR = *OFF                           dow LR is off        B01
    25 C                   IF        *INOF = *ON                            OF indicator on      B02
    26 C                   EXCEPT    Headings                               print headings        02
    27 C                   EVAL      *INOF = *OFF                           turn off OF indicatr  02
    28 C                   ENDIF                                            end IF group         E02
    29
    30  * Find low-order character in state code in the CityState field...
    31 C     ' '           SCAN      CityState:5   X                  ----60  find first space      01
    32 C                   IF        *IN60 = *ON                            blank found?         B02
    33 C                   EVAL      X = X +1                               increment X by 1      02
    34 C     2             SUBST     CityState:X   StateCode                extract StateCode     02
    35 C                                                                                          02
    36  * Convert CustName field value from lowercase to uppercase....
    37 C     LoCase:UpCase XLATE     CustName      UpperName                convert to uppercase  02
    38
    39  * Test value in StateCode field....
    40 C                   IF        StateCode <> *BLANKS                   StateCode blank?     B03
    41 C                   EXCEPT    GoodLine                               print when code       03
    42 C                   ELSE                                             false action         X03
    43 C                   EXCEPT    BadLine                                print when no code    03
    44 C                   ENDIF                                            end line 40 IF group E03
    45 C                   ENDIF                                            end line 32 IF group E02
    46
    47 C                   READ      CustFile                         ----LR  read next record      01
    48 C                   ENDDO                                            end dpw group        E01
    49
    50 OQsysprt   E            Headings       3 01
    51 O                       UDATE         Y    26
    52 O                                          47 'CUSTOMER LISTING BY'
    53 O                                          53 'STATE'
    54 O                                          63 'PAGE'
    55 O                       PAGE               68
    56 O          E            Headings       2
```

Figure 11-11 Compile listing of the **RPG IV** program that includes the **SCAN, SUBST,** and **XLATE** operations to extract a state code value from a field that includes the city name and state code.

```
57 O                                         28 'CUST#'
58 O                                         45 'NAME'
59 O                                         64 'STATE'
60 O          E          GoodLine       2
61 O                     CustomerNo         28
62 O                     UpperName          53
63 O                     StateCode          62
64 O          E          BadLine        2
65 O                     CustomerNo         28
66 O                     UpperName          53
67 O                                         67 '..NO STATE..'
```

File Description Specifications:

Line No.

6 CustFile is defined as an input (**I** in position 17), full-procedural (**F** in position 18), externally described (**E** in position 22), keyed (**K** in position 34) physical file.

7 Qsysprt is defined as an output (**O** in position 17), program-described (**F** in position 22), with 132 printer positions (132 in positions 23–27) printer file. The **OF** overflow indicator is assigned with the **OFLIND(*INOF)** keyword.

Definition Specifications:

10 X is defined as a standalone field used in the **SCAN** operation to locate the position of the blank in the CityState field value (see line 31). X is incremented on line 33 to extract the state code value from the CityState field.

11 StateCode is defined as a standalone field into which the state code value will be stored by the **SUBST** operation on line 34.

12 UpperName is defined as a standalone field into which the uppercase value of the CustName field will be stored.

13 UpCase is a **Named Constant** (**C** in position 25) with uppercase letters of the alphabet as its value.

14 LoCase is a **Named Constant** (**C** in position 25) with lowercase letters of the alphabet as its value.

Calculation Specifications:

22 The **EVAL** instruction turns on the **OF** overflow indicator to force page overflow for the first record processed.

23 This **READ** instruction reads the first record in the CustFile. If no records are stored in the file, the **LR** indicator will be turned on and will end the program after the **DOW** instruction on line 24 is executed.

24 The **DOW** group will continue to be executed until **LR** is turned on after end of the CustFile is read.

25 This **IF** instruction tests the status of the **OF** page overflow indicator. When **OF** is on, the **EXCEPT** instruction on line 26 will print the Headings format. Because **OF** was turned on with the **EVAL** instruction on line 22, page overflow will occur for the first record processed.

26 This **EXCEPT,** which is executed only if the **IF** instruction on line 25 test is true, prints the two Headings record formats.

27 This **EVAL** instruction turns off the **OF** indicator. After the Headings lines are printed on the first page, subsequent page overflow will occur when the **OF** indicator is automatically turned on when the page overflow line is detected and the **IF** instruction on line 25 tests as true.

28 This **ENDIF** operation ends the **IF** group that began on line 25.

31 The **SCAN** instruction begins scanning the CityState field at the fifth character (i.e., CityState:5) for a blank character. The position of the first blank character in the CityState value will be stored in field X. *Resulting Indicator* 60 will be turned on if a blank is found in the CityState field value.

32 This **IF** instruction tests the status of the indicator 60, which is turned on if the **SCAN** instruction is successful. When the test is true, the following instructions will be executed.

33 This **EVAL** instruction increments **X** by 1 to locate the first character of the state code.

34 The **SUBST** instruction moves two characters (*Factor 1* entry) from the X location in the CityState field to the StateCode field.

37 The **XLATE** instruction converts the alphabetic characters in the CustName field from lowercase to uppercase. The *Factor 1* entry (i.e., LoCase:Up Case), defined as **Named Constants** in the *Definition Specifications,* converts the field value to uppercase and stores the converted value in the UpperName field.

40 This **IF** instruction tests the value in StateCode for a value not equal (< >) to *BLANKS.

Figure 11-11 Compile listing of the **RPG IV** program that includes the **SCAN, SUBST,** and **XLATE** operations to extract a state code value from a field that includes the city name and state code. (Continued)

41	This **EXCEPT** instruction is executed when the StateCode field is greater than *BLANKS, and it prints the GoodLine record format on lines 60–63.
42	The **ELSE** operation begins the false action for the **IF** instruction on line 40.
43	This **EXCEPT** instruction is executed when the StateCode field is blank, and it prints the BadLine record format on lines 64–67.
44	This **ENDIF** operation ends the **IF** group that began on line 40.
45	This **ENDIF** operation ends the **IF** group that began on line 32.
47	This **READ** instruction reads the next record from the CustFile. When end of file is read, indicator **LR** will turn on and end the program when the **DOW** instruction is subsequently executed.
48	The **ENDDO** operation ends the **DOW** group and passes control back to the **DOW** instruction, where the test is made to end the progam or continue processing.
50–59	The printing of the two Headings record formats is controlled by the **EXCEPT** instruction on line 26.
60–63	The printing of the GoodLine record format is controlled by the **EXCEPT** instruction on line 41.
64–67	The printing of the BadLine record format is controlled by the **EXCEPT** instruction on line 43.

Figure 11-11 Compile listing of the **RPG IV** program that includes the **SCAN, SUBST,** and **XLATE** operations to extract a state code value from a field that includes the city name and state code. (Continued)

The %SUBST *(Substring)* Function

The **%SUBST** "built-in" **RPG IV** function provides more flexibility in extracting a substring or portion of a substring than provided by the **SUBST** operation. Examples of the **%SUBST** function are shown in Figure 11-12. (Note: *All* **RPG IV** functions must be included in an expression in an **EVAL** instruction.)

```
*.. 1 ...+... 2 ...+... 3 ...+... 4 ...+... 5 ...+... 6 ...+... 7 ...+... 8
CLON01Factor1+++++++Opcode&ExtFactor2+++++++Result++++++++Len++D+HiLoEq....
CLON01Factor1+++++++Opcode&ExtExtended-factor2+++++++++++++++++++++++++++++
 * The SCAN instruction locates the comma in the StudntName field value
 * (i.e., Mouse, Mickey) and %SUBST function extracts the LastName (Mouse).
C     ','           SCAN     StudntName     Comma
C                   EVAL     LastName = %SUBST(StudntName:1:Comma: - 1)

 * value is extracted beginning at the first character
 * extraction stops when comma is detected
 * comma is deleted from value before it is stored in LastName

 * This example %SUBST function extracts the FirstName field value from
 * the StudntName field....
      ','           SCAN     StudntName     Comma
C                   EVAL     FirstName = %SUBST(StudntName:Comma: + 2)

 * FirstName value is extracted starting with two
 * positions after the Comma's location

 * Note: In both examples a SCAN instruction located the position
 * of the comma before the related SUBST instruction....
```

Figure 11-12 Coding examples of the **RPG IV %SUBST** function.

The calculations shown in Figure 11-13 modify the **RPG IV** program in Figure 11-11 using the **SUBST** operation with the **%SUBST** function. Note that only the changed

```
....1....+....2....+....3....+....4....+....5....+....6....+....7....+....8....+....9....+..10
C * Extract state code from CityState field and store in StateCode field....
C     ' '             SCAN      CityState:5   X                  ----60   find first space
C                     IF        *IN60 = *ON                               blank found?
C                     EVAL      StateCode = %SUBST(CityState:X + 1)       extract StateCode
C
  * Extracts StateCode value beginning at the X location +
  * 1 position (blank after the comma) in CityState field
```

Figure 11-13 Modified example program section using the **%SUBST** function.

calculation instructions are shown. The remainder of the program is identical to the previously discussed program using the **SUBST** operation.

The %TRIM, %TRIML, and %TRIMR Functions

The three **RPG IV %TRIM** functions strip the leading and/or trailing blanks in a character or graphic field value and present the new value. The **%TRIM** functions perform the following:

- **%TRIM**—strips both leading and trailing blanks
- **%TRIML**—strips leading (high-order) blanks and stores the value left-justified in the field
- **%TRIMR**—strips trailing (low-order) blanks and stores the value right-justified in the field.

Without the availability of these functions, eliminating leading and/or trailing blanks in the body of a field requires the use of some combination of **RPG IV CHECK, CHECKR, SCAN,** and **EVAL** instructions. Figure 11-14 illustrates an example of how the **%TRIM** and **%TRIML** functions may be used.

```
*.. 1 ...+... 2 ...+... 3 ...+... 4 ...+... 5 ...+... 6 ...+... 7 ...+... 8
CLON01Factor1+++++++Opcode&ExtExtended-factor2+++++++++++++++++++++++++++++
 * This %TRIM function trims any leading and trailing blanks from the
 * FirstName field.  A FirstName field value of bDONALDbbb (b = a blank)
 * will be trimmed to DONALD without any blanks.  The %TRIML function will
 * trim any leading blanks in the LastName field and left-justify the value
 * (i.e., bbDUCKbbbb to DUCKbbbbbb).  The EVAL instruction concatenates
 * the FirstName and LastName field values and stores the result in the
 * CustName field (i.e., DONALD DUCKbbbbbb).  The ' ' entry after the first
 * + sign stores a blank between the FirstName and LastName values in the
 * CustName field....

C                   EVAL      CustName = %TRIM(FirstName) + ' ' +
C                                        %TRIML(LastName)
```

Figure 11-14 Coding examples of the **%TRIM** and **%TRIML** functions.

RPG IV Application Program Using the %TRIMR Function

The compile listing of the **RPG IV** program in Figure 11-15 includes the following new features:

1. A **%TRIMR** function removes low-order blanks from the City field.
2. An **EVAL** instruction concatenates the City, State, and ZipCode field values and stores the result in one field.

```
Line    <---------------------- Source Specifications ----------------------------><---- Comments ----> Do
Number ....1....+....2....+....3....+....4....+....5....+....6....+....7....+....8....+....9....+...10 Num
                           S o u r c e   L i s t i n g
     1  * This program concatenates the CITY, STATE & ZIPCODE fields....
     2 FCustomers IF   E             K DISK
        *--------------------------------------------------------------------------------------------*
        *                              RPG name          External name                                *
        * File name. . . . . . . . . : CUSTOMERS         STAN/CUSTOMERS                               *
        * Record format(s) . . . . . : CUSTRECORD        CUSTRECORD                                   *
        *--------------------------------------------------------------------------------------------*
     3 FQsysprt   O    F  132        PRINTER OFLIND(*INOF)
     4
     5 D CitStatZip      S             29
     6=ICUSTRECORD
        *--------------------------------------------------------------------------------------------*
        * RPG record format  . . . . : CUSTRECORD                                                     *
        * External format  . . . . . : CUSTRECORD : STAN/CUSTOMERS                                    *
        *--------------------------------------------------------------------------------------------*
     7=I                             A    1    5  CUSTOMERNO
     8=I                             A    6   25  CUSTNAME
     9=I                             A   26   45  STREET
    10=I                             A   46   65  CITY
    11=I                             A   66   67  STATE
    12=I                             A   68   72  ZIPCODE
    13=I                             P   73   77 2ACTBALANCE
    14 C                   EVAL      *INOF = *ON                           turn on OF indicator
    15 C                   READ      Customers                      ----LR read first record
    16 C                   DOW       *INLR = *OFF                          dow LR is off        B01
    17 C                   IF        *INOF = *ON                           OF indicator on?     B02
    18 C                   EXCEPT    Heading                               print heading         02
    19 C                   EVAL      *INOF = *OFF                          turn off OF indicatr  02
    20 C                   ENDIF                                           end IF group         E02
    21
    22  * Concatenate CITY, STATE, ZIPCODE field values....
    23 C                   EVAL      CitStatZip = %TRIMR(City) + ' ' + State + ' '                01
    24 C                             + ZipCode                             concatenate fields    01
    25 C                   EXCEPT    DetailLine                            print detail line     01
    26 C                   READ      Customers                      ----LR read next record      01
    27 C                   ENDDO                                           end DOW group        E01
    28
    29 OQsysprt   E            Heading        2  01
    30 O                       *DATE          Y       11
    31 O                                              31 'CUSTOMER LISTING'
    32 O                                              40 'PAGE'
    33 O                       PAGE                   +1
    34 O          E            DetailLine     1
    35 O                       CustName               32
    36 O          E            DetailLine     1
    37 O                       Street                 32
    38 O          E            DetailLine     3
    39 O                       CitStatZip             41
```

File Description Specifications:

Line No.

2 Customers is defined as an input (**I** in position 17), full-procedural (**F** in position 18), externally described (**E** in position 22), keyed (**K** in position 34) physical file.

3 Qsysprt is defined as an output (**O** in position 17), program-described (**F** in position 22), with 132 print positions (132 in positions 23–27) printer file. The **OF** overflow indicator is assigned with the **OFLIND(*INOF)** keyword.

Definition Specifications:

5 CitStatZip is defined as a standalone field in which the *trimmed* and *concatenated* City, State, and ZipCode field values will be stored.

Figure 11-15 RPG IV program that includes the **%TRIMR** function and concatenates the City, State, and ZipCode fields.

Calculation Specifications:

14 This **EVAL** instruction turns on the **OF** overflow indicator to force page overflow for the first record processed.

15 This **READ** instruction reads the first record in the Customers file. If no records are stored in the file, the **LR** indicator will be turned on and will end the program when the **DOW** instruction on line 16 is executed.

16 The **DOW** group will be executed until **LR** is turned on after the end of the Customers file is read.

17 This **IF** instruction tests the status of the **OF** page overflow indicator. When **OF** is on, the **EXCEPT** instruction on line 18 will print the Heading line record format. Because **OF** was turned on with the **EVAL** instruction on line 14, page overflow will occur for the first record processed.

18 This **EXCEPT** instruction, which is executed only when the **IF** instruction on line 17 test is true, prints the Heading line record format.

19 This **EVAL** instruction turns off the **OF** indicator. After the Heading line is printed on the first page, subsequent page overflow will occur when the **OF** indicator is automatically turned on when the page overflow line is detected and the **IF** instruction on line 17 test is true.

20 This **ENDIF** operation ends the **IF** group.

23–24 This **EVAL** instruction concatenates the City, State, and ZipCode field values and stores the result in the CitStatZip field. The **%TRIML** function removes any low-order blanks from the City field value. The format in this instruction is explained below:

Trims low-order blanks ↓ Performs concatenation

CitStatZip = %TRIML(City) + ' ' + State + ' ' + Zipcode

Inserts a blank between field values ↑ ↑

25 This **EXCEPT** instruction prints the three DetailLine record formats.

26 This **READ** instruction reads the next record from the Customers file. When end of file is read, indicator **LR** will turn on and will end the program when the **DOW** instruction is subsequently executed.

27 The **ENDDO** operation ends the **DOW** group and passes control back to the **DOW** instruction, where the test is made to end the program or continue processing.

Output Specifications:

29–33 The printing of the Heading record format is controlled by the **EXCEPT** instruction on line 18.

34–39 The printing of the three DetailLine record formats is controlled by the **EXCEPT** instruction on line 25.

Figure 11-15 **RPG IV** program that includes the **%TRIMR** function and concatenates the City, State, and ZipCode fields. (Continued)

A partial listing of the report generated by the **RPG IV** program in Figure 11-15 is shown in Figure 11-16.

```
9/01/1997    CUSTOMER LISTING      PAGE    1

             KAREL APPEL
             20 AMSTERDAM AVENUE
             NEW YORK NY 07450 ─┐
                                │ Concatenated
             GEORGES BRAQUE     │ field values
             300 ST CLAIR SREET │
             TRENTON NJ 05501 ──┘
```

Figure 11-16 Partial report generated by the **%TRIMR** and concatenation **RPG IV** program.

The %SIZE Function

The **%SIZE** function determines the number of bytes stored in an array, data structure, field, literal, or named constant. Figure 11-17 shows coding examples of the **%SIZE** function.

```
*.. 1 ...+... 2 ...+... 3 ...+... 4 ...+... 5 ...+... 6 ...+... 7 ...+... 8
CLON01Factor1+++++++Opcode&ExtExtended-factor2+++++++++++++++++++++++++++++
 * The following %SIZE function determines if the value in the CustName
 * field is less than or equal to 25 and print one of two output
 * records....
C                   IF     %SIZE(CustName) <= 25
C                   EXCEPT GoodLine
C                   ELSE
C                   EXCEPT BadLine
C                   ENDIF

 * The following example illustrates how a zoned numeric field size and a packed-
 * decimal numeric field size are determined with the %SIZE function....

*.. 1 ...+... 2 ...+... 3 ...+... 4 ...+... 5 ...+... 6 ...+... 7 ...+... 8
DName+++++++++++ETDsFrom+++To/L+++IDc.Keywords+++++++++++++++++++++++++++++
CLON01Factor1+++++++Opcode&ExtExtended-factor2+++++++++++++++++++++++++++++
D Zoned_Fld       S              5S 0
D Packed_Fld      S              3P 0

C                   EVAL   Fld_Length = %SIZE(Zoned_Fld)
C                   EVAL   Fld_Length = %SIZE(Packed_Fld)

* For the first %SIZE example, 5 is stored in the Fld_Length field.  In the
* second %SIZE example,  3 is stored in the Fld_Length field (the number
* of bytes occupied by the value, and not the unpacked value of 5).
```

Figure 11-17 Coding examples of the **%SIZE** function.

The %ELEM Function

The **%ELEM** function returns the number of elements in an array or table or the number of occurrences in a multiple-occurrence data structure. Figure 11-18 illustrates one example of how the **%ELEM** function may be used.

```
*.. 1 ...+... 2 ...+... 3 ...+... 4 ...+... 5 ...+... 6 ...+... 7 ...+... 8
DName+++++++++++ETDsFrom+++To/L+++IDc.Keywords+++++++++++++++++++++++++++++
CLON01Factor1+++++++Opcode&ExtExtended-factor2+++++++++++++++++++++++++++++
 * The SalesPAry is defined as Prerun with 15 elements
D SalesPAry       S              8  2 DIM(15) ASCEND FROMFILE(SalePeople)

 * The %ELEM function determines how many iterations of the DOU group will
 * be performed by storing the number of array elements as its value.  If
 * the number of elements in the array is changed, the %ELEM function
 * value will adjust accordingly.

C                   EVAL   Elements = 1
C                   DOW    Elements = %ELEM(SalesPAry)
C                   EVAL   Elements = Elements + 1
C            ..... Other instructions....
C                   ENDDO
```

Figure 11-18 Coding example of the **%ELEM** function.

RPG IV POINTER SUPPORT

Pointers are commonly used in **C** language programming but are a new addition to **RPG IV.** Transparent to the **RPG IV** programmer, pointers have been used by the AS/400 system when parameters are passed from one program to another by **CALL** instructions.

A pointer points to an address in memory indicating where an item may be found; it does *not* point to the value of the item. The value stored in the pointer will always be a 16-byte memory address of the related item.

Pointer Types and the %ADDR and %PADDR Functions

RPG IV supports two types of pointers: basing and procedure pointers. *Basing* pointers point to data; *procedure* pointers point to procedures or functions.

The **%ADDR** function stores the address of an array element, variable, or expression in an item defined as a pointer. The **%PADDR** function stores the address of a procedure in an item defined as a pointer.

Pointers are defined in the *Definition Specifications* as "standalone" items with an asterisk in the *internal data type* field (position 40). Because pointers have a default size of 16 bytes, they *do not* have to be given a size in their definition. Figure 11-19 shows examples of how basing and procedure pointers are defined and used.

Some **RPG IV** applications where pointers may be useful include the following:

1. Accessing the hundreds of *application programming interfaces (APIs)* provided with the OS/400 operating system
2. Calling other programs and accessing the address of passed data
3. Improving the performance of programs included in an **RPG IV** module.

```
*.. 1 ...+... 2 ...+... 3 ...+... 4 ...+... 5 ...+... 6 ...+... 7 ...+... 8
DName+++++++++++ETDsFrom+++To/L+++IDc.Keywords+++++++++++++++++++++++++++++
CL0N01Factor1+++++++Opcode&ExtExtended-factor2+++++++++++++++++++++++++++++
 * This instruction defines a pointer that does not point to anything...
D Pointer1        S               *

 * These instructions define an array and a pointer (Pointer1) in which the
 * address of the array is stored....
D MthArray        S              9    DIM(12)
D Pointer1        S               *   INZ(%ADDR(MthArray))

 * This instruction implicitly defines a basing pointer that holds the
 * address of the data item specified in the Factor 1 field.  The value
 * stored in MthName will be based on the address in Pointer2....
D MthName         S              9    BASED(Pointer2)

 * This instruction defines a procedure pointer with the PROCPTR keyword.
 * Pointer3 will store the address of the NewCust procedure or program.
 * Note that the %PADDR keyword must be used for procedure pointers.
D Pointer3        S               *   PROCPTR
D                                     INZ(%PADDR(NewCust))
```

Figure 11-19 Examples of basing and procedure pointers.

DATE AND TIME OPERATIONS

The **ADDDUR** *(Add Duration)*, **SUBDUR** *(Subtract Duration)*, and **EXTRCT** *(Extract Date/Time/Timestamp)* **RPG IV** operations support calculations. All three operations use the duration codes: ***YEARS** (or ***Y**), ***MONTHS** (or ***M**), ***DAYS** (or ***D**), ***HOURS** (or ***H**), ***MINUTES** (or ***MN**), ***SECONDS** (or ***S**), and ***MSECONDS** (or ***MS**) to determine how the date, time, or timestamp value is to be processed. A **TEST** *(Test Date/Time/Timestamp)* operation may be used to test the validity of the date, time, or timestamp value. Each operation is explained in the following subsections.

ADDDUR *(Add Duration)* Operation

The **ADDDUR** operation adds a duration to a date or time. Figure 11-20 explains the syntax of the **ADDDUR** operation.

```
*.. 1 ...+... 2 ...+... 3 ...+... 4 ...+... 5 ...+... 6 ...+... 7 ...+... 8 ...+... 9 ...+ ...10
CLON01Factor1+++++++Opcode&ExtFactor2+++++++Result++++++++Len++D+HiLoEq....Comments+++++++++++++
   1          2       ADDDUR          4             5                   6
                        3
```

1. *Total-* and/or *detail-time* indicators may condition an **ADDDUR** instruction.
2. *Factor 1* is optional and may contain a Date, Time, or Timestamp field, array, array element, constant, literal, or subfield. If *Factor 1* includes a field name, array, or array element, it must be defined with the same data type as the field specified in the *Result* field. If *Factor 1* is not specified, the duration (*Factor 2* entry) is added to the field in the *Result* field.
3. The **ADDDUR** operation name must be specified in the *OpCode&Ext* field.
4. *Factor 2* is required and must include two subfactors in the following format:

   Duration:Duration Code

   The first entry (before the colon) must be a duration stored in a numeric field, array element, or constant defined as an integer. The second entry (after the colon) must be a valid duration code (i.e., ***Y, *M, *D, *H, *M, *MS,** or their equivalent words) indicating the type of date or time duration.

   The duration code specified must be consistent with the *Result* field type. In other words, a date duration cannot be added to a time field or vice versa.
5. The *Result* field must be a date, time, or timestamp data type field, array, or array element. If *Factor 1* is not specified, the duration is added to the *Result* field. When the *Result* field is an array, the duration is added to each element in the array.

   If the *Result* field is a time field, the result must be a valid time. When the calculated result is greater than or equal to 24:00:00, 24 (or a multiple of 24) hours must be subtracted until the time is valid.
6. A *Resulting Indicator* may be specified in the *Lo* field (positions 73–74), which will be turned on if an error is detected when an **ADDDUR** instruction is executed.

   Note: The value in the duration item (*Factor 2* entry to the left of the required colon) may not be larger than **15** digits. Adding a duration of more than 15 digits will cause truncation or processing errors.

Figure 11-20 Syntax of the **ADDDUR** operation.

SUBDUR *(Subtract Duration)* Operation

The **SUBDUR** operation subtracts a duration from a date or time value. Figure 11-21 explains the syntax of this operation.

```
*.. 1 ...+... 2 ...+... 3 ...+... 4 ...+... 5 ...+... 6 ...+... 7 ...+... 8 ...+... 9 ...+ ...10
CLON01Factor1+++++++Opcode&ExtFactor2+++++++Result++++++++Len++D+HiLoEq....Comments+++++++++++++
   1          2       SUBDUR          4             5                   6
                        3
```

1. *Total-* and/or *detail-time* indicators may condition a **SUBDUR** instruction.
2. *Factor 1* is optional and may contain a Date, Time, or Timestamp field, array, array element, constant, literal, or subfield. If *Factor 1* includes a field name, array, or array element, it must be defined with the same data type as the field specified in the *Result* field. If *Factor 1* is not specified, the duration (*Factor 2* entry) is subtracted from the *Result* field.
3. The **SUBDUR** operation name must be specified in the *OpCode&Ext* field.
4. *Factor 2* is required and must include two subfactors in the following format:

   Duration:Duration Code

   The first entry (before the colon) must be a duration stored in a numeric field, array element, or constant defined as an integer. The second entry (after the colon) must be a valid duration code (i.e., ***Y, *M, *D, *H, *M, *MS,** or their equivalent words) indicating the type of date or time duration.

   The duration code specified must be consistent with the *Result* field type. In other words, a date duration cannot be subtracted from a time field or vice versa.

Figure 11-21 Syntax of the **SUBDUR** operation.

5. The *Result* field must be a date, time, or timestamp data type field, array, or array element. If *Factor 1* is not specified, the duration is subtracted from the *Result* field. When the *Result* field is an array, the duration is subtracted from each element in the array.

   If the *Result* field is a time field, the result must be a valid time. When the calculated result is greater than or equal to 24:00:00, 24 (or a multiple of 24) hours must be subtracted until the time is valid.

6. A *Resulting Indicator* may be specified in the *Lo* field (positions 73–74), which will be turned on if an error is detected when a SUBDUR instruction is executed.

   Note: The value in the duration item (*Factor 2* entry to the left of the required colon) may not be larger than **15** digits. Subtracting a duration of more than 15 digits will cause truncation or processing errors.

Figure 11-21 Syntax of the **SUBDUR** operation. (Continued)

Coding examples of the **ADDDUR** and **SUBDUR** operations are shown in the compile listing of the **RPG IV** program in Figure 11-22.

```
Line    <---------------------- Source Specifications ----------------------------><---- Comments ----> Do
Number ....1....+....2....+....3....+....4....+....5....+....6....+....7....+....8....+....9....+...10 Num
                         S o u r c e   L i s t i n g
     1  * This program illustrates examples of ADDDUR and SUBDUR instructions....
     2 HDATFMT(*USA) TIMFMT(*USA)                                                 format of date flds
     3
     4 FQsysprt   O    F  132         PRINTER
     5
     6  * Define date and work fields....
     7 D Loan_Date       S               D   DATFMT(*USA) INZ(D'11/25/1997')     int. Loan_Date field
     8 D Mat_Date        S               D   DATFMT(*USA)
     9 D Loan_Time       S              2  0 INZ(60)
    10 D Visit_Time      S               T   TIMFMT(*USA) INZ(T'00:00 AM')
    11 D New_Time        S               T   TIMFMT(*USA)
    12 D
    13 C     Loan_Date     ADDDUR    Loan_Time:*D  Mat_Date
    14 C                   EXCEPT    print1                                      print record
    15 C                   ADDDUR    3:*Y          Loan_Date
    16 C                   EXCEPT    Print2
    17 C     Visit_Time    ADDDUR    11:*H         New_Time
    18 C                   EXCEPT    Print3
    19 C     Mat_Date      SUBDUR    60:*D         Loan_Date
    20 C                   EXCEPT    Print4
    21 C                   EVAL      *INLR = *ON
    22
    23 OQsysprt   E            Print1         2 01
    24 O                       Mat_Date           12
    25 O          E            Print2         2
    26 O                       Loan_Date          12
    27 O          E            Print3         2
    28 O                       New_Time           12
    29 O          E            Print4         2
    30 O                       Loan_Date          12
```

Header Specifications:

Line No.

2 The **DATFMT(*USA)** keyword specifies the output format of date fields defined in the *Definition Specifications* with a **D** in the *Internal data type* field (position 40).

The **TIMFMT(*USA)** keyword specifies the output format of time fields defined in the *Definition Specifications* with a **T** in the *Internal data type* field (position 40).

Without the **DATFMT** and **TIMFMT** keywords in the *Header Specifications,* date and time formats would default to ***ISO** and not be compatible with the date and time formats defined in *Definition Specification* instructions on lines 7, 8, 10, and 11.

Figure 11-22 Compile listing of an **RPG IV** program that illustrates examples of the **ADDDUR** and **SUBDUR** operations.

File Description Specifications:

4 Qsysprt is defined as an output (**O** in position 17), program-described (**F** in position 22), with 132 print positions (132 in positions 23–27) printer file.

For simplicity, all of the data and time values are included in *Definition Specification* instructions. Consequently, no input file is specified.

Definition Specifications:

7 Loan_Date is defined as a standalone (**S** in the *Type of definition* field) date field (**D** in the *Internal data type* field). The **DATFMT(*USA)** keyword assigns the ***USA** date format (i.e., mm/dd/yyyy) to this field. The **INZ(D'11/25/1997')** keyword entry initializes the Loan_Date field to 11/25/1997.

8 Mat_Date is defined as a standalone (**S** in the *Type of definition* field) date field (**D** in the *Internal data type* field). The **DATFMT(*USA)** keyword defines this date field in the ***USA** date format.

9 Loan_Time is defined as a standalone (**S** in the *Type of definition* field) that is initialized to 60 with the **INZ(60)** keyword.

10 Visit_Time is defined as a standalone (**S** in the *Type of definition* field) time field (**T** in the *Internal data type* field). The **TIMFMT(*USA)** keyword assigns the ***USA** date format (i.e., hh:mm AM) to this field. The **INZ(T'00:00 AN')** keyword entry initializes the Visit_Time field to **00:00 AM.**

11 New_Time is defined as a standalone (**S** in the *Type of definition* field) time field (**T** in the *Internal data type* field). The **DATFMT(*USA)** keyword entry defines this time field in the ***USA** time format.

Calculation Specifications:

13 This **ADDDUR** instruction adds the value in Loan_Time (60) to the Mat_Date field. The ***D** entry after the colon in the *Factor 2* entry specifies that the value in Loan_Time is processed in days. If ***M** was specified, the value in Loan_Time would be processed in months. If ***Y** was specified, the value would be processed in years. After the instruction is executed, the value in Mat_Date will be the Loan_Date value plus the Loan_Time value incremented in days.

14 This **EXCEPT** instruction prints the Print1 record format.

15 The *Factor 2* entry, **3:*Y,** will add 3 years to the Loan_Date value when this **ADDDUR** instruction is executed.

16 This **EXCEPT** instruction prints the Print2 record format.

17 This **ADDDUR** instruction adds 11 hours (i.e., *Factor 2* entry 11:*H) to the Visit_Time field value and stores the result in the New_Time field.

18 This **EXCEPT** instruction prints the Print3 record format.

19 The **SUBDUR** instruction subtracts 60 days (i.e., *Factor 2* entry 60:*D) from the Mat_Date field and stores the result in Loan_Date.

20 This **EXCEPT** instruction prints the Print4 record format.

21 The **EVAL** instruction turns on the **LR** indicator to end the program. Because no input file is specified and end of file is not tested to turn on the **LR** indicator, this instruction must be included for this control.

Output Specifications:

23–30 The output instructions include the four record formats printed by the **EXCEPT** instructions on lines 14, 16, 18, and 20.

Figure 11-22 Compile listing of an **RPG IV** program that illustrates examples of the **ADDDUR** and **SUBDUR** operations. (Continued)

The report generated by the **RPG IV** program in Figure 11-22 is shown in Figure 11-23. Note that there are no headings and that the original value of the related output is shown as author-supplied comments to the right of the printed values.

```
01/24/1998      (60 days were added to 11/25/1997)

11/25/2000      (3 years were added to 11/25/1997)

  11:00 AM      (11 hours were added to 00:00 AM)

11/25/1997      (60 days were subtracted from 01/24/1998)
```

Figure 11-23 Commented printed report generated by the **RPG IV** program in Figure 11-22, which illustrates example **ADDDUR** and **SUBDUR** instructions.

The EXTRCT *(Extract Date/Time/Timestamp)* Operation

The **EXTRCT** operation will return

- the day, month, or year part of a date or timestamp field
- the hours, minutes, or seconds of a time or timestamp field
- the microseconds part of a timestamp field.

The syntax of the **EXTRCT** operation is detailed in Figure 11-24.

```
*.. 1 ...+... 2 ...+... 3 ...+... 4 ...+... 5 ...+... 6 ...+... 7 ...+... 8 ...+... 9 ...+ ...10
CLON01Factor1+++++++Opcode&ExtFactor2+++++++Result++++++++Len++D+HiLoEq....Comments+++++++++++++
   1        2      EXTRCT        4            5              6
                     3
```

1. *Total-* and/or *detail-time* indicators may condition an **EXTRCT** instruction.
2. *Factor 1* is not used.
3. The **EXTRCT** operation name must be specified in the *OpCode&Ext* field.
4. *Factor 2* is required and must include two subfactors in the following format:

   Date/Time/Timestamp:Duration Code

   The first entry (before the colon) must be a date, time, or timestamp field, subfield, array, array element, or table entry. The second entry (after the colon) must be a valid duration code (i.e., ***Y, *M, *D, *H, *M, *MS,** or their equivalent words) consistent with the data type specified before the colon indicating the type date, time, or timestamp duration.
5. The *Result* field may be a numeric or character field, subfield, array element, table element.
6. A *Resulting Indicator* may be specified in the *Lo* field (positions 73–74), which will be turned on if an error is detected when an **EXTRCT** instruction is executed.

Figure 11-24 Syntax of the **EXTRCT** operation.

Coding examples of **EXTRCT** instructions are shown in Figure 11-25.

```
*.. 1 ...+... 2 ...+... 3 ...+... 4 ...+... 5 ...+... 6 ...+... 7 ...+... 8
CLON01Factor1+++++++Opcode&ExtFactor2+++++++Result++++++++Len++D+HiLoEq....
 * This EXTRCT instruction extracts the month value from a date field
C                   EXTRCT    Due_Date:*M   Due_Month          2 0

 * This EXTRCT instruction extracts the day value from a date field
C                   EXTRCT    Due_Date:*D   Due_Day            2 0

 * This EXTRCT instruction extracts the year value from a date field
C                   EXTRCT    Due_Date:*Y   Due_Year           4 0

* This EXTRCT instruction extracts the hour value from a time field
C                   EXTRCT    Work_Time:*H  Work_Hrs           2 0

* This EXTRCT instruction extracts the microseconds from a Timestamp field
C                   EXTRCT    Test_Time:*MS Microsecnd         4 0
```

Figure 11-25 Coding examples of **EXTRCT** instructions.

The TEST *(Test Date/Time/Timestamp)* Operation

The **TEST** operation tests the validity of a date, time, or timestamp field value before it is subsequently used elsewhere in an **RPG IV** program. Figure 11-26 explains the syntax of the **TEST** operation.

```
*.. 1 ...+... 2 ...+... 3 ...+... 4 ...+... 5 ...+... 6 ...+... 7 ...+... 8 ...+... 9 ...+ ...10
CLON01Factor1+++++++Opcode&ExtFactor2+++++++Result++++++++Len++D+HiLoEq....Comments++++++++++++
   1      2       TEST(D/T/Z)      4             5                  6
                   3
```

1. *Total-* and/or *detail-time* indicators may condition a **TEST** instruction.

2. If the *Result* field includes a field defined as a date, time, or timestamp, *Factor 1* must be blank. However, if the *Result* field includes a field defined as numeric or character, *Factor 1* is optional and may contain any valid Date, Time, or Timestamp format.

   When *Factor 1* is blank, the date, time, or timestamp format specified in the *Header Specifications* with the **DATFMT** or **TIMFMT** keyword(s) is used. If this entry is not made, the *ISO date and time format is the default.

3. The **TEST** operation name must be entered in the *OpCode&Ext* field. An extender (i.e., **D, T,** or **Z**) must be included if the *Result* field contains a numeric or character field.

   When the extender is **D** or **T,** a *Factor 1* entry is optional. However, it must be specified if it must contain an item with a valid date or time format.

   When the extender is **Z** (Timestamp), *Factor 1* must be blank.

4. A *Resulting Indicator* must be specified in the *Lo* field (positions 73–74), which will be turned on if the value in the *Result* field is not a valid date, time, or timestamp.

Note: Character fields are tested for valid digits and separators. Numeric fields are tested only for valid digits.

Figure 11-26 Syntax of the **TEST** operation.

Coding examples of the **TEST** operation are presented in Figure 11-27.

```
*.. 1 ...+... 2 ...+... 3 ...+... 4 ...+... 5 ...+... 6 ...+... 7 ...+... 8
CLON01Factor1+++++++Opcode&ExtFactor2+++++++Result++++++++Len++D+HiLoEq....
 * This TEST instruction tests the TransDate field for a valid date.  Be-
 * cause TransDate is in a *ISO format and no DATFMT keyword is specified
 * as a Header Specification instruction, the default for all date fields
 * is a *ISO format. Consequently, the date is valid so indicator 80 will
 * not be turned on.
                   EVAL      TransDate = 19971215
C                  TEST(D)               TransDate               80

 * This TEST instruction tests the TransDate field for a *USA date format.
 * Because *USA is not in the same format as the *ISO default, indicator
 * 80 will be turned on, indicating an invalid date format.
C     *USA         TEST(D)               TransDate               80

 * This TEST instruction tests PaidDate field for a valid date format.
 * PaidDate must be defined as 10 characters to include hyphens in its
 * value.  Indicator 80 will not turn on, because the PaidDate value is in
 * the default *ISO format.
C                  EVAL      PaidDate = '1997-12-31'
C                  TEST                  PaidDate                80

 * This TEST instruction tests the StartTime value for a valid time in a
 * *HMS format.  Because the value in StartTime is in a *HMS format, in-
 * dicator 80 will not turn on.
C                  EVAL      StartTime = 183000
C     *HMS         TEST                  StartTime               80

Note: The fields used in the TEST intructions are initialized with values
by EVAL instructions.  In practice, the values would be input from fields
in a physical or logical file.
```

Figure 11-27 Coding examples of **TEST** instructions.

RPG IV Application Program Using the ADDDUR and EXTRCT Operations

A source listing of the physical file that is processed by the **RPG IV** program in Figure 11-29, which computes the due dates on loans, is shown in Figure 11-28. Note that the

```
A..........T.Name++++++RLen++TDpB......Functions++++++++++++++++++
A                                      UNIQUE
A          R LOANRECORD
A            LOAN_NO        4
A            LOAN_NAME     15
A            LOAN_DATE       L         DATFMT(*MDY) DATSEP('/')
A            LOAN_TIME      5 0
A            LOAN_AMT       8 2
A          K LOAN_NO

The L in the T field defines LOAN DATE as a date field
The DATFMT(*MDY) keyword specifies that the date value is
in an mmddyyyy format
The DATSEP('/') keyword includes the / delimiter between
the date elements (i.e., mm/dd/yyyy)
```

Figure 11-28 Source listing of the physical file processed by the example **RPG IV** progam in Figure 11-22.

LOAN_DATE field is defined as a date field by the **L** in the *T* (*Data Type* field—position 35). The **DATFMT(*USA)** keyword specifies the date format (i.e., mmddyyyy); the **DATSEP('/')** keyword assigns slashes as the date separator (i.e., mm/dd/yyyy). This coding makes the date field compatible with the standalone date fields included in the **ADDDUR** instruction in the following **RPG IV** program.

A compile listing of an **RPG IV** program that computes the due date on loans and generates a report is detailed in Figure 11-29.

```
Line   <--------------------- Source Specifications ---------------------------><---- Comments ----> Do
Number ....1....+....2....+....3....+....4....+....5....+....6....+....7....+....8....+....9....+...10 Num
                       S o u r c e   L i s t i n g
     1  * This program computes the maturity date on loans....
     2 HDATFMT(*MDY)                                                              format of date flds
     3
     4 FLoansfile IF   E           K DISK
       *----------------------------------------------------------------------------------------------*
       *                            RPG name         External name                                     *
       * File name. . . . . . . . :  LOANSFILE        STAN/LOANSFILE                                    *
       * Record format(s) . . . . :  LOANRECORD       LOANRECORD                                        *
       *----------------------------------------------------------------------------------------------*
     5 FQsysprt   O    F  132        PRINTER
     6
     7  * Define date and work fields...
     8 D Due_Date        S               D   DATFMT(*MDY)
     9 D Due_Mth         S              2
    11 D Due_Yr          S              2
    12
    13=ILOANRECORD
       *----------------------------------------------------------------------------------------------*
       * RPG record format  . . . . :  LOANRECORD                                                     *
       * External format  . . . . . :  LOANRECORD : STAN/LOANSFILE                                    *
       *----------------------------------------------------------------------------------------------*
    14=I                             A    1    4  LOAN_NO
    15=I                             A    5   19  LOAN_NAME
```

Figure 11-29 Compile listing of an example **RPG IV** program that uses the **ADDDUR** and **EXTRCT** instructions to process date type fields.

```
16=I                          *MDY/D   20   27  LOAN_DATE
17=I                               P   28   30 0LOAN_TIME
18=I                               P   31   35 2LOAN_AMT
19 C                    EXCEPT     Heading                              print heading lines
20 C                    READ       LoansFile                 ----LR     read first record
21 C                    DOW        *INLR = *OFF                         dow LR is off        B01
22 C     Loan_Date      ADDDUR     Loan_Time:*D  Due_Date               compute due date      01
23 C                    EXTRCT     Due_Date:*M   Due_Mth                extract mth value     01
24 C                    EXTRCT     Due_Date:*D   Due_Day                extract day value     01
25 C                    EXTRCT     Due_Date:*Y   Due_Yr                 extract yr value      01
26 C                    EXCEPT     Due_Line                             print record          01
27 C                    READ       LoansFile                 ----LR     read next record      01
28 C                    ENDDO                                           end DOW group        E01
29
30 OQsysprt    E              Heading         3 01
31 O                                                51 'CUSTOMER LOAN INFORMATION'
32 O           E              Heading         2
33 O                                                 7 'LOAN NO'
34 O                                                22 'DATE OF LOAN'
35 O                                                36 'TIME OF LOAN'
36 O                                                52 'MATURITY DATE'
37 O                                                60 'YEAR'
38 O                                                68 'MONTH'
39 O                                                75 'DAY'
40 O           E              Due_Line        2
41 O                          Loan_No                6
42 O                          Loan_Date             19
43 O                          Loan_Time      Z      30
44 O                                                35 'DAYS'
45 O                          Due_Date              50
46 O                          Due_Yr                59
47 O                          Due_Mth               66
48 O                          Due_Day               75
```

Header Specifications:

Line No.

2 The **DATFMT(*MDY)** keyword specifies the output format of date fields defined in the *Definition Specifications* with a **D** in the *Internal data type* field (position 40).

Without the **DATFMT** keywords in the *Header Specifications*, the date format would default to *ISO and not be compatible with the date format defined in the *Definition Specification* instruction for the Due_Date field on line 8.

File Description Specifications:

4 Loansfile is defined as an input (**I** in position 18), full-procedural (**F** in position 18), externally described (**E** in position 22), keyed (**K** in position 34) physical file.

5 Qsysprt is defined as an output (**O** in position 17), program-described (**F** in position 22), with 132 print positions (132 in positions 23–27) printer file. Because page overflow is not included in this report, no page overflow indicator is specified.

Definition Specifications:

8 Due_Date is defined as a standalone (**S** in the *Type of definition* field) date field (**D** in the *Internal data type* field). The DATFMT(*MDY) keyword assigns the *MDY date format (i.e., mm/dd/yyyy) to this field.

9 Due_Mth is defined as a standalone (**S** in the *Type of definition* field) field.

10 Due_Day is defined as a standalone (**S** in the *Type of definition* field) field.

11 Due_Yr is defined as a standalone (**S** in the *Type of definition* field) field.

Calculation Specifications:

19 This **EXCEPT** instruction prints the two Heading line record formats on lines 30–39.

20 This **READ** instruction reads the first record from the Loansfile. If no records are stored in the file, indicator **LR** will turn on and subsequently end the program when the **DOW** instruction on line 21 is executed.

Figure 11-29 Compile listing of an example **RPG IV** program that uses the **ADDDUR** and **EXTRCT** instructions to process date type fields. (Continued)

21	The **DOW** group will be executed until **LR** is turned on after end of the Loansfile is read.
22	This **ADDDUR** instruction adds the value in Loan_Time to the Due_Date field to determine the due date of a loan. The ***D** entry after the colon in the *Factor 2* entry specifies that the value in Loan_Time is processed in days. If ***M** was specified, the value in Loan_Time would be processed in months. If ***Y** was specified, the value would be processed in years. After the instruction is executed, the value in Due_Date will be the Loan_Date value plus the Loan_Time value incremented in days.
23	This **EXTRCT** instruction extracts the month value from the Due_Date composite field.
24	This **EXTRCT** instruction extracts the day value from the Due_Date composite field.
25	This **EXTRCT** instruction extracts the year value from the Due_Date composite field.
26	This **EXCEPT** instruction prints the Due_line record format on lines 40–48.
27	This **READ** instruction reads the next record from the Loansfile file. When end of file is read, indicator **LR** will turn on and the program will end when the **DOW** instruction on line 21 is subsequently executed.
28	The **ENDDO** operation ends the **DOW** group and passes control back to the **DOW** instruction, where the test is made to end the program or continue processing.
Output Specifications:	
30–39	The printing of the two Heading record formats is controlled by the **EXCEPT** instruction on line 19.
40–48	The printing of the Due_line record format is controlled by the **EXCEPT** instruction on line 26.

Figure 11-29 Compile listing of an example **RPG IV** program that uses the **ADDDUR** and **EXTRCT** instructions to process date type fields. (Continued)

The report generated by the example **RPG IV** program that processes date type fields is shown in Figure 11-30.

CUSTOMER LOAN INFORMATION

LOAN NO	DATE OF LOAN	TIME OF LOAN	MATURITY DATE	YEAR	MONTH	DAY
1000	08/11/97	60 DAYS	10/10/97	97	10	10
1001	10/20/97	30 DAYS	11/19/97	97	11	19
1003	12/20/97	30 DAYS	01/19/98	98	01	19

Figure 11-30 Report generated by the **RPG IV** program in Figure 11-29.

SUMMARY

This chapter introduces the syntax of the data manipulation operations **CHECK** *(Check)*, **CHECKR** *(Check Reverse)*, **SCAN** *(Scan String)*, **SUBST** *(Substring)*, and **XLATE** *(Translate)*.

The **CHECK** operation verifies that each character in the base string *Factor 2* item (from left to right) is included in the comparator string in the *Factor 1* item. The **CHECKR** operation verifies that each character in the base string *Factor 2* item (from right to left) is included in the comparator string in the *Factor 1* item.

The **SCAN** operation scans the characters (base string) specified in *Factor 2* for the characters stored in the item in *Factor 1*. When the **SCAN** instruction is successful, the location of the *Factor 1* value in the *Factor 2* string is stored in the *Result* field. If an array is specified in the *Result* field, every incidence of the *Factor 1* character(s) in the *Factor 2* string is stored in the array elements.

The **SUBST** operation extracts characters in the *Factor 2* substring, starting at the location specified with the *Factor 2* entry (after the colon). The number of characters moved is based on the value in the *Factor 1* item. The **XLATE** operation translates a *Factor 2* value according to the *From* and *To* entries in the *Factor 1* entry.

Functions unique to **RPG IV** include **%SUBST, %TRIM, %TRIML, %TRIMR,** and **%SIZE.** The **%SUBST** function performs the same as the **SUBST** operation except it is more flexible. **%TRIM** strips leading and trailing blanks from a value. **%TRIML** trims only leading blanks from a value. **%TRIMR** trims only trailing blanks from a value.

Concatenation of independent values is performed with the **EVAL** operation, which builds the concatenated string with plus signs between the items. The field into which the concatenated string is stored must be defined large enough to avoid truncation.

Pointers, which are new to **RPG,** point to an address in memory and not to the value of the storage position. Pointers are a default size of 16 bytes. Two functions used with pointers are **%ADDR** and **%PADDR.** The **%ADDR** function stores the address of a variable, an array element, or an expression in an item defined as a pointer. The **%PADDR** function stores the address of a procedure in an item defined as a pointer.

New **RPG IV** date and time operations include **ADDDUR** *(Add Duration),* **SUBDUR** *(Subtract Duration),* and **EXTRCT** (*Extract a Date/Time/Timestamp* element). All three operations use the duration codes ***Y, *M,** and ***D** (for date elements) and ***H, *MN, *S,** and ***MS** (for time elements).

The **ADDDUR** operation adds a duration to a date or time value, whereas the **SUBDUR** operation subtracts a duration of date or time from a date or time value. The **EXTRCT** operation returns the day, month, or year value from a date or timestamp field; or the hours, minutes, or seconds from a time or timestamp field; or the microseconds of a timestamp field. The **TEST** operation tests the validity of a date, time, or timestamp field.

Using the new **RPG IV** operations, functions, and pointers should eliminate some of the convoluted routines developed in the past to perform many of the tasks detailed in this chapter.

QUESTIONS

11-1. Name five **RPG IV** data manipulation operations.

11-2. Of the operations named in Question 11-1, which one will change an uppercase value to lowercase?

11-3. Of the operations named in Question 11-1, which one will verify characters in a base string from right to left?

11-4. Of the operations named in Question 11-1, which one will extract characters from a string?

11-5. Of the operations named in Question 11-1, which one will find the location of characters in a string?

11-6. Of the operations named in Question 11-1, which one will verify characters in a base string from left to right?

Examine the following coding and answer Questions 11-7 and 11-8:

```
*.. 1 ...+... 2 ...+... 3 ...+... 4 ...+... 5 ...+... 6 ...+... 7 ...+... 8
CLON01Factor1+++++++Opcode&ExtFactor2+++++++Result++++++++Len++D+HiLoEq....
C     ' '           CHECK     StudntName    X

C     AlphaChars    CHECKR    CustName      Array
```

11-7. For the **CHECK** instruction, what is stored in X?

11-8. For the **CHECKR** instruction, what is stored in Array (assume AlphaChars is a Named Constant that contains uppercase alphabetic characters)?

Examine the following coding and answer questions 11-9 and 11-10:

```
*.. 1 ...+... 2 ...+... 3 ...+... 4 ...+... 5 ...+... 6 ...+... 7 ...+... 8
CLON01Factor1+++++++Opcode&ExtFactor2+++++++Result++++++++Len++D+HiLoEq....
C     ', '          SCAN      StudntName    X

C     ' '           SCAN      CityStZip     Array
```

11-9. For the first **SCAN** instruction, what is stored in X?

11-10. For the second **SCAN** instruction, what is stored in Array?

Examine the following coding and answer Questions 11-11 through 11-15:

```
*.. 1 ...+... 2 ...+... 3 ...+... 4 ...+... 5 ...+... 6 ...+... 7 ...+... 8
CLON01Factor1+++++++Opcode&ExtFactor2+++++++Result++++++++Len++D+HiLoEq....
C     4             SUBST     ClientName:3  LastName          12    80

C     Size          SUBST(P)  CityStZip     HoldFld           20
```

11-11. What is the function of the *Factor 1* entry in the two **SUBST** instructions?

11-12. What is the function of the **:3** entry in *Factor 2* of the first **SUBST** instruction?

11-13. For the first **SUBST** instruction, under what conditions will indicator 80 be turned on?

11-14. For the second **SUBST** instruction, what is the function of the extender entry **(P)**?

11-15. For the second **SUBST** instruction, Size should be defined as what size?

Examine the following coding and answer Questions 11-16 and 11-17:

```
*.. 1 ...+... 2 ...+... 3 ...+... 4 ...+... 5 ...+... 6 ...+... 7 ...+... 8
CLON01Factor1+++++++Opcode&ExtFactor2+++++++Result++++++++Len++D+HiLoEq....
C     LoCase:UpCase XLATE     StudntName    PrintName         12    80

C     ',':' '       XLATE     CityStZip     NewAddress        20
```

11-16. After the first **XLATE** instruction is executed, what will be stored in PrintName?

11-17. What is the function of the second **XLATE** instruction?

11-18. Name six **RPG IV** functions, and explain the purpose of each.

11-19. What is the function of pointers in an **RPG IV** program?

11-20. What are the two types of **RPG IV** pointers? Explain how they differ.

11-21. Where are pointers defined in an **RPG IV** program? How are they defined as a pointer?

11-22. What **RPG IV** functions support pointer processing?

Examine the following coding and answer Questions 11-23 through 11-27:

```
.. 1 ...+... 2 ...+... 3 ...+... 4 ...+... 5 ...+... 6 ...+... 7 ...+... 8
DName+++++++++++ETDsFrom+++To/L+++IDc.Keywords+++++++++++++++++++++++++++++

D Location        S               *   INZ(%ADDR(CodeTable))

D Address1        S               *   PROCPTR
                                      INZ(%PADDR(Billing))
```

11-23. For the first instruction, what is stored in the Location field?

11-24. For the first instruction, explain the function of the **INZ** keyword expression.

11-25. For the second instruction, what is stored in the Address1 field?

11-26. What is the function of the **PROCPTR** keyword?

11-27. For the second instruction, explain the function of the **INZ** keyword expression.

11-28. What three **RPG IV** operations support date and time calculations?

11-29. Name seven **RPG IV** date/time durations.

Examine the following coding and answer Questions 11-30 through 11-34:

```
*.. 1 ...+... 2 ...+... 3 ...+... 4 ...+... 5 ...+... 6 ...+... 7 ...+... 8
CL0N01Factor1+++++++Opcode&ExtFactor2+++++++Result++++++++Len++D+HiLoEq....
C     CertDate      ADDDUR    6:*M          MaturDate

C     PaymtDate     SUBDUR    2:*Y          ContrtDate

C                   EXTRCT    Clock_Time:*H Hrs_Worked
```

11-30. If CertDate has a value of 6/10/1997, what value will be stored in MaturDate after the instruction is executed?

11-31. If PaymtDate has a value of 02/01/99, what value will be stored in ContrtDate after the instruction is executed?

11-32. If Clock_Time has a value of 35:31:25, what value will be stored in Hrs_Worked?

11-33. What is the default format for date fields? How may it be changed to support other date formats?

11-34. What is the function of the **TEST** operation?

PROGRAMMING ASSIGNMENTS

Programming Assignment 11-1: CUSTOMER LISTING BY LAST NAME

Write an **RPG IV** program to generate the report shown in the following printer spacing chart.

Physical File Record Format:

```
                      PHYSICAL FILE DESCRIPTION

SYSTEM: AS/400                                       DATE: Yours
FILE NAME: Yours                                     REV NO: 0
RECORD NAME: Yours                                   KEY LENGTH: None
SEQUENCE: Nonkeyed                                   RECORD SIZE: 63

                          FIELD DEFINITIONS

 FIELD     FIELD NAME    SIZE   TYPE     POSITION     COMMENTS
  NO                                    FROM    TO

  1        CUSTNAME       20     C         1     20
  2        STREET         25     C        21     45
  3        CITYSTATE      15     C        46     60
  4        ZIPCODE         5     P        61     63
```

Physical file data:

Name	Street	City/State	Zip
ALEXANDER HAMILTON	10 RESERVE STREET	NEW YORK, NY	07701
JOHN JAY	44 CONSTITUTION PLACE	RYE, NY	07744
THOMAS JEFFERSON	30 SKYLINE DRIVE	MONTICELLO, VA	05555
ANN KENSINGTON	1 DISNEY STREET	ORLANDO, FL	09000
FRANKLIN ROOSEVELT	1 FDR BOULEVARD	HYDE PARK, NY	06000
GEORGE WASHINGTON	1 APPLE TREE LANE	MT VERNON, VA	04444

Processing: Read the physical file in arrival sequence; for each record processed, extract the customer's *last* name from the CUSTNAME field and the state code from the CITYSTATE field. As shown in the printer spacing chart, print only the last name and state code for a customer. Include a counter for the number of input records processed.

Report Design:

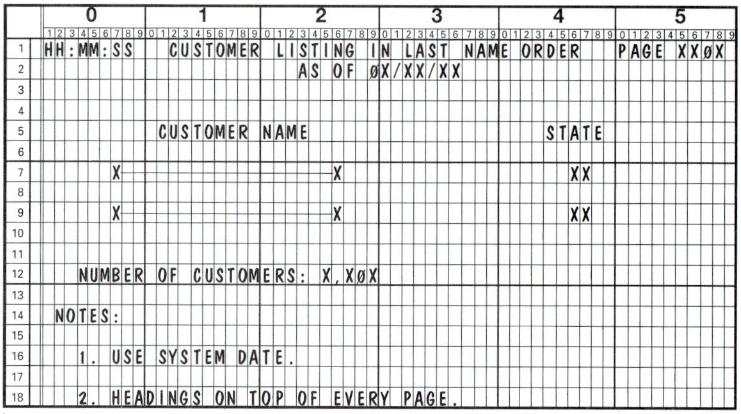

HH:MM:SS CUSTOMER LISTING IN LAST NAME ORDER PAGE XXØX
AS OF ØX/XX/XX
CUSTOMER NAME
STATE
X X XX
X X XX
NUMBER OF CUSTOMERS: X,XØX
NOTES:
1. USE SYSTEM DATE.
2. HEADINGS ON TOP OF EVERY PAGE.

Programming Assignment 11-2: PATIENT MAILING LABELS

A health clinic needs an **RPG IV** program written to generate mailing labels for their monthly billing. The labels are gummed and mounted as shown in the printer spacing chart below.

Physical File Record Format:

PHYSICAL FILE DESCRIPTION

SYSTEM: AS/400 DATE: Yours
FILE NAME: Yours REV NO: 0
RECORD NAME: Yours KEY LENGTH: None
SEQUENCE: Nonkeyed RECORD SIZE: 84

FIELD DEFINITIONS

FIELD NO	FIELD NAME	SIZE	TYPE	POSITION FROM	POSITION TO	COMMENTS
1	FIRST_NAME	12	C	1	12	
2	LAST_NAME	15	C	13	27	
3	ADDRESS1	20	C	28	47	
4	ADDRESS2	12	C	48	59	
5	CITY	20	C	60	79	
6	STATE	2	C	80	81	
7	ZIP_CODE	5	P	82	84	

Physical File Data:

First Name	Last Name	Address 1	Address 2	City	State	Zip Code
WASSILY	KANDINSKY	20 AMSTERDAM AVE	APT 35	FRANCE	KY	07450
GEORGES	BRAQUE	300 ST CLAIR ST		NEW JERSEY	NJ	05501
PAUL	CEZANNE	44 RUE PIGALLE	BLDG 10	STAMFORD	CT	06518
MARC	CHAGALL	222 QUAIL AVENUE		BRIDGEPORT	CT	06666
EDGAR	DEGAS	10 ROSE TERRACE		WESTPORT	PA	07777
BUCKMINISTER	FULLER	999 PARK AVENUE	APT 201	RYE	NY	07550

Processing: For each patient record read, concatenate the FIRST_NAME and LAST_NAME field values, with FIRST_NAME first, so that only *one space* exists between the two field values. In addition, concatenate the CITY, STATE, and ZIP_CODE field values so that a *comma and one space* are included between the CITY and STATE values and one space appears between the STATE and ZIP_CODE values.

Example:

WASSILY KANDINSKY
20 AMSTERDAM AVE
APT 35
FRANCE, KY 07450

Notice in the record format that there are two address fields (i.e., ADDRESS1 and ADDRESS2). ADDRESS2 is for supplemental information such as apartment number, box number, and office number. If the input value for this field is blank, the concatenated CITY, STATE, and ZIP_CODE line must be printed on the third line of the label and *not* the fourth. This will eliminate a blank line between the STREET line and the concatenated CITY, STATE, ZIP_CODE line when there is no value in the ADDRESS2 field.

Format of the Labels:

```
            1         2         3
   123456789012345678901234567890
 1
 2 XXXXXXXXXXXX XXXXXXXXXXXXXXXX
 3 XXXXXXXXXXXXXXXXXXXX
 4 XXXXXXXXXXXX
 5 XXXXXXXXXXXXXXXXXXXX XX XXXXX
 6
 7
 8 XXXXXXXXXXXX XXXXXXXXXXXXXXXX
 9 XXXXXXXXXXXXXXXXXXXX
10 XXXXXXXXXXXX
11 XXXXXXXXXXXXXXXXXXXX XX XXXXX
12
```

Programming Assignment 11-3: AGING ACCOUNTS RECEIVABLE

A wholesale company wants to determine how many of its company accounts are current (less than 1 month), 1 month, 2 months, and 3 months and over past due in payment of their invoices. Accounts are determined to be current or past due by computing the number of months from the related invoice date to today's date (stored in the program as a date field in an ***MDY**/ format with a value of 05/01/97). Each invoice for a customer must be separately computed. For example, if a customer has three invoices, the first may be 1 month past due; the second, 2 months past due; and the third, current.

When a company number changes (control break), print the column totals for a company. After end of file is read, print the totals for all of the companies. Refer to the printer spacing chart below for the report design.

Physical File Record Format:

```
                    PHYSICAL FILE DESCRIPTION

SYSTEM: AS/400                                  DATE: Yours
FILE NAME: Yours                                REV NO: 0
RECORD NAME: Yours                              KEY LENGTH: 5
SEQUENCE: keyed (not unique)                    RECORD SIZE: 46

                        FIELD DEFINITIONS

 FIELD     FIELD NAME   SIZE  TYPE   POSITION      COMMENTS
  NO                                 FROM   TO

  1        COMPANYNO      5    C       1      5   key field
  2        COMPNYNAME    25    C       6     30
  3        INVOICENO      4    C      31     34
  4        INV_DATE       8    L      35     42 *MDY/
  5        INV_AMOUNT     7    P      43     46 2 decimals
```

Physical File Data:

Company Number	Company Name	Invoice Number	Invoice Date	Invoice Amount
50006	THERMAL AIR SYSTEMS	2002	04/25/97	0050000
60000	MILFORD AUTO SUPPLY	3500	03/04/97	2340098
60000	MILFORD AUTO SUPPLY	3700	03/27/97	0005037
60000	MILFORD AUTO SUPPLY	3750	04/01/97	0030000
60000	MILFORD AUTO SUPPLY	3761	04/06/97	0257578
65005	DAVID MARINE ENGINEERING	4000	03/20/97	0352750
65005	DAVID MARINE ENGINEERING	4010	12/01/96	0004025
65005	DAVID MARINE ENGINEERING	4200	03/24/97	0073000
65005	DAVID MARINE ENGINEERING	4290	04/30/97	0095033
70000	AMERICAN HOME CARE	5000	02/28/97	0004427
70000	AMERICAN HOME CARE	5052	01/15/97	0015789
70000	AMERICAN HOME CARE	5100	03/15/97	0945678
70000	AMERICAN HOME CARE	5300	04/25/97	1023760

Report Design:

```
                                                                                                              1
            1         2         3         4         5         6         7         8         9         0
   12345678901234567890123456789012345678901234567890123456789012345678901234567890123456789012345678901234567 8
 1 0X/XX/XXXX                                ACCOUNTS RECEIVABLE AGING REPORT                      PAGE XX0X
 2
 3
 4  COMPANY                                  INVOICE    INVOICE                  1 MONTH      2 MONTHS     3 MONTHS
 5  NUMBER       COMPANY NAME                NUMBER     AMOUNT       CURRENT     OVERDUE      OVERDUE      & OVER
 6
 7  XXXXX  XXXXXXXXXXXXXXXXXXXXXXXXX          XXXX     XX,XX0.XX   XX,XX0.XX   XX,XX0.XX    XX,XX0.XX   XX,XX0.XX
 8
 9  XXXXX  XXXXXXXXXXXXXXXXXXXXXXXXX          XXXX     XX,XX0.XX   XX,XX0.XX   XX,XX0.XX    XX,XX0.XX   XX,XX0.XX
10
11                  COMPANY TOTALS............    XXX,XX0.XX  XXX,XX0.XX  XXX,XX0.XX   XXX,XX0.XX  XXX,XX0.XX
12
13
14                  GRAND TOTALS.............     XXX,XX0.XX  XXX,XX0.XX  XXX,XX0.XX   XXX,XX0.XX  XXX,XX0.XX
15
16 Notes:
17 1. Use the system date for the report.
18 2. Triple space between company groups.
19 3. Triple space after the last company group (before GRAND TOTALS line).
```

chapter 12

Data Validation (Batch Mode)

One of the most important functions associated with the data processing environment is ensuring the accuracy of the data. Regardless of how well structured or efficient application programs are, if the input data is not accurate, the end results will usually be unacceptable. Once "bad" data is loaded in a file, it is often difficult to correct. For example, if invalid data was included in a daily transaction file used to update a master file, it would ultimately filter throughout the system, thus making subsequent corrections difficult.

DATA VALIDATION METHODS

The procedures for maintaining the accuracy of data are referred to as *data validation*. Whether the data entry environment is batch or interactive will determine how data is validated on input. Validation functions may be implemented by one or a combination of the procedures described in the following paragraphs.

Batch Procedures External to a Data Entry Program

Data is entered from source documents directly onto such storage media as diskettes, disks, or magnetic tape by a related hardware unit. Most of these recording machines also support a separate verification function. Verification in this environment requires that an operator reference the source documents and duplicate the keying process. In this mode, the machine does not record data but compares what is already stored with what is currently being keyed. The machine locks to indicate any differences found. Then the value is checked to determine whether the original data or the currently keyed value is incorrect.

Batch Procedures Internal to a Data Entry Program

Data is entered from source documents directly onto the storage medium by the related hardware device. The file created and loaded is then processed by an **RPG IV** entry program to validate the data. Controls are included in the program to load records with errors to an error *rejection* or *abeyance* file. An *error rejection* file stores the record information for identification only, whereas the records loaded to an *error abeyance* file may be subsequently corrected by an update program or system utility.

Interactive Procedures Internal to a Data Entry Program

Data is entered via a workstation controlled by an **RPG IV** program. Some validation procedures may be supported by the screen generator software, whereas others are in the program. Popular software utilities are available, such as **SDA** and **SEU,** that provide for the design, syntax, and control of interactive screens. The standalone screens are interfaced with an **RPG IV** program with syntax and procedures unique to the computer system. See Chapters 14 and 15 for interactive processing methods.

Often, not every data entry error can be identified by the procedures just discussed. Additional validation may be provided by batch total checks, edit listings, and feedback from users.

Internal Data Validation in a Batch Environment

The following procedures are commonly included in an **RPG IV** data validation program in a batch processing environment:

1. Data type testing
   a. Numeric or alphabetic
   b. Arithmetic signs or zeros
2. Data field checking
   a. Presence or absence of data
   b. Justification of data
   c. Acceptability of data
   d. Relationship to other data
   e. Structure of the data

In this chapter, each of these validation processes is separately explained and supported by standalone programs and is then integrated into a single comprehensive data validation program.

DATA TYPE TESTING

Input data may be tested for numeric or alphabetic class but not for alphanumeric class because all characters supported by a computer may be considered alphanumeric. Numeric testing and alphabetic testing are individually discussed in the following paragraphs.

Numeric Field Testing

In the AS/400 environment when **DFU** or a *display file* record format is used to enter data into a field defined as numeric, only the digits **(0–9)** may be entered. Any attempt to enter a character other than **0** through **9** will cause an entry error. Consequently, in that scenario numeric validation is performed when the data is entered. However, data may be input from files loaded by another computer system which may include invalid numeric data and require numeric validation to prevent run-time halts or aborts. Refer to Figure 12-1 for examples of valid and invalid numeric data.

Input Field Value	Explanation
0009999	Valid numeric
1200.00	Decimal is not a numeric character

Figure 12-1 Examples of valid and invalid numeric values.

A345000	Letter is not a numeric character
123	Blank is not a numeric character
002400J	Valid numeric (low-order letter represents −1)

Note: Field is defined as 7 bytes with 2 implied decimals.

Figure 12-1 Examples of valid and invalid numeric values. (Continued)

TESTN Operation

In a batch processing environment, numeric field validation may be controlled in an **RPG IV** program by the **TESTN** operation. Figure 12-2 explains the syntax of this operation. Notice that the field specified in the *Result* field must be defined as alphanumeric. If the value passes the numeric test **(TESTN),** then it may be moved to a numeric field. If the field tested is defined on input, it may be specified as alphanumeric with one name and then redefined as numeric with another.

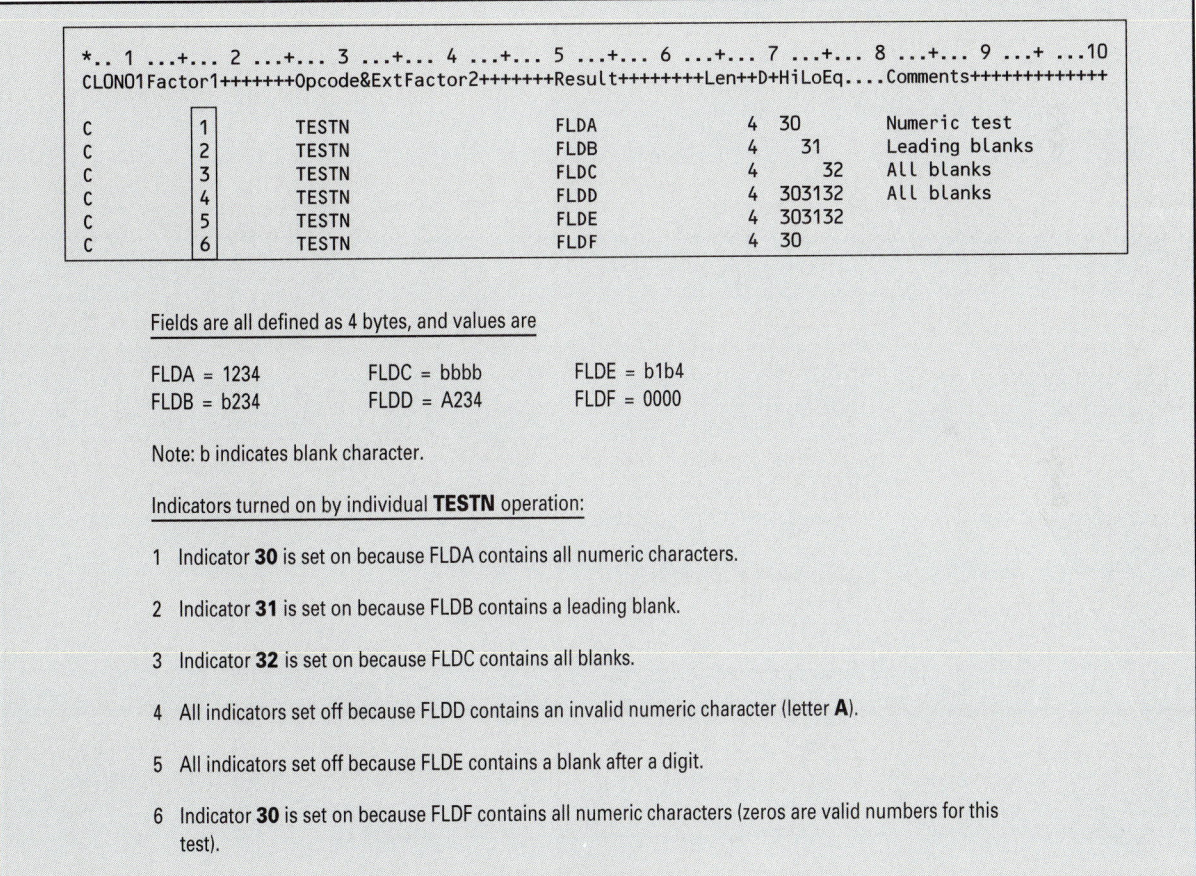

```
*.. 1 ...+... 2 ...+... 3 ...+... 4 ...+... 5 ...+... 6 ...+... 7 ...+... 8 ...+... 9 ...+ ...10
CLON01Factor1+++++++Opcode&ExtFactor2+++++++Result++++++++Len++D+HiLoEq....Comments++++++++++++
C           1       TESTN                   FLDA               4  30       Numeric test
C           2       TESTN                   FLDB               4    31     Leading blanks
C           3       TESTN                   FLDC               4      32   All blanks
C           4       TESTN                   FLDD               4  303132   All blanks
C           5       TESTN                   FLDE               4  303132
C           6       TESTN                   FLDF               4  30
```

Fields are all defined as 4 bytes, and values are

FLDA = 1234	FLDC = bbbb	FLDE = b1b4
FLDB = b234	FLDD = A234	FLDF = 0000

Note: b indicates blank character.

Indicators turned on by individual **TESTN** operation:

1 Indicator **30** is set on because FLDA contains all numeric characters.

2 Indicator **31** is set on because FLDB contains a leading blank.

3 Indicator **32** is set on because FLDC contains all blanks.

4 All indicators set off because FLDD contains an invalid numeric character (letter **A**).

5 All indicators set off because FLDE contains a blank after a digit.

6 Indicator **30** is set on because FLDF contains all numeric characters (zeros are valid numbers for this test).

Figure 12-2 TESTN operation syntax.

The example program in Figure 12-3 shows how the **TESTN** operation is used as a data validation function. Notice that all three tests (numeric, leading blanks, and all blanks) are included in the program. An application, however, may require that only one or two of the tests be specified.

```
Line    <---------------------- Source Specifications ----------------------------><---- Comments ----> Do
Number ....1....+....2....+....3....+....4....+....5....+....6....+....7....+....8....+....9....+...10 Num
                        S o u r c e   L i s t i n g
      * Validation of fields for valid numeric data with the TESTN operation
     FPf12Testn IF   E             DISK
      *--------------------------------------------------------------------------------------------*
      *                            RPG name          External name                                 *
      * File name. . . . . . . . : PF12TESTN         STAN/PF12TESTN                                *
      * Record format(s) . . . . : TESTNRECD         TESTNRECD                                     *
      *--------------------------------------------------------------------------------------------*
     FQsysprt   O    F  132        PRINTER

     D Messages        S             22    DIM(3) CTDATA                   error message array
     DCharQty          DS                                                  define data struct.
     D NumericQty                    1      8  0                           redefine CharQty
     D X               S              2  0                                 array index

    =ITESTNRECD
      *--------------------------------------------------------------------------------------------*
      * RPG record format  . . . . :  TESTNRECD                                                    *
      * External format  . . . . . :  TESTNRECD : STAN/PF12TESTN                                   *
      *--------------------------------------------------------------------------------------------*
    =I                             A    1    8  CHARQTY
     C                   EXCEPT    Heading                                 print heading record
     C                   READ      Pf12testn                          ----LR   read first record
     C                   DOW       *INLR = *OFF                            dow LR is off          B01
     C                                                                                             B01
     C                   TESTN                   CharQty          101112   numeric value test      01
     C                   SELECT                                            begin SELECT group     B02
     C                   WHEN      *IN10 = *OFF                                                   X02
     C                             AND *IN11 = *OFF                                               X02
     C                             AND *IN12 = *OFF                        all indicators off?    X02
     C                   EVAL      X = 1                                   QTY NOT NUMERIC MSG     02
     C                   EXCEPT    ErrorLine                               print error record      02
     C                   WHEN      *IN11 = *ON                             leading blanks test    X02
     C                   EVAL      X = 2                                   leading blanks msg      02
     C                   EXCEPT    ErrorLine                               print error record      02
     C                   WHEN      *IN12 = *ON                             all blanks test        X02
     C                   EVAL      X = 3                                   QTY IS BLANK MSG        02
     C                   EXCEPT    ErrorLine                               print error record      02
     C                   OTHER                                                                    X02
     C                   EXCEPT    ValidLine                               print valid record      02
     C                   ENDSL                                             end SELECT group       E02

     C                   READ      Pf12testn                          ----LR   read next record        01
     C                   ENDDO                                             end dow group          E01

     OQsysprt   E            Heading         3 01
     O                                           45 'NUMERIC VALIDATION'
     O          E            ErrorLine       2
     O                       CharQty            30
     O                       Messages(X)        55
     O          E            ValidLine       2
     O                       NumericQty         30
    * * * * *   E N D   O F   S O U R C E   * * * * *
                          .
                          .

                    C o m p i l e   T i m e   D a t a
    **CTDATA Messages
      *------------------------------------------------------------------*
      * Array . . . : MESSAGES                                           *
      *------------------------------------------------------------------*
    QTY NOT NUMERIC
    QTY HAS LEADING BLANKS
    QTY IS BLANK
 * * * * *   E N D   O F   C O M P I L E   T I M E   D A T A   * * * * *
```

Figure 12-3 Example numeric validation (**TESTN** operation) program.

Description Specifications:

Line No.

5 Messages is defined as a compile-time array (**CTDATA** keyword) with 3 elements 22 characters in length.

6 The physical file field, CharQty, is defined as a data structure so that it may be redefined as a numeric field (NumericQty) on line 7.

7 The subfield NumericQty redefines CharQty (from the physical file) as a numeric field.

8 **X,** which is defined as a standalone field, is used as the index for the Messages array.

Calculation Specifications:

12 This **EXCEPT** instruction controls printing of the Heading record format. For simplicity, page overflow control has not been included in this program.

13 This **READ** instruction reads the first record from the Pf12Testn physical file. If no records are stored in the file, indicator **LR** will be turned on and end the program when the DOW instruction on line 14 is tested.

14 The **DOW** group is executed until the end of the physical file is read (**LR** is turned on), exit from the loop is performed, and the program is ended.

16 The **TESTN** instruction tests the CharQty field (defined as character in the physical file) for valid numeric, leading blanks, all blank conditions by *Resulting Indicators* **10, 11,** and **12,** respectively. The data item specified in the *Result* field of a **TESTN** instruction must be defined as character.

17 The **SELECT** operation begins the **SELECT** group.

18–20 This compound **WHEN** instruction tests the status of *Resulting Indicators* **10, 11,** and **12.** If all are off, CharQty contains invalid numeric data.

21 This **EVAL** instruction is executed only if the previous **WHEN** instruction is true (indicators **10, 11,** and **12** are off). **X** is initialized to **1,** which will access the first element in the Messages array when the ErrorLine format (lines 38–40) is printed.

22 This **EXCEPT** instruction, which is executed only if the previous **WHEN** instruction is true, prints the ErrorLine record format on lines 38–40.

23 This **WHEN** instruction, which is executed only if the **WHEN** instruction on lines 18-20 is false, tests the status of indicator **11** (leading blank test).

24 This **EVAL** instruction is executed only if the **WHEN** instruction on line 23 is true (indicator **11** is on). **X** is initialized to 2, which will access the second element in the Messages array when the ErrorLine format (lines 38–40) is printed.

25 This **EXCEPT** instruction, which is executed only if the previous **WHEN** instruction is true, prints the ErrorLine record format on lines 38–40.

26 This **WHEN** instruction, which is executed only if the two previous **WHEN** instructions are false, tests the status of indicator **12** (all blank condition).

27 This **EVAL** instruction is executed if the **WHEN** instruction on line 26 is true. **X** is initialized to 3, which will access the third element in the Messages array when the ErrorLine (lines 38–40) is printed.

28 This **EXCEPT** instruction, which is executed only if the previous **WHEN** instruction is true, prints the ErrorLine record format on lines 38–40.

29 The instructions after this **OTHER** operation and before the **ENDSL** operation are executed only if the three previous **WHEN** instructions tests are false, indicating a valid numeric value.

30 This **EXCEPT** instruction, which is executed if the three previous **WHEN** instructions are false, prints the ValidLine record format.

31 The **ENDSL** operation ends the **SELECT** group.

33 This **READ** instruction reads the next record from the physical file. If end of file is read, the program will end when control is returned back to the **DOW** instruction on line 14 and exit from the **DOW** group is executed.

34 The **ENDDO** operation ends the **DOW** group.

Output Specifications

36–37 Printing of the Heading record format is controlled by the **EXCEPT** instruction on line 12.

38–40 Printing of the ErrorLine record format is controlled by the **EXCEPT** instructions on lines 22, 25, or 28.

Figure 12-3 Example numeric validation (**TESTN** operation) program. (Continued)

41–42	Printing of the ValidLine record format is controlled by the **EXCEPT** instruction on line 30.
43	The ****CTDATA Messages** instruction indicates the beginning of the compile-time array data. Note that supplemental diagnostic lines, generated in the compilation, have been deleted (indicated by the ellipsis) for readability.
44–46	The three elements of the Messages array are entered in these instructions. Each is accessed by the value in the index **X**.

Figure 12-3 Example numeric validation (**TESTN** operation) program. (Continued)

A copy of the data file processed by the example numeric validation program using the **TESTN** operation and the report generated are shown in Figure 12-4.

```
Data File Listing    |      Printed Report
                     |
                     |   NUMERIC VALIDATION
                     |
01450000             |  01450000
j1234500             |  j1234500  QTY NOT NUMERIC
  100000             |    100000  QTY HAS LEADING BLANKS
00099.99             |  00099.99  QTY NOT NUMERIC
12500000             |  12500000
                     |            QTY IS BLANK
```

Figure 12-4 Data file listing and report generated by the numeric validation program using the **TESTN** operation.

Alphabetic Value Testing

Valid alphabetic characters include the character blank and the letters A through Z. Few field values are purely alphabetic. For example, names of individuals, places, and things often include nonalphabetic characters (e.g., the apostrophe in O'Brien). The two-letter state code abbreviations (e.g., NY, CT, PA) are, however, one example of a field value that should always test as alphabetic.

Examples of valid and invalid alphabetic values are presented in Figure 12-5.

```
   Input
 Field Value       Explanation

     CT       Valid alphabetic value

      Y       Blank is valid alphabetic value

     12       Digits are not alphabetic

     M.       Special characters are not alphabetic

    Note: Field is defined as two-byte alphanumeric.
```

Figure 12-5 Examples of valid and invalid alphabetic values.

RPG IV does not provide a method of defining alphabetic values; fields are defined as either numeric or character. Also, because an operation is not available for the testing of alphabetic values, other controls must be used. One method is with a *Named Constant* that includes the characters the programmer wants to consider alphabetic and the

CHECK (or **CHECKR**) operation. Figure 12-6 presents an **RPG IV** program that validates a field for an alphabetic value using a Named Constant and the **CHECK** operation.

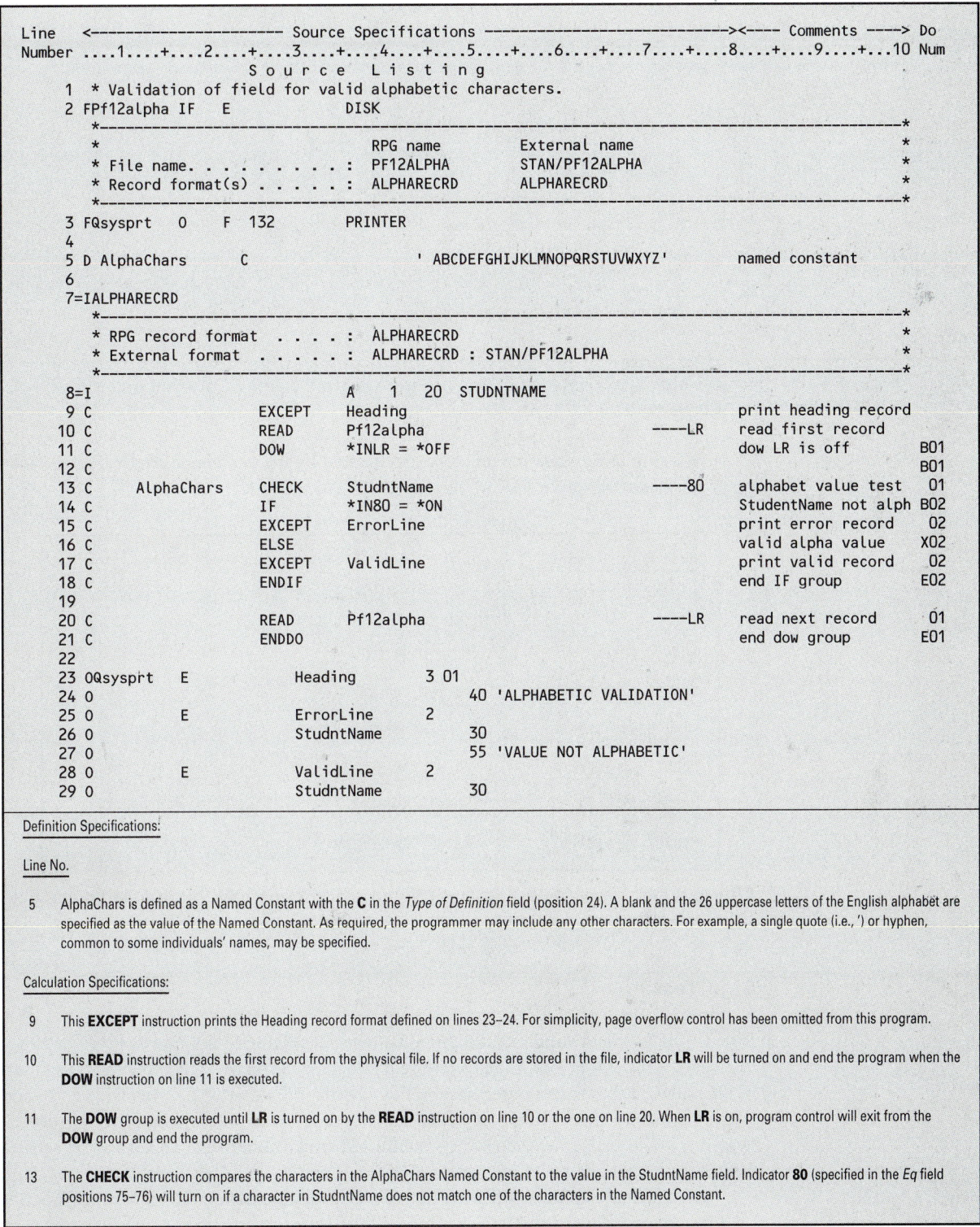

```
Line   <---------------------- Source Specifications ----------------------------><---- Comments ----> Do
Number ....1....+....2....+....3....+....4....+....5....+....6....+....7....+....8....+....9....+...10 Num
                         S o u r c e   L i s t i n g
     1  * Validation of field for valid alphabetic characters.
     2 FPf12alpha IF   E             DISK
        *--------------------------------------------------------------------------------------------*
        *                            RPG name         External name                                 *
        * File name. . . . . . . . :  PF12ALPHA        STAN/PF12ALPHA                                *
        * Record format(s) . . . . :  ALPHARECRD       ALPHARECRD                                    *
        *--------------------------------------------------------------------------------------------*
     3 FQsysprt   O    F  132        PRINTER
     4
     5 D AlphaChars      C                   ' ABCDEFGHIJKLMNOPQRSTUVWXYZ'        named constant
     6
     7=IALPHARECRD
        *--------------------------------------------------------------------------------------------*
        * RPG record format  . . . . :  ALPHARECRD                                                   *
        * External format  . . . . . :  ALPHARECRD : STAN/PF12ALPHA                                  *
        *--------------------------------------------------------------------------------------------*
     8=I                             A    1   20  STUDNTNAME
     9 C                   EXCEPT    Heading                                    print heading record
    10 C                   READ      Pf12alpha                          ----LR  read first record
    11 C                   DOW       *INLR = *OFF                               dow LR is off      B01
    12 C                                                                                          B01
    13 C     AlphaChars    CHECK     StudntName                         ----80  alphabet value test  01
    14 C                   IF        *IN80 = *ON                                StudentName not alph B02
    15 C                   EXCEPT    ErrorLine                                  print error record   02
    16 C                   ELSE                                                 valid alpha value   X02
    17 C                   EXCEPT    ValidLine                                  print valid record   02
    18 C                   ENDIF                                                end IF group        E02
    19
    20 C                   READ      Pf12alpha                          ----LR  read next record     01
    21 C                   ENDDO                                                end dow group       E01
    22
    23 OQsysprt   E            Heading        3 01
    24 O                                          40 'ALPHABETIC VALIDATION'
    25 O          E            ErrorLine      2
    26 O                       StudntName         30
    27 O                                          55 'VALUE NOT ALPHABETIC'
    28 O          E            ValidLine      2
    29 O                       StudntName         30
```

Definition Specifications:

Line No.

5 AlphaChars is defined as a Named Constant with the **C** in the *Type of Definition* field (position 24). A blank and the 26 uppercase letters of the English alphabet are specified as the value of the Named Constant. As required, the programmer may include any other characters. For example, a single quote (i.e., ') or hyphen, common to some individuals' names, may be specified.

Calculation Specifications:

9 This **EXCEPT** instruction prints the Heading record format defined on lines 23–24. For simplicity, page overflow control has been omitted from this program.

10 This **READ** instruction reads the first record from the physical file. If no records are stored in the file, indicator **LR** will be turned on and end the program when the **DOW** instruction on line 11 is executed.

11 The **DOW** group is executed until **LR** is turned on by the **READ** instruction on line 10 or the one on line 20. When **LR** is on, program control will exit from the **DOW** group and end the program.

13 The **CHECK** instruction compares the characters in the AlphaChars Named Constant to the value in the StudntName field. Indicator **80** (specified in the *Eq* field positions 75–76) will turn on if a character in StudntName does not match one of the characters in the Named Constant.

Figure 12-6 Example alphabetic data validation program using a Named Constant and the **CHECK** operation.

14–15	The **IF** instruction tests the status of indicator **80**. If it is "on," indicating an invalid character in the StudntName field, the following **EXCEPT** instruction will print the ErrorLine record format defined on lines 25–27.
16–17	The **ELSE** action of the **IF** instruction will execute when the value in StudntName contains all valid characters (indicator **80** is "off"). The following **EXCEPT** instruction will print the ValidLine record format defined on lines 28–29.
18	The **ENDIF** operation ends the **IF** group.
20	This **READ** instruction reads the next record from the physical file. When end of file is read, indicator **LR** will be turned on and end the job after the **DOW** instruction on line 11 is executed.
21	The **ENDDO** operation ends the **DOW** group and passes control back to the **DOW** instruction on line 11, where the relational test is made.

Output Specifications:

23–24	The Heading record format is printed by execution of the **EXCEPT** instruction on line 9.
25–27	The ErrorLine record format is printed by execution of the **EXCEPT** instruction on line 15.
28–29	The ValidLine record format is printed by execution of the **EXCEPT** instruction on line 17.

Figure 12-6 Example alphabetic data validation program using a Named Constant and the **CHECK** operation. (Continued)

A listing of the data file and report generated by the alphabetic data validation program are shown in Figure 12-7.

Data File Listing	Report Listing	
	ALPHABETIC VALIDATION	
SEAN O'BRIEN	SEAN O'BRIEN	VALUE NOT ALPHABETIC
DOCTOR FRANKENSTEIN	DOCTOR FRANKENSTEIN	
KING HENRY THE 5	KING HENRY THE 5	VALUE NOT ALPHABETIC
COUNT VON-LUCKNER	COUNT VON-LUCKNER	VALUE NOT ALPHABETIC
JOSE' GONZALEZ	JOSE' GONZALEZ	VALUE NOT ALPHABETIC
SIDNEY GREENSTREET	SIDNEY GREENSTREET	

Figure 12-7 Data file listing and printed report generated by the alphabetic data validation program.

Sign Testing

Sign testing is a data validation function that checks a numeric field for *positive* or *negative* value. This test is important to ensure that data is correctly signed before being used in file maintenance or report generation. For example, if a master file was updated by the addition of daily transactions, any transaction amount that was incorrectly specified as negative would cause the value to be subtracted from, rather than added to, the related master record field value.

Also included in this validation function is testing numeric field values for zero. If a field is used as a divisor and its value is zero, an exception error will occur that may cancel program execution (unless an error routine is included in the program).

Sign testing may be controlled by any of the following methods:

1. Specifying one or more indicators in the *Field Indicators Plus, Minus,* and *Zero* fields for a field in the *Input Specifications*. Then, using the indicator(s) to condition subsequent calculation and/or output instructions.
2. Testing a *Result* field item in a calculation instruction by specifying one or more indicators in the *Plus, Minus,* and *Zero* fields; then using the indicator(s) to condition subsequent calculation and/or output instructions.
3. Using one or more of the **RPG IV** structured operations (i.e., **IF, WHEN, DOU, DOW, CASxx**) in instructions that use a relational test to determine if a field value is positive, negative, or zero.

The third method (using structured operations) is included in the sign testing validation program shown in Figure 12-8.

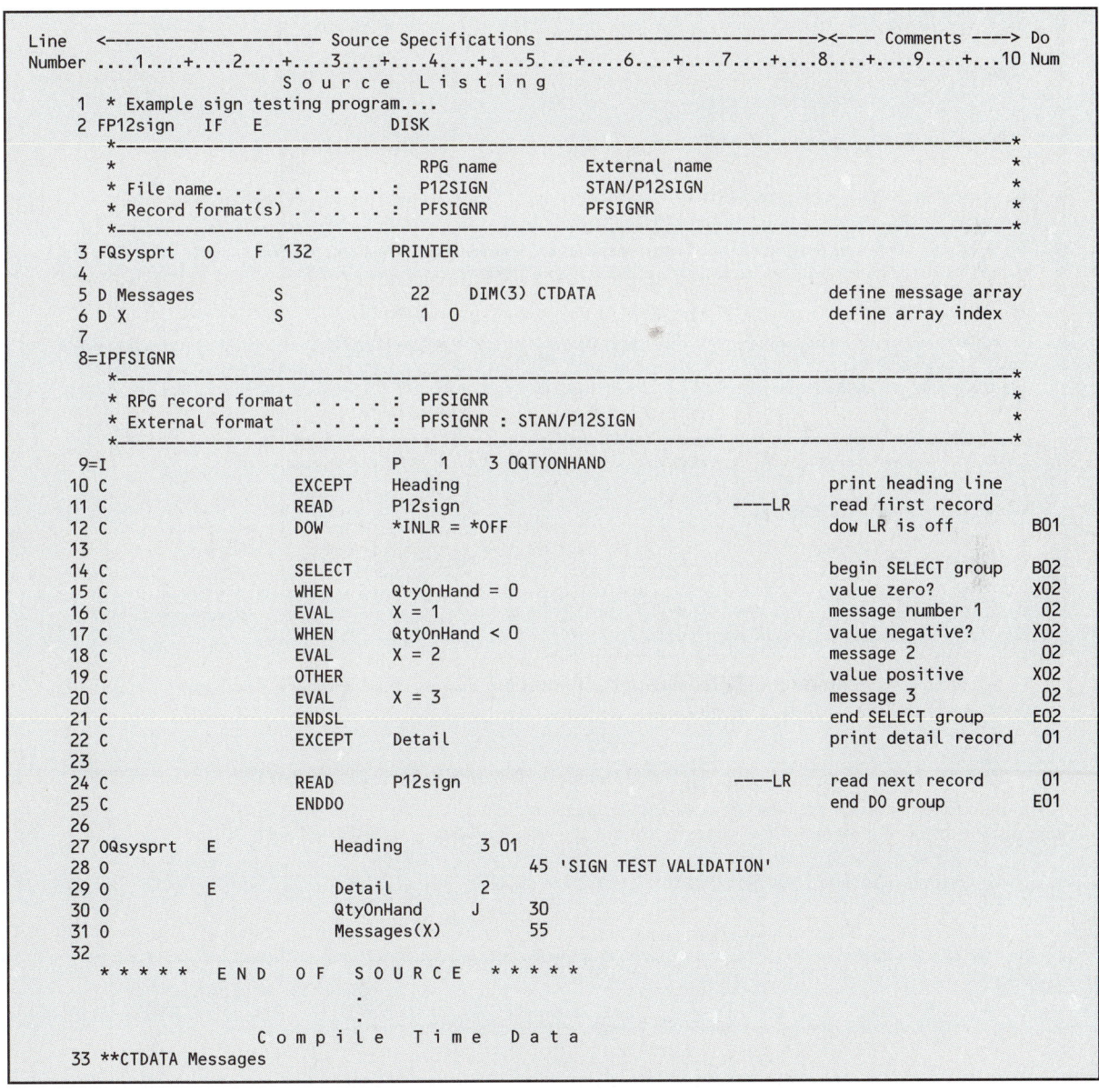

```
Line    <---------------------- Source Specifications ----------------------------><---- Comments ----> Do
Number ....1....+....2....+....3....+....4....+....5....+....6....+....7....+....8....+....9....+...10 Num
                         S o u r c e    L i s t i n g
   * Example sign testing program....
  FP12sign    IF   E             DISK
   *--------------------------------------------------------------------------------------------*
   *                                RPG name         External name                               *
   * File name. . . . . . . . . :   P12SIGN          STAN/P12SIGN                                *
   * Record format(s) . . . . . :   PFSIGNR          PFSIGNR                                     *
   *--------------------------------------------------------------------------------------------*
  FQsysprt    O    F  132            PRINTER

  D Messages        S             22    DIM(3) CTDATA                      define message array
  D X               S              1  0                                    define array index

 =IPFSIGNR
   *--------------------------------------------------------------------------------------------*
   * RPG record format  . . . . :   PFSIGNR                                                      *
   * External format  . . . . . :   PFSIGNR : STAN/P12SIGN                                       *
   *--------------------------------------------------------------------------------------------*
 =I                             P    1    3 0QTYONHAND
  C                   EXCEPT    Heading                                    print heading line
  C                   READ      P12sign                            ----LR  read first record
  C                   DOW       *INLR = *OFF                               dow LR is off         B01

  C                   SELECT                                               begin SELECT group    B02
  C                   WHEN      QtyOnHand = 0                              value zero?           X02
  C                   EVAL      X = 1                                      message number 1       02
  C                   WHEN      QtyOnHand < 0                              value negative?       X02
  C                   EVAL      X = 2                                      message 2              02
  C                   OTHER                                                value positive        X02
  C                   EVAL      X = 3                                      message 3              02
  C                   ENDSL                                                end SELECT group      E02
  C                   EXCEPT    Detail                                     print detail record    01

  C                   READ      P12sign                            ----LR  read next record       01
  C                   ENDDO                                                end DO group          E01

  OQsysprt    E            Heading        3 01
  O                                            45 'SIGN TEST VALIDATION'
  O           E            Detail         2
  O                        QtyOnHand     J     30
  O                        Messages(X)         55

   * * * * *   E N D   O F   S O U R C E   * * * * *
                                  .
                                  .
                         C o m p i l e   T i m e   D a t a
   **CTDATA Messages
```

Figure 12-8 Example sign testing validation program.

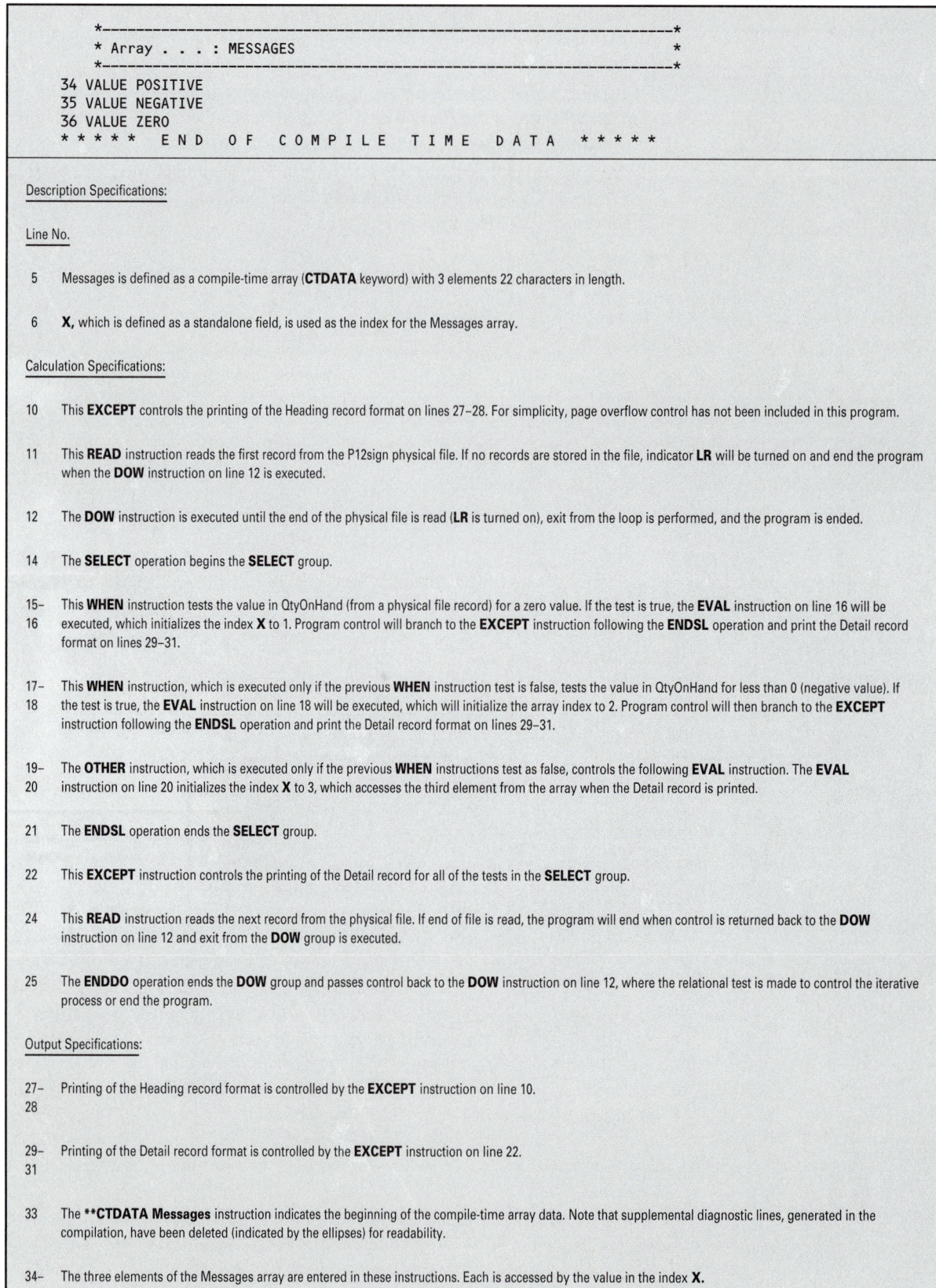

```
     *---------------------------------------------------------------------*
     * Array . . . : MESSAGES                                              *
     *---------------------------------------------------------------------*
34 VALUE POSITIVE
35 VALUE NEGATIVE
36 VALUE ZERO
* * * * *   E N D   O F   C O M P I L E   T I M E   D A T A   * * * * *
```

Description Specifications:

Line No.

5 Messages is defined as a compile-time array (**CTDATA** keyword) with 3 elements 22 characters in length.

6 **X,** which is defined as a standalone field, is used as the index for the Messages array.

Calculation Specifications:

10 This **EXCEPT** controls the printing of the Heading record format on lines 27–28. For simplicity, page overflow control has not been included in this program.

11 This **READ** instruction reads the first record from the P12sign physical file. If no records are stored in the file, indicator **LR** will be turned on and end the program when the **DOW** instruction on line 12 is executed.

12 The **DOW** instruction is executed until the end of the physical file is read (**LR** is turned on), exit from the loop is performed, and the program is ended.

14 The **SELECT** operation begins the **SELECT** group.

15–16 This **WHEN** instruction tests the value in QtyOnHand (from a physical file record) for a zero value. If the test is true, the **EVAL** instruction on line 16 will be executed, which initializes the index **X** to 1. Program control will branch to the **EXCEPT** instruction following the **ENDSL** operation and print the Detail record format on lines 29–31.

17–18 This **WHEN** instruction, which is executed only if the previous **WHEN** instruction test is false, tests the value in QtyOnHand for less than 0 (negative value). If the test is true, the **EVAL** instruction on line 18 will be executed, which will initialize the array index to 2. Program control will then branch to the **EXCEPT** instruction following the **ENDSL** operation and print the Detail record format on lines 29–31.

19–20 The **OTHER** instruction, which is executed only if the previous **WHEN** instructions test as false, controls the following **EVAL** instruction. The **EVAL** instruction on line 20 initializes the index **X** to 3, which accesses the third element from the array when the Detail record is printed.

21 The **ENDSL** operation ends the **SELECT** group.

22 This **EXCEPT** instruction controls the printing of the Detail record for all of the tests in the **SELECT** group.

24 This **READ** instruction reads the next record from the physical file. If end of file is read, the program will end when control is returned back to the **DOW** instruction on line 12 and exit from the **DOW** group is executed.

25 The **ENDDO** operation ends the **DOW** group and passes control back to the **DOW** instruction on line 12, where the relational test is made to control the iterative process or end the program.

Output Specifications:

27–28 Printing of the Heading record format is controlled by the **EXCEPT** instruction on line 10.

29–31 Printing of the Detail record format is controlled by the **EXCEPT** instruction on line 22.

33 The ****CTDATA Messages** instruction indicates the beginning of the compile-time array data. Note that supplemental diagnostic lines, generated in the compilation, have been deleted (indicated by the ellipses) for readability.

34–36 The three elements of the Messages array are entered in these instructions. Each is accessed by the value in the index **X.**

Figure 12-8 Example sign testing validation program. (Continued)

The data file processed by the sign testing validation program and the report generated are detailed in Figure 12-9.

Data File Listing	Printed Report	
	SIGN TEST VALIDATION	
00000	0	VALUE ZERO
00144	144	VALUE POSITIVE
00012-	12-	VALUE NEGATIVE

Figure 12-9 Data file listing and report generated by the sign validation program.

CHECKING DATA FIELDS

Included in data testing are procedures for the validation of data for *presence, absence, justification, acceptability, relationship,* and *structure.*

Presence of Data

This data validation function is performed to ensure that a value other than all zeros (for numeric items) or all blanks (for alphanumeric items) is stored in the field. Presence testing checks that all data for the record has been entered into the related fields. This function is used only to validate that something has been entered in the assigned field positions; it does not check the accuracy of the data.

Absence of Data

Unused fields are sometimes included in a record format to allow for uncertainties about the format's size when it was designed. These field positions may be used in validation programs to check for the justification of any field values that are located before and/or after the unused area. For example, if an unused record area did not test as blank, that would indicate that the preceding, or following, or both field values were incorrectly justified.

When an **RPG IV** program is executed, zeros are stored in all numeric fields before any data record is processed. Consequently, a justification test for numeric fields is not valid. If, however, an unused area exists before or after a numeric field, an absence test of the area may provide for a justification test for the numeric field.

Justification Checking

Alphanumeric (and alphabetic) data is usually left-justified in a related field, and any subsequent processing assumes this positioning. The *justification* of data is typically performed only on the high-order byte(s) of alphanumeric fields. For the reasons stated previously, numeric fields are *not* justification-tested.

Figure 12-10 shows a record format and stored data that include presence, absence, and justification errors.

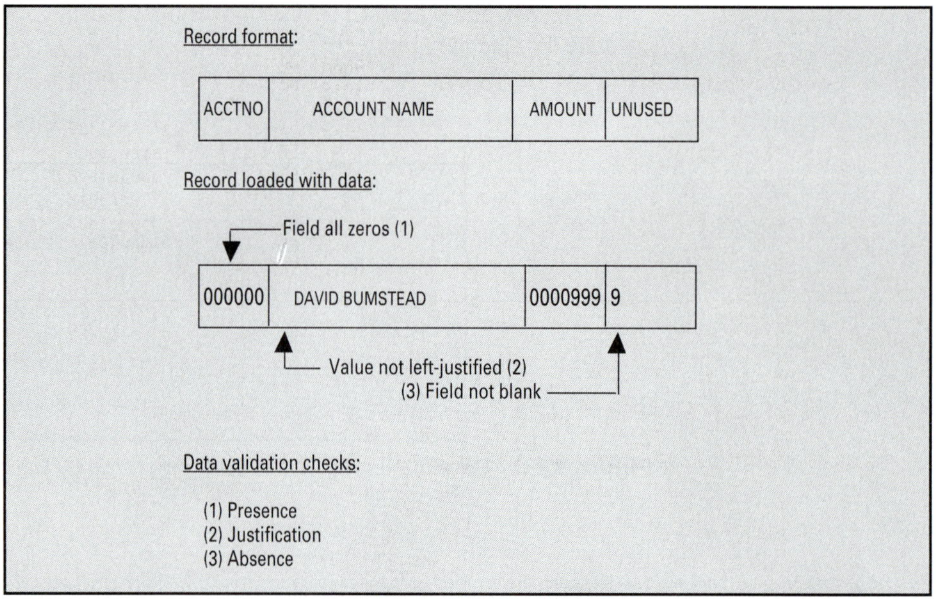

Figure 12-10 An example record that includes presence, absence, and justification validation errors.

A compile listing of an **RPG IV** program that validates the presence, absence, and justification of data is detailed in Figure 12-11.

```
Line   <--------------------- Source Specifications ----------------------------><---- Comments ----> Do
Number ....1....+....2....+....3....+....4....+....5....+....6....+....7....+....8....+....9....+...10 Num
                         S o u r c e   L i s t i n g
     1  * Example presence, absence, and justification validation program
     2
     3 FP12check  IF   E             DISK
       *--------------------------------------------------------------------------------------------*
       *                                RPG name          External name                             *
       * File name. . . . . . . . . :   P12CHECK          STAN/P12CHECK                             *
       * Record format(s) . . . . . :   P12CHECKR         P12CHECKR                                 *
       *--------------------------------------------------------------------------------------------*
     4 FQsysprt   O    F  132           PRINTER
     5
     6 D X                S              1  0                                 array index
     7 D Location         S              2  0                                 blank in ActName
     8 D Messages         S             23      DIM(3) CTDATA
     9
    10=IP12CHECKR
       *--------------------------------------------------------------------------------------------*
       * RPG record format  . . . . :   P12CHECKR                                                   *
       * External format  . . . . . :   P12CHECKR : STAN/P12CHECK                                   *
       *--------------------------------------------------------------------------------------------*
    11=I                              P     1     3 0ACTNUMBER
    12=I                              A     4    23  ACTNAME
    13=I                              P    24    27 2AMTOFSALE
    14=I                              A    28    35  UNUSED
    15 C                    EXCEPT    Heading                                   print heading line
    16 C                    READ      P12check                     ----LR       read first record
    17 C                    DOW       *INLR = *OFF                              dow LR is off        B01
    18 C                    EVAL      *IN60 = *OFF                              turn of indicator 60  01
    19
    20  * Test ActNumber for presence of a value equal to zero....
    21 C                    IF        ActNumber = *ZERO                         ActNumber zero test  B02
```

Figure 12-11 Example program for presence, absence, and justification validation of data.

```
22 C                     EVAL      X = 1                                       message 1            02
23 C                     EXSR      ErrorSR                                     branch to subroutine  02
24 C                     ENDIF                                                 end IF group         E02
25
26  * Test name for left-justification....
27 C      ' '            CHECK     ActName       Location                      find nonblank char    01
28 C                     IF        Location > 1                                nonblank location    B02
29 C                     EVAL      X = 2                                       message 2             02
30 C                     EXSR      ErrorSR                                     branch to subroutine  02
31 C                     ENDIF                                                 end IF group         E02
32
33  * Test unused field for absence of data....
34 C      ' '            CHECK     Unused                           ----70     nonblank char posi.   01
35 C                     IF        *IN70 = *ON                                 nonblank char found  B02
36 C                     EVAL      X = 3                                       Message 3             02
37 C                     EXSR      ErrorSR                                     branch to subroutine  02
38 C                     ENDIF                                                 end IF group         E02
39
40 C                     READ      P12check                         ----LR     read next record      01
41 C                     ENDDO                                                 end dow group        E01
42
43  * Subroutine that controls printing records with invalid data....
44 C     ErrorSR         BEGSR                                                 begin subroutine
45 C                     IF        *IN60 = *OFF                                indicator 60 off?    B01
46 C                     EXCEPT    PrintLine1                                  error for current rc  01
47 C                     EVAL      *IN60 = *ON                                 turn on indicator 60  01
48 C                     ELSE                                                  false action         X01
49 C                     EXCEPT    PrintLine2                                  print other error mg  01
50 C                     ENDIF                                                 end IF group         E01
51 C                     ENDSR                                                 end SR
52
53 OQsysprt    E            Heading        1 01
54 O                                               56 'PRESENCE, ABSENCE, AND'
55 O                                               75 'JUSTIFY VALIDATION'
56 O           E            PrintLine1  2  1
57 O                        ActNumber          15
58 O                        ActName            36
59 O                        AmtofSale          42
60 O                        Unused             50
61 O                        Messages(X)        93
62 O           E            PrintLine2     1
63 O                        Messages(X)        93
   * * * * *   E N D   O F   S O U R C E   * * * * *
                              .
                              .

                 C o m p i l e   T i m e   D a t a
64 **CTDATA Messages
    *-----------------------------------------------------------------------*
    * Array . . . : MESSAGES                                                *
    *-----------------------------------------------------------------------*
65 ACCT NO IS ZERO
66 NAME NOT LEFT-JUSTIFIED
67 UNUSED AREA NOT BLANK
* * * * *   E N D   O F   C O M P I L E   T I M E   D A T A   * * * * *
```

Definition Specifications:

Line No.

6 **X,** which is used as the Message array index, is defined as a one-digit integer standalone field.

7 Location, which is used as the *Result* field in the **CHECK** instruction on line 27, is defined as a two-digit integer standalone field.

8 Messages is defined as a three-element (i.e., **DIM(3)**) compile-time array (i.e., **CTDATA**) 23 characters in length.

Figure 12-11 Example program for presence, absence, and justification validation of data. (Continued)

Calculation Specifications:

15 This **EXCEPT** instruction prints the Heading record. For simplicity, page overflow is not included in this program.

16 This **READ** instruction reads the first record from the physical file. If no records are stored in the file, indicator **LR** will be turned on and end the program when the **DOW** instruction on line 17 is subsequently executed.

17 The **DOW** group will be executed while indicator **LR** is off. The **READ** instruction on line 16 or 40 will turn on **LR** when end of file is read.

18 This **EVAL** instruction turns off indicator **60,** which is used in the ErrorSR to control the printing of more than one error messge for the record currently processed.

21 This **IF** instruction tests the ActNumber field for a zero value.

22 When the **IF** test on line 21 is true, this **EVAL** instruction initializes **X** to1, which accesses the first element in the Messages array.

23 This **EXSR** instruction branches program control to the ErrorSr subroutine from which element 1 in the Messages array is printed with the input record values.

24 This **ENDIF** operation ends the **IF** group that began on line 21.

27 This **CHECK** instruction searches the ActName field for a blank character. The position of the first nonblank is stored in Location field.

28 This **IF** instruction tests the value in the Location field. If the value in Location is greater than 1, a left-justification error will be indicated in the ActName field.

29 When the **IF** test on line 28 is true, this **EVAL** instruction initializes **X** to 2, which accesses the second element in the Messages array.

30 This **EXSR** instruction branches program control to the ErrorSR subroutine from which element 2 in the Messages array is printed.

31 This **ENDIF** operation ends the **IF** group that began on line 28.

34 This **CHECK** instruction searches the *Unused* field for a blank character. When a nonblank character is found, indicator **70** will be turned on, indicating an error.

35 This **IF** instruction tests the status indicator **70.**

36 When the **IF** instruction on line 35 is true, this **EVAL** instruction initializes **X** to 3, which accesses the third element in the Messages array.

37 This **EXSR** instruction branches program control to the ErrorSR subroutine from which element 3 in the Messages array is printed.

38 This **ENDIF** operation ends the **IF** group that began on line 34.

40 This **READ** instruction reads the next record from the physical file. If end of file is read, indicator **LR** will be turned on, which will end the program when the **DOW** instruction on line 17 is subsequently executed.

41 This **ENDDO** operation ends the **DOW** group that began on line 17.

44 The **BEGSR** instruction begins the ErrorSR subroutine.

45 This **IF** instruction tests the status of indicator **60,** which is intentionally turned on by the **EVAL** instruction on line 47 to control the printing of more than one error message for the record currently processed.

46 The **EXCEPT** instruction controls the printing of the PrintLine1 and PrintLine2 record formats on lines 56–63.

47 This **EVAL** instruction turns on indicator **60,** which prevents the PrintLine1 record from printing when more than one validation error is tested in the record currently processed.

48 The **ELSE** operation controls the false action for the **IF** instruction on line 45.

49 This **EXCEPT** instruction controls the printing of the PrintLine 2 record format.

50 This **ENDIF** operation ends the **IF** group that began on line 45.

51 The **ENDSR** operation ends the ErrorSR subroutine.

Output Specifications:

53–55 Printing of the Heading record format is controlled by the **EXCEPT** instruction on line 15.

Figure 12-11 Example program for presence, absence, and justification validation of data. (Continued)

56–61	Printing of the PrintLine1 record format is controlled by the **EXCEPT** instruction on line 46. This line is printed only once for a record. When the input record generates more than one validation error, the other error messages will be printed by the PrintLine2 record.
62–63	Printing of the PrintLine2 record format is controlled by the **EXCEPT** instruction on line 49. This output is printed only when the current record processed generates more than one validation error.

Figure 12-11 Example program for presence, absence, and justification validation of data. (Continued)

A listing of the data file and report generated by the example validation program are shown in Figure 12-12.

```
Physical file listing:

00000 DAVID BUMSTEAD     00009999
20000LAMONT CRANSTON     0010000
30000 HOMER GOMEZ        0450000
40000RENE RENAULT        70000000
00000LORD SMEDLEY        1234000

Printed Report:
                         PRESENCE, ABSENCE, AND JUSTIFY VALIDATION

00000  DAVID BUMSTEAD    00009999                            ACCT NO IS ZERO
                                                             NAME NOT LEFT-JUSTIFIED
                                                             UNUSED AREA NOT BLANK

30000  HOMER GOMEZ       0450000                             NAME NOT LEFT-JUSTIFIED

40000 RENE RENAULT       70000000                            UNUSED AREA NOT BLANK

00000  LORD SMEDLEY      1234000                             ACCT NO IS ZERO
                                                             NAME NOT LEFT-JUSTIFIED
```

Figure 12-12 Data file processed and report generated by the validation program that tests for the presence, absence, and justification of data.

ACCEPTABILITY OF DATA

Range Checking

One example of *range* testing is the determination of the days, months, and/or years between two *valid* dates. If a field is defined as a date field in a physical file (i.e., **L** in the *Data Type* field—position 35), an invalid value for a date *cannot* be entered. Consequently, validation of dates may be limited to range testing instead of testing for valid day, month, year values.

The example range validation program shown in Figure 12-13 computes the days between a billing date and invoice date to determine whether an invoice is not overdue or is 30 to 59 days, or 60 to 89 days, or 90 or more days overdue.

```
Line   <--------------------- Source Specifications ----------------------------><---- Comments ----> Do
Number ....1....+....2....+....3....+....4....+....5....+....6....+....7....+....8....+....9....+...10 Num
                         S o u r c e   L i s t i n g
     * This program computes the range of days from the invoice date to the
     * billing date for not due or 30, 60, 90 and over days past due....
    HDATFMT(*USA)
    FP12BillingIF   E             DISK
     *--------------------------------------------------------------------------------------------*
     *                              RPG name        External name                                 *
     * File name. . . . . . . . . :  P12BILLING      STAN/P12BILLING                              *
     * Record format(s) . . . . . :  P2BILLINGR      P2BILLINGR                                   *
     *--------------------------------------------------------------------------------------------*
    FP12Range  IF   E             DISK
     *--------------------------------------------------------------------------------------------*
     *                              RPG name        External name                                 *
     * File name. . . . . . . . . :  P12RANGE        STAN/P12RANGE                                *
     * Record format(s) . . . . . :  P12RANGER       P12RANGER                                    *
     *--------------------------------------------------------------------------------------------*
    FQsysprt   O    F  132        PRINTER

    D X               S              1  0
    D Days            S              3  0                              days over
    D Messages        S             24     DIM(4) CTDATA

   =IP2BILLINGR
     *--------------------------------------------------------------------------------------------*
     * RPG record format  . . . . :  P2BILLINGR                                                   *
     * External format  . . . . . :  P2BILLINGR : STAN/P12BILLING                                 *
     *--------------------------------------------------------------------------------------------*
   =I                             *USA/D    1   10  BILL_DATE
   =IP12RANGER
     *--------------------------------------------------------------------------------------------*
     * RPG record format  . . . . :  P12RANGER                                                    *
     * External format  . . . . . :  P12RANGER : STAN/P12RANGE                                    *
     *--------------------------------------------------------------------------------------------*
   =I                              P     1    3 0ACTNUMBER
   =I                        *USA/D     4   13  INV_DATE
   =I                              P    14   17 2INV_AMOUNT
    C                   READ      P12Billing                       ----LR    access billing date
    C                   READ      P12range                         ----LR    read first record
    C                   EXCEPT    Heading                                    print headings

    C                   DOW       *INLR = *OFF                               dow LR is off         B01
    C     Bill_Date     SUBDUR    Inv_Date      Days:*D                      days after inv date    01
    C                   SELECT                                               begin SELECT group    B02
    C                   WHEN      Days <= 30                                 not over due?         X02
    C                   EVAL      X = 1                                      access messages 1      02
    C                   WHEN      Days > 30 AND Days < 60                    31-59 days overdue    X02
    C                   EVAL      X = 2                                      access messages 2      02
    C                   WHEN      Days >= 60 AND Days < 90                   60-89 days overdue    X02
    C                   EVAL      X = 3                                      access messages 3      02
    C                   OTHER                                                                      X02
    C                   EVAL      X = 4                                      access messages 4      02
    C                   ENDSL                                                end SELECT group      E02

    C                   EXCEPT    DetailLine                                 print detail line      01
    C                   READ      P12range                         ----LR    read next record       01
    C                   ENDDO                                                end dow group         E01

    OQsysprt   E            Heading        1
    O                                          31 'CREDIT CARD PAYMENT'
    O                                          40 'SCHEDULE'
    O          E            Heading        3
    O                                          23 'AS OF'
    O                       Bill_Date          34
    O          E            Heading        1
    O                                          10 'ACCOUNT'
    O                                          23 'INVOICE'
    O          E            Heading        2
    O                                           9 'NUMBER'
```

Figure 12-13 Example program that determines the number of days between two dates.

```
50 0                                          22 'DATE'
51 0                                          44 'PAYMENT STATUS'
52 0          E           DetailLine      2
53 0                      ActNumber          9
54 0                      Inv_Date          25
55 0                      Messages(X)       53
                             .
                             .
                 C o m p i l e   T i m e   D a t a
56 **CTDATA Messages
    *----------------------------------------------------------------------*
    * Array . . . : MESSAGES                                               *
    *----------------------------------------------------------------------*
57 NOT DUE
58 30 TO 59 DAYS OVERDUE
59 60 TO 89 DAYS OVERDUE
60 90 OR MORE DAYS OVERDUE
* * * * *   E N D   O F   C O M P I L E   T I M E   D A T A   * * * * *
```

Header Specifications:

Line No.

3 **DATFMT(*USA)** defines the date fields in an **MM/DD/YY** format instead of the default ***ISO** format.

File Description Specifications:

4 P12Billing, in which the Bill_Date value is stored, is defined as an input (**I** in position 17), full-procedural (**F** in position 18), externally described (**E** in position 22) physical file.

5 P12Range, in which the customer records are stored, is defined as an input (**I** in position 17), full-procedural (**F** in position 18), externally described (**E** in position 22) physical file.

6 Qsysprt is defined as an output (**O** in position 17), program-described (**F** in position 22) printer file with a record length of 132 characters (132 in positions 23–27).

Definition Specifications:

8 **X,** which is used as the Messages array index, is defined as a standalone one-byte integer field.

9 Days, in which the number of days between the Bill_date and the Inv_Date is stored, is defined as a standalone three-byte integer field.

10 Messages is defined as a four-element (i.e., **DIM(4)**) compile-time (i.e., **CTDATA**) array with 24 character elements.

Calculation Specifications:

18 This **READ** instruction, which is executed only once, reads the one record stored in the P12Billing file to access the Bill_Date value. Other than to satisfy syntax requirements, the **LR** indicator has no function for this instruction.

19 This **READ** instruction reads the first record in the P12Range file. If no records are stored in the file, indicator **LR** will be turned on and end the program when the **DOW** instruction on line 22 is executed.

20 This **EXCEPT** instruction prints the Heading records on lines 39–51.

22 The **DOW** group is executed until the **READ** instruction on line 19 or 36 reads the end of file, which will turn on indicator **LR** to subsequently end the program.

23 The **SUBDUR** instruction subtracts the Inv_Date value from the Bill_Date value and stores the difference in Days: ***D.** Note that Inv_Date and Bill_Date were defined as date fields (see lines 13 and 16) in their related physical files. The ***D** suffix with the Days field specifies that the number of days between the two dates is to be calculated.

24 The **SELECT** operation begins the **SELECT** group.

25–26 This **WHEN** instruction tests the value in Days for less than or equal to 30. If the test is true, the **EVAL** instruction on line 26 initializes **X** to 1, which accesses the first element in the Messages array (i.e., **NOT DUE**). Program control will branch to the first executable instruction after the **ENDSL** operation if this **WHEN** test is true.

27–28 If the **WHEN** test on line 25 is not true, this **WHEN** instruction will be executed. If the value in Days is greater than **30** and less than **60,** the **EVAL** instruction on line 28 will initialize **X** to 2 and access the second element in the Messages array (i.e., **30 TO 59 DAYS OVERDUE**). Program control will branch to the first executable instruction after the **ENDSL** operation if this **WHEN** test is true.

Figure 12-13 Example program that determines the number of days between two dates. (Continued)

29–30 If the **WHEN** test on line 27 is not true, this **WHEN** instruction will be executed. If the value in Days is greater than or equal to **60** and less than **90,** the **EVAL** instruction on line 30 will initialize **X** to 3 and access the third element in the Messages array (i.e., **30 TO 59 DAYS OVERDUE**). Program control will branch to the first executable instruction after the **ENDSL** operation if this **WHEN** test is true.

31 Instructions following the **OTHER** operation are executed only if none of the previous **WHEN** tests was true.

32 This **EVAL** instruction initializes **X** to 4 and accesses the fourth element in the Messages array (i.e., **90 OR MORE DAYS OVERDUE**). Program control will branch to the first executable instruction after the **ENDSL** operation.

33 The **ENDSL** operation ends the **SELECT** group.

35 This **EXCEPT** instruction prints the DetailLine record for any of the **WHEN** or **OTHER** conditions.

36 This **READ** instruction reads the next record from the P12Range file. If end of file is read, indicator **LR** will be turned on and end the program when the **DOW** instruction is subsequently executed.

37 The **ENDDO** operation ends the **DOW** group and sends program control back to the **DOW** instruction on line 22, where the relational test is made.

Output Specifications

39–51 The four Heading record formats are executed by the **EXCEPT** instruction on line 20. The value in Bill_Date is stored in the P12Billing file, which is read only once by the **READ** instruction on line 19.

52–55 The DetailLine record is printed by the **EXCEPT** instruction on line 35. The value in **X** determines which Messages array element is printed.

56 The ****CTDATA Messages** instruction specifies the beginning of the compile-time array.

57–60 The four elements of the Messages array are specified in these instructions.

Note: The two periods before the CompileTime Data header indicate compile-time information that has been deleted by the author for clarity.

Figure 12-13 Example program that determines the number of days between two dates. (Continued)

The report generated by the example range program is shown in Figure 12-14.

```
                 CREDIT CARD PAYMENT SCHEDULE
                       AS OF 01/10/1998

ACCOUNT        INVOICE
NUMBER           DATE          PAYMENT STATUS

  10000        11/30/1997     30 TO 59 DAYS OVERDUE

  11000        10/20/1997     60 TO 89 DAYS OVERDUE

  12000        09/10/1997     90 OR MORE DAYS OVERDUE

  13000        12/15/1997     NOT DUE
```

Figure 12-14 Report generated by the example program that determines the number of days between two dates.

Check Digits

Many account or customer numbers are large (for example, MasterCard account numbers have 16 digits), which often causes transposition or substitution errors during data entry. This problem may be controlled by including a *check digit* in the body of the number. Common methods used to develop and validate check digits are Modulus-10 and Modulus-11. Because Modulus-11 provides more control over transposition and substitution errors (it identifies over 95 percent of such errors), it is the method discussed here.

The mathematical steps for the development of a check digit are detailed in Figure 12-15.

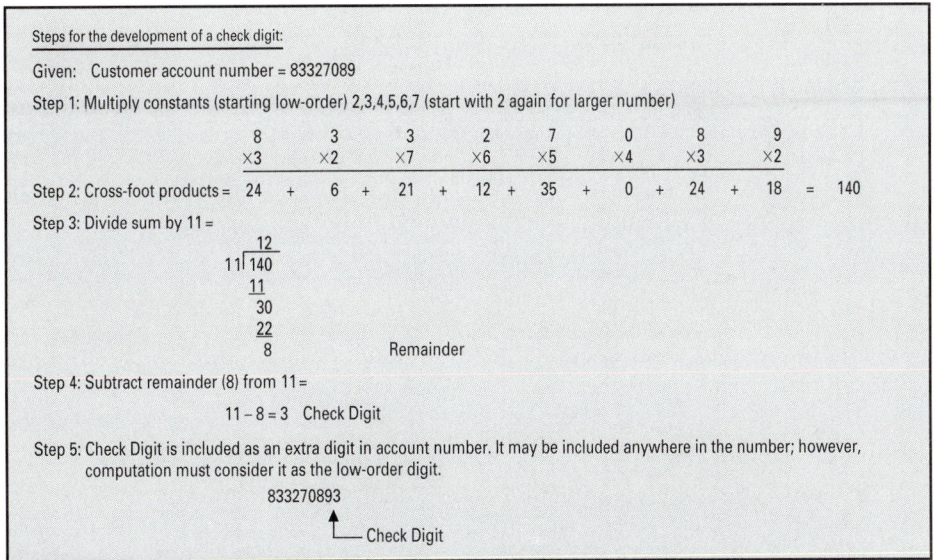

Steps for the development of a check digit:

Given: Customer account number = 83327089

Step 1: Multiply constants (starting low-order) 2,3,4,5,6,7 (start with 2 again for larger number)

8	3	3	2	7	0	8	9
×3	×2	×7	×6	×5	×4	×3	×2

Step 2: Cross-foot products = 24 + 6 + 21 + 12 + 35 + 0 + 24 + 18 = 140

Step 3: Divide sum by 11 =

```
     12
11 | 140
     11
      30
      22
       8     Remainder
```

Step 4: Subtract remainder (8) from 11 =

11 − 8 = 3 Check Digit

Step 5: Check Digit is included as an extra digit in account number. It may be included anywhere in the number; however, computation must consider it as the low-order digit.

833270893 (3 — Check Digit)

Figure 12-15 Mathematical steps for the development of a check digit by the Modulus-11 method.

Figure 12-16 contains the compile listing of an **RPG IV** program that creates a check digit by the mathematical procedures outlined in Figure 12-15 and builds a new account number with the digit included in the low-order byte.

```
Line   <---------------------- Source Specifications ----------------------------><---- Comments ----> Do
Number ....1....+....2....+....3....+....4....+....5....+....6....+....7....+....8....+....9....+...10 Num
                              S o u r c e   L i s t i n g
         * This program creates check digit for account numbers & builds the
         * new account number with the check digit in the low-order byte....

        FP12digitc IF   E             DISK
         *--------------------------------------------------------------------------------------*
         *                              RPG name           External name                        *
         * File name. . . . . . . . :   P12DIGITC          STAN/P12DIGITC                       *
         * Record format(s) . . . . :   P12DIGITXR         P12DIGITXR                           *
         *--------------------------------------------------------------------------------------*
        FQsysprt   O    F  132        PRINTER

        D                 DS
        D NumAry                        1  0 DIM(5)                    account no. array
        D Act_Number              1     5

        D Sum             S             3  0
        D Quotient        S             3  0
        D Remainder       S             3  0
        D CheckDigit      S             1  0
        D NewNumber       S             6  0                           with check digit

       =IP12DIGITXR
         *--------------------------------------------------------------------------------------*
         * RPG record format  . . . . :  P12DIGITXR                                             *
         * External format  . . . . . :  P12DIGITXR : STAN/P12DIGITC                            *
         *--------------------------------------------------------------------------------------*
       =I                               A    1    5  ACT_NUMBER
        C                   EXCEPT    Heading                          print heading line
        C                   READ      P12digitc                  ----LR  read first record
```

Figure 12-16 An example program that creates a check digit by the Modulus-11 method.

```
21 C                      DOW       *INLR = *OFF                                    dow LR is off         B01
22 C                      EVAL      Sum =                                           compute sum            01
23 C                                  NumAry(5) * 2                                 5th element * 2        01
24 C                                + NumAry(4) * 3                                 4th element * 3        01
25 C                                + NumAry(3) * 4                                 3rd element * 4        01
26 C                                + NumAry(2) * 5                                 2nd element * 5        01
27 C                                + NumAry(1) * 6                                 1st element * 6        01
28
29 C       Sum            DIV       11            Quotient          3 0            compute quotient       01
30 C                      MVR                     Remainder         3 0            save remainder         01
31 C                      EVAL      CheckDigit = 11 - Remainder                     compute check digit    01
32
33  * Build new account number with check digit in low-order digit....
34 C                      MOVEL     Act_Number    NewNumber                         move to larger field   01
35 C                      MOVE      CheckDigit    NewNumber                         store in last positn   01
36 C                      EXCEPT    DetailLine                                      print detail line      01
37
38 C                      READ      P12digitc                         ----LR        read next record       01
39 C                      ENDDO                                                     end dow group         E01
40
41 OQsysprt   E              Heading       3
42 O                                        29 'MODULUS-11 CHECK DIGIT'
43 O                                        41 'COMPUTATION'
44 O          E              Heading       2
45 O                                        15 'OLD ACCT#'
46 O                                        29 'CHECK DIGIT'
47 O                                        42 'NEW ACCT#'
48 O          E              DetailLine    2
49 O                         Act_Number     13
50 O                         CheckDigit     24
51 O                         NewNumber      41
```

Definition Specifications:

Line No.

7 The letters **DS** define the beginning of a data structure that includes the instructions on lines 8 and 9.

8 NumAry is defined as a run-time array with 5 elements (i.e., **DIM(5)**) 1 integer long.

9 The physical file field Act_Number is specified to load the NumAry with its stored value.

11 Sum is defined as a three-digit integer standalone field. The sum from step 2 in the computations shown in Figure 12-15 will be stored in this field (see lines 22–27).

12 Quotient is defined as a three-digit integer standalone field. The quotient from step 3 in the computations shown in Figure 12-15 will be stored in this field (see line 29).

13 Remainder is defined as a three-digit integer standalone field. The remainder from step 3 in the computations shown in Figure 12-15 will be stored in this field (see line 30).

14 CheckDigit is defined as a one-digit integer standalone field. The check digit from step 4 in the computations shown in Figure 12-15 will be stored in this field (see line 31).

15 NewNumber is defined as a six-digit integer standalone field. NewNumber includes the original Act_Number plus the CheckDigit in the low-order digit (see lines 34–35).

Calculation Specifications:

19 This **EXCEPT** instruction controls the printing of the Heading record formats. For simplicity, page overflow is not included in this program.

20 This **READ** instruction reads the first record from the physical file. If end of file is read, indicator **LR** will be turned on and end the program when the **DOW** instruction on line 21 is executed.

21 The **DOW** group is performed until indicator **LR** is turned on by the **READ** instruction on line 20 or 38.

Figure 12-16 An example program that creates a check digit by the Modulus-11 method. (Continued)

22–27	This **EVAL** instruction performs steps 1 and 2 shown in Figure 12-15. The numeric literals 2 through 6 must be used in the Modulus-11 formula to create a check digit.
29–30	This **DIV** instruction performs step 3 and 4 shown in Figure 12-15. The **MVR** (Move Remainder) instruction stores the remainder value in the Remainder field.
31	This **EVAL** instruction performs step 4 in Figure 12-14, the final step in computing the CheckDigit value.
34	The **MOVEL** instruction moves the five-character Act_Number value to the first five positions in the six-character NewNumber field.
35	The **MOVE** instruction moves the CheckDigit number to the sixth character in the NewNumber field, which creates the new account number.
36	This **EXCEPT** instruction controls the printing of the DetailLine record format.
38	This **READ** instruction reads the next record from the physical file. If end of file is read, indicator **LR** will be turned on and end the program when the **DOW** instruction on line 21 is subsequently executed.
39	The **ENDDO** operation ends the **DOW** group and passes control back to the **DOW** instruction, where the relational test is made to end the program or continue processing.
Output Specifications	
41–47	Printing of the Heading records is controlled by the **EXCEPT** instruction on line 19.
48–51	Printing of the DetailLine record is controlled by the **EXCEPT** instruction on line 36.

Figure 12-16 An example program that creates a check digit by the Modulus-11 method. (Continued)

Examine the report shown in Figure 12-17 and notice that the old account numbers, the computed check digits, and the new composite numbers are separately shown. The length of the new account number is six bytes.

```
MODULUS-11 CHECK DIGIT COMPUTATION

OLD ACCT#  CHECK DIGIT    NEW ACCT#
  12000         6          120006
  13000         1          130001
  14000         7          140007
  15000         2          150002
  21000         5          210005
  30000         4          300004
  40000         9          400009
```

Figure 12-17 Report generated by check digit creation program.

Validating with a Check Digit

The mathematical steps to validate an account number that includes a check digit in the low-order byte are listed in Figure 12-18.

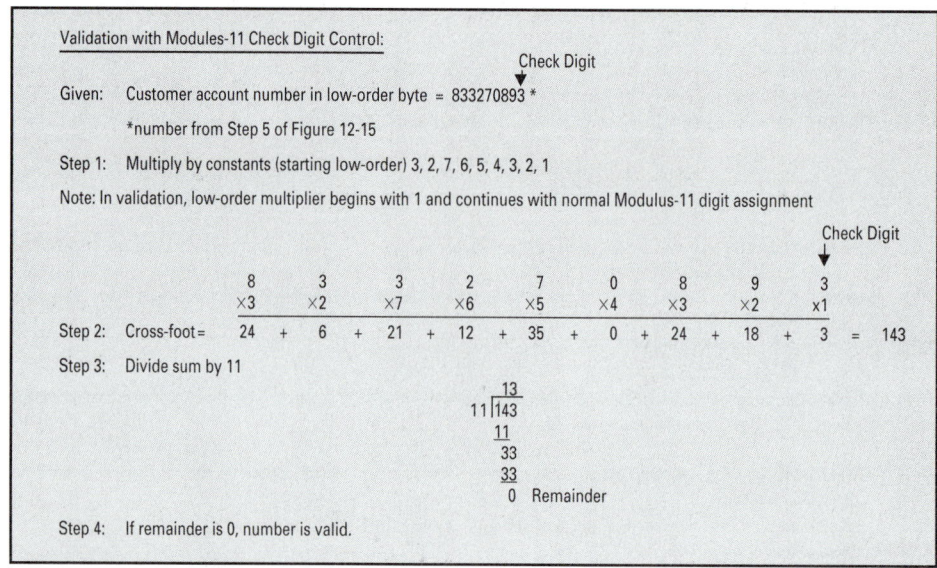

Validation with Modules-11 Check Digit Control:

Given: Customer account number in low-order byte = 833270893 * (Check Digit: 3)

*number from Step 5 of Figure 12-15

Step 1: Multiply by constants (starting low-order) 3, 2, 7, 6, 5, 4, 3, 2, 1

Note: In validation, low-order multiplier begins with 1 and continues with normal Modulus-11 digit assignment

										Check Digit	
	8	3	3	2	7	0	8	9		3	
	×3	×2	×7	×6	×5	×4	×3	×2		x1	
Step 2: Cross-foot=	24 +	6 +	21 +	12 +	35 +	0 +	24 +	18 +		3	= 143

Step 3: Divide sum by 11

```
     13
 11 |143
     11
      33
      33
       0  Remainder
```

Step 4: If remainder is 0, number is valid.

Figure 12-18 Mathematical steps to validate a number that includes a check digit in the low-order byte.

Figure 12-19 contains an **RPG IV** program that validates account numbers by the Modulus-11 check digit method.

```
Line    <---------------------- Source Specifications ----------------------------><---- Comments ----> Do
Number ....1....+....2....+....3....+....4....+....5....+....6....+....7....+....8....+....9....+...10 Num
                          S o u r c e   L i s t i n g
       * This program validates account number with the modulus-11 method....
       FP12digitv IF   E             DISK
        *--------------------------------------------------------------------------------------------*
        *                                 RPG name          External name                             *
        * File name. . . . . . . . . :   P12DIGITV         STAN/P12DIGITV                            *
        * Record format(s) . . . . . :   P12DIGITVR        P12DIGITVR                                *
        *--------------------------------------------------------------------------------------------*
       FQsysprt   O    F  132            PRINTER

       D                 DS
       D NumAry                         1  0 DIM(6)                              account no. array
       D Act_Number              1      6

       D Sum             S              3  0
       D Quotient        S              3  0
       D Remainder       S              3  0

      =IP12DIGITVR
        *--------------------------------------------------------------------------------------------*
        * RPG record format  . . . . :   P12DIGITVR                                                  *
        * External format  . . . . . :   P12DIGITVR : STAN/P12DIGITV                                *
        *--------------------------------------------------------------------------------------------*
      =I                                 A    1    6  ACT_NUMBER
       C                   EXCEPT    Heading                                      print heading line
       C                   READ      P12digitv                              ----LR read first record
       C                   DOW       *INLR = *OFF                                 dow LR is off         B01
       C                   EVAL      Sum =                                        compute sum            01
       C                               NumAry(6) * 1                              6th element * 1        01
       C                             + NumAry(5) * 2                              5th element * 2        01
       C                             + NumAry(4) * 3                              4th element * 3        01
       C                             + NumAry(3) * 4                              3rd element * 4        01
       C                             + NumAry(2) * 5                              2nd element * 5        01
       C                             + NumAry(1) * 6                              1st element * 6        01
```

Figure 12-19 Example program that validates account numbers by the Modulus-11 check digit method.

```
25
26 C      Sum           DIV      11           Quotient                     compute quotient     01
27 C                    MVR                   Remainder                    save remainder       01
28
29 C                    IF       Remainder > *ZERO                         remainder > 0?      B02
30 C                    EXCEPT   Invalid                                   print invalid acct#  02
31 C                    ENDIF                                                                  E02
32
33 C                    READ     P12digitv                          ----LR read next record     01
34 C                    ENDDO                                             end dow group       E01
35
36 OQsysprt    E            Heading       3
37 O                                           33 'MODULUS-11 CHECK DIGIT'
38 O                                           44 'VALIDATION'
39 O           E            Invalid       2
40 O                        Act_Number         18
41 O                                           43 'ACCT# INVALID'
```

Definition Specifications:

Line No.

5 The letters **DS** define the beginning of a data structure that includes the instructions on lines 6 and 7.

8 NumAry is defined as a run-time array with 6 elements (i.e., **DIM(6)**) 1 integer long.

9 The physical file field Act_Number is specified to *load* the NumAry with its stored value.

11 Sum is defined as a three-digit integer standalone field. The sum from step 2 in the computations shown in Figure 12-18 will be stored in this field (see lines 18–24).

12 Quotient is defined as a three-digit integer standalone field. The quotient from step 3 in the computations shown in Figure 12-18 will be stored in this field (see line 26).

13 Remainder is defined as a three-digit integer standalone field. The remainder from step 3 in the computations shown in Figure 12-18 will be stored in this field (see line 27).

Calculation Specifications:

15 This **EXCEPT** instruction controls the printing of the Heading record formats. For simplicity, page overflow has not been included in this program.

16 This **READ** instruction reads the first record from the physical file. If end of file is read, indicator **LR** will be turned on and end the program when the **DOW** instruction on line 17 is executed.

17 The **DOW** group is performed until indicator **LR** is turned on by the **READ** instruction on line 16 or 33.

18–24 This **EVAL** instruction performs steps 1 and 2 shown in Figure 12-18. The numeric literals 1 through 6 must be used in the Modulus-11 formula to validate an item that includes a check digit.

26–27 This **DIV** instruction performs step 3 shown in Figure 12-18. The **MVR** (Move Remainder) instruction stores the remainder value in the *Remainder* field.

29 The **IF** instruction determines if the value in the *Remainder* field is greater than zero.

30 When the **IF** test on line 29 is true, this **EXCEPT** instruction will print the invalid record format on lines 39–41.

31 The **ENDIF** operation ends the **IF** group that began on line 29.

33 This **READ** instruction reads the next record from the physical file. If end of file is read, indicator **LR** will be turned on and end the program when the **DOW** instruction on line 16 is subsequently executed.

34 The **ENDDO** operation ends the **DOW** group and passes control back to the **DOW** instruction, where the relational test is made to end the program or continue processing.

36–38 Printing of the Heading record is controlled by the **EXCEPT** instruction on line 15.

48–51 Printing of the Invalid record is controlled by the **EXCEPT** instruction on line 30.

Figure 12-19 Example program that validates account numbers by the Modulus-11 check digit method. (Continued)

The report generated in Figure 12-20 identifies the account numbers that did not pass the Modulus-11 test. An examination of the data file listing in Figure 12-20 shows that 130001 and 150002 were the only valid numbers processed. For convenience, the same account numbers developed in Figure 12-17 are used. Obviously, five of them were modified with incorrect check digits to test the function of the program in Figure 12-19.

```
Data File Listing          Printed Report

                           MODULUS-11 CHECK DIGIT VALIDATION

    120005                 120005           ACCT# INVALID
    130001
    140009                 140009           ACCT# INVALID
    150002
    200001                 200001           ACCT# INVALID
    300005
    400000                 300005           ACCT# INVALID

                           400000           ACCT# INVALID
```

Figure 12-20 Data file listing and error report generated by the Modulus-11 validation program.

Limit Checking

Limit checking is a validation function that controls a maximum (and sometimes minimum) value for a variable item. The maximum credit allowed to a customer or the maximum sales amount for a department are examples of this test. If this function was included as a validation procedure, any customer who attempted to charge a purchase would have the transaction rejected if his or her credit limit had been reached. This process would be better controlled in an interactive environment, where decisions may be made at the time of the purchase. In a batch processing mode, the information would be available only after the fact.

Relationship of Data

When possible, additional validation of data may be made by relating it to other data. For example, if a hospital charged maternity fees to a male patient, this would obviously indicate that the relationship of the service to the individual's sex had not been checked. Another application might require that some transaction codes relate to positive amounts and others to negative.

The data file processed by the example limits/relationship program and the report generated are shown in Figure 12-21.

```
Data File Listing                          Printed Report

   112000}S  (} = negative 0)       TRANSACTION CODE & SALES AMOUNT LIMIT VALIDATION
   225000JC  (J = negative 1)
   4330000C
   1000999X                         1  S  1,200.00-   SIGN NOT VALID FOR CODE
   3025000S
                                    4  C  3,300.00    SIGN NOT VALID FOR CODE
Note: 225000JC is a valid record                      INVALID DEPT NUMBER

                                    1  X      9.99    CODE NOT VALID

                                    3  S    250.00    SALES AMT OVER DEPT LIMIT
```

Figure 12-21 Data file processed and report generated by example limits/relationship validation program.

The following limits and relationship validation tests are made in the example **RPG IV** program:

1. Department numbers must be **1, 2,** or **3.**
2. Individual department sales have the following limits:

Dept #	**Maximum Sales Allowed**
1	**1,000.00**
2	**3,000.00**
3	**200.00**

3. Valid transaction codes and their functions:

Code	**Function**	**Valid Sign for Code**
S	**Sale**	+
C	**Credit**	–

If the transaction code is **S,** the Sales_Amt field value must be positive; if the code is **C,** the value must be negative to be accepted as a valid transaction.

A detailed compile listing of the example **RPG IV** program that controls limits and relationship validation functions is presented in Figure 12-22.

```
Line    <---------------------- Source Specifications ----------------------------><---- Comments ----> Do
Number ....1....+....2....+....3....+....4....+....5....+....6....+....7....+....8....+....9....+...10 Num
                              S o u r c e   L i s t i n g
   * Limits and relationship of data validation program....
   *  Valid transaction codes are:
   *    If Code = S  Transaction amount must be positive
   *    If Code = C  Transaction amount must be negative
   * Valid dept numbers are 1, 2, and 3
   * If dept number is not valid, sales limit check is not performed....
  FP12limits IF   E             DISK
   *--------------------------------------------------------------------------------------*
   *                               RPG name          External name                          *
   * File name. . . . . . . . . :  P12LIMITS         STAN/P12LIMITS                         *
   * Record format(s) . . . . . :  P12LIMITSR        P12LIMITSR                             *
   *--------------------------------------------------------------------------------------*
  FQsysprt   O    F  132          PRINTER

  D TransCodes      S              1    DIM(2) CTDATA PERRCD(2)
  D DeptCodes       S              1  0 DIM(3) CTDATA PERRCD(3)
  D DeptLimit       S              4  0 DIM(3) CTDATA PERRCD(3)
  D Messages        S             25    DIM(4) CTDATA
  D X               S              1  0                               messages array index
  D N               S              1  0                               dpt#/limit ary index

 =IP12LIMITSR
   *--------------------------------------------------------------------------------------*
   * RPG record format  . . . . :  P12LIMITSR                                               *
   * External format  . . . . . :  P12LIMITSR : STAN/P12LIMITS                              *
   *--------------------------------------------------------------------------------------*
 =I                             P    1     1 0DEPTNO
 =I                             P    2     5 2SALES_AMT
 =I                             A    6     6  TRANSCODE
  C                   EXCEPT    Heading                               print heading
  C                   READ      P12Limits                    ----LR   read first record
```

Figure 12-22 Example program that controls limits and relationship validation.

```
C                   DOW       *INLR = *OFF                              dow LR is off         B01
C                   EVAL      *IN20 = *OFF                              turn off ind. 20       01
C                   EXSR      CodeSR                                    branch to subroutine   01
C                   EXSR      SalesSR                                   branch to subroutine   01

C                   READ      P12Limits                       ----LR    read next record       01
C                   ENDDO                                               end DO group          E01

C     CodeSR        BEGSR                                               branch to subroutine
C     TransCode     LOOKUP    TransCodes                      ----50    valid transcode?
C                   SELECT                                              begin SELECT group    B01
C                   WHEN      *IN50 = *OFF                              invalid trancode?     X01
C                   EVAL      X = 1                                     messages 1             01
C                   EXSR      ErrorSR                                   branch to SR           01
C                   WHEN      TransCode = 'C' AND Sales_Amt > 0         code & amt validatin  X01
C                   EVAL      X = 2                                     messages 2             01
C                   EXSR      ErrorSR                                   branch to SR           01
C                   WHEN      TransCode = 'S' AND Sales_Amt < 0         code & amt validatin  X01
C                   EVAL      X = 2                                     messages 2             01
C                   EXSR      ErrorSR                                   branch to SR           01
C                   ENDSL                                                                     E01
C                   ENDSR                                               end subroutine

C     SalesSR       BEGSR                                               begin subroutine
C                   EVAL      N = 1                                     initialize index N
C     DeptNo        LOOKUP    DeptCodes(N)                    ----51    valid DeptNo?
C                   IF        *IN51 = *OFF                              dept no invalid?      B01
C                   EVAL      X = 3                                     messages 3             01
C                   EXSR      ErrorSR                                   branch to subroutine   01
C                   ELSE                                                                      X01
C                   IF        Sales_Amt > DeptLimit(N)                  over dept limit?      B02
C                   EVAL      X = 4                                     messages 4             02
C                   EXSR      ErrorSR                                   branch to subroutine   02
C                   ENDIF                                               end SELECT group      E02
C                   ENDIF                                               end SELECT group      E01
C                   ENDSR                                               end subroutine

C     ErrorSR       BEGSR                                               begin subroutine
C                   IF        *IN20 = *OFF                              indicator 20 off?     B01
C                   EXCEPT    PrintLine1                                                       01
C                   EVAL      *IN20 = *ON                               turn on indicator 20   01
C                   ELSE                                                                      X01
C                   EXCEPT    PrintLine2                                                       01
C                   ENDIF                                               end IF group          E01
C                   ENDSR                                               end subroutine

OQsysprt   E           Heading        3  06
O                                       28 'TRANSACTION CODE & SALES'
O                                       52 'AMOUNT LIMIT VALIDATION'
O          E           PrintLine1  2
O                      DeptNo            5
O                      TransCode        10
O                      Sales_Amt     J  22
O                      Messages(X)      50

O          E           PrintLine2  1
O                      Messages(X)      50
                          .
                          .
               C o m p i l e   T i m e   D a t a
**CTDATA TransCodes
 *---------------------------------------------------------------------*
 * Array . . . : TRANSCODES                                            *
 *---------------------------------------------------------------------*
CS
**CTDATA DeptCodes
 *---------------------------------------------------------------------*
 * Array . . . : DEPTCODES                                             *
 *---------------------------------------------------------------------*
```

Figure 12-22 Example program that controls limits and relationship validation. (Continued)

```
84 123
85 **CTDATA DeptLimit
   *-------------------------------------------------------------------*
   * Array . . . : DEPTLIMIT                                           *
   *-------------------------------------------------------------------*
86 100030000200
87 **CTDATA Messages
   *-------------------------------------------------------------------*
   * Array . . . : MESSAGES                                            *
   *-------------------------------------------------------------------*
88 CODE NOT VALID
89 SIGN NOT VALID FOR CODE
90 INVALID DEPT NUMBER
91 SALES AMT OVER DEPT LIMIT
* * * * *   E N D   O F   C O M P I L E   T I M E   D A T A   * * * * *
```

Definition Specifications:

Line No.	
10	TransCodes is defined as a compile-time array (i.e., **CTDATA**) with 2 (i.e., **DIM(2)**) 1-byte elements stored on one record (i.e., **PERRCD(2)**).
11	DeptCodes is defined as a compile-time array (i.e., **CTDATA**) with 3 (i.e., **DIM(3)**) 1-byte elements stored on one record (i.e., **PERRCD(3)**).
12	DeptLimit is defined as a compile-time array (i.e., **CTDATA**) with 3 (i.e., **DIM(3)**) 4-byte elements stored on one record (i.e., **PERRCD(3)**).
13	Messages is defined as a compile-time array (i.e., **CTDATA**) with 4 (i.e., **DIM(4)**) 25-byte elements stored on separate records (no **PERRCD** keyword specified).
14	**X,** which is used as the Messages array index, is defined as a 1-byte integer standalone field.
15	**N,** which is used as the DeptCodes array index, is defined as a 1-byte integer standalone field.

Calculation Specifications:

21	This **EXCEPT** instruction controls the printing of the Heading record format. For simplicity, page overflow has not been included in this program.
22	This **READ** instruction reads the first record from the physical file. If end of file is read, indicator **LR** will be turned on and end the program when the **DOW** instruction on line 24 is executed.
24	The **DOW** group is performed until indicator **LR** is turned on by the **READ** instruction on line 22 or 29.
25	This **EVAL** instruction turns off indicator **20,** which is used in the ErrorSR subroutine to control the output record format that will be printed.
26	This **EXSR** instruction branches program control to the CodeSR subroutine.
27	This **EXSR** instruction branches program control to the SalesSR subroutine.
29	This **READ** instruction reads the next record from the physical file. If end of file is read, indicator **LR** will be turned on and end the program when the **DOW** instruction on line 24 is subsequently executed.
30	The **ENDDO** operation ends the **DOW** group and sends program control back to the **DOW** instruction on line 24, where the relational test is made to continue processing or end the program.
32	This **BEGSR** instruction begins the CodeSR subroutine.
33	The TransCode field value from the physical file is the search argument to **LOOKUP** the valid codes in the TransCodes array. If the TransCode field value is found in the array, indicator **50** will be turned on.
34	The **SELECT** operation begins the **SELECT** group.
35	This **WHEN** instruction tests the status of indicator **50.** If it is off, indicating that the TransCode field value was not found in the array, the test will be true and execute the instructions on lines 36 and 37.
36	This **EVAL** instruction initializes the array index **X** to 1, which will access the first element in the Messages array when output is printed.
37	This **EXSR** instruction branches program control to the ErrorSR subroutine from which output is printed.
38	This **WHEN** instruction is executed only if the previous **WHEN** instruction test is false. If the value in TransCode is equal to **C** and the value in Sales_Amt is greater than **0,** the test will be true and execute the instructions on lines 39 and 40.

Figure 12-22 Example program that controls limits and relationship validation. (Continued)

39 This **EVAL** instruction initializes the array index **X** to 2, which will access the second element in the Messages array when output is printed.

40 This **EXSR** instruction branches program control to the ErrorSR subroutine from which output is printed.

41 This **WHEN** instruction is executed only if the previous **WHEN** instruction tests are false. If the value in TransCode is equal to **S** and the value in Sales_Amt is less than **0,** the test will be true and execute the instructions on lines 42 and 43.

42 This **EVAL** instruction initializes the array **X** to 2, which will access the second element in the Messages array when output is printed.

43 This **EXSR** instruction branches program control to the ErrorSR subroutine from which output is printed.

44 The **ENDSL** operation ends the **SELECT** group.

45 This **ENDSR** operation ends the CodeSR subroutine.

47 This **BEGSR** instruction begins the SalesSR subroutine.

48 This **EVAL** instruction initializes the array index **N** to 1.

49 The DeptNo field value from the physical file is used as the search argument to **LOOKUP** the DeptCodes array. The index **N,** included with the array name (i.e., **DeptCodes(N)**), will store the element number when the instruction is successful. The value in **N** is used with DeptLimit array on line 54 to access the related element for the department. Indicator **51** will be turned on if the DeptNo field value is found in the DeptCodes array.

50 This **IF** instruction tests the status of indicator **51.** When it is off, indicating an unsuccessful lookup, the test will be true and execute the following instructions.

51 This **EVAL** instruction initializes the Messages array index **X** to 3, which will access the third element in the array when the output record is printed.

52 This **EXSR** instruction branches program control to the ErrorSR subroutine from which output is printed.

53 When the **IF** instruction test on line 50 is not true, the **ELSE** operation begins the false action.

54 This **IF** instruction determines if the Sales_Amt field value is greater than the value in the DeptLimit array. The value in the N index was stored by a successful **LOOKUP** of the array on line 49. Index **N** relates the DeptCodes array with the DeptLimit array.

55 This **EVAL** instruction initializes the Messages array index **X** to 4, which will access the fourth element in the array when the output record is printed.

56 This **EXSR** instruction branches program control to the ErrorSR subroutine from which output is printed.

57 This **ENDIF** operation ends the inner **IF** group that began on line 54.

58 This **ENDIF** operation ends the outer **IF** group that began on line 50.

59 This **ENDSR** operation ends the SalesSR subroutine.

61 This **BEGSR** instruction begins the ErrorSR subroutine.

62 This **IF** instruction tests the status of indicator **20,** which was intentionally turned off by the **EVAL** instruction on line 25 which controls the printing of PrintLine2 when more than one error message is tested for the record currently processed.

63 This **EXCEPT** instruction controls the printing of the PrintLine1 record format on lines 73–77.

64 This **EVAL** instruction turns on indicator **20** to prevent the PrintLine1 record format from printing again if more than one error for the current record is tested.

65 This **ELSE** operation begins the false action for the **IF** instruction on line 62.

66 This **EXCEPT** instruction controls the printing of the PrintLine2 record format, which occurs only when more than one validation error is tested for the current record.

67 This **ENDIF** instruction ends the **IF** group that began on line 62.

68 This **ENDSR** operation ends the ErrorSR subroutine.

Output Specifications:

70–72 Printing of the Heading record format is controlled by the **EXCEPT** instruction on line 21.

Figure 12-22 Example program that controls limits and relationship validation. (Continued)

73–77	Printing of the PrintLine1 record format is controlled by the **EXCEPT** instruction on line 63. This line is printed only once for a record. When the input record generates more than one validation error, the other error message will be printed by the PrintLine 2 record.
79–80	Printing of the PrintLine2 record format is controlled by the **EXCEPT** instruction on line 66. This output is printed only when the current record processed generates more than one validation error.
81–91	The data for the four compile-time arrays is included in these instructions.

Figure 12-22 Example program that controls limits and relationship validation. (Continued)

Correspondence Checking

In inquiry or update maintenance, key fields are used to find a select record from a master file. If the corresponding key value is found in the master file, the required processing is performed. However, processing a record based on one field value may not provide enough control. Sometimes another field must be used to ensure that the correct record is accessed. For example, a wrong social security number may be assigned to a payroll transaction. It may be a valid social security number but not related to the correct employee. Consequently, subsequent processing of that record would access the wrong payroll account. Errors of this type can be reduced through the use of *correspondence checking*. In addition to the social security number, another field value from the transaction record may be used to check with a related field from a master file (or table).

An example of correspondence checking is detailed in Figure 12-23. A *prerun-time table* includes valid social security numbers, and the function table contains the first five

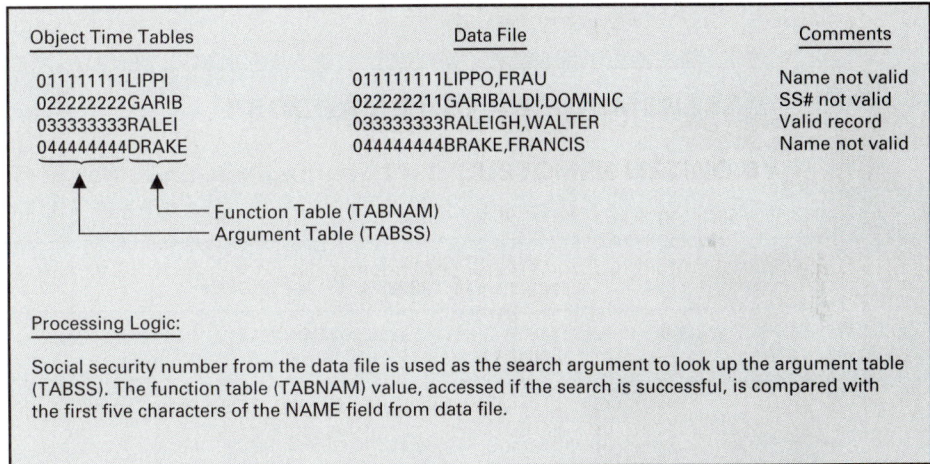

Object Time Tables	Data File	Comments
011111111LIPPI	011111111LIPPO,FRAU	Name not valid
022222222GARIB	022222211GARIBALDI,DOMINIC	SS# not valid
033333333RALEI	033333333RALEIGH,WALTER	Valid record
044444444DRAKE	044444444BRAKE,FRANCIS	Name not valid

Function Table (TABNAM)
Argument Table (TABSS)

Processing Logic:

Social security number from the data file is used as the search argument to look up the argument table (TABSS). The function table (TABNAM) value, accessed if the search is successful, is compared with the first five characters of the NAME field from data file.

Figure 12-23 Prerun-time table values and data records processed by correspondence checking program.

characters of employee names. The records in the data file include the social security number and the complete employee name. As records from the data file are processed, the social security number is used to look up the related *argument* table. If the lookup is successful, the *function* table and first five bytes of the transaction record's name field are compared. When an equal condition is indicated, the transaction corresponds to the related employee.

The report generated by the example correspondence checking program is shown in Figure 12-24. Program control performs correspondence checking only for records for which the social security number was found in the argument table. Any others are identified on the report by the following error message: SS# NOT FOUND IN TABLE.

```
                    SS#/NAME CORRESPONDENCE VALIDATION

011-11-1111   LIPPO,FRAU                  NAME DOES NOT CORRESPOND WITH SS#

022-22-2111   GARIBALDI,DOMINIC           SS# NOT FOUND IN TABLE

044-44-4444   BRAKE,FRANCIS               NAME DOES NOT CORRESPOND WITH SS#
```

Figure 12-24 Report generated by correspondence checking program.

A detailed compile listing of the example correspondence checking program is presented in Figure 12-25.

```
Line   <--------------------- Source Specifications ----------------------------><---- Comments ----> Do
Number ....1....+....2....+....3....+....4....+....5....+....6....+....7....+....8....+....9....+...10 Num
                          S o u r c e   L i s t i n g
     1  * SS Number/Name Correspondence Validation.  SS Number & first 5
     2  * characters of last name from transaction file are checked with
     3  * prerun-time tables.  TABssno contains SS Numbers & TABName
     4  * contains the first five characters of the student's last name.
     5  * If SS Number is not found in the argument table (TABssno), name
     6  * comparison is not performed.
     7 FT12ssnamesIT   F   14           DISK                                        table file
     8 FP12corrnd IF   E                DISK                                        transaction file
        *---------------------------------------------------------------------------------------------*
        *                          RPG name           External name                                   *
        * File name. . . . . . . . :  P12CORRND          STAN/P12CORRND                               *
        * Record format(s) . . . . :  P12CORRNOR         P12CORRNOR                                   *
        *---------------------------------------------------------------------------------------------*
     9 FQsysprt   O    F  132           PRINTER                                     printer file
    10
    11 D TABssno          S              9  0 DIM(4) FROMFILE(T12ssnames)
    12 D TABnames         S              5    DIM(4) ALT(TABssno)
    13 D Messages         S             33    DIM(2) CTDATA
    14 D X                S              1  0                                       messages index
    15 D FirstFive        S              5                                          first 5 characters
    16
    17=IP12CORRNOR
        *---------------------------------------------------------------------------------------------*
        * RPG record format  . . . . :  P12CORRNOR                                                    *
        * External format  . . . . . :  P12CORRNOR : STAN/P12CORRND                                   *
        *---------------------------------------------------------------------------------------------*
    18=I                                P    1    5 0SSNUMBER
    19=I                                A    6   25  STUDNTNAME
    20 C                   EXCEPT    Heading                                        print heading record
    21 C                   READ      P12corrnd                              ----LR  read first record
    22
    23 C                   DOW       *INLR = *OFF                                   dow LR is off        B01
    24 C     SSNumber      LOOKUP    TABssno                                ----60  find ss# in table     01
    25 C                   IF        *IN60 = *OFF                                   ssno found in table? B02
    26 C                   EVAL      X = 1                                          message 1             02
    27 C                   EXCEPT    ErrorLine                                      print error record    02
    28 C                   ELSE                                                     begin false action   X02
    29 C                   MOVEL     StudntName    FirstFive                        extract first 5 char  02
    30 C     FirstFive     LOOKUP    TABnames                               ----60  find name in table    02
    31 C                   IF        *IN60 = *OFF                                   name not found?      B03
    32 C                   EVAL      X = 2                                          message 2             03
    33 C                   EXCEPT    ErrorLine                                      print error record    03
    34 C                   ENDIF                                                    end inner IF group   E03
    35 C                   ENDIF                                                    end outer IF group   E02
    36
    37 C                   READ      P12corrnd                              ----LR  read next record      01
```

Figure 12-25 Example program that controls correspondence validation.

```
38 C                    ENDDO                                     end dow group      E01
39
40 OQsysprt   E            Heading        3 06
41 O                                          43 'SS#/NAME CORRESPONDENCE'
42 O                                          54 'VALIDATION'
43 O          E            ErrorLine   2
44 O                       SSnumber           15 '0   -  -    '
45 O                       StudntName         38
46 O                       Messages(X)        75
                               .
                               .
                 C o m p i l e   T i m e   D a t a
47 **CTDATA Messages
    *---------------------------------------------------------------*
    * Array . . . : MESSAGES                                        *
    *---------------------------------------------------------------*
48 SS# NOT FOUND IN TABLE
49 NAME DOES NOT CORRESPOND WITH SS#
* * * * *   E N D   O F   C O M P I L E   T I M E   D A T A   * * * * *
```

File Description Specifications:

Line No.

7 T12ssNames is defined as an input (**I** in position 17), table file (**T** in position 18), program-described (**F** in position 22), physical file with 14-byte records (**14** in positions 23–27). When **RPG IV** program is executed, the data from this table file will be loaded into memory before the other files are read.

8 P12corrnd is defined as an input (**I** in position 17), full-procedural (**F** in position 18), externally described (**E** in position 22) physical file.

9 Qsysprt is defined as an output (**O** in position 17), program-described (**F** in position 22) printer file with 132-byte records (**132** in positions 23–27).

Definition Specifications:

11 The **TAB** prefix defines TABssno as a table. It is defined with four (i.e., **DIM(4)**) elements 9 integer elements. The **FROMFILE(T12ssnames)** keyword specifies that the table data is stored in a prerun-time table.

12 The **TAB** prefix defines TABNames as a table. It is defined with four (i.e., **DIM(4)**) elements 5 character elements. The **ALT(TABssno)** specifies that elements in this table are in an alternating format with the TABssno table elements (i.e., **011111111LIPPI**).

13 Messages is defined as a compile array with two elements **(DIM(2))** 33 characters long.

14 **X,** which is used as the index for the Messages array, is defined as a standalone 1-byte integer field.

15 FirstFive, into which the first five characters of the StudntName field from a physical file record are moved, is defined as a standalone field 5 characters long.

Calculation Specifications:

20 This **EXCEPT** instruction controls the printing of the Heading record format.

21 This **READ** instruction reads the first record from the physical file (P12corrnd). If end of file is read, indicator **LR** will be turned on and end the program when the **DOW** instruction on line 23 is executed.

23 The **DOW** group is performed while indicator **LR** is off. When **LR** is turned on the by the **READ** instruction on line 21 or 37, program control will branch to line 39 and end the program.

24 The input field SSNumber is used as the search argument to **LOOKUP** the TABssno table. If the value in SSNumber is found in the table, indicator **60** will be turned on.

25 This **IF** instruction tests the status of indicator **60.** When it is off, indicating that the **LOOKUP** instruction on line 24 was not successful, the instructions on lines 26 and 27 will be executed.

26 This **EVAL** instruction initializes the Messages array index **X** to 1, which will extract the first element in the array.

27 This **EXCEPT** instruction controls printing of the ErrorLine output record.

28 The **ELSE** operation begins the false action for the **IF** instruction on line 25. Execution of the instructions on lines 29 and 30 are controlled by the **ELSE** operation.

Figure 12-25 Example program that controls correspondence validation. (Continued)

29	The **MOVEL** instruction moves the first five characters from the StudntName field into the FirstFive field that was defined as a standalone field in a Definition Specification instruction.
30	The FirstFive field value is used as the search argument to **LOOKUP** the TABNames table. If the FirstFive value is found in the table, indicator **60** will be turned on.
31	This **IF** instruction tests the status of indicator **60.** When it is off, indicating that the **LOOKUP** instruction on line 30 was not successful, the instructions on lines 32 and 33 will be executed.
32	This **EVAL** instruction initializes the Messages array index **X** to 2, which will extract the second element in the array.
33	This **EXCEPT** instruction controls printing of the ErrorLine output record.
34	This **ENDIF** operation ends the inner **IF** group that began on line 31.
35	This **ENDIF** operation ends the outer **IF** group that began on line 25.
37	This **READ** instruction reads the next record from the P12corrnd file. If end of file is read, indicator **LR** will be turned on and end the program when the **DOW** instruction on line 23 is subsequently executed.
38	The **ENDDO** operation ends the **DOW** group that began on line 23. Program control will return to the **DOW** instruction on line 23, where the decision to end the program or continue processing is determined.
Output Specifications:	
40–42	Printing of the Heading record is controlled by the **EXCEPT** instruction on line 20.
43	Printing of the ErrorLine record is controlled by the **EXCEPT** instruction on line 27 or 33.
47–49	The compile-time array and its two elements are specified in these instructions.

Figure 12-25 Example program that controls correspondence validation. (Continued)

Batch Total Validation

Batch totals, which indicate a total amount for a group of source documents, are usually developed by a user department such as sales, payroll, accounting, and so forth. The batch total is entered when the program that processes the related transaction file is executed. Transaction amounts in the file are accumulated, and at end of file the batch total previously entered is compared with the transaction file total. If the totals are equal, the transaction amounts entered are considered correct. However, if they are not equal, either the batch total and/or the transaction file data is incorrect.

Batch totals may be entered into an **RPG IV** program by any of the following methods:

1. Via a *data area* that is *implicitly* or *explicitly* accessed by an **RPG IV** program (discussed in Chapter 8)
2. Via a physical file that is input to an **RPG IV** program
3. Via an interactive program that supports a display file (introduced in Chapter 15)
4. Via a **CL** program that passes the *batch total* parameter to an **RPG IV** program (introduced in Chapter 20).

The first method, which accesses a data area, is used in the example **RPG IV** program that controls batch total validation. Refer to the compile listing in Figure 12-26, and note that a data area data structure (discussed in Chapter 8) is defined by the letter **U** in posi-

```
Line   <---------------------- Source Specifications ----------------------------><---- Comments ----> Do
Number ....1....+....2....+....3....+....4....+....5....+....6....+....7....+....8....+....9....+...10 Num
                        S o u r c e   L i s t i n g
     1  * Batch total entered via a data area and value checked with the
     2  * total of transaction amounts from the records in the pf....
     3
     4 FP12batch  IF   E            DISK
        *------------------------------------------------------------------------------------*
        *                              RPG name         External name                        *
        * File name. . . . . . . . :   P12BATCH         STAN/P12BATCH                        *
        * Record format(s) . . . . :   P12BATCHR        P12BATCHR                            *
        *------------------------------------------------------------------------------------*
     5 FQsysprt   O    F  132           PRINTER
     6
     7 D TotalAmt        S               8  2
     8 D Difference      S               8  2
     9 DC12Dta          UDS                                                 access data area
    10 D BatchNo                 1       2  0                               define data area fld
    11 D BatchAmt                3       9  2                               define data area fld
    12
    13=IP12BATCHR
        *------------------------------------------------------------------------------------*
        * RPG record format  . . . . :  P12BATCHR                                            *
        * External  format  . . . . . :  P12BATCHR : STAN/P12BATCH                            *
        *------------------------------------------------------------------------------------*
    14=I                         A    1    5  CUSTNUMBER
    15=I                         A    6   25  CUSTNAME
    16=I                         P   26   29 2TRANSAMT
    17 C                   EXCEPT    Heading
    18 C                   READ      P12batch                        ----LR   read first record
    19
    20 C                   DOW       *INLR = *OFF                             dow LR is off       B01
    21 C                   EVAL      TotalAmt = TotalAmt + TransAmt           accumulate TransAmt 01
    22 C                   READ      P12batch                        ----LR   read next record     01
    23 C                   ENDDO                                              end dow group       E01
    24
    25 C                   EVAL      Difference = TotalAmt - BatchAmt         compute difference
    26 C                   EXCEPT    TotalLine                                print TotalLine recd
    27
    28 OQsysprt   E            Heading        3 01
    29 O                                         28 'BATCH TOTAL VALIDATION'
    30 O          E            TotalLine      2
    31 O                                         15 'BATCH NUMBER:'
    32 O                       BatchNo       Z   18
    33 O          E            TotalLine      2
    34 O                                         20 'BATCH AMT ENTERED:'
    35 O                       BatchAmt      1   32
    36 O          E            TotalLine      2
    37 O                                         22 'TOTAL AMT PROCESSED:'
    38 O                       TotalAmt      1   32
    39 O          E            TotalLine      0
    40 O                                         21 'DIFFERENCE IN AMTS:'
    41 O                       Difference    J   33
```

Definition Specifications:

Line No.

7 TotalAmt, which is used to accumulate the TransAmt field values from the physical file, is defined as an 8-byte standalone field with 2 decimal positions.

8 Difference, which is used to store the difference from subtracting the BatchAmt value stored in the data area from the TotalAmt accumulated, is defined as an 8-byte standalone field with 2 decimal positions.

9 The **UDS** entry in positions 23–25 defines C12Dta as a data area data structure that is implicitly accessed and updated. The character value stored in C12Dta is separated into the 2-byte integer BatchNo field and the 7 byte–2 decimal BatchAmt field in the instructions on lines 10 and 11.

Calculation Specifications:

17 This **EXCEPT** instruction controls printing of the Heading record format.

Figure 12-26 Example batch validation program.

18 This **READ** instruction reads the first record from the physical file. If end of file is read, indicator **LR** will be turned on and end the program when the **DOW** instruction on line 20 is executed.

20 The **DOW** group is performed while indicator **LR** is off. When **LR** is turned on by the **READ** instruction on line 18 or 22, program will branch to line 25, compute the difference, and execute the **EXCEPT** instruction on line 26, which controls printing of the TotalLine record format.

21 This **EVAL** instruction adds the TransAmt field value from each input record processed to the TotalAmt field.

22 This **READ** instruction reads the next record from the physical file. If end of file is read, indicator **LR** will be turned on and subsequently exit program control from **DOW** group.

23 The **ENDDO** operation ends the **DOW** group that began on line 20. Program control will return to the **DOW** instruction on line 20, where the decision to end the program or continue processing is determined.

25 This **EVAL** instruction is executed after indicator **LR** has been turned on and exit from the **DOW** group has occurred. The value in Difference is computed by subtracting the BatchAmt value stored in the data area from the accumulated TotalAmt value.

26 This **EXCEPT** instruction controls printing of the TotalLine record format.

Output Specifications:

28–29 Printing of the Heading record is controlled by the **EXCEPT** instruction on line 17.

30–41 Printing of the TotalLine records is controlled by the **EXCEPT** instruction on line 26.

Figure 12-26 Example batch validation program. (Continued)

tion 23 (line 9). The data from the data area data structure will be *implicitly* accessed when the program is executed. At the end of the program, the data in the data structure will automatically be updated regardless of whether it has changed.

Data File Listing	Printed Report
	BATCH TOTAL VALIDATION
11111MORTIMER SNORD 0500000 22222DAFFY MOOSE 0002299 33333BUGS RABBIT 1200000 44444SYLVESTER D DOG 0084545	BATCH NUMBER: 1 BATCH AMT ENTERED: 17,868.44 TOTAL AMT PROCESSED: 17,868.44
Note: Record amounts total 17,868.44	DIFFERENCE IN AMTS: .00

Figure 12-27 Report generated by the example batch validation program and the data file listing.

Other Batch Validation Functions

Many other functions, procedures, and combinations may be included in **RPG IV** programs that control batch validation. *Record Identification Codes* and *sequence checking* are a few of the other validation processes available. However, because externally described physical files support only one record type, Record Identification Codes and sequence checking are seldom used.

The **CHAIN** operation, which will be introduced in Chapter 13, may be used to verify that an account number, customer number, and related data are valid. This could eliminate the need for check digits for existing accounts; however, the random access of a physical file with the **CHAIN** operation requires more processing time than calculation instructions.

Data Validation in an Interactive Environment

In the AS/400 environment, many of the data validation functions introduced in this chapter as program-controlled are instead supported by interactive processing. Specifically, procedures such as *numeric field testing, justification, mandatory entry, mandatory fill, check digits, range testing, value testing,* and so forth are controlled by the syntax in one or more display files processed by an **RPG IV** program. This topic will be introduced in Chapters 14 and 15.

APPLICATION RPG IV PROGRAM: BATCH VALIDATION OF AN ACCOUNTS RECEIVABLE TRANSACTION FILE

To illustrate how the batch validation functions introduced in this chapter are integrated, we discuss an application **RPG IV** program that incorporates many of them. The program specifications shown in Figure 12-28 detail the *batch validation* procedures that must be tested with the example program. Because of the complexity of the program, the instructions related to each validation function are included in separate internal subroutines.

PROGRAM SPECIFICATIONS — Page 1 of 2

Program Name: Validation Report — Program - ID: CH12VAL — Written by: SM

Purpose: Customer transactions validation report — Approved by: CM

Input files: TRANFILE

Output files: QSYSPRT

Processing Requirements:

Write an RPG IV program to generate a validation report for the customer transaction file.

Input to the program:

Use the CL command CHGJOB to change the system date for this program to 123197.

The sales transactions for customers are stored in the externally defined physical file TRANFILE. A supplemental description form details the attributes of the record format.

Include a data structure to load a run-time array with six one-byte integer elements with the value from the input field Act#. The array must be used in the Modulus-11 check digit method to validate the account numbers.

Include a compile-time array with the following five error messages:

ACCOUNT NUMBER NOT VALID
NAME NOT LEFT-JUSTIFIED
NAME CONTAINS INVALID CHARACTERS
AMOUNT NEGATIVE
INVALID YEAR

Processing:

All of the following validation functions are to be performed for every input record processed:

1. Account number (ACT#) by the Modulus-11 check digit method.

Figure 12-28 Specifications for batch validation program.

2. Customer name (NAME) for left-justification and valid alphabetic characters. Include A through Z and a blank in a Named Constant as the valid characters. Use the CHECK operation for both of these validation functions.

3. Transaction amount (AMT) for an invalid negative value.

4. Date (transaction date) year value must be equal to 97. Remember to change the session date with the CHGJOB command to 123197, or this validation function will not work for the Tranfile records processed.

Output:

A report in the format detailed in the supplemental printer spacing chart is to be generated. Only records that have validation errors are to be printed. Note that the data for a record is printed only on the line with the first error message and is not repeated for any other errors for the record.

Figure 12-28 Specifications for batch validation program. (Continued)

System Flowchart

The system flowchart in Figure 12-29 indicates that a physical file in which transaction data is stored is input to the *batch edit* program that generates a printed report. Instead of printing, output is often written to one or more physical files that are subsequently processed. This topic will be introduced when physical file maintenance is discussed in Chapter 13.

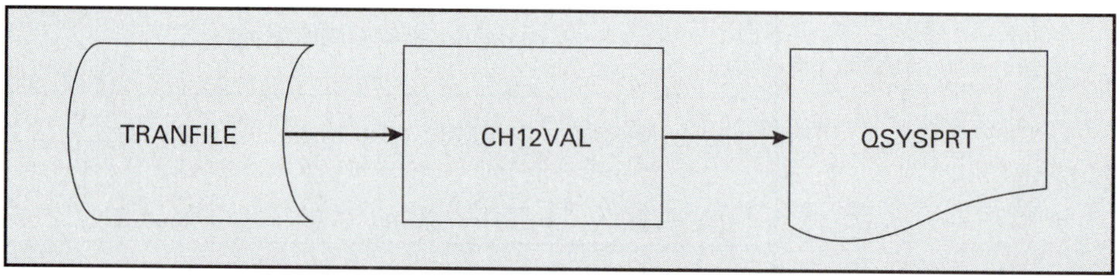

Figure 12-29 System flowchart for batch edit program.

Physical File Attributes

Figure 12-30 shows the record format of the physical file and a listing of the transaction data.

PHYSICAL FILE DESCRIPTION

SYSTEM: AS/400 DATE: 12/15/97
FILE NAME: TRANFILE REV NO: 0
RECORD NAME: TRANSR KEY LENGTH: 6
SEQUENCE: Keyed (not unique) RECORD SIZE: 32

FIELD DEFINITIONS

FIELD NO	FIELD NAME	SIZE	TYPE	POSITION FROM	TO	COMMENTS
1	ACT#	6	P	1	4	Key field
2	NAME	20	C	5	24	
3	DATE	6	P	25	28	
4	AMT	7	P	29	32	2 decimals

Figure 12-30 Physical file record format and data listing processed by the batch edit program.

Physical file data:

Account Number	Account Name	Transaction Date	Transaction Amount
120006	ALEXANDER DUMAS	013097	0002500
130000	HAROLD ROBBINS	022897	0023900-
140007	GEOFREY CHAUCE4	033196	0789000
210005	WILLIAM SHAKESPEARE	022897	0010000
300004	JACQUELINE SUSAN	013198	0056007

Figure 12-30 Physical file record format and data listing processed by the batch edit program. (Continued)

The report design shown in the printer spacing chart and listing are shown in Figure 12-31. Note that the record image is printed, not the individual fields. Also observe that the data for an error record is not repeated when there is more than one validation error.

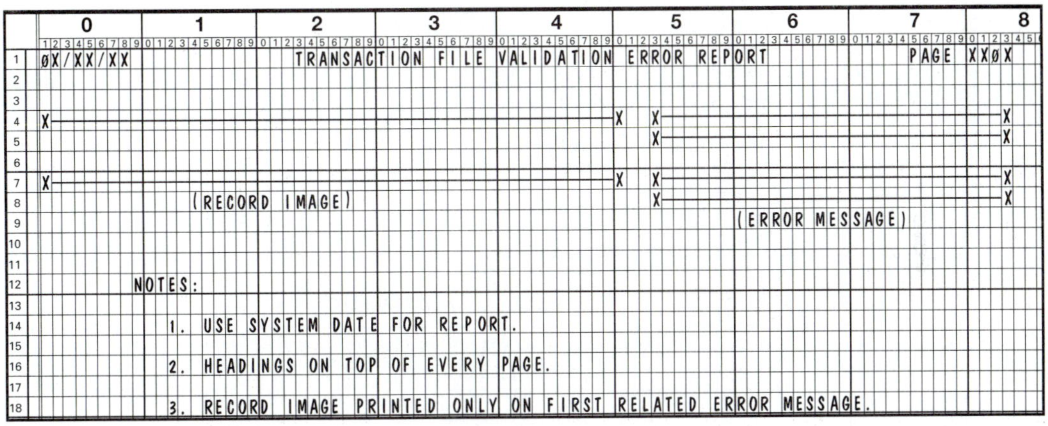


```
12/31/97              TRANSACTION FILE VALIDATION ERROR REPORT            PAGE     1

120006 ALEXANDER DUMAS      01/30/970002500          NAME NOT LEFT-JUSTIFIED

130000HAROLD ROBBINS        02/28/97002390}          ACCOUNT NUMBER NOT VALID
                                                     AMOUNT NEGATIVE

140007GEOFREY CHAUCE4       03/31/960789000          NAME CONTAINS INVALID CHARACTER
                                                     INVALID YEAR

300004JACQUELINE SUSAN      01/31/980056007          INVALID YEAR
```

Figure 12-31 Printer spacing chart and report listing generated by the batch edit program.

A detailed compile listing of the batch edit program is shown in Figure 12-32.

```
Line   <--------------------- Source Specifications ---------------------------><---- Comments ----> Do
Number ....1....+....2....+....3....+....4....+....5....+....6....+....7....+....8....+....9....+...10 Num
                        S o u r c e   L i s t i n g
     *              **** Transaction file field validation ****
     * Validation functions performed:
     *        1. Acct# validation by modulus-11 method
     *        2. Name justification
     *        3. Valid alphabetic characters and blank in the Name field
```

Figure 12-32 Compile listing of the batch edit program.

```
 *       4. Valid transaction year - must be equal to UYEAR
 *       5. Valid for positive amt value

HDATFMT(*MDY)
FTranfile  IF   E           K DISK
  *----------------------------------------------------------------------------------*
  *                             RPG name          External name                     *
  * File name. . . . . . . . :  TRANFILE          STAN/TRANFILE                     *
  * Record format(s) . . . . :  TRANFILER         TRANFILER                         *
  *----------------------------------------------------------------------------------*
FQsysprt   O    F  132         PRINTER OFLIND(*INOF)

 * Named constant of valid alphabetic chars - ActName validation....
D AlphaChars      C                   ' ABCDEFGHIJKLMNOPQRSTUVWXYZ'

D Messages        S             31    DIM(5) CTDATA
D
 * Load array with Act# value....
D                DS                                                 begin data structure
D NumAry                         1  0 DIM(6)                        account no array
D Act#                   1      6  0                                load NumAry withAct#

 * Work fields for Modulus-11 check digit validation....
D Sum             S              3  0
D Quotient        S              3  0
D Remainder       S              3  0

D Position        S              1  0                               used for justificatn
D TransYear       S              2  0                               transaction year
D X               S              1  0                               array index

=ITRANFILER
  *----------------------------------------------------------------------------------*
  * RPG record format  . . . . :  TRANFILER                                         *
  * External format  . . . . . :  TRANFILER : STAN/TRANFILE                         *
  *----------------------------------------------------------------------------------*
=I                              P    1    4 0ACT#
=I                              A    5   24  NAME
=I                         *MDY/D   25   32  DATE
=I                              P   33   36 2AMT
C                   EVAL      *INOF = *ON                           turn on OF indicator
C                   READ      Tranfile                       ----LR read first record

C                   DOW       *INLR = *OFF                          dow LR is off      B01
C                   EXSR      HeadSR                                print heading line  01
C                   EXSR      ActNoSR                               branch to subroutine 01
C                   EXSR      ActNameSR                             branch to subroutine 01
C                   EXSR      AmountSR                              branch to subroutine 01
C                   EXSR      YearSR                                branch to subroutine 01
C                   READ      Tranfile                       ----LR read next record     01
C                   EVAL      *IN60 = *OFF                          turn off print ctrl  01
C                   ENDDO                                           end dow group       E01

 * Subroutine for page overflow control....
C     HeadSR        BEGSR                                           begin subroutine
C                   IF        *INOF = *ON                           OF on?             B01
C                   EXCEPT    Heading                               print heading line  01
C                   EVAL      *INOF = *OFF                          turn off print ctrl  01
C                   ENDIF                                           end IF group        E01
C                   ENDSR                                           end subroutine

 * Subroutine to validate ActNumber with the Modulus-11 method....
C     ActNoSR       BEGSR                                           begin subroutine
C                   EVAL      Sum =                                 compute sum
C                               NumAry(6) * 1                       6th element * 1
C                             + NumAry(5) * 2                       5th element * 2
C                             + NumAry(4) * 3                       4th element * 3
C                             + NumAry(3) * 4                       3rd element * 4
C                             + NumAry(2) * 5                       2nd element * 5
C                             + NumAry(1) * 6                       1st element * 6
```

Figure 12-32 Compile listing of the batch edit program. (Continued)

```
C     Sum           DIV       11            Quotient                compute quotient
C                   MVR                     Remainder               save remainder
C                   IF        Remainder > *ZERO                     remainder > 0?      B01
C                   EVAL      X = 1                                 messages 1           01
C                   EXSR      ErrorSR                               print invalid acct#  01
C                   ENDIF                                                               E01
C                   ENDSR                                           end subroutine
 * Subroutine to check ActName for justification & valid chars....
C     ActNameSR     BEGSR                                           begin subroutine
C     ' '           CHECK     Name          Position                justification error?
C                   IF        Position > 1                          not justified?      B01
C                   EVAL      X = 2                                 Messages 2           01
C                   EXSR      ErrorSR                               branch to subroutine 01
C                   ENDIF                                           end IF group        E01
C     AlphaChars    CHECK     Name                          ----40  valid characters?
C                   IF        *IN40 = *ON                           invalid character?  B01
C                   EVAL      X = 3                                 Messages 3           01
C                   EXSR      ErrorSR                               branch to subroutine 01
C                   ENDIF                                           end IF group        E01
C                   ENDSR                                           end subroutine
 * Subroutine to check Amt for negative value....
C     AmountSR      BEGSR                                           begin subroutine
C                   IF        Amt < 0                               amount negative?    B01
C                   EVAL      X = 4                                 Messages 4           01
C                   EXSR      ErrorSR                               branch to subroutine 01
C                   ENDIF                                           end IF group        E01
C                   ENDSR                                           end subroutine
 * Subroutine to check for valid year (equal to UYEAR)....
C     YearSR        BEGSR                                           begin subroutine
C                   EXTRCT    Date:*Y       TransYear               extract year
C                   IF        TransYear <> UYEAR                    year value equal?   B01
C                   EVAL      X = 5                                 Messages 5           01
C                   EXSR      ErrorSR                               branch to subroutine 01
C                   ENDIF                                           end IF group        E01
C                   ENDSR                                           end subroutine
 * Subroutine for error messages printing....
C     ErrorSR       BEGSR                                           begin subroutine
C                   IF        *IN60 = *OFF                          indicator 60 off?   B01
C                   EXCEPT    MsgLine1                              print 1st error msg  01
C                   EVAL      *IN60 = *ON                           turn on indicator 60 01
C                   ELSE                                            false action        X01
C                   EXCEPT    MsgLine2                              print next error msg 01
C                   ENDIF                                           end IF group        E01
C                   ENDSR                                           end subroutine
OQsysprt   E            Heading        1  01
O                       UDATE         Y    8
O                                         38 'TRANSACTION FILE'
O                                         62 'VALIDATION ERROR REPORT'
O                                         78 'PAGE'
O                       PAGE              83
O          E            MsgLine1     1  1
O                       Act#               6
O                       Name              26
O                       Date              34
O                       Amt               41
O                       Messages(X)       83
O          E            MsgLine2        1
O                       Messages(X)       83
                                 .
                                 .
                     C o m p i l e   T i m e   D a t a
```

Figure 12-32 Compile listing of the batch edit program. (Continued)

```
133 **CTDATA Messages
     *---------------------------------------------------------------------*
     * Array . . . : MESSAGES                                              *
     *---------------------------------------------------------------------*
134 ACCOUNT NUMBER NOT VALID
135 NAME NOT LEFT-JUSTIFIED
136 NAME CONTAINS INVALID CHARACTERS
137 AMOUNT NEGATIVE
138 INVALID YEAR
 * * * * *   E N D   O F   C O M P I L E   T I M E   D A T A   * * * * *
```

Header Specifications:

Line No.

9 The **DATFMT(*MDY)** keyword specifies that date values will be processed in an MMDDYY format instead of the default ***ISO** format.

File Description Specifications:

10 Tranfile is defined as an input (**I** in position 17), full-procedural (**F** in position 18), externally described (**E** in position 22), keyed (**K** in position 34) physical file.

11 Qsysprt is defined as an output (**O** in position 17), program-described (**F** in position 22), printer file with 132 character records (**132** in positions 29–33). The **OFLIND(*INOF)** specifies that page overflow is controlled in the program with the **OF** indicator.

Definition Specifications:

14 AlphaChars is defined as a Named Constant (**C** in position 24) that contains a blank and the uppercase letters of the alphabet.

16 Messages is defined as a five (i.e., **DIM(5)**) 31-character element compile-time array (i.e., **CTDATA**).

19 The letters **DS** define the beginning of the data structure that includes the instructions on lines 20 and 21.

20 NumAry is defined as a run-time array with 6 elements (i.e., **DIM(6)**) 1 integer long.

21 The physical file field Act# is specified to load the NumAry array with its stored value for each record processed.

24 Sum is defined as a three-digit integer standalone field. The sum from step 2 in the computations shown in Figure 12-18 will be stored in this field (see lines 60–66).

25 Quotient is defined as a three-digit integer standalone field. The quotient from step 3 in the computations shown in Figure 12-18 will be stored in this field (see line 68).

26 Remainder is defined as a three-digit integer standalone field. The remainder from step 3 in the computations shown in Figure 12-18 will be stored in this field (see line 69).

28 Position is defined as a one-digit integer standalone field. This field is used with the **CHECK** instruction on line 79 to validate if the Name field value is left-justified.

29 TransYear is defined as a two-digit integer standalone field. This field is used with the **EXTRCT** instruction on line 102 to extract the year value from the Date field.

30 **X,** which is used as the index to access elements from the Messages array, is defined as a one-digit integer field.

Calculation Specifications:

37 This **EVAL** instruction turns on the **OF** indicator to force page overflow when the **EXCEPT** instruction on line 53 is initially executed.

38 This **READ** instruction reads the first record from the physical file. If end of file is read, indicator **LR** will be turned on and end the program when the **DOW** instruction on line 40 is executed.

40 The **DOW** group is performed until indicator **LR** is turned on by the **READ** instruction on line 38 or 46.

41–45 The five **EXSR** instructions branch program control to a subroutine where the related validation function is performed. Because none of the subroutines is conditioned, all of the validation functions are tested for every input record processed.

46 This **READ** instruction reads the next record from the physical file. If end of file is read, indicator **LR** will be turned on and end the program when the **DOW** instruction on line 40 is subsequently executed.

Figure 12-32 Compile listing of the batch edit program. (Continued)

47	This **EVAL** instruction turns off indicator **60,** which is used in the ErrorSR subroutine to determine whether the MsgLine1 or MsgLine2 record format is to be printed.
48	The **ENDDO** operation ends the **DOW** group and passes control back to the **DOW** instruction, where the relational test is made to end the program or continue processing.
51	This **BEGSR** instruction begins the HeadSR subroutine, which controls page overflow.
52	This **IF** instruction tests the status of the **OF** indicator. Page overflow was forced for the first record processed by the **EVAL** instruction on line 37. Subsequent page overflow is automatically controlled when the overflow line is sensed and the **OF** indicator is turned on.
53	This **EXCEPT** instruction controls the printing of the Heading record format. Printing of this output only occurs when the **OF** page overflow indicator is on.
54	This **EVAL** instruction turns off the **LR** indicator to prevent the Heading record from printing for every record processed.
55	This **ENDIF** operation ends the **IF** group that began on line 52.
56	This **ENDSR** operation ends the HeadSR subroutine and passes control to the **EXSR** instruction on line 42.
59	This **BEGSR** instruction begins the ActNoSR subroutine, which controls Act# validation with the Modulus-11 check digit method.
60–66	This **EVAL** instruction performs steps 1 and 2 shown in Figure 12-18. The numeric literals 1 through 6 must be used in the Modulus-11 formula to validate an item that includes a check digit.
68–69	The **DIV** instruction performs step 3 shown in Figure 12-18. The **MVR** (Move Remainder) instruction stores the remainder value in the Remainder field.
71	This **IF** instruction determines if the value in Remainder is greater than zero.
72	This **EVAL** instruction initializes the Messages array index **X** to 1, which will access the first element for printing when the **IF** test on line 71 is true (invalid Act#).
73	When the **IF** test on line 71 is true, this **EXSR** instruction will branch control to the ErrorSR subroutine, which controls printing of the MsgLine1 format on lines 125–129.
74	This **ENDIF** operation ends the **IF** group that began on line 71.
75	This **ENDSR** operation ends the ActNoSR subroutine.
78	This **BEGSR** instruction begins the ActNameSR subroutine, which validates the Name field value for left-justification and valid alphabetic characters.
79	This **CHECK** instruction searches the Name field for a blank character (*Factor 1* entry). The position of the first nonblank character is stored in the Position field.
80	This **IF** instruction tests the value stored in the Position field. When the value is greater than 1, indicating that a blank is stored in the first byte of the Position field, the instructions on lines 81 and 82 will be executed.
81	This **EVAL** instruction initializes the Messages index **X** to 2, which will access the second element when MsgLine1 or MsgLine2 is printed.
82	This **EXSR** instruction branches control to the ErrorSR subroutine from which MsgLine1 or MsgLine2 is printed.
83	This **ENDIF** operation ends the **IF** group that began on line 80.
85	This **CHECK** instruction searches the Name field for the alphabetic characters stored in the Named Constant AlphaChars. If a character is stored in the Name field that is not equal to one stored in AlphaChars, indicator **40** will be turned on.
86	This **IF** instruction tests the status of indicator **40.** An "on" condition indicates that an invalid character was found in the Name field.
87	This **EVAL** instruction initializes the Messages array index **X** to 3, which will extract the third element from the Messages array when MsgLine 1 or MsgLine 2 is printed.
88	This **EXSR** instruction branches control to the ErrorSR subroutine from which MsgLine 1 or MsgLine 2 is printed.
89	This **ENDIF** operation ends the **IF** group that began on line 86.
90	This **ENDSR** operation ends the ActNameSR subroutine.
93	This **BEGSR** instruction begins the AmountSR subroutine, which validates the Amt field value for a negative value.
94	This **IF** instruction tests the Amt field for a value less than 0 (negative value).
95	When the **IF** test on line 94 is true, this **EVAL** instruction will initialize the Messages array index **X** to 4, which will access the fourth element in the array.

Figure 12-32 Compile listing of the batch edit program. (Continued)

96 This **EXSR** instruction branches control to the ErrorSR subroutine from which MsgLine1 or MsgLine2 is printed.

97 This **ENDIF** operation ends the **IF** group that began on line 94.

98 This **ENDSR** operation ends the AmountSR subroutine.

101 This **BEGSR** instruction begins the YearSR subroutine in which the year value in the Date field is validated.

102 The **EXTRCT** instruction extracts the year value from the Date field and stores it in TransYear. Recall that Date was defined as a date field in the physical file in an MDY format (see line 35).

103 This **IF** instruction determines if the TransYear value is not equal to UYEAR. Again, recall that the program specifications required that the session date be changed from the default system date to **123197** with the **CHGJOB** command.

104 When the TransYear value is not equal to UYEAR, this **EVAL** instruction will initialize the Messages array index **X** to 5 and access the fifth element in the array.

105 This **EXSR** instruction branches control to the ErrorSR subroutine from which MsgLine1 or MsgLine2 is printed.

106 This **ENDIF** operation ends the **IF** group that began on line 103.

107 This **ENDSR** operation ends the YearSR subroutine.

110 This **BEGSR** instruction begins the ErrorSR subroutine from which MsgLine1 or MsgLine2 record formats are printed.

111 This **IF** instruction tests indicator **60** for an"off" condition. The "on" and "off" status of indicator **60** controls printing of MsgLine1 and MsgLine2. When the indicator is "off," the MsgLine1 format will be printed. On the other hand, when **60** is "on," MsgLine2 format will be printed. Recall from the specifications that the data from the input record is to be printed only on the first line with the first error message. Additional error messages are printed without the related data.

112 This **EXCEPT** instruction, which controls the printing of the MsgLine1 format, is executed only when indicator 60 is "off."

113 This **EVAL** instruction turns on indicator **60,** preventing the MsgLine1 format from printing again for the current input record.

114 The **ELSE** operation begins the false action for the **IF** group that began on line 111.

115 This **EXCEPT,** which is executed only when indicator **60** is "on," controls printing of the MsgLine2 record format, which includes only an error message.

116 This **ENDIF** operation ends the **IF** group that began on line 111.

117 This **ENDSR** operation ends the ErrorSR subroutine.

Output Specifications:

119–124 Printing of the Heading record format is controlled by the **EXCEPT** instruction on line 53.

125–130 Printing of the MsgLine1 record format is controlled by the **EXCEPT** instruction on line 112. This output is printed only for the first validation error for the current record processed.

130–132 Printing of the MsgLine2 record format is controlled by the **EXCEPT** instruction on line 115. This output is printed only if the current record processed includes more than one validation error.

133–138 The five elements for the compile-time array Messages are included in these records.

Figure 12-32 Compile listing of the batch edit program. (Continued)

SUMMARY

Data validation is important in the *batch* and/or *interactive* modes to ensure that data entered into a computerized system is accurate. The hardware and software restrictions of the computer installation usually determine when and how data is validated. Data may be validated by batch procedures external to an **RPG IV** program, by batch procedures internal to an **RPG IV** program, or by interactive procedures controlled by an **RPG IV** program. Validation procedures may be broadly classified as *data type* testing and *data field* checking.

Data type testing includes the testing of numeric fields for valid numeric characters **(0–9)** and may be supported in a batch program by the **TESTN** operation or interactively with a *Display File*. If a data entry utility such as **DFU** is used to enter data in a field defined in a physical file as numeric, nonnumeric characters cannot be entered. This would eliminate the need to validate numeric data in an **RPG IV** program.

RPG IV does not have an operation for testing alphabetic data; however, it may be controlled by including the valid alphabetic characters (both upper- and lowercase) in a Named Constant. Then validate the related field with a **CHECK** operation instruction.

Sign testing may be controlled by testing input fields in the *Input Specifications* with *Field Indicators* in the *P1, Mn,* and *Zr* fields (positions 69–74) for a positive, negative, and zero value. Or sign testing may be specified in the *Calculation Specifications* on a *Result* field with *Resulting Indicators* in the *Hi, Lo, Eq* fields (positions 71–76) for a positive, negative, or zero value. Indicators may be avoided for sign testing by including the instruction for the test(s) in an **IF** or **SELECT** group.

Data field checking includes the *presence, absence, justification, acceptability, relationship,* and *structure of data.* The presence of data validation ensures that something has been entered in the field. On the other hand, the absence of data check determines if nothing is entered in a field. Justification validation is usually performed on character fields to test if the value is entered beginning in the high-order position. The **CHECK** operation may be used to test the first byte in a field for a nonblank character to determine if the value is left-justified.

The acceptability of data includes *range checking, testing of a check digit, limit checking, correspondence checking,* and the *validation of a batch total.* These validation functions are controlled by structured **RPG IV** operations introduced in previous chapters.

QUESTIONS

12-1. Define data validation.

12-2. How may data validation procedures be implemented in a computer environment?

12-3. Explain how each of the data validation procedures named in Question 12-2 may be controlled in a computer environment.

12-4. What is the purpose of an error rejection or abeyance file?

12-5. Name and explain the validation functions included in data type testing.

12-6. By what coding methods may input data be validated as numeric?

12-7. What characters in a computer's character set are considered numeric?

12-8. Examine the following instruction and explain the function of each *Resulting Indicator:*

```
*.. 1 ...+... 2 ...+... 3 ...+... 4 ...+... 5 ...+... 6 ...+... 7 ...+... 8 ...+... 9 ...+ ...10
CLON01Factor1+++++++Opcode&ExtFactor2+++++++Result++++++++Len++D+HiLoEq....Comments+++++++++++++
                    TESTN                                        202122
```

12-9. How must the *Result* field specified in the **TESTN** operation in Question 12-8 be defined?

12-10. Explain the validation procedure(s) that may be included in an **RPG IV** program for testing a field value as alphabetic.

12-11. Name the methods by which *sign testing* may be implemented in an **RPG IV** program.

12-12. During processing, where is the sign of a number stored in a computer's memory? In a hexadecimal copy listing (over-and-under format) generated in an IBM mainframe or minicomputer environment, where is the sign identified?

12-13. When is it important to check a field value for zero?

12-14. What are some of the data validation functions that may be included in data field checking?

12-15. How is the *presence* of data checking implemented in an **RPG IV** program?

12-16. How is the *absence* of data checking supported in an **RPG IV** program?

12-17. Is *justification* checking usually performed on numeric or alphanumeric data (or both)? Explain your answer.

12-18. What data validation functions are related to the *acceptability of data* testing?

12-19. Identify an application in which *range checking* is applicable.

12-20. Refer to Question 12-19, and explain how the application may be controlled in an **RPG IV** program.

12-21. Explain the function of a *check digit*. Where is it usually stored in the related field value?

12-22. Use the Modulus-11 method to create a *check digit* for account numbers 12000 and 123456.

12-23. Use the Modulus-11 check digit method to determine if account numbers 130003 and 77003 are valid.

12-24. Name an application in which *limit checking* may be used. How is it implemented in an **RPG IV** program?

12-25. Give an example of *correspondence checking*. How may it be controlled in an **RPG IV** program?

12-26. What is a *batch total?* How may it be controlled in an **RPG IV** program?

PROGRAMMING ASSIGNMENTS

For each of the following programming assignments, a physical file must have been created and loaded with the related data records. Your instructor will tell you if you have to create the physical file and load it or if it has been prepared for the assignment.

Programming Assignment 12-1: BATCH VALIDATION OF SAVINGS ACCOUNT TRANSACTIONS

A bank wants a program created that will ensure the accuracy of all daily savings account transactions before updating a depositor's account. The program is to perform the following validation checks on the input data:

1. Transaction code
2. Transaction amount
3. Transaction date.

Details related to each of these are explained in the following paragraphs. When a validation error is found, no further checks are to be performed, and any subsequent processing for that record is to be discontinued. The related error message is to be printed on the report with the record information.

Transaction Code Validation. The valid transactions codes are

D—Deposit W—Withdrawal I—Interest Credit

A—Debit Adjustment C— Credit Adjustment

Any other code value is to be considered invalid.

Transaction Amount Validation. The following tests are to be performed on the transaction amount:

1. Invalid zero value.
2. If transaction code is D, I, or C, the amount must be positive.
3. If transaction code is W or A, the amount must be negative.

Transaction Year Validation. The year value in the transaction date must be equal to the report year.

Error Message Array. Elements include the following (processed positionally with the related error number as the index value):

INVALID TRANSACTION CODE
TRANSACTION AMOUNT ZERO
CODE INDICATES AMOUNT MUST BE POSITIVE
CODE INDICATES AMOUNT MUST BE NEGATIVE
TRANSACTION YEAR INVALID

Input of Report Date: Create a data area and load it with a report date value of 022997. Input it to the program *implicitly* with a data area data structure or *explicitly* with a second input file that includes only the report date field.

Physical File Record Format:

PHYSICAL FILE DESCRIPTION

SYSTEM: AS/400	DATE: Yours
FILE NAME: Yours	REV NO: 0
RECORD NAME: Yours	KEY LENGTH: 6
SEQUENCE: Keyed	RECORD SIZE: 17

FIELD DEFINITIONS

FIELD NO	FIELD NAME	SIZE	TYPE	POSITION FROM	POSITION TO	COMMENTS
1	TRANSCODE	1	C	1	1	D,W,I,A,C
2	ACTNUMBER	6	C	2	7	Key field
3	TRANSDATE	6	L	8	13	*MDY
4	TRANSAMT	7	P	14	17	2 decimals

Physical file data:

Transaction Code	Account Number	Transaction Date	Transaction Amount
D	100000	020196	0084000
W	200000	023197	1250000
T	300000	021097	0009250
A	400000	023097	0024567-
I	500000	021597	090000Y
C	600000	020197	0067899
D	700000	021197	0000000
W	800000	023097	0012094-
D	900000	022897	0002500-
D	910000	020897	0100000
C	980000	022998	0070000-

Report Design:

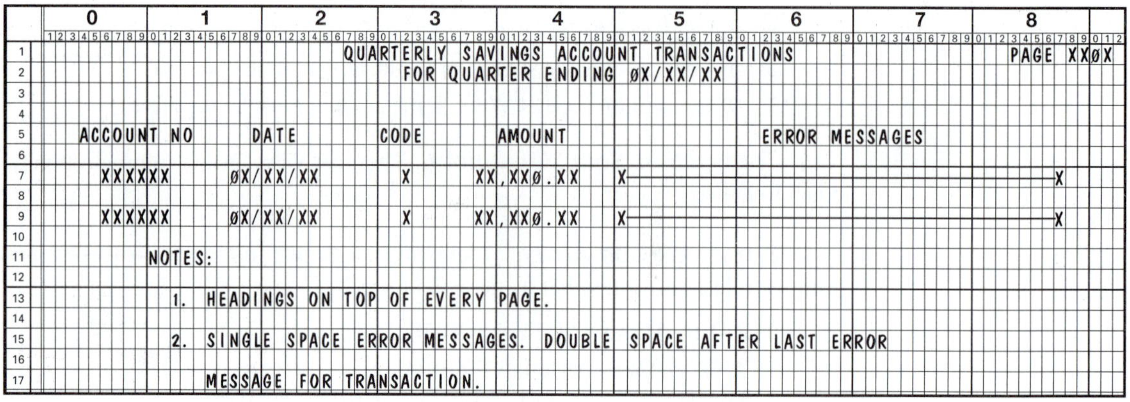

QUARTERLY SAVINGS ACCOUNT TRANSACTIONS
PAGE XXØX
FOR QUARTER ENDING ØX/XX/XX
ACCOUNT NO
DATE
CODE
AMOUNT
ERROR MESSAGES
XXXXXX ØX/XX/XX X XX,XXØ.XX X X
XXXXXX ØX/XX/XX X XX,XXØ.XX X X
NOTES:
1. HEADINGS ON TOP OF EVERY PAGE.
2. SINGLE SPACE ERROR MESSAGES. DOUBLE SPACE AFTER LAST ERROR
MESSAGE FOR TRANSACTION.

Programming Assignment 12-2: BATCH VALIDATION OF ITEM PURCHASES

A company requests a program to batch validate item purchases before accounts payable and general ledger accounts are updated.

Processing: The following validation functions must be included in the **RPG IV** program:

Item Number Validation: Use the Modulus-11 check digit method to validate that the item number is correct.

Item Name Validation:

1. Test that the name value is alphabetic. Blank, hyphen, and A through Z are to be considered alphabetic characters. *Hint: Store these characters in a Named Constant and use the* **CHECK** *operation to check the NAME field for an invalid character.*
2. Test the NAME value for left-justification.

Vendor Number Validation: Include the following valid vendor numbers in a compile-time table defined with six one-byte elements: **124568.** Using VENDORNO as the search argument, look up the table for a valid vendor number.

Cost Validation: Multiply QUANTITY by UNITCOST to determine the cost of the purchase. Validate that the purchase cost does not exceed $2,000.

Error Identification: Include the following error messages in a compile-time array:

ITEM NUMBER DOES NOT CHECK
ITEM NAME NOT ALPHABETIC
ITEM NAME NOT LEFT-JUSTIFIED
VENDOR NUMBER NOT VALID
COST EXCEEDS $2,000

The program is to be written so that every test is made.

Physical File Record Format:

```
                         PHYSICAL FILE DESCRIPTION

SYSTEM: AS/400                                  DATE: Yours
FILE NAME: Yours                                REV NO: 0
RECORD NAME: Yours                              KEY LENGTH: 5
SEQUENCE: Keyed                                 RECORD SIZE: 48

                             FIELD DEFINITIONS

FIELD    FIELD NAME    SIZE  TYPE    POSITION     COMMENTS
 NO                                  FROM   TO

 1       ITEMNUMBER       5   C        1     5    Key field
 2       ITEM_NAME       26   C        6    31
 3       PURCHDATE        6   P       32    35
 4       VENDERNO         1   P       36    36
 5       QUANTITY         3   P       37    38    0 decimals
 6       UNITCOST         6   P       39    42    2 decimals
 7       UNOFMEASUR       6   C       43    48
```

Physical file data:

Item Number	Item Name	Purchase Date	Vendor Number	Quantity	Cost Per Item	Unit of Measure
11184	BLACK TRUFFLES	040197	1	024	008500	JAR/OZ
11206	SHARK FIN SOUP	040597	4	120	001000	CAN/OZ
11304	PICKLED TRIPE	041097	3	036	000400	JAR/OZ
11509	SMOKED PHEASANT	041597	8	012	001200	CAN/PK
11606	BLACK CAVIAR	041897	5	060	003900	CAN/OZ
11703	CHOCOLATE-COVERED ANTS	042097	6	048	000650	CAN/OZ
11800	SEA WATER KEL9 SPROUTS	042897	2	144	002000	JAR/OZ
T2009	REINDEER MILK YOGURT	043097	9	010	000700	JAR/QT

Report Design: Examine the printer spacing chart and notice that the values for a record's fields are only printed on the line for the first error message. Any other error messages for the related record are to be printed without the field values. Only the records that have validation errors are to be printed.

```
 1  ØX/XX/XX                                                   ITEM PURCHASES VALIDATION REPORT                                    PAGE XXØX
 2
 3
 4  ITEM              ITEM NAME                DATE     VENDOR     QTY     COST/ITEM   UNIT OF MEAS.  ERROR MESSAGES
 5
 6  XXXXX   X-------------------------X    ØX/XX/XX     X        XØX     X,XXØ.XX       XXXXXX      X------------------------------------X
 7                                                                                                  X------------------------------------X
 8
 9  XXXXX   X-------------------------X    ØX/XX/XX     X        XØX     X,XXØ.XX       XXXXXX      X------------------------------------X
10                                                                                                  X------------------------------------X
11
12          NOTES:
13
14            1. USE SYSTEM DATE FOR REPORT.
15
16            2. PAGE OVERFLOW ON LINE 18.
17
18            3. DOUBLE SPACE AFTER LAST ERROR MESSAGE FOR RELATED RECORD.
```

chapter 13

Physical File Maintenance (Batch Mode)

The *Data Description Specifications* syntax to create physical files was discussed in Chapter 2. Recall that a physical file may be created as *keyed* or *nonkeyed* and may be defined with the following additional attributes:

1. *Keyed* file with records that have *unique* keys (duplicate keys not supported).
2. *Keyed* file that supports records with duplicate keys.
3. *Keyed* file defined so that the records are processed in a descending key order instead of the default ascending key order.
4. *Keyed* file that processes the records in a *LIFO* (last-in, first-out) key group order instead of the default *FIFO* (first-in, first-out) order.
5. *Keyed* file defined with a *composite* key that includes more than one field from the physical file record format. The file may be processed by the composite key or a partial key.
6. Other keywords support editing, relational tests, validation, referencing the record or field attributes from other files, and numerous other functions.

PHYSICAL FILE PROCESSING

Keyed and *nonkeyed* physical files may be processed by the following methods:

Keyed Physical Files:

1. In a *keyed* sequence by the **RPG IV** logic cycle, or sequentially retrieve records in a keyed order with a **READ** *(Read from a file)*, **READE** *(Read next record with an equal key)*, **READP** *(Read prior record from a data file)*, or **READPE** *(Read prior record with an equal key)* operation
2. Randomly, by a full or partial key value with the **CHAIN** operation
3. By lower and upper key limits with the records processed sequentially forward or backward by one of the **READ** operations.

Nonkeyed Physical Files:

1. In *arrival sequence* (first-in, first-out order)
2. By *relative record number* (record's position in the physical file) by a **READ** or **READP** operation.

PHYSICAL FILE MAINTENANCE

The maintenance of physical files includes the following functions:

1. *Addition* of records
2. *Update* of existing records
3. *Logical deletion* of existing records
4. *Tagging* of records for deletion (an update function)
5. *Reorganization.*

Each of these maintenance functions will be discussed, and standalone program examples will be shown, in the following sections.

Addition of Records to a Physical File

After a physical file is created, the process of loading it with data records is an add function. Under the control of an **RPG IV** program, records may be added to a physical file by the **WRITE** operation or with the compiler's logic cycle.

Record Addition with the `WRITE` Operation

The addition of records to an externally defined physical file with the **WRITE** operation does not require that *Output Specifications* be included in the program. When the **WRITE** statement is executed, the record format for the current record processed is written to the physical file after the last record stored. The syntax of the **WRITE** operation is detailed in Figure 13-1.

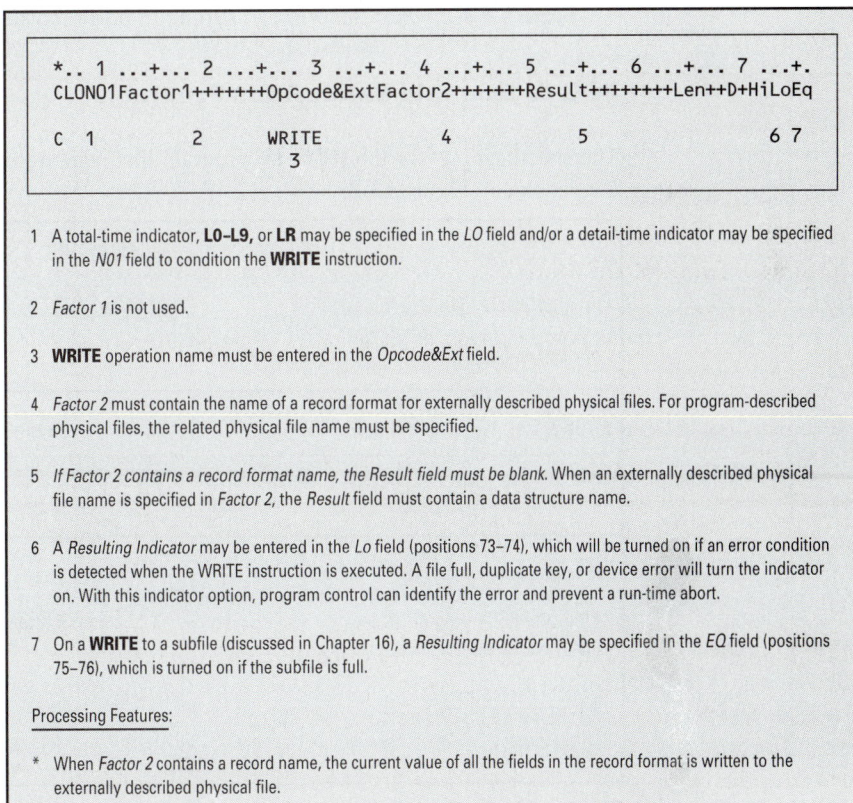

```
*.. 1 ...+... 2 ...+... 3 ...+... 4 ...+... 5 ...+... 6 ...+... 7 ...+.
CLON01Factor1+++++++Opcode&ExtFactor2+++++++Result++++++++Len++D+HiLoEq

C  1          2       WRITE          4              5               6 7
                        3
```

1 A total-time indicator, **L0–L9,** or **LR** may be specified in the *L0* field and/or a detail-time indicator may be specified in the *N01* field to condition the **WRITE** instruction.

2 *Factor 1* is not used.

3 **WRITE** operation name must be entered in the *Opcode&Ext* field.

4 *Factor 2* must contain the name of a record format for externally described physical files. For program-described physical files, the related physical file name must be specified.

5 *If Factor 2 contains a record format name, the Result field must be blank.* When an externally described physical file name is specified in *Factor 2,* the *Result* field must contain a data structure name.

6 A *Resulting Indicator* may be entered in the *Lo* field (positions 73–74), which will be turned on if an error condition is detected when the WRITE instruction is executed. A file full, duplicate key, or device error will turn the indicator on. With this indicator option, program control can identify the error and prevent a run-time abort.

7 On a **WRITE** to a subfile (discussed in Chapter 16), a *Resulting Indicator* may be specified in the *EQ* field (positions 75–76), which is turned on if the subfile is full.

Processing Features:

* When *Factor 2* contains a record name, the current value of all the fields in the record format is written to the externally described physical file.

Figure 13-1 Syntax and processing features of the **WRITE** operation.

* To add records to a disk file with a **WRITE** instruction, the character **A** must be specified in the *A* field (position 20) of the related *File Description* instruction.
* When records that use relative record numbers (not key field values) are written to a physical file, the field name specified with the **RECNO** *File Description* keyword must be updated with the relative record number of the record to be written to the file.

Figure 13-1 Syntax and processing features of the **WRITE** operation. (Continued)

File Description Syntax for Record Addition

The *File Description* syntax to add records to a physical file is detailed in Figure 13-2. Two examples are shown, one that defines the file as *output* and the other that defines output as *update/full-procedural*.

```
Physical file defined as output
(letter O in position 17)

 .. 1 ...+... 2 ...+... 3 ...+... 4 ...+... 5 ...+... 6 ...+... 7 ...+
 FFilename++IPEASFRLen+LKLen+AIDevice+.Keywords++++++++++++++++++++++++
  * Example 1:
 FCh13smstr O EA              K DISK
                                          letter A must be specified
 * Example 2:                             in position 20
FCh13smstr UF EA              K DISK

Physical file defined as update (U in position 16)
and full-procedural (F in position 17)

Note: In each example, the physical file is externally described
      (E in position 19) and keyed (K in position 34).
```

Figure 13-2 *File Description* syntax to add records to a physical file.

RPG IV Example Batch Adds Program

The specifications for the **RPG IV** program that adds transaction records to a master file are detailed in Figure 13-3.

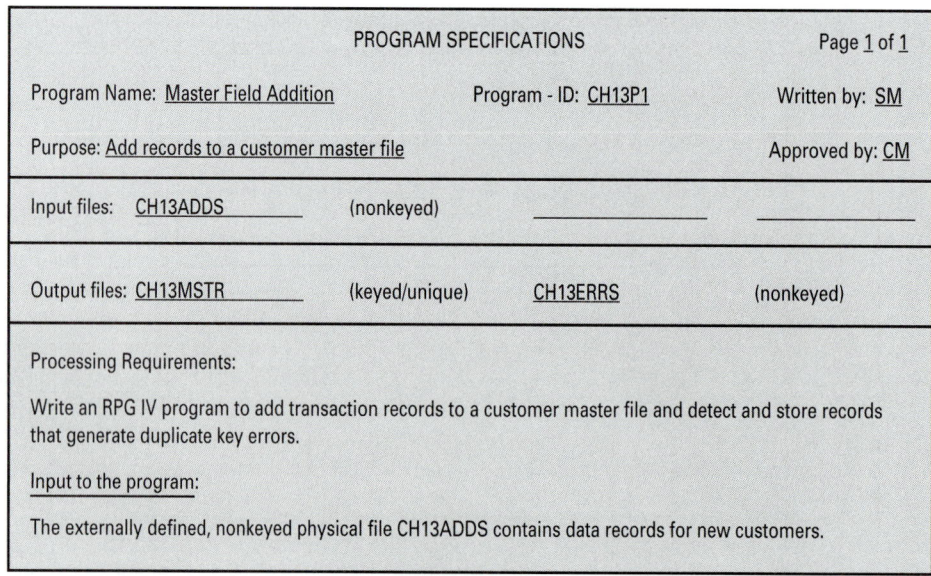

PROGRAM SPECIFICATIONS — Page 1 of 1

Program Name: Master Field Addition — Program - ID: CH13P1 — Written by: SM

Purpose: Add records to a customer master file — Approved by: CM

Input files: CH13ADDS (nonkeyed)

Output files: CH13MSTR (keyed/unique) CH13ERRS (nonkeyed)

Processing Requirements:

Write an RPG IV program to add transaction records to a customer master file and detect and store records that generate duplicate key errors.

Input to the program:

The externally defined, nonkeyed physical file CH13ADDS contains data records for new customers.

Figure 13-3 Specifications for an **RPG IV** program that adds records to a physical file.

Processing:

Read the transaction file (CH13ADDS) in arrival sequence until end of file. For every record processed, add it to the customer master file CH13MSTR. Because CH13MSTR is defined to support only unique keys, any attempt to add a record that has a key already stored in the file will result in a duplicate key error. Records with duplicate keys are to be added to the error file CH13ERRS.

Output:

Move the field values from the transaction file to the customer master fields and write the master record to the customer master file. For records that flag a duplicate key error, move the field values from the transaction file to the error record's fields and write the error record to the error file.

Figure 13-3 Specifications for an **RPG IV** program that adds records to a physical file. (Continued)

The system flowchart in Figure 13-4 indicates that three physical files are processed by the "adds" program. A transaction file (CH13ADDS) includes the "add" records, a master file (CH13MSTR) to which the records are to be added, and an error file (CH13ERRS) to which transaction records that have key values already stored in the master file *(duplicate key error)* are written.

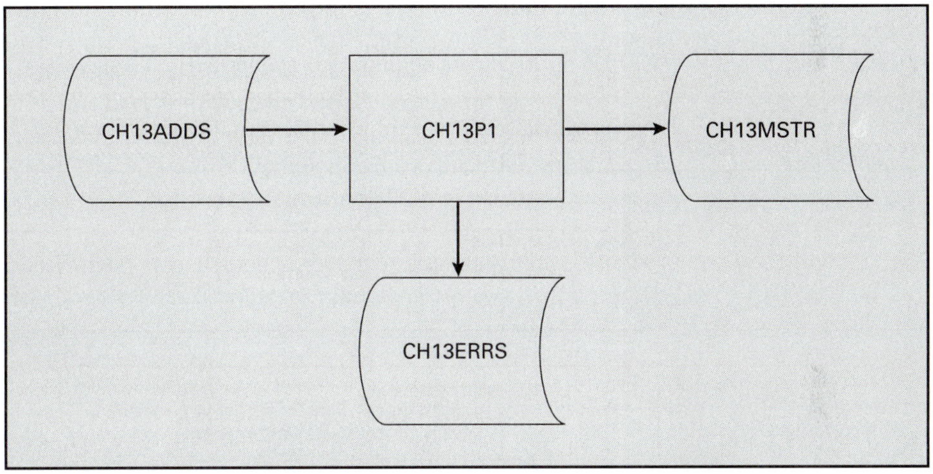

Figure 13-4 System flowchart for the "adds" program.

A listing of the transaction ("adds") file's record format and a **CPYF** *(Copy File)* utility listing of the data in *hexadecimal* format are shown in Figure 13-5.

```
                               Data Description Source
SEQNBR  *...+....1....+....2....+....3....+....4....+....5....+....6....+
   100        A          R ADDSRCD
   200        A            TCODE          1
   300        A            TACT#          5
   400        A            TNAME         30
   500        A            TDATE          6  0
   600        A            TAMT           7  2
```

Figure 13-5 Partial compile listing of the transaction file's DDS and "hexadecimal" listing of the data.

```
           RCDNBR  *...+... 1 ...+... 2 ...+... 3 ...+... 4 ...     Packed value interpreted
Character row—1    A00002STUTZ BEARCAT                     " Σ   —  as these characters
Zone row———        CFFFFFEEEEE4CCCDCCE44444444444444444402171400
Digit row———       1000022343902519313000000000000000000009F635F——  F indicates a positive
                2  A000060TTO DIESEL                      ■" c&     value; D for negative
                   CFFFFFDEED4CCCECD444444444444444444402570850
                   100006633604952530000000000000000000009F030F
                3  A00002HENRY J KAISER                    " &
                   CFFFFFCCDDE4D4DCCECD4444444444444444402072500
                   1000028559801021925900000000000000000019F700F
                4  A00023FERDINAND PORCHE                  " + ¼
                   CFFFFFCCDCCDCDC4DDDCCC444444444444402670815
                   100023659495154076938500000000000000000029F402F
                5  A00017HAROLD WINSTON                    "
                   CFFFFFCCDDDC4ECDEEDD44444444444444402670100
                   100017819634069523650000000000000000000029F000F
——————————————— 6  A00018RANSON E OLDS                   i"   -
                   CFFFFFDCDEDD4C4DDCE444444444444444402870909
Position of the    100018915265050634200000000000000000000029F008F
record in the
file (relative
record number)       Interpretation of the two packed fields:

                     0287
                     029F = 0022897 in Zoned Decimal format

                     0909
                     008F = 0090089 in Zoned Decimal format
```

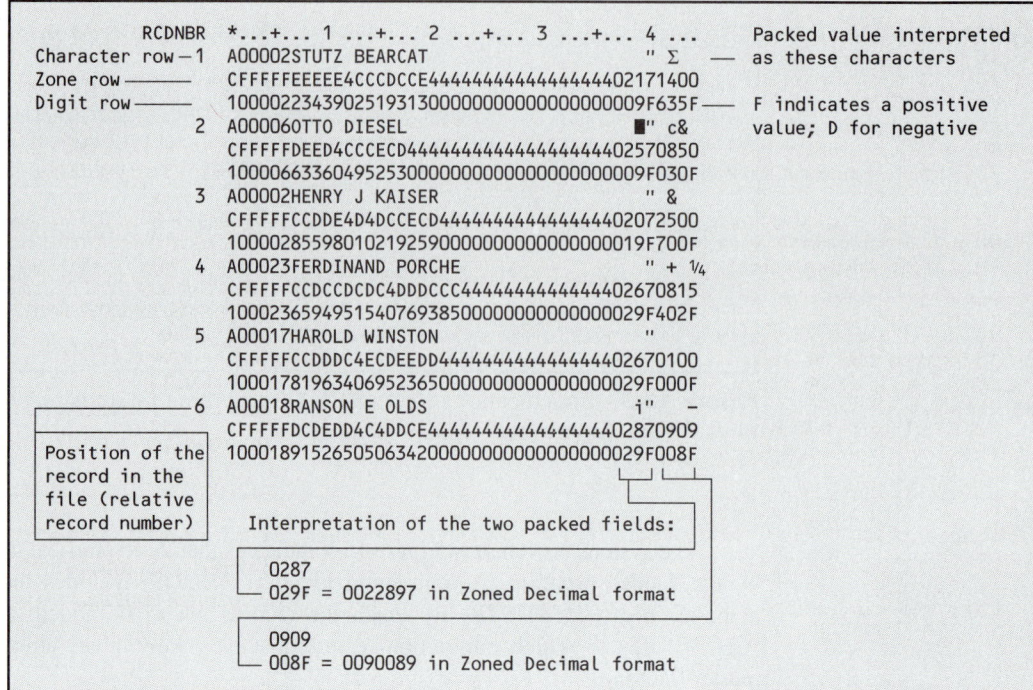

Figure 13-5 Partial compile listing of the transaction file's DDS and "hexadecimal" listing of the data. (Continued)

A listing of the master file's record format to which the transaction data is to be added and a **CPYF** listing of the data in *hexadecimal* format *before* the transaction records are added are detailed in Figure 13-6.

```
                                 Data Description Source
SEQNBR  *...+....1....+....2....+....3....+....4....+....5....+....6....+
  100        A                                      UNIQUE
  200        A          R MSTRRCD
  300        A            MCODE          1
  400        A            MACT#          5
  500        A            MNAME         30
  600        A            MDATE          6 0
  700        A            MBAL           7 2
  800        A          K MACT#

                 Key value

         RCDNBR  *...+... 1 ...+... 2 ...+... 3 ...+... 4 ...
              1   00001HENRY FORD                         ±"
                 4FFFFFCCDDE4CDDC44444444444444444444401470100
                 000001855980669400000000000000000000000009F020F
              2   00003LOUIS CHEVROLET                    i"
                 4FFFFFDDECE4CCCEDDDCE444444444444401870000
                 00000336492038559635300000000000000000009F300F
              3   00004DODGE BROTHERS                     `"
                 4FFFFFCDCCC4CDDECCDE44444444444444401771010
                 000004464750296385920000000000000000000009F900F
              4   00008STANLEY STEAMER                    " +
                 4FFFFFEECDDCE4EECCDCD444444444444401270800
                 00000823153580235145900000000000000000019F004F
              5   00009HENRY J KAISER                     "
                 4FFFFFCCDDE4D4DCCECD44444444444444401072000
```

Figure 13-6 Partial compile listing of the master file's DDS and hexadecimal listing of the data *before* adding records.

```
     000009855980102192590000000000000000000019F500F
  6   00010JOHN STUDEBAKER                        " †
     4FFFFFDDCD4EEECCCCDCD44444444444444401270640
     000010168502344521259000000000000000000019F070F
  7   00011WALTER P CHRYSLER                       "  &
     4FFFFFECDECD4D4CCDEEDCD44444444444444401670050
     000011613359070389823590000000000000000009F780F
  8   00018RANSON E OLDS                          █" n
     4FFFFFDCDEDD4C4DDCE444444444444444444401570900
     000018915265050634200000000000000000000019F050F
  9   00019MERCEDES BENZ                          i"
     4FFFFFDCDCCCCE4CCDE444444444444444444401879000
     000019459354520255900000000000000000000019F010F
 10   00020FELIX WANKEL                            " &
     4FFFFFCCDCE4ECDDCD4444444444444444444401270513
     000020653970615253000000000000000000000029F002F
```

Figure 13-6 Partial compile listing of the master file's DDS and hexadecimal listing of the data *before* adding records. (Continued)

Because the error file's (CH13ERRS) record format is identical to the transaction file (CH13ADDS) and the master file (CH13MSTR), its format is not shown. Also, before execution of the "adds" program, this file contains no data.

RPG IV "ADDS" Program Coding

A compile listing of the **RPG IV** program that "adds" transaction records to a master file is presented in Figure 13-7. Recall that the compiler-supplied instructions for input and output items are identified by a number, equal sign, and **I** (for input) or **O** (for output) (i.e., **10=I** or **42=O**). Note that the items related to the Ch13adds file are specified with the letter **I,** whereas those for the Ch13mstr and Ch13errs files are identified with the letter **O.**

```
Line    <---------------------- Source Specifications ----------------------------><---- Comments ----> Do
Number ....1....+....2....+....3....+....4....+....5....+....6....+....7....+....8....+....9....+...10 Num
                         S o u r c e   L i s t i n g
     1  * This program adds records to an existing physical file from a
     2  * transaction physical file defined as nonkeyed.  Duplicate add
     3  * records are loaded to an error file with the same format as
     4  * the transaction file.
     5
     6 FCh13adds  IF   E             DISK   ------ Transaction file
        *--------------------------------------------------------------------------------*
        *                              RPG name          External name                    *
        * File name. . . . . . . . . :  CH13ADDS          STAN/CH13ADDS                    *
        * Record format(s) . . . . . :  ADDSRCD           ADDSRCD                          *
        *--------------------------------------------------------------------------------*
     7 FCh13mstr  O   A E           K DISK   ------ Master file
        *--------------------------------------------------------------------------------*
        *                              RPG name          External name                    *
        * File name. . . . . . . . . :  CH13MSTR          STAN/CH13MSTR                    *
        * Record format(s) . . . . . :  MSTRRCD           MSTRRCD                          *
        *--------------------------------------------------------------------------------*
     8 FCh13errs  O   A E             DISK   ------ Error file
     9
        *--------------------------------------------------------------------------------*
        *                              RPG name          External name                    *
        * File name. . . . . . . . . :  CH13ERRS          STAN/CH13ERRS                    *
        * Record format(s) . . . . . :  ERRRCD            ERRRCD                           *
        *--------------------------------------------------------------------------------*
    10=IADDSRCD
        *--------------------------------------------------------------------------------*
        * RPG record format  . . . . :  ADDSRCD                                           *
        * External format  . . . . . :  ADDSRCD : STAN/CH13ADDS                           *
        *--------------------------------------------------------------------------------*
```

Figure 13-7 Compile listing of the **RPG IV** "adds" program with an explanation of each instruction.

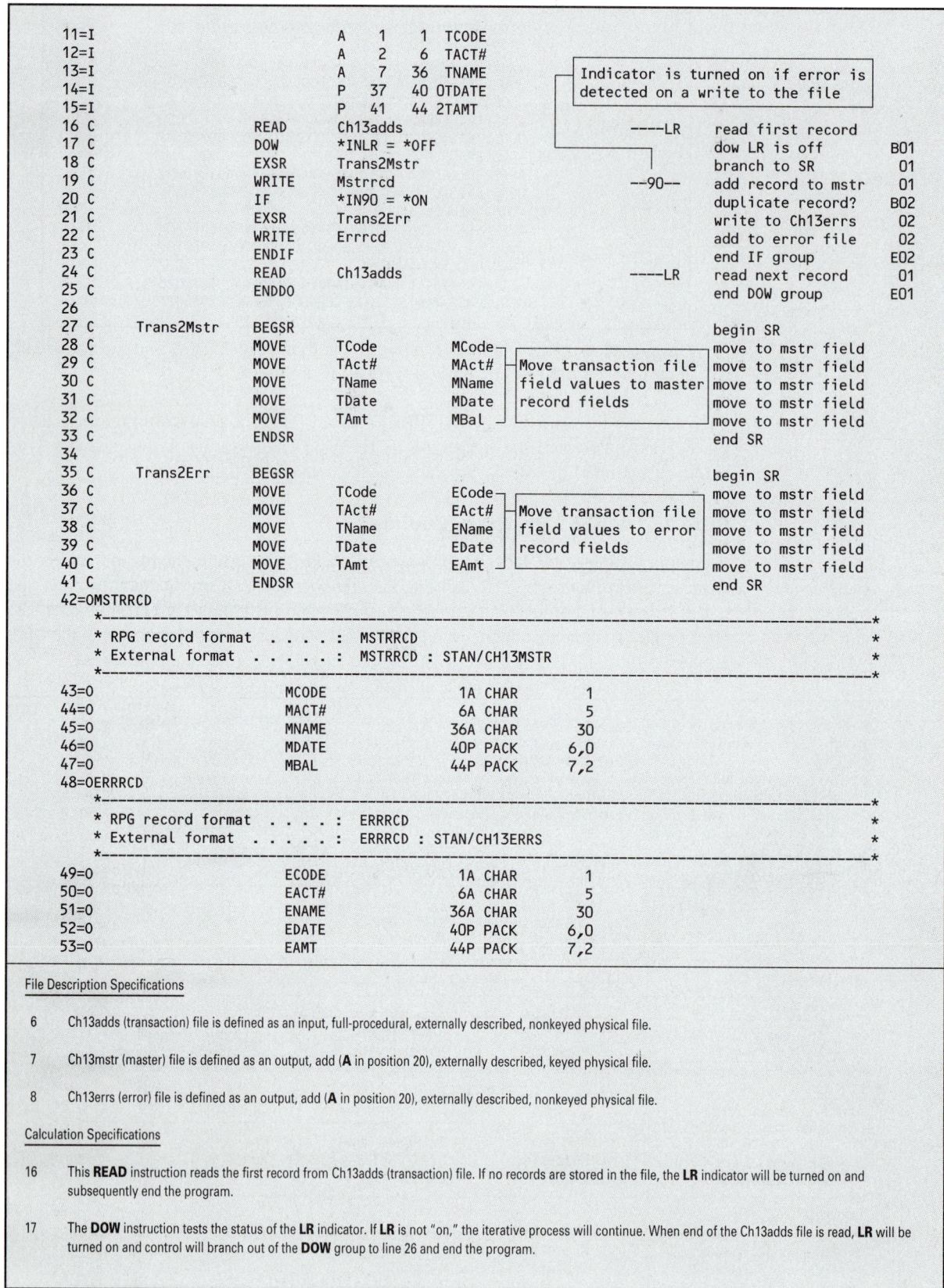

```
11=I                            A    1    1  TCODE
12=I                            A    2    6  TACT#
13=I                            A    7   36  TNAME           ┌──────────────────────────────────┐
14=I                            P   37   40 0TDATE          ┌┤Indicator is turned on if error is│
15=I                            P   41   44 2TAMT           ││detected on a write to the file   │
                                                            │└──────────────────────────────────┘
16 C                 READ       Ch13adds                    │   ----LR   read first record
17 C                 DOW        *INLR = *OFF                └──────┐     dow LR is off          B01
18 C                 EXSR       Trans2Mstr                         │     branch to SR            01
19 C                 WRITE      Mstrrcd                        --90--    add record to mstr      01
20 C                 IF         *IN90 = *ON                            duplicate record?       B02
21 C                 EXSR       Trans2Err                              write to Ch13errs        02
22 C                 WRITE      Errrcd                                 add to error file        02
23 C                 ENDIF                                             end IF group            E02
24 C                 READ       Ch13adds                       ----LR  read next record         01
25 C                 ENDDO                                             end DOW group           E01
26
27 C      Trans2Mstr BEGSR                                             begin SR
28 C                 MOVE       TCode         MCode┐┌──────────────────┐move to mstr field
29 C                 MOVE       TAct#         MAct#├┤Move transaction file│move to mstr field
30 C                 MOVE       TName         MName││field values to master│move to mstr field
31 C                 MOVE       TDate         MDate││record fields         │move to mstr field
32 C                 MOVE       TAmt          MBal ┘└──────────────────┘move to mstr field
33 C                 ENDSR                                             end SR
34
35 C      Trans2Err  BEGSR                                             begin SR
36 C                 MOVE       TCode         ECode┐┌──────────────────┐move to mstr field
37 C                 MOVE       TAct#         EAct#├┤Move transaction file│move to mstr field
38 C                 MOVE       TName         EName││field values to error │move to mstr field
39 C                 MOVE       TDate         EDate││record fields         │move to mstr field
40 C                 MOVE       TAmt          EAmt ┘└──────────────────┘move to mstr field
41 C                 ENDSR                                             end SR
42=OMSTRRCD
   *------------------------------------------------------------------------------*
   * RPG record format  . . . . :  MSTRRCD                                         *
   * External format  . . . . . :  MSTRRCD : STAN/CH13MSTR                         *
   *------------------------------------------------------------------------------*
43=O                   MCODE                1A CHAR      1
44=O                   MACT#                6A CHAR      5
45=O                   MNAME               36A CHAR     30
46=O                   MDATE               40P PACK    6,0
47=O                   MBAL                44P PACK    7,2
48=OERRRCD
   *------------------------------------------------------------------------------*
   * RPG record format  . . . . :  ERRRCD                                          *
   * External format  . . . . . :  ERRRCD : STAN/CH13ERRS                          *
   *------------------------------------------------------------------------------*
49=O                   ECODE                1A CHAR      1
50=O                   EACT#                6A CHAR      5
51=O                   ENAME               36A CHAR     30
52=O                   EDATE               40P PACK    6,0
53=O                   EAMT                44P PACK    7,2
```

File Description Specifications

6 Ch13adds (transaction) file is defined as an input, full-procedural, externally described, nonkeyed physical file.

7 Ch13mstr (master) file is defined as an output, add (**A** in position 20), externally described, keyed physical file.

8 Ch13errs (error) file is defined as an output, add (**A** in position 20), externally described, nonkeyed physical file.

Calculation Specifications

16 This **READ** instruction reads the first record from Ch13adds (transaction) file. If no records are stored in the file, the **LR** indicator will be turned on and subsequently end the program.

17 The **DOW** instruction tests the status of the **LR** indicator. If **LR** is not "on," the iterative process will continue. When end of the Ch13adds file is read, **LR** will be turned on and control will branch out of the **DOW** group to line 26 and end the program.

Figure 13-7 Compile listing of the **RPG IV** "adds" program with an explanation of each instruction. (Continued)

18	This **EXSR** instruction exits program control to the Trans2Mstr subroutine, where the Addsrcd (transaction) record field values are moved into the Mstrrcd (master) record fields.
19	This **WRITE** instruction writes (adds) the master record (loaded in the Trans2Mstr subroutine) to the Ch13mstr file. If a duplicate key, file full, or device error occurs, the **90** indicator entered in the *Lo* field (positions 73–74) will be turned on and the record will *not* be written (added) to the master file.
20–23	The **IF** instruction tests the status of the **90** indicator. If it is "on" (error detected on the **WRITE** instruction on line 19), the instructions within the **IF** group will be executed. The **EXSR** instruction on line 21 exits program control to the Trans2Err subroutine, where the Addsrcd (transaction) record field values are moved to the Errrcd (error) record fields. This **WRITE** instruction writes (adds) the Errrcd record to the Ch13errs file. The **ENDIF** operation ends the **IF** group.
24	This **READ** instruction reads the next record from the Ch13adds (transaction) file. If end of file is read, the **LR** indicator will be turned on. When control returns to the **DOW** instruction on line 17, control will exit from the **DOW** group and end the program.
25	The **ENDDO** operation ends the **DOW** group.
27–33	The instructions in the Trans2Mstr subroutine move the Ch13adds (transaction) file field values to the Ch13mstr (master) file fields. The **ENDSR** operation ends the subroutine.
27–33	The instructions in the Trans2Err subroutine move the Addsrcd (transaction) record field values to the Errrcd (error) record fields. The **ENDSR** operation ends the subroutine.
Note:	Observe that no programmer-supplied output instructions are specified in this **RPG IV** program. Because the Ch13mstr and Ch13errs file are defined as output, the compiler supplied the output record descriptions.

Figure 13-7 Compile listing of the **RPG IV** "adds" program with an explanation of each instruction. (Continued)

A **CPYF** hexadecimal listing of the Ch13mstr file *after* the "adds" program is executed is shown in Figure 13-8.

```
RCDNBR  *...+... 1 ...+... 2 ...+... 3 ...+... 4 ...
     1   00001HENRY FORD                         ±"
        4FFFFFCCDDE4CDDC444444444444444444401470100
        00000185598066940000000000000000000009F020F
    11  A00002STUTZ BEARCAT                     " Σ
        CFFFFFEEEEE4CCCDCCE44444444444444440217140
        10000223439025193130000000000000000009F635F
     2   00003LOUIS CHEVROLET                    i"
        4FFFFFDDECE4CCCEDDDCE444444444444440187000
        00000336492038559635300000000000000009F300F
     3   00004DODGE BROTHERS                     `"
        4FFFFFCDCCC4CDDECCDE4444444444444440177101
        00000446475029638592000000000000000009F900F
    12  A000060TTO DIESEL                       █" c&
        CFFFFFDEED4CCCECD4444444444444444440257085
        10000663360495253000000000000000000009F030F
     4   00008STANLEY STEAMER                   " +
        4FFFFFEECDDCE4EECCDCD444444444444440127080
        000008231535802351459000000000000000019F004F
     5   00009HENRY J KAISER                     "
        4FFFFFCCDDE4D4DCCECD4444444444444440107200
        000009855980102192590000000000000000019F500F
     6   00010JOHN STUDEBAKER                   " †
        4FFFFFDDCD4EEECCCCDCD444444444444440127064
        000010168502344521259000000000000000019F070F
     7   00011WALTER P CHRYSLER                 "  &
        4FFFFFECDECD4D4CCDEEDCD444444444444016700
        00001161335907038982359000000000000009F780F
```

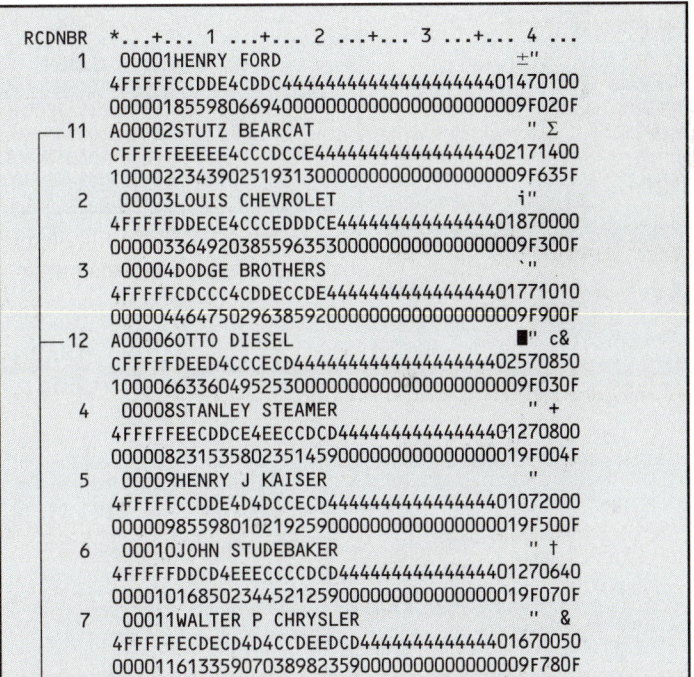

Figure 13-8 **CPYF** utility listing in hexadecimal format of the Ch13mstr file *after* execution of the "adds" program.

```
—14  A00017HAROLD WINSTON                   "
     CFFFFFCCDDDC4ECDEEDD444444444444444402670100
     10001781963406952365000000000000000029F000F
 8    00018RANSON E OLDS                  ■" n
     4FFFFFDCDEDD4C4DDCE4444444444444444401570900
     000018915265050634200000000000000000019F050F
 9    00019MERCEDES BENZ                  i"
     4FFFFFDCDCCCCE4CCDE4444444444444444401879000
     000019459354520255900000000000000000019F010F
10    00020FELIX WANKEL                    " &
     4FFFFFCCDCE4ECDDCD44444444444444444401270513
     000020653970615253000000000000000000029F002F
—13  A00023FERDINAND PORCHE                " + ¼
 |   CFFFFFCCDCCDCDC4DDDCCC4444444444444402670815
 |   1000236594951540769385000000000000000029F402F
 |
 └── Position (relative record number) of the record in
     the file.  Because the file is keyed, it is accessed
     in an ascending key-value order by the CPYF utility.

└─── Added records
```

Figure 13-8 CPYF utility listing in hexadecimal format of the Ch13mstr file *after* execution of the "adds" program.

Two Ch13adds file records, with keys 00002 and 00018, have the same key value as records already stored in the Ch13mstr file. Because the Ch13mstr file was created with the **UNIQUE** DDS keyword, records with the same key value *cannot* be added to the Ch13mstr file. Indicator **90** in the *Resulting Indicator Lo* field (positions 73–74) of the WRITE instruction will flag this error condition and prevent a run-time abort. For this **RPG IV** program, duplicate records are written to the Ch13errs file. A hexadecimal listing of the Ch13errs file after the "adds" program is executed is shown in Figure 13-9.

```
RCDNBR  *...+... 1 ...+... 2 ...+... 3 ...+... 4 ...
     1  A00002HENRY J KAISER                     " &
        CFFFFFCCDDE4D4DCCECD444444444444444402072500
        100002855980102192590000000000000000019F700F
     2  A00018RANSON E OLDS                   i"   -
        CFFFFFDCDEDD4C4DDCE4444444444444444402870909
        100018915265050634200000000000000000029F008F
```

Figure 13-9 CPYF utility listing in hexadecimal format of the Ch13errs file after execution of the "adds" program.

Update of Records in a Physical File

After records have been added to a physical file, a common maintenance function is to change the field values. With the exception of the *key* field(s), any other field in a keyed physical file may be changed by an **RPG IV** update program. For nonkeyed physical files, the value of any field may be changed.

Before "update" maintenance is introduced, the syntax of the **SETLL, CHAIN,** and **UPDATE** operations will be discussed.

The SETLL *(Set Lower Limit)* Operation

The syntax of the **SETLL** operation is explained in Figure 13-10.

```
*.. 1 ...+... 2 ...+... 3 ...+... 4 ...+... 5 ...+... 6 ...+... 7 ...+.
CLON01Factor1+++++++Opcode&ExtFactor2+++++++Result++++++++Len++D+HiLoEq

C 1          2        SETLL             4             5              6 7 8
                        3
```

1 A total-time indicator, **L0–L9,** or **LR** may be specified in the *L0* field and/or a detail-time indicator may be specified in the *N01* field to condition the **SETLL** instruction.

2 If the physical file specified in *Factor 2* is accessed by a key field, *Factor 1* must contain a field name, Named Constant, Figurative Constant, literal, or **KLIST** name.

If the physical file specified in *Factor 2* is accessed by a relative record number, *Factor 1* must contain the name of a field, literal, or Named Constant defined as a numeric integer.

3 **SETLL** operation name must be entered in the *Opcode&Ext* field.

4 *Factor 2* may contain the name of a file or a record format name. Record format names are allowed only for externally defined physical files.

5 The *Result* field is not used.

6 If a *Resulting Indicator* is specified in the *Hi* field (positions 71–72), it is set on when the key value in the item in *Factor 1* is greater than any key stored in the physical file.

7 If a *Resulting Indicator* is specified in the *Lo* field (positions 73–74), it is set on when a run-time error occurs during execution of the **SETLL** operation.

8 If a *Resulting Indicator* is specified in the *Eq* field (positions 75–76), it is set on when a record is found in the physical file with a key value equal to the key value of the item specified in *Factor 1*.

Processing Features:

* The **SETLL** operation positions the physical file at the record that has a key value or relative record number equal to or greater than the value stored in the *Factor 1* item.
* The physical file accessed must be defined as *full-procedural* (**F** in position 18) of the related *File Description* instruction.
* A **SETLL** operation does not access the record for processing, it only positions the physical file at the record. A **CHAIN** or one of the **READ** operations must subsequently access the record for processing.
* If the **SETLL** operation is not successful, the physical file is positioned at the end. The file, however, may be repositioned by executing the same or another **SETLL** instruction.

Figure 13-10 Syntax and processing features of the **SETLL** operation.

An example and the processing logic of the **SETLL** instruction are shown in Figure 13-11.

```
*.. 1 ...+... 2 ...+... 3 ...+... 4 ...+... 5 ...+... 6 ...+... 7 ...+.
CLON01Factor1+++++++Opcode&ExtFactor2+++++++Result++++++++Len++D+HiLoEq

C                     SETLL     Ch13mstr                                91
```

SETLL points to a record in the file that has a key or relative record number equal to or greater than the search key (Factor 1 item) value.

```
              00004 ─┐
                     │
                     │  00001HENRY FORD              0104910012000
                     │  00003LOUIS CHEVROLET         0108910300000
positions file here  └─ 00004DODGE BROTHERS          0107911900100
```

Figure 13-11 Coding example and processing logic of the **SETLL** operation.

```
                  00008STANLEY STEAMER                 0112910080040
                  00009HENRY J KAISER                  0110912500000
                  00010JOHN STUDEBAKER                 0112910067400
                  00011WALTER P CHRYSLER               0106910708500
                  00018RANSOM E OLDS                   0115910095000
                  00019MERCEDES BENZ                   0118919001000
                  00020FELIX WANKEL                    0122910050123

Sequential processing of the file from the SETLL position to an upper limit,
end of file, or to the beginning of the file may be controlled by a READ,
READE, READP, or REDPE operation.
```

Figure 13-11 Coding example and processing logic of the **SETLL** operation. (Continued)

The CHAIN *(Random Retrieval from a File)* Operation

The **CHAIN** operation randomly retrieves a record from a physical file based on the key value or relative record number stored in the item specified in *Factor 1* of the instruction. Figure 13-12 details the syntax of the **CHAIN** operation. Note that the retrieved record is

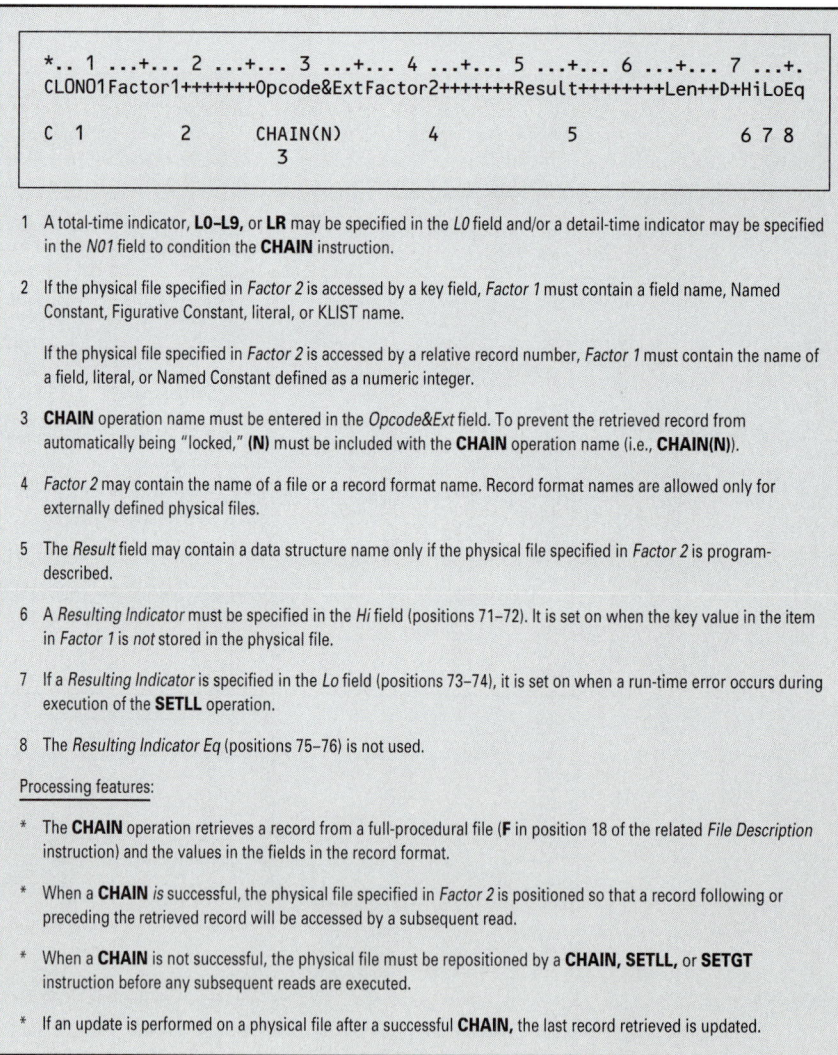

```
*.. 1 ...+... 2 ...+... 3 ...+... 4 ...+... 5 ...+... 6 ...+... 7 ...+.
CLON01Factor1+++++++Opcode&ExtFactor2+++++++Result++++++++Len++D+HiLoEq

C  1          2        CHAIN(N)       4             5               6 7 8
                          3
```

1 A total-time indicator, **L0–L9,** or **LR** may be specified in the *L0* field and/or a detail-time indicator may be specified in the *N01* field to condition the **CHAIN** instruction.

2 If the physical file specified in *Factor 2* is accessed by a key field, *Factor 1* must contain a field name, Named Constant, Figurative Constant, literal, or KLIST name.

If the physical file specified in *Factor 2* is accessed by a relative record number, *Factor 1* must contain the name of a field, literal, or Named Constant defined as a numeric integer.

3 **CHAIN** operation name must be entered in the *Opcode&Ext* field. To prevent the retrieved record from automatically being "locked," **(N)** must be included with the **CHAIN** operation name (i.e., **CHAIN(N)**).

4 *Factor 2* may contain the name of a file or a record format name. Record format names are allowed only for externally defined physical files.

5 The *Result* field may contain a data structure name only if the physical file specified in *Factor 2* is program-described.

6 A *Resulting Indicator* must be specified in the *Hi* field (positions 71–72). It is set on when the key value in the item in *Factor 1* is *not* stored in the physical file.

7 If a *Resulting Indicator* is specified in the *Lo* field (positions 73–74), it is set on when a run-time error occurs during execution of the **SETLL** operation.

8 The *Resulting Indicator Eq* (positions 75–76) is not used.

Processing features:

* The **CHAIN** operation retrieves a record from a full-procedural file (**F** in position 18 of the related *File Description* instruction) and the values in the fields in the record format.
* When a **CHAIN** *is* successful, the physical file specified in *Factor 2* is positioned so that a record following or preceding the retrieved record will be accessed by a subsequent read.
* When a **CHAIN** is not successful, the physical file must be repositioned by a **CHAIN, SETLL,** or **SETGT** instruction before any subsequent reads are executed.
* If an update is performed on a physical file after a successful **CHAIN,** the last record retrieved is updated.

Figure 13-12 Syntax and processing features of the **CHAIN** operation.

automatically "locked" until the next file processing instruction is executed for the file. To prevent a record "lock," (**N**) must be specified as an extension to the **CHAIN** operation name.

An example of the **CHAIN** instruction is shown in Figure 13-13. Note that the value stored in the search argument must be a key or relative record number.

```
*.. 1 ...+... 2 ...+... 3 ...+... 4 ...+... 5 ...+... 6 ...+... 7 ...+.
CLON01Factor1+++++++Opcode&ExtFactor2+++++++Result++++++++Len++D+HiLoEq

C      Keyfld        CHAIN     PFFile                     ┌──────────90
         │                       │                        │
         └ Search Argument       └ File or record         └ Indicator is set
                                   name                     on if a matching
                                                            key is not found
                                                            in the file
```

Figure 13-13 Example **CHAIN** instruction.

The UPDATE *(Modify Existing Record)* Operation

The **UPDATE** operation writes the last record retrieved for processing from a physical file defined as update (**U** in position 17 of the related *File Description* instruction) back to the file. Figure 13-14 details the syntax for the **UPDATE** operation.

```
*.. 1 ...+... 2 ...+... 3 ...+... 4 ...+... 5 ...+... 6 ...+... 7 ...+.
CLON01Factor1+++++++Opcode&ExtFactor2+++++++Result++++++++Len++D+HiLoEq

C  1          2      UPDATE           4             5                 6
                       3
```

1 A total-time indicator, **L0–L9,** or **LR** may be specified in the *L0* field and/or a detail-time indicator may be specified in the *N01* field to condition the **UPDATE** instruction.

2 *Factor 1* is not used.

3 **UPDATE** operation name must be entered in the *Opcode&Ext* field.

4 If the physical file to be updated is externally described, a record name must be specified in *Factor 2.* A file name is required if the physical file is program-described.

5 The *Result* field may contain a data structure name only if the physical file specified in *Factor 2* is program-described. No entry is allowed if a record name is specified in *Factor 2.*

6 A *Resulting Indicator* must be specified in the *Lo* field (positions 73–74). It is set on if an error occurs when an update to the file is executed.

Processing Features:

* Before an **UPDATE** instruction is executed, a successful **CHAIN, READ, READE, READP,** or **READPE** instruction must have retrieved the record to be updated. The record retrieved must have been "locked."

* When a record format name is specified in *Factor 2,* all of the fields in it are automatically updated. If only select fields are to be changed, the update process must be controlled by *Output Specification* instructions.

* Consecutive **UPDATE** instructions are not supported. Intervening **CHAIN** or one of the **READ** operations must be executed first.

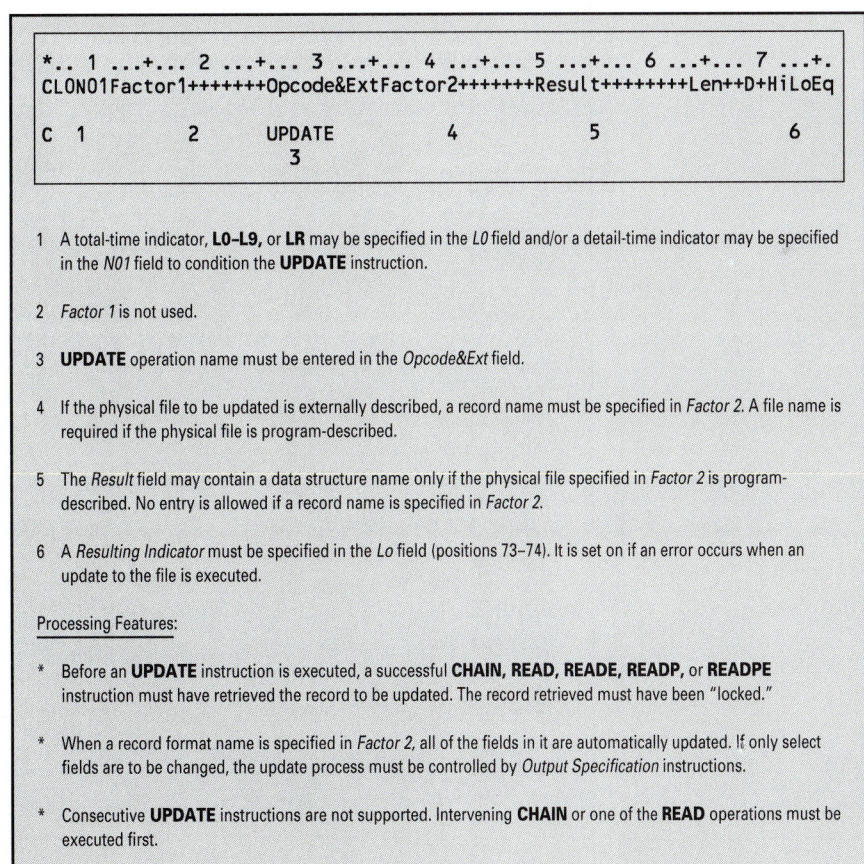

Figure 13-14 Syntax and processing features of the **UPDATE** operation.

An example **UPDATE** instruction is shown in Figure 13-15.

```
*.. 1 ...+... 2 ...+... 3 ...+... 4 ...+... 5 ...+... 6 ...+... 7 ...+.
CLON01Factor1+++++++Opcode&ExtFactor2+++++++Result++++++++Len++D+HiLoEq

C                   UPDATE    PFRecord                               92

                              Record or file          Indicator is set
                              name                    on if a runtime
                                                      error occurs

  * If a file name is specified in Factor 1, a data structure name
    must be entered in the Result field.
```

Figure 13-15 Example **UPDATE** instruction.

RPG IV Example Update Program

The specifications for an **RPG IV** program that updates records in a physical file are presented in Figure 13-16.

PROGRAM SPECIFICATIONS — Page 1 of 1

Program Name: Master File Update — Program - ID: CH13P2 — Written by: SM

Purpose: Update records in a customer master file — Approved by: CM

Input files: CH13UPS (nonkeyed) CH13MSTR (keyed/unique)

Output files: CH13MSTR (keyed/unique) CH13ERRS (nonkeyed)

Processing Requirements:

Write an **RPG IV** program to update records in a customer master file and add transaction records that do not have a matching master record to an error file.

Input to the Program:

An externally defined, nonkeyed phsyical file CH13UPS contains data records with update information. Because the master file (CH13MSTR) must be defined as an update file, the file is automatically processed as both input and output.

Processing:

Read the transaction file (CH13UPS) in arrival sequence until end of file. For every record processed, CHAIN to the customer master file CH13MSTR with the customer number field (UACT#) from the transaction file.

For a successful CHAIN, move the transaction field values in UCODE, UNAME, and UAMT to their related master record fields. Before the UNAME field value is moved, however, test it for blanks. If it tests as blank, do not move the value to the master record field. Also, move the value in UDATE to the related master record field.

In the event of an unsuccessful CHAIN, move all of the transaction record field values to the related fields in the error file (CH13ERRS) and add the record to the error file.

Output:

Update the master file with the updated record. Add error records to the error file.

Figure 13-16 Specifications for an **RPG IV** program that updates records in a physical file.

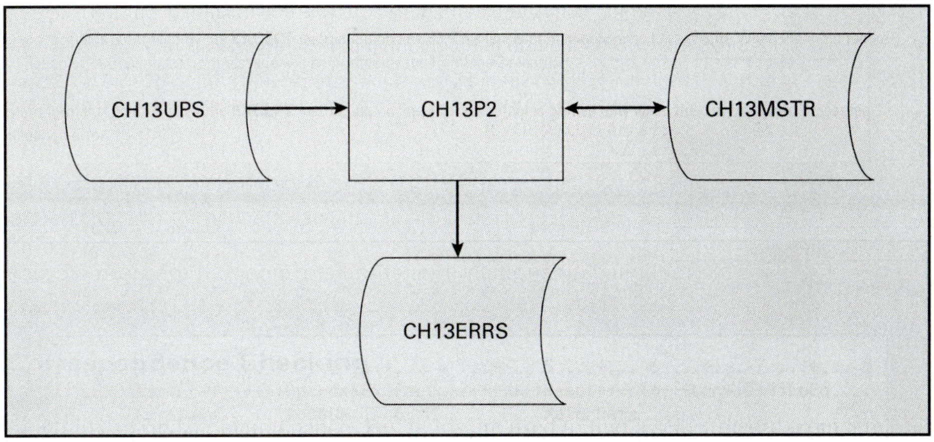

Figure 13-17 System flowchart for the "update" program.

The system flowchart in Figure 13-17 shows that three physical files are processed by the "update" program: a transaction file (CH13UPS) that contains the "update" data; a master file (CH13MSTR) in which the records are updated; and an error file (CH13ERRS) where transaction records that do not have a matching master file record are written. Note that the double-headed arrow from the **RPG IV** program to the CH13MSTR file indicates that the file is input to the program and also output (a file defined as update).

A partial compile listing of the Ch13UPS file and a **CPYF** utility listing of the data in hexadecimal format are shown in Figure 13-18.

```
                                             Data Description Source
SEQNBR  *...+....1....+....2....+....3....+....4....+....5....+....6....+
  100        A              R UPDRCD
  200        A                UCODE          1
  300        A                UACT#          5
  400        A                UNAME         30
  500        A                UDAT           6 0
  600        A                UAMT           7 2
```

```
RCDNBR  *...+... 1 ...+... 2 ...+... 3 ...+... 4 ...
     1  U00020                                  " &
        EFFFFF44444444444444444444444444444403170513
        400020000000000000000000000000000000009F002D
     2  U00011                                  "   |
        EFFFFF44444444444444444444444444444403070004
        400011000000000000000000000000000000019F000F
     3  U00001EDSEL FORD II                    r"
        EFFFFFCCECD4CDDC4CC4444444444444444403970000
        400001542530669409900000000000000000019F000F
     4  U00018                                 r"
        EFFFFF44444444444444444444444444444403970000
        400018000000000000000000000000000000029F050F
     5  U00017                                  "
        EFFFFF44444444444444444444444444444403170100
        400017000000000000000000000000000000039F000F
     6  U00005                                  "   b1/4
        EFFFFF44444444444444444444444444444403070085
        400005000000000000000000000000000000039F072F
```

Figure 13-18 Listing of the Ch13UPS file's DDS and hexadecimal listing of the data.

Hexadecimal listings of the CH13MSTR file *before* and *after* updating (execution of the Ch13P2 program) are presented in Figure 13-19.

Before Updating:

Name field changed

```
RCDNBR  *...+.|. 1 ...+... 2 ...+... 3 ...+|.. 4 ...
     1   00001HENRY FORD                      ñ¬
        4FFFFFCCDDE4CDDC444444444444444444401470100
        0000018559806694000000000000000000009F020F
    11  A00002STUTZ BEARCAT                   ¬ ä
        CFFFFFEEEEE4CCCDCCE44444444444444444402171400
        1000022343902519313000000000000000000009F635F
     2   00003LOUIS CHEVROLET                 i¬
        4FFFFFDDECE4CCCEDDDCE444444444444444401870000
        0000033649203855963530000000000000000009F300F
     3   00004DODGE BROTHERS                  `¬
        4FFFFFCDCCC4CDDECCDE444444444444444401771010
        0000044647502963859200000000000000000009F900F
    12  A000060TTO DIESEL                     ß¬ c&
        CFFFFFDEED4CCCECD444444444444444444402570850
        1000066336049525300000000000000000000009F030F
     4   00008STANLEY STEAMER                 ¬
        4FFFFFEECDDCE4EECCDCD444444444444444401270800
        0000082315358023514590000000000000000019F004F
     5   00009HENRY J KAISER                  ¬
        4FFFFFCCDDE4D4DCCECD444444444444444401072000
        0000098559801021925900000000000000000019F500F
     6   00010JOHN STUDEBAKER                 ¬ Å
        4FFFFFDDCD4EEECCCCDCD444444444444444401270640
        0000101685023445212590000000000000000019F070F
     7   00011WALTER P CHRYSLER               Ñ¬
        4FFFFFECDECD4D4CCDEEDCD44444444444444401670050
        0000116133590703898235900000000000000009F780F
    14  A00017HAROLD WINSTON                  Ñ¬
        CFFFFFCCDDDC4ECDEEDD4444444444444444402670100
        1000178196340695236500000000000000000029F000F
     8   00018RANSON E OLDS                   ß¬
        4FFFFFDCDEDD4C4DDCE44444444444444444401570900
        0000189152650506342000000000000000000019F050F
     9   00019MERCEDES BENZ                   i¬°
        4FFFFFDCDCCCCE4CCDE44444444444444444401879000
        0000194593545202559000000000000000000019F010F
    10   00020FELIX WANKEL                    ¬
        4FFFFFCCDCE4ECDDCD444444444444444444401270513
        0000206539706152530000000000000000000029F002F
    13  A00023FERDINAND PORCHE                Ñ¬   ¬
        CFFFFFCCDCCDCDC4DDDCCC444444444444402670815
        1000236594951540769385000000000000000029F402F
```

After Updating:

```
RCDNBR  *...+.|. 1 ...+... 2 ...+... 3 ...+|.. 4 ...
     1  U00001EDSEL FORD II                   `
        EFFFFFCCECD4CDDC4CC444444444444444444403170100
        4000015425306694099000000000000000000009F020F
    11  A00002STUTZ BEARCAT                   ¬ ä
        CFFFFFEEEEE4CCCDCCE44444444444444444402171400
        1000022343902519313000000000000000000009F635F
     2   00003LOUIS CHEVROLET                 i¬
        4FFFFFDDECE4CCCEDDDCE444444444444444401870000
        0000033649203855963530000000000000000009F300F
     3   00004DODGE BROTHERS                  `¬
        4FFFFFCDCCC4CDDECCDE444444444444444401771010
        0000044647502963859200000000000000000009F900F
    12  A000060TTO DIESEL                     ß¬ c&
        CFFFFFDEED4CCCECD444444444444444444402570850
        1000066336049525300000000000000000000009F030F
     4   00008STANLEY STEAMER                 ¬
        4FFFFFEECDDCE4EECCDCD444444444444444401270800
        0000082315358023514590000000000000000019F004F
     5   00009HENRY J KAISER                  ¬
        4FFFFFCCDDE4D4DCCECD444444444444444401072000
        0000098559801021925900000000000000000019F500F
     6   00010JOHN STUDEBAKER                 ¬ Å
        4FFFFFDDCD4EEECCCCDCD444444444444444401270640
        0000101685023445212590000000000000000019F070F
     7  U00011WALTER P CHRYSLER               `
        EFFFFFECDECD4D4CCDEEDCD44444444444444403170054
        4000116133590703898235900000000000000009F780F
    14  U00017HAROLD WINSTON                  `
        EFFFFFCCDDDC4ECDEEDD4444444444444444403170200
        4000178196340695236500000000000000000009F000F
     8  U00018RANSON E OLDS                   `
        EFFFFFDCDEDD4C4DDCE44444444444444444403170000
        4000189152650506342000000000000000000009F100F
     9   00019MERCEDES BENZ                   i¬°
        4FFFFFDCDCCCCE4CCDE44444444444444444401879000
        0000194593545202559000000000000000000019F010F
    10  U00020FELIX WANKEL                    `
        EFFFFFCCDCE4ECDDCD444444444444444444403190000
        4000206539706152530000000000000000000009F000F
    13  A00023FERDINAND PORCHE                Ñ¬   ¬
        CFFFFFCCDCCDCDC4DDDCCC444444444444402670815
        1000236594951540769385000000000000000029F402F
```

Records that have been updated have a U in column 1

Date field was changed to UPDATE value for all updated records

MAMT field values changed for updated records

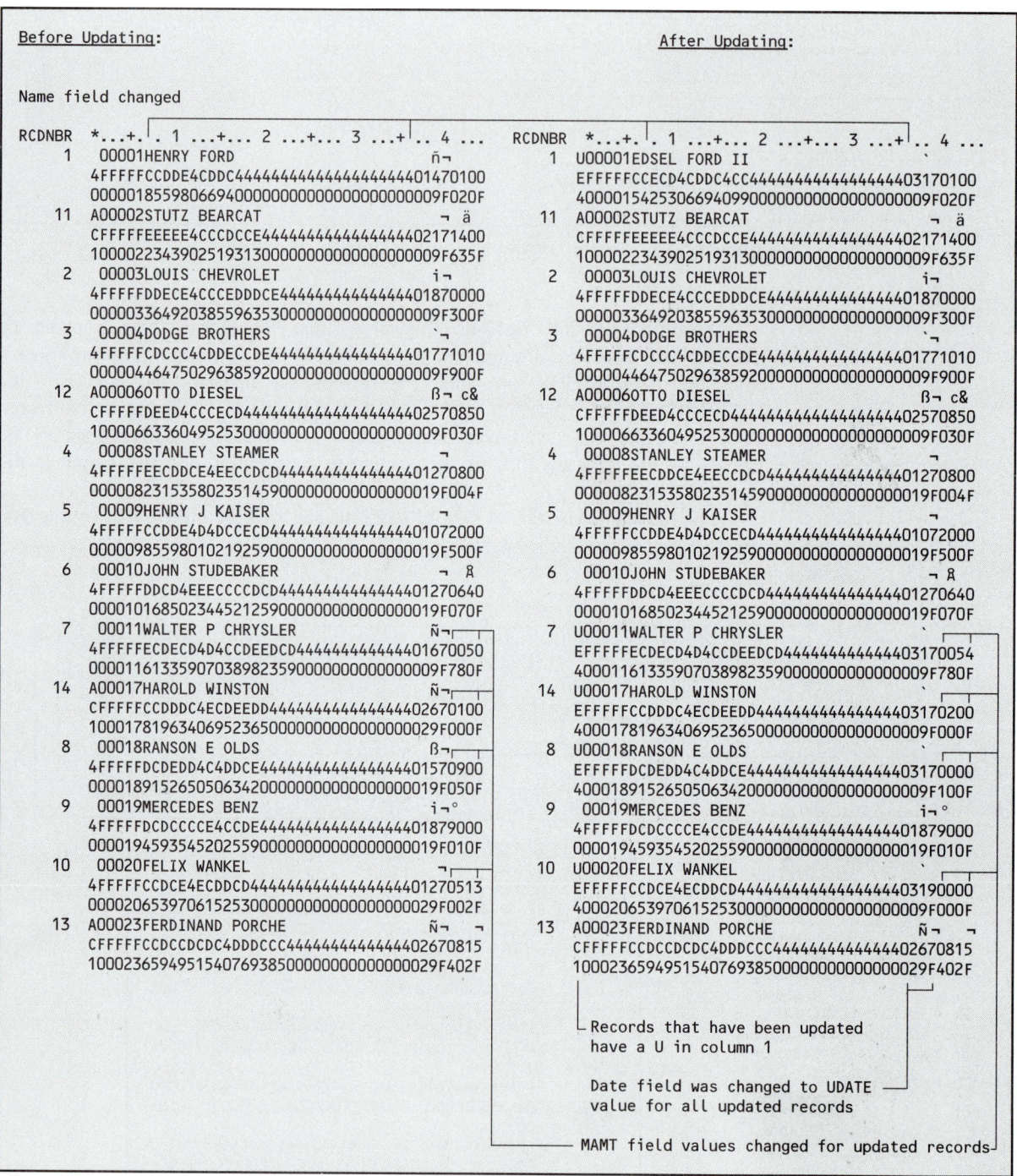

Figure 13-19 Hexadecimal listings of CH13MSTR file *before* and *after* updating.

A **CPYF** hexadecimal listing of the Ch13ERRS file after execution of the update program is shown in Figure 13-20.

```
RCDNBR  *...+... 1 ...+... 2 ...+... 3 ...+... 4 ...
     1  A00002HENRY KAISER                       ¬ &   ┬─ Error records (duplicate keys)
        CFFFFFCCDDE4DCCECD444444444444444444402072500  │  previously added by the "adds"
        1000028559802192590000000000000000000019F700F  │  program
     2  A00018RANSON E OLDS                      i¬ °⊥─┘
        CFFFFFDCDEDD4C4DDCE44444444444444444402870909
        1000189152650506342000000000000000000029F008F
     3  U00005                                   ¬  b¬ ── Error record (master record not
        EFFFFF444444444444444444444444444444403070085      found) added by the "update"
        400005000000000000000000000000000000000039F072F    program
```

Figure 13-20 **CPYF** utility listing in hexadecimal format of the Ch13ERRS file after execution of the update program.

RPG IV UPDATE Program Coding

A detailed compile listing of the **RPG IV** update program is presented in Figure 13-21.

```
Line   <---------------------- Source Specifications ----------------------------><---- Comments ----> Do
Number ....1....+....2....+....3....+....4....+....5....+....6....+....7....+....8....+....9....+...10 Num
                      S o u r c e   L i s t i n g
     1  * This program updates records in a existing physical file from a
     2  * transaction physical file defined as nonkeyed.  Transaction records
     3  * not found in the master file are written to an error file in the
     4  * same format as the transaction file.
     5
     6 FCh13ups   IF   E             DISK
        *--------------------------------------------------------------------------------------------*
        *                                RPG name           External name                          *
        * File name. . . . . . . . . :  CH13UPS            STAN/CH13UPS                           *
        * Record format(s) . . . . . :  UPDRCD             UPDRCD                                 *
        *--------------------------------------------------------------------------------------------*
     7 FCh13mstr  UF   E           K DISK ──────── Defined as update - U in position 17
        *--------------------------------------------------------------------------------------------*
        *                                RPG name           External name                          *
        * File name. . . . . . . . . :  CH13MSTR           STAN/CH13MSTR                          *
        * Record format(s) . . . . . :  MSTRRCD            MSTRRCD                                *
        *--------------------------------------------------------------------------------------------*
     8 FCh13errs  O    A E           DISK
     9
        *--------------------------------------------------------------------------------------------*
        *                                RPG name           External name                          *
        * File name. . . . . . . . . :  CH13ERRS           STAN/CH13ERRS                          *
        * Record format(s) . . . . . :  ERRRCD             ERRRCD                                 *
        *--------------------------------------------------------------------------------------------*
    10=IUPDRCD
        *--------------------------------------------------------------------------------------------*
        * RPG record format  . . . . :  UPDRCD                                                    *
        * External format  . . . . . :  UPDRCD : STAN/CH13UPS                                     *
        *--------------------------------------------------------------------------------------------*
    11=I                                 A    1    1  UCODE
    12=I                                 A    2    6  UACT#
    13=I                                 A    7   36  UNAME
    14=I                                 P   37   40 0UDAT
    15=I                                 P   41   44 2UAMT
    16=IMSTRRCD
        *--------------------------------------------------------------------------------------------*
        * RPG record format  . . . . :  MSTRRCD                                                   *
        * External format  . . . . . :  MSTRRCD : STAN/CH13MSTR                                   *
        *--------------------------------------------------------------------------------------------*
```

Figure 13-21 Compile listing of the update program.

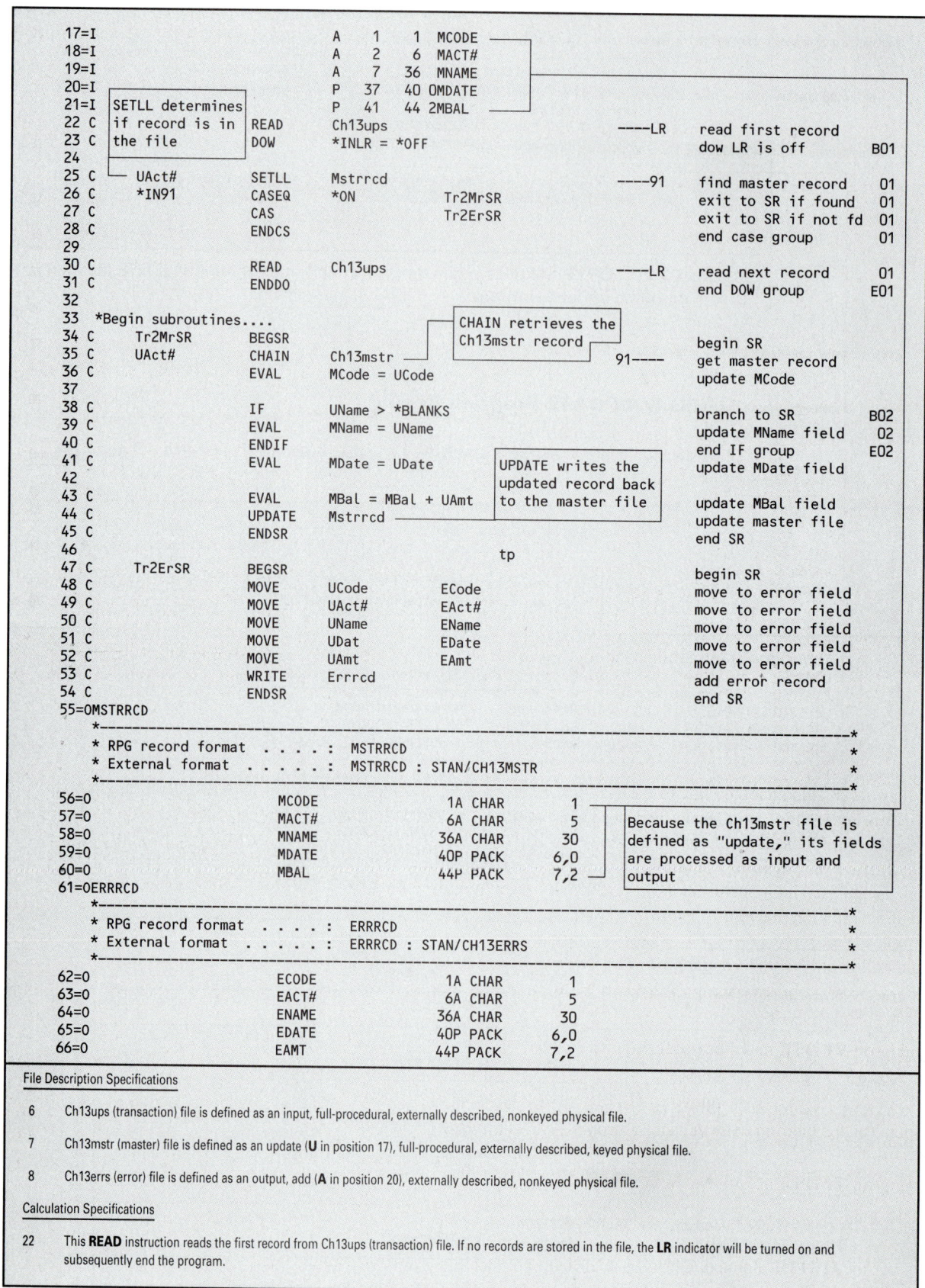

```
17=I                                      A    1    1 MCODE
18=I                                      A    2    6 MACT#
19=I                                      A    7   36 MNAME
20=I                                      P   37   40 0MDATE
21=I                                      P   41   44 2MBAL
22 C                           READ       Ch13ups                 ----LR    read first record
23 C                           DOW        *INLR = *OFF                      dow LR is off         B01
24
25 C        UAct#              SETLL      Mstrrcd                 ----91    find master record    01
26 C        *IN91              CASEQ      *ON          Tr2MrSR              exit to SR if found   01
27 C                           CAS                     Tr2ErSR              exit to SR if not fd  01
28 C                           ENDCS                                        end case group        01
29
30 C                           READ       Ch13ups                 ----LR    read next record      01
31 C                           ENDDO                                        end DOW group         E01
32
33  *Begin subroutines....
34 C      Tr2MrSR              BEGSR                                        begin SR
35 C      UAct#                CHAIN      Ch13mstr                91----    get master record
36 C                           EVAL       MCode = UCode                     update MCode
37
38 C                           IF         UName > *BLANKS                   branch to SR          B02
39 C                           EVAL       MName = UName                     update MName field    02
40 C                           ENDIF                                        end IF group          E02
41 C                           EVAL       MDate = UDate                     update MDate field
42
43 C                           EVAL       MBal = MBal + UAmt                update MBal field
44 C                           UPDATE     Mstrrcd                           update master file
45 C                           ENDSR                                        end SR
46                                                          tp
47 C      Tr2ErSR              BEGSR                                        begin SR
48 C                           MOVE       UCode        ECode                move to error field
49 C                           MOVE       UAct#        EAct#                move to error field
50 C                           MOVE       UName        EName                move to error field
51 C                           MOVE       UDat         EDate                move to error field
52 C                           MOVE       UAmt         EAmt                 move to error field
53 C                           WRITE      Errrcd                            add error record
54 C                           ENDSR                                        end SR
55=OMSTRRCD
   *------------------------------------------------------------------------------*
   * RPG record format . . . . :  MSTRRCD                                         *
   * External format . . . . . :  MSTRRCD : STAN/CH13MSTR                         *
   *------------------------------------------------------------------------------*
56=O                      MCODE             1A CHAR        1
57=O                      MACT#             6A CHAR        5
58=O                      MNAME            36A CHAR       30
59=O                      MDATE            40P PACK      6,0
60=O                      MBAL             44P PACK      7,2
61=OERRRCD
   *------------------------------------------------------------------------------*
   * RPG record format . . . . :  ERRRCD                                          *
   * External format . . . . . :  ERRRCD : STAN/CH13ERRS                          *
   *------------------------------------------------------------------------------*
62=O                      ECODE             1A CHAR        1
63=O                      EACT#             6A CHAR        5
64=O                      ENAME            36A CHAR       30
65=O                      EDATE            40P PACK      6,0
66=O                      EAMT             44P PACK      7,2
```

SETLL determines if record is in the file

CHAIN retrieves the Ch13mstr record

UPDATE writes the updated record back to the master file

Because the Ch13mstr file is defined as "update," its fields are processed as input and output

File Description Specifications

6 Ch13ups (transaction) file is defined as an input, full-procedural, externally described, nonkeyed physical file.

7 Ch13mstr (master) file is defined as an update (**U** in position 17), full-procedural, externally described, keyed physical file.

8 Ch13errs (error) file is defined as an output, add (**A** in position 20), externally described, nonkeyed physical file.

Calculation Specifications

22 This **READ** instruction reads the first record from Ch13ups (transaction) file. If no records are stored in the file, the **LR** indicator will be turned on and subsequently end the program.

Figure 13-21 Compile listing of the update program. (Continued)

23	The **DOW** instruction tests the status of the **LR** indicator. If **LR** is not "on," the iterative process will continue. When end of the Ch13ups file is read, **LR** will be turned on and control will branch out of the **DOW** group to line 32 and end the program.
25	The **SETLL** instruction determines if the key value in the UAct# field is found in the Ch13mstr file. If a record with the UAct# value is found in the Ch13mstr file, indicator **91** will be turned on. Note that the **SETLL** operation does *not* extract the record for processing.
26	If a record is found in the Ch13mstr file (indicator **91** "on"), this **CASEQ** instruction transfers control to the Tr2MrSr subroutine, where the UPDRCD field values are moved into the MSTRRCD fields.
27	If a record is not found in the Ch13mstr file (indicator **91** "off"), this **CAS** instruction transfers control to the TR2ErSR subroutine, where the UPDRCD field values are moved into the ERRRCD fields.
28	The **ENDCS** operation ends the case group.
30	This **READ** instruction reads the next record from the Ch13ups file. If end of file is read, the **LR** indicator will be turned on. When control returns to the **DOW** instruction on line 23, control will exit from the **DOW** group and end the proram.
31	The **ENDDO** operation ends the **DOW** group.
34	This **BEGSR** instruction begins the Tr2MrSR subroutine, which was accessed by the **CASEQ** instruction on line 26.
35	The record with the key value stored in the UAct# field is extracted from the Ch13mstr file by the **CHAIN** instruction. Indicator **91** will be turned on if the record is *not* found in the Ch13mstr file. Recall that the **SETLL** instruction on line 25 previously determined if the record was stored in the Ch13mstr file. However, for the **CHAIN** instruction to be syntactically correct, an indicator must be specified in the *Hi* field (positions 71–72).
36	This **EVAL** instruction stores the UCode field value in the MCode field.
38–39	The **IF** instruction tests the UName field for a blank value. If the value is greater than ***BLANK,** the **EVAL** instruction on line 39 will store the UName value in the MName field.
40	The **ENDIF** operation ends the **IF** group.
41	This **EVAL** instruction stores the Udate (system date) value in the MDate field.
43	This **EVAL** instruction adds the UAmt field value to the beginning MBAL field value.
44	The **UPDATE** instruction updates the current Mstrrcd with the new field values.
45	This **ENDSR** operation ends the Tr2MrSR subroutine.
47	This **BEGSR** instruction begins the Tr2ErSR subroutine, which was accessed by the **CAS** instruction on line 27 (no Ch13mstr record found).
48–52	This group of **MOVE** instructions moves the field values from the UPDRCD record to the ERRRCD fields.
53	The **WRITE** instruction adds the current ERRRCD to the Ch13errs file.
54	This **ENDSR** operation ends the Tr2ErSR subroutine.
Note:	Observe that no programmer-supplied output instructions are specified in this **RPG IV** program. Because the Ch13mstr file is defined as update and the Ch13errs file as output, the compiler supplied the output record descriptions (i.e., lines 55=MSTRRCD through 66=0).

Figure 13-21 Compile listing of the update program. (Continued)

DELETION OF RECORDS IN A PHYSICAL FILE

Tagging Records for Deletion

Tagging records for deletion is an update process that stores a character in a field in the body of a record. Identical to updating, the record must be retrieved by a **CHAIN** or one of the **READ** operations, a character moved into the delete field, and the record written back to its original storage position in the file. Programs that access the file usually test the related field for the delete character to avoid processing (or sometimes, to process) records *tagged* as deleted. Refer to the previously discussed update program for the syntax needed to *tag* records in a physical file as deleted.

Logical Deletion of Records

Unlike the tagging method, *logical deletion* permanently removes the record from a physical file. The syntax of the **DELETE** operation, which is used to delete records logically, is explained in Figure 13-22.

```
*.. 1 ...+... 2 ...+... 3 ...+... 4 ...+... 5 ...+... 6 ...+... 7 ...+.
CLON01Factor1+++++++Opcode&ExtFactor2+++++++Result++++++++Len++D+HiLoEq

C  1           2       DELETE          4              5            6 7
                         3
```

1 A total-time indicator, **L0–L9,** or **LR** may be specified in the *L0* field and/or a detail-time indicator may be specified in the *N01* field to condition the **DELETE** instruction.

2 *Factor 1* may have an entry, or for keyed files, it may include a field name, named constant, literal, or a **KLIST** name. If the file is accessed by relative record number, *Factor 1* must contain a numeric literal or a variable with no decimal positions.

3 **DELETE** operation name must be entered in the *Opcode&Ext* field.

4 If the physical file to be updated is externally described, a record name must be specified in *Factor 2.* A file name is required if the physical file is program-described. If *Factor 1* is not specified, a record format name (only for externally described file) must be entered in *Factor 2.*

5 The *Result* field is not used.

6 If *Factor 1* has an entry, a *Resulting Indicator* must be entered in the *Hi* field (positions 71 and 72). If *Factor 1* does not have an entry, no indicator is permitted in positions 71–72.

7 A *Resulting Indicator* may be specified in the *Lo* field (positions 73–74), which will turn on if the **DELETE** instruction is not completed successfully.

Processing features:

* Before a **DELETE** instruction is executed, a successful **CHAIN, READ, READE, READP,** or **READPE** instruction must have retrieved the record to be updated. The record retrieved must have been "locked."

* If *Factor 1* has an entry, the record accessed by the **DELETE** instruction will be logically deleted.

* The physical file in which the records are to be logically deleted must be defined as an update file (**U** in position 17 of the related *File Description* instruction).

* If a **READ** operation is immediately executed on the physical file in which a **DELETE** instruction was successfully completed, the next record is accessed.

Figure 13-22 Syntax and processing features of the **DELETE** operation.

An example **DELETE** instruction is shown in Figure 13-23. Because access to an externally described file is assumed, *Factor 1* is not used and the file's record format name is specified in *Factor 2.*

```
*.. 1 ...+... 2 ...+... 3 ...+... 4 ...+... 5 ...+... 6 ...+... 7 ...+.
CLON01Factor1+++++++Opcode&ExtFactor2+++++++Result++++++++Len++D+HiLoEq
                                                                  9192
C                    DELETE    PFRecord

When Factor 1 has no           Record name for externally
entry, record to be            described files or a file
logically deleted must         name for program-described files
have been retrieved by a
CHAIN or one of the read
operations

Indicator must be specified if Factor 1 has an entry. It is
turned on if the related record is not found in the file

Optional indicator is turned on if the DELETE instruction did
not complete successfully
```

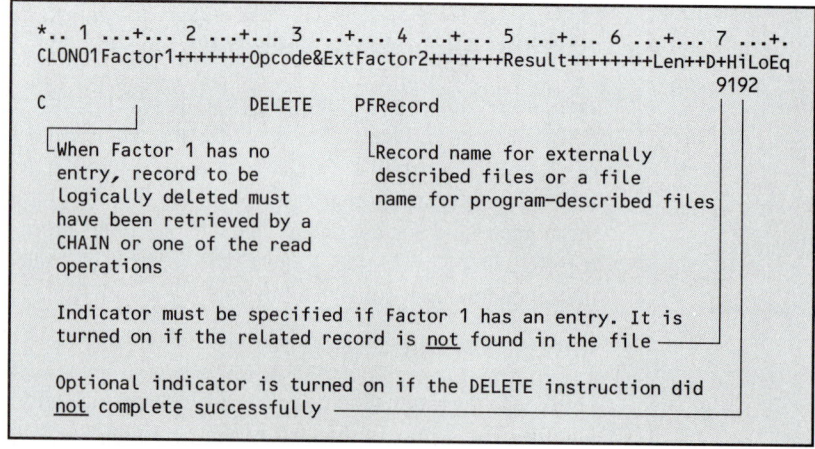

Figure 13-23 Example **DELETE** instruction.

RPG IV Example DELETE (Logical) Program

The specifications for an **RPG IV** program that logically deletes record in a physical file are presented in Figure 13-24.

PROGRAM SPECIFICATIONS — Page 1 of 1

Program Name: Master File Delete — Program-ID: CH13P3 — Written by: SM

Purpose: Logically delete records in a customer mstr file — Approved by: CM

Input files: CH13DLTS (nonkeyed) — CH13MSTR (keyed/unique)

Output files: CH13MSTR (keyed/unique) — CH13ERRS (nonkeyed)

Processing Requirements:

Write an **RPG IV** program to logically delete records in a customer master file and add transaction records that do not have a matching master record to an error file.

Input to the Program:

An externally defined, nonkeyed physical file CH13DLTS contains data records with keys of records in the master file which are to be logically deleted. Because the master file (CH13MSTR) must be defined as update, it is automatically processed as input and output.

Processing:

Read the transaction file (CH13DLTS) in arrival sequence until end of file. For every record processed, CHAIN to the customer master file CH13MSTR with the customer number field (DACT#) from the transaction file.

For a successful CHAIN, execute a **DELETE** statement to logically delete the record in the related master file.

In the event of an unsuccessful CHAIN, move all of the transaction record field values to the related fields in the error file (CH13ERRS) and add the record to the error file.

Output:

Logically delete the master file record based on the key value in the transaction file. Add any transaction records without a matching master file record to the error file (CH13ERRS).

Figure 13-24 Specifications for an **RPG IV** program that logically deletes records in a physical file.

The system flowchart in Figure 13-25 indicates that three physical files are processed by the example program: a transaction file (CH13DLTS) that includes keys for the records to be logically deleted; the master file (CH13MSTR) in which records are to be logically deleted; and an error file (CH13ERRS) where transaction records that do not have a matching master record are added.

The record format of the transaction file (CH13DLTS) and a listing of the stored data are shown in Figure 13-26.

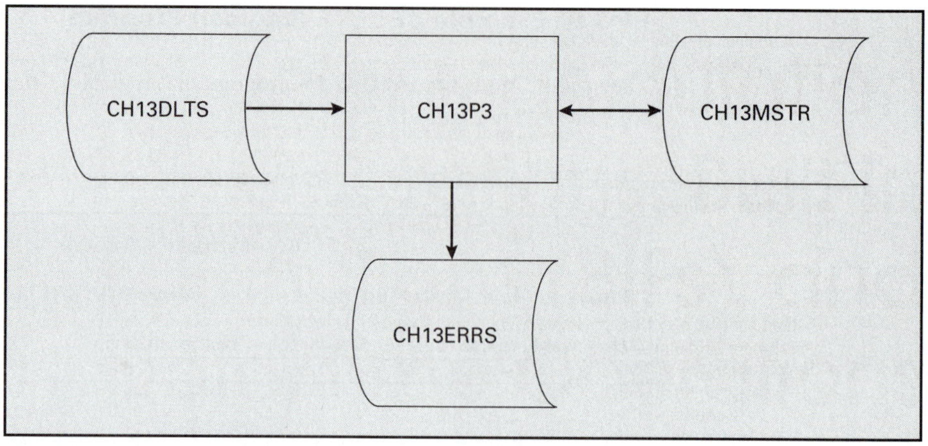

Figure 13-25 System flowchart for the **RPG IV** program that logically deletes records from a master file.

```
                             Data Description Source
SEQNBR  *...+....1....+....2....+....3....+....4....+....5....+....6....+
           A            R DLTRCD
           A              DCODE          1
           A              DACT#          5
```

```
RCDNBR  *...+.
     1  D00020
        CFFFFF
        400020
     2  D00001
        CFFFFF
        400001
     3  D00014
        CFFFFF
        400014
```

Figure 13-26 Listing of the transaction file's record format and hexadecimal listing of the data (key values).

Because the record formats of the Ch13MSTR and CH13ERRS files were previously discussed, they are not shown again.

RPG IV Logical Deletes Program Coding

A detailed compile listing of the **RPG IV** program that logically deletes records in an externally described physical file is presented in Figure 13-27.

```
Line   <---------------------- Source Specifications ----------------------------><---- Comments ----> Do
Number ....1....+....2....+....3....+....4....+....5....+....6....+....7....+....8....+....9....+...10 Num
                          S o u r c e   L i s t i n g
       * This program logically deletes records in the Ch13mstr file from a
       * transaction physical file defined as nonkeyed.  Transaction records
       * not found in the master file are written to an error file in the
       * same format as the transaction file.
```

Figure 13-27 Compile listing of a program that logically deletes records in an externally described physical file.

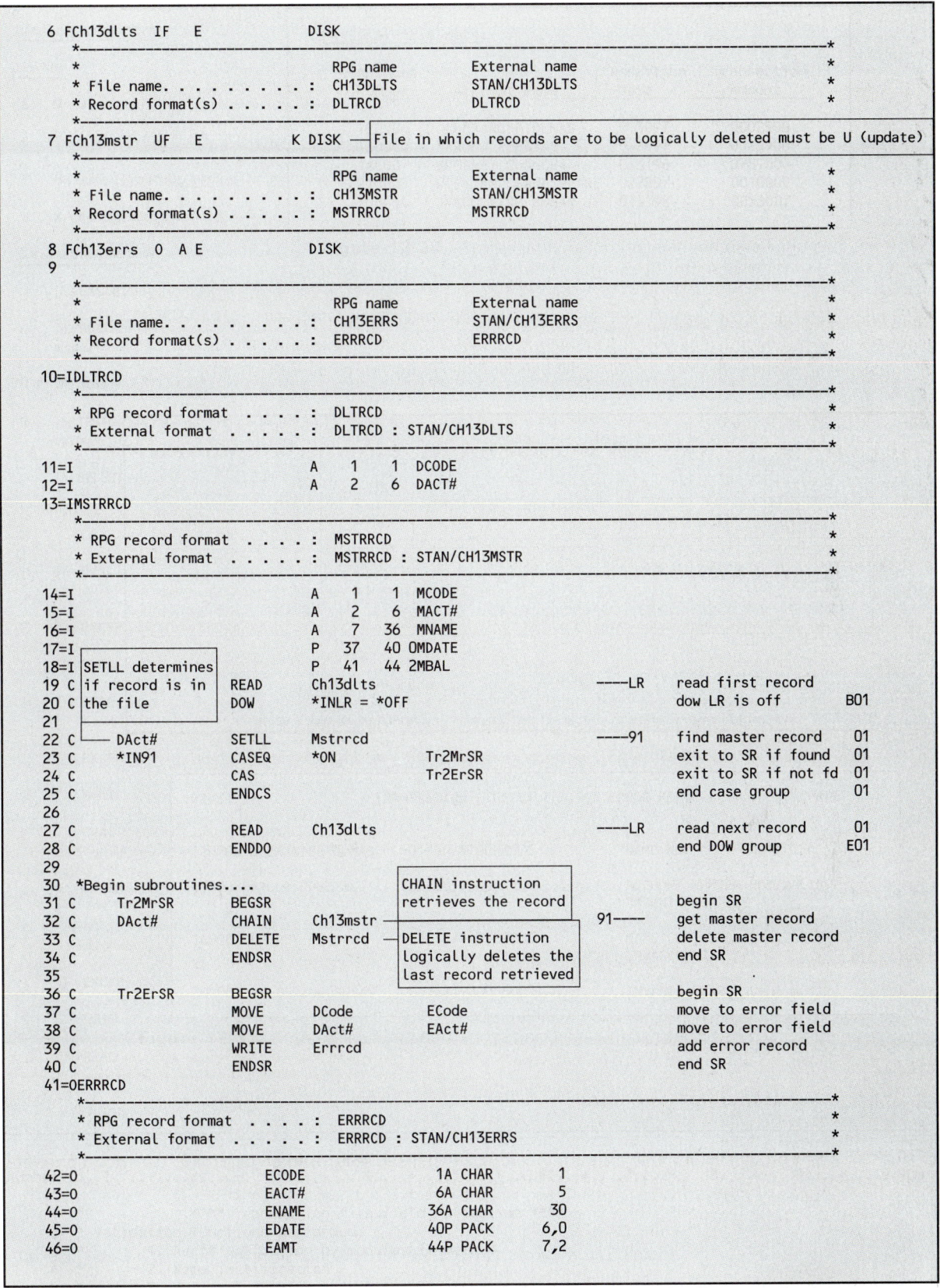

```
 FCh13dlts  IF   E            DISK
  *--------------------------------------------------------------------------*
  *                          RPG name          External name                  *
  * File name. . . . . . . . :  CH13DLTS          STAN/CH13DLTS                *
  * Record format(s) . . . . :  DLTRCD            DLTRCD                       *
  *--------------------------------------------------------------------------*
 FCh13mstr  UF   E          K DISK
  *--------------------------------------------------------------------------*
  *                          RPG name          External name                  *
  * File name. . . . . . . . :  CH13MSTR          STAN/CH13MSTR                *
  * Record format(s) . . . . :  MSTRRCD           MSTRRCD                      *
  *--------------------------------------------------------------------------*
 FCh13errs  O    A E          DISK

  *--------------------------------------------------------------------------*
  *                          RPG name          External name                  *
  * File name. . . . . . . . :  CH13ERRS          STAN/CH13ERRS                *
  * Record format(s) . . . . :  ERRRCD            ERRRCD                       *
  *--------------------------------------------------------------------------*
=IDLTRCD
  *--------------------------------------------------------------------------*
  * RPG record format  . . . . :  DLTRCD                                      *
  * External format  . . . . . :  DLTRCD : STAN/CH13DLTS                      *
  *--------------------------------------------------------------------------*
=I                          A    1    1  DCODE
=I                          A    2    6  DACT#
=IMSTRRCD
  *--------------------------------------------------------------------------*
  * RPG record format  . . . . :  MSTRRCD                                     *
  * External format  . . . . . :  MSTRRCD : STAN/CH13MSTR                     *
  *--------------------------------------------------------------------------*
=I                          A    1    1  MCODE
=I                          A    2    6  MACT#
=I                          A    7   36  MNAME
=I                          P   37   40  0MDATE
=I                          P   41   44  2MBAL
 C                READ      Ch13dlts                    ----LR   read first record
 C                DOW       *INLR = *OFF                         dow LR is off        B01

 C      DAct#     SETLL     Mstrrcd                     ----91   find master record   01
 C      *IN91     CASEQ     *ON           Tr2MrSR                exit to SR if found  01
 C                CAS                     Tr2ErSR                exit to SR if not fd 01
 C                ENDCS                                          end case group       01

 C                READ      Ch13dlts                    ----LR   read next record     01
 C                ENDDO                                          end DOW group        E01

  *Begin subroutines....
 C      Tr2MrSR   BEGSR                                          begin SR
 C      DAct#     CHAIN     Ch13mstr                    91----   get master record
 C                DELETE    Mstrrcd                              delete master record
 C                ENDSR                                          end SR

 C      Tr2ErSR   BEGSR                                          begin SR
 C                MOVE      DCode         ECode                  move to error field
 C                MOVE      DAct#         EAct#                  move to error field
 C                WRITE     Errrcd                               add error record
 C                ENDSR                                          end SR
=OERRRCD
  *--------------------------------------------------------------------------*
  * RPG record format  . . . . :  ERRRCD                                      *
  * External format  . . . . . :  ERRRCD : STAN/CH13ERRS                      *
  *--------------------------------------------------------------------------*
=O                    ECODE           1A  CHAR        1
=O                    EACT#           6A  CHAR        5
=O                    ENAME          36A  CHAR       30
=O                    EDATE          40P  PACK      6,0
=O                    EAMT           44P  PACK      7,2
```

File in which records are to be logically deleted must be U (update)

SETLL determines if record is in the file

CHAIN instruction retrieves the record

DELETE instruction logically deletes the last record retrieved

Figure 13-27 Compile listing of a program that logically deletes records in an externally described physical file. (Continued)

File Description Specifications

6 Ch13dlts (transaction) file is defined as an input, full-procedural, externally described, nonkeyed physical file.

7 Ch13mstr (master) file is defined as an update (**U** in position 17), full-procedural, externally described, keyed physical file.

8 Ch13errs (error) file is defined as an output, add (**A** in position 20), externally described, nonkeyed physical file.

Calculation Specifications

19 This **READ** instruction reads the first record from Ch13dlts (transaction) file. If no records are stored in the file, the **LR** indicator will be turned on and subsequently end the program.

20 The **DOW** instruction tests the status of the **LR** indicator. If **LR** is not "on," the iterative process will continue. When end of the Ch13edlts file is read, **LR** will be turned on and control will branch out of the **DOW** group to line 29 and end the program.

22 The **SETLL** instruction determines if the key value in the DAct# field is found in the Ch13mstr file. If a record with the DAct# value is found in the Ch13mstr file, indicator **91** will be turned on. Note that the **SETLL** operation does *not* extract the record for processing.

23 If a record is found in the Ch13 mstr file (indicator **91** "on"), this **CASEQ** instruction transfers control to the Tr2MrSr subroutine, where the related MSTRRCD record is logically deleted.

24 If a record is not found in the Ch13mstr file (indicator **91** "off"), this **CAS** instruction transfers control to the TR2ErSR subroutine, where the DLTRCD field values are moved into the ERRRCD fields.

25 The **ENDCS** operation ends the case group.

27 This **READ** instruction reads the next record from the Ch13dlts file. If end of file is read, the **LR** indicator will be turned on. When control returns to the **DOW** instruction on line 20, control will exit from the **DOW** group and end the program.

28 The **ENDDO** operation ends the **DOW** group.

31 This **BEGSR** instruction begins the Tr2MrSR subroutine, which was accessed by the **CASEQ** instruction on line 23.

32 The record with the key value stored in the DAct# field is extracted from the Ch13mstr file by the **CHAIN** instruction. Indicator **91** will be turned on if the record is *not* found in the Ch13mstr file. Recall that the **SETLL** instruction on line 22 previously determined if the record was stored in the Ch13mstr file. However, for the **CHAIN** instruction to be syntactically correct, an indicator must be specified in the *Hi* field (positions 71–72).

33 The **DELETE** instruction deletes the MSTRRCD record accessed by the **CHAIN** instruction on line 32. After this instruction is successfully executed, the logically deleted record is no longer available for processing.

34 This **ENDSR** operation ends the Tr2MrSR.

36 This **BEGSR** instruction begins the Tr2ErSR subroutine, which was accessed by the **CAS** instruction on line 24 (no Ch13mstr record found).

37–38 The two **MOVE** instructions move the field values from the UPDRCD record to the related ERRRCD record fields.

39 The **WRITE** instruction adds the current ERRRCD to the Ch13errs file.

40 This **ENDSR** operation ends the Tr2ErSR subroutine.

Figure 13-27 Compile listing of a program that logically deletes records in an externally described physical file. (Continued)

Figure 13-28 shows two **CPYF** hexadecimal listings, one *before* and one *after* records are logically deleted in the Ch13mstr file.

A hexadecimal listing of the Ch13ERRS file after execution of the logical deletion program is shown in Figure 13-29.

```
BEFORE Deleting:

RCDNBR  *...+. . 1 ...+... 2 ...+... 3 ...+ .. 4 ...
   1   00001HENRY FORD                         ñ¬          record deleted
       4FFFFFCCDDE4CDDC4444444444444444444401470100
       0000018559806694000000000000000000000009F020F
  11   A00002STUTZ BEARCAT                      ¬ ä
       CFFFFFEEEEE4CCCDCCE44444444444444444402171400
       1000022343902519313000000000000000000009F635F
   2    00003LOUIS CHEVROLET                   i¬
       4FFFFFDDECE4CCCEDDDCE4444444444444444401870000
       0000033649203855963530000000000000000009F300F
   3    00004DODGE BROTHERS                    `¬
       4FFFFFCDCCC4CDDECCDE444444444444444401771010
       0000044647502963859200000000000000000009F900F
  12   A000060TTO DIESEL                       ß¬ c&
       CFFFFFDEED4CCCECD4444444444444444444402570850
       1000066336049525300000000000000000000009F030F
   4    00008STANLEY STEAMER                    ¬
       4FFFFFEECDDCE4EECCDCD4444444444444401270800
       0000082315358023514590000000000000000019F004F
   5    00009HENRY J KAISER                     ¬
       4FFFFFCCDDE4D4DCCECD444444444444444401072000
       0000098559801021925900000000000000000019F500F
   6    00010JOHN STUDEBAKER                    ¬ Å
       4FFFFFDDCD4EEECCCCDCD444444444444401270640
       0000101685023445212590000000000000000019F070F
   7    00011WALTER P CHRYSLER                 Ñ¬ı   ı
       4FFFFFECDECD4D4CCDEEDCD4444444444401670050
       0000116133590703898235900000000000000009F780F
  14   A00017HAROLD WINSTON                    Ñ¬
       CFFFFFCCDDDC4ECDEEDD444444444444444402670100
       1000178196340695236500000000000000000029F000F
   8    00018RANSON E OLDS                     ß¬
       4FFFFFDCDEDD4C4DDCE444444444444444444401570900
       0000189152650506342000000000000000000019F050F
   9    00019MERCEDES BENZ                     i¬°
       4FFFFFDCDCCCCE4CCDE4444444444444444401879000
       0000194593545202559000000000000000000019F010F
  10    00020FELIX WANKEL                                  record deleted
       4FFFFFCCDCE4ECDDCD44444444444444444401270513
       0000206539706152530000000000000000000029F002F
  13   A00023FERDINAND PORCHE                  Ñ¬
       CFFFFFCCDCCDCDC4DDDCCC4444444444444402670815
       1000236594951540769385000000000000000029F402F

AFTER

RCDNBR  *...+... 1 ...+... 2 ...+... 3 ...+... 4 ...
  11   A00002STUTZ BEARCAT                      ¬ ä
       CFFFFFEEEEE4CCCDCCE44444444444444444402171400
       1000022343902519313000000000000000000009F635F
   2    00003LOUIS CHEVROLET                   i
       4FFFFFDDECE4CCCEDDDCE4444444444444444401870000
       0000033649203855963530000000000000000009F300F
   3    00004DODGE BROTHERS                    `
       4FFFFFCDCCC4CDDECCDE444444444444444401771010
       0000044647502963859200000000000000000009F900F
  12   A000060TTO DIESEL                       ß¬ c&
       CFFFFFDEED4CCCECD4444444444444444444402570850
       1000066336049525300000000000000000000009F030F
   4    00008STANLEY STEAMER
       4FFFFFEECDDCE4EECCDCD4444444444444401270800
       0000082315358023514590000000000000000019F004F
   5    00009HENRY J KAISER
       4FFFFFCCDDE4D4DCCECD444444444444444401072000
       0000098559801021925900000000000000000019F500F
   6    00010JOHN STUDEBAKER                     Å
       4FFFFFDDCD4EEECCCCDCD444444444444401270640
       0000101685023445212590000000000000000019F070F
   7    00011WALTER P CHRYSLER                 Ñ  &
       4FFFFFECDECD4D4CCDEEDCD4444444444401670050
       0000116133590703898235900000000000000009F780F
  14   A00017HAROLD WINSTON                    Ñ¬
       CFFFFFCCDDDC4ECDEEDD444444444444444402670100
       1000178196340695236500000000000000000029F000F
   8    00018RANSON E OLDS                     ß  n
       4FFFFFDCDEDD4C4DDCE444444444444444444401570900
       0000189152650506342000000000000000000019F050F
   9    00019MERCEDES BENZ                     i °
       4FFFFFDCDCCCCE4CCDE4444444444444444401879000
       0000194593545202559000000000000000000019F010F
  13   A00023FERDINAND PORCHE                  Ñ¬   ¬
       CFFFFFCCDCCDCDC4DDDCCC4444444444444402670815
       1000236594951540769385000000000000000029F402F
```

Figure 13-28 CPYF hexadecimal listing of the Ch13mstr file *before* and *after* records are logically deleted.

```
RCDNBR  *...+... 1 ...+... 2 ...+... 3 ...+... 4 ...
   1   A00002HENRY J KAISER                     " &
       CFFFFFCCDDE4D4DCCECD444444444444444402072500
       1000028559801021925900000000000000000019F700F
   2   A00018RANSON E OLDS                     i"    -
       CFFFFFDCDEDD4C4DDCE444444444444444444402870909
       1000189152650506342000000000000000000029F008F
   3   U00005                                   "   b¼
       EFFFFF444444444444444444444444444444403070085
       4000050000000000000000000000000000000039F072F
 ┌ 4   D00014
 │     CFFFFF44444444444444444444444444444440000000
 │     4000140000000000000000000000000000000000F000F
 │
 └ Ch13DLTS   record not found in the Ch13MSTR file
```

Figure 13-29 CPYF hexadecimal listing of the Ch13ERRS file after execution of the logical deletion program.

THE READ, READE, READP, AND READPE OPERATIONS

The **read** operations supported by the **RPG IV** compiler include **READ, READE, READP,** and **READPE.** Each operation reads one record from the data file and stores it for processing. If more than one record is to be sequentially processed, the related **read** instruction must be executed again, usually with a **DO, DOU,** or **DOW** group. Unlike the **CHAIN** operation, **read** instructions do not randomly access records from a file.

After a file is **OPEN**ed (by either the **RPG IV** logic cycle or the **OPEN** operation), and a **READ** or **READE** instruction is executed, the first record in the file is accessed. If, however, the file "pointer" is set to a select key or relative record number by a **SETLL** or **SETGT** instruction, the related **READ** or **READP** instruction will access that record for processing.

Syntax of the READ Operation

In accordance with modern **RPG IV** programming methods, the **READ** operation has been used to process the records from input files in all of the example programs discussed to date. This is the alternative to using the **RPG IV** Logic Cycle, which reads records from input files automatically without **read** operation control. Consequently, the reader is familiar with how the **READ** operation is used in **RPG IV** programs. However, additional details of the **READ** operation's syntax are explained in Figure 13-30.

```
*.. 1 ...+... 2 ...+... 3 ...+... 4 ...+... 5 ...+... 6 ...+... 7 ...+.
CLON01Factor1+++++++Opcode&ExtFactor2+++++++Result++++++++Len++D+HiLoEq

C 1           2     READ            4             5                 6 7
                     3
```

1 A total-time indicator, **L0–L9,** or **LR** may be specified in the *L0* field and/or a detail-time indicator may be specified in the *N01* field to condition the **READ** instruction.

2 *Factor 1* is not used.

3 **READ** operation name must be entered in the *Opcode&Ext* field. If file is processed as an update file, an extender (i.e., **READ(N)**) may be included with the **READ** operation name to prevent the record from being locked when it is accessed.

4 *Factor 2* must contain the name of a file or a record format from a file. A record format name may be used only with files that are externally described (**E** in position 22 of the related *File Description* instruction).

5 The *Result* field may contain the name of a data structure only if the file specified in *Factor 2* is program-described (**F** in position 22 of the related *File Description* instruction).

6 A *Resulting Indicator* may be specified in the *Lo* field (positions 73–74), which will turn on if the **READ** instruction is not completed successfully.

7 A *Resulting Indicator* must be specified in the *Eq* field (positions 75–76) that signals when end of file is read.

Processing Features:

* A file processed by a **READ** instruction must be defined as full-procedural (**F** in position 18 of the related *File Description* instruction).
* If a file is opened by the **RPG IV** Logic Cycle or an **OPEN** instruction, the file is positioned at the first record. The **READ** instruction will begin reading at that record.
* If a **SETLL, SETGT,** or **CHAIN** instruction positions the "pointer" at a record in the file, a **READ** instruction will begin the read at that record, and not the first.
* If the **READ** instruction is successful, the file is positioned at the next record that satisfies the read condition.

Figure 13-30 Syntax of the **READ** operation.

* When an end-of-file condition is tested, the *Resulting Indicator* specified in positions 75–76 will be turned on. Subsequent reads to the file must be executed only if the "pointer" is repositioned. Any attempt to read a file after the end of file is detected will cause an exception error and cancel program execution.

Figure 13-30 Syntax of the **READ** operation. (Continued)

An example **READ** instruction is shown in Figure 13-31.

```
*.. 1 ...+... 2 ...+... 3 ...+... 4 ...+... 5 ...+... 6 ...+... 7 ...+.
CLON01Factor1+++++++Opcode&ExtFactor2+++++++Result++++++++Len++D+HiLoEq

C                   READ      PFRecord                           ┌──────────LR
                              └Record or file           └Indicator is set
                               name                      on if end of file
                                                         is read

  * A data structure name must be specified in Factor 2 if the file
    is program-described.
```

Figure 13-31 Example **READ** operation instruction.

Syntax of the READE *(Real Equal Key)* Operation

The **READE** operation is similar to the **READ** operation. However, it accesses a record only if the *search argument* value (*Factor 1* entry) matches a record in the file. From its current position in the file, and if executed within a **DO, DOU,** or **DOW** group, a **READE** statement searches a file sequentially until the equal condition or end of file is tested. If a match does *not* occur or if the end of file is detected, the *required* indicator in columns 75–76 is set on. The syntax of the **READE** operation is explained in Figure 13-32.

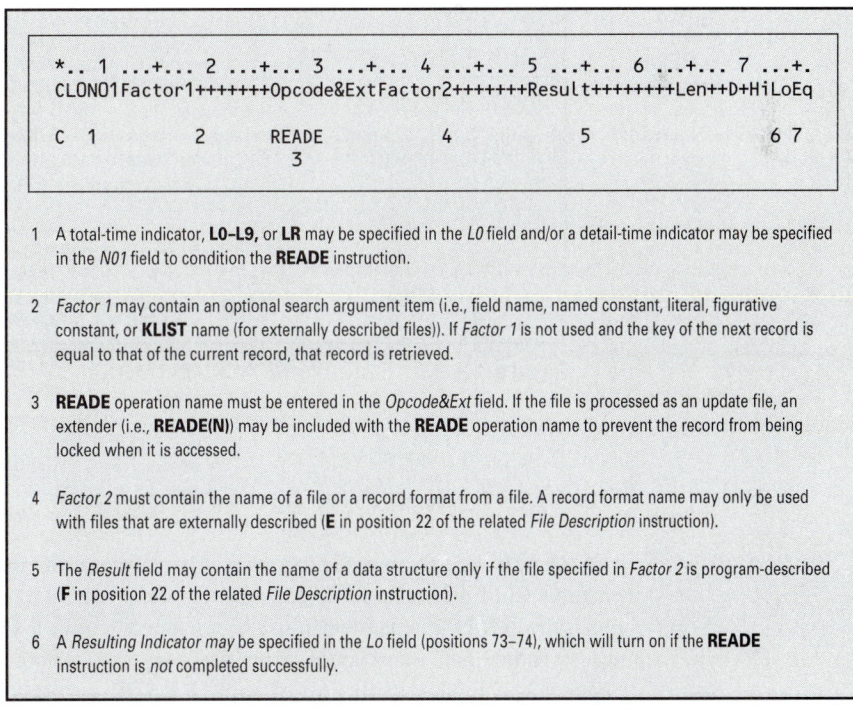

```
*.. 1 ...+... 2 ...+... 3 ...+... 4 ...+... 5 ...+... 6 ...+... 7 ...+.
CLON01Factor1+++++++Opcode&ExtFactor2+++++++Result++++++++Len++D+HiLoEq

C  1            2       READE           4             5                 6 7
                          3
```

1 A total-time indicator, **L0–L9,** or **LR** may be specified in the *L0* field and/or a detail-time indicator may be specified in the *N01* field to condition the **READE** instruction.

2 *Factor 1* may contain an optional search argument item (i.e., field name, named constant, literal, figurative constant, or **KLIST** name (for externally described files)). If *Factor 1* is not used and the key of the next record is equal to that of the current record, that record is retrieved.

3 **READE** operation name must be entered in the *Opcode&Ext* field. If the file is processed as an update file, an extender (i.e., **READE(N)**) may be included with the **READE** operation name to prevent the record from being locked when it is accessed.

4 *Factor 2* must contain the name of a file or a record format from a file. A record format name may only be used with files that are externally described (**E** in position 22 of the related *File Description* instruction).

5 The *Result* field may contain the name of a data structure only if the file specified in *Factor 2* is program-described (**F** in position 22 of the related *File Description* instruction).

6 A *Resulting Indicator may* be specified in the *Lo* field (positions 73–74), which will turn on if the **READE** instruction is *not* completed successfully.

Figure 13-32 Syntax and processing logic of the **READE** operation.

7 A *Resulting Indicator must* be specified in the *Eq* field (positions 75–76), which is turned on if the *Factor 1* item value does not equal a key stored in the file. The indicator will also be turned on when the end of file is read.

Processing Features:

* A file processed by a **READE** instruction must be defined as full-procedural (**F** in position 18 of the related *File Description* instruction).
* If a **SETLL, SETGT,** or **CHAIN** instruction positions the "pointer" at a record in the file, a **READE** instruction will begin the read at that record and not at the first.
* If the **READE** instruction is successful, the file is positioned at the next record that satisfies the read condition.
* When an end-of-file condition is tested, the *Resulting Indicator* specified in positions 75–76 will be turned on. Subsequent reads to the file must be executed only if the "pointer" is repositioned. Any attempt to read a file after end-of-file is detected will cause an exception error and cancel program execution.

Figure 13-32 Syntax and processing logic of the **READE** operation. (Continued)

An example **READE** instruction and its processing logic are shown in Figure 13-33.

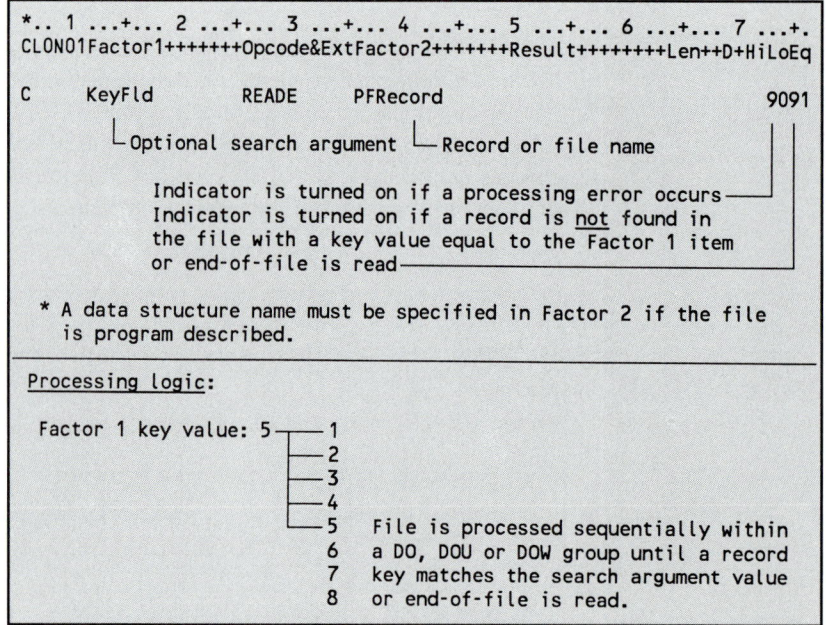

```
*.. 1 ...+... 2 ...+... 3 ...+... 4 ...+... 5 ...+... 6 ...+... 7 ...+.
CLON01Factor1+++++++Opcode&ExtFactor2+++++++Result++++++++Len++D+HiLoEq

C     KeyFld         READE      PFRecord                             9091
      └Optional search argument └─Record or file name

          Indicator is turned on if a processing error occurs
          Indicator is turned on if a record is not found in
          the file with a key value equal to the Factor 1 item
          or end-of-file is read

  * A data structure name must be specified in Factor 2 if the file
    is program described.

 Processing logic:

 Factor 1 key value: 5──1
                        ─2
                        ─3
                        ─4
                        ─5   File is processed sequentially within
                         6   a DO, DOU or DOW group until a record
                         7   key matches the search argument value
                         8   or end-of-file is read.
```

Figure 13-33 Example **READE** instruction.

The READP *(Read Prior Record)* Operation

The **READP** operation reads the *prior* record from a file defined as *full-procedural* (**F** in position 18 of the related *File Description* statement). Identical to any of the read operations, the **READP** statement must be included within a **DO, DOU,** or **DOW** group to access more than one record from the file. The syntax of the **READP** operation is explained in Figure 13-34. An example **READP** instruction and its processing logic are detailed in Figure 13-35.

```
*.. 1 ...+... 2 ...+... 3 ...+... 4 ...+... 5 ...+... 6 ...+... 7 ...+.
CLON01Factor1+++++++Opcode&ExtFactor2+++++++Result++++++++Len++D+HiLoEq

C  1          2       READP            4           5                6 7
                        3
```

1 A total-time indicator, **L0–L9,** or **LR** may be specified in the *L0* field and/or a detail-time indicator may be specified in the *N01* field to condition the **READP** instruction.

2 *Factor 1* is not used.

3 **READP** operation name must be entered in the *Opcode&Ext* field. If file is processed as an update file, an extender (i.e., **READP(N)**) may be included with the **READP** operation name to prevent the record from being locked when it is accessed.

4 *Factor 2* must contain the name of a file or a record format from a file. A record format name may be used only with files that are externally described (**E** in position 22 of the related *File Description* instruction).

5 The *Result* field may contain the name of a data structure only if the file specified in *Factor 2* is program-described (**F** in position 22 of the related *File Description* instruction).

6 A *Resulting Indicator may* be specified in the *Lo* field (positions 73–74), which will turn on if the **READP** instruction is not completed successfully.

7 A *Resulting Indicator must* be specified in the *Eq* field (positions 75–76), which is turned on when a *beginning*-of-file condition is read.

Processing Features:

* A file processed by a **READP** instruction must be defined as full-procedural (**F** in position 18 of the related *File Description* instruction).

* If a **SETLL, SETGT,** or **CHAIN** instruction positions the "pointer" at a record in the file, a **READP** instruction will begin the read at that record and not at the first.

* If the **READP** instruction is successful, the file is positioned at the next record that satisfies the read condition.

* When a beginning-of-file condition is tested, the *Resulting Indicator* specified in positions 75–76 will be turned on. Subsequent reads to the file must be executed only if the "pointer" is repositioned. Any attempt to read a file after the *beginning* of file is detected will cause an exception error and cancel program execution.

Figure 13-34 Syntax and processing logic of the **READP** operation.

```
*.. 1 ...+... 2 ...+... 3 ...+... 4 ...+... 5 ...+... 6 ...+... 7 ...+.
CLON01Factor1+++++++Opcode&ExtFactor2+++++++Result++++++++Len++D+HiLoEq

C     KeyFld        READE      PFRecord                             9192
        └Optional search argument  └Record or file name              | |
                                                                     | |
          Indicator is turned on if a processing error occurs────────┘ |
          Indicator is turned on if beginning of file is read──────────┘

  * A data structure name must be specified in Factor 2 if the file
    is program described.

Processing logic:

 SETLL, SETGT, or CHAIN
 positions pointer at a
 record─────────────┐      1
                    │      2
                    │      3
                    │      4──┐  Prior record is read by a READP
                    └──────5──┘  instruction
```

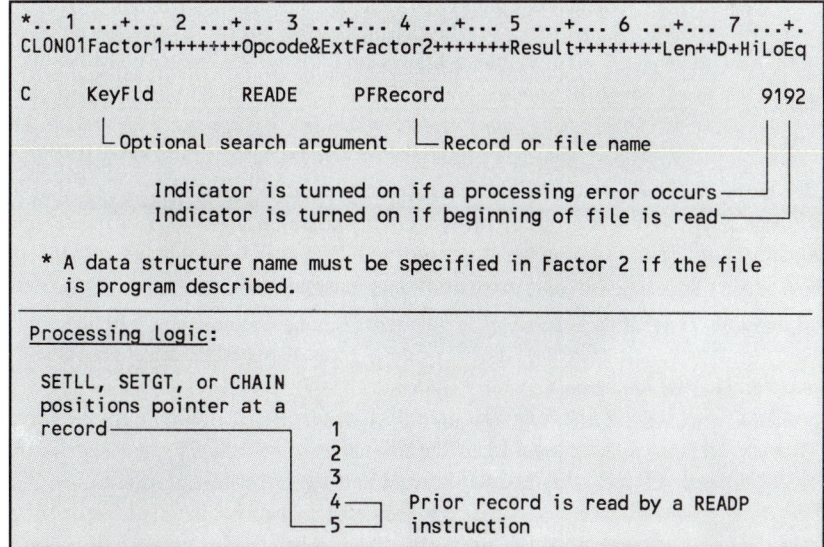

Figure 13-35 Example **READP** instruction and processing logic.

```
                                    6
                                    7
                                    8

When a file is opened explicitly by an OPEN instruction or by the RPG
IV Logic Cycle, it will be positioned at the first record.  If a READP
instruction was immediately executed, the indicator specified in posi-
tions 75-76 would be set on, indicating the beginning of file condition.
The file would have to be repositioned to continue processing.  Ident-
ical to all of the "read" operations, if more than one record is to be
read, the READP instruction must be included in a DO, DOU, or DOW group
```

Figure 13-35 Example **READP** instruction and processing logic. (Continued)

The READPE (*Read Prior Equal*) Operation

The **READPE** operation retrieves the *next prior* record sequentially from a *full-procedural* file (**F** in column 18 of the related *File Description* statement) if the key of the file's record matches the search argument value (*Factor 1* entry). Identical to all of the read operations, continued sequential processing of the file is controlled by including the **READPE** statement within a **DO, DOU,** or **DOW** group. The syntax of the **READPE** operation is explained in Figure 13-36.

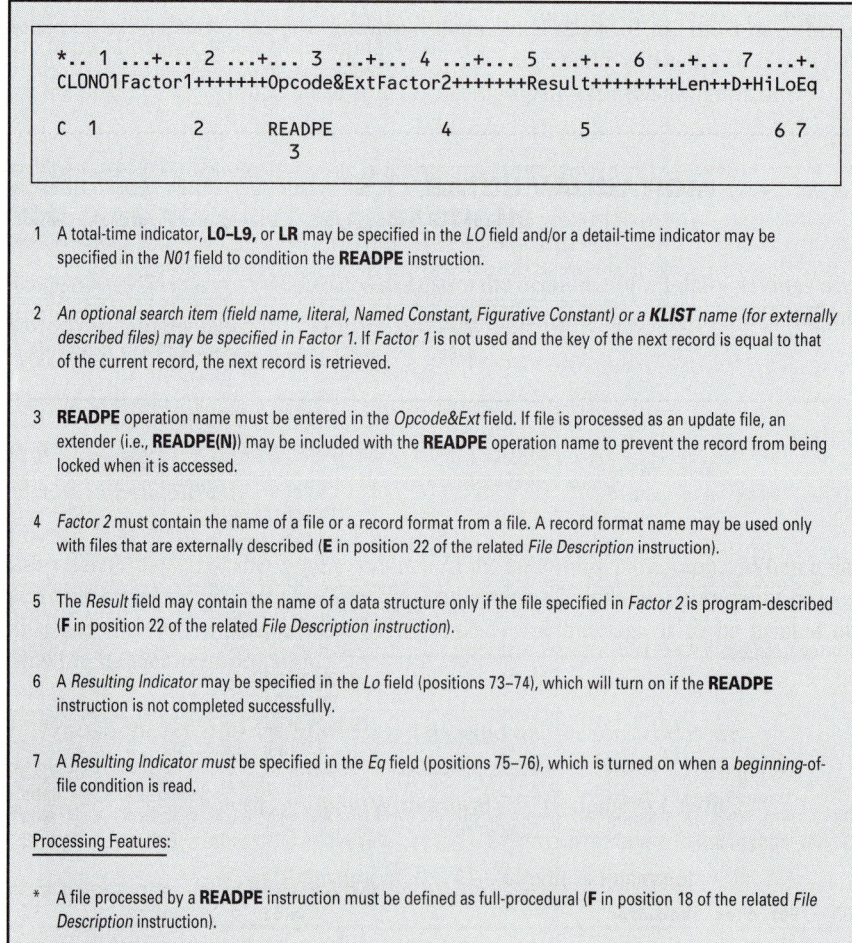

```
*.. 1 ...+... 2 ...+... 3 ...+... 4 ...+... 5 ...+... 6 ...+... 7 ...+.
CLON01Factor1+++++++Opcode&ExtFactor2+++++++Result++++++++Len++D+HiLoEq

C  1          2         READPE          4               5               6 7
                          3
```

1 A total-time indicator, **L0–L9,** or **LR** may be specified in the *L0* field and/or a detail-time indicator may be specified in the *N01* field to condition the **READPE** instruction.

2 *An optional search item (field name, literal, Named Constant, Figurative Constant) or a* ***KLIST*** *name (for externally described files) may be specified in Factor 1.* If *Factor 1* is not used and the key of the next record is equal to that of the current record, the next record is retrieved.

3 **READPE** operation name must be entered in the *Opcode&Ext* field. If file is processed as an update file, an extender (i.e., **READPE(N)**) may be included with the **READPE** operation name to prevent the record from being locked when it is accessed.

4 *Factor 2* must contain the name of a file or a record format from a file. A record format name may be used only with files that are externally described (**E** in position 22 of the related *File Description* instruction).

5 The *Result* field may contain the name of a data structure only if the file specified in *Factor 2* is program-described (**F** in position 22 of the related *File Description instruction*).

6 A *Resulting Indicator* may be specified in the *Lo* field (positions 73–74), which will turn on if the **READPE** instruction is not completed successfully.

7 A *Resulting Indicator must* be specified in the *Eq* field (positions 75–76), which is turned on when a *beginning*-of-file condition is read.

Processing Features:

* A file processed by a **READPE** instruction must be defined as full-procedural (**F** in position 18 of the related *File Description* instruction).

Figure 13-36 Syntax and processing logic of the **READPE** operation.

- If a **SETLL, SETGT,** or **CHAIN** instruction positions the "pointer" at a record in the file, a **READPE** instruction will begin the read at that record and not at the first.
- If the **READPE** instruction is successful, the file is positioned at the next record that satisfies the read condition.
- When a beginning-of-file condition is tested, the *Resulting Indicator* specified in positions 75–76 will be turned on. Subsequent reads to the file must be executed only if the "pointer" is repositioned. Any attempt to read a file after the *beginning* of file is detected will cause an exception error and cancel program execution.

Figure 13-36 Syntax and processing logic of the **READPE** operation. (Continued)

An example **READPE** instruction and its processing logic are shown in Figure 13-37.

```
*.. 1 ...+... 2 ...+... 3 ...+... 4 ...+... 5 ...+... 6 ...+... 7 ...+.
CLON01Factor1+++++++Opcode&ExtFactor2+++++++Result++++++++Len++D+HiLoEq

C      KeyFld         READPE     PFRecord                            9192

        └Optional search argument   └─Record or file name

              Indicator is turned on if a processing error occurs
              Indicator is turned on if beginning of file is read
              or if the search argument key is not in the file

   * A data structure name must be specified in Factor 2 if the file
     is program described.

Processing logic:

  SETLL, SETGT, or CHAIN
  positions pointer at a
  record                         1
                                 2
                                 3
                                 4       Prior record is read by a READPE
                                 5       instruction for an "equal" key
                                 6       condition
                                 7
                                 8

When a file is opened explicitly by an OPEN instruction or by the RPG
IV Logic Cycle, it will be positioned at the first record.  If a READPE
instruction was immediately executed, the indicator specified in posi-
tions 75-76 would be set on, indicating the beginning of file condition.
The file would have to be repositioned to continue processing.  Ident-
ical to all of the "read" operations, if more than one record is to be
read, the READPE instruction must be included in a DO, DOU, or DOW group
```

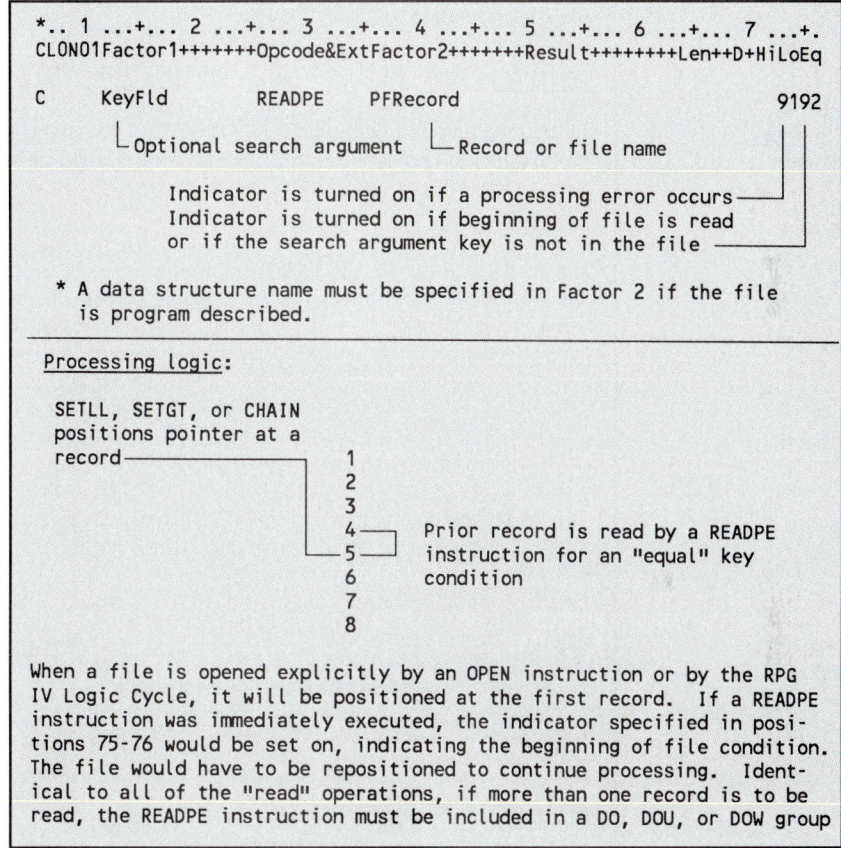

Figure 13-37 Example **READPE** instruction and processing logic.

An **RPG IV** application program will be introduced using records from one input file to process the records in another input file using the **READE** operation.

RPG IV APPLICATION PROGRAM: STUDENT TRANSCRIPTS

The specifications for an **RPG IV** application program that generates student transcripts are detailed in Figure 13-38.

PROGRAM SPECIFICATIONS — Page 1 of 1

Program Name: Student Transcripts — Program - ID: CH13P4 — Written by: SM

Purpose: Generate temporary student transcripts — Approved by: CM

Input files: CH13SMST (keyed) CH13SCRS (keyed)

Output files: QSYSPRT (printer)

Processing Requirements:

Write an **RPG IV** program to generate temporary student transcripts for all of the students stored in the master file CH13SMST.

Input to the program:

An externally defined, keyed physical file, CH13SMST contains general student data (i.e., name, address, major, etc.), and the keyed file, CH13SCRS, includes year-to-date course records.

Processing:

Read the student master file (CH13SMST) in arrival sequence until end of file. For each master record accessed, read the related records from the course file (CH13SCRS). A student may have no, one, or more course records. Consequently, a "do" loop must be coded to access all of the course records related to a student. The student master and course files are matched by the student's social security number.

Compute each student's cumulative point average based on the following:

A = 4 points, B = 3 points, C = 2 points, D = 1 point, F = 0 points

Step 1: Multiply the course credits (CREDIT) by the points for the letter grade. For example, a 3-credit course that earned an A would result in 12 points (3 credits × 4 points).

Step 2: For each student accumulate the total points and total credits.

Step 3: After the last course record for a student is processed, divide the total points by the total credits to determine the student's cumulative point average.

Convert the term date from its stored YYMMDD format to an MMDDYY format by multiplying it by 100.0001.

Output:

Generate a temporary transcript for each student in the master file in the format shown in the attached printer spacing chart. For students who have no course records, print a transcript and include the error message **NO COURSE RECORDS FOUND**.

Figure 13-38 Specifications for Student Transcripts program.

The system flowchart shown in Figure 13-39 indicates that two input files as well as printer output are processed by the program.

A listing of the student master file's (CH13SMST) record format and a **CPYF** utility listing of the data in hexadecimal format are shown in Figure 13-40.

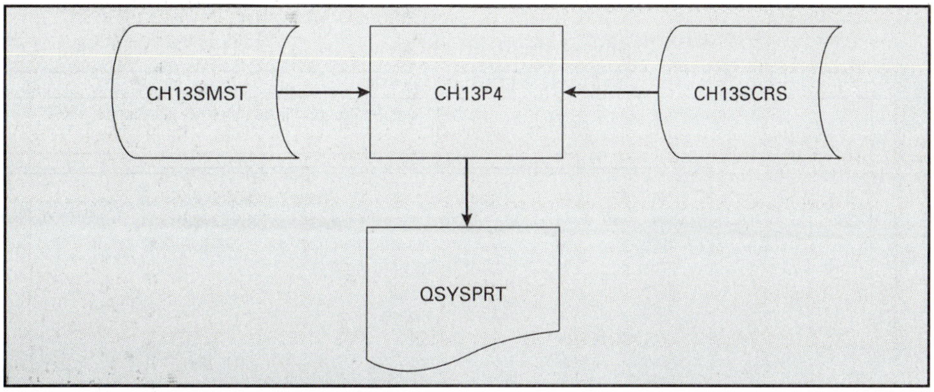

Figure 13-39 System flowchart for Student Transcripts program.

```
                              Data Description Source
SEQNBR  *...+....1....+....2....+....3....+....4....+....5....+
   100      A                                      UNIQUE
   200      A          R SMSTRRCD
   300      A            SS#            9  0
   400      A            SNAME         20
   500      A            SADD1         20
   600      A            SADD2         15
   700      A            SCITY         20
   800      A            SSTATE         2
   900      A            SZIP           5  0
  1000      A            SMAJOR        20
  1100      A          K SS#
```

```
RCDNBR  *...+... 1 ...+... 2 ...+... 3 ...+... 4 ...+... 5 ...+... 6 ...+... 7 ...+... 8 ...+... 9 ...+... 0
     1       SELMA ALABAMA        1640 PARK AVENUE    APT 10              NORWALK             CT e|DATA PROCESSING
        01111ECDDC4CDCCCDC4444444FFFF4DCDD4CECDEC4444CDE4FF444444444DDDECDD4444444444444CE084CCEC4DDDCCEECDC
        1111F2534101312141000000016400719201555450000173010000000000569613200000000000003365F413107963522957
        44444
        00000
     2       ALI BABA             25 BURNT PLAINS                         DARIEN              CT e COMPUTER SCIENC
        01233CDC4CCCC444444444444FF4CEDDE4DDCCDE444444444444444444444CCDCCD44444444444444CE083CDDDEECD4ECCCDC
        1233F139021210000000000002502495307319520000000000000000000041995500000000000000003365F364743590239553
        E
        C4444
        50000
     3     ái¬ANDY PANDA          26 PEARSALL PLACE   SUITE 30            STAMFORD            CT e DATA PROCESSING
        02455CDCE4DCDCC4444444444FF4DCCDECDD4DDCCC444EECEC4FF4444444EECDCDDC444444444444CE080CCEC4DDDCCEECDC
        2455F154807154100000000002607519213307313500024935030000000023146694000000000000003365F413107963522957
        44444
        00000
     6      r MAE WEST            853 WOOD AVENUE     APT 45              BRIDGEPORT          CT - COMPUTER SCIENC
        03790DCC4ECEE44444444444FFF4EDDC4CECDEC44444CDE4FF444444444CDCCCDDDE444444444CE061CDDDEECD4ECCCDC
        3789F4150652300000000000853066640155545000001730450000000000299475769300000000003360F364743590239553
        E
        C4444
        50000

      4    Çh±TOM  THUMB          102 VIRGINIA AVENUE                     GREENWICH           CT   COMPUTER SCIENC
        01688EDD4ECEDC4444444444FFF4ECDCCDCC4CECDEC4444444444444444CDCCDECCC4444444444CE070CDDDEECD4ECCCDC
        4688F3640384420000000000102059979591015554500000000000000007955569380000000000003364F364743590239553
        E
        C4444
        50000
     5    é r=CLARK KENT          7 BOOT SHOP LANE                        NEW CANNAN          CT í| DATA PROCESSING
        05199CDCDD4DCDE444444444F4CDDE4ECDD4DCDC444444444444444444DCE4CCDDCD444444444CE054CCEC4DDDCCEECDC
        5199F3319202553000000000070266302867031550000000000000000000556031551500000000003365F413107963522957
        44444
        00000
```

Figure 13-40 Listing of the student master file's record format and hexadecimal listing of the data.

A listing of the student course file's (CH13SCRS) record format and a hexadecimal listing of the data are shown in Figure 13-41. Note that the data is in a *composite key* (CSS#, CDATE, CNO) order.

```
                                     Data Description Source
SEQNBR  *...+....1....+....2....+....3....+....4....+....5....+....6.
   100        A                                          UNIQUE
   200        A          R SCRRECRD
   300        A            CSS#            9  0
   400        A            CNAME          20
   500        A            CNO             6
   600        A            CDATE           6  0
   700        A            CINST#          3  0
   800        A            CMARK           1
   900        A            CREDIT          1  0
  1000        A          K CSS#   ┐
  1100        A          K CDATE ─┤  Composite key. Records may be
  1200        A          K CNO    ┘  accessed by the three key fields,
                                     or by CSS#, or by CSS# and CDATE
```

```
RCDNBR  *...+... 1 ...+... 2 ...+... 3 ...+...
     1        ENGLISH COMPOSITION ACD100    ¼ C
        01111CDCDCEC4CDDDDECECDD4CCCFFF072530C3
        1111F5573928036476293965013410091 1F0F3F
    21        INTRO TO PROGRAMMINGDPS100  ¼  |A|
        01111CDEDD4ED4DDDCDCDDCDCCDEFFF072514C4
        1111F9539603607967914495747210091 1F0F1F
     3        COLLEGE ALGEBRA I   MTH100  ¼ C
        01111CDDDCCC4CDCCCDC4C444DECFFF072511C3
        1111F3633575013752910900043810091 1F6F3F
     4        INTO TO RPG/400     DPS200 +Ω   A|
        01111CDED4ED4DDC6FFF44444CDEFFF085121C4
        1111F9536036097714000000047220090 2F2F1F
     5        COBOL I             DPS210 +Ω   B
        01111CDCDD4C444444444444CDEFFF085121C4
        1111F3626309000000000000047221090 2F2F2F
     6        COMPUTER SCIENCE I  CSC101  ¼ B
        01233CDDDEECD4ECCCDCC4C44CECFFF072510C3
        1233F3647435902395535090032310191 1F9F2F
     7        COMPUTER SCIENCE II CSC202 +Ω   C
        01233CDDDEECD4ECCCDCC4CC4CECFFF085110C3
        1233F3647435902395535099032320290 2F8F3F
     8        CALCULUS I          MTH201 +Ω  "B
        01233CCDCEDEE4C444444444DECFFF085117C3
        1233F3133434209000000000043820190 2F6F2F
     9     ß  INTRO TO PROGRAMING DSP100  ¼  |B|
        02455CDEDD4ED4DDDCDCDCDC4CEDFFF072514C4
        2455F9539603607967914957042710091 1F0F2F
    10     ß  MICROCOMPUTERS I    DSP110  ¼ A
        02455DCCDDCDDDEECDE4C4444CEDFFF072520C3
        2455F4939636474359209000042711091 1F0F1F
    11    r-COMPUTER SCIENCE I  CSC101  ¼ A
        03799CDDDEECD4ECCCDCC4C44CECFFF072510C3
        3789F3647435902395535090032310191 1F9F1F
    12    r-PASCAL I            CSC120  ¼   B|
        03799DCECCD4C444444444444CECFFF072510C4
        3789F7123130900000000000003231209 11F8F2F
    13    h ENGLISH COMPOSITION ACD101  ¼ F
        01688CDCDCEC4CDDDDECECDD4CCCFFF072530C3
        4688F5573928036476293965013410191 1F0F6F
    22    h CALCULUS I          MTH201  ¼"D
        01688CCDCEDEE4C444444444DECFFF072517C3
        4688F3133434209000000000043820191 1F6F4F
    14    h PHYSICS I           SCS101 ¼¼C
        01688DCEECCE4C4444444444ECEFFF072505C3
        4688F7882932090000000000023210191 1F7F3F
    16    h PROGRAMMING I       CSC210 +θ   B|
        01688DDDCDCDDCDC4C444444CECFFF085212C4
        4688F7967914495709000000032321090 1F8F2F
    15    h COMPUTER SCIENCE II CSC202 +Ω   A|
        01688CDDDEECD4ECCCDCC4CC4CECFFF085110C4
        4688F3647435902395535099032320290 2F8F1F
    17    r-INTRO TO PROGRAMMINGDPS100  ¼  |C
        05199CDEDD4ED4DDDCDCDDCDCCDEFFF072514C3
        5199F9539603607967914495747210091 1F0F3F
    18    r-MICROCOMPUTERS I    DSP110  ¼  C
        05199DCCDDCDDDEECDE4C4444CEDFFF072520C3
        5199F4939636474359209000042711091 1F0F3F
    19    r-AMERICAN STUDIES    ACD210 +Ω  -B
        05199CDCDCCCD4EEECCCE4444CCCFFF085129C3
        5199F1459931502344952000013421090 2F9F2F
    20    r-ENGLISH LITERATURE  ACD300 +Ω   C
        05199CDCDCEC4DCECDCEEDC44CCCFFF085130C3
        5199F5573928039359134950013430090 2F0F3F
```

Figure 13-41 Compile listing of the student course file's record format and a hexadecimal listing of the data.

The design of the report is detailed in the printer spacing chart shown in Figure 13-42.

The transcript program is written to process all six students in the master file (CH13SMST). However, because of space limitations, only two transcripts are presented in Figure 13-43: one for a student with course records and the other for a student with no course records.

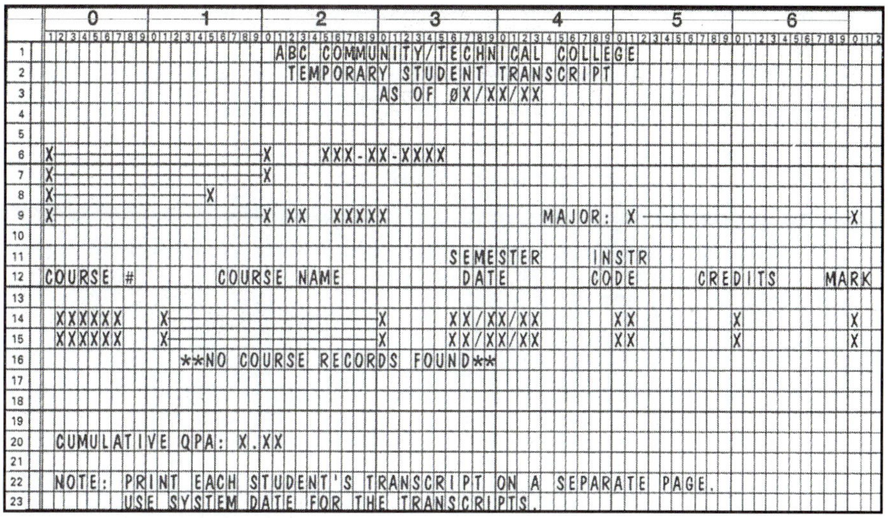

Figure 13-42 Report design for the Student Transcripts program.

```
                    ABC COMMUNITY/TECHNICAL COLLEGE
                     TEMPORARY STUDENT TRANSCRIPT
                            AS OF  5/31/98


SELMA ALABAMA              011-11-1111
1640 PARK AVENUE
APT 10
NORWALK                 CT  06854           MAJOR: DATA PROCESSING

                                     SEMESTER    INSTR
COURSE #        COURSE NAME            DATE       CODE     CREDITS    MARK
 ACD100    ENGLISH COMPOSITION       12/15/97      300        3         C
 DPS100    INTRO TO PROGRAMMING      12/15/97      104        4         A
 MTH100    COLLEGE ALGEBRA I         12/15/97      161        3         C
 DPS200    INTO TO RPG/400           05/21/98      221        4         A
 DPS210    COBOL I                   05/21/98      221        4         B




 CUMULATIVE QPA: 3.11
```

```
                    ABC COMMUNITY/TECHNICAL COLLEGE
                     TEMPORARY STUDENT TRANSCRIPT
                            AS OF  5/31/98


MAE WEST                   033-77-8990
853 WOOD AVENUE
APT 45
BRIDGEPORT              CT  06601           MAJOR: COMPUTER SCIENCE

                                     SEMESTER    INSTR
COURSE #        COURSE NAME            DATE       CODE     CREDITS    MARK

             **NO COURSE RECORDS FOUND**
```

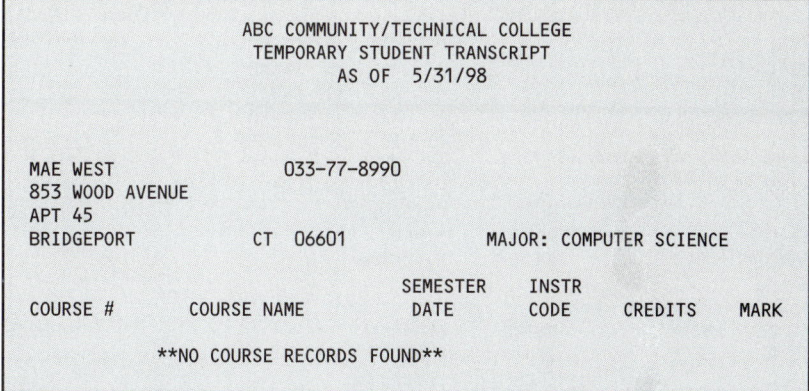

Figure 13-43 One good and one error transcript generated by the Student Transcripts program.

RPG IV STUDENT TRANSCRIPTS PROGRAM CODING

A detailed compile listing of the Student Transcripts **RPG IV** program is presented in Figure 13-44.

```
Line   <---------------------- Source Specifications ----------------------------><---- Comments ----> Do
Number ....1....+....2....+....3....+....4....+....5....+....6....+....7....+....8....+....9....+...10 Num
                     S o u r c e   L i s t i n g
    * This program generates student transcripts - input from a student master file (Ch13smst) --
    * records accessed by a READ instruction and a course file (Ch13scrs) -- record accessed by
    * READE instructions.
   FCh13smst  IF   E           K DISK
    *--------------------------------------------------------------------------------------------*
    *                                 RPG name         External name                             *
    * File name. . . . . . . . . :   CH13SMST         STAN/CH13SMST                             *
    * Record format(s) . . . . . :   SMSTRRCD         SMSTRRCD                                  *
    *--------------------------------------------------------------------------------------------*
   FCh13scrs  IF   E           K DISK
    *--------------------------------------------------------------------------------------------*
    *                                 RPG name         External name                             *
    * File name. . . . . . . . . :   CH13SCRS         STAN/CH13SCRS                             *
    * Record format(s) . . . . . :   SCRRECRD         SCRRECRD                                  *
    *--------------------------------------------------------------------------------------------*
   FQsysprt   O    F  132        PRINTER OFLIND(*INOF)

    * Define work fields....
   D Points          S              2  0
   D TotCredits      S              4  0
   D TotPoints       S              4  0
   D CumPtAvg        S              3  2
   D MmDdYy          S               D   DATFMT(*MDY/)
   D YyMmDd          S               D   DATFMT(*YMD)

    * Process Ch13mstr until end-of-file is read....
  =ISMSTRRCD
    *--------------------------------------------------------------------------------------------*
    * RPG record format  . . . . :   SMSTRRCD                                                    *
    * External format  . . . . . :   SMSTRRCD : STAN/CH13SMST                                    *
    *--------------------------------------------------------------------------------------------*
  =I                              P     1     5 OSS#
  =I                              A     6    25  SNAME
  =I                              A    26    45  SADD1
  =I                              A    46    60  SADD2
  =I                              A    61    80  SCITY
  =I                              A    81    82  SSTATE
  =I                              P    83    85 OSZIP
  =I                              A    86   105  SMAJOR
  =ISCRRECRD
    *--------------------------------------------------------------------------------------------*
    * RPG record format  . . . . :   SCRRECRD                                                    *
    * External format  . . . . . :   SCRRECRD : STAN/CH13SCRS                                    *
    *--------------------------------------------------------------------------------------------*
  =I                              P     1     5 OCSS#
  =I                              A     6    25  CNAME
  =I                              A    26    31  CNO
  =I                              P    32    35 OCDATE
  =I                              P    36    37 OCINST#
  =I                              A    38    38  CMARK
  =I                              P    39    39 OCREDIT
   C                   READ      Ch13smst                           ----LR    read 1st master rcd
   C                   DOW       *INLR = *OFF                                 dow 80 is off        B01
   C                   EXCEPT    HeadLine                                     print heading lines   01

    * Find course record for current student...
   C     SS#           SETLL     Ch13scrs                           ----80    find record           01
   C                   IF        *IN80 = *OFF                                                      B02
   C                   EXCEPT    ErrorLine                                    print error message   02
   C                   ELSE                                                   record found         X02
```

Figure 13-44 Compile listing of the Student Transcripts program.

```
 * Process Ch13scrs until no more course records for the student....
C     SS#           READE     Ch13scrs                               ----81  get record          02
C                   DOW       *IN81 = *OFF                                   dou 80 is on        B03
 * Compute cumulative QPA...
C                   SELECT                                                   begin select group  B04
C                   WHEN      CMark = 'A'                                                        X04
C                   EVAL      Points = Credit * 4                            A mark Points       04
C                   WHEN      CMark = 'B'                                                        X04
C                   EVAL      Points = Credit * 3                            B mark points       04
C                   WHEN      CMark = 'C'                                                        X04
C                   EVAL      Points = Credit * 2                            C mark Points       04
C                   WHEN      CMark = 'D'                                                        X04
C                   EVAL      Points = Credit * 1                            D mark Points       04
C                   OTHER                                                                        X04
C                   EVAL      Points = 0                                     F mark points       04
C                   ENDSL                                                    end SELECT group    E04
C                   MOVE      CDATE         YyMmDd                                               03
C                   MOVE      YYMmDd        MmDdYy                           new date format     03
C                   EXCEPT    DetailLine                                     print course        03
C                   EVAL      TotCredits = TotCredits + Credit               accumulate credits  03
C                   EVAL      TotPoints = TotPoints + Points                 accumulate points   03
C     SS#           READE     Ch13scrs                               ----81  get record          03
C                   ENDDO                                                    end dow group       E03
C                   EVAL      CumPtAvg = TotPoints / TotCredits              compute pt average  02
C                   EXCEPT    AvgLine                                        print cum pt avg    02
 * Initialize fields for next student....
C                   EVAL      TotCredits = 0                                 initialize field    02
C                   EVAL      TotPoints = 0                                  initialize field    02
C                   ENDIF                                                    end IF group        E02
C                   READ      Ch13smst                               ----LR  next student master 01
C                   ENDDO                                                    end dow group       E01
OQsysprt   E            HeadLine       1 01
O                                           43 'ABC COMMUNITY/TECHNICAL'
O                                           51 'COLLEGE'
O          E            HeadLine       1
O                                           38 'TEMPORARY STUDENT'
O                                           49 'TRANSCRIPT'
O          E            HeadLine       3
O                                           34 'AS OF'
O                       UDATE         Y     43
O          E            HeadLine       1
O                       SName               20
O                       SS#                 35 '0   -  -    '
O          E            HeadLine       1
O                       SAdd1               20
O          E            HeadLine       1
O                       SAdd2               15
O          E            HeadLine       2
O                       SCity               20
O                       SState              23
O                       SZip                30
O                                           49 'MAJOR:'
O                       SMajor              70
O          E            HeadLine       1
O                                           43 'SEMESTER'
O                                           52 'INSTR'
O          E            HeadLine       2
O                                            8 'COURSE #'
O                                           26 'COURSE NAME'
O                                           40 'DATE'
O                                           51 'CODE'
O                                           63 'CREDITS'
O                                           71 'MARK'
O          E            DetailLine     1
```

Figure 13-44 Compile listing of the Student Transcripts program. (Continued)

```
113 O                    Cno                7
114 O                    CName             30
115 O                    MmDdYy            43
116 O                    CInst#            51
117 O                    Credit            60
118 O                    CMark             70
119 O         E          ErrorLine      2
120 O                                      31 '**NO COURSE RECORDS'
121 O                                      39 'FOUND**'
122 O         E          AvgLine    3
123 O                                      16 'CUMULATIVE QPA:'
124 O                    CumPtAvg      1   21
```

File Description Specifications

4 Ch13smst (master) file is defined as an input, full-procedural, externally described, keyed physical file.

5 Ch13scrs (course) file is defined as an input, full-procedural, externally described, keyed physical file.

6 Qsysprt is defined as a printer file. Overflow indicator **OF** is assigned by the **OFLIND(*INOF)** keyword.

Definition Specifications

9–12 Work fields Points through CumPtAvg are defined with these instructions.

13 MmDdYy is defined as a standalone date field (**D** in position 40). The **DATFMT(*MDY/)** keyword presents and edits the field in an **MM/DD/YY** format.

14 YyMmDd is defined as a standalone date field (**D** in position 40). The **DATFMT(*YMD)** keyword presents the field in a **YYMMDD** format.

Calculation Specifications

34 This **READ** instruction reads the first record from Ch13smst (master) file. If no records are stored in the file, the **LR** indicator will be turned on and subsequently end the program.

35 This **DOW** group controls the sequential reading of the Ch13smst file. When end of file is read by the **READ** operation on line 34 or 77 and **LR** is turned on, control will branch out of the **DOW** group to line 79 and end the program.

36 This **EXCEPT** instruction prints the HeadLine record formats on lines 80–111. Because student transcripts will not exceed one page, page overflow control is not included in the program.

39 The **SETLL** instruction determines if the key value in the SS# field is equal to the key in a record in the Ch13smst file. If a record with the SS# value is found in the Ch13smst file, *Resulting Indicator* **80** will be turned on. Note that the **SETLL** operation does *not* extract the record for processing.

40–42 The **IF** instructions test the status of indicator **80**. If a record with a matching key is not found in the Ch13scrs file, the **EXCEPT** instruction on line 41 is executed, which transfers control to line 119 and prints the error message ****NO COURSE RECORDS FOUND****. If a record with a matching key is found in the Ch13scrs file, the instructions following the **ELSE** operation on line 42 will be executed.

45 This **READE** instruction reads the current record (one found by the **SETLL** instruction on line 39) in the Ch13scrs file for a key value equal to the value in the SS# input field from the Ch13smst file.

46 This **DOW** instruction tests the status of indicator **81**. If it is "off," the instructions within this **DOW** group are executed. If indicator **81** is "on," which indicates that a different student's course record has been read, control will branch out of this **DOW** group to line 70.

49 The **SELECT** operation begins the "select" group.

50–51 This **WHEN** instruction tests the CMark field from the SCRRECRD record for the character **A.** If the test is "true," the **EVAL** instruction on line 51 is executed, which computes the value for Points by multiplying the Credits field from the SCRRECRD record by 4.

52–53 This **WHEN** instruction tests the CMark field from the SCRRECRD record for the character **B.** If the test is "true," the **EVAL** instruction on line 53 is executed, which computes the value for Points by multiplying the Credits field from the SCRRECRD record by 3.

54–55 This **WHEN** instruction tests the CMark field from the SCRRECRD record for the character **C.** If the test is "true," the **EVAL** instruction on line 55 is executed, which computes the value for Points by multiplying the Credits field from the SCRRECRD record by 2.

56–57 This **WHEN** instruction tests the CMark field from the SCRRECRD record for the character **D.** If the test is "true," the **EVAL** instruction on line 57 is executed which computes the value for Points by multiplying the Credits field from the SCRRECRD record by 1.

58–59 If none of the previous **WHEN** instructions tests "true," the instruction following this **OTHER** operation will be executed. The **EVAL** instruction on line 59 initializes the Points field to zero (0).

Figure 13-44 Compile listing of the Student Transcripts program. (Continued)

60	The **ENDSL** operation ends the **SELECT** group.
62–63	This **MOVE** instruction moves the CDATE field value, input in a YYMMDD format, into YyMmDd, which was defined as a date field (**D** in position 40) on line 14. The second **MOVE** instruction moves and converts the YYMMDD format into an edited MM/DD/YY format. MmDdYy was defined as a date field in an MM/DD/YY edited format with the **DATFMT(*MDY/)** keyword on line 13.
64	This **EXCEPT** instruction prints the DetailLine record format on lines 112–118.
65	This **EVAL** instruction computes a value for TotCredits by adding Credit to TotCredits for each course record processed for the current student.
66	This **EVAL** instruction computes a value for TotPoints by adding Points to TotPoints for each course record processed for the current student.
67	This **READE** instruction reads another record from the Ch13scrs file. Control returns to the **DOW** instruction on line 46, where the status of indicator **81** is tested. If **81** is "off" (keys match), the iterative process will continue. If indicator **81** is "on" (keys do not match), control will branch out of the **DOW** group to line 70.
68	The **ENDDO** operation ends the inner **DOW** group that began on line 46.
70	This **EVAL** instruction is executed after the last course record for the current student is processed (exit from the inner DOW group). The value for CumPtAvg is computed by dividing TotPoints by TotCredits.
71	This **EXCEPT** instruction prints the AvgLine record format on lines 122–124.
74–75	TotCredits and TotPoints are initialized to zeros by these **EVAL** instructions before the next student master record from the Ch13smst file is processed.
76	The **ENDIF** operation ends the **IF** group that began on line 40.
77	This **READ** operation reads either a new student record from the Ch13smst file or end of file.
78	This **ENDDO** operation ends the outer **DOW** group that began on line 35.
80–111	The HeadLine record formats are printed by the **EXCEPT** instruction on line 36.
112–118	The DetailLine record format is printed by the **EXCEPT** instruction on line 64.
122–124	The AvgLine record format is printed by the **EXCEPT** instruction on line 71.

Figure 13-44 Compile listing of the Student Transcripts program. (Continued)

OTHER RPG IV FILE CONTROL OPERATIONS

Some of the other **RPG IV** file control operations that will be discussed in this chapter are **OPEN, CLOSE, SETGT,** and **KLIST.**

The OPEN *(Open File for Processing)* Operation

Instead of files automatically **OPEN**ing under the control of the **RPG IV** logic cycle, files may be explicitly **OPEN**ed by an **OPEN** operation. Figure 13-45 details the syntax related to this operation.

```
*.. 1 ...+... 2 ...+... 3 ...+... 4 ...+... 5 ...+... 6 ...+... 7 ...+.
CLON01Factor1+++++++Opcode&ExtFactor2+++++++Result++++++++Len++D+HiLoEq

C  1           2      OPEN          4             5               6
                        3
```

Figure 13-45 Syntax and processing features of the **OPEN** operation.

1 A total-time indicator, **L0–L9,** or **LR** may be specified in the *L0* field and/or a detail-time indicator may be specified in the *N01* field to condition the **OPEN** instruction.

2 *Factor 1* is not used.

3 **OPEN** operation name must be entered in the *Opcode&Ext* field.

4 A file name must be specified in *Factor 2.* However, it *cannot* be defined as a primary, secondary, or table file (**P, S,** or **T** in position 18 of the related *File Description* instruction). Only full-procedural, combined, and output files are supported with the **OPEN** operation.

5 The *Result* field is not used.

6 A *Resulting Indicator may* be specified in the *Lo* field (positions 73–74), which will turn on if the **OPEN** instruction is not completed successfully.

Processing Features:

* If a file is to be opened for the first time by an **OPEN** instruction, the **USROPN** keyword must be specified with related *File Description* instruction.
* If a file is opened automatically by the **RPG IV** logic cycle and later closed by a **CLOSE** instruction, it may be reopened by an **OPEN** instruction without specifying a **USROPN** keyword.
* Multiple **OPEN** instructions are valid, providing the file is closed with a **CLOSE** instruction before it is reopened.
* If an **OPEN** instruction is executed for a file that is already open, a processing error will occur.

Figure 13-45 Syntax and processing features of the **OPEN** operation. (Continued)

An example **OPEN** statement and its related *File Description* coding are presented in Figure 13-46.

File Description instruction:

```
.. 1 ...+... 2 ...+... 3 ...+... 4 ...+... 5 ...+... 6 ...+... 7 ...+... 8
FFilename++IPEASFRLen+LKlen+AIDevice+.Keywords++++++++
FCh13scrs  IF   E           K DISK    USROPN ------- keyword must be in-
                                                     cluded if file is
            |└File must be defined as full procedural to be explicitly
            |              -or-                      opened for the first
            └─C (combined) or O (output)             time
```

Calculation instruction:

```
*.. 1 ...+... 2 ...+... 3 ...+... 4 ...+... 5 ...+... 6 ...+... 7 ...+.
CL0N01Factor1+++++++Opcode&ExtFactor2+++++++Result++++++++Len++D+HiLoEq

C                   OPEN      Ch13scrs                               90

   File is explicitly opened─────┘                                    |
                                                                      |
         Indicator is turned on if a processing error occurs──────────┘
```

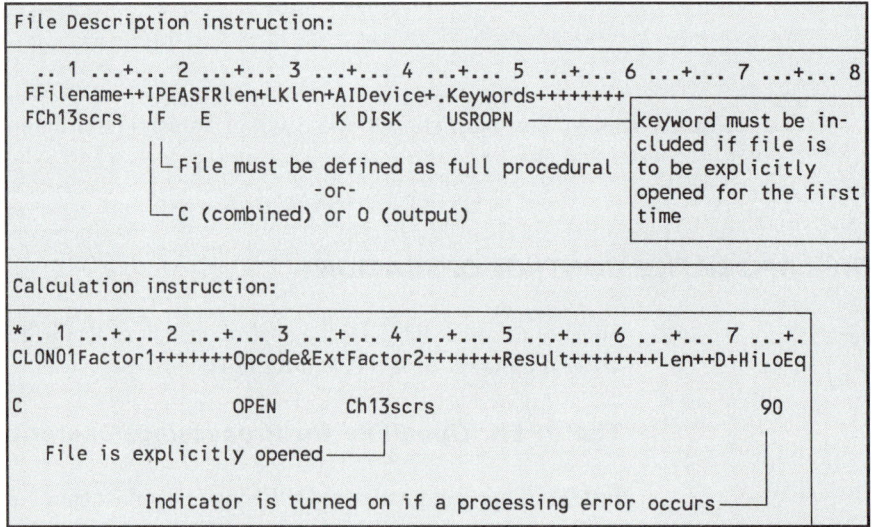

Figure 13-46 Example **OPEN** instruction and related *File Description* coding.

The CLOSE *(Close Files)* Operation

The **CLOSE** operation closes one or more files or devices and disconnects them from the related program. Once a file is closed with a **CLOSE** statement, it cannot be referenced again in the program unless an explicit **OPEN** statement for the file is executed. One file or all of the files specified in the program may be closed by one **CLOSE** operation. To close all of the files at one time, the keyword ***ALL** must be entered in *Factor 2* of the **CLOSE** statement. Figure 13-47 details the syntax of the **CLOSE** operation.

```
*.. 1 ...+... 2 ...+... 3 ...+... 4 ...+... 5 ...+... 6 ...+... 7 ...+.
CLON01Factor1+++++++Opcode&ExtFactor2+++++++Result++++++++Len++D+HiLoEq

C  1          2       CLOSE          4           5                  6
                        3
```

1 A total-time indicator, **L0–L9,** or **LR** may be specified in the *L0* field and/or a detail-time indicator may be specified in the *N01* field to condition the **CLOSE** instruction.

2 *Factor 1* is not used.

3 **CLOSE** operation name must be entered in the *Opcode&Ext* field.

4 A file name must be specified in *Factor 2.* However, it *cannot* be defined as a table file (**T** in position 18 of the related *File Description* instruction). In lieu of a file name, the keyword ***ALL,** which will close all of the files opened in the program, may be specified in *Factor 2.*

5 The *Result* field is not used.

6 A *Resulting Indicator may* be specified in the *Lo* field (positions 73–74), which will turn on if the **CLOSE** instruction is not completed successfully.

Processing Features:

* A **CLOSE** instruction executed on a file already closed will *not* cause an error condition.
* A **CLOSE** instruction may be specified for a file that is *implicitly* or *explicitly* opened.

Figure 13-47 Syntax and processing features of the **CLOSE** operation.

An example **CLOSE** instruction that closes all of the files defined in the **RPG IV** program and another that closes only one file are shown in Figure 13-48.

```
*.. 1 ...+... 2 ...+... 3 ...+... 4 ...+... 5 ...+... 6 ...+... 7 ...+.
CLON01Factor1+++++++Opcode&ExtFactor2+++++++Result++++++++Len++D+HiLoEq
 * The following instruction closes all of the opened files:
C                     CLOSE     *ALL                                90
                                                                     |
 * The following instruction closes only the specified file:
C                     CLOSE     Ch13scrs                            90
                                                                     |
            Indicator is turned on if a processing error occurs------┘
```

Figure 13-48 Example **CLOSE** instructions.

The SETGT *(Set Greater Than)* Operation

The **SETGT** operation positions a file at a record with a key or relative record number that is *greater than* the value of the key or relative record number specified in the item in *Factor 1*. Figure 13-49 explains the syntax of the **SETGT** operation.

```
*.. 1 ...+... 2 ...+... 3 ...+... 4 ...+... 5 ...+... 6 ...+... 7 ...+.
CLON01Factor1+++++++Opcode&ExtFactor2+++++++Result++++++++Len++D+HiLoEq

C  1          2       SETGT          4           5                  6
                        3
```

Figure 13-49 Syntax and processing features of the **SETGT** operation.

1 A total-time indicator, **L0–L9,** or **LR** may be specified in the *L0* field and/or a detail-time indicator may be specified in the *N01* field to condition the **SETGT** instruction.

2 If the file is accessed by a key value, *Factor 1* must contain a field name, Named Constant, Figurative Constant, literal, or **KLIST** name.

If the file is accessed by relative record number, *Factor 1* must contain a numeric field, integer literal, or Named Constant with no decimal positions.

3 The **SETGT** operation name must be entered in the *Opcode&Ext* field.

4 A file name or record name must be specified in *Factor 2.* A record name may be specified only for externally described files. In any case, the file must have been defined as full-procedural (**F** in position 18 of the related *File Description* instruction).

5 The *Result* field is not used.

6 A *Resulting Indicator* may be specified in the *Hi* field (positions 71–72), which will be turned on if *no* record is found in the file wih a key or relative record number that is greater than the search argument specified in *Factor 1.*

6 A *Resulting Indicator may* be specified in the *Lo* field (positions 73–74), which will turn on if the **SETGT** instruction is not completed successfully.

Processing Features:

* The **SETGT** operation positions the file at a record that has a key value or relative record number *greater than* the value stored in the *Factor 1* item (search argument).
* If the **SETGT** instruction is not successful, the file is positioned at the end. It may be repositioned, however, by executing another **SETGT** or the same **SETGT** instruction with a different search argument value.
* A **SETGT** instruction does not *access* the record for processing; it *positions* the file at a record. A **CHAIN** or one of the read operations must access the record for processing.

Figure 13-49 Syntax and processing features of the **SETGT** operation. (Continued)

An example **SETGT** instruction and its processing logic are detailed in Figure 13-50.

```
*.. 1 ...+... 2 ...+... 3 ...+... 4 ...+... 5 ...+... 6 ...+... 7 ...+.
CLON01Factor1+++++++Opcode&ExtFactor2+++++++Result++++++++Len++D+HiLoEq
C     SS#           SETGT     Ch13scrs                           8081

 Indicator is turned on if a key or relative record greater than
 the search argument (Factor 1 value) is not found in the file
 Indicator is turned on if a processing error occurs
```

```
SETGT points to a record in the file that has a key or relative record
number greater than the search key (Factor 1 entry) value.

      00009

               00001HENRY FORD                     0104910012000
               00003LOUIS CHEVROLET                0108910300000
               00004DODGE BROTHERS                 0107911900100
               00008STANLEY STEAMER                0112910080040
               00009HENRY J KAISER                 0110912500000
               00010JOHN STUDEBAKER                0112910067400
               00011WALTER P CHRYSLER              0106910708500
               00018RANSOM E OLDS                  0115910095000
               00019MERCEDES BENZ                  0118919001000
               00020FELIX WANKEL                   0122910050123
 File is positioned
 at this record

Sequential processing of the file from the SETGT position to an upper
limit, end of file, or to the beginning of the file) may be controlled
by a READ, READE, READP, or READPE operation.
```

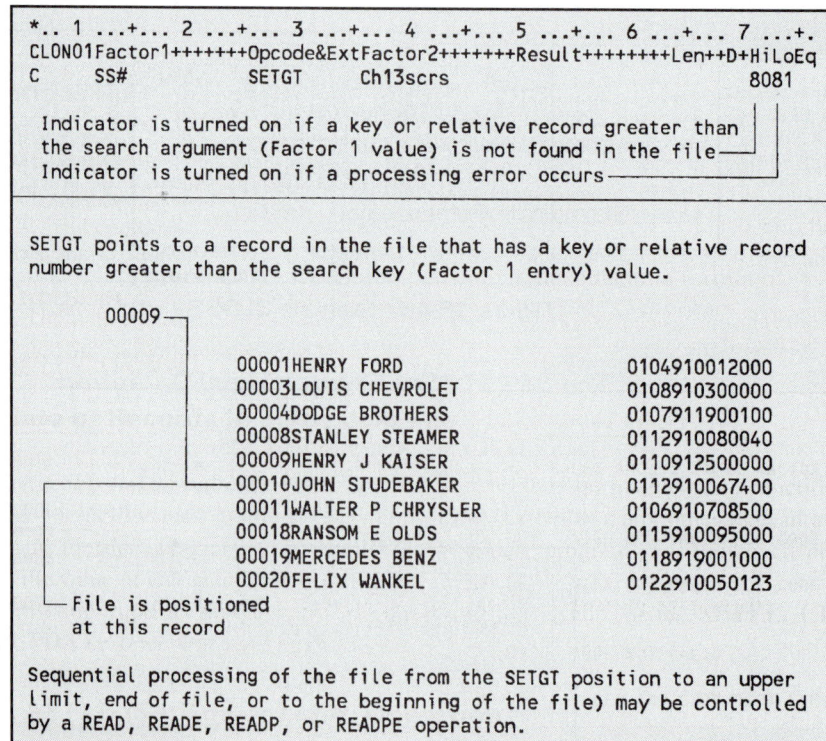

Figure 13-50 Example **SETGT** instruction and processing logic.

THE KLIST (DEFINE A COMPOSITE KEY) AND KFLD (DEFINE PARTS OF A KEY) OPERATIONS

The KLIST Operation

KLIST is a *declarative* operation that names a list of **KFLDs.** The **KLIST** name may be used as the search argument (*Factor 1* entry) to retrieve records from files defined with composite key fields. Figure 13-51 explains the syntax and processing features of the **KLIST** operation.

```
*.. 1 ...+... 2 ...+... 3 ...+... 4 ...+... 5 ...+... 6 ...+... 7 ...+.
CLON01Factor1+++++++Opcode&ExtFactor2+++++++Result++++++++Len++D+HiLoEq

C  1          2        KLIST              4           5             6
                         3
```

1 A **KLIST** instruction may be conditioned by a total-time indicator (**L0–L9,** or **LR**) entered in the *L0* field. Detail-time indicators are *not* permitted in the *N01* field.

2 *Factor 1* must contain a programmer-supplied **KLIST** name.

3 The **KLIST** operation name must be entered in the *Opcode&Ext* field.

4 *Factor 2* is not used.

5 The *Result* field is not used.

6 *Resulting Indicator* fields are not used.

Processing Features:

* A **KLIST** name may be specified as a *Factor 1* search argument only for externally described files (*Factor 2* entry).
* A **KLIST** instruction must be immediately followed by at least one **KFLD** instruction.
* A **KLIST** group is ended when a non-**KFLD** instruction is encountered.
* A **KLIST** name may be used as the search argument (*Factor 1* entry) for a **CHAIN, DELETE, READE, READPE, SETLL,** or **SETGT** instruction.
* The same **KLIST** name may be used as the search argument to access multiple files multiple times.

Figure 13-51 Syntax and processing features of the **KLIST** operation.

The KFLD *(Define Parts of a Key)* Operation

KFLD is also a declarative operation that identifies the field that is part of the search argument specified in *Factor 1* of the related **KLIST** instruction. The **KLIST** and **KFLD** operations must be used together; neither is valid if used alone. The syntax and processing features of the **KLFD** operation are discussed in Figure 13-52.

```
*.. 1 ...+... 2 ...+... 3 ...+... 4 ...+... 5 ...+... 6 ...+... 7 ...+.
CLON01Factor1+++++++Opcode&ExtFactor2+++++++Result++++++++Len++D+HiLoEq

C  1          2        KFLD               4           5             6
                         3
```

Figure 13-52 Syntax and processing features of the **KFLD** operation.

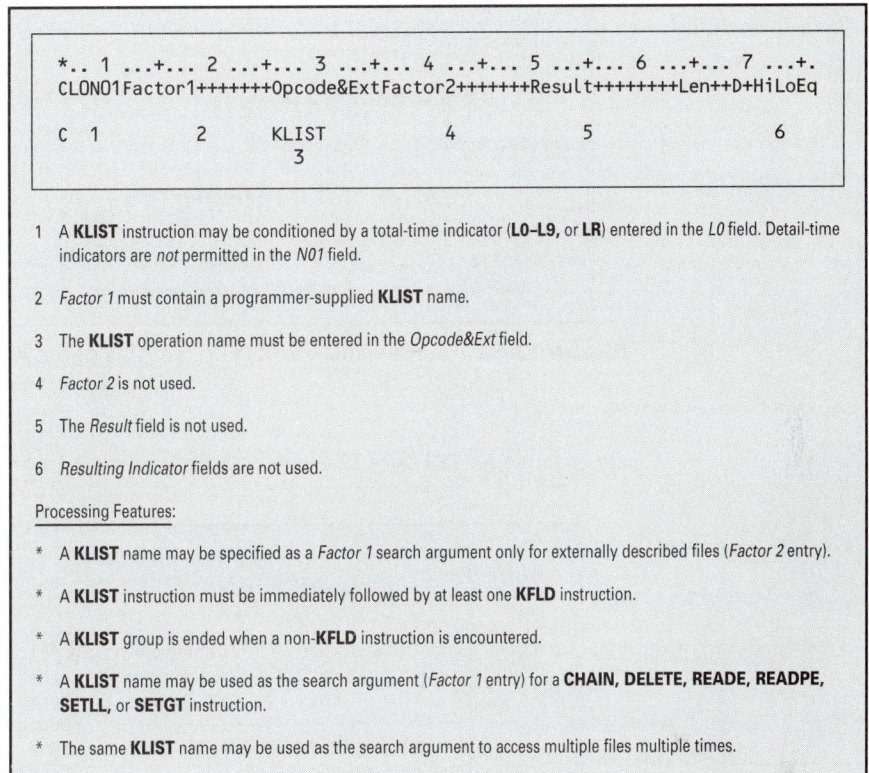

1 A **KFLD** instruction may be conditioned by a total-time indicator (**L0–L9,** or **LR**) entered in the *L0* field. Detail-time indicators are *not* permitted in the *N01* field.

2 *Factor 1* is not used.

3 The **KFLD** operation name must be entered in the *Opcode&Ext* field.

4 *Factor 2* is not used.

5 The *Result* field must contain the name of a field that is part of the **KLIST** *Factor 1* item. An array or table name is not permitted.

Each **KFLD** entry must be defined with the same attributes and be in the same order as the corresponding key in the related physical or logical file. The **KFLD** name, however, does *not* have to be the same as the related key field in the physical or logical file.

6 *Resulting Indicator* fields are not used.

Processing Features:

* At least one **KFLD** instruction must follow a **KLIST** instruction.
* A **KFLD** instruction may be specified only as part of a **KLIST** group.
* A **KLIST** group ends when a non-**KFLD** instruction is encountered.

Figure 13-52 Syntax and processing features of the **KFLD** operation. (Continued)

An example **KLIST/KFLD** group is shown in Figure 13-53.

```
*.. 1 ...+... 2 ...+... 3 ...+... 4 ...+... 5 ...+... 6 ...+... 7 ...+.
CLON01Factor1+++++++Opcode&ExtFactor2+++++++Result++++++++Len++D+HiLoEq

C     EmpKeyFld     KLIST
C                   KFLD          DeptNumber
C                   KFLD          SectionNo
C                   KFLD          EmpNumber
```

Stores DeptNumber, SectionNo, and EmpNumber values

Fields must be in the same order as the related record format. The may have different names, but must have the same attributes as the corresponding field

Figure 13-53 Example **KLIST/KFLD** instruction group.

REORGANIZING DATA IN PHYSICAL FILE MEMBERS

The **RGZPFM** *(Reorganize Physical File Member)* command performs the following functions:

- Removes deleted records and compresses the file, which changes the following relative record numbers (record positions in file).
- Records are added to a physical file after the last record and are usually loaded in a random key order. The **RGZPFM** command resequences the file in a key-value order. The **KEYFILE** parameter of the command must be used for this control.
- A physical file member can be reorganized in the following ways:

  1. By key fields of the physical file
  2. By key fields of a logical file based on a physical file.

An **RGZPFM** display is shown in Figure 13-54. Note that the only user-entered parameters for this example are CH13MSTR and SMYERS; the others are defaults. For a comprehensive discussion of this command, refer to IBM's related *Control Language Manual.*

```
                    Reorganize Physical File Mbr (RGZPFM)

Type choices, press Enter.
Data base file . . . . . . . . .  CH13MSTR      Name
  Library  . . . . . . . . . . .    SMYERS      Name, *LIBL, *CURLIB
Member . . . . . . . . . . . . .  *FIRST        Name, *FIRST, *LAST
Source update options  . . . . .  *SAME         *SAME, *SEQNBR, *DATE
Source sequence numbering:
  Starting sequence number . . .  1.00          0.01-9999.99
  Increment number . . . . . . .  1.00          0.01-9999.99
Key file:
  Logical file . . . . . . . . .  *FILE         Name, *NONE, *FILE
    Library  . . . . . . . . . .                Name, *LIBL, *CURLIB
  Member . . . . . . . . . . . .                Name
Record format  . . . . . . . . .  *ONLY         Name, *ONLY

                                                                  Bottom

F3=Exit   F4=Prompt   F5=Refresh   F12=Cancel   F13=How to use this display
F24=More keys
```

Figure 13-54 RGZPFM (*Reorganize Physical File Member*) display.

The results of executing a **RGZPFM** command are shown in Figure 13-55. Note that the *before* and *after* listings are generated by using the **DSPPFM** command and pressing the Print key to print each display. Because a hexadecimal format was not selected, the **DSPPFM** utility displayed "unreadable characters" in the right margin of each display for the packed fields. Copies of the *before* and *after* displays are presented only to show how the **RGZPFM** command reorganized the physical file in an ascending key-value order.

```
              Before RGZPFM                                      After RGZPFM

 *...+....1....+....2....+....3....+....4....     *...+....1....+....2....+....3....+....4....
  00003LOUIS CHEVROLET                  i¬       ┌A00002STUTZ BEARCAT                      ¬ ä
  00004DODGE BROTHERS                   `¬       │ 00003LOUIS CHEVROLET                    i¬
  00008STANLEY STEAMER                  ¬ ⊣      │ 00004DODGE BROTHERS                     `¬
  00009HENRY J KAISER                   ¬ Ř      │A00006OTTO DIESEL                        ß¬ c&
  00010JOHN STUDEBAKER                ╥`  &¦     │ 00008STANLEY STEAMER                    ¬ ⊣
 U00011WALTER P CHRYSLER              ╥`         │ 00009HENRY J KAISER                     ¬
 U00018RANSON E OLDS                  i¬°        │ 00010JOHN STUDEBAKER                    ¬ Ř
  00019MERCEDES BENZ                  ¬ ä        │U00011WALTER P CHRYSLER                ╥`
┌A00002STUTZ BEARCAT                  ß¬ c&      │U00017HAROLD WINSTON                   ╥`
├A00006OTTO DIESEL                    Ñ¬ ⊣ ¬     │U00018RANSON E OLDS                    ╥`
│A00023FERDINAND PORCHE                          │ 00019MERCEDES BENZ                    i¬°
├U00017HAROLD WINSTON                 ╥`         ├A00023FERDINAND PORCHE                 Ñ¬ ⊣¬
│                                     │          │
└── Key fields are not in      Packed field values   └ Key fields in ascending order
    ascending order            are not readable in
                               a character format
```

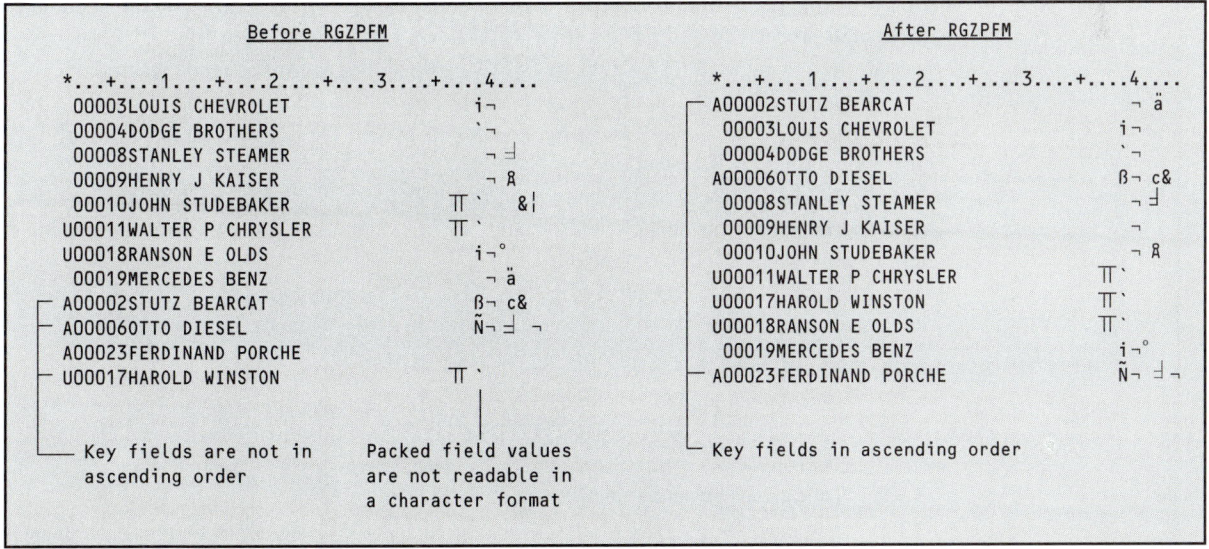

Figure 13-55 *Before* and *after* **DSPPFM** command displays showing the result of executing the **RGZPFM** command.

SUMMARY

Physical file maintenance includes

1. Adding records
2. Updating (changing) field values in the body of a record
3. Deleting records (logical and tagging methods)
4. Reorganizing files.

Adding records to a physical file requires use of the **WRITE** operation and defining the file as output or update. *Keyed* physical files defined as unique will not support the addition of records with the same key value (duplicate key error). However, keyed physical files not defined as unique will support records that are added with the same key value.

In *update* maintenance, one or more field values of a record are changed. Except for key fields, any field values may be changed. The physical file to be updated must be defined as an *update* file (**U** in position 17) and *full-procedural* (**F** in position 18) of the related *File Description* statement. Update processing requires use of the **UPDATE** operation.

Deletion of records in a physical file may be done by the *tagging* or *logical* method. The tagging method is an update process in which a record is accessed, a character is moved to a designated field, and the record is written back to its storage area. Logical deletion requires use of the **DELETE** operation, which logically deletes a record from the file. Any subsequent processing of the file will not read records that are deleted by the **DELETE** operation.

The **CHAIN** operation randomly retrieves a record from a physical file. The *Factor 1* entry (*search argument*) must contain either a key field value or a relative record number.

A **SETLL** operation "points" to a record in the file with a key value or relative record number value equal to or greater than the *Factor 1* entry of the statement. The **SETGT** operation "points" to a record in the file greater than the key or relative number value in the *Factor 1* item.

The **READ** operation reads one record in a physical file from the current record location *forward*. A **READE** operation also reads one record in a file but searches for a record with a key or relative record number equal to the key or relative number value in the *Factor 1* entry of the statement. The **READP** operation reads a record from the current record location *backward*. A **READPE** operation reads *backward* and searches for a record with a key or relative record number equal to the *Factor 1* entry of the statement. Sequential processing of the file with a **READ, READE, READP,** or **READPE** operation is controlled by either a **DO, DOU,** or **DOW** group and/or multiple "read" statements.

Physical files are usually opened and closed automatically by the **RPG IV** *Logic Cycle*. However, they may be *explicitly* opened by the **OPEN** operation and explicitly closed by the **CLOSE** operation.

The **KLIST** operation defines a group of fields specified in **KFLD** statements to build a composite key field. Values in the **KFLD** statements are stored in the *Factor 1* item of the related **KLIST** operation.

Physical files are reorganized by the **RGZPFM** command. This command removes deleted records from a file and sequences the file in a key-value order.

QUESTIONS

13-1. Name the maintenance functions for physical files.

13-2. How must the physical file be defined in an **RPG IV** program to support each maintenance function?

13-3. Name the **RPG IV** operations to perform each maintenance function.

Examine the following calculation statement and answer Questions 13-4 through 13-8:

```
*.. 1 ...+... 2 ...+... 3 ...+... 4 ...+... 5 ...+... 6 ...+... 7 ...+.
CLON01Factor1+++++++Opcode&ExtFactor2+++++++Result++++++++Len++D+HiLoEq
C                   WRITE     ABC                                  80
```

13-4. What maintenance function does the **WRITE** operation support?

13-5. What is the ABC *(Factor 2)* entry?

13-6. When does the *Resulting Indicator* specified in the *Lo* field turn on? Name the specific conditions that may set the indicator on.

13-7. How must a physical file be defined in an **RPG IV** program to support a **WRITE** instruction?

13-8. After execution of a **WRITE** instruction, where are the records stored in the physical file?

13-9. What **CL** command will generate a listing of a file? What **CL** command will display the records in a data file?

13-10. How does a hexadecimal **(*HEX)** display or listing differ from a character **(*CHAR)** display?

Examine the following calculation statement and answer Questions 13-11 through 13-16:

```
*.. 1 ...+... 2 ...+... 3 ...+... 4 ...+... 5 ...+... 6 ...+... 7 ...+.
CLON01Factor1+++++++Opcode&ExtFactor2+++++++Result++++++++Len++D+HiLoEq
C     AAA           SETLL     XYZ                                8081
```

13-11. Explain the function of the **SETLL** operation.

13-12. What is stored in the AAA (*Factor 1*) entry?

13-13. What is the XYZ (*Factor 2*) entry?

13-14. When is *Resulting Indicator* **80** set on?

13-15. When is *Resulting Indicator* **81** set on?

13-16. What record will be "pointed to" by a **SETLL** statement?

Examine the following calculation statement and answer Questions 13-17 through 13-21:

```
*.. 1 ...+... 2 ...+... 3 ...+... 4 ...+... 5 ...+... 6 ...+... 7 ...+.
CLON01Factor1+++++++Opcode&ExtFactor2+++++++Result++++++++Len++D+HiLoEq
C     EmpNumber     CHAIN     ZYX                                90
```

13-17. Explain the function of the **CHAIN** operation.

13-18. What is stored in the EmpNumber (*Factor 1*) entry?

13-19. What is the ZYX (*Factor 2*) entry?

13-20. When does *Resulting Indicator* **90** turn on?

13-21. How must a physical file be defined to support a **CHAIN** instruction?

Examine the following calculation statement and answer Questions 13-22 through 13-26:

```
*.. 1 ...+... 2 ...+... 3 ...+... 4 ...+... 5 ...+... 6 ...+... 7 ...+.
CLON01Factor1+++++++Opcode&ExtFactor2+++++++Result++++++++Len++D+HiLoEq
C                   UPDATE    ABCDE                                85
```

13-22. Explain the function of the **UPDATE** operation.

13-23. What must be specified in *Factor 2* (ABCDE entry)?

13-24. When does *Resulting Indicator* **85** entered in the *Lo* field turn on?

13-25. How must a physical file be defined to support an **UPDATE** instruction?

13-26. Before an **UPDATE** instruction is executed, what other functions have to be performed in the **RPG IV** program?

Examine the following calculation statement and answer Questions 13-27 through 13-31:

```
*.. 1 ...+... 2 ...+... 3 ...+... 4 ...+... 5 ...+... 6 ...+... 7 ...+.
CLON01Factor1+++++++Opcode&ExtFactor2+++++++Result++++++++Len++D+HiLoEq
C                   DELETE    CDEFG                                80
```

13-27. Explain the function of the **DELETE** operation.

13-28. What must be specified in *Factor 2* (CDEFG entry)?

13-29. When does *Resulting Indicator* **80** in the *Lo* field turn on?

13-30. How must a physical file be defined to support a **DELETE** instruction?

13-31. Before a **DELETE** instruction is executed, what other functions have to be performed in the **RPG IV** program?

13-32. Explain the processing features of the **READ** and **READE** operations.

Examine the following calculation statement and answer Questions 13-33 through 13-35:

```
*.. 1 ...+... 2 ...+... 3 ...+... 4 ...+... 5 ...+... 6 ...+... 7 ...+.
CLON01Factor1+++++++Opcode&ExtFactor2+++++++Result++++++++Len++D+HiLoEq
C     SSNumber      READE     ABCDE                                  81
```

13-33. What is stored in the *Factor 1* (SSNumber) entry?

13-34. What is specified in the *Factor 2* (ABCDE) entry?

13-35. Under what conditions will *Resulting Indicator* **81** in the *Eq* field be turned on?

Examine the following calculation statement and answer Questions 13-36 through 13-38:

```
*.. 1 ...+... 2 ...+... 3 ...+... 4 ...+... 5 ...+... 6 ...+... 7 ...+.
CLON01Factor1+++++++Opcode&ExtFactor2+++++++Result++++++++Len++D+HiLoEq
C     ActNumber     READPE    CDEFG                                  81
```

13-36. What is stored in the *Factor 1* (ActNumber) entry?

13-37. What is specified in the *Factor 2* (CDEFG) entry?

13-38. Under what conditions will *Resulting Indicator* **80** in the *Eq* field be turned on?

13-39. What **RPG IV** operation explicitly opens a file? Which operation explicitly closes a file?

13-40. If the open and close functions for a file are to be explicitly controlled in a program, what additional coding is required in the **RPG IV** program?

13-41. How does the processing controlled by a **SETGT** operation differ from that controlled by the **SETLL** operation?

Examine the following calculation statement and answer Questions 13-42 through 13-45:

```
*.. 1 ...+... 2 ...+... 3 ...+... 4 ...+... 5 ...+... 6 ...+... 7 ...+.
CLON01Factor1+++++++Opcode&ExtFactor2+++++++Result++++++++Len++D+HiLoEq
C     PartNumber    KLIST                                            81
C                   KFLD                    PlantNo
C                   KFLD                    BinNo
C                   KFLD                    ItemNo
```

13-42. What is the function of the **KLIST** and **KFLD** operations?

13-43. After execution of the **KLIST** statement, what is stored in PartNumber?

13-44. Where must PlantNo, BinNo, and ItemNo be initially defined?

13-45. What "ends" a **KLIST** group?

13-46. Which **CL** command reorganizes a physical file?

13-47. Name some of the functions performed by execution of the **CL** command answered for Question 13-46.

PROGRAMMING ASSIGNMENTS

For each of the following programming assignments, more than one physical file must have been created. Two must be loaded with the related data records. Your instructor will inform you if you have to create the physical files and load them or if they have been prepared for the assignment.

Programming Assignment 13-1: SAVINGS ACCOUNT MASTER FILE ADDITION

Write an **RPG IV** program to add records to a Savings Account Master file. Three physical files are required for this assignment: a Savings Account Master file; a transaction file; and a file for error records. The File/Record attributes of each file and the related data for the Savings Account Master and transaction (Adds) files are detailed in the following sections.

Savings Account Master File/Record Format:

```
                    PHYSICAL FILE DESCRIPTION

SYSTEM: AS/400                                   DATE: Yours
FILE NAME: Yours                                 REV NO: 0
RECORD NAME: Yours                               KEY LENGTH: 5
SEQUENCE: Keyed (Unique)                         RECORD SIZE: 82

                        FIELD DEFINITIONS

FIELD    FIELD NAME    SIZE  TYPE    POSITION     COMMENTS
 NO                                 FROM    TO

 1       DELETECODE      1    C        1     1   D=deleted
 2       ACCTNUMBER      5    C        2     6   Key field
 3       NAME           31    C        7    37
 4       STREET         20    C       38    57
 5       CITY           16    C       58    73
 6       STATE           2    C       74    75
 7       ZIPCODE         5    P       76    78   0 decimals
 8       ACTBALANCE      6    P       79    82   2 decimals
```

Savings Account Master Data:

Acct#	Account Name	Street	City	State	Zip	Deposit Amount
21345	JOHN DOE	212 ELM STREET	BRIDGEPORT	CT	06610	120000
31121	LOUISE LESSER	12 APPLES ROAD	BAHA	CA	92100	081299
48891	JUDY JOHNSON	114 EASY DRIVE	RALEIGH	NC	44410	006017
50000	DAVE HOOTEN	8 STRIKE LANE	LOS ANGELES	CA	90000	064111

51540	MARIE BLAKE	GREEN PASTURE RD	NEWARK	NJ	07733	940013
63141	JOSEPH WELCH	110 DILL STREET	NEW YORK	NY	10000	077777
71510	JOHN HINES	220 HIGH DRIVE	KEENE	ND	58847	000940

Transaction (Adds) File/Record Format:

PHYSICAL FILE DESCRIPTION

SYSTEM: AS/400	DATE: Yours
FILE NAME: Yours	REV NO: 0
RECORD NAME: Yours	KEY LENGTH: 5
SEQUENCE: Keyed (Unique)	RECORD SIZE: 81

FIELD DEFINITIONS

FIELD NO	FIELD NAME	SIZE	TYPE	POSITION FROM	POSITION TO	COMMENTS
1	ACCTNUMBER	1	C	1	5	Key field
2	NAME	31	C	6	36	
3	STREET	20	C	37	56	
4	CITY	16	C	57	72	
5	STATE	2	C	73	74	
6	ZIPCODE	5	P	75	77	0 decimals
7	DEPOSIT	6	P	78	81	2 decimals

Transaction File (Adds) Data:

Acct#	Account Name	Street	City	State	Zip	Deposit
80000	SIDNEY GREENSTREET	10 CASTLE LANE	ALCATRAZ	CA	92220	100000
10000	PETER LORRE	9 DREARY DRIVE	HUNGRY	AL	99999	004500
71510	JOHN HINES	220 HIGH DRIVE	KEENE	ND	58847	075950
60000	BORIS KARLOFF	1 INNER SANCTUM	MISERABLE	AK	10000	549000

Error File: The error file, where transaction records that have key equal to records already stored in the Savings Account Master (duplicate key error) are written, must be created with the same record format as the transaction file.

After the program is executed, generate hexadecimal listings of the Savings Account Master and error files with the **CPYF** command.

Programming Assignment 13-2: SAVINGS ACCOUNT MASTER FILE UPDATE AND LOGICAL DELETION OF RECORDS

Programming Assignment 13-1 must have been completed, or the master file previously created and loaded with data, before this assignment is started.

Write an **RPG IV** program to *update* and *logically delete* records in the Savings Account Master file with data from a transaction file. In addition, generate the edit report shown in the supplemental printer spacing chart. *Before* the program is executed, print a **CPYF** listing of the Savings Account Master file in hexadecimal format.

Transaction File/Record Format:

PHYSICAL FILE DESCRIPTION

SYSTEM: AS/400	DATE: Yours
FILE NAME: Yours	REV NO: 0
RECORD NAME: Yours	KEY LENGTH: 5
SEQUENCE: Keyed (not unique)	RECORD SIZE: 82

FIELD DEFINITIONS

FIELD NO	FIELD NAME	SIZE	TYPE	POSITION FROM	POSITION TO	COMMENTS
1	TRCODE	1	C	1	1	U or D
2	TACTNO	5	C	2	6	Key field
3	TNAME	31	C	7	37	
4	TSTREET	20	C	38	57	
5	TCITY	16	C	58	73	
6	TSTATE	2	C	74	75	
7	TZIPCODE	5	P	76	78	0 decimals
8	TAMOUNT	6	P	79	82	2 decimals

Transaction File Data:

Trans Code	Acct#	Account Name	Street	City	State	Zip	Trans Amount
D	61000						
U	80000						200000
U	21345	JOHN DOEST	10 ROSE TERRACE	TRUMBULL	VT	07779	
U	40000						015000
U	63141						077777-
D	48891						

Note: Blank field values are <u>not</u> to be used to update the related field(s) in the Savings Account Master file.

Records that include a **U** in the transaction code field contain update data, and those with a **D** indicate that the record is to be logically deleted. Update records that have a blank value in a field are not to change the related master record field!

Report Design:

```
ØX/XX/XX                               SAVING ACCOUNTS EDIT REPORT                                    PAGE XXØX

BEFORE UPDATING:

 X    XXXXX  X                         X  X                       X  X                   X  XX  XXXXX   X,XXØ.XX

 X    XXXXX ....ACCOUNT NOT FOUND....

AFTER UPDATING:

 X    XXXXX  X                         X  X                       X  X                   X  XX  XXXXX   X,XXØ.XX

    NOTES:

      1. HEADINGS ON TOP OF EVERY PAGE.

      2. USE SYSTEM DATE FOR REPORT.

      3. WHEN AN ACCOUNT IS NOT FOUND DO NOT PRINT AFTER UPDATE OUTPUT LINES.
```

Print a **CPYF** listing in hexadecimal format *after* the program is executed, and compare the before and after listings for the update and delete results.

Programming Assignment 13-3: CEREAL BRANDS MASTER FILE ADDITION

Write an **RPG IV** program to add records to a Cereal Brands Master file. Two physical files are required for this assignment: the Cereal Brands Master file and a transaction (adds) file. *A printed report is also to be generated.* The File/Record attributes of each file and the related data for the Cereal Brands Master and transaction (Adds) files are detailed in the following sections.

Cereal Brands Master Record Format:

PHYSICAL FILE DESCRIPTION

SYSTEM: AS/400 | DATE: Yours
FILE NAME: Yours | REV NO: 0
RECORD NAME: Yours | KEY LENGTH: 5
SEQUENCE: Keyed (Unique) | RECORD SIZE: 63

FIELD DEFINITIONS

FIELD NO	FIELD NAME	SIZE	TYPE	POSITION FROM	TO	COMMENTS
1	DELCODE	1	C	1	1	D=deleted
2	BRANDNO	5	C	2	6	Key field
3	BRANDNAME	20	C	7	26	
4	SIZE	3	P	27	28	
5	UNIT	2	C	29	30	
6	MFGR	15	C	31	45	
7	LASTPDATE	6	P	46	49	
8	UNITCOST	6	P	50	53	4 decimals
9	QTYONHAND	5	P	54	56	0 decimals
10	AVGCOST	6	P	57	60	4 decimals
11	UNITSP	4	P	61	63	2 decimals

Cereal Brands Master File Data:

Brand#	Brand Name	Size	Measure	Manufacturer	Date	Unit Cost	On Hand	Average Cost	Unit SP
C1100	TOTAL	012	OZ	GENERAL MILLS	060795	016111	00360	016111	0183
C1134	KIX	014	OZ	GENERAL MILLS	060795	019990	00480	019990	0239
C4889	BRAN CHEX	014	OZ	RALSTON	071195	012899	00840	012899	0149
C5150	RICE CHEX	012	OZ	RALSTON	051195	014550	01200	014550	0169
C6314	RAISIN BRAN	020	OZ	KELLOGG	071295	018840	00960	018840	0209
C6550	CORN FLAKES	018	OZ	KELLOGG	061595	010000	02400	010000	0118
C6900	FROSTED FRAKES	010	OZ	KELLOGG	061595	010910	01800	010910	0129
C7000	GRAPE-NUT FLAKES	012	OZ	POST	061695	012788	02400	012788	0139
C7100	FRUIT & FIBER	014	OZ	POST	051895	016220	01200	016220	0189
C7440	ALPHA-BITS	015	OZ	POST	052095	017050	04800	017050	0195
C8000	CAP'N CRUNCH	016	OZ	QUAKER	072195	017233	06000	017233	0199
C8100	PUFFED WHEAT	006	OZ	QUAKER	062295	010000	12000	010000	0119

Transaction (Adds) File Record Format:

PHYSICAL FILE DESCRIPTION

SYSTEM: AS/400 | DATE: Yours
FILE NAME: Yours | REV NO: 0
RECORD NAME: Yours | KEY LENGTH: 5
SEQUENCE: Keyed (Unique) | RECORD SIZE: 62

FIELD DEFINITIONS

FIELD NO	FIELD NAME	SIZE	TYPE	POSITION FROM	POSITION TO	COMMENTS
1	ABRANDNO	5	C	1	5	Key field
2	ANAME	20	C	6	25	
3	ASIZE	3	P	26	27	
4	AMEASURE	2	C	28	29	
5	AMFGR	15	C	30	44	
6	APURDATE	6	P	45	48	
7	ALASTPRICE	6	P	49	52	4 decimals
8	AQTYONHND	5	P	53	55	0 decimals
9	AUNITCOST	6	P	56	59	4 decimals
10	AUNITSP	4	P	60	62	2 decimals

Physical File Data:

Brand#	Brand Name	Size	Measure	Manufacturer	Last Purchase Date	Last Purchase Price	Amount On Hand	Avg Cost/ Unit	SP Price/ Unit
C5200	SUN FLAKES	015	OZ	RALSTON	082295	019900	00600	019900	0219
C1134	CHEERIOS	020	OZ	GENERAL MILLS	082195	025500	12000	025500	0279
C9000	SHREDDED WHEAT SS	012	OZ	NABISCO	082495	011500	01080	011500	0125
C8100	PAC-MAN	013	OZ	GENERAL MILLS	082595	017899	24000	017899	0199
C1200	TREATS	014	OZ	KELLOGG'S	083095	028895	07200	028895	0349

Report Design:

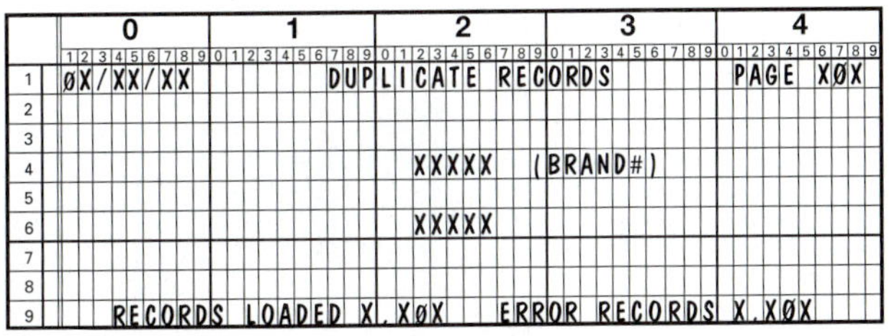

Programming Assignment 13-4: CEREAL BRANDS MASTER FILE UPDATE AND LOGICAL DELETION OF RECORDS

Programming Assignment 13-3 must have been completed, or the master file previously created and loaded with data, before this assignment is started.

Write an **RPG IV** program to *update* and *logically delete* records in the Cereal Brands Master file with data from two transaction files. One file includes purchase and sales transactions, and the other contains "change" data and the key values of records that are to be logically deleted.

The following update functions are to be performed:

From the purchase/sales transaction file, a record with a **P** code indicates a purchase transaction that requires the following moving average computations:

Step 1: Determine Total Quantity and Cost after Purchase:

	AVG. PRICE/UNIT	*	QTY. ON HAND	TOTAL
Values in master record	1.0000	*	12000	12000
Values in transaction record	1.1000	*	08000	08800
Totals			20000	20800

Step 2: Determine New Average Cost per Unit:

Total Cost/Total Qty. = 20800/20000 = 1.0400 (new avg. cost)

In addition to changing the average cost for purchase transactions, the last purchase date, the last purchase price, and the quantity on hand in the related master records are to be updated with the transaction file data.

Transaction records coded with an **S** indicate sales transactions that require that the related master record quantity on hand field be reduced by the quantity field value of the sale. No other computations are needed.

*Sales and Purchases (**S** and **P**) Transaction File/Record Format:*

PHYSICAL FILE DESCRIPTION

SYSTEM: AS/400	DATE: Yours
FILE NAME: Yours	REV NO: 0
RECORD NAME: Yours	KEY LENGTH: 5
SEQUENCE: Keyed (non-unique)	RECORD SIZE: 17

FIELD DEFINITIONS

FIELD NO	FIELD NAME	SIZE	TYPE	POSITION FROM	POSITION TO	COMMENTS
1	TRANSCODE	1	C	1	1	P or S
2	BRANDNO	5	C	2	6	Key field
3	SORPQTY	5	P	7	9	0 decimals
4	PURCOST	6	P	10	13	2 decimals
5	PURDATE	6	P	14	17	

Note: S (sales records) must have zeros stored in the PURCOST and PURDATE fields.

<u>Physical File Data</u>:

Trans Code	Brand#	Quantity	Purchase Cost	Purchase Date
P	C2121	00400	019000	091597
P	C8000	02000	017000	092197
S	C6550	00500	000000	000000
S	C8900	10000	000000	000000
S	C7440	00800	000000	000000
S	C1200	07600	000000	000000

*Changes (**C**)/Deletes (**D**) Transaction File/Record Format:*

PHYSICAL FILE DESCRIPTION

SYSTEM: AS/400	DATE: Yours
FILE NAME: Yours	REV NO: 0
RECORD NAME: Yours	KEY LENGTH: 5
SEQUENCE: Keyed (not unique)	RECORD SIZE: 63

FIELD DEFINITIONS

FIELD NO	FIELD NAME	SIZE	TYPE	POSITION FROM	POSITION TO	COMMENTS
1	CCODE	1	C	1	1	C
2	CBRANDNO	5	C	2	6	Key field
3	CNAME	20	C	7	26	
4	CSIZE	3	P	27	28	
5	CMEASURE	2	C	29	30	
6	CMFGR	15	C	31	45	
7	CLPDATE	6	P	46	49	
8	CUNITCOST	6	P	50	53	4 decimals
9	CQTYONHAND	5	P	54	56	0 decimals
10	CAVGCOST	6	P	57	60	4 decimals
11	CUNITSP	4	P	61	63	2 decimals

Physical File Data:

Trans Code	Brand#	Brand Name	Size	Measure	Manufacturer	Last Purchase Date	Last Purchase Price	Amount On Hand	Avg Cost/ Unit	SP Price/ Unit
C	C1100						017000			0190
D	C7100									
C	C4889		012			081597				
C	C8100	PUFFED RICE								
C	C1300								020000	
D	C7440									

Generate an edit report for transaction records not found in the master file in the following format:

Report Design:

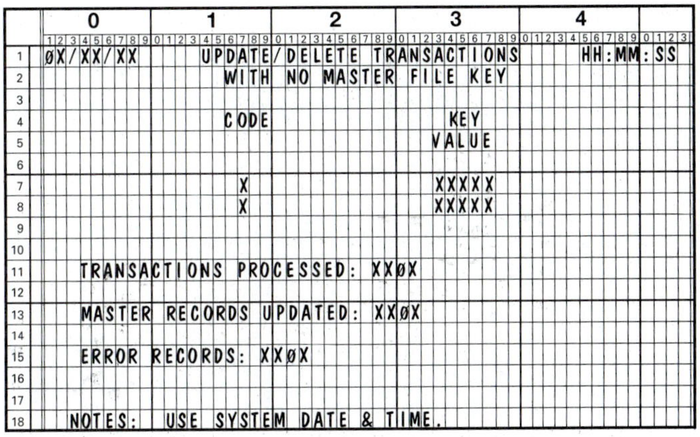

ØX/XX/XX
UPDATE/DELETE TRANSACTIONS
HH:MM:SS
WITH NO MASTER FILE KEY
CODE
KEY
VALUE
X
X
XXXXX
XXXXX
TRANSACTIONS PROCESSED: XXØX
MASTER RECORDS UPDATED: XXØX
ERROR RECORDS: XXØX
NOTES: USE SYSTEM DATE & TIME.

Print a **CPYF** hexidecimal listing of the master file *before* and *after* the records are updated and deleted. Compare the listings to check the execution results of your program.

chapter 14

Display Files

A *display file* defines the format of one or more records that will be shown on a display device. The record format usually includes fields, constants, indicators, and keywords. Display files are initially developed in source code and then compiled to create an object. A display file may contain a maximum of 1,024 record formats with no more than 32,763 characters in each format. They may include entries at the *File*, *Record*, *Field*, and *Help Levels*.

The record format(s) in a display file **(DSPF)** may be created by the following two methods:

1. Design a screen format on a form, complete the DDS coding, enter the code via **SEU,** and compile with the **CRTDSPF** command.
2. Design and code a screen format using the *Screen Design Aid* **(SDA)** utility.

The procedures and syntax for creating display files using the *Screen Design Aid* **(SDA)** utility are detailed in Appendix D. This chapter follows the familiar **SEU** method for creating display files.

CREATING A DISPLAY FILE RECORD

The steps required to create a display file using the **SEU** method are as follows:

1. Design the record format on a CRT layout form (or print chart).
2. Code the record format on DDS forms (may be skipped).
3. Enter the DDS instructions via **SEU.**
4. Save, compile (**CRTDSPF** command), debug, and optionally test with the **SDA** test utility.

Each of the steps is detailed in upcoming sections.

Designing the Record Format

The **DSPF** record design shown in Figure 14-1 will be used as the input/output medium to add, update, inquiry, and logically delete records from a physical file.

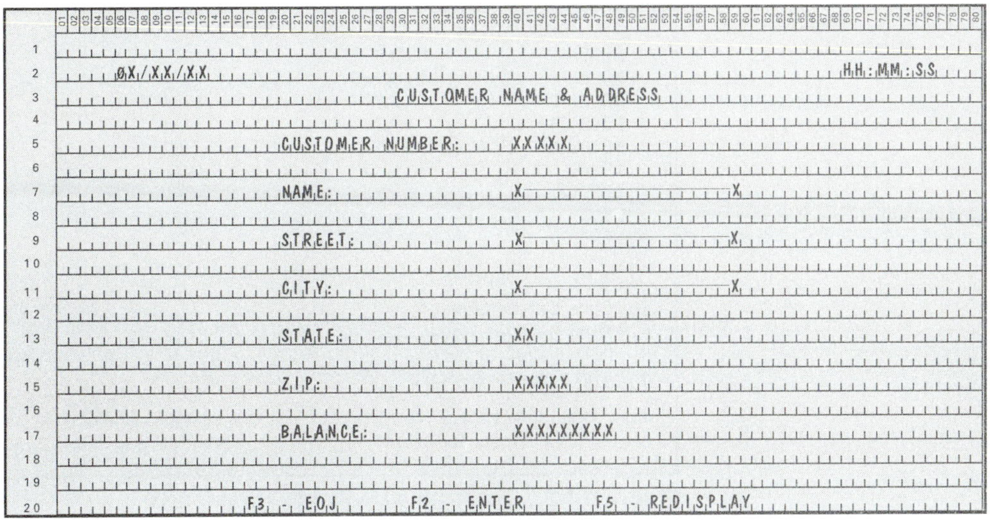

Figure 14-1 Display file record design.

Data Description Specification Syntax for Display Files

Similar to physical files, the instructions for display files are entered on SEU **DDS** record formats. Entries may be made at the *File*, *Record*, *Help*, *Field*, *Select/Omit Levels*. A list of keywords unique to a display file is presented in Figure 14-2. Note that some keywords are only functional at the *File* **(F)**, *File/Record* **(FR)**, *File/Record/Field* **(FRD)**,

R ALARM	D EDTMSK	R MDTOFF	R SFLCSRRRN
D ALIAS	D EDTWRD	D MLTCHFLD	R SFLCTL
F ALTHELP	FRD ENTFLDATR	R MNUBAR	R SFLDLT
R ALTNAME	R ERASE	D MNUBARCHC	R SFLDROP
F ALTPAGEDWN	R ERASEINP	R MNUBARDSP	R SFLDSP
F ALTPAGEUP	D ERRMSG	D MNUBARSEP	R SFLDSPCTL
FR ALWGPH	D ERRMSGID	FR MNUBARSW	R SFLEND
R ALWROL	F ERRSFL	FR MNUCNL	R SFLENTER
R ASSUME	D FLDCSRPRG	FR MOUBTN	R SFLFOLD
D AUTO	D FLTFXDEC	FR MSGALARM	R SFLINZ
D BLANKS	D FLTPCN	D MSGCON	R SFLLIN
R BLINK	R FRCDTA	D MSGID	R SFLMLTCHC
D BLKFOLD	R GETRETAIN	F MSGLOC	R SFLMODE
FR CAnn	FR GRDATR	D NOCCSID	R SFLMSG
FR CFnn	R GRDBOX	F OPENPRT	R SFLMSGID
RD CHANGE	R GRDCLR	R OVERLAY	D SFLMSGKEY
D CHCACCEL	R GRDLIN	RD OVRATR	R SFLMSGRCD
D CHCAVAIL	R GRDRCD	RD OVRDTA	R SFLNXTCHG
D CHCCTL	FR HELP	FR PAGEDOWN	R SFLPAG
D CHCSLT	H HLPARA	FR PAGEUP	D SFLPGMQ
D CHCUNAVAIL	H HLPBDY	F PASSRCD	D SFLRCDNBR
D CHECK	H HLPCLR	FR PRINT	R SFLRNA
FRD CHGINPDFT	R HLPCMDKEY	R PROTECT	D SFLROLVAL
ID CHKMSGID	FH HLPDOC	D PSHBTNCHC	R SFLRTNSEL
ID CHOICE	H HLPEXCLD	D PSHBTNFLD	D SFLSCROLL
D CHRID	F HLPFULL	R PULLDOWN	R SFLSIZ
FR CLEAR	D HLPID	R PUTOVR	R SFLSNGCHC
R CLRL	FH HLPPNLGRP	RD PUTRETAIN	R SLNO
D CMP	FH HLPRCD	D RANGE	D SNGCHCFLD
D CNTFLD	FR HLPRTN	F REF	D SYSNAME
D COLOR	F HLPSCHIDX	D REFFLD	RD TEXT
D COMP	R HLPSEQ	R RETKEY	D TIME
FR CSRINPONLY	F HLPSHELF	R RETCMDKEY	R UNLOCK
R CSRLOC	FR HLPTITLE	R RETLCKSTS	D USER
D DATE	FR HOME	R RMVWDW	R USRDFN
D DFT	F INDARA	FR ROLLDOWN	F USRDSPMGT

Figure 14-2 Display file keywords.

D DFTVAL	FRD INDTXT	FR ROLLUP	R USRRSTDSP
D DLTCHK	FR INVITE	R RTNCSRLOC	FRD VALNUM
D DLTEDT	R INZINP	R RTNDTA	D VALUES
D DSPATR	R INZRCD	R SETOF	FR VLDCMDKEY
R DSPMOD	R KEEP	R SETOFF	FR WDWBORDER
F DSPRL	R LOCK	R SFL	R WDWTITLE
F DSPSIZ	R LOGINP	D SFLCHCCTL	R WINDOW
D DUP	R LOGOUT	R SFLCLR	FRD WRDWRAP
D EDTCDE	D LOWER	D SFLCSRPRG	

F File Level Keyword
R Record Level Keyword
H Help Level Keyword
D Field Level Keyword

More than one letter to the left of the keyword indicates that it is supported at more than one level (e.g., FRD).

Figure 14-2 Display file keywords. (Continued)

Record/Field (**RD**), or *Field* (**D**) level. Any keyword not entered at the correct level will cause an SEU syntax error when entering the instruction.

Of the current 179 keywords, only a few will be used in this chapter's display file examples. For an explanation of the function of each keyword, refer to IBM's most recent *AS/400 DDS Reference* manual.

The display file syntax for the record design in Figure 14-1 is detailed in the SEU source listing in Figure 14-3. Note that keywords are entered at the *File*, *Record*, and *Field Levels*.

```
SEQNBR*...+... 1 ...+... 2 ...+... 3 ...+... 4 ...+... 5 ...+... 6 ...+... 7 ...+... 8
        A                                      REF(STAN/CUSTMASTER)
        A                                      PRINT
        A                                      CA03(03 'EOJ')                File Level
        A                                      CF02(02 'ENTER')
        A                                      CA05(05 'REDISPLAY')
        A          R MASTERRCD                 CHGINPDFT(CS)                 Record Level
        A                                  2  6DATE EDTCDE(Y)
        A                                  2 69TIME
        A                                  3 30'CUSTOMER NAME & ADDRESS'
        A                                  5 20'CUSTOMER NUMBER:'
        A            CUSTNUMBERR     D  B  5 40
        A  99                                  ERRMSG('DUPLICATE RECORD' 99)
        A                                  7 20'NAME:'
        A            CUSTNAME  R        B  7 40
        A                                  9 20'STREET:'
        A            STREET    R        B  9 40
        A                                 11 20'CITY:'
        A            CITY      R        B 11 40                              Field Level
        A                                 13 20'STATE:'
        A            STATE     R        B 13 40
        A                                 15 20'ZIP:'
        A            ZIPCODE   R     D  B 15 40
        A                                 17 20'BALANCE:'
        A            ACTBALANCER        B 17 40
        A                                 20 17'F3 - EOJ         F2 - ENTER        F5-
        A                                       - REDISPLAY'
```

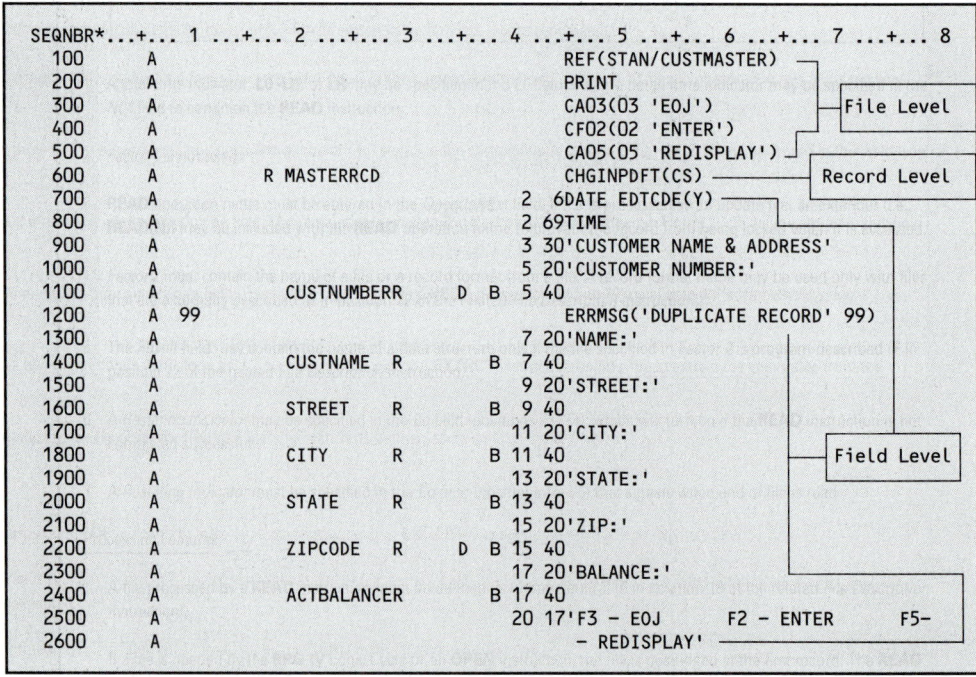

Figure 14-3 DDS coding for an example of display file record format.

File Level Keywords

The *File Level* keywords used in the example display file record format are explained in Figure 14-4.

```
SEQNBR*...+... 1 ...+... 2 ...+... 3 ...+... 4 ...+... 5 ...+... 6 ...+... 7 ...+... 8
      .....AAN01N02N03T.Name++++++RLen++TDpBLinPosFunctions++++++++++++++++++++++++++++

  100      A                                    REF(STAN/CUSTMASTER)
  200      A                                    PRINT
  300      A                                    CA03(03 'EOJ')
  400      A                                    CF02(02 'ENTER')
  500      A                                    CA05(05 'REDISPLAY')
```

File Level (Lines 100 to 500):

Line No. Functions (Columns 45–80)

1 The keyword **REF** (Reference) retrieves the field descriptions from a previously described record format. Its format is shown below:

REF([library-name]/data-base-file-name/ [record name])

As indicated by the brackets [ ], the library-name and record-name entries are optional. The library-name entry is needed only if the database file referenced is not in a library included in your library list. The record-name entry is required if the referenced database file has more than one record format, which is not relevant for physical files.

2 The keyword **PRINT** controls the printing of a displayed screen when the print key is pressed on the keyboard. Without this entry the screen image could not be printed at the operator's discretion. Its format is shown below:

PRINT [(response-indicator ['text']) I (*PGM) I (*PGM) I ([library-name/]printer-file name)]

The following examples indicate ways to format the **PRINT** keyword:

PRINT—Stores the screen image to the user's output queue. The Reset key must be pressed to continue.

PRINT (01 "Press print key')—Tells the operator what to do and passes control to the program, which determines the action to be taken.

PRINT (*PGM)—Control is automatically returned to your program after the Print key is pressed.

PRINT(library-name/printer-file-name)—Spools output to the specified printer file.

3 The keyword **CA03** (Command Attention key) assigns the Command Key 3 to some display file function and turns on an optional response indicator. Command Attention keys 01 through 24 may be assigned at the *File* or *Record Level.* They do *not,* however, provide for the transmission of input data from display file to an **RPG IV** program. The format of the **CA** keyword is shown below:

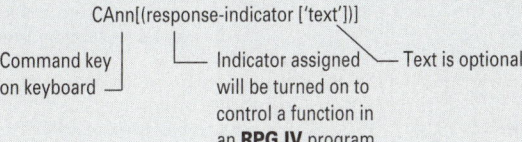

CAnn[(response-indicator ['text'])]

Command key on keyboard — Indicator assigned will be turned on to control a function in an **RPG IV** program — Text is optional

Note that the response indicator specified does not have to be the same as the **CA** key.

When a **CA** key is pressed during program execution, all other command keys are turned off.

CA03(03 'EOJ') will be used to control end-of-job processing and **CA05(05 'REDISPLAY')** for redisplay in an example **RPG IV** program discussed in Chapter 15.

4 The keyword **CF02** (Command Function key) assigns the Command Key 2 to some screen control function and turns on an optional response indicator. Command function keys 01 through 24 may be assigned at the *File* or *Record Level.* The Command Function keyword **(CF)** differs from the Command Attention keyword **(CA)** in that it does provide for the transmission of data from a display file to a program. The format of a **CF** keyword is shown below:

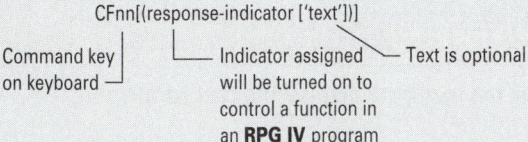

CFnn[(response-indicator ['text'])]

Command key on keyboard — Indicator assigned will be turned on to control a function in an **RPG IV** program — Text is optional

Note that the response indicator specified does not have to be the same assigned to the **CF** key.

Figure 14-4 *File Level* keywords for the example display file record format.

If more than one record format was included in the display file, keywords at the *File Level* would apply to all of the records unless overridden with an alternative keyword at the *Record* or *Field Level*. For example, **PRINT, CA03, CF02,** and **CF05** keywords could have been specified at the *Record Level* and be functional only for that record format. Then, if additional record formats were added to the display file, those keywords would not apply to them.

Record Level Keywords

The one *Record Level* keyword included in the example display file is explained in Figure 14-5.

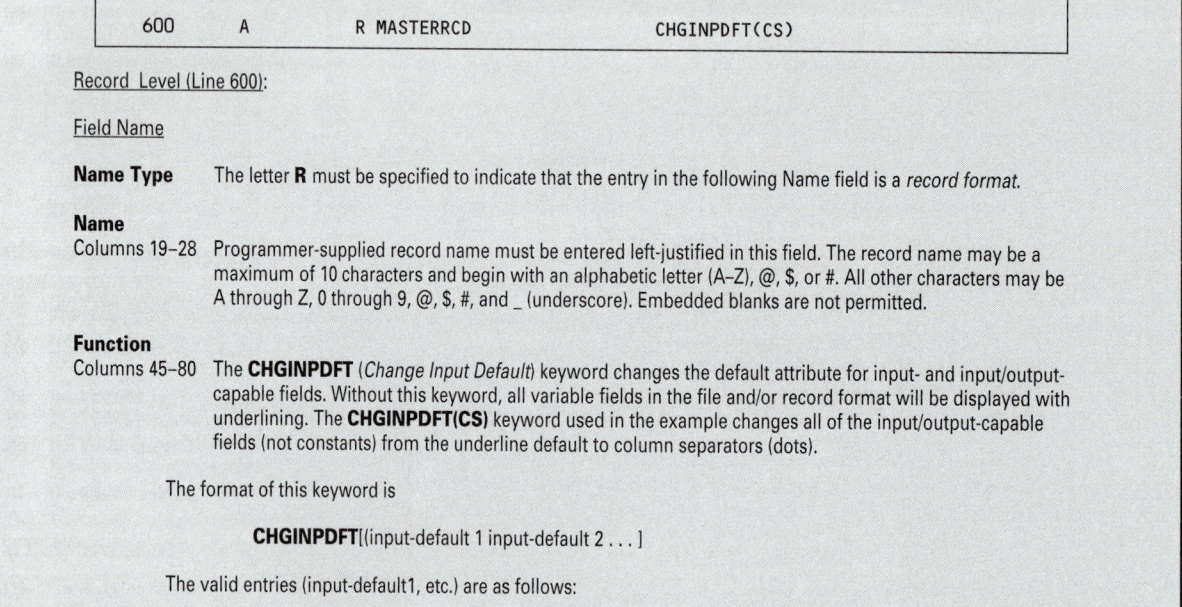

```
SEQNBR*...+... 1 ...+... 2 ...+... 3 ...+... 4 ...+... 5 ...+... 6 ...+... 7 ...+... 8
     .....AAN01N02N03T.Name++++++RLen++TDpBLinPosFunctions++++++++++++++++++++++++++++

 600       A            R MASTERRCD                  CHGINPDFT(CS)
```

Record Level (Line 600):

Field Name

Name Type The letter **R** must be specified to indicate that the entry in the following Name field is a *record format.*

Name
Columns 19–28 Programmer-supplied record name must be entered left-justified in this field. The record name may be a maximum of 10 characters and begin with an alphabetic letter (A–Z), @, $, or #. All other characters may be A through Z, 0 through 9, @, $, #, and _ (underscore). Embedded blanks are not permitted.

Function
Columns 45–80 The **CHGINPDFT** (*Change Input Default*) keyword changes the default attribute for input- and input/output-capable fields. Without this keyword, all variable fields in the file and/or record format will be displayed with underlining. The **CHGINPDFT(CS)** keyword used in the example changes all of the input/output-capable fields (not constants) from the underline default to column separators (dots).

The format of this keyword is

CHGINPDFT[(input-default 1 input-default 2 . . .]

The valid entries (input-default1, etc.) are as follows:

Value	Equivalent DDS Keyword	Function
none	none	Remove underlining
BL	DSPATR (BL)	Blinking field
CS	DSPATR (CS)	Column separators (dots)
HI	DSPATR (HI)	High intensity
RI	DSPATR (RI)	Reverse image
UL	DSPATR (UL)	Underline
FE	CHECK (FE)	Field exit
LC	CHECK (LC)	Lowercase
ME	CHECK (ME)	Mandatory enter
MF	CHECK (MF)	Mandatory fill

A *File Level* **CHGINPDFT** changes all of the input- and input/output-capable fields in all of the record formats to the designated parameter value. **CHGINPDFT** keywords at the *Record Level* will override any specified at the *File Level.* Similarly, *Field Level* **CHGINPDFT** entries will override those previously specified at the *File* and *Record Levels.* In other words, any lower-level **CHGINPDFT** keyword will override any specified at a higher level.

Figure 14-5 *Record Level* keyword for the example display file record format.

Field Level Keywords and Entries

Because of the number of keywords and syntax related to *Field Level* entries for the example display file, the instructions are discussed in separate sections.

System Date and Time (DATE/TIME Keywords)

The **DATE** keyword accesses the system date in an MMDDYY format. Standard date editing (i.e., MM/DD/YY) is not included and must be separately specified with an **EDTCDE** *(edit code)* or **EDTWRD** *(edit word)* keyword.

System time, which is accessed by the **TIME** keyword, displays in an HH:MM:SS format with the colons automatically inserted. An explanation of how these keywords are used in the example display file is detailed in Figure 14-6.

```
SEQNBR*...+... 1 ...+... 2 ...+... 3 ...+... 4 ...+... 5 ...+... 6 ...+... 7 ...+... 8
     .....AAN01N02N03T.Name++++++RLen++TDpBLinPosFunctions++++++++++++++++++++++++++++

  700     A                                  2  6DATE EDTCDE(Y)
  800     A                                  2 69TIME
```

Field level (lines 700–800)

Line 700

<u>Location/Line Field</u>

Columns 39–41 The **2** right-justified in this field indicates the line on which the **DATE** value will be displayed.

<u>Location/Pos Field</u>

Columns 42–44 The **6** right-justified in this field indicates the starting position of the **DATE** value that will be displayed on the line specified in the *Line* field.

<u>Functions</u>

Column 45–80 The keyword **DATE** accesses the system data in an MMDDYY format and will display the value in accordance with the *Location* field entries. Note that **DATE** is <u>*predefined*</u> as a six-byte numeric field.

Columns 45–80 The keyword **EDTCDE** controls editing of **DATE** or any numeric field specified in the *Name* field entry. Edit codes specified within parentheses are identical to those supported by **RPG IV** (1, 2, 3, 4, A, B, C, D, J, K, L, M, Y, and Z). **EDTCDE(Y)** edits the **DATE** value by suppressing the leading zero for months 01 through 09 and inserts two slashes (/) for an MM/DD/YY format. The keyword **EDTCDE** may be included on the same line as the item edited or on the next line.

When unique editing is required, as for social security or telephone numbers, an **EDTWRD** keyword may be used. Again, the structure of an **EDTWRD** is identical to the **RPG IV** syntax for edit words. The example shown below illustrates how **DATE** is edited using the **EDTWRD** keyword.

EDTWRD('0 / / ')

For a review of edit codes and edit words, refer to Chapter 4.

Line 800

<u>Location</u>

Columns 38–44 Line **(2)** and starting **(69)** positions are specified for the **TIME** value.

<u>Functions</u>

Columns 45–80 The **TIME** keyword accesses the system time in an HH:MM:SS format. Because the colons (:) are included in the **TIME** values, an edit word is not needed. **TIME** is predefined as a numeric field; therefore, an **EDTWRD** may be specified in any valid format.

Figure 14-6 **DATE** and **TIME** keyword entries in the example display file.

The other *Field Level* keywords, constants, and fields used in the example display file's record format are explained in Figure 14-7.

```
SEQNBR*...+... 1 ...+... 2 ...+... 3 ...+... 4 ...+... 5 ...+... 6 ...+... 7 ...+... 8
      .....AAN01N02N03T.Name++++++RLen++TDpBLinPosFunctions++++++++++++++++++++ ++++++

   900     A                                  3 30'CUSTOMER NAME & ADDRESS'
  1000     A                                  5 20'CUSTOMER NUMBER:'
  1100     A          CUSTNUMBERR       D  B  5 40
  1200     A  99                                    ERRMSG('DUPLICATE RECORD' 99)
  1300     A                                  7 20'NAME:'
  1400     A          CUSTNAME  R          B  7 40
  1500     A                                  9 20'STREET:'
  1600     A          STREET    R          B  9 40                          Field Level
  1700     A                                 11 20'CITY:'
  1800     A          CITY      R          B 11 40
  1900     A                                 13 20'STATE:'
  2000     A          STATE     R          B 13 40
  2100     A                                 15 20'ZIP:'
  2200     A          ZIPCODE   R       D  B 15 40
  2300     A                                 17 20'BALANCE:'
  2400     A          ACTBALANCER          B 17 40
  2500     A                                 20 17'F3 - EOJ       F2 - ENTER      F5-
  2600     A                                      - REDISPLAY'
```

Lines 900–1000

Location

Columns 38–44 Indicates the line and column locations where the constants will display.

Columns 45–80 Any constants must be enclosed in single quotes and will display exactly as they are specified in the **DSPF** coding. Display attributes **(DSPATR)** including reverse image, highlighting, underlining, blinking, and so forth may be specified for any constant or field.

Line 1100

Name

Columns 19–28 The field name **(CUSTNUMBER)** referenced from the physical file (see line 100) is entered here. Independent fields may be also defined in a display file.

Length

Columns 30–34 Because the field was referenced from a physical file, it does not have to be defined in the display file. However, if the field was not referenced, its length would have to be entered. Numeric fields may be defined with a maximum of 31 bytes, and character fields with 256.

The attributes of individual fields may be accessed from any DDS-supported file by the following *Field Level* keyword:

REFFLD([record-format-name/]referenced-field-name [{*SRC | [library-name/]data-base-file-name}])

If the program that supports the **DSPF** file is executing in the same library as the referenced file, the keyword may be shortened to the following format:

REFFLD (referenced-field-name)

Note that the letter **R** must be specified in the *Reference* field (position 29) to access the attributes of any field referenced from a file by the **REF** or **REFFLD** keyword.

Data Type

Column 35 **D** specified for this field is the data type/keyboard shift attribute for a display file field. The letter **D** allows only positive numbers to be entered in the CUSTNUMBER and ZIPCODE fields. Because the low-order sign position is suppressed, only the Field Exit, Field+, and Dups keys are permitted to enter the field value.

Specifying a **D** for this field requires that the user enter only the digits 0–9. Furthermore, because a sign position is not displayed, the user is less likely to be confused by the extra digit position.

Figure 14-7 Other *Field Level* entries used in the example display file.

Other valid column 35 entries are:

Entry	Meaning	Valid Data Type
Blank	Default	
X	Alphabetic only	Character
A	Alphanumeric shift	Character
N	Numeric shift	Character or numeric
S	Signed numeric	Numeric
Y	Numeric only	Numeric
W	Katakana (Japanese)	Character
I	Inhibit keyboard entry	Character or numeric
D	Digits only	Character or numeric
M	Numeric only character	Character
F	Floating point	Numeric

Refer to the *Data Description Specifications* Manual (Display File chapter) for an explanation of these entries.

Decimal Positions

Columns 36–37 Because all of the field attributes are referenced from the CUSTMASTER physical file, no entry has to be specified. When a numeric field is defined in the display file, the number of related decimal positions must be included in this field. Recall that the number of decimal positions for a numeric field processed by an **RPG IV** program is limited to 9. For character fields this area must be blank.

Usage

Column 38 The **B** specified indicates that the field is defined both as an input and an output field. Values may be input from the screen to a program or output from a program to a screen as required in update or deletion processing.

Other options include:

O—Output from a program to the screen as required by inquiry processing.

I—Input from the screen to a program as required by data entry processing or adding records to an existing file.

Location

Columns 39–44 *Line* and *Pos* entries define the line and starting positions, respectively, of the field value.

Line 1200

Functions

Columns 45–80 The **ERRMSG** keyword controls the display of the error text specified within the parentheses and single quotes. A conditioning indicator(s) must be specified in columns 8 through 16, which is turned on when the related error condition is flagged during execution of an **RPG IV** program; controls the display of the error message.

The format of the **ERRMSG** keyword is illustrated below:

ERRMSG ('message-text' [response-indicator])

Programmer-supplied ↗ ↑ Conditioning indicator (columns 8 through 16) is specified here and will turn off when the Reset key is pressed

In the example shown, indicator **99** will be turned on in an **RPG IV** program if an attempt is made to **WRITE** a record to a physical file defined with unique keys with a key already stored in the file. When the related error occurs, the programmer-supplied text in the body of the **ERRMSG** keyword will display in reverse image at the bottom (line 2400) of the screen and the cursor will move to the input field that generated the error. The Reset key must be pressed to continue.

If more than one **ERRMSG** keyword is specified and the errors tested occur at the same time, only the first **ERRMSG** text will be displayed.

Lines 1300–2400

The constant and field entries on these lines follow the syntax explained above. Note that the ZIPCODE field also includes a **D** in the *Data Type* field, which will eliminate the low-order sign position from this packed numeric item.

Columns 45–80 The **EDTCDE(Z)** keyword suppresses all leading zeros in the displayed field. Without this keyword, zeros will be included when the display file's record format is displayed.

Figure 14-7 Other *Field Level* entries used in the example display file. (Continued)

Lines 2500–2600

The constant entered on line 2500 differs from the others in that it continues to another line. Continuation of an entry is controlled by including a minus sign (–) or plus sign (+) at the end of the item. The entry is continued on the next line without any leading quote. Note that **SEU** will indicate an error (reverse-image display) for line 2500 when the ENTER key is pressed. Completing the statement on line 2600 will correct the syntax error.

Figure 14-7 Other *Field Level* entries used in the example display file. (Continued)

SEU Entry and Compilation of Display Files

If the *Programmer Menu* is used to access **SEU, 8** must be entered in the *Selection* field, the display file name in the *Parm* field, and **DSPF** for the member type. To compile the display file, **3** must be entered in the *Selection* field of the Programmer Menu with the *Parm* and *Type* entries. If any of the default parameters are to be changed, the **CRTDSPF** command has to be entered on the command line of any display and **F4** pressed. The programmer can then select the parameters to be changed.

If **PDM** is used to develop a display file, refer to Appendix B for the procedures that must be followed.

Figure 14-8 shows the listing generated from compilation of the example display file. Note that the Expanded Source listing, which provides supplemental information, is shown.

```
5763SS1 V3R1M0  940909              Data Description              STAN/NEWCUSTMRS         12/04/97  8:51:17         Page    1
File name . . . . . . . . . . . . . . . . . . . . . :   NEWCUSTMRS
  Library name  . . . . . . . . . . . . . . . . . . :   STAN
File attribute  . . . . . . . . . . . . . . . . . . :   Display
Source file containing DDS  . . . . . . . . . . . . :   QDDSSRC
  Library name  . . . . . . . . . . . . . . . . . . :   STAN
Source member containing DDS  . . . . . . . . . . . :   NEWCUSTMRS
Source member last changed  . . . . . . . . . . . . :   12/04/97    8:50:53
Source listing options  . . . . . . . . . . . . . . :   *SOURCE     *LIST          *NOSECLVL
DDS generation severity level . . . . . . . . . . . :   20
DDS flagging severity level . . . . . . . . . . . . :   00
Authority . . . . . . . . . . . . . . . . . . . . . :   *LIBCRTAUT
Replace file  . . . . . . . . . . . . . . . . . . . :   *YES
Text  . . . . . . . . . . . . . . . . . . . . . . . :   fig14-3 -example dspf record format
Compiler  . . . . . . . . . . . . . . . . . . . . . :   IBM AS/400 Data Description Processor
                               Data Description Source
SEQNBR  *...+....1....+....2....+....3....+....4....+....5....+....6....+....7....+....8  Date
   100      A                                      REF(STAN/CUSTMASTER)                   12/02/97
   200      A                                      PRINT                                  12/02/97
   300      A                                      CA03(03 'EOJ')                         12/02/97
   400      A                                      CF02(02 'ENTER')                       12/02/97
   500      A                                      CA05(05 'REDISPLAY')                   12/02/97
   600      A            R MASTERRCD               CHGINPDFT(CS)                          12/02/97
   700      A                                  2  6DATE EDTCDE(Y)                         12/02/97
   800      A                                  2 69TIME                                   12/02/97
   900      A                                  3 30'CUSTOMER NAME & ADDRESS'              12/02/97
  1000      A                                  5 20'CUSTOMER NUMBER:'                     12/02/97
  1100      A              CUSTNUMBERR     D  B  5 40                                     12/02/97
  1200      A  99                                  ERRMSG('DUPLICATE RECORD' 99)          12/04/97
  1300      A                                  7 20'NAME:'                                12/02/97
  1400      A              CUSTNAME  R        B  7 40                                     12/02/97
  1500      A                                  9 20'STREET:'                              12/02/97
  1600      A              STREET    R        B  9 40                                     12/02/97
  1700      A                                 11 20'CITY:'                                12/02/97
  1800      A              CITY      R        B 11 40                                     12/02/97
  1900      A                                 13 20'STATE:'                               12/02/97
  2000      A              STATE     R        B 13 40                                     12/02/97
  2100      A                                 15 20'ZIP:'                                 12/02/97
  2200      A              ZIPCODE   R     D  B 15 40                                     12/02/97
  2300      A                                 17 20'BALANCE:'                             12/02/97
  2400      A              ACTBALANCER        B 17 40                                     12/02/97
  2500      A                                 20 17'F3 - EOJ       F2 - ENTER      F5-    12/02/97
  2600      A                                      - REDISPLAY'                           12/02/97
                  * * * * *   E N D   O F   S O U R C E   * * * * *
```

Figure 14-8 Compile listing of the example display file.

```
5763SS1 V3R1M0  940909              Data Description                STAN/NEWCUSTMRS          12/04/97  8:51:17         Page    2
                                    Expanded Source
                                                                                        Field        Buffer position
SEQNBR  *...+....1....+....2....+....3....+....4....+....5....+....6....+....7....+....8 length         Out       I
   200                                          PRINT CA03(03 'EOJ') +
   400                                          CF02(02 'ENTER') +
   500                                          CA05(05 'REDISPLAY')
                                                DSPSIZ(*DS3)
              * Option indicator output buffer positions:
              *  *IN99 0001
              * Response indicator input buffer positions:
              *  *IN02 0002    *IN03 0001    *IN05 0003    *IN99 0004
   600                R MASTERRCD               CHGINPDFT(CS)
   700                                      2  6DATE EDTCDE(Y)                      8
   800                                      2 69TIME                                8
   900                                      3 30'CUSTOMER NAME & ADDRESS'          23
  1000                                      5 20'CUSTOMER NUMBER:'                 16
  1100                  CUSTNUMBER    5D 0B  5 40                                  5            2        5
 * Referenced Field . . . . . . . . . . . :  CUSTNUMBER
 *   Format . . . . . . . . . . . . . . . :  CUSRECORD
 *   File . . . . . . . . . . . . . . . . :  CUSTMASTER
 *   Library . . . . . . . . . . . . . . . :  STAN
  1200          99                              ERRMSG('DUPLICATE RECORD' 99)
  1300                                      7 20'NAME:'                             5
  1400                  CUSTNAME     20A  B  7 40                                  20            7       10
 * Referenced Field . . . . . . . . . . . :  CUSTNAME
 *   Format . . . . . . . . . . . . . . . :  CUSRECORD
 *   File . . . . . . . . . . . . . . . . :  CUSTMASTER
 *   Library . . . . . . . . . . . . . . . :  STAN
  1500                                      9 20'STREET:'                           7
  1600                  STREET       20A  B  9 40                                  20           27       30
 * Referenced Field . . . . . . . . . . . :  STREET
 *   Format . . . . . . . . . . . . . . . :  CUSRECORD
 *   File . . . . . . . . . . . . . . . . :  CUSTMASTER
 *   Library . . . . . . . . . . . . . . . :  STAN
  1700                                     11 20'CITY:'                             5
  1800                  CITY         20A  B 11 40                                  20           47       50
 * Referenced Field . . . . . . . . . . . :  CITY
 *   Format . . . . . . . . . . . . . . . :  CUSRECORD
 *   File . . . . . . . . . . . . . . . . :  CUSTMASTER
 *   Library . . . . . . . . . . . . . . . :  STAN
  1900                                     13 20'STATE:'                            6
  2000                  STATE         2A  B 13 40                                   2           67       70
 * Referenced Field . . . . . . . . . . . :  STATE
 *   Format . . . . . . . . . . . . . . . :  CUSRECORD
 *   File . . . . . . . . . . . . . . . . :  CUSTMASTER
 *   Library . . . . . . . . . . . . . . . :  STAN
  2100                                     15 20'ZIP:'                              4
  2200                  ZIPCODE       5D 0B 15 40                                   5           69       72
 * Referenced Field . . . . . . . . . . . :  ZIPCODE
 *   Format . . . . . . . . . . . . . . . :  CUSRECORD
 *   File . . . . . . . . . . . . . . . . :  CUSTMASTER
 *   Library . . . . . . . . . . . . . . . :  STAN
5763SS1 V3R1M0  940909              Data Description                STAN/NEWCUSTMRS          12/04/97  8:51:17         Page    3
                                    Expanded Source
                                                                                        Field        Buffer position
SEQNBR  *...+....1....+....2....+....3....+....4....+....5....+....6....+....7....+....8 length         Out      In
  2300                                     17 20'BALANCE:'                          8
  2400                  ACTBALANCE    8S 2B 17 40                                   8           74       77
 * Referenced Field . . . . . . . . . . . :  ACTBALANCE
 *   Format . . . . . . . . . . . . . . . :  CUSRECORD
 *   File . . . . . . . . . . . . . . . . :  CUSTMASTER
 *   Library . . . . . . . . . . . . . . . :  STAN
  2500                                     20 17'F3 - EOJ        F2 - ENTER      F5 --  44
  2500                                          REDISPLAY'
             * * * * *   E N D   O F   E X P A N D E D   S O U R C E   * * * * *
5763SS1 V3R1M0  940909             Data Description                STAN/NEWCUSTMRS          12/04/97  8:51:17         Page    4
                                    Message Summary
   Total         Informational      Warning        Error        Severe
                    (0-9)           (10-19)       (20-29)      (30-99)
       0              0                0             0            0
 * CPC7301       00            Message . . . . :   File NEWCUSTMRS created in library STAN.
                  * * * * *   E N D   O F   C O M P I L A T I O N   * * * * *
```

Figure 14-8 Compile listing of the example display file. (Continued)

A Print key listing of the display file's record format displayed by the *Test* function of **SDA** (see Appendix D for the required steps) is shown in Figure 14-9. If the *Test* func-

```
12/07/97                                                     9:34:52
                       CUSTOMER NAME & ADDRESS

          CUSTOMER NUMBER:    99999

          NAME:               BBBBBBBBBBBBBBBBBBBB

          STREET              BBBBBBBBBBBBBBBBBBBB

          CITY:               BBBBBBBBBBBBBBBBBBBB

          STATE:              BB

          ZIP:                99999

          BALANCE:            99999999

        F3 - EOJ      F2 - ENTER      F5 - REDISPLAY
```

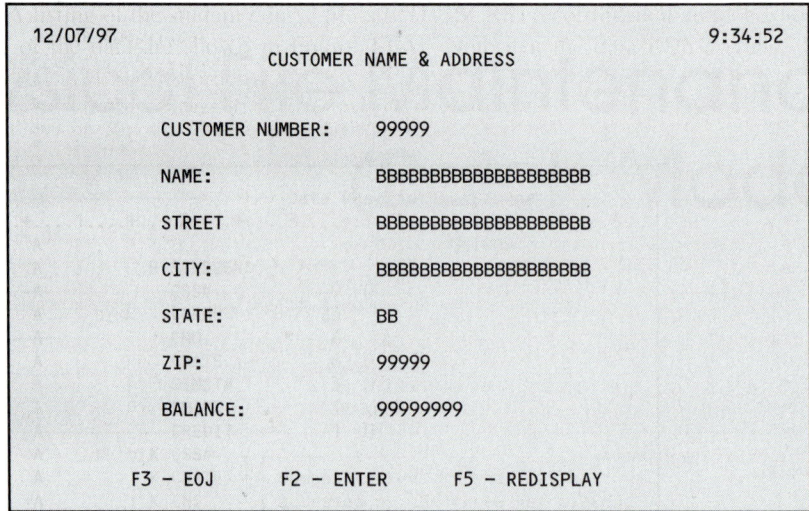

Figure 14-9 SDA display of the example display file's record format.

tion of **SDA** was not used to review the displayed record format, it could not be tested until the related **RPG IV** program was written, compiled, debugged, and tested.

In the **SDA** *Test* mode, the **B**s indicate that the variable field is defined as character with **B Usage** (input and output). The **9**s indicate that the field is defined as numeric with **B Usage**.

Character fields defined with **I Usage** (input) will display with one or more **I**s indicating the field size and type. Input numeric fields would be identified by one or more **3**s.

On the other hand, character fields defined with **O Usage** (output) will display one or more **O**s indicating the field size and type. Output numeric fields are displayed with one or more **6**s.

DISPLAY FILE ENHANCEMENTS

A modified version of the previous example display file is shown in Figure 14-10; it includes the following changes:

1. The **REF(STAN/CUSTMASTER)** keyword instruction and related **R**s in column 29 have been deleted for every field. This change requires that the fields be defined in the display file with entries in the *Length* and *Decimal Positions* (when numeric) fields.
2. The **MSGLOC** *(Message Location)* keyword is added at the *File Level*, which will display the **ERRMSG** text on line 2200 instead of default line 2400.
3. The **TEXT('Customer Master Record')** has been added at the *Record Level.*
4. The keyword entries, **PRINT** through **CA05(05 'REDISPLAY'),** previously specified at the *File Level* have to move to the *Record Level*. If additional record formats were added to the display file, the functions controlled by those keywords would not be applicable to them.
5. The **CHGINPDFT(CS)** *(Change Input Default–Column Separators)* keyword has been changed to **CHGINPDFT(RI)** so that the variable field sizes are displayed in reverse image (light background with dark foreground characters) instead of the default underline attribute.
6. **DSPATR** *(Display Attribute)* keywords provide highlighting **(HI)** to the variable field constants and underlining **(UL)** to the one heading line.

```
SEQNBR *...+....1....+....2....+.... ....+....4....+....5....+....6....+....7....+....8
 100      A                                          MSGLOC(22)
 200      A          R MASTERRCD2                    TEXT('Customer Master Record')
 300      A                                          PRINT
 400      A                                          CA03(03 'EOJ')
 500      A                                          CF02(02 'ENTER')
 600      A                                          CA05(05 'REDISPLAY')
 700      A                                          CHGINPDFT(RI)
 800      A                                      2  6DATE EDTCDE(Y)
 900      A                                      2 69TIME
1000      A                                      3 30'CUSTOMER NAME & ADDRESS' DSPATR(UL)
1100      A                                      5 20'CUSTOMER NUMBER:' DSPATR(HI)
1200      A            CUSTNO         5  0B  5 40
1300      A  99                                      ERRMSG('DUPLICATE RECORD' 99)
1400      A                                      7 20'NAME:' DSPATR(HI)
1500      A            CNAME         20   B  7 40
1600      A                                      9 20'STREET:' DSPATR(HI)
1700      A            CSTREET       20   B  9 40
1800      A                                     11 20'CITY:' DSPATR(HI)
1900      A            CCITY         20   B 11 40
2000      A                                     13 20'STATE:' DSPATR(HI)
2100      A            CSTATE         2   B 13 40
2200      A                                     15 20'ZIP:' DSPATR(HI)
2300      A            CZIPCODE       5  0B 15 40
2400      A                                     17 20'BALANCE:' DSPATR(HI)
2500      A            CBALANCE       8  2B 17 40
2600      A                                     20 16'F3 - EOJ       F2 - ENTER       F5-
2700      A                                          - REDISPLAY'
```

New fields defined in the DSPF

New Entries

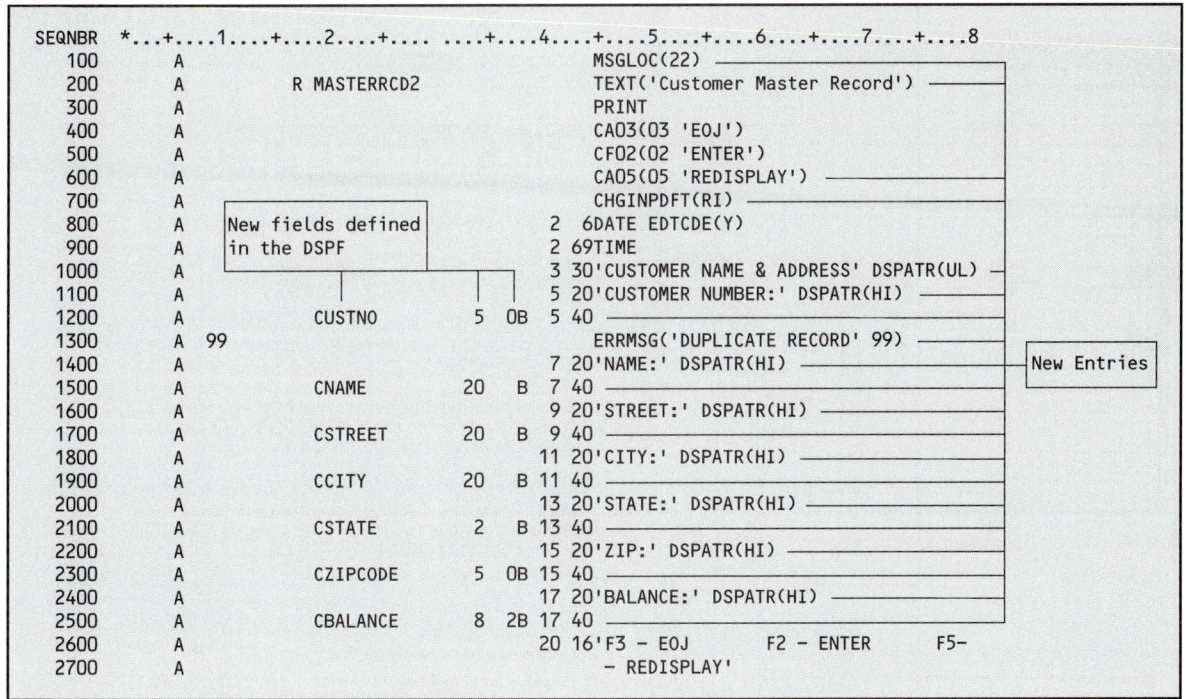

Figure 14-10 Modified example display file.

The new keywords and/or keyword options included in the modified display file will be discussed further in the following paragraphs.

The TEXT Keyword

The **TEXT** keyword is only specified for program documentation in that it supplies a descriptive comment for a record format or field. All of the record formats and fields in any DDS file type may be supplemented with a **TEXT** keyword. The text (included between the single quotes) appears only on a source or compiled source listing and is not displayed in the record format. Upper- or lower- (or both) case letters and any other valid characters may be specified in the text.

CHGINPDFT *(Change Input Default)* Keyword

As mentioned before, the **CHGINPDFT** keyword changes input **(I Usage)** and input/output **(B Usage)** fields from the default underline display to the attribute(s) specified. The **CHGINPDFT(RI)** on line 700 of Figure 14-10 changes the default underline attribute for *all* of the fields (CUSTNO through CBALANCE) to reverse image.

The DSPATR *(Display Attribute)* Keyword

Display attributes are controlled in a display file by the **DSPATR** and **CHGINPDFT** keywords. The functions controlled by the *Field Level* **DSPATR** keyword for *all* fields include *blinking* **(BL),** *column separators* **(CS),** *high intensity* **(HI),** *nondisplay* **(ND),** *position cursor* **(PC),** *reverse image* **(RI),** and *underline* **(UL).** In addition, input-capable fields also support **MDT** (*set changed data tag*), **OID** (*operator identification*), **PR** (*protect field value from input*), and **SP** (*select by light pen*). Figure 14-11 explains the features of each attribute.

CHGINPDFT display attribute functions are limited to blinking **(BL),** column separators **(CS),** high intensity **(HI),** reverse image **(RI),** and underlining **(UL)** at the *File*, *Record*, and *Field Levels*.

Display Attribute	Meaning	Explanation
For All Fields:		
* BL	Blinking Field	Field (or constant) will blink when displayed.
CS	Column Separator	Display dots equal to the size of the field.
* HI	High Intensity	Highlights the field (or constant) when it is displayed.
* ND	Nondisplay	Prevents field (or constant) from being displayed. Often used for passwords and other security-sensitive data.
PC	Position Cursor	Positions the cursor at the first (high-order) position of the related field. If specified for more than one field, the cursor will position at the first field defined with this attribute.
* RI	Reverse Image	Reverses the image of this field (or constant) from the screen's image. For example, if the screen is light-on-dark, the field will display as dark-on-light, or vice versa.
* UL	Underline	Underlines a field or constant. All input-capable fields (**I** or **B Usage**) default to underlining. This default may be overridden with a **CHGINPDFT** keyword specified at the *File or Record Level* or with individual **DSPATR** keywords.
For Input-Capable Fields Only:		
MDT	Set Modified Data Tag	Ensures that a field value is read from the screen.
OID	Operator Identification	Allows magnetic strip reader OID in the field.
PR	Protect	Prevents the workstation user from entering data into an input-capable field (**I** or **B Usage**).
SP	Select by Light Pen	Allows this field to be selected by light pen.

* Indicates that the attribute may be used with constants.

Figure 14-11 DSPATR and **CHGINPDFT** keyword display attributes.

DATA VALIDATION KEYWORDS

Display file keywords that support *data validation* interactively include **CHECK, COMP, RANGE,** and **VALUES.** The syntax of each keyword will be discussed in the following sections.

The CHECK Keyword

For validity checking, the codes that may be specified with the **CHECK** keyword are detailed in Figure 14-12.

CHECK Code	Meaning
AB	Allow blanks
ME	Mandatory enter
MF	Mandatory fill
M10	IBM Modulus-10 self-check algorithm
M11	IBM Modulus-11 self-check algorithm
VN	Validate name
VNE	Validate name extended

Figure 14-12 CHECK keyword edit codes for validity checking.

The function of each edit code is explained in the following paragraphs.

AB (Allow Blanks) CHECK Keyword Code

This code usually supplements another so that blanks will be allowed as an alternative value to satisfy the validity check. For example, if an account number field is validated with the **M11** (Modulus-11) code and the data entered does not pass the test, the user may enter blanks to satisfy the validity check and continue to the next field or exit from the screen. Without the **AB** code, any further action would not be possible and the user would have to press the Shift and System Req keys to exit from the screen and program. An example of how the **CHECK** keyword code is specified is shown in Figure 14-13.

```
SEQNBR*...+... 1 ...+... 2 ...+... 3 ...+... 4 ...+... 5 ...+... 6 ...+... 7 ...+... 8
     .....AAN01N02N03T.Name++++++RLen++TDpBLinPosFunctions++++++++++++++++++++++++++++

          A            INPUTFLD  R            12 20CHECK(AB M11)
```

Figure 14-13 CHECK(AB) keyword coding example.

In addition to validity checking, the **CHECK** keyword may be used for *keyboard and cursor* control. Refer to IBM's *Data Description Reference* manual for an explanation of those functions.

ME (*Mandatory Enter*) CHECK Keyword Code

When specified, the **CHECK** keyword's **ME** code requires that at least one character (a blank is valid) be entered in the field. Note that when none of the fields in the current display has been changed, the *mandatory entry* function is not enforced. If all of the fields in the record format are to support mandatory entry, **DSPATR** (**MDT**) must be specified for at least one field, or a **CHECK** keyword would have to be specified for each field. Figure 14-14 illustrates the syntax for the **CHECK(ME)** keyword.

```
SEQNBR*...+... 1 ...+... 2 ...+... 3 ...+... 4 ...+... 5 ...+... 6 ...+... 7 ...+... 8
     .....AAN01N02N03T.Name++++++RLen++TDpBLinPosFunctions++++++++++++++++++++++++++++

          A            INPUTFLD  R            20 20CHECK(ME)
```

Figure 14-14 CHECK(ME) keyword coding example.

The MF (*Mandatory Fill*) CHECK Keyword Code

The **CHECK** keyword's **MF** code requires that if any character(s) in the field is changed, each position in the field must include a character. In other words, if the field is defined as five positions, five characters must be entered. Figure 14-15 shows the syntax for the **CHECK(MF)** keyword.

```
SEQNBR*...+... 1 ...+... 2 ...+... 3 ...+... 4 ...+... 5 ...+... 6 ...+... 7 ...+... 8
     .....AAN01N02N03T.Name++++++RLen++TDpBLinPosFunctions++++++++++++++++++++++++++++

          A            INPUTFLD  R            20 30CHECK(MF)
```

Figure 14-15 CHECK(MF) keyword coding example.

M10 *(Modulus-10)* and M11 *(Modulus-11)* CHECK Keyword Codes

Chapter 12 introduced and explained the mathematics of the Modulus-11 method (see Figure 12-18) for validating numeric fields that include a check digit in the low-order byte. Because the Modulus-11 method provides for a greater percent of error detection (transpositional and substitution errors) than the Modulus-10 method, it is discussed in this text. Specifying the **CHECK(M11)** keyword with a numeric field that has a check digit included in its value will automatically compute the mathematical steps previously shown in Figure 12-18. To control any values that do not pass the M11 test, the **AB** (*Allow Blanks*) code should be included in the keyword. An example **CHECK(AB M11)** statement is illustrated in Figure 14-16.

```
SEQNBR*...+... 1 ...+... 2 ...+... 3 ...+... 4 ...+... 5 ...+... 6 ...+... 7 ...+... 8
     .....AAN01N02N03T.Name++++++RLen++TDpBLinPosFunctions++++++++++++++++++++++++++++

          A             ACTNUMBER R             14 15CHECK(M11 AB)
```

Figure 14-16 CHECK(M11) keyword coding example.

The VN (Validate Name) CHECK Keyword Code

The **VN** keyword validates that the first character of a field defined as character is a $, #, @, or A through Z with a *keyboard shift* (column 35) of **A, N, X, W,** or **I.** Any remaining field entries may be **$, #, @, A** through **Z, 0** through **9,** or underscore (_) with no embeded blanks. Figure 14-17 illustrates an example **CHECK(VN)** keyword.

```
SEQNBR*...+... 1 ...+... 2 ...+... 3 ...+... 4 ...+... 5 ...+... 6 ...+... 7 ...+... 8
     .....AAN01N02N03T.Name++++++RLen++TDpBLinPosFunctions++++++++++++++++++++++++++++

          A             ADDRESS   R             14 15CHECK(VN)
```

Figure 14-17 CHECK(VN) keyword coding example.

The VNE (*Validate Name Extended*) CHECK Keyword Code

The **VNE** code validates that the first byte in a character field (keyboard shift of **A, N, X, W,** or **I**) is **A** through **Z, a** through **z, #, $,** or **@**. Any remaining characters must be **A** through **Z, a** through **z, $, _ ,** a comma or a period. The size of the related character field is limited to 10 characters. In the validation process, lowercase letters will be converted to uppercase. An example of the **CHECK(VNE)** keyword is shown in Figure 14-18.

```
SEQNBR*...+... 1 ...+... 2 ...+... 3 ...+... 4 ...+... 5 ...+... 6 ...+... 7 ...+... 8
     .....AAN01N02N03T.Name++++++RLen++TDpBLinPosFunctions++++++++++++++++++++++++++++

          A             CUSTNAME  R             14 15CHECK(VNE)
```

Figure 14-18 CHECK(VNE) keyword coding example.

The COMP (*Comparison*) Keyword

The **COMP** keyword, which may also be specified as **CMP,** validates that the value specified is **EQ** *(Equal)*, **NE** *(Not equal to)*, **LT** *(Less than)*, **NL** *(Not less than)*, **GT** *(Greater than)*, **NG** *(Not greater than)*, **LE** *(Less than or equal to)*, or **GE** *(Greater than* *or equal to)* the related field value. Depending on whether the field is defined as numeric or character, the value in the **COMP** keyword must be the same type (numeric or character). Character values must be enclosed in single quotes. Valid numeric values include **0** through **9** and a leading sign (+ or –). Numeric values that do not include a sign are compared as positive. Figure 14-19 illustrates two coding examples of the **COMP** keyword.

```
SEQNBR*...+... 1 ...+... 2 ...+... 3 ...+... 4 ...+... 5 ...+... 6 ...+... 7 ...+... 8
     .....AAN01N02N03T.Name++++++RLen++TDpBLinPosFunctions++++++++++++++++++++++++++++

          * Numeric field comparison:
          A          YTDSS      R            12 1OCOMP(LT 57600)
          * Character field comparison:
          A          STATECODE R             15 1OCOMP(EQ 'CT')
```

Figure 14-19 COMP keyword coding examples.

The RANGE Keyword

The **RANGE** keyword validates that the data in a field value is *equal to or greater than the lower value and less than or equal to the higher value* specified in the **RANGE** keyword. The format of the keyword is

RANGE (low-value high-value)

When the related field is defined as character, the low and high values must both be enclosed in single quotes. The quotes are omitted for numeric fields. Figure 14-20 details two examples of the **RANGE** keyword.

```
SEQNBR*...+... 1 ...+... 2 ...+... 3 ...+... 4 ...+... 5 ...+... 6 ...+... 7 ...+... 8
     .....AAN01N02N03T.Name++++++RLen++TDpBLinPosFunctions++++++++++++++++++++++++++++

          * Numeric field range example:
          A          SALESAMT   R            12 1ORANGE(25 2000)
          * Character field range example:
          A          COUNTY     R            15 1ORANGE('FAIRFIELD' 'TOLLAND')
```

Figure 14-20 RANGE keyword coding examples.

The VALUES Keyword

The **VALUES** keyword validates that a field value is equal to one of the values included in the specified list. It is similar to the **COMP** keyword in that a relational test is made. However, the **VALUES** keyword only performs an *equal test* on a *list* of values, whereas the **COMP** keyword may include any of the relational tests, but only for one value. The format of the keyword is

VALUES (value-1 [value-2 ... [value-100]])

One hundred values may be specified, each separated by at least one blank. A **VALUES** keyword specified with character fields must have each value in the list enclosed in single quotes. Numeric values are specified without quotes. Identical to any relational comparison function, the value list must be the same type as the related field. Figure 14-21 shows two coding examples of the **VALUES** keyword.

```
SEQNBR*...+... 1 ...+... 2 ...+... 3 ...+... 4 ...+... 5 ...+... 6 ...+... 7 ...+... 8
     .....AAN01N02N03T.Name++++++RLen++TDpBLinPosFunctions++++++++++++++++++++++++++++

                * Numeric field VALUES example:
               A            DEPTNO     R            9 12VALUES(10 15 18 30)
                * Character field VALUES example:
               A            TRANSCODE R           12 30VALUES('DP' 'WT' 'CR' 'DB')
```

Figure 14-21 **VALUES** keyword coding examples.

Example Display File Modified with Validation Keywords

A source listing of the example display file modified with validation keywords and a supplemental explanation of the processing that occurs when a validation error is detected are detailed in Figure 14-22.

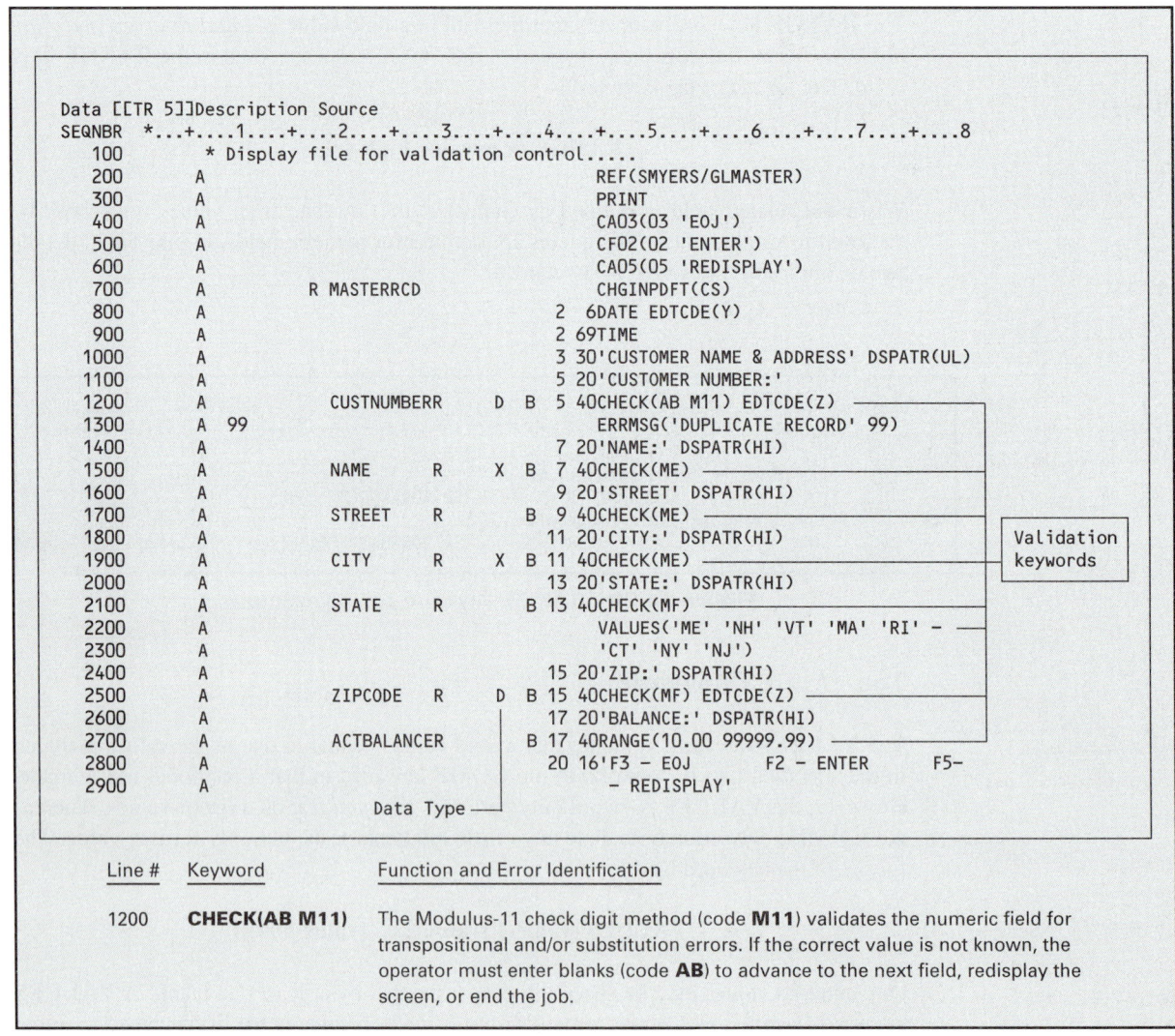

```
Data [[TR 5]]Description Source
SEQNBR  *...+....1....+....2....+....3....+....4....+....5....+....6....+....7....+....8
   100       * Display file for validation control.....
   200      A                                      REF(SMYERS/GLMASTER)
   300      A                                      PRINT
   400      A                                      CA03(03 'EOJ')
   500      A                                      CF02(02 'ENTER')
   600      A                                      CA05(05 'REDISPLAY')
   700      A          R MASTERRCD                 CHGINPDFT(CS)
   800      A                                  2  6DATE EDTCDE(Y)
   900      A                                  2 69TIME
  1000      A                                  3 30'CUSTOMER NAME & ADDRESS' DSPATR(UL)
  1100      A                                  5 20'CUSTOMER NUMBER:'
  1200      A            CUSTNUMBERR      D  B  5 40CHECK(AB M11) EDTCDE(Z)
  1300      A  99                                  ERRMSG('DUPLICATE RECORD' 99)
  1400      A                                  7 20'NAME:' DSPATR(HI)
  1500      A            NAME       R     X  B  7 40CHECK(ME)
  1600      A                                  9 20'STREET' DSPATR(HI)
  1700      A            STREET     R        B  9 40CHECK(ME)
  1800      A                                 11 20'CITY:' DSPATR(HI)              Validation
  1900      A            CITY       R     X  B 11 40CHECK(ME)                      keywords
  2000      A                                 13 20'STATE:' DSPATR(HI)
  2100      A            STATE      R        B 13 40CHECK(MF)
  2200      A                                      VALUES('ME' 'NH' 'VT' 'MA' 'RI' -
  2300      A                                      'CT' 'NY' 'NJ')
  2400      A                                 15 20'ZIP:' DSPATR(HI)
  2500      A            ZIPCODE    R     D  B 15 40CHECK(MF) EDTCDE(Z)
  2600      A                                 17 20'BALANCE:' DSPATR(HI)
  2700      A            ACTBALANCER         B 17 40RANGE(10.00 99999.99)
  2800      A                                 20 16'F3 - EOJ          F2 - ENTER          F5-
  2900      A                                       - REDISPLAY'
                                   Data Type
```

Line #	Keyword	Function and Error Identification
1200	**CHECK(AB M11)**	The Modulus-11 check digit method (code **M11**) validates the numeric field for transpositional and/or substitution errors. If the correct value is not known, the operator must enter blanks (code **AB**) to advance to the next field, redisplay the screen, or end the job.

Figure 14-22 Example display file modified with validation keywords.

Usually, all of the field values in the display are entered before the related function or ENTER key is pressed and any validation errors identified. Every field that is specified with a validation keyword will be validated sequentially beginning with the first field.

The system-supplied message generated on line 24 for an **M11** error is

The value for the field does not meet modulus 10 or 11 check.

1500 **CHECK(ME)**

The mandatory entry code **(ME)** for this character field requires that at least one character be entered to pass the validation criteria. *Note that if nothing is entered in the field, the mandatory entry function will not be enforced.* Supplemental to this keyword, *Keyboard Shift* **X** is entered in the *Data Type* field (column 35), which allows only the characters **A** through **Z, a** through **z,** comma, period, dash, or space to be entered.

When an error is detected, a system-supplied error number 0021 is displayed on line 2400. Pressing the Help key will display the following message on line 2400:

Mandatory enter field must have data entered.

1700 &
1900 **CHECK(ME)**

The mandatory entry code **(ME)** is entered for these fields, requiring that at least one valid character be entered. Because the STREET value usually includes numbers, the *Keyboard Shift* **X** is omitted in the *Data Type* field (column 35). However, it is specified with the CITY field.

2100 **CHECK(MF)** &
2200 **VALUES(...)**

The mandatory fill keyword, **CHECK(MF),** specified with this field requires that every position in the field must include a character. *Note that if no character is entered in this field, the mandatory fill function will not be enforced.* When an error is detected, the message number 0021 displays on line 2400. Pressing the Help key will display the following error message on line 2400:

The field must be filled before exiting. Key used not valid.

The **VALUES** keyword requires that either ME, NH, VT, MA, RI, CT, NY, or NJ be entered in this field. Any other value will generate the following system-supplied message on line 2400:

Value for field is not valid.

The operator may access the valid values by pressing the Help key.

2500 **CHECK(MF)**

The mandatory fill code specified with this field requires that a character be entered in all of the field positions. The *Keyboard Shift* **D** in the *Data Type* field (column 35) restricts the characters entered to 0 through 9.

2700 **RANGE(10.00 99999.99)**

This keyword requires that the data entered must be greater than or equal to the lower value (10.00) and less than or equal to the greater value (99999.99). When an error is detected, the following system-supplied message will be displayed:

Valid range for the field is 1000 to 9999999.

Figure 14-22 Example display file modified with validation keywords. (Continued)

SUMMARY

Display files define the format of one or more records that will be shown on a display device. The instructions for display files may be entered via **SEU**, or the record formats may be "painted" on the screen using the **SDA** utility. With either method the source member must be compiled to generate an object. A display file may include 1,024 record formats and include entries at the *File*, *Record*, *Help*, and *Field Levels*.

The display of *constants* may be changed from their default *low-intensity* image by the **DSPATR** keyword and the *underline* default for *variables* with the **CHGINPDFT** keyword. Attributes included with the **DSPATR** keyword may be specified for any constant or variable. However, the **CHGINPDFT** keyword is functional only with input- or input/output-capable fields.

The display attributes supported are **BL** (blinking field), **CS** (column separators), **HI** (high-intensity), **ND** (nondisplay), **PC** (position cursor), **RI** (reverse image), **UL** (underline), **MDT** (set modified data tag), **PR** (protect), **OID** (operator identification), and **SP** (select by light pen).

Command Attention **(CAnn)** and *Command Function* **(CFnn)** keywords provide programmer-supplied end-of-job and other controls between the display file and an **RPG IV** or **CL** program. Function keys assigned with **CAnn** *do not* support the passing of data from the display file to the **RPG IV** or **CL** program, whereas those specified with **CFnn** *do*.

The keywords that support data validation include **CHECK, COMP** (or **CMP**), **VALUES,** and **RANGE.** Each has its own syntax and related controls. In addition to these keywords, a *Keyboard Shift* entry in the *Data Type* field (column 35) can restrict the type of data entered. System-supplied error messages (or error numbers) are displayed on line 2400 of the screen if a validation error is detected after the related function key or the ENTER key is pressed. Additional information may be accessed about the error by pressing the Help key. To exit from the error condition and correct or ignore the validation error, the Reset key must be pressed.

QUESTIONS

14-1. What are display files? For what processing functions are they used?

14-2. By what methods may display files be created?

14-3. How many record formats may be included in a display file?

14-4. Explain the procedures for entering the DDS coding for a display file using the Programmer Menu.

14-5. Explain the function of the following display file keywords:

PRINT	DSPATR	EDTWRD	DATE
CAnn	ERRMSG	REF	TIME
CFnn	EDTCDE	REFFLD	CHGINPDFT

14-6. How does the processing controlled by the **CAnn** and **CFnn** keywords differ?

14-7. Explain the function of each part of the following keyword:

CF04(04 'update record')

14-8. Is the following entry valid for the maintenance function specified?

CA02(02 'add record')

14-9. Where may the fields specified in a display file be defined?

14-10. In what format is the **DATE** value accessed? The **TIME** value?

14-11. What is the default display attribute for input and input/output fields? How may this default attribute be globally changed?

14-12. What is the default display attribute for constants? How is this attribute globally changed?

14-13. Name the available display attributes. Explain the function of each one.

14-14. Write the keyword to change the default attribute for *all* of the input/output fields in a display file's record format to reverse image.

14-15. Write the keyword to position the cursor at the related field when the screen is displayed and to provide blinking.

14-16. Refer to a DDS specification and explain the **O, I,** and **B** values that may be entered in the *Usage* field (column 38).

14-17. Refer to Question 14-16 and relate a physical file maintenance function to the **O, I,** and **B** entries for the *Usage* field.

14-18. Refer to a DDS form or **SEU** format and explain the function of the following *Data Type* (column 35) entries: **A, P, S, X, D, Y.**

14-19. What is the function of the **Line** and **Pos** field entries on the form for display files?

14-20. What levels of coding may be specified in a display file?

14-21. Write the keyword to access the field attributes of all the fields in the record format of the physical file INVENTRY stored in the PARTS library.

14-22. Write the keyword to access the attributes of the PTNAME field defined in the record format of the INVENTRY physical file stored in the PARTS library.

14-23. With the keywords specified for Questions 14-21 and 14-22, what must be entered in column 29?

Questions 14-24 through 14-26 relate to the following instruction:

```
SEQNBR*...+... 1 ...+... 2 ...+... 3 ...+... 4 ...+... 5 ...+... 6 ...+... 7 ...+... 8
     .....AANO1NO2NO3T.Name++++++RLen++TDpBLinPosFunctions++++++++++++++++++++++++++++

          A            PARTNO     R          I  4 10
          A  90                                     ERRMSG('DUPLICATE KEY' 90)
```

14-24. What is the function of the indicator specified in columns 9 and 10? Where and under what conditions is it set on?

14-25. What happens if indicator **90** is set on?

14-26. How is indicator **90** turned off?

14-27. May more than one **ERRMSG** be included in a record format of a display file?

14-28. What is the default line for the **ERRMSG** text? What keyword is used to change the line on which the text will display?

14-29. Name the display file keywords used for data validation.

14-30. Write the keyword to validate that the field value passes the Modulus-11 test and to provide for exit from the field if the value is incorrect and the correct entry is unknown.

14-31. Write the keyword to test that a SALES field value is not less than 25.00 and not greater than 3000.00.

14-32. Write the keyword to validate that a COURS# field has all of its characters entered.

14-33. Write the keyword to validate that the value in DEPT# is equal to 10, 15, 20, or 25.

14-34. Write the keyword to validate that the value in LGRADE is not greater than 8.

PROGRAMMING ASSIGNMENTS

For each of the following programming assignments, a physical file must have been created (but not loaded with data). Your instructor will inform you if you have to create the physical file or if it has already been created.

Programming Assignment 14-1: DISPLAY FILE FOR ENTRY OF NEW CUSTOMER ACCOUNTS

Before the display file is started, the following physical file must have been created:

```
                    PHYSICAL FILE DESCRIPTION

SYSTEM: AS/400                                DATE: Yours
FILE NAME: Yours                              REV NO: 0
RECORD NAME: Yours                            KEY LENGTH: 5
SEQUENCE: Keyed  (Unique)                     RECORD SIZE: 68

                        FIELD DEFINITIONS

 FIELD    FIELD NAME   SIZE  TYPE    POSITION     COMMENTS
  NO                                FROM    TO

  1       CUSTNUMBER     5    P        1     3   Key field
  2       CUSTNAME      24    C        4    27
  3       STREET        20    C       28    47
  4       CITY          20    C       48    57
  5       STATE          2    C       58    59
  6       ZIPCODE        5    P       60    62
  7       CREDLIMIT      7    P       63    66   0 decimals
  8       CREDRATING     2    C       67    68
```

From the following CRT layout form, create a display file record format based on the following requirements:

1. Reference the field attributes from the physical file created for this assignment.
2. Specify **B** (input and output) in the *Usage* field (position 38) for all of the fields.
3. Specify the **PRINT, CA,** and **CF** keywords at the *Record Level.*
4. Include the display attributes indicated in the CRT layout form.
5. Include the error message **'RECORD ALREADY EXISTS'** for the CUSTNUMBER field.
6. Use **SDA** to test your *compiled* display record format.

```
 1   MM/DD/YY                       CUSTOMER ENTRY                            HH:MM:SS
 2
 3
 4     CUSTOMER NUMBER: XXXXX       NAME: X-----------------------X
 5
 6     STREET: X------------------X
 7
 8     CITY: X------------------X      STATE: XX        ZIP: XXXXX
 9
10     CREDIT LIMIT: XXXXXXX                                        CREDIT RATING: XX
11
12
13       CMD KEY 3 - EOJ          CMD KEY 2 - ENTER          CMD KEY 5 - IGNORE
14
15     NOTES:
16       1. HIGHLIGHT ALL CONSTANTS.
17       2. UNDERLINE CONSTANT ON LINE 1.
18       3. REVERSE IMAGE ALL VARIABLE FIELDS.
19       4. INCLUDE THE ERRMSG 'RECORD ALREADY EXISTS' FOR THE CUSTOMER NO. FIELD.
```

Programming Assignment 14-2: VALIDATION OF NEW CUSTOMER ACCOUNTS

Modify Programming Assignment 14-1 to include the following validation functions:

1. Modulus-11 validation for the CUSTNUMBER field
2. Mandatory entry for the CUSTNAME field and test that the data type is alphabetic
3. Mandatory entry for the STREET field
4. Mandatory entry for the CITY field and test that the data type is alphabetic
5. Values entered for the STATE field are OH, MI, NY, IL, PA, NY, and CA
6. Mandatory fill for the ZIPCODE field
7. Test that the data entered for the CREDLIMIT field is from 500 to 5000
8. Test that the values entered in the CREDRATING field are A, A–, B, B–, and C.

Use ***SDA*** *to test your modified display file record format for the validation functions.*

Programming Assignment 14-3: MODIFICATION OF ASSIGNMENT 14-1 OR 14-2 TO INCLUDE A SECOND RECORD FORMAT

Modify either Assignment 14-1 or 14-2 to include a second record format with the following format:

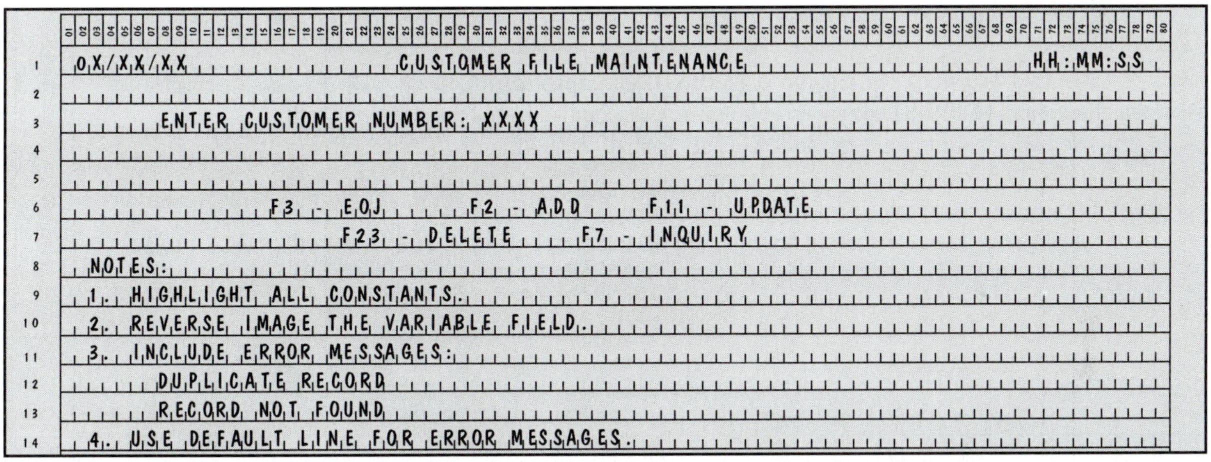

0X/XX/XX
CUSTOMER FILE MAINTENANCE
HH:MM:SS
ENTER CUSTOMER NUMBER: XXXXX
F3 - EOJ
F2 - ADD
F11 - UPDATE
F23 - DELETE
F7 - INQUIRY
NOTES:
1. HIGHLIGHT ALL CONSTANTS.
2. REVERSE IMAGE THE VARIABLE FIELD.
3. INCLUDE ERROR MESSAGES:
DUPLICATE RECORD
RECORD NOT FOUND
4. USE DEFAULT LINE FOR ERROR MESSAGES.

In addition, modify the first record format (either 14-1 or 14-2) as follows:

1. Protect the CUSTNUMBER field.
2. Position cursor at the CUSTNAME field.
3. Remove the constant CMD KEY 3 and center the two remaining line 13 constants.
4. Remove the **ERRMSG** keyword.
5. Use **SDA** to test both record formats.

Programming Assignment 14-4: STUDENT COURSE FILE MAINTENANCE

Before the display file is started, the following physical file must be created:

```
                         PHYSICAL FILE DESCRIPTION

SYSTEM: AS/400                                          DATE: Yours
FILE NAME: Yours                                        REV NO: 0
RECORD NAME: Yours                                      KEY LENGTH: 21
SEQUENCE: Keyed  (Unique)                               RECORD SIZE: 39

                            FIELD DEFINITIONS

 FIELD     FIELD NAME    SIZE  TYPE      POSITION      COMMENTS
  NO                                    FROM    TO

  1        SSNUMBER        9    P          1     5    Key fld 1
  2        COURSENO        6    C          6    11    Key fld 2
  3        COURSENAME     20    C         12    31
  4        TERMDATE        6    P         32    35    Key fld 3
  5        INSTCODE        3    P         36    37
  6        CREDIT          1    P         38    38
  7        MARK            1    C         39    39
```

From the following CRT layout forms, create two display file record formats based on the following requirements:

1. Define display file field names *different* from the related physical file in the maintenance record format. Refer to the physical file for the field attributes.
2. Specify **B** (input and output) in the *Usage* field (position 38) for all of the fields in the maintenance display record and **I** (input) for the fields in the prompt display record format.
3. Specify the **PRINT** keyword at the *File Level* and the **CA** and **CF** keywords in their related display formats at the *Record Level.*
4. Include the display attributes indicated in the CRT layout forms.
5. In the prompt display, include the error messages **DUPLICATE RECORD** for addition maintenance and **RECORD NOT FOUND** for the update and delete maintenance functions and inquiry processing.
6. Include a seven-character MODE field on line 2 of the maintenance display record. This field will be loaded in the program with the related maintenance function currently performed (i..e, **ADDS, UPDATE, DELETE,** or **INQUIRY**).
7. Use **SDA** to test your *compiled* display record formats.

Prompt Display Design:

```
     0000000001111111111222222222233333333334444444444555555555566666666667777777777
     1234567890123456789012345678901234567890123456789012345678901234567890123456789 0
 1   0X/XX/XX                  COURSE FILE MAINTENANCE                       HH:MM:SS
 2
 3
 4      ENTER:
 5
 6      SS NUMBER: XXXXXXXXX      COURSE NUMBER: XXXXXX          TERM DATE: XXXXXX
 7
 8
 9                     F3 - EOJ      F2 - ADD      F11 - UPDATE
10                          F23 - DELETE      F7 - INQUIRY
11    NOTES:
12     1. HIGHLIGHT ALL CONSTANTS.
13     2. REVERSE IMAGE ALL VARIABLES.
14     3. DISPLAY ERROR MESSAGES ON LINE 8:
15            DUPLICATE RECORD
16            RECORD NOT FOUND
```

Maintenance Display Design:

```
 1  OX/XX/XX                 COURSE FILE MAINTENANCE                 HH:MM:SS
 2                                  XXXXXXXX
 3
 4
 5       STUDENT NO: XXXXXXXXX                      COURSE NO: XXXXXX
 6
 7       COURSE NAME: X                     X          TERM DATE: XXXXXX
 8
 9       INSTRUCTOR CODE: XXX         CREDITS: X              MARK: X
10
11
12            F2 - ENTER                               F10 - IGNORE
13
14  NOTES:
15  1. HIGHLIGHT ALL CONSTANTS.
16  2. REVERSE IMAGE ALL VARIABLES.
17  3. UNDERLINE CONSTANT ON LINE 1:
18  4. MODE FOUND ON LINE 2 WOULD BE LOADED IN THE
19     PROGRAM WITH RELATED MAINTENANCE CONSTANT.
20  5. PROTECT THE STUDENT NO., COURSE NO., & TERM DATE FIELDS.
21  6. POSITION CURSOR AT THE COURSE NAME FIELD.
```

Programming Assignment 14-5: PARTS INVENTORY MASTER FILE MAINTENANCE

The following physical file must be created before this display file is started:

PHYSICAL FILE DESCRIPTION

SYSTEM: AS/400 | DATE: Yours
FILE NAME: Yours | REV NO: 0
RECORD NAME: Yours | KEY LENGTH: 5
SEQUENCE: Keyed (Unique) | RECORD SIZE: 54

FIELD DEFINITIONS

FIELD NO	FIELD NAME	SIZE	TYPE	POSITION FROM	POSITION TO	COMMENTS
1	PARTNUMBER	5	C	1	5	Key field
2	PARTNAME	20	C	6	25	
3	AMTONHAND	6	P	26	29	
4	AMTORDERED	6	P	30	33	
5	AVGCOST	7	P	34	37	2 decimals
6	AMTALLOCTD	6	P	38	41	
7	EOQ	6	P	42	45	
8	SAFTYSTOCK	6	P	46	49	
9	LEADTIME	3	P	50	51	
10	WAREHLOCTN	3	C	52	54	

From the following CRT layout forms, create two display file record formats based on the following requirements:

1. Define display file field names *different* from the related physical file in the maintenance record format. Refer to the physical file for the field attributes.

2. Specify **B** (input and output) in the *Usage* field (position 38) for all of the fields in the maintenance display record and **I** (input) for the one field in the prompt display record format.
3. Specify the **PRINT** keyword at the *File Level* and the **CA** and **CF** keywords in their related display formats at the *Record Level.*
4. Include the display attributes indicated in the CRT layout forms.
5. In the prompt display, include the error messages **DUPLICATE RECORD** for addition maintenance and **PART NUMBER NOT FOUND** for the update and delete maintenance and inquiry processing.
6. Include a seven-character MODE field on line 1, upper right-hand corner of the maintenance display record. This field will be loaded in the program with the related maintenance function currently performed (i.e., **ADDS, UPDATE, DELETE,** or **INQUIRY**).
7. Include the following validation functions only for adds maintenance. This requires that the related validation keywords in the maintenance format be conditioned by the indicator that controls adds maintenance. Maintenance functions to include in the maintenance format are listed below:
   a. Mandatory entry for the PARTNUMBER and PARTNAME fields.
   b. Mandatory entry for the AVGCOST field and suppress the low-order sign position.
   c. Mandatory entry for the EOQ field and suppress the low-order sign position.
   d. Mandatory entry for the LEADTIME field and suppress the low-order sign position.
   e. Mandatory entry for the SAFTYSTOCK field and suppress the low-order sign position.
   f. Mandatory fill for the WAREHLOCTN field and validate that the characters entered are only alphabetic.
   g. Use **SDA** to test your compiled display record formats.

Prompt Display Design:

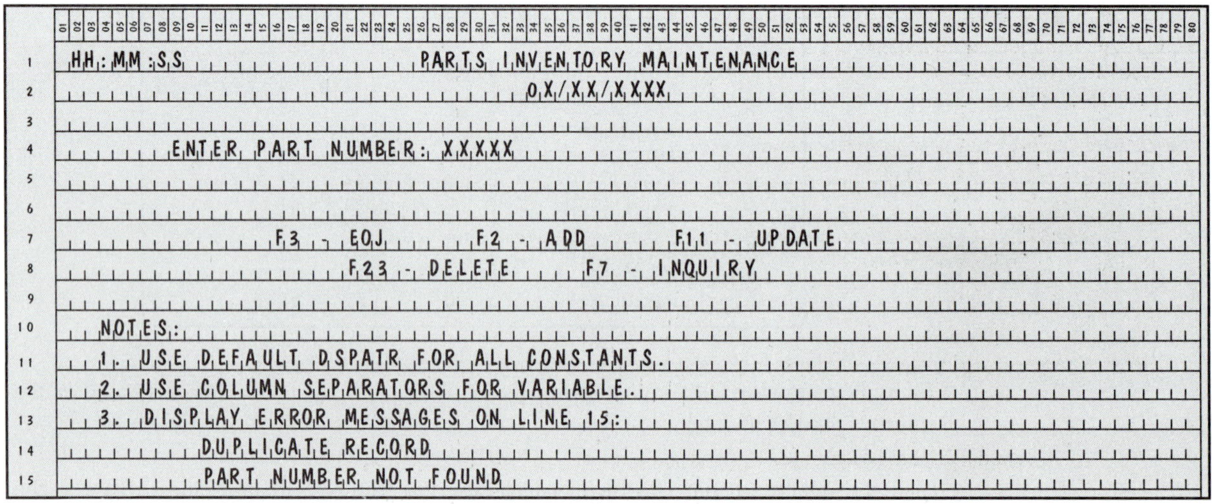

```
 1  HH:MM:SS                    PARTS INVENTORY MAINTENANCE
 2                                        0X/XX/XXXX
 3
 4        ENTER PART NUMBER: XXXXX
 5
 6
 7               F3 - EOJ        F2 - ADD       F11 - UPDATE
 8                    F23 - DELETE     F7 - INQUIRY
 9
10    NOTES:
11    1. USE DEFAULT DSPATR FOR ALL CONSTANTS.
12    2. USE COLUMN SEPARATORS FOR VARIABLE.
13    3. DISPLAY ERROR MESSAGES ON LINE 15:
14             DUPLICATE RECORD
15             PART NUMBER NOT FOUND
```

Maintenance Display Design:

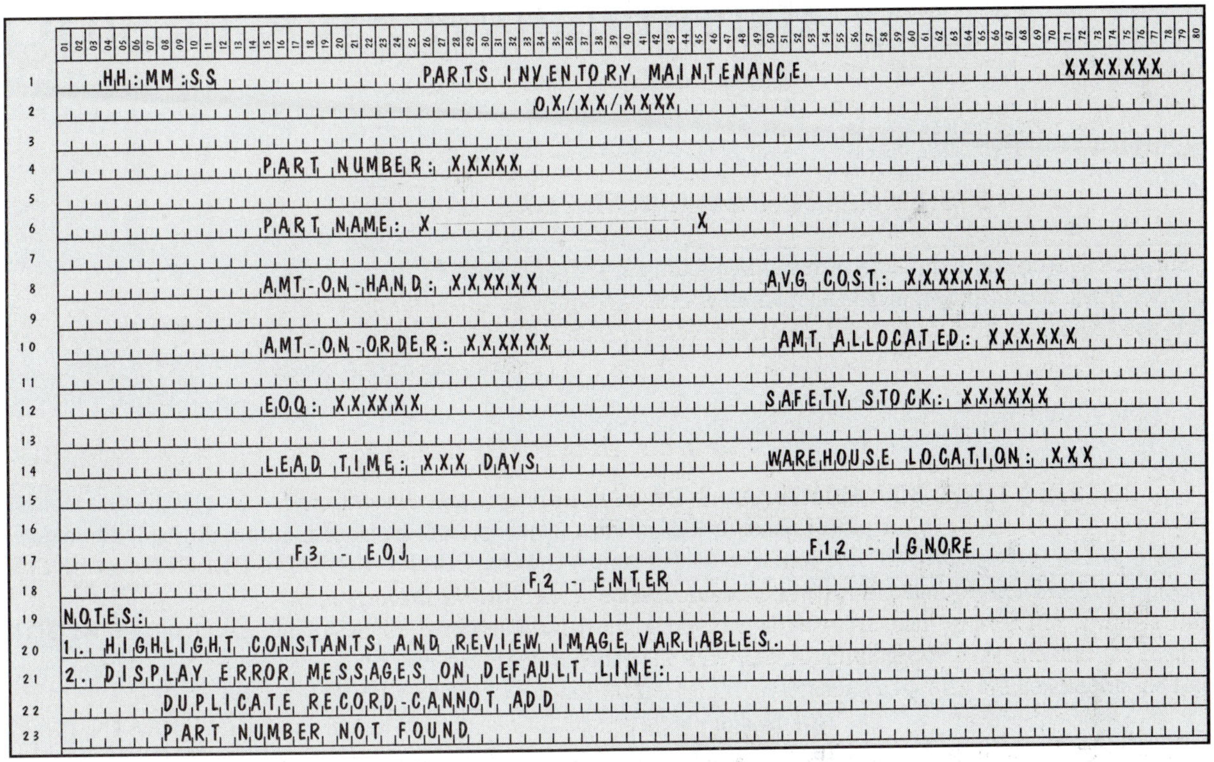
HH:MM:SS
PARTS INVENTORY MAINTENANCE
XXXXXXXX
0X/XX/XXXX
PART NUMBER: XXXXX
PART NAME: X X
AMT-ON-HAND: XXXXXX
AVG COST: XXXXXXX
AMT-ON-ORDER: XXXXXX
AMT ALLOCATED: XXXXXX
EOQ: XXXXXX
SAFETY STOCK: XXXXXX
LEAD TIME: XXX DAYS
WAREHOUSE LOCATION: XXX
F3 - EOJ
F12 - IGNORE
F2 - ENTER
NOTES:
1. HIGHLIGHT CONSTANTS AND REVIEW IMAGE VARIABLES.
2. DISPLAY ERROR MESSAGES ON DEFAULT LINE:
DUPLICATE RECORD-CANNOT ADD
PART NUMBER NOT FOUND

chapter 15

Interactive Processing

An **RPG IV** program is *interactive* when it processes one or more display files and one or more physical and/or logical files. Interactive programs that control physical file maintenance and inquiry use the same **WRITE, CHAIN, UPDATE, DELETE** and **SETLL** operations introduced in Chapter 13 for batch maintenance.

The following syntax must be considered when coding an interactive **RPG IV** program:

1. All display files accessed must be defined as *workstation* **(WORKSTN)** files.
2. The **EXFMT** *(Write/Then Read Format)* operation (or separate **WRITE** and **READ** statements) must be specified to process any display file's record format.
3. Usually one or more **DOU** or **DOW** groups are included to control the iterative (looping) control needed with interactive processing.
4. The indicators assigned to the *Command Attention* **(CAnn)** and *Command Function* **(CFnn)** keys in a display file are tested for an ***ON** or ***OFF** condition in the **RPG IV** program to control a specific processing function (i.e., end-of-job, redisplay, file addition, file inquiry, record deletion, and record update).

The **RPG IV** syntax required to process display files and access their record formats for physical file maintenance will be discussed in the following sections.

File Description Syntax for Workstation Files

Any display file defined in an **RPG IV** program must be assigned to a **WORKSTN** *(Workstation)* file. The *File Description* syntax for a **WORKSTN** file is explained in Figure 15-1.

```
.. 1 ...+... 2 ...+... 3 ...+... 4 ...+... 5 ...+... 6 ...+... 7 ...+
FFilename++IPEASFRLen+LKLen+AIDevice+.Keywords+++++++++++++++++++++++++

FGldf1     CF   E             WORKSTN
```

1. The display file name must be left-justified in the *Filename* field (positions 7–16).

Figure 15-1 *File Description Specification* syntax for **WORKSTN** files.

2. A **C** (for combined input and output), **I** (for input), or **O** (for output) file may be specified in position 17.
3. An **F** (full-procedural), **P** (primary), **S** (secondary), and a **blank** (for a file that has **O** in position 15) may be entered in position 18.
4. An **E** (externally defined) or an **F** (program-described) may be entered in position 22.
5. **WORKSTN** must be entered in the *Device* field (positions 32–42).

Notes:

1. The entries for the example shown define the display file as combined (supports input and output processing), full-procedural, and externally defined.
2. The **EXFMT** operation is valid only with externally defined display files.

Figure 15-1 *File Description Specification* syntax for **WORKSTN** files. (Continued)

The EXFMT *(Write/Then Read Format)* Operation

The **RPG IV EXFMT** operation is valid only for **WORKSTN** files defined in a *File Description* statement as *combined* (**C** in position 17), *full-procedural* (**F** in position 18), and *externally defined* (**E** in position 22). An **EXFMT** instruction is a combined **WRITE** (to the CRT) followed by a **READ** (from the CRT). Separate **WRITE** and **READ** statements may be specified in lieu of an **EXFMT** statement. A unique feature of the **EXFMT** operation is that it holds the display on the CRT after it has been written. The operator must press either a function key or the ENTER key to continue. Figure 15-2 details the syntax of this operation.

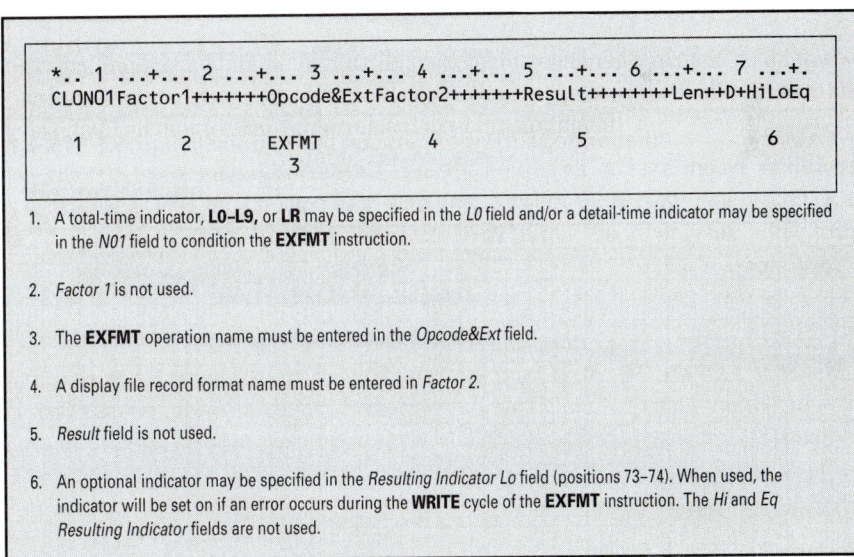

```
*.. 1 ...+... 2 ...+... 3 ...+... 4 ...+... 5 ...+... 6 ...+... 7 ...+.
CL0N01Factor1+++++++Opcode&ExtFactor2+++++++Result++++++++Len++D+HiLoEq

   1         2         EXFMT         4              5                 6
                         3
```

1. A total-time indicator, **L0–L9,** or **LR** may be specified in the *L0* field and/or a detail-time indicator may be specified in the *N01* field to condition the **EXFMT** instruction.
2. *Factor 1* is not used.
3. The **EXFMT** operation name must be entered in the *Opcode&Ext* field.
4. A display file record format name must be entered in *Factor 2.*
5. *Result* field is not used.
6. An optional indicator may be specified in the *Resulting Indicator Lo* field (positions 73–74). When used, the indicator will be set on if an error occurs during the **WRITE** cycle of the **EXFMT** instruction. The *Hi* and *Eq Resulting Indicator* fields are not used.

Figure 15-2 Syntax of the **EXFMT** operation.

Other **RPG IV** operations that are valid for **WORKSTN** files are detailed in Figure 15-3, with their required *File Description Specification* position 17 and 18 entries.

File Description Specifications Positions		Calculation Positions
17	18	26–35
I	P/S	CLOSE, ACQ, REL, NEXT, POST, FORCE
I	P/S	WRITE,[1] CLOSE, ACQ, REL, NEXT, POST, FORCE
1	F	READ, OPEN, CLOSE, ACQ, REL, NEXT, POST
C	F	READ, WRITE,[1] EXFMT,[2] OPEN, CLOSE, ACQ, REL, NEXT, POST, UPDATE,[3] CHAIN,[3] READC[3]
O	Blank	WRITE,[1] OPEN, CLOSE, ACQ, REL, POST
Note: [1]The **WRITE** operation is not valid for a program-described file used with a format name.		
Note: [2]If the **EXFMT** operation is used, the file must be externally described (an **E** in position 19 of the *File Description* specifications).		
Note: [3]For subfile record formats, the **UPDATE, CHAIN,** and **READC** operations are also valid.		

Figure 15-3 Valid **RPG IV** operations for **WORKSTN** files. (Courtesy of IBM)

The CLEAR Operation

When fields in a display file's record format are defined with a *Usage* (position 38 of the DDS specifications) of **O** (output) or **B** (input/output), they are not always initialized to blanks or zeros after a display. This would be confusing to a user doing inquiry, update, or deletion processing when some or all of the previous record's values are redisplayed.

The **CLEAR** operation clears the fields or elements in a record format, data structure, array, table, or subfield to blanks (for character fields) or zeros (for numeric fields). Indicators are automatically set to "O" (off). Depending how the instruction is formatted, it clears fields, elements, and indicators individually or globally (all fields, elements, and indicators) at one time. Figure 15-4 explains the syntax of the **CLEAR** operation.

```
*.. 1 ...+... 2 ...+... 3 ...+... 4 ...+... 5 ...+... 6 ...+... 7 ...+.
CLON01Factor1+++++++Opcode&ExtFactor2+++++++Result++++++++Len++D+HiLoEq

   1       2         CLEAR          4            5                6
                       3
```

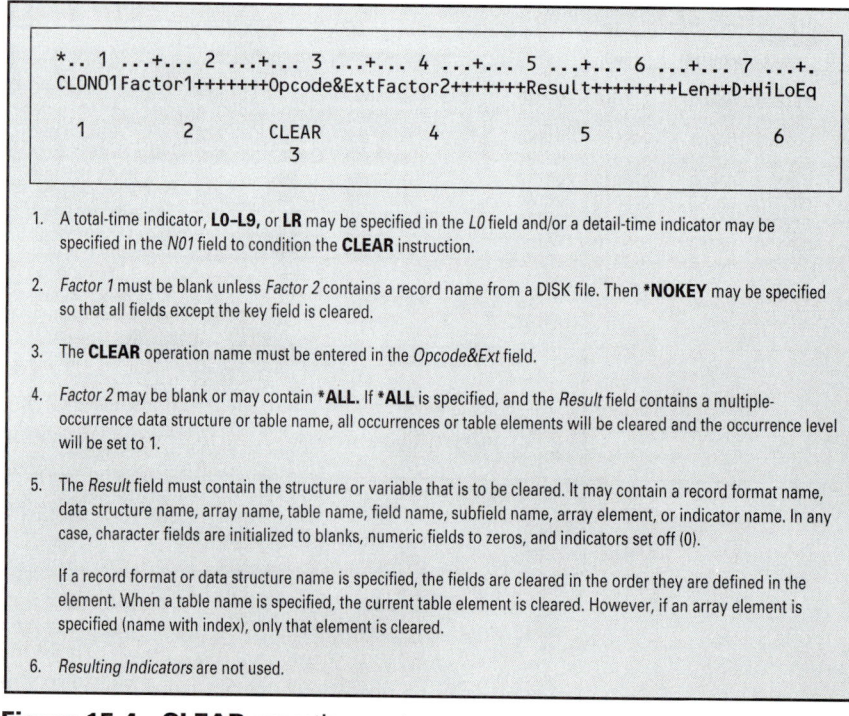

1. A total-time indicator, **L0–L9,** or **LR** may be specified in the *L0* field and/or a detail-time indicator may be specified in the *N01* field to condition the **CLEAR** instruction.
2. *Factor 1* must be blank unless *Factor 2* contains a record name from a DISK file. Then ***NOKEY** may be specified so that all fields except the key field is cleared.
3. The **CLEAR** operation name must be entered in the *Opcode&Ext* field.
4. *Factor 2* may be blank or may contain ***ALL.** If ***ALL** is specified, and the *Result* field contains a multiple-occurrence data structure or table name, all occurrences or table elements will be cleared and the occurrence level will be set to 1.
5. The *Result* field must contain the structure or variable that is to be cleared. It may contain a record format name, data structure name, array name, table name, field name, subfield name, array element, or indicator name. In any case, character fields are initialized to blanks, numeric fields to zeros, and indicators set off (0).

   If a record format or data structure name is specified, the fields are cleared in the order they are defined in the element. When a table name is specified, the current table element is cleared. However, if an array element is specified (name with index), only that element is cleared.
6. *Resulting Indicators* are not used.

Figure 15-4 **CLEAR** operation syntax.

Six **RPG IV** programs that support interactive processing will be discussed in the remainder of this chapter in the following order:

1. Addition of records to a physical file
2. Inquiry of records in a physical file
3. Update of records in a physical file
4. Logical deletion of records in a physical file
5. Combined addition, update, and deletion maintenance
6. Data validation.

RPG IV PROGRAM: INTERACTIVE ADDITION OF RECORDS

The display file that is processed by the program that adds records to a physical file defined with unique keys is shown in Figure 15-5. Note that it includes the following features:

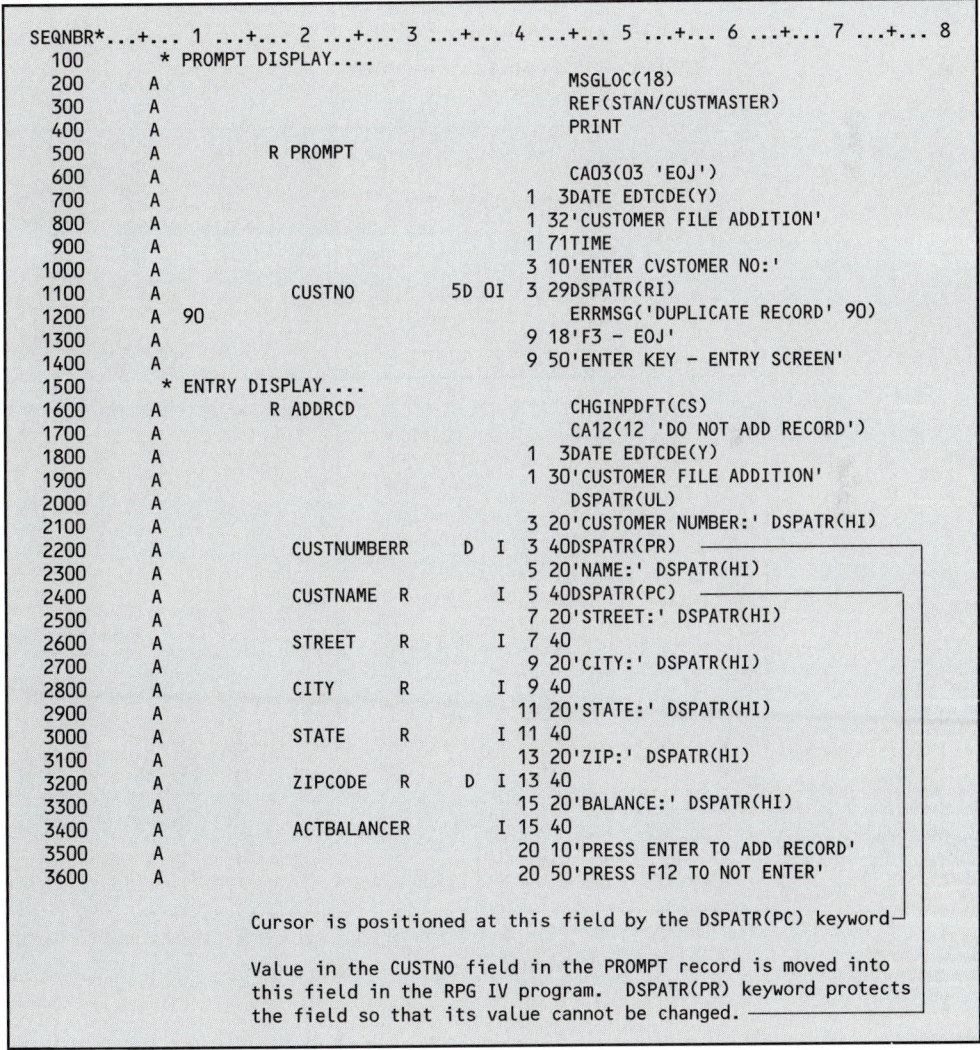

```
SEQNBR*...+... 1 ...+... 2 ...+... 3 ...+... 4 ...+... 5 ...+... 6 ...+... 7 ...+... 8
      * PROMPT DISPLAY....
     A                                      MSGLOC(18)
     A                                      REF(STAN/CUSTMASTER)
     A                                      PRINT
     A          R PROMPT
     A                                      CA03(03 'EOJ')
     A                                  1  3DATE EDTCDE(Y)
     A                                  1 32'CUSTOMER FILE ADDITION'
     A                                  1 71TIME
     A                                  3 10'ENTER CVSTOMER NO:'
     A            CUSTNO         5D 0I  3 29DSPATR(RI)
     A  90                                  ERRMSG('DUPLICATE RECORD' 90)
     A                                  9 18'F3 - EOJ'
     A                                  9 50'ENTER KEY - ENTRY SCREEN'
      * ENTRY DISPLAY....
     A          R ADDRCD                    CHGINPDFT(CS)
     A                                      CA12(12 'DO NOT ADD RECORD')
     A                                  1  3DATE EDTCDE(Y)
     A                                  1 30'CUSTOMER FILE ADDITION'
     A                                      DSPATR(UL)
     A                                  3 20'CUSTOMER NUMBER:' DSPATR(HI)
     A            CUSTNUMBERR      D  I  3 40DSPATR(PR)
     A                                  5 20'NAME:' DSPATR(HI)
     A            CUSTNAME  R         I  5 40DSPATR(PC)
     A                                  7 20'STREET:' DSPATR(HI)
     A            STREET    R         I  7 40
     A                                  9 20'CITY:' DSPATR(HI)
     A            CITY      R         I  9 40
     A                                 11 20'STATE:' DSPATR(HI)
     A            STATE     R         I 11 40
     A                                 13 20'ZIP:' DSPATR(HI)
     A            ZIPCODE   R      D  I 13 40
     A                                 15 20'BALANCE:' DSPATR(HI)
     A            ACTBALANCER         I 15 40
     A                                 20 10'PRESS ENTER TO ADD RECORD'
     A                                 20 50'PRESS F12 TO NOT ENTER'
```

Cursor is positioned at this field by the DSPATR(PC) keyword

Value in the CUSTNO field in the PROMPT record is moved into this field in the RPG IV program. DSPATR(PR) keyword protects the field so that its value cannot be changed.

Figure 15-5 Display file for "adds" maintenance.

1. Two record formats are coded. One is a PROMPT record in which a customer number is entered to determine if the key value already exists. Error identification (i.e., **DUPLICATE RECORD**) is controlled in this record format. The PROMPT screen is used to identify duplicate keys before the second record format is displayed, data entered, and then the record rejected because of a duplicate key condition. If the physical file supported duplicate keys, this record format would not be needed for add maintenance.
2. All of the fields in the ADDRCD record format are defined with an **I** usage, which supports input only (from the display to the program). In the **RPG IV** program, the CUSTNO value from the PROMPT display is moved into the CUSTNUMBER field in the ADDRCD display. To prevent the CUSTNUMBER value from being changed, the field is protected with the **DSPATR(PR)** keyword and the cursor is positioned at the CUSTNAME field with the **DSPATR(PC)** keyword.
3. *Command Attention* **(CA)** and *Command Function* **(CF)** keys are specified at the *Record Level,* which limits a specific function to each record type. End-of-job control and access to the ADDRCD record is controlled in the PROMPT record. The decision to write the current record to the physical file or to ignore the entry is controlled in the ADDRCD record.

A Print key copy of the displays generated from execution of the related **RPG IV** program is shown in Figure 15-6.

```
12/16/97                 CUSTOMER FILE ADDITION                 13:28:27

     ENTER CUSTOMER NO: 20000




          F3 - EOJ                              ENTER KEY - ENTRY SCREEN
```

PROMPT display

```
12/16/97                 CUSTOMER FILE ADDITION

               CUSTOMER NUMBER:      20000

               NAME:                 EDGAR POE

               STREET:               10 DREARY LANE

               CITY:                 HOPELESS

               STATE:                CA

               ZIP:                  09901

               BALANCE:                 35000


     PRESS ENTER TO ADD RECORD                  PRESS F12 TO NOT ENTER
```

ADDRCD display

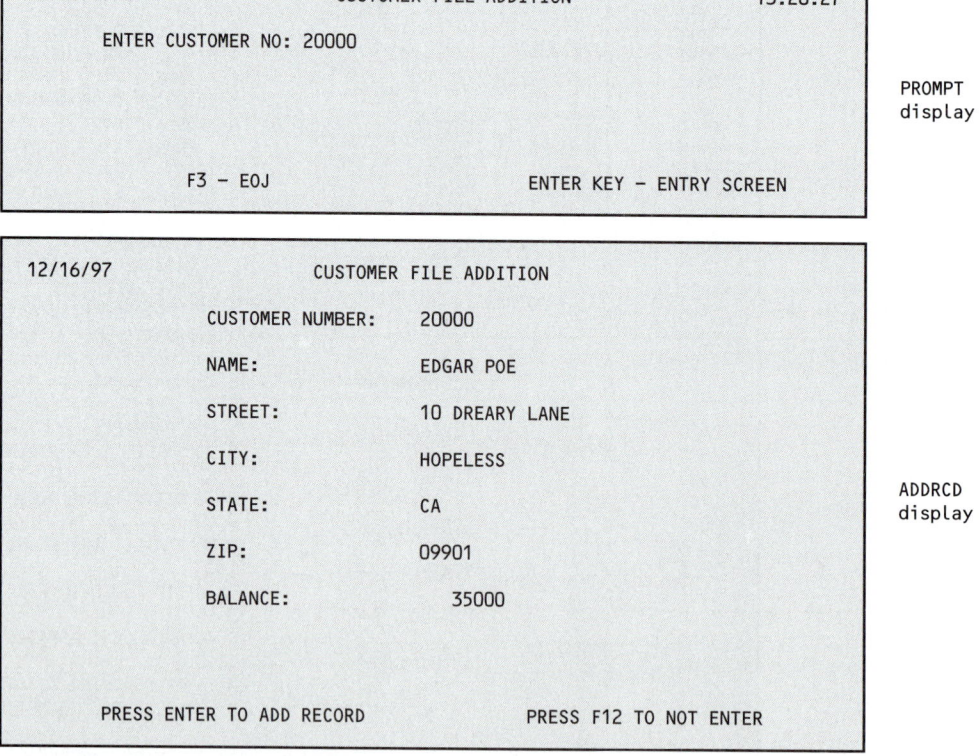

Figure 15-6 Print key copy of the display file's two record formats for "adds" maintenance.

The **RPG IV** program that adds records to a physical file includes the following operations:

DOU group
EXFMT instruction
CAS instruction
SETLL instruction
IF group
WRITE instruction

A compile listing of the program and a supplemental line-by-line explanation of the instructions are presented in Figure 15-7.

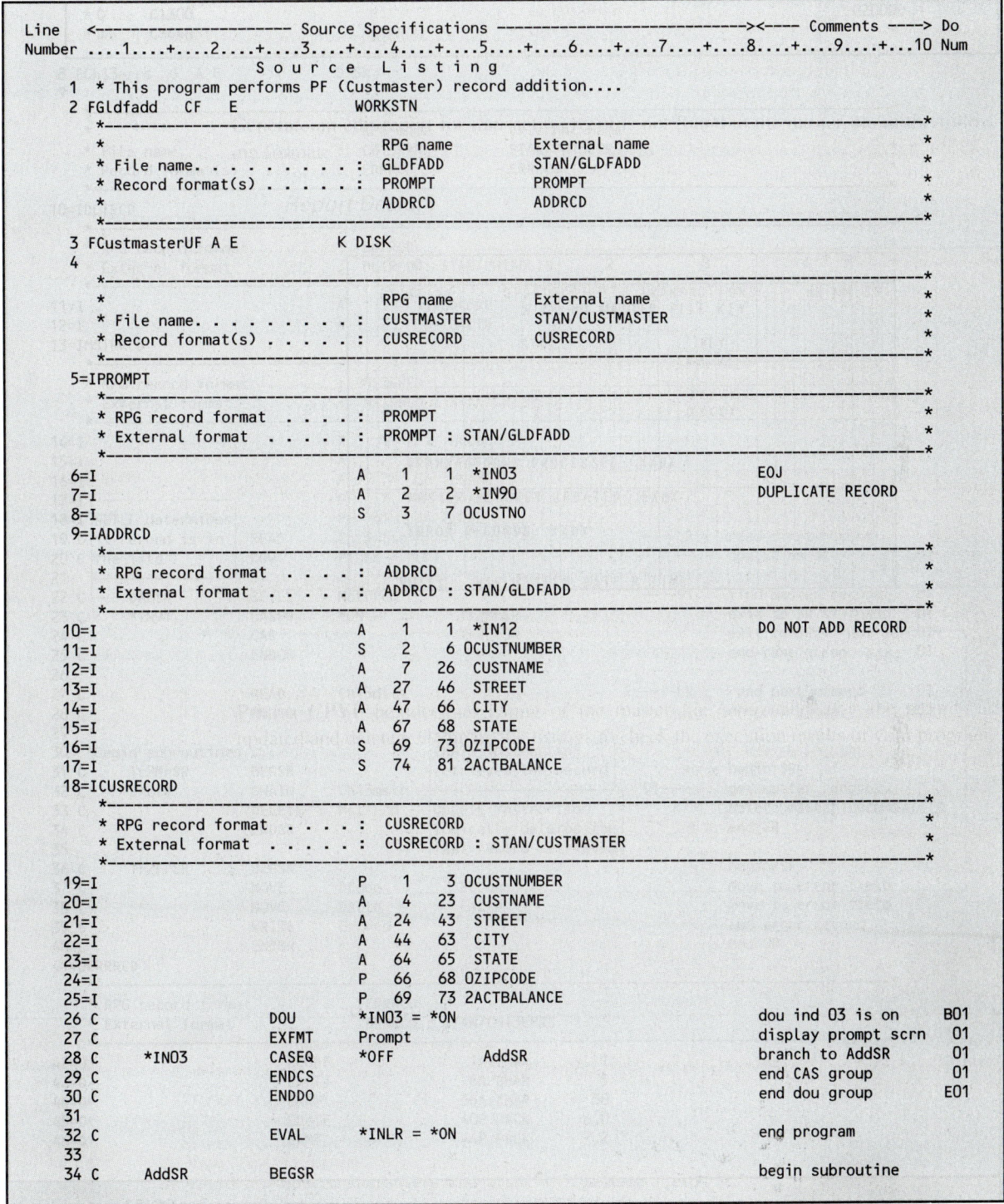

```
Line   <---------------------- Source Specifications ----------------------------><---- Comments ----> Do
Number ....1....+....2....+....3....+....4....+....5....+....6....+....7....+....8....+....9....+...10 Num
                              S o u r c e   L i s t i n g
     1  * This program performs PF (Custmaster) record addition....
     2 FGldfadd   CF   E              WORKSTN
       *--------------------------------------------------------------------------------------------*
       *                                  RPG name          External name                           *
       * File name. . . . . . . . . :    GLDFADD           STAN/GLDFADD                            *
       * Record format(s) . . . . . :    PROMPT            PROMPT                                  *
       *                                  ADDRCD            ADDRCD                                  *
       *--------------------------------------------------------------------------------------------*
     3 FCustmasterUF A E           K DISK
     4
       *--------------------------------------------------------------------------------------------*
       *                                  RPG name          External name                           *
       * File name. . . . . . . . . :    CUSTMASTER        STAN/CUSTMASTER                         *
       * Record format(s) . . . . . :    CUSRECORD         CUSRECORD                               *
       *--------------------------------------------------------------------------------------------*
     5=IPROMPT
       *--------------------------------------------------------------------------------------------*
       * RPG record format  . . . . :    PROMPT                                                    *
       * External format  . . . . . :    PROMPT : STAN/GLDFADD                                     *
       *--------------------------------------------------------------------------------------------*
     6=I                              A    1    1  *IN03                        EOJ
     7=I                              A    2    2  *IN90                        DUPLICATE RECORD
     8=I                              S    3    7 0CUSTNO
     9=IADDRCD
       *--------------------------------------------------------------------------------------------*
       * RPG record format  . . . . :    ADDRCD                                                    *
       * External format  . . . . . :    ADDRCD : STAN/GLDFADD                                     *
       *--------------------------------------------------------------------------------------------*
    10=I                              A    1    1  *IN12                        DO NOT ADD RECORD
    11=I                              S    2    6 0CUSTNUMBER
    12=I                              A    7   26  CUSTNAME
    13=I                              A   27   46  STREET
    14=I                              A   47   66  CITY
    15=I                              A   67   68  STATE
    16=I                              S   69   73 0ZIPCODE
    17=I                              S   74   81 2ACTBALANCE
    18=ICUSRECORD
       *--------------------------------------------------------------------------------------------*
       * RPG record format  . . . . :    CUSRECORD                                                 *
       * External format  . . . . . :    CUSRECORD : STAN/CUSTMASTER                               *
       *--------------------------------------------------------------------------------------------*
    19=I                              P    1    3 0CUSTNUMBER
    20=I                              A    4   23  CUSTNAME
    21=I                              A   24   43  STREET
    22=I                              A   44   63  CITY
    23=I                              A   64   65  STATE
    24=I                              P   66   68 0ZIPCODE
    25=I                              P   69   73 2ACTBALANCE
    26 C                   DOU       *IN03 = *ON                           dou ind 03 is on      B01
    27 C                   EXFMT     Prompt                                display prompt scrn    01
    28 C     *IN03         CASEQ     *OFF          AddSR                   branch to AddSR        01
    29 C                   ENDCS                                           end CAS group          01
    30 C                   ENDDO                                           end dou group         E01
    31
    32 C                   EVAL      *INLR = *ON                           end program
    33
    34 C     AddSR         BEGSR                                           begin subroutine
```

Figure 15-7 Detailed compile listing of the "adds" maintenance program.

```
35 C      Custno        SETLL     Custmaster                          ----90   record exists?
36 C                    IF        *IN90 = *OFF                                 duplicate record?    B01
37 C                    EVAL      Custnumber = Custno                          pf fld to dspf fld    01
38 C                    EXFMT     Addrcd                                       display screen        01
39 C                    IF        *IN12 = *OFF                                 ignore entry?        B02
40 C                    WRITE     Cusrecord                           --90--   add record to pf      02
41 C                    ENDIF                                                 end line 1900 IF grp E02
42 C                    ENDIF                                                 end line 1500 IF grp E01
43 C                    ENDSR                                                 end subroutine
     *--------------------------------------------------------------------------------------*
     * RPG record format  . . . . :  PROMPT                                                  *
     * External format  . . . . . :  PROMPT : STAN/GLDFADD                                   *
     *--------------------------------------------------------------------------------------*
45=O                         *IN90               1A CHAR        1           DUPLICATE RECORD
46=OADDRCD
     *--------------------------------------------------------------------------------------*
     * RPG record format  . . . . :  ADDRCD                                                  *
     * External format  . . . . . :  ADDRCD : STAN/GLDFADD                                   *
     *--------------------------------------------------------------------------------------*
47=O                         CUSTNUMBER          5S ZONE      5,0
48=OCUSRECORD
     *--------------------------------------------------------------------------------------*
     * RPG record format  . . . . :  CUSRECORD                                               *
     * External format  . . . . . :  CUSRECORD : STAN/CUSTMASTER                             *
     *--------------------------------------------------------------------------------------*
49=O                         CUSTNUMBER          3P PACK      5,0
50=O                         CUSTNAME           23A CHAR       20
51=O                         STREET             43A CHAR       20
52=O                         CITY               63A CHAR       20
53=O                         STATE              65A CHAR        2
54=O                         ZIPCODE            68P PACK      5,0
55=O                         ACTBALANCE         73P PACK      8,2
```

File Description Specifications

Line No.

2 **WORKSTN** file (Gldfadd) is defined as combined (**C** in position 17), full-procedural (**F** in position 18), and externally defined (**E** in position 22).

3 Custmaster is defined as an update (**U** in position 17), full-procedural (**F** in position 18), externally defined (**E** in position 22), and keyed (**K** in position 34) physical file. The **A** in position 20 indicates that records may be added. Because the **SETLL** instruction on line 35 determines if the current record exists before attempting to add it, the physical file must be defined as update to support this operation. If the optional **SETLL** instruction was not specified, the file could have been defined as output (**O** in position 17).

Calculation Specifications

26 The **DOU** group controls the display of the PROMPT and ADDRCD formats and the addition of records to the physical file. The iterative processing (looping) continues until the operator presses **F3,** which sets on indicator **03,** when in the PROMPT display to end the job. The relational test for the **DOU** instruction is made at the related **ENDDO** operation on line 30. Consequently, the **DOU** group will be executed at least once.

27 The **EXFMT** instruction *writes* the PROMPT record to the screen and holds it there. After the operator enters a customer number and presses the ENTER key, the value *read* and a blank ADDRCD record, or a DUPLICATE RECORD error message, are displayed. The operator may end the job by pressing **F3.**

28 The **CASEQ** instruction tests the status of the **03** indicator. If it is "off," control branches to the AddSR subroutine.

29 The **ENDCS** operation ends the **CASEQ** group.

30 The **ENDDO** operation ends the **DOUEQ** group. Recall that the relational test is made here and *not* at the **DOUEQ** instruction on line 26. When indicator **03** is "on," control will exit from the **DOUEQ** group and execute the instruction on line 32 to end the job.

32 The **EVAL** instruction turns on the **LR** indicator to end the job.

34 The **BEGSR** instruction begins the AddSR subroutine.

35 The Custno value from the PROMPT screen, specified in the **SETLL** instruction, searches the Custmaster file for a duplicate key condition. If a duplicate key is found, *Resulting Indicator* **90** will be set on.

36 This **IF** instruction tests the status of indicator **90.** If it is "off," which indicates that a duplicate key is *not* stored in the file, the instructions on lines 37 and 38 will be executed. Otherwise, control will branch to the **ENDIF** operation on line 42.

Figure 15-7 Detailed compile listing of the "adds" maintenance program. (Continued)

37 The **EVAL** instruction initializes the Custnumber field in the ADDRCD display with the Custno field value from the PROMPT display. This ensures that the customer number entered will be unchanged in the physical file's record format when it is written to the file. Recall that the Custnumber field is protected in the ADDRCD record and the cursor positioned at the Custname field.

38 This **EXFMT** instruction writes the ADDRCD display on the screen and holds it so that data may be entered. After entering the data, the operator may press the ENTER key to read the display file and write the record to the physical file, or press **F12** at any time not to enter the data. In either case, program control will redisplay the PROMPT screen.

39 This **IF** instruction tests the status of indicator **12.** When it is "off," the Cusrecord record will be written to the physical file by the **WRITE** instruction on line 40, the nested **IF** group ended, and control returned to the **ENDDO** instruction on line 30, where the end-of-job test is made. When indicator **12** is "on," the **WRITE** instruction on line 40 will not be executed and the record will *not* be written to the physical file.

Because the field names in the display file's ADDRCD record are the same as those in the physical file (Custmaster), the field values do not have to be moved from the display file to the physical file's fields.

40 The **WRITE** instruction writes the CUSRECORD display record to the physical file. *Resulting Indicator* **90** will turn on if a processing error occurs.

41 This **ENDIF** instruction ends the **IF** group that began on line 39.

42 This **ENDIF** instruction ends the **IF** group that began on line 36.

43 The **ENDSR** operation ends the AddSR internal subroutine.

Figure 15-7 Detailed compile listing of the "adds" maintenance program. (Continued)

A **DSPPFM** *(Display Physical File Member)* command display of the physical file will show that the "add" records are stored at the end of the file. However, because the physical file is keyed, a **CPYF** *(Copy File)* listing will place the "add" records in their key sequence location(s).

RPG IV PROGRAM: INTERACTIVE INQUIRY OF RECORDS

A source listing of the display file processed by a program that inquiries records in a physical file defined with unique keys is shown in Figure 15-8.

```
SEQNBR*...+... 1 ...+... 2 ...+... 3 ...+... 4 ...+... 5 ...+... 6 ...+... 7 ...+... 8
     * PROMPT DISPLAY....
     A                                      MSGLOC(18)
     A                                      REF(STAN/CUSTMASTER)
     A                                      PRINT
     A          R PROMPT
     A                                      CA03(03 'EOJ')
     A                                  1  3DATE EDTCDE(Y)
     A                                  1 32'CUSTOMER FILE INQUIRY'
     A                                  1 71TIME
     A                                  3 10'ENTER CVSTOMER NO:'
     A            CUSTNO         5D 0I  3 29DSPATR(RI)
     A  91                                  ERRMSG('RECORD NOT FOUND' 91)
     A                                  9 18'F3 - EOJ'
     A                                  9 50'ENTER KEY - INQUIRY'
     * ENTRY DISPLAY....
     A          R INQRCD
     A                                  1  3DATE EDTCDE(Y)
     A                                  1 30'CUSTOMER FILE INQUIRY'
     A                                      DSPATR(UL)
     A                                  3 20'CUSTOMER NUMBER:' DSPATR(HI)
     A            CUSTNUMBERR     D  O  3 40DSPATR(PR)
     A                                  5 20'NAME:' DSPATR(HI)
     A            CUSTNAME  R        O  5 40DSPATR(PC)
     A                                  7 20'STREET:' DSPATR(HI)
     A            STREET    R        O  7 40
     A                                  9 20'CITY:' DSPATR(HI)
     A            CITY      R        O  9 40
     A                                 11 20'STATE:' DSPATR(HI)
```

Figure 15-8 Display file for inquiry processing.

```
     A            STATE       R          O 11 40
     A                                     13 20'ZIP:' DSPATR(HI)
     A            ZIPCODE     R       D  O 13 40
     A                                     15 20'BALANCE:' DSPATR(HI)
     A            ACTBALANCER            O 15 40
     A                                     20 10'PRESS ENTER TO CONTINUE'
```

O usage supports output only; from the program to the display record

Figure 15-8 Display file for inquiry processing. (Continued)

Note that the following features are included:

1. Two record formats are coded. One is a PROMPT record in which a customer number is entered to determine if a record with that key value is stored in the physical file. Error identification (i.e., **RECORD NOT FOUND**) is controlled in this record format.
2. The *Command Attention* key, **CA03,** is defined at the *Record Level* in the PROMPT record to control end-of-job processing. The job is continued when a CUSTNO value is entered and the ENTER key pressed.
3. The second (INQRCD) record format defines all of the fields with **O** *Usage,* which supports the display of values *from* the program *to* this record format. Control is returned to the PROMPT display by pressing the ENTER key.

A Print key copy of the displays generated from execution of the **RPG IV** inquiry program is shown in Figure 15-9.

```
12/28/97                 CUSTOMER FILE INQUIRY                  14:30:00

     ENTER CUSTOMER NO: 12345



           F3 - EOJ                        ENTER KEY - INQUIRY
```

Prompt display

```
12/28/97               CUSTOMER FILE INQUIRY

              CUSTOMER NUMBER:       12345

              NAME:                  KAREL APPEL

              STREET                 20 AMSTERDAM AVENUE

              CITY:                  NEW YORK

              STATE:                 NY

              ZIP:                   07450

              BALANCE:               00125000


     PRESS ENTER TO CONTINUE
```

INQRCD display

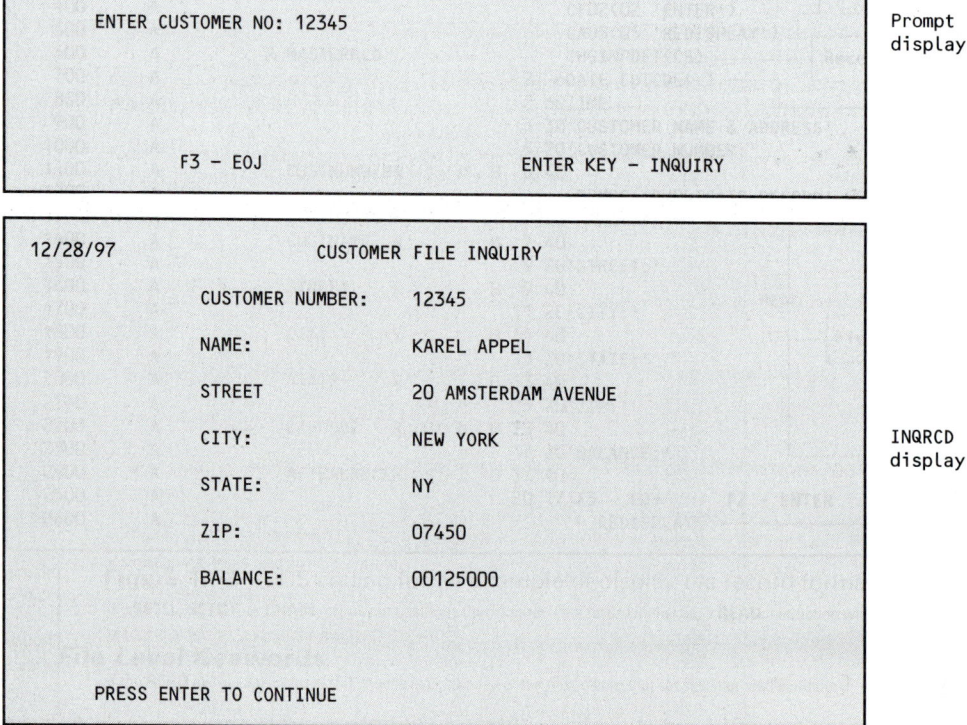

Figure 15-9 Print key copy of the display file's two record formats for file inquiry.

The **RPG IV** inquiry program includes the following operations:

DOUEQ group — **CHAIN** statement
EXFMT statement — **IFEQ** statement
CASEQ statement

A compile listing of the **RPG IV** inquiry program and a supplemental line-by-line explanation of the instructions are detailed in Figure 15-10.

```
Line   <---------------------- Source Specifications ----------------------------><---- Comments ----> Do
Number ....1....+....2....+....3....+....4....+....5....+....6....+....7....+....8....+....9....+...10 Num
                            S o u r c e   L i s t i n g
     1  * This program performs PF (Custmaster) interactive inquiry....
     2 FGldfinq   CF   E             WORKSTN
       *--------------------------------------------------------------------------------*
       *                              RPG name           External name                   *
       * File name. . . . . . . . :   GLDFINQ            STAN/GLDFINQ                    *
       * Record format(s) . . . . :   PROMPT             PROMPT                          *
       *                              INQRCD             INQRCD                          *
       *--------------------------------------------------------------------------------*
     3 FCustmasterIF   E           K DISK
     4
       *--------------------------------------------------------------------------------*
       *                              RPG name           External name                   *
       * File name. . . . . . . . :   CUSTMASTER         STAN/CUSTMASTER                 *
       * Record format(s) . . . . :   CUSRECORD          CUSRECORD                       *
       *--------------------------------------------------------------------------------*
     5=IPROMPT
       *--------------------------------------------------------------------------------*
       * RPG record format  . . . . :  PROMPT                                            *
       * External format  . . . . . :  PROMPT : STAN/GLDFINQ                             *
       *--------------------------------------------------------------------------------*
     6=I                             A    1    1  *IN03                        EOJ
     7=I                             A    2    2  *IN91                        RECORD NOT FOUND
     8=I                             S    3    7 0CUSTNO
     9=IINQRCD
       *--------------------------------------------------------------------------------*
       * RPG record format  . . . . :  INQRCD                                            *
       * External format  . . . . . :  INQRCD : STAN/GLDFINQ                             *
       *--------------------------------------------------------------------------------*
    10=ICUSRECORD
       *--------------------------------------------------------------------------------*
       * RPG record format  . . . . :  CUSRECORD                                         *
       * External format  . . . . . :  CUSRECORD : STAN/CUSTMASTER                       *
       *--------------------------------------------------------------------------------*
    11=I                             P    1    3 0CUSTNUMBER
    12=I                             A    4   23  CUSTNAME
    13=I                             A   24   43  STREET
    14=I                             A   44   63  CITY
    15=I                             A   64   65  STATE
    16=I                             P   66   68 0ZIPCODE
    17=I                             P   69   73 2ACTBALANCE
    18 C                   DOU       *IN03 = *ON                               dou ind 03 is on      B01
    19 C                   EXFMT     Prompt                                    display prompt scrn    01
    20 C     *IN03         CASEQ     *OFF          InqSR                       branch to AddSR        01
    21 C                   ENDCS                                               end CAS group          01
    22 C                   ENDDO                                               end dou group         E01
    23
    24 C                   EVAL      *INLR = *ON                               end program
    25
    26 C     InqSR         BEGSR                                               begin subroutine
    27 C     Custno        CHAIN     Custmaster                       91----   get pf record
    28 C                   IF        *IN91 = *OFF                              duplicate record?     B01
    29 C                   EXFMT     Inqrcd                                    display inqrcd         01
    30 C                   ENDIF                                               end IF group          E01
    31 C                   ENDSR                                               end subroutine
    32=OPROMPT
```

Figure 15-10 Compile listing of the interactive "inquiry" program.

```
       *--------------------------------------------------------------------------------*
       * RPG record format . . . . : PROMPT                                              *
       * External format . . . . . : PROMPT : STAN/GLDFINQ                               *
       *--------------------------------------------------------------------------------*
33=0                    *IN91              1A CHAR        1              RECORD NOT FOUND
34=OINQRCD
       *--------------------------------------------------------------------------------*
       * RPG record format . . . . : INQRCD                                              *
       * External format . . . . . : INQRCD : STAN/GLDFINQ                               *
       *--------------------------------------------------------------------------------*
35=0                    CUSTNUMBER         5S ZONE      5,0
36=0                    CUSTNAME          25A CHAR       20
37=0                    STREET            45A CHAR       20
38=0                    CITY              65A CHAR       20
39=0                    STATE             67A CHAR        2
40=0                    ZIPCODE           72S ZONE      5,0
41=0                    ACTBALANCE        80S ZONE      8,2
```

File Description Specifications

Line No.

2 **WORKSTN** file (Gldfinq) is defined as combined (**C** in position 17), full-procedural (**F** in position 18), and externally defined (**E** in position 22).

3 Custmaster is defined as an input (**I** in position 17), full-procedural (**F** in position 18), externally defined (**E** in position 22), and keyed (**K** in position 34) physical file. Inquiry processing requires that the physical file be defined as **I** (input) or **U** (update).

Calculation Specifications

18 The **DOU** group controls the display of the Prompt and Inqrcd formats and the random access of records in the physical file. The iterative processing (looping) continues until the operator presses **F3,** which sets on indicator **03,** when in the Prompt display to end the job. The relational test for the **DOU** statement is made at the related **ENDDO** instruction on line 22. Consequently, the **DOU** group will be executed at least once.

19 The **EXFMT** instruction *writes* the Prompt record to the screen and holds it there. After the operator enters a customer number and presses the ENTER key, the Inqrcd record format, or **RECORD NOT FOUND** error message, will display. The operator may end the job by pressing **F3.**

20 The **CASEQ** instruction tests the status of the **03** indicator. If it is "off," control branches to the InqSR subroutine.

21 The **ENDCS** operation ends the **CASEQ** group.

22 The **ENDDO** operation ends the **DOUEQ** group. Recall that the relational test is made here and *not* at the **DOUEQ** instruction on line 18. When indicator **03** is "on," control will exit from the **DOUEQ** group and execute the instruction on line 24 to end the job.

24 The **EVAL** instruction turns on the **LR** indicator to end the job.

26 The **BEGSR** instruction begins the InqSR subroutine.

27 The Custno value from the PROMPT screen, specified in the **CHAIN** instruction, searches the Custmaster file for an equal key condition. If a physical file record with the same key is found, it is moved into memory for processing. *Resulting Indicator* **90** is turned on if the **CHAIN** is not successful (record-not-found condition).

28 The **IF** instruction tests the status of indicator **91.** If it is "off," which indicates that a Custmaster file record was found with the same key value as the Custno field, the instruction on line 29 will be executed. Otherwise, control will branch to the **ENDIF** operation on line 30.

29 This **EXFMT** instruction writes the Inqrcd display on the screen for review. The operator may continue the inquiry process, or end the job, by pressing the ENTER key to display the PROMPT record.

30 This **ENDIF** instruction ends the **IF** group that began on line 28.

31 The **ENDSR** operation ends the InqSR subroutine.

Figure 15-10 Compile listing of the interactive "inquiry" program. (Continued)

Instead of using the **DSPPFM** or **CPYF** command to view the records in a physical file, which may be difficult for the user to read, an inquiry program is usually more "user-friendly." However, the **DSPPFM** and **CPYF** commands are generic and may be used with any physical file, whereas an inquiry program is applicable only for one file.

RPG IV PROGRAM: INTERACTIVE UPDATE OF RECORDS

The display file processed by a program that updates records in a physical file defined with *unique* keys is shown in Figure 15-11.

```
SEQNBR*...+... 1 ...+... 2 ...+... 3 ...+... 4 ...+... 5 ...+... 6 ...+... 7 ...+... 8
      * PROMPT DISPLAY....
     A                                      MSGLOC(18)
     A                                      PRINT
     A          R PROMPT
     A                                      CA03(03 'EOJ')
     A                                  1  3DATE EDTCDE(Y)
     A                                  1 32'CUSTOMER FILE UPDATE'
     A                                  1 71TIME
     A                                  3 10'ENTER CVSTOMER NO:'
     A            CUSTNO         5D 0I  3 29DSPATR(RI)
     A  91                                  ERRMSG('RECORD NOT FOUND' 91)
     A                                  9 18'F3 - EOJ'
     A                                  9 50'ENTER KEY - UPDATE'
      * ENTRY DISPLAY....
     A          R UPDRCD
     A                                      CA12(12 'DO NOT UPDATE')
     A                                      CHGINPDFT(RI)
     A                                  1  3DATE EDTCDE(Y)
     A                                  1 30'CUSTOMER FILE UPDATE'
     A                                      DSPATR(UL)
     A                                  3 20'CUSTOMER NUMBER:' DSPATR(HI)
     A            UUSTNUMBER     5D  B  3 40DSPATR(PR)
     A                                  5 20'NAME:' DSPATR(HI)
     A            UUSTNAME      20   B  5 40DSPATR(PC)
     A                                  7 20'STREET:' DSPATR(HI)
     A            USTREET       20   B  7 40
     A                                  9 20'CITY:' DSPATR(HI)
     A            UCITY         20   B  9 40
     A                                 11 20'STATE:' DSPATR(HI)
     A            USTATE         2   B 11 40
     A                                 13 20'ZIP:' DSPATR(HI)
     A            UZIPCODE       5D 0B 13 40
     A                                 15 20'BALANCE:' DSPATR(HI)
     A            UCTBALANCE     8  2B 15 40
     A                                 20 10'PRESS ENTER TO UPDATE'
     A                                 20 50'PRESS F12 TO NOT UPDATE'

     B supports output (from) and
     input (to) the RPG IV program
```

Figure 15-11 Display file for interactive "update" maintenance.

1. Two record formats are coded. One is a PROMPT record in which a customer number is entered to determine if a record with that key value is stored in the physical file. Error identification (i.e., **RECORD NOT FOUND**) is controlled in this record format.
2. The *Command Attention* key, **CA03,** defined at the *Record Level* in the PROMPT record, controls end-of-job processing. The job is continued when a CUSTNO value is entered and the ENTER key is pressed.
3. The second (UPDRCD) record format defines all of the fields with **B** *Usage,* which supports the input and output of values to and from this display to the program. In an interactive update process, a record must be retrieved, displayed (output), values changed, display read (input), and the screen record written back to the same record location in the physical file.

   The record is updated when the operator presses the ENTER key. If the decision is made not to update, the operator presses **F12.** For either case, control redisplays the PROMPT screen and the operator decides whether to end the job or continue the update process.
4. Instead of referencing the field attributes from the physical file, new field names are defined in the UPDRCD format. This is important in update maintenance to ensure that the changed data is written back to the file. In the **RPG IV** program,

the field values from the retrieved physical file record are moved to the related display record fields. Then, after the data is changed, the display record's field values are moved back to the fields in the physical file's record format.

A Print key copy of the PROMPT and UPDRCD displays generated from execution of the **RPG IV** update program is shown in Figure 15-12. Note that two UPDRCD displays are shown, one *before* values are changed and the other *after* they have been changed. When the operator presses the ENTER key, the physical file's record will be updated with the new values.

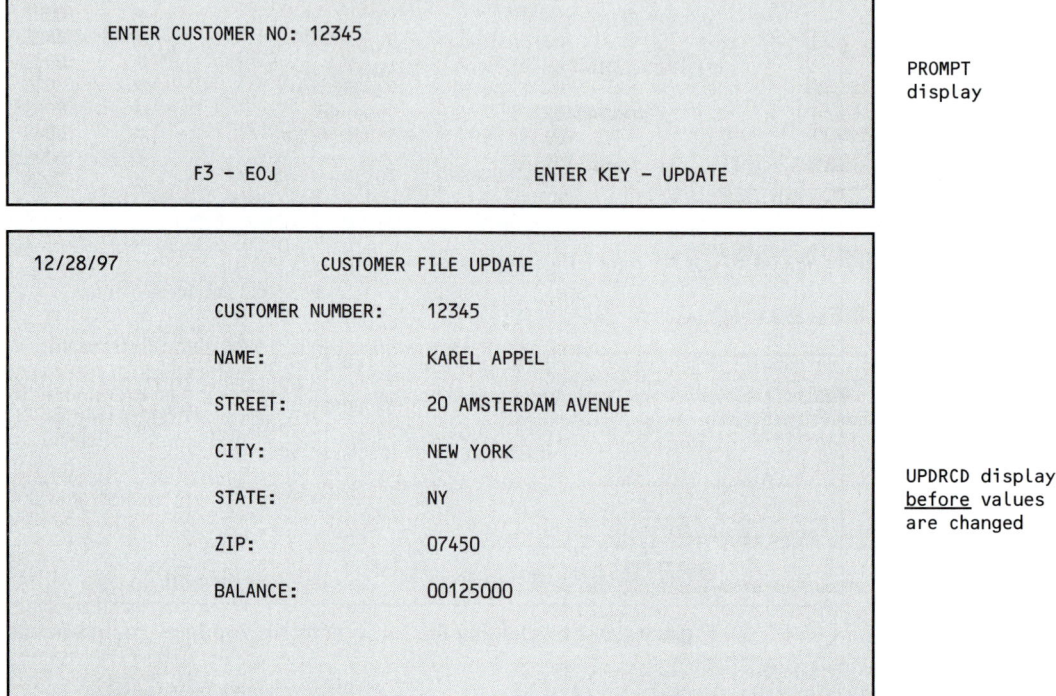

```
12/30/97                  CUSTOMER FILE UPDATE                  15:20:10

      ENTER CUSTOMER NO: 12345

              F3 - EOJ                     ENTER KEY - UPDATE
```

PROMPT display

```
12/28/97                CUSTOMER FILE UPDATE

                CUSTOMER NUMBER:     12345

                NAME:                KAREL APPEL

                STREET:              20 AMSTERDAM AVENUE

                CITY:                NEW YORK

                STATE:               NY

                ZIP:                 07450

                BALANCE:             00125000

      PRESS ENTER TO CONTINUE                PRESS F12 - TO NOT UPDATE
```

UPDRCD display <u>before</u> values are changed

```
12/28/97                CUSTOMER FILE UPDATE

                CUSTOMER NUMBER:     12345

                NAME:                KAREL APPEL

                STREET:              9 SECOND HILL LANE

                CITY:                TRENTON

                STATE:               NJ

                ZIP:                 08330

                BALANCE:             00125000

      PRESS ENTER TO UPDATE                  PRESS F12 TO NOT UPDATE
```

UPDRCD display <u>after</u> values are changed

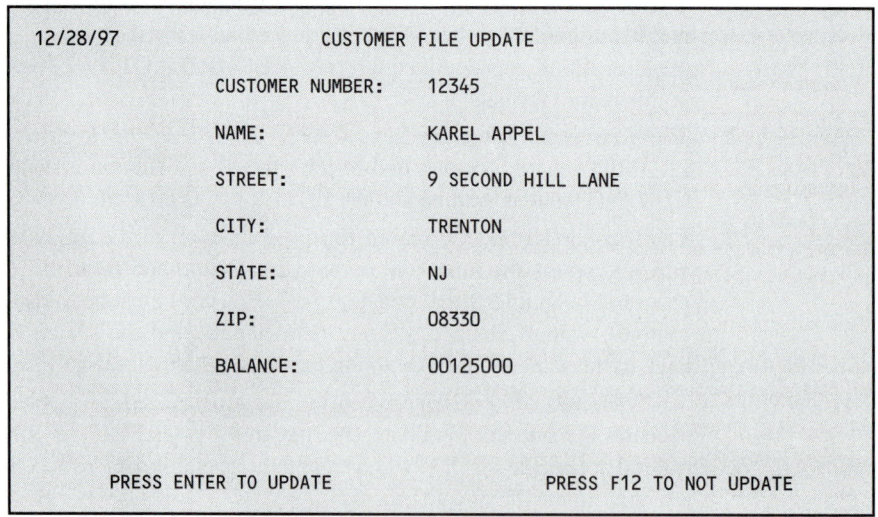

Figure 15-12 Print key copy of the display file's PROMPT display and before and after update values are entered in the UPDRCD display.

A compile listing of the "update" **RPG IV** program and a supplemental line-by-line explanation of the instructions are detailed in Figure 15-13. Note that the **RPG IV** program includes the following operations:

DOU group	**CHAIN** instruction
EXFMT instruction	**IF** instruction
CAS instructions	**UPDATE** instructions
EXSR instructions	

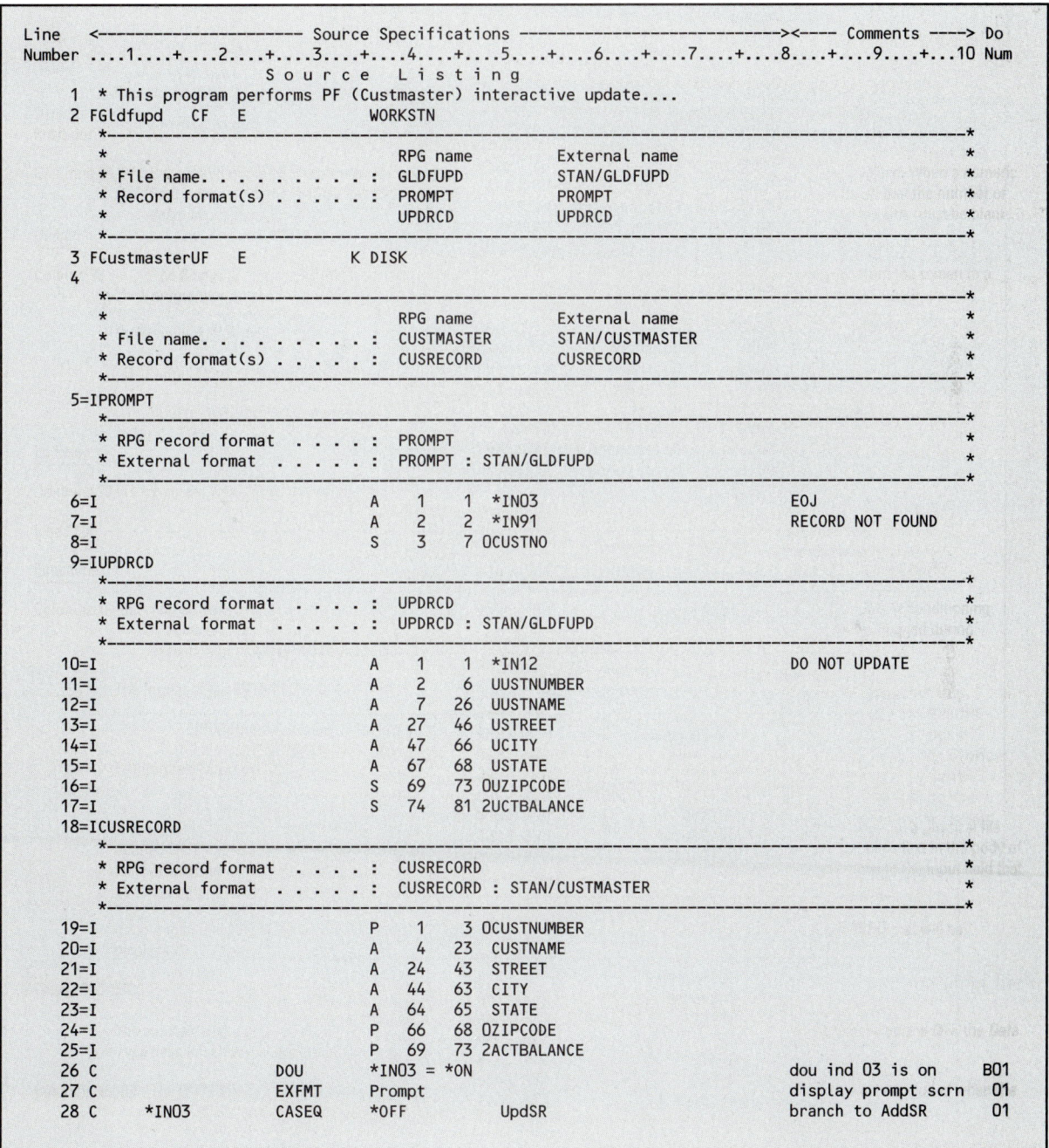

```
Line    <---------------------- Source Specifications ----------------------------><---- Comments ----> Do
Number ....1....+....2....+....3....+....4....+....5....+....6....+....7....+....8....+....9....+...10 Num
                            S o u r c e   L i s t i n g
     1 * This program performs PF (Custmaster) interactive update....
     2 FGldfupd   CF   E             WORKSTN
       *--------------------------------------------------------------------------------------------*
       *                                RPG name           External name                            *
       * File name. . . . . . . . . :   GLDFUPD            STAN/GLDFUPD                             *
       * Record format(s) . . . . . :   PROMPT             PROMPT                                   *
       *                                UPDRCD             UPDRCD                                   *
       *--------------------------------------------------------------------------------------------*
     3 FCustmasterUF   E           K DISK
     4
       *--------------------------------------------------------------------------------------------*
       *                                RPG name           External name                            *
       * File name. . . . . . . . . :   CUSTMASTER         STAN/CUSTMASTER                          *
       * Record format(s) . . . . . :   CUSRECORD          CUSRECORD                                *
       *--------------------------------------------------------------------------------------------*
     5=IPROMPT
       *--------------------------------------------------------------------------------------------*
       * RPG record format  . . . . :   PROMPT                                                      *
       * External format  . . . . . :   PROMPT : STAN/GLDFUPD                                       *
       *--------------------------------------------------------------------------------------------*
     6=I                             A    1    1  *IN03                          EOJ
     7=I                             A    2    2  *IN91                          RECORD NOT FOUND
     8=I                             S    3    7 0CUSTNO
     9=IUPDRCD
       *--------------------------------------------------------------------------------------------*
       * RPG record format  . . . . :   UPDRCD                                                      *
       * External format  . . . . . :   UPDRCD : STAN/GLDFUPD                                       *
       *--------------------------------------------------------------------------------------------*
    10=I                             A    1    1  *IN12                          DO NOT UPDATE
    11=I                             A    2    6  UUSTNUMBER
    12=I                             A    7   26  UUSTNAME
    13=I                             A   27   46  USTREET
    14=I                             A   47   66  UCITY
    15=I                             A   67   68  USTATE
    16=I                             S   69   73 0UZIPCODE
    17=I                             S   74   81 2UCTBALANCE
    18=ICUSRECORD
       *--------------------------------------------------------------------------------------------*
       * RPG record format  . . . . :   CUSRECORD                                                   *
       * External format  . . . . . :   CUSRECORD : STAN/CUSTMASTER                                 *
       *--------------------------------------------------------------------------------------------*
    19=I                             P    1    3 0CUSTNUMBER
    20=I                             A    4   23  CUSTNAME
    21=I                             A   24   43  STREET
    22=I                             A   44   63  CITY
    23=I                             A   64   65  STATE
    24=I                             P   66   68 0ZIPCODE
    25=I                             P   69   73 2ACTBALANCE
    26 C                   DOU       *IN03 = *ON                                 dou ind 03 is on     B01
    27 C                   EXFMT     Prompt                                      display prompt scrn   01
    28 C     *IN03         CASEQ     *OFF          UpdSR                         branch to AddSR       01
```

Figure 15-13 Compile listing of the "update" maintenance program.

```
 C                  ENDCS                                                 end CAS group       01
 C                  ENDDO                                                 end dou group      E01

 C                  EVAL      *INLR = *ON                                 end program

 C     UpdSR        BEGSR                                                 begin subroutine
 C     Custno       CHAIN     Custmaster                      91----      get pf record
 C                  IF        *IN91 = *OFF                                duplicate record?  B01
 C                  EXSR      Pftodf                                      pf to df subroutine 01
 C                  EXFMT     Updrcd                                      display inqrcd      01
 C                  IF        *IN12 = *OFF                                do not update?     B02
 C                  EXSR      Dftopf                                      df to pf            02
 C                  UPDATE    Cusrecord                       --90--      update pf record    02
 C                  ENDIF                                                 end IF group       E02
 C                  ENDIF                                                 end IF group       E01
 C                  ENDSR                                                 end subroutine

 * Move pf field values to df fields....

 C     Pftodf       BEGSR                                                 begin subroutine
 C                  MOVE      Custnumber    Uustnumber
 C                  MOVE      Custname      Uustname
 C                  MOVE      Street        UStreet
 C                  MOVE      City          Ucity
 C                  MOVE      State         Ustate
 C                  MOVE      Zipcode       Uzipcode
 C                  MOVE      Actbalance    Uctbalance
 C                  ENDSR

 C     Dftopf       BEGSR                                                 begin subroutine
 C                  MOVE      Uustnumber    Custnumber
 C                  MOVE      Uustname      Custname
 C                  MOVE      Ustreet       Street
 C                  MOVE      Ucity         City
 C                  MOVE      Ustate        State
 C                  MOVE      Uzipcode      Zipcode
 C                  MOVE      Uctbalance    Actbalance
 C                  ENDSR
=OPROMPT
   *---------------------------------------------------------------------------------------*
   * RPG record format . . . . :  PROMPT                                                   *
   * External format . . . . . :  PROMPT : STAN/GLDFUPD                                    *
   *---------------------------------------------------------------------------------------*
=O                      *IN91            1A CHAR       1                RECORD NOT FOUND
=OUPDRCD
   *---------------------------------------------------------------------------------------*
   * RPG record format . . . . :  UPDRCD                                                   *
   * External format . . . . . :  UPDRCD : STAN/GLDFUPD                                    *
   *---------------------------------------------------------------------------------------*
=O                      UUSTNUMBER       5A CHAR       5
=O                      UUSTNAME        25A CHAR      20
=O                      USTREET         45A CHAR      20
=O                      UCITY           65A CHAR      20
=O                      USTATE          67A CHAR       2
=O                      UZIPCODE        72S ZONE     5,0
=O                      UCTBALANCE      80S ZONE     8,2
=OCUSRECORD
   *---------------------------------------------------------------------------------------*
   * RPG record format . . . . :  CUSRECORD                                                *
   * External format . . . . . :  CUSRECORD : STAN/CUSTMASTER                              *
   *---------------------------------------------------------------------------------------*
=O                      CUSTNUMBER       3P PACK     5,0
=O                      CUSTNAME        23A CHAR      20
=O                      STREET          43A CHAR      20
=O                      CITY            63A CHAR      20
=O                      STATE           65A CHAR       2
=O                      ZIPCODE         68P PACK     5,0
=O                      ACTBALANCE      73P PACK     8,2
```

Figure 15-13 Compile listing of the "update" maintenance program. (Continued)

File Description Specifications:

Line No.

2 Gldfupd is defined as a combined (**C** in position 17), full-procedural (**F** in position 18), and externally defined (**E** in position 22) **WORKSTN** file.

3 Custmaster is defined as an update (**U** in position 17), full-procedural (**F** in position 18), externally defined (**E** in position 22), keyed (**K** in position 34) physical file.

Calculation Specifications:

26 The **DOU** group controls the display of the PROMPT format, the entry of a Custno value, the display of the Updrcd format, any change to the data, update of records in the physical file, and end-of-job control. The iterative processing (looping) continues after the operator presses **F3,** which sets on indicator **03,** to end the job. The relational test for the **DOU** instruction is made at **ENDDO** instruction on line 30. Consequently, the **DOU** group will be executed at least once.

27 The **EXFMT** instruction *writes* the PROMPT record to the screen and holds it there until the operator presses ENTER or the **F3** key.

28 The **CASEQ** instruction tests the status of indicator **03.** If it is "off," control will branch to the **BEGSR** instruction on line 34. If indicator **03** is "on," control will branch to the **ENDDO** instruction on line 30, test the status of the **03** indicator at the **ENDDO** operation, and end the program by executing the **EVAL** instruction on line 32.

29 The **ENDCS** operation ends the **CASEQ** group that began on line 28.

30 The **ENDDO** operation ends the **DOU** group that began on line 26.

32 The **EVAL** instruction turns on the **LR** indicator to end the program.

34 This **BEGSR** instruction begins the Pftodf subroutine in which the physical file's Cusrecord field values are **MOVED** into the display file's Addrcd record fields.

35 The **CHAIN** instruction random searches the Custmaster file for a key equal to the value in the Custno field. Recall that the Custno value was entered as the response in the Prompt display. If a record with an equal key value is *not* found in the Custmaster file, *Resulting Indicator* **91** will be set on.

36 The **IF** instruction tests the status of indicator **91.** When it is "off," instructions on lines 37–39 will be executed. If it is "on," control will branch to the **ENDSR** operation on line 44.

37 This **EXSR** instruction branches control to the Pftodf subroutine that begins on line 48.

38 This **EXFMT** instruction displays the Updrcd record "filled in" with the field values from the Custmaster file's Cusrecord.

39 This **IF** instruction tests the status of indicator **12.** If the user presses **F12,** the update process will be ignored, control will be returned to the Prompt display, and the current Cusrecord values in the Updrcd display will not be updated. However, if the user presses the ENTER key instead of **F12,** control will execute the **EXSR** instruction on line 40 and branch to the Dftopf subroutine.

40 This **EXSR** instruction passes control to the Dftopf subroutine.

41 The **UPDATE** instruction updates the current Cusrecord whose original or changed values are displayed in the display file's Updrcd record format.

42 This **ENDIF** operation ends the **IF** group that began on line 39.

43 This **ENDIF** operation ends the **IF** group that began on line 36.

44 This **ENDSR** operation ends the UpdSR subroutine that began on line 34.

48 This **BEGSR** instruction begins the Pftodf subroutine.

49–55 These **MOVE** instructions move the physical file's current Cusrecord record values to their related display file's Addrcd record fields.

56 This **ENDSR** operation ends the Pttodf subroutine that began on line 48.

58 This **BEGSR** instruction begins the Dftopf subroutine.

59–65 These **MOVE** instructions move the display file's Updrcd record values to the related physical file's Cusrecord fields before updating with the **UPDATE** instruction on line 41.

66 This **ENDSR** operation ends the Dftopf subroutine that began on line 58.

Figure 15-13 Compile listing of the "update" maintenance program. (Continued)

RPG IV PROGRAM: INTERACTIVE LOGICAL DELETION OF RECORDS

The display file processed by a program that logically deletes records in a physical file defined with unique keys is shown in Figure 15-14.

```
SEQNBR*...+... 1 ...+... 2 ...+... 3 ...+... 4 ...+... 5 ...+... 6 ...+... 7 ...+... 8
      * PROMPT DISPLAY....
     A                                      MSGLOC(6)
     A                                      REF(STAN/CUSTMASTER)
     A                                      PRINT
     A          R PROMPT
     A                                      CA03(03 'EOJ')
     A                                  1  3DATE EDTCDE(Y)
     A                                  1 32'CUSTOMER FILE DELETES'
     A                                  1 71TIME
     A                                  3 10'ENTER CVSTOMER NO:'
     A            CUSTNO         5D 0I  3 29DSPATR(RI)
     A 91                                   ERRMSG('RECORD NOT FOUND' 91)
     A                                  9 18'F3 - EOJ'
     A                                  9 50'ENTER KEY - DELETE'
      * DELETE SCREEN....
     A          R DLTRCD
     A                                      CA12(12 'DO NOT DELETE')
     A                                      CHGINPDFT(RI)
     A                                  1  3DATE 9EDTCDE(Y)
     A                                  1 30'CUSTOMER FILE DELETES'
     A                                      DSPATR(UL)
     A                                  3 20'CUSTOMER NUMBER:' DSPATR(HI)
     A            CUSTNUMBERR     D  B  3 40DSPATR(PR)
     A                                  5 20'NAME:' DSPATR(HI)
     A            CUSTNAME  R        O  5 40DSPATR(PC)
     A                                  7 20'STREET:' DSPATR(HI)
     A            STREET    R        O  7 40
     A                                  9 20'CITY:' DSPATR(HI)
     A            CITY      R        O  9 40
     A                                 11 20'STATE:' DSPATR(HI)
     A            STATE     R        O 11 40
     A                                 13 20'ZIP:' DSPATR(HI)
     A            ZIPCODE   R     D  O 13 40
     A                                 15 20'BALANCE:' DSPATR(HI)
     A            ACTBALANCER        O 15 40
     A                                 20 10'PRESS ENTER TO DELETE RECORD'
     A                                 20 50'PRESS F12 TO NOT DELETE'
```

Defined with B usage

Defined with O usage

Figure 15-14 Display file for logical deletion maintenance.

Note that the following features are included:

1. Two record formats are coded. One is a PROMPT record in which a customer number is entered to determine if a record with that key value is stored in the physical file. Error identification (i.e., **RECORD NOT FOUND**) is controlled in this record format.
2. The *Command Attention* key, **CA03,** defined at the *Record Level* in the PROMPT record, controls end-of-job processing. The job is continued when a CUSTNO value is entered and the ENTER key is pressed.
3. The second (DLTRCD) record format defines the CUSTNUMBER field with **B** *Usage,* which supports the input and output of its value so that the key value may be written to the screen and then read, to logically delete the retrieved record. All

of the other fields are defined with an **O** *Usage* (output only) so that their values may be displayed but not changed. There is no reason for changing field values when the record is to be logically deleted. The record is logically deleted when the operator presses the ENTER key. If the decision is made not to delete the record, **F12** is pressed. In either case, control redisplays the **PROMPT** screen, and the operator decides whether to end the job or continue the deletion process.

A Print key copy of the PROMPT and DLTRCD displays generated from execution of the **RPG IV** update program is shown in Figure 15-15.

```
12/01/97                    CUSTOMER FILE DELETES                    11:15:00

    ENTER CUSTOMER NO: 12345



           F3 - EOJ                         ENTER KEY - DELETE
```

PROMPT display

```
12/01/97                  CUSTOMER FILE DELETES

              CUSTOMER NUMBER:     12345

              NAME:                KAREL APPEL

              STREET:              20 AMSTERDAM AVENUE

              CITY:                NEW YORK

              STATE:               NY

              ZIP:                 07450

              BALANCE:             00125000


    PRESS ENTER TO DELETE RECORD          PRESS F12 TO NOT DELETE
```

DLTRCD display

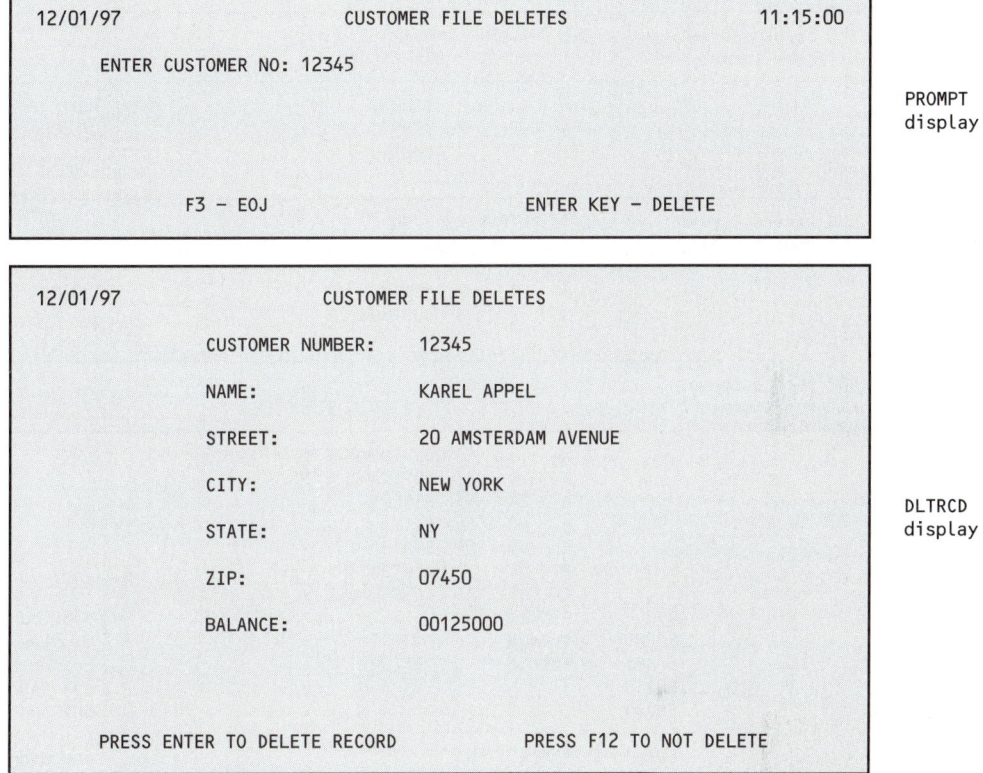

Figure 15-15 Print key copy of the display file's PROMPT and DLTRCD displays.

The compile listing of the **RPG IV** program that logically deletes records in the Custmaster file is detailed in Figure 15-16. Note that the following operations are included:

DOU instruction	**CHAIN** instruction
EXFMT instructions	**IF** instructions
CAS instruction	**DELETE** instruction
EXSR instructions	

```
Line   <---------------------- Source Specifications ----------------------------><---- Comments ----> Do
Number ....1....+....2....+....3....+....4....+....5....+....6....+....7....+....8....+....9....+...10 Num
                           S o u r c e   L i s t i n g
     1  * This program performs PF (Custmaster) interactive logical deletes...
```

Figure 15-16 Compile listing of the logical deletion maintenance program.

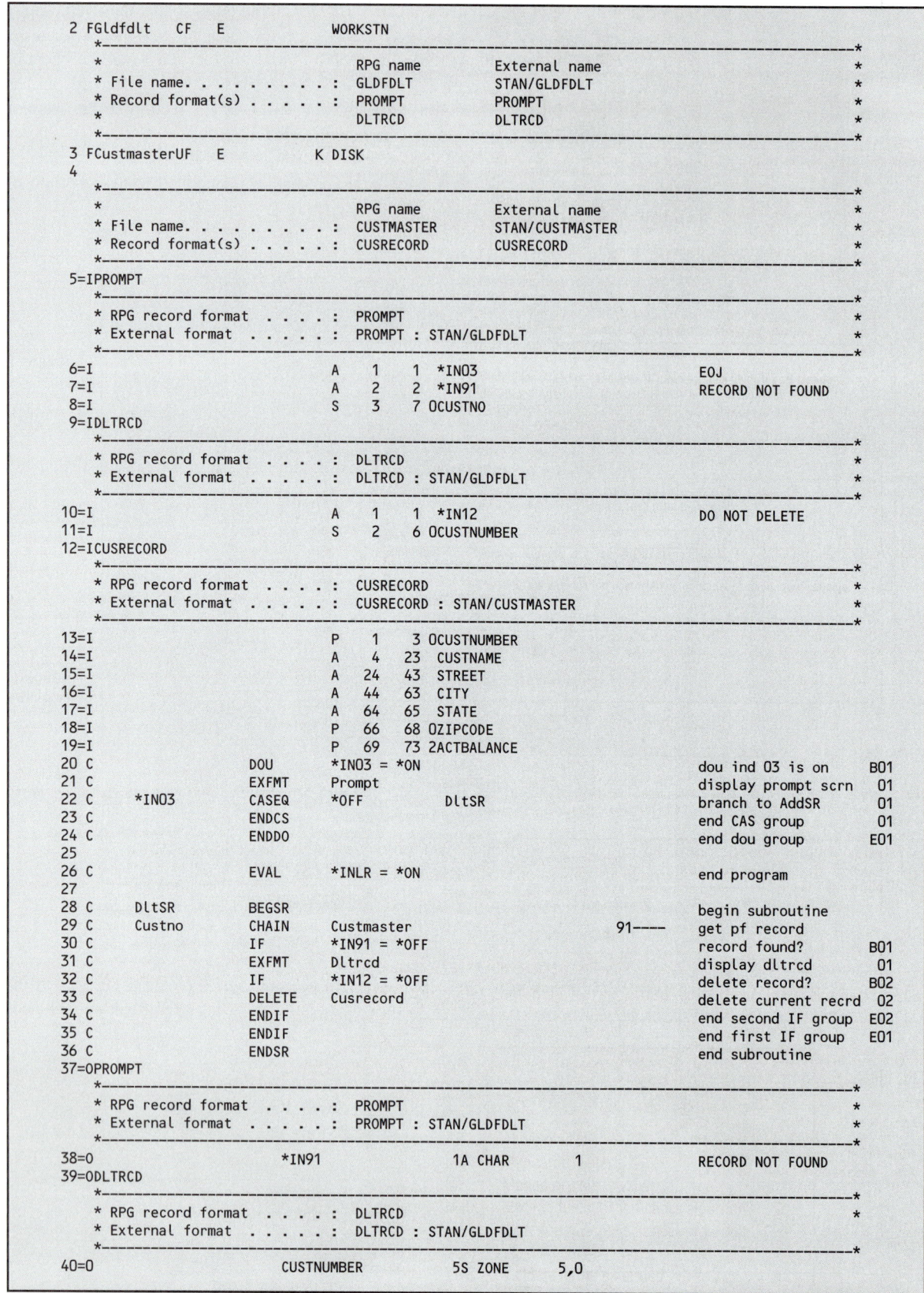

```
 2 FGldfdlt   CF   E                WORKSTN
   *--------------------------------------------------------------------------------------------*
   *                                 RPG name          External name                            *
   * File name. . . . . . . . . :    GLDFDLT           STAN/GLDFDLT                             *
   * Record format(s) . . . . . :    PROMPT            PROMPT                                   *
   *                                 DLTRCD            DLTRCD                                   *
   *--------------------------------------------------------------------------------------------*
 3 FCustmasterUF   E            K DISK
 4
   *--------------------------------------------------------------------------------------------*
   *                                 RPG name          External name                            *
   * File name. . . . . . . . . :    CUSTMASTER        STAN/CUSTMASTER                          *
   * Record format(s) . . . . . :    CUSRECORD         CUSRECORD                                *
   *--------------------------------------------------------------------------------------------*
 5=IPROMPT
   *--------------------------------------------------------------------------------------------*
   * RPG record format  . . . . :    PROMPT                                                     *
   * External format  . . . . . :    PROMPT : STAN/GLDFDLT                                      *
   *--------------------------------------------------------------------------------------------*
 6=I                            A    1     1  *IN03                        EOJ
 7=I                            A    2     2  *IN91                        RECORD NOT FOUND
 8=I                            S    3     7 0CUSTNO
 9=IDLTRCD
   *--------------------------------------------------------------------------------------------*
   * RPG record format  . . . . :    DLTRCD                                                     *
   * External format  . . . . . :    DLTRCD : STAN/GLDFDLT                                      *
   *--------------------------------------------------------------------------------------------*
10=I                            A    1     1  *IN12                        DO NOT DELETE
11=I                            S    2     6 0CUSTNUMBER
12=ICUSRECORD
   *--------------------------------------------------------------------------------------------*
   * RPG record format  . . . . :    CUSRECORD                                                  *
   * External format  . . . . . :    CUSRECORD : STAN/CUSTMASTER                                *
   *--------------------------------------------------------------------------------------------*
13=I                            P    1     3 0CUSTNUMBER
14=I                            A    4    23  CUSTNAME
15=I                            A   24    43  STREET
16=I                            A   44    63  CITY
17=I                            A   64    65  STATE
18=I                            P   66    68 0ZIPCODE
19=I                            P   69    73 2ACTBALANCE
20 C                  DOU       *IN03 = *ON                                dou ind 03 is on     B01
21 C                  EXFMT     Prompt                                     display prompt scrn   01
22 C     *IN03        CASEQ     *OFF          DltSR                        branch to AddSR       01
23 C                  ENDCS                                                end CAS group         01
24 C                  ENDDO                                                end dou group        E01
25
26 C                  EVAL      *INLR = *ON                                end program
27
28 C     DltSR        BEGSR                                                begin subroutine
29 C     Custno       CHAIN     Custmaster                      91----     get pf record
30 C                  IF        *IN91 = *OFF                               record found?        B01
31 C                  EXFMT     Dltrcd                                     display dltrcd        01
32 C                  IF        *IN12 = *OFF                               delete record?       B02
33 C                  DELETE    Cusrecord                                  delete current recrd  02
34 C                  ENDIF                                                end second IF group  E02
35 C                  ENDIF                                                end first IF group   E01
36 C                  ENDSR                                                end subroutine
37=OPROMPT
   *--------------------------------------------------------------------------------------------*
   * RPG record format  . . . . :    PROMPT                                                     *
   * External format  . . . . . :    PROMPT : STAN/GLDFDLT                                      *
   *--------------------------------------------------------------------------------------------*
38=O                      *IN91               1A CHAR         1            RECORD NOT FOUND
39=ODLTRCD
   *--------------------------------------------------------------------------------------------*
   * RPG record format  . . . . :    DLTRCD                                                     *
   * External format  . . . . . :    DLTRCD : STAN/GLDFDLT                                      *
   *--------------------------------------------------------------------------------------------*
40=O                      CUSTNUMBER          5S ZONE       5,0
```

Figure 15-16 Compile listing of the logical deletion maintenance program. (Continued)

```
41=0        CUSTNAME       25A CHAR      20
42=0        STREET         45A CHAR      20
43=0        CITY           65A CHAR      20
44=0        STATE          67A CHAR       2
45=0        ZIPCODE        72S ZONE     5,0
46=0        ACTBALANCE     80S ZONE     8,2
```

File Description Specifications

Line No.

2 **WORKSTN** file (Gldfdlt) is defined as combined (**C** in position 17), full-procedural (**F** in position 18), and externally defined (**E** in position 22).

3 Custmaster is defined as an update (**U** in position 17), full-procedural (**F** in position 18), externally defined (**E** in position 22), and keyed (**K** in position 34) physical file. Deletion processing requires that the physical file be defined as **U** (update).

Calculation Specifications

20 The **DOU** group controls the display of the Prompt and Dltrcd formats and the deletion of records in the physical file. The iterative processing (looping) continues until the operator presses **F3,** which sets on indicator **03,** when in the Prompt display to end the job. The relational test for the **DOU** statement is made at the related **ENDDO** instruction on line 24. Consequently, the **DOU** group will be executed at least once.

21 The **EXFMT** instruction *writes* the Prompt record to the screen and holds it there. After the operator enters a customer number and presses the ENTER key, the Dltrcd record format, or RECORD NOT FOUND error message, will display. The operator may end the job by pressing **F3.**

22 The **CASEQ** instruction tests the status of the **03** indicator. If it is "off," control branches to the DltSR subroutine.

23 The **ENDCS** operation ends the **CASEQ** group.

24 The **ENDDO** operation ends the **DOU** group. Recall that the relational test is made here and *not* at the **DOU** instruction on line 20. When indicator 03 is "on," control will exit from the **DOU** group and execute the instruction on line 26 to end the job.

26 The **EVAL** instruction turns on the **LR** indicator to end the job.

28 The **BEGSR** instruction begins the DltSR subroutine.

29 The Custno value from the PROMPT screen, specified in the **CHAIN** instruction, searches the Custmaster file for an equal key condition. If a physical file record with the same key is found, it is moved into memory for processing. *Resulting Indicator* **91** is turned on if the **CHAIN** is not successful (record not found condition).

30 This **IF** instruction tests the status of indicator **91.** If it is "off," which indicates that a Custmaster file record was found with the same key value as the Custno field, the instruction on line 31 will be executed. Otherwise, control will branch to the **ENDSR** operation on line 36.

31 This **EXFMT** instruction writes the Dltrcd display on the screen for review. The operator may delete the displayed physical file record by pressing the ENTER key or ignore the deletion process by pressing **F12.** in any case, control will return to the Prompt display from which the user may end the program or continue the record deletion process.

32 This **IF** instruction tests the status of indicator **12,** which was turned on if the operator pressed the **F12** key to ignore the transaction. If it is on, control will branch to line 35. However, when indicator **12** is "off," the **DELETE** instruction on line 33 will be executed.

33 The **DELETE** instruction logically deletes the physical file record that is displayed in the Dltrcd screen.

34 This **ENDIF** instruction ends the **IF** group that began on line 32.

35 This **ENDIF** instruction ends the **IF** group that began on line 30.

36 The **ENDSR** operation ends the DltSR internal subroutine.

Figure 15-16 Compile listing of the logical deletion maintenance program. (Continued)

As shown in Figure 15-17, the result of logically deleting a record may be tested from the PROMPT display by entering the customer number of a record determined to be deleted and pressing the ENTER key. If the record has been successfully deleted, the error message **RECORD NOT FOUND** will display on line 6 of the PROMPT display. The Reset key must be pressed to continue processing.

```
12/01/97                  CUSTOMER FILE DELETES                 11:25:00

       ENTER CUSTOMER NO: 12345


RECORD NOT FOUND




                F3 - EOJ                        ENTER KEY - DELETE
```

PROMPT display

Error message displayed when a record with the entered key value is not found in the file.

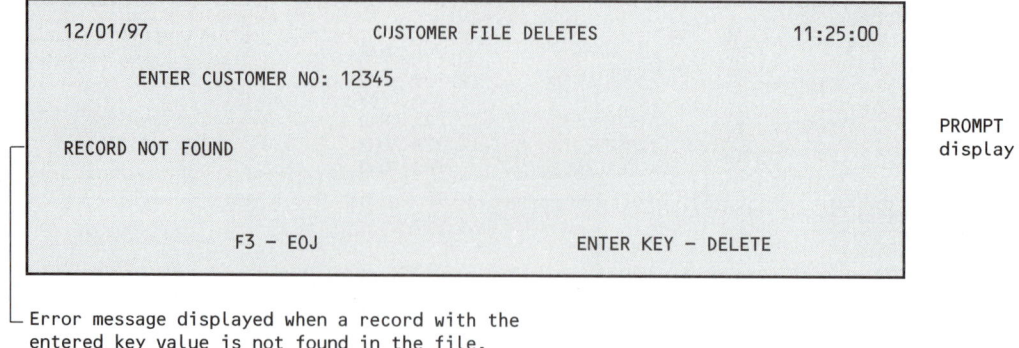

Figure 15-17 PROMPT display when a record is not found in the physical file.

RPG IV PROGRAM: COMBINED MAINTENANCE

The previous program examples in this chapter each supported only one maintenance function. Sometimes it may be advantageous to combine record addition, update, and deletion maintenance in one program. The changes needed in the display file and **RPG IV** program to support the three maintenance functions are discussed in the following sections.

Examine Figure 15-18, and note that the following syntax is included in the display file to support all of the maintenance functions:

```
SEQNBR*...+... 1 ...+... 2 ...+... 3 ...+... 4 ...+... 5 ...+... 6 ...+... 7 ...+... 8
     * PROMPT DISPLAY....
     A                                      MSGLOC(04)
     A                                      REF(STAN/CUSTMASTER)
     A                                      CHGINPDFT(RI)
     A                                      PRINT
     A          R PROMPT
     A                                      CA03(03 'EOJ')
     A                                      CF10(10 'ADD RECORD')
     A                                      CF11(11 'UPDATE RECORD')
     A                                      CF23(23 'DELETE RECORD')
     A                                  1  3DATE EDTCDE(Y)
     A                                  1 28'CUSTOMER FILE MAINTENANCE'
     A                                  1 71TIME
     A                                  3 10'ENTER CVSTOMER NO:'
     A            CUSTNO         5D 0I  3 29DSPATR(RI)
     A  90                                  ERRMSG('DUPLICATE KEY - CANNOT ADD -
     A                                      RECORD' 90)
     A  91                                  ERRMSG('RECORD NOT FOUND - CANNOT -
     A                                      UPDATE' 91)
     A  92                                  ERRMSG('RECORD NOT FOUND - CANNOT -
     A                                      DELETE' 92)
     A                                  9 10'F3 - EOJ                F10 - ADD -
                                              F11 - UPDATE'
     A                                 11 31'F23 - DELETE'
     * MAINTENANCE SCREEN....
     A          R MAINTRCD
     A                                      CA12(12 'REDISPLAY')
     A                                  1  3DATE EDTCDE(Y)
     A                                  1 28'CUSTOMER FILE MAINTENANCE'
     A                                      DSPATR(UL)
     A            MODE           6    0  1 72
```

Access to all of the maintenance functions is controlled from the PROMPT record

An ERRMSG is specified for each maintenance function

A constant is moved to this output field in the program to indicate the maintenance function

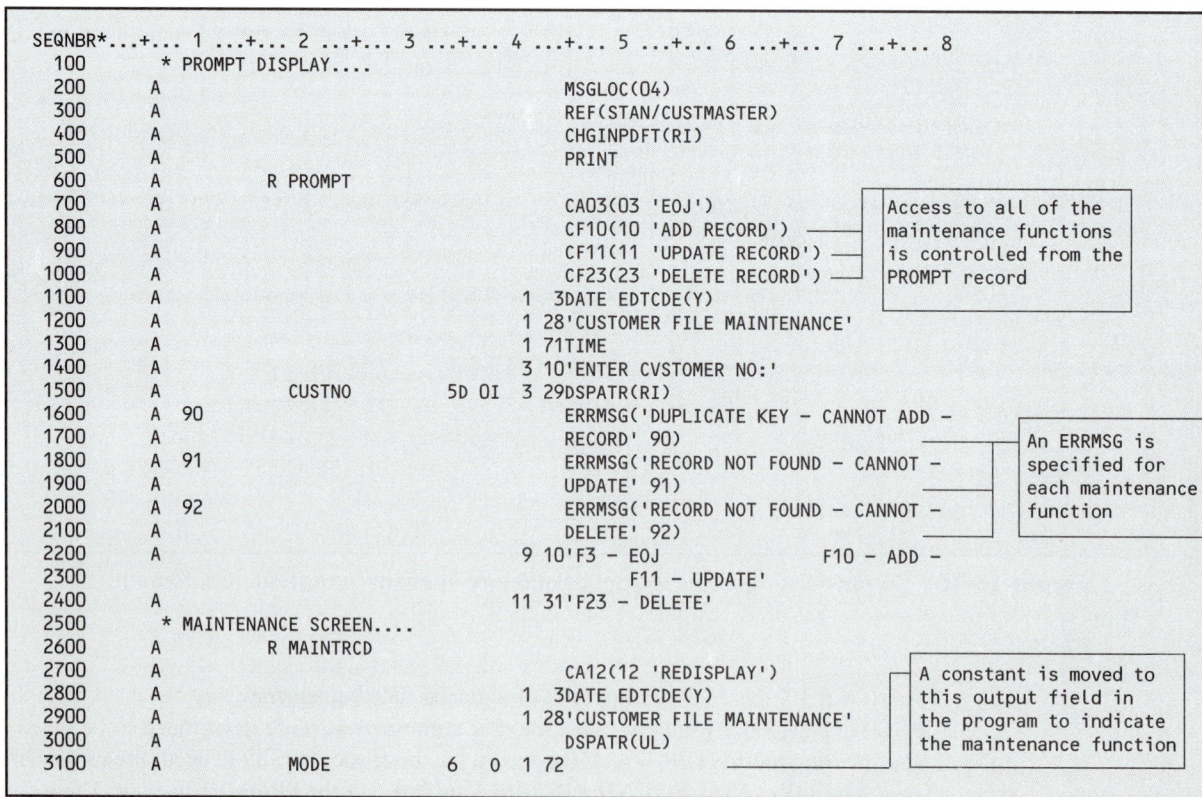

Figure 15-18 Display file for combined (addition, update, and deletion) physical file maintenance.

```
     A                                  3 20'CUSTOMER NUMBER:' DSPATR(HI)
     A            CUSTNUMBERR      D  B  3 40DSPATR(PR)
     A                                  5 20'NAME:' DSPATR(HI)
     A            CUSTNAME  R         B  5 40DSPATR(PC)
     A                                  7 20'STREET:' DSPATR(HI)
     A            STREET    R         B  7 40
     A                                  9 20'CITY:' DSPATR(HI)
     A            CITY      R         B  9 40
     A                                 11 20'STATE:' DSPATR(HI)
     A            STATE     R         B 11 40
     A                                 13 20'ZIP:' DSPATR(HI)
     A            ZIPCODE   R      D  B 13 40
     A                                 15 20'BALANCE:' DSPATR(HI)
     A            ACTBALANCER         B 15 40
     A                                 18 12'ENTER KEY - ENTER TRANSACTION'
     A                                 18 46'F12 - DO NOT ENTER'
```

Field is protected

Cursor is positioned at this field

To support the input and output of data to and from the RPG IV program, all fields (except MODE) are defined with a B usage

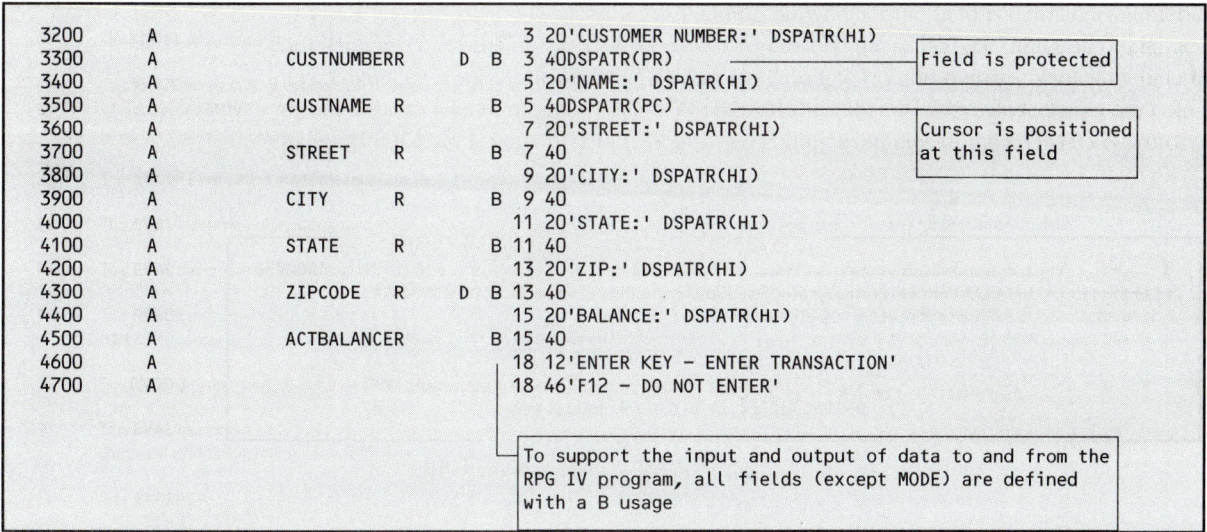

Figure 15-18 Display file for combined (addition, update, and deletion) physical file maintenance. (Continued)

1. Additional *Command Function Keys* are specified in the PROMPT display screen including CF10 *(Add Record)*, CF11 *(Update Record)*, and CF23 *(Delete Record)*. End-of-job processing is controlled by Command Attention Key **03.**

   Three **ERRMSG** statements are specified to identify the error generated by each maintenance function. Additional constants are included at the bottom of the screen indicating the key action the operator must take to perform the selected function or end the job.

2. A MODE field is defined in the MAINTRCD record format to which a maintenance function constant is moved in the **RPG IV** program. The constant **ADD, UPDATE,** or **DELETE** will display on line 1 beginning in position 72 of the MAINTRCD screen.

   With the exception of the MODE and CUSTNUMBER fields, the others are referenced from the physical file, CUSTMASTER.

   Because the MODE field value is only to be displayed (output), it is defined with an **O** *Usage*. The CUSTNUMBER field is the same as that defined in the PROMPT format and will display the value entered in the PROMPT display. To prevent the value from being changed, a **DSPATR(PR)** keyword is assigned, and the cursor is positioned at the CUSTNAME field with the **DSPATR(PC)** keyword.

   A maintenance transaction is completed by the operator pressing the **ENTER** key. The transaction may be ignored by pressing **F12.**

A Print key listing of the PROMPT and MAINTRCD displays is shown in Figure 15-19. When the operator presses one of the maintenance function keys (**F11** for this example), the same screen MAINTRCD format will display for all of them. The user is reminded of the maintenance mode he or she is currently in by the **UPDATE, ADD,** or **DELETE** constant in the upper right corner of the MAINTRCD display. The application could have been developed by including a different record format for each maintenance function, each with its own display attributes.

```
12/15/97                CUSTOMER FILE MAINTENANCE                8:36:38

    ENTER CUSTOMER NO: 12345



     F3 - EOJ                F10 - ADD            F11 - UPDATE

                          F23 - DELETE
```

```
12/15/97                CUSTOMER FILE MAINTENANCE               UPDATE
                  CUSTOMER NUMBER:    12345

                  NAME:               KAREL APPEL

                  STREET:             20 AMSTERDAM AVENUE

                  CITY:               NEW YORK

                  STATE:              NY

                  ZIP:                 7450

                  BALANCE:               125000

         ENTER KEY - ENTER TRANSACTION     F12 - DO NOT ENTER
```

Constant is moved in the program to the MODE field

Field value is accessed from the prompt screen and protected so that it cannot be changed

Cursor is positioned at the NAME field

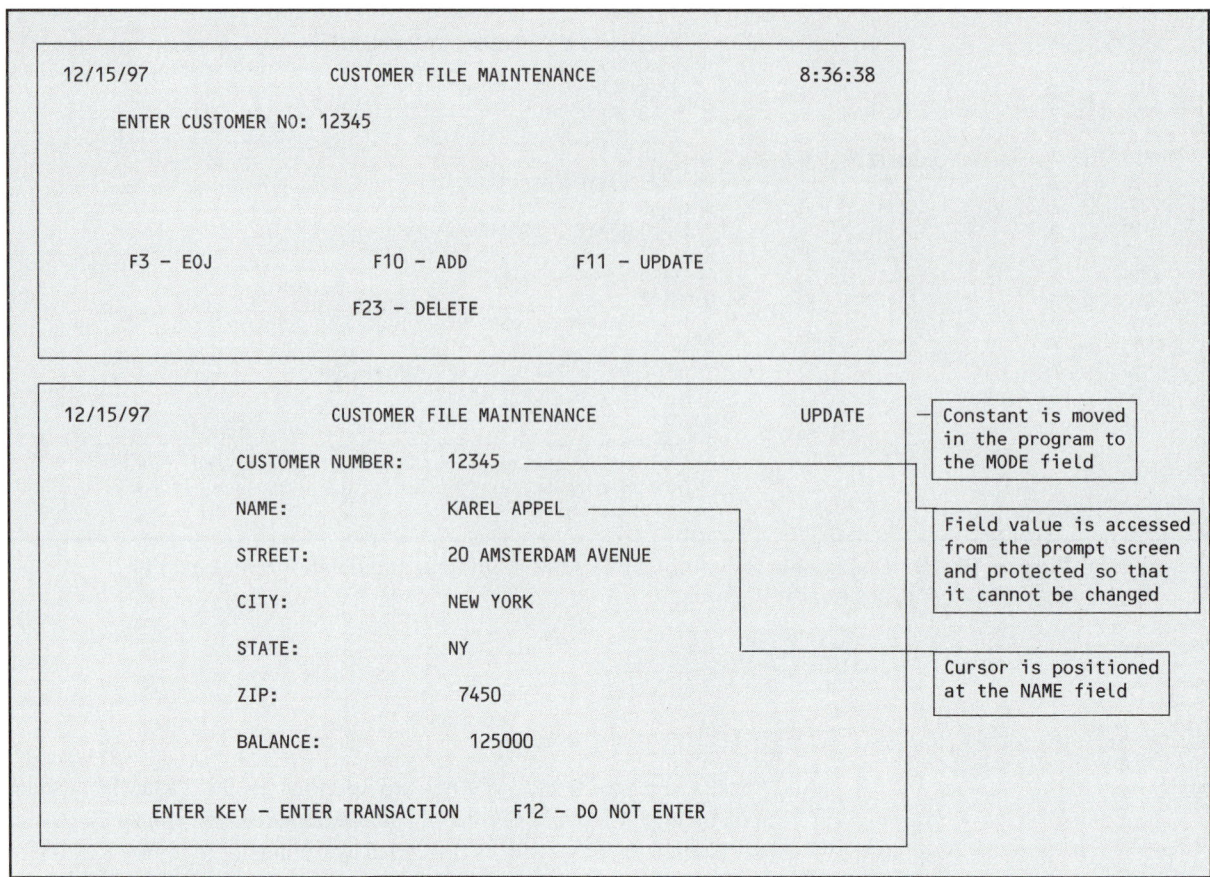

Figure 15-19 Print key listing of the display file's PROMPT and MAINTRCD formats for combined maintenance interactive processing.

A compile listing of the **RPG IV** program that supports record addition, update, and logical deletion maintenance, supplemented with a line-by-line explanation of the syntax, is presented in Figure 15-20.

```
Line   <---------------------- Source Specifications ----------------------------><---- Comments ----> Do
Number ....1....+....2....+....3....+....4....+....5....+....6....+....7....+....8....+....9....+...10 Num
                         S o u r c e   L i s t i n g
     1  * This program performs PF (Custmaster) interactive maintenance
     2 FGldfmaint CF   E             WORKSTN
        *--------------------------------------------------------------------------------------------*
        *                            RPG name         External name                                    *
        * File name. . . . . . . . :  GLDFMAINT        STAN/GLDFMAINT                                   *
        * Record format(s) . . . . :  PROMPT           PROMPT                                           *
        *                            MAINTRCD         MAINTRCD                                         *
        *--------------------------------------------------------------------------------------------*
     3 FCustmasterUF A E           K DISK
     4
     5  * Define data structure for clearing fields for record addition
        *--------------------------------------------------------------------------------------------*
        *                            RPG name         External name                                    *
        * File name. . . . . . . . :  CUSTMASTER       STAN/CUSTMASTER                                  *
        * Record format(s) . . . . :  CUSRECORD        CUSRECORD                                        *
        *--------------------------------------------------------------------------------------------*
```

Figure 15-20 Compile listing of the **RPG IV** program that includes combined maintenance.

```
  6 DDffields        DS
  7 D Custnumber                    5  0
  8 D Custname                     20
  9 D Street                       20
 10 D City                         20
 11 D State                         2
 12 D Zipcode                       5P 0
 13 D Actbalance                    8P 2
 14
 15=IPROMPT
    *---------------------------------------------------------------------------------------*
    * RPG record format  . . . . :  PROMPT                                                  *
    * External format  . . . . . :  PROMPT : STAN/GLDFMAINT                                 *
    *---------------------------------------------------------------------------------------*
 16=I                           A    1    1 *IN03                       EOJ
 17=I                           A    2    2 *IN10                       ADD RECORD
 18=I                           A    3    3 *IN11                       UPDATE RECORD
 19=I                           A    4    4 *IN23                       DELETE RECORD
 20=I                           A    5    5 *IN90                       DUPLICATE KEY - CANNOT ADD RECORD
 21=I                           A    6    6 *IN91                       RECORD NOT FOUND - CANNOT UPDATE
 22=I                           A    7    7 *IN92                       RECORD NOT FOUND - CANNOT DELETE
 23=I                           S    8   12 0CUSTNO
 24=IMAINTRCD
    *---------------------------------------------------------------------------------------*
    * RPG record format  . . . . :  MAINTRCD                                                *
    * External format  . . . . . :  MAINTRCD : STAN/GLDFMAINT                               *
    *---------------------------------------------------------------------------------------*
 25=I                           A    1    1 *IN12                       REDISPLAY
 26=I                           S    2    6 0CUSTNUMBER
 27=I                           A    7   26  CUSTNAME
 28=I                           A   27   46  STREET
 29=I                           A   47   66  CITY
 30=I                           A   67   68  STATE
 31=I                           S   69   73 0ZIPCODE
 32=I                           S   74   81 2ACTBALANCE
 33=ICUSRECORD
    *---------------------------------------------------------------------------------------*
    * RPG record format  . . . . :  CUSRECORD                                               *
    * External format  . . . . . :  CUSRECORD : STAN/CUSTMASTER                             *
    *---------------------------------------------------------------------------------------*
 34=I                           P    1    3 0CUSTNUMBER
 35=I                           A    4   23  CUSTNAME
 36=I                           A   24   43  STREET
 37=I                           A   44   63  CITY
 38=I                           A   64   65  STATE
 39=I                           P   66   68 0ZIPCODE
 40=I                           P   69   73 2ACTBALANCE
 41 C                  DOW       *IN03 = *OFF                           dou 03 is on        B01
 42 C                  EXFMT     Prompt                                 display prompt scrn  01
 43 C                  CLEAR                   Dffields                 clear sd fields      01
 44 C     *IN10        CASEQ     *ON           AddSR                    branch to AddSR      01
 45 C     *IN11        CASEQ     *ON           UpSR                     branch to UpSR       01
 46 C     *IN23        CASEQ     *ON           DelSR                    branch to DelSR      01
 47 C                  ENDCS                                            end CAS group        01
 48 C                  ENDDO                                            end dou group       E01
 49
 50 C                  EVAL      *INLR = *ON                            end program
 51
 52  * Begin AddSr (add record) subroutine....
 53 C     AddSR        BEGSR                                            begin subroutine
 54 C     Custno       SETLL     Custmaster                    90----   check for dup record
 55 C                  IF        *IN91 = *OFF                           duplicate record?   B01
 56 C                  MOVE      'ADD   '      MODE                     initialize mode fld  01
 57 C                  EVAL      Custnumber = Custno                    move df to pf field  01
 58 C                  EXFMT     Maintrcd                               display inqrcd       01
 59 C     *IN12        CABEQ     *ON           Skip1                    do not add record?   01
 60 C                  WRITE     Cusrecord                     --99--   add record to pf     01
 61 C                  ENDIF                                            end IF group        E01
```

Figure 15-20 Compile listing of the **RPG IV** program that includes combined maintenance. (Continued)

```
 62 C     Skip1        ENDSR                                                end AddSR subroutine
 63
 64  * Begin UpSR (update) subroutine
 65 C     UpSR         BEGSR                                                begin UpSR subroutin
 66 C     Custno       CHAIN     Custmaster                         91----  get pf record
 67 C                  IF        *IN91 = *OFF                               pf record found?    B01
 68 C                  MOVE      'UPDATE'      Mode                         initialize mode      01
 69 C                  EXFMT     Maintrcd                                   dsp maintrcd screen  01
 70 C     *IN12        CABEQ     *ON           Skip2                        do not update        01
 71 C                  UPDATE    Cusrecord                                  update pf record     01
 72 C                  ENDIF                                                end IF group        E01
 73 C     Skip2        ENDSR                                                end UpSR subroutine
 74
 75  * Begin DelSR (delete) subroutine....
 76 C     DelSR        BEGSR                                                begin DelSR
 77 C     Custno       CHAIN     Custmaster                         92----  get pf record
 78 C                  IF        *IN92 = *OFF                               pf record found?    B01
 79 C                  MOVE      'DELETE'      Mode                         initialize mode      01
 80 C                  EXFMT     Maintrcd                                   dsp maintrcd screen  01
 81 C     *IN12        CABEQ     *ON           Skip3                        do not update        01
 82 C                  DELETE    Cusrecord                                  update pf record     01
 83 C                  ENDIF                                                end IF group        E01
 84 C     Skip3        ENDSR                                                end UpSR subroutine
 85=OPROMPT
     *--------------------------------------------------------------------------------------*
     * RPG record format . . . . :  PROMPT                                                   *
     * External format . . . . . :  PROMPT : STAN/GLDFMAINT                                  *
     *--------------------------------------------------------------------------------------*
 86=O                    *IN90           1A CHAR        1        DUPLICATE KEY - CANNOT ADD RECORD
 87=O                    *IN91           2A CHAR        1        RECORD NOT FOUND - CANNOT UPDATE
 88=O                    *IN92           3A CHAR        1        RECORD NOT FOUND - CANNOT DELETE
 89=OMAINTRCD
     *--------------------------------------------------------------------------------------*
     * RPG record format . . . . :  MAINTRCD                                                 *
     * External format . . . . . :  MAINTRCD : STAN/GLDFMAINT                                *
     *--------------------------------------------------------------------------------------*
 90=O                    MODE            6A CHAR        6
 91=O                    CUSTNUMBER     11S ZONE      5,0
 92=O                    CUSTNAME       31A CHAR       20
 93=O                    STREET         51A CHAR       20
 94=O                    CITY           71A CHAR       20
 95=O                    STATE          73A CHAR        2
 96=O                    ZIPCODE        78S ZONE      5,0
 97=O                    ACTBALANCE     86S ZONE      8,2
 98=OCUSRECORD
     *--------------------------------------------------------------------------------------*
     * RPG record format . . . . :  CUSRECORD                                                *
     * External format . . . . . :  CUSRECORD : STAN/CUSTMASTER                              *
     *--------------------------------------------------------------------------------------*
 99=O                    CUSTNUMBER      3P PACK      5,0
100=O                    CUSTNAME       23A CHAR       20
101=O                    STREET         43A CHAR       20
102=O                    CITY           63A CHAR       20
103=O                    STATE          65A CHAR        2
104=O                    ZIPCODE        68P PACK      5,0
105=O                    ACTBALANCE     73P PACK      8,2
```

File Description Specifications:

Line No.

2 **WORKSTN** file (Gldfmaint) is defined as combined (**C** in position 17), full-procedural (**F** in position 18), and externally defined (**E** in position 22).

3 Custmaster is defined as an update (**U** in position 17), full-procedural (**F** in position 18), externally defined (**E** in position 22), and keyed (**K** in position 34) physical file. The **A** in position 20 is needed to support record addition. Because update and delete maintenance require that the same record be read from and written back to the physical file, it must be defined as update. In addition, because **RPG IV** file processing operations are used (i.e., **CHAIN, SETLL, UPDATE,** and **DELETE**), the file must be defined as full-procedural.

Figure 15-20 Compile listing of the **RPG IV** program that includes combined maintenance. (Continued)

Definition Specifications:

6–13 The data structure, Dffields, defines the Maintcrd format's fields that are to be initialized to blanks and zeros by the **CLEAR** operation before it is displayed again. If the Maintrcd record format in the display file was specified in lieu of a data structure, all indicators would be set off—a condition not wanted for this application.

Because the fields in the MAINTRCD display record are defined with a **B** usage (both input and output), the previously entered values would redisplay for "adds" maintenance. To avoid user confusion, the fields are cleared after a record is added to the physical file. This condition will not occur for update or deletion maintenance.

Calculation Specifications:

41 The **DOW** group controls the display of the Prompt and Maintrcd formats and the maintenance function selected. The iterative processing (looping) continues until the operator presses **F3,** which sets on indicator **03,** when in the Prompt display to end the job. The relational test for the **DOW** is made at the instruction.

42 This **EXFMT** instruction *writes* the Prompt record to the screen and holds it there. After the operator enters a customer number and presses one of the designated command keys, the variable is *read* and the Maintcrd record or one of the error messages displayed. The operator ends the job from the Prompt display by pressing **F3.**

43 The **CLEAR** instruction clears all of the fields defined in the data structure specified in *Factor 2* (Dffields) to blanks (for character fields) and zeros (for numeric fields). Because the controlling indicators were not specified in the data structure, they are not turned off by the **CLEAR** instruction.

44 When the operator presses **F10,** which sets on indicator **10,** this **CASEQ** instruction branches program control to the AddSR subroutine, where the instructions to add a record to the physical file are performed.

45 When the operator presses **F11,** which sets on indicator **11,** this **CASEQ** instruction branches program control to the UpSR subroutine, where the instructions to update the displayed physical file record are performed.

46 When the operator presses **F23,** which sets on indicator **23,** this **CASEQ** instruction branches program control to the DelSR subroutine, where the instructions to logically delete the displayed physical file record are performed.

If the ENTER or **F3** key is pressed, program control will ignore the **CAS** group, execute the **ENDDO** operation, and pass control back to the **DOW** instruction on line 41, where the relational test is made to end the job or continue the maintenance process.

47 The **ENDCS** operation ends the **CAS** group.

48 The **ENDDO** operation ends the **DOW** group that began on line 41.

50 This **EVAL** instruction turns on the **LR** indicator to end the program.

53 Beginning of the AddSR subroutine, which is branched to by the **CASEQ** instruction on line 44.

54 The Custno value from the Prompt display is specified in the **SETLL** instruction to determine if the "add" record is already stored in the physical file. If it is stored, indicator **90** will be set on.

55 The status of indicator **90** (specified with the **SETLL** instruction) is tested in this **IF** instruction. If it is "off," the instructions on lines 56–58 will be executed. If **90** is "on," control will branch to the **ENDSR** statement on line 62.

56 The literal 'ADD ' is moved to the MODE field defined in the Maintrcd display record.

57 This **EVAL** instruction initialized the Custnumber field with the Custno value entered in the Prompt display.

58 This **EXFMT** instruction displays a blank Maintrcd record with the Custnumber value included from the Prompt display. The operator may enter the field information and add the record to the physical file or ignore the adds process by pressing **F12.**

59 The status of indicator **12** is tested with this **CABEQ** instruction, which allows the operator to either complete the adds process or abort it by skipping to the **ENDSR** instruction on line 62.

60 The **WRITE** instruction writes (adds) the displayed Cusrecord record to the physical file.

61 The **ENDIF** operation ends the **IF** group that began on line 55.

62 The **ENDSR** instruction ends the AddSR subroutine and is the Skip 1 label for the **CABEQ** instruction on line 59.

65 This **BEGSR** instruction begins the UpSR subroutine which was branched to by the **CAS** instruction on line 45.

66 The Custno value entered in the Prompt display is used in the **CHAIN** instruction to randomly access the record to be updated. If the record *is* found (same key value), indicator **91** will *not* be turned on.

Figure 15-20 Compile listing of the **RPG IV** program that includes combined maintenance. (Continued)

67 This **IF** instruction tests the status of indicator **91.** When it is "on" (record-not-found condition), control will branch to the **ENDSR** instruction on line **73.**

68 The literal 'UPDATE' is moved to the MODE field defined in the Maintrcd display record.

69 This **EXFMT** instruction displays the Maintrcd screen "filled in" with field values from the accessed physical file record.

70 The status of indicator **12** is tested with this **CABEQ** instruction. If it is "on," the operator pressed **F12** not to update the displayed record; control branches to the **ENDSR** instruction on line 73.

71 The **UPDATE** instruction writes the changed physical file record (Cusrecord) back to its original disk storage location.

72 The **ENDIF** operation ends the **IF** group that began on line 67.

73 The **ENDSR** statement ends the UpSR routine and is the Skip2 label for the **CABEQ** instruction on line 70.

76 This **BEGSR** instruction is branched to by the **CASEQ** instruction on line 46.

77 The Custno value entered in the Prompt display is used in this **CHAIN** instruction to access the physical file record to be deleted. If the record *is* found (same key value), indicator **92** will *not* be turned on.

78 When this **IF** instruction tests as "true" (indicator **92** is "off"), the instructions on lines 79–80 will be executed.

79 The literal 'DELETE' is moved to the MODE field defined in the Maintrcd display record.

80 This **EXFMT** instruction displays the Maintrcd screen "filled in" with field values from the accessed physical file record.

81 The status of indicator **12** is tested with this **CABEQ** instruction. If **12** is "on," the operator pressed **F12** not to delete the current record, which transfers control to the **ENDSR** instruction on line 84.

82 The **DELETE** instruction logically deletes the Cusrecord record in the physical file.

83 The **ENDIF** operation ends the **IF** group that began on line 78.

84 This **ENDSR** instruction ends the DelSR subroutine and is the Skip3 label for the **CABEQ** instruction on line 81.

Note: No programmer-supplied output instructions are included in this program. All output is controlled by **RPG IV** file processing operations.

Figure 15-20 Compile listing of the **RPG IV** program that includes combined maintenance. (Continued)

RPG IV PROGRAM: INTERACTIVE DATA VALIDATION

Chapter 14 introduced and explained the syntax of the keywords that may be specified in a display file to support interactive data validation. A source listing of the example display file shown in Figure 15-21 includes the **CHECK, VALUES,** and **RANGE** keywords to control the required validation functions.

```
SEQNBR*...+... 1 ...+... 2 ...+... 3 ...+... 4 ...+... 5 ...+... 6 ...+... 7 ...+... 8
  100        * DISPLAY FILE FOR VALIDATION CONTROL....
  200      A                                      REF(STAN/CUSTMASTER)
  300      A                                      PRINT
  400      A                                      CA03(03 'EOJ')
  500      A                                      CF02(02 'ENTER')
  600      A                                      CA05(05 'REDISPLAY')
  700      A                                      CHGINPDFT(RI)
  800      A          R ADDRECORD
  900      A                                  2  6DATE EDTCDE(Y)
 1000      A                                  3 33'NEW CUSTOMER ENTRY' DSPATR(UL)
```

Figure 15-21 Display file modified with validation keywords.

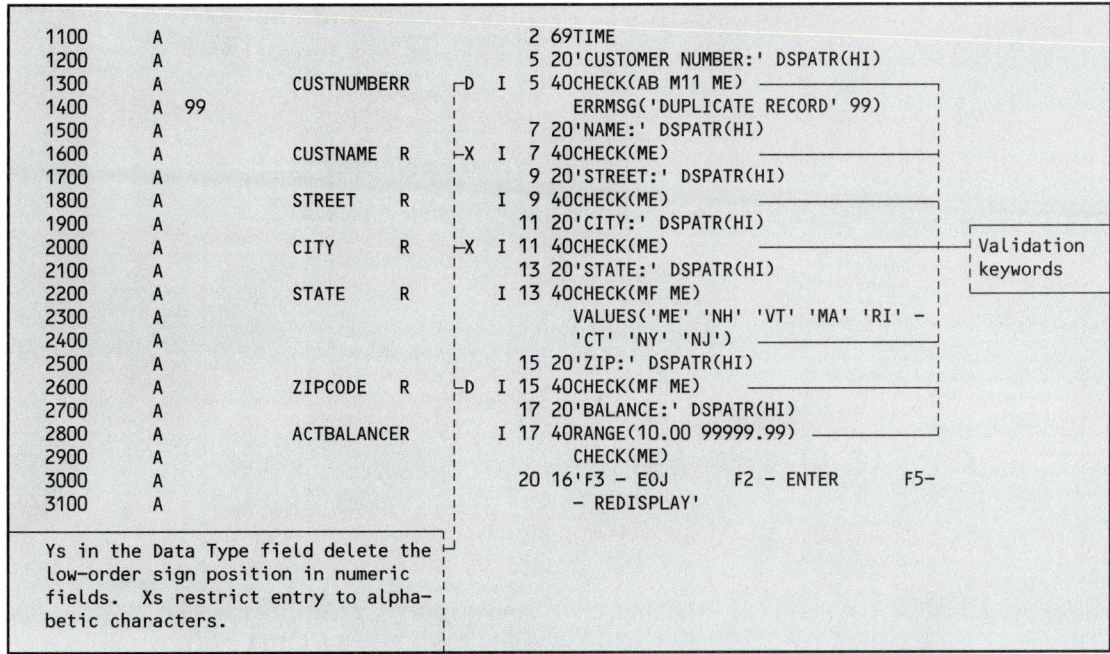

```
     A                                 2 69TIME
     A                                 5 20'CUSTOMER NUMBER:' DSPATR(HI)
     A            CUSTNUMBERR    D  I  5 40CHECK(AB M11 ME)
     A  99                                  ERRMSG('DUPLICATE RECORD' 99)
     A                                 7 20'NAME:' DSPATR(HI)
     A            CUSTNAME  R    X  I  7 40CHECK(ME)
     A                                 9 20'STREET:' DSPATR(HI)
     A            STREET    R       I  9 40CHECK(ME)
     A                                11 20'CITY:' DSPATR(HI)
     A            CITY      R    X  I 11 40CHECK(ME)
     A                                13 20'STATE:' DSPATR(HI)
     A            STATE     R       I 13 40CHECK(MF ME)
     A                                      VALUES('ME' 'NH' 'VT' 'MA' 'RI' -
     A                                      'CT' 'NY' 'NJ')
     A                                15 20'ZIP:' DSPATR(HI)
     A            ZIPCODE   R    D  I 15 40CHECK(MF ME)
     A                                17 20'BALANCE:' DSPATR(HI)
     A            ACTBALANCER       I 17 40RANGE(10.00 99999.99)
     A                                      CHECK(ME)
     A                                20 16'F3 - EOJ      F2 - ENTER      F5-
     A                                      - REDISPLAY'
```

Validation keywords

Ys in the Data Type field delete the low-order sign position in numeric fields. Xs restrict entry to alphabetic characters.

Figure 15-21 Display file modified with validation keywords. (Continued)

A Print key listing of the **ADDRECORD** display is shown in Figure 15-22. Note that only one record format is included in the display file instead of two as in the previous examples in this chapter.

```
12/26/97                                                    9:46:06
                          NEW CUSTOMER ENTRY

              CUSTOMER NUMBER:     40000

              NAME:                SALVATORE DALI

              STREET:              2 CUBIST LANE

              CITY:                WESTPORT

              STATE:               CT

              ZIP:                 06498

              BALANCE:                80000

          F3 - EOJ        F2 - ENTER       F5 - REDISPLAY
```

Figure 15-22 Print key copy of the display file's record format that includes data validation.

Use of one record format for physical file addition requires the user to enter all of the data before adding the record. For physical files that support records with duplicate keys, this presents no inconvenience. However, for physical files created with the **UNIQUE** keyword, it may be inconvenient.

An examination of the compile listing of the **RPG IV** program in Figure 15-23 that controls the interactive validation of data entry indicates that it is similar to the program that supports record addition without validation (see Figure 15-7). As compared to the

```
Line   <---------------------- Source Specifications ----------------------------><---- Comments ----> Do
Number ....1....+....2....+....3....+....4....+....5....+....6....+....7....+....8....+....9....+...10 Num
                         S o u r c e   L i s t i n g
     1  *This program performs PF (Custmaster) record addition with validation
     2 FGldfvalid CF   E             WORKSTN
       *--------------------------------------------------------------------------------------*
       *                             RPG name          External name                          *
       * File name. . . . . . . . :  GLDFVALID         STAN/GLDFVALID                         *
       * Record format(s) . . . . :  ADDRECORD         ADDRECORD                              *
       *--------------------------------------------------------------------------------------*
     3 FCustmasterUF A E           K DISK
     4
       *--------------------------------------------------------------------------------------*
       *                             RPG name          External name                          *
       * File name. . . . . . . . :  CUSTMASTER        STAN/CUSTMASTER                        *
       * Record format(s) . . . . :  CUSRECORD         CUSRECORD                              *
       *--------------------------------------------------------------------------------------*
     5=IADDRECORD
       *--------------------------------------------------------------------------------------*
       * RPG record format  . . . :  ADDRECORD                                                *
       * External format  . . . . :  ADDRECORD : STAN/GLDFVALID                               *
       *--------------------------------------------------------------------------------------*
     6=I                             A    2    2  *IN02                    ENTER
     7=I                             A    1    1  *IN03                    EOJ
     8=I                             A    3    3  *IN05                    REDISPLAY
     9=I                             A    4    4  *IN99                    DUPLICATE RECORD
    10=I                             S    5    9 0CUSTNUMBER
    11=I                             A   10   29  CUSTNAME
    12=I                             A   30   49  STREET
    13=I                             A   50   69  CITY
    14=I                             A   70   71  STATE
    15=I                             S   72   76 0ZIPCODE
    16=I                             S   77   84 2ACTBALANCE
    17=ICUSRECORD
       *--------------------------------------------------------------------------------------*
       * RPG record format  . . . :  CUSRECORD                                                *
       * External format  . . . . :  CUSRECORD : STAN/CUSTMASTER                              *
       *--------------------------------------------------------------------------------------*
    18=I                             P    1    3 0CUSTNUMBER
    19=I                             A    4   23  CUSTNAME
    20=I                             A   24   43  STREET
    21=I                             A   44   63  CITY
    22=I                             A   64   65  STATE
    23=I                             P   66   68 0ZIPCODE
    24=I                             P   69   73 2ACTBALANCE
    25 C                   DOU       *IN03 = *ON                           dou ind 03 is on     B01
    26 C                   EXFMT     Addrecord                             display entry screen  01
    27 C                   IF        *IN02 = *ON                           compound IF group    B02
    28 C                             AND Custnumber > *ZEROS                                    B02
    29 C                             AND Custname > *BLANKS                                     B02
    30 C                             AND Street > *BLANKS                                       B02
    31 C                             AND City > *BLANKS                                         B02
    32 C                             AND State > *BLANKS                                        B02
    33 C                             AND Zipcode > *ZEROS                                       B02
    34 C                                                                                        B02
    35 C                   EXSR      EntrySR                               branch to subroutine  02
    36 C                   ENDIF                                           end IF group         E02
    37 C                   ENDDO                                           end dou group        E01
    38
    39 C                   EVAL      *INLR = *ON                           end program
    40
    41 C     EntrySR       BEGSR                                           begin subroutine
    42 C                   WRITE     Cusrecord                   --99--    add record to pf
    43 C                   ENDSR                                           end subroutine
    44=OADDRECORD
       *--------------------------------------------------------------------------------------*
       * RPG record format  . . . :  ADDRECORD                                                *
       * External format  . . . . :  ADDRECORD : STAN/GLDFVALID                               *
       *--------------------------------------------------------------------------------------*
    45=O                   *IN99              1A CHAR         1             DUPLICATE RECORD
    46=OCUSRECORD
```

Figure 15-23 Compile listing of the program that supports the interactive validation of data entry.

```
     *--------------------------------------------------------------------------------------*
     * RPG record format  . . . . :  CUSRECORD                                              *
     * External format  . . . . . :  CUSRECORD : STAN/CUSTMASTER                            *
     *--------------------------------------------------------------------------------------*
  47=0                         CUSTNUMBER            3P PACK       5,0
  48=0                         CUSTNAME             23A CHAR        20
  49=0                         STREET               43A CHAR        20
  50=0                         CITY                 63A CHAR        20
  51=0                         STATE                65A CHAR         2
  52=0                         ZIPCODE              68P PACK       5,0
  53=0                         ACTBALANCE           73P PACK       8,2
```

File Description Specifications:

Line No.

2 Gldfvalid is defined as a combined (**C** in position 17), full-procedural (**F** in position 18), externally defined (**E** in position 22) **WORKSTN** (display) file.

3 Custmaster is defined as an output (**O** in position 17), externally defined (**E** in position 22), keyed (**K** in position 34) physical file. The **A** in column 20 supports the addition of records to the file.

Calculation Specifications:

25 The **DOU** group controls the display of the Addrecord, the entry of data, and the addition of records to the physical file. The iterative processing (looping) continues until the operator presses **F3,** which sets on indicator **03,** to end the job. The relational test for the **DOU** instruction is made at the **ENDDO** operation on line 37. Consequently, the **DOU** group will be executed at least once.

26 The **EXFMT** instruction *writes* the Addrecord display to the screen and holds it there until the operator presses either **F3** to end the program or **F2** to add the displayed record to the physical file.

27–33 If indicator **02** is "on" and Custnumber is greater than zero, and Custname is greater than blanks, and Street is greater than blanks, and City is greater than blanks, and State is greater than blanks, and Zipcode is greater than zero, the **EXSR** instruction on line 35 will be executed, which branches control to the EntrySR subroutine, which includes instructions to add the displayed record to the physical file.

The testing of the numeric fields for zeros and the character fields for blanks in this compound **IF** instruction prevent a blank record from being written to the physical file.

If any of the **"AND"** relationship tests are false, the record will not be added and control will skip to the **ENDDO** operation, then return to the **DOU** instruction on line 25, and redisplay the Addrecord with the **EXFMT** instruction on line 26. Again, the user will decide whether to end the program or to continue the record addition process.

35 The **EXSR** instruction branches control to the EntrySR subroutine.

36 The **ENDIF** operation ends the **IF** instruction that began on line 27.

37 The **ENDDO** operation ends the **DOU** group. Recall that the relational test is made at this instruction and not at the related **DOU.**

39 The **EVAL** instruction turns on indicator **LR** to end the program.

41 The **BEGSR** instruction begins the EntrySR subroutine.

42 The **WRITE** instruction writes (adds) the displayed Cusrecord to the physical file.

43 The **ENDSR** operation ends the EntrySR subroutine.

Figure 15-23 Compile listing of the program that supports the interactive validation of data entry. (Continued)

batch validation program in Chapter 12 (see Figure 12-32), interactive data validation significantly simplifies the program's syntax. Now all of the validation functions are controlled in the display file and not in the RPG IV program.

After each system-supplied validation error message or number is displayed, the operator may press the Help key (or on PCs, the Shift and Scroll Lock keys) to access supplemental information about the error. The Reset key (or on PCs, the Ctrl key) must be pressed after each error to continue processing.

SUMMARY

Unlike batch processing, *interactive processing* connects the user directly with database file(s) and facilitates immediate access to authorized data. The creation (source and object) of display files is necessary to support *interactive processing* in the AS/400 environment.

Any display file processed by an **RPG IV** program must be defined in a *File Description Specifications* statement as a full-procedural, externally described **WORKSTN** (workstation) file.

The record formats in a display file are accessed in an **RPG IV** program by an **EXFMT** operation, which controls the writing of a format by the program to the screen and then the reading from the screen to the program. In lieu of the **EXFMT** operation, separate **WRITE** and **READ** statements may be specified to write and read a display file's record format.

Error identification is controlled and displayed by one or more **ERRMSG** keywords specified at the *Field Level* in the record format of a display file. The conditioning indicator specified with the **ERRMSG** keyword will control the display of the text. Indicators included in **WRITE, CHAIN,** and **SETLL** statements are set on when an error occurs. The indicators are specified with their related **ERRMSG** keyword to control the display of the error message text.

The first four programs discussed in the chapter separately support addition, update, logical deletion maintenance, and inquiry processing. A fifth program combines addition, update, and deletion maintenance. The sixth program controls the interactive validation of data.

In an **RPG IV** program, addition maintenance is performed with the **WRITE** operation, update with the **CHAIN** and **UPDATE** operations, and logical deletion with the **CHAIN** and **DELETE** operations. Inquiry processing is executed with the **CHAIN** operation.

When the fields in a display file's record format are defined with an **O** or **B** *Usage,* they usually have to be initialized to blanks and zeros before the format is redisplayed. This prevents the previously entered values from appearing when the format is displayed again. The **CLEAR** operation, which may be specified with a field, record, data structure, array name, array element, or table name, will initialize character fields to blanks and numeric fields to zeros.

QUESTIONS

Examine the following statement and answer Questions 15-1 through 15-5:

```
.. 1 ...+... 2 ...+... 3 ...+... 4 ...+... 5 ...+... 6 ...+... 7 ...+
FFilename++IPEASFRLen+LKLen+AIDevice+.Keywords+++++++++++++++++++++++++

FDsplyfile CF   E             WORKSTN
```

15-1. What is the function of the letter **C** in position 17?

15-2. In lieu of the **C** in position 17, what other entries may be specified? Explain their functions.

15-3. What control is supported by the **F** in position 17? May any other entry be specified for display files?

15-4. What is the function of the letter **E** in position 22? May any other entry be specified for display files?

15-5. What physical device is supported by the **WORKSTN** device name?

Examine the following statement and answer Questions 15-6 through 15-9:

```
*.. 1 ...+... 2 ...+... 3 ...+... 4 ...+... 5 ...+... 6 ...+... 7 ...+.
CLON01Factor1+++++++Opcode&ExtFactor2+++++++Result++++++++Len++D+HiLoEq

C                   EXFMT     DFR1                                  80
```

15-6. What is the function of the **EXFMT** operation? May any other **RPG IV** operations be specified to provide the same control?

15-7. What does the DFR1 entry in *Factor 2* refer to? May any other entry be specified?

15-8. When does the indicator **(80)** specified in positions 73–74 turn on? What does this indicator usually control?

15-9. What occurs if the **EXFMT** statement is executed successfully?

15-10. How should a physical file that supports "adds-only" processing be defined? Under what conditions would the file be defined as an update file?

15-11. What **RPG IV** operation supports the addition of records to a physical file? Identify the processing errors that may occur when the statement is executed. How may these errors be identified in the related display file?

15-12. What is specified in *Factor 2* of the operation named in Question 15-11?

15-13. How should a physical file that supports "update" processing be defined?

15-14. What **RPG IV** operations support the update of records in a physical file? Identify the processing errors that may occur when these statements are executed. Which operation is coordinated with an **ERRMSG** keyword in a display file's record format?

15-15. What is specified in *Factor 2* of the operations named in Question 15-14?

15-16. How should a physical file that supports "logical deletion" processing be defined?

15-17. What **RPG IV** operations support the logical deletion of records in a physical file? Identify the processing errors that may occur when these statements are executed. Which operation is coordinated with an **ERRMSG** keyword in a display file's record format?

15-18. What is specified in *Factor 2* of the operations named in Question 15-17?

15-19. How should a physical file that supports "inquiry" processing be defined?

15-20. What **RPG IV** operation supports physical file inquiry? Identify the processing errors that may occur when this statement is executed.

15-21. What is specified in *Factor 2* of the operation named in Question 15-20?

15-22. What is the function of the **CLEAR** operation? With what file type(s) may it be specified?

15-23. What may be specified in *Factor 2* of a **CLEAR** statement?

PROGRAMMING ASSIGNMENTS

Before any of these assignments are started, the related physical and display files from the assignments for Chapter 14 must be completed.

Programming Assignment 15-1: VALIDATION OF NEW CUSTOMER ACCOUNTS

Before this program is started, Assignments 14-1, 14-2, and 14-3 must be completed. Then write an **RPG IV** program to add records to the physical file created for Assignment 14-1. When testing the program, enter all of the data in the second display record and press **F2** to check each field for its validation test. If the customer number does not pass the Modulus-11 test, enter blanks to continue the validation of other fields. When an error occurs for the other fields, correct it with your own data so that all of the fields can be validated. However, do *not* add the corrected record to the physical file. Print a **CPYF** hexidecimal listing of the physical file after all of the data has been entered.

Physical File Data:

Customer Number	Name	Street	City	State	Zip	Limit	Rating
12343	JOHN FIRESTONE	20 TYRE LANE	AKRON	OH	05456	2000	B
13005	WILLIAM GOODYEAR	19 TUBE ROAD	DETROIT	MI	06606	5000	A
14100	JOHN KELLY	100 PATCH PLACE	FRANKFORT	KY	07701	7000	A+
21008	JAMES GOODRICH	81 VALVE TERRACE	CHICAGO	IL	04404	3000	B
35009	CLAUDE MICHELIN	1 PARIS PLACE	FRANCE	PA	05500	6000	C
44008	ANTHONY PIRELLI	33 FIAT BOULEVARD	ROME	NY	06608	4000	A-
47104	TOYO KOGO THE 2ND	12 HIROSHIMA ROAD	TOKYO2	CA	09900	0100	D
50008	JAMES COOPER	55 FLAT STREET	COOPERSTOWN	NY	06620	0500	C
60003	WILLIAM BRIDGESTONE	80 WHEEL DRIVE	AGOURA	CA	09940	2000	B-
65005	HENRY ATLAS	210 LUG AVENUE	GREENWICH	CT	06649	3000	B

Programming Assignment 15-2: CUSTOMER FILE INQUIRY

Assignment 15-1 must have been completed before this program is started. Modify the headings in the two display record formats to **CUSTOMER INQUIRY,** and change the **ERRMSG** instruction in the first prompt display record to **RECORD NOT FOUND.**

Inquiry records with customer numbers **12343, 14000, 44008,** and **65005.**

Programming Assignment 15-3: CUSTOMER FILE UPDATE

Assignment 15-1 must have been completed before this program is started. Modify the headings in the two display record formats to **CUSTOMER UPDATE,** and change the **ERRMSG** instruction in the first prompt display record to **RECORD NOT FOUND.**

Update Data: Check each record after updating by redisplaying the same record.

	Record 1	Record 2	Record 3	Record 4
CUSTNO	65005	20000	13005	60003
NAME				
STREET	150 TREAD PLACE		WALTER DUNLOP	99 BALANCE LANE
CITY	ORLANDO			PITTSBURGH
STATE	FL			PA
ZIP	08801			07701
LIMIT		2000		3000
RATING		B		A-

* If the data for a field is blank, the original values are not to be changed!

Programming Assignment 15-4: CUSTOMER FILE RECORD DELETION

Assignment 15-1 must have been completed before this program is started. Modify the headings in the two display record formats to **CUSTOMER DELETION,** and change the **ERRMSG** instruction in the first prompt display to **RECORD NOT FOUND.**

Delete records with key values **50008** and **14000** from the physical file. Check the accuracy of the deletion process by trying to access the deleted record(s) with this program.

Programming Assignment 15-5: STUDENT COURSE FILE MAINTENANCE

Before this assignment is started, Assignments 14-4 and 14-5 must be completed. Then, write an **RPG IV** program to support addition, update, and logical deletion maintenance.

Adds Maintenance: After the **RPG IV** program is completed, add the following data to the physical file created for Assignment 14-4. Note that the prompt display includes an error message for a **DUPLICATE RECORD** condition. This, and **RECORD NOT FOUND** error control, must be specified in the program.

Physical File Data: Except for a duplicate key condition, enter all of the data in the second display record and press **F2** to check each field for its validation test. If an error occurs for a field, correct it with your own data so that all of the fields can be validated. However, do *not* add the corrected record to the physical file. Print a **CPYF** hexidecimal listing of the physical file after all of the valid data has been entered.

SSNO	COURSE NUMBER	COURSE NAME	TERM DATE	INSTRUCTOR CODE	CREDIT	MARK
011111111	ACD101	ENGLISH COMPOSITION	052297	300	3	B
011111111	DPS100	INTRO TO PROGRAMMING	121597	104	4	I
011111111	MTH100	ALGEBRA I	121597	161	3	C
011223333	DPS200	INTRO TO RPG/400	052297	221	4	A
011223333	DPS210	COBOL I	121597	221	4	B
022334444	CSC101	COMPUTER SCIENCE I	052297	190	4	B
022334444	CSC202	COMPUTER SCIENCE II	121597	189	4	F
033445555	MTH201	CALCULUS I	052297	167	5	D
044556666	CSC210	INTRO TO C	052297	200	4	A
044556666	CSC310	ADVANCED C	121597	200	4	B
055667777	DPS110	MICROCOMPUTERS I	121597	100	4	A
066778888	CSC101	COMPUTER SCIENCE I	052297	190	4	X

Update Maintenance: For update maintenance, the composite SSNUMBER/COURSENO/TERMDATE entered from the prompt display is used to randomly access the related physical file record. If the record is found, the entry screen must be displayed "filled in" with the data from the physical file. When a record is not found, the error message **RECORD NOT FOUND** (provided for in the display file) will display in the prompt screen.

Update Data:

	Record 1	Record 2	Record 3	Record 4
SSNUMBER	011111111	011233333	011111111	066778888
COURSENO	DPS100	DSP200	ACD101	CSC101
COURSENAME			ENGLISH I	
TERMDATE	121597	121097	052297	
NSTCODE				221
CREDIT				
MARK	C	B		F

Deletion Maintenance: For deletion maintenance, the composite key SS-NUMBER/COURSENO/TERMDATE entered from the prompt screen randomly accesses the physical file for the stored record. If the record is found, the entry screen must be displayed "filled in" with the data from the physical file. When the record is *not* found, the error message **RECORD NOT FOUND** (provided for in the display file) must be displayed in the prompt screen.

Logically delete records with composite key values **03344555 MTH201 052297** and **044556666 CSC202 052597.** Test your program by trying to delete the record(s) again.

Inquiry Processing: For *inquiry* processing, the composite SSNUMBER/COURSENO/TERMDATE must be entered in the prompt screen to randomly access the physical file for the stored record. If the record is found, the second screen format must be displayed "filled in" with the data from the physical file. When the record is not found, the error message **RECORD NOT FOUND** (provided for in the display file) must be displayed in the prompt screen.

Inquiry records with composite key values **055667777 DPS110 121597** and **011111111 ACD102 052297.** Display of any stored record will test the inquiry function.

Programming Assignment 15-6: PARTS INVENTORY MASTER FILE MAINTENANCE

Before this assignment is started, Assignment 14-6 must have been completed. Write an **RPG IV** program to include adds, update, and logical deletion maintenance and inquiry processing. The command key pressed in the prompt display will determine the maintenance function processed or end-of-program control.

Adds Maintenance: For adds maintenance, the physical file must be checked for a duplicate PARTNUMBER key before the second record is displayed. If the record is already stored in the physical file, the error message **DUPLICATE RECORD** must be displayed in the prompt screen.

Adds Data:

Part#	Part Name	Amount On Hand	Amount On Order	Avg Cost /Unit	Amount Allocated	EOQ	Safety Stock	Lead Time	Warehouse Location
A2345	AC SPARK PLUG	000000	012000	0000075	005000	001440	002000	014	ABC
B6789	FRAM OIL FILTERS	004000	001200	0000324	001875	001875	000500	031	DEF
C5555	POINT SETS	000500	000000	0000227	000000	001000	002000	015	AAA
D9876	LOCKING GAS CAP	000325	001000	0000455	000400	002400	000400	090	GHI
E3459	LIQUID CAR WASH	010224	000000	0000125	050000	004000	003000	015	BBB
C5555	ARMOR-ALL	036000	001200	0000325	004800	003000	005000	010	EFG

Update Maintenance: For update maintenance, the PARTNUMBER value entered in the prompt display randomly accesses the physical file for the stored record. If the record is found, the second record format must be displayed "filled in" with the field values from the physical file. When the record is not found, the error message **PART NUMBER NOT FOUND** (included in the display file) must be displayed in the prompt screen.

Update Data: Check the update process by redisplaying the record previously changed.

	Record 1	Record 2	Record 3
PARTNUMBER	E3459	A2345	F6666
PARTNAME		AC SPARK PLUGS	
AMTONHAND		500	
AMTORDERED		4500	
AVGCOST			
AMTAVAIL		0	
EOQ			
SAFTYSTOCK			
LEADTIME	30		
WAREHLOCTN		CCC	DDD

Deletion Maintenance: For *deletion* maintenance, the part number key value entered from the prompt display randomly accesses the physical file for the stored record. If the record is found, the second screen must be displayed "filled in" with the date from the physical file. When the record is *not* found, the error message **PART NUMBER NOT FOUND** must be displayed in the prompt screen.

Logically delete the records with key values **D9876** and **E4448.**

Check the results of the deletion processing by trying to recall a record assumed to be deleted.

Inquiry Processing: For *inquiry* processing, the part number entered from the prompt display randomly accesses the physical file for the stored record. If it is found, the second screen must be displayed "filled in" with data from the physical file. When the record is *not* found, the error message **PART NUMBER NOT FOUND** (provided for in the display file) must be displayed in the prompt screen.

Inquiry records with key values **B6789** and **C6666.**

chapter 16

Subfiles

A *subfile* is a group of records that is loaded and read from or written to a display device file. Examples of subfile applications follow:

1. For inquiry processing, a subfile may be created to which a group of records read from a physical file is loaded.
2. For update processing, a subfile may be used to store a group of records read from a physical file. All or select records may be updated. Under control of an **RPG IV** program (**READC** operation), only the changed records are written back to the physical file.
3. For adds processing, a subfile may be built to load the new records that may be edited before adding them to an existing physical file.
4. For deletion processing, a subfile may be created to load a group of records that may be logically deleted or tagged for deletion.

The processing logic for subfiles included in **RPG IV** programs that control inquiry, update, or deletion maintenance is detailed in Figure 16-1.

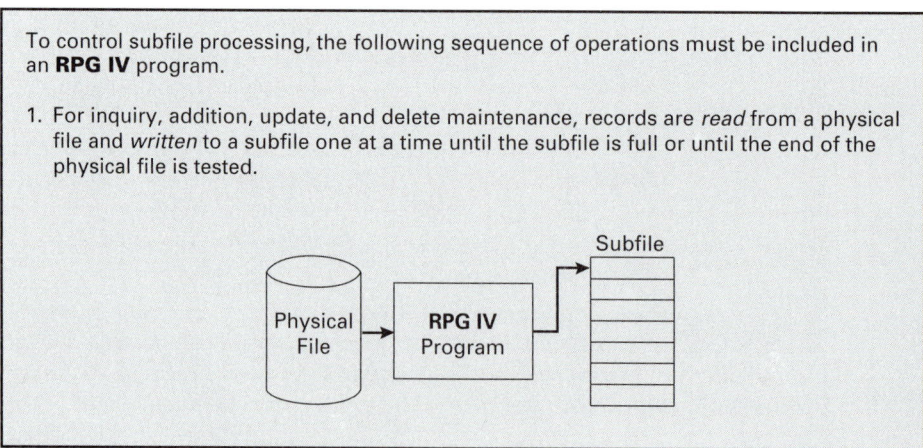

To control subfile processing, the following sequence of operations must be included in an **RPG IV** program.

1. For inquiry, addition, update, and delete maintenance, records are *read* from a physical file and *written* to a subfile one at a time until the subfile is full or until the end of the physical file is tested.

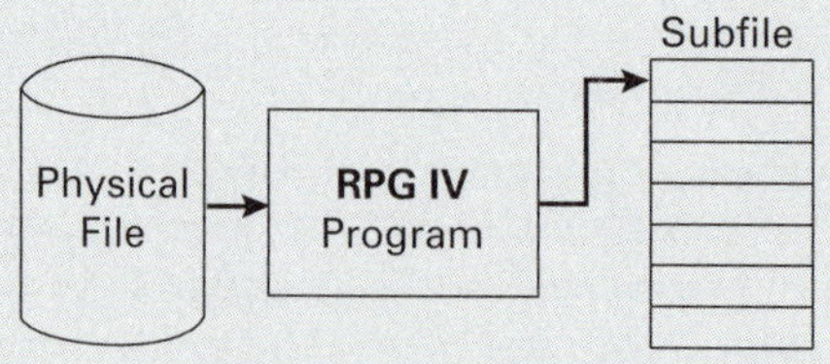

Figure 16-1 Subfile processing logic.

2. After the subfile is full or the physical file is at end, all the records in the subfile are displayed by one operation.

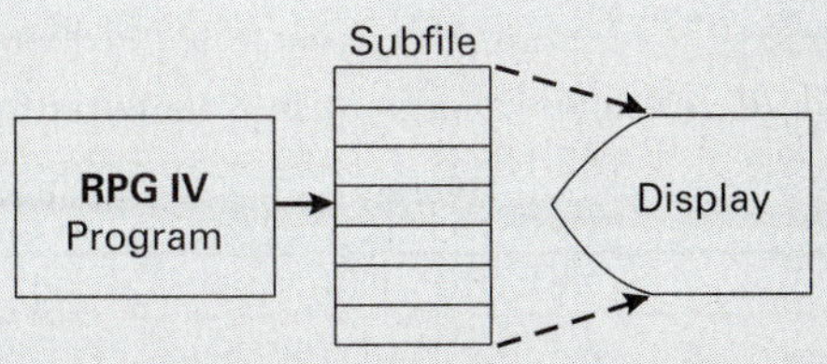

3. Depending on the maintenance application, the displayed records may be individually reviewed, changed, or deleted.

4. For addition, update, and deletion processing, each record is read from the subfile and the related physical file modified accordingly.

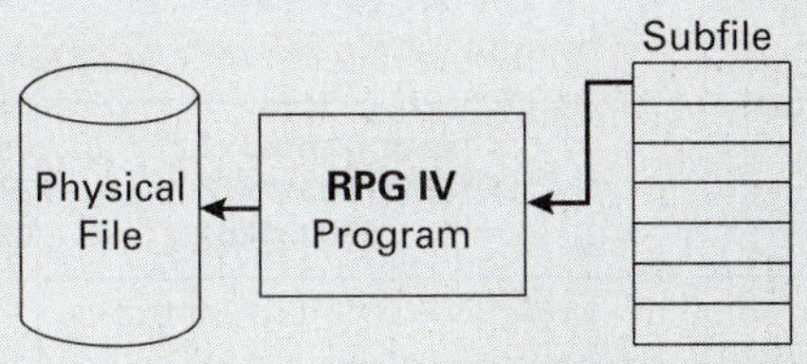

Note: In lieu of the procedure illustrated, add records may be loaded directly to a subfile from a display file that supports input processing.

Figure 16-1 Subfile processing logic. (Continued)

Similar to any display file, subfiles are coded as DDS specifications using either **SEU** *(Source Entry Utility)* or **SDA** *(Screen Design Aid)*. All subfiles must include a ***subfile record format*** and a related ***subfile control record format*** in the DDS coding. The function of each format is explained in the next paragraph.

The subfile record format defines the fields in the subfile record. **RPG IV** programs that control subfile processing use the subfile record format to read the subfile (input), write records to the subfile (output), and perform update operations to the subfile. Processing of the subfile record format is performed between the subfile and the **RPG IV** program. The display is not changed on operations to a subfile record format.

The subfile control record format describes any heading syntax and controls unique subfile functions such as size, clearing, and initialization. DDS coding requires that the subfile record format description precede the control record format instructions. An **RPG IV** program must access the control record format in order to write the complete subfile to the display unit and to read the subfile from the display unit.

The minimum *Data Description Specification* (DDS) keywords required in the definition of a subfile are **SFL, SFLCTL, SFLSIZ, SFLPAG,** and **SFLDSP.** The function of each is explained in the following paragraphs.

- **SFL:** A *Record Level* keyword that specifies the subfile record format, which consists of variable data items. The instructions for the format must immediately precede the subfile control record format.
- **SFLCTL:** A *Record Level* keyword that specifies the subfile control record format in which display, clearing, and initialization functions are controlled.

- **SFLSIZ:** A *Record Level* control record keyword that specifies the number of records that may be loaded in the subfile. The maximum allowed for a subfile is 9,999.
- **SFLPAG:** A *Record Level* control record keyword that specifies the number of records that may be displayed on the CRT at the same time.
- **SFLDSP:** A *Record Level* control record keyword that displays the subfile when the **RPG IV** program issues an output operation to the control record format. The **SFLDSP** instruction must be conditioned by one or more indicators set on in the **RPG IV** program at the appropriate time in the processing cycle.

Other special-purpose DDS keywords for subfiles that must be specified at the *Record Level* in the control record format include the following:

- **SFLCLR:** Clears a subfile of all records before new records are loaded. The subfile is not deleted by execution of this keyword, only cleared.
- **SFLINZ:** Initializes all records in a subfile. Alphanumeric fields are initialized with blanks and numeric fields with zeros.
- **SFLDLT:** Deletes a subfile. It is used when more than one subfile is controlled by an **RPG IV** program and one or more are no longer needed. Because the number of subfiles that may be active at any time is limited to 24, this keyword may be specified to delete subfiles so that others may be included in the processing cycle.
- **SFLDSPCTL:** Displays constants and fields defined within the control record instruction format. This keyword is usually conditioned by an indicator that is turned on in an **RPG IV** program at the appropriate time in the processing cycle.
- **SFLEND:** A *Record Level* control record keyword that displays a plus sign in the lower right area of the screen. The plus sign indicates that more records are stored in the subfile than can be displayed at one time on the screen. Pressing the Roll Up key displays the next group of records in the subfile. A plus sign will not display if no records are left in the subfile. Recall that the number of records displayed on the screen is controlled by the value included with the **SFLPAG** keyword. **SFLEND** is usually conditioned by an indicator.
- **SFLRNA:** This keyword is used with **SFLINZ** for program-controlled initialization of a subfile with no active records. A workstation user may key data into the related blank subfile records. **SFLRNA** must be specified when the **SFLINZ** keyword is included in the coding of a subfile.
- **SFLMSG:** Specifies a subfile record error that is included in the control record format and displays on the error message line (default 24) unless the location is changed by an **MSGLOC** keyword.
- **SFLDROP:** Controls the folding of records when they are too long to display at one time on the screen. This keyword is used with a command key that the workstation operator may press to display the folded format of the subfile record.
- **SFLLIN:** Displays the subfile data in a horizontal format versus a vertical format. Records are displayed in columns in lieu of vertical lines. The number of records per page specified in the **SFLPAG** keyword will determine how many columns of data are displayed on each page of the subfile. The format of the keyword is **SFLLIN(spaces);** the **spaces** parameter indicates the number of spaces between each record.

For an explanation of the function of other subfile keywords, refer to the system's current DDS manual.

SUBFILE APPLICATION PROGRAM: INQUIRY PROCESSING

The specifications for a program that processes a subfile for the inquiry of a physical file are detailed in Figure 16-2.

PROGRAM SPECIFICATIONS — Page 1 of 1

Program Name: Customer File Inquiry — Program-ID: CH16INQ — Written by: SM

Purpose: Inquiry of the customer file using a subfile — Approved by: CM

Input files: CUSTOMERS (keyed) SFLINQ (display file)

Output files: SFLINQ (display file)

Processing Requirements:

Write an **RPG IV** program to inquiry records from the customer master file utilizing a subfile.

Input to the program:

Create a display file that includes a prompt screen, a subfile record, a subfile control record, and a command-line record. The designs of the prompt screen and subfile are included in supplemental forms. Define the subfile to store 10 records with 8 per page.

The Prompt screen, which will be executed first, is included for the entering of a customer number. The entry (key value) specifies the record at which the reading of the physical file is to begin.

The subfile must be coded with the subfile record statements first, followed by the subfile control record, and then the command-line format.

Processing:

Read the physical file (beginning at the student number entered) and sequentially write the records to the subfile. The loading process is to continue until the subfile is full or the physical file is "at end."

Output:

Display the three subfile record formats on the screen and provide control to return to the Prompt screen to continue inquiry or end the job.

Figure 16-2 Specifications for an application program that controls the inquiry file with a subfile.

The system flowchart shown in Figure 16-3 indicates that the program accesses records from a physical file and stores them in a subfile for review.

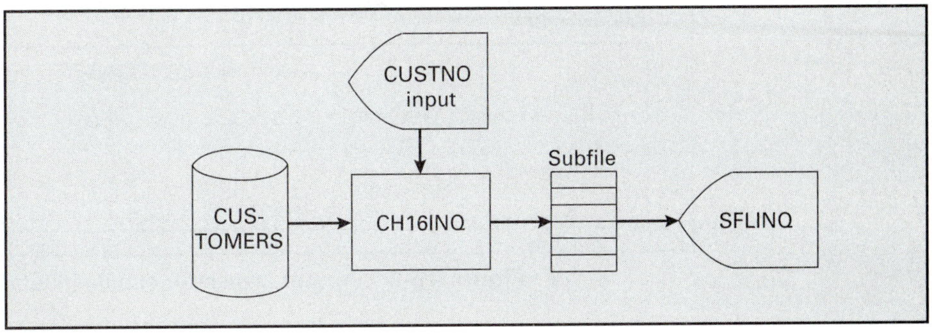

Figure 16-3 System flowchart for a program that accesses records from a physical file for inquiry with subfile control.

The structure of the physical file (CUSTOMERS) processed by the subfile inquiry application program is shown in Figure 16-4. Also included is a listing of the data stored in the file.

```
                       PHYSICAL FILE DESCRIPTION

SYSTEM: AS/400                                   DATE: 9/30/97
FILE NAME: CUSTOMERS                             REV NO: 0
RECORD NAME: CUSTRECORD                          KEY LENGTH: 5
SEQUENCE: Keyed (Unique)                         RECORD SIZE: 75

                           FIELD DEFINITIONS

 FIELD   FIELD NAME    SIZE  TYPE     POSITION     COMMENTS
  NO                                  FROM   TO

  1      CUSTOMERNO      5    C          1    5  Key field
  2      CUSTNAME       20    C          6   25
  3      STREET         20    C         26   45
  4      CITY           20    C         46   65
  5      STATE           2    C         66   67
  6      ZIPCODE         5    P         68   70
  7      ACTBALANCE      8    P         71   75 2 decimals

12345KAREL APPEL         20 AMSTERDAM AVENUE NEW YORK           NY0745000125000
23456GEORGES BRAQUE      300 ST CLAIR STREET TRENTON            NJ0550100010000
34567PAUL CEZANNE        44 RUE PIGALLE      STAMFORD           CT0651808190000
45678MARC CHAGALL        222 QUAIL AVENUE    BRIDGEPORT         CT0666600092600
56789EDGAR DEGAS         10 ROSE TERRACE     WESTPORT           PA0777700784599
67890MAX ERNST           1 FRANKFURT DRIVE   FRANKFORT          KY0555100050000
78900BUCKMINSTER FULLER  999 PARK AVENUE     NEW YORK           NY0755503300010
89000JULIO GONZALEZ      101 SMITH LANE      GREENWICH          CT0644400065478
90000HECTOR HYPPOLITE    888 PEACHTREE AVENUEATLANTA            GA0333212000000
91000PIERRE JEANERET     90 CHATEAU DRIVE    GENEVA             NY0777700000945
```

Figure 16-4 Physical file (CUSTOMERS) structure and listing of the stored data processed by the subfile inquiry program.

The design of the Prompt screen included in the display file is shown in Figure 16-5.

```
1                              CUSTOMER FILE INQUIRY
2
3          ENTER CUSTOMER NUMBER: XXXXX
4
5
6                   F3 - END-OF-JOB    ENTER TO DISPLAY
```

```
PROMPT display (with customer number entered):

                         CUSTOMER FILE INQUIRY

          ENTER CUSTOMER NUMBER: 56789


                  F3 - END-OF-JOB    ENTER TO DISPLAY
```

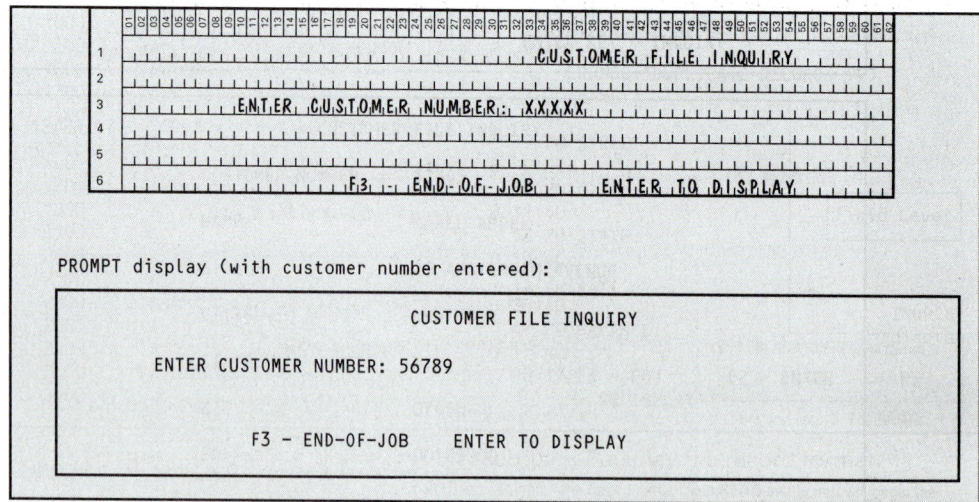

Figure 16-5 Prompt screen for subfile inquiry program.

The format of the subfile, which is displayed when the inquiry program is executed, is illustrated in Figure 16-6. Notice that Xs represent the size and location of the variable field data. As shown in the last section of Figure 16-6, the Xs are replaced with field values when the subfile is executed under program control.

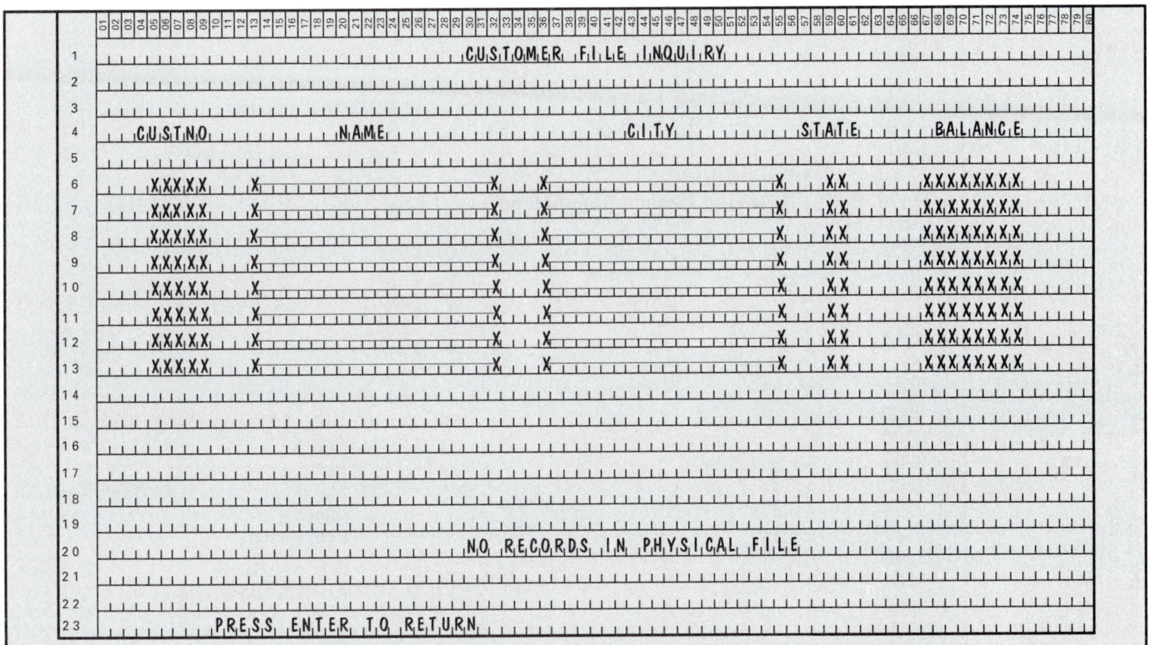

Subfile display:

```
                     CUSTOMER FILE INQUIRY


CUSTNO          NAME                CITY          STATE     BALANCE

12345   KAREL APPEL          NEW YORK             NY      00125000
23456   GEORGES APPEL        TRENTON              NJ      00010000
34567   PAUL CEZANNE         STAMFORD             CT      08190000
45678   MARC CHAGALL         BRIDGEPORT           CT      00092600
56789   EDGAR DEGAS          WESTPORT             PA      00784599
67890   MAX ERNST            FRANKFORT            KY      00050000
78900   BUCKMINSTER FULLER   NEW YORK             NY      03300010
89000   JULIO GONZALEZ       GREENWICH            CT      00065478    +
```

Figure 16-6 Display format of the subfile controlled by the inquiry program.

Subfile DDS Syntax—Inquiry Program

The instructions for a subfile may be explicitly entered with **SEU** (Source Entry Utility) or may be generated by **SDA** (Screen Design Aid) through a series of prompt screens. In any case, the structure of the subfile and the function of its keywords are the same. As in previous chapters, DDS source code will be entered via **SEU.**

A listing of the display file (SFINQ), which includes record formats for the Prompt screen (PROMPT), subfile record (SM01SFR), subfile control record (SM01CTL), and command message record (CMDLINE), is presented in Figure 16-7. An explanation of the function of each instruction is also included.

Notice the following two important coding features in the syntax of the subfile:

1. The keyword **OVERLAY** is included in the subfile control record format so that the subfile's variables and constants will not erase the message lines

```
SEQNBR*...+... 1 ...+... 2 ...+... 3 ...+... 4 ...+... 5 ...+... 6 ...+... 7 ...+... 8
   100     A                                        PRINT
   200     A                                        REF(STAN/CUSTOMERS)
   300      * Prompt Record Definition....
   400     A          R PROMPT
   500     A                                        CA03(03 'END OF JOB')
   600     A                                    1 34'CUSTOMER FILE INQUIRY'
   700     A                                    3 10'ENTER CUSTOMER NUMBER:'
   800     A            CUSTNO          5    I  3 33
   900     A                                    6 18'F3 - END-OF-JOB'
  1000     A                                    6 38'ENTER TO DISPLAY'
  1100      * Subfile Record Definition....
  1200     A          R SM01SFR                     SFL
  1300     A            CUSTOMERNOR          O  6  5
  1400     A            CUSTNAME  R          O  6 13
  1500     A            CITY      R          O  6 36
  1600     A            STATE     R          O  6 59
  1700     A            ACTBALANCER          O  6 67
  1800      * Subfile Control Record Ddefinition....
  1900     A          R SM01CTL                     SFLCTL(SM01SFR)
  2000     A                                        SFLSIZ(10)
  2100     A                                        SFLPAG(8)
  2200     A  80                                    SFLCLR
  2300     A  81                                    SFLDSP
  2400     A  81                                    SFLDSPCTL
  2500     A  81                                    SFLEND(*MORE)
  2600     A                                        OVERLAY
  2700     A                                    1 30'CUSTOMER FILE INQUIRY'
  2800     A                                    4  4'CUSTNO'
  2900     A                                    4 20'NAME'
  3000     A                                    4 43'CITY'
  3100     A                                    4 57'STATE'
  3200     A                                    4 68'BALANCE'
  3300      * Command Line Record Definition....
  3400     A          R CMDLINE
  3500     A  70                               20 30'NO RECORDS IN PHYSICAL FILE'
  3600     A                                   23 10'PRESS ENTER TO RETURN'
```

Line No.

100 The keyword **PRINT** allows use of the Print key to print a copy of the screen image.

200 The keyword **REF** references the field attributes in the physical file CUSTOMERS.

400–1000 The instructions included in this group relate to a Prompt screen in which the operator enters a customer number to begin an inquiry of the physical file or end the job.

1200 The letter **R** in position 17, the programmer-supplied record name SM01SFR (positions 19–28), and the **SFL** keyword define this statement as the subfile record format.

1300–1700 The physical file (CUSTOMERS) field attributes included in the subfile record format are referenced by the letter **R** in position 29. Individual field line (positions 39–41) and column locations (positions 42–44) are specified for each field entry. The **6** entry for line number indicates the beginning line on which the first record will be displayed. Subsequent records will automatically be displayed on the following lines. Because this subfile only supports inquiry processing, the letter **O** (output from the program to the screen) is specified in the *Usage* field (position 38) for all of the data items.

1900 The letter **R** in position 17, the programmer-supplied name SM01CTL (positions 19–28), and supporting keywords define this entry as the subfile control record format.

The **SFLCTL(SM01SFR)** keyword defines the record format as the control record for the subfile record SM01SFR specified on line 1200.

2000 The **SFLSIZ(10)** keyword defines the size of the subfile. For this example, the file will store 10 records. A subfile may store a maximum of 9,999 records.

2100 The **SFLPAG(8)** keyword specifies how many subfile records are to be displayed at one time on the screen. This number specified does not include the constants or variables that may be described on the subfile control record.

Figure 16-7 Syntax for display file (SFLINQ), including record formats for PROMPT, SM01SFR, SM01CTL, and CMDLINE.

2200	The **SFLCLR** keyword clears the subfile before it is loaded. Indicator **80** is turned on in the **RPG IV** program, and the clearing function is performed when the control record is executed by an **EXFMT SM01CTL** instruction.
2300	The **SFLDSP** keyword displays the subfile record values when indicator **81** is set on in the **RPG IV** program and an **EXFMT SM01CTL** statement is executed. The number of records displayed on the screen is determined by the **SFLPAG(8)** keyword.
2400	**SFLDSPCTL** displays the constants included in the subfile control record (SM01CTL) when indicator **81** is set on in the **RPG IV** program and an **EXFMT SM01CTL** statement executed.
2500	**SFLEND** controls the display of a + (plus sign) to the right of the last subfile record displayed on the screen. The + sign indicates that more records are included on the following page. When there are no more records in the subfile, the + sign does not display. This keyword is accessed when indicator **81** is set on in the **RPG IV** program and the control record executed by an **EXFMT SM01CTL** statement.
2600	The **OVERLAY** keyword prevents the CMDLINE constants from being cleared when the control record (SM01CTL) is displayed. Each record format will automatically display 24 lines unless the **OVERLAY** keyword is specified. Overlaying formats must begin on lines not used by a previously displayed record.
2700–3200	The constants included in these statements are displayed when an **EXFMT SM01CTL** statement that controls the display of the subfile control record is executed in the **RPG IV** program.
3400	Display of the constants included in the CMDLINE record format are controlled with a **WRITE CMDLINE** statement in the **RPG IV** program. This record format is displayed *before* the subfile control record.
3500	Indicator **70,** set on in the **RPG IV** program by a **READ** statement when no records are stored in the physical file, conditions the constant NO RECORDS IN PHYSICAL FILE. Display of this constant is controlled by the **WRITE CMDLINE** statement in the **RPG IV** program. If **70** is on, the statement will be executed.
3600	The constant PRESS ENTER TO RETURN display is controlled by the **WRITE CMDLINE** statement in the **RPG IV** program. As coded, it will display beginning in column 10, line 23 of the screen.

Figure 16-7 Syntax for display file (SFLINQ), including record formats for PROMPT, SM01SFR, SM01CTL, and CMDLINE. (Continued)

(CMDLINE format) after they are displayed. In the **RPG IV** program, the message line(s) is (are) displayed by a **WRITE** statement before the subfile control record format (SM01CTL) is executed by an **EXFMT** operation. Because processing is so fast, the sequence of the record displays will not be seen by the operator. All the variables in the subfile record (one page) and constants in the subfile control record and command line appear to display simultaneously.

2. A separate record format (CMDLINE) must be included for the command-line constants (error and action messages) and is displayed before the other subfile record formats.

The relationship of the subfile record, control record, and command-line record formats are illustrated in Figure 16-8. The subfile control record (SM01CTL) includes the constants (two heading lines) and control keywords; the subfile record (SM01SFR) defines variable fields and stores the data; and the command record (CMDLINE) file defines the message lines. All these subfile components are displayed simultaneously in the **RPG IV** program by either a **WRITE** or **EXFMT** operation.

```
SEQNBR*...+... 1 ...+... 2 ...+... 3 ...+... 4 ...+... 5 ...+... 6 ...+... 7 ...+
  100       A                                      PRINT
  200       A                                      REF(STAN/CUSTOMERS)
  300       A* PROMPT SCREEN..........
  400       A          R PROMPT
  500       A                                      CA03(03 'END OF JOB')
  600       A                                  1 34'CUSTOMER FILE INQUIRY'
  700       A                                  3 10'ENTER CUSTOMER NUMBER:'
```

Figure 16-8 Relationship of subfile coding to subfile display.

```
     A                CUSTNO         5  I  3 33
     A                                     6 18'F3 - END-OF-JOB'
     A                                     6 38'ENTER TO DISPLAY'
     A* SUBFILE DEFINITION.....
     A          R SM01SFR                      SFL
     A                CUSTOMERNOR          O  6  5
     A                CUSTNAME  R          O  6 13
     A                CITY      R          O  6 36
     A                STATE     R          O  6 59
     A                ACTBALANCER          O  6 67
     A* CONTROL RECORD.........
     A          R SM01CTL                      SFLCTL(SM01SFR)
     A                                         SFLSIZ(10)
     A                                         SFLPAG(8)
     A  80                                     SFLCLR
     A  81                                     SFLDSP
     A  81                                     SFLDSPCTL
     A  81                                     SFLEND
     A                                     1 30'CUSTOMER FILE INQUIRY'
     A                                     4  4'CUSTNO'
     A                                     4 20'NAME'
     A                                     4 43'CITY'
     A                                     4 57'STATE'
     A                                     4 68'BALANCE'
     A                                          OVERLAY
     A          R CMDLINE
     A  70                                20 30'NO RECORDS IN PHYSICAL FILE'
     A                                    23 10'PRESS ENTER TO RETURN'
```

```
                         CUSTOMER FILE INQUIRY

  CUSTNO          NAME                  CITY            STATE    BALANCE

   12345     KAREL APPEL            NEW YORK              NY     00125000
   23456     GEORGES BRAQUE         TRENTON               NJ     00010000
   34567     PAUL CEZANNE           STAMFORD              CT     08190000
   45678     MARC CHAGALL           BRIDGEPORT            CT     00092600
   56789     EDGAR DEGAS            WESTPORT              PA     00784599
   67890     MAX ERNST              FRANKFORT             KY     00050000
   78900     BUCKMINSTER FULLER     NEW YORK              NY     03300010
   89000     JULIO GONZALEZ         GREENWICH             CT     00065478    +

PRESS ENTER TO RETURN
```

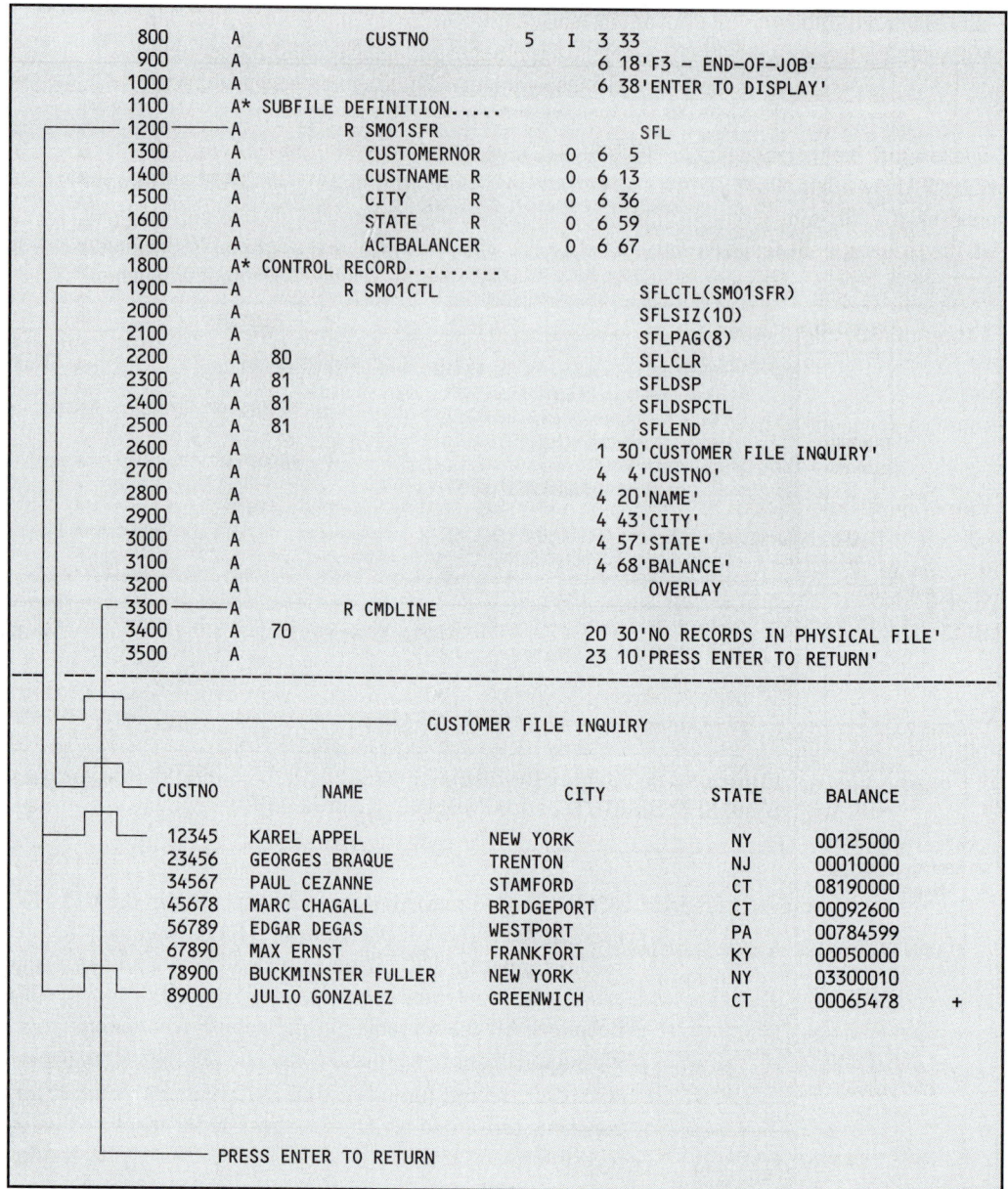

Figure 16-8 Relationship of subfile coding to subfile display. (Continued)

RPG IV-Subfile Inquiry Program

A line-by-line explanation of the function of each instruction supplements the **RPG IV** compile listing in Figure 16-9.

```
Line   <---------------------- Source Specifications ----------------------------><---- Comments ----> Do
Number ....1....+....2....+....3....+....4....+....5....+....6....+....7....+....8....+....9....+...10 Num
                   S o u r c e   L i s t i n g
   * Customers file inquiry with a subfile....
  FSflinq    CF   E             WORKSTN SFILE(Sm01sfr:Sfrrno)
   *--------------------------------------------------------------------------------------*
   *                        RPG name       External name                                   *
```

Figure 16-9 Compile listing of an **RPG IV** program that processes a subfile for inquiry of a physical file.

```
     * File name. . . . . . . . . :  SFLINQ            STAN/SFLINQ                         *
     * Record format(s) . . . . . :  PROMPT            PROMPT                              *
     *                               SM01SFR           SM01SFR                             *
     *                               SM01CTL           SM01CTL                             *
     *                               CMDLINE           CMDLINE                             *
     *---------------------------------------------------------------------------------*
   3 FCustomers IF   E           K DISK
   4
     *---------------------------------------------------------------------------------*
     *                               RPG name          External name                       *
     * File name. . . . . . . . . :  CUSTOMERS         STAN/CUSTOMERS                      *
     * Record format(s) . . . . . :  CUSTRECORD        CUSTRECORD                          *
     *---------------------------------------------------------------------------------*
   5 D Sfrrno          S              4  0                          define sf counter
   6
   7=IPROMPT
     *---------------------------------------------------------------------------------*
     * RPG record format  . . . . :  PROMPT                                               *
     * External format  . . . . . :  PROMPT : STAN/SFLINQ                                 *
     *---------------------------------------------------------------------------------*
   8=I                            A    1    1  *IN03                END OF JOB
   9=I                            A    2    6  CUSTNO
  10=ISM01SFR
     *---------------------------------------------------------------------------------*
     * RPG record format  . . . . :  SM01SFR                                              *
     * External format  . . . . . :  SM01SFR : STAN/SFLINQ                                *
     *---------------------------------------------------------------------------------*
  11=I                            A    1    5  CUSTOMERNO
  12=I                            A    6   25  CUSTNAME
  13=I                            A   26   45  CITY
  14=I                            A   46   47  STATE
  15=I                            S   48   55 2ACTBALANCE
  16=ISM01CTL
     *---------------------------------------------------------------------------------*
     * RPG record format  . . . . :  SM01CTL                                              *
     * External format  . . . . . :  SM01CTL : STAN/SFLINQ                                *
     *---------------------------------------------------------------------------------*
  17=ICMDLINE
     *---------------------------------------------------------------------------------*
     * RPG record format  . . . . :  CMDLINE                                              *
     * External format  . . . . . :  CMDLINE : STAN/SFLINQ                                *
     *---------------------------------------------------------------------------------*
  18=ICUSTRECORD
     *---------------------------------------------------------------------------------*
     * RPG record format  . . . . :  CUSTRECORD                                           *
     * External format  . . . . . :  CUSTRECORD : STAN/CUSTOMERS                          *
     *---------------------------------------------------------------------------------*
  19=I                            A    1    5  CUSTOMERNO
  20=I                            A    6   25  CUSTNAME
  21=I                            A   26   45  STREET
  22=I                            A   46   65  CITY
  23=I                            A   66   67  STATE
  24=I                            A   68   72  ZIPCODE
  25=I                            P   73   77 2ACTBALANCE
  26 C                  EXFMT     Prompt                            display prompt rcd
  27 C                  DOW       *IN03 = *OFF                      dow 03 is off      B01
  28 C                  EVAL      *IN80 = *ON                       sfl clear control   01
  29 C                  WRITE     Sm01ctl                           clear subfile       01
  30 C                  EVAL      *IN80 = *OFF                      turn off indicatr 80 01
  31 C                  EVAL      SFRRNO = *ZERO                    initialize counter  01
  32 C                  SETOFF                             7071--   turn off indicators 01
  33 C     Custno       SETLL     Customers                         positn to = or > key 01
  34 C                  READ      Customers                ----70   read a pf record    01
  35
  36  * If one or more records are stored in the physical file, load the
  37  * subfile until end of the physical file is read or subfile is full..
  38
  39 C                  IF        *IN70 = *OFF                      no pf records test  B02
```

Figure 16-9 Compile listing of an **RPG IV** program that processes a subfile for inquiry of a physical file. (Continued)

```
40 C                   DOW       *IN71 = *OFF                       sf load control     B03
41 C                   EVAL      Sfrrno = Sfrrno + 1                increment counter    03
42 C                   WRITE     Sm01sfr                    ----71  write rcd to subfile 03
43 C                   IF        *IN71 = *OFF                       subfile full?       B04
44 C                   READ      Customers                  ----71  read a pf record     04
45 C                   ENDIF                                        end line 21 IF group E04
46 C                   ENDDO                                        end dow group       E03
47 C                   ENDIF                                        end line 18 IF group E02
48
49  * Display subfile or message if no records in the physical file....
50
51 C                   WRITE     Cmdline                            display constants    01
52 C                   EVAL      *IN81 = *ON                        turn on dsp indicatr 01
53 C                   EXFMT     Sm01ctl                            display subfile      01
54 C                   EVAL      *IN81 = *OFF                       turn off dsp indcatr 01
55 C                   EXFMT     Prompt                             dsp prompt screen    01
56 C                   ENDDO                                        end line 7 dow group E01
57
58 C                   EVAL      *INLR = *ON                        eoj control
59=OPROMPT
    *--------------------------------------------------------------------------------*
    * RPG record format  . . . . :  PROMPT                                            *
    * External format  . . . . . :  PROMPT : STAN/SFLINQ                              *
    *--------------------------------------------------------------------------------*
60=OSM01SFR
    *--------------------------------------------------------------------------------*
    * RPG record format  . . . . :  SM01SFR                                           *
    * External format  . . . . . :  SM01SFR : STAN/SFLINQ                             *
    *--------------------------------------------------------------------------------*
61=O                       CUSTOMERNO          5A CHAR         5
62=O                       CUSTNAME           25A CHAR        20
63=O                       CITY               45A CHAR        20
64=O                       STATE              47A CHAR         2
65=O                       ACTBALANCE         55S ZONE       8,2
66=OSM01CTL
    *--------------------------------------------------------------------------------*
    * RPG record format  . . . . :  SM01CTL                                           *
    * External format  . . . . . :  SM01CTL : STAN/SFLINQ                             *
    *--------------------------------------------------------------------------------*
67=O                       *IN80               1A CHAR         1
68=O                       *IN81               2A CHAR         1
69=OCMDLINE
    *--------------------------------------------------------------------------------*
    * RPG record format  . . . . :  CMDLINE                                           *
    * External format  . . . . . :  CMDLINE : STAN/SFLINQ                             *
    *--------------------------------------------------------------------------------*
70=O                       *IN70               1A CHAR         1
```

File Description Specifications:

Line No.

2 Sflinq is defined as a combined (**C** in position 17), full-procedural (**F** in position 18), externally described (**E** in position 22), **WORKSTN** (workstation) display file.

The **SFILE(Sm01sfr:Sfrrno)** keyword indicates that this display file supports a subfile (**SFILE** keyword), with a subfile record name **Sm01sfr,** and **Sfrrno** as the subfile record counter. Note that a colon must be included between the subfile record name and the subfile record counter. With the exception of the **SFILE** keyword, the other entries are programmer-supplied.

3 Customers is defined as an input (**I** in position 17), full-procedural (**F** in position 18), externally described (**E** in position 22), keyed (**K** in position 34) physical file.

Definition Specifications:

5 Sffrno is defined as a standalone field, which is used as the subfile record counter.

Calculation Specifications:

26 This **EXFMT** instruction displays the Prompt record and holds it on the screen for a user response (**F3** to end the job or enter a customer no.).

Figure 16-9 Compile listing of an **RPG IV** program that processes a subfile for inquiry of a physical file. (Continued)

27 This **DOW** group is executed if the user does not press **F3,** which will turn on indicator **03** to end the job. When **F3** is pressed, control will branch to the **EVAL** instruction on line 58 to end the job.

28 This **EVAL** instruction turns on indicator **80,** which is specified in the **SFLCLR** keyword in the subfile control record to control the subfile clearing function.

29 The subfile control record (Sm01ctl) is written by this **WRITE** instruction to clear the subfile.

30 This **EVAL** instruction turns off indicator **80** to prevent the subfile from being cleared when the next **WRITE** or **EXFMT** instruction is executed.

31 This **EVAL** instruction initializes the subfile record counter, Sfrrno, to zero.

32 The **SETOFF** instruction is a housekeeping function that turns off indicators **70** and **71** used in the **READ** and **WRITE** instructions.

33 This **SETLL** instruction searches the physical file (Customers) for a record with a key value equal to or greater than that stored in the Custno field. The Custno field value was entered by the user in the Prompt display.

34 This **READ** instruction reads the first record from the physical file (Customers). If no records are stored in the file, indicator **70** will be turned on.

39 This **IF** instruction tests the status of indicator **70,** which was specified with the **READ** instruction on line 34. When it is off (records stored in the physical file), the next instruction will be executed. However, if indicator **70** is on (no records stored in Customers), control will branch to the **WRITE** instruction on line 51 and display the error message **NO RECORDS IN PHYSICAL FILE.**

40 This **DOW** group controls the writing of the physical file's records to the subfile and the reading of additional records. When the subfile is full or the physical file is at end, control will exit from this **DOW** group to line 51. Indicator **71** will be turned on in the **WRITE** instruction on line 42 if the subfile is full or in the **READ** instruction on line 44 if the physical file is at end.

41 This **EVAL** instruction increments the subfile record counter (Sfrrno) by 1.

42 This **WRITE** instruction loads the current Customer file record to the subfile (Sm01sfr) to the position determined by the value in Sfrrno. If the value in Sfrrno is 1, the record is written to the first record position in the subfile. When the value in Sfrrno is 2, the record is written to the second storage position, and so forth. Indicator **71,** specified in the *Eq* field (positions 75–76), will turn on if the subfile is full (as determined by the **SFLSIZ(10)** keyword).

43 This **IF** instruction tests the status of indicator **71,** which may have been turned on by the **WRITE** instruction on line 42 if the subfile was full. When **71** is off, the instructions within this **IF** group will be executed. However, if **71** is on, control branches to the **WRITE** instruction on line 51.

44 This **READ** instruction reads another record from the physical file (Customers). If the file is "at end," indicator **71** will be turned on, which will subsequently end the program when the **DOW** instruction on line 40 is executed.

45 This **ENDIF** operation ends the **IF** group that began on line 43.

46 This **ENDDO** operation ends the **DOW** group that began on line 40.

47 This **ENDIF** operation ends the **IF** group that began on line 39.

51 This **WRITE** instruction displays the constants included in the Cmdline record format. If indicator **70,** specified in the **READ** instruction on line 34, is on, the error message **NO RECORDS IN PHYSICAL FILE** will display with the other constants.

52 This **EVAL** instruction turns on indicator **81,** which conditions the **SFLDSP, SFLDSPCTL,** and **SFLEND** keywords in the subfile control record. Then, when the **EXFMT** instruction on line 53 is executed, the subfile control record constants, the subfile record field values, and the continuation symbol will be displayed simultaneously with the Cmdline constants. Because of the computer's processing speed, it appears that the Cmdline record, Sm01sfr, and Sm01ctl record constants display at the same time.

53 This **EXFMT** instruction displays the subfile control record constants, subfile record field values, and the continuation symbol. If indicator **81** was not previously turned on by the **EVAL** instruction on line 52, none of these items would display.

54 This **EXFMT** instruction turns off indicator **81.**

55 This **EVAL** instruction displays the Prompt record again so that the user may continue the inquiry process or end the job.

56 This **ENDDO** operation ends the **DOW** group that began on line 27.

58 This **EVAL** instruction turns on indicator **LR** to end the program.

Figure 16-9 Compile listing of an **RPG IV** program that processes a subfile for inquiry of a physical file. (Continued)

An examination of the compile listing in Figure 16-9 and the related line-by-line explanation of the instructions will show that previously discussed **RPG IV** syntax unique to interactive processing has been included. Other than the **WRITE** and **EXFMT** instructions that control the display of the subfile components, the only unfamiliar coding is included in the *File Description Specification* instruction for the **WORKSTN** (display) file. An explanation of the syntax of this instruction is given in Figure 16-10.

```
.. 1 ...+... 2 ...+... 3 ...+... 4 ...+... 5 ...+... 6 ...+... 7 ...+
FFilename++IPEASFRLen+LKLen+AIDevice+.Keywords+++++++++++++++++++++++++

FSFLinq    CFE                    WORKSTN SFILE(Sm01sfr:Sfrrno)
```

SFLinq is defined as a combined (**C** in position 17), full-procedural (**F** in position 18), externally described (**E** in position 19), **WORKSTN** (workstation) file.

The **SFILE** keyword specifies that this display file includes a subfile. **Sm01sfr** is the subfile record format name defined in the display file. A colon must follow the subfile record format name. **Sfrrno** is a programmer-supplied subfile record counter that must be incremented in the **RPG IV** program when a physical file record is added to the subfile.

Figure 16-10 *File Description* entries that define a **WORKSTN** (display) file that includes a subfile.

SUBFILE APPLICATION PROGRAM: UPDATE PROCESSING

Instead of accessing and updating one physical file record at a time, subfiles may be used effectively to access a group of records for selective changes. The processing is similar to functions supported by some third-party utilities, such as REVUE, except that it is controlled by a user **RPG IV** program. Perhaps more important, however, is that the displayed records are in a format specifically designed for and familiar to the end user, who is not typically a programmer.

The system flowchart illustrated in Figure 16-11 details the processing sequence controlled by an **RPG IV** program that updates a physical file via a subfile. An explanation of the processing steps is given in the following paragraphs:

1. Records are read from the physical file in the **RPG IV** program by a **READ** statement and written to the subfile by a **WRITE** instruction.
2. After the subfile is loaded (or the physical file is at its end), it is displayed by an **EXFMT** instruction.
3. The user scans the records and makes necessary changes.

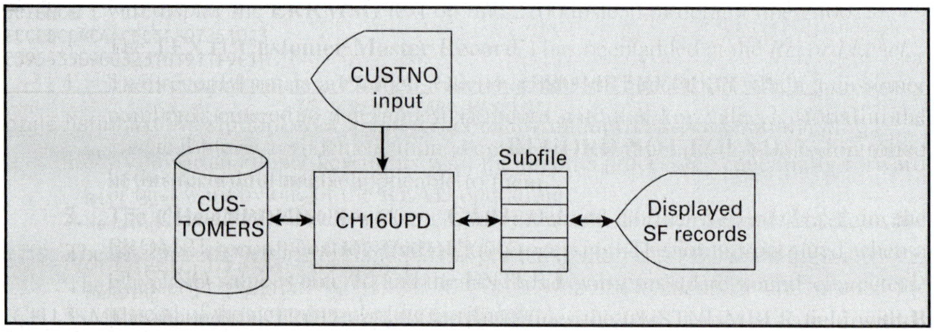

Figure 16-11 System flowchart for an **RPG IV** program that updates a physical file with subfile control.

4. Only the records that have been changed are processed by the **RPG IV** program with a **READC** *(Read Change)* operation. When any byte in the body of a record is changed, a *Modified Data Tag* (**MDT**) is automatically turned on by the system to identify the record for update processing. Therefore, if only one record is changed in the subfile, that record alone is processed in the update of the physical file—not every record in the subfile. This feature saves both input and output resources and processing time.
5. The CUSTOMERNO field from each record read by the **READC** instruction is used to **CHAIN** to the physical file and locate the address of the record before it is updated by an **UPDATE** operation.

DDS Coding—Subfile Update Program

Modifications to the DDS coding for the subfile inquiry application to support update processing are identified in Figure 16-12 and explained in the following paragraphs.

```
SEQNBR*...+... 1 ...+... 2 ...+... 3 ...+... 4 ...+... 5 ...+... 6 ...+... 7 ...+... 8
     A                                      PRINT
     A                                      REF(STAN/CUSTOMERS)
      * Prompt Record Definition....
     A          R PROMPT
     A                                      CA03(03 'END OF JOB')
     A                                 1 34'CUSTOMER FILE UPDATE'
     A                                 3 10'ENTER CUSTOMER NUMBER:'
     A            CUSTNO         5   I 3 33
     A                                 6 18'F3 - END-OF-JOB'
     A                                 6 38'ENTER TO DISPLAY'
      * Subfile Record Definition....
     A          R SM02SFR                   SFL
     A            SUSTOMERNOR          B  6  5REFFLD(CUSTOMERNO) DSPATR(PR)
     A            SUSTNAME  R          B  6 13REFFLD(CUSTNAME) DSPATR(PC)
     A            SCITY     R          B  6 36REFFLD(CITY)
     A            SSTATE    R          B  6 59REFFLD(STATE)
     A            SCTBALANCER          B  6 67REFFLD(ACTBALANCE)
      * Subfile Control Record Definition..........-
     A          R SM02CTL                   SFLCTL(SM02SFR)
     A                                      SFLSIZ(10)
     A                                      SFLPAG(8)
     A  80                                  SFLCLR
     A  81                                  SFLDSP
     A  81                                  SFLDSPCTL
     A  81                                  SFLEND(*MORE)
     A                                      OVERLAY
     A                                 1 30'CUSTOMER FILE UPDATE'
     A                                 4  4'CUSTNO'
     A                                 4 20'NAME'
     A                                 4 43'CITY'
     A                                 4 57'STATE'
     A                                 4 68'BALANCE'
      * Command Line Record Definition....
     A          R CMDLINE
     A  70                            20 30'NO RECORDS IN PHYSICAL FILE'
     A                                23 10'PRESS ENTER TO UPDATE'
```

To support update processing, Usage entry is specified with B (input and output).

Field names unique to the subfile are specified. Physical file is referenced for field attributes.

Constants changed

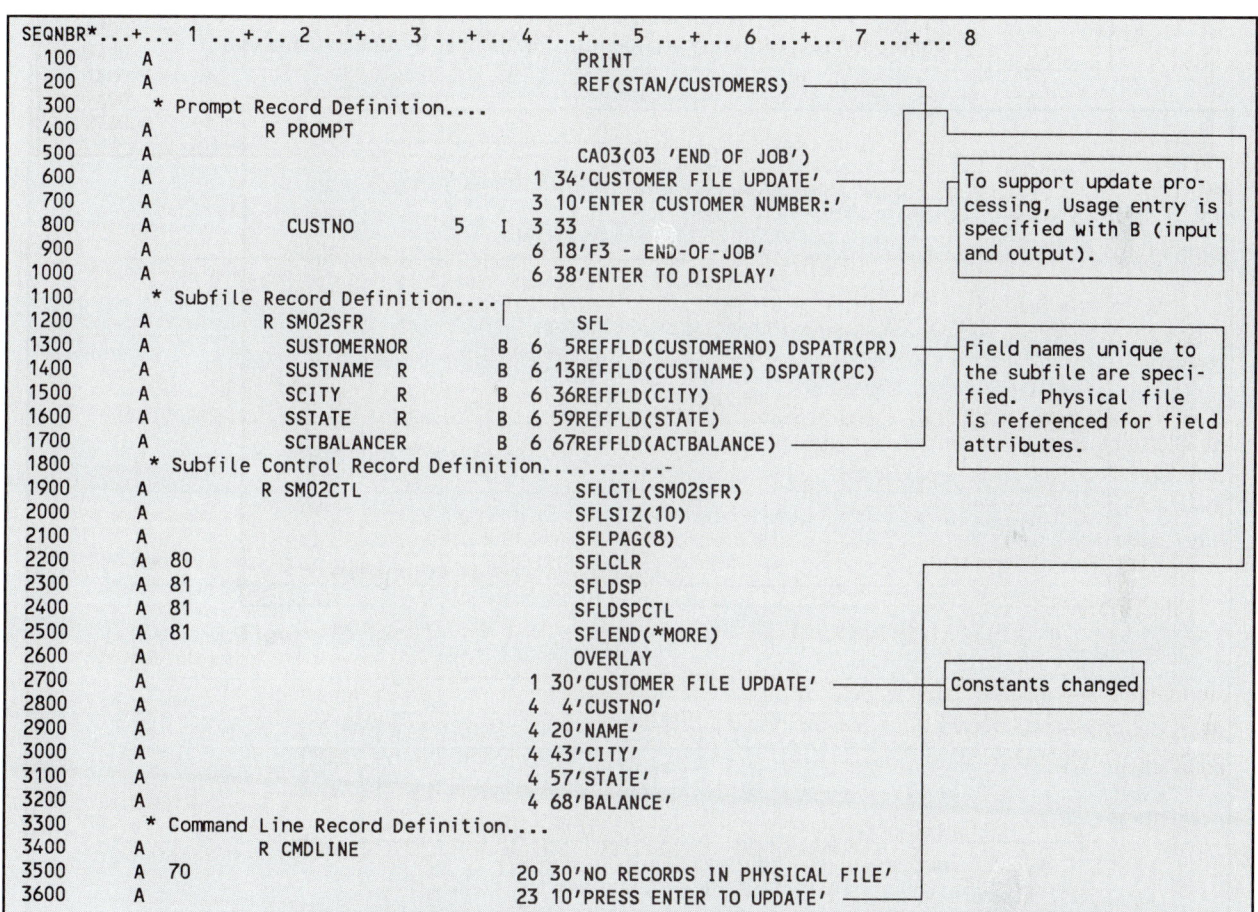

Figure 16-12 DDS subfile syntax to support the update processing of a physical file.

Instead of specifying the physical file's field names that were used in the inquiry program, new fields have been defined in the subfile's record format. This is a necessary change because once the physical file's records are accessed and loaded to the subfile, their storage addresses have been lost and the records must be randomly accessed again before updating.

If the same field names were used in both the physical file and subfile definitions, the second access of the physical file's records would replace any changed subfile values, and the physical file's records would be updated with their original field values.

Consequently, it is necessary to move the physical file's field values to the subfile fields before loading the subfile and, then, after modifying records in the subfile, move the subfile field values to their related physical file fields before updating the physical file.

Another change needed in the DDS coding to support update processing is in the *Usage* (column 38) field for the subfile record data items in which **B** (both input and output) is specified instead of **O** (output only). This entry controls both the output of field values from the program to the screen and the input from the screen to the program.

The last change in the DDS coding replaces the constants on lines 600 and 2700 from CUSTOMER FILE INQUIRY to CUSTOMER FILE UPDATE.

RPG IV Subfile Update Program

An examination of the **RPG IV** program in Figure 16-13 indicates that coding for the update processing of a physical file via subfile control is similar to the previously discussed inquiry application. Any changes and additions to convert the inquiry program to support update processing are identified in the line-by-line explanation.

```
Line    <---------------------- Source Specifications ----------------------------><---- Comments ----> Do
Number ....1....+....2....+....3....+....4....+....5....+....6....+....7....+....8....+....9....+...10 Num
                         S o u r c e   L i s t i n g
     1  * Customers file update with a subfile....
     2 FSflupd    CF   E             WORKSTN SFILE(Sm02sfr:Sfrrno)
        *--------------------------------------------------------------------------------------------*
        *                                RPG name          External name                            *
        * File name. . . . . . . . . :   SFLUPD            STAN/SFLUPD                              *
        * Record format(s) . . . . . :   PROMPT            PROMPT                                   *
        *                                SM02SFR           SM02SFR                                  *
        *                                SM02CTL           SM02CTL                                  *
        *                                CMDLINE           CMDLINE                                  *
        *--------------------------------------------------------------------------------------------*
     3 FCustomers UF   E           K DISK
     4
        *--------------------------------------------------------------------------------------------*
        *                                RPG name          External name                            *
        * File name. . . . . . . . . :   CUSTOMERS         STAN/CUSTOMERS                           *
        * Record format(s) . . . . . :   CUSTRECORD        CUSTRECORD                               *
        *--------------------------------------------------------------------------------------------*
     5 D Sfrrno          S              4  0                                    define sf counter
     6
     7=IPROMPT
        *--------------------------------------------------------------------------------------------*
        * RPG record format  . . . . :   PROMPT                                                     *
        * External format  . . . . . :   PROMPT : STAN/SFLUPD                                       *
        *--------------------------------------------------------------------------------------------*
     8=I                            A    1    1  *IN03                          END OF JOB
     9=I                            A    2    6  CUSTNO
    10=ISM02SFR
        *--------------------------------------------------------------------------------------------*
        * RPG record format  . . . . :   SM02SFR                                                    *
        * External format  . . . . . :   SM02SFR : STAN/SFLUPD                                      *
        *--------------------------------------------------------------------------------------------*
    11=I                            A    1    5  SUSTOMERNO
    12=I                            A    6   25  SUSTNAME
    13=I                            A   26   45  SCITY
    14=I                            A   46   47  SSTATE
    15=I                            S   48   55 2SCTBALANCE
    16=ISM02CTL
        *--------------------------------------------------------------------------------------------*
        * RPG record format  . . . . :   SM02CTL                                                    *
```

Figure 16-13 Compile listing of an **RPG IV** program that processes a subfile for the update of a physical file.

```
     * External format  . . . . . :  SM02CTL : STAN/SFLUPD                                        *
     *--------------------------------------------------------------------------------------------*
ICMDLINE
     *--------------------------------------------------------------------------------------------*
     * RPG record format  . . . . :  CMDLINE                                                      *
     * External format  . . . . . :  CMDLINE : STAN/SFLUPD                                        *
     *--------------------------------------------------------------------------------------------*
ICUSTRECORD
     *--------------------------------------------------------------------------------------------*
     * RPG record format  . . . . :  CUSTRECORD                                                   *
     * External format  . . . . . :  CUSTRECORD : STAN/CUSTOMERS                                  *
     *--------------------------------------------------------------------------------------------*
I                            A    1    5  CUSTOMERNO
I                            A    6   25  CUSTNAME
I                            A   26   45  STREET
I                            A   46   65  CITY
I                            A   66   67  STATE
I                            A   68   72  ZIPCODE
I                            P   73   77 2ACTBALANCE
C                  EXFMT     Prompt                                   display prompt rcd
C                  DOW       *IN03 = *OFF                             dow 03 is off      B01
C                  EVAL      *IN80 = *ON                              sfl clear control   01
C                  WRITE     Sm02ctl                                  clear subfile       01
C                  EVAL      *IN80 = *OFF                             turn off indicatr 80 01
C                  EVAL      SFRRNO = *ZERO                           initialize counter  01
C                  SETOFF                                 707172      turn off indicators 01
C     Custno       SETLL     Customers                                positn to = or > key 01
C                  READ      Customers                    ----70      read a pf record    01

 * If one or more records are stored in the physical file, load the
 * subfile until the end of the physical file is read or subfile is full....

C                  IF        *IN70 = *OFF                             no pf records test  B02
C                  DOW       *IN71 = *OFF                             sf load control     B03
C                  EXSR      pf2sfSR                                  branch to subroutine 03
C                  EVAL      Sfrrno = Sfrrno + 1                      increment counter   03
C                  WRITE     Sm02sfr                      ----71      write rcd to subfile 03
C                  IF        *IN71 = *OFF                             subfile full?       B04
C                  READ      Customers                    ----71      read a pf record     04
C                  ENDIF                                              end line 21 IF group E04
C                  ENDDO                                              end dow group        E03
C                  ENDIF                                              end line 18 IF group E02

 * Display subfile or message if no records in the physical file....

C                  WRITE     Cmdline                                  display constants    01
C                  EVAL      *IN81 = *ON                              turn on dsp indicatr 01
C                  EXFMT     Sm02ctl                                  display subfile      01
C                  EVAL      *IN81 = *OFF                             turn off dsp indcatr 01

 * Update physical file record(s) with modified subfile records....

C                  DOW       *IN72 = *OFF AND *IN70 = *OFF            end of sf and pf?    B02
C                  READC     Sm02sfr                      ----72      read a sf record      02
C                  IF        *IN72 = *ON                              sf at end?           B03
C                  LEAVE                                              exit dow group        03
C                  ENDIF                                              end IF online 43     E03

C     Sustomerno   CHAIN     Customers                    99----      get pf record         02
C                  IF        *IN99 = *ON                              pf record not found? B03
C                  LEAVE                                              exit dow group        03
C                  ENDIF                                              end line 48 IF group E03

C                  EXSR      Sf2pfSR                                  branch to subroutine  02
C                  UPDATE    Custrecord                               update pf record      02
C                  ENDDO                                              end line 41 dow grp  E02
C                  EXFMT     Prompt                                   display prompt scrn   01
C                  ENDDO                                              end line 8 dow grp   E01
```

Figure 16-13 Compile listing of an **RPG IV** program that processes a subfile for the update of a physical file. (Continued)

```
75
76 C                   EVAL      *INLR = *ON                                  end of job control
77
78  * Move pf field values to sf fields before display of subfile....
79
80 C     Pf2sfSR       BEGSR                                                  begin subroutine
81 C                   MOVE      Customerno    Sustomerno
82 C                   MOVE      Custname      Sustname
83 C                   MOVE      City          Scity
84 C                   MOVE      State         Sstate
85 C                   MOVE      Actbalance    Sctbalance
86 C                   ENDSR                                                  end Pf2sfSR subroutn
87
88  * Move sf field values to pf fields before update....
89
90 C     Sf2pfSR       BEGSR                                                  begin subroutine
91 C                   MOVE      Sustomerno    Customerno
92 C                   MOVE      Sustname      Custname
93 C                   MOVE      Scity         City
94 C                   MOVE      Sstate        State
95 C                   MOVE      Sctbalance    Actbalance
96 C                   ENDSR                                                  end Sf2pfSR subroutn
97=OPROMPT
    *---------------------------------------------------------------------------------------*
    * RPG record format . . . . :  PROMPT                                                    *
    * External format  . . . . . :  PROMPT : STAN/SFLUPD                                      *
    *---------------------------------------------------------------------------------------*
98=OSM02SFR
    *---------------------------------------------------------------------------------------*
    * RPG record format . . . . :  SM02SFR                                                   *
    * External format  . . . . . :  SM02SFR : STAN/SFLUPD                                     *
    *---------------------------------------------------------------------------------------*
99=O                         SUSTOMERNO            5A CHAR        5
100=O                        SUSTNAME             25A CHAR       20
101=O                        SCITY                45A CHAR       20
102=O                        SSTATE               47A CHAR        2
103=O                        SCTBALANCE           55S ZONE      8,2
104=OSM02CTL
    *---------------------------------------------------------------------------------------*
    * RPG record format . . . . :  SM02CTL                                                   *
    * External format  . . . . . :  SM02CTL : STAN/SFLUPD                                     *
    *---------------------------------------------------------------------------------------*
105=O                        *IN80                 1A CHAR        1
106=O                        *IN81                 2A CHAR        1
107=OCMDLINE
    *---------------------------------------------------------------------------------------*
    * RPG record format . . . . :  CMDLINE                                                   *
    * External format  . . . . . :  CMDLINE : STAN/SFLUPD                                     *
    *---------------------------------------------------------------------------------------*
108=O                        *IN70                 1A CHAR        1
109=OCUSTRECORD
    *---------------------------------------------------------------------------------------*
    * RPG record format . . . . :  CUSTRECORD                                                *
    * External format  . . . . . :  CUSTRECORD : STAN/CUSTOMERS                               *
    *---------------------------------------------------------------------------------------*
110=O                        CUSTOMERNO            5A CHAR        5
111=O                        CUSTNAME             25A CHAR       20
112=O                        STREET               45A CHAR       20
113=O                        CITY                 65A CHAR       20
114=O                        STATE                67A CHAR        2
115=O                        ZIPCODE              72A CHAR        5
116=O                        ACTBALANCE           77P PACK      8,2
```

File Description Specifications:

Line No.

2 Sflupd is defined as a combined (**C** in position 17), full-procedural (**F** in position 18), externally described (**E** in position 22), **WORKSTN** (workstation) display file.

Figure 16-13 Compile listing of an **RPG IV** program that processes a subfile for the update of a physical file. (Continued)

The **SFILE(sm02sfr:Sfrrno)** keyword indicates that this display file supports a subfile (**SFILE** keyword), with a subfile record name **Sm02sfr,** and **Sfrrno** as the subfile record counter. Note that a colon must be included between the subfile record name and the subfile record counter. With the exception of the **SFILE** keyword, the other entries are programmer-supplied.

3 Customers is defined as an update (**U** in position 17), full-procedural (**F** in position 18), externally described (**E** in position 22), keyed (**K** in position 34) physical file.

Definition Specifications:

5 Sffrno is defined as a standalone field, which is used as the subfile record counter.

Calculation Specifications:

26 This **EXFMT** instruction displays the Prompt record and holds it on the screen for a user response (**F3** to end the job or enter a customer no.).

27 This **DOW** group is executed if the user does not press **F3,** which will turn on indicator **03** to end the job. When **F3** is pressed, control will branch to the **EVAL** instruction on line 76 to end the job.

28 This **EVAL** instruction turns on indicator **80,** which is specified in the **SFLCLR** keyword in the subfile control record to control the subfile clearing function.

29 The subfile control record (Sm02ctl) is written by this **WRITE** instruction to clear the subfile.

30 This **EVAL** instruction turns off indicator **80** to prevent the subfile from being cleared when the next **WRITE** or **EXFMT** instruction is executed.

31 This **EVAL** instruction initializes the subfile record counter, Sfrrno, to zero.

32 The **SETOFF** instruction is a housekeeping function that turns off indicators **70, 71,** and **72** used in the **READ** and **WRITE** instructions.

33 This **SETLL** instruction searches the physical file (Customers) for a record with a key value equal to or greater than that stored in the Custno field. The Custno field value was entered by the user in the Prompt display.

34 This **READ** instruction reads the first record from the physical file (Customers). If no records are stored in the file, indicator **70** will be turned on.

39 This **IF** instruction tests the status of indicator **70,** which was specified with the **READ** instruction on line 34. When it is off (records stored in the physical file), the next instruction will be executed. However, if indicator **70** is on (no records stored in Customers), control will branch to the **WRITE** instruction on line 52 and display the error message **NO RECORDS IN PHYSICAL FILE.**

40 This **DOW** group controls the writing of the physical file's records to the subfile and the reading of additional records. When the subfile is full or the physical file is at the end, control will exit from this **DOW** group to line 52. Indicator **71** will be turned on in the **WRITE** instruction on line 43 if the subfile is full or by the **READ** instruction on line 45 if the physical file is at the end.

41 This **EXSR** instruction branches control to the Pf2sfSR subroutine, where the current physical file's record field values are moved to the related subfile fields.

42 This **EVAL** instruction increments the subfile record counter (Sfrrno) by 1.

43 This **WRITE** instruction loads the current Customer file record to the subfile (Sm02sfr) to the position determined by the value in Sfrrno. If the value in Sfrrno is 1, the record is written to the first record position in the subfile. When the value in Sfrrno is 2, the record is written to the second storage position, and so forth. Indicator **71,** specified in the *Eq* field (positions 75–76), will turn on if the subfile is full as determined by the **SFLSIZ(10)** keyword.

44 This **IF** instruction tests the status of indicator **71** which may have been turned on by the **WRITE** instruction on line 43 if the subfile was full. When **71** is off, the instructions within this **IF** group will be executed. However, if **71** is on, control branches to the **WRITE** instruction on line 52.

45 This **READ** instruction reads another record from the physical file (Customers). If the file is "at end," indicator **71** will be turned on, which will subsequently end the program when the **DOW** instruction on line 40 is executed.

46 This **ENDIF** operation ends the **IF** group that began on line 44.

47 This **ENDDO** operation ends the **DOW** group that began on line 40.

48 This **ENDIF** operation ends the **IF** group that began on line 39.

52 This **WRITE** instruction displays the constants included in the Cmdline record format. If indicator **70,** specified in the **READ** instruction on line 34, is on, the error message **NO RECORDS IN PHYSICAL FILE** will display with the other constants.

53 This **EVAL** instruction turns on indicator **81,** which conditions the **SFLDSP, SFLDSPCTL,** and **SFLEND** keywords in the subfile control record. Then, when the **EXFMT** instruction on line 54 is executed, the subfile control record constants, the subfile record field values, and the continuation symbol will be displayed simultaneously with the Cmdline constants. Because of the computer's processing speed, it will appear that the Cmdline record, Sm02sfr, and Sm02ctl record constants all display at the same time.

Figure 16-13 Compile listing of an **RPG IV** program that processes a subfile for the update of a physical file. (Continued)

54	This **EXFMT** instruction displays the subfile control record constants, subfile record field values, and the continuation symbol. If indicator **81** was not previously turned on by the **EVAL** instruction on line 53, none of these items would display.
55	This **EVAL** instruction turns off indicator **81.**
59	This **DOW** group will execute if indicators **72** and **70** are off. Indicator **72** will turn on when the **READC** instruction on line 60 tests the end of the subfile. Indicator **70** will turn on when the **READ** instruction on line 34 tests the end of the physical file.
60	The **READC** instruction reads a changed record from the subfile memory area. Subfile records that have not been changed by the user will not be processed. Indicator **72** will turn on if the subfile is at the end.
61	This **IF** instruction tests the status of indicator **72,** which was included in the **READC** instruction on line 60 to test for an end-of-subfile condition. If indicator **72** is on, the **LEAVE** operation on line 62 will be executed and will branch control to line **73.** When indicator **72** is off, the instructions on lines 70 and 71 will be executed and the physical file updated with the current subfile record.
62	The **LEAVE** operation will be executed if indicator **72** is on (subfile at end condition) and will branch control to the **EXFMT Prompt** instruction on line 73.
63	This **ENDIF** operation ends the **IF** group that began on line 61.
70	This **EXSR** instruction branches control to the Sf2pfSR subroutine where the subfile field values are moved to the related physical file's fields before updating the current physical file record.
71	The **UPDATE** instruction updates the current physical file record (Custrecord).
72	This **ENDDO** operation ends the **DOW** instruction that began on line 59.
73	This **EXFMT** instruction displays the Prompt record again so that the user may continue the update process or end the job.
74	This **ENDDO** operation ends the **DOW** group that began on line 27.
76	This **EVAL** instruction turns on indicator **LR** to end the program.
80	This **BEGSR** instruction begins the Pf2sfSR subroutine.
81–85	The field values from the current Customers file record are moved into their related subfile fields.
86	This **ENDSR** operation ends the Pf2sfSR subroutine.
90	This **BEGSR** instruction begins the Sf2pfSR subroutine.
91–95	The field values from the current subfile record are moved into their related physical file fields.
96	This **ENDSR** operation ends the Sf2pfSR subroutine.

Figure 16-13 Compile listing of an **RPG IV** program that processes a subfile for the update of a physical file. (Continued)

READC *(Read Next Changed Record)*

The syntax of the **READC** operation used in the previously discussed **RPG IV** subfile update program is explained in Figure 16-14. Note that the **READC** operation is functional only for **WORKSTN** files that include one or more subfile record formats.

```
*.. 1 ...+... 2 ...+... 3 ...+... 4 ...+... 5 ...+... 6 ...+... 7 ...+.
CLON01Factor1+++++++Opcode&ExtFactor2+++++++Result++++++++Len++D+HiLoEq

C 1          2      READC            4              5            6 7
                      3
```

Figure 16-14 Syntax of the **READC** *(Read Next Changed Record)* operation.

1 A total-time indicator, **L0–L9,** or **LR** may be specified in the *L0* field and/or a detail-time indicator may be specified in the *N01* field to condition the **READC** instruction.

2 *Factor 1* is not used.

3 The **READC** operation name must be entered in the *Opcode&Ext* field.

4 *Factor 2* must contain the name of a record format defined as a subfile by the **SFILE** keyword in the *File Description Specification* instruction for the related **WORKSTN** file.

5 The *Result* field is not used.

6 A *Resulting Indicator* may be specified in the *Lo* field (positions 73–74), which will turn on if the **READC** instruction is not completed successfully.

7 A *Resulting Indicator* must be specified in the *Eq* field (positions 75–76) that turns on when there are no more "changed" records in the subfile.

Processing features:

* The **READC** operation is valid only for externally described **WORKSTN** files that include subfiles.
* The **READC** operation reads only the "changed" records in a subfile.
* For the **READC** operation to be functional, a subfile must be specified in a **SFILE** keyword in a *File Description Specification* instruction for a **WORKSTN** file.

Figure 16-14 Syntax of the **READC** *(Read Next Changed Record)* operation. (Continued)

The results of subfile update processing are shown in Figure 16-15. The top section identifies two subfile records that will be changed; the bottom section is a redisplay of the

```
Display of Subfile Before Update of Physical File:

                        CUSTOMER FILE UPDATE

 CUSTNO         NAME                 CITY          STATE      BALANCE

  12345   KAREL APPEL          NEW YORK              NY      00125000
  23456   GEORGES BRAQUE       TRENTON               NJ      00010000  -Changed from 10000
  34567   PAUL CEZANNE         STAMFORD              CT      08190000    to 20000
  45678   MARC CHAGALL         BRIDGEPORT            CT      00092600
  56789   EDGAR DEGAS          WESTPORT              PA      00784599
  67890   MAX ERNST            FRANKFORT             KY      00050000  -Changed from 50000
  78900   BUCKMINSTER FULLER   NEW YORK              NY      03300010    to 69000
  89000   JULIO GONZALEZ       GREENWICH             CT      00065478     +

Re-display of Subfile After Physical File Records Are Updated:

                        CUSTOMER FILE UPDATE

 CUSTNO         NAME                 CITY          STATE      BALANCE

  12345   KAREL APPEL          NEW YORK              NY      00125000
  23456   GEORGES BRAQUE       TRENTON               NJ      00020000  -Record changed
  34567   PAUL CEZANNE         STAMFORD              CT      08190000
  45678   MARC CHAGALL         BRIDGEPORT            CT      00092600
  56789   EDGAR DEGAS          WESTPORT              PA      00784599
  67890   MAX ERNST            FRANKFORT             KY      00069000  -Record changed
  78900   BUCKMINSTER FULLER   NEW YORK              NY      03300010
  89000   JULIO GONZALEZ       GREENWICH             CT      00065478     +
```

Figure 16-15 Before and after results of updating a physical file with a subfile.

same data after the physical file (Customers) has been updated. Again, only the subfile records changed by the user will be processed by a **READC** instruction and updated in the physical file.

SUBFILE APPLICATION PROGRAM: ADDITION PROCESSING

Interactive data validation procedures may be enhanced by first loading the input data to a subfile. Then the user may review the records for errors before they are added to a physical file. The system flowchart shown in Figure 16-16 details the file processing associated with the addition of records to a physical file via a subfile. The sequence of processing steps shown in Figure 16-16 is controlled by the **RPG IV** program and includes the following:

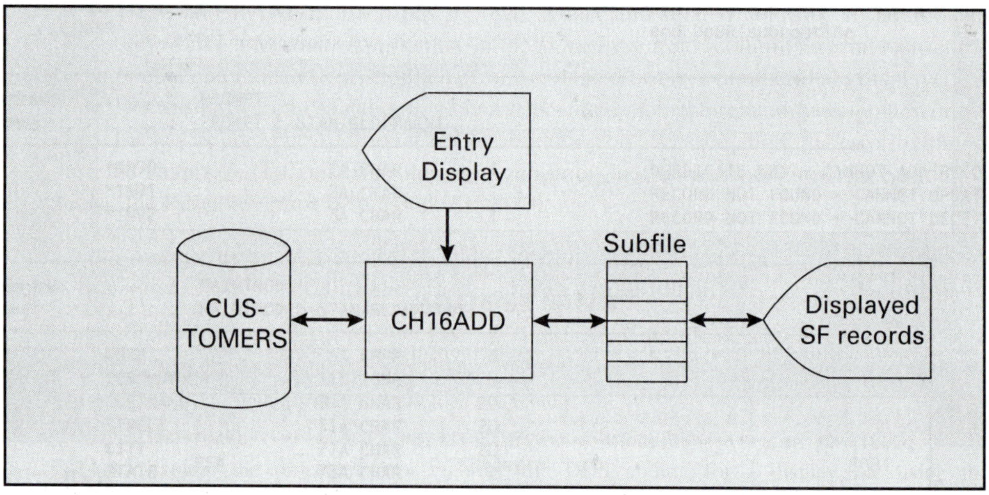

Figure 16-16 System flowchart for an **RPG IV** program that adds records to a physical file via a subfile.

1. Records are input via a separate display file record format and loaded to the subfile.
2. The subfile is displayed and the records are reviewed by the user. Any necessary changes are made.
3. The subfile records are added to the physical file.

DDS Coding—Subfile Adds Program

Formats of the four records, ENTRY, SM03SFR, SM03CTL, and CMDLINE, included in the display file SFLADD are shown in Figure 16-17. The constants defined on line 23 of the subfile are defined as the fourth record format in the display file.

Entry Record Format:

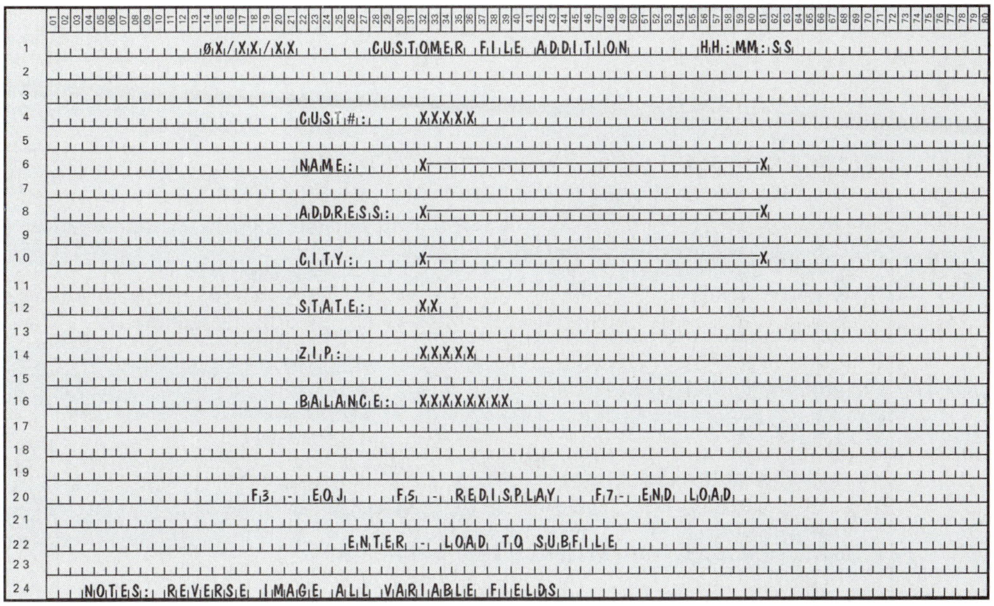

Subfile Record Formats:

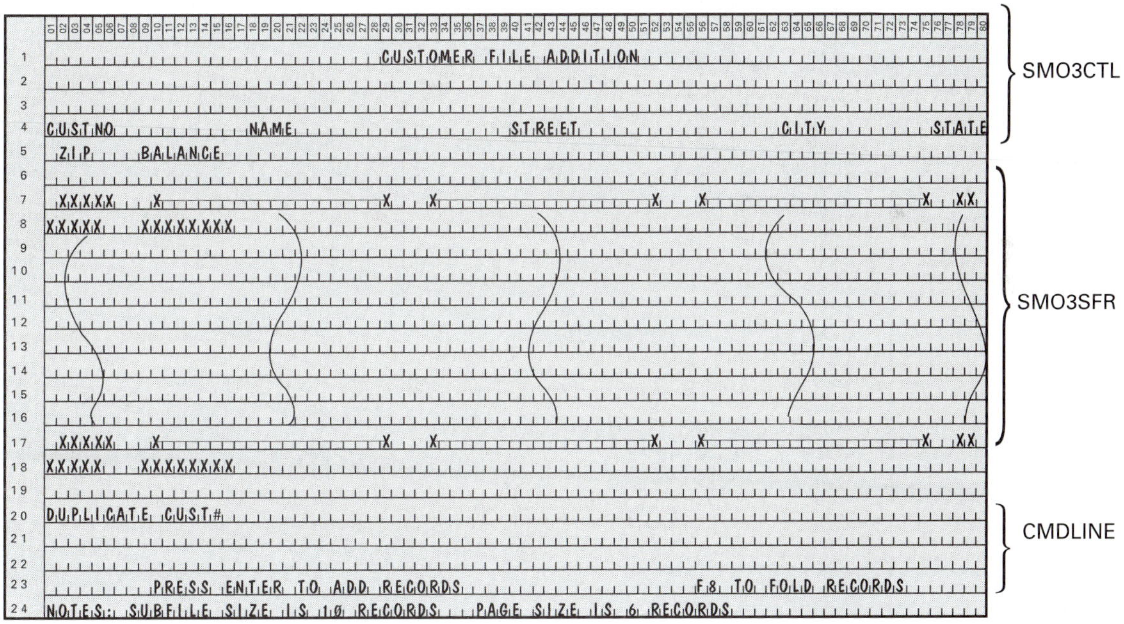

Figure 16-17 Record formats defined in the display file SFLADD.

A source listing and a line-by-line explanation of the DDS coding of the display file SFADD processed by the subfile addition program appear in Figure 16-18. Notice that three keywords not used in the previous subfile programs have been specified in this application. Included is the subfile record keyword **SFLNXTCHG** and the subfile control record keywords **SFLNRA** and **SFLINZ.** The function of each is explained in the text that supplements Figure 16-18.

```
SEQNBR*...+... 1 ...+... 2 ...+... 3 ...+... 4 ...+... 5 ...+... 6 ...+... 7 ...+... 8
     A                                      PRINT
     A                                      REF(STAN/CUSTOMERS)
      * Entry Record Definition....
     A          R ENTRY                     CHGINPDFT(RI)
     A                                      CA03(03 'END OF JOB')
     A                                      CA05(05 'REDISPLAY')
     A                                      CA07(07 'END OF SF LOAF')
     A                                  1 14DATE EDTCDE(Y)
     A                                  1 56TIME
     A                                  1 28'CUSTOMER FILE ADDITION'
     A                                  4 22'CUST#:'
     A            CUSTOMERNOR       I   4 32
     A                                  6 22'NAME:'
     A            CUSTNAME  R       I   6 32
     A                                  8 22'STREET:'
     A            STREET    R       I   8 32
     A                                 10 22'CITY:'
     A            CITY      R       I  10 32
     A                                 12 22'STATE:'
     A            STATE     R       I  12 32
     A                                 14 22'ZIP:'
     A            ZIPCODE   R       I  14 32
     A                                 16 22'BALANCE:'
     A            ACTBALANCER       I  16 32
     A                                 20 17'F3 - EOJ      F5 - REDISPLAY-
     A                                      F7 - END LOAD'
     A                                 22 26'ENTER - LOAD TO SUBFILE'
      * Subfile Record Definition....
     A          R SM03SFR                   SFL
     A                                      SFLNXTCHG
     A            CUSTOMERNOR       B   7  2
     A  99                                  DSPATR(RI)
     A            CUSTNAME  R       B   7 10
     A            STREET    R       B   7 33
     A            CITY      R       B   7 56
     A            STATE     R       B   7 78
     A            ZIPCODE   R       B   8  1
     A            ACTBALANCER       B   8  9
      * Subfile Control Record Definition....
     A          R SM03CTL                   SFLCTL(SM03SFR)
     A                                      SFLRNA
     A                                      SFLSIZ(10)
     A                                      SFLPAG(6)
     A  80                                  SFLCLR
     A  80                                  SFLINZ
     A  81                                  SFLDSP
     A  81                                  SFLDSPCTL
     A  81                                  SFLEND
     A                                      SFLDROP(CF08)
     A  99                                  SFLMSG('DUPLICATE CUST#' 99)
     A                                      OVERLAY
     A                                  1 29'CUSTOMER FILE ADDITION'
     A                                  4  1'CUSTNO'
     A                                  4 18'NAME'
     A                                  4 40'STREET'
     A                                  4 63'CITY'
     A                                  4 76'STATE'
     A                                  5  2'ZIP'
```

Figure 16-18 DDS syntax for the display file that supports the subfile addition program.

```
5900      A                                    5  9'BALANCE'
6000        * Command Line Record Definition....
6100      A          R CMDLINE
6200      A                                   23 10'PRESS ENTER TO ADD RECORDS'
6300      A                                   23 55'F8 TO FOLD RECORDS'
```

Line No.

100 **PRINT** keyword, specified at the *File Level,* supports printing of any of the three screen images when the **Print** key is pressed.

200 The field attributes of the physical file CUSTOMERS are referenced by the **REF(STAN/CUSTOMERS)** keyword.

400 The **ENTRY** display record is defined at the *Record Level.* The **CHGINPDFT(RI)** keyword changes all of the variables (not constants) in this record format from the underline default display to reverse image.

500–700 The *Command Attention* and *Function* keys are defined in these instructions. **CA03** controls end of job: **CF05** redisplays this record format without adding the record to the subfile; and **CA07** enables the operator to stop loading the subfile. As specified in the line 2700 constant, the ENTER key will add the displayed record to the subfile.

800–2700 These instructions define the display record that supports the entry of data and subsequent loading to the subfile.

2900 **SM03SFR** is defined as a subfile record format by the **SFL** keyword.

3000 The **SFLNXTCHG** keyword enables a **READC** instruction in an **RPG IV** program to process all of the subfile records as "changed."

3100–3800 The attributes of the fields in the physical file (CUSTOMERS) are referenced (letter **R** in position 29) in these instructions. Because the physical file was defined as supporting only **UNIQUE** keys, any attempt to add a record with a duplicate key will cause a **WRITE** error. Indicator **99,** assigned to the **WRITE** instruction (positions 73–74) in the **RPG IV** program, identifies this error. When **99** is on, the CUSTOMERNO value will display in reverse image by the **DSPATR(RI)** keyword on line 3200.

4000 The **SFLCTL(SM03SFR)** keyword defines record format **SM03CTL** as the subfile control record for the subfile record **SM03SFR.**

4100 Keyword **SFLRNA** initializes the subfile with no active records. This keyword is used in conjunction with **SFLINZ,** which actually performs the initialization function.

4200 **SFLSIZ(10)** specifies that the subfile is to store a maximum of 10 records.

4300 **SFLPAG(6)** specifies that 6 records are to be displayed on each page of the subfile.

4400 **SFLCLR** clears the subfile area before the subfile is created. This action is performed in the **RPG IV** program when indicator **80** is turned on and the subfile control record is executed by a **WRITE** instruction.

4500 **SFLINZ** initializes alphanumeric fields to blanks and numeric fields to zeros in all of the subfile records with one operation when indicator **80** is set on in the **RPG IV** program and the subfile control record is executed.

Because the **READC** operation is used to read records from a subfile, the records must be changed to support this function. When the input records are added to a subfile initialized by a **SFLINZ** oeration, they are flagged as "changed" and may then be processed by a **READC** instruction. For this program example, all of the subfile records are added to a physical file.

Without the **SFLRNA/SFLINZ** keywords, none of the subfile records would be "flagged" as changed. Consequently, no records would be read by a **READC** operation and none added to the physical file.

4600–4800 Indicator **81,** turned on in the **RPG IV** program, conditions the following subfile functions:

- **SFLDSP** Displays the subfile records
- **SFLDSPCTL** Displays the constants and any variables specified in the subfile control record format
- **SFLEND** Displays a + (plus sign) to the right of the last subfile record on the current page, indicating that another page of records is stored in the subfile.

4900 The **SFLDROP(CF08)** keyword controls the folding of subfile control and record formats when the constants and/or variables require a display of more than 80 columns on a standard CRT. The command function or attention key specified with this keyword (**CF08** for this example) must be pressed to cause the subfile records to change from a truncated to a folded format (continued on next line specified). Note that the constants in the control record format will automatically wrap to the line specified. However, **F8** *must* be pressed to continue the subfile record field values on another line. Notice in the control record format, lines 5800 and 5900, that the constants ZIP and BALANCE are defined on line 5 immediately below the other constants on line 4. This coding places these constants on line 5 when the subfile control record is displayed.

Figure 16-18 DDS syntax for the display file that supports the subfile addition program. (Continued)

Refer to the subfile record format, lines 3700 and 3800, and notice that the variables ZIPCODE and ACTBALANCE are defined to display on line 8 below the other related field variables on line 7. This coding places these variables on the following line only when **F8** is pressed and the **SFLDROP** instruction is executed.

The line location in the subfile record identifies the location of the first record. Other records are sequentially displayed on subsequent lines of the screen limited by the **SFLPAG** keyword.

5000 **SFLMSG** performs the same function as an **ERRMSG** keyword. When the **WRITE** instruction in the **RPG IV** program attempts to add a record that has a key value already stored in the physical file, indicator **99** specified in positions 73–74 of the **WRITE** instruction will be turned on. Because this keyword is conditioned by the **99** indicator, the message **DUPLICATE CUST#** will be displayed when the indicator is on. Indicator **99,** which is included in parentheses of the **SFLMSG** keyword, turns off the indicator when any key is subsequently pressed.

5100 **OVERLAY** prevents the previously displayed **CMDLINE** record from being written over when the subfile control record is output. Because processing of the subfile control record, subfile record, and command record are so fast, it will appear as if they display simultaneously. However, the constants in the **CMDLINE** record are displayed first by the **RPG IV** program followed by the constants in the **SM03CTL** record, and field values in the **SM03SFR** record.

5200–5900 Column headings are defined in these instructions. When the **SM03CTL** record is executed by an **EXFMT** instruction, the headings will display in their specified locations.

6100–6300 Record format **CMDLINE** includes constants that are displayed at the bottom of the subfile to inform the operator what actions to take to add the subfile records to the physical file or fold the truncated field values on to the next display line.

Figure 16-18 DDS syntax for the display file that supports the subfile addition program. (Continued)

RPG IV Subfile Addition Program

A detailed source listing of the **RPG IV** program that adds records to a physical file via a subfile is presented in Figure 16-19.

```
Line   <---------------------- Source Specifications ----------------------------><---- Comments ----> Do
Number ....1....+....2....+....3....+....4....+....5....+....6....+....7....+....8....+....9....+...10 Num
                         S o u r c e   L i s t i n g
     1 * Customers file addition with a subfile....
     2 FSfladd    CF   E             WORKSTN SFILE(Sm03sfr:Sfrrno)
       *---------------------------------------------------------------------------------------------*
       *                                RPG name          External name                              *
       * File name. . . . . . . . . :  SFLADD            STAN/SFLADD                                *
       * Record format(s) . . . . . :  ENTRY             ENTRY                                      *
       *                                SM03SFR           SM03SFR                                    *
       *                                SM03CTL           SM03CTL                                    *
       *                                CMDLINE           CMDLINE                                    *
       *---------------------------------------------------------------------------------------------*
     3 FCustomers O   A E           K DISK
     4
       *---------------------------------------------------------------------------------------------*
       *                                RPG name          External name                              *
       * File name. . . . . . . . . :  CUSTOMERS         STAN/CUSTOMERS                             *
       * Record format(s) . . . . . :  CUSTRECORD        CUSTRECORD                                 *
       *---------------------------------------------------------------------------------------------*
     5 D Sfrrno          S              4  0                          define sf counter
     6
     7=IENTRY
       *---------------------------------------------------------------------------------------------*
       * RPG record format  . . . . :  ENTRY                                                        *
       * External format  . . . . . :  ENTRY : STAN/SFLADD                                          *
       *---------------------------------------------------------------------------------------------*
     8=I                              A    1    1  *IN03                 END OF JOB
```

Figure 16-19 Compile listing of the **RPG IV** program that adds records to a physical file via a subfile.

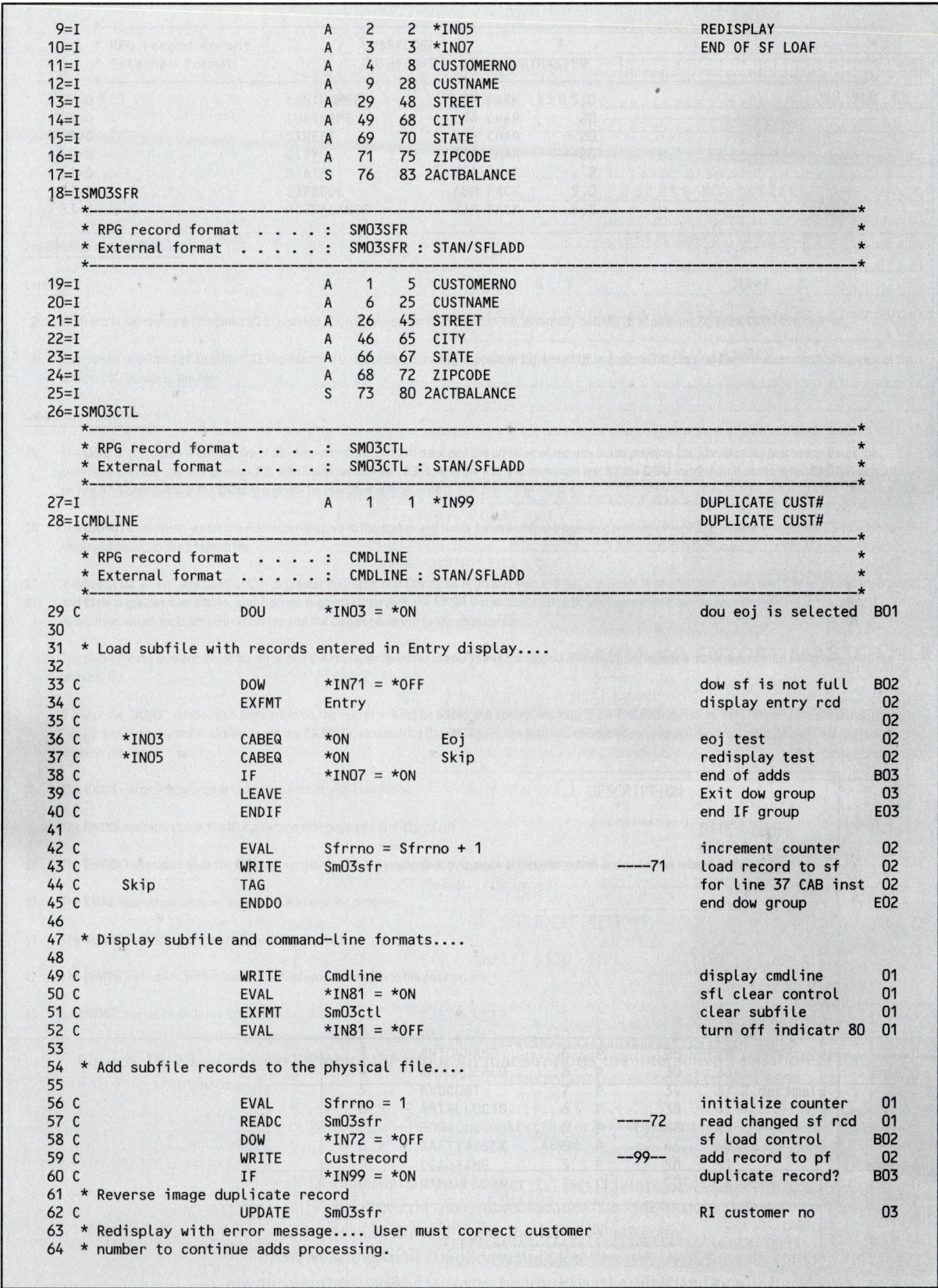

```
     9=I                          A    2    2 *IN05                     REDISPLAY
    10=I                          A    3    3 *IN07                     END OF SF LOAF
    11=I                          A    4    8 CUSTOMERNO
    12=I                          A    9   28 CUSTNAME
    13=I                          A   29   48 STREET
    14=I                          A   49   68 CITY
    15=I                          A   69   70 STATE
    16=I                          A   71   75 ZIPCODE
    17=I                          S   76   83 2ACTBALANCE
    18=ISM03SFR
       *---------------------------------------------------------------------------*
       * RPG record format . . . . :  SM03SFR                                       *
       * External format . . . . . :  SM03SFR : STAN/SFLADD                         *
       *---------------------------------------------------------------------------*
    19=I                          A    1    5 CUSTOMERNO
    20=I                          A    6   25 CUSTNAME
    21=I                          A   26   45 STREET
    22=I                          A   46   65 CITY
    23=I                          A   66   67 STATE
    24=I                          A   68   72 ZIPCODE
    25=I                          S   73   80 2ACTBALANCE
    26=ISM03CTL
       *---------------------------------------------------------------------------*
       * RPG record format . . . . :  SM03CTL                                       *
       * External format . . . . . :  SM03CTL : STAN/SFLADD                         *
       *---------------------------------------------------------------------------*
    27=I                          A    1    1 *IN99                     DUPLICATE CUST#
    28=ICMDLINE                                                         DUPLICATE CUST#
       *---------------------------------------------------------------------------*
       * RPG record format . . . . :  CMDLINE                                       *
       * External format . . . . . :  CMDLINE : STAN/SFLADD                         *
       *---------------------------------------------------------------------------*
    29 C                 DOU       *IN03 = *ON                          dou eoj is selected  B01
    30
    31  * Load subfile with records entered in Entry display....
    32
    33 C                 DOW       *IN71 = *OFF                         dow sf is not full   B02
    34 C                 EXFMT     Entry                                display entry rcd     02
    35 C                                                                                      02
    36 C     *IN03       CABEQ     *ON           Eoj                    eoj test              02
    37 C     *IN05       CABEQ     *ON           Skip                   redisplay test        02
    38 C                 IF        *IN07 = *ON                          end of adds          B03
    39 C                 LEAVE                                          Exit dow group        03
    40 C                 ENDIF                                          end IF group         E03
    41
    42 C                 EVAL      Sfrrno = Sfrrno + 1                  increment counter     02
    43 C                 WRITE     Sm03sfr                  ----71      load record to sf     02
    44 C     Skip        TAG                                            for line 37 CAB inst  02
    45 C                 ENDDO                                          end dow group        E02
    46
    47  * Display subfile and command-line formats....
    48
    49 C                 WRITE     Cmdline                              display cmdline       01
    50 C                 EVAL      *IN81 = *ON                          sfl clear control     01
    51 C                 EXFMT     Sm03ctl                              clear subfile         01
    52 C                 EVAL      *IN81 = *OFF                         turn off indicatr 80  01
    53
    54  * Add subfile records to the physical file....
    55
    56 C                 EVAL      Sfrrno = 1                           initialize counter    01
    57 C                 READC     Sm03sfr                  ----72      read changed sf rcd   01
    58 C                 DOW       *IN72 = *OFF                         sf load control      B02
    59 C                 WRITE     Custrecord               --99--      add record to pf      02
    60 C                 IF        *IN99 = *ON                          duplicate record?    B03
    61  * Reverse image duplicate record
    62 C                 UPDATE    Sm03sfr                              RI customer no        03
    63  * Redisplay with error message.... User must correct customer
    64  * number to continue adds processing.
```

Figure 16-19 Compile listing of the **RPG IV** program that adds records to a physical file via a subfile. (Continued)

```
65 C                 EVAL      *IN81 = *ON                                  sfl clear control    03
66 C                 EXFMT     Sm03ctl                                      display subfile      03
67 C                 EVAL      *IN81 = *OFF                                 turn off indicatr 80 03
68 C                 ELSE                                                                       X03
69 C                 EVAL      Sfrrno = Sfrrno + 1                          increment counter    03
70 C                 ENDIF                                                                      E03
71 C                 READC     Sm03sfr                            ----72    read changed sf rcd  02
72 C                 ENDDO                                                  end dow group       E02
73
74 C                 EXSR      ClearSR                                      branch to subroutine 01
75 C     Eoj         TAG                                                    for line 36 CAB inst 01
76 C                 ENDDO                                                  end dou group       E01
77
78 C                 EVAL      *INLR = *ON                                  end job
79
80  * Subroutine to clear subfile and initialize record counter....
81
82 C     ClearSR     BEGSR                                                  begin subroutine
83 C                 EVAL      *IN80 = *ON                                  turn on dsp indicatr
84 C                 WRITE     Sm03ctl                                      clear subfile
85 C                 EVAL      *IN80 = *OFF                                 turn off dsp indcatr
86 C                 EVAL      Sfrrno = *ZERO                               initialize counter
87 C                 SETOFF                                       7172--   turn off indicators
88 C                 ENDSR                                                  end ClearSR subroutn
89=OENTRY
   *---------------------------------------------------------------------------------------*
   * RPG record format . . . . :  ENTRY                                                    *
   * External format . . . . . :  ENTRY : STAN/SFLADD                                      *
   *---------------------------------------------------------------------------------------*
90=OSM03SFR
   *---------------------------------------------------------------------------------------*
   * RPG record format . . . . :  SM03SFR                                                  *
   * External format . . . . . :  SM03SFR : STAN/SFLADD                                    *
   *---------------------------------------------------------------------------------------*
91=O                      *IN99               1A CHAR        1
92=O                      CUSTOMERNO          6A CHAR        5
93=O                      CUSTNAME           26A CHAR       20
94=O                      STREET             46A CHAR       20
95=O                      CITY               66A CHAR       20
96=O                      STATE              68A CHAR        2
97=O                      ZIPCODE            73A CHAR        5
98=O                      ACTBALANCE         81S ZONE      8,2
99=OSM03CTL
   *---------------------------------------------------------------------------------------*
   * RPG record format . . . . :  SM03CTL                                                  *
   * External format . . . . . :  SM03CTL : STAN/SFLADD                                    *
   *---------------------------------------------------------------------------------------*
100=O                     *IN80               1A CHAR        1
101=O                     *IN81               2A CHAR        1
102=O                     *IN99               3A CHAR        1              DUPLICATE CUST#
103=OCMDLINE
   *---------------------------------------------------------------------------------------*
   * RPG record format . . . . :  CMDLINE                                                  *
   * External format . . . . . :  CMDLINE : STAN/SFLADD                                    *
   *---------------------------------------------------------------------------------------*
104=OCUSTRECORD
   *---------------------------------------------------------------------------------------*
   * RPG record format . . . . :  CUSTRECORD                                               *
   * External format . . . . . :  CUSTRECORD : STAN/CUSTOMERS                              *
   *---------------------------------------------------------------------------------------*
105=O                     CUSTOMERNO          5A CHAR        5
106=O                     CUSTNAME           25A CHAR       20
107=O                     STREET             45A CHAR       20
108=O                     CITY               65A CHAR       20
109=O                     STATE              67A CHAR        2
110=O                     ZIPCODE            72A CHAR        5
111=O                     ACTBALANCE         77P PACK      8,2
```

Figure 16-19 Compile listing of the **RPG IV** program that adds records to a physical file via a subfile. (Continued)

File Description Specifications:

Line No.

2 Sfladd is defined as a combined (**C** in position 17), full-procedural (**F** in position 18), externally described (**E** in position 22), **WORKSTN** (workstation) display file.

The **SFILE(Sm03sfr:Sfrrno)** keyword indicates that this display file supports a subfile (**SFILE** keyword), with a subfile record name **Sm03sfr,** and **Sfrrno** as the subfile record counter. Note that a colon must be included between the subfile record name and the subfile record counter. With the exception of the **SFILE** keyword, the other entries are programmer-supplied.

3 Customers is defined as an output (**O** in position 17), full-procedural (**F** in position 18), externally described (**E** in position 22), keyed (**K** in position 34) physical file. The **A** in position 20 supports record addition.

Definition Specifications:

5 Sfrrno is defined as a standalone field, which is used as the subfile record counter.

Calculation Specifications:

29 This **DOU** group is performed until the operator presses **F3** while the Entry record is displayed.

33 This **DOW** group is performed while the subfile is *not* full (indicator **71** is off). Indicator **71** is turned on in the **WRITE** instruction on line 43 when the subfile is full as controlled by the **SFLSIZ(10)** keyword in the subfile control record.

34 This **EXFMT** instruction displays the **Entry** record and holds it on the screen so that data may be entered, or the job ended **(F3),** or the **Entry** screen redisplayed **(F5),** or the subfile displayed **(F7).**

36 This **CABEQ** instruction tests the status of indicator **03,** which is turned on if **F3** was pressed to end the job. When **03** is on, control will branch to the **Eoj TAG** instruction on line 75. If **03** is not on, the following **CASEQ** instruction will be tested.

37 If the operator changes his or her mind about entering the current record, **F5** must be pressed, which will turn on indicator **05,** execute this **CABEQ** instruction, pass control to the **Skip TAG** instruction on line 44, then to the **ENDDO** operation on line 45, and back to the **DOW** instruction on line 33 to continue or end the adds process.

38 This **IF** instruction tests the status of indicator **07,** which is turned on if the operator presses **F7** to display the subfile. When **07** is on, the **LEAVE** operation on line 39 will branch control to line 49 and execute the **WRITE, EVAL,** and **EXFMT** instructions on lines 49 through 51, displaying the **Cmdline, Sm03ctl,** and **Sm03sfr** record formats.

39 The **LEAVE** operation branches control out of this **DOW** group to line 49.

40 This **ENDIF** operation ends the **IF** group that began on line 38.

42 This **EVAL** instruction increments the subfile record counter **(Sfrrno)** by 1.

43 This **WRITE** instruction writes the "filled in" **Entry** record to the subfile.

44 This **TAG** instruction is the Skip label for the **CABEQ** instruction on line 37.

45 This **ENDDO** operation ends the **DOW** group that began on line 33.

49 The constants in the **Cmdline** record format are displayed by this **WRITE** instruction.

50 This **EVAL** instruction turns on indicator **81,** which controls the display of the subfile record and subfile control record formats.

51 This **EXFMT** instruction displays the subfile control record constants and subfile record field values. Indicator **81,** which was turned on with the **EVAL** instruction on line 50, conditioned the subfile control record keywords: **SFLDSP, SFLDSPCTL,** and **SFLEND.**

52 This **EVAL** instruction turns off indicator **81.**

56 This **EVAL** instruction initializes the subfile record counter **(Sfrrno)** to 1 *before* "changed" records are read in the subfile.

57 The **READC** instruction reads the "changed" records in the subfile. Because of the **SFLNXTCHG** keyword in the subfile record coding in the display file, all of the records are tagged as "changed."

58 The **DOW** group controls the reading of the subfile records and adding them to the physical file until end of the subfile is read (indicator **72** is on).

Figure 16-19 Compile listing of the **RPG IV** program that adds records to a physical file via a subfile. (Continued)

59 This **WRITE** instruction adds the "changed" subfile record to the physical file. If a duplicate record condition occurs, the record will not be added, indicator **99** will be turned on, which will display the customer number in error and the error message **DUPLICATE CUST#** when the **EXFMT** instruction on line 66 is executed.

60 This **IF** instruction tests the status of indicator **99,** which was used to test for a duplicate record condition in the **WRITE** instruction on line 59.

62 When the **IF** instruction on line 60 test is "true," the **UPDATE** instruction will reverse image the customer number in error. Note that this instruction *does not* redisplay the subfile records; it only executes the reverse image function.

65 This **EVAL** instruction turns on indicator **81** that conditions the keywords **SFLDSP, SFLDSPCTL,** and **SFLEND** in the subfile control record (Sm03ctl).

66 This **EXFMT** instruction displays the subfile field values, constants, and + sign. When a duplicate customer number was tested in the **WRITE** instruction on line 59, the customer number in error and the error message **DUPLICATE CUST#** will display with the other field values.

67 This **EVAL** instruction turns off indicator **81.**

68 The instructions following this **ELSE** operation are executed if the test for the **IF** instruction on line 60 is false (no duplicate record condition).

69 This **EVAL** instruction increments the subfile record counter **(Sfrrno)** by 1.

70 This **ENDIF** operation ends the **IF** group that began on line 60.

71 This **READC** instruction reads another "changed" record from the subfile. If the subfile is at end, indicator **72** will be turned on. When control returns to the **DOW** instruction on line 58, the relational test will be "false," transferring control to the **EVAL** instruction on line 78 to end the program.

72 This **ENDDO** operation ends the **DOW** group that began on line 58.

74 The **EXSR** instruction branches control to the ClearSR subroutine, where the subfile is cleared and the subfile record counter is initialized to zero.

75 This **Eoj TAG** instruction is the label for the **CABEQ** instruction on line 36.

76 This **ENDDO** operation ends the **DOU** group that began on line 29. If **F3** was pressed to end the job, the **DOU** test at this instruction will exit the **DOU** group and execute the **EVAL** instruction on line 78 to end the job.

78 This **EVAL** instruction turns on indicator **LR** to end the job.

82 The **BEGSR** instruction begins the ClearSR subroutine.

83 This **EVAL** instruction turns on indicator **80,** which conditions the **SFLCLR** and **SFLINZ** keywords in the subfile control record to clear the subfile and initialize the fields to zeros and blanks.

84 This **WRITE** instruction executes the subfile control record **(Sm03ctl)** to clear and initialize the subfile record field values.

85 This **EVAL** instruction turns off indicator **80.**

86 This **EVAL** instruction initializes the subfile record counter **(Sfrrno)** to zero.

87 The **SETOFF** instruction is a housekeeping function that turns off indicators **71** and **72** used in the **WRITE** and **READC** instructions.

88 The **ENDSR** operation ends the ClearSR subroutine.

Figure 16-19 Compile listing of the **RPG IV** program that adds records to a physical file via a subfile. (Continued)

Execution of the subfile addition program generates the displays illustrated in Figure 16-20. The first display shown (**Entry** record) supports the entry of data to load the subfile; the second is a display of the subfile (**Sm03sfr, Sm03ctl,** and **Cmdline** records) after it is loaded. Under control of the subfile display, the user has the option to move the cursor to any record and modify one or all of the field values. To see the truncated subfile record field values (ZIPCODE and ACTBALANCE), the operator must press **F8.** This action folds the two hidden field values onto the next line for review and/or change. As explained in Figure 16-18, folding the subfile record field values is controlled by the **SFLDROP** keyword in the subfile control record format **Sm03ctl.**

Displayed Entry Record Format:

```
        12/01/97      CUSTOMER FILE ADDITION        11:15:00

                  CUST#:      20000

                  NAME:       PAUL GAUGUIN

                  STREET:     12 TAHITI PLACE

                  CITY:       PACIFIC

                  STATE:      CA

                  ZIP:        09900

                  BALANCE:        10012


              F3 - EOJ     F5 - REDISPLAY    F7 - END LOAD

                    ENTER - LOAD TO SUBFILE
```

Displayed SM03CTL, SM03SFR, and CMDLINE Subfile Record Formats:

```
                       CUSTOMER FILE ADDITION

CUSTNO            NAME                 STREET                CITY         STATE
 ZIP      BALANCE

 20000     PAUL GAUGUIN          12 TAHITI PLACE           PACIFIC              CA
09900 00010012
 35000     EDWARD MONET          4 IMPRESSIONIST ROAD      MILAN                PA
04444 00089500
 40000     HENRI MATISSE         44 RUE PIGALLE            FRANCE               KY
07777 00034910
 90000     PIERRE RENOIR         96 MONTCLAIR DRIVE        PARIS                NY
01111 00100000                                                                     +



         PRESS ENTER TO ADD RECORDS                      F8 TO FOLD RECORDS
```

Figure 16-20 Displays of the **Entry** and the subfile's **SM03SFR, SM03CTL,** and **CMDLINE** records.

WINDOWS

Windowing is the superimposing of one or more displays within the body of one or more existing displays. Figure 16-21 illustrates a window format displayed within the body of an underlying display. The syntax for windows may be supplied by the programmer or with special keywords supplied by DDS for display files.

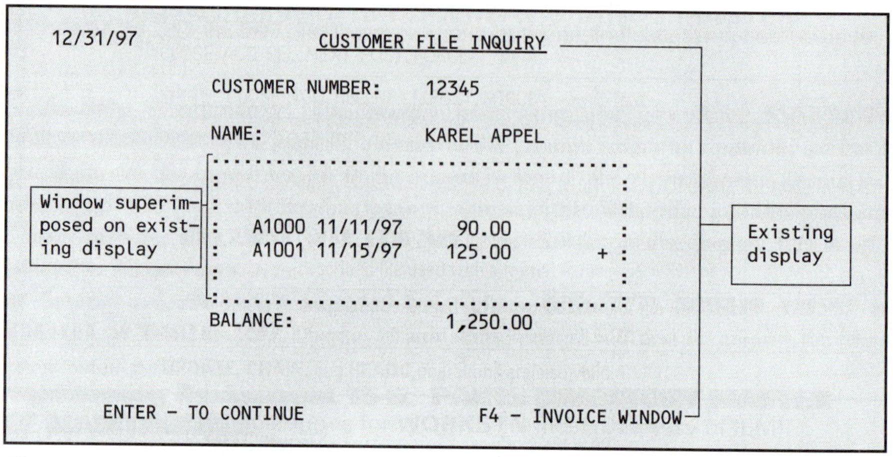

Figure 16-21 Window example.

Window Keywords

Display file keywords unique to windows are **WINDOW, WDWBORDER, WDWTITLE, RMVWDW,** and **USRRSTDSP.** The function of each keyword is explained in Figure 16-22. For a detailed discussion of the window keywords, refer to the chapter for display files in IBM's latest DDS manual.

Keyword	Function
WINDOW	Defines the display file record as a window format. The row, column, width, and height of the window are defined with this keyword.
WDWBORDER	Defines the window border attributes including ***CHAR, *DSPATR,** and ***COLOR.** Supplies the top and bottom lines and left and right border characters.
WDWTITLE	Defines the text, color, and display attributes for a title that will be displayed within the top or bottom border of a window
RMVWDW	Removes all window formats from the display before the current window is displayed.
USRRSTDSP	Removes the underlying display before the related window is displayed. Use of this keyword supports any number of window displays at one time. The limit is 12 if this keyword is not specified.

Figure 16-22 DDS keywords for windows.

The `WINDOW` Keyword

The syntax for the two formats of the **WINDOW** keyword and its parameters and functions are detailed in Figure 16-23.

The following two formats of the **WINDOW** keyword are supplied by DDS:

Format 1:

```
WINDOW(starting-line starting-column lines columns [*NOMSGLIN | *MSGLIN])

WINDOW(7 20 5 28)
```

Format 2:

```
WINDOW(*DFT lines columns [*NOMSGLIN | *MSGLIN])

WINDOW(*DFT 5 28)
```

Parameter	Function
starting-line	Defines the line number where the window's top left corner is positioned. In lieu of a digit, the entry may be a variable name defined as a three-byte packed field with 0 decimal positions in the DDS program. The name must include an ampersand (&) prefix.
starting-column	Defines the column number where the window's top left corner is positioned. In lieu of a digit, the entry may be a variable name defined as a three-byte packed field with 0 decimal positions in the DDS program. The name must include an ampersand (&) prefix.
***DFT**	This entry may be used to replace the programmer-supplied starting-line and starting-column values. When specified, the system will determine where to position the window.
lines	Defines the number of lines for the window. The value specified does not include the two border (upper and lower) lines. A numeric literal must be specified for this value.
columns	Defines the number of columns used by the window. The value specified does not include the window borders. A numeric literal must be specified for this value.
***NOMSGLIN**	An optional entry that controls the display of status messages on the last line of the window. If specified, the last line of the window is reserved for application messages. When not specified, the last line is reserved for system-supplied messages.

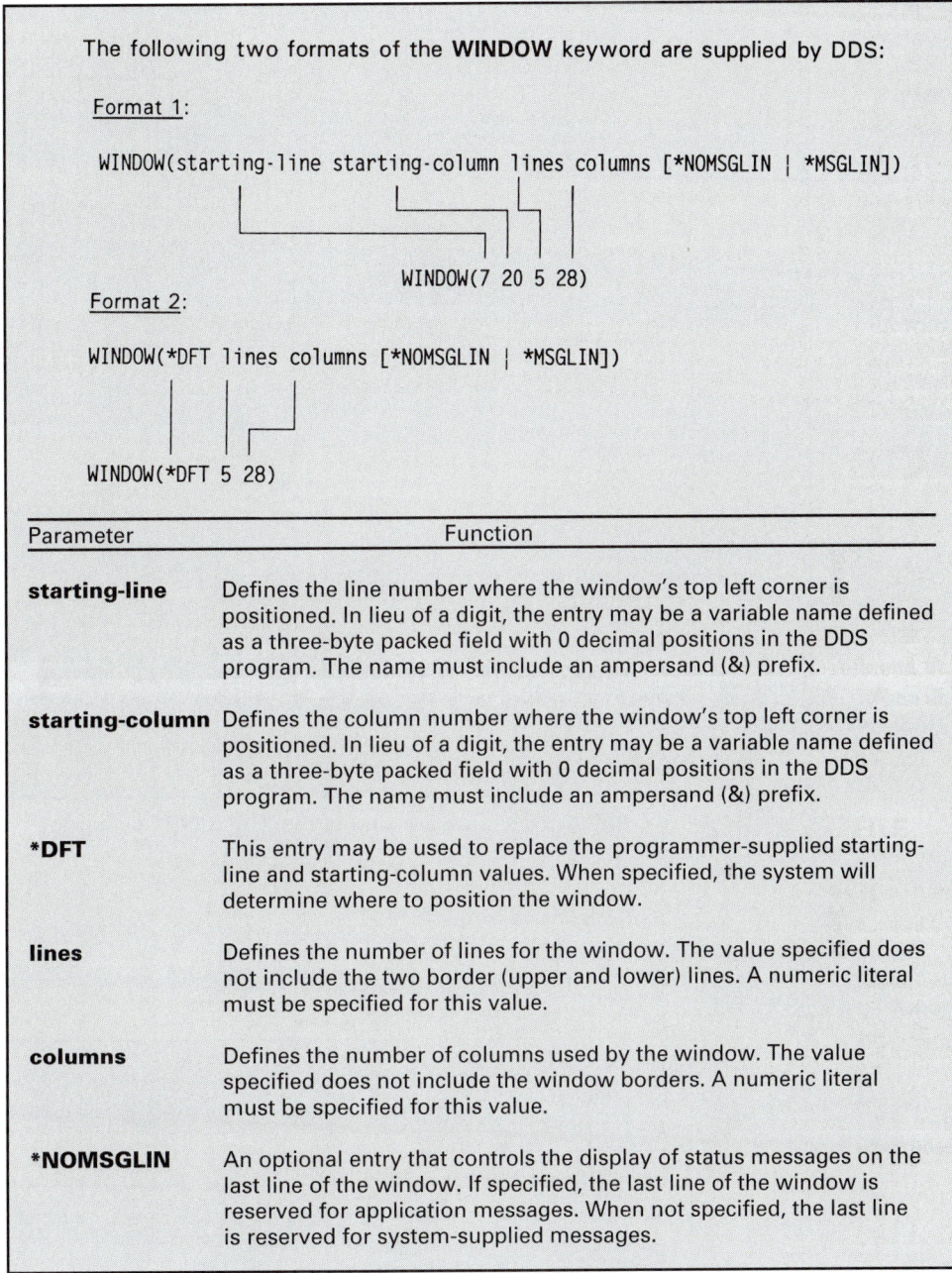

Figure 16-23 Syntax of the **WINDOW** keyword.

Figure 16-24 shows the relationship of the entries in a **WINDOW** keyword to its related display.

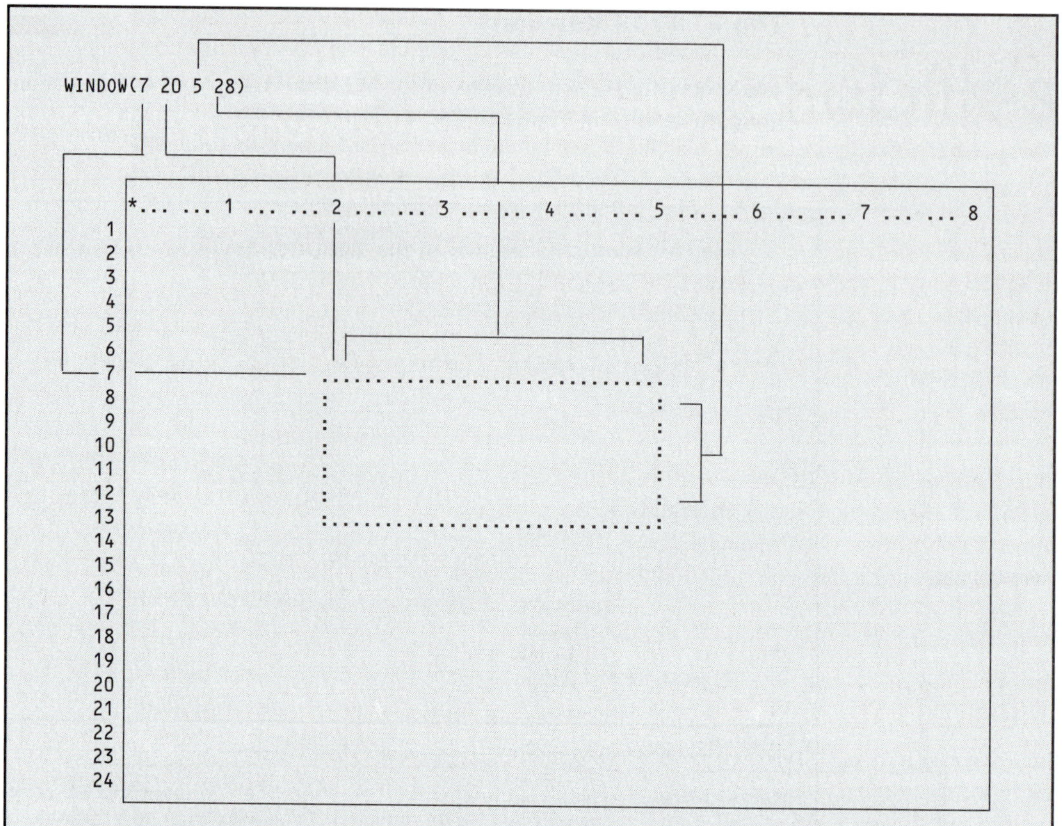

Note: The number of horizontal values is 4 greater than the 28 WINDOW entry. Two extra characters are automatically inserted for the one-byte character attribute. The additional two characters are provided to accommodate the usable window area, which does not include the borders. The vertical borders include one extra character than the 5 specified in the WINDOW keyword. This provides for five usable lines within the border.

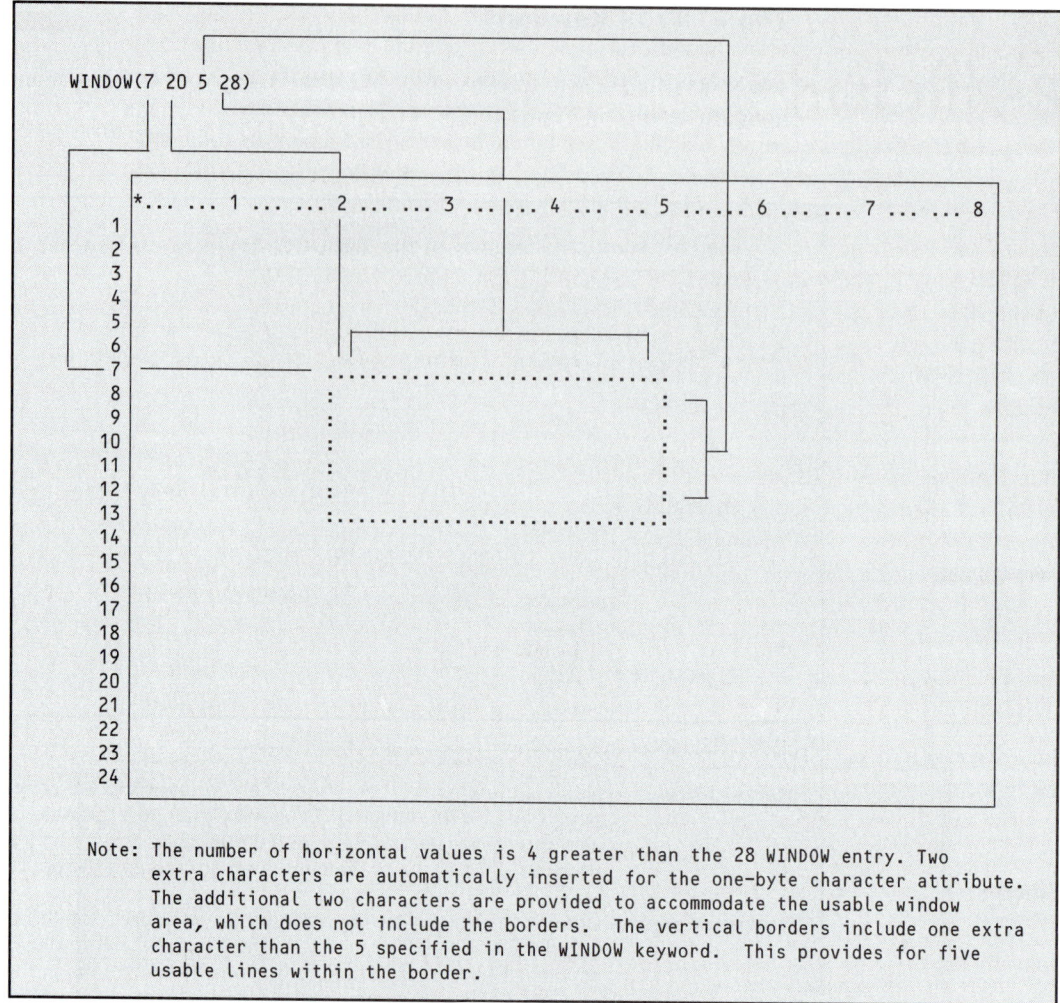

Figure 16-24 Relationship of the **WINDOW** keyword to a display.

The WDWBORDER Keyword

The syntax and parameters of the **WDWBORDER** keyword are explained in Figure 16-25.

WDWBORDER Format:

WDWBORDER((ctrl-parm1 options) (ctrl-parm2 options) (crtl-parm3 options))

Parameter	Options	Function
***CHAR**	any 8 characters	A window border must include 8 characters that have the following functions in the indicated order: 1. Top left corner 2. Top row border 3. Top right corner 4. Left column border 5. Right column border 6. Bottom left corner 7. Bottom row border 8. Bottom right corner

Figure 16-25 **WDWBORDER** parameters and options.

		Example: WDWBORDER((*CHAR'+ - + | | + - +'))
***DSPATR**	BL, CS, HI, ND, RI, UL	Only one display attribute may be specified for a window border. All are valid for monochrome or color displays. HI (highlight) is the default for monochrome displays and normal for color. Example: WDWBORDER((*DSPATR RI))
***COLOR**	BLU, GRN, PNK, RED, TRQ, WHT, YLW	Only one color may be specified for a window border. The color parameter is ignored by monochrome displays. Example: WDWBORDER((*COLOR GRN))

Figure 16-25 WDWBORDER parameters and options. (Continued)

The relationship of the **WDWBORDER** keyword and its related display is shown in Figure 16-26.

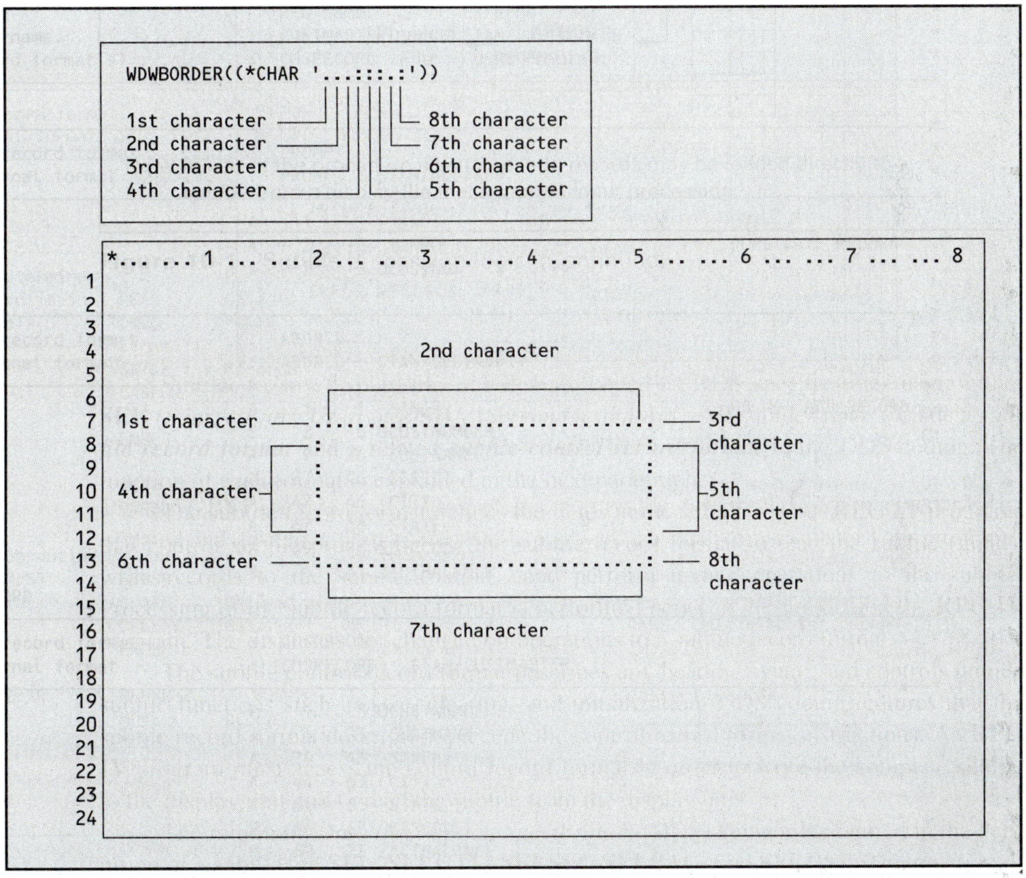

Figure 16-26 Relationship of the **WDWBORDER** keyword to a display.

The format **WDWBORDER** ((***CHAR** '...:::.:')) is only one of any number of ***CHAR** parameter options that may be used. A programmer may specify any combination of characters that he or she finds acceptable for the window borders. Figure 16-27 illustrates a few other window border patterns that are often used.

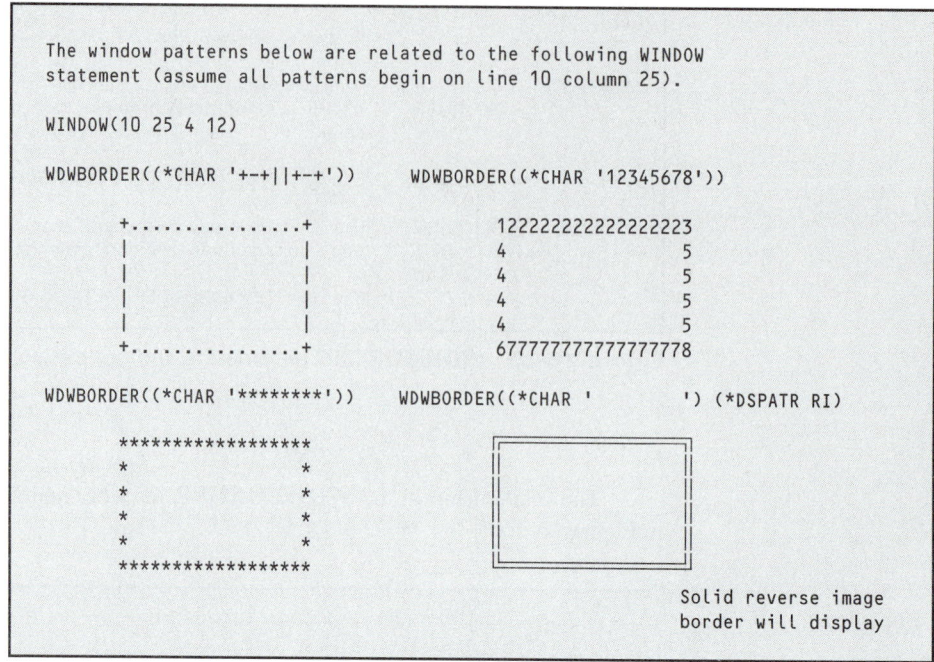

```
The window patterns below are related to the following WINDOW
statement (assume all patterns begin on line 10 column 25).

WINDOW(10 25 4 12)

WDWBORDER((*CHAR '+-+||+-+'))        WDWBORDER((*CHAR '12345678'))

      +...............+                     122222222222222223
      |               |                     4                5
      |               |                     4                5
      |               |                     4                5
      |               |                     4                5
      +...............+                     677777777777777778

WDWBORDER((*CHAR '********'))       WDWBORDER((*CHAR '        ') (*DSPATR RI)

      ******************
      *                *
      *                *
      *                *
      *                *
      ******************
```

Solid reverse image
border will display

Figure 16-27 Window border pattern examples.

EXAMPLE SUBFILE PROGRAM USING WINDOWING

A source listing of a display file that includes five record formats is shown in Figure 16-28.

The function of the record formats included in the display file are explained in the following paragraphs.

```
SEQNBR*...+... 1 ...+... 2 ...+... 3 ...+... 4 ...+... 5 ...+... 6 ...+... 7 ...+... 8
         * Customers/Invoices inquiry with windowing....

        A                                      MSGLOC(04)
        A                                      REF(STAN/CUSTOMERS)
        A                                      PRINT
         * Prompt display....
        A          R PROMPT
        A                                      CA03(03 'END OF JOB')
        A                                  1  3DATE EDTCDE(Y)
        A                                  1 32'CUSTOMER FILE INQUIRY'
        A                                  1 71TIME
        A                                  3 10'ENTER CUSTOMER NO:'
        A            CUSTNUM        5   I  3 29DSPATR(RI)
        A  99                                  ERRMSG('RECORD NOT FOUND' 99)
        A                                  9 18'F3 - EOJ'
        A                                  9 50'ENTER KEY - INQUIRY'
         * Inquiry display....

        A          R INQRCD
        A                                      CF04(04 'DISPLAY WINDOW')
        A                                  1  3DATE EDTCDE(Y)
        A                                  1 30'CUSTOMER FILE INQUIRY' DSPATR(UL)
        A                                  3 20'CUSTOMER NUMBER:' DSPATR(HI)
        A            CUSTOMERNOR        O  3 40
        A                                  5 20'NAME:' DSPATR(HI)
        A            CUSTNAME  R        O  5 40
        A                                  7 20'STREET:' DSPATR(HI)
```

Display for entering
a customer number

Figure 16-28 Source listing of the display file that processes a subfile with windows.

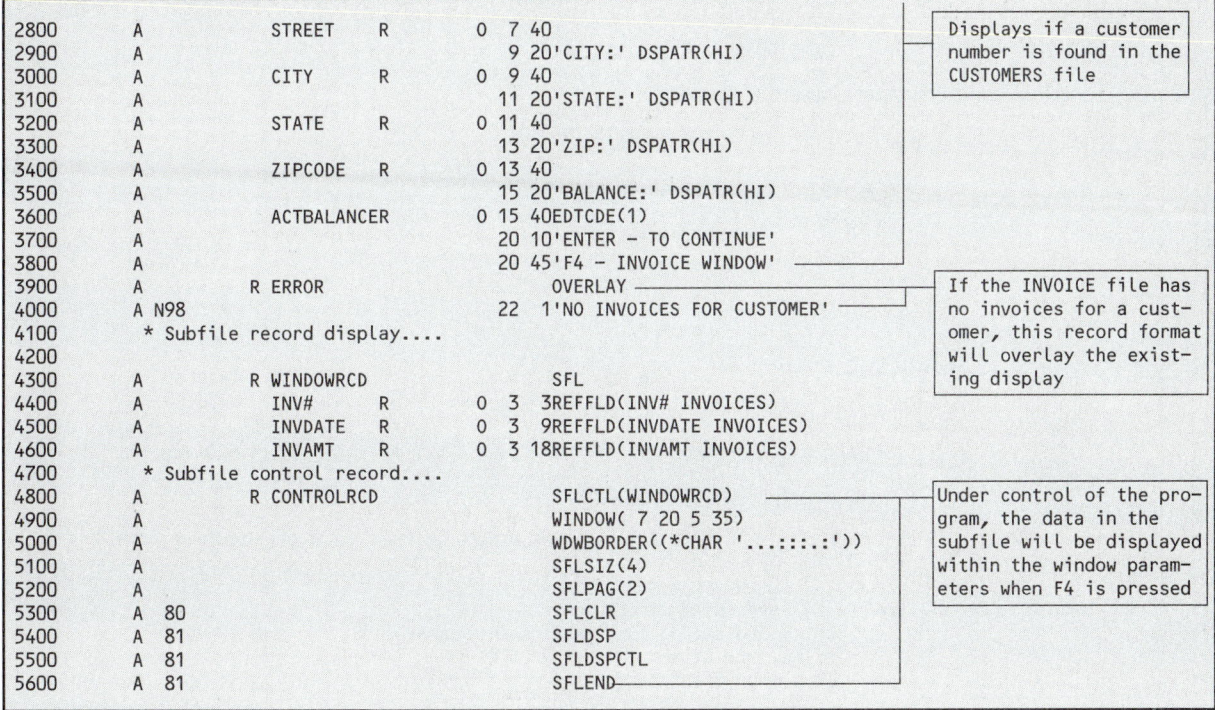

```
2800    A          STREET     R     0  7 40
2900    A                              9 20'CITY:' DSPATR(HI)
3000    A          CITY       R     0  9 40
3100    A                             11 20'STATE:' DSPATR(HI)
3200    A          STATE      R     0 11 40
3300    A                             13 20'ZIP:' DSPATR(HI)
3400    A          ZIPCODE    R     0 13 40
3500    A                             15 20'BALANCE:' DSPATR(HI)
3600    A          ACTBALANCER      0 15 40EDTCDE(1)
3700    A                             20 10'ENTER - TO CONTINUE'
3800    A                             20 45'F4 - INVOICE WINDOW'
3900    A        R ERROR                   OVERLAY
4000    A N98                         22  1'NO INVOICES FOR CUSTOMER'
4100     * Subfile record display....
4200
4300    A        R WINDOWRCD               SFL
4400    A          INV#       R     0  3  3REFFLD(INV# INVOICES)
4500    A          INVDATE    R     0  3  9REFFLD(INVDATE INVOICES)
4600    A          INVAMT     R     0  3 18REFFLD(INVAMT INVOICES)
4700     * Subfile control record....
4800    A        R CONTROLRCD              SFLCTL(WINDOWRCD)
4900    A                                  WINDOW( 7 20 5 35)
5000    A                                  WDWBORDER((*CHAR '...:::.:'))
5100    A                                  SFLSIZ(4)
5200    A                                  SFLPAG(2)
5300    A  80                              SFLCLR
5400    A  81                              SFLDSP
5500    A  81                              SFLDSPCTL
5600    A  81                              SFLEND
```

Displays if a customer number is found in the CUSTOMERS file

If the INVOICE file has no invoices for a customer, this record format will overlay the existing display

Under control of the program, the data in the subfile will be displayed within the window parameters when F4 is pressed

Figure 16-28 Source listing of the display file that processes a subfile with windows. (Continued)

- **PROMPT record**—First record displayed. Provides for the entry of a customer number, error message display **(RECORD NOT FOUND),** and end-of-job control.
- **INQRCD record**—Second record displayed after customer number is entered via the PROMPT screen accesses the related record in the physical file. This display writes over the PROMPT screen. Error message on line 4000 is displayed when the user presses **F4** to display subfile window and no records for the customer are stored in INVOICES. If records are stored in INVOICES, the subfile window will display with two records shown. User may roll to examine any other invoices stored in the subfile for the customer.
- **WINDOWRCD record**—Defines the subfile record format. Because only one **REF** keyword may be included in a display file, **REFFLD** keywords must reference the field attributes of INVOICES, the second physical file processed by the program. The data from INVOICES is the input to the subfile window.
- **CONTROLRCD record**—Defines the subfile control record, which references the subfile record WINDOWRCD and controls the display of the window and the subfile's data; both within the INQRCD display.

The display images are shown in Figure 16-29.

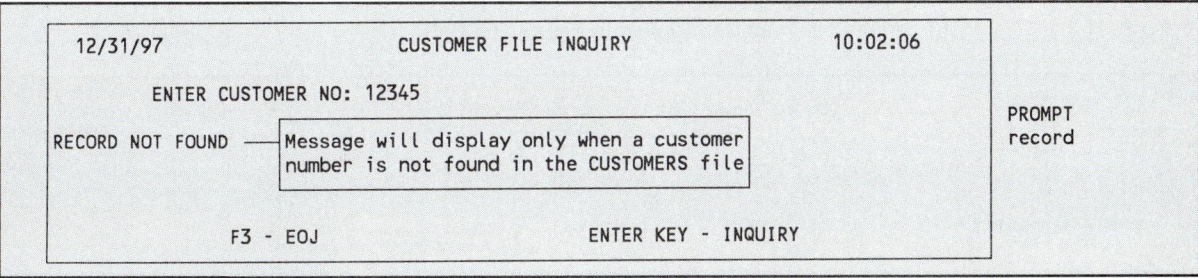

```
 12/31/97              CUSTOMER FILE INQUIRY              10:02:06

          ENTER CUSTOMER NO: 12345
                                                                      PROMPT
RECORD NOT FOUND ---Message will display only when a customer         record
                    number is not found in the CUSTOMERS file


              F3 - EOJ                  ENTER KEY - INQUIRY
```

Figure 16-29 Record images of the display file that supports windowing.

```
12/31/97              CUSTOMER FILE INQUIRY

                CUSTOMER NUMBER:     45678

                NAME:                MARC CHAGALL

                STREET:              222 QUAIL AVENUE

                CITY:                BRIDGEPORT

                STATE:               CT

                ZIP:                 06666

                BALANCE:                 926.00                 INQRCD
                                                                record



       ENTER - TO CONTINUE               F4 - INVOICE WINDOW

    NO INVOICES FOR CUSTOMER  —— Message will display only when F4 is
                                 pressed and no invoices for the cust-
                                 omer are stored in the INVOICES file.
```

```
12/31/97              CUSTOMER FILE INQUIRY

                CUSTOMER NUMBER:     12345

                NAME:                KAREL APPEL
                :.....................................:
                :                                     :
                :   A1000 11/11/97      90.00         :     INQRCD, WINDOWR,
                :   A1001 11/15/97     125.00       + :     and CONTROLR
                :                                     :     records
                :.....................................:

                BALANCE:                 1,250.00

 Window is displayed when operator
 presses F4 and the INVOICES file
 contains records for the customer

       ENTER - TO CONTINUE               F4 - INVOICE WINDOW
```

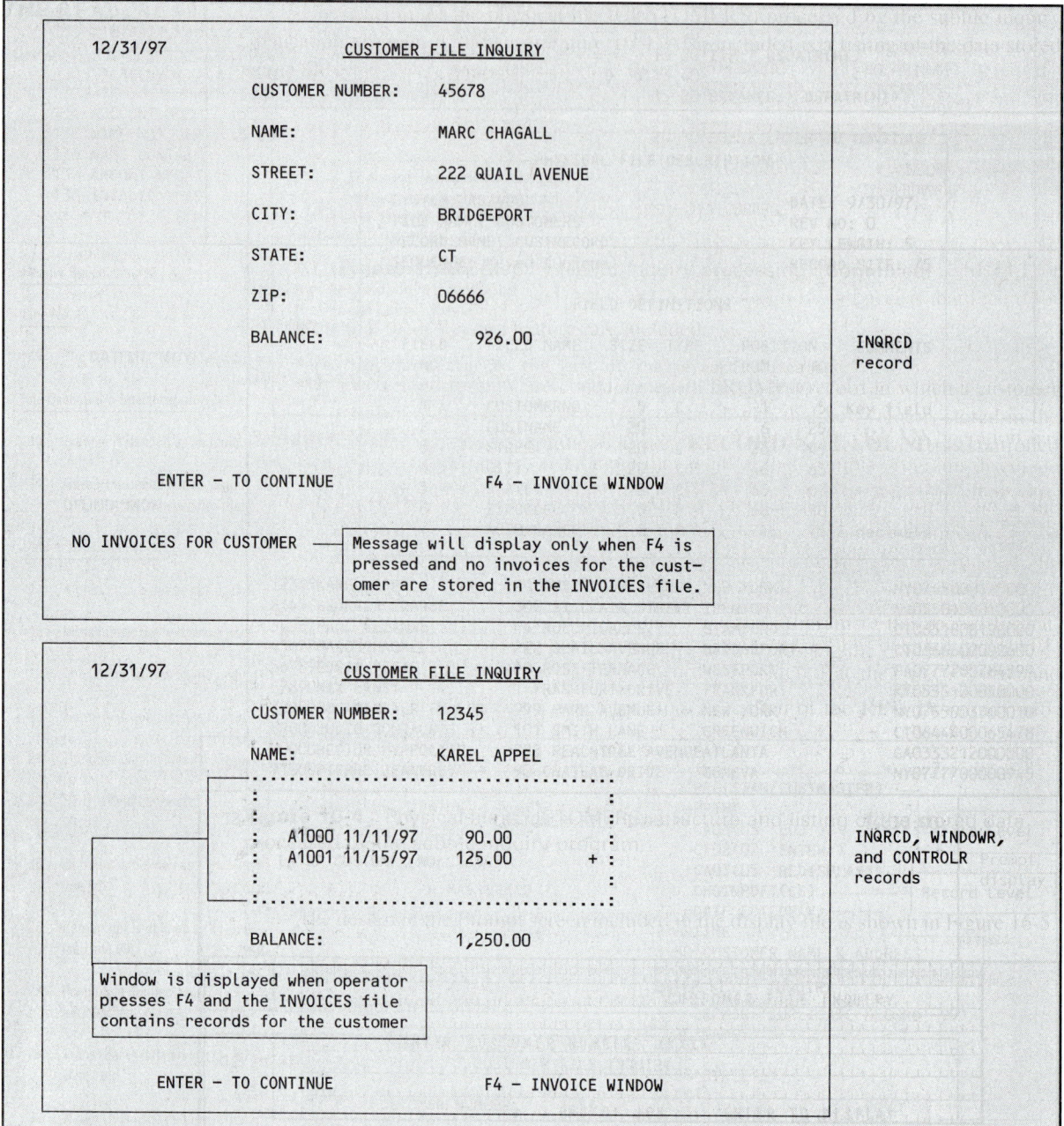

Figure 16-29 Record images of the display file that supports windowing. (Continued)

A detailed compile listing of the **RPG IV** program that processes the display file that supports windowing is presented in Figure 16-30.

```
Line   <--------------------- Source Specifications ----------------------------><---- Comments ----> Do
Number ....1....+....2....+....3....+....4....+....5....+....6....+....7....+....8....+....9....+...10 Num
                          S o u r c e   L i s t i n g
       * Customers file inquiry of two files with windowing....

       FSflwindow CF   E              WORKSTN SFILE(Windowrcd:Sfrrno)
```

Figure 16-30 Compile listing of an **RPG IV** program that processes a subfile that supports windowing.

```
     *--------------------------------------------------------------------------------------*
     *                             RPG name         External name                           *
     * File name. . . . . . . . :  SFLWINDOW        STAN/SFLWINDOW                          *
     * Record format(s) . . . . :  PROMPT           PROMPT                                  *
     *                             INQRCD           INQRCD                                  *
     *                             ERROR            ERROR                                   *
     *                             WINDOWRCD        WINDOWRCD                               *
     *                             CONTROLRCD       CONTROLRCD                              *
     *--------------------------------------------------------------------------------------*
   4 FCustomers IF   E           K DISK
     *--------------------------------------------------------------------------------------*
     *                             RPG name         External name                           *
     * File name. . . . . . . . :  CUSTOMERS        STAN/CUSTOMERS                          *
     * Record format(s) . . . . :  CUSTRECORD       CUSTRECORD                              *
     *--------------------------------------------------------------------------------------*
   5 FInvoices  IF   E           K DISK
   6
     *--------------------------------------------------------------------------------------*
     *                             RPG name         External name                           *
     * File name. . . . . . . . :  INVOICES         STAN/INVOICES                           *
     * Record format(s) . . . . :  INVRCD           INVRCD                                  *
     *--------------------------------------------------------------------------------------*
   7 D Sfrrno          S              4  0                                  record counter
   8
   9=IPROMPT
     *--------------------------------------------------------------------------------------*
     * RPG record format  . . . :  PROMPT                                                   *
     * External format  . . . . :  PROMPT : STAN/SFLWINDOW                                  *
     *--------------------------------------------------------------------------------------*
  10=I                            A    1    1  *IN03                        END OF JOB
  11=I                            A    2    2  *IN99                        RECORD NOT FOUND
  12=I                            A    3    7  CUSTNUM
  13=IINQRCD
     *--------------------------------------------------------------------------------------*
     * RPG record format  . . . :  INQRCD                                                   *
     * External format  . . . . :  INQRCD : STAN/SFLWINDOW                                  *
     *--------------------------------------------------------------------------------------*
  14=I                            A    1    1  *IN04                        DISPLAY WINDOW
  15=IERROR                                                                 DISPLAY WINDOW
     *--------------------------------------------------------------------------------------*
     * RPG record format  . . . :  ERROR                                                    *
     * External format  . . . . :  ERROR : STAN/SFLWINDOW                                   *
     *--------------------------------------------------------------------------------------*
  16=IWINDOWRCD                                                             DISPLAY WINDOW
     *--------------------------------------------------------------------------------------*
     * RPG record format  . . . :  WINDOWRCD                                                *
     * External format  . . . . :  WINDOWRCD : STAN/SFLWINDOW                               *
     *--------------------------------------------------------------------------------------*
  17=I                            A    1    5  INV#
  18=I                            S    6   11 0INVDATE
  19=I                            S   12   18 2INVAMT
  20=ICONTROLRCD
     *--------------------------------------------------------------------------------------*
     * RPG record format  . . . :  CONTROLRCD                                               *
     * External format  . . . . :  CONTROLRCD : STAN/SFLWINDOW                              *
     *--------------------------------------------------------------------------------------*
  21=ICUSTRECORD
     *--------------------------------------------------------------------------------------*
     * RPG record format  . . . :  CUSTRECORD                                               *
     * External format  . . . . :  CUSTRECORD : STAN/CUSTOMERS                              *
     *--------------------------------------------------------------------------------------*
  22=I                            A    1    5  CUSTOMERNO
  23=I                            A    6   25  CUSTNAME
  24=I                            A   26   45  STREET
  25=I                            A   46   65  CITY
  26=I                            A   66   67  STATE
  27=I                            A   68   72  ZIPCODE
  28=I                            P   73   77 2ACTBALANCE
  29=IINVRCD
```

Figure 16-30 Compile listing of an **RPG IV** program that processes a subfile that supports windowing. (Continued)

```
     *--------------------------------------------------------------------------------------------*
     * RPG record format  . . . . :  INVRCD                                                       *
     * External format  . . . . . :  INVRCD : STAN/INVOICES                                       *
     *--------------------------------------------------------------------------------------------*
30=I                                A    1    5 CUSTNO
31=I                                A    6   10 INV#
32=I                                P   11   14 0INVDATE
33=I                                P   15   18 2INVAMT
34 C                      EXFMT     Prompt                                display prompt rcd
35 C                      DOW       *IN03 = *OFF                          end of job?         B01
36 C      Custnum         CHAIN     Customers                   99----    get pf record        01
37 C                      IF        *IN99 = *OFF                          record found?       B02
38
39  * Display Inqrcd record with related customer data....
40 C                      EXFMT     Inqrcd                                display Inqrcd rcd   02
41 C                      EVAL      *IN80 = *ON                           turn on clear indctr 02
42 C                      WRITE     Controlrcd                            execute sfl clear    02
43 C                      EVAL      *IN80 = *OFF                          turn off indicator   02
44
45 C                      EVAL      Sfrrno = *ZERO                        Initialize counter   02
46 C                      SETOFF                                71----    turn off indicator   02
47
48  * If no records for customer in Invoices and F4 is pressed
49  * (window requested), display error message at bottom of screen....
50 C      Custnum         SETLL     Invoices                    ----98     find record         02
51 C                      IF        *IN98 = *OFF AND *IN04 = *ON          rcd not fnd & 04 on B03
52 C                      EXFMT     ERROR                                 display error msg    03
53 C                      ENDIF                                           end IF group        E03
54
55  * If records for customer in Invoices & subfile not at end & Invoices
56  * not at end, load subfile with a record....
57 C                      DOW       *IN98 = *ON AND *IN71 = *OFF          rcd fd & fle not end B03
58 C      Custnum         READE     invoices                    ----71    read equal pf record 03
59 C                      EVAL      Sfrrno = Sfrrno + 1                   increment counter    03
60 C                      IF        *IN71 = *OFF                          eof Invoices test   B04
61 C                      WRITE     Windowrcd                   ----71    load subfile         04
62 C                      ENDIF                                           end IF group        E04
63 C                      ENDDO                                           end dow group       E03
64
65  * If records at found in Invoices and F4 pressed, display subfile....
66 C                      IF        *IN98 = *ON AND *IN04 = *ON           rcd fnd & F4 pressed B03
67 C                      EVAL      *IN81 = *ON                           sf display indicator 03
68 C                      EXFMT     Controlrcd                            display sf window    03
69 C                      EVAL      *IN81 = *OFF                          turn off dsp indcatr 03
70 C                      ENDIF                                           end line 66 IF group E03
71 C                      ENDIF                                           end line 37 IF group E02
72
73  * Display Prompt record to continue inquiry or end the program....
74 C                      EXFMT     Prompt                                display prompt rcd   01
75 C                      ENDDO                                           end line 35 DOW grp  E01
76
77 C                      EVAL      *INLR = *ON                           end of job control
78=OPROMPT
     *--------------------------------------------------------------------------------------------*
     * RPG record format  . . . . :  PROMPT                                                       *
     * External format  . . . . . :  PROMPT : STAN/SFLWINDOW                                      *
     *--------------------------------------------------------------------------------------------*
79=O                       *IN99               1A CHAR        1           RECORD NOT FOUND
80=OINQRCD
     *--------------------------------------------------------------------------------------------*
     * RPG record format  . . . . :  INQRCD                                                       *
     * External format  . . . . . :  INQRCD : STAN/SFLWINDOW                                      *
     *--------------------------------------------------------------------------------------------*
81=O                       CUSTOMERNO          5A CHAR        5
82=O                       CUSTNAME           25A CHAR       20
83=O                       STREET             45A CHAR       20
84=O                       CITY               65A CHAR       20
85=O                       STATE              67A CHAR        2
86=O                       ZIPCODE            72A CHAR        5
87=O                       ACTBALANCE         80S ZONE      8,2
```

Figure 16-30 Compile listing of an **RPG IV** program that processes a subfile that supports windowing. (Continued)

```
88=OERROR
    *--------------------------------------------------------------------------------*
    * RPG record format  . . . . :  ERROR                                            *
    * External format  . . . . . :  ERROR : STAN/SFLWINDOW                           *
    *--------------------------------------------------------------------------------*
89=O                          *IN98                 1A CHAR        1
90=OWINDOWRCD
    *--------------------------------------------------------------------------------*
    * RPG record format  . . . . :  WINDOWRCD                                        *
    * External format  . . . . . :  WINDOWRCD : STAN/SFLWINDOW                       *
    *--------------------------------------------------------------------------------*
91=O                          INV#                  5A CHAR        5
92=O                          INVDATE              11S ZONE       6,0
93=O                          INVAMT               18S ZONE       7,2
94=OCONTROLRCD
    *--------------------------------------------------------------------------------*
    * RPG record format  . . . . :  CONTROLRCD                                       *
    * External format  . . . . . :  CONTROLRCD : STAN/SFLWINDOW                      *
    *--------------------------------------------------------------------------------*
95=O                          *IN80                 1A CHAR        1
96=O                          *IN81                 2A CHAR        1
```

File Description Specifications:

Line No.

3 Sflwindow is defined as a combined (**C** in position 17), full-procedural (**F** in position 18), externally described (**E** in position 22), **WORKSTN** (workstation) display file.

The **SFILE(Windowrcd:Sfrrno)** keyword indicates that this display file supports a subfile (**SFILE** keyword), with a subfile record name **Windowrcd,** and **Sfrrno** as the subfile record counter. Note that a colon must be included between the subfile record name and the subfile record counter. With the exception of the **SFILE** keyword, the other entries are programmer-supplied.

4 Customers is defined as an input (**I** in position 17), full-procedural (**F** in position 18), externally described (**E** in position 22), keyed (**K** in position 34) physical file. Records for each customer are stored in this file.

5 Invoices is defined as an input (**I** in position 17), full-procedural (**F** in position 18), externally described (**E** in position 22), keyed (**K** in position 34) physical file. Invoice records for each customer are stored in this file.

Definition Specifications:

7 Sfrrno is defined as a standalone field which is used as the subfile record counter.

Calculation Specifications:

34 This **EXFMT** instruction displays the Prompt screen in which a customer number may be entered or **F3** pressed to end the job.

35 This **DOW** group is performed until the operator presses **F3** while the Prompt screen is displayed to pass control to line 77 to end the job. If **F3** is not pressed, control will continue with the next instruction.

36 The **CHAIN** instruction uses the Custnum value, entered in the Prompt screen, to search the Customers file for an equal key. If the record is found, indicator **99,** entered in the *Resulting Indicator Hi* field (positions 71–72), will *not* be turned on.

37 This **IF** instruction tests the status of indicator **99** specified with the previous **CHAIN** instruction. An "off" condition indicates that a record in the Customers file was found with a key equal to the value in Custnum. An "on" condition indicates that a record was not found with a key equal to the value in the Custnum field. When **99** is turned on, the error message **RECORD NOT FOUND** will display in the Prompt screen.

40 When the **IF** test on line 37 is true, this **EXFMT** instruction will display the Inqrcd screen "filled in" with field values from the current Customers file record.

41 This **EVAL** instruction turns on indicator **80,** which is specified in the display file's Controlrcd record to control clearing of the subfile before any records from the Invoices file are loaded.

42 This **WRITE** instruction executes the subfile's control record (Controlrcd), which clears the subfile (Windowrcd) storage area in memory.

43 This **EVAL** instruction turns off indicator **80.**

45 This **EVAL** instruction initializes the subfile record counter (Sfrrno) to zero.

46 The **SETOFF** instruction is a housekeeping function that turns off indicator **71.**

50 The **SETLL** instruction uses the Custnum value, input in the Prompt screen, to position the "pointer" in the Invoices file to a record with the same key value. *Resulting Indicator* **98,** entered in the *Eq* field (positions 75–76), will turn on if a record with the same key value is found.

51 This compound **IF** instruction tests the status of indicator **98,** specified with the **SETLL** instruction on line 51, and indicator **04,** turned on when the operator presses **F4** to display the subfile. When indicator **98** is "off," indicating that no records are stored in the Invoices file for the current customer, and indicator **04** is on, an error message will display at the bottom of the Inqrcd screen.

Figure 16-30 Compile listing of an **RPG IV** program that processes a subfile that supports windowing. (Continued)

52	This **EXFMT** instruction is executed when the compound **IF** instruction is "true," which displays the error message **NO INVOICES FOR CUSTOMER** at the bottom of the Inqrcd screen.
53	This **ENDIF** operation ends the **IF** group that began on line 51.
57	This **DOW** instruction is executed if a record was found in the Invoices file for the current customer (indicator **98** is "on") and the Invoices file is *not* at end or the subfile is *not* full (indicator **71** off for either condition).
58	The **READE** instruction reads a record from the Invoices file equal to the key value in the Custnum field. *Resulting Indicator* **71,** entered in the *Eq* field (positions 75–76), will turn on when an equal key is *not* found or when an end-of-file condition is read in the Invoices file.
59	This **EVAL** instruction increments the subfile record counter **(Sffrno)** by 1 so that the current record will be loaded into its related subfile's relative record position.
60	This **IF** instruction tests the status of indicator **71.** When it is off, the **READE** instruction on line 58 was successful (an equal customer number was found or the Invoices file is *not* at the end).
61	This **WRITE** instruction adds an Invoices file record to the subfile. *Resulting Indicator* **71,** entered in the *Eq* field (positions 75–76), will turn on when the subfile is full.
62	This **ENDIF** operation ends the **IF** group that began on line 60.
63	This **ENDDO** operation ends the **DOW** group that began on line 57. Control is returned back to the **DOW** instruction on line 57, where the relational test is made.
66	This compound **IF** instruction tests the status of indicator **98** (specified with the **SETLL** instruction on line 50) and indicator **04,** turned on when the operator presses **F4** from the Inqrcd display. Indicator **98** is turned on when one record for the related customer is found in the Invoices file. Indicator **04** is turned on when the operator presses **F4** to display the subfile.
67	This **EVAL** instruction turns on indicator **81,** which conditions the keywords **SFLDSP, SFLDSPCTL,** and **SFLEND** in the subfile control record (Controlrcd). The keywords control display of the subfile records, constants, and + (plus sign), indicating more records.
68	This **EXFMT** instruction executes the subfile control record (Controlrcd), which displays two subfile records and the window border characters.
69	This **EVAL** instruction turns on indicator **81.**
70	This **ENDIF** operation ends the **IF** group that began on line 66.
71	This **ENDIF** operation ends the **IF** group that began on line 37.
74	This **EXFMT** instruction displays the Prompt record. The user may enter another customer number and continue the inquiry process by pressing ENTER, or end the job by pressing **F3.**
75	This **ENDDO** operation ends the **DOW** group that began on line 35 and passes control back to the **DOW** instruction where the end-of-job test is made (indicator **03** on?).
77	This **EVAL** instruction turns on indicator **LR** to end the program. This instruction is branched to when the **DOW** instruction on line 35 tests a "false" condition—indicator **03** is "on" after the operator presses **F3.**

Figure 16-30 Compile listing of an **RPG IV** program that processes a subfile that supports windowing. (Continued)

SUMMARY

A *subfile* is a temporary area in memory that records may be written to and read from a display file device. They may be used for any of the physical file maintenance functions when more than one record is to be displayed at one time.

Subfiles are created like any display file, with **SEU** or **SDA.** However, they must include special keywords that control their loading, display, and processing functions. At least *two* record formats must be specified in the display file that supports a subfile. The *subfile record,* which must be coded first in the DDS, defines the areas where the data is stored, and the *subfile control record* defines the processing functions. Subfile functions, including the number of records to display on the screen, number of records to be stored in the subfile, clearing of the screen, display of the subfile's data, display of constants, display of page continuation symbol, and overlay of an existing screen, are some of the functions that may be specified in the subfile control record.

An **RPG IV** program that processes a subfile must define it in the *File Description* statement for the related display file. A field for a record counter, the **SFILE** keyword, and the subfile record name must be specified in the definition of the display file. In the program, the *control record format* is usually executed first to clear the subfile area. Then the subfile is loaded and the control record format displayed again. Indicators that were assigned to select keywords in the subfile control record must be set on in the **RPG IV** program before the control record is executed.

Windowing is supported on the AS/400 by the keywords **WDWBORDER, WINDOW, USRRSTDSP,** and **RMVWDW.** Windows have horizontal and vertical borders that are superimposed on an existing display. The **RPG IV** program coding for windows follows standard display and, when specified, subfile processing logic.

QUESTIONS

16-1. Define a subfile as related to the AS/400 environment.

16-2. For what processing functions may a subfile be used?

16-3. How may a subfile be created?

16-4. Name the minimum number of record formats that must be included in the definition of a subfile. In what order must they be specified?

16-5. Refer to Question 16-4 and explain the function of each record format.

16-6. What is the minimum number of keywords that must be included in the definition of a subfile?

The following subfile terms relate to Questions 16-7 through 16-21:

Match the following keywords to their related definition:

a. SFL	**e. SFLDSP**	**i. SFLRNA**	**m. SFLMSG**
b. SFLCTL	**f. SFLCLR**	**j. SFLDSPCTL**	**n. SFLDROP**
c. SFLSIZ	**g. SFLINZ**	**k. SFLEND**	**o. SFLNXTCHG**
d. SFLPAG	**h. SFLDLT**	**l. SFLLIN**	

16-7. ___ Deletes a subfile from the current processing environment.

16-8. ___ Used in conjunction with another keyword that actually performs the initialization of a subfile's field values.

16-9. ___ Specifies the number of spaces between columns of subfile records when the subfile is displayed horizontally.

16-10. ___ Determines the number of records that may be stored in the subfile.

16-11. ___ Indicates the number of subfile records that may be displayed on the screen at one time.

16-12. ___ Specifies that the record format defined is a subfile control record format.

16-13. ___ Controls display of the records stored in the subfile record format.

16-14. ___ Initializes alphanumeric fields in the subfile to blanks and numeric fields to zeros.

16-15. ___ Supports the folding of truncated subfile record format field values.

16-16. ___ Identifies the subfile record format.

16-17. ___ Controls display of the constants and variables defined in the subfile control record format.

16-18. ___ Identifies on the CRT that more records are included in the subfile.

16-19. ___ Is the control record format keyword that supports the display of an error message.

16-20. ___ Enables **RPG IV** program to identify subfile records that have been modified.

16-21. ___ Clears the subfile of all records.

16-22. For inquiry processing, what *Usage* must be assigned to the subfile record's fields? What *Usage* is specified for update and for addition processing?

16-23. What **RPG IV** operation is used to read records from a subfile? In what resulting indicator field(s) must the indicator(s) be specified? What is the function of the indicator(s)?

Examine the following File Description Specifications and answer Questions 16-24 through 16-27:

```
.. 1 ...+... 2 ...+... 3 ...+... 4 ...+... 5 ...+... 6 ...+... 7 ...+
FFilename++IPEASFRlen+LKlen+AIDevice+.Keywords++++++++++++++++++++++++

FDemofile  CF   E             WORKSTN SFILE(Test:RR)
```

16-24. What is the function of the **SFILE** keyword?

16-25. What does the **Test** entry represent? Where is it defined?

16-26. What is the function of the colon symbol?

16-27. What is the function of the **RR** entry? Where is it defined?

16-28. When a subfile is cleared, is the control record format or the subfile record format included in the **WRITE** statement?

16-29. When a subfile is displayed, is the control record format or the subfile record format included in the **EXFMT** statement?

16-30. Name the **RPG IV** operation that loads records to a subfile. What is the function of the indicator(s) that must be specified in the resulting indicator field(s)? In which resulting indicator field(s) must it be included?

16-31. As related to display files, define windowing.

16-32. What DDS keywords support windowing? Explain the functions of each.

16-33. Explain the function of each entry in the following statement:

WINDOW(10 30 8 40)

16-34. Explain the function of each entry in the following statement:

WDWBORDER ((*CHAR '12345678') (*DSPATR RI))

16-35. Refer to Question 16-34 and draw how the window will display.

16-36. What special **RPG IV** operations are required to process a window? May a window only be specified with subfiles?

PROGRAMMING ASSIGNMENTS

Before the assignments are started for this chapter, create a physical file with the following attributes:

PHYSICAL FILE DESCRIPTION

SYSTEM: AS/400	DATE: Yours
FILE NAME: Yours	REV NO: 0
RECORD NAME: Yours	KEY LENGTH: 5
SEQUENCE: Keyed (Unique)	RECORD SIZE: 54

FIELD DEFINITIONS

FIELD NO	FIELD NAME	SIZE	TYPE	POSITION FROM	POSITION TO	COMMENTS
1	PARTNO	5	C	1	5	Key field
2	PARTNAME	20	C	6	25	
3	AMTONHAND	6	P	26	29	0 decimals
4	AMTONORDER	6	P	30	33	0 decimals
5	AVGCOST	7	P	34	37	2 decimals
6	AMTALCATED	6	P	38	41	0 decimals
7	EOQ	6	P	42	45	0 decimals
8	SAFTYSTOCK	6	P	46	49	0 decimals
9	LEADTIME	3	P	50	51	0 decimals
10	WARELOCATN	3	C	52	54	

Physical File Data:

Part#	Part Name	Amount On Hand	Amount On Order	Avg Cost/ Unit	Amount Allocated	Economic Order Qty	Safety Stock	Lead Time	Warehouse Location
A2345	AC SPARK PLUGS	000000	018000	0000075	005000	000150	002000	014	ABC
B6789	FRAM OIL FILTRS	004000	001200	0000325	000480	001200	000500	031	DEF
C5555	POINT SETS	000600	000000	0000850	000000	000100	000100	015	AAA
D9876	LOCKING GAS CAP	000024	000012	0000499	000012	000012	000012	090	GHI
E3459	LIQUID CAR WASH	000360	000120	0000179	000480	000072	000200	016	BBB
E4555	TURTLE WAX	001200	000480	0000236	000900	000240	000500	030	BBC
F6666	CHAMOIS (LARGE)	000600	000120	0000397	000240	000048	000100	120	BBD
G7800	ARMOR ALL	002800	000840	0000219	001400	000240	000700	025	CCC
H1000	NO TOUCH FOAM	001350	000360	0000275	000800	000120	000300	030	CCD
H2100	GAS LINE AF	004000	001200	0000051	003000	000480	001000	020	DDD
I3120	NU FINISH WAX	001300	000600	0000419	001000	000240	000240	010	DEG
J4000	WD-40 (SMALL)	002500	001200	0000181	000900	000120	000300	015	EFG

Programming Assignment 16-1: INQUIRY PROCESSING WITH A SUBFILE

Create a subfile to *inquiry* process the physical file described above. The record formats for the display file are detailed below.

Prompt Screen Format:

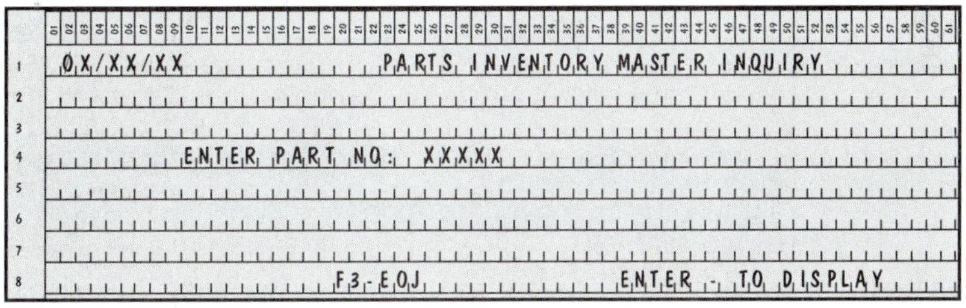

Subfile Formats (Subfile Record, Subfile Control, and Command Line):

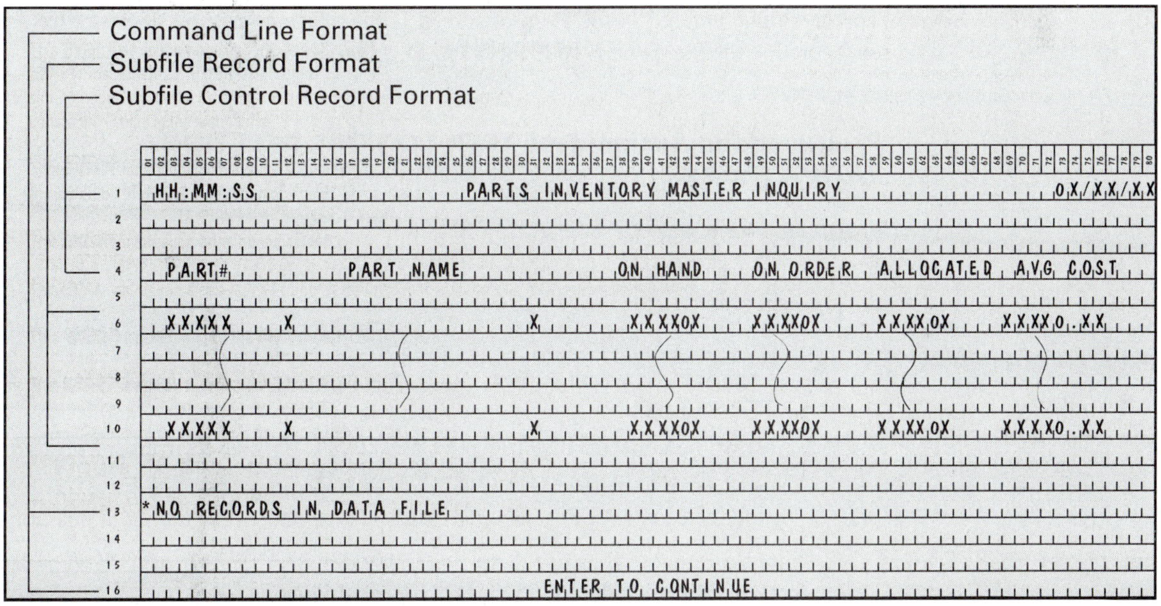

The key value entered in the Prompt screen is the starting key and does *not* have to be one stored in the file. Hence, code the **RPG IV** program with this control.

Programming Assignment 16-2: UPDATE PROCESSING WITH A SUBFILE

The physical file, display file, and subfile formats for this assignment are identical to those in Assignment 16-1. If Assignment 16-1 was completed, it must be modified to support update processing. However, if the assignment was not completed, refer to the specifications for Assignment 16-1.

In either case, the following changes must be made to Assignment 16-1 to support update processing:

1. Change the constant on line 1 in both screens to PARTS INVENTORY MASTER UPDATE.
2. Move the constant ENTER TO CONTINUE on line 16 from starting position 33 to 20 and change to ENTER TO UPDATE.
3. Add the constant **F5**—IGNORE UPDATE to line 16 beginning in position 49.
4. Fields in the subfile record must be defined with a **B** *Usage* (input/output).

Field	Record 1	Record 2	Record 3	Record 4
PARTNO........	E3459	B6789	C5500	A2345
PARTNAME......		FRAM OIL FILTERS		CHAMPION SPARK PLUGS
AMTONHAND.....	000480			018000
AMTONORDER....	000000		004000	004800
AVGCOST.......		0000370		
AMTALCATED....				002000

Note: Fields in the transaction records that <u>do not</u> have a value are <u>not</u> to be updated!

The key value entered in the Prompt screen is the starting key and does not have to be one stored in the file. Hence, code the **RPG IV** program with this control.

Programming Assignment 16-3: LOGICAL DELETION WITH A SUBFILE

Assignment 16-2 must be completed before this program is started. The following modifications must be made to Assignment 16-2 to support the logical deletion of records in the physical file:

1. Change the constant on line 1 in both screens to: PARTS INVENTORY MASTER DELETION.
2. Move the constant ENTER TO CONTINUE on line 16 from starting position 33 to 20 and change to ENTER TO DELETE.
3. Add the constant **F5**—IGNORE DELETE to line 16 beginning in position 49.

Delete records with key values **C5500, D9876,** and **J4000.**

Programming Assignment 16-4: ADDITION PROCESSING WITH A SUBFILE

Refer to completed Assignment 16-1, 16-2, or 16-3, and modify the display file, subfile, and **RPG IV** program to support the addition of records to a physical file with a subfile.

Add Data:

```
Field             Record 1                   Record 2                 Record 3

Part#..........   A1000 ..............       C5000 ............       D9876
Part Name......   PRESTONE DE-ICER....       CHAMOIS (LARGE)....      LOCKING GAS CAP
Amt-on-hand....   000000 ............        000000 ...........       000000
Amt-on-order...   000144 ............        000120 ...........       000144
Avg-cost/unit..   0000259 ...........        0000675 ..........       0000115
Amt-allocated..   000000 ............        000012 ...........       000000
EOQ............   000144 ............        000120 ...........       000024
Safety Stock...   000100 ............        000024 ...........       000012
Lead time......   010 ...............        015 ..............       090
```

Programming Assignment 16-5: WINDOWING WITH A SUBFILE

Create the following physical file of vendor information and load it with the data indicated. The data from this file will be input to the subfile for display in the window.

Physical File Record Format:

```
                    PHYSICAL FILE DESCRIPTION

     SYSTEM: AS/400                           DATE: Yours
     FILE NAME: Yours                         REV NO: 0
     RECORD NAME: Yours                       KEY LENGTH: 5
     SEQUENCE: Keyed (not unique)             RECORD SIZE: 61

                        FIELD DEFINITIONS

      FIELD    FIELD NAME   SIZE  TYPE    POSITION     COMMENTS
       NO                                 FROM   TO

       1       PARTNO          5   C         1    5   Key field
       2       VNAME          15   C         6   20
       3       VADDRS         15   C        21   35
       4       VCITY          15   C        36   50
       5       VSTATE          2   C        51   52
       6       VZIP            5   P        53   55
       7       VTEL#          10   P        56   61

Physical File Data:

Part                                                                Telephone
Number   Vendor Name       Address          City          State  Zip     Number

A2345   GENERAL MOTORS     1 PLUG LANE      DETROIT        MI   07702  3133334444
A2345   GM-AC DIVISION     2 SPARK PLACE    LANSING        MI   07704  5171234567
A2345   GM-PARTS SUPPLY    9 GOODWRENCH ST  MOUNT VERNON   NY   09901  9144569876
X9999   JOHNSON & SONS     2 FIXUM BLVD     RACINE         WI   04400  4146785432
H1000   ARMOR ALL CO       7 FOAM DRIVE     FRESNO         CA   05500  2099990090
```

Modify the display file completed for Assignment 16-1 to include a window that supports a subfile. Define the window to begin on line 11, column 22, with 6 lines and 35 columns. Use a border design of your choice. The subfile must store three records, with two records per page. Include only the VNAME and VTEL# field values from the vendor file in the subfile. Edit the VTEL# value as **'0(   )-   -   '.**

If a vendor is not found for a part number, display **NO VENDOR FOR PART** on line 24, column 31 of the inquiry screen, and prevent the window from displaying.

Indicate in the inquiry screen that the window may be displayed if the user presses **F8.**

chapter 17

Logical Files

A *logical file* is a database file used to access the data stored in one or more physical files. The features unique to logical files include the following:

1. Logical files do not contain data.
2. Access paths (indexes) may be built by logical files to process the data stored in one or more physical files in an arrival sequence or in any single- or multiple-field (key) value order.
3. Any physical file may be processed by any number of logical files.
4. Two or more logical files may share the same access path.
5. Omit and select criteria may be specified in a logical file to process only the required physical file data.
6. A logical file may include multiple record formats. Each format, however, must relate to one or more physical files and include at least one key field.
7. Any one logical file with multiple record formats may process the data from more than one physical file as though all the data were stored in the same physical file.
8. A logical file with multiple record formats may be used to process the data from more than one physical file. The physical file record formats accessed may be of different lengths.
9. During processing, a physical file's field attributes may be changed by a logical file. However, the data stored in the physical file will not be modified.

Logical files may be specified as either *nonjoin* or *join*. A *nonjoin* logical file processes each record individually from one or more physical files. *Join* logical files, however, create a single record from the selected fields from two or more physical files.

The type of logical file (nonjoin or join) specified is determined in the related DDS coding. In the following text, the processing logic and DDS syntax for nonjoin logical files are introduced first, followed by the coding requirements associated with join logical files.

NONJOIN LOGICAL FILES (ONE-RECORD FORMAT)

All logical files are formatted and defined by DDS coding. The DDS coding for nonjoin logical files is specified in the following order:

1. *File Level* entries (optional)
2. *Record Level* entries

3. *Field Level* entries (optional)
4. *Key Field Level* entries (optional)
5. *Select/Omit Level* entries (optional)

Accessing One Physical File by a Logical File

Processing Logic. In the traditional computer environment, keyed files are processed in an order different from the base index either by sorting the file with a Sort/Merge utility or by specifying alternate indexes when the file is initially created. Logical files eliminate the restrictions imposed by those methods by building access paths that process a physical file(s) by any select field or fields included in the physical file's record format.

Figure 17-1 illustrates the logic associated with processing of a physical file (created with CUST# as the key) by a logical file that will process it in a STATE code order. The term *access path* refers to a separate index built and maintained by the related logical file.

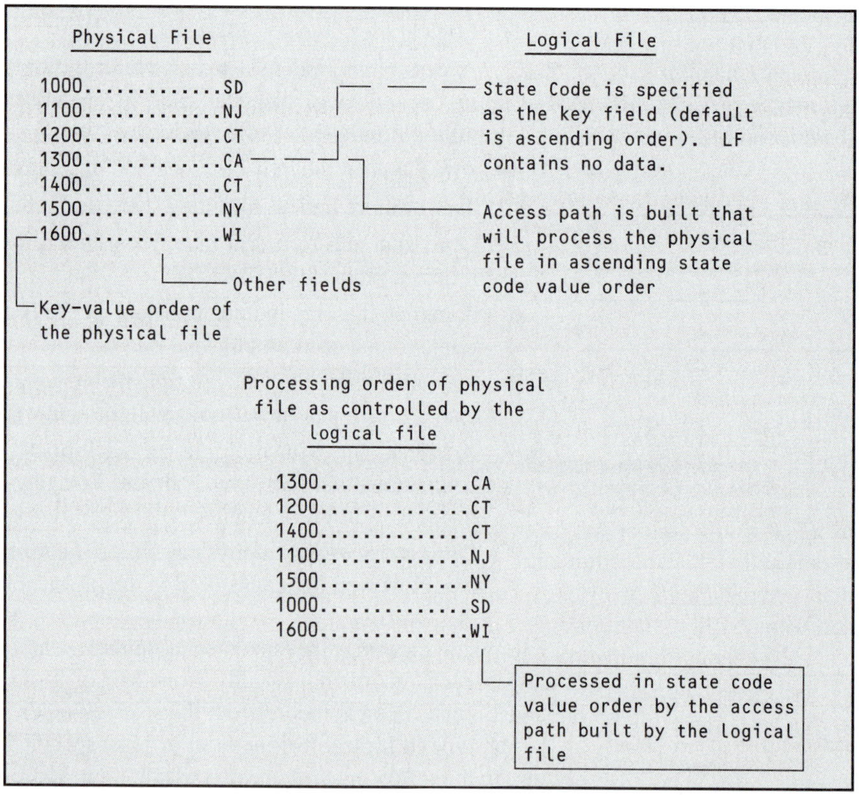

Figure 17-1 Processing logic of the access path created by a logical file (one-record format).

Data Description Specifications Coding (Nonjoin Logical File)

Logical files (**LF**) are created according to DDS syntax that is entered and stored via **SEU. LF** must be entered in the TYPE field on the Programmer Menu to initiate the required **SEU** format. Similar to physical and display files, logical files must be compiled and an object created. Figure 17-2 details the syntax to control the processing shown in Figure 17-1.

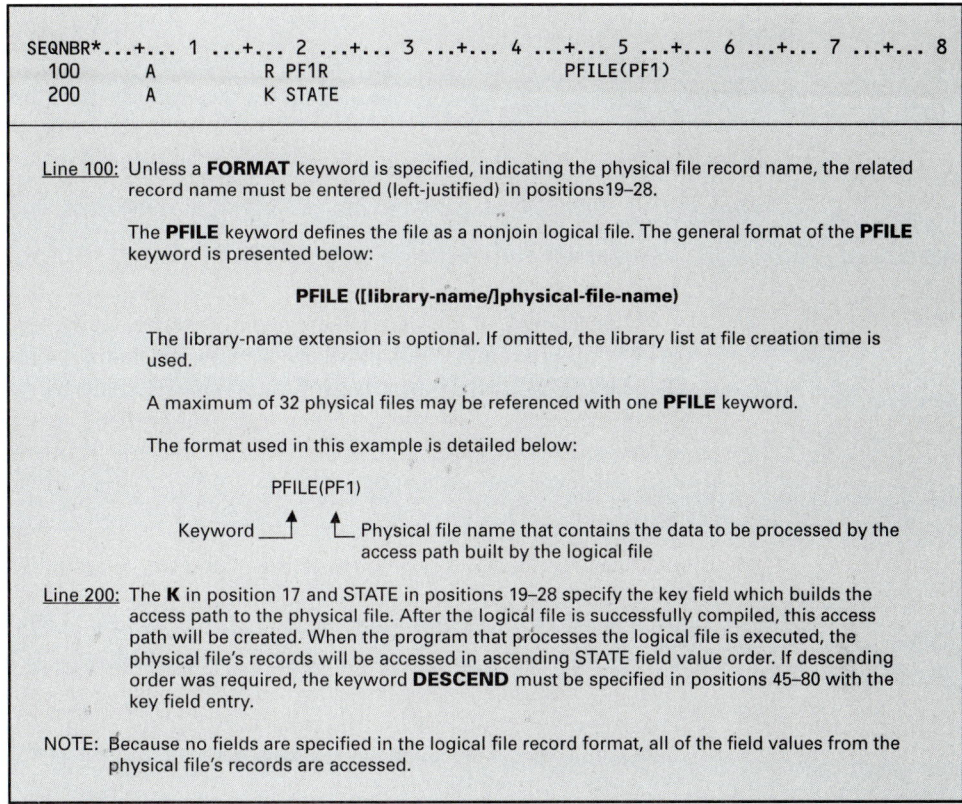

```
SEQNBR*...+... 1 ...+... 2 ...+... 3 ...+... 4 ...+... 5 ...+... 6 ...+... 7 ...+... 8
  100       A          R PF1R                          PFILE(PF1)
  200       A          K STATE
```

Line 100: Unless a **FORMAT** keyword is specified, indicating the physical file record name, the related record name must be entered (left-justified) in positions19–28.

The **PFILE** keyword defines the file as a nonjoin logical file. The general format of the **PFILE** keyword is presented below:

PFILE ([library-name/]physical-file-name)

The library-name extension is optional. If omitted, the library list at file creation time is used.

A maximum of 32 physical files may be referenced with one **PFILE** keyword.

The format used in this example is detailed below:

PFILE(PF1)

Keyword ↑ ↑ Physical file name that contains the data to be processed by the access path built by the logical file

Line 200: The **K** in position 17 and STATE in positions 19–28 specify the key field which builds the access path to the physical file. After the logical file is successfully compiled, this access path will be created. When the program that processes the logical file is executed, the physical file's records will be accessed in ascending STATE field value order. If descending order was required, the keyword **DESCEND** must be specified in positions 45–80 with the key field entry.

NOTE: Because no fields are specified in the logical file record format, all of the field values from the physical file's records are accessed.

Figure 17-2 DDS syntax for a logical file that processes one physical file in a STATE code order.

RPG IV Program Control of a Nonjoin Logical File

An **RPG IV** program that processes the logical file shown in Figure 17-2 is detailed in Figure 17-3. Because the logical file is designated as a primary (**P** in position 17 of the *File Descriptions* instruction), it will access the related physical file consecutively in an ascending key-value (STATE code) order.

```
.. 1 ...+... 2 ...+... 3 ...+... 4 ...+... 5 ...+... 6 ...+... 7 ...+
FFilename++IPEASFRLen+LKLen+AIDevice+.Keywords+++++++++++++++++++++++++

FLFILE1    IP   E             K DISK       ———— Logical file is defined here
FPTFILE1   O    E               PRINTER         (not physical file).  K in
                    .                           column 34 will process physical
                    .                           file in a consecutive key order
  Calculation instructions as needed.           (STATE in logical file)
                    .
                    .
  Because the logical file and printer
  file are both externally defined,
  input or output specifications do
  not have to be specified.
```

Figure 17-3 **RPG IV** progam that processes a logical file in ascending key-value order.

```
Printed report:

        1300...................CA  ---- Report is printed in
        1200...................CT       ascending state code
        1400...................CT       order as controlled
        1100...................NJ       by the logical file
        1500...................NY
        1000...................SD
        1600...................WI

  Cust# --┘        └-- Other field values
```

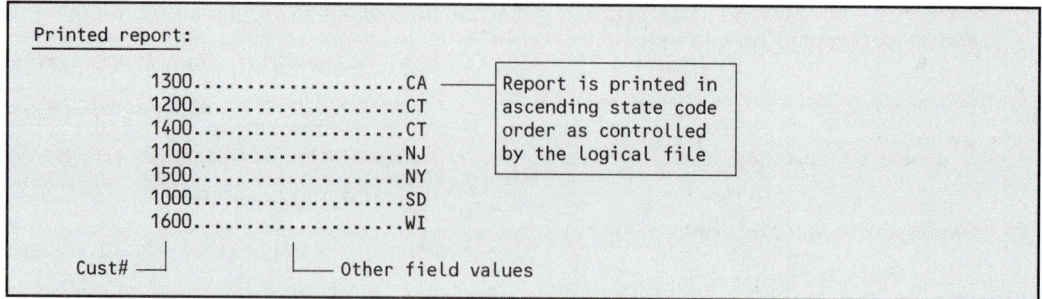

Figure 17-3 **RPG IV** progam that processes a logical file in ascending key-value order. (Continued)

If the physical file were to be randomly processed, the letter **P** must be replaced by an **F** (full-procedural file). Then, operations including **CHAIN, READ, READE, READP, SETLL, SETGT, DELET,** and **WRITE** could be supported by the program. Because the logical and printer files are externally defined, no input or output instructions are required in the program. Calculations must include instructions to control page overflow and any report computations.

Accessing More Than One Physical File with a Nonjoin Logical File

More than one physical file may be accessed with one logical file. If the record formats are not common to all the physical files, separate **PFILE** keywords must be specified. Figure 17-4 details the processing logic that supports the access of two physical files that have differing record formats. The records are merged for processing in the order that the physical files are specified in the logical file.

```
     PF1                                  PF2

  1000MICKEY MOUSE..........          1000MEN'S ............
  1100DONALD DUCK...........          1000WOMEN'S WEAR.......
  1200BUGS BUNNY............          1000SMALL APPLIANCES...
                                      1100GARDEN EQUIPMENT...
                                      1200CHILDREN'S WEAR....
                                      1200FURNITURE..........

                  Processing order of the physical
                     files as controlled by the
                           logical file

               1000MICKEY MOUSE.......... --  Records from the physical
               1000MEN'S WEAR............ --  files are merged in their
               1000WOMEN'S WEAR.......... --  common key-value order
               1000SMALL APPLIANCES...... --
               1100DONALD DUCK........... --
               1100GARDEN EQUIPMENT......
               1200BUGS BUNNY............
               1200CHILDREN`S WEAR.......
               1200FURNITURE.............
```

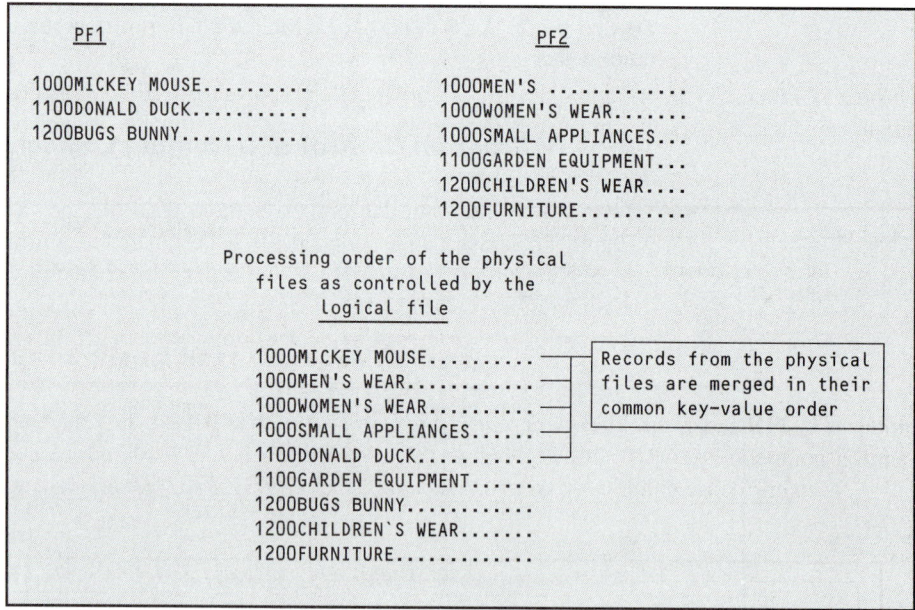

Figure 17-4 Processing logic for two physical files that have different record formats with one logical file.

The DDS coding for the logical file that controls the processing of the two physical files is presented in Figure 17-5.

```
SEQNBR*...+... 1 ...+... 2 ...+... 3 ...+... 4 ...+... 5 ...+... 6 ...+... 7 ...+... 8
  100      A          R PF1R                          PFILE(PF1)
  200      A          K CUST#
  300       *
  400      A          R PF2R                          PFILE(PF2)
  500      A          K CUSTNO
```

Record from PF1 will be read first followed a related record from PF2.

Records from each physical file will be read and merged in an ascending customer number order.

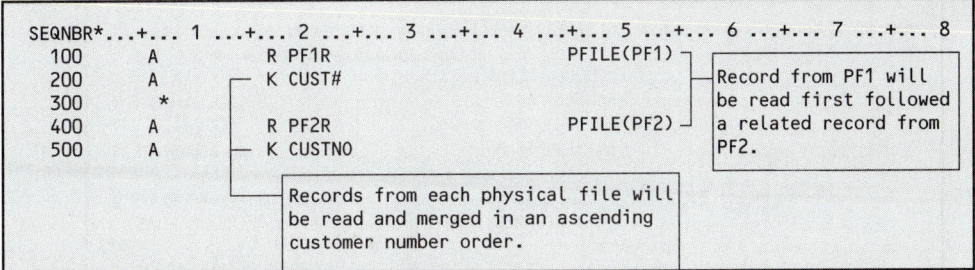

Figure 17-5 DDS coding for a logical file that processes two physical files having different record formats.

A partial listing of the **RPG IV** program that processes the logical file that accesses two physical files with different record formats is shown in Figure 17-6. The coding is identical to that explained for the processing of one physical file. The merging of the records from the two physical files is controlled by the logical file and not by the program.

```
.. 1 ...+... 2 ...+... 3 ...+... 4 ...+... 5 ...+... 6 ...+... 7 ...+
FFilename++IPEASFRLen+LKLen+AIDevice+.Keywords+++++++++++++++++++++++++

FLFILE2    IP   E           K DISK
FPTFILE2   O    E             PRINTER
                .
                .
Calculation instructions as needed.
                .
                .
Because the logical file and printer
file are both externally defined,
input or output specifications do
not have to be included.
```

Logical file is defined here (not physical file). K in column 34 will process the physical files in a consecutive customer number key value order. First physical file specified in logical file will be processed first, followed by related record(s) in the second physical file.

Printed report:

```
1000 MICKEY MOUSE..........
1000 MEN'S WEAR............
1000 WOMEN'S WEAR..........
1000 SMALL APPLIANCES......
1100 DONALD DUCK...........
1100 GARDEN EQUIPMENT......
1200 BUGS BUNNY............
1200 CHILDREN'S WEAR.......
1200 FURNITURE.............
```

Records from each file are merged. The first physical file specified in the logical file is processed first.

Figure 17-6 **RPG IV** program that processes one logical file that accesses two physical files.

Merging Records from Two Physical Files and Resequencing One Physical File

The example illustrated in Figure 17-7 details the processing logic for a nonjoin logical file that accesses two physical files by a common key and then resequences the records in the second physical file.

```
 PF1                                      PF2

1000MICKEY MOUSE..........         1000MEN'S WEAR.........970901
1100DONALD DUCK...........         1000WOMEN'S WEAR.......971012
1200BUGS BUNNY............         1000SMALL APPLIANCES...970831
                                   1100GARDEN EQUIPMENT...971001
                                   1200CHILDREN'S WEAR....971002
                                   1200FURNITURE..........970920

                  Processing order of the Physical
                    Files as controlled by the
                           Logical File

                  1000MICKEY MOUSE..........
                  1000SMALL APPLIANCES......970831
                  1000MEN'S WEAR............970901
                  1000WOMEN'S WEAR..........971012
                  1100DONALD DUCK...........
                  1100GARDEN EQUIPMENT......971001
                  1200BUGS BUNNY............
                  1200FURNITURE.............970920
                  1200CHILDREN'S WEAR.......971002

Physical files processed            Second physical file is
in a merged ascending               processed in ascending
customer number key order           date order within each
                                    customer group
```

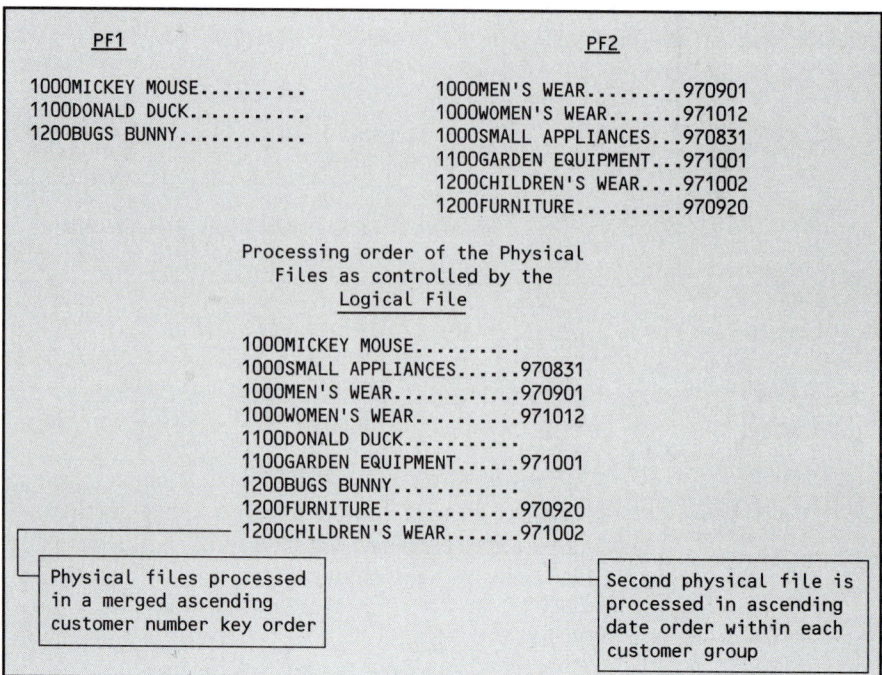

Figure 17-7 Processing logic for a logical file that accesses two physical files by a common key and then resequences the second physical file within a customer group.

The DDS coding for the logical file that controls the processing explained in Figure 17-7 is presented in Figure 17-8. Because the physical file PF1 does not include a date field in its record format, a ***NONE** word must be specified to offset the related **DATE** field in the record format of PF2. Then the merging process will be executed with a PF1 record first, followed by any number of related records (with the same customer number) from the PF2 file in an ascending date order.

```
SEQNBR*...+... 1 ...+... 2 ...+... 3 ...+... 4 ...+... 5 ...+... 6 ...+... 7 ...+... 8
  100      A          R PF1R                          PFILE(PF1)
  200      A          K CUST#
  300      A          K *NONE                                     Both physical files
  400      A*                                                     will be processed in
  500      A          R PF2R                          PFILE(PF2)  ascending customer
  600      A          K CUSTNO                                    number order
  700      A          K DATE

                      Second physical file is processed
                      in an ascending date order within
                      a customer group
```

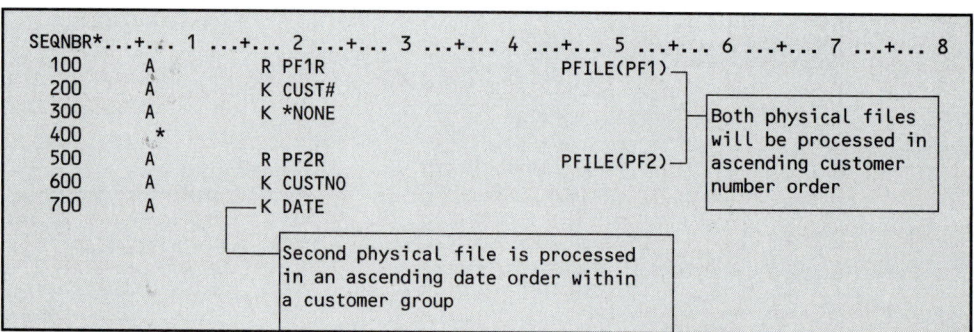

Figure 17-8 DDS coding for a logical file that processes two physical files by a common key and then resequences the records in the second physical file by a second key.

Merging Records from Two Physical Files and Resequencing Both Files Within Two Groups

Figure 17-9 details the processing logic associated with the processing of two physical files and the resequencing of both files within two groups. Notice that STATE is related only to PF1, CUST# to both files, and DATE only to PF2.

```
          PF1                                    PF2

1000MICKEY MOUSE........CA             1000MEN'S WEAR.........970901
1100DONALD DUCK.........CT             1000WOMEN'S WEAR.......971012
1200BUGS BUNNY..........CT             1000SMALL APPLIANCES...970831
                                       1100GARDEN EQUIPMENT...971001
                                       1200CHILDREN'S WEAR....971002
                                       1200FURNITURE..........970920

                         Processing order of the Physical
                            Files as controlled by the
                                   Logical File

                      CA...1000MICKEY MOUSE..........
                           1000SMALL APPLIANCES......970831
                           1000MEN'S WEAR............970901
                           1000WOMEN'S WEAR..........971012
                      CT...1100DONALD DUCK...........
                           1100GARDEN EQUIPMENT......971001
                      CT...1200BUGS BUNNY............
                           1200FURNITURE.............970920
                           1200CHILDREN'S WEAR.......971002

PF1 processed in ascend-    PF1 and PF2 are processed in    PF2 is processed in as-
ing state code order.       ascending customer number or-   cending date order within
Field is not included       der within each state group     a customer number group
in PF2.
```

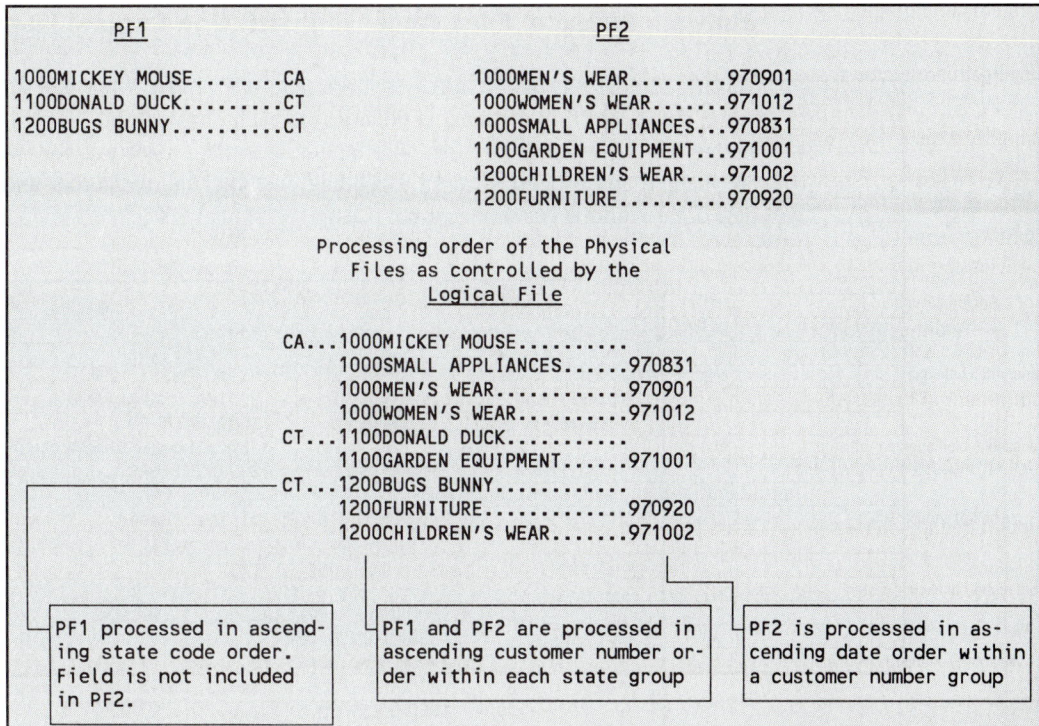

Figure 17-9 Processing logic for a logical file that accesses two physical files by three key fields.

The DDS coding that supports the processing shown in Figure 17-9 is detailed in Figure 17-10. When a related key field is missing in one of the physical files, the special word ***NONE** is included in that position. The effect of this coding on the order of processing is as follows:

Physical File	Key Position in DDS Coding 1	2	3
PF1	STATE	CUST#	*NONE
PF2	*NONE	CUSTNO	DATE

```
SEQNBR*...+... 1 ...+... 2 ...+... 3 ...+... 4 ...+... 5 ...+... 6 ...+... 7 ...+... 8
  100      A          R PF1R                        PFILE(PF1)
  200      A          K STATE
  300      A          K CUST#
  400      A          K *NONE ------------------------------ Matches DATE in PF2R
  500       *
  600      A          R PF2R                        PFILE(PF2)
  700      A          K *NONE ------------------------------ Matches STATE in PF1R
  800      A          K CUSTNO
  900      A          K DATE
```

Figure 17-10 DDS coding for a logical file that processes two physical files by three key fields.

The processing sequence may be paralleled to that of sorting, with STATE/*NONE as the major field level, CUST#/CUSTNO as the intermediate field level, and *NONE/DATE as the minor field level.

Multiple Physical Files Accessed with One Logical File Record

When a logical file record accesses more than one physical file in a single **PFILE** keyword, the record formats must be identical to each physical file. In the example shown in Figure 17-11, two physical files that include transaction records for two separate weeks are merged and processed in an ascending customer number order and in a descending date order within a customer group.

```
            WEEK1                                         WEEK2

1100JEWELRY.........970825            1000MEN'S WEAR.........970901
1000MEN'S SHOES.....970826            1000WOMEN'S WEAR.......970912
1200CARPETING.......970827            1000SMALL APPLIANCES...970930
1000COSMETICS.......970828            1100GARDEN EQUIPMENT...970902
                                      1200CHILDREN'S WEAR....970905
                                      1200FURNITURE..........970920

                      Processing order of the Physical
                         Files as controlled by the
                               Logical File

                      1000SMALL APPLIANCES......970930
                      1000WOMEN'S WEAR..........970912
                      1000MEN'S WEAR............970901
                      1000COSMETICS.............970828
                      1000MEN'S SHOES...........970826
                      1100GARDEN EQUIPMENT......970902
                      1100JEWELRY...............970825
                      1200FURNITURE.............970920
                      1200CHILDREN'S WEAR.......970905
                      1200CARPETING.............970827

Physical files are processed in          Physical files are pro-
a merged ascending customer              cessed in a descending
number order (major field)               date order (minor field)
                                         within each merged cust-
                                         omer number group
```

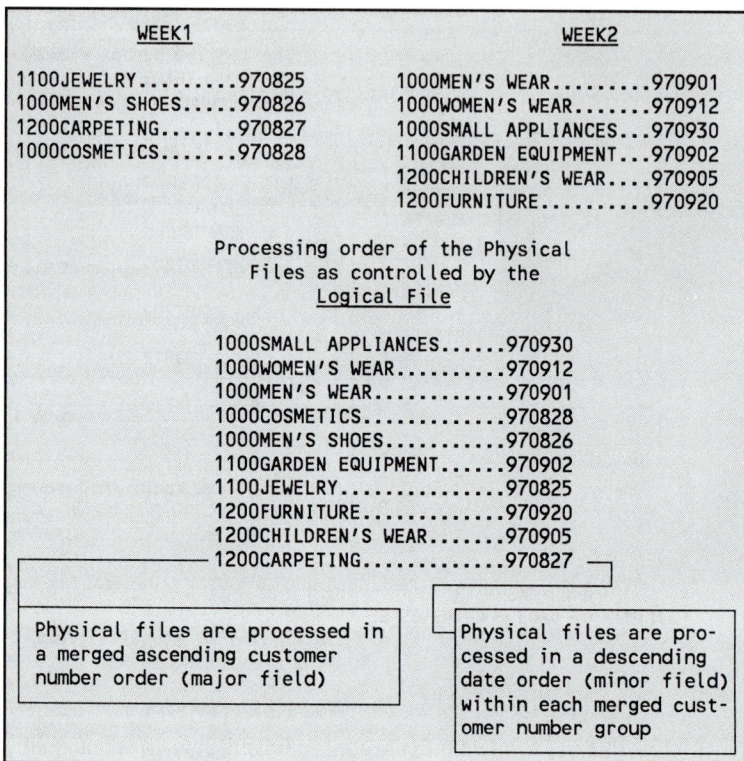

Figure 17-11 Processing logic for the access of two physical files with identical record formats.

The syntax included in a logical file to support the merging of two physical files that have identical record formats is detailed in Figure 17-12. The first file specified in the **PFILE** keyword will be processed first.

```
SEQNBR*...+... 1 ...+... 2 ...+... 3 ...+... 4 ...+... 5 ...+... 6 ...+... 7 ...+... 8
  100       A          R WEEKR                      PFILE(WEEK1 WEEK2)
  200       A          K CUSTNO
  300       A          K DATE                       DESCEND
```

Figure 17-12 DDS coding for a logical file that processes two physical files with identical record formats.

Selecting Fields from a Physical File

The previous examples of logical files have assumed that all the fields from the physical files are accessed. This default action may be changed by specifying only select fields from the physical file in the related logical file record format. The DDS syntax for a logical file with this control is shown in Figure 17-13.

```
SEQNBR*...+... 1 ...+... 2 ...+... 3 ...+... 4 ...+... 5 ...+... 6 ...+... 7 ...+... 8
  100       A            R LFR1                      PFILE(PF1)
  200       A              NAME                                  The logical file will
  300       A              STATE                                 access only the fields
  400       A            K STATE                     DESCEND     from the physical file
  500       A            K NAME                                  that are specified
                                 STATE will be processed
                                 in a descending order and
                                 NAME in an ascending order
```

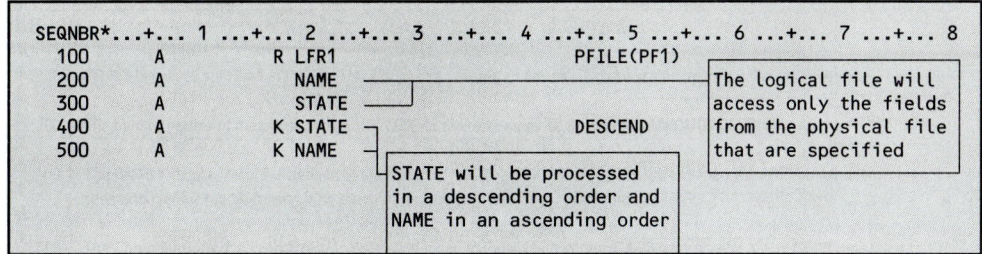

Figure 17-13 Logical file syntax for accessing select fields from a physical file.

The syntax in the **RPG IV** program to process a logical file that accesses select fields from a physical file is identical to the examples previously shown.

Nonjoin Logical File Summary

Logical files do not include data. Their function is to build access paths to one or more related physical files that will process the data in an order different from that specified by the physical file(s).

The processing of one physical file by a logical file may be compared to that of sorting. Any field(s) included in the physical file may be specified as a key (or keys) in the logical file. This control will process the physical file in any required order by any field or field values.

In addition, the base key sequence of a physical file may be ignored and the file processed in an arrival sequence by a logical file. This processing is controlled by not specifying any key field in the related logical file.

Unless otherwise controlled in an **RPG IV** program, the records from two or more physical files are sorted and merged in an order controlled by fields referenced as keys in the logical file.

Nonjoin logical files may specify more than one record format. If two or more physical files with *different* record formats are to be accessed by a logical file, separate **PFILE** keywords must be specified. When the record formats are the same, only one **PFILE** keyword is required. A maximum of 32 physical files may be referenced in one **PFILE** keyword.

When two or more physical files with different record formats are accessed by a logical file, ***NONE** may be specified as a key field substitute for either of the following conditions:

1. The related key fields from the physical files do not have the same attributes.
2. The key fields from the physical files have the same attributes, but they are not to be merged and sequenced together.

APPLICATION PROGRAM: PROCESSING THREE PHYSICAL FILES WITH A NONJOIN LOGICAL FILE

The specifications presented in Figure 17-14 detail the processing requirements for an **RPG IV** program that reads a logical file that accesses three physical files.

PROGRAM SPECIFICATIONS — Page 1 of 1

Program Name Credit card report — Program-ID CH17P1 — Written By S. Myers

Purpose Generate a credit card activity report — Approved By The Boss

Input files (directory names):
Physical Files CUSMAST, CUSTRAN, and CUSPAID
Logical File CUSHIST

Output files (directory names):
QSYSPRT

Processing Narrative:

Create a logical file that will access the three physical files, CUSMAST, CUSTRAN, and CUSPAID, in an ascending order by customer number and transaction date. Complete an **RPG IV** program to process the logical file and generate a report that includes information from all of the physical files.

Input:

An access path is to be built by a logical file that processes the three physical files in a customer number/transaction date composite key order. Because the CUSMAST record format does not include a transaction date field, the keyword ***NONE** is to be substituted in the composite key for that file.

Customer number and transaction date are to be used as the keys for the CUSTRAN file, and customer number and payment date for the CUSPAID file.

For all of the composite keys, customer number is the major key element (specified first) and date the minor.

The CUSMAST file includes address, credit limit, and beginning balance for each account. CUSTRAN contains records for charge transactions that have occurred for each account. CUSPAID includes records that store information for payments on account.

Processing:

Define the logical file in a *File Description* statement as an input, primary, and externally defined keyed file. The logical file is to be processed using full-procedure control. Include separate internal subroutines in the program for charge and payment processing. Determine the ending balance for each account by adding charge amounts to the beginning balance and subtracting payments.

Output:

Generate the report format shown in the supplemental printer spacing chart. The printing of each customer group is to be controlled when a change in customer number is tested.

Figure 17-14 Specifications for an **RPG IV** program that processes a logical file that accesses three physical files.

The system flowchart in Figure 17-15 shows that three physical files, CUSMAST, CUSTRAN, and CUSPAID, are accessed by the logical file CUSHIST, which is read by the program CH17P1.

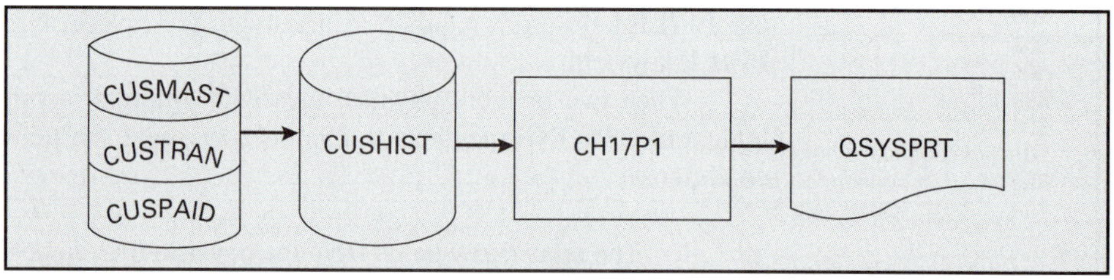

Figure 17-15 System flowchart for an **RPG IV** program that processes a logical file that accesses three physical files.

Figure 17-16 shows the record formats for the three physical files (CUSMAST, CUSTRAN, and CUSPAID) accessed by the logical file CUSHIST. Because the *Data Description* (top section) is identical for all three physical files (except for the file name), it has been omitted from all of the listings. Observe that all the files have the customer number as the *major* key field, with CUSTRAN and CUSPAID defined with transaction date as a *minor* key field.

CUSMAST Physical File Description:

```
                              Data Description Source

SEQNBR  *...+....1....+....2....+....3....+....4....+....5....+....6....+....7....+....8  Date
   100       A* CUSMAST FILE                                                             08/11/97
   200       A          R MASTR                                                          08/11/97
   300       A            CUST#          5                                               08/11/97
   400       A            NAME          15                                               08/11/97
   500       A            ADDR          20                                               08/11/97
   600       A            CITY          10                                               08/11/97
   700       A            STATE          2                                               08/11/97
   800       A            ZIP            5 0                                             08/11/97
   900       A            LIMIT          5 0                                             08/11/97
  1000       A            BEGBAL         7 2                                             08/11/97
  1100       A          K CUST#                                                          08/11/97
```

CUSTRAN Physical File Description:

```
SEQNBR  *...+....1....+....2....+....3....+....4....+....5....+....6....+....7....+....8  Date
   100       A* CUSTRAN FILE                                                             08/11/97
   200       A          R CHARGR                                                         08/11/97
   300       A            CUSTNO         5                                               08/11/97
   400       A            NAME          15                                               08/11/97
   500       A            PAYEE         12                                               08/11/97
   600       A            PADDR         15                                               08/11/97
   700       A            PCITY         12                                               08/11/97
   800       A            PSTAT          2                                               08/11/97
   900       A            PZIP           5 0                                             08/11/97
  1000       A            AMT            7 2                                             08/11/97
  1100       A            CDATE          6 0                                             08/11/97
  1200       A          K CUSTNO                                                         08/11/97
  1300       A          K CDATE                                                          08/11/97
```

CUSPAID Physical File Description:

```
SEQNBR  *...+....1....+....2....+....3....+....4....+....5....+....6....+....7....+....8  Date
   100* CUSPAID FILE                                                                     08/11/97
   200                  R PAIDR                                                          08/11/97
   300                    CUSTN          5                                               08/11/97
   400                    NAME          15                                               08/11/97
   500                    PAMT           7 2                                             08/11/97
   600                    PDATE          6 0                                             08/11/97
   700                  K CUSTN                                                          08/11/97
   800                  K PDATE                                                          08/11/97
```

Figure 17-16 Record formats of the physical files accessed by the logical file CUSHIST.

A printer spacing chart that details the format of the report and a listing generated by the program that processes a nonjoin logical file are presented in Figure 17-17.

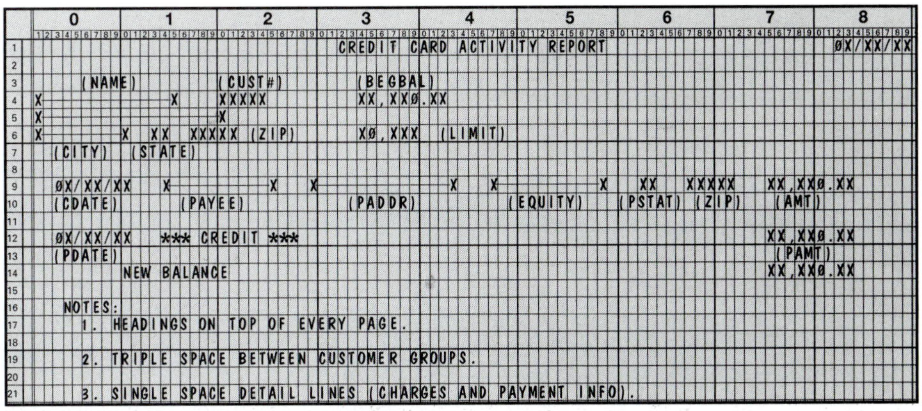

Figure 17-17 Printer spacing chart and report generated by the **RPG IV** program that processes a nonjoin logical file.

```
                                   CREDIT CARD ACTIVITY REPORT                       8/31/97


HENRY FORD             10000            3,250.00
10 DEARBORN AVENUE
HARTFORD     CT  06100                 10,000


    8/09/97    *** CREDIT ***                                                          320.00
    8/11/97    FAGAN'S             200 BOSTON AVE       STRATFORD     CT    06497       85.25
    8/15/97    STONEHENGE          RTE 7                WILTON        CT    06640      120.00

           NEW BALANCE                                                               3,135.25



LOUIS CHEVROLET        11000            1,950.15
15 MOTOR PLACE
BRIDGEPORT   CT  06601                  2,000


    8/01/97    *** CREDIT ***                                                           20.00

           NEW BALANCE                                                               1,930.15



HORACE DODGE           12000            2,478.89
9 CHASSIS BOULEVARD
NEW HAVEN    CT  06607                  3,000

    8/04/97    CALDORS             HAWLEY LANE CTR      TRUMBULL      CT    06601      100.00

           NEW BALANCE                                                               2,578.89



WALTER CHRYSLER        13000              500.00
30 SPARKPLUG LANE
STRATFORD    CT  06497                  1,500


    8/05/97    *** CREDIT ***                                                           75.00

           NEW BALANCE                                                                 425.00
```

Figure 17-17 Printer spacing chart and report generated by the **RPG IV** program that processes a nonjoin logical file. (Continued)

Nonjoin Logical File Syntax

The syntax for the nonjoin logical file that accesses three physical files is explained in Figure 17-18.

```
SEQNBR*...+... 1 ...+... 2 ...+... 3 ...+... 4 ...+... 5 ...+... 6 ...+... 7 ...+...
  100       A           R MASTR                          PFILE(CUSMAST)
  200       A           K CUST#
  300       A           K *NONE
  400        *
  500       A           R CHARGR                         PFILE(CUSTRAN)
  600       A           K CUSTNO
  700       A           K CDATE
  800        *
  900       A           R PAIDR                          PFILE(CUSPAID)
 1000       A           K CUSTN
 1100       A           K PDATE
```

Figure 17-18 Syntax for a nonjoin logical file that accesses three physical files.

SEQUENCE NUMBER	
100	The record format (MASTR) in the physical file CUSMAST is included left-justifed in positions 19–28. A **PFILE(CUSMAST)** keyword identifies the physical file accessed. A different physical file record format may be referenced in positions 19–28 if the **FORMAT** keyword is specified after the **PFILE** keyword statement as shown below: **FORMAT ([library-name/]physical-file-name)**
200	CUST# is defined as one of the key fields by which the physical file (CUSMAST) will be accessed. This field matches the customer number fields in the other physical file record formats.
300	Because the other physical files are accessed by two key fields, the keyword ***NONE** must be specified for the CUSMAST file to indicate that the record format does not have a matching second key (date) field. CUST# will be processed as the major field and ***NONE** as the minor. Because the ***NONE** value will always be spaces, the records from this file will be processed first for the customer group.
500	The record format (CHARGR) in the physical file CUSTRAN is included left-justified in positions 19–28. A **PFILE(CUSTRAN)** keyword identifies the physical file accessed.
600	CUSTNO is defined as one of the key fields by which the physical file (CUSTRAN) will be accessed. This field matches the customer number fields in the other physical file record formats.
700	The value of the date field **(*NONE, CDATE, PDATE)** in each physical file record will determine the order in which the records are processed. **CDATE** is defined in the CHARGR record format as the minor key field.
900	The record format (PAIDR) in the physical file CUSPAID is included left-justified in positions 19–28. A **PFILE(CUSPAID)** keyword identifies the physical file accessed.
1000	CUSTN is defined as one of the key fields by which the physical file (CUSPAID) will be accessed. This field matches the customer number fields in the other physical file record formats.
1100	The value of the date field **(*NONE, CDATE, PDATE)** in each physical file record will determine the order in which the records are processed within the customer group. **PDATE** is defined in the **PAIDR** record format as the minor key field.

Figure 17-18 Syntax for a nonjoin logical file that accesses three physical files. (Continued)

The first listing (expanded listing not shown) generated from compilation of the nonjoin logical file processed by the application program is presented in Figure 17-19.

```
File name . . . . . . . . . . . . . . . . . . . . . :  CUSHIST
  Library name  . . . . . . . . . . . . . . . . . . :  SMYERS
File attribute  . . . . . . . . . . . . . . . . . . :  Logical
Source file containing DDS  . . . . . . . . . . . . :  QDDSSRC
  Library name  . . . . . . . . . . . . . . . . . . :  SMYERS
Source member containing DDS  . . . . . . . . . . . :  CUSHIST
Source member last changed  . . . . . . . . . . . . :  10/11/97  10:30:33
Source listing options  . . . . . . . . . . . . . . :  *SOURCE    *LIST       *NOSECLVL
DDS generation severity level . . . . . . . . . . . :  20
DDS flagging severity level . . . . . . . . . . . . :  00
File type . . . . . . . . . . . . . . . . . . . . . :  *DATA
Authority . . . . . . . . . . . . . . . . . . . . . :  *LIBCRTAUT
Replace file  . . . . . . . . . . . . . . . . . . . :  *NO
```

Figure 17-19 First listing (expanded not shown) generated from compilation of the nonjoin logical file.

```
Text . . . . . . . . . . . . . . . . . . . . . . :   ch 17 - logical file - nonjoin
Compiler . . . . . . . . . . . . . . . . . . . . :   IBM AS/400 Data Description Processor

                          Data Description Source

SEQNBR  *...+....1....+....2....+....3....+....4....+....5....+....6....+....7....+....8  Date

   100        A            R MASTR                    PFILE(CUSMAST)                   10/11/97
   200        A            K CUST#                                                     10/11/97
   300        A            K *NONE                                                     10/11/97
   400         *                                                                       10/11/97
   500        A            R CHARGR                   PFILE(CUSTRAN)                   10/11/97
   600        A            K CUSTNO                                                    10/11/97
   700        A            K TDATE                                                     10/11/97
   800         *                                                                       10/11/97
   900        A            R PAIDR                    PFILE(CUSPAID)                   10/11/97
  1000        A            K CUSTN                                                     10/11/97
  1100        A            K DATE                                                      10/11/97
```

Figure 17-19 First listing (expanded not shown) generated from compilation of the nonjoin logical file. (Continued)

The processing logic controlled by the nonjoin logical file read by the application program is presented in Figure 17-20.

```
   CUSMAST              CUSTRAN                CUSPAID

10000...........    10000.......081197    10000.......080997
11000...........    12000.......080497    11000.......080197
12000...........    10000.......081597    13000.......080597
13000...........

              Order in which the records are processed:

              10000           -  CUSMAST record
              10000080997     -  CUSPAID record
              10000081197     -  CUSTRAN record
              10000081597     -  CUSTRAN record
              11000           -  CUSMAST record
              11000080197     -  CUSPAID record
              12000           -  CUSMAST record
              12000080497     -  CUSTRAN record
              13000           -  CUSMAST record
              13000080597     -  CUSPAID record

The logical file controls the processing of three physical
files in ascending customer number order and in ascending
date order within each customer group.  Because the value of
the *NONE field for the CUSMAST record is spaces, a record
from the master file is processed first for each customer
group.  Then the records from the other two physical files
are selected for processing in an ascending date value order.
```

Figure 17-20 Processing logic for the **RPG IV** program that processes a nonjoin logical file.

RPG IV Program That Processes a Nonjoin Logical File

Figure 17-21 contains a compile listing of an **RPG IV** program that processes a nonjoin logical file that accesses three physical files.

```
Line    <---------------------- Source Specifications ----------------------------><---- Comments ----> Do
Number ....1....+....2....+....3....+....4....+....5....+....6....+....7....+....8....+....9....+...10 Num
                        S o u r c e   L i s t i n g
     1  * This program processes three physical files accessed by a nonjoin logical file....
```

Figure 17-21 Compile listing of an **RPG IV** program that processes a nonjoin logical file that accesses three physical files.

```


 FCushist   IF   E             K DISK
  *--------------------------------------------------------------------------------*
  *                             RPG name         External name                      *
  * File name. . . . . . . . :  CUSHIST          STAN/CUSHIST                       *
  * Record format(s) . . . . :  MASTR            MASTR                              *
  *                             CHARGR           CHARGR                             *
  *                             PAIDR            PAIDR                              *
  *--------------------------------------------------------------------------------*
 FQsysprt   O    F  132          PRINTER OFLIND(*INOF)

  * Work field (Owed) & holding field for control break test (HoldCust#)
 D Owed            S              7 2
 D HoldCust#       S              5

=IMASTR
  *--------------------------------------------------------------------------------*
  * RPG record format  . . . . :  MASTR                                             *
  * External format  . . . . . :  MASTR : STAN/CUSHIST                              *
  *--------------------------------------------------------------------------------*
=I                             A    1    1  RECORDID
=I                             A    2    6  CUST#
=I                             A    7   21  NAME
=I                             A   22   41  ADDR
=I                             A   42   51  CITY
=I                             A   52   53  STATE
=I                             P   54   56 0ZIP
=I                             P   57   59 0LIMIT
=I                             P   60   63 2BEGBAL
=ICHARGR
  *--------------------------------------------------------------------------------*
  * RPG record format  . . . . :  CHARGR                                            *
  * External format  . . . . . :  CHARGR : STAN/CUSHIST                             *
  *--------------------------------------------------------------------------------*
=I                             A    1    1  RECORDID
=I                             A    2    6  CUSTNO
=I                             A    7   21  NAME
=I                             A   22   33  PAYEE
=I                             A   34   48  PADDR
=I                             A   49   60  PCITY
=I                             A   61   62  PSTAT
=I                             P   63   65 0PZIP
=I                             P   66   69 2AMT
=I                             P   70   73 0CDATE
=IPAIDR
  *--------------------------------------------------------------------------------*
  * RPG record format  . . . . :  PAIDR                                             *
  * External format  . . . . . :  PAIDR : STAN/CUSHIST                              *
  *--------------------------------------------------------------------------------*
=I                             A    1    1  RECORDID
=I                             A    2    6  CUSTN
=I                             A    7   21  NAME
=I                             P   22   25 2PAMT
=I                             P   26   29 0PDATE
 C                   READ      Cushist                                ----LR   read first LF record
 C                   EXSR      HouseKepSR                                      branch to SR
 C
 C                   DOW       *INLR = *OFF                                    dow ind 80 is off     B01

  * Heading control....
 C                   IF        *INOF = *ON                                     OF "on"?              B02
 C                   EXCEPT    Hdging                                          print heading lines    02
 C                   EXCEPT    CustHdg                                                                02
 C                   EVAL      *INOF = *OFF                                    turn off OF indicatr   02
 C                   ENDIF                                                     end IF group          E02

  * When change in customer number occurs (control break) branch to SR
```

Figure 17-21 Compile listing of an **RPG IV** program that processes a nonjoin logical file that accesses three physical files. (Continued)

```
C                   IF        Cust# <> HoldCust#                                 control fld break?  B02
C                   EXSR      Custbreak                                          branch to SR        02
C                   EXCEPT    CustHdg                                            print customer hdg  02
C                   ENDIF                                                        end IF group       E02

 * Test for record type (Chargr or Paidr) and exit to related SR....
C     RecordID      CASEQ     'C'           ChargSR                              branch to subroutine 01
C     RecordID      CASEQ     'P'           PaytSR                               branch to subroutine 01
C                   ENDCS                                                        end CAS group       01

C                   READ      Cushist                                ----LR      read next record    01
C                   ENDDO                                                        end DOW group      E01
C                   EXSR      CustBreak

 * Begin subroutines....
C     HouseKepSR    BEGSR                                                        begin subroutine
C                   EVAL      HoldCust# = Cust#                                  Initialize HoldCust#
C                   EVAL      Owed = Begbal                                      initialize Owed fld
C                   EVAL      *INOF = *ON                                        turn on OF indicator
C                   ENDSR                                                        end HouseKepSr

C     CustBreak     BEGSR                                                        begin CustBreak SR
C                   EXCEPT    Balance                                            print cust owed amt
C                   EVAL      HoldCust# = Cust#                                  initialize HoldCust#
C                   EVAL      Owed = Begbal                                      store Begbal in Owed
C                   ENDSR                                                        end CustBreak SR
C
C     ChargSR       BEGSR                                                        begin Chargsr SR
C                   EXCEPT    Charge                                             print charge record
C                   EVAL      Owed = Owed + Amt                                  increment Owed field
C                   ENDSR                                                        end Chargsr subroutn
C
C     PaytSR        BEGSR                                                        begin Paytsr SR
C                   EXCEPT    Paymt                                              print payment record
C                   EVAL      Owed = Owed - Pamt                                 decrement Owed field
C                   ENDSR                                                        end Paytsr SR

OQsysprt   E            Hdging         3 01
O                                           51 'CREDIT CARD ACTIVITY'
O                                           58 'REPORT'
O                       Udate         Y     80
O          E            CustHdg        1
O                       Name                15
O                       Cust#               24
O                       Begbal        1     42
O          E            CustHdg        1
O                       Addr                20
O          E            CustHdg              3
O                       City                10
O                       State               14
O                       Zip                 21
O                       Limit         1     39
O          E            Charge         1
O                       Cdate         Y     10
O                       Payee               25
O                       Paddr               43
O                       Pcity               58
O                       Pstat               63
O                       Pzip                71
O                       Amt           1     83
O          E            Paymt          1
O                       Pdate         Y     10
O                                           27 '*** CREDIT ***'
O                       Pamt          1     83
O          E            Balance      1 3
O                                           20 'NEW BALANCE'
O                       Owed          1     83
```

Figure 17-21 Compile listing of an **RPG IV** program that processes a nonjoin logical file that accesses three physical files. (Continued)

File Description Specifications:

Line No.

4 Cushist is defined as an input (**I** in position 17), full-procedural (**F** in position 18), externally described (**E** in position 22), keyed (**K** in position 34) logical file. Note that the *File Description* syntax for a logical file is identical to that of a physical file.

5 Qsysprt is defined as an output (**O** in position 17), program-described (**F** in position 22), printer file. Overflow indicator **(OF)** is defined with the **OFLIND(*INOF)** keyword.

Definition Specifications:

8 Owed is defined as a standalone field into which the Begbal value from the Cusmast file is moved.

9 HoldCust# is defined as a standalone field into which the Cust# value from the Cusmast file is moved to check for a change in customer number so that the end balance of the previous customer can be printed before the heading lines for the next customer.

Calculation Specifications:

38 This **READ** instruction reads the first record from the Cushist (logical) file. If end of file is read, indicator **LR** will be turned on.

39 This **EXSR** instruction branches control to the HouseKepSR subroutine, where the Cust# value from the first MASTR record is moved into the HoldCust# field. The Owed field is initialized with the value in the Begbal field from the MASTR record and overflow indicator **OF** is turned on.

41 Instructions within the **DOW** group control subsequent reads and all other processing functions. Exit from the DOW group is controlled when indicator **LR** is turned on, which takes place when the **READ** instruction on line 38 or on line 61 reads end of file.

44 This **IF** instruction tests the status of indicator **OF**, which was initially turned on in the HouseKepSR subroutine for the first logical record processed. Subsequent page overflow is "flagged" when the overflow line is detected and indicator **OF** automatically turned on.

45 When the relational test in the **IF** instruction is true, this **EXCEPT** will branch control to the output instructions and print the Hdging record format on the first line of the report.

46 This **EXCEPT** instruction will branch control to output and print the CustHdg record formats on instruction lines 92 through 102. The data included for this output is from a MASTR record.

47 This **EVAL** instruction turns off indicator **OF**, which is automatically turned on when the page overflow line is subsequently tested.

48 This **ENDIF** operation ends this **IF** group, which began on line 44.

51 This **IF** instruction compares the value in Cust# (from the MASTR record) with the value stored in HoldCust#. If the values are not equal, the following **EXSR** instruction is executed.

52 The **EXSR** instruction branches control to the CustBreak subroutine, where control break (change in Cust#) instructions are executed.

53 This **EXCEPT** instruction prints the CustHdg output records on lines 92 through 102, which includes MASTR record data for the current customer.

54 This **ENDIF** operation ends the **IF** group that began on line 51.

57 This **CASEQ** instruction compares the value in the RecordID field (included in the three record formats) with the character literal **C**. When the relational test is "true" (values are equal), control branches to the ChargSR subroutine, where instructions for customer charges are performed.

58 This **CASEQ** instruction compares the value in the RecordID field (included in the three record formats) with the character literal **P**. When the relational test is "true" (values are equal), control branches to the PaytSR subroutine, where instructions for customer payments are performed.

59 The **ENDCS** operation ends the **CAS** group.

61 This **READ** instruction reads the next record from the logical file. When end of file is read, indicator **LR** will be turned on to subsequently end the program.

62 The **ENDDO** operation ends the **DOW** group that began on line 41.

63 This **EXSR** instruction branches control to the CustBreak subroutine so that the New Balance value for the last customer will print. Without this instruction, the last line for the last customer group in the logical file would not be printed.

66 This **BEGSR** instruction begins the HouseKepSR subroutine.

Figure 17-21 Compile listing of an **RPG IV** program that processes a nonjoin logical file that accesses three physical files. (Continued)

67 This **EVAL** instruction initializes the HoldCust# field with the value from the Cust# field from the current MASTR record.

68 This **EVAL** instruction initializes the Owed field with the value in Begbal from the current MASTR record.

69 This **EVAL** instruction turns on indicator **OF**, to control page overflow for the first logical file record processed.

70 This **ENDSR** operation ends the HouseKepSR subroutine.

72 This **BEGSR** instruction begins the CustBreak subroutine.

73 This **EXCEPT** instruction prints the Balance record format on lines 115 through 117. The NEW BALANCE value is printed after all of the related customer's charge and payment records are processed and the new Owed amount is calculated.

74 This **EVAL** instruction initializes the HoldCust# field with the Cust# field value from the current MASTR record.

75 This **EVAL** instruction initializes the Owed field with the value in Begbal from the current MASTR record.

76 This **ENDSR** operation ends the CustBreak subroutine.

78 This **BEGSR** instruction begins the ChargSR subroutine.

79 This **EXCEPT** instruction prints the values in the Charge record format on lines 103 through 110.

80 This **EVAL** operation increments the Owed field value with the Amt field value from the current CHARGR record processed.

81 This **ENDSR** operation ends the ChargSR subroutine.

83 This **BEGSR** instruction begins the PaytSR subroutine.

84 This **EXCEPT** instruction prints the Paymt record format on lines 111 through 114.

85 This **EVAL** operation decrements the Owed field value with the Amt field value from the current PAIDR record processed.

86 This **ENDSR** operation ends the PaytSR subroutine.

Output Specifications:

88–91 The Hdging record values are printed by the **EXCEPT** instruction on line 45.

92–102 The three CustHdg record values are printed by the **EXCEPT** instructions on lines 46 and 53. Field values are from the MASTR record merged in the logical file in an ascending customer number/date (i.e., CUST#/*NONE) order.

103–110 The Charge record values are printed by the **EXCEPT** instructions on line 79. Field values are from the CHARGR record merged in the logical file in an ascending customer number/date (CUSTNO/CDATE) order.

111–114 The Paymt record values are printed by the **EXCEPT** instructions on line 84. Field values are from the PAIDR record merged in the logical file in an ascending customer number/date (CUSTN/PDATE) order.

115–117 The Balance record values are printed by the **EXCEPT** instructions on line 73. The final value in Owed is computed on line 75, 80, or 85 after the last record for the customer group is processed.

Figure 17-21 Compile listing of an **RPG IV** program that processes a nonjoin logical file that accesses three physical files. (Continued)

JOIN LOGICAL FILES

Join logical files concatenate the fields from the records in two or more physical files and process them as one record. The advantages of join logical files include the following:

1. *Increased productivity.* Because multiple **READ** operations are not required with join logical files, the coding in **RPG IV** programs is simplified.
2. *Improved performance.* Because a join logical file builds only one record for processing, program performance is improved. Only one **READ** (or **CHAIN**)

operation has to be specified instead of the multiple **READs** (or **CHAINs**) required for nonjoin logical file processing. Furthermore, if a program has fewer open data paths, the job's **PAG** *(Process Access Group)* size is reduced. This saves main storage and facilitates faster program loading.

3. *More flexible database.* Compared to *nonjoin* logical files, join logical files parallel the design and processing features related to a true database structure. Hence, more-complex accesses may be built around the existing database.

Features of Join Logical Files. The features unique to join logical files supported by IBM's AS/400 computer are the following:

1. Join logical files are **READ**-only files and may not be used in update processing.
2. Join logical files support only *inner* and *left outer joins. Outer join processing* is not supported.
3. They may reference from 2 to 32 physical files. The physical files specified may be in key or arrival sequence. A common key (or keys) is not required to link the files. In addition, because the same physical file may be specified as the base file more than once, it may be joined to itself.
4. Any key field specified must be included in the primary file.
5. *Select/omit* criteria may be specified for any field in a join logical file.

Join Logical File Keywords. The steps in building a join logical file include the following:

1. Name all the physical files that will be accessed by the join logical file.
2. Specify the fields that will relate the physical files to each other.
3. Define all the fields from each physical file that will be included in the join logical file's record format.

The creation of a join logical file depends on a knowledge of the seven keywords: **JFILE, JOIN, JFLD, JREF, JDUPSEQ, JDFTVAL,** and **DYNSLT.** The function and syntax of each of these keywords are explained in the following paragraphs.

JFILE *Keyword (Record Level):* This *Record Level* (which requires the letter **R** in position 17 of the *Data Description* statement) keyword is used to identify the physical files to be accessed in a join logical file. At least 2 physical files and no more than 32 may be specified in one **JFILE** keyword.

The general format of the **JFILE** keyword follows:

JFILE([library-name/]physical-file-name [..32])

The first file included in a **JFILE** keyword is called the *primary file,* and it is this file from which the join processing starts.

When a user formats a **JFILE** keyword, the physical file that has the smallest number of data records should be specified first (as the primary file). The sequence in which the physical files are specified in the **JFILE** keyword can affect both performance and the results of join logical file processing.

JOIN *Keyword (Join Level):* The **JOIN** keyword is required in the coding for a join logical file to join two physical files for processing. If three physical files are accessed by the join logical file, two **JOIN** keywords must be specified; if four physical files are accessed, three **JOIN** statements must be included, and so forth. The general format of a **JOIN** keyword is as follows:

JOIN(from-file to-file)

The from-file and to-file entries may be the names or relative numbers of two physical files that were included in the **JFILE** keyword. In the first example that follows, relative numbers 1 and 2 are used in the alternative coding in the **JOIN** keyword. To join the third file to the master file, the second example uses 1 and 3.

JFILE(CUSMAST CUSTRAN CUSPAID)

The **JOIN** keyword may be formatted as

JOIN(CUSMAST CUSTRAN) -or- JOIN(1 2)

and

JOIN(CUSMAST CUSPAID) -or- JOIN(1 3)

When duplicate physical file names are specified in a **JFILE** keyword, the **JOIN** keyword must use the relative number format. Definition of the **JOIN** keyword requires that the letter **J** be included in position 17 of the DDS statement.

***JFLD** Keyword (Join Level):* A **JFLD** keyword identifies the *from* field and the *to* field that will join two physical files. The related fields must have the same attributes (type, size, and decimal positions), but they do not need to have the same name. Any *from* field and *to* field that does not have the same attributes may be redefined in the join logical file. Any fields specified in a **JFLD** keyword must have been defined in the related physical file. Consequently, join fields do not have to be defined in the join logical file. The general format of the **JFLD** keyword is

JFLD(from-field-name to-field-name)

Notice that only two fields may be specified in a **JFLD** keyword. If the physical files are to be joined by other fields, then additional **JFLD** keywords must be defined.

***JREF** Keyword (Field Level):* The **JREF** keyword is used when the physical files accessed by the join logical file have some or all of the same field names. **JREF** is used to identify the physical file in which the field is related. The general format of the **JREF** keyword is

JREF(file-name|relative-file-number)

A file name or the relative position of the file's name in the **JFILE** keyword may be included in the **JREF** statement. The related field name must be entered in the Name field (positions 19–28) of the DDS statement.

***JDUPSEQ** Keyword (Join Level):* A **JDUPSEQ** keyword specifies the order in which the records from physical files that have duplicate join fields will be processed. The general format of the **JDUPSEQ** keyword is

JDUPSEQ(sequencing-file-name[*DESCEND])

If ***DESCEND** is included in the keyword, the duplicate records (same field value) will be retrieved in a descending order instead of an ascending default order.

***JDFTVAL** Keyword (File Level):* The **JDFTVAL** keyword enables primary file records that do not have matching secondary file records to be included in the join. Without the

JDFTVAL keyword, any primary file record that did not have a matching secondary file record would be skipped. The general format of the **JDFTVAL** keyword is

JDFTVAL

***DYNSLT** Keyword (File Level):* The **DYNSLT** keyword is required when the **JDFTVAL** keyword is specified in a join logical file. When specified, it causes record selection to occur when a record is read before instead of after it is stored. The general format of the **DYNSLT** keyword is

DYNSLT

JOIN Logical File Coding Examples

The DDS coding for the first join logical file example is shown in Figure 17-22. Two physical files (HISTORY and COURSES) are accessed by the join logical file and joined by student number fields that are common to both files. The processing result indicates that the physical files are retrieved in an ascending student number order. Multiple records from the COURSES file are grouped within their related student number.

The processing results in Figure 17-22 do not indicate a printed report but rather the order in which the records from the physical files are retrieved by the join logical file. Only one record will be read from the HISTORY (primary) file and stored. Then, one or more records will be retrieved from the COURSES file in an arrival sequence until the student number changes.

```
SEQNBR*...+... 1 ...+... 2 ...+... 3 ...+... 4 ...+... 5 ...+... 6 ...+... 7 ...+... 8
 100       A          R JOINRCD
 200       A                                         JFILE(HISTORY COURSES)
 300       A          J                              JOIN(1 2)
 400       A                                         JFLD(STUD# STUDNO)
 500       A                        .
 600       A                        .
 700       A        Fields are included as required
 800       A                        .
 900       A                        .
```

HISTORY File

STUD#
100
200
300

COURSES File

STUDNO	DATE
200	980520
300	971223
200	971220
100	970520
200	981223

Processing Results

STUD#	DATE
100	970520
200	980520
200	971220
200	981223
300	971223

Processed by the JFLD keyword in an ascending STUD# order

Duplicate records are accessed in arrival sequence

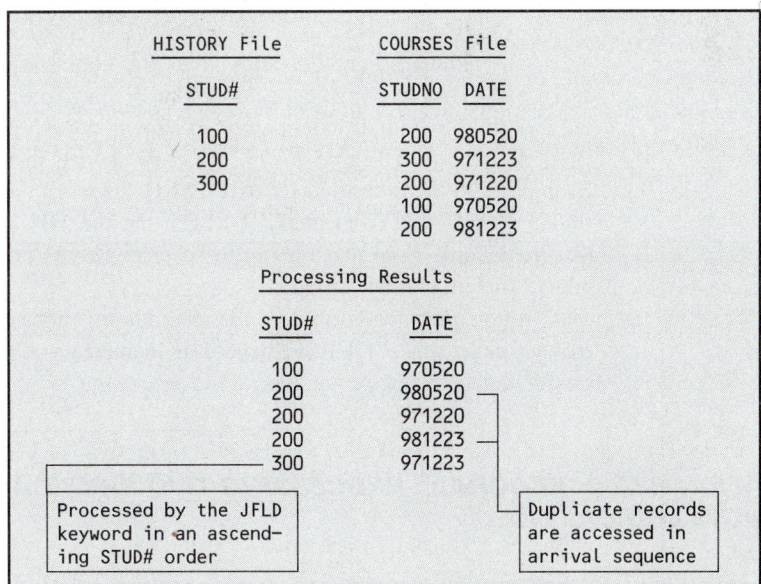

Figure 17-22 Join logical file syntax and processing results—Example 1.

The DDS coding for the second join logical file example is shown in Figure 17-23.

```
SEQNBR*...+... 1 ...+... 2 ...+... 3 ...+... 4 ...+... 5 ...+... 6 ...+... 7 ...+... 8

  100      A           R JOINRCD
  200      A                                           JFILE(HISTORY COURSES)
  300      A           J                               JOIN(1 2)
  400      A                                           JFLD(STUD# STUDNO)
  500      A                                           JDUPSEQ(DATE)
  600      A                            .
  700      A                            .
  800      A         Fields are included as required
  900      A                            .
 1000      A                            .
```

```
              HISTORY File          COURSES File

                 STUD#              STUDNO   DATE

                  100                200   980520
                  200                300   971223
                  300                200   971220
                                     100   970520
                                     200   981223

                        Processing Results

                        STUD#         DATE

                         100         970520
                         200         971220 ──┐
                         200         980520   │
                         200         981223 ──┤
       ┌──────────────── 300         971223   │
       │                                      │
 Processed by the JFLD                  Processed by the JDUPSEQ
 keyword in an ascend-                  keyword in an ascending
 ing STUD# order                        date order within a STUD#
                                        group
```

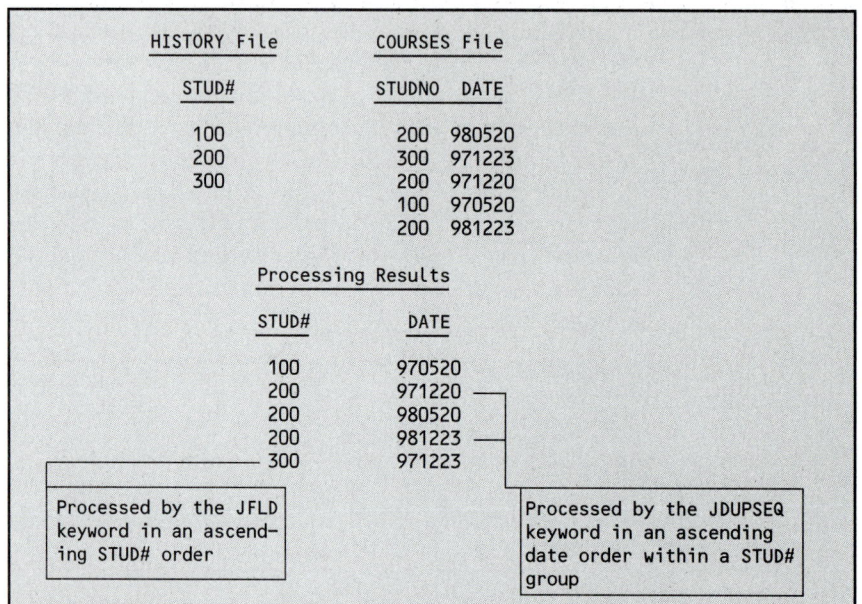

Figure 17-23 Join logical file syntax and processing results—Example 2.

Two physical files (HISTORY and COURSES) are accessed by the join logical file and joined by student number fields that are common to both files. In addition, the **JDUPSEQ(DATE)** statement accesses the records from the COURSES file in an ascending date order within a student group as shown in the processing results in Figure 17-23.

As shown in Figure 17-23, the only change in the join logical file syntax from Example 1 is the addition of a **JDUPSEQ** keyword. When more than one record for a student is retrieved from the COURSES file, the **JDUPSEQ(DATE)** keyword indicates that the records from that file are to be processed in an ascending date order within the related student number group.

If you relate the HISTORY file record to the miles digit on an automobile's speedometer and regard the COURSES record as increments of tenths of a mile, you may have a clearer understanding of join logical file processing.

APPLICATION RPG IV PROGRAM: PROCESSING TWO PHYSICAL FILES WITH A JOIN LOGICAL FILE

An application program that processes two physical files with a join logical file is presented in this section. Other than this application having only one transaction file (for both charges and payments), the documentation is identical to that specified for the previously discussed nonjoin logical file. The two physical file record formats processed by the join logical file example are shown in Figure 17-24.

CUSMAST Physical File Description:

```
                         Data Description Source

SEQNBR  *...+....1....+....2....+....3....+....4....+....5....+....6....+....7....+....8  Date
   100        A* CUSMAST FILE                                                          08/11/97
   200        A          R MASTR                                                       08/11/97
   300        A            CUST#          5                                            08/11/97
   400        A            NAME          15                                            08/11/97
   500        A            ADDR          20                                            08/11/97
   600        A            CITY          10                                            08/11/97
   700        A            STATE          2                                            08/11/97
   800        A            ZIP            5 0                                          08/11/97
   900        A            LIMIT          5 0                                          08/11/97
  1000        A            BEGBAL         7 2                                          08/11/97
  1100        A          K CUST#                                                       08/11/97
```

TRANS Physical File Description:

```
SEQNBR  *...+....1....+....2....+....3....+....4....+....5....+....6....+....7....+....8  Date
   100        A* CUSTRAN FILE                                                          08/11/97
   200        A          R CHARGR                                                      08/11/97
   300        A            RECORDID       1                                            08/11/97
   400        A            CUSTNO         5                                            08/11/97
   500        A            NAME          15                                            08/11/97
   600        A            PAYEE         12                                            08/11/97
   700        A            PADDR         15                                            08/11/97
   800        A            PCITY         12                                            08/11/97
   900        A            PSTATE         2                                            08/11/97
  1000        A            PZIP           5 0                                          08/11/97
  1100        A            AMT            7 2                                          08/11/97
  1200        A            DATE           6 0                                          08/11/97
  1300        A          K CUSTNO                                                      08/11/97
  1400        A          K CDATE                                                       08/11/97
```

Figure 17-24 Record formats of the physical files accessed by the join logical file.

Join Logical File Syntax

Figure 17-25 details the syntax for the join logical file processed by the application program. Notice the sequence in which the join logical file keywords are specified. Syntax errors will result in compilation if the keywords are not specified in the indicated order.

```
SEQNBR*...+... 1 ...+... 2 ...+... 3 ...+... 4 ...+... 5 ...+... 6 ...+... 7 ...+... 8
   100       A                                      JDFTVAL
   200       A          R CHISTR
   300       A                                      JFILE(CUSMAST TRANS)
   400       A          J                           JOIN(CUSMAST TRANS)
   500       A                                      JFLD(CUST# CUSTNO)
   600       A                                      JDUPSEQ(DATE)
   700       A            NAME                      JREF(1)
   800       A            CUST#
   900       A            BEGBAL
  1000       A            ADDR
  1100       A            CITY
  1200       A            STATE
  1300       A            ZIP
  1400       A            LIMIT
  1500       A            DATE
```

Figure 17-25 Syntax for a join logical file that accesses two physical files.

```
1600     A            PAYEE
1700     A            PADDR
1800     A            PCITY
1900     A            PSTATE
2000     A            PZIP
2100     A            AMT
2200     A            RECORDID                   JREF(2)
2300     A          K CUST#
```

SEQUENCE NUMBER

100 The **JDFTVAL** statement controls the processing of a primary (physical) file record when the secondary (physical) file does not have a related record (same key field value(s)).

200 The letter **R** in position 17 identifies this entry as the join logical file's record format. Unlike nonjoin logical files, this entry cannot be a record name from one of the physical files.

Only one record format name may be specified for a join logical file.

300 The **JFILE** keyword joins CUSMAST and TRANS for access by the join logical file. This entry must be made at the record level—on the same line as the record name or as a separate entry on the next coding line.

The first file specified in the **JFILE** keyword is the primary file, and the other file is the secondary.

400 The letter **J** must be entered in position 17 with a **JOIN** keyword. This entry identifies which pair of physical files are to be joined for processing. At least one **JOIN** keyword is required in a join logical file.

500 The **JFLD** keyword joins the two files specified in the preceding **JOIN** statement by common fields (CUST# and CUSTNO). This entry must immediately follow a related **JOIN** keyword.

600 The **JDUPSEQ(DATE)** controls the processing of records from the TRANS file in an ascending transaction date order within the customer group.

700–2100 Because the NAME field is included in the record formats of the CUSMAST and TRANS files, a **JREF(1)** keyword must be specified to indicate from which physical file the value is to be used. The 1 entry included with the **JREF** keyword indicates the file is referenced by its relative position in the **JFILE** keyword.

The fields to be included in the join logical file processing are specified in these entries. Lines 700 through 1400 include fields from the CUSMAST file with the remaining fields from the TRANS file.

2200 Because the RECORDID field is included in the CUSMAST and TRANS files, the **JREF(2)** keyword must be used to identify the file from which the value will be extracted. The **2** in parentheses indicates that the RECORDID value will be accessed from the TRANS file.

2300 CUST# is defined as the key field, which will cause the join logical file to process both files in ascending customer number order. However, because of the **JDFTVAL** keyword, transaction records will be accessed in an ascending date order within the customer group.

Figure 17-25 Syntax for a join logical file that accesses two physical files.

The first listing (expanded listing not shown) generated from compilation of the join logical file is presented in Figure 17-26.

```
5763SS1 V3R1M0  940909              Data Description              STAN/JOINLF              8/19/97
File name . . . . . . . . . . . . . . . . . . . . . . :  JOINLF
  Library name  . . . . . . . . . . . . . . . . . . . :  STAN
File attribute  . . . . . . . . . . . . . . . . . . . :  Logical
Source file containing DDS  . . . . . . . . . . . . . :  QDDSSRC
  Library name  . . . . . . . . . . . . . . . . . . . :  STAN
Source member containing DDS  . . . . . . . . . . . . :  JOINLF
Source member last changed  . . . . . . . . . . . . . :  08/19/97  14:19:03
Source listing options  . . . . . . . . . . . . . . . :  *SOURCE    *LIST       *NOSECLVL
DDS generation severity level . . . . . . . . . . . . :  20
DDS flagging severity level . . . . . . . . . . . . . :  00
File type . . . . . . . . . . . . . . . . . . . . . . :  *DATA
Authority . . . . . . . . . . . . . . . . . . . . . . :  *LIBCRTAUT
Replace file  . . . . . . . . . . . . . . . . . . . . :  *NO
Text  . . . . . . . . . . . . . . . . . . . . . . . . :  Figure 17-25 - join logical file
Compiler  . . . . . . . . . . . . . . . . . . . . . . :  IBM AS/400 Data Description Processor
                                    Data Description Source
```

Figure 17-26 First listing (expanded listing not shown) generated from compilation of the join logical file.

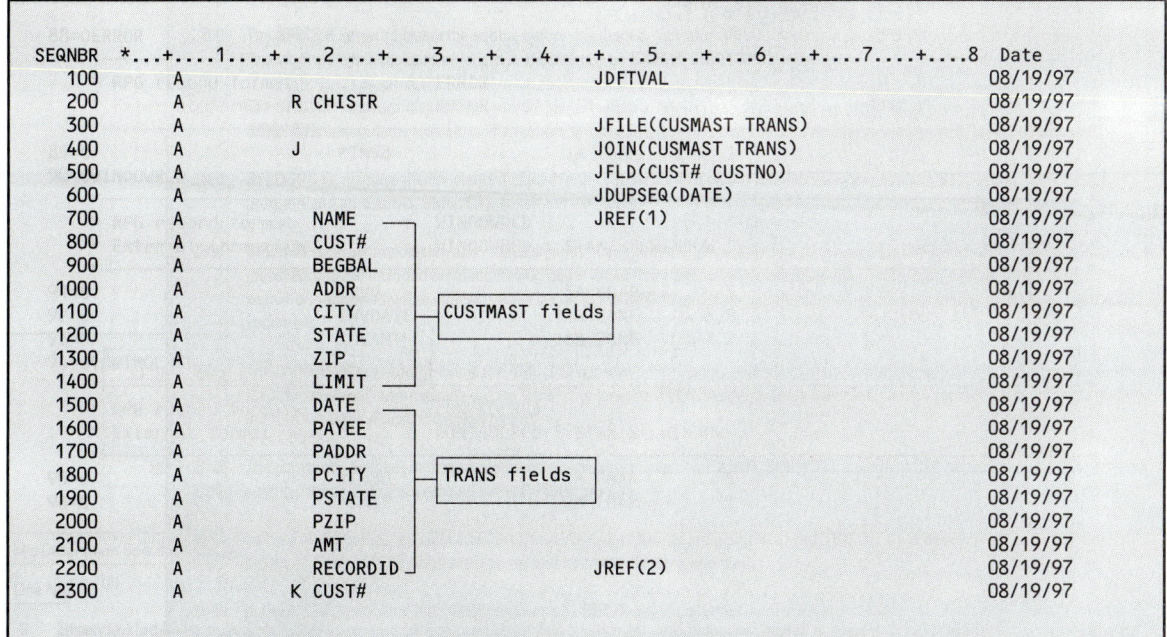

```
SEQNBR  *...+....1....+....2....+....3....+....4....+....5....+....6....+....7....+....8  Date
  100        A                                      JDFTVAL                                 08/19/97
  200        A          R CHISTR                                                            08/19/97
  300        A                                      JFILE(CUSMAST TRANS)                    08/19/97
  400        A          J                           JOIN(CUSMAST TRANS)                     08/19/97
  500        A                                      JFLD(CUST# CUSTNO)                      08/19/97
  600        A                                      JDUPSEQ(DATE)                           08/19/97
  700        A            NAME    --+               JREF(1)                                 08/19/97
  800        A            CUST#     |                                                       08/19/97
  900        A            BEGBAL    |                                                       08/19/97
 1000        A            ADDR      |                                                       08/19/97
 1100        A            CITY      |-- CUSTMAST fields                                     08/19/97
 1200        A            STATE     |                                                       08/19/97
 1300        A            ZIP       |                                                       08/19/97
 1400        A            LIMIT   --+                                                       08/19/97
 1500        A            DATE    --+                                                       08/19/97
 1600        A            PAYEE     |                                                       08/19/97
 1700        A            PADDR     |                                                       08/19/97
 1800        A            PCITY     |-- TRANS fields                                        08/19/97
 1900        A            PSTATE    |                                                       08/19/97
 2000        A            PZIP      |                                                       08/19/97
 2100        A            AMT       |                                                       08/19/97
 2200        A            RECORDID--+               JREF(2)                                 08/19/97
 2300        A          K CUST#                                                             08/19/97
```

Figure 17-26 First listing (expanded listing not shown) generated from compilation of the join logical file. (Continued)

The processing logic controlled by the join logical file read by the application program is detailed in Figure 17-27.

```
        CUSMAST                   TRANS

     09000............       10000.......090197
     10000............       10000.......090597
     11000............       10000.......090797
     12000............       11000.......090197
     13000............       12000.......091097
                             13000.......090597

          Order in which the records are processed:

In storage, the first matching records (same customer number) from each
file are processed as one record (concatenated):

                      10000¦090197

              CUSMAST ____|    |____ TRANS

Because another record for CUST# 10000 is read from the TRANS file, the
10000 record from the CUSMAST file remains in storage. The second 10000
record from the TRANS file is concatenated with the CUSMAST record for
processing.

                      10000¦090597

              CUSMAST ____|    |____ TRANS

Note that CUST# 09000 in the CUSMAST file does not have a matching record
in the TRANS file. Because the JDFTVAL keyword was specified in the JOIN
logical file format, the CUSMAST record without a matching TRANS record
will be processed. Without the JDFTVAL keyword, the 09000 record would
not be accessed.
```

Figure 17-27 Processing logic for a join logical file that accesses two physical files.

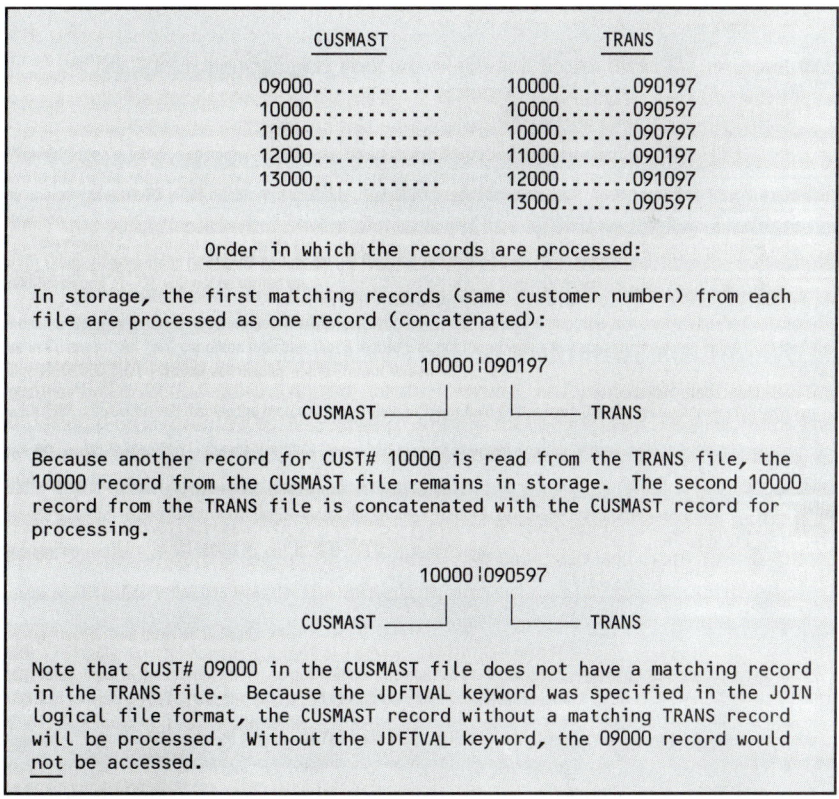

RPG IV Program Coding

Figure 17-28 contains a compile listing of the **RPG IV** program that reads a join logical file that processes two physical files.

```
Line   <---------------------- Source Specifications ----------------------------><---- Comments ----> Do
Number ....1....+....2....+....3....+....4....+....5....+....6....+....7....+....8....+....9....+...10 Num
                          S o u r c e   L i s t i n g
        * This program processes two physical files accessed by a join
        * logical file....

       FJoinLF    IF   E             K DISK
        *----------------------------------------------------------------------------------------*
        *                                RPG name            External name                      *
        * File name. . . . . . . . . :   JOINLF              STAN/JOINLF                        *
        * Record format(s) . . . . . :   CHISTR              CHISTR                             *
        *----------------------------------------------------------------------------------------*
       FQsysprt   O    F  132           PRINTER OFLIND(*INOF)

        * Work field (Owed) & holding field for control break test (HoldCust#)
       D Owed            S              7  2
       D HoldCust#       S              5

      =ICHISTR
        *----------------------------------------------------------------------------------------*
        * RPG record format  . . . . :   CHISTR                                                 *
        * External format  . . . . . :   CHISTR : STAN/JOINLF                                   *
        *----------------------------------------------------------------------------------------*
      =I                                 A    1   15  NAME
      =I                                 A   16   20  CUST#
      =I                                 P   21   24 2BEGBAL
      =I                                 A   25   44  ADDR
      =I                                 A   45   54  CITY
      =I                                 A   55   56  STATE
      =I                                 P   57   59 0ZIP
      =I                                 P   60   62 0LIMIT
      =I                                 P   63   66 0DATE
      =I                                 A   67   78  PAYEE
      =I                                 A   79   93  PADDR
      =I                                 A   94  105  PCITY
      =I                                 A  106  107  PSTATE
      =I                                 P  108  110 0PZIP
      =I                                 P  111  114 2AMT
      =I                                 A  115  115  RECORDID
       C                   READ      JoinLF                                 ----LR  read first LF record
       C                   EXSR      HouseKepSR                                     branch to SR
       C
       C                   DOW       *INLR = *OFF                                   dow ind 80 is off   B01

        * Heading control....
       C                   IF        *INOF = *ON                                    OF "on"?            B02
       C                   EXCEPT    Hdging                                         print heading lines 02
       C                   EXCEPT    CustHdg                                                            02
       C                   EVAL      *INOF = *OFF                                   turn off OF indicatr 02
       C                   ENDIF                                                    end IF group        E02

        * Test for a change in customer number....
       C                   IF        Cust# <> HoldCust#                             control fld break?  B02
       C                   EXSR      Custbreak                                      branch to SR        02
       C                   EXCEPT    CustHdg                                        print customer hdg  02
       C                   ENDIF                                                    end IF group        E02

        * Test for record type (Chargr or Paidr) and exit to related SR....
       C     RecordID      CASEQ     'C'           ChargSR                          branch to subroutine 01
       C     RecordID      CASEQ     'P'           PaytSR                           branch to subroutine 01
       C                   ENDCS                                                    end CAS group       01
```

Figure 17-28 Compile listing of the **RPG IV** program that reads a join logical file.

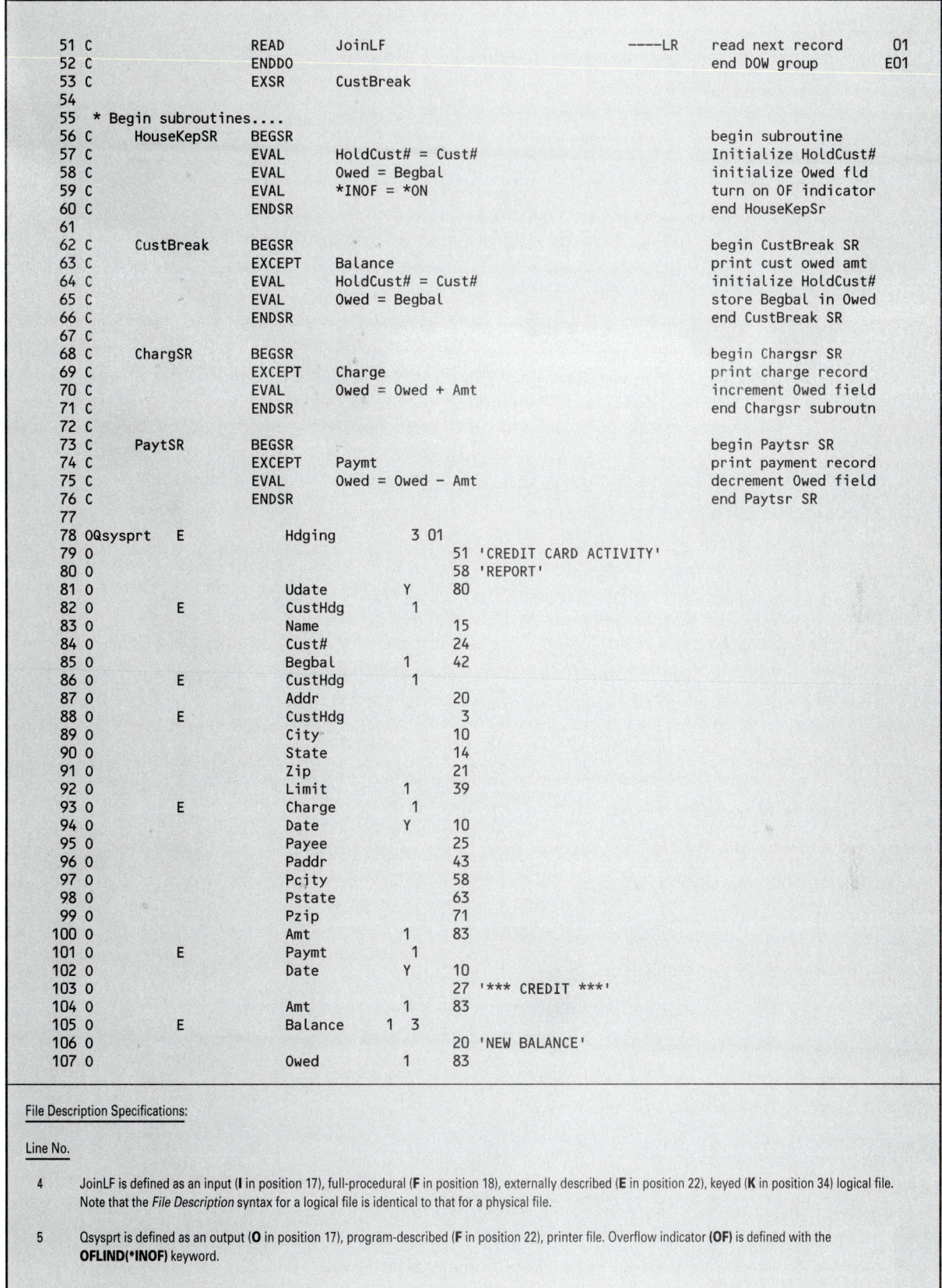

```
 51 C                   READ      JoinLF                             ----LR   read next record       01
 52 C                   ENDDO                                                end DOW group         E01
 53 C                   EXSR      CustBreak
 54
 55  * Begin subroutines....
 56 C     HouseKepSR    BEGSR                                                begin subroutine
 57 C                   EVAL      HoldCust# = Cust#                          Initialize HoldCust#
 58 C                   EVAL      Owed = Begbal                              initialize Owed fld
 59 C                   EVAL      *INOF = *ON                                turn on OF indicator
 60 C                   ENDSR                                                end HouseKepSr
 61
 62 C     CustBreak     BEGSR                                                begin CustBreak SR
 63 C                   EXCEPT    Balance                                    print cust owed amt
 64 C                   EVAL      HoldCust# = Cust#                          initialize HoldCust#
 65 C                   EVAL      Owed = Begbal                              store Begbal in Owed
 66 C                   ENDSR                                                end CustBreak SR
 67 C
 68 C     ChargSR       BEGSR                                                begin Chargsr SR
 69 C                   EXCEPT    Charge                                     print charge record
 70 C                   EVAL      Owed = Owed + Amt                          increment Owed field
 71 C                   ENDSR                                                end Chargsr subroutn
 72 C
 73 C     PaytSR        BEGSR                                                begin Paytsr SR
 74 C                   EXCEPT    Paymt                                      print payment record
 75 C                   EVAL      Owed = Owed - Amt                          decrement Owed field
 76 C                   ENDSR                                                end Paytsr SR
 77
 78 OQsysprt   E            Hdging         3 01
 79 O                                           51 'CREDIT CARD ACTIVITY'
 80 O                                           58 'REPORT'
 81 O                       Udate          Y    80
 82 O          E            CustHdg         1
 83 O                       Name                15
 84 O                       Cust#               24
 85 O                       Begbal         1    42
 86 O          E            CustHdg         1
 87 O                       Addr                20
 88 O          E            CustHdg              3
 89 O                       City                10
 90 O                       State               14
 91 O                       Zip                 21
 92 O                       Limit          1    39
 93 O          E            Charge          1
 94 O                       Date           Y    10
 95 O                       Payee               25
 96 O                       Paddr               43
 97 O                       Pcity               58
 98 O                       Pstate              63
 99 O                       Pzip                71
100 O                       Amt            1    83
101 O          E            Paymt           1
102 O                       Date           Y    10
103 O                                           27 '*** CREDIT ***'
104 O                       Amt            1    83
105 O          E            Balance      1  3
106 O                                           20 'NEW BALANCE'
107 O                       Owed           1    83
```

File Description Specifications:

Line No.

4 JoinLF is defined as an input (**I** in position 17), full-procedural (**F** in position 18), externally described (**E** in position 22), keyed (**K** in position 34) logical file. Note that the *File Description* syntax for a logical file is identical to that for a physical file.

5 Qsysprt is defined as an output (**O** in position 17), program-described (**F** in position 22), printer file. Overflow indicator **(OF)** is defined with the **OFLIND(*INOF)** keyword.

Figure 17-28 Compile listing of the RPG IV program that reads a join logical file. (Continued)

Definition Specifications:

8 Owed is defined as a standalone field into which the Begbal value from the Cusmast file is moved.

9 HoldCust# is defined as a standalone field into which the Cust# value from the Cusmast file is moved to check for a change in customer number so that the end balance of the previous customer can be printed before the heading lines for the next customer.

Calculation Specifications:

28 This **READ** instruction reads the first record from the Join LF (logical) file. If end of file is read, indicator **LR** will be turned on.

29 This **EXSR** instruction branches control to the HouseKepSR subroutine, where the Cust# value from the first MASTR record is moved into the HoldCust# field. The Owed field is initialized with the value in the Begbal field from the MASTR record and overflow indicator **OF** is turned on.

31 Instructions within the **DOW** group control subsequent reads and all other processing functions. Exit from the **DOW** group is controlled when indicator **LR** is turned on, when the **READ** instruction on line 28 or 51 reads end of file.

34 This **IF** instruction tests the status of indicator **OF,** which was initially turned on in the HouseKepSR subroutine for the first logical record processed. Subsequent page overflow is "flagged" when the overflow line is detected and indicator **OF** automatically turned on.

35 When the relational test in the **IF** instruction is true, this **EXCEPT** will branch control to the output instructions and print the Hdging record format on the first line of the report.

36 This **EXCEPT** instruction will branch control to output and print the CustHdg record formats on instruction lines 82 through 92. The data included for this output is from a MASTR record.

37 This **EVAL** instruction turns off indicator **OF,** which is automatically turned on when the page overflow line is subsequently tested.

38 This **ENDIF** operation ends this **IF** group, which began on line 34.

41 This **IF** instruction compares the value in Cust# (from the MASTR record) with the value stored in HoldCust#. If the values are not equal, the following **EXSR** instruction is executed.

42 The **EXSR** instruction branches control to the CustBreak subroutine, where control break (change in Cust#) instructions are executed.

43 This **EXCEPT** instruction prints the CustHdg output records on lines 82 through 92, which include MASTR record data for the current customer.

44 This **ENDIF** operation ends the **IF** group that began on line 41.

47 This **CASEQ** instruction compares the value in the RecordID field (included in the three record formats) with the character literal **C.** When the relational test is "true" (values are equal), control branches to the ChargSR subroutine, where instructions for customer charges are performed.

48 This **CASEQ** instruction compares the value in the RecordID field (included in the three record formats) with the character literal **P.** When the relational test is "true" (values are equal), control branches to the PaytSR subroutine, where instructions for customer payments are performed.

49 The **ENDCS** operation ends the **CAS** group.

51 This **READ** instruction reads the next record from the logical file. When end of file is read, indicator **LR** will be turned on to subsequently end the program.

52 The **ENDDO** operation ends the **DOW** group that began on line 31.

53 This **EXSR** instruction branches control to the CustBreak subroutine so that the New Balance value for the last customer will print. Without this instruction, the <u>last</u> line for the <u>last</u> customer group in the logical file would not be printed.

56 This **BEGSR** instruction begins the HouseKepSR subroutine.

57 This **EVAL** instruction initializes the HoldCust# field with the value from the Cust# field from the current MASTR record.

58 This **EVAL** instruction initializes the Owed field with the value in Begbal from the current MASTR record.

59 This **EVAL** instruction turns on indicator **OF,** to control page overflow for the first logical file record processed.

60 This **ENDSR** operation ends the HouseKepSR subroutine.

62 This **BEGSR** instruction begins the CustBreak subroutine.

63 This **EXCEPT** instruction prints the Balance record format on lines 105 through 107. The NEW BALANCE value is printed after all of the related customer's charge and payment records are processed and the new Owed amount is calculated.

64 This **EVAL** instruction initializes the HoldCust# field with the Cust# field value from the current MASTR record.

65 This **EVAL** instruction initializes the Owed field with the value in Begbal from the current MASTR record.

Figure 17-28 Compile listing of the **RPG IV** program that reads a join logical file. (Continued)

66	This **ENDSR** operation ends the CustBreak subroutine.
68	This **BEGSR** instruction begins the ChargSR subroutine.
69	This **EXCEPT** instruction prints the values in the Charge record format on lines 93 through 100.
70	This **EVAL** operation increments the Owed field value with the Amt field value from the current CHARGR record processed.
71	This **ENDSR** operation ends the ChargSR subroutine.
73	This **BEGSR** instruction begins the PaytSR subroutine.
74	This **EXCEPT** instruction prints the Paymt record format on lines 101 through 104.
75	This **EVAL** operation decrements the Owed field value with the Amt field value from the current PAIDR record processed.
76	This **ENDSR** operation ends the PaytSR subroutine.
<u>Output Specifications:</u>	
78–81	The Hdging record values are printed by the **EXCEPT** instruction on line 35.
82–92	The three CustHdg record values are printed by the **EXCEPT** instructions on lines 36 and 43. Field values are from the MASTR record merged in the logical file in an ascending customer number/date (i.e., CUST#/*NONE) order.
93–100	The Charge record values are printed by the **EXCEPT** instruction on line 69. Field values are from the CHARGR record merged in the logical file in an ascending customer number/date (CUSTNO/CDATE) order.
101–104	The Paymt record values are printed by the **EXCEPT** instruction on line 74. Field values are from the PAIDR record merged in the logical file in an ascending customer number/date (CUSTN/PDATE) order.
105–107	The Balance record values are printed by the **EXCEPT** instruction on line 63. The final value in Owed is computed on line 58, 65, or 70 after the last record for the customer group is processed.

Figure 17-28 Compile listing of the **RPG IV** program that reads a join logical file. (Continued)

Except for the logical file name and line numbers, the **RPG IV** syntax for the join logical file program is identical to that for the nonjoin logical file program earlier shown in Figure 17-21.

Because the report generated by the **RPG IV** program that reads a join logical file is identical to that shown in Figure 17-17 for the nonjoin logical file, it is not repeated again.

SELECT/OMIT FIELD NAMES

Records in a physical file may be selected or omitted for processing by a nonjoin or join logical file that includes one or more *select* and/or *omit* fields. The rules related to this control are explained in Figure 17-29.

1. Select fields are identified in a logical file's record format by an **S** in position 17; omit fields are identified by an **O.** Select and omit fields must follow all field and key field level entries.
2. Select and omit fields may only be specified if key fields are defined for the logical file's record format or if the **DYNSLT** (*Dynamic Select*) keyword is assigned at the file level. If the application does not require a key field, ***NONE** may be specified to satisfy the key field requirement.

Figure 17-29 Rules for logical file select/omit fields.

3. A blank in position 17 of the statement immediately following a select or omit field indicates that the field is in an **AND** relationship with the previous **S** or **O** field. A following field with an **S** or **O** indicates that it is in an **OR** relationship.
4. If both **S** and **O** fields are included in a logical record, the order in which they are specified is important. Select and omit statements are processed in the order in which they are coded. A record is either selected or omitted as specified, and any remaining select/omit statements are ignored.
5. If both select and omit statements are included in a logical file's record format, records not meeting the selection tests may be selected or omitted by the **ALL** keyword.
6. If the **ALL** keyword is not specified, records that do not meet the selection criteria are omitted and records that do not meet the omission criteria are selected.
7. A field name may not be included in an **ALL** statement. However, as appropriate, an **S** or **O** must be specified in position 17.
8. Valid keywords that may be used with **S** or **O** fields are **COMP, RANGE,** and **VALUES.**

Figure 17-29 Rules for logical file select/omit fields. (Continued)

Examples that explain the syntax and processing logic of select and omit fields for logical files are illustrated in Figure 17-30.

Example 1:

```
SEQNBR *...+....1....+....2....+....3....+....4....+....5....+....6....+....7....+....8

              * Select statement on line 300 processes only the physical file (TRANS)
              * records that have a C stored in the CODE field.   All other records are
              * ignored.
  100         A          R CHARGR                       PFILE(TRANS)
  200         A          K CUSTNO
  300         A          S CODE                         COMP(EQ 'C')
```

Example 2:

```
SEQNBR *...+....1....+....2....+....3....+....4....+....5....+....6....+....7....+....8

              * Select statement on line 300 processes only the physical file (TRANS)
              * records that have a C or P stored in the CODE field.   All other records
              * are ignored.
  100         A          R CHARGR                       PFILE(TRANS)
  200         A          K CUSTNO
  300         A          S CODE                         VALUES('C' 'P')
```

Example 3:

```
SEQNBR *...+....1....+....2....+....3....+....4....+....5....+....6....+....7....+....8

              * Select statement on line 300 is in an AND relationship with the implied
              * select statement on line 400.  Physical file records will be processed
              * that have a C or P stored in the CODE field and have an AMT value from
              * 100.00 to 500.00.   All other records are ignored.
  100         A          R CHARGR                       PFILE(TRANS)
  200         A          K CUSTNO
  300         A          S CODE                         VALUES('C' 'P')
  400         A            AMT                          RANGE(100.00 500.00)
```

Figure 17-30 Syntax and processing logic of select and omit fields.

Example 4:

```
SEQNBR *...+....1....+....2....+....3....+....4....+....5....+....6....+....7....+....8

                * Omit statement on line 300 is in an OR relationship with the omit state-
                * ment on line 400.  Physical file records will not be processed that have
                * a C stored in the CODE field or have an AMT value less than 100.00.  All
                * other records will be selected for processing.
   100      A           R CHARGR                    PFILE(TRANS)
   200      A           K CUSTNO
   300      A           O CODE                      COMP(EQ 'C')
   400      A    ┌───── O AMT                       COMP(LT 100.00)
  ┌──────────────┘
  └─ OR relationship is indicated for two or more select/omit statements when an S
     and/or O entry is included in position 17.
```

Example 5:

```
SEQNBR *...+....1....+....2....+....3....+....4....+....5....+....6....+....7....+....8

                * Omit statement on line 300 is in an AND relationship with the omit state-
                * ment on line 400.  Physical file records will not be processed that have
                * a P stored in the CODE field and an AMT value greater than 101.00.  The
                * ALL statement on line 500 explicitly specifies that all other records
                * will be selected for processing.
   100      A           R CHARGR                    PFILE(TRANS)
   200      A           K CUSTNO
   300      A           O CODE                      COMP(EQ 'P')
   400      A    ┌─────   AMT                       COMP(GT 101.00)
   500      A    │      S                           ALL
                 │
  ┌──────────────┘
  └─ AND relationship is indicated for two or more select/omit statements when an S
     and/or O entry is not included in position 17.
```

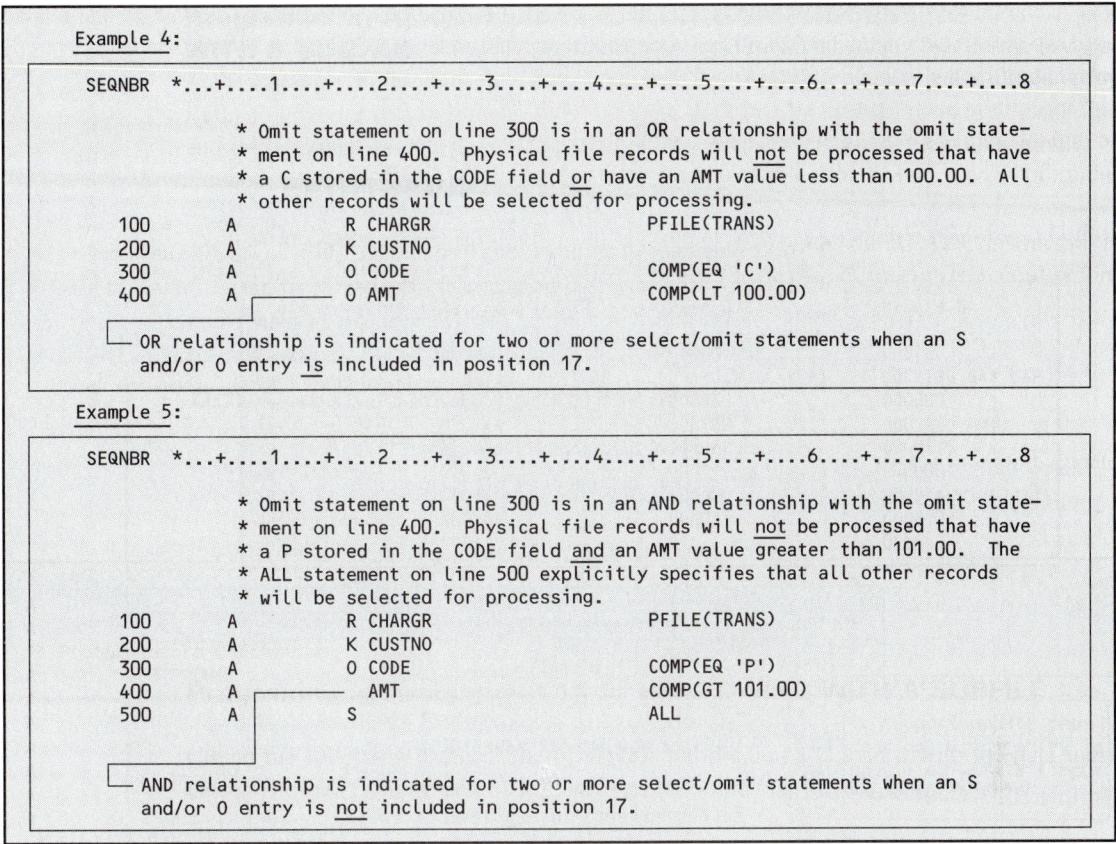

Figure 17-30 Syntax and processing logic of select and omit fields. (Continued)

SUMMARY

A *logical file* is a database file that accesses the data stored in one or more physical files. When created over a physical file, an *access path,* which includes the processing criteria, is built. Logical files do not contain data and, unlike physical files, may include more than one record format.

Two types of logical files supported by the AS/400 are *nonjoin* and *join. Nonjoin logical files* may process either one physical file or two or more by merging the records. *Join logical files* support only one record format and are used only when two or more physical files are to be processed together. A join logical file creates one record in storage from two or more matched records (same key values) from the physical files. Join logical files are "read-only." Consequently, they may not be used to update the related physical files.

The code for a logical file is included in *Data Description Specifications* and is entered via **SEU.** Identical to other DDS file types, the logical file source must be compiled to generate an object. Once a logical file is created over a physical file, the physical file cannot be deleted unless the logical file is deleted first.

Records from one or more physical files may be selected or omitted from processing by a nonjoin or join logical file's *select/omit* control. Select and omit fields must follow all field and key field entries and are identified by an **S** (for *select*) or **O** (for *omit*) in position 17 of the DDS statement(s). Select/omit criteria are controlled by **COMP, RANGE,** and **VALUES** keywords, which may be specified individually or in an **AND** or **OR** relationship.

An **RPG IV** program that processes a logical file must include its name in positions 7–16 of the *File Description* statement and define it as externally described (**E** in position

22). If the logical file is keyed, a **K** must be entered in position 34, or the related physical file(s) will be processed in arrival sequence.

QUESTIONS

17-1. Name some of the processing functions for which logical files are used.

17-2. As compared to the sorting of files, what are the advantages of logical files?

17-3. Is data stored in a logical file? On what specifications form is the syntax for a logical file included? Does the compilation of a logical file delete the data in the related physical file(s)?

17-4. Name the two types of logical files. How do they differ in processing logic?

17-5. When a logical file references one or more physical files, what is automatically built by each logical file to control processing?

17-6. What is the function of a **PFILE** keyword?

Examine the following DDS coding and answer Questions 17-7 through 17-12:

```
SEQNBR*...+... 1 ...+... 2 ...+... 3 ...+... 4 ...+... 5 ...+... 6 ...+... 7 ...+... 8
 100      A          R FORMAT                    PFILE(GLACCTS)
 200      A          K BALANCE
```

17-7. What is the function of the letter **R** in position 17 of line 100?

17-8. What does the entry in the *Name* field (positions 19–28) reference?

17-9. What does the entry GLACCTS in the **PFILE** keyword reference?

17-10. Explain the function of the entry on line 200.

17-11. In what order will the physical file be processed?

17-12. What fields will be accessed in the record format of the physical file?

Examine the following DDS coding and answer Questions 17-13 through 17-16:

```
SEQNBR*...+... 1 ...+... 2 ...+... 3 ...+... 4 ...+... 5 ...+... 6 ...+... 7 ...+... 8
 100      A          R PF2R                      PFILE(PF1)
 200      A                                      FORMAT(PF2)
 300      A          K ACCT#                     DESCEND
 400      A*
 500      A          R PF4R                      PFILE(PF3)
 600      A                                      FORMAT(PF4)
 700      A          K ACTNO                     DESCEND
```

17-13. How many physical files will be accessed by the nonjoin logical file?

17-14. What is the function of the **FORMAT** keyword?

17-15. Where are the field names in positions 19–28 defined?

17-16. What is the function of the **DESCEND** keyword?

Examine the following DDS coding and answer Questions 17-17 through 17-19:

```
SEQNBR*...+... 1 ...+... 2 ...+... 3 ...+... 4 ...+... 5 ...+... 6 ...+... 7 ...+... 8
 100      A          R GLRECD                    PFILE(GLEDGER)
 200      A          K ACCT#
 300      A          K NONE
 400      A*
 500      A          R TRRECD                    PFILE(GLTRANS)
 600      A          K ACTNO
 700      A          K TDATE
```

17-17. How many physical files are accessed by the nonjoin logical file?

17-18. What is the function of the ***NONE** keyword on line 300?

17-19. Within an account group, which of the physical files will be processed first, second, and third? What controls this processing?

17-20 Explain the function of the following join logical file keywords:

JFILE	**JFLD**	**JDUPSEQ**
JOIN	**JREF**	**DYNSLT**

17-21. Identify the level of the join logical file keywords listed in Question 17–20—*file, record, field,* or *join.*

Examine the following DDS coding and answer Questions 17-22 through 17-24:

```
SEQNBR*...+... 1 ...+... 2 ...+... 3 ...+... 4 ...+... 5 ...+... 6 ...+... 7 ...+... 8
 100       A           R JRECRD                     JFILE(SUMMARY ITEMS)
 200       A           J                            JOIN(SUMMARY ITEMS)
 300       A                                        JFLD(INV# INV#)
 400       A             CUST#
 500       A             INV#                       JREF(1)
 600       A             DESCRP
 700       A             QTY
 800       A             UCOST
```

17-22. How many record formats are being joined into one record? Which physical file is considered primary?

17-23. By what value and order will the physical files be processed?

17-24. What is the function of the **JREF(1)** keyword?

17-25. How would a **JDFTVAL** keyword control change the processing of the physical files?

17-26. What is the function of select/omit control for logical files?

17-27. Name the keywords supported with logical file select/omit control.

17-28. Explain the function of each of the keywords named in Question 17-27.

17-29. How is an **OR** relationship between two or more select/omit statements specified? How is an **AND** relationship indicated?

17-30. *Examine the following related statements and explain the processing logic:*

```
SEQNBR*...+... 1 ...+... 2 ...+... 3 ...+... 4 ...+... 5 ...+... 6 ...+... 7 ...+... 8
 100       A           R CUSTMR                     PFILE(CUSTMERS)
 200       A           K CUSTNO
 300       A           S STATE                      VALUES('CT' 'NY' 'NJ')
 400       A             BALANCE                    COMP(GT 5000.00)
 500       A           O RATING                     RANGE('A' 'C')
```

PROGRAMMING ASSIGNMENTS

For each of the following programming assignments, more than one physical file must have been created and loaded with data. Your instructor will inform you if you have to create the physical files and load them or if they have been prepared for the assignment.

Programming Assignment 17-1: STUDENT TRANSCRIPTS (USING A NONJOIN LOGICAL FILE)

Write an **RPG IV** program to process a student master file and a student course file to generate temporary transcripts. A nonjoin logical file is to be created to access the two physical files.

Student Master File Record Format:

PHYSICAL FILE DESCRIPTION

SYSTEM: AS/400	DATE: Yours
FILE NAME: Yours	REV NO: 0
RECORD NAME: Yours	KEY LENGTH: 9
SEQUENCE: Keyed (Unique)	RECORD SIZE: 105

FIELD DEFINITIONS

FIELD NO	FIELD NAME	SIZE	TYPE	POSITION FROM	POSITION TO	COMMENTS
1	SS#	9	P	1	5	Key field
2	SNAME	20	C	6	25	
3	SADD1	20	C	26	45	
4	SADD2	15	C	46	60	
5	SCITY	20	C	61	80	
6	SSTATE	2	C	81	82	
7	SZIP	5	P	83	85	
8	SMAJOR	20	C	86	105	

SS#	SNAME	SADDR	SADD2	SCITY	SSTATE	SZIP	SMAJOR
011111111	HENRY CHURCHILL	1640 PARK AVENUE	APT 10	NORWALK	CT	06854	DATA PROCESSING
011223333	GEORGE ROOSEVELT	25 BURNT PLAINS		DARIEN	CT	06853	COMPUTER SCIENCE
022445555	NELSON FORD	26 PEARSALL PLACE	SUITE 30	STAMFORD	CT	06850	DATA PROCESSING
033778990	WILLIAM CARTER	853 WOOD AVENUE	APT 45	BRIDGEPORT	CT	06601	COMPUTER SCIENCE
041668888	PHILIP BUSH	102 VIRGINIA AVENUE		GREENWICH	CT	06740	COMPUTER SCIENCE
055119999	FRANK TRUMAN	7 BOOT SHOP LANE		NEW HAVEN	CT	06554	DATA PROCESSING
066227777	FREDERICK GRANT	14 GETTYSBURG PLACE		BRISTOL	CT	06770	DATA PROCESSING

Student Course File Record Format:

PHYSICAL FILE DESCRIPTION

SYSTEM: AS/400	DATE: Yours
FILE NAME: Yours	REV NO: 0
RECORD NAME: Yours	KEY LENGTH: 21
SEQUENCE: Keyed (Unique)	RECORD SIZE: 53

FIELD DEFINITIONS

FIELD NO	FIELD NAME	SIZE	TYPE	POSITION FROM	POSITION TO	COMMENTS
1	CSS#	9	P	1	5	Major key
2	CNAME	20	C	6	25	
3	CNO	6	C	26	45	Minor key 2
4	CDATE	6	P	46	49	Minor key 1
5	CINST#	3	P	50	51	
6	CMARK	1	C	52	52	
7	CREDIT	1	P	53	53	

Physical File Data:

CSS#	CNAME	CNO	CDATE	CINST#	CMARK	CREDIT
011111111	ENGLISH COMPOSITION	ACD101	961215	300	C	3
011111111	INTRO TO PROGRAMMING	DPS100	961215	104	A	4

Processing: A nonjoin logical file must be created to merge the student master file in an ascending student number order with the course file in ascending student number and ascending term date order. For each student, a temporary transcript is to be printed.

011111111	COLLEGE ALGEBRA I	MTH100	971215	161	C	3
011111111	INTRO TO RPG/400	DPS200	970521	221	A	4
011111111	COBOL I	DPS210	970521	221	A	4
011223333	COMPUTER SCIENCE I	CSC101	961215	190	B	4
011223333	COMPUTER SCIENCE II	CSC202	970521	180	C	4
011223333	CALCULUS I	MTH201	970521	167	B	3
022445555	INTRO TO PROGRAMMING	DPS100	961215	104	C	4
022445555	MICROCOMPUTERS I	DPS110	961215	200	A	4
033778999	COMPUTER SCIENCE I	CSC101	962115	190	C	4
033778999	PASCAL I	CSC120	961215	180	A	4
041668888	ENGLISH COMPOSITION	ACD101	961215	300	F	3
041668888	CALCULUS I	MTH201	961215	167	D	3
041668888	PHYSICS I	SCS101	961215	075	C	4
041668888	COMPUTER SCIENCE II	CSC202	970521	180	C	4
041668888	C PROGRAMMING I	CSC210	970521	182	B	4
055119999	MICROCOMPUTERS I	DPS110	961215	200	A	4
055119999	AMERICAN STUDIES	ACD210	970521	299	A	3
055119999	ENGLISH LITERATURE	ACD210	970521	300	B	3

Compute each student's cumulative grade point average based on the following:

A = 4 points, B = 3 points, C = 2 points, D = 1 point, F = 0 points

Step 1: Multiply the course credits by the points for the letter grade. For example, a 3-credit course that earned an A would result in 12 points (3 credits × 4 points).

Step 2: For each student accumulate the total points and total credits.

Step 3: After the last course record for a student is processed, divide the total points by the total credits to determine the student's cumulative point average.

Because the term date is stored in a YYMMDD format, it must be converted to an MMDDYY format before printing.

Output: Generate a temporary transcript for each student in the master file in the format shown in the attached printer spacing chart. For students that have no course records, print a transcript and include the error message ****NO COURSE RECORDS FOUND**** in the course section.

Report Design:

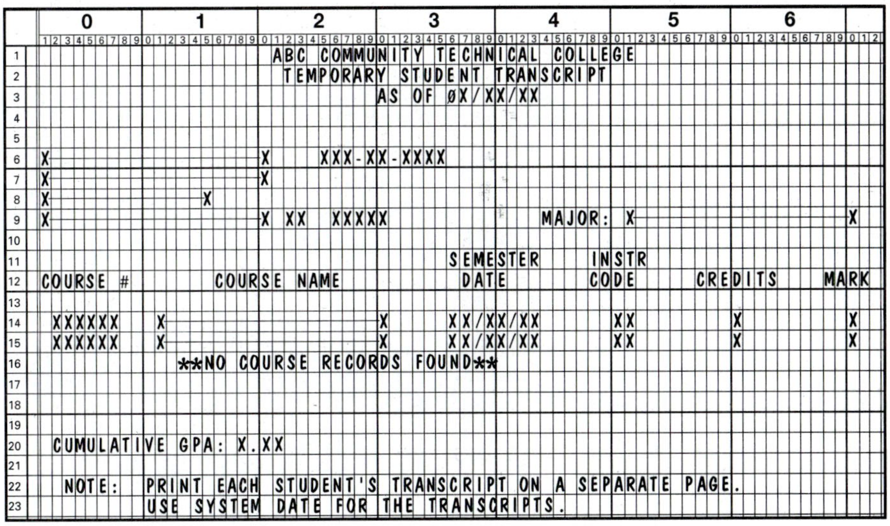

ABC COMMUNITY TECHNICAL COLLEGE
TEMPORARY STUDENT TRANSCRIPT
AS OF ØX/XX/XX
XXX-XX-XXXX
MAJOR:
SEMESTER DATE
INSTR CODE
COURSE #
COURSE NAME
CREDITS
MARK
XXXXXX
XX/XX/XX
XX
NO COURSE RECORDS FOUND
CUMULATIVE GPA: X.XX
NOTE: PRINT EACH STUDENT'S TRANSCRIPT ON A SEPARATE PAGE.
USE SYSTEM DATE FOR THE TRANSCRIPTS.

Programming Assignment 17-2: STUDENT TRANSCRIPTS (USING A JOIN LOGICAL FILE)

If Programming Assignment 17-1 was completed, modify it to process the physical files with a join logical file. However, if the assignment was not completed, refer to the specifications in Assignment 17-1 and process the physical files using a join logical file instead of with a nonjoin logical file.

Programming Assignment 17-3: MONTHLY SALES REPORT (USING A NONJOIN LOGICAL FILE)

Write an **RPG IV** program to generate the monthly sales report detailed in the attached printer spacing chart. Two physical files with the following record formats are to be processed by a nonjoin logical file.

Physical File Record Format:

PHYSICAL FILE DESCRIPTION

SYSTEM: AS/400 DATE: Yours
FILE NAME: Yours REV NO: 0
RECORD NAME: Yours KEY LENGTH: 3
SEQUENCE: Keyed (Unique) RECORD SIZE: 29

FIELD DEFINITIONS

FIELD NO	FIELD NAME	SIZE	TYPE	POSITION FROM	POSITION TO	COMMENTS
1	SALP#	3	P	1	2	Key field
2	BRNCH#	2	P	3	4	
3	SPNAME	20	C	5	24	
4	MHTODT	9	P	25	29	2 decimals

Physical File Data:

SALP#	BRNCH#	SPNAME	MHTODT
123	10	RICHARD H MACY	001232415
234	10	JOHN GIMBEL	000863579
345	10	JOHN WANAMAKER	001000000
456	20	BERT ALTMAN	000080000
567	20	ROGER PEET	003200000
678	30	JOHN PENNEY	010856700

Salesperson Transaction File Record Format:

PHYSICAL FILE DESCRIPTION

SYSTEM: AS/400 DATE: Yours
FILE NAME: Yours REV NO: 0
RECORD NAME: Yours KEY LENGTH: 3
SEQUENCE: Keyed (not unique) RECORD SIZE: 13

FIELD DEFINITIONS

FIELD NO	FIELD NAME	SIZE	TYPE	POSITION FROM	POSITION TO	COMMENTS
1	SALPNO	3	P	1	2	Key field
2	BRNHNO	2	P	3	4	
3	UNITSP	5	P	5	7	2 decimals

```
  4        QTYSLD          3   P          8      9  0 decimals
  5        SALDAT          6   P         10     13  0 decimals
```

Physical File Data:

SALPNO	BRNHNO	UNITSP	QTYSLD	SALDAT
345	10	01200	500	110197
123	10	10000	020	110197
678	30	01850	240	110197
234	10	09000	100	110297
456	20	02800	050	110297
567	20	35000	006	110397
123	10	00500	200	110397
123	10	60000	002	110497
345	10	50000	010	110497
678	30	09999	050	110497
456	20	14000	012	110697
678	30	01999	360	110697

Processing:

Step 1: Create a nonjoin logical file that will access the records from the two physical files in an ascending branch (major key) and salesperson (minor key) number order.

Step 2: For each transaction record, multiply the selling price per unit by the quantity sold to determine the daily sales dollar amount. Add this dollar sales amount to a weekly sales accumulator.

Step 3: When the salesperson number changes (a control break), add the accumulated week's total for the salesperson to the month-to-date value from the master record and print the line that includes the salesperson number, name, weekly sales amount, and the accumulated monthly total.

Step 4: When a control break is tested, add the accumulated weekly sales and monthly sales for a salesperson to their related branch totals (see printer chart).

Step 5: When the branch number changes (a control break), the branch's weekly and monthly totals are to be added to the related company accumulators (see printer chart) and the total branch sales line printed. The company totals are to be printed at **LR** time on a separate page.

Step 6: Create a data area into which the report date value 110697 is to be stored. Access the data area to extract the date for line 2 of the report (see printer chart).

Report Design:

```
                                  WEEKLY SALES REPORT BY SALESMAN & BRANCH             PAGE XXØX
                                       FOR THE WEEK ENDING ØX/XX/XX


                   BRANCH ØX

                     SALESMAN NO      SALESMAN NAME             WEEKLY SALES    MONTHLY SALES

                         XXX       X-----------------X           XXX,XXØ.XX     X,XXX,XXØ.XX
                         XXX       X-----------------X           XXX,XXØ.XX     X,XXX,XXØ.XX


                                       TOTAL BRANCH SALES      X,XXX,XXØ.XX    XX,XXX,XXØ.XX

                                       TOTAL COMPANY SALES    XX,XXX,XXØ.XX   XXX,XXX,XXØ.XX

                   NOTES:

                     1. EACH BRANCH'S SALES INFORMATION ON A SEPARATE PAGE.

                     2. HEADINGS PRINTED ON TOP OF EVERY PAGE.
```

Programming Assignment 17-4: MONTHLY SALES REPORT (USING A JOIN LOGICAL FILE)

If Programming Assignment 17-3 was completed, modify it to process the physical files with a join logical file. On the other hand, if the assignment was not completed, refer to the specifications in Assignment 17-3 and process the physical files using a join logical file instead of using a nonjoin logical file.

chapter 18

Printer Files

All of the previously discussed programs that included printed output have specified the system-supplied printer file shell **QSYSPRT** (**QPRINT** may also be used) as the output file. Use of the "print shell" required that the syntax for a report be included by the traditional method, in the *Output Specifications* of the **RPG IV** program.

Instead of the syntax for report formats being hard-coded in an **RPG IV** program, they may be externally described by a programmer-defined *printer file*. The syntax for printer files is entered, debugged, and compiled by exactly the same procedures followed for the other DDS file types. If the Programmer Menu is used to access **SEU, PRTF** must be entered as the selection type. Compared to the traditional method of coding report formats, printer files offer the following advantages:

1. **RPG IV** programs include less coding and are therefore easier to maintain.
2. If more than one program uses the same report format, the coding does not have to be duplicated in each program.
3. Modifications have to be made to only one source member and not to every program that references the report format.
4. Because the **RPG IV** built-in processing cycle for output control cannot be followed, page overflow, line count, and page numbering must be controlled by programmer-supplied statements. This requirement eliminates many of the problems associated with **RPG IV**-controlled printed output. For example, overflow lines cannot be specified with exception lines (**E** in position 17) for standard **RPG IV** controlled output. In addition, programmer-controlled output parallels the logic familiar to procedure-oriented languages such as COBOL, BASIC, and so forth.

Printer File Keywords

The keywords valid for printer files (**PRTF**) are listed in Figure 18-1. For a comprehensive discussion of all the valid **PRTF** keywords, refer to the *Data Description Specifications* manual. Only those specified in the example printer file are summarized in the following paragraphs.

DATE *Keyword.* **DATE** is a *Field Level* keyword that accesses and prints the current job date. The standard format is MMDDYY, which may be edited by an **EDTCDE** *(Edit Code)* or **EDTWRD** *(Edit Word)* keyword.

	ALIAS	**	DRAWER	**	OVERLAY
	BARCODE		EDTCDE	***	PAGNBR
	BLKFOLD		EDTWRD	**	PAGRTT
**	BOX	**	ENDPAGE	**	PAGSEQ
****	CDEFNT		FLTFIXDEC		POSITION
	CHRID		FLTPCN	*	PRTQLTY
*	CHRSIZ	*	FONT	***	REF
	COLOR	**	GDF		REFFLD
*	CPI	*	HIGHLIGHT	*	SKIPA
	CVTDTA	*****	INDARA	*	SKIPB
	DATE	*****	INDTXT	*	SPACEA
*****	DFNCHR	**	LINE	*	SPACEB
*	DFT	**	LPI	*	TEXT
	DLTEDT		MSGCON		TIME
					TRNSPY
					TXRTT
					UNDERLINE

blank - Field Level
* - Field and Record Level
** - Record Level
*** - File Level
**** - File and Record Level
***** - Field, Record, and Field Level

Figure 18-1 Printer **(PRTF)** file keywords.

EDTCDE *Keyword.* **EDTCDE** *(Edit Code)* is a *Field Level* keyword that controls the editing of output-capable numeric fields. The edit code options, which are identical to those available in **RPG IV,** include 1, 2, 3, 4, A, B, C, D, J, K, L, M, Y, and Z. Examples of the syntax and edited results for three **EDTCDE** keywords are shown in Figure 18-2.

```
SEQNBR*...+... 1 ...+... 2 ...+... 3 ...+... 4 ...+... 5 ...+... 6 ...+... 7
     .....AAN01N02N03T.Name++++++RLen++TDpBLinPosFunctions++++++++++++++++++

  100      A             DATE           6  0   1  1EDTCDE(Y)
  200      *
  300      A             AMT            8  2  10 50EDTCDE(1 $)
  400      *
  500      A             BALNCE         7  2  15 50EDTCDE(J *)
```

Line No.	Value in Storage	EDTCDE Specified	Edited Result
100	090198	Y	9/01/98
300	00150000	1 $	$1,500.00
500	000250}	J *	***25.00-

Notes:

1 Line 100 EDTCDE controls the suppression of leading zeros and the insertion of slashes.

2 Line 300 EDTCDE controls the suppression leading zeros and a floating dollar sign to the left of the first significant digit. An EDTWRD would have to be used to control a fixed dollar sign to the left of the field value.

3 Line 500 EDTCDE controls the suppression of leading zeros and replacement with asterisks. } indicates a negative 0. When the field value is negative the low-order zero and minus sign will print or display. On a PC or IBM keyboard, pressing the minus key after the value is entered will supply a minus sign over the low-order digit.

Figure 18-2 Example **EDTCDE** keywords with edited results.

The table presented in Figure 18-3 summarizes all the valid **EDTCDE** *(Edit Code)* keyword options and their editing functions. An **EDTCDE** (or **EDTWRD**) is valid only for numeric fields specified as a *Data Type* **S** (signed) or **P** (packed) in position 35 of the DDS form.

Edit Code	Commas[1] Printed	Decimal Points[1] Printed	Signs Printed When Negative Number	Blank Value of QDECFMT System Value	I Value of QDECFMT System Value	J Value of QDECFMT System Value	Leading Zero Suppressed
1	Yes	Yes	No sign	.00 or 0	,00 or 0	0,00 or 0	Yes
2	Yes	Yes	No sign	Blanks	Blanks	Blanks	Yes
3		Yes	No sign	.00 or 0	,00 or 0	0,00 or 0	Yes
4		Yes	No sign	Blanks	Blanks	Blanks	Yes
A	Yes	Yes	CR	.00 or 0	,00 or 0	0,00 or 0	Yes
B	Yes	Yes	CR	Blanks	Blanks	Blanks	Yes
C		Yes	CR	.00 or 0	,00 or 0	0,00 or 0	Yes
D		Yes	CR	Blanks	Blanks	Blanks	Yes
J	Yes	Yes	– (Minus)	.00 or 0	,00 or 0	0,00 or 0	Yes
K	Yes	Yes	– (Minus)	Blanks	Blanks	Blanks	Yes
L		Yes	– (Minus)	.00 or 0	,00 or 0	0,00 or 0	Yes
M		Yes	– (Minus)	Blanks	Blanks	Blanks	Yes
N	Yes	Yes	– (Minus)	.00 or 0	,00 or 0	0,00 or 0	Yes
O	Yes	Yes	– (Minus)	Blanks	Blanks	Blanks	Yes
P		Yes	– (Minus)	.00 or 0	,00 or 0	0,00 or 0	Yes
Q		Yes	– (Minus)	Blanks	Blanks	Blanks	Yes
Y[2]							Yes
Z[3]							Yes

Notes:

1 The QDECFMT system value determines the decimal point character (period as used in the U.S.), the character used to separate groups of three digits (comma as used in the U.S.), and the type of zero suppression (depending on comma and period placement). For more information on the QDECFMT system value, see the *Work Management* book.

2 The Y edit code suppresses the farthest left zero of a date field that is three to six digits long, and it suppresses the two farthest left zeros of a field that is seven positions long. The Y edit code also inserts slashes (/) between the month, day, and year according to the following pattern:

nn/n
nn/nn
nn/nn/n
nn/nn/nn
nnn/nn/nn

If the Date keyword is specified with EDTCDE(Y), the separator character used is the job attribute, DATSEP at run time. If a separator character is not specified on the DATSEP job attribute, the system value, QDATSEP, is used (where slash (/) is the default value). If, at file creation time, DATFMT is JUL (Julian), the date is formatted as nnnnn. If EDTCDE(Y) is specified, the date is formatted as nn/nnn, where the slash (/) represents the job date separator.

3 The Z edit code removes the sign (plus or minus) from a numeric field. The sign of the units column is changed to a hexadecimal F before the field is written.

Figure 18-3 Summary of all valid **EDTCDE** codes and editing functions *(Courtesy of IBM).*

`EDTWRD` *Keyword.* When the edit requirements cannot be satisfied by an **EDTCDE,** an **EDTWRD** must be specified. An **EDTWRD** is a *Field Level* keyword that may be specified with numeric fields defined as *Data Type* **S** or **P.**

An **EDTWRD** *(Edit Word)* consists of three parts: the body; the status; and the expansion; as shown in the following format.

The *body* of an **EDTWRD** is the area that allocates space for the digits from the sending field. It must be formatted equal to or greater than the size of the field to be edited. When floating dollar signs are included, the body of the edit word must be one space larger than the related numeric field. The body of the edit word ends with the low-order position that may be replaced by a digit.

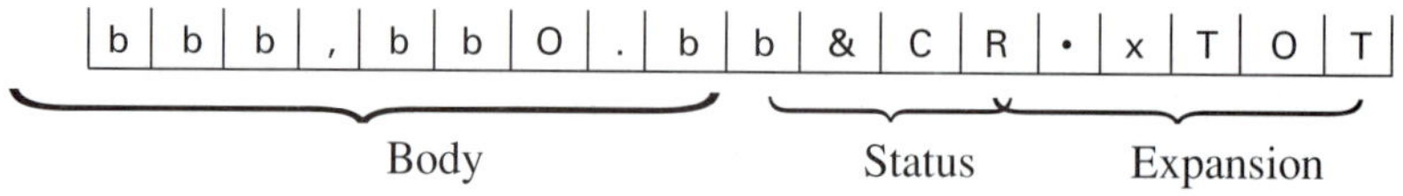

The *status* is an optional part of an **EDTWRD** that immediately follows the body and supports a minus sign or a CR (credit) symbol. If the numeric field value is negative and a minus sign is included in this area, a minus sign will print (or display) after the low-order digit. On the other hand, if CR is specified and the value is negative, CR will print or display in the area. When the field value is positive (a plus sign), blanks will print in the positions allocated to the status section. If a minus sign or credit symbol is not specified, a status entry is not part of an **EDTWRD.**

The *expansion* area of an **EDTWRD** begins after the status section, or after the body if the status is not specified. The characters included in this area will print or display every time the instruction is executed; it does not depend on the field value. Blanks are not permitted in the expansion area. If blanks are required, they must be specified by ampersands (&). Examples of **EDTWRD** formats and their edited results are shown in Figure 18-4. In addition to the parentheses, **EDTWRD**s must also be enclosed in single quotes.

```
SEQNBR*...+... 1 ...+... 2 ...+... 3 ...+... 4 ...+... 5 ...+... 6 ...+... 7 ...+... 8
      .....AAN01N02N03T.Name++++++RLen++TDpBLinPosFunctions++++++++++++++++++++++++++

  100      A            FIELDA         7S 2   7 50EDTWRD('  ,  0.  -')
  200       *
  300      A            FIELDB         7S 2  10 50EDTWRD('   , $0.  -')
  400       *
  500      A            FIELDC         7S 2  12 50EDTWRD('  ,  *.  &CR')
  600       *
  700      A            FIELDD         7S 2  14 50EDTWRD('  ,   .  -&NET DUE')
  800       *
  900      A            SSNUMBER       9  0  16 50EDTWRD('U   -  -    ')
 1000       *
 1100      A            TELEPHONE     10  0  18 50EDTWRD('0(   )-  -    ')
 1200       *
 1300      A            COUNTER        5  0  20 50EDTWRD('    0')
```

Sequence Number	Data Value in Storage	EDTWRD Format	Edited Result	Comments
100	010000} ▲	'bb,bb0.bb-'	1,000.00-	Minus will print only when value is negative. 0 in the body of the edit word indicates extent of zero suppression.
300	0000199 ▲	'bbb,b$0.bb'	$1.99	Floating $ sign requires extra high-order digit position in edit word format. A fixed dollar sign is specified by placing it in the extra-high order position.
500	000004R ▲	'bb,bb*.bb&CR'	******.49 CR	Asterisk replaces all high-order zeros with asterisks to the extent of its location in the body of the edit word. The ampersand provides a space before the status part. CR prints because the value is negative (R = –9). If the value was positive, two spaces would be included in those positions.

Figure 18-4 **EDTWRD** formats and editing example.

700	1250000 ▲	'bb,bb0.bb-&NET&DUE'	12,500.00 NET DUE	Because the value is positive, the minus sign does not print. The space after the status and in the expansion part are controlled by ampersands. NET DUE, which is in the expansion area, follows the status for this example. If a status was not specified, the expansion value would follow the body. Regardless of the value of the edited item, the expansion entry will print.
900	011223333	'0bbb-bb-bbbb'	011-22-3333	To prevent suppression of the leading zero in the social security number, a 0 must be specified in an extra high-order position in the body of the edit word.
1100	2039998888	'0(bbb)•bbb•bbbb'	(203)-999-8888	To prevent suppression of the leading parenthesis, a 0 must be specified in an extra high-order position in the body of the edit word.
1300	00000 ▲	'bbbb0'		Complete zero suppression may be specified by placing a 0 in the low-order position in the body of an edit word.

b's in body part of edit word indicate spaces.

▲ Indicates implied decimal position in stored value

Figure 18-4 EDTWRD formats and editing example. (Continued)

PAGNBR *(Page Number) Keyword.* The **PAGNBR** keyword predefines a four-byte numeric integer field. Its value is automatically initialized to zeros when the program is executed and is incremented by 1 before printing a page. Page numbers are not incremented beyond 9999, but **PAGNBR** may be reset to 1 by conditioning the related instruction with an indicator. Figure 18-5 illustrates two coding examples of the **PAGNBR** keyword.

```
SEQNBR*...+... 1 ...+... 2 ...+... 3 ...+... 4 ...+... 5 ...+... 6 ...+... 7 ...+... 8
      .....AAN01N02N03T.Name++++++RLen++TDpBLinPosFunctions++++++++++++++++++++++++++++
             * EXAMPLE 1:
             *
            A          R HDG1
            A                               1124'PAGE'
            A                                  +1PAGNBR EDTCDE(Z)
             * EXAMPLE 2:
             *
            A          R HDG1
            A                               1124'PAGE'
            A 10                               +1PAGNBR EDTWRD('   0')
```

Example 1:

The constant PAGE is optional. The +1 entry in the Pos field indicates the number of spaces to be included between the previous constant or field and the beginning of the field or constant currently defined. Also notice that **EDTCDE(Z)** is specified to suppress leading zeros in the PAGNBR value.

Example 2:

The constant PAGE and PAGNBR value locations are identical to Example 1. However, here the PAGNBR line is conditioned by an indicator **(10).** Regardless of the ON or OFF status of the indicator, the PAGNBR value will be incremented and printed on every page. When the status of the indicator changes (from ON to OFF or OFF to ON), the PAGNBR value will be reset to 1 and automatic incrementation continued. To illustrate how an **EDTWRD** may be used for PAGNBR editing, it is specified for this example.

Figure 18-5 Examples of the **PAGNBR** keyword.

SKIPA *(Skip After) Keyword.* The **SKIPA** *(Skip After)* keyword, which may be specified at the *File, Record,* or *Field Level,* controls skipping to a specific line *after* one or more lines are printed. If the specified line number has been passed, control will advance the paper to the next page and begin printing on the line indicated. When **SKIPA** is specified at the *File Level,* skipping will be performed *after* all the records defined in the **PRTF** have been printed. If **SKIPA** is assigned at the *Record Level,* skipping will be performed *after* all the lines related to the record format are printed. Finally, when **SKIPA** is included at the *Field Level,* skipping will be executed *after* the related field value is printed.

SKIPB *(Skip Before) Keyword.* The **SKIPB** *(Skip Before)* keyword may be specified at the *File, Record,* or *Field Level.* It controls skipping to a specified line *before* the next line is printed. If the designated line has been passed, control will advance the paper to the next page and begin printing on the specified line. When **SKIPB** is specified at the *File Level,* skipping will be performed *before* all the records defined in the **PRTF** have been output. If **SKIPB** is assigned at the *Record Level,* skipping will be performed *before* any of the lines related to the record format are printed. Finally, when **SKIPB** is included at the *Field Level,* skipping will be executed *before* the related field value is printed.

SPACEA *(Space After) Keyword.* The **SPACEA** keyword controls line spacing *after* a record or line is printed. It may be specified only at the *Record* or *Field Level.* The valid parameters for this keyword are as follows:

- 0 No spacing
- 1 Space one line
- 2 Space two lines
- 3 Space three lines

If **SPACEA** is specified at the *Record Level,* spacing occurs *after* all the lines related to that record have been printed. When used at the *Field Level,* spacing is performed *after* the field value is printed.

A line number assignment (positions 39–41) cannot be specified along with a **SPACEA** keyword. If they are used together, the compilation of the **PRTF** will flag the line numbers as errors. If a line number or a **SPACEA** keyword is not used, overprinting will result.

SPACEB *(Space Before) Keyword.* The **SPACEB** keyword controls line spacing *before* a record or line is printed. It may be specified only at the *Record* or *Field Level.* The valid parameters for this keyword are as follows:

- 0 No spacing
- 1 Space one line
- 2 Space two lines
- 3 Space three lines

If **SPACEB** is specified at the *Record Level,* spacing occurs before the first line related to that record is printed. When used at the *Field Level,* spacing is performed before the field value is printed.

A line number assignment (positions 39–41) cannot be specified along with a **SPACEB** keyword. If they are used together, the compilation of the **PRTF** will flag line numbers as errors. If a line number or the **SPACEB** keyword is not specified, overprinting will result.

Examples of SKIPA, SKIPB, SPACEA, SPACEB Keywords Control

The parameter included with a **SKIPA, SKIPB, SPACEA,** or **SPACEB** keyword is coded in the following general format:

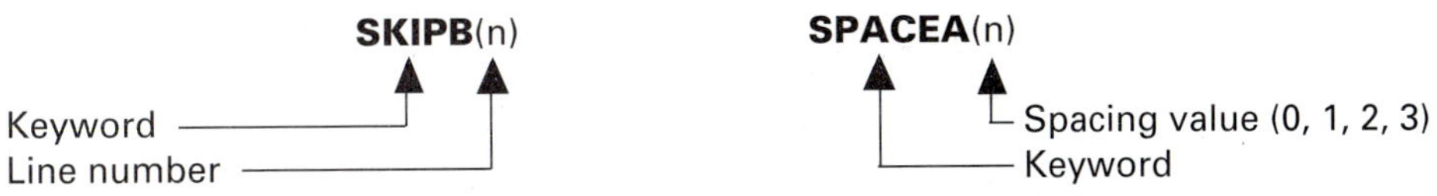

Coding examples and the processing functions of the **SKIPB** and **SPACEA** keywords are illustrated in Figure 18-6.

```
SEQNBR*...+... 1 ...+... 2 ...+... 3 ...+... 4 ...+... 5 ...+... 6 ...+... 7 ...+... 8
      .....AAN01N02N03T.Name++++++RLen++TDpBLinPosFunctions++++++++++++++++++++++++++++

  100    A          R HDG1                         SKIPB(6)
  200    A                                       40'HEADING LINE ONE'
  300    A          R HDG2                         SKIPB(10)
  400    A                                       40'HEADING LINE TWO'
  500    A          R DETAIL                       SPACEB(2)
  600    A             .
  700    A             .
  800    A          R TOTAL                        SPACEB(3)
  900    A             .
```

Line No. On Page	Value Printed	Keyword Specified	Comments
Line 100	HEADING LINE ONE	SKIPB(6)	If printer carriage is beyond line 6 on the previous page, paper will advance to line 6 of the next page before printing the line.
Line 300	HEADING LINE TWO	SKIPB(10)	Keyword advances paper to line 10 of the same page before printing the line.
Line 500	DETAIL LINE	SPACEB(2)	Keyword advances the paper two lines before printing a detail line.
	. . .		
Line 800	TOTAL LINE	SPACEB(3)	Keyword advances paper three lines before printing the total line.

Notes:

1. Any combination of **SKIPA, SKIPB, SPACEA,** and **SPACEB** may be specified to meet page and line requirements.
2. Execution of skipping and spacing is controlled in an **RPG IV** program by referencing the related **PRTF** file record and/or field name.

Figure 18-6 SKIPB and **SPACEB** syntax and processing functions.

TIME (Current System Time)

TIME is a *Field-Level*–only keyword that prints the current system time as a constant in an edited HH:MM:SS format. Other edited formats may be specified by an **EDTWRD** or user-defined edit code. Conditioning indicators may be used to control the printing of a specific **TIME** value format. Figure 18-7 shows two examples of the syntax and processing results for this keyword. An application program that accesses a printer file **(PRTF)** instead of including *Output Specifications* to generate a report is introduced in the following subsections.

```
SEQNBR*...+... 1 ...+... 2 ...+... 3 ...+... 4 ...+... 5 ...+... 6 ...+... 7 ...+... 8
       .....AANO1NO2NO3T.Name++++++RLen++TDpBLinPosFunctions++++++++++++++++++++++++++++
          * EXAMPLE 1:
         A                                 2TIME
          *
          * EXAMPLE 2:
         A                                 2TIME EDTWRD('0 &HRS& &MINS& &SECS')
```

Figure 18-7 Two examples of the syntax and processing results for the **TIME** keyword.

Example Printer File

The report design in Figure 18-8 will be used to illustrate the syntax for a printer file **(PRTF)**.

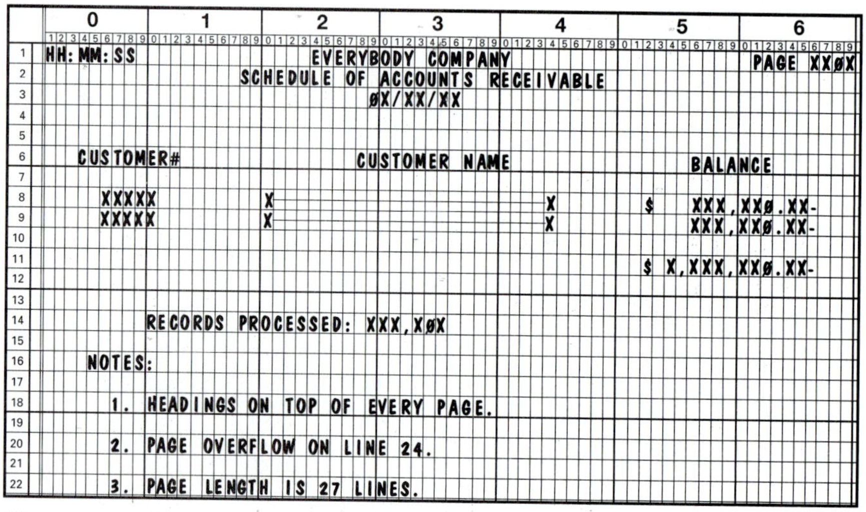

Figure 18-8 Report design for a printer file.

The *Data Description Specifications* statements for the report design are shown in Figure 18-9.

```
SEQNBR  *...+....1....+....2....+....3....+....4....+....5....+....6....+....7....+....8
          * Example Printer (PRTF) File....
         A                                      REF(STAN/ARMASTER)
         A          R HDGS                      SKIPB(6)
         A                                     1TIME
         A                                    24'EVERYBODY COMPANY'
         A                                    61'PAGE'
         A                                    +1PAGNBR EDTCDE(Z) SPACEA(1)
         A                                    18'SCHEDULE OF ACCOUNTS RECEIVABLE'
         A                                      SPACEA(1)
         A                                    29DATE EDTCDE(Y) SPACEA(3)
         A                                     4'CUSTOMER'
         A                                    28'CUSTOMER NAME'
         A                                    56'BALANCE' SPACEA(2)
         A                                    52'$' SPACEA(0)
         A          R DETAIL
         A            CUSTOMERNOR              6
         A            CUSTNAME  R             20
         A            ACTBALANCER             56EDTCDE(J) SPACEA(1)
```

Figure 18-9 *Data Description Specification* instructions for example printer file **(PRTF)**.

```
1900      A          R TOTALS
2000      A                                        SPACEB(1)
2100      A            TOTAL           9  2      54EDTWRD('$&  ,    ,  0.  -')
2200      A                                        SPACEA(3)
2300      A                                      10'RECORDS PROCESSED:'
2400      A            RECORDS         6  0      29EDTCDE(1)
```

Figure 18-9 *Data Description Specification* instructions for example printer file **(PRTF).** (Continued)

An examination of the DDS coding in Figure 18-9 will indicate the following features:

1. Three record formats, HDGS, DETAIL, and TOTALS, are defined. The HDGS format includes top-of-page control and line spacing. The DETAIL and TOTALS record formats include line spacing only.
2. The **SPACE(0)** keyword on line 1400 prevents spacing after the $ is printed so that the first DETAIL record will print on the same line (see Figure 18-10).
3. Because line spacing is controlled with the **SPACEA** and **SPACEB** keywords, the Line reference (positions 39–41) does not have to be specified. In any case, however, the *Pos* entry (columns 42–44) must be included.
4. Field attributes are referenced from the related physical file. Two non-database fields, *TOTAL* and *RECORDS*, are defined in the DDS coding for the printer file.

A source listing of the example printer file and its relationship to the printed report are illustrated in Figure 18-10.

```
SEQNBR  *...+....1....+....2....+....3....+....4....+....5....+....6....+....7....+....8
  100      * Example PRTF file.....
  200     A                                       REF(SMYERS/GLMASTER)
  300     A          R HDGS                       SKIPB(6) ----------------- Skipping Control
  400     A                                      1TIME
  500     A                                    24'EVERYBODY COMPANY'
  600     A                                    61'PAGE'
  700     A                                    +1PAGNBR EDTCDE(Z) SPACEA(1)
  800     A                                    18'SCHEDULE OF ACCOUNTS RECEIVABLE'
  900     A                                       SPACEA(1)
 1000     A                                    29DATE EDTCDE(Y) SPACEA(3)
 1100     A                                     4'CUSTOMER#'
 1200     A                                    28'CUSTOMER NAME'
 1300     A                                    56'BALANCE' SPACEA(2) ------- Spacing Control
 1400     A                                    52'$' SPACEA(0)
 1500     A          R DETAIL
 1600     A            CUSTOMERNOR                6
 1700     A            CUSTNAME  R               20
 1800     A            ACTBALANCER               56EDTCDE(J) SPACEA(1)
 1900     A          R TOTALS
 2000     A                                       SPACEB(1)
 2100     A            TOTAL         9  2      52EDTWRD('$&  ,   ,  0.  -')
 2200     A                                       SPACEA(3)
 2300     A                                    10'RECORDS PROCESSED:'
 2400     A            RECORDS       6  0      29EDTCDE(1)

Printed Report:                                               Keyword/PRTF Line Ref

 13:32:54              EVERYBODY COMPANY              PAGE    1 — SKIPB(6)  Line 100
              SCHEDULE OF ACCOUNTS RECEIVABLE —————————————————— SPACEA(1)  Line 500
```

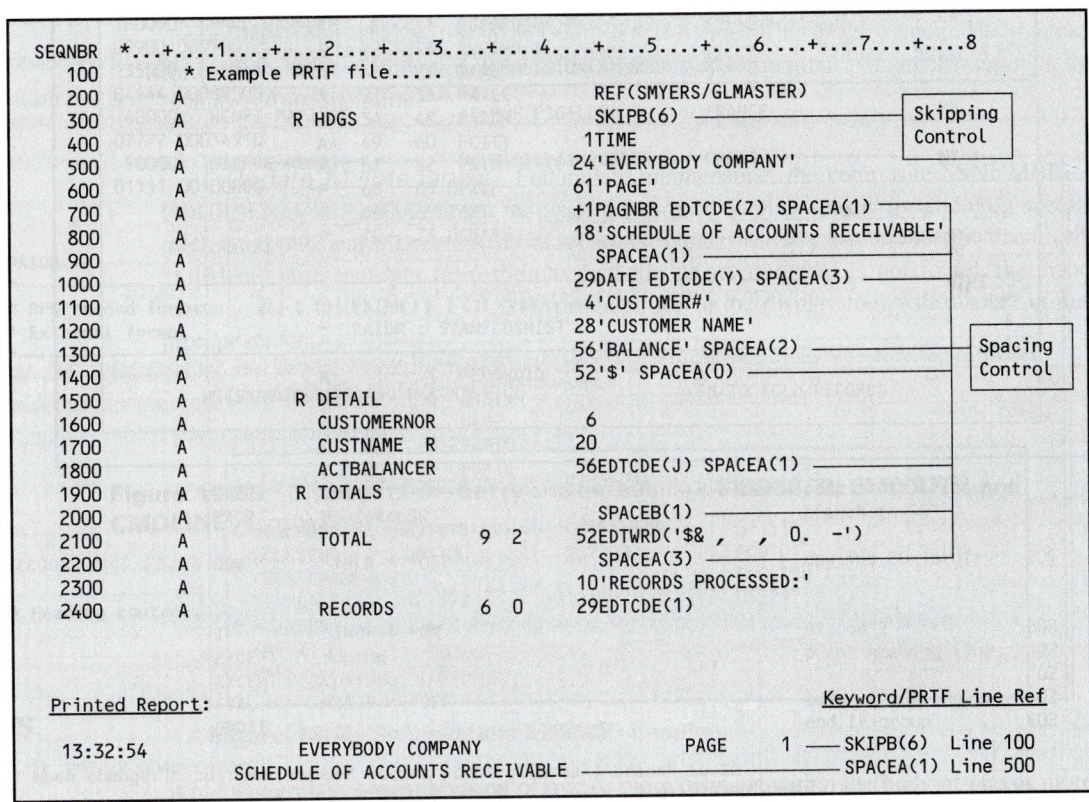

Figure 18-10 Relationship of **SKIPA, SPACEA,** and **SPACEB** keyword line control to the report.

```
                    12/20/97 ─────────────────────────────── SPACEA(1) Line 700

  CUSTOMER#          CUSTOMER NAME            BALANCE ─────── SPACEA(3) Line 800
                                                      ─────── SPACEA(0) Line 1200
     12345          KAREL APPEL            $     1,250.00 ─── SPACEA(2) Line 1100
     23456          GEORGES BRAQUE                 100.00 ─── SPACEA(1) Line 1600
     34567          PAUL CEZANNE                81,900.00          "       "
     45678          MARC CHAGALL                   926.00          "       "
     56789          EDGAR DEGAS                  7,854.99          "       "
     67890          MAX ERNST                      500.00          "       "
     78900          BUCKMINSTER FULLER          33,000.10          "       "
     89000          JULIO GONZALEZ                 654.78          "       "

- - - - - - - - - - - - - - - - - - - - - - - - - - - - - - - - - - - - -

13:32:54           EVERYBODY COMPANY                PAGE    2 ── SKIPB(6)  Line 600
               SCHEDULE OF ACCOUNTS RECEIVABLE ──────────────── SPACEA(1) Line 500
                        12/20/97 ─────────────────────────────── SPACE(1)  Line 700

  CUSTOMER#          CUSTOMER NAME            BALANCE ─────── SPACEA(3) Line 800
                                                      ─────── SPACEA(0) Line 1200
     90000          HECTOR HYPPOLITE       $   120,000.00 ─── SPACEA(2) Line 1100
     91000          PIERRE JEANERET                  9.45 ─── SPACEA(1) Line 1600
     92000          WASSILY KANDINSKY          375,000.00          "       "
     93000          CHARLES CORBUSIER              250.00          "       "

                                           $   621,445.32 ─── SPACEB(1) Line 1800

        RECORDS PROCESSED:      12 ───────────────────────── SPACEA(3) Line 2000

Note: The keyword/line references indicate position of printer carriage after related instruction
      is executed.
```

Figure 18-10 Relationship of **SKIPA, SPACEA,** and **SPACEB** keyword line control to the report. (Continued)

EXAMPLE RPG IV PRINTER FILE PROGRAM

Page overflow cannot be controlled by an overflow indicator in **RPG IV** programs that process printer files. Consequently, page overflow must be controlled by programmer-supplied instructions. The page overflow items needed in any program that processes a printer file include:

1. A standalone field that includes a value for the number of lines per page. The field value may be initialized in a *Definition* or *Calculation Specification* instruction.
2. A standalone field for a line counter. This field must be incremented with the appropriate integer every time a line or lines is printed.
3. **WRITE** instructions to control the output of the printer file's record formats.

The processing logic for programmer-controlled page overflow and record format **(HDGS, DETAIL,** and **TOTALS)** output for the example printer file is illustrated in Figure 18-11.

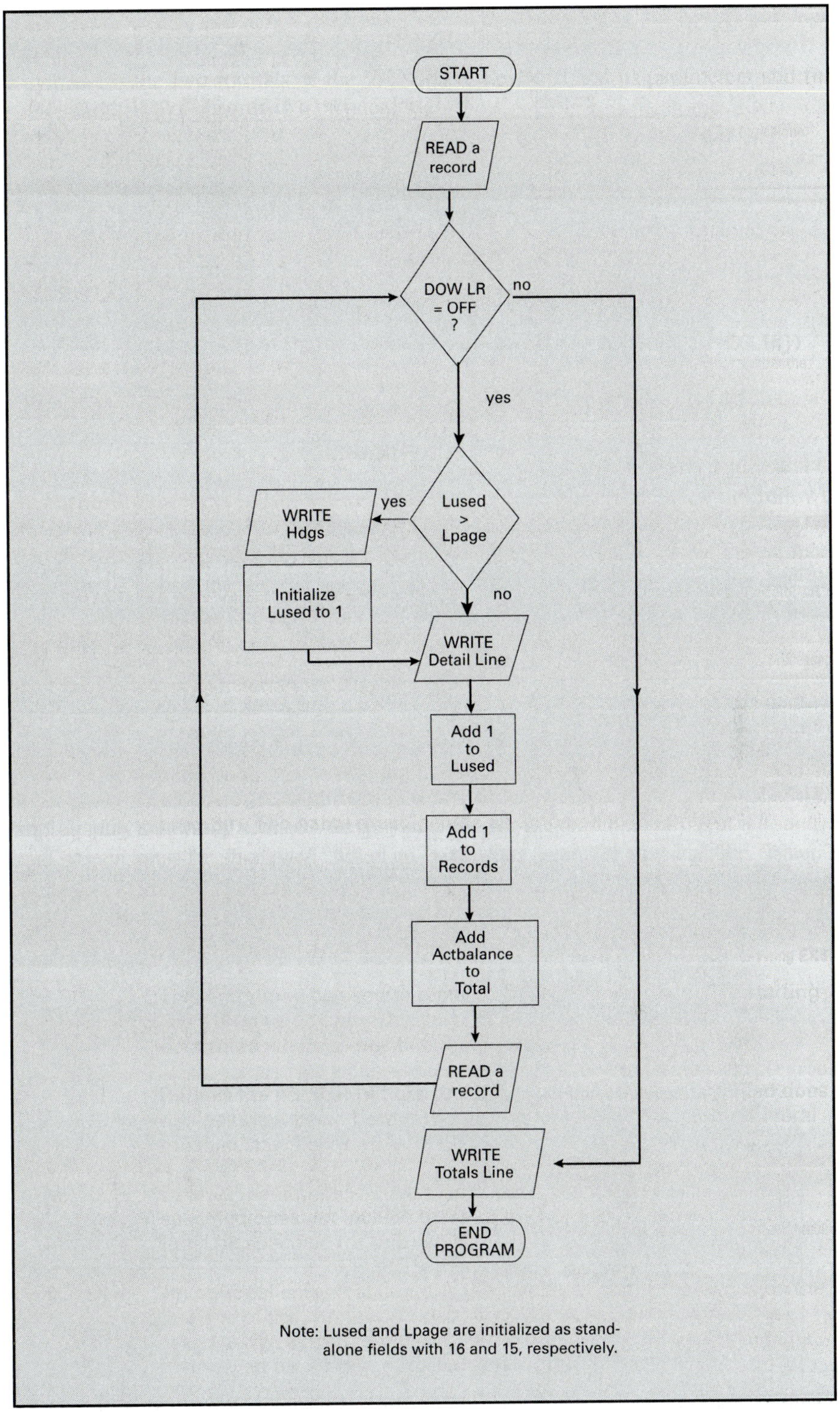

Figure 18-11 Processing logic flowchart for programmer-controlled page overflow and record format output for a printer file.

A compile listing of the **RPG IV** program that processes a printer file and a line-by-line explanation of the instructions are detailed in Figure 18-12.

```
Line    <---------------------- Source Specifications ----------------------------><---- Comments ----> Do
Number ....1....+....2....+....3....+....4....+....5....+....6....+....7....+....8....+....9....+...10 Num
                      S o u r c e   L i s t i n g
     1  * This program processes a printer file....
     2
     3 FARMaster  IF   E           K DISK
       *--------------------------------------------------------------------------------------------*
       *                              RPG name          External name                             *
       * File name. . . . . . . . . : ARMASTER          STAN/ARMASTER                             *
       * Record format(s) . . . . . : ARRECORD          ARRECORD                                  *
       *--------------------------------------------------------------------------------------------*
     4 FCh18prtf1 O    E             PRINTER
     5
     6  * Define and initialize fields for page overflow control...
       *--------------------------------------------------------------------------------------------*
       *                              RPG name          External name                             *
       * File name. . . . . . . . . : CH18PRTF1         STAN/CH18PRTF1                            *
       * Record format(s) . . . . . : HDGS              HDGS                                      *
       *                              DETAIL            DETAIL                                    *
       *                              TOTALS            TOTALS                                    *
       *--------------------------------------------------------------------------------------------*
     7 D LUsed          S              2  0 INZ(16)
     8 D LPage          S              2  0 INZ(15)
     9
    10=IARRECORD
       *--------------------------------------------------------------------------------------------*
       * RPG record format  . . . . : ARRECORD                                                    *
       * External format  . . . . . : ARRECORD : STAN/ARMASTER                                    *
       *--------------------------------------------------------------------------------------------*
    11=I                             A    1    5  CUSTOMERNO
    12=I                             A    6   25  CUSTNAME
    13=I                             A   26   45  STREET
    14=I                             A   46   65  CITY
    15=I                             A   66   67  STATE
    16=I                             P   68   70 0ZIPCODE
    17=I                             P   71   75 2ACTBALANCE
    18 C                   READ      ARMaster                           ----LR   Read first record
    19 C                   DOW       *INLR = *OFF                                 dow ind LR is off   B01
    20
    21  * Test for page overflow and initialize line counter if true..
    22 C                   IF        LUsed > LPage                                page overflow test  B02
    23 C                   WRITE     Hdgs                                         write PRTF Hdgs rcd  02
    24 C                   EVAL      LUsed = 8                                    initialize line ctr  02
    25 C                   ENDIF                                                  end IF group        E02
    26
    27  * Print Detail record from PRTF.  Increment line ctr, total records,
    28  * and Actbalance.  Read next record from ARMaster....
    29 C                   WRITE     Detail                                       print detail record  01
    30 C                   EVAL      LUsed = LUsed + 1                            increment line ctr   01
    31 C                   EVAL      Records = Records + 1                        increment record ctr 01
    32 C                   EVAL      Total = Total + Actbalance                   increment total fld  01
    33 C                   READ      ARMaster                           ----LR   read next record     01
    34 C                   ENDDO                                                  end dow group       E01
    35
    36  * Print Total record from PRTF after end of file is read....
    37 C                   WRITE     Totals                                       print Totals record
    38=OHDGS
       *--------------------------------------------------------------------------------------------*
       * RPG record format  . . . . : HDGS                                                        *
       * External format  . . . . . : HDGS : STAN/CH18PRTF1                                       *
       *--------------------------------------------------------------------------------------------*
    39=ODETAIL
       *--------------------------------------------------------------------------------------------*
       * RPG record format  . . . . : DETAIL                                                      *
       * External format  . . . . . : DETAIL : STAN/CH18PRTF1                                     *
       *--------------------------------------------------------------------------------------------*
    40=O                       CUSTOMERNO          5A CHAR         5
    41=O                       CUSTNAME           25A CHAR        20
    42=O                       ACTBALANCE         34S ZONE       9,2
```

Figure 18-12 Compile listing of the example **RPG IV** program that processes a printer file.

```
43=OTOTALS
    *---------------------------------------------------------------------------------------*
    * RPG record format  . . . . :  TOTALS                                                  *
    * External format  . . . . . :  TOTALS : STAN/CH18PRTF1                                  *
    *---------------------------------------------------------------------------------------*
44=O                          TOTAL                9S ZONE      9,2
45=O                          RECORDS             15S ZONE      6,0
```

File Description Specifications:

Line No.	
3	ARMaster is defined as an input (**I** in position 17), full-procedural (**F** in position 18), externally described (**E** in position 22), keyed (**K** in position 34) physical file.
4	Ch18prtf1 is defined as an output (**O** in position 17), externally described (**E** in position 22) printer file.

Definition Specifications:

7	LUsed is defined as a standalone field 2 integers in length. The **INZ** keyword initializes the field value to 16 (i.e., **INZ(16)**). This field is used as the line counter to determine when page overflow is to occur.
8	LPage is defined as a standalone field 2 integers in length. The **INZ** keyword initializes the field value to 15 (i.e., **INZ(15)**). This field determines the report's page length, which may be easily changed by specifiying a different initialization value.

Calculation Specifications:

18	This **READ** instruction reads the first record from the ARMaster physical file. If no records are stored in the file, the **LR** indicator specified in the *Eq* field (positions 75–76) will be turned on.
19	The **DOW** instruction tests the status of the **LR** indicator; which will be turned on by the **READ** instruction on line 18 or 33. When **LR** is on, control will branch to the **WRITE** instruction on line 37, print the Totals record and end the program.
22	The **IF** instruction determines if the value in LUsed is greater than the value in LPage. For the first record processed, page overflow will occur because the LUsed and LPage field were initialized in "standalone" fields in *Definition Specification* instructions with LUsed having a greater value than LPage. Subsequent page overflow will occur by incrementing the LUsed field for every printer file record output and performing this relational test.
23	This **WRITE** instruction prints the printer file's Hdgs record format on the top of a new page.
24	This **EVAL** instruction initializes the Lused (line counter) field to 8. Because the Hdgs record format requires 8 print lines, the LUsed field is initialized to 8 after the Hdgs record format is printed on a new page.
25	The **ENDIF** operation ends the **IF** group that began on line 22.
29	This **WRITE** instruction prints the printer file's Detail record format. The Detail record is printed for every ARMaster record processed regardless of the result of the page overflow test.
30	This **EVAL** instruction increments the LUsed (line counter) field by 1. Because Detail output is single-spaced, LUsed is incremented by 1.
31	This **EVAL** instruction increments the Records field by 1 for every ARMaster record processed. The Records field value is printed after end of file is read.
32	This **EVAL** instruction adds the Actbalance field value to the Total field for every ARMaster record processed. The Total value is printed after end of file is read.
33	This **READ** instruction reads the next record from the ARMaster file. If end of file is read, the **LR** indicator will be turned on, which will subsequently end the program when the **DOW** instruction is executed on line 19.
34	The **ENDDO** operation ends the **DOW** group that began on line 19. The relational test for exiting the **DOW** group is performed at the **DOW** instruction on line 19 and not at this operation.
37	This **WRITE** instruction prints the printer file's Totals record format after the end of file is read and indicator **LR** was turned on.

Figure 18-12 Compile listing of the example **RPG IV** program that processes a printer file. (Continued)

PRINTER FILE (PRTF) COMMAND PARAMETERS

External parameters for printer files are assigned by the **CRTPRTF** *(Create Printer File)* command. Controls, including form size, lines per inch, characters per inch, page overflow, forms alignment, print quality, font type, and so forth, may be specified by a series of prompt screens generated when **CRTPRTF** is entered on a command line and **F4** is pressed. Displays 1 and 2 of the seven accessed by the **CRTPRTF** command are shown in Figure 18-13. Some of the parameters are valid only for select printers. Most of them, however, are valid for laser printers, some for serial printers, and a few for line printers.

```
                        Create Printer File (CRTPRTF)

 Type choices, press Enter.

 File . . . . . . . . . . . . . .   CH18PRF2      Name
   Library  . . . . . . . . . . .     *CURLIB     Name, *CURLIB
 Source file  . . . . . . . . . .   *NONE         Name, *NONE
   Library  . . . . . . . . . . .                 Name, *LIBL, *CURLIB
 Source member  . . . . . . . . .   *FILE         Name, *FILE
 Generation severity level  . . .   20            0-30
 Flagging severity level  . . . .   0             0-30
 Device specification:
   Printer  . . . . . . . . . . .   *JOB          Name, *JOB, *SYSVAL
 Printer device type  . . . . . .   *SCS          *SCS, *IPDS, *USERASCII...
 Text 'description' . . . . . . .   ch 18 - printer file 2



                                                                        Bottom
 F3=Exit   F4=Prompt   F5=Refresh   F10=Additional parameters   F12=Cancel
 F13=How to use this display        F24=More keys
--------------------------------------------------------------------------------
                        Create Printer File (CRTPRTF)

 Type choices, press Enter.


                           Additional Parameters
 Source listing options . . . . .                 *SRC, *NOSRC, *SOURCE...
              + for more values
 Page size:
   Length--lines per page . . . .   66            .001-255.000
   Width--positions per line  . .   132           .001-378.000
   Measurement method . . . . . .   *ROWCOL       *ROWCOL, *UOM
 Lines per inch . . . . . . . . .   6             6, 3, 4, 7.5, 7,5, 8, 9, 12
 Characters per inch  . . . . . .   10            10, 5, 12, 13.3, 13,3, 15...
 Front margin:
   Offset down  . . . . . . . . .   *DEVD         0-57.790, *DEVD
   Offset across  . . . . . . . .                 0-57.790


                                                                       More...
 F3=Exit   F4=Prompt   F5=Refresh   F12=Cancel   F13=How to use this display
 F24=More keys
```

Figure 18-13 **CRTPRTF** *(Create Printer File)* command displays 1 and 2.

PRINTER FILE (PRTF) SHELLS

In lieu of including the syntax for a report in a printer file, programmers may prefer to follow traditional *Output Specifications* coding procedures. Normally, this would prevent many of the options available in the **CRTPRTF** command from being specified. The problem may be resolved by creating a printer file "shell" with the **CRTPRTF** command and include no DDS source code in the member. The coding for the report would be included in the *Output Specifications* of the **RPG IV** program. A compile listing of an example program that supports this method is shown in Figure 18-14.

```
Line   <---------------------- Source Specifications ---------------------------><---- Comments ----> Do
Number ....1....+....2....+....3....+....4....+....5....+....6....+....7....+....8....+....9....+...10 Num
                          S o u r c e   L i s t i n g
         * This program processes a printer file shell....

       FARMaster  IF   E           K DISK
         *-------------------------------------------------------------------------------------------*
         *                                RPG name          External name                            *
         * File name. . . . . . . . . :  ARMASTER          STAN/ARMASTER                            *
         * Record format(s) . . . . . :  ARRECORD          ARRECORD                                 *
         *-------------------------------------------------------------------------------------------*
       FCh18prtf2 O    F  132        PRINTER OFLIND(*INOF)

         * Define system time format....
       D Hhmmss          S               T   TIMFMT(*HMS:)

         * Define work fields....
       D Records         S              6  0
       D Total           S              9  2
       D Time            S              6  0

       IARRECORD
         *-------------------------------------------------------------------------------------------*
         * RPG record format  . . . . :  ARRECORD                                                   *
         * External format  . . . . . :  ARRECORD : STAN/ARMASTER                                   *
         *-------------------------------------------------------------------------------------------*
       I                             A    1    5  CUSTOMERNO
       I                             A    6   25  CUSTNAME
       I                             A   26   45  STREET
       I                             A   46   65  CITY
       I                             A   66   67  STATE
       I                             P   68   70 0ZIPCODE
       I                             P   71   75 2ACTBALANCE
       C                   TIME                    Time                         access system time
       C                   MOVE      Time          Hhmmss                       time to output fld
       C                   EVAL      *INOF = *ON                                turn on OF indicator
       C                   READ      ARMaster                           ----LR   Read first record
       C                   DOW       *INLR = *OFF                               dow ind LR is off     B01

       C                   IF        *INOF = *ON                                page overflow test    B02
       C                   EXCEPT    Headings                                   print heading lines    02
       C                   EVAL      *INOF = *OFF                               turn off OF indicatr   02
       C                   ENDIF                                                end IF group          E02

       C                   EXCEPT    Detail                                     print detail line      01
       C                   EVAL      Total = Total + Actbalance                 increment Total fld    01
       C                   EVAL      Records = Records + 1                      increment records fd   01
       C                   READ      ARMaster                           ----LR  read next record       01
       C                   ENDDO                                                end dow group         E01

         * Print Total output after end of file is read....
       C                   EXCEPT    TotalLines                                 print Totals record

       OCh18prtf2 E            Headings       1  6
       O                       Hhmmss               8
       O                                           40 'EVERYBODY COMPANY'
       O                                           64 'PAGE'
       O                       PAGE                69
       O          E            Headings       1
       O                                           37 'SCHEDULE OF ACCOUNTS'
       O                                           48 'RECEIVABLE'
       O          E            Headings       3
       O                       *DATE         Y     36
       O          E            Headings       2
       O                                           12 'CUSTOMERS'
       O                                           40 'CUSTOMER NAME'
       O                                           62 'BALANCE'
       O          E            Headings       0
       O                                           52 '$'
```

Because the PRTF is a shell (no DDS format), it must be program-described (F in position 22) and record length in (132) in positions 23-27). Note that page overflow indicator control is supported.

Figure 18-14 Compile listing of an **RPG IV** program that processes a printer file shell.

```
58 O          E          Detail        1
59 O                     CustomerNo         10
60 O                     Custname           44
61 O                     Actbalance     J   66
62 O          E          TotalLines  1
63 O                                        52 '$'
64 O                     Total          J   66
65 O          E          TotalLines  2
66 O                                        27 'RECORD PROCESSED:'
67 O                     Records        2   35
```

File Description Specifications:

Line No.

3 ARMaster is defined as an input (**I** in position 17), full-procedural (**F** in position 18), externally described (**E** in position 22), keyed (**K** in position 34) physical file.

4 Ch18prtf2 is defined as an output (**O** in position 17), program-described (**F** in position 22) printer file. The **OFLIND(*INOF)** keyword assigns **OF** as the overflow indicator. Because Qsysprt or Qprint is not specified as the default printer file, the program will automatically search for an externally described printer file **(PRTF).** No special syntax is needed to access a **PRTF** shell.

7 Hhmmss is defined as a standalone field with a time format (**T** in the *internal data type* field position 40). The keyword **TIMFMT(*HMS:)** will edit the Hhmmss field in an Hh:mm:ss format.

10–12 Records, Total, and Time are defined as standalone work fields.

Calculation Specifications:

22 The **TIME** instruction accesses the system time and stores the value in the standalone field Time. The **TIME** operation is used in an **RPG IV** program to extract the system time.

23 The value in Time is moved to the time format Hhmmss defined on line 7. This instruction will present the system time in an Hh:mm:ss format for printing.

24 This **EVAL** instruction turns on the **OF** page overflow indicator so that the paper will advance to a new page before printing the first Headings line.

25 This **READ** instruction reads the first record from the ARMaster file. If no records are stored in the file, indicator **LR** will be turned on, which will end the program when the following **DOW** instruction is executed.

26 The **DOW** instruction is executed when indicator **LR** is off. If **LR** is turned on by the **READ** instruction on line 25 or 36, control will exit from the **DOW** group to the **EXCEPT** instruction on line 40, print the Total record output, and end the program.

28 The **IF** instruction tests the status of indicator **OF.** When **OF** is on, the following **EXCEPT** instruction on line 29 will be executed.

29 This **EXCEPT** instruction prints the Headings record formats on lines 42–57.

30 This **EVAL** instruction turns off indicator **OF.** After the first record has been processed and the Headings records printed on the first page, subsequent page overflow will be controlled when the page overflow line is tested and the **OF** indicator automatically turned on.

31 The **ENDIF** operation ends the **IF** group that began on line 28.

33 This **EXCEPT** instruction prints the Detail line for the current record processed. Regardless of the page overflow test, this instruction will be executed for every ARMaster file record processed.

34 This **EVAL** instruction adds the Actbalance from the current ARMaster file record to the Total field. The Actbalance value from each record will be added to the Total field.

35 This **EVAL** instruction adds 1 to the Records field. Every ARMaster file record processed will add 1 to the Records field.

36 This **READ** instruction reads the next record from the ARMaster file. When end of file is read, indicator **LR** will be turned on, which will subsequently end the program.

37 The **ENDDO** operation ends the **DOW** group and passes control back to the **DOW** instruction on line 26, where the end-of-program test is made.

40 This **EXCEPT** instruction is executed after exit from the **DOW** group (end of file read and **LR** turned on). The Total record format on lines 64–67 is printed by this instruction.

Figure 18-14 Compile listing of an **RPG IV** program that processes a printer file shell. (Continued)

Output Specifications:

42–57	The Headings record formats are printed when the **EXCEPT** instruction on line 29 is executed.
58–61	The Detail record format is printed when the **EXCEPT** instruction on line 33 is executed.
62–67	The Total record format is printed when the **EXCEPT** instruction on line 40 is executed.

Figure 18-14 Compile listing of an **RPG IV** program that processes a printer file shell. (Continued)

SUMMARY

In the **RPG IV** environment, the syntax for printed reports may be specified by the following methods:

1. Included in the **RPG IV** program's *Output Specifications*
2. Included in a printer file using unique DDS syntax
3. Create a printer file "shell" to support select printer features (e.g., print quality, font type, and so forth) not accessible in standard **RPG IV** coding. The syntax for the report is coded in the program's *Output Specifications.*

The *Data Description Specifications* for printer files include special keywords. Skipping and line spacing are controlled by the **SKIPA, SKIPB, SPACEA,** and **SPACEB** keywords. Constants are defined in exactly the same way as they are for display files. Fields may be defined in the DDS, or their attributes may be referenced from a file by the **REF** or **REFFLD** keyword. Usually, more than one record format is included in a printer file for heading, detail, and total lines. Because page overflow indicators **(OA–OG, OV)** are *not* supported by printer files, this control must be included in calculation statements in the **RPG IV** program. Furthermore, headings, detail, and total lines are printed by **WRITE** statements with the select printer file's record format specified in *Factor 2.*

QUESTIONS

18-1. What are printer files?

18-2. As compared to standard **RPG IV** *Output Specifications* coding for reports, what are the advantages of printer files? Are there any disadvantages?

18-3. How are printer files created?

18-4. Where and how are printer files defined in an **RPG IV** program?

18-5. What is the function of each of the following printer file keywords?

DATE	**EDTWRD**	**SPACEB**
SPACEA	**SKIPA**	**SKIPB**
TIME	**PAGNBR**	**EDTCDE**

18-6. Where in the DDS form are the keywords in Question 18-5 specified?

18-7. In what format is the **DATE** value accessed?

18-8. In what format is the **TIME** value accessed?

18-9. What is the maximum value that may be specified with the **SPACEA** and **SPACEB** keywords?

18-10. What is the result of processing if **SKIPB(06)** is specified and the printer carriage is on line 1? On line 10?

18-11. Format **EDTCDE** keywords to generate the indicated edited result for the following examples:

	Value in Storage	Edited Output	EDTCDE Format
a.	00000▲00	.00	
b.	092291	9/22/91	
c.	12500▲00)	125,000.00–	
d.	000000▲00		

▲Indicates implied decimal position

18-12. Format **EDTWRD** keywords to generate the indicated edited result for the following examples:

	Value in Storage	Edited Output	EDTWRD Format
a.	00150▲00	$ 150.00	
b.	00150▲00	$150.00	
c.	011223333	011-22-3333	
d.	011223333	011 22 3333	
e.	2038380601	(203)-838-0601	
f.	000009▲00	*****9.00 CREDIT	
g.	00001	1	
h.	093091	9/30/91	
i.	250▲00)	2,500.00–	

▲ Indicates implied decimal position

Assume all dollar values are to include commas in the EDTWRD when large enough.

18-13. How is page overflow controlled in an **RPG IV** program when printer files are used for report formats?

18-14. Explain the processing logic of the following calculation instructions:

```
*.. 1 ...+... 2 ...+... 3 ...+... 4 ...+... 5 ...+... 6
CLON01Factor1+++++++Opcode&ExtExtended-factor2+++++++++
                    IF        *IN10 <> *ON
                    EVAL      LineCounter = 55
                    EVAL      PageLength  = 54
                    EVAL      *IN10 = *ON
                    ENDIF
```

18-15. Explain the processing logic of the following calculation instructions:

```
*.. 1 ...+... 2 ...+... 3 ...+... 4 ...+... 5 ...+... 6 ...+
CLON01Factor1+++++++Opcode&ExtExtended-factor2+++++++++++++++
                    IF        LineCounter >= PageLength
                    WRITE     HeadingLine
                    EVAL      LineCounter = 6
                    ENDIF
                    WRITE     DetailLine
                    EVAL      LineCounter = LineCount + 2
```

18-16. Refer to Question 18-15 and explain where HeadingLine and DetailLine are defined. How are they defined? What general syntax is included in each?

18-17. What is the function of the **CRTPRTF** command? Name some of the controls that may be specified by this command.

18-18. Under what conditions may the syntax for a report be included in the *Output Specifications* and a related printer file be specified in the *File Description Specifications*?

PROGRAMMING ASSIGNMENTS

The programming assignments for this chapter will require you refer to assignments in other chapters. If the referenced assignment had not been previously completed, create the physical file, load the data, create a printer file from the report design, and write the **RPG IV** program to generate the report. If the assignment had been completed, create a printer file for the report design and modify the program accordingly.

Programming Assignment 18-1: SALES JOURNAL

Refer to Programming Assignment 6-1 for the specifications.

Programming Assignment 18-2: SALESPERSON SALARY/COMMISSION REPORT

Refer to Programming Assignment 6-2 for the specifications.

Programming Assignment 18-3: VOTER REPORT BY TOWN, COUNTY, AND STATE TOTALS

Refer to Programming Assignment 7-2 for the specifications.

Programming Assignment 18-4: INCOME STATEMENT BY QUARTERS

Refer to Programming Assignment 10-2 for the specifications.

chapter 19

Calling Programs in the ILE RPG IV Environment

RPG IV MODULAR PROGRAMMING

Instead of creating large **RPG IV** programs, the trend today is to divide them into a logical number of *modular* programs or procedures. Field addresses in storage are passed *to* and received *from* standalone *modules* as required.

Modular programming has the following advantages:

- Small modular programs or procedures are easier to maintain than large **RPG IV** programs.
- Modular programs or procedures may be shared by other programs (**ILE RPG IV, ILE COBOL, ILE C,** and **ILE CL**) without consuming a large amount of memory, which may lead to performance degradation.
- Small modular programs or procedures are easier to debug and test than large **RPG IV** programs.
- Development time may be decreased by assigning more than one programmer a separate module or modules for an application.

In the *Integrated Language Environment* **(ILE),** other programs and procedures may be "called" with the **CALL** operation using *dynamic binding* or with the **CALLB** operation using *static binding*. The processing features of each method are explained in the following sections.

The `CALL` *(Call a Program)* Operation and Dynamic Binding

Before the introduction of the *Integrated Language Environment*, program and procedure modules had to be called with the **CALL** operation using *dynamic binding*. In that environment, traditional **RPG/400** programs were compiled with the **CRTRPGPGM** command, which was the default using the compile options with the Programmer Menu or Program Development Manager.

Now in the **ILE** environment, **RPG IV** (or **ILE COBOL, ILE C, ILE CL**) programs that are to be dynamically bound must be compiled with the **CRTBNDRPG** *(Create Bound RPG)* command. If the Programmer menu is used to develop programs, this command must be entered on the command line and **F4** pressed to access the command's displays when more parameters, other than the source program name, are required. However, if the Program Development Manager is used to develop programs, option 15 will automatically compile programs with the **CRTBNDRPG** command.

With dynamic binding, a "called" program is placed into memory only when a **CALL** instruction to that program or procedure is "issued" by the "calling" program. Note that the *addresses* of the parameters are passed between the modules and not the values in the storage positions. Figure 19-1 illustrates the logic of the dynamic binding of four **RPG IV** objects.

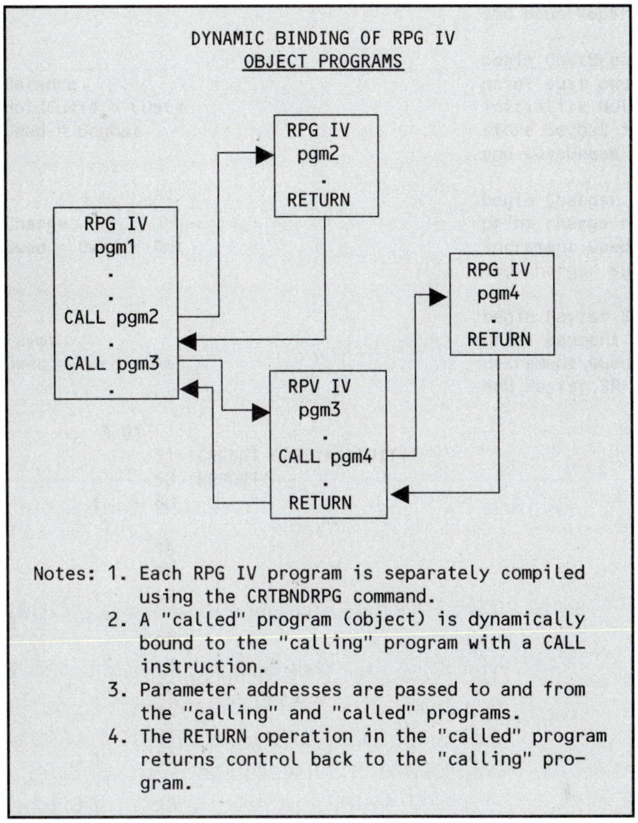

Figure 19-1 Processing logic of the dynamic binding of four **RPG IV** programs.

Because a "calling" program must find the "called" program and build a number of internal procedures, dynamic binding is usually less efficient in performance times and generates more machine instructions than static binding. One advantage to dynamic binding, however, is that changes may be made to a called or calling program without modifying any of the other related programs.

The Passing of Parameter Addresses to a Called Program

Regardless of the binding method used in modular programming, parameter addresses are sent to a called program with a **PLIST** operation followed by one or more **PARM** instructions and a **CALL** (for dynamic binding) or **CALLB** (for static binding) command. The parameter addresses are received by the called program with a **PLIST** instruction followed by one or more positionally related **PARM** instructions.

The parameter addresses are returned from the called program to the calling program when a **RETURN** operation is encountered or indicator **LR** is turned on in the called program. The syntax of the **PLIST, PARM,** and **COPY** operations is explained in the following sections.

The PLIST *(Identify a Parameter List)* Operation

The declarative **PLIST** operation identifies a parameter list (one or more **PARM** instructions) that immediately follows. Figure 19-2 details the syntax related to the **PLIST** operation.

```
*.. 1 ...+... 2 ...+... 3 ...+... 4 ...+... 5 ...+... 6 ...+... 7 ...+... 8 ...+... 9 ...+ ...10
CLON01Factor1+++++++Opcode&ExtFactor2+++++++Result++++++++Len++D+HiLoEq....Comments+++++++++++++
  1 2         3          PLIST
                           4         5              5         5     5
```

1 A *Control Level Indicator* **(L0–L9)** may be specified in the *L0* field to place the parameter list within total-time calculations.

2 Conditioning indicators in the *N01* field are *not* permitted.

3 *Factor 1* must contain the name of a programmer-supplied parameter list in the calling program. ***ENTRY** must be specified in the called program's **PLIST** instruction. Only one ***ENTRY** parameter list may be in a program or procedure.

4 The **PLIST** operation name must be entered left-justified in the *Opcode&Ext* field.

5 The *Factor 2, Result* field, *Len,* and *Hi, Lo,* and *Eq* fields are not used.

Processing Features:

* A **PLIST** operation may be specified anywhere in calculations, including between subroutines and within total-time calculations.

* A parameter list is ended when an instruction other than **PARM** is encountered.

Figure 19-2 Syntax and processing features of the **PLIST** operation.

The PARM *(Identify Parameters)* Operation

The declarative **PARM** operation defines the parameters that are included in a **PLIST** (parameter list). **PARM** instructions may be placed anywhere in calculations providing they immediately follow the **PLIST, CALL,** or **CALLB** operation to which they refer. One **PARM** instruction, or as many as 255 for a **CALL** instruction, or 399 for a **CALLB** or **PLIST** instruction, may be specified in an **RPG IV** program. Parameter addresses of the fields or literals in the **PARM** instructions are passed from the calling program to one or more called programs. The syntax of the **PARM** operation is detailed in Figure 19-3.

```
*.. 1 ...+... 2 ...+... 3 ...+... 4 ...+... 5 ...+... 6 ...+... 7 ...+... 8 ...+... 9 ...+ ...10
CLON01Factor1+++++++Opcode&ExtFactor2+++++++Result++++++++Len++D+HiLoEq....Comments+++++++++++++
  1 2         3         PARM
                          4       5           6        7    7
```

1 A *Control Level Indicator* **(L0–L9)** may be specified in the *L0* field to place the parameter list within total-time calculations.

2 Conditioning indicators in the *N01* field are *not* permitted.

3 *Factor 1* is optional. If specified, the entry must be the same type (numeric or character) as the *Result* field. A literal or Named Constant *cannot* be specified.

4 The **PARM** operation name must be entered left-justified in the *Opcode&Ext* field.

5 *Factor 2* is optional. If specified, the entry must be the same type (numeric or character) as the *Result* field.

6 The *Result* field entry may contain only a field name, data structure, or array name.

7 The *Len,* and *Hi, Lo,* and *Eq* fields are not used.

Figure 19-3 Syntax and processing features of the **PARM** operation.

Processing Features:

Calling Program:

* If *Factor 2* is *not* specified, the address of the *Result* field item is passed to the called program and values are returned to the same *Result* field item in storage.

* If a *Factor 2* item *is* specified, its value will be moved to the *Result* field item and its address passed to the called program and returned to the calling program.

* If a *Factor 1* item is specified, when control from the called program is returned to the calling program, the value in the *Result* field item will also be stored in the *Factor 1* entry.

Called Program:

* A value received from a calling program is stored in the *Result* field item of the called program. Note that the first **PARM**'s *Result* field item in the calling program will be stored in the first **PARM**'s *Result* field item in the called program. Because of this positional relationship, it is important that the *Result* field items in both programs are in the same order. Note, however, that the field names do not have to be the same.

* If a *Factor 1* item is specified, the value in the related *Result* field is also stored in it.

* If a *Factor 2* item is specified, the value stored in it is placed in the *Result* field before the program returns to the calling program.

Figure 19-3 Syntax and processing features of the **PARM** operation. (Continued)

The CALL *(Call a Program)* Operation

With dynamic binding, a called program is bound to the calling program by a **CALL** instruction that passes control from the calling program to the called program. The syntax of the **CALL** operation is explained in Figure 19-4.

```
*.. 1 ...+... 2 ...+... 3 ...+... 4 ...+... 5 ...+... 6 ...+... 7 ...+... 8 ...+... 9 ...+ ...10
CLON01Factor1+++++++Opcode&ExtFactor2+++++++Result++++++++Len++D+HiLoEq....Comments++++++++++++
C 1 2        3       CALL           5          6               7 8 9
                      4
```

1 A *Control Level Indicator* **(L0–LR)** may be specified in the *LO* field to place the **CALL** instruction within total-time calculations.

2 Conditioning indicators in the *N01* field are not permitted.

3 *Factor 1* is not used.

4 The **CALL** operation name must be left-justified in the *Opcode&Ext* field.

5 *Factor 2* must contain a character entry specifying the name of the program to be called. The entry may be the name of a field, named constant, array, or a literal that contains the name of the program to be called. A library name may be optionally included (i.e., **(library/pgmname)).** A literal, indicating the called program's name, must be enclosed in single quotes.

6 The *Result* field may contain a programmer-supplied name of a **PLIST** to communicate values between the calling and called programs. If a **PARM** instruction immediately follows a **CALL** instruction, or if the "called" program does not access parameters, this entry may be omitted.

7 The *Resulting Indicator Hi* field is not used.

8 A *Resulting Indicator* may be specified in the *Lo* field, which will be turned on if an error is returned from the called program.

9 A *Resulting Indicator* may be specified in the *Eq* field, which will be turned on if the called program is an **RPG IV** program, that returns with the LR indicator on.

Figure 19-4 Syntax of the **CALL** operation.

Examples of how a **CALL** operation may be used with **PARM** instructions are shown in Figure 19-5.

Example 1:

```
*.. 1 ...+... 2 ...+... 3 ...+... 4 ...+... 5 ...+... 6 ...+... 7 ...+... 8 ...+... 9 ...+ ...10
CLON01Factor1+++++++Opcode&ExtFactor2+++++++Result++++++++Len++D+HiLoEq....Comments+++++++++++++
 * When one or more PARM instructions immediately follow a CALL instruction, a PLIST name is not
 * required in the Result field.  PROG1 will be "called" and the values in Field1 and Field2
 * passed to it.....
C                   CALL      'PROG1'
C                   PARM                    Field1
C                   PARM                    Field2
```

Example 2:

```
*.. 1 ...+... 2 ...+... 3 ...+... 4 ...+... 5 ...+... 6 ...+... 7 ...+... 8 ...+... 9 ...+ ...10
CLON01Factor1+++++++Opcode&ExtFactor2+++++++Result++++++++Len++D+HiLoEq....Comments+++++++++++++
 * When instructions other than PARMs are included between a CALL operation and its related
 * PARM instructions, a PLIST name is required in the Result field.  The related PLIST instruc-
 * tion must include the name in Factor 1. If a PLIST name is included in the Result field of
 * the CALL operation, the CALL operation may be placed before or after its related PARM in-
 * structions....
C                   CALL      'PROG2'       List
C                     .
C                     .
C     List          PLIST
C                   PARM                    Field1
C                   PARM                    Field2
```

Example 3:

```
*.. 1 ...+... 2 ...+... 3 ...+... 4 ...+... 5 ...+... 6 ...+... 7 ...+... 8 ...+... 9 ...+ ...10
CLON01Factor1+++++++Opcode&ExtFactor2+++++++Result++++++++Len++D+HiLoEq....Comments+++++++++++++
 * The "called" program name may be stored in a field, a named constant, or an array element
 * defined as character....
C                   CALL      ProgName
C                   PARM                    Field1
C                   PARM                    Field2
```

Figure 19-5 Examples of **CALL** instructions and their relationship with **PLIST** and **PARM** instructions.

Syntax Required in the Called Program

To receive parameter values from a calling program, the called program must specify an instruction with ***ENTRY** in *Factor 1* and the **PLIST** operation name in the *OpCode&Ext* field. The **PARM** fields that follow must be in the same order as those sent from the calling program. However, the field names in the called program *do not* have to be the same as those in the calling program. Figure 19-6 illustrates parameter entries common to a called program.

In Example 1, when control returns back to the calling program, all of the field values and the status of any indicators will be retained in the called program. If the same program is called again, any field values and indicator conditions will be preserved. However, the system resources used by the called program will remain active until the calling program has ended.

In Example 2, turning on indicator **LR** will release the system resources allocated to the called program. Any of the field values or indicator conditions in the called program will be lost after the parameter values are passed. If control is passed again to the called program in the same run, the called program will have to be restarted.

The decision on whether to use the Example 1 or Example 2 approach depends on the application. If a called program is to be accessed more than once in the same run, the

Example 1:

```
*.. 1 ...+... 2 ...+... 3 ...+... 4 ...+... 5 ...+... 6 ...+... 7 ...+... 8 ...+... 9 ...+ ...10
CLON01Factor1+++++++Opcode&ExtFactor2+++++++Result++++++++Len++D+HiLoEq....Comments+++++++++++++
 * The *ENTRY PLIST instruction identifies the entry point for the following parameter list in
 * the called program.  The fields in the PARM instruction Result fields must be in the same
 * order as those in the calling program, but they do not have to have the same names.  Values
 * in the Result fields (Field1 and Field2) are passed back to the calling program when the
 * RETURN operation is encountered.

C     *ENTRY        PLIST
C                   PARM                    Field1
C                   PARM                    Field2
C                   RETURN
```

Example 2:

```
*.. 1 ...+... 2 ...+... 3 ...+... 4 ...+... 5 ...+... 6 ...+... 7 ...+... 8 ...+... 9 ...+ ...10
CLON01Factor1+++++++Opcode&ExtFactor2+++++++Result++++++++Len++D+HiLoEq....Comments+++++++++++++
 * Turning on the LR indicator before the RETURN operation releases the system's resources
 * allocated by the called program.

C     *ENTRY        PLIST
C                   PARM                    Field1
C                   PARM                    Field2
C                   EVAL      *INLR = *ON
C                   RETURN
```

Figure 19-6 Syntax examples in the called program.

syntax of Example 1 should probably be used. On the other hand, if a called program is accessed only once in the same run, Example 2 will release the system resources allocated by the called program.

The Relationship Between the Calling and Called Programs

Optional *Factor 1* and *Factor 2* entries in a **PARM** instruction in the calling and called programs will determine what values are stored in the *Result* field items and passed to and received from a called program. Figure 19-7 illustrates two examples of how **PARM** instruction *Result* field values are passed to and received from a called program.

Notice in Figure 19-7 that the Code *(Result)* field (line 5) value in the calling program is passed to the Code1 *(Result)* field (line 2) in the called program. When control is returned to the calling program, the value in Code1 is passed to and stored in Code. The original value in Code will be lost with this method of transferring parameters.

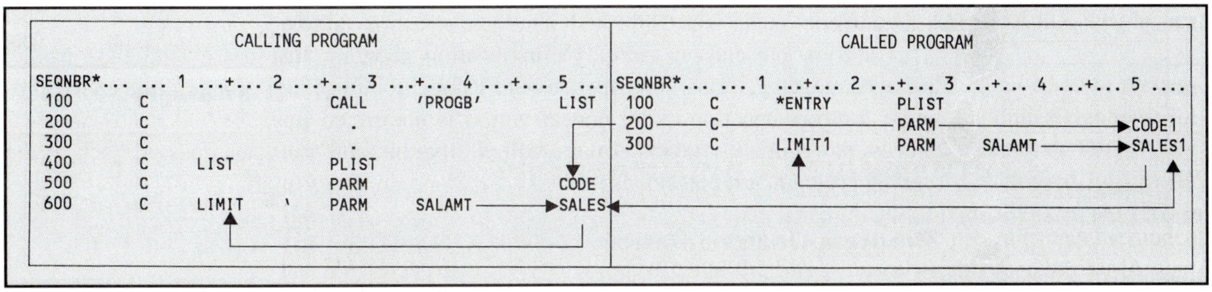

Figure 19-7 **PARM** field relationships between the calling and called programs.

Line No.	Explanation	Line No.	Explanation
100	**CALL** statement calls PROGB and passes the values stored in the **PARM** statement's *Result* field.	100	***ENTRY** in *Factor 1* identifies the parameter list being received by the called program.
400	The **PLIST** instruction indicates the beginning of a parameter list definition (LIST). If the **PARM** statements immediately followed the **CALL** statement, a **PLIST** statement would not be required.	200	The value passed from the calling program is stored in the CODE1 field. When PROGB returns control back to the calling program, the value in CODE1 will be passed back to the calling program.
500	The value in the CODE field is passed to the called program. When control returns to the calling program, the value in CODE will reflect the value returned from PROGB in CODE1.	300	When control is transferred from the calling program to the called program (PROGB), the value passed is stored in the *Result* field item (SALES1 for this example) and then automatically moved to LIMIT1 (the *Factor 1* field). When PROGB returns control to the calling program, the value in SALAMT (the *Factor 2* field) is moved to SALES (the *Result* field).
600	When PROGB is called, the value in SALAMT is moved to the SALES field and then passed to PROGB. When PROGB returns control to the calling program, the value in SALES is moved to LIMIT, the *Factor 1* field.		

Notes:

1. Coding examples assume fields are previously defined.
2. Related field names in calling and called programs may be the same. However, for clarity, it may be expedient to use different names in each program.
3. Field values are passed to and from the calling and called programs positionally. Hence, the first **PARM** field specified in the calling program must be specified in the first **PARM** statement of the called program.
4. Parameter lists are ended when a statement other than a **PARM** is encountered.
5. From the called program, values are passed back to the calling program when the **RETURN** operation (if specified) is encountered or when **LR** turns on.

Figure 19-7 **PARM** field relationships between the calling and called programs. (Continued)

In the calling program, the **PARM** instruction on line 600 moves the SalAmt (*Factor 2*) field value to the Sales (*Result*) field before sending it to the called program. After control returns to the calling program, the new value in the Sales field is moved into the Limit (*Factor 1*) field. This method retains the original value in the SalAmt field for any additional processing.

In the called program, the **PARM** instruction on line 300 receives the Sales field value from the calling program and stores it in the Sales1 *(Result)* field. Then it automatically moves the value into the Limit1 *(Factor 1)* field. Before control is returned to the calling program, the value in the SalAmt *(Factor 2)* field is moved to the Sales1 *(Result)* field. This method retains the original value passed in the Limit1 field. The method used will usually depend on the processing requirements.

APPLICATION PROGRAM: CALLING A PROGRAM USING DYNAMIC BINDING

This section presents an **RPG IV** application program that passes the Last_Name, First_Name, City, State, and Zipcode field values from a calling program to a called program for concatenation. After concatenation is performed (e.g., STANLEY E MYERS and NORWALK, CT 06854) by the called program, and the values passed back to the calling program, a report line is printed.

Program Documentation

The specifications for this application are detailed in Figure 19-8.

PROGRAM SPECIFICATIONS — Page 1 of 1

Program Name: Customer Address List   Program-ID: CUSTLIST   Written by: SM

Purpose: Print customer address listing   Approved by: CM

Input files: CADDRS

Output files: QSYSPRT

Processing Requirements:

Write two RPG IV programs to generate a customer address listing.

Input to the program:

The externally described physical file, CADDRS, contains customer names and addresses with the attributes shown in the attached physical file description form.

Processing:

Read the physical file in keyed sequence until end of file. For every record processed, pass the LAST_NAME, MID_INIT, FIRST_NAME, CITY, STATE, and ZIPCODE field parameters to the RPG IV program CATENATE. The called program must be written to concatenate the FIRST_NAME, MID_INIT, and LAST_NAME with one space between each field value. In addition, the called program must also provide for the concatenation of the CITY, STATE, and ZIPCODE fields so that a comma and one space are included after the CITY value and one space is included between the STATE and ZIPCODE values.

The CATENATE program is stored as an object in a library in your library list.

Output:

A supplemental printer spacing chart shows the report design.

Figure 19-8 Specifications for an application that calls a program.

Figure 19-9 presents a system flowchart that identifies the programs executed and files processed by the calling application.

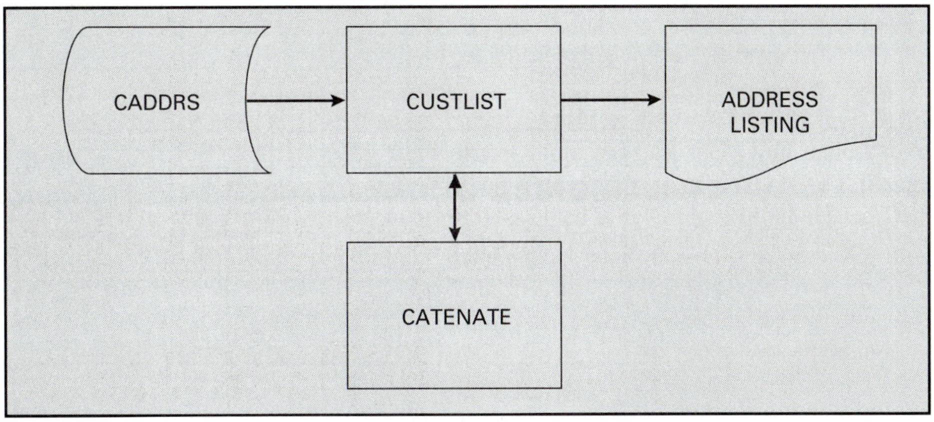

Figure 19-9 System flowchart for an applications program that calls a program.

The record format of the physical file and listing of the data are presented in Figure 19-10.

PHYSICAL FILE DESCRIPTION

SYSTEM: AS/400	DATE: 12/11/97
FILE NAME: CADDRS	REV NO: 0
RECORD NAME: CADDRSR	KEY LENGTH: 5
SEQUENCE: Keyed	RECORD SIZE: 73

FIELD DEFINITIONS

FIELD NO	FIELD NAME	SIZE	TYPE	POSITION FROM	POSITION TO	COMMENTS
1	CUSTNUMBER	5	C	1	5	Key Field
2	LAST_NAME	15	C	6	20	
3	MID_INIT	1	C	21	21	
4	FIRST_NAME	12	C	22	33	
5	STREET	18	C	34	51	
6	CITY	15	C	52	66	
7	STATE	2	C	67	68	
8	ZIPCODE	5	C	69	73	

Physical File Data:

Customer Number	Last Name	Initial	First Name	Street	City	State	Zip
10000	APPEL	E	KAREL	20 AMSTERDAM AVE	NEW YORK	NY	07450
11000	BRAQUE	F	GEORGES	300 ST CLAIR ST	TRENTON	NJ	05501
12000	CEZANNE	C	PAUL	44 RUE PIGALLE	STAMFORD	CT	06518
13000	CHAGALL	W	MARC	222 QUAIL AVENUE	BRIDGEPORT	CT	06666
14000	DEGAS	T	EDGAR	10 ROSE TERRACE	WESTPORT	PA	07777
15000	ERNST	S	MAX	1 FRANKFURT DRIVE	FRANKFURT	KY	05551
16000	FULLER	H	BUCKMINSTER	999 PARK AVE	NEW YORK	NY	07550
17000	GONZALEZ	G	JULIO	101 SMITH LANE	GREENWICH	CT	06444
18000	HYPPOLITE	H	HECTOR	888 PEACHTREE AVE	ATLANTA	GA	03332
19000	JEANERET	R	PIERRE	90 CHATEAU DRIVE	GENEVA	NY	07777
20000	KANDINSKY	F	WASSILY	13 WARSAW LANE	LOS ANGELES	CA	09990
21000	CORBUSIER	C	CHARLES	10 PARIS PLACE	ENGLEWOOD	NJ	07632

Figure 19-10 Physical file record format and data listing for application call program.

The report design is detailed in the printer spacing chart in Figure 19-11. Also included is the printed report generated by the application call program. Note as a result

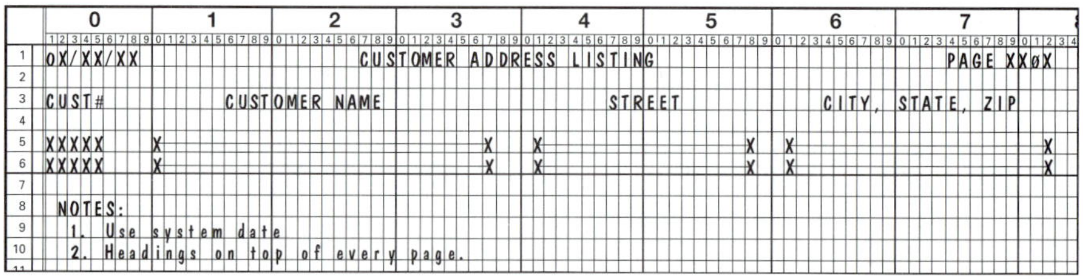


```
12/28/97                 CUSTOMER ADDRESS LISTING                    PAGE    1

CUST#          CUSTOMER NAME                    STREET          CITY, STATE, ZIP

10000     KAREL E APPEL                    20 AMSTERDAM AVE    NEW YORK, NY 07450
```

Figure 19-11 Report design and printed output generated by the application call program.

11000	GEORGES F BRAQUE	300 ST CLAIR ST	TRENTON, NJ 05501
12000	PAUL C CEZANNE	44 RUE PIGALLE	STAMFORD, CT 06518
13000	MARC W CHAGALL	222 QUAIL AVENUE	BRIDGEPORT, CT 06666
14000	EDGAR T DEGAS	10 ROSE TERRACE	WESTPORT, PA 07777
15000	MAX S ERNST	1 FRANKFURT DRIVE	FRANKFORT, KY 05551
16000	BUCKMINSTER H FULLER	999 PARK AVENUE	NEW YORK, NY 07550
17000	JULIO G GONZALEZ	101 SMITH LANE	GREENWICH, CT 06444
18000	HECTOR H HYPPOLITE	888 PEACHTREE AVE	ATLANTA, GA 03332
19000	PIERRE R JEANERET	90 CHATEAU DRIVE	GENEVA, NY 07777
20000	WASSILY F KANDINSKY	13 WARSAW LANE	LOG ANGELES, CA 09990
21000	CHARLES C CORBUSIER	10 PARIS PLACE	ENGLEWOOD, NJ 07632

Figure 19-11 Report design and printed output generated by the application call program. (Continued)

of the called program's concatenation process, the field values of a customer's first name, middle initial, and last name are concatenated with one space between the values. In addition, the field values of city, state, and zip code are concatenated with one space (except for the comma and space after the city value) between the values.

Compile Listing of the RPG IV Calling Program (Dynamic Binding)

A detailed compile listing of the calling program that dynamically binds another **RPG IV** program is presented in Figure 19-12.

```
Line   <---------------------- Source Specifications ----------------------------><---- Comments ----> Do
Number ....1....+....2....+....3....+....4....+....5....+....6....+....7....+....8....+....9....+...10 Num
                            S o u r c e   L i s t i n g
         * This calling program passes parameters to a called program
         * that concatenates name and address elements for a report

       FCaddrs    IF   E           K DISK
         *------------------------------------------------------------------------------------------*
         *                               RPG name          External name                            *
         * File name. . . . . . . . . :  CADDRS            STAN/CADDRS                              *
         * Record format(s) . . . . . :  CADDRSR           CADDRSR                                  *
         *------------------------------------------------------------------------------------------*
       FQsysprt   O    F  132           PRINTER OFLIND(*INOF)

       D Full_Name       S             28                                    first, md, last name
       D Full_Addrs      S             22                                    st, city, zipcode

      =ICADDRSR
         *------------------------------------------------------------------------------------------*
         * RPG record format  . . . . :  CADDRSR                                                    *
         * External format  . . . . . :  CADDRSR : STAN/CADDRS                                      *
         *------------------------------------------------------------------------------------------*
      =I                                A    1    5  CUSTNUMBER
      =I                                A    6   20  LAST_NAME
      =I                                A   21   21  MID_INIT
      =I                                A   22   33  FIRST_NAME
      =I                                A   34   51  STREET
      =I                                A   52   66  CITY
      =I                                A   67   68  STATE
      =I                                A   69   73  ZIPCODE
       C                   EVAL      *INOF = *ON                             turn on OF indicator

       C                   READ      Caddrs                           ----LR read first record
       C                   DOW       *INLR = *OFF                            dow LR is off       B01
       C                   EXSR      HeadingSR                               branch to subroutine 01
       C                                                                                         01
         * Call program and pass parameter values....
```

Figure 19-12 Compile listing of the calling program.

```
26 C                      CALL      'CATENATE'                                      call program          01
27 C                      PARM      First_Name     Full_Name                        pass first name       01
28 C                      PARM                     Mid_Init                         pass middle initial   01
29 C                      PARM                     Last_Name                        pass last name        01
30 C                      PARM      City           Full_Addrs                       pass city             01
31 C                      PARM                     State                            pass state            01
32 C                      PARM                     ZipCode                          pass zip code         01
33 C                      EXCEPT    DetailLine                                      print detail line     01
34
35 C                      READ      Caddrs                                ----LR    read next record      01
36 C                      ENDDO                                                     end dow group        E01
37
38 C     HeadingSR        BEGSR                                                     begin subroutine
39 C                      IF        *INOF = *ON                                     OF on?               B01
40 C                      EXCEPT    Heading                                                               01
41 C                      EVAL      *INOF = *OFF                                    turn off OF indicatr  01
42 C                      ENDIF                                                     end IF group         E01
43 C                      ENDSR                                                     end subroutine
44
45 OQsysprt   E            Heading          2 01
46 O                       UDATE          Y      8
47 O                                             50 'CUSTOMER ADDRESS LISTING'
48 O                                             77 'PAGE'
49 O                       PAGE                  82
50 O          E            Heading          2
51 O                                              5 'CUST#'
52 O                                             28 'CUSTOMER NAME'
53 O                                             52 'STREET'
54 O                                             79 'CITY, STATE, ZIP'
55 O          E            DetailLine       1
56 O                       CustNumber             5
57 O                       Full_Name             37
58 O                       Street                58
59 O                       Full_Addrs            82
```

File Description Specifications:

Line No.

4 Caddrs is defined as an input (**I** in position 17), full-procedural (**F** in position 18), externally described (**E** in position 22), keyed (**K** in position 34) physical file.

5 Qsysprt is defined as an output (**O** in position 17), program-described (**F** in position 22) printer file with a record size of 132. The ***INOF** page overflow indicator is specified with the **OFLIND(*INOF)** keyword.

Definition Specifications:

7 Full_Name is defined as a standalone, 28-byte character field. Its size is defined to hold the concatenated First_Name, Mid_Init, and Last_Name values. The First_Name value is moved left-justified into this field (see line 27) whose address is accessed by the called program to extract the value, concatenate the three field values, and return it to its storage area to be accessed by the calling program.

8 Full_Addrs is defined as a standalone, 22-byte character field. Its size is defined to hold the concatenated City, State, and ZipCode values. The City value is moved left-justified into this field (see line 30) whose address is accessed by the called program to extract the value, concatenate the three field values, and return it to its storage area to be accessed by the calling program.

Calculation Specifications:

19 This **EVAL** instruction turns on the **OF** indicator to force page overflow for the first record processed.

21 This **READ** instruction reads the first record from the physical file. If no records are stored in the file, the **LR** indicator will be turned on and will subsequently end the program when the **DOW** instruction on line 22 is executed.

22 The **DOW** instruction begins the iterative group that is continually processed until indicator **LR** (end-of-file condition) is turned on by the **READ** instruction on line 21 or 35.

23 The **EXSR** instruction branches control to the HeadingSR subroutine.

26 The **CALL** instruction dynamically "binds" the calling program to the called program, which will access the addresses of the field values in the related **PARM** instructions.

Figure 19-12 Compile listing of the calling program. (Continued)

27 This **PARM** instruction moves the value in the First_Name field left-justified into the Full_Name field and passes its address to the "called" program.

28 This **PARM** instruction passes the address of the Mid_Init field to the called program.

29 This **PARM** instruction passes the address of the Last_Name field to the called program.

30 This **PARM** instruction moves the value in the City field left-justified into the Full_Addrs field and passes its address to the called program.

31 This **PARM** instruction passes the address of the State field to the called program.

32 This **PARM** instruction passes the address of the ZipCode field to the called program. The **PARM** group ends when an instruction other than a **PARM** is encountered.

33 After the field values in the Full_Name and Full_Addrs are concatenated by the called program and control is returned to the calling program, this **EXCEPT** instruction prints the DetailLine record format for the current input record.

35 This **READ** instruction reads the next record from the physical file. If end of file is read, the **LR** indicator will be turned on and will end the program when control is passed back to the **DOW** instruction on line 22.

36 The **ENDDO** operation returns control to the **DOW** instruction on line 22, where the decision to continue processing or exit from the **DOW** group is made.

38 The **BEGSR** instruction begins the HeadingSR subroutine, which is accessed by the **EXSR** instruction on line 23.

39 The **IF** instruction tests the status of the **OF** indicator, which will be on for the first record processed (see line 19). Subsequent page overflow will occur automatically when the overflow line is detected.

40 This **EXCEPT** instruction controls printing of the Heading record formats.

41 This **EVAL** instruction turns off the **OF** indicator to prevent page overflow from occurring for each record processed.

42 The **ENDIF** operation ends the **IF** group that began on line 39.

43 The **ENDSR** operation ends the Heading SR subroutine that began on line 38.

Output Specifications:

45–54 The two Heading record formats, which are controled by the **EXCEPT** instruction on line 40, are defined in these instructions.

55–59 The DetaiLine record format, which is printed by the **EXCEPT** instruction on line 33, is defined in these instructions.

Figure 19-12 Compile listing of the calling program. (Continued)

Compile Listing of the Called Program

A detailed compile listing of the called program (Catenate) that concatenates the Full_Name and Full_Addrs field values is presented in Figure 19-13.

```
Line    <--------------------- Source Specifications ---------------------------><---- Comments ----> Do
Number ....1....+....2....+....3....+....4....+....5....+....6....+....7....+....8....+....9....+...10 Num
                          S o u r c e   L i s t i n g
       * This called program concatenates name and address elements
       * received from a calling program....

       * Define parameters passed from calling program....
      D Full_Name       S             25
      D Mid_Init        S              1
      D Last_Name       S             15
      D Full_Addrs      S             22
      D State           S              2
      D ZipCode         S              5

```

Figure 19-13 Compile listing of the called program.

```
12  * Receive parameter values from calling program....
13
14 C     *ENTRY       PLIST                                         begin parameter list
15 C                  PARM                    Full_Name
16 C                  PARM                    Mid_Init
17 C                  PARM                    Last_Name
18 C                  PARM                    Full_Addrs
19 C                  PARM                    State
20 C                  PARM                    ZipCode
21
22  * Concatenate elements of the Full_Name field....
23
24 C                  EVAL      Full_Name = %TRIM(Full_Name) + ' ' + Mid_Init
25 C                            + ' ' + Last_Name                  concatenate full nam
26
27  * Concatenate elements of the Full_Addrs field....
28 C                  EVAL      Full_Addrs = %TRIM(Full_Addrs) + ', ' + State
29 C                            + ' ' + ZipCode                    concatenate full add
30 C                  RETURN                                       return values
```

*Note: Because this **RPG IV** program does not include any input or output file, no File Description Specification instructions are required.

Definition Specifications:

Line No.

5–10 Full_Name, Mid_Init, Last_Name, Full_Addrs, State, and ZipCode are defined as standalone fields used in the **PARM** instructions on lines 15 through 20 to access the addresses of the related fields from the calling program. For this example, the calling and called programs have the same parameter field names. This is not a requirement in passing parameters, provided that the fields are positionally related (the first field from the calling program is the first field in the called program and so forth).

14 The special word ***ENTRY** in *Factor 1* of the **PLIST** instruction specifies the beginning of a parameter list in the called program. A parameter group may be placed anywhere in calculations; however, only *one* ***ENTRY PLIST** instruction may be included in a called program.

15 This **PARM** instruction accesses the address of the Full_Name field from the calling program. The First_Name field value was moved left-justified into the Full_Name field in the calling program. The Mid_Init and Last_Name values will be concatenated and the value returned to the storage area by the called program and accessed by the calling program.

16–17 These **PARM** instructions access the addresses of the Mid_Init and Last_Name fields from the calling program.

18 This **PARM** instruction accesses the address of the Full_Addrs field from the calling program. The City field value was moved left-justified into the Full_Addrs field in the calling program. The State and ZipCode field values will be concatenated and the value returned to the storage area by the called program and accessed by the calling program.

19–20 These **PARM** instructions access the addresses of the State and Zipcode fields from the calling program.

24–25 This **EVAL** instruction concatenates the First_Name, Mid_Init, and Last_Name field values in the Full_Name field as shown below:

```
     Full_Name = %TRIM(Full_Name) + ' ' + Mid_Init + ' ' + Last_Name

  KARL K APPEL =      KARL               K                APPEL
```

* The **%TRIM** function trims any low-order spaces from the First_Name value stored in the Full_Name field.
* The + ' ' entries add a space after the **L** in **KARL** in the Full_Name field.
* The + **Mid_Init** entries add **K** after the first space in the Full_Name field.
* The + ' ' entries add a space after the Mid_Init value **K** in the Full_Name field.
* The + **Last_Name** entries add **APPEL** after the second space in the Full_Name field, concatenating the three field values as shown above in the Full_Name value.

28–29 This **EVAL** instruction concatenates the City, State, and ZipCode field values in the Full_Addrs field as shown below:

Figure 19-13 Compile listing of the called program. (Continued)

```
        Full_Addrs = %TRIM(Full_Addrs) + ' , ' + State + ' ' + ZipCode

NEW YORK, NY 07450 =          NEW YORK                 NY            07450
```

* The **%TRIM** function trims any low-order spaces from the City value stored in the Full_Addrs field.

* The + **' , '** entries add a comma and space after the **K** in **NEW YORK** in the Full_Addrs field.

* The + **State** entries add **NY** after the first space in the Full_Addrs field.

* The + **' '** entries add a space after the State value **NY** in the Full_Addrs field.

* The + **ZipCode** entries add **07450** after the second space in the Full_Addrs field, concatenating the three field values as shown above in the Full_Addrs value.

30 The **RETURN** operation returns the six parameter values to their related storage areas whose addresses will be accessed and values extracted by the calling program.

Figure 19-13 Compile listing of the called program. (Continued)

Note that no input or output files are defined in the called program. An **RPG IV** program is syntactically correct if only one calculation instruction is specified.

After the concatenation process in the called program is completed, control is returned to the calling program when a **RETURN** operation is encountered or when an instruction that turns on indicator **LR** is executed.

Note that the field addresses from the calling program are passed positionally to the called program. The address of the first field parameter in the calling program is the first accessed by the called program, and so forth. Because of this positional processing feature, the related field names do not have to be the same.

STATIC BINDING

Static binding may be controlled by two kinds of calls: *bound by copy* and *bound by reference*. Both methods require that the **CALLB** *(Call a Bound Procedure)* operation be used to implement the binding of two or more program and/or procedure modules. Figure 19-14 details the syntax of the **CALLB** operation.

```
*.. 1 ...+... 2 ...+... 3 ...+... 4 ...+... 5 ...+... 6 ...+... 7 ...+... 8 ...+... 9 ...+ ...10
CLON01Factor1+++++++Opcode&ExtFactor2+++++++Result++++++++Len++D+HiLoEq....Comments+++++++++++++
C 1 2      3        CALLB           5             6               7 8 9
                      4
```

1 A *Control Level Indicator* **(L0–LR)** may be specified in the *L0* field to place the **CALLB** instruction within total-time calculations.

2 Conditioning indicators in the *N01* field are not permitted.

3 *Factor 1* is not used.

4 The **CALLB** operation name must be left-justified in the *Opcode&Ext* field. The operation extender **D** may be used to include operation descriptors.

5 *Factor 2* must contain a character entry specifying the name of the procedure to be called. The entry may be the name of a field, named constant, array, or a literal that contains the name of the program to be called. A library name may be optionally included (i.e., **(library/pgmname)**)—enclosed in single quotes if a literal or stored in an item defined as character.

6 The *Result* field may contain a programmer-supplied name of a **PLIST** to communicate values between the calling and called programs. If a **PARM** instruction immediately follows a **CALLB** instruction or if the called program does not access parameters, this entry may be omitted.

7 The *Resulting Indicator Hi* field is not used.

8 A *Resulting Indicator* may be specified in the *Lo* field, which will be turned on if an error is returned from the called program.

9 A *Resulting Indicator* may be specified in the *Eq* field, which will be turned on if the called program is an **RPG IV** program that returns with the LR indicator on.

Figure 19-14 Syntax of the **CALLB** operation.

The logic of static binding with the *by-Copy* method is shown in Figure 19-15.

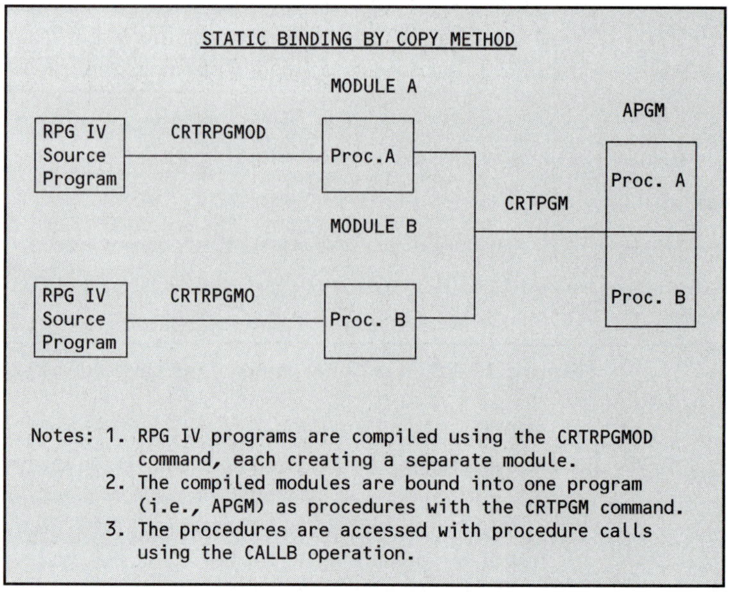
STATIC BINDING BY COPY METHOD
MODULE A
APGM
RPG IV Source Program
CRTRPGMOD
Proc.A
Proc. A
CRTPGM
MODULE B
RPG IV Source Program
CRTRPGMO
Proc. B
Proc. B
Notes: 1. RPG IV programs are compiled using the CRTRPGMOD command, each creating a separate module.
2. The compiled modules are bound into one program (i.e., APGM) as procedures with the CRTPGM command.
3. The procedures are accessed with procedure calls using the CALLB operation.

Figure 19-15 Processing logic of the "static binding-by-copy" method.

Note the following features of static binding by copy:

1. A module is created by compiling an **RPG IV** source program with the **CRTRPGMOD** command.
2. The module object created contains translated but not executable code.
3. The modules must be bound into a program by the **CRTPGM** command to be executable.
4. After the modules are bound into a program, any of them may be deleted.
5. If a source program is changed, it must be recompiled and all of the related modules bound together again with the **CRTPGM** command.
6. **COBOL, C, CL,** and **RPG IV** source programs may be compiled into modules with their respective **CRTCBLMOD, CRTCMOD, CRTCLMOD,** and **CRTRPGMOD** commands and bound into one executable program with the **CRTPGM** command.

APPLICATION PROGRAM: CALLING A PROGRAM—STATIC BINDING

Bound-By-Copy Method

The documentation for this version of the application is identical to that previously presented for the Dynamic Binding example. The only modification needed in the **RPG IV** program shown in Figure 19-12 to support Static Binding is to change the **CALL** instruction on line 26 to **CALLB.** No other changes are required in the calling or called programs. Remember, however, that all **RPG IV** source programs that are to be statically bound must be compiled with option **15** (Create a module) in the Programmer Development Manager or with the **CRTRPGMOD** command from the Programmer Menu.

After the modules are created by successful compilation of the **RPG IV** source programs, they must be bound together as procedures into one program using the **CRTPGM** *(Create Program)* command. The displays for this command are accessed by entering

CRTPGM on a command line and pressing **F4.** Figure 19-16 shows the first page filled in with the entries needed for the application modified for static binding by copy. Other optional parameters are not shown.

```
                         Create Program (CRTPGM)

Type choices, press Enter.

Program . . . . . . . . . . .   CUSTLIST2     Name
  Library . . . . . . . . . .     *CURLIB     Name, *CURLIB
Module . . . . . . . . . . . .   CUSTLIST2     Name, generic*, *PGM, *ALL
  Library . . . . . . . . . .     *CURLIB     Name, *LIBL, *CURLIB...
              + for more values   CATENATE
                                    *CURLIB
Text 'description' . . . . . . .   create a program from two modules
_____                                                              Bottom




F3=Exit   F4=Prompt   F5=Refresh   F10=Additional parameters   F12=Cancel
F13=How to use this display        F24=More keys
```

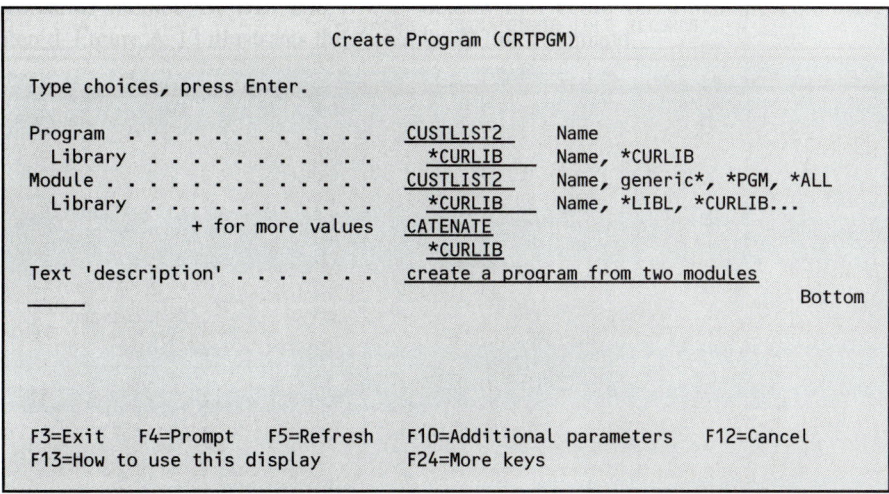

Figure 19-16 **CRTPGM** *(Create Program)* display.

After the procedures are bound together, they are executed by calling the program name (CUSTLIST2) specified on line 1 of the **CRTPGM** display. The report generated will be identical to that shown in Figure 19-11.

Bound-By-Reference Method

The Static Bound-By-Reference method is commonly used with *service programs.* A service program is a collection of commonly used procedures from one or more module objects.

The steps required to create a service program and bind it to an **RPG IV *MODULE** with the Bound-By-Reference method are summarized in the following sections.

Step 1: Write the **RPG IV** program(s) that will be accessed by the service program and compile it (them) with the **CRTRPGMOD** command to create the individual ***MODULE**(s). For the continuing example, the called program is now named CATMOD (not CATENATE) and the calling program PGMCLIST (not CUSTLIST2).

Step 2: Write the source for the service program with the syntax shown in Figure 19-17 using a special *binder language* accessed in **SEU** by the source type **END.**

```
SEQNBR*...+... 1 ...+... 2 ...+... 3 ...+... 4 ...+... 5 ...+... 6 ...+... 7 ...+... 8
  100              STRPGMEXP  SIGNATURE(*GEN)
  200                 EXPORT  SYMBOL('CATMOD')
  300              ENDPGMEXP
```

Line No.

100 The **STRPGMEXP SIGNATURE(*GEN)** command identifies the beginning of the list of exports from the service program.

200 The **EXPORT** command identifies the symbol (module, procedure, data item) name to be exported (controlled) by the service program. The **SYMBOL('CATMOD')** keyword specifies the module, procedure, or data item to be exported. Any number of **EXPORT** instructions may be specified, each identifying a different module, procedure, or data item.

300 The **ENDPGMEXP** command identifies the end of the list of exports from the service program.

* A service program is created in **SEU** by specifying **BND** for the source type.

Figure 19-17 Source code for the example service program.

Step 3: Create the service program, with the **CRTSRVPGM** command. The first page of the command's display is shown in Figure 19-18. SRVCAT is the name of the service program source shown in Figure 19-17. CATMOD is the **RPG IV *MODULE** previously compiled using the **CRTRPGMOD** command. All of the other parameters are defaults.

```
                    Create Service Program (CRTSRVPGM)

Type choices, press Enter.

Service program . . . . . . . . > SRVCAT        Name
  Library . . . . . . . . . . . >   STAN        Name, *CURLIB
Module . . . . . . . . . . . . . > CATMOD        Name, generic*, *SRVPGM, *ALL
  Library . . . . . . . . . . . >   STAN        Name, *LIBL, *CURLIB...
              + for more values
                                >   *LIBL
Export . . . . . . . . . . . . .   *SRCFILE      *SRCFILE, *ALL
Export source file . . . . . . . > QSRVSRC       Name, QSRVSRC
  Library . . . . . . . . . . . >   STAN        Name, *LIBL, *CURLIB
Export source member . . . . . .   *SRVPGM       Name, *SRVPGM
Text 'description' . . . . . . . > 'service program for CATMOD bind by reference'
e'

                                                                    Bottom
F3=Exit   F4=Prompt   F5=Refresh   F10=Additional parameters   F12=Cancel
F13=How to use this display        F24=More keys
```

Figure 19-18 CRTSRVPGM *(Create Service Program)* command display for example.

Step 4: Create a program with the **CTRPGM** command to bind the service program to the calling program into a run-time unit. Figure 19-19 shows the **CRTPGM** *(Create Program)* display with the entries needed for the example application.

```
                          Create Program (CRTPGM)

Type choices, press Enter.

Program . . . . . . . . . . . . > PGMCLIST      Name
  Library . . . . . . . . . . . >   STAN        Name, *CURLIB
Module . . . . . . . . . . . . .   *PGM          Name, generic*, *PGM, *ALL
  Library . . . . . . . . . . .                 Name, *LIBL, *CURLIB...
              + for more values

Text 'description' . . . . . . .   *ENTMODTXT


                        Additional Parameters

Bind service program . . . . . . > SRVCAT        Name, generic*, *NONE, *ALL
  Library . . . . . . . . . . .     STAN        *LIBL,
              + for more values
                                    *LIBL

                                                                    Bottom
F3=Exit   F4=Prompt   F5=Refresh   F12=Cancel   F13=How to use this display
F24=More keys
```

Figure 19-19 CRTPGM display parameters to bind the service program to the calling program into a run-time unit.

Step 5: Execute the calling program (PGMCLIST) with option **4** on the Programmer Menu, or **14** in the Program Development Manager, or with the **CALL** command on any command line to generate the report shown in Figure 19-11.

One of the major advantages of a service program is that it may be changed without always recreating the **ILE** programs (**RPG IV, COBOL, C,** or **CL**) that use the updated service program.

SUMMARY

Modular programming means dividing a large **ILE RPG IV** program into a logical number of small programs. Field addresses of common data items in memory are passed to and from the modules to access and process the stored values.

Programs that "call" each other may be bound with dynamic or static binding. With *dynamic binding*, a called program is placed into memory only when it is called by the "calling" program. The called program is bound to the calling program by a **CALL** operation and the addresses of the data items are passed by **PARM** operations. The addresses of the updated data items are passed from the called program back to the calling program when a **RETURN** operation is executed or when indicator **LR** is turned on.

PARM instructions are positional; the first address passed from the calling program is the first address received by the called program. Providing that the related parameters have the same field attributes, the names *do not* have to be the same. When dynamic binding is used, all of the related **ILE RPG IV** programs must be compiled with the **CRTBNDRPG** *(Create Bound RPG)* command and bound together with the **CRTPGM** *(Create Program)* command.

Static binding creates one executable program from the related modules. Programs may be bound by the *bound-by-copy* or *bound-by-reference* method. For either method, **ILE RPG IV** programs must be compiled with the **CRTRPGMOD** *(Create RPG Module)* command. All of the modules must be integrated into a run-time unit with the **CRTPGM** command.

Called programs are accessed by the calling program with the **CALLB** operation. Identical to dynamic binding, the addresses of parameters are passed with **PARM** instructions.

The static binding bound-by-reference method is commonly used with *service programs.* A service program is a collection of commonly used procedures from one or more module objects. The source for a service program is created with a unique bind language accessed from **SEU** with the source type **END.** Service programs must be compiled with the **CRTSRVPGM** *(Create Service Program)* command and included in a run-time unit with the **CRTPGM** command.

QUESTIONS

19-1. What is modular programming? What are its advantages?

19-2. What types of binding may be used to "call" other programs?

19-3. For the binding methods explained for Question 19-2, what **CL** commands are required to compile the **RPG IV** programs to be bound?

19-4. When is an **RPG IV** program a "calling" or "called" program?

19-5. To pass parameters to a called program, what **RPG IV** operations are required in the calling program for each binding method?

19-6. What **RPG IV** operations must be inclued in the called program to receive parameters from the calling program?

19-7. In the called program, when is control returned to the calling program?

19-8. Do the parameter names have to be the same in the calling and called programs? Explain your answer.

19-9. What values are passed between the calling and called programs?

Examine the following coding specified in a calling program and answer Questions 19-10 through 19-15:

```
*.. 1 ...+... 2 ...+... 3 ...+... 4 ...+... 5 ...+... 6 ...+... 7 ...+... 8
CLON01Factor1+++++++Opcode&ExtFactor2+++++++Result++++++++Len++D+HiLoEq....

C                   CALL      'Prog2'       Pass
C                     .
C                     .
C     Pass          PLIST
C                   PARM                    Value
C     Rating        PARM      Charge        Amount
```

19-10. What is the function of the **CALL** instruction?

19-11. Other than a character literal, what may be specified in *Factor 2* of a **CALL** instruction? What does the entry represent?

19-12. When is a *Result* field entry *not* required in a **CALL** instruction?

19-13. What is the function of the **PLIST** instruction? When is it not required?

19-14. What is the function of the first **PARM** instruction?

19-15. What is the function of the *Factor 1* and *Factor 2* entries in the second **PARM** instruction?

Examine the following coding specified in a called program and answer Questions 19-16 through 19-19:

```
*.. 1 ...+... 2 ...+... 3 ...+... 4 ...+... 5 ...+... 6 ...+... 7 ...+... 8
CLON01Factor1+++++++Opcode&ExtFactor2+++++++Result++++++++Len++D+HiLoEq....

C     *ENTRY        PLIST
C                   PARM                    Value1
C     Rating        PARM      Charge        Amt1
C                     .
C                     .
C                   RETURN
```

19-16. What is the function of the **PLIST** instruction?

19-17. What is the function of the first **PARM** instruction?

19-18. Explain the function of the *Factor 1*, *Factor 2*, and *Result* field entries in the second **PARM** instruction.

19-19. What is the function of the **RETURN** operation?

19-20. If a **RETURN** operation is not specified in a "called" program, what other control may be included for the processing answered for Question 19-19 to occur?

19-21. What is a *service program*?

19-22. How is the source for a service program created?

19-23. What **CL** command is used to create the service program's object?

19-24. What is the last step in the development of a service program?

Examine the following coding specified in a called program and answer Questions 19-25 through 19-28:

```
SEQNBR*...+... 1 ...+... 2 ...+... 3 ...+... 4 ...+... 5 ...+... 6 ...+... 7 ...+... 8
 100           STRPGMEXP  SIGNATURE(*GEN)
 200              EXPORT  SYMBOL('INTEREST')
 300           ENDPGMEXP
```

19-25. What is the function of the **STRGMEXP** instruction?

19-26. What is the function of the **EXPORT** instruction? How many may be included in *one* service program?

19-27. What is the function of the **ENDPGMEXP** operation?

19-28. The three operations used in this coding are part of what language?

PROGRAMMING ASSIGNMENTS

For each of the following programming assignments, a physical file must have been created and loaded with the related data records. Your instructor will inform you if you have to create the physical file and load it or if it has been prepared for the assignment.

Programming Assignment 19-1: CREDIT SALES REPORT

This assignment requires the completion of *two* **RPG IV** programs. One will be a *calling* program that generates a Credit Sales Report after passing values to and receiving values from a *called* program. The processing steps include the following:

1. The calling program must pass the UMONTH, UYEAR, and SALE AMOUNT values to the called program.
2. The called program must test the UMONTH value and move the related month name to a field that must be defined large enough to include the month name, the constant 19, and the UYEAR value. To access the month name, nested **IF** statements or a **SELECT** group must be specified in the called program.
3. The month name, the constant 19, and the UYEAR value are to be concatenated in the called program. One space is to be included after the month name, with no space between 19 and the UYEAR value as shown below:

June 19XX

system year value

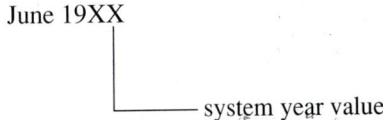

4. The sales amount value passed from the calling program is to be tested in the called program to determine the applicable sales discount. Sales discounts are determined as follows:

Sales Amount Range	*Sales Discount Percent*
5000 to 10000	1.5%
10001 to 30000	2.5%
30001 to 50000	4.0%
50001 and over	5.0%

5. After the date elements have been concatenated and the sales discount computed in the called program, the values are to be passed back to the calling program.
6. The calling program must generate the report shown in the supplemental printer spacing chart.

Physical File Record Format:

```
                    PHYSICAL FILE DESCRIPTION

SYSTEM: AS/400                                  DATE: Yours
FILE NAME: Yours                                REV NO: 0
RECORD NAME: Yours                              KEY LENGTH: 4
SEQUENCE: Nonkeyed                              RECORD SIZE: 41

                      FIELD DEFINITIONS

FIELD    FIELD NAME    SIZE  TYPE     POSITION     COMMENTS
 NO                                  FROM   TO

 1       ACTNUMBER       4    C         1    4   Key field
 2       ACTNAME        25    C         5   29
 3       SALESDATE       6    P        30   33
 4       INVOICENO       5    P        34   36
 5       SALE_AMT        8    P        37   41   2 decimals

Physical File Data:
                                                   Sales
Acct#    Account Name        Sale Date  Invoice#   Amount

1000   IVAN SNODSMITH        0103??     13568     00620099
1200   THERESA PIRES         0105??     13569     07098014
1300   RALPH SCADDED         0108??     13570     04574026
1400   HENRY CARLSON         0115??     13571     02990089
1500   JUAN HERNANDEZ        0122??     13572     10032415
1600   IRA FINKELSTEIN       0128??     13573     00462018

                                   Replace ?? with your
                                   session or job year
```

Report Design:

```
 1  HH:MM:SS                         CREDIT SALES REPORT                       PAGE XXØX
 2                                     FOR XXXXXXXXX 19XX
 3
 4
 5                  ACCOUNT                                    INVOICE
 6    SALE DATE     NUMBER          ACCOUNT NAME               NUMBER       SALE AMOUNT
 7
 8    ØX/XX/XX      XXXX     X---------------------------X      XXXXX       XXX,XXØ.XX
 9
10    ØX/XX/XX      XXXX     X---------------------------X      XXXXX       XXX,XXØ.XX
11
12
13                                        TOTAL CREDIT SALES.....X,XXX,XXØ.XX
```

Programming Assignment 19-2: MORTGAGE PAYMENT SCHEDULE

This assignment requires the completion of *two* **RPG IV** programs. A calling program will read an input file of mortgage data and pass parameters from each record to a called program. The called program must compute the monthly mortgage payment and total interest to be paid on the loan and return this information to the calling program, which will generate the report shown in the following printer spacing chart.

Physical File Record Format:

PHYSICAL FILE DESCRIPTION

SYSTEM: AS/400	DATE: Yours
FILE NAME: Yours	REV NO: 0
RECORD NAME: Yours	KEY LENGTH: 5
SEQUENCE: Keyed	RECORD SIZE: 36

FIELD DEFINITIONS

FIELD NO	FIELD NAME	SIZE	TYPE	POSITION FROM	TO	COMMENTS
1	LOAN_NO	5	C	1	5	Key field
2	MORTGAGOR	20	C	6	25	
3	TIMEINYRS	2	P	26	27	0 decimals
4	INT_RATE	5	P	28	30	5 decimals
5	PRINCIPAL	6	P	31	34	0 decimals
6	PAYTPERYR	2	P	35	36	0 decimals

Physical File Data:

Loan#	Mortgagor	Time In Yrs	Rate	Principal	Payments Per Year
12345	HENRY W. LONGFELLOW	05	06450	020000	12
13333	EDGAR A. POE	30	08000	056000	12
22222	GEOFFREY CHAUCER	10	09000	060000	12
22333	JOHN MILTON	15	07250	200000	24

Processing:

The calling program must read all of the records in the physical file and pass a seven-integer interest field (initialized to zero) and the TIMEINYRS, INT_RATE, PRINCIPAL, and PAYTPERYR values from each record to the called program. The called program must compute the monthly mortgage payment and the total interest to be paid on the loan based on the following computations:

Step 1: Determine the constant fixed monthly payment from the following formula:

$$\text{Monthly Payment} = \left(\frac{P}{\dfrac{1 - \dfrac{1}{(1+i)^n}}{i}} \right)$$

where:

$i =$ annual mortgage rate. Must be divided by number of interest payments per year to determine application's interest rate period per month.

$n =$ total number of payment periods for the year.

$P =$ balance of the mortgage principal.

Step 2: Calculate the interest amount of the monthly payment using the following formula for simple interest:

$$I = \frac{P \times R \times T}{12}$$

where:

I = simple interest amount.

P = principal amount. The balance of the principal will decline after each monthly payment.

R = annual interest rate.

T = time for the life of the mortgage. If payments are monthly, time is expressed as total number of months for the mortgage loan.

Note: Because payments are monthly, 12 is used as a denominator in the formula.

Step 3: The amount of the monthly payment applicable to the payment of the principal (reducing the principal) is determined as follows:

principal payment = monthly payment – interest amount

Step 4: The end-of-month principal balance is determined by subtracting the monthly principal payment (step 3) amount from the previous principal balance. The new balance is used for the next month's computation of the principal and interest parts of the monthly payment.

Step 5: Accumulate the monthly interest payment for each loan and move the total to the interest field parameter sent from the calling program.

The called program must pass the computed monthly mortgage payment and total interest for the life of the loan back to the calling program to generate the report format shown below.

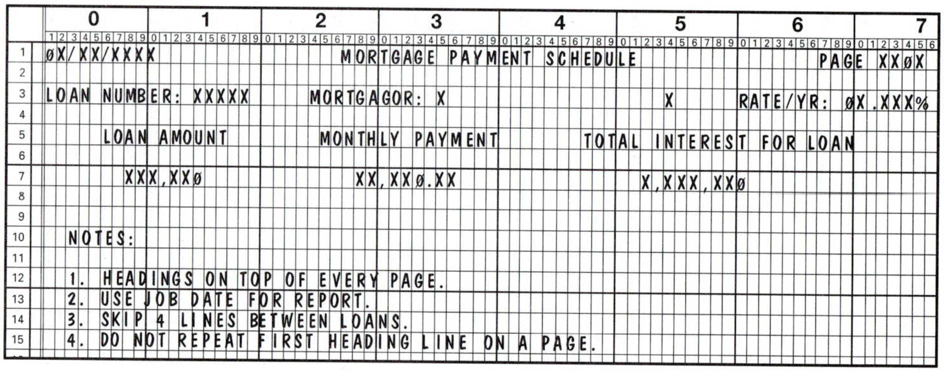

ØX/XX/XXXX MORTGAGE PAYMENT SCHEDULE PAGE XXØX
LOAN NUMBER: XXXXX MORTGAGOR: X X RATE/YR: ØX.XXX%
LOAN AMOUNT MONTHLY PAYMENT TOTAL INTEREST FOR LOAN
XXX,XXØ XX,XXØ.XX X,XXX,XXØ
NOTES:
1. HEADINGS ON TOP OF EVERY PAGE.
2. USE JOB DATE FOR REPORT.
3. SKIP 4 LINES BETWEEN LOANS.
4. DO NOT REPEAT FIRST HEADING LINE ON A PAGE.

Programming Assignment 19-3: MODIFICATION OF ASSIGNMENT 19-1 OR 19-2

Modify either Programming Assignment 19-1 or 19-2 by compiling and modifying the programs using a method different than originally used. For example, if dynamic binding was used, modify with static binding with the copy or reference method.

chapter 20

Control Language Programming

The AS/400 Control Language allows the programmer to communicate with OS/400, the AS/400 operating system. There are well over one thousand commands for the programmer to select from. To simplify command usage, IBM adopted standard naming conventions. These naming conventions were briefly discussed in Chapter 1.

All commands begin with a three-letter *verb* indicating the type of action the programmer wants to take. Examples of verbs are as follows:

STR	**Start**	**END**	**End**
EDT	**Edit**	**CHG**	**Change**
WRK	**Work with**	**ADD**	**Add**
DSP	**Display**	**CRT**	**Create**
DLT	**Delete**	**CLR**	**Clear**

Verbs such as those listed above are combined with a *subject* to create a command. Subjects are generally represented by three or four letters, although they may be shorter or longer. A few example subjects are listed below:

OUTQ	**Output Queue**	**WTR**	**Writer**
PGM	**Program**	**OBJ**	**Object**
LIB	**Library**	**LIBL**	**Library List**
PFM	**Physical File Member**	**MSG**	**Message**
JOB	**Job**	**F**	**File**

The combination of verbs with subjects produces commands similar to those that follow:

WRKOUTQ	**Work with Output Queue**
SNDMSG	**Send Message**
EDTLIBL	**Edit Library List**
DLTF	**Delete File**
CLRPFM	**Clear Physical File Member**
DSPPGM	**Display Program**

Sometimes additional information is needed to make the command meaningful. *Modifiers* may be added to the subject to clarify the meaning of the command. For example:

WRKACTJOB	**Work with Active Jobs**
CRTCLPGM	**Create CL Program**
STRPRTWTR	**Start a Print Writer**
SNDBRKMSG	**Send a Break Message**

Most commands have additional parameters which provide the operating system with specific information (such as *which* **CL** program to create or *where* to send the break message). Some parameters, known as *required parameters,* must have a value entered. Other parameters, known as *optional parameters,* contain default values that the programmer may choose to use or override. Each command has a specific order in which it expects to receive parameter values; thus, each command's parameters may be entered in a *positional* format. When using a positional format to enter a command, a space is used as the parameter delimiter, and each of the command's parameters is assigned a value based on that value's position in the command string (see Figure 20-1).

```
Positional Format

    COMMAND   PARM1  PARM2  PARM3 . . .

    DSPJOBD   SMYERS/PGM1   *PRINT

Keyword Format

    COMMAND   KEYWORD1(PARM1)  KEYWORD2(PARM2)  KEYWORD3(PARM3) . . .

    DSPJOBD   JOBD(SMYERS/PGM1)  OUTPUT(*PRINT)
```

Figure 20-1 Command syntax formats.

If a command has a large number of parameters, using the positional format to enter the command may become confusing. Another method of specifying parameter values (also shown in Figure 20-1) identifies each parameter by *keyword.* Keywords may be thought of as parameter names. By specifying a keyword with an associated value, the programmer may enter the parameter values in any order. Also, the programmer may choose to enter only the parameters for which values must be specified, and accept the default values for the remaining parameters.

CL PROGRAMMING

Many commands may be entered on the command line and run interactively. However, the AS/400's Control Language is a flexible programming language that allows the programmer to combine commands into programs, store them in source files, and compile them into system objects.

The programmer uses **SEU** *(the Source Entry Utility)* to enter the Control Language Program **(CLP).** Programs are stored as source-type **CLP** and, although the IBM default source file for **CL** programs is **QCLSRC,** programs may be stored in any source file. While entering the **CL** commands, the programmer may request the command prompt screens by pressing **F4.** This simplifies the program entry and allows the programmer to verify command parameters. The resulting source code may then be used to create a **CLP** object using the **CRTCLPGM** *(Create CL Program)* command (or option 3 of the Programmer Menu) or selecting option 14 from a **PDM** source member display.

Figure 20-2 illustrates the basic **CLP** structure. Comments may appear anywhere within the program, even spanning several lines, and are denoted by the slash-asterisk (/*) and the asterisk-slash (*/) that surround the comment text.

The **PGM** *(Program)* statement is required and indicates the beginning of a **CLP.** It may or may not include a list of parameters that are passed into the program upon execution. These parameters are positional, and any variables listed must be defined in the *Declaration Section* of the program.

All program variables must be declared in the Declaration Section of the program using the **DCL** *(Declare Variable)* statement. Variable names begin with an ampersand

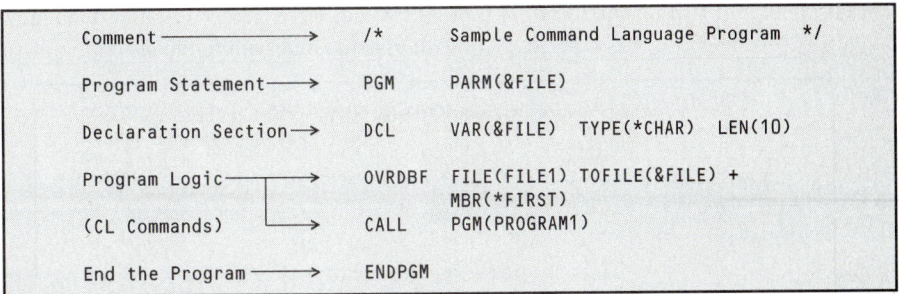

```
Comment ------------->        /*       Sample Command Language Program  */

Program Statement---->        PGM      PARM(&FILE)

Declaration Section-->        DCL      VAR(&FILE)  TYPE(*CHAR)  LEN(10)

Program Logic-------->        OVRDBF   FILE(FILE1) TOFILE(&FILE) +
                                       MBR(*FIRST)
(CL Commands)   ----->        CALL     PGM(PROGRAM1)

End the Program ----->        ENDPGM
```

Figure 20-2 Basic structure of a **CL** program.

(**&**) and may be up to 10 characters in length. Variables may be character (***CHAR**), decimal (***DEC**), or Boolean logical (***LOG**) data type. A **VALUE** clause may be added to the **DCL** statement to assign an initial value to the variable.

The programmer may also declare *one* externally defined file (a display file, physical file, or logical file) using the **DCLF** *(Declare File)* statement for processing by the program.

Almost any Control Language command may be used to form the *Program Logic* portion of the **CLP.** Commands may be specified as either positional or keyword syntax. A plus sign (+), as shown in the **OVRDBF** command in Figure 20-2, indicates that the command continues on the next line.

The optional **ENDPGM** *(End Program)* command indicates that all program processing is complete.

CALLING MULTIPLE PROGRAMS

CL programs are often used to execute consecutive programs. When the processing of one program is dependent upon another program's having been run, a **CLP** that executes the programs in the appropriate order may prove useful. Figure 20-3 illustrates this concept.

```
100-   PGM
200-   CLRPFM     FILE(WORKFILE) MBR(*FIRST)
300-   CALL       PGM(BLDFILE)   /* BUILD WORK FILE */
400-   CALL       PGM(PRTRPT)    /* PRINT WORK FILE */
500-   ENDPGM
```

Figure 20-3 **CLP** to execute two programs.

Like the skeleton program shown in Figure 20-2, the example **CLP** shown in Figure 20-3 begins with a **PGM** statement (at line 100). However, unlike the skeleton program, the program in Figure 20-3 has no variable declarations. This program does not require any variables, so none have been defined.

The first command issued by the program is **CLRPFM** *(Clear Physical File Member)* (line 200). This command removes all data from the specified member (in this case, ***FIRST,** the first member) of a physical file (in this example, WORKFILE).

Next, the first program is executed by the **CALL** command at line 300. The comment on line 300 indicates that this program will output records to WORKFILE. Once the first program, BLDFILE, has completed, the second program will be executed. Again a **CALL** command on line 400 is issued, this time to run the program PRTRPT, which reads the WORKFILE and prints a report.

By creating the example **CLP** program, the programmer has ensured that the programs will be executed in the appropriate order. If, as in this example, none of the programs requires operator interaction, the **CLP** may be submitted to the batch subsystem

(QBATCH) for execution in batch mode. To submit the previous program (PRTRPTCL), a **SBMJOB** *(Submit Job)* command such as the following would be used:

```
SBMJOB JOB(BATCH_JOB) CMD(CALL PGM(PRTRPTCL)) JOBD(QBATCH)
```

PASSING PARAMETERS

CLP programs are frequently used to retrieve and pass parameters between programs. Figure 20-4 contains a simple Control Language program that retrieves a date range from

```
SEQNBR  *...+... 1 ...+... 2 ...+... 3 ...+... 4 ...+... 5 ...+... 6
   100- /* PASS DATES FROM DATA AREA TO PROGRAM */
   200- PGM
   300- DCL          VAR(&DATES) TYPE(*CHAR) LEN(20)
   400- DCL          VAR(&FROM)  TYPE(*CHAR) LEN(10)
   500- DCL          VAR(&TO)    TYPE(*CHAR) LEN(10)
   600- RTVDTAARA    DTAARA(DATES)  RTNVAR(&DATES)
   700- CHGVAR       VAR(&FROM)  VALUE(%SST(&DATES  1 10))
   800- CHGVAR       VAR(&TO)    VALUE(%SST(&DATES 11 10))
   900- CALL         PGM(RPGPGM1) PARM(&FROM &TO)
  1000- ENDPGM
```

Figure 20-4 Control Language program **(CLP)** that passes parameters to an **RPG IV** program.

a data area and passes the dates as parameters to a report program. Three program variables have been defined. The first, *&DATES,* will hold the 12 characters of data found in the data area DATES. The remaining two variables, *&FROM* and *&TO,* will each eventually hold a date value in numeric format.

Information stored in the data area DATES is retrieved by using the **RTVDTAARA** *(Retrieve Data Area)* command. The retrieved information is stored in a specified variable field, in this example, *&DATES.*

The **CHGVAR** *(Change Variable)* command is used to move data from one variable to another and to convert the data from character to numeric format. The receiving field is specified in the **VAR** parameter, and a sending field or constant is specified in the **VALUE** parameter. Because the *&DATES* field is defined as character data, it is possible to use the *substring* function **(%SST)** to extract the individual date elements. The format of the *substring* function and its use are depicted in Figure 20-5.

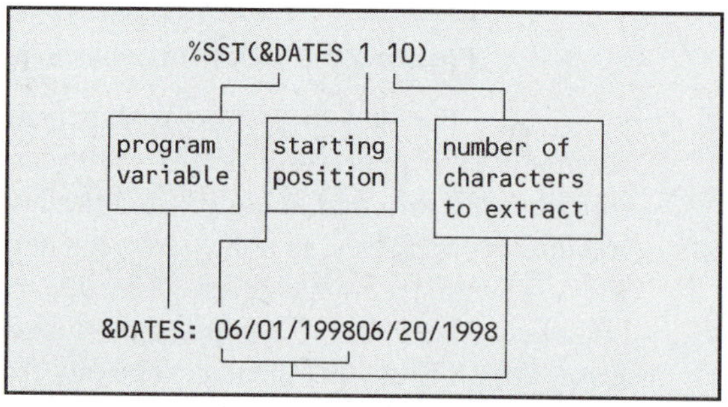

Figure 20-5 Syntax of the substring function.

Once the dates have been separated into the variables *&FROM* and *&TO* (at lines 700 and 800), they are available for passing as parameters when the program RPGPGM1 is called. Parameters passed to a program via the **CALL** statement are positional, with a space as the delimiter. In the example shown in Figure 20-6, the called program RPGPGM1 will first receive the *&FROM* date, and then the *&TO* date value, as two 10-position numeric data fields.

```
Line   <---------------------- Source Specifications ----------------------------><---- Comments ----> Do
Number ....1....+....2....+....3....+....4....+....5....+....6....+....7....+....8....+....9....+...10 Num
                           S o u r c e   L i s t i n g
       * RPG IV "called" program that receives to and from dates (stored
       * in a data area) accessed from a CL program and generates a per-
       * formance report....
      HDATFMT(*USA/)
      FSalesMstr IF   E             DISK
       *--------------------------------------------------------------------------------------------*
       *                                RPG name        External name                               *
       * File name. . . . . . . . . :  SALESMSTR       STAN/SALESMSTR                              *
       * Record format(s) . . . . . :  SALESRCD        SALESRCD                                    *
       *--------------------------------------------------------------------------------------------*
      FQsysprt   O    F  132        PRINTER OFLIND(*INOF)

       * Load run-time array with input field values....
      D                 DS
      D SalesAry                      7S 2 DIM(5)
      D  SalesPer1              1     7S 2
      D  SalesPer2              8    14S 2
      D  SalesPer3             15    21S 2
      D  SalesPer4             22    28S 2
      D  SalesPer5             29    35S 2

       * Define total array (run time)...
      D TotalAry        S             8  2 DIM(5)

       * Define work fields....
      D MonthTotal      S             8  2                                 define mth total fld
      D WeekTotal       S             8  2                                 define week totl fld

       * Define parameter fields from CL program....
      D $From           S            10
      D $To             S            10

       * Receive from and to date parameters from CL program...
      =ISALESRCD
       *--------------------------------------------------------------------------------------------*
       * RPG record format  . . . . :  SALESRCD                                                    *
       * External format  . . . . . :  SALESRCD : STAN/SALESMSTR                                   *
       *--------------------------------------------------------------------------------------------*
      =I                            *USA/D    1   10  WEEKENDING
      =I                                 P   11   14 2SALESPER1
      =I                                 P   15   18 2SALESPER2
      =I                                 P   19   22 2SALESPER3
      =I                                 P   23   26 2SALESPER4
      =I                                 P   27   30 2SALESPER5
      C     *ENTRY        PLIST                                            begin PLIST
      C                   PARM                    $From                    receive from date
      C                   PARM                    $To                      receive to date

      C                   EVAL      *INOF = *ON                            turn on OF indicator
      C                   READ      SalesMstr                      ----LR  read first record
      C                   DOW       *INLR = *OFF                           dow LR is off         B01
      C                   IF        *INOF = *ON                            page overflow on?     B02
      C                   EXCEPT    Headings                               print heading rcrds    02
      C                   EVAL      *INOF = *OFF                           turn off OF indicatr   02
      C                   ENDIF                                            end IF group          E02

       * Compute report totals....
      C                   XFOOT     SalesAry      WeekTotal                cross-foot array       01
      C                   EVAL      TotalAry = TotalAry + SalesAry         accum SalesPer total   01
      C                   EXCEPT    DetailLine                             print detail line      01
      C                   READ      SalesMstr                      ----LR  read next record       01
      C                   ENDDO                                            end dow group         E01

       * Cross-foot salesperson totals and print total line....

      C                   XFOOT     TotalAry      MonthTotal               cross-foot totals
```

Figure 20-6 Compile listing of the **RPG IV** program that receives parameters from a **CL** program.

```
58 C                 EXCEPT    TotalLine                              print total line
59
60 OQsysprt   E            Headings        1 01
61 O                       *DATE          Y     10
62 O                                            40 'SALES PERFORMANCE'
63 O                                            62 'REPORT BY SALESPERSON'
64 O                                            85 'PAGE'
65 O                       PAGE                 90
66 O          E            Headings        3
67 O                                            29 'FOR'
68 O                       $From                41
69 O                                            44 'TO'
70 O                       $To                  56
71 O          E            Headings        1
72 O                                             6 'WEEK'
73 O                                            39 'SALESPERSON  SALESPERSON'
74 O                                            65 'SALESPERSON  SALESPERSON'
75 O                                            89 'SALESPERSON     WEEKLY'
76 O          E            Headings        2
77 O                                             7 'ENDING'
78 O                                            34 '#1              #2'
79 O                                            60 '#3              #4'
80 O                                            88 '#5            TOTAL'
81 O          E            DetailLine      2
82 O                       WeekEnding           10
83 O                       SalesAry             81 '  ,  0.  &&&&'
84 O                       WeekTotal      1     91
85 O          E            TotalLine          1
86 O                                             7 'TOTALS'
87 O                       TotalAry             80 '   ,  0.  &&&'
88 O                       MonthTotal     1     91
```

```
 6/20/1998              SALES PERFORMANCE REPORT BY SALESPERSON                  PAGE    1
                           FOR  06/01/1998 TO  06/20/1998

   WEEK       SALESPERSON SALESPERSON SALESPERSON SALESPERSON SALESPERSON      WEEKLY
  ENDING           #1          #2          #3          #4          #5          TOTAL

 06/04/1998        80.00      145.30      351.40      124.00       52.24       752.94

 06/11/1998       543.00      570.00    5,800.01      585.00      630.00     8,128.01

 06/18/1998        90.00      400.00      525.00      535.00    7,540.00     9,090.00

  TOTALS          713.00    1,115.30    6,676.41    1,244.00    8,222.24    17,970.95
```

Figure 20-6 Compile listing of the **RPG IV** program that receives parameters from a **CL** program. (Continued)

As can be seen in Figure 20-6, the **RPG IV** coding necessary to receive the parameters passed by the **CL** program is the same as that required to receive parameters from another **RPG IV** program. A *parameter list* **(PLIST)** is defined at line 36 to receive the parameters upon program initialization **(*ENTRY).** Data fields to receive the data are defined as parameter fields using the **PARM** operation at lines 37 and 38. The length and type of data specified for these fields must match the **CLP** definition of the fields being passed. Once received, the data in the parameter fields may be processed like any other data by the program. Upon completion of the called program (when the **LR** indicator is turned on or a **RETURN** operation is encountered), the values in the parameter data fields are returned to the calling **CLP.**

Once the called program RPGPGM1 has finished executing, processing is complete. An **ENDPGM** statement indicates the end of the **CL** program (see Figure 20-4). Because *dynamic binding* (see Chapter 19 for an explanation of the binding methods) was elected, the **CLP** program had to be compiled with the **CRTBNDCL** command and the **RPG IV** "called" program with the **CRTBNDRPG** command. The programs are bound when the **CLP** program is executed.

PROCESSING A DISPLAY FILE

As mentioned before, Control Language programs may be used to process one externally defined file. Figure 20-7 shows a **CLP** that presents a display screen (also shown in

```
          SCROOGE                                                10/18/99
                                                                  9:15:22
                             GRINDSTONE MILLWORKS
                              ORDER ENTRY/UPDATE

                         1.  Monday's Orders
                         2.  Tuesday's Orders
                         3.  Wednesday's Orders
                         4.  Thursday's Orders
                         5.  Friday's Orders
                         6.  ALL Orders

                        Select an order batch

      F3 - Exit
```

```
               PGM
               DCLF      FILE(BATCHES) RCDFMT(SELECT)
               DCL       VAR(&IN03)    TYPE(*CHAR) LEN(1)
               DCL       VAR(&CHOICE) TYPE(*CHAR) LEN(1)
               /*  DISPLAY & READ THE SCREEN  */
       DSPLY:  SNDRCVF   RCDFMT(SELECT)
               IF        COND(&IN03 *EQ '1') THEN(GOTO EXIT)
               /*  PROCESS SELECTION    */
               IF        COND(&CHOICE *EQ '1')  THEN(+
                         OVRDBF FILE(ORDERS) TOFILE(*FILE) MBR(MONDAY))
               IF        COND(&CHOICE *EQ '2')  THEN(+
                         OVRDBF FILE(ORDERS) TOFILE(*FILE) MBR(TUESDAY))
               IF        COND(&CHOICE *EQ '3')  THEN(+
                         OVRDBF FILE(ORDERS) TOFILE(*FILE) MBR(WEDNESDAY))
               IF        COND(&CHOICE *EQ '4')  THEN(+
                         OVRDBF FILE(ORDERS) TOFILE(*FILE) MBR(THURSDAY))
               IF        COND(&CHOICE *EQ '5')  THEN(+
                         OVRDBF FILE(ORDERS) TOFILE(*FILE) MBR(FRIDAY))
               IF        COND(&CHOICE *EQ '6')  THEN(+
                         OVRDBF FILE(ORDERS) TOFILE(*FILE) MBR(*ALL))
               /*  EXECUTE PROGRAM  */
               CALL      PGM(EDITORDS)
               DLTOVR    FILE(ORDERS)
               GOTO      CMDLBL(DSPLY)
       EXIT:   ENDPGM
```

Figure 20-7 Processing a display file.

Figure 20-7) from which the user may select a batch of orders to be processed. Each day's orders are stored in a separate member of the ORDERS physical file. Based on the day of the week chosen, the appropriate orders will be selected for processing.

The **CLP** begins with the **PGM** statement, indicating that this is a program, followed by the declaration of the display file with the **DCLF** *(Declare File)* statement. Only one file may be defined in a Control Language program, and its declaration must be placed after the **PGM** statement and before any other command statements. The **DCLF** command shown in Figure 20-7 indicates that the program will use the record format SELECT in the BATCHES file. The record contains the variables *&IN03* (associated with

F3 to end processing) and *&CHOICE* (which contains the selected option). The display file has been coded with a **VALUES** clause, which will edit the *&CHOICE* field and prevent an invalid value from being entered.

The **SNDRCVF** *(Send/Receive File)* command on line 500 is used to display, and then read, the SELECT screen. A *label,* **DSPLY,** allows processing to loop back up and redisplay the screen.

Seven **IF** statements are used to test for specific conditions and take appropriate action. The general format of the **IF** command is illustrated in Figure 20-8. Character constants used for comparison must be enclosed in apostrophes, while numeric constants are entered without them. Note that various relationships may be tested:

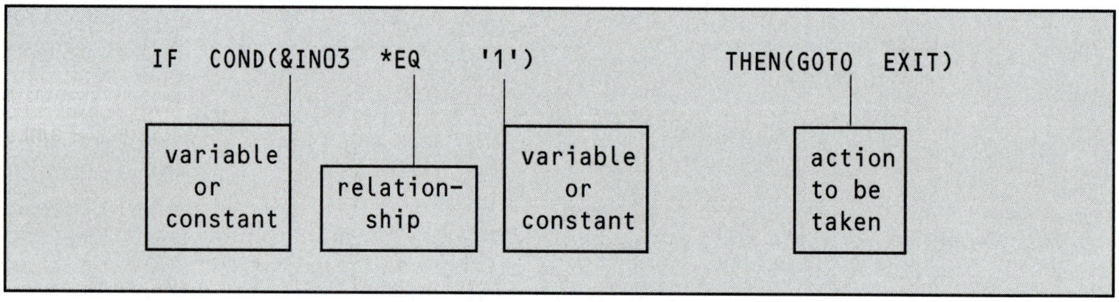

Figure 20-8 The **IF** command.

***EQ**	**Equal to**	***NE**	**Not equal to**
***GT**	**Greater than**	***GE**	**Greater than or equal to**
***LT**	**Less than**	***LE**	**Less than or equal to**

Although not shown in this example, compound **IF** statements are possible. Multiple conditions may be joined using ***AND** and ***OR** to produce more sophisticated testing.

The first **IF** statement, located at line 600, tests *&IN03* to determine if the user has requested that the program end. If the indicator is *ON* (the condition is true), control is passed to the statement labeled **EXIT** (the **ENDPGM** statement). The remaining **IF** statements determine the value entered in *&CHOICE* and, using the **OVRDBF** *(Override Data Base File)* command, direct the ORDERS file to access the appropriate physical file member (i.e., Monday through Friday, or all members).

Finally, the edit program EDITORDS is called on line 2100. Then the file override is removed using the **DLTOVR** *(Delete Override)* command (line 2200), and control is returned to the **SNDRCVF** *(Send/Receive File)* command at line 500 to display the selection screen again. Only when **F3** is pressed and *&IN03* is set ON will control pass to the **ENDPGM** *(End Program)* statement and end the program.

PROCESSING A DATABASE FILE

Database files may also be processed by **CL** programs. Figure 20-9 shows a **CLP** that sequentially reads the REPORTS file. Records in the file contain a program name, a brief description of the program, and a list of parameters necessary to execute the program. As each record is read, the report program is submitted to run in batch mode. When all records in the REPORTS file have been read and an end-of-file condition is sensed, a message indicating how many programs were processed is sent to the system operator's message queue.

Similar to the other example programs shown in this chapter, the program in Figure 20-9 begins with a **PGM** statement and a declarative section. Within the declarative section, the file REPORTS is defined using the **DCLF** *(Declare File)* statement specify-

```
100          **------------------------------------------------------------
200          ** REPORTS - REPORTS TO BE RUN BY CL PROGRAM
300          **------------------------------------------------------------
400         A          R PGMREC
500         A            PGM            10
600         A            TITLE          35
700         A            PARMS          80
800         A          K PGM
                       * * * * *   E N D   O F   S O U R C E   * * * * *
```

```
    100-          PGM
    200-          DCLF         FILE(REPORTS) RCDFMT(PGMREC)
 A00001-          DCL          VAR(&PGM)    TYPE(*CHAR) LEN(10)
 A00002-          DCL          VAR(&TITLE)  TYPE(*CHAR) LEN(35)
 A00003-          DCL          VAR(&PARMS)  TYPE(*CHAR) LEN(80)
    300-          DCL          VAR(&MSG)    TYPE(*CHAR) LEN(80)
    400-          DCL          VAR(&CMD)    TYPE(*CHAR) LEN(80)
    500-          DCL          VAR(&COUNT)  TYPE(*DEC)  LEN(3 0)
    600-          DCL          VAR(&NUMBR)  TYPE(*CHAR) LEN(3)
    700-          /* READ FILE */
    800-          OVRDBF       FILE(REPORTS) TOFILE(*FILE) NBRRCDS(1) SEQONLY(*YES 1)
    900- READ:    RCVF         RCDFMT(*FILE)
   1000-          MONMSG       MSGID(CPF0864)  EXEC(DO)
   1100                        CHGVAR  VAR(&NUMBR) VALUE(&COUNT)
   1200                        GOTO CMDLBL(EXIT)
   1300                        ENDDO
   1400-          /*  SUBMIT REPORT PROGRAM  */
   1500-          IF           COND(&PARMS *EQ '      ') THEN(+
   1600-                       CHGVAR VAR(&CMD) VALUE('CALL' *BCAT &PGM)
   1700-          ELSE         CHGVAR VAR(&CMD) VALUE('CALL ' *CAT &PGM *CAT +
   1800-                       ' PARM(''' *CAT &PARMS *CAT ''')')
   1900-          SBMJOB       JOB(&PGM) CMD(&CMD) JOBD(QBATCH)
   2000-          CHGVAR       VAR(&COUNT) VALUE(&COUNT + 1)
   2100-          GOTO         CMDLBL(READ)
   2200- EXIT:    CHGVAR       VAR(&MSG) VALUE('Processing complete. ' *CAT &NUMBR +
   2300                          *CAT ' programs executed.')
   2300-          SNDPGMMSG    MSG(&MSG)  TOPGMQ(QSYSOPR) MSGTYPE(*INFO)
   2400-          ENDPGM
```

Figure 20-9 Processing a database file.

ing record format PGMREC. The physical file's record format PGMREC contains three fields *(PGM, TITLE,* and *PARMS),* which, when the **CL** program is compiled, generate variable declaration **(DCL)** statements. Four additional variables *(&MSG, &CMD, &COUNT,* and *&NUMBR)* have been added for use by the program (lines 300 to 600).

An **OVRDBF** *(Override Data Base File)* command is issued on line 800 for the REPORTS file to itself. The **NBRRCDS** *(Number Records)* parameter of the **OVRDBF** command specifies that one record at a time is to be moved from auxiliary storage (disk) into main storage for processing. The **SEQONLY** *(Sequential Only)* parameter shown in the example indicates that the file will be processed sequentially and that one record at a time will be transferred from the database to the program's internal buffer.

It is the **RCVF** *(Receive File)* command on line 900 that reads the database file. Data is placed into the appropriate variables based on the record format specified in the **RCDFMT** *(Record Format)* parameter. In the example, ***FILE** has been specified as the record format to be used. This is a special entry that indicates that there is only one record format in the specified database file and that, whatever its name, it is the format that is to be used.

If an end-of-file condition is experienced when the program executes the **RCVF** *(Receive File)* command, the system issues an error message. The program monitors for this message, CPF0864, using the **MONMSG** *(Monitor Message)* command. When the system issues the CPF0864 message, the **MONMSG** command will execute the command specified in the **EXEC** *(Execute)* parameter. In the example shown in Figure 20-9, the command specified in the **EXEC** parameter is a **DO** command. This allows several commands to be performed. All of the commands listed between the **DO** and the **ENDDO** statements will be executed. In this instance, the value in the variable *&COUNT* will be converted from numeric format to character format and stored in the variable *&NUMBR* by the **CHGVAR** *(Change Variable)* command. Then the **GOTO** command will cause program control to branch to the statement labeled **EXIT** (statement number 2200) before processing continues.

If a record was found (that is, the end of file does not occur), processing continues with the formatting of a message. The ***BCAT** *(Concatenate with a Leading Blank)* function, as illustrated in Figure 20-10, allows literal values to be joined with program variables to produce a desired character string. Note in Figure 20-10 that although the variable *&PGM* is 10 characters long, only the portion of the variable that contains data is used. Notice also that the value of each variable or literal value which was preceded by a ***BCAT** in the **VALUE** clause of the **CHGVAR** command is preceded by a blank in the *&CMD* variable. Using the concatenate function in the **VALUE** clause of the **CHGVAR** *(Change Variable)* command results in the entire character string's being stored in the variable *&CMD*.

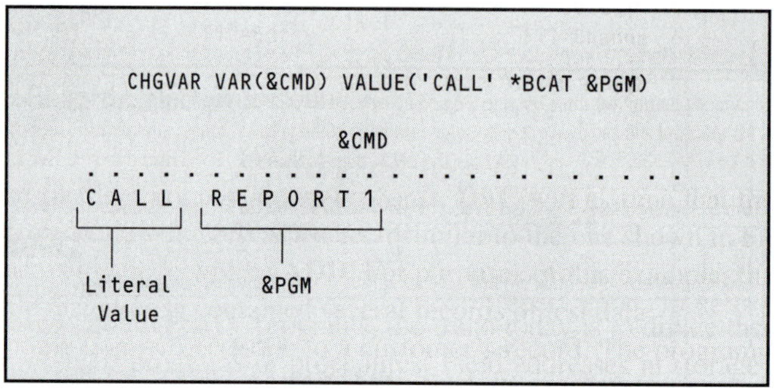

Figure 20-10 The ***BCAT** *(Concatenate with Leading Blank)* function.

An **IF** command checks to see whether parameters have been specified. If no parameters were specified, a simple **CALL** command is constructed using the ***BCAT** function and stored in the *&CMD* variable. Otherwise, if parameters are to be included, the list of parameters contained in the variable *&PARMS* is included in the **CALL** command.

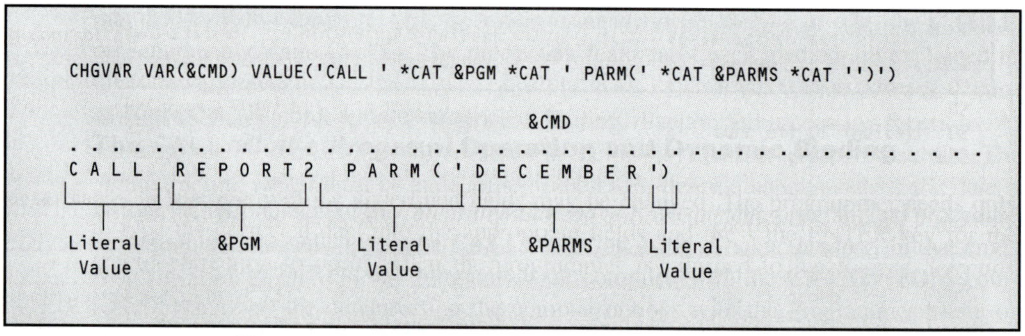

Figure 20-11 The ***CAT** *(Concatenate)* function.

The ***CAT** function (illustrated in Figure 20-11) is used to construct the command string. Notice in Figure 20-11 that some of the literal values specified contain spaces intended to separate them from the value stored in the *&PGM* variable. However, when constructing the parameter list, no spaces are included.

Other than the inclusion of a leading blank, the ***CAT** and ***BCAT** functions process data in the same way, and either one may be used to concatenate program variables and literal values into character strings. Also note that where a single apostrophe would normally be placed within the character string, two apostrophes have been keyed. This indicates to OS/400 that the apostrophe is to be included as part of the character string and is not to be confused with the apostrophes surrounding the character data.

A **SBMJOB** *(Submit Job)* command is issued at line 1900 of the program (Figure 20-9) to submit the program specified in the *&PGM* variable for processing in batch mode.

Next the *&COUNT* variable is incremented using the **CHGVAR** command, and the **GOTO** command transfers control back to the **READ** label (at statement 900) to read the next record.

Only when an end-of-file condition is encountered will the program execute statements 2200 through 2400. Recall that when an end-of-file condition is sensed by the **MONMSG** *(Monitor Message)* command at statement 1000, the value in the *&COUNT* variable is converted from numeric to character format and stored in the variable *&NUMBR*. Then the program branches to statement 2200 as a result of the **GOTO** command on line 1200.

Once again, the **CHGVAR** command is used to create a character string. This time the ***CAT** *(Concatenate)* function is used to include the value currently in the *&NUMBR* variable in the message text stored in *&MSG*. The message is then sent to the system operator's message queue by the **SNDPGMMSG** *(Send Program Message)* command on line 2300, and the program ends with the **ENDPGM** statement.

CREATING USER COMMANDS

CL programs may be used to create commands similar to the OS/400 commands. The **CRTTESTF** *(Create Test File)* command (shown in Figure 20-12) is a user-defined command that copies 25 records from a specified file into a file by the same name in the programmer's current library. It can be very useful when creating small files for testing programs.

```
100-        CMD     PROMPT('Create Test File')
200-        PARM    KWD(LIVEFILE)  TYPE(*CHAR) LEN(10) +
300                 MIN(1) PROMPT('Live File to Copy:')
```

Figure 20-12 Source for **CRTTESTF** *(Create Test File)* command.

Command parameters are defined in a command source (source type CMD) similar to the example shown in Figure 20-12 and are entered via **SEU.** Six types of command definition statements exist:

Statement	Function
CMD	Defines the prompt text to be used for the command. Only one CMD statement per command definition is allowed.
PARM	Defines the parameter to be passed to the command processing program **(CPP).** Several (to a maximum of 75) parameters may be defined, and the order in which they appear within the command source is the order in which they will appear on the command prompt.
ELEM	Defines the elements of a list of values which may be entered for a parameter (for example, the command may require that a list of library names be entered).

QUAL Defines a qualifier for a parameter (for example, an object's library name).

DEP Defines a dependency (for example, if PARM1 is equal to ***YES,** then PARM1 must also be specified).

PMTCTL Allows control of prompting based on a variety of criteria (for example, display additional prompts when **CF10** is pressed).

The example shown in Figure 20-12 contains only the **CMD** statement and one **PARM** statement. The **CMD** statement indicates that the prompt text "Create Test File" (defined by the keyword **PROMPT**) will appear at the top of the command prompt screen. The **PARM** statement contains several keywords. **KWD** stands for *keyword* and indicates that the word LIVEFILE will be used to indicate this parameter when entering the command parameters in keyword format. The **TYPE** keyword defines the type of data being defined for this parameter, in this case ***CHAR** or character data. **LEN** specifies the length of the parameter (10 positions in this example). The LIVEFILE parameter will be a required parameter because a minimum entry, **MIN(1),** has been specified. And finally, "Live File to Copy" has been specified as the prompt text for the parameter **(PROMPT).** Later, when the **CRTCMD** *(Create Command)* command is executed, the command source shown in Figure 20-12 will be used to generate a command object called **CRTTESTF.**

The **CLP CRTTESTFC** (shown in Figure 20-13) is used to process the **CRTTESTF** command. **CRTTESTFC** was created in the same way that any other Control Language program is created. However, as can be seen in Figure 20-14, when the **CRTCMD** *(Create Command)* command was executed to create the **CRTTESTF** command, **CRTTESTFC** was specified as the **CPP** *(Command Processing Program)* in the *Program to process command* prompt.

```
              PGM          PARM(&FILE)
              CPYF         FROMFILE(&FILE) TOFILE(*CURLIB/&FILE) +
                            MBROPT(*REPLACE) CRTFILE(*YES) TORCD(25)
              ENDPGM
```

Figure 19-13 CLP CRTTESTFC (**CPP** for **CRTTESTF**) command.

Figure 20-14 contains all of the **CRTCMD** *(Create Command)* command prompts. Only the *Command, Program to process the command, Source file,* and *Source member* parameters are required parameters. The remaining parameters may be defaulted. Many of the prompt responses displayed contain default values. However, the programmer has elected to change a few of these parameters.

In this example the programmer chose not to include a *validity checking* program. Had the programmer chosen to do so, a validity checking program could have been specified at the *Validity checking program* prompt. OS/400 will verify that all required parameters are entered for the command, that each parameter is of the data type and length specified in the command definition, that each parameter value meets any defined optional requirements (such as a list of valid values, a range of values, or a relational comparison to a value), and that conflicting parameters are not entered. Beyond this, any parameter verification must be done in either a validity checking program or within the **CPP.** Verifying that the command prompt entries are logically valid (such as checking the validity of a date entry) is frequently done in a validity checking program to ensure that only valid entries are passed to the **CPP.** Validity checking programs may be written in **CL** or in another language (like **RPG IV**).

Users will be able to execute the **CRTTESTF** command regardless of their current processing mode because the programmer specified ***ALL** to the *Mode in which valid* prompt. This means, for example, that even if the programmer is in debug mode (has

```
                         Create Command (CRTCMD)
Type choices, press Enter.
 Command . . . . . . . . . . . . > CRTTESTF        Name
   Library . . . . . . . . . . . >   SMYERS        Name, *CURLIB
 Program to process command . . . > CRTTESTFC      Name, *REXX
   Library . . . . . . . . . . . >   SMYERS        Name, *LIBL, *CURLIB
 Source file . . . . . . . . . . > QCMDSRC         Name
   Library . . . . . . . . . . . >   SMYERS        Name, *LIBL, *CURLIB
 Source member . . . . . . . . . > CRTTESTF        Name, *CMD
 Text 'description' . . . . . . .  *SRCMBRTXT
                          Additional Parameters
 Validity checking program . . .  *NONE            Name, *NONE
   Library . . . . . . . . . .                     Name, *LIBL, *CURLIB
 Mode in which valid . . . . . .  *ALL             *ALL, *PROD, *DEBUG, *SERVICE
              + for more values
 Where allowed to run . . . . . . *ALL             *ALL, *BATCH, *INTERACT...
              + for more values
 Allow limited users . . . . . .  *NO              *NO, *YES
 Maximum positional parameters  .  *NOMAX          0-75, *NOMAX
 Message file for prompt text . . *NONE            Name, *NONE
   Library . . . . . . . . . .                     Name, *LIBL, *CURLIB
 Message file . . . . . . . . . . QCPFMSG          Name
   Library . . . . . . . . . . .    *LIBL          Name, *LIBL, *CURLIB
 Help panel group . . . . . . . . *NONE            Name, *NONE
   Library . . . . . . . . . . .                   Name, *LIBL, *CURLIB
 Help identifier . . . . . . . .  *NONE            Character value, *CMD, *NONE
 Help search index . . . . . . .  *NONE            Name, *NONE, *SYSTEM
   Library . . . . . . . . . . .                   Name, *LIBL, *CURLIB
 Current library . . . . . . . .  *NOCHG           Name, *NOCHG, *CRTDFT
 Product library . . . . . . . .  SMYERS           Name, *NOCHG, *NONE
 Prompt override program . . . .  *NONE            Name, *NONE
   Library . . . . . . . . . . .                   Name, *LIBL, *CURLIB
 Authority . . . . . . . . . . .  *USE             Name, *LIBCRTAUT, *USE...
 Replace command . . . . . . . .  *YES             *YES, *NO
```

Figure 20-14 The **CRTCMD** *(Create Command)* command.

issued the **STRDBG** *(Start Debug)* command) the command may be executed. The programmer has also specified that the **CRTTESTF** command may be executed interactively, in batch, or in a **CL** program by entering ***ALL** to the *Where allowed to run* prompt.

Users whom the Security Officer has indicated as being limited on their user profiles are not allowed to execute certain commands. The programmer's response of ***NO** to the *Allow limited users* prompt will prevent these users from executing the **CRTTESTF** command.

The *Maximum positional parameters* prompt allows the programmer to specify the maximum number of parameters that may be entered positionally for the command. The default is ***NOMAX** *(no maximum),* which allows all command parameters to be entered positionally. The **CRTTESTF** command has only one parameter, so the programmer may enter either 1 or ***NOMAX** for this prompt.

Prompt text may be stored in a message file. The **CRTTESTF** command prompt text is stored in the command source member, so the programmer has accepted the default value of ***NONE** for the *Message file for prompt text* parameter.

The QCPFMSG file contains all of the messages used by OS/400. If an error occurs, a message is retrieved from this file and displayed. Other *message files* exist for various AS/400 products, and programmers may define their own message files to be used with their programs. The *Message file* parameter allows the programmer to specify which message file is to be used should an error occur while processing the **CRTTESTF** command. In the example, the programmer has chosen to accept the default value and use the QCPFMSG file.

The *Help panel group, Help identifier,* and *Help search index* parameters contain information used by OS/400 to identify help text screens for the command. The example **CRTTESTF** command has no associated help text; therefore, the programmer has allowed the default value of ***NONE** to remain for all three of these parameters.

A command may need a different current library while processing, so the programmer has the option of specifying the desired current library for the command. Any library on the system may be specified. In the example, the **CRTTESTF** command expects the current library to be the programmer's development library and no change is desired, so the programmer has specified ***NOCHG** *(No Change)* in response to the *Current library* prompt.

Note that a product library was specified in the *Product library* prompt. As you will recall from the discussion of library lists in Chapter 1, a product library is placed before the user portion of the library list. Specifying a product library ensures that the library containing the objects needed by the **CPP** will be included in the individual's library list.

The *prompt override program* replaces the default values for selected parameters on the prompt display with current actual values. The program name may be specified in the *Prompt override program* parameter. However, the example does not have a prompt override program, so the programmer has responded to the prompt with ***NONE.**

The value specified in the *Authority* parameter defines the authority the programmer is granting to other people who wish to use the **CRTTESTF** command. Specifying ***USE** allows others to use the command but not make changes to it.

Specifying ***YES** to the *Replace command* parameter allows the system to replace an older version of the **CRTTESTF** command with the most current version.

Figure 20-15 shows the resulting **CRTTESTF** command. OS/400 does not differentiate between the user-defined command and the Control Language command. Both

```
                         Create Test File (CRTTESTF)
Type choices, press Enter.
Live File to Copy: . . . . . . .   ORDERS       Character value



                                                                        Bottom
F3=Exit   F4=Prompt   F5=Refresh   F12=Cancel   F13=How to use this display
F24=More keys
```

Figure 20-15 CRTTESTF *(Create Test File)* command prompt screen.

recognize **F3** as a cancel request, and typing either command and pressing **F4** will result in a prompt screen. No additional coding to process the command keys is required. Thus, user-defined commands are useful as user interfaces to Control Language programs.

Additional information about creating user-defined commands may be found in IBM's *Programming: Control Language Programming Guide* manual.

SUMMARY

The AS/400 Control Language allows the programmer to interface with OS/400, the AS/400 operating system. IBM developed naming conventions that make Control Language easy to use. Command names are a combination of three-letter *verbs* and *subjects* (and occasionally *modifiers)* that produce meaningful commands such as **CRTCLPGM** *(Create CL Program)* or **WRKOUTQ** *(Work with Output Queue).*

Commands generally have associated parameters that provide the operating system with additional information for processing the command. *Required parameters* must have a value entered in order for the command to process. Other parameters, known as *optional parameters,* contain default values which the programmer may choose to use or override.

Each command expects to receive its parameter values in a specific order. Parameters may be entered in the specified order, separated by spaces, in what is known as *positional format.* An alternative method of specifying command parameters identifies each parameter by name, or *keyword.* Specifying a *keyword,* with an associated value in parentheses, allows the programmer to enter command parameters in any order.

CL commands may be combined to create programs. **CL** programs have a basic structure, which includes a *Program Statement,* a *Declaration Section,* a *Program Logic* section, and an *End of Program* section. The *Program Statement,* or **PGM** command, is required and indicates the beginning of a **CLP.** The **DCL** *(Declare Variable)* and **DCLF** *(Declare File)* statements are used to define variables and files within the Declaration Section. The Program Logic section may contain almost any **CL** command and its appropriate parameters. The **ENDPGM** *(End Program)* command is used to indicate that program processing is complete. Comments may appear anywhere throughout the program.

CL programs may be used for a variety of purposes. Examples within the chapter illustrate using a **CLP** to execute a series of programs in a specific order, to pass parameters into a program, to process a display file, and to read and process a database file. The *Substring* **(%SST)** and *Concatenate* **(*CAT** and ***BCAT)** functions were detailed, and several new commands (and their associated parameters) were introduced.

User-defined commands may use **CLP**s as **CPP**s *(Command Processing Programs).* Because OS/400 does not differentiate between user-defined commands and Control Language commands, user-defined commands are useful as user interfaces to Control Language programs.

QUESTIONS

20-1. Explain the IBM naming conventions for AS/400 commands.

20-2. What is the difference between *required* and *optional* parameters?

20-3. What are the two methods of formatting a command and its parameters?

20-4. Which command is required at the beginning of every **CL** program?

20-5. Write the declaration statement for a program variable for a date field that is six numeric positions (no decimal positions) with an initial value of 063098.

20-6. What symbol is used to indicate that a command's parameters continue on the next line of a program?

20-7. Which command indicates the end of a **CL** program?

20-8. Write the command to extract the value stored in the sixth position of a 10-byte character variable called *&TEN* and store it in a variable named *&SIX.*

20-9. Which command is used to display, and then read, a display file format?

20-10. Write the **IF** command to determine if the value in *&COST* is greater than 100.00, and if so, to call program TOOMUCH.

20-11. Which command reads a database file?

20-12. When reading a database file in a **CLP,** how is an end-of-file condition sensed?

20-13. Use the ***BCAT** function to create a *VALUE* parameter for a **CHGVAR** command that will join the value stored in *&DAY* with the literal 'Today is'.

20-14. Change the *VALUE* parameter defined in Question 20-13 to use the ***CAT** function.

20-15. Which command is used to close a file?

20-16. Write the command to convert the value in a numeric field *&SUM* to character data and store it in a variable called *&TOTAL.*

20-17. Which parameter on the **CRTCMD** command links the user-defined command to the **CL** program that will process the command?

PROGRAMMING ASSIGNMENTS

The following programming assignments require the use of three programs that the student has already written. We recommend using the Sales Journal from Programming Assignment 6-1, the Salesperson Salary/Commission Report from Programming Assignment 6-2, and the Income Statement from Programming Assignment 10-2. However, any **RPG IV** programs the student has already created may be used.

Programming Assignment 20-1: CONSECUTIVE PROGRAM PROCESSING

Select three programs from previous programming assignments. Write a **CLP** to consecutively execute the three selected programs.

Programming Assignment 20-2: THE SALES DEPARTMENT REPORT MENU

```
JANE                                                12/15/97
                                                    10:13:47
                  WORLD-WIDE COCONUTS, INC
                  SALES DEPARTMENT REPORTS

            1.  Sales Journal
            2.  Sales Person Salary/Commission Report
            3.  Income Statement


Selection: ___

F3 - Exit
```

Design a display file similar to the one shown above. Use **F3** as the "exit" key. Allow the user to enter an option 1 through 3. Then write the **CL** program to output the display file, read the user's selected option, and execute the appropriate program.

Programming Assignment 20-3: THE PROGRAM FILE

```
                  PHYSICAL FILE DESCRIPTION

SYSTEM: AS/400                                DATE: Yours
FILE NAME: PGMS                               REV NO: 0
RECORD NAME: Yours                            KEY LENGTH: 10
SEQUENCE: Keyed                               RECORD SIZE: 35

                      FIELD DEFINITIONS

 FIELD    FIELD NAME   SIZE  TYPE    POSITION      COMMENTS
  NO                                FROM    TO

  1       ZPGM          10    C        1    10    Program
  2       ZDESC         25    C       11    35    Description
```

Define and create the physical file PGMS (shown above). Use **DFU** to load the names and descriptions of three **RPG IV** programs. Then write a **CLP** to read the file **PGMS** and execute the program specified in the program name field.

Programming Assignment 20-4: THE RUNPGMS COMMAND

Write the command source to create a command **RUNPGMS** *(Run Programs)*. The command will have no parameters. Use the **CLP** created in Programming Assignment 20-3 as the command processing program **(CPP).**

appendix a

Source Entry Utility (SEU)

The *Source Entry Utility* (**SEU**) is a full-screen editor that provides for the entry and update of any source member type. Specifically, when in an edit mode, records may be inserted, deleted, changed, and/or moved. In addition, character strings may be found and/or replaced.

SEU may be accessed by any of the following methods:

- Entering **STRSEU** on any command line and pressing **F4,** which accesses a display where parameter values are entered
- Choosing option 8 or 5 on the Programmer Menu
- Choosing option 2 *(Edit)* or 5 *(Display)* on the *Work with Members* display in **PDM.**

EDITING MEMBERS

When **SEU** is entered by one of the preceding methods, the Edit screen shown in Figure A-1 will display. The syntax supported will depend on the member type entered (i.e., **PF, DSPF, PRTF, LF, CL, CLP, RPG, TXT**) when **SEU** is accessed.

```
Columns . . . :    1  71              Edit                        SMYERS/QDDSSRC
SEU==>                                                                    GLACTS
FMT PF .. .A..........T.Name++++++RLen++TDpB......Functions+++++++++++++++++++
        ** ************ Beginning of data ************************************
'''''''
'''''''
'''''''
'''''''
'''''''
'''''''
'''''''
'''''''
'''''''
'''''''
'''''''
'''''''
'''''''
'''''''
'''''''
           ****************** End of data ****************************************

F3=Exit   F4=Prompt   F5=Refresh   F9=Retrieve   F10=Cursor
F16=Repeat find       F17=Repeat change          F24=More keys

Line format for a PF is automatically displayed when that DDS type is
specified in the PROGRAMMER MENU, PDM, or the STRSEU command

Indicates source file - QDDSSRC for this display

Indicates member type entered in the PROGRAMMER MENU, PDM, or the
STRSEU command
```

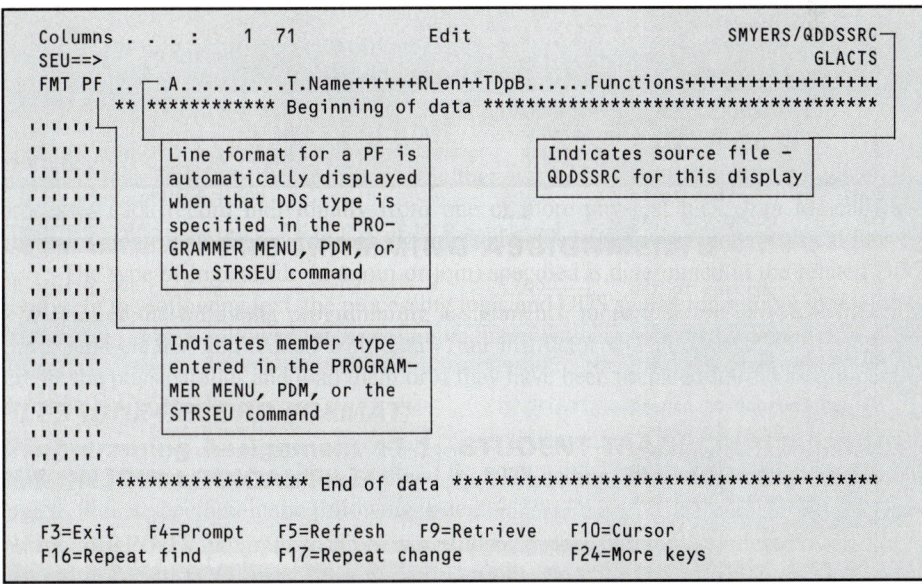

Figure A-1 Edit display for a new physical file member.

In the example in Figure A-1, **PF** (physical file) was entered as the format for the type prompt in one of the methods to access **SEU.** If a logical file was to be edited, **FMT LF** would be shown; **FMT H** as the first specification type for an **RPG IV** program; **FMT DP** for a display file, and so forth. The fields available and the syntax checking supported will depend on the member and/or line type specified.

Entering Source Code

Physical files, display files, logical files, and printer files are all developed as members of a *Data Description Specification* source file. When the source code is entered, the statements for these member types are automatically assigned the letter **A** in column 6. However, the fields supported are not common to all of the member types. For example, physical files do not support the DDS fields related to line and position locations, whereas display and printer files do. The syntax checker will identify any syntactical errors when the source code is entered.

For **RPG IV** programs, however, each specifications form has its own *format line* or *prompt* that must be accessed to support the syntax for a specific statement.

Figure A-2 shows the Prompt Selection display, which summarizes the AS/400 member types supported by **SEU.** Entering **P?** or **IP?** in the sequence area of the Edit

```
                              Select Format

 Type choice, press Enter.

  Format type . . . . . . . . . . .           Values listed below

    ILE RPG/400:      H,F,FX,I,IX,J (I cont),JX,D,C,CX,O,OD,P (O cont),
                      * (Comment)
    ILE COBOL/400:    CB,C*
    REFORMAT/SORT:    RH,RR,RF,RC
    DDS:              LF (Logical file),PF (Physical file),
                      BC (Interactive Communications Feature file),
                      DP (Display and Printer file),
                      A* (Comment)
    MNU:              MS,MH,MD,MC (MD cont),CC (Comment)
    FORTRAN:          FT, F*
    Other:            NC (No syntax checking),** (Free format)



 F12=Cancel
```

Figure A-2 Prompt Selection display for AS/400 member types.

screen and pressing ENTER will access this display. Enter **F?** or **IF?** for the identical Format Selection display. Entering the type in the Prompt or Format type field and pressing ENTER will display it in the member being edited. Note that **RPG IV** has 14 prompt/line types; each is either a complete, or a section of a, specification.

FORMAT LINES AND PROMPTS

Format Lines

Source code for any member type may be entered using *format lines* and/or *prompts*. An example of a format line for a physical file is shown in Figure A-3. The format displayed includes only the fields valid for a physical file. If a display file was edited, only the fields

```
Columns . . . :    1  71            Edit                          SMYERS/QDDSSRC
SEU==>                                                                    GLACTS
FMT PF .....A..........T.Name++++++RLen++TDpB......Functions++++++++++++++++++

       *************** Beginning of data *************************************

0001.00      A                                     UNIQUE
0002.00      A          R GLACTSR
 FMT PF .....A..........T.Name++++++RLen++TDpB......Functions++++++++++++++++++
'''''''      A            ACTNO          5A        COLHDG('ACCOUNT NUMBER')
       ****************** End of data ****************************************
```

A statement may be inserted using a format line as a reference by entering **IF** in the sequence area and pressing ENTER. The format line will display above a blank line. Note that the programmer must enter the required column 6 specification character along with the other field entries. The example shown occurs after the syntax is entered and before ENTER is pressed.

Figure A-3 Format line for a physical file member.

supported by that member type would be included on the format line. Understand that a format line is only a guide to the field locations for the statement. Entries are made on the line under the format.

A format line may be inserted above an existing statement by entering an **F** in the sequence number area of the Edit display and pressing ENTER. However, if a new instruction is inserted using a format line as a reference, **IF** must be entered. After the programmer presses ENTER, the format line will display first followed by a blank line for the instruction. Insertion of blank lines will continue until the ENTER key, without entering a statement, **F5,** or **F12** is pressed.

The format line initially displayed will depend on the member type selected. For example, physical, logical, display, and printer files have only two format line types: **A** for the instructions and * for comments. On the other hand, **RPG IV** has 14 line formats. Figure A-4 details the commands to request a format line.

Command	Function
F	Places the format line above for the related statement.
F?	Displays the Prompt Selection screen, from which a format line may be selected.
Fff	Places the format line entered for the **ff** entry above the current record.
IF	Inserts a format line for the current record type above the statement.
IF?	Displays the Format Selection screen, from which a format line may be selected, and inserts a blank record below the selected format line.
Iff	Places the format line entered for the **ff** entry above a blank record.

Note: All of these commands are entered in the sequence area of the Edit display and executed by pressing the ENTER key.

Figure A-4 Codes for requesting a format line.

Prompts

A *prompt* displays the fields in a line type for *Data Description* members or any of the **RPG IV** specifications after the **********End of data********** delimiter. An example of the prompt for a physical file is shown in Figure A-5. Note that a line is included under each field name, indicating its size.

```
 Columns . . . :    1  71              Edit                        SMYERS/QDDSSRC
 SEU==>                                                                    GLACTS
 FMT PF .....A..........T.Name++++++RLen++TDpB......Functions+++++++++++++++++
        *************** Beginning of data *************************************
0001.00        A                                         UNIQUE
0002.00        A             R GLACTSR
0003.00        A               ACTNO            3A
'''''''
        ***************** End of data ****** *********************************
                                                When the Enter key is pressed,
                                                prompt line values are moved
                                                to related line in listing and
                                                a new prompt line displays

 Prompt type . . .   PF       Sequence number . . .   '''''''

 Name                                        Data      Decimal
 Type         Name         Ref      Length   Type      Positions     Use
  _         ACTNO______     _       ____3     A          __           _

 Functions
 ____________________________________________

 F3=Exit   F4=Prompt   F5=Refresh          F11=Previous record
 F12=Cancel            F23=Select prompt   F24=More keys
```

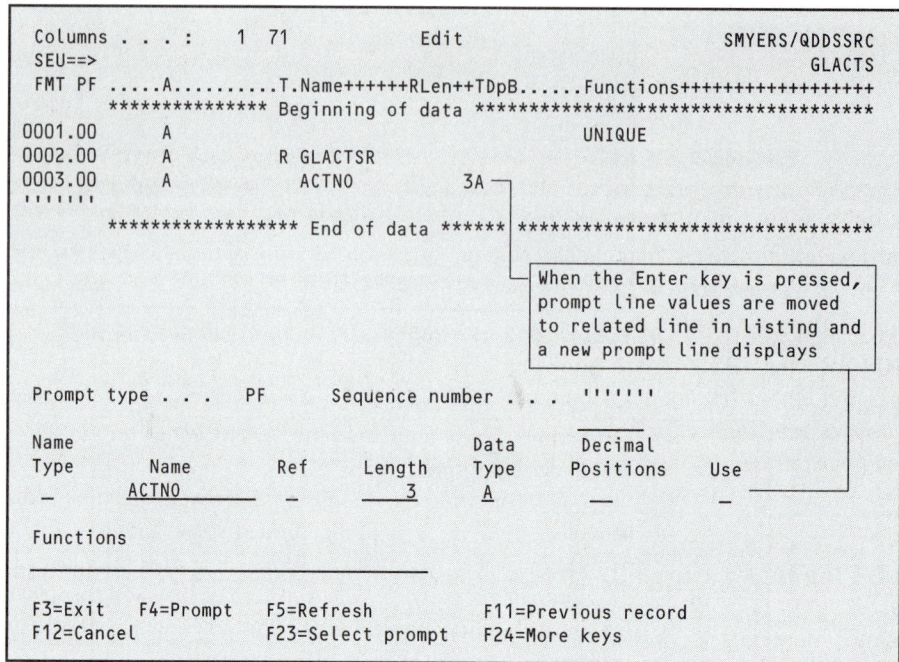

Figure A-5 Prompt example for a physical file member.

A statement may be modified using a prompt by entering a **P** in the sequence number area and pressing ENTER. New statements may be entered by typing **IP** in the sequence number area and pressing ENTER. When the instruction is completed and the ENTER key pressed, it is transferred to its line location in the source member and a *new prompt* is displayed. Exit from the prompt mode is executed by pressing **F5** *(Refresh)* or **F12** *(Previous)*. Figure A-6 summarizes the prompt commands. In addition to the commands shown in Figure A-6, a prompt may be requested by pressing **F4.**

The following line commands are used to place an existing record in a prompt:

Command	Function
P	Places the record in a prompt that has the same format as the record.
P?	Displays the Prompt Selection screen for selection of a prompt type. The record is displayed in the selected prompt.
Pff	**ff** specifies the prompt line to be displayed with the record. When editing an **RPG IV** program, **PF** will display the prompt for the *File Description*, **PC** for the *Calculation Specifications* prompt, and so forth.

The following line commands insert a blank line and place it in a prompt:

IP	Inserts a blank line after the record and provides for a prompt with the format of the existing record. Related code may be entered in the prompt line(s).

Figure A-6 Prompt commands.

IP?	Displays the Prompt Selection screen for the selection of a prompt type. A blank line is inserted after the existing record with the prompt type selected. Related code may be entered on the prompt line(s).
IPff	**ff** specifies the prompt line to be displayed with the blank record. When editing an **RPG IV** program, **IPE** will display the *Extension Specifications* prompt in which the code may be entered.

Figure A-6 Prompt commands. (Continued)

OTHER LINE COMMANDS

Other line commands are used to insert, delete, and move records. All of the commands must be entered in the sequence number area of the related record(s) and executed by pressing the ENTER key.

COPY Line Commands

COPY line commands are used to copy one or more records to some other location(s) in the source member currently being edited. Figure A-7 summarizes the **COPY** line commands and their target commands.

Copy Commands

Command	Function
C	Copies the record to a target line designated with an A, B, O, or OO.
CC	Copies the group (**CC** placed on first record and last record) beginning on a target line designated with an A, B, O, or OO.
Cn	Copies *n* records, starting with this record, to beginning with a target line designated with an A, B, O, or OO.
CR	Copies this record to target lines specified by multiple A, B, O, or OO lines.
CRn	Copies *n* records, starting with this record, to multiple A, B, O, or OO lines.
CCR	Copies this block of records (identified by two **CCR** commands) to multiple target lines designated by A, B, O, or OO lines.

Target Line Commands

A	Move, copy, or include the specified records after this line.
B	Move, copy, or include the specified records before this line.
An	Move, copy, or include the specified records after this record and repeat the line *n* – 1 times.
Bn	Move, copy, or include the specified records before this record and repeat the line *n* – 1 times.
O	Overlay this record with the first record specified by the Copy, Copy Repeat, or Move line command.

Figure A-7 **COPY** line commands.

On	Overlay the specified records on this record, and repeat the lines $n - 1$ times.
OO	Overlay all records in this block (defined by two **OO** commands) with the records defined by a Copy, Copy Repeat, or Move line command.

Note: Target commands may be entered before or after their related copy command(s).

Figure A-7 **COPY** line commands. (Continued)

An example **COPY** command that copies an instruction to an *after* **(A)** target in a source member is shown in Figure A-8.

```
Before COPY is executed (C entered on line 0002.00 and target A on 0005.00):

 FMT **  ...+... 1 ...+... 2 ...+... 3 ...+... 4 ...+... 5 ...+... 6 ...+... 7
        *************** Beginning of data ************************************
0001.00 Instruction 1
C 02.00 Instruction 2 ──  Letter C will copy this record
0003.00 Instruction 3     after target A record
0004.00 Instruction 4
A 05.00 Instruction 5 ──
0006.00 Instruction 6
        ****************** End of data ****************************************

After COPY is executed:

 FMT **  ...+... 1 ...+... 2 ...+... 3 ...+... 4 ...+... 5 ...+... 6 ...+... 7
        *************** Beginning of data ************************************
0001.00 Instruction 1
0002.00 Instruction 2
0003.00 Instruction 3
0004.00 Instruction 4
0005.00 Instruction 5      Instruction 2 is copied to the inserted record
0005.01 Instruction 2 ──   number 0005.01 immediately after 0005.00
0007.00 Instruction 6
        ****************** End of data ****************************************
```

Figure A-8 Example **COPY** command that copies an instruction to an *after* **(A)** target.

A **COPY** line command that copies a group of instructions to a *before* **(B)** target is detailed in Figure A-9.

```
Before COPY is executed (CC entered on lines 0001.00 and 0003.00 with target B
on 0006.00):

 FMT **  ...+... 1 ...+... 2 ...+... 3 ...+... 4 ...+... 5 ...+... 6 ...+... 7
        *************** Beginning of data ************** **********************
CC 1.00 Instruction 1 ──
0002.00 Instruction 2      The two CC commands will copy
CC 3.00 Instruction 3 ──   the group of records (1-3) be-
0004.00 Instruction 4      fore statement 0006.00
0005.00 Instruction 5
B 06.00 Instruction 6 ──
        ****************** End of data ***************************************
```

Figure A-9 Example **COPY** command that copies a group of instructions to a *before* **(B)** target.

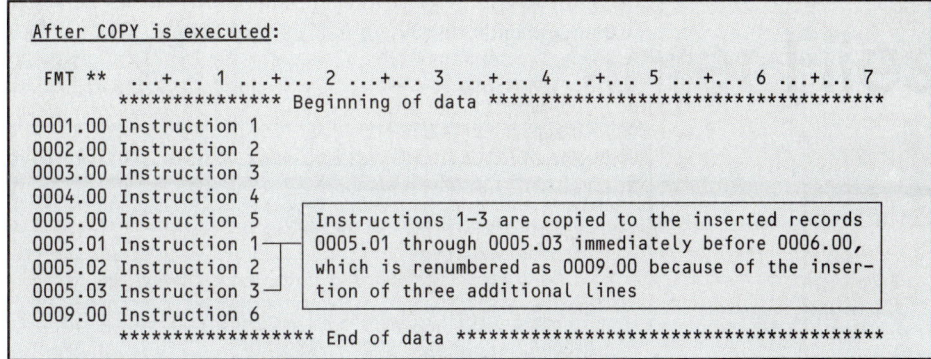

```
After COPY is executed:

 FMT **   ...+... 1 ...+... 2 ...+... 3 ...+... 4 ...+... 5 ...+... 6 ...+... 7
        *************** Beginning of data ************************************
0001.00 Instruction 1
0002.00 Instruction 2
0003.00 Instruction 3
0004.00 Instruction 4
0005.00 Instruction 5    Instructions 1-3 are copied to the inserted records
0005.01 Instruction 1    0005.01 through 0005.03 immediately before 0006.00,
0005.02 Instruction 2    which is renumbered as 0009.00 because of the inser-
0005.03 Instruction 3    tion of three additional lines
0009.00 Instruction 6
        ****************** End of data ***************************************
```

Figure A-9 Example **COPY** command that copies a group of instructions to a *before* **(B)** target. (Continued)

MOVE *LINE COMMANDS*

MOVE line commands are used to move an instruction or instructions in the source member to a location *before* or *after* one or more target instruction(s). Figure A-10 summarizes the **MOVE** line commands and their target commands, which are identical to those discussed for the **COPY** line command.

Move Commands

Command	Function
M	Moves the record to a target line designated with an A, B, O, or OO.
MM	Moves the group (**MM** placed on first record and last record) beginning on a target line designated with an A, B, O, or OO.
Mn	Moves *n* records, starting with this record, to beginning with a target line designated with an A, B, O, or OO.

Target Line Commands

A	Move, copy, or include the specified records after this line.
B	Move, copy, or include the specified records before this line.
An	Move, copy, or include the specified records after this record and repeat the line *n* – 1 times.
Bn	Move, copy, or include the specified records before this record and repeat the line *n* – 1 times.
O	Overlay this record with the first record specified by the Copy, Copy Repeat, or Move line command.
On	Overlay the specified records on this record, and repeat the lines *n* – 1 times.
OO	Overlay all records in this block (defined by two **OO** commands) with the records defined by a Copy, Copy Repeat, or Move line command.
Note:	Target commands may be entered before or after their related move commands.

Figure A-10 **MOVE** line commands.

An example **MOVE** line command that moves an instruction to an *after* **(A)** target in a source member is shown in Figure A-11.

```
Before MOVE is executed (M entered on line 0002.00 and target A on 0005.00):

 FMT **   ...+... 1 ...+... 2 ...+... 3 ...+... 4 ...+... 5 ...+... 6 ...+... 7
            *************** Beginning of data *************************************
0001.00 Instruction 1
M 02.00 Instruction 2 ──┬ Letter M will move the record
0003.00 Instruction 3   │ 2 after target A record
0004.00 Instruction 4   │
A 05.00 Instruction 5 ──┘
0006.00 Instruction 6
            ****************** End of data ****************************************

After MOVE is executed:

 FMT **   ...+... 1 ...+... 2 ...+... 3 ...+... 4 ...+... 5 ...+... 6 ...+... 7
            *************** Beginning of data *************************************
0001.00 Instruction 1
0003.00 Instruction 3
0004.00 Instruction 4
0005.00 Instruction 5     Instruction 2 is moved to the inserted record
0005.01 Instruction 2 ─── number 0005.01 immediately before 0006.00
0006.00 Instruction 6
            ****************** End of data ****************************************
```

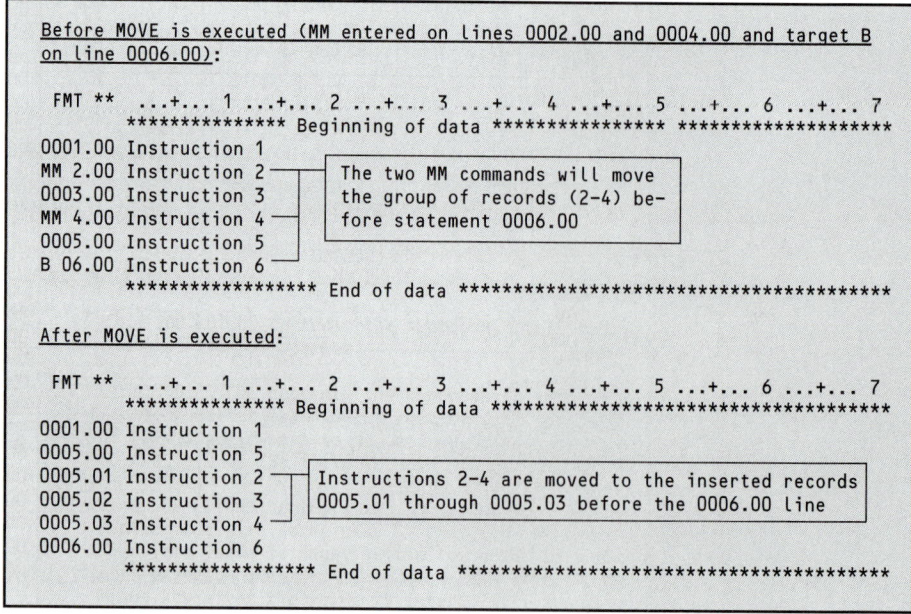

Figure A-11 Example **MOVE** line command that moves an instruction to an *after* **(A)** target.

A **MOVE** line command that moves a group of instructions to a *before* **(B)** target is detailed in Figure A-12.

```
Before MOVE is executed (MM entered on lines 0002.00 and 0004.00 and target B
on line 0006.00):

 FMT **   ...+... 1 ...+... 2 ...+... 3 ...+... 4 ...+... 5 ...+... 6 ...+... 7
            *************** Beginning of data **************** ********************
0001.00 Instruction 1
MM 2.00 Instruction 2 ─┬─ The two MM commands will move
0003.00 Instruction 3  │  the group of records (2-4) be-
MM 4.00 Instruction 4 ─┤  fore statement 0006.00
0005.00 Instruction 5  │
B 06.00 Instruction 6 ─┘
            ****************** End of data ****************************************

After MOVE is executed:

 FMT **   ...+... 1 ...+... 2 ...+... 3 ...+... 4 ...+... 5 ...+... 6 ...+... 7
            *************** Beginning of data *************************************
0001.00 Instruction 1
0005.00 Instruction 5
0005.01 Instruction 2 ─┬─ Instructions 2-4 are moved to the inserted records
0005.02 Instruction 3  │  0005.01 through 0005.03 before the 0006.00 line
0005.03 Instruction 4 ─┘
0006.00 Instruction 6
            ****************** End of data ****************************************
```

Figure A-12 Example **MOVE** command that moves a group of instructions to a *before* **(B)** target.

DELETE LINE COMMANDS

Delete line commands delete one or more existing records from a source member. The commands include **D, DD,** and **Dn. D** deletes the record on which the command is entered. Figure A-13 illustrates the use of the **D** line command.

```
Before DELETE is executed (D entered on line 0002.00):

 FMT **   ...+... 1 ...+... 2 ...+... 3 ...+... 4 ...+... 5 ...+... 6 ...+... 7
          *************** Beginning of data *************************************
0001.00 Instruction 1
D 02.00 Instruction 2 ---| D will delete record 2 |
0003.00 Instruction 3
0004.00 Instruction 4
0005.00 Instruction 5
0006.00 Instruction 6
          ****************** End of data ****************************************

After DELETE is executed:

 FMT **   ...+... 1 ...+... 2 ...+... 3 ...+... 4 ...+... 5 ...+... 6 ...+... 7
          *************** Beginning of data *************************************
0001.00 Instruction 1
0003.00 Instruction 3     | Record 2 is deleted |
0004.00 Instruction 4
0005.00 Instruction 5
0006.00 Instruction 6
       ****************** End of data ****************************************
```

Figure A-13 Example delete command for deleting one record.

DD entered on separate records deletes the specified group of records. **Dn** (**n** indicating the number of records) will delete the specified number of records, including the record on which the command is entered. Target line commands are *not* used with delete commands.

Figure A-14 illustrates use of the **Dn** line command.

```
Before DELETE is executed (D3 entered on line 0002.00):

 FMT **   ...+... 1 ...+... 2 ...+... 3 ...+... 4 ...+... 5 ...+... 6 ...+... 7
          *************** Beginning of data *************************************
0001.00 Instruction 1
D3 2.00 Instruction 2 -------| D3 will delete records 2-4. At  |
0003.00 Instruction 3        | least one space must follow the |
0004.00 Instruction 4        | D3 command                      |
0005.00 Instruction 5
0006.00 Instruction 6
          ****************** End of data ****************************************

After DELETE is executed:

 FMT **   ...+... 1 ...+... 2 ...+... 3 ...+... 4 ...+... 5 ...+... 6 ...+... 7
          *************** Beginning of data *************************************
0001.00 Instruction 1
0005.00 Instruction 5        | Records 2-4 are deleted |
0006.00 Instruction 6
          ****************** End of data ****************************************
```

Figure A-14 Example of record deletion with the **Dn** command.

WINDOW COMMAND

Different horizontal sections of the Edit display may be viewed by the *Window* command. The command includes **W** and **Wn. W** shows the data beginning in position 1 (default position) of the display, and **Wn,** with **n** as the variable for the first alternative position of the display. For example, if **W10** is entered in the sequence area, the data is moved to the left so that the first position displayed is 10, followed by the other characters. *It is important that at least one blank follow a* **W** *or* **Wn** *command, or the remaining sequence numbers will be considered as part of the command.* In lieu of using a Window command, key **F19** *(Scroll left)* will position the records to the left and **F20** *(Scroll right)* will position them to the right.

FINDING/REPLACING CHARACTER STRINGS

The shortcut method of finding a character string in the edit member is to enter the string in the **SEU==>** line and press **F16.** The member will be searched until the first matching string is found. Pressing **F16** again will continue the **Find** function until the next string is found or the **End of data reached** message is displayed.

Strings may also be found and/or replaced with a new value by accessing the Find/Change Services display shown in Figure A-15 from the Edit screen by pressing **F14.** The string to find is entered in the *Find* field, and **F16** must be pressed to start the search. When the string is found in the member, **F16** must be pressed again to continue.

```
                         Find/Change Options

 Type choices; press Enter.

   Find . . . . . . . . . . . . .   ____________________________________
   Change . . . . . . . . . . . .   ____________________________________
   From column number  . . . . . .  1__           1-80
   To column number  . . . . . . .  80_           1-80 or blank
   Occurrences to process  . . . .  1             1=Next, 2=All
                                                  3=Previous
   Records to search . . . . . . .  1             1=All, 2=Excluded
                                                  3=Non-excluded
   Kind of match . . . . . . . . .  2             1=Same case
                                                  2=Ignore case
   Allow data shift  . . . . . . .  Y             Y=Yes, N=No
   Search for date . . . . . . . .  95/12/12      YY/MM/DD or YYMMDD
     Compare . . . . . . . . . . .  _             1=Less than
                                                  2=Equal to
                                                  3=Greater than
 F3=Exit    F5=Refresh          F12=Cancel    F13=Change session defaults
 F15=Browse/Copy options        F16=Find      F17=Change
```

Figure A-15 Find/Change Services display.

Replace is executed by entering the current string in the *Find* field and the new value in the *Change* field and pressing **F17.** To continue to replace the string throughout the document, **F17** must be continually pressed. However, a global replace may be executed by changing the default for the *Occurrences to process* field value from 1 to 2.

EXITING FROM SEU

When in the Edit screen, exit from **SEU** is executed by pressing **F3,** which displays the Exit display in Figure A-16. A detailed explanation of each field is included at the bottom of the figure. From the Exit display, a member is saved by pressing the **ENTER** key, *not* the **F3** key.

```
                              Exit
Type choices, press Enter.
Change/create member . . . . . . .   Y               Y=Yes, N =No
  Member . . . . . . . . . . . . .   CH17P1         Name, F4 for list
  File . . . . . . . . . . . . . .   QRPGSRC        Name, F4 for list
    Library . . . . . . . . . . .      SMYERS       Name
  Text . . . . . . . . . . . . . .   ch 17 - sfl inquiry program

  Resequence member. . . . . . . .   Y               Y=Yes, N=No
   Start. . . . . . . . . . . . . .  0001.00         0000.01-9999.99
   Increment . . . . . . . . . . .   01.00           00.01-99.99

 Print member. . . . . . . . . . .   N               Y=Yes, N=No

 Return to editing . . . . . . . .   N               Y=Yes, N=No

 Go to member list . . . . . . . .   N               Y=Yes, N=No


F3=Exit    F4=Prompt  F5=Refresh  F12=Cancel
```

Change/Create member

Y (Yes) will automatically be specified when any character in the edited member has been changed. When a member is accessed and no changes are made, the default is **N.**

Member

The default is the name of the member currently edited. To make a copy of the member, a new name must be entered and **Y** must be specified for the *Change/Create Member* field to save the new member.

File

The default is the source file name specified when entering **SEU.** Default source file names include **QDDSSRC** for **PF, DSPF, LF, PRTF** members; **QRPGLESRC** for **RPG IV** programs; **QCLSRC** for **CL** programs; and **QCMDSRC** for commands.

Library

The default is the library name specified when the **SEU** session began. It may be changed to store the member in a different library, providing that the programmer has authority to access the referenced library.

Text

Text may be entered to describe the member. If text was entered when the **SEU** session began, it will automatically be included on this line.

Resequence number

The default is **Y,** which will resequence the statements upon exit from this display. Sequence numbers for the statements in the member automatically begin with 0001.00 and increment by 1.00 unless the programmer specifies a different value for each entry. **N** must be specified if the statements in the member are not to be resequenced. During the edit process, copy, delete, move, and insert line commands will change the default sequence numbering of statements. Resequencing will reorder the source statements.

Start

If the default **Y** was assumed for the Resequence number, the programmer may change the beginning sequence number. Otherwise, 0001.00 is the beginning default value.

Figure A-16 Exit display.

Increment

If **Y** was entered (or accepted as the default), the 01.00 default value for this field may be changed with a number from 00.01 to 99.99.

Print member

The default for this field is **N.** To print a copy of the member (without compilation), **Y** must be entered.

Return to editing

N is the default for this field. However, if there are syntax errors, control will automatically return to the **SEU** Edit display. Providing that there are no syntax errors, **Y** will save the current version of the member and, in any case, return control to the Edit display.

Go to member list

The default is **N.** A **Y** entry will access the Work with Members Using SEU display, which lists the members of the type currently edited stored in the referenced library.

Figure A-16 Exit display. (Continued)

SPLITTING THE EDIT AND BROWSE DISPLAYS

"Splitting" an Edit display enables the programmer to work with *two* members at the same time. When in the Edit display, pressing **F15** will access the Browse/Copy Options display shown in Figure A-17.

```
                         Browse/Copy Options

Type choices, press Enter.

  Selection . . . . . . . . . .   1              1=Member
                                                 2=Spool file
                                                 3=Output queue
  Copy all records  . . . . . .   N              Y=Yes, N=No
  Browse/copy member  . . . . .   CH17P2         Name, F4 for list
    File  . . . . . . . . . . .     QRPGSRC      Name, F4 for list
      Library . . . . . . . . .       SMYERS     Name, *CURLIB, *LIBL

  Browse/copy spool file  . . .   CH17P1         Name, F4 for list
    Job . . . . . . . . . . . .     CH17P1       Name
      User  . . . . . . . . . .       SMYERS     Name, F4 for list
      Job number  . . . . . . .       *LAST      Number, *LAST
    Spool number  . . . . . . .     *LAST        Number, *LAST, *ONLY

  Display output queue  . . . .   QPRINT         Name, *ALL
    Library . . . . . . . . . .     *LIBL        Name, *CURLIB, *LIBL

F3=Exit        F4=Prompt        F5=Refresh        F12=Cancel
F13=Change session defaults     F14=Find/Change options
```

Selection

The default **1** will access a source member, which will be displayed in the lower section of the split Edit display. **2** will access a Spool file, and **3** will view a member in the Output queue.

Figure A-17 Browse/Copy Options display.

Copy all records

The default for this field is **Y** (Yes), which enters **CC** in the first and last record of the browsed member. Specifying **N** (No) gives the programmer the option to select the records to be copied from the browsed member into the edited member.

Browse/Copy member

The name of the member to browse must be entered in this field. If the cursor is in this field, pressing **F4** will access the Select Member display to find the member to be browsed.

File

The name of the source file in which the member is stored must be specified in this field. The default is the source file for the member currently being edited or the last value entered for the edit session.

Library

The default for this field is the library that contains the member being edited or the last value entered for the edit session. Otherwise, the library that contains the requested member must be entered.

Browse/copy spool file

The default for this field is the name of the member currently edited. Otherwise, the member name to be viewed must be entered.

Job

The default for this field is the name of the member currently edited. Otherwise, the name of the job that created the spooled file must be entered.

User

The default for this field is the current user's ID. Otherwise, specify the user's profile name.

Job number

The default for this field is ***LAST.** Otherwise, specify the six-digit number of the job that created the spool file.

Spool number

The default for this field is ***LAST.** Otherwise, specify the five-digit number of the spooled file.

Display output queue

The default for this field is **QPRINT**. Otherwise, specify the name of the output queue.

Library

The default for this field is ***LIBL.** Otherwise, specify the name of the library for the output queue.

Figure A-17 Browse/Copy Options display. (Continued)

With the exception of the *Browse/copy member* entry, all other entries may or may not be accepted at their default values. The function of each field is explained in Figure A-17. Pressing the ENTER key will return control back to the Edit display in a "split" format. The number of lines displayed for the edited member in the top section and those for the browsed member in the bottom section depends on the cursor's location when the Browse/Copy Options display was accessed.

The result of returning back to the Edit display is shown in Figure A-18. **F6** may be used to move the "split line" to the cursor's location and display more or fewer lines for either section.

```
Columns . . . :     1  71              Edit                          SMYERS/QRPGSRC
SEU==>                                                                       CH17P1
FMT *  ..... *. 1 ...+... 2 ...+... 3 ...+... 4 ...+... 5 ...+... 6 ...+... 7
        *************** Beginning of data ************************************
0001.00       * Customer master inquiry with a subfile....
0002.00       *
0003.00       FCH17INQ CF  E                   WORKSTN
0004.00       F                                    SFRRN1KSFILE SM01SFR
0005.00       FP1PF1   IF  E            K      DISK
0006.00       C                   EXFMTPROMPT                              dspf prompt
------------------------------------------------------------------------------------
Columns . . . :     1  71              Browse                        SMYERS/QRPGSRC
SEU==>                                                                       CH17P2
        *************** Beginning of data ************************************
0001.00       * Customer master update with a subfile....
0002.00       *
0003.00       FCH17UPD CF  E                   WORKSTN
0004.00       F                                    SFRRN1KSFILE SM02SFR
0005.00       FP1PF1   UF  E            K      DISK
0006.00       C                   EXFMTPROMPT                              dspf prompt

F3=Exit   F5=Refresh   F9=Retrieve   F10=Cursor   F12=Cancel
F16=Repeat find        F17=Repeat change          F24=More keys
```

Figure A-18 "Split" Edit display—edited member in the top and browsed member in the bottom section.

With the exception of prompts, any of the line commands are valid in either section of the Edit display. Roll up and Roll down keys may be used to view records in either section. **F12** will return control to the single format for the edited member.

Change Session Defaults

While in the Edit display, the edit session defaults may be changed by pressing **F13** to access the *Change Session Defaults* display shown in Figure A-19. From this display, the input of uppercase only or both upper- and lowercase characters, syntax checking,

```
                         Change Session Defaults

Type choices, press Enter.

  Amount to roll . . . . . . . . . . .   H          H=Half, F=Full
                                                    C=Cursor, D=Data
                                                    1-999
  Uppercase input only . . . . . . . .   Y          Y=Yes, N=No
  Tabs on  . . . . . . . . . . . . . .   N          Y=Yes, N=No
  Increment of insert record . . . . .   0.01       0.01-999.99
  Full screen mode . . . . . . . . . .   N          Y=Yes, N=No

  Source type  . . . . . . . . . . . .   RPG
  Syntax checking:
    When added/modified  . . . . . . .   Y          Y=Yes, N=No
    From sequence number . . . . . . .              0000.00-9999.99
    To sequence number . . . . . . . .              0000.00-9999.99
  Set records to date  . . . . . . . .     / /      YY/MM/DD or YYMMDD
                                                                  More...
F3=Exit       F5=Refresh     F12=Cancel
F14=Find/Change options      F15=Browse/Copy options
```

Figure A-19 Change Session Defaults display.

Amount to roll

Entry specifies the number of lines to roll up or down when the Page Up or Page Down key is pressed. The default **H** indicates that a half-page will roll, and **F** a full page.

Uppercase input only

The default **Y** indicates that only uppercase is supported in the Edit session. Entering **N** will support upper- and lowercase.

Tabs on

The default **N** disables the tab settings. **Y** will enable them.

Increment of insert records

The default .01 will increment inserted records by .01. The increment may be changed from 0.01 to 999.99.

Full-screen mode

The default **N** indicates that the Edit session is not in a full-screen mode. **Y** will provide for this.

Source type

Indicate the source file type.

When added/modified

The default **Y** indicates that syntax checking related to the source type is supported. **N** disables syntax checking.

From sequence number

The default is to support syntax checking for all records in the member. When a value is entered, the *When added/modified* entry is ignored and syntax checking begins at the specified sequence number.

To sequence number

This entry is valid if a statement number was entered for the *From* sequence number field.

Set records to date

A date entered here will include the value in the right margin of each source record and override the default system date.

Figure A-19 Change Session Defaults display. (Continued)

sequence numbering of statements, and how many lines the Page keys display may be controlled. An explanation of each prompt is included in Figure A-19.

Accessing a List of Members

A list of the members stored in the source file (i.e., QDDSSRC, QRPGLESRC, QCLSRC, QCMDSRC, QTXTSRC, or user-named) currently accessed may be displayed by entering **Y** in the *Go to member list* field in the Exit display and pressing ENTER. This action will access the Work with Members Using SEU display shown in Figure A-20.

From this display, the user may edit, delete, browse, or print a member by entering the related number (2, 4, 5, or 6) in the *Opt* field before a member's name.

```
                         Work with Members Using SEU

Source file . . . . . .   QRPGSRC                    Library . . . . .   SMYERS
Position to . . . . . . . . . . . . . . . . . . . . . . . . . . .
New member  . . . . . . . . . . . . . . . . . . . . . . . . . . .
  Type for new member . . . . . . . . . . . . . . . . . . . . . .   RPG
  Text  . . . . . . . . .

Type options, press Enter.
   2=Edit       4=Delete       5=Browse         6=Print

Opt Member        Type          Text
    CATENATE      RPG           chapter 7 - called program
    CH10P1        RPG           ch10p1 - sales report program
    CH11P2        RPG           ch11p2 - modified performance report
    CH11P2ID      RPG           ch11p2 - modified for infds
    CH11P3        RPG           ch11p3 - canned soup report
    CH11P4        RPG           ch11p4 - multiple-occurrence data structure
    CH11P5        RPG           ch11p5 - customer listing using SCAN & SUBST oper.
    CH11P6        RPG           ch11p5 - customer listing using SCAN & SUBST oper.
                                                                          More...
 F3=Exit            F5=Refresh            F12=Cancel           F14=Display date
 F15=Sort by date                         F17=Subset
```

Figure A-20 Work with Members Using SEU display.

All of the features of **SEU** have not been covered in this appendix. For a comprehensive review of **SEU,** consult the latest release of IBM's **SEU** manual. The SEU function keys discussed in this appendix are summarized in Figure A-21. For information regarding other **SEU** function keys, refer to the AS/400's most current *Source Entry Utility* Manual.

Key	Name	Function
F3	Exit	Exits from **SEU** to the Exit screen. ENTER must be pressed to save the member.
F4	Prompt	Displays a prompt for a record or command.
F4	List	Presents a list of members. Valid only in the Member field of the Browse/Copy or Browse Services display.
F5	Refresh	Resets the values on the display to the values that were there before ENTER was last pressed or when the display was first shown.
F6	Move split Line	Splits the display at the cursor point.
F12	Previous	Presents a prior display.
F13	Change Defaults	Edit defaults may be changed in this display. May be accessed only when in the Edit display.
F14	Find/Change Services	Call the Find/Change Options display. Valid only in the Edit display.
F15	Browse/Copy	Access another member for complete or partial copying into the current split Edit display. May only be accessed when in the Edit display.
F16	Find	Starts the search when in the Find/Change Options display.
F17	Change	Performs the change function. Valid only when in the Find/Change Option display.

Figure A-21 Summary of the **SEU** function keys discussed in this appendix.

appendix b

Programming Development Manager (PDM)

The *Programming Development Manager,* better known as **PDM,** is a system tool intended to simplify software development and maintenance. To begin using **PDM,** the programmer may enter the command **STRPDM** *(Start Programming Development Manager)* on a command line or select the *Programming* option from the AS/400 Main menu and then select the option to *Start the Programming Development Manager.* A menu similar to the one shown in Figure B-1 is displayed. From this menu, four options are available for selection. Also included are other processes activated by pressing command function keys.

```
            AS/400 Programming Development Manager (PDM)
Select one of the following:
     1. Work with libraries
     2. Work with objects
     3. Work with members
     9. Work with user-defined options



Selection or command
===> ___________________________________________________________
F3=Exit      F4=Prompt        F9=Retrieve        F10=Command entry
F12=Cancel   F18=Change defaults
```

Figure B-1 **PDM** Main menu.

Most of the command function keys are self-explanatory. **F3** allows the programmer to exit the current display. **F4** displays command prompts for any command entered on the command line (or as a standard option on a list display). **F9** retrieves the previous command entered and displays it on the command line. **F10** begins a command entry **(QCMD)** session. **F12** cancels the current display and returns to the previous display. With one exception, the meaning of each of these command keys remains consistent throughout all **PDM** displays.

The exception is **F18,** *Change Defaults.* Default values for several parameters in frequently used programming commands are stored for each user by **PDM.** These values have been reviewed by the Security Officer and are consistent with the individual company's programming environment. If this is the first time the programmer has used **PDM,** he or she should review these default values and tailor them to his or her specific needs. To review and modify these values, the programmer would press **F18.**

As Figure B-2 shows, there are nine parameters to review. First is the *Object library*. This is the default library in which to store objects created via **PDM.** It may be a specific library, the programmer's current library **(*CURLIB),** or the library containing the source file in which the source member being compiled resides **(*SRCLIB).** The programmer may also specify whether or not an existing object of the same name and type should be replaced in the *Replace object* parameter, and whether the compile should be submitted to batch or run interactively in the *Compile in batch* parameter.

```
                              Change Defaults
 Type choices, press Enter.
   Object library . . . . . . .   *CURLIB       Name, *CURLIB, *SRCLIB
   Replace object . . . . . . .   Y             Y=Yes, N=No
   Compile in batch . . . . . .   Y             Y=Yes, N=No
   Run in batch . . . . . . . .   N             Y=Yes, N=No
   Job description  . . . . . .   SMYERS        Name, *USRPRF, F4 for list
     Library  . . . . . . . . .     SMYERS      Name, *CURLIB, *LIBL
   Change type and text . . . .   Y             Y=Yes, N=No
   Option file  . . . . . . . .   QAUOOPT       Name
     Library  . . . . . . . . .     QGPL        Name, *CURLIB, *LIBL
   Member . . . . . . . . . . .   QAUOOPT       Name
   Full screen mode . . . . . .   N             Y=Yes, N=No

 F3=Exit      F4=Prompt      F5=Refresh      F12=Cancel
```

Figure B-2 Change Defaults display.

For options other than compiles, the programmer may indicate whether he or she wishes the processes to run interactively or in batch with the *Run in batch* parameter. Jobs submitted for batch processing require a *Job description*. Here the programmer may indicate a particular job description or reference the job description specified in the programmer's user profile **(*USRPRF).**

The ability of the programmer to modify the type and text description fields of an object or member via the **PDM** displays is controlled by the entry in the *Change type and text* parameter.

The file specified in the *Option file* parameter will be used to interpret the two-position user-defined codes the programmer may enter on the **PDM** displays. The QAUOOPT file in the **QGPL** library contains the IBM-defined options. If a programmer wishes to modify these options or define new options, it is recommended that he or she copy the QAUOOPT file into his or her own development library. Then modifications may be made to the copy in the development library without affecting other PDM users. In such a case, the library specified for the *Option file* parameter should be changed to the programmer's development library. Then the programmer's own version of the file would be accessed as the *Option file*.

Finally, activation of *Full-screen mode* produces a display that lists only object or member names and their associated types, without descriptions. This is difficult for the programmer to use and is therefore seldom seen. For our purposes we have chosen not to use this display. As a result, none of the sample screen displays in this appendix is a full-screen mode display.

Three types of screen displays are used throughout **PDM:** the *subset definition display;* the *list display;* and the *command-specific display*. The subset definition allows the programmer to define selection criteria for the items to be displayed on the list display. The list display presents a list of selected items and allows the programmer to process them using various options. Based on the option specified, a command-specific display may appear. Samples of these displays are presented over the next few pages as the **PDM** Main menu options are discussed in detail.

The next thing a new **PDM** user should do is review the user-defined option file. To do this the programmer would select option 9 from the **PDM** Main menu, *Work with* *user-defined options.* A screen similar to Figure B-3 would appear to allow the programmer to specify which option file to work with.

```
                     Specify Option File to Work With
      Type choices, press Enter.
        File . . . . . . . . . .    QAUOOPT         Name
          Library . . . . . . . .     QGPL          *LIBL, *CURLIB, name
        Member  . . . . . . . . .   QAUOOPT         Name




      F3=Exit       F5=Refresh       F12=Cancel
```

Figure B-3 Select user option file display.

The screen displays the option file specified in the programmer's default values, but this may be overridden. For our example we will be using the IBM default option file, QAUOOPT, in the **QGPL** library.

Pressing the ENTER key brings us to a display similar to the one shown in Figure B-4. Here the user-defined options and their associated commands are displayed. Note that some of the commands have variables associated with command parameters. These variables are defined by **PDM.** For example, **&L** represents the library being displayed, **&N** stands for the name of the item (either an object or a file member) being displayed, **&F** refers to the file whose members are currently being displayed, and **&T** represents the object type specified on the display. Several other predefined substitution variables exist. By using these predefined variables, a programmer may construct flexible commands for use with the **PDM** list displays.

```
                        Work with User-Defined Options
 File . . . . . . . :   QAUOOPT            Member . . . . . . :   QAUOOPT
   Library  . . . . :     QGPL
 Type options, press Enter.
   2=Change          3=Copy          4=Delete          5=Display
 Opt  Option  Command
 __     C     CALL &O/&N
 __     CC    CHGCURLIB CURLIB(&L)
 __     CL    CHGCURLIB CURLIB(&N)
 __     CD    STRDFU OPTION(2)
 __     CM    STRSDA OPTION(2) SRCFILE(&L/&F) ??SRCMBR()
 __     CS    STRSDA OPTION(1) SRCFILE(&L/&F) ??SRCMBR()
 __     DM    DSPMSG
 __     EA    EDTOBJAUT OBJ(&L/&N) OBJTYPE(&T)
 __     GO    GO &L/&N
                                                                        More...
 Parameters or command
 ===> ____________________________________________________________________________
 F3=Exit            F4=Prompt            F5=Refresh          F6=Create
 F9=Retrieve        F10=Command entry                        F24=More keys
```

Figure B-4 Work with User-Defined Options display.

To create a new user-defined option, the programmer would press **F6.** A screen similar to the one shown in Figure B-5 would display. The new two-character code would be entered in the *Option* parameter, and the command to be executed would be entered on the *Parameters* or *command* line. Prompting is available for any command entered in the *Command* parameter to ensure that all appropriate parameters are included.

For example, if the programmer wished to create an option to edit his or her user library list, he or she might enter **EL** as the option and specify **EDTLIBL** *(Edit Library List)* as the command to be executed whenever **EL** is entered. No additional parameters are required for this command, and so the programmer would not need to specify any

```
                      Create User-Defined Option

 Type option and command, press Enter.
  Option . . . . . . . . . ___        Option to create
  Command . . . . . . . . . ________________________________________
________________________________


F3=Exit        F4=Prompt        F12=Cancel
```

Figure B-5 Create User-Defined Option display.

variables, and prompting is not necessary. Pressing the ENTER key would create the option and return the programmer to the previous screen.

Other options are available from the *Work with User-Defined Options* display. Entering a **2** next to any of the options on the display will allow the programmer to change that option. A screen such as the one shown in Figure B-6 will be displayed. The programmer may enter the desired modification on this screen. Pressing the ENTER key causes the user-defined option to be updated with the specified change and the programmer to then be returned to the previous screen.

```
                      Change User-Defined Option
 Type changes, press Enter.
    Option . . . . . . . . .   _C   Value to change to
    Command . . . . . . . . .  CALL &O/&N
_____________________________________________________


 F3=Exit        F4=Prompt        F12=Cancel
```

Figure B-6 Change User-Defined Option display.

To copy an option from one file to another or to the same file but under a different option name, the programmer would enter a **3** next to the option on the *Work with User-Defined Options* display. A screen similar to the one shown in Figure B-7 would be displayed.

```
                      Copy User-Defined Options

 From file . . . . . . . :   QAUOOPT
   From library  . . . . :    QGPL
 From member . . . . . . :   QAUOOPT
 Type the file, library, and member to receive copied options.
   To file . . . . . . . .   QAUOOPT         Name, F4 for List
     To library  . . . . .    SMYERS
   To member . . . . . . .   QAUOOPT
 To rename copied option, type New Option, press Enter.
 Option    New Option
   EL        EL
   __        __
   __        __
                                                          Bottom
 F3=Exit      F5=Refresh      F12=Cancel
```

Figure B-7 Copy User-Defined Options display.

In our example the programmer has selected the user-defined option **EL** to be copied. It is to be copied from the QAUOOPT file in **QGPL** to the QAUOOPT file in SMYERS and will retain the code of **EL** to execute the specified command. Once the

ENTER key is pressed, the option will be copied to the specified file and the programmer will be returned to the *Work with User-defined Options* display.

Entering a **4** next to an option on the *Work with User-defined Options* display indicates that the specified option is to be deleted. A confirmation screen similar to the one shown in Figure B-8 will be displayed. To confirm the deletion, the programmer must press the ENTER key. To cancel the deletion process, the programmer must press **F12.** Either action returns the programmer to the *Work with User-defined Options* display.

```
                   Confirm Delete of User-Defined Options
File . . . . . . . :    QAUOOPT
  Library . . . . . :     QGPL
Member . . . . . . :    QAUOOPT

Press Enter to confirm your choices for Delete.
Press F12=Cancel to return to change your choices.
Option        Command
  EL          EDTLIBL

                                                             Bottom
F12=Cancel
```

Figure B-8 Delete confirmation display.

To display an option in detail, the programmer would enter a **5** next to the option on the *Work with User-defined Options* display. A screen similar to the one shown in Figure B-9 would be displayed. The programmer could press **F3, F12,** or the ENTER key to return to the previous screen. From there the programmer would press **F12** to return to the **PDM** Main menu.

```
                        Display User-Defined Option
Type changes, press Enter.
   Option . . . . . . . . .    C
   Command . . . . . . . . .   CALL &O/&N


F3=Exit                       F12=Cancel
```

Figure B-9 Display User-Defined Option display.

Having become familiar with the **PDM** processing defaults assigned to him or her, as well as with the *User-Defined Options* available to work with, the programmer is now prepared to utilize the main functions of **PDM.** We will now discuss the more commonly accessed **PDM** functions.

When option 1, *Work with libraries,* is selected from the **PDM** Main menu, a selection screen such as the one shown in Figure B-10 is displayed. This allows the programmer to specify which libraries are to be listed. A variety of subsets is possible. To list all libraries found on the system, the programmer would enter ***ALL** in the *List type* prompt. Other possible entries include all of the libraries in the programmer's user library list (***USRLIBL),** all libraries except for operating system libraries (***ALLUSR),** the programmer's current library (***CURLIB),** the name of a specific library, a generic name that would display a group of libraries (such as **A*,** which would display all libraries with names beginning with the letter **A**), or all libraries in the programmer's library list (***LIBL).**

```
                    Specify Libraries to Work With
Type choice, press Enter.
  Library . . . . . . . . . . .   *LIBL       *LIBL, name, generic*, *ALL,
                                              *ALLUSR, *USRLIBL, *CURLIB




      F3=Exit      F5=Refresh      F12=Cancel
```

Figure B-10 Library subset specification display.

For our example we have requested that the libraries in the programmer's library list be displayed. Figure B-11 shows the *Work with Libraries Using* **PDM** display. Note that the libraries listed represent all four parts of the programmer's library list (the system library list **(SYS),** the product library **(PROD),** the current library **(CUR),** and the user library list **(USR)**). From this display, a number of options are possible. Standard options *(Change, Copy, Display,* etc.) are displayed above the list. Any of these options may be entered in an *Opt* field, and the associated process will occur. User-defined options may also be entered in *Opt* fields, adding to the flexibility of the list display. Commands may be entered on the *Parameters or command* line for execution. Or, command function keys may be used to perform any of the functions listed.

```
                       Work with Libraries Using PDM
List type . . . . . . .   *LIBL
Type options, press Enter.
  2=Change                    3=Copy        5=Display        7=Rename
  8=Display description       9=Save        10=Restore       12=Work with ...
Opt  Library      Type        Text
 __  QSYS         *PROD-SYS   System Library
 __  QSYS2        *PROD-SYS   System Library for CPI's
 __  QUSRSYS      *PROD-SYS   SYSTEM LIBRARY FOR USERS
 __  QHLPSYS      *PROD-SYS
 __  QPDA         *PROD-PRD
 __  SMYERS       *TEST-CUR   Stan Myers' development library
 __  FILELIB      *PROD-USR   Production File Library
 __  PROGLIB      *PROD-USR   Production Software Library
 __  QGPL         *PROD-USR   General Purpose Library
                                                                  More...
Parameters or command
===> ____________________________________________________________________
F3=Exit          F4=Prompt            F5=Refresh          F6=Add to list
F9=Retrieve      F10=Command entry    F23=More options    F24=More keys
```

Figure B-11 Work with Libraries Using PDM display.

The programmer is encouraged to explore the options and command function keys in order to determine just how flexible **PDM** is. In all cases, **F3** will return the programmer to the previous display without executing the command associated with the current display. Eventually the programmer will return to the **PDM** Main menu.

Selection of option 2, *Work with objects,* from the **PDM** Main menu will display a screen similar to that found in Figure B-12. The programmer has the option of entering a specific library name or selecting the current library **(*CURLIB)** for the *Library* parameter. Various entries may be combined in the *Name, Type,* and *Attribute* parameters in order to produce the desired object subset. The example in Figure B-12 requests that all files in the SMYERS library be displayed. The display shown in Figure B-13 is the result of this selection. Note that a variety of files is shown, including logical files **(LF-DTA),** physical files containing data **(PF-DTA),** and physical files containing source code **(PF-SRC).**

```
                    Specify Objects to Work With
Type choices, press Enter.
  Library . . . . . . . . . .  SMYERS      *CURLIB, name
  Object:
    Name . . . . . . . . . . . *ALL        *ALL, name, *generic*
    Type . . . . . . . . . . . *FILE       *ALL, *type
    Attribute  . . . . . . . . *ALL        *ALL, attribute, *generic*,
                                                    *BLANK

F3=Exit     F5=Refresh     F12=Cancel
```

Figure B-12 Specify Objects to Work With display.

Again, standard options *(Change, Copy, Display,* etc.) are displayed above the list. Any standard or user-defined option may be entered in an *Opt* field and the associated process will occur. Commands may be entered on the *Parameters or command* line for execution. Or command function keys may be used to perform any of the functions listed.

```
                    Work with Objects Using PDM
Library . . . . .   SMYERS           Position to . . . . . . . . ________
                                     Position to type  . . . . . ________
Type options, press Enter.
  2=Change       3=Copy          4=Delete       5=Display      7=Rename
  8=Display description          9=Save         10=Restore     11=Move ...
Opt  Object      Type         Attribute    Text
 __  APLVEND     *FILE        LF-DTA       AP Vendor by Vendor Name
 __  APLVEND2    *FILE        LF-DTA       AP Vendor by Vendor Number
 __  APPVEND     *FILE        PF-DTA       AP Vendor Master File
 __  QCLSRC      *FILE        PF-SRC       source for CL programs
 __  QDDSSRC     *FILE        PF-SRC       source for DDS
 __  QRPGSRC     *FILE        PF-SRC       source for RPG programs
 __  WRKFILE     *FILE        PF-DTA       Workfile for report
 __  ZEROBAL     *FILE        PF-DTA       Zero Balance Accounts
                                                               More...
Parameters or command
===> ___________________________________________________________________
F3=Exit          F4=Prompt            F5=Refresh          F6=Create
F9=Retrieve      F10=Command entry    F23=More options    F24=More keys
```

Figure B-13 Work with Objects Using PDM display.

The third option from the **PDM** Main menu, *Work with members,* allows the programmer to access file members and is most often used to access source members in a source file. A screen similar to the one shown in Figure B-14 allows the programmer to specify the file and members to be displayed. The example specifies the QRPGLESRC file in the SMYERS library and requests that all members be displayed.

```
                    Specify Members to Work With
Type choices, press Enter.
  File . . . . . . . . . .   QRPGLESRC   Name, F4 for list
    Library . . . . . . . .    SMYERS    *LIBL, *CURLIB, name
  Member:
    Name . . . . . . . . .   *ALL        *ALL, name, *generic*
    Type . . . . . . . . .   *ALL        *ALL, type, *generic*, *BLANK

F3=Exit     F4=Prompt     F5=Refresh     F12=Cancel
```

Figure B-14 Specify Members to Work With display.

Similar to other major list displays, Figure B-15 shows standard options listed above the member display. Note that option **2** now specifies **Edit** instead of **Change.** Selecting option 2 will initiate an **SEU** *(Source Entry Utility)* session using the member indicated.

```
                         Work with Members Using PDM
File  . . . . . .   QRPGSRC
  Library . . . .     SMYERS              Position to  . . . . .__________
Type options, press Enter.
  2=Edit          3=Copy        4=Delete       5=Display       6=Print
  7=Rename        8=Display description        9=Save          13=Change text ...
Opt  Member       Type          Text
 __  APR820       RPG           AP Vendor Maintenence
 __  ARR121       RPG           AR Status Report
 __  COMRPT023    RPG           COMMISSION REPORT
 __  HOLDFLAG1    RPG           Release records for tape
 __  OER726       RPG           Order Entry Quote List
 __  OER729       RPG           Order Entry Purge Quote File
 __  PRR327       RPG           Payroll Time Card Edit Report
 __  SAR010       RPG           Sales Analysis  Weekly Sales Report
 __  SAR045       RPG           Sales Analysis  On-line Inquiry
                                                                      More...
Parameters or command
===> ____________________________________________________________________

F3=Exit           F4=Prompt            F5=Refresh          F6=Create
F9=Retrieve       F10=Command entry    F23=More options    F24=More keys
```

Figure B-15 Work with Members Using PDM display.

Other useful options exist. If the programmer were to press **F23** *(More options),* a different set of standard options will appear, as shown in Figure B-16. Option **14** can be used to compile a source member (the create command to be used is determined by the

```
                         Work with Members Using PDM
File  . . . . . .   QRPGSRC
  Library . . . .     SMYERS              Position to  . . . . .__________
Type options, press Enter.
  14=Compile            16=Run procedure          17=Change using SDA
  19=Change using RLU   25=Find string ...
Opt  Member       Type          Text
 __  APR820       RPG           AP Vendor Maintenance
 __  ARR121       RPG           AR Status Report
 __  COMRPT023    RPG           COMMISSION REPORT
 __  HOLDFLAG1    RPG           Release records for tape
 __  OER726       RPG           Order Entry Quote List
 __  OER729       RPG           Order Entry Purge Quote File
 __  PRR327       RPG           Payroll Time Card Edit Report
 __  SAR010       RPG           Sales Analysis  Weekly Sales Report
 __  SAR045       RPG           Sales Analysis  On-line Inquiry
                                                                      More...
Parameters or command
===> ____________________________________________________________________

F3=Exit           F4=Prompt            F5=Refresh          F6=Create
F9=Retrieve       F10=Command entry    F23=More options    F24=More keys
```

Figure B-16 Work with Members Using PDM display.

Type field displayed next to the member name). If the source member is for a display file (type **DSPF),** then option **17** could be used to initiate an **SDA** *(Screen Design Aid)* session. If the source member is for a printer file, option **19** could be used to initiate an **RLU** *(Report Layout Utility)* session.

With its flexible user-defined options and simple list format, the *Programming Development Manager* can be a powerful tool for the programmer to use. The programmer is encouraged to explore **PDM** and become familiar with its various capabilities.

appendix c

Data File Utility (DFU)

The AS/400 *Data File Utility,* better known as **DFU,** allows the programmer to quickly generate an interactive program to add, delete, and change records in a database file. To access this utility, the programmer enters the **STRDFU** *(Start Data File Utility)* command from any command entry line. A menu similar to the one shown in Figure C-1 will be displayed.

```
                    AS/400 Data File Utility (DFU)
Select one of the following:
     1. Run a DFU program
     2. Create a DFU program
     3. Change a DFU program
     4. Delete a DFU program
     5. Update data using temporary program


Selection or command
===> 5
F3=Exit   F4=Prompt   F9=Retrieve   F12=Cancel
                                    (C) COPYRIGHT IBM CORP. 1981, 1991.
```

Figure C-1 **DFU** Main menu.

DFU programs may be created and stored for later use. This is a good idea if the programmer intends to use the **DFU** program frequently. However, the programmer most often uses a **DFU** program to fix an occasional problem or to create test data. Under those circumstances, the **DFU** program is not intended for repeated use. A temporary **DFU** may be created by selecting option **5** from the **DFU** Main menu.

The programmer is then prompted with a screen similar to the one shown in Figure C-2 to specify the data file and member to be updated. Either a physical file or a logical file may be specified here.

```
                     Update Data Using Temporary Program
Type choices, press Enter.
  Data file . . . . . . . . .   CUSTOMERS    Name, F4 for list
    Library . . . . . . . . .    SMYERS      Name, *LIBL, *CURLIB
  Member  . . . . . . . . . .   CUSTOMERS    Name, *FIRST, F4 for list




F3=Exit     F4=Prompt     F12=Cancel
```

Figure C-2 Data File Selection screen.

The file's database definition is used to construct the temporary program. After a brief wait, during which time the **DFU** program is being generated, a screen will appear. If the file already contains data, **DFU** assumes that the programmer wishes to change an existing record. The **DFU** program will therefore present a record selection screen similar to the one shown in Figure C-3, and the default processing mode will be **CHANGE.**

```
WORK WITH DATA IN A FILE                             Mode . . . . :    CHANGE
Format . . . . :   CUSTOMERS                         File . . . . :    CUSTOMERS
CUST#:             ____




F3=Exit                      F5=Refresh                 F6=Select format
F9=Insert                    F10=Entry                  F11=Change
```

Figure C-3 Record Selection screen.

However, if the file does not contain any records, **DFU** will assume that the programmer intends to enter data and will present a screen similar to the one shown in Figure C-5, and the default processing mode will be **ADD.** For purposes of this example, the programmer has chosen a file that already contained several records of test data.

First, a correction will be made to a customer's record. The programmer enters the desired customer number, in this case **11111,** on the *Record Selection* screen. This key value is used to locate the appropriate customer record. If the file selected for processing was not a keyed access file, the *Record Selection* screen would allow the programmer to specify the relative record number of the desired record. Either way, a record from the file is retrieved and displayed on a screen similar to the one shown in Figure C-4.

```
WORK WITH DATA IN A FILE                             Mode . . . . :    CHANGE
Format . . . . :   CUSTOMERS                         File . . . . :    CUSTOMERS
CUST#:             11111
LAST NAME:         LONGFELLOW
FIRST NAME:        HENRY
MIDDLE INITIAL:    W
ADDRESS LINE 1:    88 HIAWATHA DRIVE
ADDRESS LINE 2:
CITY:              WILLOWTON
STATE:             PA
ZIP CODE:          01624

F3=Exit                      F5=Refresh                 F6=Select format
F9=Insert                    F10=Entry                  F11=Change
```

Figure C-4 Record Update screen.

Data in any of the underlined fields may be changed. The programmer needs only to type the corrected data into the appropriate fields and press the ENTER key for the record correction to occur. Then the programmer is returned to the *Record Selection* screen (Figure C-3).

As noted along the bottom of each screen, several command function keys are available throughout the **DFU** program processing. Pressing **F3** will end the **DFU** program, and pressing **F5** will clear entries made in data fields and reset them to their original values. **F6** allows the programmer to change to a different screen format (this option does not apply for the temporary **DFU** because only one format is generated). **F9, F10,** and **F11** allow the programmer to change processing modes. To enter additional test records, the programmer now presses **F10** to switch to **ENTRY** mode. The **DFU** program now displays a screen similar to the one shown in Figure C-5.

```
WORK WITH DATA IN A FILE                              Mode . . . . :   ENTRY
Format . . . . :    CUSTOMERS                         File . . . . :   CUSTOMERS
CUST#:           _____
LAST NAME:       __________________
FIRST NAME:      _____________
MIDDLE INITIAL:  _
ADDRESS LINE 1:  ______________________
ADDRESS LINE 2:  ______________________
CITY:            _____________
STATE:           __
ZIP CODE:        ___

F3=Exit                  F5=Refresh                F6=Select format
F9=Insert                F10=Entry                 F11=Change
```

Figure C-5 Add Record screen.

The programmer may now enter data in the fields provided (as shown in Figure C-6). When the ENTER key is pressed, the record will be added to the file.

```
WORK WITH DATA IN A FILE                              Mode . . . . :   ENTRY
Format . . . . :    CUSTOMERS                         File . . . . :   CUSTOMERS
CUST#:            22220
LAST NAME:        STEVENSON
FIRST NAME:       ROBERT
MIDDLE INITIAL:   L
ADDRESS LINE 1:   127 GREEN FARM RD.
ADDRESS LINE 2:
CITY:             TOWNSEND
STATE:            VT
ZIP CODE:         22213

F3=Exit                  F5=Refresh                F6=Select format
F9=Insert                F10=Entry                 F11=Change
```

Figure C-6 Add Record screen with data entered.

To delete a record from a file via **DFU,** the programmer must enter the mode. To do this the programmer presses **F23.** Once in the **DELETE** mode, a screen similar to the one displayed in Figure C-7 allows the programmer to select the record to be deleted.

```
WORK WITH DATA IN A FILE                              Mode . . . . :   DELETE
Format . . . . :    CUSTOMERS                         File . . . . :   CUSTOMERS
CUST#:            _____

F3=Exit                  F5=Refresh                F6=Select format
F9=Insert                F10=Entry                 F11=Change
```

Figure C-7 Delete Record screen.

DFU retrieves the specified record and displays it for visual verification on a screen similar to the one shown in Figure C-8. If this is not the correct record, the programmer may cancel the record deletion by pressing **F12** and returning to the *Delete Record Selection* screen (Figure C-7). Otherwise, to physically remove the record, the programmer must confirm the deletion by pressing **F23.**

```
 WORK WITH DATA IN A FILE                              Mode . . . . :   DELETE
 Format . . . . :   CUSTOMERS                          File . . . . :   CUSTOMERS
 CUST#:             32247
 LAST NAME:         EMERSON
 FIRST NAME:        RALPH
 MIDDLE INITIAL:    W
 ADDRESS LINE 1:    726 GREAT POND DRIVE
 ADDRESS LINE 2:
 CITY:              WALDON
 STATE:             MA
 ZIP CODE:          60490
Record deletion pending

 F3=Exit                 F5=Refresh                F6=Select format
 F9=Insert               F10=Entry                 F11=Change
```

Figure C-8 Delete Record screen.

The programmer may toggle between functions by pressing **F10** (for **ENTRY** mode), **F11** (for **CHANGE** mode), and **F23** (for **DELETE** mode). All modifications are immediately reflected in the file.

When the programmer has completed all of the file modifications, he or she may end the **DFU** program by pressing **F3.** A screen summarizing the processing (see Figure C-9) will be displayed. Pressing the ENTER key will allow the **DFU** processing to complete, and an audit listing of the programmer's transactions will be printed.

```
                           End Data Entry
   Number of records processed
     Added . . . . . :           1
     Changed . . . . :           1
     Deleted . . . . :           1

 Type choice, press Enter.
   End data entry . . . . . . .  Y           Y=Yes,  N=No


 F3=Exit       F12=Cancel
```

Figure C-9 End Data Entry screen.

appendix d

Screen Design Aid Utility (SDA)

The *Screen Design Aid* (**SDA**) utility provides an easy method to design, create, and maintain *display files, menus,* and *online help information.* Because the user does not need to know the complex and detailed syntax required when the *Source Entry Utility* (**SEU**) is used to create and maintain display files, the processes are simplified with **SDA.**

SDA may be accessed by any of the following methods.

1. From any menu that includes a command line by typing the Control Language (**CL**) command **STRSDA** and pressing ENTER.
2. Selecting Option **9** on the PM and pressing ENTER. Unless otherwise set up, the PM may be accessed by entering the **CL** command **STRPGMMNU** on the command line on any menu and pressing ENTER.
3. Selecting Option **17** when in the PDM (**PDM**) utility and pressing ENTER. **PDM** may be accessed by entering **STRPDM** on the command line of any display and pressing ENTER.

Upon entering the **SDA** environment, the first menu that displays is shown in Figure D-1.

```
                         AS/400 Screen Design Aid (SDA)

 Select one of the following:

      1. Design screens
      2. Design menus
      3. Test display files










 Selection or command
 ===> 1

 F1=Help   F3=Exit   F4=Prompt   F9=Retrieve   F12=Cancel
                                       (C) COPYRIGHT IBM CORP. 1981, 1992.
```

Figure D-1 Initial **SDA** display with Option **1** selected.

This initial menu includes the following options:

1. *Design screens*—Controls the creation or maintenance of the record(s) in a display file.
2. *Design menus*—Controls the creation and maintenance of interactive menus.
3. *Test display files*—Controls the testing of successfully compiled display files and menus.

Steps in the Creation of a Display File

The following steps create a display file with a one-record format:

1. Select Option **1** *(Design screens)*—type **1** on the command line (Figure D-1).
2. Press the ENTER key, and the display shown in Figure D-2 will appear.

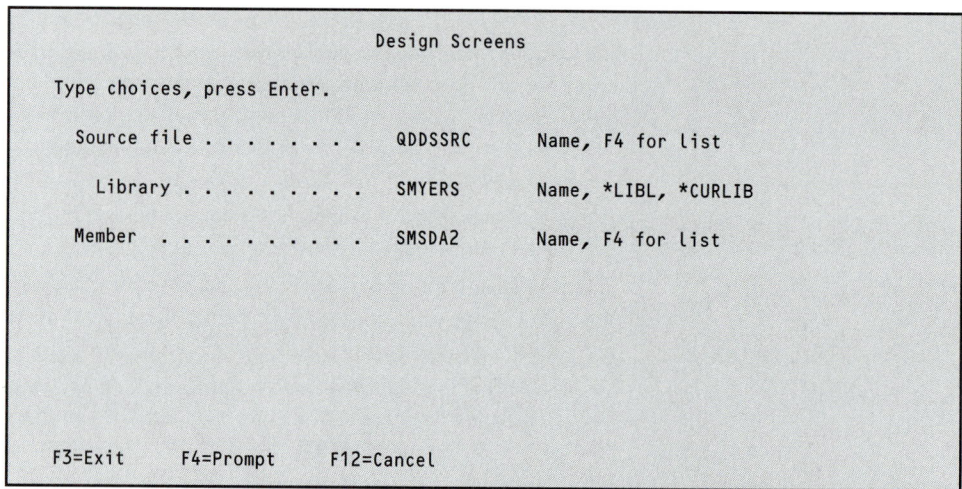

```
                              Design Screens

 Type choices, press Enter.

   Source file . . . . . . . .   QDDSSRC      Name, F4 for list

     Library . . . . . . . . .   SMYERS       Name, *LIBL, *CURLIB

   Member  . . . . . . . . . .   SMSDA2       Name, F4 for list






 F3=Exit      F4=Prompt      F12=Cancel
```

Figure D-2 Design Screens display with variables entered.

Definitions of the entries in the display in Figure D-2 are explained below.

- *Source file*—The IBM default is **QDDSSRC;** the installation has the option of programmers' assigning their own base source files.
- *Library*—The default is ***LIBL,** or the user may enter the specific library in which the display file's source will be stored.
- *Member*—The name of the display file to be created is entered on this line. If an existing display file is to be changed, **F4** may be pressed for a list of the files in the library specified on the preceding line.
- The three command keys listed at the bottom of the display provide the following control:
  - *F3 = Exit*—Returns control to the previous screen without executing the current changes (if any).
  - *F4 = Prompt*—Displays list of existing files as explained above.
  - *F12 = Cancel*—Cancels any entries and returns control to the previous screen.

Press ENTER, and the *Work with Display Record* screen shown in Figure D-3 will display.

```
                        Work with Display Records

File . . . . . . :    QDDSSRC               Member . . . . . . :   SMSDA2
  Library . . . . :     SMYERS              Source type  . . . :   DSPF

Type options, press Enter.
  1=Add            2=Edit comments        3=Copy          4=Delete
  7=Rename         8=Select keywords      12=Design image

Opt  Order     Record        Type      Related Subfile  Date        DDS Error
1              SMSDA2R
  (No records in file)




                                                                       Bottom
F3=Exit                            F12=Cancel      F14=File-level keywords
F15=File-level comments            F17=Subset      F24=More keys
```

Figure D-3 Work with Display Records screen.

Assuming that *File Level* keywords are required for the example display file to be created, **F14** must be pressed to display the screen shown in Figure D-4.

```
                           Select File Keywords
Member . . . :    SMSDA2

Type choices, press Enter.
                                          Y=Yes
  General keywords . . . . . . . .         Y
  Indicator keywords . . . . . . .         Y
  Print keywords . . . . . . . . .         Y
  Help keywords . . . . . . . . . .
  Display sizes . . . . . . . . . .
  Alternate keywords . . . . . . .
  DBCS conversion . . . . . . . . .
  Window Borders  . . . . . . . . .



F3=Exit    F12=Cancel
```

Figure D-4 Select File Keywords display with three options *(General, Indicator, Print keywords)* selected.

In response to the *General keywords* selection, type **Y** on the *General, Indicator,* and *Print keywords* lines to access each of those displays sequentially. Press the ENTER key, and the *Select General Keywords* display shown in Figure D-5 will appear.

```
                         Select General Keywords

Member . . . :    SMSDA2

Type choices, press Enter.
                                             Keyword     Y=Yes    Indicators/+
  Invite devices for later read . . . . . .  INVITE        _      ___ ___ ___
  Allow graphics  . . . . . . . . . . . . .  ALWGPH        _      ___ ___ ___
```

Figure D-5 Select General Keywords display.

```
Sound alarm on messages . . . . . . . . .  MSGALARM      _     ___ ___ ___
Separate indicators area  . . . . . . . .  INDARA        _
Manage display in S/36 mode . . . . . . .  USRDSPMGT     _
Allow blanks  . . . . . . . . . . . . . .  CHECK(AB)     _
Move cursor right-left, top-bottom  . . .  CHECK(RLTB)   _
Move cursor right to left . . . . . . . .  CHECK(RL)     _
Change input defaults . . . . . . . . . .  CHGINPDFT     Y
  Select parameters . . . . . . . . . . .                Y
Write error messages to subfile . . . . .  ERRSFL        _
Reference database file . . . . . . . . .  REF           SMPF1_____   Name
  Library . . . . . . . . . . . . . . . .                SMYERS____   Name
  Record  . . . . . . . . . . . . . . . .                SMPF1R____   Name
Record to pass unformatted data . . . . .  PASSRCD       __________   Name

F3=Exit   F12=Cancel
```

Figure D-5 Select General Keywords display. (Continued)

The display default (underline for variables) is changed by entering a **Y** *(Yes)* for the **CHGINPDFT** *(Change Input Defaults)* keyword entry. Selection of this option will override any default display attributes in all of the record formats in the display file. Specific display attributes are assigned at the *File Level* by entering **Y** for the *Select parameters* response and pressing ENTER. The screen shown in Figure D-6 will appear,

```
                         Select Display Attributes_

Constant  . . . :
Length  . . . . :                       Row . . . :      Column . . . :

Type choices, press Enter.
                                          Keyword  Y=Yes   Indicators/+
  Field conditioning . . . . . . . . . .
  Display attributes:                     DSPATR
    High intensity . . . . . . . . . . .   HI       _     ___ ___ ___
    Reverse image  . . . . . . . . . . .   RI       _
    Column separators  . . . . . . . . .   CS       Y     ___ ___ ___
    Blink  . . . . . . . . . . . . . . .   BL       _     ___ ___ ___
    Nondisplay . . . . . . . . . . . . .   ND       _     ___ ___ ___
    Underline  . . . . . . . . . . . . .   UL       _     ___ ___ ___
    Position cursor  . . . . . . . . . .   PC       _     ___ ___ ___


F3=Exit   F12=Cancel
```

Figure D-6 Select Display Attributes display.

where one or more display attributes may be selected. Note that *Column separators* **(CS)** has been selected, which will display dots indicating the size of the variable fields (not constants) in the record format of the example display file.

If database file field names are to be used in the display file, the related physical file name must be entered on the *Reference database file* **REF** line of the display shown in Figure D-5. Note that to the right of the **REF** keyword, **SMPF1** is specified by the programmer. **SMYERS** is entered for the *Library* selection and **SMPF1R** (physical file's record name) for the *Record* selection.

Pressing the ENTER key displays the *Define Indicator Keywords* screen illustrated in Figure D-7. Note that *Command Attention Key 3* **(CA03)** is assigned indicator **03** for EOJ (end-of-job control in the **RPG IV** program). *Command Function Key 2* **(CF02)** is assigned indicator **02** for ENTER DATA control, and *Command Attention Key 5* **(CA05)**

```
                          Define Indicator Keywords

 Member . . . :    SMSDA2

 Type keywords and parameters, press Enter.
   Conditioned keywords:        CFnn CAnn CLEAR PAGEDOWN/ROLLUP PAGEUP/ROLLDOWN
                                HOME HELP HLPRTN
   Unconditioned keywords:      INDTXT VLDCMDKEY

 Keyword    Indicators/+ Resp Text
 CA03____ ___ ___ ___     03  EOJ
 CF02____ ___ ___ ___     02  ENTER DATA
 CA05____ ___ ___ ___     05  REFRESH



                                                                     Bottom
 F3=Exit    F12=Cancel
```

Figure D-7 Define Indicator Keywords display with command keys/indicators specified.

indicator **05,** for REFRESH processing. Any command key and related indicators could be specified for the required screen controls. However, recall that **CA** *(Command Attention)* defines function keys *which do not pass data to or from the display file to the* ***RPG IV*** *program,* whereas **CF** *(Command Function) keys do pass data.* Pressing ENTER advances control to the *Define Print Keywords* display shown in Figure D-8.

```
                           Define Print Keywords

 Member . . . :    SMSDA2

 Type choices, press Enter.
                                       Keyword
   Enable keyword . . . . . . . . . .  PRINT     Y                Y=Yes
     Indicators . . . . . . . . . . .            ___ ___ ___

   Program handles print:
     Response indicator . . . . . . .            __               01-99
     Text . . . . . . . . . . . . . .            _________________________________
 ___________________________

   System handles print:
     Print file . . . . . . . . . . .            ____________     Name, *PGM
       Library  . . . . . . . . . . .            ____________     Name,
                                                                  *LIBL, *CURLIB
    Leave print file open until
       display file is closed . . . .  OPENPRT   _                Y=Yes

 F3=Exit    F12=Cancel
```

Figure D-8 Define Print Keywords display with **PRINT** option selected.

The letter **Y** entered on the *Enable keyword PRINT* line enables the Print Screen key, which when pressed will print the image of the record format currently displayed. Pressing ENTER *twice* returns control back to the *Work with Display Records* screen.

Before a screen is designed, a record must be defined in the display file to store the coding entries. To add a record to the display file, **1** (for *Add)* must be entered in the *Opt* field of the *Work with Display Records* screen as shown in Figure D-9.

```
                         Work with Display Records

File  . . . . . . :   QDDSSRC                     Member . . . . . . :   SMSDA2
  Library . . . . :     SMYERS                    Source type  . . . :   DSPF

Type options, press Enter.
  1=Add            2=Edit comments            3=Copy          4=Delete
  7=Rename         8=Select keywords         12=Design image

Opt  Order    Record          Type      Related Subfile   Date          DDS Error

 1      10   ________       _______




                                                                          Bottom
F3=Exit                      F12=Cancel       F14=File-level keywords
F15=File-level comments      F17=Subset       F24=More keys
```

Figure D-9 Work with Display Records screen with option **1** *(Add)* specified to add a record format.

Pressing ENTER displays the *Add New Record* screen illustrated in Figure D-10. Previously entered variables including the source file name, library name, member name, source type, and so forth are included in this display.

```
                              Add New Record

File  . . . . . . :   QDDSSRC                     Member . . . . . . :   SMSDA2
  Library . . . . :     SMYERS                    Source type  . . . :   DSPF

Type choices, press Enter.

  New record . . . . . . . . . . . . . . .   SMSDA2R        Name

  Type . . . . . . . . . . . . . . . . . .   RECORD         RECORD, USRDFN
                                                            SFL,    SFLMSG
                                                            WINDOW, WDWSFL




F3=Exit      F5=Refresh      F12=Cancel
```

Figure D-10 Add New Record display.

Unless entered on the previous display, a record name must be specified for the *New record* response and RECORD for *Type*. Pressing ENTER returns control back to the *Work with Display Record* screen shown in Figure D-11.

```
                         Work with Display Records

File  . . . . . . :   QDDSSRC                     Member . . . . . . :   SMSDA2
  Library . . . . :     SMYERS                    Source type  . . . :   DSPF

Type options, press Enter.
  1=Add            2=Edit comments            3=Copy          4=Delete
  7=Rename         8=Select keywords         12=Design image
```

Figure D-11 Work with Display Record with option **12** *(Design image)* selected.

```
 Opt  Order    Record          Type      Related Subfile  Date        DDS Error

 12      10    SMSDA2R         RECORD                     08/14/95




                                                                        Bottom
F3=Exit                         F12=Cancel     F14=File-level keywords
F15=File-level comments         F17=Subset     F24=More keys
```

Figure D-11 Work with Display Record with option **12** *(Design image)* selected. (Continued)

At this point in the display file's creation, the named record format may be designed ("painted") on the CRT. From the *Work with Display Record* screen, entering **12** in the *Opt* field for Option **12** *(Design image)* and pressing ENTER will display the blank Work Screen shown in Figure D-12.

```
 Work screen for record SMSDA2R: Press Help for function keys.
```

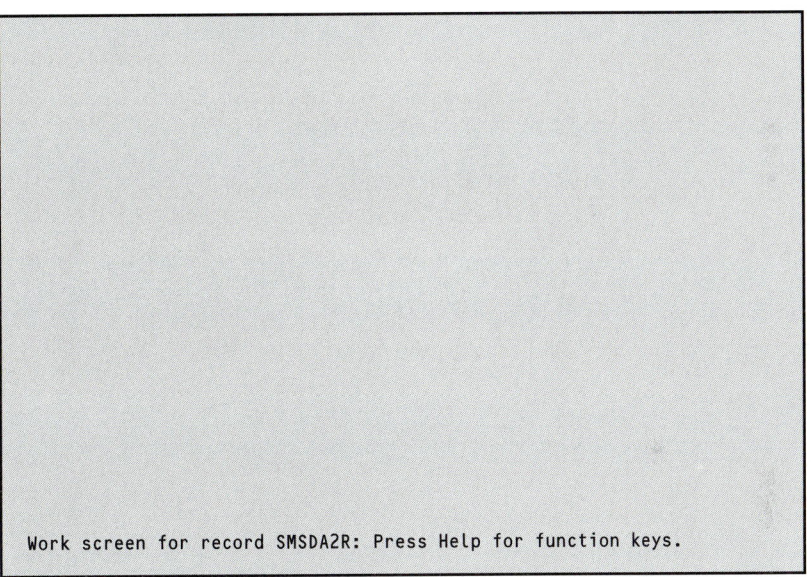

Figure D-12 Blank Work Screen.

Then, to extract the physical file's fields to be used in the display file's record format, **F10** must be pressed to access the *Select Database Files* display shown in Figure D-13. Because a database file was referenced in the *Select General Keywords* display in Figure D-5, the variables *(Database File, Library,* and *Record)* are carried over to this display.

```
                           Select Database Files

 Type options and names, press Enter.
   1=Display database field list
   2=Select all fields for input (I)
   3=Select all fields for output (O)
   4=Select all fields for both (B) input and output
```

Figure D-13 Select Database Files display with option **2** *(Select all fields for input)* specified.

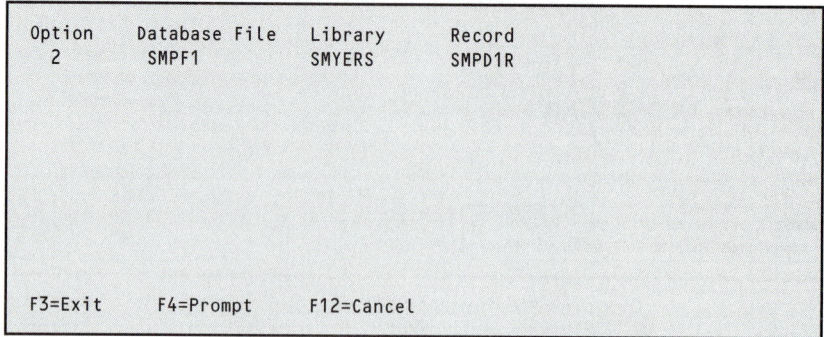

```
Option    Database File    Library      Record
  2        SMPF1            SMYERS       SMPD1R





F3=Exit     F4=Prompt       F12=Cancel
```

Figure D-13 Select Database Files display with option **2** *(Select all fields for input)* specified. (Continued)

Because the display file record is to provide the input to an **RPG IV** *add* program, option **2** was selected. If *inquiry-only* processing was required, option **3** would be specified. On the other hand, if *update* processing was supported, option **4** (both) would be required. Option **2, 3,** or **4** will access all of the fields in the related physical file. If, however, only some of the fields included in the physical file were needed, **1** would be entered as the option. After pressing ENTER, a list of the fields in the physical file's record format would display, from which the user could select only the fields needed for the display file's record format.

Pressing ENTER returns control back to the blank *Work Screen* with the physical file's fields displayed horizontally across the bottom as shown in Figure D-14. If more fields were included than could fit across the row, a + (plus sign) would appear at the right of the field list. Any other fields may be displayed by pressing the Page Down key.

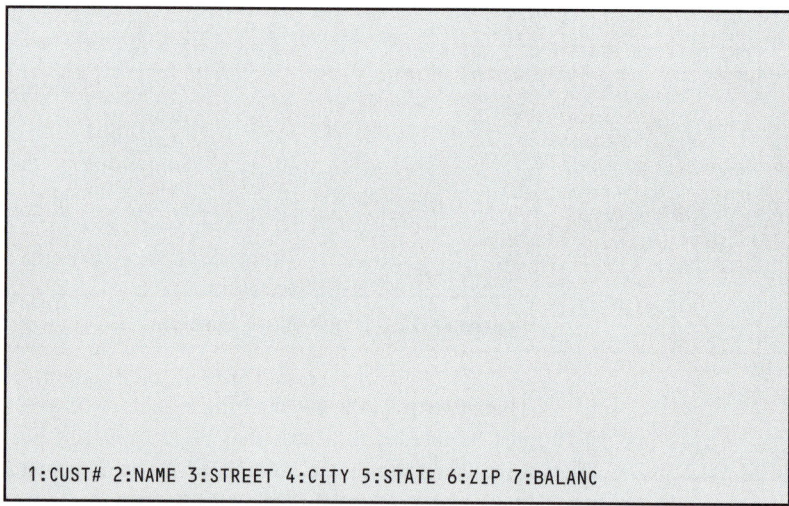

```










 1:CUST# 2:NAME 3:STREET 4:CITY 5:STATE 6:ZIP 7:BALANC
```

Figure D-14 Work Screen with database field names included.

The user begins the layout process by entering constants and variables on the screen. Because the physical file referenced in Figure D-5 provides the field names, field sizes, and field constants, the "painting" process is simplified. To illustrate the relationship between the physical file and the display file, the record format of the physical file SMPF1 is presented in Figure D-15.

```
                              Data Description Source
SEQNBR  *...+....1....+....2....+....3....+....4....+....5....+....6....+....7....+
  100         A                                          UNIQUE
  200         A          R SMPF1R
  300         A            CUST#           5A            COLHDG('CUSTOMER NO')
  400         A            NAME           20A            COLHDG('CUSTOMER NAME')
  500         A            STREET         20A            COLHDG('STREET ADDRESS')
  600         A            CITY           20A            COLHDG('CITY ADDRESS')
  700         A            STATE           2A            COLHDG('STATE ADDRESS')
  800         A            ZIP             5P 0          COLHDG('ZIP CODE')
  900         A            BALANC          8P 2          COLHDG('BALANCE')
 1000         A          K CUST#
```

Figure D-15 Physical file (SMPF1) record format.

To provide a more detailed description of the data items, each field includes a **COLHDG** *(Column Heading)* keyword. The text included in a **COLHDG** keyword is the constant for the related field. If the **COLHDG** keywords were not specified, field names would be used as the constants.

In the *Work Screen* shown in Figure D-16, all of the constant and field entries for the display file record are entered before the ENTER key is pressed. At the option of the programmer, each item may be separately entered and ENTER pressed after every entry.

```
... ... 1 ... ... 2 ... ... 3 ... ... 4 ... ... 5 ... ... 6 ... ... 7 ... ... 8
2 *DATE                          'NEW CUSTOMER ENTRY'                     *TIME
3
4
5                                &1L
6
7                                &2L
8
9                                &3L
10
11                               &4L
12
13                               &5L
14
15                               &6L
16
17                               &7L
18
19
20              'F3 - EOJ            F2 - ENTER            F5 - REFRESH'
21
22
23
 1:CUST# 2:NAME 3:STREET 4:CITY 5:STATE 6:ZIP 7:BALANC
```

Figure D-16 Work Screen with all of the constants and fields specified (before ENTER is pressed).

The following syntax is included in the *Work Screen* for building the display file's record:

1. When the *Work Screen* displays, the cursor will be positioned at row 1, column 2. Note that *row 1, column 1* is reserved by **SDA** for a Record Identification Code and cannot be used. The cursor may be moved to any position on the screen by up, down, right, or left arrow keys.
2. Pressing **F14** will access a "ruler," which displays vertical row and horizontal column numbers as shown in Figure D-16. The position of the cursor determines where the vertical row and column numbers appear. For this display, the cursor was positioned at Row 1, Column 2. The "ruler" may be disabled by pressing **F14** again.

3. A field for the system date is specified by the reserved word ***DATE** (upper- or lowercase) and the system time by ***TIME.** The format for ***DATE** is MM/DD/YY and for ***TIME** is HH:MM:SS.
4. The constant NEW CUSTOMER ENTRY is enclosed in single quotes. Constants may be entered without the quotes; however, if the entry has to be moved to another position on the screen, each word would have to be individually moved. In contrast, if a multiple-word constant is included in leading and ending quotes, it can be moved as a unit. The same restrictions apply to the deletion of constants or assignment of display attributes (underlining, reverse image, highlighting, and so forth).
5. **&1L** through **&7L** reference the fields specified at the bottom of the screen. In addition to the field size, type (numeric or character), and usage **(I, O,** or **B),** the text in the **COLHDG** keyword included in the physical file will be displayed to the left of the related field format as shown in Figure D-17.

```
... ... 1 ... ... 2 ... ... 3 ... ... 4 ... ... 5 ... ... 6 ... ... 7 ... ... 8
2 DD/DD/DD                               NEW CUSTOMER ENTRY                     TT:TT:TT
3
4
5                       CUSTOMER NO:  IIIII
6
7                     CUSTOMER NAME:  IIIIIIIIIIIIIIIIIII
8
9                    STREET ADDRESS:  IIIIIIIIIIIIIIIIIII
10
11                     CITY ADDRESS:  IIIIIIIIIIIIIIIIIII
12
13                    STATE ADDRESS:  II
14
15                         ZIP CODE:  33333-
16
17                          BALANCE:  33333333-
18
19
20                         F3 - EOJ          F2 - ENTER          F5 - REFRESH
21
22
23
24
```

Figure D-17 Work Screen display after all entries are made and the ENTER key is pressed.

If the **COLHDG** text was to be included at the right of the field format, entries **&1R** through **&7R** would be specified. On the other hand, if the **COLHDG** text was to be included over the field formats, **&1C** through **&7C** would be entered. Note that all of the items are not required to have the same format. Each field may be individually formatted.

6. The row of constants at the bottom of the screen are enclosed as a group within single quotes.

When the ENTER key is pressed, the *Work Screen* presented in Figure D-17 is redisplayed in the format shown.

Notice that the following conditions have occurred:

1. ***DATE** and ***TIME** items are displayed in an edited format.
2. Single quotes around each constant have disappeared.
3. The **COLHDG** text included in the field definitions in the physical file SMPF1 is included at the left of each variable and terminated with an **SDA**-supplied

colon. If the **COLHDG** keyword was not specified for each data item, the field names would be used as the related constant.

4. The horizontal line of the field names at the bottom of the screen has disappeared.
5. Because the fields were specified to support input in the *Select Database Files* display in Figure D-13, the character fields are identified by Is and the numeric fields by **3**s. If output was selected, **O**s would be assigned to the character fields and **6**s to the numeric. On the other hand, if both (input and output) was selected, the character fields would be identified by **B**s and the numeric by **9**s.

   Because the numeric fields were defined in the physical file as packed, a minus sign is included in the low-order position in the display of the *ZIP* and *BALANC* fields. The sign position does not increase the field size of the data stored on disk.

Moving Screen Items

Screen items (constants or variables) may be moved by the following methods.

1. The > (greater than) symbol will move an item to the right the number of columns equal to the number of > characters specified after the ENTER key is pressed.
2. The < (less than) symbol will move an item to the left the number of columns equal to the number of < characters specified after the ENTER key is pressed.
3. Typing a - (hyphen) before an item and an = (equal sign) somewhere on a used area on the screen will move the item beginning at the = location after ENTER is pressed.

When using any of the move functions, basic screen creation rules must be followed: At least one space must be included between items, and they may not overlap each other. A sign position included at the end of a numeric field is considered a character, and anything following it must include at least one leading space.

Deleting Screen Items

Any screen item previously entered may be deleted by typing an upper- or lowercase **D** before it and pressing ENTER.

Specifying Display Attributes

Display attributes for constants or variables may be assigned by entering the related attribute letter in the space preceding the item and pressing ENTER. Figure D-18 lists the letter equivalents for each display attribute.

Letter	Display Attribute
H	Highlight
R	Reverse Image
S	Column Separators (dots)
B	Blink
U	Underline (default for variables)
N	Nondisplay

Figure D-18 Display attribute letter equivalents.

Another method to assign display attributes requires that an * (asterisk) be entered in the space before a screen item. After ENTER is pressed, the *Select Field Keywords* display shown in Figure D-19 will appear. Note that the name of the field, its length, and

```
                          Select Field Keywords

Constant  . . . :   NEW CUSTOMER ENTRY
Length  . . . . :   18                     Row . . . : 2    Column . . . : 34

Type choices, press Enter.
                                     Y=Yes   For Field Type
  Display attributes . . . . . . .    Y      All except Hidden
  Colors . . . . . . . . . . . . .           All except Hidden


  General keywords . . . . . . . .           All types



  TEXT keyword . . . . . . . . . .  _____________________________________
_____

F3=Exit   F12=Cancel
```

Figure D-19 Select Field Keywords screen with display attributes option selected.

Row/Column position on the screen are included at the top of the display. To access the *Select Display Attributes* screen shown in Figure D-20, where one or more attributes may be selected, **Y** must be entered on the *Display attribute* line and ENTER pressed.

From the *Select Display Attributes* screen illustrated in Figure D-20, one or more compatible display attributes may be selected by specifying **Y** on the related line(s).

```
                        Select Display Attributes

Constant  . . . :   NEW CUSTOMER ENTRY
Length  . . . . :   18                     Row . . . : 2    Column . . . : 34

Type choices, press Enter.
                                           Keyword   Y=Yes   Indicators/+
  Field conditioning . . . . . . . . . .                     __ __ __
  Display attributes:                       DSPATR
    High intensity . . . . . . . . . . .      HI       _     __ __ __
    Reverse image  . . . . . . . . . . .      RI       _     __ __ __
    Column separators  . . . . . . . . .      CS       _     __ __ __
    Blink  . . . . . . . . . . . . . . .      BL       _     __ __ __
    Nondisplay . . . . . . . . . . . . .      ND       _     __ __ __
    Underline  . . . . . . . . . . . . .      UL       Y     __ __ __
    Position cursor  . . . . . . . . . .      PC       _     __ __ __



F3=Exit   F12=Cancel
```

Figure D-20 Select Display Attributes screen with one selection specified **(UL).**

Pressing ENTER will return control to the *Work Screen* with the attributes enabled. Additional attributes, which cannot be assigned on the *Work Screen,* such as Protect Field, Position Cursor, and Modified Tag, may be specified on the *Select Field Keywords* (General keywords line) display.

Deleting Display Attributes

Any attribute assigned to an item (constant or variable) may be deleted by typing a − (minus sign) in the space before the item, followed by the attribute letter over the first character of the item and pressing ENTER. If more than one attribute had been assigned and all were to be deleted, the same procedure would have been followed except that the letter A would have replaced the individual attribute characters.

Adding Independent Fields

Fields not included in a related database may be added to the *Work Screen* by the syntax detailed in Figure D-21. After the required format is typed and ENTER pressed, the item is displayed as shown in the *Result* column.

```
Screen
 Entry       Result              Comment

 +I(10)      IIIIIIIII     Character defined input field

 +O(12)      OOOOOOOOOOOO  Character defined output field

 +B(8)       BBBBBBBB      Character defined input/output (both)
                           field

 +3(5,0)     33333-        Numeric defined input field

 +6(6,2)     6666.66       Numeric defined output field

 +9(5,0)     99999-        Numeric defined input/output (both)
  |  |                     field
  |  └─ Field size and decimal position for numeric items
  └──── Field type (character I, O, B) and (numeric 3, 6, 9)

 Note: 3s define numeric input, 6s numeric output, and 9s numeric
       input/output (both) fields.
```

Figure D-21 Screen entries to add independent fields.

An example of adding a field, **+3(7,0),** to the current *Work Screen* is illustrated in Figure D-22.

```
... ... 1 ... ... 2 ... ... 3 ... ... 4 ... ... 5 ... ... 6 ... ... 7 ... ... 8
 2 DD/DD/DD                           NEW CUSTOMER ENTRY                  TT:TT:TT
 3
 4
 5                CUSTOMER NO:  IIIII
 6
 7              CUSTOMER NAME:  IIIIIIIIIIIIIIIIIII
 8
 9             STREET ADDRESS:  IIIIIIIIIIIIIIIIIII
10
11               CITY ADDRESS:  IIIIIIIIIIIIIIIIIII
12
13              STATE ADDRESS:  II                           Attributes of the
14                                                           added input field
15                   ZIP CODE:  33333-
16
17                    BALANCE:  33333333-     'CREDIT LIMIT:' +3(7,0) ──────┘
18
19
20                   F3 - EOJ           F2 - ENTER           F5 - REFRESH
21
22
23
```

Figure D-22 Work Screen with field addition syntax specified.

After ENTER is pressed, the *Work Screen* is redisplayed with the "added" field formatted as shown in Figure D-23.

```
... ... 1 ... ... 2 ... ... 3 ... ... 4 ... ... 5 ... ... 6 ... ... 7 ... ... 8
2 DD/DD/DD                         NEW CUSTOMER ENTRY                    TT:TT:TT
3
4
5              CUSTOMER NO:  IIIII
6
7            CUSTOMER NAME:  IIIIIIIIIIIIIIIIIII
8
9           STREET ADDRESS:  IIIIIIIIIIIIIIIIIII
10
11            CITY ADDRESS:  IIIIIIIIIIIIIIIIIII
12
13           STATE ADDRESS:  II
14                                                                Format of the
15                ZIP CODE:  33333-                               dded field
16
17                 BALANCE:  33333333-        CREDIT LIMIT:   3333333-
18
19
20                 F3 - EOJ            F2 - ENTER          F5 - REFRESH
21
22          SDA supplied
23          field name
 1:FLD001
```

Figure D-23 Work Screen after add field is entered and the ENTER key pressed.

Note that an **SDA**-supplied field name, FLD001, is included at the lower left corner of the screen. Additional user-defined "add" fields would be assigned FLD002, FLD003, and so forth.

Default field names may be changed by placing the cursor in the space preceding the field. Pressing **F4** will display the *Work with Fields* screen. To access the field name to be changed, press the Roll Up key until the field name to be changed is found. Figure D-24 illustrates the *Work with Fields* display *after* field FLD001 has been changed to LIMIT.

```
                               Work with Fields

Record . . . :   SMSDA2R

Type information, press Enter.
  Number of fields to roll . . . . . . . . . . . . . . . . .    6

Type options, change values, press Enter.
  1=Select keywords    4=Delete field

Option    Order   Field       Type Use  Length  Row/Col  Ref Condition  Overlap
 _         190    CREDIT LIM   C           13    17 050
 _         200    LIMIT             I     7,0    17 066

 Field name changed
 from FLD001 to LIMIT
 by programmer
                                                                   Bottom
 Add                                H            Hidden
 Add                                M            Message
 Add                                P            Program-to-system

F3=Exit   F6=Sort by row/column   F12=Cancel
```

Figure D-24 Work with Fields display after a default "add" field name (FLD001) is changed to LIMIT.

Specifying Error Messages

Error messages may be specified for field items by placing an asterisk in the space before the field. Pressing ENTER will display the *Select Field Keywords* display shown in Figure D-25.

```
                              Select Field Keywords

 Field . . . . . :   CUST#                   Usage . . :  I
 Length  . . . . :   5                       Row . . . :  5    Column . . . :  33

 Type choices, press Enter.
                                       Y=Yes   For Field Type
   Display attributes  . . . . . . .           All except Hidden
   Colors  . . . . . . . . . . . . .     _     All except Hidden
   Keying options  . . . . . . . . .     _     Input or Both
   Validity check  . . . . . . . . .     _     Input or Both, not float
   Input keywords  . . . . . . . . .     _     Input or Both
   General keywords  . . . . . . . .     _     All types

   Database reference  . . . . . . .     _     Hidden, Input, Output, Both
   Error messages  . . . . . . . . .     Y     Input, Output, Both


   TEXT keyword  . . . . . . . . . .   CUSTOMER NO______________________

 F3=Exit   F12=Cancel
```

Figure D-25 Select Field Keywords display after **Y** is entered for Error messages choice.

Typing a **Y** on the *Error messages* line and pressing ENTER will display the *Define Error Messages* screen presented in Figure D-26. For this example, an error mes-

```
                              Define Error Messages

 Field . . . . . :   CUST#                   Usage . . :  I
 Length  . . . . :   5                       Row . . . :  5    Column . . . :  33

 Type parameters, press Enter.

   Indicators/+      ERRMSG - Message Text                        More   Ind
   99 ___ ___        DUPLICATE KEY                                _____   99



                                                                     Bottom

   Indicators/+      ERRMSGID  File          Library    Ind    Name



                                                                     Bottom
 F3=Exit   F12=Cancel
```

Figure D-26 Define Error Messages display after entries are specified.

sage is assigned to the CUST# field. Indicator **99** is entered for the *Indicator/+* response; the message **DUPLICATE KEY** for the *ERRMSG—Message Text* entry; and **99** for the *Ind* column entry.

The *Indicator/+* **99** entry is assigned at the option of the programmer. Because the database file was defined as supporting only **UNIQUE** keys (refer to Figure D-15), any attempt to add a record with CUST# key value already stored in the file will cause a processing error. To control this, the **WRITE** statement in the related **RPG IV** program must include **99** in columns 73 and 74 of the calculation instruction. When a duplicate key is tested, **99** will be set on by the program and cause the error message **DUPLICATE KEY** to display on line 24 of the screen. The **99** entry for the *Ind* column entry will set the indicator off after the **Reset** key is pressed. Pressing ENTER *twice* will return control to the *Work Screen.*

Changing a Field's Keying Options

When a numeric field is stored as packed and is subsequently referenced in a display file, a sign position will be included after the last digit. Under some conditions, this may be confusing to the user. In the example presented here, *ZIP* (zip code) was defined as packed in the physical file and when displayed will include a sign position in the low-order position as shown previously in Figure D-17.

The sign position may be deleted on the displayed field by entering an asterisk in the space preceding the *ZIP* field and pressing ENTER. The *Select Field Keywords* screen will display and the *Keying options* selection made by entering a **Y** on the related line as shown in Figure D-27.

```
                          Select Field Keywords

Field . . . . . :   ZIP                     Usage . . :  I
Length  . . . . :   5,0                     Row . . . :  15    Column . . . :  33

Type choices, press Enter.
                                  Y=Yes    For Field Type
  Display attributes  . . . . . .   _      All except Hidden
  Colors  . . . . . . . . . . . .   _      All except Hidden
  Keying options  . . . . . . . .   Y      Input or Both
  Validity check  . . . . . . . .   _      Input or Both, not float
  Input keywords  . . . . . . . .   _      Input or Both
  General keywords  . . . . . . .   _      All types

  Database reference  . . . . . .   _      Hidden, Input, Output, Both
  Error messages  . . . . . . . .   _      Input, Output, Both


  TEXT keyword  . . . . . . . . .   ZIP CODE ____________________


F3=Exit    F12=Cancel
```

Figure D-27 Select Field Keywords display after option is entered.

Pressing ENTER again displays the *Select Keying Options* screen shown in Figure D-28. Entering a **Y** for the *Keyboard shift* attribute response and pressing ENTER will delete the sign position in the *ZIP* field and return control back to the *Work Screen.*

```
                          Select Keying Options

Field . . . . . :   ZIP                     Usage . . :  I
Length  . . . . :   5,0                     Row . . . :  15    Column . . . :  33

Type choices, press Enter.

                                          Keyword  Y=Yes  Indicators/+
  Keying options:                          CHECK
    Mandatory entry . . . . . . . . . .     ME      _     ___ ___ ___
    Automatic record advance  . . . . .     ER      _     ___ ___ ___
```

Figure D-28 Select Keying Options display after **Y** is entered.

```
    Mandatory fill . . . . . . . . . . . .    MF      _    ___ ___ ___
    Field exit key required . . . . . . .     FE      _    ___ ___ ___
    Right adjust blank fill . . . . . . .     RB      _    ___ ___ ___
    Right adjust zero fill  . . . . . . .     RZ      _    ___ ___ ___


  Keyboard shift attribute  . . . . . . .           Y      S N Y I D
                             Y deletes low-order minus
                             sign position in field                       _
 F3=Exit    F12=Cancel
```

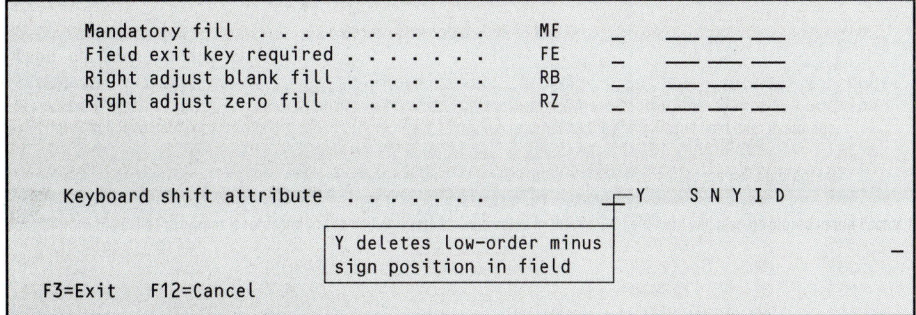

Figure D-28 Select Keying Options display after **Y** is entered. (Continued)

Saving and Compiling a Display File

To save the DDS source code, press **F3** until the *Exit SDA Work Screen* shown in Figure D-29 displays.

```
                              Exit SDA Work Screen

 Select one of the following:

     1. Save work since last Enter and exit work screen
     2. Exit without saving any work done on the work screen
     3. Resume work screen session


 Selection
     1

 F12=Cancel
```

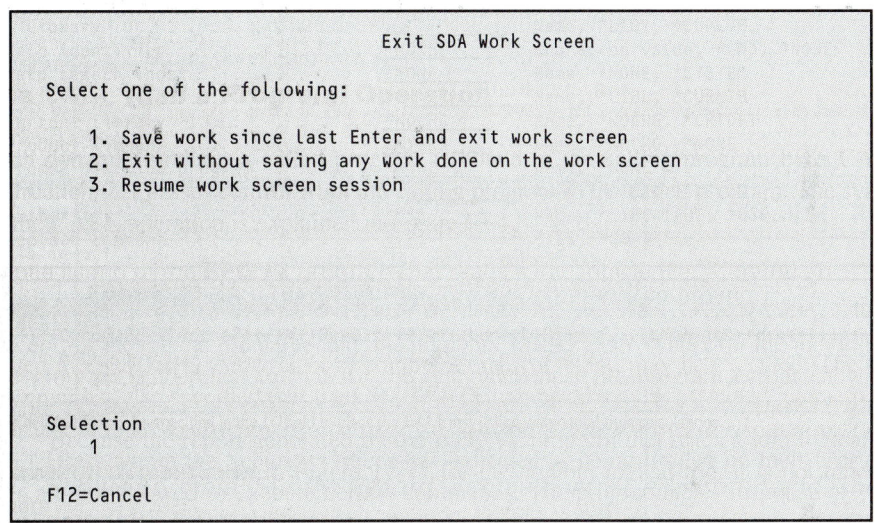

Figure D-29 Exit SDA Work Screen with selection **1** specified.

Selecting **1** and pressing ENTER will display the *Save DDS—Create Display File* screen shown in Figure D-30.

```
                         Save DDS - Create Display File

 Type choices, press Enter.

   Save DDS source . . . . . . . . . . . .   Y             Y=Yes
     Source file . . . . . . . . . . . . .   QDDSSRC       F4 for list
       Library . . . . . . . . . . . . . .   SMYERS        Name, *LIBL ...
     Member . . . . . . . . . . . . . . . .  SMSDA2        F4 for list
     Text . . . . . . . . . . . . . . . . .  sda example

   Create display file . . . . . . . . . .   Y             Y=Yes
     Prompt for parameters . . . . . . . .                 Y=Yes
     Display file . . . . . . . . . . . . .  SMSDA2        F4 for list
       Library . . . . . . . . . . . . . .   SMYERS        Name, *CURLIB
     Replace existing file . . . . . . . .                 Y=Yes
```

Figure D-30 Save DDS—Create Display file screen.

```
   Submit create job in batch . . . . . . .  Y            Y=Yes

   Specify additional
     save or create options . . . . . . . .  _            Y=Yes

 F3=Exit   F4=Prompt   F12=Cancel
```

Figure D-30 Save DDS—Create Display file screen. (Continued)

After the defaults are taken or changes made, pressing ENTER twice will save, compile, and create an object (if there are no terminal errors). A listing that may be reviewed and/or printed will be generated in the user's print queue.

Every feature of **SDA** has not been introduced (e.g., menus and subfiles) in this appendix. For a comprehensive discussion of **SDA,** refer to the newest release of IBM's *AS/400 SDA* manual.

Testing a Display File's Record Format

After the display file has been successfully compiled, any record format included may be tested by the *Test display files* option **(3)** on the AS/400 *Screen Design Aid* **(SDA)** display shown in Figure D-31.

```
                         AS/400 Screen Design Aid (SDA)

 Select one of the following:

      1. Design screens
      2. Design menus
      3. Test display files

 Selection or command
 ===> 3

 F1=Help   F3=Exit   F4=Prompt   F9=Retrieve   F12=Cancel
                                    (C) COPYRIGHT IBM CORP. 1981, 1992.
```

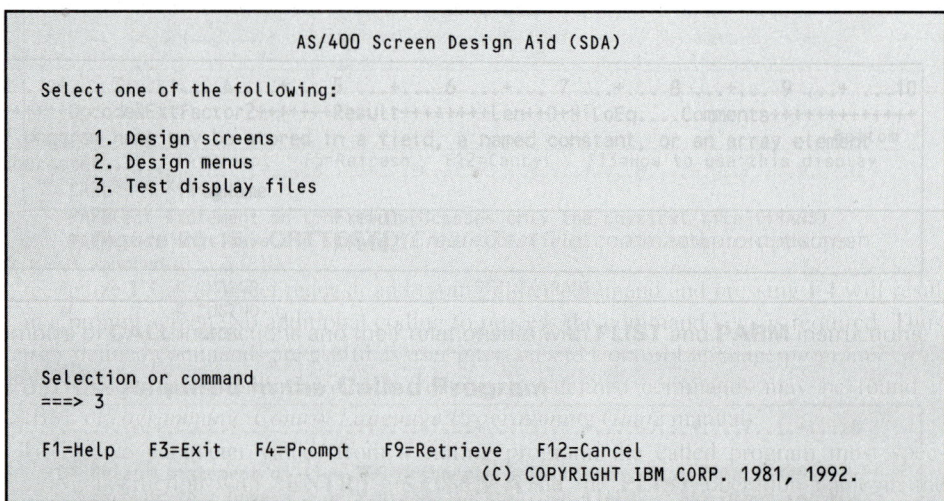

Figure D-31 AS/400 Screen Design Aid **(SDA)** display with option **3** selected.

The *Test display files* option supports the following functions:

1. Tests record formats in the display file to observe how they appear on the screen
2. Tests any data validation checks of input fields
3. Displays the values in the input buffer that pass data and indicator status
4. Displays the values in the output buffer and the status (ON or OFF) of the indicator(s).

To advance to the next display, press ENTER. The *Test Display File* screen shown in Figure D-32 will display where the user must respond to the prompts: *Display File,*

```
                              Test Display File

 Type choices, press Enter.

   Display file . . . . . . . . . . . . .   SMSDA2       Name, F4 for list
     Library  . . . . . . . . . . . . . .   SMYERS       Name,
                                                         *LIBL ...
   Record to be tested  . . . . . . . . .   SMSDA2R      Name,
                                                         F4 for list
   Additional records to display  . . . .   ________     Name




 F3=Exit     F4=Prompt      F12=Cancel
```

Figure D-32 Test Display File screen with required entries.

Library, and *Record to be tested.* An entry (or entries) may be made for the *Additional records to display* prompt if the display file includes more than one record and additional formats are to be tested.

If the name of the display file record format to be tested is not known, a list of the record name(s) may be displayed by pressing **F4.**

Pressing ENTER will display the *Set Test Output Data* screen shown in Figure D-33. Because the display file's record format was defined to process *input* only (from the display file to the **RPG IV** program), no fields are included in the *output* buffer. The ***IN99** *Field* entry identifies the conditioning indicator **(99)** specified with the **ERRMSG** keyword in the display file. Note that the status of the **99** indicator is passed from the **RPG IV** program (included with the **WRITE** instruction to test for duplicate records) to the display file. Consequently, it is automatically specified as output. The **0** entry under the *Value* column indicates that the **99** indicator is OFF. If *Output* and/or *Both* fields were defined, the related field name(s) and their display format would be included in the *Set Test Output Data* display.

```
                             Set Test Output Data

 Record . . . :    SMSDA2R

 Type indicators and output field values, press Enter.

 Field          Value
 *IN99          0:




                                                                      Bottom

 F3=Exit    F12=Cancel
```

Figure D-33 Set Test Output Data display.

```
8/14/95                    NEW CUSTOMER ENTRY                  9:53:00

            CUSTOMER NO:  98765

          CUSTOMER NAME:  MICKEY THE MOOSE

         STREET ADDRESS:  1 DEER LANE

           CITY ADDRESS:  YELLOWSTONE

          STATE ADDRESS:  WY

               ZIP CODE:  19901

                BALANCE:    250000         CREDIT LIMIT:      3000

              F3 - EOJ           F2 - ENTER          F5 - REFRESH
```

Figure D-34 Work screen after data is entered.

Pressing ENTER will display the *Work screen* shown in Figure D-34.

After the test data is entered, as shown in Figure D-34, and **F2** is pressed, the *Display Test Input Data* screen shown in Figure D-35 will appear.

```
                        Display Test Input Data

Record . . . :    SMSDA2R

View indicators and input field values.

Field          Value
*IN03          0:
*IN02          1:
*IN05          0:
*IN99          0:
CUST#          98765:
NAME           MICKEY THE MOOSE          :
STREET         1 DEER LANE               :
CITY           YELLOWSTONE               :
STATE          WY:
ZIP            19901:
BALANC         00250000:
LIMIT          0003000:
                                                          Bottom
Press Enter to continue

F3=Exit   F12=Cancel    F14=Display input buffer
```

Figure D-35 Display Test Input Data screen.

Examine Figure D-35 and note the following:

1. The status (**0** for OFF and **1** for ON) of the indicators defined in the record format is included. Because **F2** was pressed, the related ***IN02** indicator is **1** (ON) and indicators ***IN03** and ***IN05** are **0** (OFF).
2. The field values entered are included. Note that the **:** (colon) at the end of each field is a delimiter indicating its size.

When the test is completed, pressing **F3** several times will exit **SDA.**

appendix e

Program Debugging

Programming errors may be classified into two types: *compile-time* errors and *execution* (or *run-time)* errors. The debugging methods for each type will be discussed in the following sections.

COMPILE-TIME ERRORS

Compile-time errors are syntax errors that fall into one of the following broad categories:

1. Incorrect syntax, such as placing an entry in the wrong field
2. Undefined and referenced fields
3. Specifying a field in calculations, or as edited output, that was not defined as numeric
4. Undefined and unreferenced indicators
5. Specifying total-time before detail-time calculations and/or output.

Note that some of the syntax errors will be "flagged" by **SEU** when the source instructions are entered. For example, if an indicator is omitted in the *Eq* field in a **READ** instruction or if a closing quote is omitted in a constant in an output instruction, **SEU** will reverse image the line and force the programmer to make the necessary correction(s).

Severity errors generated during compilation of an **RPG IV** program are classified as **Information (00), Warning (10), Error (20),** or **Severe Error (30+).** A severity error of **20** or above will prevent compilation of an **RPG IV** program.

Furthermore, any syntax error may generate more than one severity error. For example, if field ABC is defined (name, size, and type), but specified as BAC, two compile errors would be generated. Field ABC will be identified as an *unreferenced* field (**Warning** error) and BAC as an *undefined* field, causing a **Severe Error.**

A compile listing of an **RPG IV** program that has 15 syntax errors (7 **Information,** 0 **Warning,** 1 **Error,** and 7 **Severe Errors**) is detailed in Figure E-1.

```
5763RG1 V3R1M0  940909 RN        IBM ILE RPG/400          STAN/CH5R1ERR          S1012CFA   12/05/97 15:27:34        Page      1
 Command . . . . . . . . . . . . :   CRTBNDRPG
   Issued by . . . . . . . . . . :     SMYERS
 Program . . . . . . . . . . . . :   CH5R1ERR
   Library . . . . . . . . . . . :     STAN
 Text 'description' . . . . . . . :   *SRCMBRTXT
```

Figure E-1 Compile listing of an **RPG IV** program with syntax errors.

```
Source Member . . . . . . . . . . :  CH5R1ERR
Source File . . . . . . . . . . . :  QRPGLESRC
  Library . . . . . . . . . . . . :    STAN
  CCSID . . . . . . . . . . . . . :    65535
Text 'description' . . . . . . . :  CH5R1 - Soup brands report with errors
Last Change . . . . . . . . . . . :  12/05/97  15:23:01
Generation severity level . . . . :  10
Default activation group . . . . :  *YES
Compiler options . . . . . . . . :  *XREF      *GEN       *NOSECLVL  *SHOWCPY
                                     *EXPDDS    *EXT       *NOEVENT
Debugging views . . . . . . . . . :  *STMT
Output . . . . . . . . . . . . . :  *PRINT
Optimization level . . . . . . . :  *NONE
Source listing indentation . . . :  *NONE
Type conversion options . . . . . :  *NONE
Sort sequence . . . . . . . . . . :  *HEX
Language identifier . . . . . . . :  *JOBRUN
Replace program . . . . . . . . . :  *NO
User profile . . . . . . . . . . :  *USER
Authority . . . . . . . . . . . . :  *LIBCRTAUT
Truncate numeric . . . . . . . . :  *YES
Fix numeric . . . . . . . . . . . :  *NONE
Target release . . . . . . . . . :  V3R1M0
Allow null values . . . . . . . . :  *NO

5763RG1 V3R1M0  940909 RN        IBM ILE RPG/400         STAN/CH5R1ERR              S1012CFA    12/05/97 15:27:34          Page      2
Line   <--------------------- Source Specifications ----------------------------><---- Comments ----> Do  Page  Change Src Seq
Number ....1....+....2....+....3....+....4....+....5....+....6....+....7....+....8....+....9....+...10 Num Line  Date   Id Number
                         S o u r c e   L i s t i n g
     1 FSoupmstr  IF   E             DISK                                                             960214      000100
       *--------------------------------------------------------------------------------------------*
       *                             RPG name          External name                                 *
       * File name. . . . . . . . :  SOUPMSTR          STAN/SOUPMSTR                                 *
       * Record format(s) . . . . :  SOUPR             SOUPR                                         *
       *--------------------------------------------------------------------------------------------*
     2 FQsysprt   O    F  132        PRINTER                                                          960214      000200
     3                                                                                                960214      000300
     4  * Define work fields....                                                                      960214      000400
RNF2318 00      2 000200  Overflow indicator OA is assigned to PRINTER file QSYSPRT. — Informational error
     5 DCaseProfit        S              4  2                                                         960214      000500
     6 DDecimalPct        S              5  5                                                         960214      000600
     7 DPrintPct          S              5  3                                                         960214      000700
     8 DTotlAvgPct        S              6  3                                                         960214      000800
     9 DRecords           S              4  0                                                         960214      000900
    10 DAveragePct        S              5  3                                                         960214      001000
    11                                                                                                960214      001100
    12  * Begin calculations....                                                                      960214      001200
    13=ISOUPR                                                                                                     1000001
       *--------------------------------------------------------------------------------------------*  1
       * RPG record format . . . . :  SOUPR                                                          *  1
       * External format . . . . . :  SOUPR : STAN/SOUPMSTR                                          *  1
       *--------------------------------------------------------------------------------------------*  1
    14=I                             A    1   20  SOUPBRAND                                                       1000002
    15=I                             P   21   23 2SPPERCASE                                                       1000003
    16=I                             P   24   26 2CSTPERCASE                                                      1000004
    17 C                   EXCEPT    Heading                                   print heading lines        961205      001300
    18                                                                                                960214      001400
    19 C                   READ      Soupmstr                           ----80 read first record          961205      001500
    20 C                   DOW       *INLR = *OFF                              dow while LR is off    B01  960214      001600
    21 C                   EVAL      CasProfit = SpPerCase - CstPerCase                               01  961205      001700
    22 C                   EVAL      DecimalPct = CaseProfit / CstPerCase      decimal percent        01  960214      001800
    23 C                   EVAL      PrintPct = DecimalPct * 100               Printable Percent      01  960214      001900
    24 C                   EXCEPT    Detailine                                 print detail line      01  960214      002000
    25 C                   EVAL      TotlAvgPct = TotlAvgPct + PrintPct        Total Avg Percent      01  960214      002100
    26 C                   EVAL      Records = Records + 1                     no of records read     01  960214      002200
    27 C                   READ      Soupmstr                           ----80 read another record    01  961205      002300
    28 C                   ENDDO                                               end dow group          E01  960214      002400
    29                                                                                                960214      002500
    30 C                   EVAL(H)   AveragePct = TotlAvgPct / Records         total average pct          960214      002600
    31 C                   EXCEPT    Totaline                                  print total line           960214      002700
```

Figure E-1 Compile listing of an **RPG IV** program with syntax errors. (Continued)

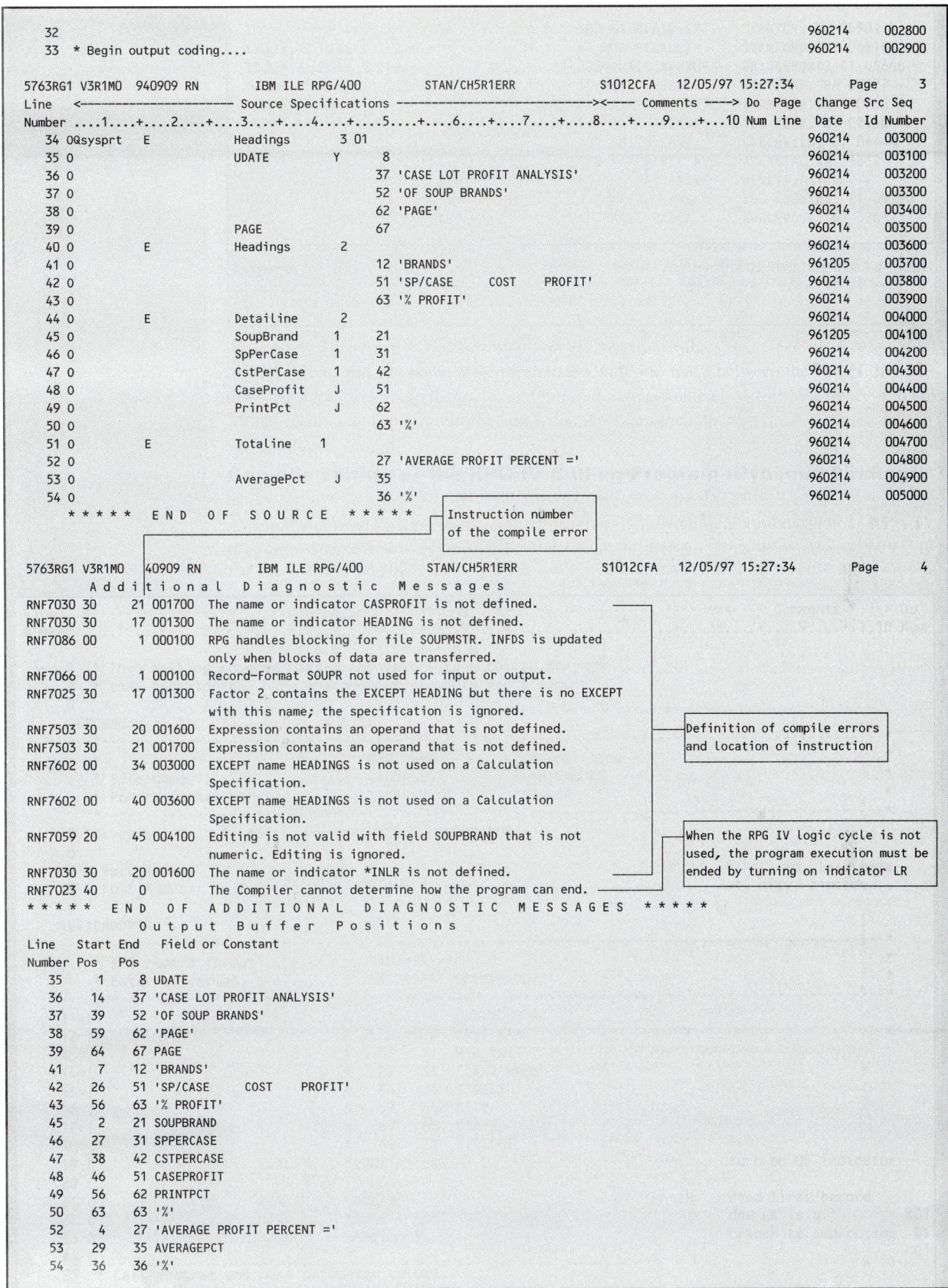

```
    32                                                                                    960214    002800
    33  * Begin output coding....                                                         960214    002900

5763RG1 V3R1M0  940909 RN       IBM ILE RPG/400         STAN/CH5R1ERR        S1012CFA   12/05/97 15:27:34      Page     3
Line   <---------------------- Source Specifications ----------------------------><---- Comments ----> Do  Page  Change Src Seq
Number ....1....+....2....+....3....+....4....+....5....+....6....+....7....+....8....+....9....+...10 Num Line  Date   Id Number
    34 OQsysprt   E           Headings       3 01                                         960214    003000
    35 O                      UDATE          Y     8                                      960214    003100
    36 O                                          37 'CASE LOT PROFIT ANALYSIS'           960214    003200
    37 O                                          52 'OF SOUP BRANDS'                     960214    003300
    38 O                                          62 'PAGE'                               960214    003400
    39 O                      PAGE                67                                      960214    003500
    40 O          E           Headings       2                                            960214    003600
    41 O                                          12 'BRANDS'                             961205    003700
    42 O                                          51 'SP/CASE      COST     PROFIT'       960214    003800
    43 O                                          63 '% PROFIT'                           960214    003900
    44 O          E           Detailine      2                                            960214    004000
    45 O                      SoupBrand      1    21                                      961205    004100
    46 O                      SpPerCase      1    31                                      960214    004200
    47 O                      CstPerCase     1    42                                      960214    004300
    48 O                      CaseProfit     J    51                                      960214    004400
    49 O                      PrintPct       J    62                                      960214    004500
    50 O                                          63 '%'                                  960214    004600
    51 O          E           Totaline     1                                              960214    004700
    52 O                                          27 'AVERAGE PROFIT PERCENT ='           960214    004800
    53 O                      AveragePct     J    35                                      960214    004900
    54 O                                          36 '%'                                  960214    005000
      * * * * *   E N D   O F   S O U R C E   * * * * *

5763RG1 V3R1M0  940909 RN       IBM ILE RPG/400         STAN/CH5R1ERR        S1012CFA   12/05/97 15:27:34      Page     4
          A d d i t i o n a l   D i a g n o s t i c   M e s s a g e s
RNF7030 30      21 001700  The name or indicator CASPROFIT is not defined.
RNF7030 30      17 001300  The name or indicator HEADING is not defined.
RNF7086 00       1 000100  RPG handles blocking for file SOUPMSTR. INFDS is updated
                           only when blocks of data are transferred.
RNF7066 00       1 000100  Record-Format SOUPR not used for input or output.
RNF7025 30      17 001300  Factor 2 contains the EXCEPT HEADING but there is no EXCEPT
                           with this name; the specification is ignored.
RNF7503 30      20 001600  Expression contains an operand that is not defined.
RNF7503 30      21 001700  Expression contains an operand that is not defined.
RNF7602 00      34 003000  EXCEPT name HEADINGS is not used on a Calculation
                           Specification.
RNF7602 00      40 003600  EXCEPT name HEADINGS is not used on a Calculation
                           Specification.
RNF7059 20      45 004100  Editing is not valid with field SOUPBRAND that is not
                           numeric. Editing is ignored.
RNF7030 30      20 001600  The name or indicator *INLR is not defined.
RNF7023 40       0         The Compiler cannot determine how the program can end.
* * * * *   E N D   O F   A D D I T I O N A L   D I A G N O S T I C   M E S S A G E S   * * * * *
                O u t p u t   B u f f e r   P o s i t i o n s
Line    Start End    Field or Constant
Number  Pos    Pos
    35      1    8 UDATE
    36     14   37 'CASE LOT PROFIT ANALYSIS'
    37     39   52 'OF SOUP BRANDS'
    38     59   62 'PAGE'
    39     64   67 PAGE
    41      7   12 'BRANDS'
    42     26   51 'SP/CASE      COST     PROFIT'
    43     56   63 '% PROFIT'
    45      2   21 SOUPBRAND
    46     27   31 SPPERCASE
    47     38   42 CSTPERCASE
    48     46   51 CASEPROFIT
    49     56   62 PRINTPCT
    50     63   63 '%'
    52      4   27 'AVERAGE PROFIT PERCENT ='
    53     29   35 AVERAGEPCT
    54     36   36 '%'
```

Instruction number of the compile error

Definition of compile errors and location of instruction

When the RPG IV logic cycle is not used, the program execution must be ended by turning on indicator LR

Figure E-1 Compile listing of an **RPG IV** program with syntax errors. (Continued)

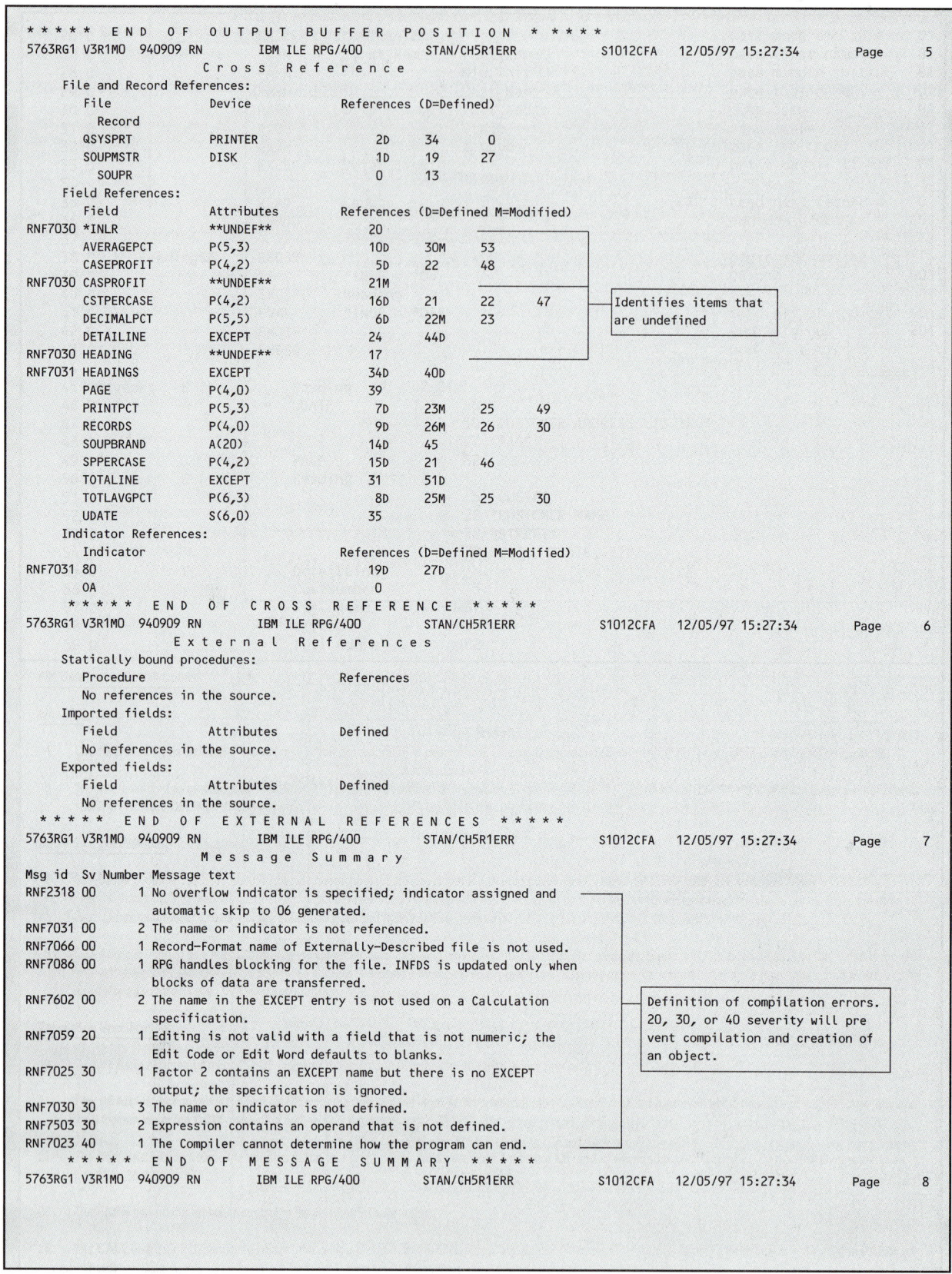

```
* * * * *   E N D   O F   O U T P U T   B U F F E R   P O S I T I O N   * * * * *
5763RG1 V3R1M0  940909 RN        IBM ILE RPG/400         STAN/CH5R1ERR          S1012CFA   12/05/97 15:27:34       Page     5
                                 C r o s s   R e f e r e n c e
     File and Record References:
        File                Device              References (D=Defined)
          Record
        QSYSPRT             PRINTER                  2D       34       0
        SOUPMSTR            DISK                     1D       19      27
          SOUPR                                      0        13
     Field References:
        Field               Attributes          References (D=Defined M=Modified)
RNF7030 *INLR               **UNDEF**               20
        AVERAGEPCT          P(5,3)                  10D      30M      53
        CASEPROFIT          P(4,2)                   5D      22       48
RNF7030 CASPROFIT           **UNDEF**               21M
        CSTPERCASE          P(4,2)                  16D      21       22       47     Identifies items that
        DECIMALPCT          P(5,5)                   6D      22M      23              are undefined
        DETAILINE           EXCEPT                  24       44D
RNF7030 HEADING             **UNDEF**               17
RNF7031 HEADINGS            EXCEPT                  34D      40D
        PAGE                P(4,0)                  39
        PRINTPCT            P(5,3)                   7D      23M      25       49
        RECORDS             P(4,0)                   9D      26M      26       30
        SOUPBRAND           A(20)                   14D      45
        SPPERCASE           P(4,2)                  15D      21       46
        TOTALINE            EXCEPT                  31       51D
        TOTLAVGPCT          P(6,3)                   8D      25M      25       30
        UDATE               S(6,0)                  35
     Indicator References:
        Indicator                               References (D=Defined M=Modified)
RNF7031 80                                          19D      27D
        OA                                           0
     * * * * *   E N D   O F   C R O S S   R E F E R E N C E   * * * * *
5763RG1 V3R1M0  940909 RN        IBM ILE RPG/400         STAN/CH5R1ERR          S1012CFA   12/05/97 15:27:34       Page     6
                              E x t e r n a l   R e f e r e n c e s
     Statically bound procedures:
        Procedure                               References
        No references in the source.
     Imported fields:
        Field               Attributes          Defined
        No references in the source.
     Exported fields:
        Field               Attributes          Defined
        No references in the source.
  * * * * *   E N D   O F   E X T E R N A L   R E F E R E N C E S   * * * * *
5763RG1 V3R1M0  940909 RN        IBM ILE RPG/400         STAN/CH5R1ERR          S1012CFA   12/05/97 15:27:34       Page     7
                                 M e s s a g e   S u m m a r y
Msg id  Sv Number Message text
RNF2318 00      1 No overflow indicator is specified; indicator assigned and
                  automatic skip to 06 generated.
RNF7031 00      2 The name or indicator is not referenced.
RNF7066 00      1 Record-Format name of Externally-Described file is not used.
RNF7086 00      1 RPG handles blocking for the file. INFDS is updated only when
                  blocks of data are transferred.
RNF7602 00      2 The name in the EXCEPT entry is not used on a Calculation        Definition of compilation errors.
                  specification.                                                   20, 30, or 40 severity will pre
RNF7059 20      1 Editing is not valid with a field that is not numeric; the       vent compilation and creation of
                  Edit Code or Edit Word defaults to blanks.                       an object.
RNF7025 30      1 Factor 2 contains an EXCEPT name but there is no EXCEPT
                  output; the specification is ignored.
RNF7030 30      3 The name or indicator is not defined.
RNF7503 30      2 Expression contains an operand that is not defined.
RNF7023 40      1 The Compiler cannot determine how the program can end.
     * * * * *   E N D   O F   M E S S A G E   S U M M A R Y   * * * * *
5763RG1 V3R1M0  940909 RN        IBM ILE RPG/400         STAN/CH5R1ERR          S1012CFA   12/05/97 15:27:34       Page     8
```

Figure E-1 Compile listing of an **RPG IV** program with syntax errors. (Continued)

```
                    F i n a l   S u m m a r y
 Message Totals:
   Information  (00) . . . . . . . :         7 ─┐
   Warning      (10) . . . . . . . :         0  │      ┌─────────────────────────────┐
   Error        (20) . . . . . . . :         1  ├──────┤Specifies number of errors at│
   Severe Error (30+)  . . . . . . :         7 ─┘      │the related severity level   │
   ------------------------------------   -------      └─────────────────────────────┘
   Total . . . . . . . . . . . . . :        15
 Source Totals:
   Records . . . . . . . . . . . . :        54
   Specifications  . . . . . . . . :        46
   Data records  . . . . . . . . . :         0
   Comments  . . . . . . . . . . . :         3
        * * * * *   E N D   O F   F I N A L   S U M M A R Y   * * * * *
Compilation stopped. Severity 40 errors found in program.
        * * * * *   E N D   O F   C O M P I L A T I O N * * * * *
```

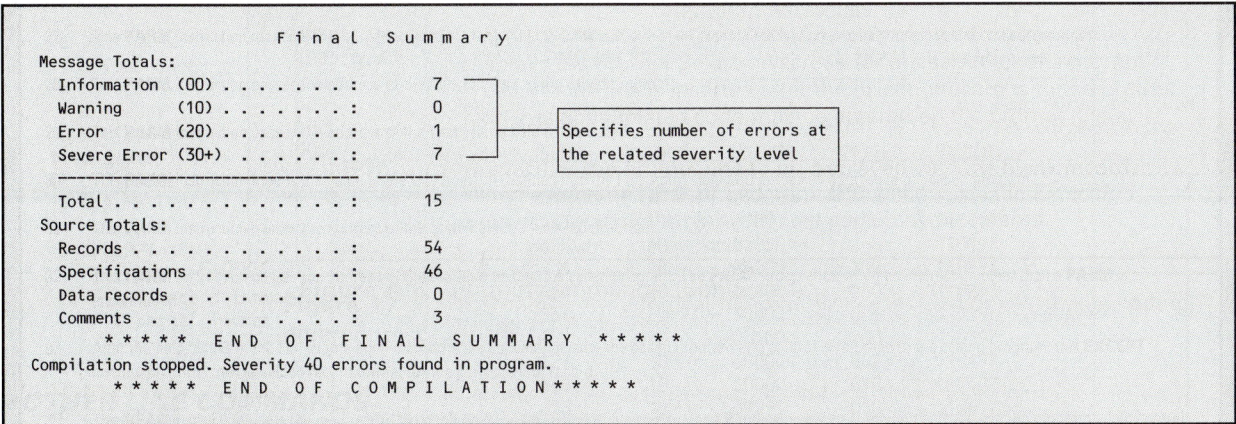

Figure E-1 Compile listing of an **RPG IV** program with syntax errors. (Continued)

Often, the correction of one syntax error will eliminate more than one error. Several **Information (00)** errors may be included in a compilation. Sometimes they are impossible to eliminate (e.g., Record-format name of externally described file is not used) and may usually be ignored. However, *all* compile errors should be reviewed by the programmer.

After a programmer learns the syntax of the **RPG IV** language, compile-time errors are relatively easy to locate and correct.

RUN-TIME ERRORS

Run-time errors, which cause halts or abends (abnormal ends) during execution of a compiled program, are usually logic or data errors that are more difficult to find. Some errors included in this category are the following:

1. Divide by zero
2. Conditioning of an instruction with the wrong indicator
3. Decimal data error
4. Neverending (perpetual) loop
5. Unconditional branch
6. Unidentified record type
7. Array index error
8. Incorrect output results.

Some run-time errors may be difficult, if not impossible, to locate by standard procedures such as checking the program's syntax, studying the logic, and so forth.

Including an informational data structure or a program-status data structure, both discussed in Chapter 8, in an **RPG IV** program may help to locate and interpret run-time errors.

PROGRAM DUMP

Often, when a run-time error occurs, the system operator will receive a message similar to the message shown in Figure E-2, which enables him or her to produce a *program dump*. The operator options provided are **C, G, D,** and **F,** indicating the following actions:

C cancel the program
G continue the program at the RPG cycle's GETIN phase
D produce a formatted program dump
F produce a full formatted program dump.

```
                         Display Program Messages
Job 013459/SMYERS/DSP03 started on 12/08/96 at 22:40:17 in subsystem QCTL in
Decimal-data error in field (C G D F).


Type reply, press Enter.
  Reply . . . D ______________________________________________________

F3=Exit   F12=Cancel
```

Figure E-2 Run-time program error message display providing dump actions.

A program dump may be very useful in the run-time debugging process. If a **D** or **F** option is selected, the dump listing may be found with the **WRKOUTQ QEZDEBUG** command. As with any *Work with Output Queue* display, option **5** will display the listing and **2** will provide for changes to print the listing.

In lieu of a system-supplied program dump, the **RPG IV DUMP** operation may be included in the program at a select location. This may help to debug a specific routine or sequence of instructions.

In order for the program dump to be complete, it is important that the **DBG VIEW(*NONE)** option is *not* selected when the **RPG IV** source program is compiled with either the **CRTRPGMOD** *(Create RPG module)* or **CRTBNDRPG** *(Create Bound RPG)* command.

Areas of a Program Dump

The two main areas of a program dump include the *Program Status Area* and the *INFDS FILE FEEDBACK AREA*. The parts that help in the debugging process are explained and coordinated by letter references in the formatted program dump (option D) listing in Figure E-3.

```
Program Status Area:                                                      Page    1
Procedure Name . . . . . . . .
Program Name . . . . . . . . . . . . :  CUSTADDRES ──── A) Check to ensure this is the correct program
  Library . . . . . . . . . . . . . . :  STAN
Module Name. . . . . . . . . . . . . :  CUSTADDRES
Program Status . . . . . . . . . . . :  00907
          Decimal-data error in field (C G D F). ──── B) Cause of the error
Previous Status  . . . . . . . . . . :  00000
Statement in Error . . . . . . . . . :  00000027 ──── C) Compile listing instruction in error
RPG Routine  . . . . . . . . . . . . :  *DETC
Number of Parameters . . . . . . . . :
Message Type . . . . . . . . . . . . :  MCH
Additional Message Info  . . . . . . :  1202
Message Data . . . . . . . . . . . . :
          Decimal data error. ──────────── D) Additional error message information
Status that caused RNX9001 . . . . . :
Last File Used . . . . . . . . . . . :
Last File Status . . . . . . . . . . :
Last File Operation  . . . . . . . . :
Last File Routine  . . . . . . . . . :
Last File Statement  . . . . . . . . :
```

Figure E-3 Program dump listing (Option **D** selected).

```
Last File Record Name . . . . . . . . :
Job Name . . . . . . . . . . . . . . . :   DSP03
User Name  . . . . . . . . . . . . . . :   SMYERS
Job Number . . . . . . . . . . . . . . :   013440
Date Entered System  . . . . . . . . . :   12081996
   Century . . . . . . . . . . . . . . :   19
Date Started . . . . . . . . . . . . . :   *N/A*
Time Started . . . . . . . . . . . . . :   *N/A*
Compile Date . . . . . . . . . . . . . :   120896
Compile Time . . . . . . . . . . . . . :   222302
Compiler Level . . . . . . . . . . . . :   0001
Source File  . . . . . . . . . . . . . :   QRPGLESRC
   Library . . . . . . . . . . . . . . :   STAN
Member . . . . . . . . . . . . . . . . :   CUSTADDRES
- - - - - - - - - - - - - - - - - - - - - - - - - - - - - - - - - - - - - - - - - - - - - - - - -
                                                                                       Page    2
INFDS FILE FEEDBACK
File . . . . . . . . . . . . . . . . . :   QSYSPRT   E) Which file(s) is/are open
File Open  . . . . . . . . . . . . . . :   YES       F) Indicates which files(s) are at end
File Status  . . . . . . . . . . . . . :   00000     G) Indicates if an error occurred on the file.  00000 indicates no error
File at EOF  . . . . . . . . . . . . . :   NO
File Operation . . . . . . . . . . . . :   WRITEF
File Routine . . . . . . . . . . . . . :   HEADING   H) Indicates what the last RPG IV operation was on each file
Statement Number . . . . . . . . . . . :   00000019
Record Name  . . . . . . . . . . . . . :             I) Where in the RPG IV program each file was last used
Message Identifier . . . . . . . . . . :
OPEN FEEDBACK
ODP type . . . . . . . . . . . . . . . :   SP
File Name  . . . . . . . . . . . . . . :   QSYSPRT   J) Which file and member were in use when the error occurred
   Library . . . . . . . . . . . . . . :   QSYS
Member . . . . . . . . . . . . . . . . :   Q798857674
Spool File . . . . . . . . . . . . . . :   Q04079N001
   Library . . . . . . . . . . . . . . :   QSPL
Spool File Number  . . . . . . . . . . :   11
Primary Record Length  . . . . . . . . :   132
Input Block Length . . . . . . . . . . :   0
Output Block Length  . . . . . . . . . :   132
Device Class . . . . . . . . . . . . . :   PRINTER
Lines per Page . . . . . . . . . . . . :   66
Columns per Line . . . . . . . . . . . :   132
Allow Duplicate Keys . . . . . . . . . :   *N/A*
Records to Transfer  . . . . . . . . . :   1
Overflow Line  . . . . . . . . . . . . :   60
Block Record Increment . . . . . . . . :   0
File Sharing Allowed . . . . . . . . . :   NO
Device File Created with DDS . . . . . :   NO
IGC or graphic capable file. . . . . . :   NO
File Open Count. . . . . . . . . . . . :   1
Separate Indicator Area. . . . . . . . :   NO
User Buffers . . . . . . . . . . . . . :   NO
Open Identifier. . . . . . . . . . . . :   Q04079N001
Maximum Record Length. . . . . . . . . :   0
ODP Scoped to Job. . . . . . . . . . . :   NO
Maximum Program Devices. . . . . . . . :   1
Current Program Device Defined . . . . :   1
Device Name  . . . . . . . . . . . . . :   *N
Device Description Name. . . . . . . . :   *N
Device Class . . . . . . . . . . . . . :   '02'X
Device Type. . . . . . . . . . . . . . :   '08'X
COMMON I/O FEEDBACK
Number of Puts . . . . . . . . . . . . :   1
Number of Gets . . . . . . . . . . . . :   0
Number of Put/Gets . . . . . . . . . . :   0
Number of other I/O  . . . . . . . . . :   0
Current Operation  . . . . . . . . . . :   '05'X
Record Format  . . . . . . . . . . . . :
                                           '00000000000000000000'X
Device Class and Type. . . . . . . . . :   '0208'X
Device Name  . . . . . . . . . . . . . :   *N
Length of Last Record  . . . . . . . . :   132
```

Figure E-3 Program dump listing (Option **D** selected). (Continued)

```
Number of Records Retrieved. . . . . . :   132
---------------------------------------------------------------------------------
                                                                      Page    3
Last I/O Record Length . . . . . . . . :   0
Current Block Count. . . . . . . . . . :   0
PRINTER FEEDBACK:
Current Line Number. . . . . . . . . . :   3
Current Page . . . . . . . . . . . . . :   1                      K) Field values in last
Major Return Code. . . . . . . . . . . :   00                        record processed
Minor Return Code. . . . . . . . . . . :   00
Output Buffer:
   0000   40404040 40404040 4040D4C9 C3D2C5E8 40D4D6E4 E2C54040 40404040 40404040   *    MICKEY MOUSE          *
   0020   40404040 40404040 40404040 40F240C3 C8C5C5E2 C540E2E3 D9C5C5E3 40404040   *       2 CHEESE STREET    *
   0040   40404040 40404040 404040C4 C9E2D5C5 E8E6D6D9 D3C44040 4040C6D3 40404040   *     DISNEYWORLD     FL   *
   0060   F7F7F0F1 40404040 40404040 40404040 40404040 40404040 40404040 40404040   *7701                      *
   0080   40404040                                                                 *                          *
---------------------------------------------------------------------------------
                                                                      Page    4
INFDS FILE FEEDBACK
File . . . . . . . . . . . . . . . . . :   CUSTADDR
File Open  . . . . . . . . . . . . . . :   YES
File at EOF  . . . . . . . . . . . . . :   NO
File Status  . . . . . . . . . . . . . :   00000
File Operation . . . . . . . . . . . . :   READ F
File Routine . . . . . . . . . . . . . :   *DETC
Statement Number . . . . . . . . . . . :   00000013
Record Name  . . . . . . . . . . . . . :   01
Message Identifier . . . . . . . . . . :
OPEN FEEDBACK
ODP type . . . . . . . . . . . . . . . :   DB
File Name  . . . . . . . . . . . . . . :   CUSTADDRES
   Library . . . . . . . . . . . . . . :   STAN
Member . . . . . . . . . . . . . . . . :   CUSTADDRES
Primary Record Length  . . . . . . . . :   48
Secondary Record Length  . . . . . . . :   0
Input Block Length . . . . . . . . . . :   4160
Output Block Length  . . . . . . . . . :   0
Device Class . . . . . . . . . . . . . :   DATABASE
Access Type  . . . . . . . . . . . . . :   ARRIVAL SEQ
Allow Duplicate Keys . . . . . . . . . :   *N/A*
Source File  . . . . . . . . . . . . . :   NO
Records to Transfer  . . . . . . . . . :   67
Block Record Increment . . . . . . . . :   61
File Sharing Allowed . . . . . . . . . :   NO
Commit Active  . . . . . . . . . . . . :   NO
Commit Record Locking Level. . . . . . :   NO
Database Member. . . . . . . . . . . . :   NO
IGC or graphic capable file. . . . . . :   NO
End-of-file Delay Processing . . . . . :   NO
File Open Count. . . . . . . . . . . . :   1
Based Physical Files Opened. . . . . . :   1
Multiple Member Processing . . . . . . :   NO
Logical Join File. . . . . . . . . . . :   NO
File on Remote System. . . . . . . . . :   NO
File on System/38. . . . . . . . . . . :   NO
User Buffers . . . . . . . . . . . . . :   NO
Open Identifier. . . . . . . . . . . . :
                                           '00000000000000000000'X
CCSID. . . . . . . . . . . . . . . . . :   37
Null Capable Field File. . . . . . . . :   NO
Variable Length Fields File. . . . . . :   NO
CCSID Substitution chars may Exist . . :   NO
ODP Scoped to Job. . . . . . . . . . . :   NO
Maximum Program Devices. . . . . . . . :   1
Current Program Device Defined . . . . :   1
Device Name  . . . . . . . . . . . . . :   DATABASE
COMMON I/O FEEDBACK
Number of Puts . . . . . . . . . . . . :   0
Number of Gets . . . . . . . . . . . . :   1
Number of Put/Gets . . . . . . . . . . :   0
```

Figure E-3 Program dump listing (Option **D** selected). (Continued)

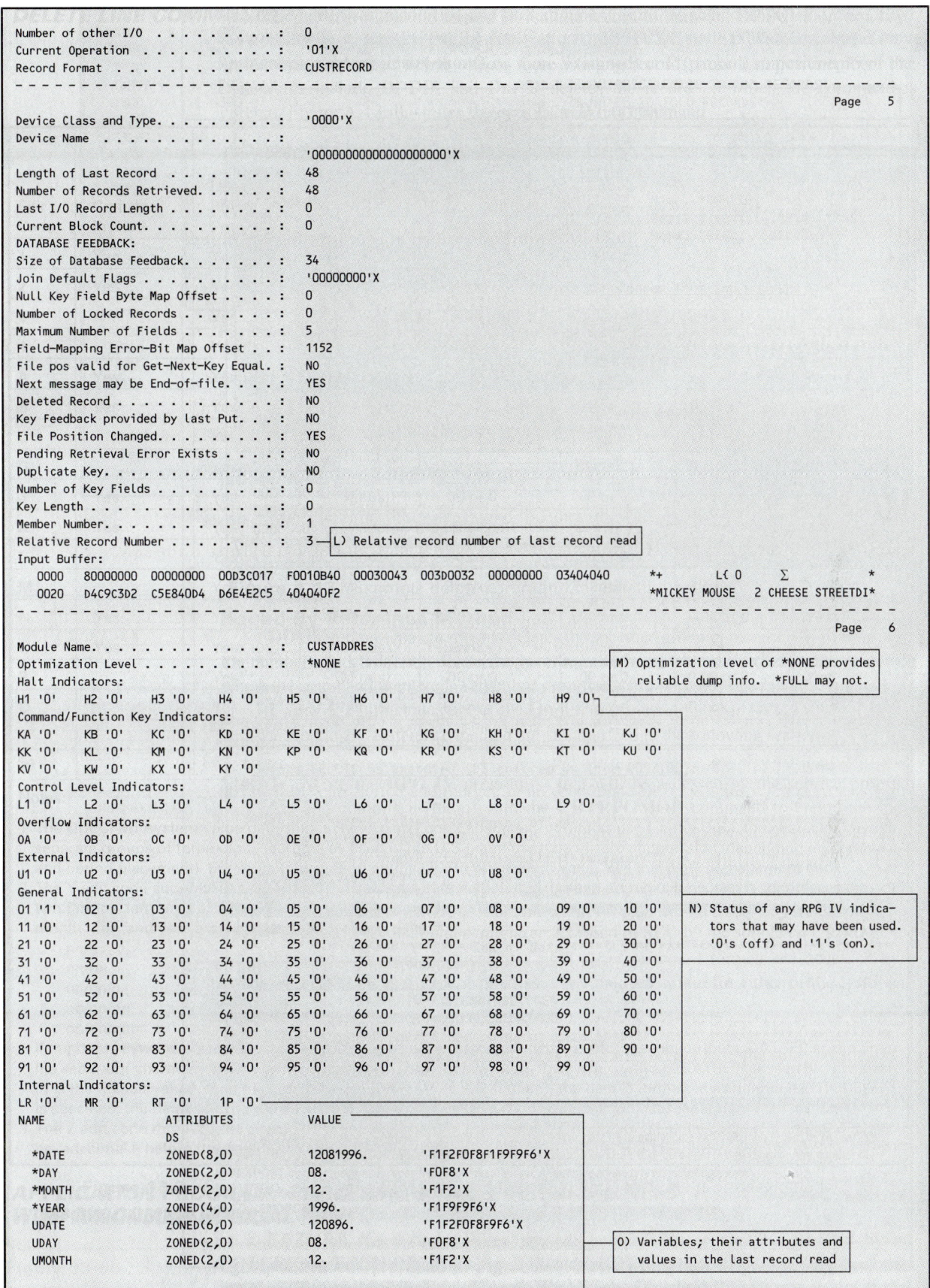

```
Number of other I/O . . . . . . . . . :   0
Current Operation . . . . . . . . . . :   '01'X
Record Format . . . . . . . . . . . . :   CUSTRECORD
- - - - - - - - - - - - - - - - - - - - - - - - - - - - - - - - - - - - - - - - - - - - - - - - - - - - - -
                                                                                              Page    5
Device Class and Type. . . . . . . . . :   '0000'X
Device Name . . . . . . . . . . . . . :
                                          '00000000000000000000'X
Length of Last Record . . . . . . . . :   48
Number of Records Retrieved. . . . . . :   48
Last I/O Record Length . . . . . . . . :   0
Current Block Count. . . . . . . . . . :   0
DATABASE FEEDBACK:
Size of Database Feedback. . . . . . . :   34
Join Default Flags . . . . . . . . . . :   '00000000'X
Null Key Field Byte Map Offset . . . . :   0
Number of Locked Records . . . . . . . :   0
Maximum Number of Fields . . . . . . . :   5
Field-Mapping Error-Bit Map Offset . . :   1152
File pos valid for Get-Next-Key Equal. :   NO
Next message may be End-of-file. . . . :   YES
Deleted Record . . . . . . . . . . . . :   NO
Key Feedback provided by last Put. . . :   NO
File Position Changed. . . . . . . . . :   YES
Pending Retrieval Error Exists . . . . :   NO
Duplicate Key. . . . . . . . . . . . . :   NO
Number of Key Fields . . . . . . . . . :   0
Key Length . . . . . . . . . . . . . . :   0
Member Number. . . . . . . . . . . . . :   1
Relative Record Number . . . . . . . . :   3—L) Relative record number of last record read
Input Buffer:
   0000   80000000  00000000  00D3C017  F0010B40  00030043  003D0032  00000000  03404040     *+          L{ 0      Σ        *
   0020   D4C9C3D2  C5E840D4  D6E4E2C5  404040F2                                               *MICKEY MOUSE   2 CHEESE STREETDI*
- - - - - - - - - - - - - - - - - - - - - - - - - - - - - - - - - - - - - - - - - - - - - - - - - - - - - -
                                                                                              Page    6
Module Name. . . . . . . . . . . . . . :   CUSTADDRES
Optimization Level . . . . . . . . . . :   *NONE ——————————— M) Optimization level of *NONE provides
                                                                  reliable dump info.  *FULL may not.
Halt Indicators:
H1 '0'   H2 '0'   H3 '0'   H4 '0'   H5 '0'   H6 '0'   H7 '0'   H8 '0'   H9 '0'
Command/Function Key Indicators:
KA '0'   KB '0'   KC '0'   KD '0'   KE '0'   KF '0'   KG '0'   KH '0'   KI '0'   KJ '0'
KK '0'   KL '0'   KM '0'   KN '0'   KP '0'   KQ '0'   KR '0'   KS '0'   KT '0'   KU '0'
KV '0'   KW '0'   KX '0'   KY '0'
Control Level Indicators:
L1 '0'   L2 '0'   L3 '0'   L4 '0'   L5 '0'   L6 '0'   L7 '0'   L8 '0'   L9 '0'
Overflow Indicators:
OA '0'   OB '0'   OC '0'   OD '0'   OE '0'   OF '0'   OG '0'   OV '0'
External Indicators:
U1 '0'   U2 '0'   U3 '0'   U4 '0'   U5 '0'   U6 '0'   U7 '0'   U8 '0'
General Indicators:
01 '1'   02 '0'   03 '0'   04 '0'   05 '0'   06 '0'   07 '0'   08 '0'   09 '0'   10 '0'   N) Status of any RPG IV indica-
11 '0'   12 '0'   13 '0'   14 '0'   15 '0'   16 '0'   17 '0'   18 '0'   19 '0'   20 '0'      tors that may have been used.
21 '0'   22 '0'   23 '0'   24 '0'   25 '0'   26 '0'   27 '0'   28 '0'   29 '0'   30 '0'      '0's (off) and '1's (on).
31 '0'   32 '0'   33 '0'   34 '0'   35 '0'   36 '0'   37 '0'   38 '0'   39 '0'   40 '0'
41 '0'   42 '0'   43 '0'   44 '0'   45 '0'   46 '0'   47 '0'   48 '0'   49 '0'   50 '0'
51 '0'   52 '0'   53 '0'   54 '0'   55 '0'   56 '0'   57 '0'   58 '0'   59 '0'   60 '0'
61 '0'   62 '0'   63 '0'   64 '0'   65 '0'   66 '0'   67 '0'   68 '0'   69 '0'   70 '0'
71 '0'   72 '0'   73 '0'   74 '0'   75 '0'   76 '0'   77 '0'   78 '0'   79 '0'   80 '0'
81 '0'   82 '0'   83 '0'   84 '0'   85 '0'   86 '0'   87 '0'   88 '0'   89 '0'   90 '0'
91 '0'   92 '0'   93 '0'   94 '0'   95 '0'   96 '0'   97 '0'   98 '0'   99 '0'
Internal Indicators:
LR '0'   MR '0'   RT '0'   1P '0'
NAME          ATTRIBUTES          VALUE
              DS
  *DATE       ZONED(8,0)          12081996.       'F1F2F0F8F1F9F9F6'X
  *DAY        ZONED(2,0)          08.             'F0F8'X
  *MONTH      ZONED(2,0)          12.             'F1F2'X
  *YEAR       ZONED(4,0)          1996.           'F1F9F9F6'X
  UDATE       ZONED(6,0)          120896.         'F1F2F0F8F9F6'X
  UDAY        ZONED(2,0)          08.             'F0F8'X           O) Variables; their attributes and
  UMONTH      ZONED(2,0)          12.             'F1F2'X              values in the last record read
```

Figure E-3 Program dump listing (Option **D** selected). (Continued)

```
  UYEAR             ZONED(2,0)          96.                'F9F6'X
CITY                CHAR(13)            'DISNEYWORLD  '
                    VALUE IN HEX        'C4C9E2D5C5E8E6D6D9D3C44040'X
CUSTNAME            CHAR(15)            'MICKEY MOUSE   '
                    VALUE IN HEX        'D4C9C3D2C5E840D4D6E4E2C5404040'X
STATE               CHAR(2)             'FL'               'C6D3'X
STREET              CHAR(15)            '2 CHEESE STREET'
                    VALUE IN HEX        'F240C3C8C5C5E2C540E2E3D9C5C5E3'X
ZIPCODE             PACKED(7,0)         _307701.           'D307701F'X
         * * * * *   E N D   O F   R P G   D U M P   * * * * *

P) Invalid numeric value in the ZipCode
   field caused the decimal data error
```

Figure E-3 Program dump listing (Option **D** selected). (Continued)

By identifying the location of the run-time error in the program dump and examination of the compile listing, the *Decimal-data* error can be found. The compile listing in Figure E-4 indicates that a program-described physical file (Custaddres) is processed which requires that the fields be defined in *Input Specification* instructions. Note that the ZipCode field location in positions 45–48 overlaps the previous State field in positions 44–45. This error includes a nonnumeric character in the high-order position of the ZipCode value, causing the Decimal-data error.

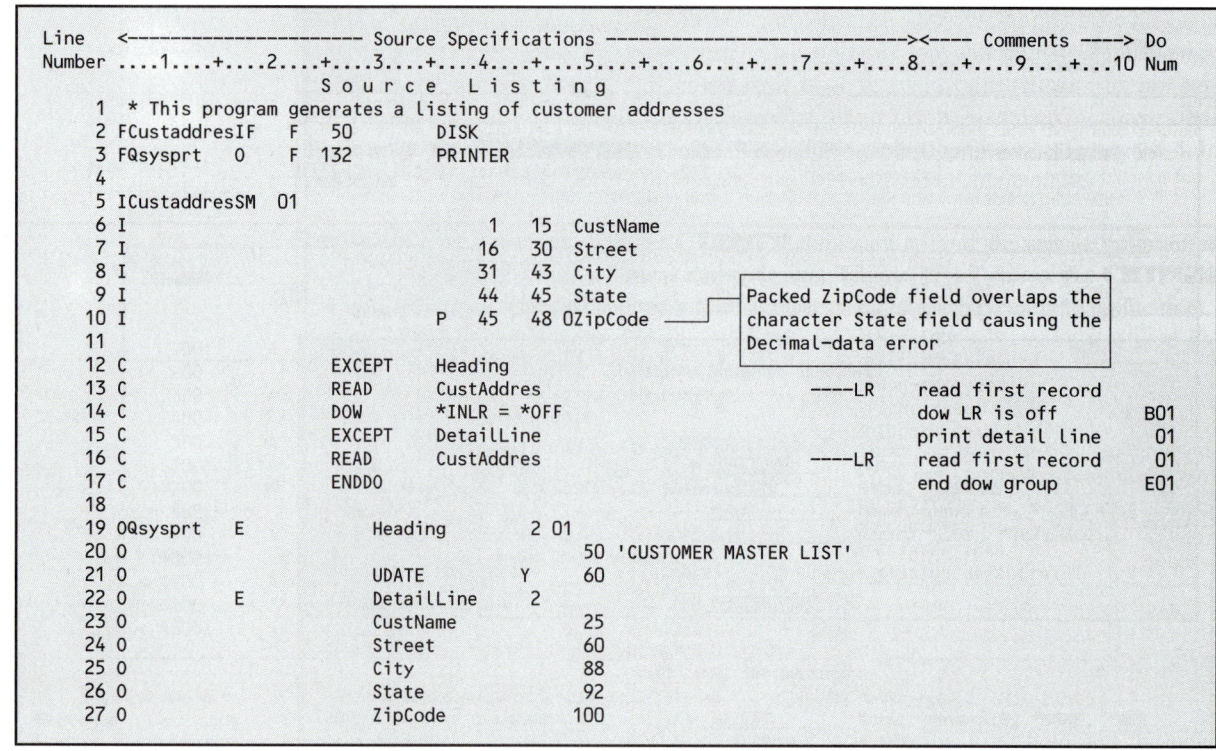

```
Line   <---------------------- Source Specifications ----------------------------><---- Comments ----> Do
Number ....1....+....2....+....3....+....4....+....5....+....6....+....7....+....8....+....9....+...10 Num
                         S o u r c e   L i s t i n g
     1  * This program generates a listing of customer addresses
     2 FCustaddresIF   F   50        DISK
     3 FQsysprt   O    F  132        PRINTER
     4
     5 ICustaddresSM  01
     6 I                                   1   15  CustName
     7 I                                  16   30  Street
     8 I                                  31   43  City
     9 I                                  44   45  State
    10 I                              P   45   48 0ZipCode

    Packed ZipCode field overlaps the
    character State field causing the
    Decimal-data error

    11
    12 C                    EXCEPT    Heading
    13 C                    READ      CustAddres                       ----LR    read first record
    14 C                    DOW       *INLR = *OFF                               dow LR is off       B01
    15 C                    EXCEPT    DetailLine                                 print detail line    01
    16 C                    READ      CustAddres                       ----LR    read first record    01
    17 C                    ENDDO                                                end dow group       E01
    18
    19 OQsysprt   E            Heading        2 01
    20 O                                         50 'CUSTOMER MASTER LIST'
    21 O                       UDATE         Y   60
    22 O          E            DetailLine     2
    23 O                       CustName          25
    24 O                       Street            60
    25 O                       City              88
    26 O                       State             92
    27 O                       ZipCode          100
```

Figure E-4 Compile listing of the **RPG IV** program that generated the Decimal-data error dump.

Only one simple example of debugging a program using a dump has been shown here. Many other, more-complex run-time errors may be located by this method.

INTERACTIVE DEBUGGING

Run-time errors that do or do not cause a program dump may be located by the AS/400's interactive debugging tools. Before interactive debugging of an **RPG IV** program is started, a ***SOURCE, *ALL, *LIST, *STMT, *COPY,** or ***NONE** option must be entered in the **DBGVIEW** (debugging view) parameter of the **CRTBNDRPG** or **CRTRPGMOD** compile command. The function of each parameter is explained below.

***SOURCE** (or ***ALL**)—Contains the **RPG IV** program's root source instructions in the debugging view.

***LIST**—Is similar to the ***SOURCE** view. The parameter **OPTION(SHOWCPY)** will include the /COPY members in the listing. **OPTION(*EXPDDS)** will include the record and field attributes of any externally described files in the debugging view listing.

***STMT**—This default view does not include the source member instructions in the debugging view. A compile listing must be available to identify the instruction numbers in the source program. This parameter should be used only if there are storage constraints or if the source code is to be kept from the user.

***COPY**—Contains the instructions from the root source member and instructions from any copy members.

***NONE**—Will prevent any source member instructions or data from appearing in the debugging view.

Starting an Interactive Debugging Session

To begin an interactive debugging session, the programmer must issue the **STRDBG** *(Start Debug)* command, which will return the display shown in Figure E-5.

```
                              Start Debug (STRDBG)

Type choices, press Enter.
Program . . . . . . . . . . .   ch5r1         Name, *NONE
  Library . . . . . . . . . .     stan        Name, *LIBL, *CURLIB
               + for more values
Default program . . . . . . .   *PGM          Name, *PGM, *NONE
Maximum trace statements . . .  200           Number
Trace full . . . . . . . . . .  *STOPTRC      *STOPTRC, *WRAP
Update production files . . .   *NO           *NO, *YES

                                                                      Bottom
F3=Exit   F4=Prompt   F5=Refresh   F10=Additional parameters   F12=Cancel
F13=How to use this display        F24=More keys
```

Parameter	Explanation
Program	RPG IV source member name must be specified.
Library	Related library (or generic) name must be specified.
+ more values	Up to 10 other source member names may be specified with their related libraries.
*PGM	Default for program modules.
Maximum trace statements	Number of trace statements to include.
Trace full	***STOPTRC** will stop the trace when the maximum number of trace statements is encountered. ***WRAP** will continue the trace.
Update production files	The default is ***NO.** If production files are to be updated during the debugging process, specify ***YES.**

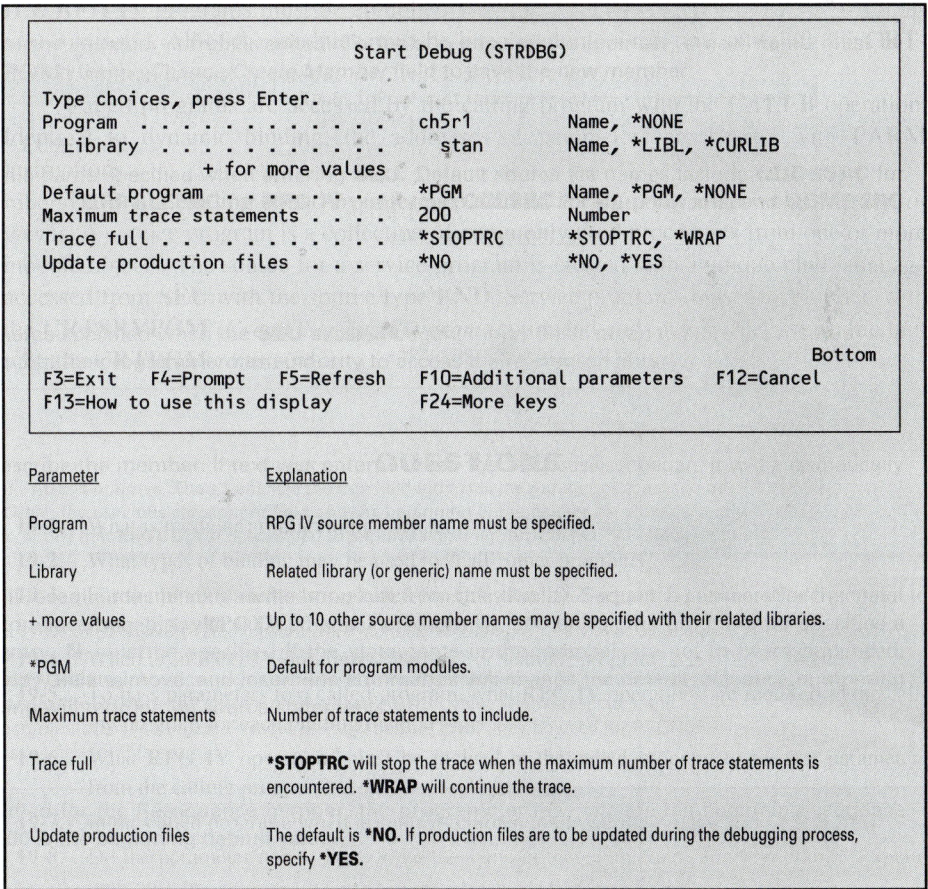

Figure E-5 The **STRDBG** *(Start Debug)* command display.

If the debugging view ***SOURCE, *ALL**, ***COPY,** or ***LIST** was specified in the **CRTBNDRPG** or **CRTRPGMOD** command, pressing the ENTER key will display the source listing shown in Figure E-6. The default ***STMT** view will *not* display a source listing.

With the ***STMT** debugging view, a compile listing of the **RPG IV** program would have to be available to set breakpoints and assign other ILE source debugger functions.

On a microcomputer keyboard, the source member may be reviewed by pressing the Page Down key to advance one display and pressing Page Up to back up one display.

After the source member is displayed, interactive debugging may be performed by one or a combination of the following functions:

- Changing the View of a Module
- Setting and Removing Breakpoints
- Stepping Through the Program Object
- Displaying Data and Expressions
- Displaying the Contents of an Array
- Displaying the Contents of a Table
- Displaying the Contents of a Data Structure
- Displaying Indicators
- Changing the Value of Fields
- Displaying the Attributes of a Field
- Equating a Name with a Field, Expression, or Command
- Using Debug Built-in Functions

All of these functions may be performed by entering the related debug command on the **Debug . . .** line above the list of command key options in the *Display Module Source* display (see Figure E-6). Some may be executed by pressing a select command key. Each of these interactive debugging functions is discussed in the following sections.

```
                          Display Module Source

 Program:    CH5R1          Library:    STAN                Module:    CH5R1

      1        FSoupmstr  IF   E                 DISK
      2        FQsysprt   O    F  132            PRINTER
      3
      4         * Define work fields....
      5        DCaseProfit        S                 4  2
      6        DDecimalPct        S                 5  5
      7        DPrintPct          S                 5  3
      8        DTotlAvgPct        S                 6  3
      9        DRecords           S                 4  0
     10        DAveragePct        S                 5  3
     11
     12         * Begin calculations....
     13        C                    EXCEPT    Headings
     14
     15        C                    READ      Soupmstr
                                                                    More...
 Debug . . .   _____________________________________________________________

 F3=End program   F6=Add/Clear breakpoint   F10=Step   F11=Display variable
 F12=Resume       F13=Work with module breakpoints     F24=More keys
```

Figure E-6 Debugging view ***SOURCE** display (first page).

Changing the View of a Module

If debugging view ***ALL** was initially specified in the **CRTBNDRPG** or **CRTRPGMOD** command, it may be changed from the *Display Module Source* display by pressing the **F15** command key. This action will display the *Select View* window shown in Figure E-7 from which the debugging view may be changed to **Source, Listing,** or **Copy.** Note that the ***ALL** view will default to a **Source** view in this window.

```
                          Display Module Source
 ......................................................................
 :                              Select View                           :
 :                                                                    :
 :  Current View . . . :        ILE RPG/400 Source View              :
 :                                                                    :
 :  Type option, press Enter.                                         :
 :    1=Select                                                        :
 :                                                                    :
 :  Opt      View                                                     :
 :   _         ILE RPG/400 Listing View                               :
 :   _         ILE RPG/400 Source View                                :
 :   _         ILE RPG/400 Copy View                                  :
 :                                                                    :
 :                                                           Bottom   :
 :  F12=Cancel                                                        :
 :                                                                    :
 :....................................................................:
                                                                More...
 Debug . . .  ______________________________________________________

 F3=End program    F6=Add/Clear breakpoint   F10=Step   F11=Display variable
 F12=Resume        F13=Work with module breakpoints     F24=More keys
```

Figure E-7 Changing a view of a module **(Select View)** window.

If **1** was entered next to the *Listing View* option and the ENTER key was pressed, the *Display Module Source* screen would appear in a **Listing** view.

SETTING AND REMOVING BREAKPOINTS

Breakpoints are used in interactive debugging to halt execution of the program object at a specific instruction. *Unconditional breakpoints* stop execution of the program at a specific instruction. *Conditional breakpoints* stop execution of the program when the specified condition occurs at the related breakpoint instruction.

When using breakpoints, the following processing occurs:

- An unconditional breakpoint will occur before the related instruction is executed.
- A conditional breakpoint for an instruction will occur after the conditional expression is evaluated.

Unconditional Breakpoints

When in the *Display Module Source* display (debug mode), unconditional breakpoints may be set by either of the following two methods:

- Place the cursor on the instruction at which the breakpoint is to occur and press **F6.**
- Or enter the debug **BREAK line-number** command on the **Debug . . .** line and press ENTER.

Unconditional breakpoints may be removed by either of the following two methods:

- Place the cursor on the instruction from which the breakpoint is to be removed and press **F6.**
- Or enter the debug **CLEAR line-number** command on the **Debug . . .** line and press ENTER.

Conditional Breakpoints

Conditional breakpoints may be set by either of the following two methods:

- When in the *Display Module Source* screen, press **F13** to display the *Work with Module Breakpoints* screen shown in Figure E-8. Option **1,** the line number of the instruction at which the breakpoint is to occur, and the condition must be entered. After the breakpoint is entered, **F12** must be pressed to return to the *Display Module Source* screen.

```
                       Work with Module Breakpoints
                                                    System:   S1012CFA
Program  . . . :    CH5R1                 Library  . . . :   STAN
  Module . . . :      CH5R1               Type . . . . . :   *PGM

Type options, press Enter.
  1=Add    4=Clear

Opt     Line        Condition
 1      15          *INLR = '1'

                                                                  Bottom
Command
===>
F3=Exit   F4=Prompt   F5=Refresh   F9=Retrieve   F12=Cancel
Breakpoint added to line 15   (Message will display after F12 is pressed)
```

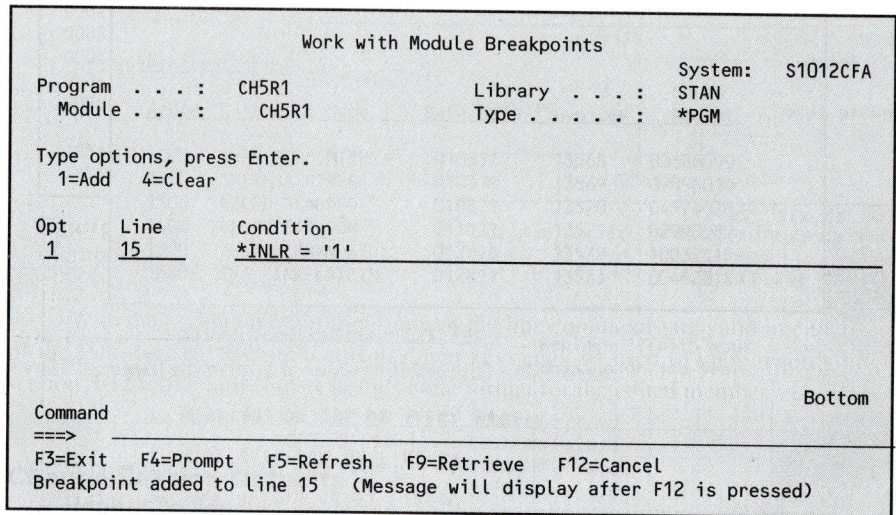

Figure E-8 Setting a conditional breakpoint with the Work with Module Breakpoints display.

- Or enter the debug **BREAK line-number WHEN expression** command on the **Debug . . .** line and press ENTER. A conditional breakpoint example for the program shown in Figure E-6 using the **BREAK** command is shown below.

  BREAK 15 WHEN *INLR = *ON

  The relational tests >, <, =, >=, <=, and <> may be used in the **expression** entry of a conditional breakpoint **BREAK** command.

Conditional breakpoints may be removed by either of the following two methods:

- When in the *Display Module Source* screen, press **F13** to display the *Work with Module Breakpoints* display shown in Figure E-8. Enter Option **4** and the line number of the instruction at which the breakpoint was set. Pressing **F12** will remove the conditional breakpoint and return control to the *Display Module Source* screen.
- Or enter the debug **CLEAR line-number** command on the **Debug . . .** line and press ENTER.

All unconditional and conditional breakpoints may be removed at one time from a program by entering the **CLEAR PGM** debug command on the **Debug . . .** line in the *Display Module Source* screen and pressing ENTER.

After one or more breakpoints are set, **F3** must be pressed to leave the ILE source debugger. Then the related program must be **CALL**ed, which will display the *Display Module Source* screen and stop execution when the first breakpoint is encountered. Pressing **F12** will resume program execution to the next breakpoint or end that processing cycle. At this point, the debugging options discussed in the following sections may be performed.

STEPPING THROUGH THE PROGRAM OBJECT

After a breakpoint is encountered, a specific number of instructions may be run and the program stopped again. This *step* control may be performed by the following methods.

- Pressing **F10** will execute the next instruction and stop again.
- The **STEP number-of-statements** debug command will run the specified number of instructions before execution is stopped again. For example, if **STEP 10** is entered on the **Debug . . .** line of the *Display Module Source* screen, the next 10 instructions will be executed before the program execution is stopped.

DISPLAYING DATA AND EXPRESSIONS

Displaying Data in a Field

Data stored in a field, data structure, array, or table and an expression may be displayed by the following methods:

- Place the cursor on a variable and press the **F11** *(Display Variable)* key. Figure E-9 illustrates a *Display Module Source* screen after the cursor was placed on the CaseProfit field and **F11** was pressed. Note that the name of the variable and its value are displayed at the bottom of the screen.
- Enter the **EVAL variable-name** debug command on the **Debug . . .** line in the *Display Module Source* screen and press ENTER. For example, to display the value in CaseProfit, the debug command would be **EVAL CaseProfit.**

```
                          Display Module Source
Program:   CH5R1         Library:   STAN            Module:   CH5R1
    16      C                     DOW       *INLR = *OFF
    17      C                     EVAL      CaseProfit = SpPerCase - CstPerCase
    18      C                     EVAL      DecimalPct = CaseProfit / CstPerCas
    19      C                     EVAL      PrintPct = DecimalPct * 100
    20      C                     EXCEPT    Detailine
    21      C                     EVAL      TotlAvgPct = TotlAvgPct + PrintPct
    22      C                     EVAL      Records = Records + 1
    23      C                     READ      Soupmstr
    24      C                     ENDDO
    25
    26      C                     EVAL(H)   AveragePct = TotlAvgPct / Records
    27      C                     EXCEPT    Totaline
    28
    29      * Begin output coding....
    30      OQsysprt   E              Headings       3 01
                                                                   More...
Debug . . .   _______________________________________________________________

F3=End program   F6=Add/Clear breakpoint   F10=Step   F11=Display variable
F12=Resume       F13=Work with module breakpoints     F24=More keys
CASEPROFIT = 02.52
```

Figure E-9 Field name and value displayed after placing the cursor on a field and pressing **F11**.

Because only one breakpoint was set for this example, pressing **F12** will end this processing cycle and read the next record. Placing the cursor on the CaseProfit field again and pressing **F11** will present the value for this processing cycle.

To recall the previous CaseProfit values, pressing the ENTER key displays the *Evaluate Expression* screen shown in Figure E-10. The additional values shown for CaseProfit were assessed by pressing the **F12** key to resume processing. For this example, the values came from the next record read from the physical file.

```
                         Evaluate Expression

Previous debug expressions
> EVAL CaseProfit
  CASEPROFIT = 00.00
> EVAL CaseProfit
  CASEPROFIT = 01.44
> EVAL CaseProfit
  CASEPROFIT = 02.52
                                                              Bottom
Debug . . .  _____________________________________________________

F3=Exit   F9=Retrieve   F12=Cancel   F19=Left   F20=Right   F21=Command entry
```

Figure E-10 Evaluate Expression display showing field values for the selected processing cycles.

Displaying the Values in an Array

All of the values in the elements of an array, or select element values, or a range of contiguous element values may be displayed in the interactive debugging mode. Figure E-11 lists a segment of a program (from Chapter 10; Figure 10-18) that processes an array (SalesAry). The result at the bottom of the *Display Module Source* screen is shown after a breakpoint has been set, the program called, and an **EVAL** command entered on the **Debug . . .** line.

```
                         Display Module Source

Program:   CH10R1        Library:   STAN            Module:   CH10R1
     31       C                     EVAL       *INOF = *OFF
     32       C                     ENDIF
     33
     34       C                     XFOOT      SalesAry        WeekTotal
     35       C                     EXCEPT     DetailLine
     36       C                     EVAL       TotalAry = TotalAry + SalesAry
     37       C                     READ       Ch10p1
     38       C                     ENDDO
     39
     40       C                     XFOOT      TotalAry        MonthTotal
     41       C                     EXCEPT     TotaLine
     42
     43        * Begin output....
     44       OQsysprt   E                Heading          1 01
     45       O                           UDATE           Y       8
                                                                More...
Debug . . .  _____________________________________________________

F3=End program   F6=Add/Clear breakpoint   F10=Step   F11=Display variable
F12=Resume       F13=Work with module breakpoints     F24=More keys
SALESARY(3) = 00351.40
```

Figure E-11 Value in an array element shown after the **EVAL SalesAry(3)** debug command has been entered.

To access the value in one element of an array, the debug command **EVAL array-name (element-number)** must be entered and the ENTER key pressed. As shown in Figure E-11, the array name, element number, and value are displayed at the bottom of the *Display Module Source* screen.

To access the values in *all* elements of an array at one time, the **EVAL** command and the array name (e.g., **EVAL SalesAry**) have to be entered on the **Debug . . .** line. After the ENTER key is pressed, the *Evaluate Expression* display shown in Figure E-12 will automatically appear, showing the values in every element of the array.

```
                        Evaluate Expression

Previous debug expressions
> EVAL SALESARY
  SALESARY(1) = 00080.00
  SALESARY(2) = 00145.30
  SALESARY(3) = 00351.40
  SALESARY(4) = 00124.00
  SALESARY(5) = 00052.24
                                                          Bottom
Debug . . .   _____________________________________________________

F3=Exit   F9=Retrieve   F12=Cancel   F19=Left   F20=Right   F21=Command entry
```

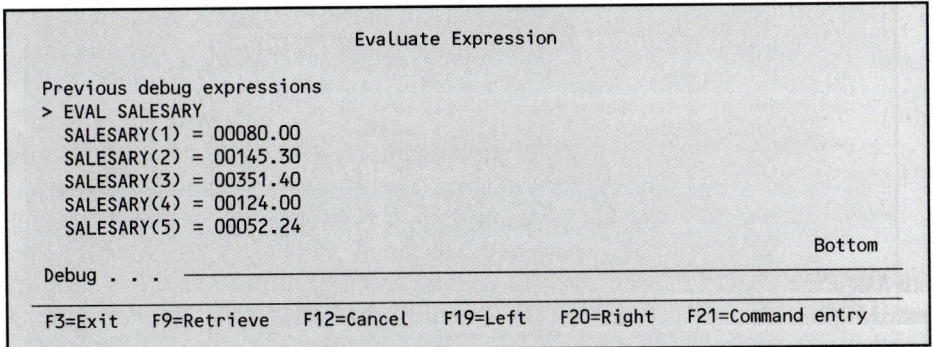

Figure E-12 Evaluate Expression display after the **EVAL SalesAry** debug command is entered and the ENTER key pressed.

If a contiguous range of elements is to be accessed in the debug mode, the **EVAL** command, array name, and beginning and ending element numbers must be specified. For example, if the values in elements 2 and 3 are to be displayed in the SalesAry, the debug command **EVAL SalesAry(2 . . 3)** must be entered on the **Debug . . .** line. After the ENTER key is pressed, the *Evaluate Expression* display will appear, showing the values in the range of elements.

Displaying the Values in a Table

To display the value in the current table element, the **EVAL Table-Name** debug command must be entered on the **Debug . . .** line of the *Display Module Source* display and the ENTER key pressed.

If the values in all elements of a 12-element table are to be displayed, the **EVAL table-name(1 . . 12)** debug command must be entered on the **Debug . . .** line of the *Display Module Source* display. After the ENTER key is pressed, the *Evaluate Expression* display will appear, showing the values stored in all elements of the table.

Displaying the Contents of a Data Structure

The values stored in a data structure may be displayed by entering the **EVAL** command and the data structure name (e.g., **EVAL DS1**) on the **Debug . . .** line of the *Display Module Source* screen. After the ENTER key is pressed, the *Evaluate Expression* display will appear, showing all of the values stored in the subfields of the data structure. To view the contents of a single subfield of a data structure, enter the **EVAL** command and the subfield name. After the ENTER key is pressed, the subfield value will be displayed at the bottom of the *Display Module Source* screen.

Displaying Indicators

The "on" (**1**) or "off" (**0**) status of all indicators available to the **RPG IV** program may be obtained by entering the **EVAL *IN** command on the **Debug . . .** line of the *Display*

Module Source screen. After the ENTER key is pressed, the *Evaluate Expression* screen will display, showing the status of the **RPG IV** indicators **01** through **99.**

To display the status of *one* indicator, the **EVAL *INxx** (**xx** = indicator name) command must be entered on the **Debug . . .** line. After the ENTER key is pressed, the status of the single indicator will be displayed at the bottom of the *Display Module Source* screen.

If the status of the range of indicators **01** through **08** were required, for example, the command **EVAL(1 . . 8)** would be entered. After the ENTER key had been pressed, the *Evaluate Expression* screen would be displayed, showing the status of the range of indicators.

Changing the Value of Fields

The value of a field may be changed by the **EVAL field-name = value** command entered on the **Debug . . .** line of the *Display Module Source* screen. For example, if the value of the SpPerCase field was to be changed to 7.00, the debug command **EVAL SpPerCase = 7.00** would be entered on the **Debug . . .** line. After the ENTER key had been pressed, **SPPERCASE = 07.00** would be displayed at the bottom of the screen. When **F12** was pressed, the related instruction would include the new field value.

Displaying the Attributes of a Field

The attributes of a field, array, table, data structure, indicator, or pointer may be displayed at the bottom of the *Display Module Source* screen by entering the **ATTR variable-name** command on the **Debug . . .** line. For example, if the attributes of the CaseProfit field were to be determined, the **ATTR CaseProfit** command would be entered. After the ENTER key had been pressed, the message **TYPE = PACKED(4,2), LENGTH = 3 BYTES** would be displayed at the bottom of the screen.

Equating a Name with a Field, Expression, or Command

In order to shorten entries, the **EQUATE** debug command may be used to equate a name with a field, expression, or command. For example, if the command **EVAL RCD-COUNT** was to be shortened, the command **EQUATE RC EVAL RCDCOUNT** would be entered on the **Debug . . .** line and the ENTER key pressed. Note that the abbreviated **RC** entry may be anything the programmer selects. Then, each time **RC** is entered on the debug command line, the **EVAL RCDCOUNT** command will be performed. The **DISPLAY EQUATE** command will display the **EQUATE** commands entered for the current interactive debugging session.

USING BUILT-IN DEBUGGER FUNCTIONS

The ILE source debugger includes the following built-in functions:

%SUBSTR—Substring a string field

%INDEX—Change the index of a table or multiple-occurrence data structure

%ADDR—Retrieve the address of a field.

The %SUBSTR Function

The **%SUBSTR** built-in debugging function supports the substringing of a string (field, table, or array) defined as *character* or *graphic*. Specifically, **%SUBSTR** may be used to

- Display part of a character field
- Assign part of a character field
- Use part of a character field in a conditional break expression.

Figure E-13 illustrates the four formats of **%SUBSTR** instructions that appear individually at the bottom of the *Display Module Source* screen.

```
> EVAL TransDate
  TRANSDATE = '19980131'                        ———— value stored in field
** Display the first four characters of TransDate **
> EVAL %substr (TransDate 1 4)                  ———— %substr function
  %SUBSTR (TRANSDATE 1 4) = '1998'              ———— displayed result

> EVAL CustName
  CUSTNAME = 'MICKEY MOUSE'                     ———— value stored in field
** Set LastName equal to last five characters of the CustName field **
  EVAL LastName=%substr(CustName 8 12)          ———— %substr function
  LASTNAME=%SUBSTR(CUSTNAME 8 12) = 'MOUSE'     ———— displayed result

> EVAL TabMonth(8)
  TABMONTH(8) = AUGUST                          ———— value stored in field
** Display first three characters of eighth TabMonth element **
> EVAL %substr(TabMonth(8) 1 3)                 ———— %substr function
  %SUBSTR(TABMONTH(8) 1 3) = 'AUG'              ———— displayed result

> EVAL OldDate
  OLDDATE = 'JUNE 15, 1998'          ——┐
> EVAL NewDate                         ├——values stored in fields
  NEWDATE = 'SEPTEMBER 31, 1998'     ——┘
** Set characters 11-12 of NewDate equal to characters 6-7 of OldDate **
  EVAL %substr(NewDate 11 12) = %substr(OldDate 6 7)  ——%substr function
  %SUBSTR(NEWDATE 11 12) = %SUBSTR(OLDDATE 6 7) = '15'—displayed result
> EVAL NEWDATE = 'SEPTEMBER 15, 1998'
```

Figure E-13 Examples of the **%SUBSTR** function.

A summary of the **%SUBSTR** functions assigned in a debugging session may be displayed by pressing the ENTER key after an instruction has been entered.

The %INDEX Function

The interactive debugging **%INDEX** function may be used to change the index of a table or a multiple-occurrence data structure. For example, the debug command **EVAL TabMonth=%INDEX(12),** entered on the *Display Module Source* screen's **Debug . . .** line will change the current table element to 12. Entering **EVAL TabMonth** and pressing ENTER will display the value of the new element.

The %ADDR Function

The interactive debugging **%ADDR** function is used to find the address of an item in memory. For example, the debug command **EVAL %ADDR(TABMthNo)** displays **%ADDR(TABMONTH) = SSP: C0019E000780** on the bottom of the *Display Module Source* screen. The **SSP:C0019E000780** entry indicates the memory address of the TABMONTH storage area. This address may be used to manipulate any pointers used in the **RPG IV** program.

With any of the interactive debug commands or functions discussed, they are enabled only after the related program is "called." Failure to "call" the program will display the **Identifier does not exist** error message at the bottom of the *Display Module Source* screen when a debug command or function is entered.

Ending the Debug Session

After the debugging session is completed for a program, it must be ended by the **END-DBG** command. If another program is to be debugged or if **STRDBG** is entered again for the same program without entering the **ENDDBG** command (after exiting from the debugging mode), the error message **Command STRDBG not valid in this mode** will be displayed at the bottom of the *Display Module Source* screen.

appendix f

The RPG Logic Cycle

All RPG compilers have a "built-in" logic cycle that controls the opening and closing of files and the reading and writing of records. In addition, many of the processing functions such as first page print control, heading, detail- and total-time output, and control break operations are automatically provided by the logic cycle. Because the modern trend is not to use the logic cycle, **RPG IV** programs introduced in this text have not used it. All of the file, record, and processing functions have been controlled by **RPG IV** operations similar to the requirements of other high-level languages (e.g., **COBOL, BASIC, PL-1**).

RPG LOGIC CYCLE PROGRAMMING

When a system processes data, it must do the processing in a particular order. This logical order is provided by:

- The **RPG IV** compiler
- Your program code.

The logic the compiler supplies is called the **program cycle.** When you let the compiler provide the logic for your programs, it is called **cycle programming.** The program cycle is a series of steps that your program repeats until an end-of-file condition is reached. Depending on the specifications you code, the program may or may not use each step in the cycle.

If you want to have files controlled by the cycle, the information that you code on RPG specifications in your source program need not specify when records for these files are read. The compiler supplies the logical order for these operations, and some output operations, when your source program is compiled.

If you do not want to have files controlled by the cycle, you must create an end-of-file condition, usually by setting on the last record (**LR**) indicator.

1. RPG processes all heading and detail lines (H or D in position 17 of the output specifications).
2. RPG reads the next record and sets on the record identifying and control level indicators.
3. RPG processes total calculations (conditioned by control level indicators L1 through L9, an LR indicator, or an L0 entray).
4. RPG processes all total output lines (identified by a T in position 17 of the output specifications).
5. RPG determines it the LR indicator is on. If it is on, the program ends.

6 The fields of the selected input records move from the record to a processing area. RPG sets on field indicators.

7 RPG processes all detail calculations (not conditioned by control level indicators in positions 7 and 8 of the calculation specifications). It uses the data from the record at the beginning of the cycle.

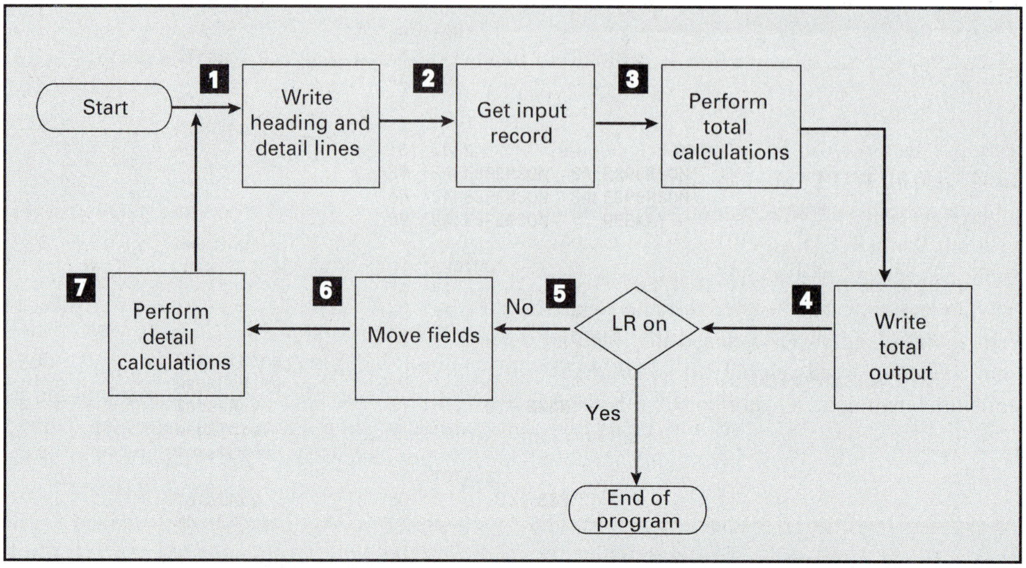

Figure F-1 RPG Program Logic Cycle (Courtesy of IBM.)

The First Cycle

The first and last time through the program cycle differ somewhat from other cycles. Before reading the first record the first time through the cycle, the program does three things:

- handles imput parameters, opens files, initializes program data
- writes the records conditioned by the 1P (first page) indicator
- processes all heading and detail output operations.

For example, heading lines printed before reading the first record might consist of constant or page heading information, or special fields such as **PAGE** and ***DATE.** The program also bypasses total calculations and total output steps on the first cycle.

The Last Cycle

The last time a program goes through the cycle, when no more records are available, the program sets the LR (last record) indicator and the L1 through L9 (control level) indicators to **on.** The program processes the total calculations and total output, then all files are closed, and then the program ends.

Index